Other books by Don Gold:

ZOO

A Behind-the-Scenes Look at the Animals and the People Who Care for Them

DON GOLD

CB

CONTEMPORARY
BOOKS

CHICAGO · NEW YORK

Library of Congress Cataloging-in-Publication Data

Gold, Don.
   Zoo : a behind-the-scenes look at the animals and
the people who care for them.

   1. Zoo animals.   2. Zoo keepers.   3. Lincoln
Park Zoo.   I. Title.
QL77.5.G65   1988   590'.74'777311   88-23761
ISBN 0-8092-4617-1

Quotation from *Cancer Ward* by Alexander Solzhenitsyn,
translated by Nicholas Bethell and David Burg. Translation
© 1968, 1969 by The Bodley Head Ltd. Reprinted by
permission of Farrar, Straus and Giroux, Inc.

Illustrations by Joe Hindley

Copyright © 1988 by Don Gold
All rights reserved
Published by Contemporary Books, Inc.
180 North Michigan Avenue, Chicago, Illinois 60601
Manufactured in the United States of America
Library of Congress Catalog Card Number: 88-23761
International Standard Book Number: 0-8092-4617-1

Published simultaneously in Canada by Beaverbooks, Ltd.
195 Allstate Parkway, Valleywood Business Park
Markham, Ontario L3R 4T8 Canada

For
Alexander
and
Lola

CONTENTS

If we stop loving animals, aren't we bound to stop loving humans too?

—Alexander Solzhenitsyn
The Cancer Ward

1

Zoo:
Ark and Covenant

For animals, humans have been loving, threatening, and often unreliable friends. Fickle, opportunistic, needy, they have petted animals and slain them, built monuments to them and eaten them. People have covered their chilled bodies with animal fur and fitted animals with sweaters to guard against the wicked winds of winter. It is no wonder that some animals cling to humans and others run wildly away from them.

It is not surprising, either, that the history of zoos is strewn with ambiguities. To look at zoos is to look at the ways in which humans have confronted animals. A search into the distant corners of history can be revelatory.

From the murky past, some scraps emerge. As early as 4500 B.C., in what is now Iraq, pigeons were kept in captivity. Groups of elephants were assembled in India in 2500 B.C. During that same period, hoofed animals—antelopes—wore collars; they can be seen in drawings in Egyptian tombs. We know that the Egyptians treated some animals as sacred: lion, baboon, ibis, among others. Animal parks existed in that ancient society; the prevalent attitude toward animals was reverent.

By 1000 B.C., there were zoos in China. Halfway around the world, the biblical King Solomon was fond of the apes and peacocks given to him as tribute every three years; he was a part-time zoologist. He was not the only ruler with a passion for animals. Assurbanipal, who ruled Assyria (669–633 B.C.), and Nebuchadnezzar, the King of Babylonia in the sixth century B.C., sponsored royal zoos.

The Greeks had been displaying captured animals several centuries before Aristotle wrote *The History of Animals* in the fourth century B.C. Aristotle, wise in many matters, knew about zoos; so did his pupil, Alexander the Great, who caught animals on his expeditions and shipped them home.

The Romans joined in centuries later. But their use of animals was not benign. Their devotion to blood sports led to the slaughter of animals. Bull elephants fought each other, to the delight of Roman spectators. Big cats were tossed into an arena to destroy each other. Peacocks, sacred in other cultures, were roasted and served. In one series of games that lasted four months, 10,000 gladiators did battle, and 11,000 animals were killed.

Charlemagne, in the eighth century A.D., proudly displayed captured animals. In England four centuries later, Henry I opened a zoo near Oxford; in it, he displayed lions, lynx, leopards, and camels. In France, Philip VI opened a zoo, with lions and leopards, in the Louvre in 1333.

When Cortez arrived in Mexico, he discovered a zoo (in 1519)—a massive collection served by more than 300 keepers and a corps of nurses serving as veterinarians. There were birds in huge aviaries, iguanas, monkeys, bears, and jaguars. Other explorers seized animals to stock urban zoos in Europe and North Africa. In 1665, animals were on display at Versailles; it was an early case of animals as the basis for scientific research and education. Eventually, that zoo was moved to Paris.

In 1752, the Imperial Menagerie was founded at the

Schonbrunn Palace in Vienna. It was officially opened in 1765 and is still open today. It was built by the Holy Roman Emperor Francis I for his wife, Maria Theresa, who had a fondness for dining while surrounded by camels, zebras, and elephants.

Ten years later, a zoo was opened in Madrid. By 1793, the Muséum d'Histoire Naturelle was flourishing in Paris.

For centuries, animals had been herded into cages for the pleasure of rulers and governments. The welfare of the captured creatures was secondary to the delight of the observers.

Then, in 1826, a pivotal development occurred. The London Zoological Society was founded, the first of its kind, and a major trend toward scientific inquiry was begun. Other societies were to follow; meetings were held regularly, publications were born.

In 1828, a zoo was built in Regent's Park in London. In 1847, the term *Zoological Gardens* (in London) was shortened to *zoo*, and the word quickly became universal. The United States Congress funded a National Zoological Park in Washington, D.C., in 1890.

In 1907, another crucial development took place that was to influence zoos everywhere. Carl Hagenbeck, an animal dealer in Hamburg, took a chunk of his profits and opened his own zoo in Stellingen. Hagenbeck was a man with a vision. His zoo did not resemble any other zoo.

He described his mission: "I desired, above all things, to give the animals the maximum of liberty. I wished to exhibit them not as captives, confined to narrow spaces, and looked at between bars, but as free to wander from place to place within as large limits as possible, and with no bars to obstruct the view and serve as a reminder of captivity."

Hagenbeck's dream proved to be contagious. The traditional tile cages with cement floors and bars persisted, and still do, but zoos all over the world realized the validity of his intent.

As the decades of the twentieth century passed, zoos

grew in size and number. World War II intervened; it was to deter progress. However, it also was to enhance the perception of zoo directors. From the evil of war, a realization was born.

Robert Bendiner, in his excellent book *The Fall of the Wild, the Rise of the Zoo* wrote about it:

> By the mid-1940s many of the zoos from England to Japan had been wrecked or starved out. Zoo people everywhere became acutely aware of what the wisest of them already knew, that populations in the wild were drastically low, and were due to become less and less available to zoos as newly established states in Africa and Asia either slaughtered their wildlife without restriction or began to clamp down on its export. For the first time animal counts were undertaken from the air, along with field studies of breeding habits and animal behavior in the wild, many of them under the aegis of the world's great zoological societies. All of which produced a great ferment among zoo personnel everywhere, and a surge in breeding programs that in turn inspired advances in zoo building, animal grouping, veterinary medicine, ethology, and other scientific research.

Bendiner defined the zoos' obligation to breed animals in terms of three objectives: "to relieve pressure on the wild . . . to raise animals with a view to reintroducing them into the wild . . . to serve as an ultimate haven, the scene of a last-resort effort to save and propagate endangered species as a scientific and aesthetic boon to future man."

Today, there are more than 1,000 zoos in the world, more than 140 in the United States. Zoos exchange information, do research, breed animals, educate the public, and do battle against the forces that endanger species all over the world. Some conduct themselves ethically and effectively; some do not. Some are vulnerable to the criticism of animal rights' activists; some are not. When animals are taken for granted, zoos decay. In our time, most zoos know that many of their sins may be visible, and they guard against them. Their work is costly, but their purpose drives them on.

Lord Zuckerman, the president of the Zoological Society of London, edited the book *Great Zoos of the World*. In his introduction, he wrote:

> Civic pride in a well-run zoo park, however magnificent it may be, is not enough. If those who are responsible for managing zoos do not agree with the minority who are opposed to zoos, they at least have to show that they are just as humane in their attitude toward wild animals. They have to show that they treat their public educational programmes seriously. Their keeper staff has to be properly trained. They should be able to demonstrate—not to the world of amateurs who write about zoos, but to the scientific world—that they are seriously concerned with research of the quality and kind which yields knowledge that is not only relevant to the health and breeding of wild animals, but also to man's own well-being. And finally; they should be able to show that they have a contribution to make to the preservation of species which have either become extinct in the wild or which are now endangered.

The standards that Lord Zuckerman posed test the success of all zoos. The historic course of zoos—jailing animals for the often mocking delight of tourists—has been in transition in the second half of this century. In striving for the profoundly humane, zoos have complicated their mission, and have ennobled it. There will be frustrations ahead for all zoo directors; animals will be in need, and money may be in short supply.

One zoo moving through its transitional period to what its staff hopes will be the best of times is the Lincoln Park Zoo in Chicago.

Its special history began 120 years ago, with two pairs of swans.

In the summer of 1868, New York's Central Park managers, in a small burst of generosity, donated two pairs of mute swans to the developing landscape of Lincoln Park, for display on one of the park's ponds. In time, the swans bred a colony of thirteen. By 1873, in fact, that early animal collection had grown to twenty-seven mammals and forty-eight birds. In 1874, the locals began to refer to the assortment as a zoo, making it one of the first zoos in the United States. (Philadelphia's zoo is the only one disputing the claim of Lincoln Park's to being the first zoo.)

That same year, the zoo made its first purchase, a bear for $10, and became known officially as the Lincoln Park Zoological Gardens, the name it's kept ever since. It continued to spend money to acquire animals; in 1877, it spent $275 for two more bears, two peafowl, a kangaroo, a condor, and a goat.

Three years later, dens were built for wolves and foxes. Buffalo and polar bears were added, and in 1882 a small mammal house was built. Until 1888, the work was done by a group of zoo loyalists; that year, the zoo's first director, Cyrus DeVry, was hired. (He served until 1919.)

As the turn of the century approached, more animals were obtained, more exhibits were built, and more money was spent.

By 1908 the zoo, on ten acres of choice parkland, had 782 birds and mammals, 117 species in all. The lion house, a large classic Victorian building with a great hall, opened in 1912; the first giraffes arrived at the zoo two years later. The early 1920s brought the reptile house. During the depression of the thirties, the animals were fed at night; no one wanted to antagonize those people who were without food. (They were permitted to sleep on the zoo grounds.)

By then, the primate house, another Victorian building, had been built, and Bushman, a lowland gorilla who was to grow to more than 500 pounds and become famous, was in it.

During World War II, Judy, a female Indian elephant, arrived and became a crowd favorite for almost thirty years; she came to the zoo from the Brookfield Zoo in a western suburb. She walked across the city, with police and keepers as escorts. When she died in 1971, she was sixty-eight, and few zoo visitors had not seen her.

In 1945, a new era began, with the arrival of R. Marlin Perkins as director. People all over the country who did not know about the Lincoln Park Zoo did know about Perkins. He hosted the weekly television show "Zoo Parade" for years; he knew that television could serve his cause, and he was right. Thanks to his work, the zoo became famous beyond the borders of Chicago.

During Perkins's reign, other improvements took place. The zoo rookery, a miniwildlife refuge in the heart of the zoo, opened. Perkins acquired four lowland gorillas in Africa. (One of them, Sinbad, was as mammoth as Bushman.)

In 1959, the Lincoln Park Zoological Society was formed; it had seventy-seven founding members—and was to grow to more than thirteen thousand. Within a few years, it had a master plan, and the Chicago Park District, which had supported the zoo, had a supplementary source of funding, a fact that was to generate intensive activity over the years.

In 1960, the children's zoo building was completed, the first year-round children's zoo building in the country. Two years later, Dr. Lester E. Fisher, who had been a consulting veterinarian at the zoo, succeeded Perkins as director. He merged his vision of the zoo with that of the zoo society, and reform and renovation became the bywords of the zoo.

New exhibits were born: the Farm in the Zoo, the sea lion pool, outdoor areas for lions and tigers, a small mammal house. The first baby gorilla was born, the beginning of a program that was to become the world's leader in breeding gorillas in captivity.

In the seventies, funds from the city and the zoo society—a total investment of $23 million—spurred a building campaign designed to produce better, larger habitats for animals, areas set aside for breeding, and better viewing by zoo visitors. The landscape of the zoo was transformed.

The Kroc Animal Hospital–Commissary (built with a

large donation from the founder of the McDonald's chain), the modernistic great ape house, the climate-controlled flamingo dome, the waterfowl lagoon, the Crown-Field Center (housing the offices of the zoo staff and the zoo society along with education facilities), the penguin-seabird house, the antelope-zebra area, and the large mammal habitat were all put in place between 1976 and 1982. The master plan was not completed, however. There was more to be done. A $10 million Landmark Campaign was undertaken to renovate the farm, the children's zoo, the lion house, and the primate house. The funds would support a redesign of the bird house and the creation of a new bird of prey habitat. As 1987 wound down, much of the work was in progress; much of the planning had been done.

The Lincoln Park Zoo today remains a part of the Chicago Park District, but almost half of its funds come from the work of the zoo society. Les Fisher continues to be in charge, twenty-five years after he took over.

The zoo is placed on thirty-five acres of choice parkland not far from Lake Michigan. It is one of the few free zoos in the country; visitors don't pay to enter or to view any of the exhibits. It is open every day of the year, from nine to five. Its design is ingenious; thirty-five acres is not a large space, yet in walking along the pathways at the zoo, the visitor never feels cramped, hemmed in by buildings. By comparison, the San Diego Zoo is on 125 acres, New York's Bronx Zoo on 265.

More than 4 million visitors enter the zoo each year; only the National Zoo in Washington, D.C., can match that total, and few zoos in the world are in that league. The visitors come to see the more than 2,000 animals on display. (As habitats grow in size, that number will be reduced, carefully and selectively, by the zoo staff.) Almost half of them are mammals, a quarter are birds, another quarter are reptiles.

In 1987, $8,603,435 was spent on the zoo by the park district and the zoo society. The money supported more than buildings, services, utilities, and animals. The zoo

staff—including administration, curators, and keepers—
numbered close to 100 (the zoo society staff was 40). In the
zoo's budget estimate for fiscal 1988, some entries revealed
that few employees work at the zoo for profit.

Les Fisher, at the top of the salary scale, earned $74,796.
The assistant director, Dennis Meritt, earned $44,244.
Veterinarian Tom Meehan received a salary of $41,580;
his assistant veterinarian, Peregrine Wolff, was paid
$33,696. For the zoo's five curators, pay ranged from
$32,000 to $33,000, while the upper limit for the full-time
keepers was $21,812. Others on the zoo staff earned less
than that.

It is not surprising that many of the zoo employees
dream about winning the state lottery.

The truth, of course, is that the zoo has little to do with
money, with numbers or dates or even its history. The
zoo's story is about people and animals and how they do or
do not get along. It is about love and disappointment and
the temptations of the anthropomorphic.

There is a steady stream of gossip at the zoo, and the
usual resentments of subordinates against superiors. What
unites them all, and what keeps the gall from rising to do
harm, is the commonly held belief that the fate of the
animals is what matters most.

In that sense, the zoo is a continuing case study in the
relationship of humans to animals. But the effort is not an
easy one. The curators and administrators are inundated by
paperwork, by management decisions, by planning sessions, renovation projects, and frequent staff meetings.
Keepers spend much of their time in the basic labor of
their jobs, the daily drudgery of cleaning cages and feeding
animals. Fortunately, most of them are conscientious. One
factor in that is the presence of women as keepers; before
1972, there were none, then the civil service exam was
opened to women. By 1987 almost half of the keepers were
women. They brought with them qualifications that the
patronage army did not always demonstrate: a college
education and a zeal for caring for animals. Old-guard

male keepers who viewed the job simply as a job were challenged, often successfully, by the women who brought a new perspective to caring for animals.

When all the bureaucratic distractions are swept aside and all the menial tasks accomplished, what remains is that essential measure of a zoo's performance: the well-being of the animals and the devotion of the staff to those animals.

There is much to consider.

In the pages of the journal kept each day at the zoo's main office, a sample of the events that command attention reveals the range of emotions involved:

- A trumpeter swan was sent to the Milwaukee Zoo as a donation. "This bird will be incorporated into the Wisconsin recovery plan for trumpeters and will be released later in 1987."
- A snow leopard was sent, on a breeding loan, to the Oklahoma Zoo.
- A Nicobar pigeon was sent on a breeding loan to the Cleveland Metropark Zoo.
- A baselisk lizard died.
- Three piglets were born at the farm.
- A short-tailed bat died.
- An Arabian oryx was born, a male weighing thirteen pounds.
- Mumbi, a female lowland gorilla, underwent surgery for peritonitis. "Critically ill."
- Another Arabian oryx, a female, was born. She was rejected by her mother and was placed with another nursing female (the mother of the male born earlier). The newborn was "apparently adopted" and "was observed nursing from the surrogate."
- A giraffe was born: "normal birth, seen nursing from female." It was the first viable giraffe birth in the zoo's history.
- A Burmese python laid sixty eggs.
- Two moustached tamarins were born at the small mammal house. One was killed by the parents; the other was pulled to be hand-reared.

- A Mexican beaded lizard was found dead. "Saved head for Education. Body too decomposed to necropsy."
- A piglet died at the farm.
- There was a minor electrical fire in the great ape house; the building was closed for the day.
- A trumpeter swan egg was hatched at the bird house. It was the first hatching of that species in recent times.

The entries go on and on; the set of journals reaches back for years. A lion fell into the moat. A keeper was injured by a hostile animal. A wolf escaped from its exhibit. The clipped, unemotional entries state a series of interrelated truths about life in the zoo. It can be a joyful place, a sad place, a dangerous place. Always it is a challenging place.

That is what keeps it going. The staff are there (often at night and on weekends as well) not for the money; they could earn more driving a cab or collecting garbage. They are not there for the status, although some positions provide that. Most of them get up early, to arrive before 8 A.M., and bring their concerns home with them at night, because they are fascinated by animals. And because they know that a bonding can take place between them and the animals.

That bonding, that passion, can at times border on obsession. Anthropomorphism does exist at the zoo. Most of the zoo staff know what Bent Jorgensen, director of the Copenhagen Zoo, once said: "A tiger is a tiger and not a human in a tiger skin. It is unfair to treat animals as human beings, it is unfair to animals."

Yet, despite the danger of loving an animal too well, that love thrives. For those who work in a zoo, zoos are the best place for animals in this dehumanizing world.

Jon R. Luoma, in his book *A Crowded Ark*, noted:

A compelling case could be made that, if one considers the best interests of animals as individuals, they are *better off* in zoos than in the wild. Animals in the wild are subject to a Homeric catalogue of parasites and diseases. In good zoos, they receive, from extensively trained staff veterinarians, far better medical care than many of the earth's humans ever will enjoy. They are free from sudden, painful death by predation. They live longer lives, their toenails clipped, cataracts removed, lacerations stitched, boils lanced, bumblefoot salved, and hunger sated with carefully balanced, sometimes vitamin-enriched foods.

Yet, Luoma qualified his verdict: "It is still a box with wild animals living in it rather than where they should be." However, as he pointed out, " 'where they should be' isn't there anymore."

It is a dilemma faced by those who work in a zoo. Most agree that a wild untainted by the presence of humans and their destructive fury would be best for animals. Zoos save animals from that fury, from extinction. Yet zoo workers appreciate what Heini Hediger, the well-known director of the Zurich Zoo, once wrote:

In the zoo, where the animal is protected from surprise attacks by the bars, and where every inmate has ample food provided daily, both of these main activities [avoiding enemies, seeking food] disappear. Thus a vacuum—an occupational blank, as it were—is caused, which may lead in the worst cases to complete boredom . . . a distorted or even morbid manner, resulting in all kinds of stereotyped movements; running to and fro hour after hour; endless walking in circles, or all sorts of silly behavior and grimacing, even self-mutilation.

Finally, there are those who feel that zoos are barbaric denials of the rights of animals. In their book *Zoo Culture*, Bob Mullan and Garry Marvin wrote:

Zoos are institutions established for human pleasure, but it is pleasure that can quite clearly be problematic. For zoos represent the power of human beings to command the presence of living creatures which would normally absent themselves from human gaze. Confined in the zoo in an alien environment, they are 'displaced' creatures, and the human visitor must at some level recognize this, for there is clearly a disjunction between the animal's environment in the zoo and that in which it would live if allowed. In a subtle way, anthropomorphism disguises this fact by humanizing the animal, thus suggesting that it is in its appropriate environment.

The debate has raged on for decades, and will continue to simmer. It is not central to the lives of those who work at the zoo, but most of them know that the ideological struggle persists, and they pursue compromise solutions. They keep their attention on the animals.

Someday the wild may be restored, although that is not likely, and zoos may cease to exist (not likely either). It is more probable that the best zoos will prosper and will continue to be the only contact most people will have with animals. At Lincoln Park, the staff takes that responsibility seriously.

*S*unrise in late spring. The zoo is quiet. The grounds don't open until 8 A.M. The buildings open an hour later. The animals have their privacy. Then the first humans arrive, to bring the place to life. A veterinarian with a sick leopard on her mind. A curator working on a research paper without the accompaniment of a ringing phone. A great ape keeper clutching a baby chimp she is raising at home, to feed it during the night when no one would be at the zoo to feed it there.

In the small mammal house, the creatures of the night—owl monkeys, armadillos, civets, bats, and others—have been awake while others slept. Now they will sleep. The animals who have been kept indoors—the lions, tigers, polar bears—can emerge into the sunlight and rest or play as their spirits move them.

The first joggers pound through the zoo. Businesspeople bearing attaché cases strut deliberately along, choosing to share their early morning time expeditiously with the animals they pass. The first contingents of mothers and children arrive; the day will bring hordes of them.

The sea lions bask motionless atop the rock formation in their pool, expressing a contentment beyond words. Inside the buildings the animals stir, make their sounds, stare at the world.

Lights go on. Piles of food are carried into kitchens. The administrative staff arrives, dressed to stay clean. A photocopier wheezes. Typewriters begin to clatter. Keepers turn on their hoses, chop food for the animals, walk past cages, looking for pleasure—the presence of a newborn—or trouble—the signs of sickness.

In the distance, the hum of traffic deepens.

The city and the zoo have come to life.

2

AMONG THE MAMMALS

Even in the land of the American dream, it is rare for a boyhood wish to become a grown man's occupation. For Mark Rosenthal, the zoo's curator of mammals, it happened.

He was born in 1946 and grew up just a few blocks from the zoo. His mother took him there regularly; it was his favorite outing. When he was ten, he met Marlin Perkins, the zoo director and the host of the TV series "Zoo Parade." "If you want fun, work in a zoo," Perkins told him, oversimplifying the reality to coddle a young boy's fantasy.

At twenty-two, Mark got his bachelor's degree in zoology from Southern Illinois University; during his summers there, he worked at the Lincoln Park Zoo's children's zoo. After graduation, he took the Chicago Park District exam for animal keeper. He finished first.

After a year in the keeper's job, he was named associate curator in 1969—and embarked on a master's in zoology at Northeastern Illinois State University. The year he got that degree, 1975, he was named curator of mammals, at age twenty-nine. He has been curator ever since.

15

Mark's domain was vast. He governed the large mammal house, the small mammal house, the wolves-bears habitat, the primate house, the lion house, the great ape house, and the antelope-zebra area.

It was the zoo equivalent of being the mayor of New York City. In order to manage it, he had to delegate authority and rely upon the skills of the keepers who reported to him. Fortunately, they had dependable skills.

A tall (6′2″), dark, husky (210 pounds), and bespectacled bachelor, Mark spent more time at the zoo than he did in his nearby apartment.

On a gray, uncharacteristically cool Monday in June, he got to work before 8 A.M. and went to the zoo office in the modern bunker that housed it, the Crown-Field Center. He checked the red daily journal that the staff kept to note events of importance. There wasn't much in it that day. A lizard had been donated to the zoo. A red wallaby was sent on a breeding loan to another zoo.

Mark phoned the keepers who reported to him, to find out who was on duty, who was not—and who was assigned to care for the elephants. He walked over to the small mammal house, where he lingered in the kitchen, sampled a few grapes, and chatted with the senior keeper. The keeper reported a broken window—minor vandalism—in the cage of a springhaas (a rabbit-like rodent). The window needed repair, and the keeper had to file a work order to get it done. Mark walked out into the exhibit area and checked the damage. The glass was cracked but not yet dangerous to animal or visitors.

He resumed his walk along the curved walkway to his cramped office in the large mammal house. On a blackboard outside the door to his office, the keepers had noted, "Maddis, spectacled bear, has a bad right eye. Jocko, Jr., maned wolf, is very sick." He knew that the staff veterinarians would have detailed reports on both later.

One of the daily keeper reports on his desk noted that one of the sea lions wasn't eating.

"Could be pregnant," he murmured. "Or could be sick."

A saki monkey had given birth.

"That's exciting, because it rarely happens in captivity," he noted.

His office was packed. Copies of *Wildlife Review*. Files, a typewriter, a tape recorder, a collection of well-worn pipes and some tobacco. A "trouble" alarm box and a separate fire alarm box. A pile of booklets: "Lincoln Park Zoological Gardens International Studbook for the Spectacled Bear." The "studbook keeper" was credited: Mark Rosenthal. It was a kind of pedigree book for the breed of bear that most intrigued him. The spectacled bear, from South America, was an endangered species; Mark had assembled a small collection of them at the zoo, and the breeding program had been successful. As editor of the studbook, he provided information on the bears—where they could be found in captivity, which ones had died, and which ones had been born—for all those interested in the fate of the species.

A young woman keeper walked into Mark's office to let him know that one of the vets would be coming over to see the sick wolf. The phone rang. A keeper was needed at the lion house; Mark had to shift one from the farm. He was responsible for half of the keepers at the zoo.

Some of them were happy to work for him; others were not. His critics found him to be imperious; his loyalists found him to be concerned. His personality did not reflect extremes: spontaneous laughter or sudden rage. He remained stoical under pressure, often expressionless in emotionally charged situations. Some keepers assumed he could not manage everything he had been asked to manage, responsibilities collected over the years. Friendly keepers were pleased to help him manage; critics were not.

He tended to staff the large mammal house, where he spent time in his office, with docile, uncomplaining keepers. He spent time, as well, at the great ape house, where the senior keeper, Pat Sass, was an old friend and a fan. He was literal in dealing with keepers he knew might oppose him on the most trivial of matters. He did not try to court them.

His large physical presence and his noncommittal demeanor were taken as a taunt by some, as a comfort by others. For his part, he did not engage in criticism of the keepers in the company of others. Some of his keepers did not share that sense of tact.

Despite the low-level irritants, Mark worked at managing his realm. There was little time for revolts at the zoo; there was too much work to be done.

Mark sat in his office and contemplated an event that could have brought negative publicity to the zoo—but didn't. The previous Friday, a wolf had escaped, somehow managing to scale a ledge in its outdoor habitat and leap into some bushes on the outside. A visitor had spotted it and had summoned a keeper. The keeper got help; the wolf—not looking for a fight—was cornered. The vets arrived and darted (tranquilized) it. The procedure went smoothly, but when Mark was told about it on Monday, he said, "Anything with teeth can be dangerous. We marshalled our forces, and this time it worked out well. The wolf didn't get hurt. The public didn't get hurt. A keeper didn't get hurt."

Still sitting at his desk, he seemed weary.

"I don't like Mondays," he sighed. "You walk in, and they've got twenty thousand things for you to do." One of those 20,000 things: a DeBrazza's guenon, a monkey, gave birth on Friday night. He would have to take a look at mother and child.

He had walked and talked and conferred, and it was only 9 A.M., with a full day ahead. He grabbed his walkie-talkie and headed out of his office. He strolled along the behind-the-scenes area in the large mammal house. He approached two sea lions in small, separate pools.

"Hi, Rocky!" Mark shouted. The small sea lion came out of the water, obviously recognizing him. Rocky was a one-year-old, raised since birth at the zoo. When it was born, its mother had abandoned it; the keepers had hand-raised it, taught it to live in water (newborn sea lions cannot swim), weaned it to solid food. Now, Rocky was eating fish and was getting used to a variety of people and sounds. Mark had moved one of the nonaggressive females from the main pool, Omega, to be Rocky's neighbor in the holding area. If all went well, both sea lions would join the group in the main pool.

Mark continued his stroll. He passed the giraffes, calm and inquisitive. A rhino lumbered across its holding pen toward him. He reached over the wall and patted it. He visited the marmoset breeding room, a holding area for the tiny monkeys. Roaches had invaded the room; it was a serious problem. Marmosets eat roaches, which contain worms that can kill marmosets. Surgery must be done to remove the parasites.

Down the hall, Bozie—a twelve-year-old female elephant from Sri Lanka—was getting a scrub and a bath from a pair of keepers.

"The keepers are trained in-house to manage the elephants," Mark pointed out. "The elephants are trained, too, to respond to voice commands. It's like training dogs, only we use an ankus, that short pole with the curved hook on the end of it. It's not sharp. It is, really, just an extension of the keeper's arm. It makes a point, but with love. You can't abuse an elephant, because it is very large and could be seriously hostile. It must exist in a controlled situation."

Bozie stared at Mark; the knowing quality of her sleepy eyes begged for anthropomorphic interpretation, but Mark did not volunteer any as he returned the gaze. He did not believe that he could easily read the minds of mammals. As elephant and man looked at each other, one of the keepers handed her keys to the elephant, who grasped them in its trunk.

"Drop them," the keeper instructed.

The elephant dropped the keys.

The second keeper asked Bozie to lift a leg. Bozie obliged.

"We're going to mate Bozie with a male at the Springfield, Missouri, zoo," Mark announced. "We'll get her there in a special elephant truck. Uneventfully, we hope."

As he spoke, Bozie had opened her mouth on command, and was kneeling.

Mark ended his tour of the large mammals; he had other visits to pay.

At the zoo office, he chatted with the registrar, the computer specialist who kept the zoo's animal inventory up to date. Then, he walked to the primate house, where he chatted with the senior keeper, who was preparing food for the animals. Mark sampled a banana. On the wall, a list of foods was posted: apples, celery, grapes, lettuce, spinach, oranges, nuts, sweet potatoes, smelt, eggs, escarole, onions.

As Mark walked behind the scenes—the inner corridor behind the cages—he spotted a female mandrill "soliciting" a male, backing up to him.

"She's pregnant, so it's not sexual. She's being submissive, letting him know that she knows he's the boss," Mark said.

He headed for the antelope-zebra area, to a room filled with video equipment. When the wolf escaped, a summer helper in the education department had a video camera and recorded the incident. Mark popped the cassette into a video recorder and watched.

"A woman ran up and said, 'Mister keeper, there's a fox running around!' I looked and saw the maned wolf. We contained it. We used the emergency procedure for animal capture. The vet darted it, it fell asleep, and we shipped it off to the hospital," the keeper recited.

Mark was satisfied with the keeper's performance, in life and on tape.

He walked briskly back to his own office. He phoned a woman at the Louisville Zoo; she needed his advice about caring for a tamarin. Two keepers, both young women, entered to let him know that the sick maned wolf was not in such great shape. "It's deaf and blind," one of them said. The tentative diagnosis was neurological; the wolf could have a brain tumor.

The hours passed. After a brief lunch at a modest restaurant in the park (but not at the zoo; few zoo workers ate at the zoo concessions), Mark plunged into the pile of paperwork that obscured the surface of his desk: forms, work orders, reports, journals, correspondence, and more.

"I was closer to the animals as a keeper than I am as a curator," he sighed.

At 3 P.M., Mark attended a meeting in a classroom at the Crown-Field Center, a discussion about the redesign of the primate house. Also present were Les Fisher, his second-in-command Dennis Meritt, and Chuck Harris, the zoo society's project manager for building design and renovation.

For two hours, the foursome talked about the preliminary plans for transforming the old-fashioned primate house into a more naturalistic exhibit—fewer animals in larger habitats. One suggestion was raised: simply replace the bars and mesh with glass.

"It'll still look like a jail," Dennis stressed. "It's silly to put in glass with the same old tile cages."

Les liked the notion of building vertical spaces for the monkeys, following the example set in the modernistic great ape house. "In most zoos, the gorillas sit on their asses. When the height potential is there, it generates activity," he said.

"Sight lines are important," Mark added. "But we don't want visitors to see only dangling *tushes*."

"Whatever we do, remember this: we don't have space as a great advantage in this zoo. But we do have intimacy. You can get close to an animal here," Les pointed out.

"It's also very important to hear the animals," Mark said. "That's why we put mikes in the ape house. They're behind glass, sure, but they can be heard."

The conversation rambled and, at 5 P.M., wound down to silence. There would be many other meetings like that one; the changing face of the zoo was a common concern and would continue to be until all the major renovations were done.

Mark dealt with the city bureaucracy by being patient.

He remembered a small mammal exhibit he had worked on. Most of the difficult work was done; all that remained

was for a park district crew to return to remove one final
load of earth from the exhibit. He asked for that.

Two years later, they showed up.

He remembered, as well, visiting one of the park district
executives in his office. The executive opened a large file
drawer and pointed to a thick stack of work orders.

"See those? The people who sent them in never called
again to find out about them. If they didn't care, why
should I? It's one way of finding out what's urgent and what
isn't. You people at the zoo keep calling, so we get those
jobs done," he said.

Sometimes, Mark thought.

It was useless to be impulsive, to expect work to be done
within minutes, Mark knew. He courted the workers—the
painters and carpenters and electricians and ironworkers
and plumbers—who belonged to the park district force. He
hoped that when he declared a situation to be an emergency, they would believe him.

It was important, Mark believed, to remain calm, retain
information, and stay in touch with the people who worked
for him. It was important, too, to appear to be in charge,
even when you weren't. Troops needed a commander, he
felt, so it was vital to assume the role, even if you didn't feel
like leading at a given moment.

A sensible manager dispensed with trivia, whenever
possible, with a minimal expenditure of effort.

A keeper meeting in the large mammal house on a
muggy day in June: to work on a clogged drain in the wolf
habitat, a woman keeper needed a pair of waders; the only
pair around was torn and leaked. Mark knew that there
might be a spare pair at the bird house.

"How energetic are you?" he asked the keeper.

She smiled demurely but didn't head for the door.

"We're burning daylight," he said. "Let's move on."

She moved, languorously.

Mark passed her on his way out the door.

He visited the newborn DeBrazza's guenon. He had seen
it before, but a visitor had stopped him to call his attention

to what she deemed parental neglect on the part of the newborn's mother. Mark notified the senior keeper in the primate house to keep visitors away from the cage. At times, monkeys were disturbed by close-up visitors. When Mark got to the cage, the mother was holding her baby.

"The baby is in the right position," Mark said to the keeper.

"Yes, the baby's doing real good," the keeper agreed. "I don't see anything wrong."

"Sensitize your people to keep an eye on them. Maybe you can get a docent to sit here and keep an eye out, too," Mark suggested. Docents—volunteer teachers—could be employed on such missions (but the keepers objected when docents wanted to play hands-on roles with the animals).

Mark moved along, to the great ape house. He enjoyed observing the apes, and he enjoyed chatting with the senior keeper, Pat Sass, who kept him informed about the animals, their joys and their stresses. Pat had been at the zoo for twenty-five years; she had known Mark since he was a young boy wanting to work at the zoo.

Mark learned that Terra, a twenty-four-year-old female gorilla on loan from the Milwaukee Zoo, was pregnant again. The gorilla breeding program was one of the most productive and most famous in the world; it was one of Les Fisher's continuing passions. An occasional frustration did arise. Terra had been introduced to Otto with breeding in mind. But Otto, a massive and occasionally troublesome gorilla, didn't like her and wouldn't collaborate. Frank, a more cooperative male, welcomed the opportunity. Their unions produced two babies, one alive, one stillborn. This would be Terra's third offspring. But Pat knew that Otto could be mean.

"If Otto bothers her, chases her, we ought to keep her away from him during her last trimester," Pat told Mark. "She gets riled up and doesn't turn the other cheek. He could hurt her."

As they spoke, a female chimp in a nearby cage clutched her baby. She turned around, her back to Mark, and she looked at him over her shoulder. Mark scratched her back, satisfying her wish.

In the main areas of the building, gorillas, chimps, and orangutans (in their separate exhibits) leaped, bellowed, banged against the glass, scampered around noisily.

Mark made his way up a narrow staircase to the top of the building, which opened to the outside area for the gorillas. Most of the building was, in fact, underground, but the gorillas could cavort in the sunlight or simply bask in it.

Frank's troop of lowland gorillas was outside; a small, animated baby rode on its mother's back. A female gorilla sat calmly, munching on grass it plucked delicately from the earth, blade by blade. There were three troops in all, led by males Otto, Frank, and Koundu. In the wild, those males would lead, find food, settle disputes, protect the troop against the dangers of the wild, and breed. At the zoo, their role was less demanding: they governed and they bred.

Pat Sass and her keeper staff kept their eyes on the apes and recorded pertinent observations in their daily keeper reports. Frank was one of their favorite subjects:

"Frank bent out of shape about something today. He did not go up; did not move over into nursery. Charged at girls; knocked Hope over and has been slamming into doors. The ultimate pain in the !*@!*!

"Debbie and Kumba got into a screaming, swiping fight at 4:30 P.M. Frank let them fight for a little while, then ran in between the two of them and pushed them in opposite directions. Could not see any bashes, etc., on either one. No blood dripping from anyone. No one favoring anything. They did not resume fighting after Frank intervened."

Mark appreciated the apes; they were smart, imaginative, responsive. When he went to the great ape house, he could get close to them, inches away, with only wire mesh between him and them. It was a throwback to his time as a keeper. Keepers participated; they were on the front line.

Curators were observers, analysts, supervisors. A curator could be a critic, but usually after the fact, not as an eyewitness; it made some curators uncomfortable, like the parent asked to discipline a child who had been unruly while the parent had been at work. The keepers were the game players, on the field; the curators commented from the press box. There was a difference.

Mark passed a small orangutan, a baby recovering from a broken hand inflicted by an overzealous older animal. It was in a playpen, clutching a small blanket, like one of its counterparts in the world of humans. The keepers realized that it had been injured when she held her hand strangely and whined. In the wild, animals resist expressing pain; it makes them vulnerable to preying adversaries. At the zoo, they were less guarded. In the case of the baby orangutan, surgery had repaired the hand.

Mark reached over into the playpen and gently scratched the orangutan's head. It peered up at him and made a nodding motion.

It was time to move on; the luxury of getting to know an animal was the keepers' reward, not his.

He walked quickly into the antelope-zebra building. The senior keeper told him that all was in order, that the yards had been cleaned early that morning. Two keepers not in sight were walking a camel, he told Mark. Such routine matters were important to Mark; cleaning and feeding were forms of drudgery, but they were essential, and Mark did not take them for granted. Better to be a pest about them, he felt.

When he got back to the large mammal house, the keepers were at their midmorning break, devouring micro-waved pizza. Mark grabbed a slice and a can of Pepsi, then retreated into his office. He spent the next ninety minutes shuffling papers at his desk, before driving off to lunch in his 1985 Plymouth Horizon, with the license plate ZOO MAN.

After lunch, as he returned to his office, he noticed the

rows of small children in identical T-shirts. "It must be summer," he said. "The school groups are gone, and the day campers are here."

Inside the building, he could hear music coming from a radio near the indoor giraffe area.

"For years around here, the keepers were told to whisper when they were around the hoofed animals—the gazelles, the zebras, the antelope, the deer, the giraffes, the rhinos. So if there *was* any noise, the animals would go crazy. No more. We want them to get used to sounds. So when a keeper drops a shovel, the elephant will know what it is and won't get excited. It makes sense," he said.

Meetings.

It would be easy to assume, from afar, that a zoo curator sits around petting animals. That is a fallacy.

Mark worked—as manager, supervisor, researcher, and conservationist-educator—but he did not have time to fondle animals. He spent as much time with humans as he did with animals. On another sweltering summer day, he had several meetings to fill the day.

At 8 A.M., he attended a keepers' meeting in the auditorium of the Crown-Field Center. Les Fisher presided.

The room was half-filled with people dressed in the familiar keeper colors, khaki and brown. Stragglers continued to enter after Les had begun.

"Are the others coming by elephant?" he asked. His manner was fatherly, relaxed, folksy. But there was often a message in his wit.

Although the meeting was called a keepers' meeting, it rarely became a vehicle for keeper complaints or disputes; those centered in Les's own office, where grievances could be aired privately. Les opposed open warfare; he preferred to be the zoo's ultimate ombudsman.

He used the keepers' meeting to keep the keeper staff informed, to remind them that they were the core of the zoo family.

As Mark sat in the back row, barely noticed, it was Les's

show. He told the keepers that planning was proceeding on schedule for the changes to be made at the bird, primate, and lion houses. The children's zoo renovation, under construction, would be ready in four months, he hoped. A few snickers in the audience symbolized the cynicism that accompanied all such announcements.

There was a "scary fire in the ape house," he told those who hadn't already heard about it. "We had trouble finding the source of it for a few minutes. Happily, nothing bad happened. A supplementary heater was smoking." He wanted to use that event to make a point: recognize that emergencies can occur and be ready for them.

"Think of the staff and the safety of the public first," he urged. "But know how to save the animals. Keep thinking about how you'd react to a fire. And repair faulty equipment before it causes a tragedy."

Mark had known about the fire; he was grateful that it had not turned into something horrifying. He knew how difficult it would be to lead the apes out of that building to safety. The thought of making such an attempt troubled him.

Les went on. Some topiary figures of animals were being installed in front of the penguin-seabird house. "If we're successful, it'll be fun," he said. "It's just a little thing, of course, but if you see someone abusing them, scare them off."

He pointed out that the selection of a new concessionaire for food at the zoo was still in progress. The winning bidder would improve the quality of food sold at the zoo; it couldn't be worse than it had been. But all that was months away.

He introduced Gene Brimer, a new employee reporting to Mark; Gene was an experienced pest control expert (he disliked the term "exterminator" because he felt that he never truly obliterated the foe). He would take on the roaches, mice, rats, and other creatures attacking the zoo grounds and the animals. There were mice visible, running around cages in the small mammal house, in the bird house, and elsewhere.

"The visitors will see them," Les said, wearily, like a father telling a child how important it was to keep the room clean. "We must make a dent in the problem."

Brimer, a personable, gray-haired veteran of such wars, nodded and smiled, more as a sign of courage than joy in the nature of the fray.

The meeting ended just before 9 A.M. Mark strolled through the building for his next meeting, Les's weekly staff gathering in the conference room.

It opened with Mark in his role as visual-aid producer. With the help of a docent, he had put together a ten-minute slide-and-audio presentation: a guide for keepers on the potential dangers in their work. Its message was blunt:

- Animals protect their space.
- You can't predict their reactions, no matter how well you think you know them.
- Elephants are the most threatening. They can cuddle you to death, just by leaning against you.
- Animals kick, bite, and use their horns and tusks.
- Always carry a tool for self-defense, and always be aware—in advance—of an escape route.
- Don't be casual. A jaguar can kill with one blow of its paw to the head. Even rodents can bite and scratch. A parrot can crack a hard nut with its beak; it can crack a finger just as easily. Talons are designed to tear flesh; they work. An alligator can move at a speed of forty miles per hour. A tiger can be provoked by something as subtle as a keeper's shampoo, a new and strange scent.

The soundtrack recited the unadorned advice, while graphic photos—some from newspapers—made the points.

When Mark finished his presentation, he announced that it was truly a low-budget production. He'd gotten it done for a total expenditure of $50. Now, he hoped, all the keepers would view it and learn from it.

Les again presided at the meeting. He repeated much of what he had told the keepers earlier. He then discussed the results of a recent keeper exam conducted by the park district. Approximately six hundred people took the test, and only thirty passed it. Most of those who passed were existing keepers who wanted to turn their temporary status into permanent status—and many of them didn't do too well on the test. In other words, as Les explained, the test may have been unrealistically tough—but there was nothing to be done about that. At least new keepers to be added to the permanent roster would be those already on the job.

Les paused, sighed, and mentioned some papers that had been on his desk when he left the night before and were gone when he got to work in the morning.

"It's part of the never-ending silliness at the zoo," he said, with a pained smile on his face.

An animal rights zealot had contacted him, he said, wanting to know how many animals had died, and why they had died, in the past twenty years. "There are no secrets at the zoo," he said, but he added that information from the precomputer age might take months to collect.

The group around the conference table—Mark and the other curators, the assistant director (Dennis Meritt), the veterinarians, and a representative from the zoo society staff—squirmed almost in unison. Few of them wanted to oppose the good intentions of the animal rights legions; few of them wanted to be obedient to them either.

The meeting lapsed into small talk about troublesome employees. Given the bureaucratic red tape, it wasn't easy to fire anyone; serious infractions had to be documented carefully and that often took months. One example: an alcoholic who had agreed to accept treatment was slated to be back at work after a prolonged absence. There was concern about his ability to function. Another employee had pleaded for a promotion that couldn't be granted; no vacancy existed. A third, formerly at the zoo, had left the zoo business for another field. The consensus of those present was that the move elevated the quality of the zoo profession.

The meeting ended an hour after it began, but for Mark, who sat impassively through most of the staff meeting, jotting notes on a ruled pad, it was simply time to attend another meeting. That one was in Les's office, with Clarence Wright, curator of reptiles, and representatives from the zoo staff and the zoo society.

The American Association of Zoological Parks and Aquariums was going to hold a regional conference in Chicago in April 1988, and three local institutions—Lincoln Park Zoo, Brookfield Zoo, and the Shedd Aquarium—would host it.

What ideas could Les and his staff contribute to the organization of that conference? What workshops might be useful?

Among the suggestions: a workshop on pest control, another on the use of video to study animal behavior (an activity of importance to Mark), a panel on construction and renovation, others on marketing, fund-raising (for which the zoo society was respected), outreach programs (the zoo was the first in America to set up a traveling zoo), publications, keeper in-service training (like Mark's slide show).

The conversation lagged; the conference wasn't soon enough for those present to be eager and inventive.

"How about a workshop on egg management?" Mark asked.

The others looked at him incredulously.

"You know, what to do with eggs. How to dye them at Easter," he added with a faint giggle.

It brought the meeting to a close, subject to be considered again at a later date.

It was close to lunchtime, and Mark needed a break.

The conference room had been turned into the setting for a party to celebrate Pat Sass's twenty-fifth anniversary at the zoo. Mark could toast Pat and munch on the food available.

He never wore a jacket, but almost always wore a tie. In keeping with a tradition set by Les Fisher, many of his ties were animal prints. For Pat's party, he wore his monkey tie.

After the party, he headed back to the large mammal house and his office. As he entered the modern building, with its wide, winding walkway past spacious exhibits, a woman with a small child in tow stopped him. Her sunglasses had fallen into the moat at the elephant exhibit. Could they be retrieved?

Yes, Mark told her. He asked one of the keepers to do it.

He phoned an electronics supplier to solicit a bid for video equipment to monitor the outdoor area at the great ape house. He called a state agency to request an application for certification for the new staff pest control expert, Gene Brimer. Despite Gene's view of his work, Mark referred to him as "the exterminator."

The he headed to the bear line, behind the scenes.

He noticed that the large wooden stockade doors to the bear line had been left open. So had an inner heavy metal door. A nearby sign read: BEARS AND WOLVES ARE DANGEROUS.

Mark spoke into his walkie-talkie, trying to find the person who hadn't locked the doors. (A large inner door and those on the individual bear dens prevented the bears and wolves from emerging, but for Mark, there was a principle at stake.)

His walkie-talkie crackled; a keeper had responded to his call. He asked her to come to the bear line, and within a few minutes, she did. He showed her the open doors. She took his demonstration to be an accusation and denied that she had left the doors open.

"Well, let's find out who did," he said. "It makes me crazed."

He entered the bear line; it was like entering a prison, with heavy metal doors throughout and long, dark corridors, thick concrete walls, bars, peepholes, large padlocks, closed-circuit TV. He moved past the empty dens; most of the bears were outside, and two wolves inside were sleeping. He looked at the floor, then tugged at his walkie-talkie again. A keeper answered.

"There's mouse crap all over," he said, his voice rising, but stopping short of anger.

He moved on, along the corridor past the bears and wolves. Below a slot on one den, a sign read: DANGER. BEAR CAN REACH PAW OUT! In that slot, a large wet nose protruded, an open mouth displayed spikelike teeth grinding against the bar in the slot, a clawed paw barely visible. Mark stopped. He patted the paw, gingerly. It belonged to one of the spectacled bears he had collected; the zoo had seven of them, with six others out on breeding loan.

He went outdoors, to check the bears' outdoor habitat. A mother bear, Goggles, and her daughter, Annie, were running around the exhibit, which had been designed to duplicate the South American setting that the species knew well: high clifflike walls made of Gunite (a mixture of cement, sand, and water sprayed to specifications and used throughout the zoo to duplicate rock formations), trees, dirt, pools—separated from the public by a deep dry moat.

When Mark leaned toward them at the railing that faced the exhibit, the two bears stopped and looked at him. He made a fluttering sound, imitating their own sound. They paid attention to him.

He smiled. "I do a good monkey imitation, too," he said.

He couldn't linger; he had another meeting to attend. He went to the antelope-zebra house, to the video room, where he met with Pat Sass and a pair of docents. They discussed a chimp behavior study, inspired by Jane Goodall's celebrated research, that would involve docent observers in the great ape house. They would watch the chimps and make notes about their behavior. All the work would, if successful, compare chimps' behavior in captivity to Goodall's findings on chimp behavior in the wild. Some believed that chimps in zoos played to the crowds. The study might confirm that.

Although he hoped to leave early for a relaxing cruise on

Lake Michigan on a cousin's boat, Mark sat through the meeting patiently; he liked those present, and the project intrigued him. But when the meeting did end, he thanked those who attended and headed out of the building toward his car.

All days weren't gratifying. There were days dominated by nagging frustrations.

On such a day, with a searing June sun overhead, he had made plans to record on videotape the behavior of a pair of trumpeter swans. The nesting pair, particularly sensitive in that mode, had attacked several flamingos, killing two of them by breaking one's neck and traumatizing another beyond medical rescue. Nesting swans did indeed protect their turf—their offspring were at stake—but this pair presented a challenge to Mark. He felt that a tape of the swans being aggressive would be instructive.

He informed those whose help would be needed. Several keepers would be present, alongside the waterfowl lagoon. A friend of Mark's—the wife of an orthopedic surgeon who had operated on some of the apes—would operate the video camera. Mark would direct. Kathy Brown, the senior keeper in the bird house, who had been attacked by the swans recently (but not seriously wounded) would be on hand, with a large push broom to protect herself. The swans' wings had long been pinioned, clipped, to prevent them from flying, from escaping.

The swans were about to be transferred to Indian Boundary Zoo, a satellite zoo run by Lincoln Park. The value of videotaping the swans made Mark's decision to proceed an urgent one. He told the participants to be on the site at 1:30 P.M.

At his office that morning, he mediated a dispute between two women elephant keepers in the large mammal house. There weren't specific grievances; it was more a matter of temporary incompatibility. He set up a meeting with one of them, Pat, a middle-aged, calm, experienced keeper. The other, Robin, young and feisty, was not at work that day. Larry, the senior keeper, sat in on Mark's meeting with Pat.

From Mark's viewpoint, it was vital for keepers working together to maintain a sense of détente. There was the safety factor; distracted keepers were vulnerable keepers. Large mammals could be lethal.

They met behind closed doors, and when they emerged, Mark hugged Pat reassuringly. Later, he told her, they'd meet with Robin.

It was time for another test: to put together the two sea lions—Rocky and Omega—being held in the separate pools in the holding area at the large mammal house.

If the two sea lions could overcome their fear or reticence, if they would swim in the same pool, he could put them together in a larger pool, in the hippo yard. If that worked, he could move them to a holding pool in the sea lion pool complex. If they were compatible there, he could open the gate into the main pool.

There were risks. "They're like gorillas, in the sense that there are no social graces among sea lions, if you're new to the troop. We can't predict how it will go," he said.

He peered at the two sea lions from behind the wall that separated them from the behind-the-scenes corridor. The two pools were surrounded by a wide concrete deck, providing plenty of room for the sea lions to move around. A small platform, painted red, offered one the opportunity to perch. There was a small two-step staircase for a similar purpose.

Rocky was in his pool; a keeper was tossing fish to him. Omega was being fed, too. Then one of the young women keepers entered the area and unlocked the gate between the two pool areas. Rocky came out of the water and bounced around the floor toward the open space, then retreated to his own pool. Omega did the same, not crossing the border where the gate had been.

Minutes passed as both sea lions emerged from their pools, approached the midpoint, peered at each other, and retreated. Rocky tentatively crossed over to Omega's side, then quickly waddled back to his own.

Mark watched, impatient; he had other work to do. He asked the keepers to watch the pair and let him know what developed. He returned to his office and began sorting through the papers on his desk: forms, letters, work orders, daily keeper reports from all the mammal houses. As he did, a thunderstorm came to life overhead, and a single streak of lightning triggered a loud thunderclap.

And the power failed in the large mammal house.

It was not the first time that had happened. Mark was not shocked. He used his walkie-talkie to inform the main zoo office of the power failure; he reached Larry, the senior keeper, and urged him to check on the moods of the animals in the large mammal house. A few minutes later, Larry responded: no problems to report.

The park district power house was nearby, and the electricians in it would be at work tracing the source of the failure. The rain, which had been heavy, was lessening. Mark made sure that all the keepers on duty had flashlights. He grabbed a Lincoln Park Zoo rain slicker from a hook and headed out to lunch.

When he returned, the power was still off, but the keepers and the animals were undaunted. He went to visit the sea lions. Several keepers and a docent were monitoring matters, but there was little to monitor. Rocky was out of the water, attempting to hide behind the small staircase, his head down. Omega was sitting on the red platform, a few feet away from him. They had achieved one objective: they were on the same side of the gate.

Omega had shared Rocky's pool with him, a keeper told Mark, but just briefly. If Mark was disappointed by the minimal progress, he didn't express it to the keepers.

It was time to videotape the trumpeter swans.

The swans—elegant, graceful birds—stood proudly near the pond, where dozens of ducks and geese had gathered. The swans paid little attention to the other birds. They were conversing face-to-face. They trumpeted at each other, lowered their long necks and raised them in unison; the choreography was precise and beautiful.

Mark signaled to Kathy Brown, and Kathy approached the swans, broom ahead of her. The swans' chatter became more animated as Kathy approached, carefully. The birds became agitated and began to flap their wings, not in emulation of flight, but as weapons of self-defense. Mark's camerawoman was ready, camera pointed at the scene, motor running.

Kathy moved closer to the swans, poking the broom at them. The birds retreated, slowly. Kathy continued to move toward them. The swans stopped, ready for a confrontation. One flapped its wings at the broom, then was joined by the second. Kathy backed up. The swans appeared to celebrate with loud trumpeting.

Mark's camera-wielding friend noticed it first: one of the swans had been injured. In flapping its wing against the broom, it had lacerated it and was bleeding. The smudges of blood were evident against the impeccable whiteness of the bird's feathers.

The two swans moved toward the pond and stepped into it, gliding away, trumpeting at each other, a communication no one there could interpret.

"She'll wash it off in the water," Kathy said.

"Keep an eye on her," Mark instructed.

The swans glided off, side by side, toward the middle of the pond. Yes, nesting swans protect their own, Mark knew, and that—as it turned out—was not a fact out of a textbook. Mark had seen it proved in life and had captured it on videotape.

If he regretted the injury to the swan, he didn't articulate it at that moment.

A few days later, the swans were transferred to Indian Boundary, and the flamingos were safe again. But Kathy had second thoughts about the "ugly" role she had played. Had she been tempted to provoke those swans? She considered that possibility for months.

When Mark got to his office the next morning, he was told that Rocky and Omega were not exactly friendly.

Rocky had stopped eating. And when Omega entered his pool, Rocky would leave it. Mark asked the keepers to try another tack: keep the sea lions together during the day and apart at night for a week.

A few minutes later, Mark learned that the sick maned wolf might have distemper; a second maned wolf also was a candidate for the dangerous disease. The keeper who informed Mark was concerned that the wolf might unknowingly transmit the disease to other animals. Peri Wolff, the assistant vet, was consulted; she wasn't sure that was likely, but she was taking the outbreak seriously.

Mark then met with the two disputing keepers, Pat and Robin, and senior keeper Larry. He held the meeting in the context of a discussion about caring for the elephants, the two keepers' main assignment.

Bozie, the female elephant who had been at the zoo for eleven years, since she was one year old, had never been easy to control.

"She's a six-thousand-pound brat," Robin said. "It's a case of an elephant behaving like a twelve-year-old kid. She can't be allowed to get away with her bad behavior. I say, don't be nice to her. Let her know what's OK and what isn't. After all, one of us could get hurt. You can't take for granted what these animals will or won't do. She'll test you, like kids do, to see how far she can go."

Patiently, slowly, Mark steered the conversation to the disagreement between the two keepers. Without blaming either one, he stressed the need for a team effort.

"I want to go beyond the problems and take care of the elephants. If you're emotional out there, you're going to get in trouble," he told them.

Pat responded, "If we could just go to each other instead of leaping at each other, things wouldn't fester. I don't mean to hurt her feelings, but she was upset. Let's try to discuss it."

"We should communicate," Robin declared. "If I have a beef with you, I should talk to you about it."

"Count to ten," Larry suggested.

"I don't want shouting matches," Pat said.

"Sometimes I do things, and I'm not even aware that I did them," Robin offered.

"When you're together, grow together," Mark told the group. "Be professionals. Make that commitment."

The two women began to talk about their differences.

"You were hyper with me. And when you are, I go boom, boom, boom," Pat said.

"When I get pissed, I let you know about it," Robin replied. "I admit when I'm wrong, and then I forget about it."

"We lost control," Larry interjected. "It got out of hand. When you're both hot, we all lose communication."

"I have to walk away from this knowing I've got a team here, and that's not simple," Mark said. "All I can ask is that we have respect for each other."

"Things can be worked out," Robin volunteered. "I'm willing to try. Sometimes it's impossible not to have personal things affect you."

No one asked her to elaborate.

"The day Bozie drops a baby here, no one out there will know how much work we've done here. But *we* will," Mark said, attempting to propel the conversation to a higher level.

The three keepers went off together, toward the elephants.

Mark went back to his desk, slumped in his chair, and glared at the paper on his desk.

What was it that Marlin Perkins had said to him when Mark was a boy? "If you want fun, work at a zoo."

Mark smiled, got up, and went out of the building to the midday sun, the chains of hand-holding children, the loving young couples, and a few small kids who might, someday, want to work at a zoo.

FIRST PERSON: MARK ROSENTHAL

The first time I came to the zoo, I must have been four

years old, five years old. When I was born, my parents lived right across from the zoo. My mother, like all the mothers around, would take her kid and go to the zoo, and that was a day out with the kid. I remember coming to the zoo every day. I mean every day.

When I was in grammar school, I always loved collecting pictures of animals and collecting the old postcards that they sold at the zoo, reading about animals. When I was in grammar school, I remember taking books out of the library, classic texts about zoos and working in zoos and working with animals. I think I always knew somehow that I enjoyed being with animals. It seemed pleasant; it seemed natural. I wanted to work with living animals. I didn't want to work in a museum with dead animals. I thought I wanted to be a vet. When I got to college, I went into pre-vet, and right away it was eighteen hours of work, and I wasn't in the mood to study. I flunked out. So I went into zoology. I went to junior college to build up my grades, and I did excellently. I was ready. When you're ready to study, you do it.

My parents thought it was strange for a Jewish boy to want to work in a zoo, but they always wanted me to be happy and to do what I wanted to do.

The first job I got at the zoo was working summers in the children's zoo. I was still going to college, so it was summer break. Every day I'd go to explore places in the zoo. Every lunchtime I'd go to a different place that I hadn't been to before. The last day I'm working with Debbie, a baby gorilla, and of course Pat, the senior keeper, who knew me before I started here; she knew me when I was a snot-nosed kid. And Debbie bit me, a puncture wound. Something happened, I don't know what; she bit my hand. It wasn't serious, but it was a puncture wound. And I said to myself, I gotta get a tetanus shot. But I was leaving, I was going to school the next day. Well, I'll go the health service, no problem.

So I went down to the health service at school. I knocked at the door, and the nurse came over. "I need a tetanus shot." "Oh, OK, come on in, come on in." She sat me down, asked my name, what year I was in, and the pertinent information. She said, "What bit you?" I said, "A gorilla bit me." So she was thinking, "Another smart-mouthed student." She said, "OK, that's pretty funny. Why don't we start from the beginning. You were bitten by an animal?" I said, "Yes, I was." She said, "What was it?" I said, "It was a gorilla."

I knew she was losing patience quickly, so I said, "Let me tell you what I did during the summer." "That's great," she said, "oh, that's so interesting, and blah blah blah," and then she said, "Would you wait here just a moment?" And I said, "I'm not going anywhere. I'm waiting for my shot." She went out, came back, and there were two doctors and a nurse with her. And one asked, "You were bitten by a gorilla yesterday?" I said yes, and I told my story again. And they put it in my record, so from that day on whenever I'd go to the health service for a scrape, I always had to explain the gorilla bite.

After college, the animal keeper exam came up, the civil service thing. I took it, passed, and was an animal keeper. And then there was another opening. I applied for that, and I got it. A job as a zoologist, a kind of assistant curator. There I was, a young zoologist who was in charge of keepers who had been there thirty years, guys that could have eaten me up and spit me out, because I had no background, no confidence in what I was doing. Academically, I knew more than they did, but that wasn't the test. Luckily for me, a number of senior people took me under their wing and said things like, "Just shut up and listen, and we'll get you through this." And I learned, made mistakes, and hoped that some of them were not bad enough to get me canned. It worked out.

Les Fisher promoted me to curator. His philosophy of management is very open-ended, very flexible. To some people, that's the kiss of death, because they need to know what to do. I'm not perfect, no one is, but that ability to let people be on their own, but be responsible, well, not many directors of zoos would allow you that freedom, especially in your formative years. Even if your actions were correct, there'd be a tighter rein on your responsibilities. Curators do many things on their own at Lincoln Park, not because the director told them they had to. If you deliver the goods, Les is happy. I think that somehow intuitively he knows if you're doing a good job or not doing a good job. Certain things were requested of you; if you followed through on those things, it was pretty obvious that you were responding to directives. And we picked up extra things that we would do and want to do.

I have a great interest in video. Now, that's not defined as my job. Anybody can use the video room. It's not *my* video room; I don't want it to be my video room. All the Marlin Perkins films, we have those kinescopes as part of our archives. No one said to me, your assignment is to work with Marlin and see if you can catalogue them. It was a three-year project. We have two hundred twenty of these films.

The zoo was always a very positive place for me. People always ask me at parties, or if they don't know me, "What do you do?" "I'm Mark Rosenthal, and I'm a curator at Lincoln Park Zoo." Almost always their reaction is, "That must be great, how wonderful, what is a curator?" I always say it's like being a curator of an art museum. You manage a collection. I tell people what I really do, and they ask, "How do you do all that?" I don't know. You learn about certain things. I mean, I work with nutrition. I'm not the nutrition expert of the world. I work with the vets; we do research projects. I deal with all kinds of keepers and personnel. We put exhibits together, we design things. I'm learning a lot more. I'm not a videotape editor. I can do a little of it, and I'm learning, but when we needed to really get it done, I got the services of somebody who knew what was going on. So to me I'm a manager, manager of a collection, and I've been free to expand that a great deal.

If there's any snag in the job, it's that we don't get paid enough money. When I met Marlin Perkins when I was very young, and my mother cornered him in the zoo, she said to him, "Here's my ten-year-old kid, and he always wants to work with animals." Marlin said, "If you want to have fun, that's a great job; if you want to make money, go into something else." In certain ways, he was right. Of course Marlin had it all, so he could talk. On one hand, I think that's one of the problems: we don't get paid enough for what we do. On the other hand, I'm a big enough boy to know that I could go and do something else that paid more, and then I don't have to crab about it. I truly believe that in the next year or so, just being good little soldiers and presenting our side of it, we will get what we feel is the type of salary that a major zoo should be paying its curators, what major zoos in the United States do pay their curators. The keepers deserve everything they get, but they have a union. I don't have a union. I happen to be single. I've often wondered how married people on a keeper level with kids do things. I've been able to make do with my salary, and I can't complain. On the other hand, I know I'm not being paid what I feel I'm worth. I say that not as curator, but for all the curators.

Being a curator and retiring as a curator is certainly not the worst thing in the world one can do. I've thought that maybe being a director gives you that end point of creativity and that it might be an interesting career move. I am not sure I yet have what I consider all the skills to be a director, and that's more of financial management, things that have nothing to do with animals.

I think that you develop relationships with certain animals. God help you if you didn't, because why would you want to be here? When I was a young zoologist at the zoo, the only elephant that had been in Lincoln Park Zoo was Judy. I worked with her a little, and one day we came in, and Judy was down on the ground. I had seen other animals live and die. When the first couple that I was working with died, it left an impact, but it passed, and I went on to do other things. Well, we worked all day on Judy trying to get her up, and she wouldn't get up. There was something wrong. We later found out it was a blood vessel that had burst in the brain, and she'd had a stroke, but at the time we didn't know that. And so many people came in; the repair and construction forces were called in. How do you lift this elephant, how can we have a sling, what can we do? She was obviously trying to respond to commands, but couldn't. We worked all day, brought all kinds of people in, a lot of energy was exerted. And then in the end, that day she died. And that was a very sad time. It was losing an animal friend that I had known, more as a young child growing up, than as one who had directly worked with her, but that day of intense trying to save her was very emotional at the end. As the years go by, you see so many animals die and be born. The joy of seeing my first gazelle born was a special joy, wonderful, but the feeling of the thirty-eighth gazelle is different from the first. And the death of a first animal as opposed to the four hundredth animal that you've lost is different.

When I was a summer volunteer, still a kid, a curator told me, enjoy your time with the animals, because the higher you go in any job, the further away you are from that which brought you there. If you really want to work with animals, then you don't want to be a curator. I do interact with them, but it's not on a daily basis. I'm more removed.

I do get in and work with the elephants; I try to keep up with that every once in a while. That gives me direct feedback. Maybe that's why I like elephants, because you know exactly where you stand. I mean, they're either listening to you, or they're not. You're either in charge of what's going on, or you're not. A relationship is built up. They respect you. You use certain tricks to get them to respect you, because you are little and they are big. Everybody can't go in and work the elephants. You have to pay your dues, and I think that is what makes me accepted by the elephant keepers, because I paid my dues, and they know that. I'm not as good as they are, because they do it every day.

Some animals recognize me, and that's enjoyment. A bat

does not recognize me, but the chimps do, the gorillas recognize me. When Sinbad the gorilla died, that was very sad. I had worked with Sinbad. I mean I'd been a keeper hosing out the cages, and he had thrown stuff at me, and I knew him. There are not many personalities in a zoo. They all may have house names, or the majority may be known to their own individual keepers, but when Sinbad died, it was in the newspapers, the headlines. It won't be when Mark goes, but when Sinbad died, it was. Certain animals have that individual personality that the public likes. And usually it's mammals. That's not to say disparaging things about birds or reptiles, but . . .

Of course, we do have our critics. Someone says to me, "You know that giraffe that you have, he's not free."

Where is he free?

"What do you mean, where is he free? Don't be stupid. In the wilds he's free, in Africa."

But he's not free in the wild, he's not free in Africa.

"What do you mean?"

What I mean is, this animal has certain biological needs that are a fact of nature, that keep him or her or it in a certain area. Giraffes don't travel all over Africa, they have territories. They don't deviate from those territories; in fact, they're very regimented within those territories. There are constraints. Whatever those are, be they made by man or be they biological, there are constraints. Why don't I go off and live on an island? If I had a lot of money, maybe that's what I would do. But maybe I wouldn't, because of my family, because of this or that. So when people throw the word *free* around, I try to make them define what free means. I think that wherever we get our animals, from captivity or from the wild, we have an obligation to do the right thing, because they have not chosen to be at Lincoln Park Zoo; we have made a conscious decision to bring them here.

When I hear critics attack the zoo, I think of what British author Gerald Durrell wrote in his book *Beasts in My Belfry*:

It is hard to argue with these people [people who do not like to see animals 'imprisoned']; they live in a euphoric state where they believe that an animal in a zoo suffers as though it were in Dartmoor and an animal in its natural surroundings is living in a 'Garden of Eden' where the lamb can lie down with the lion without starting in friendship and ending up as dinner. It is useless to point out the ceaseless drudgery of finding adequate food supplies each day in the wilds, of the constant strain on the nerves of avoiding enemies, of the battle against disease and parasites, of the fact that in some species there is a more than 50% mortality rate among the young in the first 6 months. 'Ah,' these bemused animal lovers will say when these are pointed out to them 'but they are *free*.' You point out that animals have strict territories that are governed by three things: food, water and sex! Provide all these successfully within a limited area and the animals will stay there.

But the people seem to be obsessed with this word, freedom, particularly when applied to animals. They never seem to worry about the freedom of the bank clerks of Streathem, the miners of Durham, the factory hands of Sheffield, the carpenters of Hartley Wintney, or the head waiters of Soho, yet if a careful survey were conducted on these and other similar species, you would find that they are confined by their jobs and by convention as securely as any zoo inmate.

We have to give our animals the best conditions that we can for them to live in, and that's a very basic thing. I would be the first to admit if someone said, "Ah, but there are bad zoos." That's right, and hopefully through education and through other reforms, some of them through national organizations, you can make those bad zoos be better zoos. If you treat an animal with respect, give it the type of food that the animal needs, give it the proper lodging that it's within your power to do, meet the biological needs that it has as an animal, I think the public will see the animals as representatives of their kind in the wild. Part of a zoo's mission is to give people an appreciation of the animal world around them. Many people live in cities, and it's as strange to an African kid in Nairobi to know what a lion is as it is for a kid here to know about cows and where milk comes from.

A gorilla family living together and interacting one and five-eighths inches away from the public gives the public a greater appreciation of the size, the scope, the speed, the intimacy. Why are zoos around? Well, one reason zoos are around is that people have an affinity for animals. They like being around animals, they like being near animals, they like to know the animals are around. I don't want to say it's some inward genetic quality that is within all of us, but it certainly is something that is learned, however it has evolved. I mean when men were hunters, there was this affinity, there was this need for a relationship with animals. You killed, you revered what you killed. Why? Because the animal gave you life. The Eskimos do it today; that's their philosophy. I think people have a positive feeling about being around animals.

Sure, animals die here as they die in the wild, but on the other hand, as the wild shrinks, I think zoos play an ultimately greater part than they ever have before, and the fact that they realize it makes it even more important, because in certain ways they're just coming to discover their destiny. Zoos will never be the saviors of all the animals in the world. No way; it can't happen. But on the other hand, they can play an integral part in the whole equation. They will play their part.

What is their part? Managing isolated populations for the long-term good. We get information from the wild; we hopefully give it back. More and more zoos will find that niche in the conservation of animals, and they will exploit it in a positive way and be part of that mass of people doing whatever they can to bring their expertise to save living things.

I learn about the animals every day. With the great apes, you have animals that are intelligent, very strong, and in the chimpanzees and gorillas, you have a sense of family. So when you're exhibiting those kinds of animals or you're working with them, you have to consider their strength and their thinking ability and the different personalities of the animals. We have some gorillas, males, that like certain females, and others like other females, and certain females don't get along with other females. So in group composition, that individual personality of the animal has to be considered, just as it would be in the wild.

Apes are smart. For example, we put together this termite mound, which essentially was a device for chimpanzees, who could take pieces of twigs, push the twigs down into a small hole, and come out with a honeylike substance, and they'd get just a little of it. Now, this was imitating something that was seen in the wild by Jane Goodall, where the chimps would use simple tools, and they would stick them into termite mounds, termites would come out at the end of them, they'd eat the termites. We put the mound in, put the ketchup, honey, whatever it was we were using, and then we put the twigs in, and the keeper said, "Shall we put the twigs in the holes?" And I said, "No, just leave them in the cage." Within ten minutes, the chimps had taken the twigs and were using them in the holes to get the food. They'd never seen the device before. I'm sure they smelled a honey substance or odor, I think they knew there was something down there; the question was how did they get it? They took these twigs, and all of a sudden one played around with it and stuck it in and came out with a reward, and that was that.

Yes, they're smart. If there's a whole group of people, and I walk over, they'll come over to me, if it's other people they don't know. They'll give me a greeting. Chimpanzees have a way of greeting one another. Sometimes it'll take the form of a hand held out, waving it. Sometimes it'll take the form of coming up to the bars and presenting themselves, submitting, showing you their rear, a form of submission saying, "I submit to you, and you don't have to do anything more than acknowledge it."

The gorillas and chimps can be very tough, if they're aggressive. If they run away from you, that's one thing; if they're running at you, that's another thing. We had a young gorilla that had taken one of the ropes somehow and wrapped it around his arm and twisted it so tightly that he couldn't untwist it, and he was caught and was crying. We had to move all of the other gorillas out of the exhibit, but that took time, because they were concerned about their friend, and they didn't want to leave. We couldn't just go in until they left. We went up on the top of the exhibit, cut the rope, so there was no longer any pressure. And then we had to go in and remove it from the animal. Now he was a small animal, so it wasn't like we were really worried. On the other hand, sometimes you have to tranquilize them. With Donna the chimp, whose baby we took for hand-raising, the only way we could get that kid away from Donna was to tranquilize her. It gave us an opportunity to check her medically. She wasn't about to leave the kid, but she wasn't about to take care of it either. And we didn't want her to drag the kid all over and do it some harm.

The newborns keep us busy. Bonding is very important. When we have zebras born, or any hoofed stock, we try to keep mom with the kid for at least twenty-four hours alone, to have that child bond on that particular female, and make sure it's a strong bond, rather than throw them out with the herd right away. Then, of course, you also can monitor the animals, depending on the species. Is it nursing? We've used the closed-circuit time lapse a lot for those kinds of things with zebras. What's the behavior of the kid the first couple of hours? That's been very handy for us to have, and I think very good for keepers to see also.

We have a seventy-two-hour protocol for the great apes when they have babies, and that's based on when Mary the gorilla had a baby many years ago. The doctor said it could go five days without nursing, and then, at the end of those five days, as a maximum, if you had a problem and it wasn't nursing, you had to take it. Well that was OK, you still could bring it back, and it wouldn't be the end of the world. At the end of five days, she wasn't nursing it; we pulled the baby to the nursery, and we lost it. We felt maybe kids can last five days in extreme circumstances, but why should that be a protocol, let's back it up three days. Now we still have some latitude, and then we'll make a decision, so we came up with the seventy-two-hour protocol, and that's been reasonably successful. You have to monitor things very specifically. Certainly with a kid, with first-time mothers.

The sea lions are very active animals; I think that's why the exhibit attracts a lot of people. I think that they're intelligent, curious, and energetic animals. They're doing one of two things, generally: they're sleeping and sunning themselves, or they're in the water, patrolling, moving around. They're very much afraid of things that are new or strange to them. When we have divers go into the pool to clean the bottom, pick up pennies, they'll always stay away from the divers. After an hour or so of someone being in the tank, they'll start coming closer, but it's more inquisitive than it is aggressive. They can be hostile, but that's rare.

If it has teeth, it can bite, and it depends on the situation. Mothers defending their babies can be very aggressive. Big beach masters, big males, defending their harems, can be tough at certain times of the year on dry land. So you'd have to be aware of those and be sensitive to that, and usually you can work around it.

One of the things that we've tried to do with the small mammal house is show the diversity of the small mammals that are in the world. When I walk through the building, what always catches my eye is the African crested porcupine. It really is a very striking animal, not as small as the elephant shrew, but certainly very striking. The other creatures that people like among the small mammals are the smaller primates, the marmosets and the saki monkeys.

If the elephants aren't the smartest, they're among the smartest of all the animals. They show an intelligence; they learn very quickly and respond to dozens of commands, verbal commands, that the keepers through training reinforce. They are not above solving problems and making the keepers think all the time. Anytime you have an animal that thinks and is as big as an elephant, then the keepers always have to be one step ahead. They can never lose their temper or their cool; they have to be thinking all the time.

Elephants will test you. So will chimpanzees and gorillas and other thinking animals. A good example is in the children's zoo. We would have chimpanzees there that we were raising. Pat Sass was keeper then at the children's zoo, and she'd walk in and work with the chimps. She'd tell them, through training, "Sit on your shelf so I can clean," and they'd sit on the shelf. She'd give them a treat. And then when she'd leave, they would go swinging around. Well, whenever anybody else came into the exhibit and was going to clean it, he or she would say the same thing: "Sit on the shelf." Well, the chimps would sit on the shelf, but this was another person, so how far can we push this person? Well, they might stand up on the shelf. And then if the person didn't say anything right away, they would swing a little, and then they'd swing a little more, and if the person didn't perceive it as a problem, they'd just go beyond, beyond, beyond. They knew they didn't have to listen. Pat would walk by, see it, walk through the door and say, "Go sit on the shelf." They were on the shelf. They can differentiate between people they know and people they are going to test.

Camels are stubborn and not very inquisitive. We have traditionally halter-broken the young camels and used them as exhibit animals to be close to people. But as they get older, we don't do that. Camels can be mean; camels can spit. That's when they really get upset.

Giraffes are kind of beautiful, elegant, nondescript animals. I mean, they're there, they're majestic, they're tall, they're fleet of foot, many positive things, but because there are no vocalizations in the giraffe adults and because they're not hyper animals like the seals, jumping and running and so forth—they're stately—they have a very positive regalness, but they don't have much of a personality. Maybe every keeper who works with them would beg to differ with me, and they probably are very responsive to the keepers they know. But that takes time.

In most cases, keepers do achieve some kind of rapport with their animals. It can be as simple as when you open the door to clean the cage, and the animal tends to move to a certain spot. And then you do your cleaning, never interacting with the animal. On the other hand, with small mammals, you might be cleaning an exhibit, and the animal will hop on your shoulder. Never going farther than your shoulder, going back to the exhibit. But it will not bite you. Others are too skittish, or you have to move them into holding areas while you clean their area; you wouldn't want to go in with them because that might bother them too much, and they might try to escape. Not to freedom, but away from your presence and then get into trouble.

Rhinos are another matter—very powerful, in short bursts of energy. They are not too good in the eyesight department; they're much better smellers. They tend to like regularity. You start throwing new things into their routine, and it takes them a while to adjust.

Pygmy hippos are very fast, aggressive animals who are a no-nonsense kind of animal. You leave them alone, they'll leave you alone. You push them, and they'll show their teeth and are not afraid to fight.

Bears are very smart. In circuses, bears pick up tricks right away. Very sharp. So the intelligence is there. And they're very inquisitive; they'll check all the locks and

check all the perimeters of their exhibit and will be me-
thodical about it. The problem with bears always seems to
be that, for some reason, they're very difficult to read.
When your cat's ears go down and its mouth opens up, it's
generally an aggressive kind of thing, a defensive thing,
you have a feel for what's going on. You may not know
exactly what's happening but you kind of have a feel. With
bears, they don't telegraph those feelings as much. And so,
to me, if any animal is going to be really a dangerous
animal in a zoo, a bear would be. Bears are powerful, they
may not be afraid of people, they're potentially dangerous,
they're big, they have teeth, they can be fast. If I were
locked into an open space with a bear or a lion, I'd rather be
in with a lion. I might have more of a chance.

Timber wolves are very social animals, timid at times
but inquisitive. They want to investigate things that are in
their exhibit all the time. They're very defensive about
their territory. We had an unfortunate incident with a
Doberman pinscher last year that ran into the zoo and
somehow got in between the public railing and the edge of
the timber wolf yard. Some keepers tried to catch it, but it
bit one of the keepers. We had to capture the dog because it
might have had rabies. Before we could do that, the dog
jumped into the timber wolf yard to get away from us, and
as it did, all the wolves attacked it immediately and killed it.
It was very quick, very fast. The maned wolves tend to be
different. They're more laid-back; they're not a troop animal or a group animal, just pairs.

Polar bears are smart, too. Remember, they're a major
predator in the area that they live in. They have to be a
thinking animal, to be immensely strong; some of the seals
that they pull up out of the air holes that the seals are in
weigh hundreds of pounds, and the bear does it easily.

In the primate house, I like to watch Admiral; he's a
wanderoo macaque. He's the oldest wanderoo we have.
And he'll jut his chin out. That may be a behavioral greeting to people. Or, on the other hand, sometimes male
primates will constantly flash their teeth and yawn, and

open their mouth to show you what their weapons are. It's a visual signal to let you know, "This is off limits, and these are my weapons." Mandrills will do it a lot; people mistake it for yawning.

I like the marmosets. Small, colorful, squirrel-like, very interesting, very hyper little guys. The family situation: mom, dad, usually two to three kids, and there may be another litter after that, that would be their family troop.

It's an old joke: A lion's walking down the pathway, and he sees this baboon, and he roars out to the baboon, "Who's king of the jungle?" The baboon is not near a tree; none of his troop is around, he's afraid. And he says, "Oh, your majesty, you are, of course." The lion says, "That's right, I'm the king." And he walks a little farther down, and he sees a zebra, and he says to the zebra, "Zebra, who's the king of the jungle?" And the zebra looks at him, and he's not near his herd, and there's no defense, and he's a prey animal, so he says, "Oh, your majesty, you're the king of the beasts." The lion says, "That's right, I certainly am." And he walks farther, and he comes to an elephant. And he roars at the elephant, "Elephant, who's the king of the beasts?" And the elephant looks down at him and picks him up with his trunk and throws him down on the ground and kicks some dirt on him and walks down the road. The lion gets up, brushes himself off, and yells down to the elephant walking away, "Hey, just 'cause you didn't know the answer, you don't have to get upset."

The elephant is the true king of the beasts.

Among the big cats, I find the leopards most interesting, and the tigers more interesting than the lions. Certainly, as a social animal, the lion's more interesting, because it's one of the few that forms a social grouping. When I have talked to trainers of cats, they have often said that a lion can be bullied at times and might have to be dominated, but a tiger needs to be talked to; they're a little more sensitive. You can't just shout them down, because they're going to be upset for a long time. That's similar to elephants: African elephants tend to be a bit more flighty, you can hurt their feelings with a word, where Asian elephants tend to be animals you really have to dominate, and they have to know that you are the person giving the orders.

Keepers can build up a rapport with hoofed stock—antelope, gazelles, members of the herd. It takes a long time, but it's possible for a keeper working every day with animals to build up a rapport. It depends on the keeper. In Europe they do it a lot. Here in the United States, it's more of a remote control thing: animals in, animals out. You're managing them remote control, not hands-on. But it is possible for a keeper to build up associations with the hoofed stock, absolutely. Of course, we tend not to walk among them for a number of reasons. One, we don't want them to flee from us and get hurt, go through barriers because they're excited. The other thing is that the animals, the antelopes and the zebras, unless they're conditioned and unless you visit them on a regular basis and condition them to something, they're not going to be responsive to the keeper. Being familiar with them may put you in dangerous situations. A good example is the guy who every day goes to the paddock where the deer are, and he goes in with the deer and he rakes the yard. Every day he takes a bagel, and he throws it away, and the male deer goes and eats the bagel. So this guy can do his work, he throws him another bagel. Now the guy goes on vacation, and the relief guy comes on. And the regular keeper doesn't bother to communicate to the relief guy that he gives the deer a bagel every day. So the relief guy comes in and starts to work, and the deer comes over, he's expecting his bagel. This guy doesn't know anything because there's been no communication, so he doesn't give him any food. The deer gets upset. I want my bagel. Well, he may do something, be aggressive toward the guy. He has antlers.

Deer, or any bull animal in rut, in a season where he's breeding females, has to be considered dangerous, and you don't just go in with them, because they will have their full array of weapons. So you have to be respectful.

We have many missions. There has been a trend in the last couple of years to have species-survival programs, to use all of the zoos in the United States as pools of animals, to breed animals, rather than one zoo or two zoos doing it exclusively. The pool becomes larger then. We all try to work for a minimum number of animals to be born every year to replace those that die. To continue the genetic diversity, we use all of the zoos in cooperative programs. And I think the majority of zoos have gone along with that. Lincoln Park can't do it all, but to certain animals we want to make long-term commitments. Apes. Bears. Maned wolves. Black rhinoceroses. Pygmy hippos, certain of the lemur species, and tamarin species. A lot of those tend to be listed as endangered. Also, we want to continue to show animals that are not endangered, and we try to maintain breeding programs on some, but not all of them.

You cooperate with other zoos. Before you start, you sign a breeding loan agreement with the other zoo. Everything is very specifically spelled out. If the animal dies while at the other zoo, you don't expect them to accept any kind of responsibility for replacing the animal, and they of course will assure you that they will feed and care for it correctly, and then you work out some division of offspring.

But I don't spend all my time on major projects. Sometimes a ringing phone makes me busy. We once got phone calls from the press asking about a report that a kangaroo had been spotted by two police officers in Chicago. Then, we got calls from all over the city reporting this kangaroo, and the radio stations were picking up on it; it was a good story. People swore that they were seeing kangaroos in their back yards, and we started plotting them on a graph. The kangaroo would have had to have been in a teleport machine to get to some of the places, in a time limit, through the city. It turned out to be a hoax.

We got a call that there was a snakelike animal in the engine block of a car on the South Side. The police called

us. They wanted to know if someone who was familiar
with snakes could go down to the South Side to this garage
and investigate it. The police picked up our reptile curator,
and I wanted to go along just for the ride. We zipped down
there. Big crowd. Eddie—the curator—fiddled in the engine
block for a while, and he actually pulled out, not a snake,
but a lizard, a Tegu lizard, a lizard from central South
America. And it's a big animal, a foot and a half, two feet,
something like that. As Eddie was working on it, he was
bending over the engine block, and the crowd of hundreds
of people were all around him in a circle, looking, and
when he pulled that out of the engine block and held it up,
you know, because he's tussling, and he finally gets it up, it
was like throwing a stone in a pond and watching the
ripples go out. The circle of people was about a hundred
feet from him. And we bagged it, and then took it back to
the zoo. How it got in the engine God only knows.

Years ago, we got a call that there was this large cat on
LaSalle Street, killing pigeons. A big cat. Our veterinarian
called me, and we went to investigate. Sure enough, high in
a tree, we saw a bobcat. I mean it was distinctive, bigger
than a housecat; you could see it, so we called the fire
department and said, "There is something up there, and we
can tranquilize it or try to snare it, but we need a snorkel."
They brought out the snorkel unit with all the firefighters
that have to come with it, and it had to be approved by
downtown. We had all the capture equipment, and a small
crowd was there, mostly firefighters. And we said, "Well,
we've got to have somebody go up and shoot it, with the
tranquilizer gun, or try to lasso it or do something." The
firefighters said, "We'll get you up there, but we won't do
anything else. You have to send somebody." So we sent the
reptile curator up there. He went up there, and he saw that
the shot would be too dangerous, so he put a catch pole on
it, and ripped it out of the tree. It was holding on with all its
claws, and it was dangling there from the catch pole making choking noises. We got it down; the vet worked on it,

revived it, and we put it in a cage, and it went to Indian Boundary Zoo.

That's one way to acquire an animal. There are more conventional ways. We don't deal with private individuals. That's been a general policy. Nor do we sell to the general public; that's been a policy, too. We generally sell through accepted avenues, and we pick up animals through accepted avenues, so we know where they are and where they come from, and get a good health history on them. Many times we get calls from people wanting to know more about exotic pets. We try to dissuade them from having anything exotic. The official zoo advice is not to have exotic pets. We don't recommend it, and indeed we don't recommend it because a lot of times calls that we get from people to donate animals to the zoo are because they took exotic animals as pets, and they didn't really have an idea of what would happen when they grew up, or how much work it would be, or that they're potentially dangerous. So we wind up with them.

When I first came to the zoo, I worked as a keeper on the bear line. We had spectacled bears; they were small, the only bears in South America. There wasn't much known about them, compared to other bears, and it just seemed to me that they were interesting and had a story to tell. One could add to the information about them, one could help out in answering questions about them. We weren't doing much with them.

One of the things that the zoo can do, as opposed to people in the field studying animals, is to add certain things to the literature with the animals that we have at the zoo, in a research-conservation kind of way. And when you get animals that are endangered and you can add to the information, it seems that you should do it. And we can't do it with all, so you tend to pick animals that interest you for whatever reason. The bears? Maybe it's because I had a teddy bear like everybody else. God only knows.

You can't work with creatures day after day and not feel

something for the animals in your care. Obviously, the keeper on the line has that direct contact with the animal every day and would be more emotional or caring than the pathologist who finally dissects the creature and learns what some of the problems are, who's never really worked with it. You do get jaded to certain things. It's not that you're uncaring; it's just that some things become matter-of-fact routines.

My first death had to do with a dehorning of a deer at Indian Boundary. Antlers fall off anyway, and there's a methodology, and you tranquilize the animal. That deer died under the anesthesia we were giving it. And that bothered me. I mean, my first animal, and I administered the stuff, and we had a consulting vet who told us what to do. I was just devastated. When you're dealing with a hundred and fifty bats in an exhibit, and you find one dead, it's still a concern, it still goes to pathology, you still want to learn why it happened, but there is less affinity to one of one hundred fifty bats than there is to one deer. That's the fact.

Animals get out; I guess it's inevitable. A lot of times it's human error which allows that to happen. One night I got a call at midnight from a zoo security guard, and he said, "The lions are out." And I said, "Out where?" The kind of call you really need at midnight. "Out where? Out on the grounds or out in the building, where?" "Out in the building." I said, "Well, then they're contained. I don't know how they got out, but they are contained, and we'll slowly deal with it and find the best solution."

So I ran to the zoo and found the security guard. He had been making rounds in the lion house and had seen some of the lions chewing on a rubber hose. The keeper must have left the rubber hose, the water hose, too close to the door, and the lions had somehow reached out and grabbed it and were biting off pieces of it. He was going to be a good guy, go in the back area, pull the hose away so they couldn't get more of it. The truth of what had happened was the keeper had neglected to lock a lock for some reason; the lions had pushed against the door, gotten out, and grabbed the hose and were bringing it back in. So when he went in the back, he turned a corner and walked straight into a male lion looking at him. They scared each other. The lion ran one way because he was scared, and the guard ran the other way, and that's when he called me.

Of course, it was a police emergency, and I called the director of the zoo right away when I got there, and some other keepers for help to get some backup. Les Fisher's line was busy, so I took care of things at the zoo and got everything squared away. And police started coming in droves. They secured the outside; they weren't allowing reporters in. Les Fisher arrived and said, "Why didn't you call me?" I said, "Well, I tried, but your line was busy." The police had asked for the heavy weapons truck to come to the zoo, and that's monitored by all the TV and radio and so forth, so they called Les Fisher up right away and asked him to comment on lions being loose at the zoo. He didn't know anything, and no one could get through to him because the press was calling. We made sure all the lions who were going back and forth in the back area behind their den returned to their exhibit. Then the guard who originally had called me and I went in. I had a fire extinguisher with me because that makes a lot of noise and has a lot of foam, and it scares a lot of animals. The guard had a gun, a shotgun, and we went in and closed the door and resecured the animals. That was it; there was no big deal. But there was, for about an hour and a half, two hours, a little tension, trying to make sure everything worked out OK.

Another day I was sleeping late and was going to take an hour or so before I got to work. I got a call at eight o'clock in the morning. "You'd better get here right away." "Why?" "Polar bear's out." Well, that's not good. Polar bears, anything that's a predator, like a cat, especially bears, can be very unpredictable. I was at the zoo in three minutes. And indeed one of the polar bears had scaled a light ice ladder that had formed from a hose throwing water. This polar bear female had gotten just the right footing. A keeper had seen her scale the ice, couldn't get her to go down, so he called everybody.

We shut the zoo down and got everybody out. The polar bear was not out in the general public area, but it was in a secondary area, obviously out of its cage, though behind the scenes. We got the capture equipment out. We're all trained to use it in emergencies. I loaded up, shot the bear in the rump with the standard dose that we have for just such an emergency, and the bear started to go to sleep. I put another dart into it, and the bear went to sleep. The keepers then rolled it on a tarp and put her into the den, where she slept it off. But for half an hour it was pretty good excitement there; we had a lot of police, we were trying to direct them, make sure that they didn't get in our way but were around. We wanted to contain the situation and make sure everybody was safe.

We had a heavy weapon in case it was needed, but it turned out it wasn't. The darts always work. It's a question of how fast. If an animal is stressed, that amount of concentrated drug may not work as well as if the animal's in a relaxed state. So you have to take that into consideration. I figured I'd done everything I could do that day. I wasn't ready to just go back to doing paperwork.

When I was videotaping those two trumpeter swans, I knew that what had happened was just a minor injury, one that didn't need the vet to look at it. Of course, we called the vet anyway. Anytime we do filming like that, it has to be opportunistic, and I knew that they were going to be moving those swans to Indian Boundary, and that the birds were probably going to be agitated. So there's always a risk; you try to minimize the risk by doing it the proper way. It was opportunistic to get an animal to respond that may again, down the road, save keepers from being hurt by an aggressive animal or to save an animal from being hurt by a keeper misreading it or not handling it correctly. In that context, everything was OK. We don't want to have any animal hurt, regardless of when we handle it.

3

FLYING OBJECTS

Kevin Bell went into the family business: birds.

Kevin was born in New York City in 1952, the son of Joseph Bell, distinguished curator of birds (and chairman of the department of ornithology) at New York's Bronx Zoo. Kevin's father, who died in 1986, was more than a curator of birds; he was a woodcarver, a painter, and an author. His text for *Metropolitan Zoo*, a volume of works depicting animals from the collection of the Metropolitan Museum of Art in New York, is a respected commentary on animals and on art.

His father passed along to Kevin a knowledge of birds and a fondness for them. Kevin did not need to choose a career; he knew, from an early age, what it would be.

He got his bachelor's degree in biology from Syracuse University and his master's in zoology from the State University of New York. While he was still in graduate school, he heard about the search for a curator of birds at the Lincoln Park Zoo, and that zoo's director, Les Fisher, heard about Kevin from a mutual friend. Kevin joined the zoo staff in February 1976.

Once depicted on television and in the New York press as "Kevin Bell, the little boy who grew up in the zoo," the adult Kevin was ready to assume command of the bird population at the zoo. Eleven years later, he was firmly in charge.

A slim (150 pounds) six-footer with a brown beard, Kevin's angular frame was often seen in motion around the zoo. As one keeper observed, "If Mark Rosenthal looks like a mammal, Kevin certainly looks like a bird." Kevin spent long hours at the zoo. A bachelor, he also had a social life: for a while he lived with assistant veterinarian Peri Wolff and before that had been known to fraternize with some of the best-looking women keepers.

His social life had to suffer; it was not unusual to find him at the zoo before 6 A.M., in jeans and dress shirt, with sleeves rolled up. He often worked late and on weekends as well. His was a job clogged with paperwork and phone calls.

His neat office in the bird house was lined with the elements of his trade. Two incubators warmed eggs about to hatch. Design plans for the renovation of the bird house abounded. Reference books, a typewriter, and various journals added to the pragmatic decor.

On one cloudy summer day, he arrived at work a few minutes before 6 A.M. The sea lions were resting atop the rocks in their pool area. The lions were stretching, welcoming the day in their outdoor habitat. The monkeys had begun to chatter. Except for a few dedicated joggers, Kevin had little human company.

In his office, he discovered that one of the old incubators had failed; the motor had burned out. Before it could be repaired, a trumpeter swan's egg was lost. One of Kevin's missions was to breed those swans, then release them in the wild of northern Michigan. He couldn't bring back the unhatched swan, but he could attempt to revive the incubator; he phoned for an electrician.

He got up, discouraged, and walked around the vastness of the empty bird house; only the birds' eyes were on him.

He walked past the sterile glass-and-tile cages and the central free-flight area for birds; he deplored the old-fashioned barren confinement for them and looked forward to the redesign, a drastic shift to naturalistic habitats.

In 1983, he had suggested the specifications for that renovation. Outside the bird house, a large complex of cages would house birds of prey. The well-known architectural firm Skidmore, Owings and Merrill would design it. The main cage would be thirty-five feet high, one-hundred feet long, forty feet deep. It would contain a large cliff, a waterfall, a pool, and appropriate plantings. There would be two vulture species in large groups, some storks, and, in smaller cages, eagles, large owls, and hawks—all with access to heated dens and nesting areas on the cliffs (made of Gunite sprayed over a steel frame and contoured by hand to match the look of the wild). It would be ready, he hoped, in the spring of 1988. After that, the bird house itself would be renovated. The birds now in it would be sent to other zoos. Most of them wouldn't be retrieved. The new bird house would have birds suited to the new habitats.

He walked out of the bird house and strolled toward the flamingo dome, where the flamingos wintered. Inside the dome, tiny young ducks—summer transients—quacked and moved rapidly in a holding tub.

"We let them fly away in the fall. We don't need them," he said.

Outside the dome, beside the waterfowl lagoon, the flamingos gathered, a design in pink—tall, stately, ever-watchful. Kevin looked at them.

"Graceful creatures. Ours are Chilean flamingos," he said. "They appear to be very delicate, but their life in the wild was actually rather rugged. They live at high altitudes and can withstand very cold temperatures and very harsh climates. One of the reasons we don't allow them outside in winter isn't because of the temperature, but because the pond freezes. They can get into trouble walking on ice."

A large group of ducks and geese were noisy and busy on

that pond. The waterfowl area was a haven for North American waterfowl; their presence attracted migratory birds. When waterfowl were born at the zoo, they joined those migratory birds in the fall.

"We have only one species of goose, the emperor goose, and one swan species, the trumpeter swan. Plenty of birds pass through here. Warblers pass through in the spring and in the fall. Certain species we see only for a couple of days, and then they're gone; others can be seen for weeks. Some are around all summer. Then they're gone. They'll fly all the way into Central America, the Caribbean, and beyond, even to South America," he said.

The bird house, the penguin-seabird house, the flamingo dome, the waterfowl lagoon, and the zoo rookery—the small nature preserve at the edge of the zoo grounds—composed Kevin's domain. So did the Indian Boundary Zoo, a little zoo in a park on the city's Northwest Side. Once or twice a week, Kevin borrowed a park district pickup truck and drove to that zoo.

On that summer day, with the clouds fading and the sun beginning to bake the city, he made his way through nagging traffic and annoying road repairs to Indian Boundary. As he approached the park, he spotted a nun in her habit, playing tennis on a park court. He smiled.

At the satellite zoo, he made rounds. It didn't take long.

"This is a tough zoo to manage," he said. "There's no nighttime protection for the animals, so we have to bring them in at night."

He passed a pair of yaks; their mood was between relaxed and sluggish. He spotted a pair of trumpeter swans that had been at the main zoo. He greeted them with a wave. The swans trumpeted. One of them had arrived with a small scrape on its wing, a souvenir of an encounter with Mark Rosenthal's videotaping project.

"It's healed," Kevin noted.

A few chubby pheasants shared the pen with the swans. "They won't intimidate the swans," Kevin said. "Nothing scares them."

Nearby, three alpacas were basking in the sun. Next to

them, in their own pen, three reindeer demonstrated their wisdom by splashing in a pool. In a third pen, pygmy goats, some chickens, and a rabbit played out their communal existence.

Inside the small zoo building, Kevin was greeted by two housecats and a temporary keeper filling in for the regular keeper, who had a day off.

"Those yaks are nice animals," the keeper told Kevin. "We should get more of them."

"Talk to your curator," Kevin said, referring to Mark Rosenthal.

"Those swans honk a lot," the keeper told Kevin, waiting for a response. There was none. "But they don't bother us," the keeper went on.

Kevin entered the alpacas' pen; slowly, they moved away from him. So did the reindeer, when he entered their pen.

Kevin conferred briefly with the keeper, walked briskly around, and then, satisfied that there weren't any problems for him to deal with, got into his pickup and drove away.

Overhead, within view, a small, slender bird in shades of green and gray flew by.

"Quaker parakeet," Kevin said, pointing at the bird. "It was probably released into the wild of Chicago by an owner who got tired of it. Most parakeets that you buy in pet stores are expensive, as much as five hundred or even a thousand dollars. But the quaker may go for just forty-nine ninety-five. They're colorful, but what the buyers don't know is that they're not as likely to talk as the more costly ones. They're just noisy. And most of them are adults, not likely to be tamed. A year after it's been bought, the owner gets tired of it and tries to sell it or give it to a zoo. When there aren't any takers, the owner just releases it.

Fortunately, they form groups; there are others out there. I've seen a group at the tennis courts on Fifty-fifth Street. And they survive. They build a stick nest, a community nest. In New York, you'll see them with missing toes. Frostbite. But if there's food, they survive, even in winter.

"We don't take any birds unless we have a need for them

or know a zoo that does. If you do take one, it has to be quarantined for thirty days. That's a bother."

Kevin didn't have much time for city bird-watching. He preferred to see them in Iceland. He had gone there eight times, to observe and capture the baby puffins he'd admired ever since he wrote his master's thesis about them.

The wild seabirds intrigued him. Most of each year, they lived at sea. In summer, they returned to land to raise their young. That's when Kevin wanted to be there. His efforts had been captured in a film, *Arctic Window*, an Emmy-Award–winning documentary familiar to viewers of public television.

Back at the Lincoln Park Zoo a few minutes after he left Indian Boundary, Kevin headed for the penguin-seabird house, one of the new buildings and one of the buildings that existed because of his zeal.

He entered the building, followed the curve of the walkway, and confronted the penguin exhibit, along with a crowd of mothers and small children. Behind the glass, another civilization had been preserved.

The penguins, which can't fly, were romping around their habitat and swimming in their pool. (Penguins can swim at speeds up to thirty miles per hour.) Their chilly exhibit duplicated their home in the wild: ice formations and water. Some of them, the rockhoppers, were collected from the wild (from the island of Tristan da Cunha, in the South Atlantic) and were reproducing at the zoo. Most of the others—including the chinstraps and the macaronis—were on loan from the San Diego Zoo, which had them in abundance. All were subantarctic, from the southern edge of South America, including the Falkland Islands.

The three species of penguins at the zoo—out of the eighteen species in the world—had more in common than they had differences, and that made them compatible in the zoo exhibit. The macaronis were the largest, the rockhoppers the smallest, the chinstraps in between—but all were knee-high to a tall keeper. The macaronis and rockhoppers were easily spotted; they were crested penguins, with gold tufts of feathers on the sides of their heads. The chinstraps were penguins most familiar to viewers who looked for the familiar tuxedo appearance, the dark back and the white front.

The penguins' zoo environment was controlled, with proper lighting defined day and night. The exhibit was cooled to thirty-five degrees; the 18,000-gallon pool was kept at forty degrees. Most of the penguins had been hand-raised in captivity; adjustment to life indoors had not been difficult.

"For the wild ones, it takes a while for them to eat dead fish—which we fortify with vitamins and minerals—instead of catching live ones," Kevin said. "But we do duplicate sunrise and sunset, long and short days as well. Some of these penguins are quite tame, even in the wild. If they haven't been hunted by humans, they don't fear people.

"It's true that wild-caught birds tend to be more stand-offish. If you went into the exhibit and walked up to the birds, the hand-raised birds would probably stand there and let you walk right up to them. They'd probably chew your shoelace or peck at your pants leg. The wild-caught birds would avoid you, even jump into the water if you got close to them. We go in there to trim their nails or their bills. When we grab a hand-raised bird, it usually won't try to bite us. A wild-caught bird might, and it can inflict a fairly severe wound, so you've got to be careful. They can hit you with their flippers, too. After all, they are birds that sort of fly underwater, so those flippers are powerful. A good whack from a flipper can make you black and blue.

"They don't usually breed until they're four or five years old. But when they're ready, they'll do it right in the exhibit. We provide the rocks, and they make rock nests with them."

Kevin was delighted by the antics of the penguins, and so were the children peering in at them. But his pride was the seabird exhibit, which shared the building with the penguins.

He had personally collected all the seabirds in the

glassed-in exhibit. There were dozens of black and white and gray shapes against the eighteen-foot-high indoor cliff and in the 10,000-gallon pool in front of it. The birds—the common murre, the razorbill, and the common puffin— were swimming, diving, strutting, and observing as Kevin approached them.

"We found them all in southwest Iceland, where there are millions of them," he said. "Most of them are collected as chicks, one to three weeks old, and are raised here at the zoo. They're not at all tame, by the way."

A wave machine sent waves across the pool, and filtered the water as well. A misting system, controlled lighting, and a consistent temperature of forty-five to fifty degrees made the environment familiar to the birds.

"We had to modify the exhibit," Kevin pointed out. "We started with a closed system and found out that the water filtration system couldn't deal with the number of birds we had. The amount of fecal material that went into the water was so great that the system couldn't handle it. So we changed the system, to skim a lot of water off the surface and send it out to the sewer system, particularly when we hosed down the exhibit. Now we add fresh water regularly.

"We had a health problem, too, at first. We attributed it to the fish we were feeding them, a common freshwater smelt from Lake Michigan. Researchers told us that there were heavy metals in the fish. Dangerous. So we switched to saltwater fish, and that solved it."

The puffins were his favorites. He had appreciated them in the wild and now could appreciate them in captivity. But once they came to the zoo, they were there to stay.

"Puffins are a very heavy-bodied bird, with small wings," he explained. "In the wild there may not be suffi- cient wind at times, and that means they have a hard time flying. They rely on the sea breeze to get them up into the air, and it takes them a long stretch to gain altitude. We can't achieve that for them here. Fortunately, we won't release them back into the wild. This is their home now."

It was an important conclusion: the birds' lives depended upon Kevin and the conscientious keepers who cared for the exhibit.

He left the penguin-seabird colonies and walked back to the bird house. A few people were strolling around the cavernous building, some of them accompanied by walking birds.

Kevin permitted himself a rare leisurely walk around the building. As he moved along, birds caught his eye and inspired comment.

A pair of Major Mitchell's cockatoos: "That's an old male we've had for years, with a female that's on loan to us from the Cleveland Zoo. What is fascinating is that the two birds look alike to the average person. But if you look at them very closely, the female is the one with the lighter-color eye."

The galah, a cockatoo: "It's very common in Australia. It's even shot there, because of the damage it can do to grain crops. Here it's fairly rare. A pair of these would cost a zoo anywhere from three to four thousand dollars. They can be tamed; most cockatoos can be tamed, especially if they're hand-raised. If they're wild-caught, they're a little more skittish."

Rothschild's mynah: "An endangered species, almost extinct on its native island, Bali. But there is a species survival program, breeding them in captivity for release back on Bali. The first release will be done very soon."

Nicobar pigeons: "They're not endangered, but they are threatened. We started out with six in 1976, and we've produced close to sixty from those six. Fascinating birds. Originally from Nicobar Island in the Bay of Bengal, now found all over the South Pacific. They can be aggressive with each other during the breeding season, especially the males, which chase each other around. They'll nest in the trees, but they like to walk around on the ground, too.

"They're a heavy-bodied pigeon, larger than our domestic pigeon. They have very long hackles, which are long feathers that surround the neck, chest, and upper back. They are colorful, from green to coppery bronze to blue and purple—metallic colors.

"Here at the zoo, most of the Nicobars have two bands around their legs. A metal band with a number on it for identifying the bird in our collection. And a plastic, colored band that allows us, at a distance, to determine which birds are which. To keep track of individuals."

The white-crested laughing thrush: "Asian birds. Popular because they make a very loud sort of laughing sound. We feed them mealworms, crickets, waxworms, some meat, some fruit. There are cricket ranches that sell crickets to us. And places that produce worms—mice, too."

The blue-crowned conure: "One of the parrots. Slim-bodied birds. We don't know a lot about this particular species. We got them when they were confiscated by the government at a port of entry. Someone was trying to bring them in without the proper paperwork. That paperwork never was forthcoming, so now the birds are ours."

The tawny frogmouth: "From Australia. They look like owls, but they're not related to owls at all. They don't have grasping feet, for example; they have perching feet. They have a huge gaping mouth; they can eat small mice or large insects by crushing them with their bills.

"They're nocturnal. Their coloration enables them to blend in with the bark on a tree. During the day, if you walk around here and look for them, it's hard to find them. They are absolutely still and blend in. When it starts to get dark in here, that's when they wake up."

He paused. He could hear a mild commotion between a parent bird and its baby.

"When birds are successful at reproducing, parent birds will chase some of their older chicks out of the area. Aggressively, especially when the parent wants to renest. They'll tolerate a youngster up to a point, but when that youngster gets old enough, they'll chase it out, even roughly. In the wild, they chase out the chicks to head out and colonize a new area."

He resumed his stroll.

"There's a Shama thrush feeding her chick in a log," he observed. The birds were in a small glassed-in cell.

"That spare setting inhibits reproduction. They're helped by more space, more plants. They'll respond better in a naturalistic habitat. There's no depth to these old cages. When the keeper enters to put down some food, the bird flies out of range but can't go very far. It's possible that placid birds, birds that do well in these old cages, we won't want to exhibit in our new setting. Temperamental birds, which may not adapt well, are more fascinating."

He passed a blacksmith plover sitting on an egg.

"Hi, mom!" he hollered. Another plover, nearby, guarding the mother, shrieked an alarm call.

A Jackson's hornbill, from East Africa, was facing the wall at the back of its cage, peering down.

"Looking for a roach to eat," Kevin said.

In the free-flight area in the middle of the building, a Nicobar pigeon, in metallic copper and green, sat surveying the invented landscape: thickly overgrown, with a miniature stream along the outer edges and a waterfall.

"One of the things that goes into planning a free-flight like this is the number of different strata. You have limited ground space, so you have to limit the number of birds who live on the forest floor. Then you have those birds that inhabit the low shrubbery or the water areas. You have to figure out how many birds you can have and then work your way right up to the top of the exhibit," he explained.

Across the room, Sammy—a white cockatoo and a venerable resident of the bird house—called out, "Hello." Sammy had been donated to the zoo more than fifteen years ago by a wealthy woman with a fondness for birds and for zoos. Whenever she returned to visit him, she fed him Godiva chocolates. She died, but the bird survived, and at age thirty it showed few signs of weariness. Old age in birds never surprised Kevin; there was a cockatoo at the San Diego Zoo that was sixty-five, and he knew of a condor that lived to seventy-five.

"It's the only tame bird we have," Kevin said of Sammy. "It'll sit on your arm and take food from you."

When he completed his circle around the bird house, he walked outside, into the summer heat. A common city pigeon flashed by, in a familiar nosedive. Kevin grimaced.

"It's ironic," he said. "There are many pigeons and doves, and some of them are very difficult to keep in captivity. That one adapted. To spread disease and be a nuisance. They're like rats. Dirty. Another dirty urban animal leaving its remains. I get calls from people who want us to kill them. I tell them to call the city's animal control people. Killing animals isn't our business."

By eight o'clock the next morning, Kevin had been at work for two hours. As he often did, he went to the reception desk in the Crown-Field Center to pick up his mail, memos from other staff members, anything that had accumulated in his box. He sat at the desk, alone, sorting out what he'd found, assessing employee time sheets, working in solitude.

The building was quiet, the only time in the day that it would be. As Kevin looked at the pile of paperwork and thought about his schedule for the day, Mark Rosenthal came in.

Mark was concerned.

The previous day, a prominent local orthopedic surgeon (best known for treating valuable and frequently fragile athletes) had operated on Lenore, an eighteen-year-old female gorilla with a wrist infection. Efforts to treat the infection with antibiotics had failed because Lenore wouldn't sit still, literally, to permit insertion of an IV line. Treating animals is not like treating cooperative humans. A plate implanted in her wrist did not thwart the growth of the infection, either. The decision was made—based on consultation with Mark and senior keeper Pat Sass—to amputate Lenore's left hand, wrist, and part of her forearm. It took the surgeon more than an hour to complete the operation.

Mark had just come from visiting Lenore. He talked about it to Kevin.

Lenore was up, alert, and had taken her medicine. Most

important, she hadn't picked at the incision beneath the heavily bandaged arm; it remained intact.

But Mark had unanswered questions. Would Lenore adapt to the loss of her hand once she was returned to the other gorillas? How would the others treat her? Other animals in the zoo, including monkeys, had survived amputations and had thrived. But the riddles of animal behavior did not inspire precise answers.

Kevin was interested, and sympathetic, but the paperwork beckoned; he wanted to get through as much of it as possible before Les Fisher's 9 A.M. staff meeting.

Kevin was curator of birds, but the birds had to get in line for his attention. His administrative responsibilities often devoured hours of his time. He was in charge of many of the items used by the zoo; the inventories were his responsibility. When a broom was needed, he ordered it from the storehouse. He authorized the replacement of missing or broken tools.

All the zoo's purchasing, other than food, was his to govern. He approved all the orders for familiar implements: shovels, rakes, hoses and nozzles, heavy-duty cleaners and disinfectants, chemicals to attack rodents and pests, paper towels by the mile each year, keeper uniforms (Ike jackets, parkas, jumpsuits for the elephant keepers and the vets). The unfamiliar orders were on his agenda, too. An artist's carving tool—an Exacto knife—was used to clean elephants' feet. The timber wolves enjoyed dog rawhide bones. There had to be a supply of Pampers on hand to diaper zoo-raised primates. There was a budget code system to master. He sent purchase orders to the park district; all such requests from zoo staff came to him.

He supervised the timekeeping system. There were daily time sheets and semimonthly summaries to check regularly.

And there were the daily keeper reports waiting for him every morning at the bird house. A sampling:

- "Buffalo weavers definitely doing something, but what?"
- "Terns ate 36 fish."

- "All 3 Blacksmith plover eggs missing. Probably eaten by mice."
- "Male starfinch missing from last cage on west run. Did not look real good yesterday. Maybe died up in the pot hanging from the ceiling. Will check.
- "Went up and checked hanging pot for starfinch, and he was there. Not real sure what he died from. Old age?"
- "School kids today are horrible. Three-quarters of the groups had no supervisors."
- "Have seen only four Inca terns all day. A $1.25 hot dog to anyone who can find the fifth."
- "Flamingo #78-103 attacked by swan, dragged in water west of flamingo nest island. Swan had it by neck and back, submerging it. I threw seaweed at them, and it escaped. Called Dr. Meehan, took it to hospital. No bleeding, but it was shaking and unable to stand.

  "P.S. Died next day."
- "The sunbitterns have taken over the Nicobar nest in rubber tree and thrown the Nicobars out."

The reports informed Kevin, baffled him, amused him. And they contributed to the paper load in his life. He spent as much as six hours a day reviewing the architectural plans for the bird of prey exhibit and the redesign of the bird house. Every meeting on those subjects—and they were frequent—required his comments later. Paper generated paper.

There were reports describing any incidents involving the public, reports of employee accidents, animal inventory forms, updated whenever an animal died, was born, or was sent to another zoo.

His mailbox was filled with literature from zoos of the world, much of it forwarded to him by Les Fisher. There were letters from curators at other zoos. Newsletters, journals, reports on various conservation projects. He consoled himself with a rationalization: all the paper related to one of the zoo's four objectives: conservation, recreation, education, research.

Les Fisher liked to convene his Wednesday 9 A.M. staff meeting on time. He knew that those attending were busy, and so was he. On one hot Wednesday in June, Kevin attended a staff meeting that was to give zoo librarian Joyce Shaw a chance to make a presentation to the curators, the vets, and others in attendance.

Although she had been the librarian for several years, Joyce had not before been asked to report on her activities. Her office was the small, dreary, two-room suite off the north entrance to the sixty-year-old primate house; it had been Les Fisher's office, before the Crown-Field Center was built. As a library, it was a tight fit.

Joyce was thirty-two, tall, blond, bespectacled, an attractive, smart, chain-smoking single parent with a cynical view of the zoo administration. She was underpaid and unhappy about it. She had come to the zoo from a job at the Field Museum (the city's eminent natural history museum) three years ago to bring order to the library. It hadn't been easy.

The library's confined space had to accommodate more than 100 journal-magazine subscriptions, more than 2,000 monographs, English-language zoo publications from England to Australia, a large slide collection, videotapes, and a poster collection.

Joyce's only help was provided by one part-time volunteer. She intended to use her command appearance at the staff meeting to make her case. The library, she reminded all present, was used by the zoo staff, the zoo society staff (she was paid by the zoo society), and a broad range of outsiders. She had to field questions, informed and uniformed, that kept her phone ringing frequently. The air conditioner worked but wheezed; the copying machine was unreliable. Calmly, she seemed to be conveying a message: If the zoo wanted an effective library, it would have to support it. And her.

Les Fisher knew that the zoo could not expand to provide a new building for the library; the park district had prohibited that sort of expansion in the zoo's limited space. But he did not want to clash bluntly with Joyce's ambition for a modern library.

"You know," he said, "a library is a new idea for the zoo. We used to have books scattered around all over the place. And we'd lose them. Our library ought to be service-oriented to the public, but our limitations are there. It's possible that the renovation of the primate house may leave us without a library."

His voice was calm, soft, unthreatening.

Joyce paid attention to him. "We do have a good collection of specialized, unique material that's not duplicated anywhere else in the city," she pointed out. "It's nice to be a research library. It's great to help employees working on research projects."

Les listened, paused, and commented. The others in the room were less attentive; Joyce had her supporters and her critics.

"We just haven't got room in this zoo for everything that needs room," Les sighed. "It may be solved someday. But we may have to assign priorities. Do we want to store more journals than we use? Do we even need a poster collection? I have no personal wisdom on this matter.

"Except this: The keepers shouldn't use the library as the primate house lunchroom. Get rid of that candy that you've got over there. We want to try to keep the place free of vermin."

Joyce lapsed into silence, and the meeting ended.

In the corridor outside of the conference room, she paused and articulated her devotion: "I love libraries, and I love this stupid little zoo library. I feel it strongly. My place is here. I keep seeing its potential. I guess it comes down to this: it's my job to care, even if nobody else gives a damn."

The staff filed out of the room, heading out of the building toward their own work.

One of the staff members who knew Les well turned to another.

"Know what the point of all that was?" he asked.

"No."

"Don't eat lunch in the library."

Kevin walked over to his mail box. He had removed a batch of papers from it early in the morning. It was filled again. He seized the new batch and headed for the door.

FIRST PERSON: KEVIN BELL

When I first heard that I was moving into the Bronx Zoo, I was five years old. I probably wasn't completely aware of what it all meant. It was like being close to a circus all the time. Certainly, after I was there for a period of time, it truly was a remarkable experience. From my earliest memories, it meant getting up as early as I possibly could in the morning. That's probably one of the reasons I get up so early now. I mean it was so exciting to go out and make the rounds with my dad, and go and work with incubators and do the fun stuff of working with the animals before I went to school. And then after school trying to get home as fast as I possibly could. When I was growing up, I probably didn't have as many outside friends as most kids, because after school when a lot of kids were doing things, I always wanted to come home to the zoo right away.

I knew all the keepers as well as I knew my own family. As time went on, and I had a little bit more experience working around the zoo, my role changed from one of sheer enjoyment, of doing things that I liked, to projects that my dad gave me to work on. I actually became involved. When they would get a certain type of bird in from the wild, and they wanted someone to work with it, my dad would just assign it to me. I would work with it in the morning before I went to school, and I'd start working with it again when I came home. It never seemed like work to me; it was always fun. And working alongside my dad added something to the whole experience.

My father was an excellent animal person overall. I wish that someday I become the naturalist that he was, because his knowledge of botany, of natural history, was just fantastic. But his experience dealing with people was different from my experience. I can remember when I left New York, my dad told me, "You're going to work at Lincoln Park, so make sure that you don't allow anybody there to call you by your first name. Remember, you're in charge, and everybody refers to you as Mr. Bell, not as Kevin." Well, of course, at Lincoln Park, there was a very laid-back attitude. The Bronx Zoo was very formal, and he was from the old school; keepers dressed a certain way, the staff members dressed a certain way, and they were addressed properly. He didn't have a work day. He literally worked whenever he needed to, any time of the day or night, just to make sure that whatever he was working on was done in a proper way. Also, living on the grounds meant that he was totally involved in the zoo for twenty-four hours a day. Our phone at home was the nighttime zoo phone, so everybody who had a question about raising birds, or having an opossum in their back yard, would call our number.

My dad openly said that he was not going to direct me into the animal field, but I think there was nothing that made him feel better than when I did enter the animal field. I think he consciously wanted to give me as much experience as he possibly could so that if I did choose that field, I would be as prepared as I possibly could be. I think he knew that I was going to end up in zoos, and end up in birds. He was very strong about my attending graduate school; he was always a little self-conscious about that, because he hadn't done it.

I think deep down inside I always knew that I was going to be involved with zoos. With birds. I think birds are a challenge, maybe more of a challenge in some cases than mammals even. Mammals are very popular; a lot of people know about mammals. There aren't as many people who have experience in birds. There are still birds being discovered, there are still birds, enormous numbers of birds, that have never been worked with, that people know almost nothing about. I think with birds, more than with mammals, reproduction is a good indicator not only of the health of the bird but also of the fact that you've created the proper stimuli in order to get it. You are able to feel you've created that set of circumstances necessary to get birds to reproduce.

Some birds can be very personable, like the penguins; you can almost see that there is a relationship between the keeper and the animals themselves. With birds on the other end of the scale, a lot of the perching birds, unless they're really raised as pet birds or they're hand-raised, they tend not to have the interaction with their keepers and curators that you might see with some of the mammals. But the affection is there. If you talk with the bird keepers, you'll find that they know their individual birds.

Take the Nicobar pigeons. I've got a few people who could identify every one of those birds, of the twenty-five or thirty birds out there, tell you the history of the bird, when it hatched out, how many chicks it's sired. They really know the ins and outs of a bird; whether it tends to be a good mother or tends not to be a good mother. They know the animals; there's a tremendous feeling for the animals. But, again, the animals are not the type that are going to come up and necessarily take food from your hand.

In a lot of cases, that's good, because with birds you don't want an imprinted bird that's more interested in a human than in a bird of its same species. Of course, tame birds sometimes can be better to work with than wild birds. A true wild parrot tends to be so skittish that in a captive situation it never really settles down in the sense that it will reproduce. A tamer bird, provided it isn't totally imprinted, will be willing to overlook a keeper coming into its cage to put the food pan down, to clean up, and then leave. In most cases, if they're in a breeding situation, they're not going to come over and sit on the keeper's shoulder. They're going to tolerate the keeper, but they're also going to be very protective of their nests and stay fairly aloof. It's certainly not like the interaction between a keeper and an elephant or between a gorilla and a gorilla keeper.

There are birds that I happen to like more than others. Species that either I have worked with or I'm fascinated by.

The seabirds, whether the puffins, the murres, the razor-bills, have always been a keen interest of mine. They're colonial nesters, they live in huge numbers, they're not really that well studied. We're really starting to learn more and more about them. Well, to me the most gratifying thing is this: You have a species that maybe hasn't been worked with that much in captivity. But you've gone ahead and you've done all the research on the bird in the wild that you can, in terms of reading all the literature. If you can see them in the wild, that's great, but at least you've covered it in the literature. Then you look around, and you see that in captivity there's no way to duplicate exactly what they have in the wild. You start to look at as many artificial factors that you can put in that closely simulate what they have in the wild, and when you're able to do that and get the bird to successfully reproduce, I think it's a tremendous feeling of accomplishment.

There are incredibly beautiful birds: the whole group of hummingbirds and sunbirds; there are some absolutely breathtaking birds, breathtaking birds of paradise. But there's also a tremendous amount of beauty in some of the common waterfowl that occur in this area. I mean, the mallard duck, as common as it is, is a very beautiful bird. To say one is more beautiful is to say you prefer green or blue or you prefer metallic or flat. There is certainly a beautiful array of colors and shapes in the bird.

Some birds have more intelligence, in terms of learning capabilities. But in general, birds are not a smart group; I guess that's the best way to put it.

The reason that zoos are here, the primary reason, is to do something for the public. If we didn't have any public coming through our gates, zoos would close down. We're not a forest preserve; we're not a wildlife park, although we'd like to be. It would make our job a lot easier if we could just keep animals and do what would be best for them and not necessarily best for the public. But I think our job is to get a message across to the people who are coming in here. Not only show people the variety of birds, but the variety of habitats that the birds live in, and show

how they are specifically adapted to those habitats. That's what we're going to stress in our new bird facility. So that people will get an awareness of environments and an animal's place in the environment, and the need to protect the environment and therefore protect the bird.

Reproduction is crucial because animals are not available from the wild the way they once were. If you don't reproduce, you're not going to have any animals in your zoo, not any birds anyway. Now, fortunately, we're in a situation where animals that are reproduced in zoos will be released back into the wild. That's certainly a very important aspect of our job. There are complications; there are always complications. The habitat is not what it was, and you're trying to take a bird and send it to something that is no longer there.

There's a bird that's not really endangered, called an oil bird, that occurs in Trinidad and lives only in caves. Well, the tourists have come there so much to see the oil birds that the oil birds tended to leave the caves. So you have a situation where the cave is still there, but it's just not usable for the birds. The birds are just diminishing; they're going someplace else, but they're not reproducing if they're not going into the caves. The habitat is very important and has to be maintained, and I think that's why again, we have to teach more about preserving habitats rather than just about birds. Once people learn to protect the land, then the rest will come afterward. If you educate the people here, that's going to help the situation in the wild a little bit. If you establish breeding programs here and somewhere down the road have animals to release into the wild, that's all part of conservation. More and more zoos are becoming actively involved in supporting conservation projects around the world. They're sending people out to study the animals in the wild, to study what the animals need, what their habitats are, the essential parts of their habitat, and why the numbers may be diminishing. Then we have that information that we can relate to the public. It's all really closely tied together.

One of the nice aspects of our zoo, but also a limiting

aspect, is our space. Some of our habitats can't be quite as large as we'd like them to be. There are a lot of birds that will never be exhibited at Lincoln Park. We don't have the open area for ostriches, for rheas, for emus, for cassowaries. There's a certain aspect that we'll be missing because of our limited size. It would be nice to have an area where people could go on a monorail and actually see what the animals would be like if they were out in an open valley. But then one of the nice things about our zoo is the fact that people can come here and in a couple of hours see most of the zoo, experiencing a lot of different aspects of the zoo in a short period of time. At some of the bigger places, they see only part of the zoo, they tire themselves out, and then they go home.

I think there are a number of poor zoo facilities around the country; there's no sense in hiding that fact. There are a number of facilities that for budgetary reasons or whatever don't have adequate conditions for everything. But now our parent organization, the American Association of Zoological Parks and Aquariums (AAZPA), has developed a program of accrediting zoos, so that zoo people themselves go around to each zoo, to each member institution, and look very critically, a lot more critically than anybody else would look at it. If zoos aren't accredited, they have a certain amount of time to correct the conditions that created the nonaccredited status, or they're more or less kept outside the zoo community, and we won't send animals there or deal with them.

Things that would be objectionable would involve having animals in inadequate facilities with inadequate care. For example, if there was no shade for an animal that requires shade, and it was forced to stay out in the sun all the time, maybe was not given free running water, things like that would bother me the most.

In ten years, hopefully, Lincoln Park Zoo's bird collection will have made a complete turnabout from when I got here, which was more than ten years ago. It was an extremely large collection, one of the largest collections around, but very overcrowded and with virtually no reproduction whatsoever. Birds were not kept in any particular order. There was no real management plan for the collection. Our new bird house will put us up there where we will feel good about the collection, in terms of what we're doing, what we're telling the public, our reproductive program, and the information that we'll be able to share with other zoos, based on what we've learned from keeping the birds here.

At this point I really don't have any ambition to be a zoo director. It's a whole different ball game now than it was years ago, and more and more you find people who aren't even animal people who are directors because it's a job of fund-raising, a job of public relations, not a real animal job. I'm still interested in the animal aspect of it. Sure, being a curator is frustrating at times because there is such a tremendous amount of nonanimal work, of paperwork. But most of the paperwork is still related to animals. Some days, from eight to five you're in meetings constantly. As a curator you can still come in at six, or stay until eight at night, and spend that time doing whatever you want. You can walk around the collection, you can think of things that you want to do with the collection, and so the time's there. And, you know, as busy as you are, you can always find the time for the animals.

4

LOOKING FOR MR. WRIGHT

Clarence Wright returned to his post as curator of reptiles from vacation in his hometown, Tulsa, Oklahoma. He knew that he was back at work when, at 7:45 A.M., he confronted a large stack of paperwork that had piled up in his box at the zoo office. The feeling was confirmed when he met with several reptile house keepers a few moments later.

They gathered around him in the vestibule of the old reptile house, not air-conditioned and heated almost unbearably by the morning summer sun. They recited a litany of events that had occurred while Clarence was away.

An alligator had died. Several apes had been born. (Clarence was interested in all zoo animals, not simply reptiles.) The ceiling of the primate house had been damaged—chunks had fallen, but no one had been injured—during the annual lakefront air show. Apparently, the sonic booms from low-flying jets had shaken the old building. It had been closed for repairs; the bird house and the lion house had been closed as well, to be checked.

Over the weekend, vandals had broken into the zoo between 4 and 6 A.M. and had done some damage to one of the gift shops.

That incident triggered a memory. When Clarence had worked at the Tulsa Zoo, vandals had entered the zoo and had released all the chimps. When Clarence drove into the parking lot, seven chimps were there to greet him. One moved toward him, menacingly, its arms outstretched in its attack mode. Clarence knew that he couldn't wrestle it into submission. He glared at the chimp, stretched out his own arms, and moved toward the chimp, emulating the chimp's stance. The chimp looked at Clarence and fled in fright back to its cage, shutting the cage door behind it.

Clarence left his briefing and took a quick tour of the main floor of the reptile house—an oval of glassed-in cages. Two pythons were in a courtship ritual; the male was licking the female. As Clarence walked along the tile floor in the oppressive heat, an oft-felt sense of depression came upon him.

"The building needs new lighting and new temperature controls," he said. "It's too cold in winter and too hot in summer. The humidity can't be properly controlled, and that affects some species, like frogs and toads, whose breeding is ruled by humidity. This building is sixty-five years old."

Clarence was sturdily built: six feet tall and 200 pounds. His blond hair, thinning, was matched by a trimmed moustache. His dress was casual: jeans, simple shirts, ties with animal motifs. Peering through his glasses, he demonstrated a demeanor—reinforced by a faint Oklahoma-southern accent—like that of a kindly neighbor in a Tennessee Williams play. Clarence did not like to shout or lose control. He tried to remain calm. His toughness was not obvious, but it was there.

Two of the keepers who served him were Art, a lively, informed, short, trimly built guy, and Caryn, a tall, tanned brunette with pigtails, long earrings, and dark red nail polish. They treated Clarence with affection, although in his first year on the job, he had initiated reforms in the reptile house that affected the way they had always worked. He was thirty-nine, and they knew that he knew his work and appreciated theirs.

They joked about the dead alligator; there was no mourning for it. Caryn complained about a perpetual problem: low water pressure in the building. She couldn't hose down anything. She did have some good news: a fire-bellied toad and an arrow-poison frog had laid eggs. Within days, they should hatch.

A Gila monster had died.

"I'd like to know what the hell happened to that kid," Art said, as if musing about the death of a friend. He rambled on. "The Cuban boa is not eating, but it's awfully hot out there. And in here."

They talked about repairs needed in the reptile house and the customary wait for park district laborers to show up to make them. "Christ wouldn't have been born if He had to wait for our carpenters to build a creche," Art said.

Clarence and the two keepers walked down a narrow stairway to the gray, decaying basement area, filled with displays for the public, holding areas for the animals, and keeper facilities. In an open plastic jug live crickets fluttered, waiting to serve as food for lizards. A bucket collected a leak from the ceiling; the source of the leak remained a mystery. They paused in front of the alligator exhibit. The seven alligators in it were placid, if not enervated. The exhibit was cramped, unadorned, uninteresting.

"One's got one eye. Another has a cut tail. And a third has a couple of broken legs," Caryn recited. "And there's shit in there that I can't clean without water pressure."

Her comment did not surprise Clarence. The alligator exhibit troubled him; the creatures were crowded into a dark, unadorned space. The one-eyed alligator had lost the eye in a fight with another alligator; the one with the cut tail had lost its battle as well. The alligator with the broken legs would heal itself. It was often easier to allow that to happen; treating an alligator was extremely difficult. And minor wounds did heal in time without intervention by the vets.

Clarence spotted a tortoise egg being fertilized in an incubator.

"Watch the temperature in there," Clarence instructed. "If it fluctuates, you kill the embryo."

A red-legged tarantula ambled toward the front of its case to peer at Clarence. It was common to house spiders in the reptile building; the temperature, humidity, and food served them, too.

Clarence paused in a passageway, looked around, and scowled. Everywhere he looked, it seemed, he saw the potential for change.

"There's so much to be done," he sighed. "We've got to redo our record systems. That's major work. We've got to sex the animals and make sure that our IDs are correct. Some species have been mislabeled in the past. We had a specialist visit us not long ago and take a look at a sign on an exhibit: 'Orinoco Crocodile.' He said, 'No, that's not an Orinoco crocodile. It's an American saltwater croc from Florida.' He was right. It'll take time, a year or two, just to make all the changes I want to make, but it'll get done."

He resumed his walk, passing a large cage that contained a green iguana from Mexico. It was poised on a large branch, motionless. "People buy them in pet stores," he noted. "But they're really very delicate, and few of them make it."

He peeked at the boa who hadn't been eating.

"We fed it three live mice, and it didn't eat them, so we'll switch to dead food. I don't really like to feed them live rats and mice. They can kill snakes. They eat right through to the spine. If this boa isn't eating after three weeks, we'll try mice legs or just open up a mouse to get the odor out and tempt the snake. We can force-feed it if we have to, with special food in a syringe inserted in its mouth; that's a last resort, because you can tear the lining of the throat. But some snakes can go for months without food. Adult pythons have fasted for two years."

He walked over to a small cage and picked up a desert iguana. It did not struggle.

"It's not well. When you know an animal, you know its responses, even if it moves just a little. A snake's eyes may move just a bit, but that's a signal of recognition. If you see an animal every day, you know its subtle behavior, and you can spot sickness early enough to treat it."

He continued his rounds past salamanders, toads, frogs, tortoises, iguanas, and an Asian land turtle, in a cage with the iguanas. "They're both vegetarians," he said. "They get along."

In a nearby cage, a group of Yacare caimans, a crocodile-like creature from South America, moved slowly. "They reproduce well in zoos, but they're difficult to exhibit," he noted. "They need a lot of space, something we don't have right now. We'll have to put these out on loan.

"I've never met a nice caiman. They're vicious. American alligators are more social, not as aggressive, more predictable. You can even feed one by hand. It's an animal that recognizes you."

He moved into a narrow room, where mice were raised as live food. "We're better off buying them instead of raising them, and we can do just that, buying them twice a week to feed the reptiles. Mice are thirty-five cents each, rats ninety-five cents."

Clarence finished his tour and returned to his office on the main floor. It was small, almost claustrophobic. He had a desk, a chair, a file cabinet, a typewriter; there wasn't room for more. But whatever the frustrations he faced almost daily, he was pleased to be at the zoo as a curator. For him, getting there hadn't been easy.

He grew up in Tulsa. During his summers in college, he worked as a laborer at the Tulsa Zoo. He got his degree: a bachelor's in zoology from Oklahoma State University. (Later, he got a teaching certificate as well.) He served as a full-time keeper, as curator of reptiles and amphibians, and as curator of small mammals and primates at the Tulsa Zoo. In 1985, he moved on, to become zoo curator—a complex, administrative job—at the Lowry Park Zoo in Tampa, Florida. In 1986, he headed north, to Chicago and the Lincoln Park Zoo, first as assistant curator, then as curator of reptiles and amphibians.

When Les Fisher offered the job at the zoo, "I took it immediately, no question about it. An honor," Clarence recalled. "I was hired to clean up the reptile house." A bachelor, Clarence felt he had the time—he liked working on weekends, and didn't mind working nights, either—and the energy to do what Les wanted done.

His tiny office was silent, until the phone rang.

The caller confirmed shipment of a batch of tortoises due in from Bermuda. They originated in South America and had been confiscated in Bermuda—their papers were not in order—and had been acquired by the zoo.

"Thirteen? I was expecting six or seven," Clarence bellowed into the phone. He'd have to quarantine the tortoises. If they carried any disease, he didn't want them to spread it to the other animals. And he didn't have space for thirteen tortoises.

He presented the dilemma to Caryn; she was feeding animals in the basement.

"Thirteen!" she shouted. "Where are we going to keep them? And how big do they get? They shit unbelievably every day. We'd better get some Astroturf, so I can clean it. My God, their shit is horrible-smelling. And we'll get roaches."

She was right about the odor, Clarence knew. The foot-long oblong tortoises were vegetarians; in the wild, they were able to consume as much roughage as they needed, creating normal stool. The zoo could not duplicate that diet, despite its best effort. He did better with other reptiles; the stench that troubled Caryn was not a common one.

"If we get rid of some caimans, we can make room for the tortoises," Clarence told her calmly.

The phone in the keeper area clanged. Caryn picked it up, listened, then yelled, "Artie!" Art came up and took the phone from her as she whispered, "How do you identify a caterpillar?"

"Does it have a little horn?" Art said into the phone. "Red or white? On your tomato plant? Is it moving much? Uh huh. Probably tomato hornworms," he said. "They eat leaves and turn into moths that feed on nectar at night. Get a book called *Insect Friends* or something like that." He paused and grinned. "Just look for 'em and pick 'em off. If you want to, bring 'em to Art at the reptile house."

Clarence smiled at the exchange, waved, and walked up the stairs back to his office. A mound of paperwork rested on his desk; he stared at it. He had other things on his mind.

"This is the only building that wasn't scheduled for renovation," he said. He was a man suffering from neglect. "There isn't much interest here in reptiles. Elsewhere there is. The Dallas Zoo collection is world-renowned. An excellent facility. Fort Worth and Houston are, too. St. Louis is the best of the old and the best of the new.

"Here, we're saddled with so many surplus animals. We don't need them, and nobody else wants them either.

"Then, there's that sexing problem. We shipped a male rattlesnake to a zoo that had asked for a female. We shipped an entirely different snake to a zoo that was shocked when it didn't get what it asked for. That's the way it was here.

"Now, we work harder and do better. There are six hundred animals in the reptile house. We can't be ignorant. One keeper used tongs to lift an aggressive lizard. No. Never. You can hurt it. We're learning. I have weekly meetings with the keepers. I hope to conduct actual classes with them, too. To teach. You know, you can't tell how an animal's doing by opening the cage and shutting it. The animal must come first around here.

"It's true that some reptiles shrivel away and die if you don't work at getting them to eat. You force-feed a reptile if you have to, to keep it alive. But it all takes time, and affection.

"At this zoo, the keepers are thought of as generic, interchangeable. They don't have to specialize. Well, they should. They do in other zoos. An ape keeper takes care of apes. I'm used to working with people who have a burning desire to work with reptiles.

"I have to do what's best for the collection. I want to expand its scope, if not its numbers. Here's my ideal. Tortoises on the floor, frogs in the water, massive toads, tree-dwelling snakes—all integrated into a lush tropical setting, including the insects of the region, insects that wouldn't be consumed. That tells a better story than we're telling now. An entire ecosystem.

"I want this to be a research institute, a center for the breeding of reptiles. Breeding is vital. Some snakes breed only at certain times of the year, in season. We have to know what we're doing. For example, we have to introduce the male into the female's territory—her exhibit—at the right time. The first day is the most important if courtship is to be successful. The male will run over her body with his to stimulate her. His penis—actually a double penis—locks into her, and they can copulate like that from hours to several days. The male dominates. We have to know about such things.

"We could get rid of one-third or one-half of the collection, as I see it. I'd like to pull the whole building down and start all over again. But that won't happen. So I'm hoping to do some serious planning for a renovation, and I hope that someone here takes it as seriously as I do. It's my mission."

Clarence had gotten up from his desk chair and was leaning across the desk, gesturing, sweating, imploring an unseen benefactor. But he did not shout.

The next morning, once again, Clarence was roaming the halls of the reptile house, assessing the well-being of the animals. He was an animal person; his view of his work was closer to a keeper's than to a curator's. He believed in a hands-on approach; he didn't mind getting dirty.

The summer heat was unrelenting, but it did not deter

Clarence. He roamed around the basement holding areas; there seemed to be more reptiles stored there than there were on public display.

He spotted a boa who might be sick, a tortoise plagued by parasites, and a lizard who hadn't eaten properly in days. He reached down into the lizard's cage and picked it up gently.

"This is one of those cases in which the creature would be better off in the wild than it is here," he said. "It was wild when it was found and shipped to us, and it's not adjusting well to captivity. Maybe I can arrange for it to be sent back. It'll be happier, and so will I."

He made a mental note to visit the hoofed-stock enclosure; he had sent some radiated tortoises (named for the "wheel" design on their shells), a rare species from Madagascar, to an outdoor pen at the hoofed-stock area. He wanted the tortoises to get some direct sunlight to enhance the breeding process. Sunlight could be duplicated by a special fluorescent light, but the reptile house would have to be rewired for that, so Clarence chose the real thing. By putting them in sunlight in summer, he would help get them through the long, gray midwestern winter. Late summer was the best time for breeding. Later, Clarence would have breeding boxes, filled with soil, built for them; they needed the soil in which to lay their eggs. Without it, they would not lay the eggs and could die of egg impaction.

He walked behind the exhibits on the main floor. He could feel the heat from the sun, and it bothered him.

"This building should be air-conditioned," he lamented to no one in particular. "It's destructive to the animals. That's why the mortality is so high in here."

As he passed the backs of cages holding poisonous snakes—each one marked with a conspicuous red dot—he was aware of the pull cord that ran at eye level across the entire bank of cages. A keeper hadn't been bitten in years (and not fatally then), but if one were, that cord was crucial.

Once bitten, a keeper would have to pull that cord,

similar to those found on big-city buses. It would sound an alarm.

It was important to memorize the rest of the drill. Sit down and relax. The first keeper to respond would take charge and call an ambulance. A snake-bite specialist at a nearby hospital would be alerted. On the back of each cage, a coded letter designated the proper antitoxin to be used. The antitoxins were kept in the reptile house refrigerator. One keeper would bring the antitoxin to the hospital; another would capture the animal.

"The problem isn't easy to predict," Clarence said. He had never been bitten; that was rare for a professional. "A snake can adjust the amount of venom it produces, from none to a lot. With a rattlesnake, within five minutes you can feel an ache and see redness. It's serious. But there are some venoms we simply can't read well. It can take a few hours to work, and then it can kill you. Another complication is that the antitoxin is horse serum, so you have to be tested for sensitivity to it. That's done at the hospital."

As Clarence spoke, a rattlesnake in a cage near him began to rattle.

"He's alerting the predator—me—that's all. But he probably doesn't want to hurt me. Tomorrow is feeding day for him. He's smart enough to know that he's going to get fed." (Unlike many zoo animals, reptiles are not fed daily; they're fed once, twice, or three times a week, depending on the species.)

"In captivity, they rattle from excitement," Clarence continued, looking at the snake. "If they're captive-born, they don't become afraid of you. They feed better, too, when they're hand-raised, and they're less stressed.

"Stress is a perpetual factor at a zoo. Animals can behave neurotically. Take some of the gorillas in captivity. They can have a regurgitation neurosis. They vomit, then eat it. We don't see that here, but you do in some zoos, and the visitors are shocked by it. You don't see that in the wild. In zoos, you see primates masturbating, and you don't see that in the wild either."

He peered at an Asiatic cobra. It was pale gray.

"It's supposed to be a kind of lustrous black, and it was when we got it, but now it's sick. It had a tumor on the side of its hood, and our vet removed it. But then it changed color. I've never seen a snake do that. Maybe some chemical change in its body produced that tumor—and the change in color."

Several mangrove snakes slithered around their cages.

"We have tons of those," he said. "I'm going to have them sexed, then get rid of some of them."

In the next cage, an eastern indigo snake, found in the southeastern United States, rested, all three feet of it. It was a male and was black.

"He's really tame," Clarence said. "He never bites. I can even pick him up. Sadly, the pet industry made these snakes a threatened species. They were sold to people who didn't know how to take care of them, and the snakes died."

A Gila monster glared at Clarence. It was an exception, one of two of the only venomous lizards in the world. (The other is the beaded lizard.) This one had had a long trip from its home in the Southwest (Arizona and New Mexico are the homes of the Gila monster), but it was doing well in captivity. As Clarence returned its stare, the Gila monster closed its eyes.

"Hey, kiddo, wake up," Clarence said to it. It had fallen asleep curled up in its water bowl.

"He's a slow-moving reptile, but a powerful one. They don't have fangs like snakes," Clarence pointed out, "just sharp teeth. The poison runs from ducts in the gums and is chewed into the victim. It's deadly. When a Gila bites, it hangs on. There's swelling, discoloration before death. There's no antitoxin for it, but I don't think about that. It's one of my favorite creatures. And we have eight of them."

On the back of the next exhibit, there was a plastic mask and instructions for the use of emergency eyewash.

"A spitting cobra," Clarence pointed out. "A black-necked cobra from central Africa. Accurate up to twelve feet. I don't like to deal with something that can get you from afar. They aim for the eyes. You just don't open that cage without putting on that mask first. I'd like to get rid of it, frankly, but they're tough snakes to place."

The cobra's venom could damage one's eyesight if the victim didn't wash out the eye immediately. But it was lethal only if it entered an open wound. The cobra's strike was not considered to be an aggressive move; it was the cobra's defense against an attacking animal—to blind it and permit the cobra to escape.

Clarence walked back to his office. As he opened the door, a tiny green lizard skittered across the floor. Clarence waved at it. It was an anole, purchased (thirty-five cents each) as food for a snake. It was an escapee determined to survive, and Clarence was disinclined to deter it from its mission.

His mind was on the snakes.

"A snake doesn't go after an animal it can't consume," he said. "Snakes strike out in self-defense, of course, and they kill for food. That's it. They're remarkable in some ways. Some of them can sense changes in temperature of less than one degree. A snake can analyze the body heat of its victim within 1/10,000th of a degree and conclude how much venom will be needed to kill it. The heat of an animal's footprints can lead a snake to it; the warmer it is, the closer the snake is to it. Remember, the initial bite doesn't kill the prey. The snake must follow it and see it fall. And the snake does just that."

Clarence was restless in his confining office space. He headed out into the warm day, to the hoofed-stock area, where he tracked down the tortoises, in a pen by themselves, eating. One tortoise had almost fallen into a deep pan containing food, but had not stopped eating.

"Pizza pans, that's what we need. Low, flat pizza pans," Clarence mumbled to himself.

He watched the tortoises, who moved very slowly. Some people like them as pets, he noted, but what makes a good pet is not always easy to determine, once you've listed dogs and cats.

"People want wild animals to behave like pets. It doesn't

turn out like that. Animals have temperaments. They can be stressed. When they're irritable, they can attack. And when a wild animal attacks, it's not like getting scratched by a house cat. They can chew an arm off. Or kill. I don't push animals. You can read them, their moods. A good keeper picks up on that."

On his way back to the reptile house, Clarence stopped to visit some friends, human and animal, at the great ape house. His interest in animals didn't end with reptiles; he was a familiar sight to keepers throughout the zoo.

As he strolled around the center core of the exhibit, he spotted Koundu, a large, lively male gorilla bounding around his habitat. Koundu spotted Clarence and, with a carrot in his mouth, came over to where Clarence and a keeper were standing. Koundu stuck the carrot, still in his mouth, through the mesh cage toward the keeper, a young man.

"He's trading. He wants to give me the carrot in exchange for something sweet. He loves raisins, adores peanut butter. If you fake eating the carrot, he'll take it back from you. That's his way of sharing," the keeper said, pretending to munch the carrot.

A second keeper, another young man, joined them.

"Did you hear? Shauri's baby died last night," he said to Clarence.

"No, I hadn't," Clarence sighed. He had known that the likable chimp was pregnant, but hadn't heard about the birth.

"At 5:45 last night, in the zoo hospital. Pneumonia. They took blood from its father and transfused it, but no luck. It was anemic. They tried antibiotics, too, but it probably had a congenital bacterial infection. Nothing would have worked."

There was a pause in the conversation. An unstated sense of mourning silenced the three men.

Clarence headed back to the reptile house. The shipment of tortoises from Bermuda was due to arrive at night, and he would stay late to build two simple pens for them in the basement of the reptile house.

The next morning, Clarence sat in the zoo office conference room, waiting for Les Fisher's weekly staff meeting to begin. He wore a short-sleeved white shirt and tie, his customary corduroy jeans; the short sleeves were his admission that the Chicago summer was affecting him.

Les Fisher convened the meeting on time. Before consulting his notes, the informal agenda he brought to the meetings, he asked Kevin Bell, "Would a loon eat a baby duck? My mother-in-law thought she saw one do it."

"Sure," Kevin answered.

The first item on the agenda: the continuing problem of the few alcoholics on the zoo staff and what to do about them. He urged those present to remember the need to confirm in writing any objectionable behavior.

"If people are impaired, it will show up in their work," Les said. He notified the group that the park district administration was now giving offenders just two incidents of substance abuse before taking significant action.

He moved on.

"Moats. We have stuff growing in the lion house moats," he said. "Eventually, the moat might crack. Weeds. That thistle stuff. The moats at the large mammal area have almost tree-sized things in them. The roots could create a problem. Take a look, please."

Mark Rosenthal made a note on his pad.

For the first time in years, vandals had entered the zoo after hours and had done some damage. They had entered the large mammal house through the outdoor tapir yard. The tapirs may have been unnerved by being awakened, but they had not been harmed, Mark noted, and had not, apparently, harmed the intruders. The vandals either had a key or were gifted at breaking locks; they had gone directly to the gift shop inside the large mammal house and had stolen whatever they could carry.

"There were film packages, hats, and T-shirts littered in the tapir yard. I guess when they saw the animals, they dropped some of their loot and ran," Kevin reported. The discovery of the break-in had been reported to him early in the morning.

"Instant panic," Dennis Meritt observed. As assistant director, he felt responsible for the safety of all the animals. "We're lucky. We could have had some dead giraffes. They're flighty animals, and they panic in the face of the unusual. They've been known to run into walls and kill themselves. Lucky that the people who broke in didn't confront the giraffes."

"I guess this weather's debilitating to both man and beast," Les said, indicating that some keepers had urged him to order T-shirts to replace their khaki uniform shirts. He wanted to help, but there wasn't any money in the budget for T-shirts.

Mark reported that a consultant in elephant training would be in residence all day, training the keepers who worked with the elephants. Don Meyer, the consultant, was based in southern Wisconsin and was a familiar figure at the zoo. He had worked with animals for years, had run a zoo, and had been a zoo curator. He had a positive approach to elephants, to caring for them, that Mark shared. It was Meyer's method to train the keepers to handle the elephants; they, not the animals, were his students. He stressed the importance of keepers talking to each other, the value of standardizing the way the elephants were treated. The elephants had to know—as trained dogs did—what was right and what was wrong. Meyer sought to teach the keepers to avoid confusion, which could lead to trouble. A troubled elephant was a serious threat. The keepers were taught to call the elephants by name, to give them clear commands. The use of the ankus and ropes prodded the elephants without harming them. Good behavior was rewarded, with a food "treat" at first, then words of praise. The system had been invaluable in managing the elephants under Mark's care.

The meeting ended, and Clarence went back to the reptile house. The tortoises had arrived from Bermuda, and they were in their pens. Clarence wanted to take a look at them. On his way, he told Art, busy cleaning cages, to "keep them moist; they dehydrate."

Clarence walked through the basement; he passed a cage

containing a black Tegu lizard. A keeper had attached a homemade sign, THIS ANIMAL NOW BITES. When Clarence passed the cage, the lizard leaped toward the glass, crashed into it, and bounced off, its tongue flicking out wildly.

The Tegu was young, but its behavior mimicked that of an adult. Normally the young were docile, the older ones aggressive. Tegus grew to be more than two feet long from nose to tip of their long tail. A Tegu's black and gold striped appearance kept it concealed in nature. In the wild, it would not chase a larger creature; it would try to get away. Its bite was like a band-saw slash; it gripped the flesh and tore with a sawing motion. This Tegu did not succeed in taunting Clarence, or even in getting his attention. Clarence's mind was elsewhere.

Clarence suspected that the arrival of the tortoises would unnerve the keepers, who felt that they had enough reptiles to care for already.

"We'll have some anxiety attacks. But it doesn't do any good to fret. We have to stay calm. We're overstocked and understaffed. It'll take a year to get rid of our surplus and get properly organized.

"We advertise in the zoo association journal for surplus and wanted animals. Reptile departments keep in touch with each other, too. In due time, everything will be taken care of, but right now those tortoises will inspire some anxiety."

When he got to the two pens, a male tortoise had mounted a female and was clucking happily. He did not dally; his mission was accomplished quickly. Within seconds, a second pair joined them in initiating their new home. Group sex among tortoises. Clarence looked on and smiled; he was pleased to discover that their anxiety level was not high.

It was feeding day. The reptile house was closed when live food—chicks, rabbits, rats, mice—was fed, so children's dreams would not be corrupted.

Clarence passed Art, at work in the basement.

"We're up to the kazoo in rats," Art said.

"Give some extras to the pythons. They'll eat 'em,"

Clarence suggested. "Anyway, I want to cancel the rat shipments and get rid of that rat room. Let's order weekly instead of collecting them down here."

As Clarence and Art chatted, a pair of white rabbits, doomed to be dinner for large snakes, were twitching in a carrier nearby. Large chickens would be on the snake menu as well; the gators and the Gila monsters preferred chicks.

"That rabbit," Art said, pointing to the carrier, "I'll just toss it into the anaconda cage. Believe me, the anaconda will take it. It'll take me, too, if I'm not careful. By the way, Clarence, the puff adder is eating very little. And it defecates just once a month. It's getting fatter and fatter."

Clarence looked at Art with an expression that seemed to say, "That's your problem, Art."

"One of these days, I hope to convert to dead food," Clarence proclaimed. "It's better for the keepers and the animals. A dying rabbit still has the teeth to bite a snake. I've seen it happen."

Again, he had snakes on his mind. He knew all the charges against them. He'd heard that man, the commanding upright presence, has a deeply rooted aversion to any crawling species. It is, some said, biological. He knew, as well, that snakes represent evil in many societies. Nevertheless, he sustained an admiration for them, a respect, and, at times, a profound fear.

"If a king cobra bites an appendage, cut it off. Quickly. That's how dangerous they are. The king cobra has a large venom gland, and when it bites, it holds on and pumps. Don't forget, it's an eighteen-foot snake with a tablespoon of venom in it. If a person gets all that venom, it's terminal. Even newborn snakes have venom, and it's in a concentrated form, which makes it extremely dangerous. What some people don't realize is that even a scratch from a big, or even a small, snake can do harm. It doesn't always take a bite."

He was distracted by the scampering of the black Tegu lizard in its cage.

"We got that one when it was a baby," he said. "That

sucker is going to be mean as shit when he grows up."

He paused in front of the large cage holding the green iguana; as usual, the iguana was reclining along a tree branch, surveying the basement of the reptile house with its fixed glare. Clarence returned the glare, then moved on.

Along the way, he passed cages with snakes and lizards. Occasionally, he would get a phone call from someone who wanted to buy one as a pet. It annoyed him.

"When you think about all the creatures captured in the wild that go to pet shops and on to owners, you ought to know that ninety-nine percent of them die before they've had a chance to live a long, happy life.

"Visit a wild-animal wholesaler, and see a new shipment. Count the dead animals, dead before they can even be sold. The people who ship them in, the worst of them, use the smallest containers to ship them. It's cheaper. When iguanas are packed that way, they trample each other to death, and others die simply because they're so severely stressed. So many die that the price of the survivors goes up. This green one here would cost eighty-nine dollars in a pet store."

When Clarence had lived in Tulsa with his parents, he kept as many as 200 reptiles and amphibians in the house. Some of them remained in that house, cared for by his parents. When Clarence visited home, he visited more than his parents.

"In the old days, when I lived there, they had the run of the house in some cases," he recalled. "I had two iguanas five feet long that certainly did. I guess you could say that they were paper-trained house pets, but I hate to use the word *pet*. I'd rather talk about what I call captive behavior. These creatures aren't pets. They're wild animals that may be able to adjust to their new environment.

"I remember my iguanas crawling up onto my lap, to get my body warmth. They recognized me by my scent. They'd come to me but would stay away from strangers. They can be taught. But within limitations."

He resumed his walk, pausing in front of a cage holding a

leopard gecko, a small, spotted desert lizard from Pakistan.

"If I have to use that word *pet*," he said, "this would be my favorite for kids. It will allow them to hold it. It can be hand-fed. It's very clean, like a cat. It eats live crickets and baby mice, which you can buy. And cleaning its cage is not difficult. If they're used to you, they'll lick your hand. They need some rocks to hide under, some water and some food and a warm room—they like heat—and if you ever need a vet, you can find one who specializes in reptiles. You can buy a gecko for fifty dollars."

Clarence picked up the gecko. It shot feces at him and urinated in his hand.

Clarence looked sternly at the nervous lizard.

"Mine *never* do that," he said.

And then he laughed.

FIRST PERSON: CLARENCE WRIGHT

When I was twelve, through a lot of the Walt Disney films, I realized that what I was really interested in was wildlife and animals. As a child I was different from most kids. I never really played with a group. I always was pretty much by myself, doing my own things. Then, when I was twelve, I found a purpose in my life. I started devoting more time to observing wildlife. We lived in a remote area; I think the nearest human was probably about ten miles away, so I was able to do a lot of field observations, and I developed a comfortable feeling with nature. More than I did around people.

I remember buying books; the first book was *Born Free*, which I read two or three times. And then, after I saw Walt Disney's film on otters, I read *Ring of Bright Water*. At that time, I started purchasing small reptiles. I was thirteen when I purchased my first caiman in a pet shop. Like most kids at that age, I knew nothing about it; no one seemed to know anything about it. I lost that first caiman because I didn't know exactly what I was doing. I also was interested in local wildlife, and I raised a baby coyote. I raised it successfully to adulthood.

When I was fourteen, my brother was driving past a nature center—run by Hugh and Zelta Davis—in a little town called Catoosa, Oklahoma, between Tulsa and Claremore. I went out there almost everyday; my brother would take me out there. He was very understanding. The third time I went, I was going to pay fifty cents to get in, but Mrs. Davis said, "No, no, you don't have to worry about it. You've seen this place more than most people will see it in their lifetime." She said, "Just come on in and enjoy yourself."

At that time, they had a tremendous collection of reptiles, all kinds of cobras, a large selection of alligators, about a hundred and fifty alligators, all running loose in a five-acre fenced-in area.

I was one of these quiet people who would just observe. I observed body movements, behavior among alligators. I started learning a lot about the behavior of reptiles. They also had a very good collection of native mammals, bobcats and mountain lions and a fantastic prairie dog pound.

I started reading like you wouldn't believe, and the book collection grew. Today it numbers about thirty thousand dollars' worth of books. It was a fascination that has not stopped. Today, it's a pioneering thing for me to learn as much as I can about natural history. At that time, I decided that I wanted to either go into wildlife conservation work, be a game ranger, or be a zoo person.

From the time I was about fourteen, I worked every summer. I worked at the nature center, and I went out there on weekends. I spent a lot of time at the Davises' home, which was just across the street from the nature center. Their house was like a natural history museum; they had all kinds of skins, skulls. It was just a real comfortable place for me. I learned a wealth of information from Mr. Davis. He got me involved in going out and catching alligators; when I was about sixteen, we went to Arkansas and collected some alligators down in that area.

So I learned a lot about how to handle animals and about the laws of conservation.

After I was graduated from high school, I was torn whether to go in the zoo business or be in some other kind of business. I worked with my dad for about a year. Hugh Davis, who did not have a degree, told me, "If you're going to make zoos a career, you have to have at least a bachelor's degree." And he said, "As far as I'm concerned, you can take the degree and stick it, but you definitely have to get it." So I decided that I was going to have to. Well, I'm the first in my family to have a bachelor's degree. My parents never felt it was a waste of time, but they just didn't really encourage me to do it.

The money wasn't there; I had to earn it all. But the desire and interest were all there. I started working at the zoo during the summer at college, and those four summers I worked as a laborer, but I worked with animals, too. After that, a keepership at the Tulsa Zoo popped up, right after I was graduated. I worked with reptiles.

I was very green. The zoo was like an open encyclopedia to me because there was so much to learn about the behavior of animals in captivity. And, of course, I read all the literature.

You know, if you get your technique down, you can do it all, cleaning and taking care of the animals. And you learn the animals so well you know when they're going to shit. So you gear your time for it. At that time we had approximately five hundred animals in the collection, lines of three-tier cages, little box cages with full-grown reptiles—western diamondbacks, rattlesnakes, cobras, and on and on.

I was a kind of working curator. That's the reason why I'm really not used to wearing a shirt and a tie. I'm used to filling in for absent keepers and still doing my other work. Most of the paperwork I either did at home or did before or after work. They knew they had someone who was far beyond most keepers. In one of the zoo publications my second summer there, the director mentioned my name and said I was a future zoo director. That got me so much flak from everybody. A lot of them were jealous. I didn't just work hard. I had the abilities and knowledge to look at a new situation and work through it. Common sense. To me, common sense is to look at something and do the best you can with the situation.

That zoo was primitive enough so that every situation that came along I could solve fairly easily. I was comfortable in the whole zoo. It wasn't because of the desire to please somebody; it was the desire to work with the animals and make them comfortable. I was trying to please myself. I still hold to that; I do the best I can with a job, and if it reflects positively, fine. I don't want to say I don't care, it's just that I don't look for recognition for doing a good job.

I was finally promoted to supervisor of reptiles, a curator's job. Within two years in that reptile department, I turned it around. I turned it around to where the animals were being cared for very well, we had reproduction going on, of reptiles that had never before bred in the Tulsa Zoo. We had three endangered species that bred for the first time. I was very excited about the department. And at that time I wanted to switch over to mammals, even though I was comfortable over at reptiles. But I wanted to switch over to mammals because my interest was otters, and I had a big interest in primates. They created a department for me, a primate section and a small mammal section.

I'd been curator of small mammals for about two years, and there was a lot of political stuff going on. They hired a general curator. I thought, "Well, I can live through anything." Well, that wasn't true. I thought I could survive. After all, I was married to the Tulsa Zoo; I mean, I was putting in twelve hours a day, and I'd be there seven days a week, because I loved doing it. I was doing all kinds of research projects. My parents were in Tulsa, and I wanted to stay with my parents. I was still living with my parents, so I tried to weather it for about eight months. The new guy was going in and moving animals around in my department. We didn't get along.

I had a major research project going with Asian small-clawed otters at the Tulsa Zoo. At the American Association of Zoological Parks and Aquariums, they asked me to be the coordinator and studbook keeper for that species. It was the first mammal model species survival plan that the AAZPA ever had, and they said they were probably going to use it as a model for the other mammals. It's a big deal. We had people coming in from other parts of the country to see the program. And when the new guy got on board, he took the whole program lightly, and he told me, "You don't have time for this program anymore," and he threw it out. Just like that, just threw the whole thing out. I gave two weeks' notice. I'd committed almost twelve years of my life to that facility, and the zoo director didn't even talk to me about what happened.

I went back to school and got a teaching certificate. The Tampa Zoo advertised in the AAZPA newsletter. I went down, and the interview with the director went very well. Sure enough, he called me. At that time I was supporting my parents, like I am now, and the salary was nineteen five, which is nothing. And I was to be a zoo curator, which is like a general curator. But I thought, here is a zoo that was an old roadside zoo, bars and stuff like that, that they were going to bulldoze down to build a brand-new zoo. And I thought, "God, here I would be second in charge; I could really design a zoo the way I want it done." Again, I was working seven days a week. I did it because I love doing it. I was working twelve and thirteen hours, seven days a week, and I enjoyed it.

After a year and a half, I needed a salary increase, because nineteen five a year is not very good. I was doing the general curator stuff, all the paperwork, and all the computer stuff. I was supervising the keepers, hiring keepers, doing the curator stuff of getting animals in, getting rid of animals, and we still had a zoo, we still had a temporary zoo I was overseeing. I decided I just had to have more money. Luckily, that's when the job came open at Lincoln Park. I applied for it, and it took them about six months to process it; out of seventy applications they narrowed it down to me.

Otters are my favorite animals. I think it's their outlook on life. It is "Get as much joy out of life as you can." They constantly play; they get so much out of every little thing they have, whether it's a little marble, or whether it's a stone. They take their time and enjoy life.

I had otters from the time I was nineteen, at home. I know otter behavior. Almost by glancing, seeing what they're doing, I can tell you what they are thinking. It's not being anthropomorphic. I interpret it as animal behavior, not human behavior. I literally lived with North American otters in my home, so if they were sleeping at the foot of my bed, I was hearing sounds from them that normal people wouldn't hear by just having them in a zoo and observing them. There were vocalizations that had never been recorded before; I recorded them. Low guttural sounds that meant that otters have nightmares, and they'll start twitching and making little guttural sounds.

Otters that have grown up with me read my face. They look at your face and eyes. My female Millie follows me around; she's always looking up at my face. I can give her a facial signal that I want to play, and she'll jump up and start playing. If I'm in a bad mood, they still may push me. I remember telling Millie not to open the drawers in the highboy. She knew she wasn't supposed to go there, but then I started doing something else, and I actually saw her in the corner of my eye sneak around until she thought she was out of my vision, go to the drawer, and pop that drawer open and crawl in, quickly, quickly.

They are very affectionate. Millie will, if I'm standing, stand up and put her arms around my leg, and then I'll stroke her. And if she wants to be picked up, she'll push her head against my hand while I'm stroking her, and then I'll hold her. They express some affection by grooming. I'll start petting her, and she'll start grooming my neck. Though she's an otter, she realizes that I hand-raised her from a baby. I introduced her to other otters; she knows she's an otter, and she enjoys it and gets along very well with a man.

My main interest, when I first got involved, was to breed

otters. And to understand their behavior. I'm an otter specialist for the International Union for the Conservation of Nature. I do a lot of behavioral observation. I don't have Asian small-clawed otters now; I have North Americans. Vocalization is different between the two species. The Asian small-clawed otters, all they can do is make bird chirps. The North American otters have bird chirps, but they also have a humming sound. You can talk to them that way, and they'll hum back. I think they're even more affectionate than the Asians. Asians are very temperamental; if they're into something and you swat them, they'll turn around and chew your leg off. And North Americans, if you swat them, they walk off. I learned very quickly how to read Asians, because I got bit many times. My otters I kept mainly in the house. Now these three Asians that I had, I did not want to do that. They were tame, but they weren't tame enough.

Asian small-clawed otters run in bands of up to twenty individuals. We're finding out they have extended families, meaning that the sons and daughters stay with the family group for a long time, up to two generations. And they actually help care for the offspring that are born. We're finding out all this new stuff.

Psychologists believe that people feel comfortable around mammals because they are mammals. Also, the fur has a lot to do with the psychological security of a person, who can touch the fur of an animal; it's more soft and gentle to the touch than a scale. Humans feel more comfortable around mammals. Reptiles have gotten a bad rap, because when most people think of reptiles, they automatically think venomous. I don't care if it's a lizard or an amphibian—when I grew up, I was scared of reptiles. When I was twelve years old, before I got to know Hugh Davis, I was scared of reptiles. Somebody showed me a garter snake, and I was unbelievably scared. A lot of the proliferation of the reptiles' image is done by parents, in teaching their kids that all reptiles are bad. Toads give you warts, you know, you don't pick up toads. I was scared of toads. When Hugh

Davis came along and taught me about reptiles, and how to deal with them and their behavior, I realized that it was all bunk.

Do snakes recognize people? If you have a different body odor than other people, they may sense that, but as far as true recognition, no. I don't feel they can recognize an individual: "Gee, this person feeds me, and I want to be good to this person." It doesn't have that kind of intelligence. It doesn't have a sense of remorse; if it bites you, it bites you out of self-defense.

Now, lizards—when you get higher up into some of the lizards—are very aware of people and their shapes and body forms. I think they can recognize a little more than the snake. Supposedly snakes were the last to evolve, so they're the newest type of reptile. Tortoises and crocodilians are the oldest; supposedly that's where snakes and lizards came from. Lizards are more cognizant of their environment. They're more visual than snakes.

You can work with snakes and tame them by just handling them. It's because they get habituated to your handling them. You deal with them every day, you handle them every day, and they know you're not going to do them any harm by repetitive touching. But they're not affectionate.

A lizard may come over and just be curious, and that's the word that I use when they come over to look at you; curious. It's not that they're going to show you affection. I can pretty safely say of all reptiles that there's no affection. They're driven by mating, by courtship, by instincts. You'll hear people say, "Oh, my lizard recognizes me, and he comes over, and he gets up." Well, if they think a little bit, if it's a cool day, the lizard gets up and rests on your body because it's getting body heat from you. And you can calm a reptile down that's cool, that's a little excited, by just putting him on your arm and letting him rest. He'll lie there because he's getting the warmth.

Each reptile has a personality the way all animals do. Even snakes have their own little quirky personalities. You may have one snake that is really curious, when you walk by, to see if you've got any food. And the other one's just lying there, couldn't care less about its world. You may put the food in, and the snake who's curious will grab it and eat it with no problem; for the other you have to dangle it, and he doesn't care. Some rattlesnakes will be interested in just exploring their world. They'll move around and are looking at it. Others will strike the glass constantly because they're so nervous and upset. When you get a wild-caught reptile, you want to try to get a reptile that is the most adaptive to captivity. There have been reptiles brought in that have been so nervous about being in captivity they die. They literally won't eat; they die. With animals like that, if they're local animals, I'll take them back out and turn them loose.

There's so little known about reptiles, in behavior, court-ship, and reproduction, that it's still an open field. We have come a long way in ten, fifteen years, on the care of reptiles and amphibians in captivity. Animals that now are kept so easily, ten years ago you'd be lucky if you could keep one alive, because of the lack of knowledge of the care of that animal. A prime example is green tree pythons, which we don't have here, but I had in Tulsa. If you kept them alive, you were lucky. Now, everybody's learned to reproduce them. Individuals and institutions and research facilities are doing the pioneering work; that adds to the whole body of the care of these animals.

As far as crocodilians go, the alligators have the broadest perspective and broadest personality of all crocodilians. They are aware of their environment. They're more curi-ous about things. I think curiousness is a sign of intelli-gence. If an animal's curious enough to go look over and see what's going on, it tells me that it has enough mental ability to synthesize. Since I grew up at the nature center and they had over a hundred alligators, I could see the behavioral differences in each individual alligator.

We had a female that was a delicate petite alligator who liked the food a certain way, and if it wasn't a certain way, she just wouldn't eat it. We had one named Betty, who was an eight-foot female, very heavy-set. I'll never forget, Zelta Davis was feeding this animal late in the evening, and she had sunglasses on, so she really couldn't see where the mouth was. She would just tap it on the snout, and it would open its mouth, and she'd throw the food in. Well, Betty came lumbering up on the land and was waiting there patiently, and she had her mouth open. And instead of tapping the top part of the snout, Mrs. Davis tapped on the lower part, and of course Betty clamped down and was in the process of pulling her into the water slowly. Betty had her mouth shut and didn't realize what she was pulling on. Mrs. Davis took her hand and said "let go" and slapped Betty. Betty just let go. Like, "What did I do?" and went back in the water. Of course, we had more food, but she wouldn't come up, not for a week after that.

I think tortoises have been given a bad rap as far as being dull and dim-witted. In their own way, they have the ability to be interested in their environment if they are given a chance to have an environment. Unfortunately, when you give them a brick wall, that's not much of an environment. I think a lot of reptiles are that way; if they're kept in small little glass cages, they lose interest, and they look dull. But tortoises are a lot smarter than we give them credit for. First of all, they've survived beyond all the dinosaurs and all the prehistoric mammals, so they've got to have some basic instincts. More than anything, they're majestic in many ways. They seem to have their own purpose in life, they don't care about anything else, they know where they stand.

Some psychologists believe that people are more at ease with objects or animals that are round and really don't have a shape. And tortoises have that round appearance, nonthreatening. There's another point: they're vegetarians, they don't eat meat. Another fascination is that they are a beautiful animal, there are a lot of beautiful colors in them. I'm fascinated by their behavior—courtship behavior has not been well documented in a lot of the tortoises—and reproduction. My fascination with all the reptiles has evolved into trying to set up an enriching environment. The quality of life is super important, for the snake as well as the elephant. Unfortunately reptiles in zoos have been kept in a very limited environment, and I think that's the reason why you get this thing that just lies there and does nothing.

My dream is to develop habitats that pretty much simulate where the animals are from. I know there's no way to totally simulate them, because of our space limitations, but we can give more space and incorporate a very active environment, with flowing water, live plants, soil, and bark chips instead of just gravel, giving them a lot of nooks and crannies they can get involved with and move around in. We can give them all kinds of options that they don't have in a square box. You can incorporate several different species in one exhibit. Some zoos have done it. There's enough known now about reptile care; they won't eat one another.

You can actually feed the animal by hand-feeding or putting the food in a location where the animal in the wild would normally feed. For example, the green iguana lies in the trees and eats fruit off the trees. You have a food dish that is in a bushy area of an exhibit on a log, and you can put out the food pan, and the iguana knows that it can feed there; it doesn't have to go to the ground to eat, which is really not normal. When the dandelions were blooming, I asked the reptile people to feed them to the tortoises. Well, you know, it's extra work, and they don't like doing it. But when you give them a variety of food like that, their whole interest picks up. Gee, this is different, I love it. And they eat it. So their behavior starts developing, they start getting a broader interest. And they can go over, and here's this waterfall coming down, and they can crawl in the pool, or they can crawl underneath the waterfall and get splashed on to get stimulation. If they can do that, they've got some options.

A classic example is our great apes facility; the activity of those gorillas and orangs and chimps is phenomenal. You go to some zoos, and they have the apes set off where the public looks on, and the apes are just sitting there doing nothing. Ours is designed to promote movement, and upward movement, and social connections. They can climb and move and manipulate ropes; I have never seen such an active group of animals.

The major uncertainty I have is what direction this zoo wants the reptile collection to go. Do they want to renovate the building? Do they really understand about giving the animals environmental stimulation? Or do they want just a big box? By having a habitat and environmental stimulation, you can get more activity from your animals and more interest in life. I think our zoo's reptile collection will be equal to others in the United States, probably in two to three years, if we go down the path of renovation and development of new facilities, and taking on the new kind of husbandry that it's going to need to get there. Right now, I feel we are a long way from being on a par with the other great zoos as far as the reptile collection goes.

In five years, I would like to be either a field biologist with a Ph.D., doing field research on otters, or a director of a zoo that is very open and able to contribute to world conservation. My whole purpose in life is world conservation, to develop and help save habitats, to develop habitats if they've been destroyed.

In my life, the animals are number one, whether they're in the wild or in captivity, and I will do all I can in my power, if I have to do it myself, to make sure animals are cared for properly. If it means saving a habitat, I would do all I could to save the habitat. I go by my own drumbeat, and I do what I think is best for the animals. And if that means getting in and scrubbing a cage, I'll do it. When I quit my job in Tulsa, I adopted a philosophy of life: I was going to do the best I could; I was always going to be kind to people, no matter how bad they were to me. And this relates to my whole being. I'm going to always give love, and I think it will always come back.

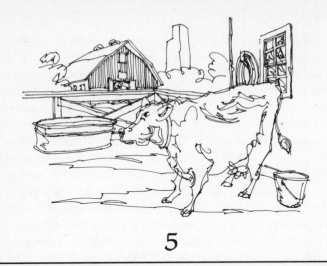

5

Farmer's Daughter

Picture a typical farmer: a middle-aged man in well-worn overalls, workshirt, weathered boots, and a cap with the emblem of a farm equipment company, surveying vast fields of waving grain.

Then picture the "farmer" who oversees the Farm in the Zoo, five acres of red barns and patches of grass. That farmer was LuAnne Metzger. At age twenty-eight, she was tall (5'8"), trim, athletic; her hair was bronze-colored, her eyes royal blue, her summertime tan calculatedly deep. She wore two pairs of earrings: a pair of small diamond studs and a pair of gold hoops. Her clothing was impeccably fashionable.

LuAnne had come a long way from Carlock, Illinois, a very small town (population less than 500) her family had lived in for generations—and she'd done it in a relatively short time.

She grew up in a house that doubled as the local funeral parlor; when she was born and required a room, she displaced the casket display. Her father was an independent insurance agent who also raised sheep and beef cattle. (He was a minor partner in the funeral home.)

After high school, she went to the University of Illinois, where she majored in agricultural communications; she was graduated in 1980. While she was at college, she spent summers as an intern with the United States Department of Agriculture in Chicago; after graduation, she worked for that department's office of information. A budget cut eliminated her job after five months. She did not mourn.

"They offered me the chance to go to New York to work," she remembered. "But I hated that city. As it turned out, I hated doing everything in triplicate as well."

She got a call from an editor at a new farm newspaper based in Bloomington, Illinois. She was tempted by the combination of journalism and farming.

She had grown up showing sheep and cattle at county and state fairs and had a collection of trophies to prove it. She knew about farming. For the newspaper, she covered fourteen counties. The experience paid off and led to another phone call. That conversation took her to Des Moines, Iowa, to be beef editor of *Wallace's Farmer* ("Iowa's Farm Progress Publication"), founded by Henry Wallace of Progressive Party fame.

For LuAnne, that was an exciting time; she covered crops, too, and was the first woman editor the publication had hired.

"The pay was better. In fact, I could live on it. I could live on my own," she recalled. "Our readers lived and died with *Wallace's Farmer*," she added. "It was a great job. Sure, Iowa was a little hickish compared to Illinois, but I worked with great people, and I had a company car. I even found an Iowa farm boy, who had become a grain trader. But when he decided to take a job in Chicago, I knew I'd have to quit my job.

"I interviewed with public relations firms in Chicago. No fun in them. I came to the conclusion that I wanted to be on a farm again. I didn't want a nine-to-five job. Then I picked up a copy of the University of Illinois newsletter for agriculture grads, and I saw the listing for the farm curator's job at the zoo, so I applied."

She got the job in February 1986 and married the grain trader seven months later.

The Farm in the Zoo was funded by the zoo society, not by the park district. LuAnne worked for the society, but those who reported to her worked for the city bureaucracy. At first, that caused resentment; the keepers wanted to report to a curator who owed allegiance to the park district, not to the zoo society, which some saw as a group of fluttering socialites. No doubt they objected to taking orders from a young new curator, a young new female curator as well.

A year and a half after LuAnne was hired, the situation had calmed down—or gone underground. Keepers griped at times, but LuAnne was in charge.

Her daily commute from a western suburb to her cluttered basement office in the primate house took several hours a day out of her life, but she was often at work before 7 A.M.

"I wound up here by a fluke, but I love it," she said, seated behind her old desk covered with zoo paperwork. "I don't miss the procrastination and pain of meeting deadlines. I like agriculture, and I like the chance to teach urban kids about it."

When she took the job, she was told the Farm in the Zoo would be renovated. The work, in fact, was well under way, and she played a guiding role.

"That encouraged me to take the job. Now I've got a commitment here. I know what I want this farm to be in two years, in five years. I want visitors to see activities and demonstrations, food tastings, folk music, storytellers, and more. I want them to leave here with a basic fact: food doesn't come from a grocery store. I want classes held here and all sorts of things going on. I want this to be a lump of coal that becomes a diamond."

The farm consisted of five red barns: a main exhibit hall and barns for poultry, horses, dairy cattle, and livestock.

The animals she governed included six dairy cows (each producing a calf every year), three to four dairy goats and their kids, a sow and her litter, four sheep and lambs, four beef steers, six horses and ponies, and a collection of chickens. Some stayed on as tenants; others moved on to market.

Every morning, LuAnne would dig into the paperwork in her primate house office, check her box at the zoo center, attend meetings related to the renovation, then head for the farm itself on the southern edge of the zoo.

Early one summer morning, she headed for the farm to make rounds. In the dairy barn, two piglets were nursing with wild abandon on their mammoth sow. "One of the meanest animals—along with the dairy bull—on the farm," LuAnne noted.

Six dairy cows were in an outdoor pen, standing around stoically. A brown-and-white Guernsey calf was in an outdoor pen with two piglets; they seemed oblivious to each other. In another adjoining pen, sheep and goats pranced.

Inside the dairy barn, a sign was posted: "Each day the average cow drinks 25 gallons of water, eats 26 pounds of hay and 20 pounds of grain, to produce 7 gallons of milk." At the zoo's farm, the milking process was for the public's delight; the milk produced by the milking machines, open to view, was used to feed the calves and other young animals.

As LuAnne walked around the dairy barn, she was met by Tom Meehan, the zoo's veterinarian. He was there to visit the mother of the calf in the outdoor pen. The Guernsey was not in good shape.

"After the birth, which was unassisted, she went down," LuAnne said. The expression meant that the animal dropped to the ground and couldn't get up on her own, a serious sign in other animals at the zoo as well.

"We almost lost her. She was close to being euthanized. We put some feed and water in front of her and left for the day. I really thought I'd find a stiff cow in the morning, but she drank the water and ate the feed, and by eight in the morning, she was standing."

Tom was checking the cow's right front hoof for signs of healing; earlier, he'd removed an abscess from it. He unwrapped the hoof, cleaned and treated the area, and bandaged it again. LuAnne watched him work in silence. So did the Guernsey.

A horde of flies had entered the barn. LuAnne swiped at them unsuccessfully, then motioned to one of the keepers on duty: "Please spray for flies. They're biting." The keeper, a middle-aged woman, nodded and disappeared.

LuAnne went outside and entered the pen with the Guernsey calf; she petted it, and it nuzzled her knee. A few yards away, a goat bleated. Two piglets wallowed in a pool of muddy water, a few feet away from the calf; one defecated in the water. A group of morning zoo visitors watched it all with pleasure. In the distance, modern highrise buildings bordered the zoo; the sound of traffic mixed with the sounds of the animals, a living incongruity.

LuAnne resumed her stroll through the farm.

"Imagine. Five acres of farmland. And I don't pay any taxes. Just a few headaches, that's all," she said, as she passed a patch of worn grass that she wanted to turn into a garden. "We'll grow vegetables, soybeans, corn, alfalfa, and wheat, just for city kids to see.

"You know what's funny? I wasn't a zoo person when I was growing up. I didn't watch all those animal shows on public television. I'm even allergic to hay. But now that I'm here, I want to learn. I want to know about the other animals. So when I have time, I go to the bird house. I go to see the great apes. I sit in on staff meetings with my eyes and ears wide open. I'm fascinated by the people who work here. It's quite a gamut. Weird, different people trying to work as a team."

She knew that she was unlike most of them, but she was determined to succeed despite the differences. Most of the others were zealous in protecting their animals; as a child, on a farm, she had learned another lesson. Calves became veal. Pigs became bacon. The zoo got its sow from a farmer when that sow was pregnant, so visitors could see the birth, and the piglets produced. But after the birth, the pigs went back to that farm—and a fate in contradiction to that of the other zoo animals.

The farm raised chickens, too, and the chicks were shipped to the reptile house, to serve as food. That was not recited to visitors, but LuAnne did have to field protests from informed and angry callers.

"I've had calls from people who call me a murderer," she said. "For God's sake, I loved steers. I saved pictures of me with my favorite steers before they went to slaughter. It's either them or us. Everything eats something, and if the reptiles prefer chicks, well, that's how it is. When we raise all these animals here, I watch the docents love them. I know that our steers are sold and slaughtered and our lambs go to market. But I watch the docents loving those animals, and I'm touched by it. I hate to be the bad guy. But I really don't think I am. I think I'm sensible, realistic, not heartless.

"If a cow or a ewe doesn't give birth in a year, we ship it out. On a real farm, you have to keep culling them. That's selective breeding, to breed for the best milk producers, the best meat, the best wool, the best-looking. Here, we want them to look good, and we want them to be well nourished, but we don't have to turn a profit. That's the advantage and the big difference from running a real farm. My profit is in the people who come here and enjoy the exhibits and the animals and go away a little smarter about farms than they were when they got here."

In 1964, when the Farm in the Zoo opened—thanks to the fund-raising mastery of the zoo society—it was part of a major effort to upgrade the entire zoo. The zoo society was just five years old then, developing its fiscal muscles, and LuAnne was six. By the time LuAnne arrived at the zoo, it had grown, the society had raised millions of dollars to support that growth, and the farm had achieved a level of popularity that made it a common stop for two million visitors annually.

They came to see the cows milked, as they were on real

dairy farms. They came to see poultry, horses, and livestock—and exhibits that explained farm life to street-smart city dwellers.

For LuAnne, the farm functioned, but it wasn't easy to compete with the more exotic collections in the rest of the zoo. Cows weren't wild animals. And LuAnne, new to the business of zoos, was uneasy at first.

"I felt lost," she recalled. "I knew how things got done at newspapers and magazines, but I wasn't a zoo professional. I didn't know how you got office supplies at the zoo. The staff welcomed me; they were friendly. But the keepers were another matter. I felt an icy stare between them and me.

"By the time I arrived, it seemed to me that the farm was being ignored. I was the first full-time curator at the farm. Early on, I met a guy who was supposed to be helping me. He hated women, Jews, blacks, you name it. It was a chilling time.

"As I saw it, the farm had become the zoo's Siberia. If you messed up, that's where you were sent. A zoo professional with knowledge of mammals probably wouldn't have wanted to work at the farm. Fortunately, I didn't know any better.

"It was survival of the fittest. I stuck it out. There were some rough times. I found ways to get along with the keepers. Some of the old-timers, who weren't going to change, retired. I never expected them to change. But I was ready to change.

"It took a while for me to learn about the place. I'm still learning. It's funny, but I've always been the young kid on every job I've ever had. I've had to get used to working with seasoned professionals. One way was to learn how important it was to say, 'I don't know. I'll find out and let you know.' In other words, I didn't want to fake knowledge."

She sat on a bench in the small grassy area in the center of the farm, surrounded by the barns. She knew her weaknesses and how they played into the hands of her critics. She had pride, and she knew her strengths.

She knew farm animals. She knew the six major breeds of dairy cattle: Ayrshire, Guernsey, Jersey, Holstein, Milking Shorthorn, and Brown Swiss. She knew that most dairy cows are artificially inseminated and that a cow would calve once a year. She knew, too, that most older dairy cows were sold to make hamburger, although a few might live to be fifteen years old.

She was a mobile reservoir of farm facts; she enjoyed providing useful information to neophytes. She had written a guide for the docents, so when they lectured at the farm, what they said would be correct:

"Pigs are young swine of either sex, under six months old. Hogs are swine older than six months or of greater than two hundred pounds. When mature, females (sows), may weigh up to four hundred pounds, boars up to six hundred pounds."

Sows at the zoo farm—and at real ones—delivered about a dozen piglets. They were the delight of young visitors. For LuAnne, pigs of any size or shape were transients.

"We only have pigs for a month at a time. But that's long enough to know that the maternal instinct makes a sow nasty. Pick up one of the piglets and watch out. The real challenge is to keep all the piglets alive. The sow will lie down on one, and that piglet will scream. We'll pound on the sow, but if we get her real mad, it's even worse."

Goats were another matter. Their history extended back into prehistoric times. LuAnne pointed to a rambunctious goat in a pen nearby.

"The poor man's cow, that's what they're called," she said. They require less feed than cows, which makes them valuable in underdeveloped countries.

One of the goats in the pen was attempting to chew the fence imprisoning it.

"Goats eat walls," she said, with the hint of a laugh denting her customary low-key demeanor.

"They'll eat fiberglass. It takes a lot to kill a goat. They're the delinquents of the farm. They're cute, and people love them, but if you watch them regularly, it's another matter. I saw a kid lose his plastic Cubs helmet in the goat pen, and the goat even tried to chew that."

In the next pen, several sheep moved stolidly, side by side. For the docents, LuAnne had written some guidelines, distinguishing among "sheep raised for mutton (mature meat), for wool, for fur (Karakul) and for hair (Barbados). All breeds produce lamb (young meat), and most produce wool."

While she was charmed by their appearance, LuAnne was convinced that "sheep are dumb farm animals. They flock together. They're skittish. Trying to catch one is hard. Also, they have sensitive digestive systems. They live or they die. A sickly looking sheep is bad news waiting to happen."

She got up and walked toward the poultry barn; the sound of chickens filled the air. She stopped at the entrance and listened to the noise.

"They're no problem. They have a short life here, thanks to the appetite of the reptiles. When they lay eggs, the keepers eat the eggs for lunch. We keep those chickens that lay eggs; we don't sell them or their eggs. When we're done with them, off they go the reptile house. I guess you could call us the terminal market."

The horse barn was being renovated; the horses had been sent to barns in the area until it was completed. LuAnne felt ambivalent about horses. They were beautiful animals; they were dumb animals.

"They are just not as smart as some would have us believe," she said. She conceded that some had splendid memories. The zoo had been home to a Clydesdale, one of the massive brewery horses, who had been patient with petting children. When the barn was ready to be opened again, LuAnne planned to stock it with several well-known breeds.

"We used to have sorry horses, with bad feet and legs,

who were given to the zoo. Now, some are donated and some I've bought. I'm the one who decides what we'll be willing to accept," she noted, implying the difference between the farm's past and present.

She turned toward the barn for beef cattle. The names were familiar: Angus, Hereford, Shorthorn. They can weight up to 2,500 pounds, so LuAnne did not think of them as playful animals. For most of them, the future held a quality grade: prime and choice were familiar to supermarket shoppers.

She spoke of the animals the way a farm manager might speak of them. She never succumbed to anthropomorphic fantasies. Being farm curator was a job—and she liked the job. She wasn't in the business of preserving endangered species, but she could educate the uneducated masses. That, for her, was enough. She had been a farm girl and now was in the big city. She wanted to combine the best of the two lifestyles.

As she got into an electric cart to drive across the zoo to the zoo office, she waved at two keepers—a man and a woman—standing in the doorway to the dairy barn. She drove off, disappearing over the bridge that spanned the lagoon beside the farm.

"She doesn't like to get her hands dirty," one of the keepers said.

"She doesn't have to," the other replied. "She's smart."

FIRST PERSON: LUANNE METZGER

I grew up in a small town. Sheltered, very sheltered. Things were a lot simpler than they are in the city. Everything revolved around the family and the work that we did on the farm. In little towns everyone knows what you're doing, sometimes before you're doing it. You always kept an eye on what others thought about, what other people would think of you.

It was a town of three hundred people, two churches.

You either went to one church or the other, and a lot of people were related to each other.

I grew up with farm animals, living on a farm. It seemed natural that I wanted to join FFA, Future Farmers of America, and take ag classes. I was always in 4-H as I was growing up, boys' 4-H. Girls' 4-H at the time was sewing, cooking, baby-sitting, things like that. I didn't do that. I grew up working on the farm and being with the animals, and that just seemed the natural place for me. When I went to high school, I wanted to join FFA and take ag classes, and I was the first girl to do so at our chapter, and our chapter was a large one—one hundred twenty, one hundred thirty boys. I think the instructor and adviser truly believed that I joined just so I could be with lots of boys. And as I began taking tests and doing well, he found out that I truly had an interest and aptitude for it.

When I became an officer of the chapter, it was always standard policy that the officers, when they were seniors, got to go to Kansas City for the national convention. There was a little bit of a furor, because I was the only girl—who would chaperon me? They'd have to take another girl to share a room with me; I couldn't bunk in with the guys. They tried to tell me I couldn't go, when I'd earned the right, because I was a girl. Well, I ended up going; they took another girl.

I think it was the way I was raised. I wasn't pampered because I was a girl. My sister and I were on the farm, and there was work to be done. We did it equally. When we went to the fairs in the summer, it was pull your equal weight, take care of your own livestock, do your work.

I remember being around animals from the earliest time. There are pictures of us as young children with my brother's prize ram, and it'd be my brother and my sister and me standing there. The house was always filled with trophies and animal awards that my brother and sister earned at fairs and shows. I had an affection for the farm animals that we worked with and showed. You spend every day taking care of them. But I always had that sense of realism, that these animals were going to a terminal market, that that's what we were raising them for.

I still have a problem with people who say we murder animals, because they look at it with such tunnel vision. I try to let them know that no one cares for their animals more than a farmer. Even though they may be marketing them and in the end slaughtering them, no one cares more for them because that is their livelihood. A healthy, happy animal is a good productive animal.

Wild animals—the other zoo animals—have their place. It's important that we understand them and try to learn how we can cohabit with them and quit pushing them out of their habitats. But to become so attached to them, and almost give them human characteristics and feelings, I think is wrong. Of course, I think I'm still in the learning stage about what a zoo should do and should be to the public and to the animals. I came here ignorant about zoos and wild animals, and I'll be the first to admit it. People would stop me at the zoo and ask me if we had some sort of animal, and the first few weeks I had to say I didn't know. I'm still formulating my view. I think there's a purpose and a need for zoos.

Two years ago, I never thought I'd be here. I was a journalism major, and I thought I would always be writing or photographing or something along that line. Now, after being here almost two years, I can't see myself leaving for a while. I've set some goals.

The farm was basically nothing; it sat here for twenty, twenty-five years. It was nice, it was pleasant, some cute little farm animals, but there was nothing happening. It was very static. With the renovation, we've given ourselves some new, updated facilities without structurally changing too much. We're going to be a lot more consumer-oriented. Not only do I want people to come here and enjoy the animals, I want them to understand the purpose of these animals, why they're here, that milk does not come from the corner grocery store; milk comes from a cow, and that's why we do milking demonstrations. I want them to understand why we raise beef cattle, why the dairy calf is taken off of its mother. I want them to at least learn one piece of something, so that maybe when they see a sheep covered with wool they'll realize that that's where a sweater came from.

There are different levels of information that we may want to set up: something very basic for the six-, seven-, ten-year-olds, and then a higher level of information. We'll do market buys, where we tell what are the best buys at the supermarket that week, whether it's that sweet corn is cheap now, or hamburger or beef is cheap—so stock up if you can—or how to buy a chicken.

My father thinks a zoo's a dumb place for a farm, but I think they're impressed at what I'm trying to do here. But they come from a small town where a farm doesn't look like what our farm does here. We brought my grandmother up here once. She was more impressed with meeting the elephants. She was very interested in seeing what I was doing; she grew up in a totally different time, when almost everybody was a farmer, and she can't imagine that people don't know what a cow is, or what it does. But my job is to explain farm animals to people who've never seen a farm.

I start with the pigs, swine, hogs, whatever you want to call them. They're my favorite, because they're the one thing we didn't have on our farm. We had a horse and a pony, we had chickens running loose, we had beef cattle, we had sheep. Dairy cattle were too much work; I didn't want to be around those. But I was always interested in pigs. My mother had shown pigs as a young girl in 4-H. I'd always wanted to show one. I finally got that wish four or five years ago at the state fair; a hog producer gave me one of his animals to show, and that was one of the highlights of my life. I think pigs are intelligent animals, highly intelligent. More intelligent than dogs and cats. They're easily trained, very easily. When I was growing up, we had puppies, and I remember how hard they were to paper-train. We had a baby pig that was donated to the farm last September. We took it home one weekend, and it was amazing: within a couple of hours, once she'd checked out our whole apartment, she was using the paper. We called her Freckles; she was red with little dark freckles. My husband worked on a hog farm when he was growing up, with ten thousand of these things, and we'd been married one week when I told him I wanted to bring home a piglet. He said, "Don't do this to me." But once I got it home, it was like a boy and his pig; they would walk down to get the mail. We took her to a party that night at a friend's apartment. People thought it was a dog; it minded better than our neighbor's poodle.

They're just highly intelligent, the only farm animal that won't overeat, despite the bad connotations, you know: don't eat like a pig. Or your room looks like a pig sty. Pigs, if they're given enough space in their pen, will have zones. They'll have their bedding area, they'll have their eating area, and then where they defecate. And those last two, if they have enough space, will not meet. I think they've gotten a very bad rap, that pigs stink and wallow in the mud. The only reason they wallow in the mud is they have sweat glands only around their nose area, and they're hot. There's nothing better than cool mud. They're very much like humans in their digestive system, in their heart-respiratory system. Heart valves from pigs have been used in humans. They're used to do health studies, because they'll eat the same type of things we do. They eat corn and soybean meal, in a different form, but it's the same type of products that we eat.

We've got two piglets on the farm now, and they've not been worked with that much, but they've been imprinted on a little bit. They hear you coming, and they're standing, trying to crawl up the gate and snorting at you that they want out. They want to come see you. Pigs don't like to be picked up; they squeal like crazy. But they like to be rubbed behind the ears. They'll start snorting and stretch out, and then they'll roll over and let you rub their bellies. They'll go to sleep and let kids pet them.

As lovable and friendly as Freckles was, however, she

had a mind-set that if she didn't want to go that way, she wouldn't. Pigs also have sweet tooths; they like fruit and blueberry muffins. There are even pigs that race for Oreo cookies.

Beef cattle are smart animals, not super intelligent but not dumb, either. They don't relate to humans as individuals, and I think part of that is that you don't work with them. Beef cattle are raised on the range or in a lot; it's not one-on-one, handler-animal contact. But I know how intelligent some of our own beef cows were. They would have their calves out in the woods, and sometimes we wouldn't see their calves for weeks. We had some cows that would walk one way, and you'd follow them, thinking, "I'm gonna find this calf," and you know darn well that their calf was lying the other way, and they weren't going to go back to their calf, they were protecting it. They may be domesticated animals, but they still have some wild left in them that they protect their young. They're trainable enough that you can break them to lead, you can break them to stand for you. People who truly work with their animals and show them can put a halter on them, drop the halter, walk all the way around it, brush the animal, set its feet, come back, and the animal hasn't moved. It's a matter of personality. There are other ones that we've worked with for a whole summer and never quite got them to mind us and work well.

Dairy cattle can be very docile, and that's because you work with them. They're milked twice a day; they have people walking around. They are intelligent. They may be in a barn with five hundred stalls in it, stanchions for each of the dairy cows. They're released to go out into the drydock to be milked, and when a cow walks back in, she'll walk to her own stanchion. It's hard to get a cow to go into a stanchion that isn't hers, so there must be some level of intelligence there. But not much affection. With beef cattle and dairy cattle, if they're tame, you can brush them, and they enjoy it and they'll stand for you, but I don't see much affection from them. Maybe in a young calf. Ours at the zoo have been worked with. If a calf has been raised out on a farm somewhere where it wasn't handled, it wasn't worked, more than likely if it heard you say something, it would run the other way. One of ours has been imprinted on; we take it out and lead it, we talk to it as we give it its bucket of milk, and we call it by name, so we can work on it.

When I was ten, twelve, thirteen, somewhere around there, I saw my sister get kicked in the face by one of our horses, one that was very tame. She came up behind it, and it got scared and hit her in the face with both rear hooves. So I've always had a healthy respect for horses. I stay away from them, and I honestly don't know much about them. I'm probably somewhat scared of them. Horses are not smart animals. They're one of our least intelligent, but the advantage that horses have is they're able to retain about ninety percent of what they learn. They have a memory. If you keep working with them, it sort of gets ingrained in them; they remember. There are horses that are more highly trained, but horses are, as a group, somewhat dim-witted. That's why they are so good for riding, because they've got the memory retention, and they're dumb enough to let you tell them where to go and what to do.

Sheep are sweet, but they're dumb animals. One sheep walks off one way, and they all follow. It could be down a ditch, and they'll just keep going. Trying to round up sheep is like a circus. They all run, and then they split off and run around. They're so dumb, and they're scared of you. As we were growing up, we'd have dog attacks on our sheep every so often. The ones that were not even touched by a dog would stand in a corner of a barn shaking for two to three weeks. We lost some sheep after that just because they wouldn't eat, they wouldn't drink; they were so scared, you would have to carry the water and the feed back to them. They're very skittish, scared animals.

Chickens are just feathered fowl. They're destined to lay eggs and then go to chicken soup. We raised chickens on our farm just because my father enjoyed them. I have no fond memories of chickens. I never got brave enough to reach underneath a hen and grab the eggs out from underneath her. Even though she doesn't hurt much, I didn't like to get pecked. I remember trying to chase them around with an old wire chicken catcher to catch the young roosters for dinner. Not a good memory.

All the memories may not be perfect, but I never forget where I came from. I want nice things, but my house is filled with antiques, country things that I enjoy telling people about. If anyone asks me, I tell where I'm from. I think people need to know about it. I think that's part of the problem that agriculture has today—city folks are ignorant about agriculture, and they don't want to know. And I know that farmers are ignorant about city people, and they don't want to know about them—their customers. I see myself as a bridge between the two. I work with ag groups, and I want to get them involved at the farm, because I think they should be here. With millions of visitors a year, and the consumers of tomorrow coming through, they need to be here.

I always know where I came from, and it's always going to be part of me. I don't think I could live in the city itself. I prefer the suburbs. But I don't think I could live on a farm, either. I've gotten used to all the conveniences; I've gotten used to going to a museum and enjoying it, running over to the mall if I need something. I can ride my bike to the grocery store, and it's a supermarket, not the little grocery that I grew up near, which was wonderful but didn't have all the options. I like the choices. I can do anything on a weekend. And I also like the fact that I'm not tied to a farm. When I was growing up, we didn't have vacations; the fairs were our family vacations. I don't want to go back to that. But I don't want to leave it totally. I'm walking a line.

6

TEACHER'S PETS

For most of the key employees at the zoo, working with animals had roots in a childhood yearning. That wasn't the case for Judy Kolar, the curator of education.

As a child, she didn't have a pet; her mother had been bitten by a dog and had no fondness for animals. In fact, Judy had never contemplated a career at the zoo until she came to work there in 1977.

What she had been preparing for was a career in education. A native Chicagoan, she had both a bachelor's degree and a master's degree in education from the National College of Education in Evanston, Illinois. She had been a teacher in a north suburban school, a program coordinator for the Chicago public school system, and chairman of the special education department—dealing with the needs of students with learning disabilities—at a city high school.

When she accepted Les Fisher's offer to be curator of education, she easily made the transition to providing knowledge about animals to those in search of that knowledge, from students and teachers to casual zoo visitors.

A tall (5'9"), trim, chic divorcée, Judy was based in a small, neat office in the Crown-Field Center. At forty-seven, with hazel eyes and brown hair flecked with gray, she was a stunning figure; her cool manner enhanced the overall impression that she was in charge.

She ran an education department staffed by seven persons, several of them supported by the zoo society, the rest on the park district payroll. The department produced a wide array of activities, an assortment that had expanded dramatically under her direction.

Among them were zoo classes for school children, from toddlers to high school students. They ranged from films to observation of the animals to supervised hands-on contact with live animals.

For students in all grades, there were forty-five-minute tours of the zoo, introducing the zoo and its commitment to the conservation of wildlife. There was a hands-on zoo for blind and partially sighted students, and a zoology class taught by the zoo staff for high school students.

For the general public, Judy and her staff provided workshops for students, families, and adults interested in in-depth studies of wildlife. Films, slide and video presentations brought visitors an awareness of the lives of animals in the wild and the behind-the-scenes workings of the zoo itself.

The department provided the movable carts often seen at the zoo in good weather, informally teaching visitors using touchable items, such as feathers, eggs, and snakeskins.

The zoo's outreach program included the traveling zoo, which brought the zoo to those who couldn't get to it (during the spring and summer); two vans transported animals and instructors to Chicago's parks, hospitals, nursing homes, senior citizen centers, day camps, and libraries. During the school year, the Zoo-to-You program used the vans to bring the zoo to fourth- and fifth-grade classrooms in city schools, with live animals—small mammals, birds, and reptiles.

The education department was active in the graphic

design of zoo exhibits, educational concepts for the children's zoo, and various publications.

For more than fifteen years, the bulk of the teaching effort had been conducted by docents, the zoo society's corps of unpaid teachers. There were 200 of them, out of a total volunteer group of 400. The docents went through a fifteen-week course in vertebrate biology, teaching techniques, and animal handling, followed by a written exam and on-the-job training. They made a commitment to the zoo—four hours on one day a week, for at least one hundred hours a year—and that enabled them to serve Judy and her staff with zeal and wisdom on a continuing basis.

Finally, Judy worked closely with the zoo society in obtaining grants, such as the $45,000 it received from the Joyce Foundation to expand the Zoo-to-You program and $100,000 from Citicorp to fund a learning center in the renovated children's zoo.

All of these responsibilities made for clogged days in Judy's life. She did not clean cages or chop food or worry about sick animals, but she was usually at work by 8 A.M. Meetings filled her days. Planning provided the main thrust of her career.

"We don't invite people to the zoo simply to have them stare or sit," she said. "The zoo is a unique resource." She planned ways to keep them alert, to keep them thinking about the zoo and its animals.

There were programs and events to offer: an introduction to animals for "tiny tots"; "Animal Talk," a three-year-old's guide to what animals say; "Zookeepers and Their Animal Friends," a presentation by Pat Sass, senior keeper at the great ape house; "Zoo Photography," for families with children eight and up. The zoo lecture series offered evenings with Les Fisher, curator of mammals Mark Rosenthal, great ape keeper Peter Clay, and others.

For Judy, all the hours of preparation paid off.

"It's fun. It's recreation. But it's more than that," she said. "It's the conservation of captive populations. It's the breeding of endangered species. This place is special, for it's staff and what they're involved in.

"My office used to be in the great ape house. A wonderful place to work. It took me no time to learn that the animals were the focus of the zoo. I swear to God those apes were talking to me. I'd look up and see a chimp staring at me through a slot in the wall. I was almost in the exhibit.

"But what matters to me most is not just watching the animals. The education I've gotten here, that's what matters. The openness of the staff, the keepers. They want to tell their stories, to share them. They told them to me. Biology. Ecology. And I learned.

"Respect for animals—you develop that here. Those apes peeking into my office. You need that one-on-one to have that respect. You know, animals are up-front with you. There's no bullshit, no manipulation. I've learned a lot about nature, the most orderly of societies. You know what it's capable of. Animals have a role in life, and you know what it is. If we could relate to each other that way, maybe our disturbances would go away."

For Judy, there had to be quiet time to study animals. It was observation with a purpose.

"Looking at an ape or an armadillo, I ask, 'What's your hidden secret that the world should know about you? What was your life like in the wild?' I'm not talking about being anthropomorphic now. It's that one-on-one feeling that enables you to achieve some understanding of them. Each animal has special features. Why claws? Why a shell? To help us anticipate the questions that the public brings to us, to help us interpret animals for them, that's what those quiet times mean to me."

While Judy sat behind her desk, two docents were on the move, rushing past her doorway to a Zoo-to-You appointment.

Mary Patton was a new docent. She was a grandmother and a retired lawyer, a feisty blonde with time to spare and a conspicuous sense of determination. But she was nervous. It was her first Zoo-to-You mission, bringing small animals—and a lecture about them—to the fourth and fifth grades at a parochial school.

Fortunately, Mary had help. Accompanying her was Charlene Ehlscheid, a docent with fourteen years of service, a registered nurse whose docent time was a needed change of pace. A cheerful redhead with dangling giraffe earrings, she was not nervous; she'd done it before, and she assured Mary that it would go well.

The cast of animal characters they were taking along included Blossom, an opossum; a rabbit named Butch; a ball python; and a kestral (a gray-beige sparrow hawk) named Jasper. Each one was in a carrying case, and the entire group of animals and docents were driven to St. Henry's School by driver Art Cotton in the colorfully painted traveling zoo van.

Along the way, Charlene remembered a Zoo-to-You visit she had made to a ghetto elementary school.

"I asked the class, 'Why does a snake have so many babies?' " she recalled.

A small boy waved his hand.

"Powerful sperm," he proclaimed.

As the van moved through traffic, the two docents chatted.

"The opossum is my favorite," Mary volunteered. "She is so beautiful. I love her."

When they arrived at the school, they were directed to the fifth-grade class. The students were well behaved, sitting on their small chairs behind their small desks. The room was filled with their artwork. On the blackboard, the teacher had written, "No recess if not quiet."

The class was a United Nations assortment of ethnic origins, unified in the girls' white blouses and plaid skirts and the boys' yellow shirts and brown slacks.

"Your mouths are sealed, and you're going to listen," the teacher said sternly.

"We like children and we like animals," Charlene began. She told them that the zoo was free, that it belonged to them, and that they should care for it. The zoo is the place, she said, where they can learn about animals and have fun learning.

Charlene posed questions for the class to answer. They were eager.

"Why do birds go south?"

"For food."

She took the kestral from its cage, and it sat on her gloved left hand. It defecated, and the children giggled.

"He has to eliminate, just as you do," she said, with a serene smile. She did not explain the nature of stress in animals.

She walked around the room with the bird on her hand; the children's faces brightened. The bird had a damaged wing and could not be released into the wild, she pointed out; she assured the students that the bird would be cared for in the zoo.

Mary took over, to talk about mammals.

"We're the brightest of all the mammals," she said. "But which one is the biggest? The tallest?"

The children knew: the elephant, the giraffe.

She carefully extracted the opossum from its traveling case. Blossom, a tidy gray bundle of fur with a long, pink-tipped nose, seemed less than eager to participate, but Mary grasped it firmly. She allowed the children to pet it. They squealed.

She returned Blossom to its case, as Charlene cradled the ball python in her arms.

"We brought a snake today," Mary announced. The children exhaled loudly, in mock or real fear. "Don't worry," Mary comforted them. "It's harmless to us. It kills by squeezing its prey, and we're too big."

The ball python remained coiled in Charlene's arms, its tongue flicking out.

One chubby Hispanic boy cheered the snake. Others moved away when Charlene approached.

"If you don't choose to pet it, that's fine, but don't create a scene," the teacher said firmly.

"Its forked tongue helps it taste and smell," Mary instructed. "And it's deaf."

After an hour, it was time to move on to the fourth grade.

Mary and Charlene introduced the class to the relationship between an animal's habitat and its food supply.

"What if we all ate nothing but hamburger?" Mary asked.

"We'd get sick," a small blond boy snapped.

"True," Mary said. "And there wouldn't be any food left."

"You can read animals like books," she added. "Look at their eyes, ears, nose, teeth, legs, tail, and you find out how they live and how they eat.

She plucked the opossum from its carrier gingerly. The class sighed.

"She's got a big nose—better than her eyes or ears—so she can smell her food. And with her fifty teeth, she can eat almost anything. Even your garbage. She's what we call an opportunistic omnivore. She likes to live in the hollows of trees. And you wouldn't even notice her there," Mary said.

She encouraged the children to pet the opossum.

"When you pet a wild animal, never pet its head," she advised.

Blossom began to quiver.

"She's shivering because she's scared," Mary said, sensing that the animal was stressed. "So we'll put her back in her case." Mary seemed relieved to deposit Blossom inside the case.

Charlene introduced the rabbit to the class. Again, the class sighed in unison. Butch—gray and white and soft and furry—behaved properly. When Charlene placed it on a long table, it made no effort to move. The children rushed up and petted Butch; the rabbit did not resist.

Then it was time to pack up and leave.

The two docents urged the children to go to their library and study about animals—and to go to the zoo whenever they could. The message was well received. The children applauded.

Back in the van, the two women relaxed as Art—an experienced driver accustomed to hearing the sounds of animals in the back of the van—drove slowly back to the zoo. For Charlene, it had been another in a series of gratifying trips. For Mary, it had been the first, and it had worked out well. For both, there would be many more to come.

In her office, Judy was alone, checking plans for the graphics for the lion house once it had been renovated. Joan Friedman, the assistant curator, stopped by, and the conversation led Judy to comment on the use of graphics at the zoo.

"Our graphics aren't an encyclopedia of information," she said. "We know that the average visitor spends a minute or less in front of a graphic. That's OK. We set our own limitations, and we don't go beyond them. Short, succinct, accurate information to motivate them to study. At least we give them some basic understanding of the animal and the meaning of that animal to the environment.

"If an exhibit changes, the graphics must change. Animals come, animals go. We can use temporary signs for new animals. Sometimes we have to; a permanent sign can cost five thousand dollars.

"I've been heavily into all this for five years, and I'll be involved with it for another five. It's a ten-year campaign, the renovation of the zoo, and it's changing the face of the zoo."

Later that day, she met with three members of her staff: Joan; Sue, a full-time teacher on the staff; and Vanessa, a recent college graduate serving a one-year internship in the education department. They discussed a series of portable displays they hoped to have in the learning center at the renovated children's zoo.

Special boxes were being designed to display learning materials about animal diets. Other exhibits would show the beaks and feet of birds, the eggs of birds, and reptiles.

Such displays could cause problems.

"Will the children wonder, when they see beaks and feet, if we're chopping up animals?" one of the women asked.

"Should we use the entire stuffed animal instead?" another proposed.

"Let's go for real parts," Judy decided.

She liked to get children to sit down with her, on the grass, so that she could show them such exhibits, to see what questions they might ask.

"Did you kill the animals?" was one question heard.

Judy was prepared: "No, they died of natural causes, like people do. We save their bodies to teach you about them."

But she knew that there could be a reaction when you took a child who had just seen a live animal and showed it a dead one.

"If the kids' questions persist, there is fear to deal with, or a fascination with death," Joan noted. "If you address their questions, they accept your answers. You can remind them about a dog that died. Or a grandparent."

"In truth, sometimes you lie," Sue said. "When they ask you what happens to the chicks on the farm, you don't tell them that they're fed to the reptiles."

After the meeting ended, Judy went back to her office. At times, she liked to tie all the pieces together—to link the graphics to the displays to the needs of visitors and more. The more closely they all meshed, the better the thrust of the efforts made by the education department.

"We're trying to create an awareness and respect for wildlife," she said. "That's the foundation. Not just the wildlife here in the zoo, either, but the wildlife in its own environment. What does it mean for an animal not to be? Extinction. Some people say, 'So what?' But to me, it matters. Education at the zoo has a bias: conservation. But we don't rush to convert the unconverted. We give facts. We urge consideration. We never tell people that they're wrong if they think that zoos are bad. We give them options to think about."

Perpetual self-scrutiny went with the territory.

"I think we've been successful, but we evaluate our programs all the time," she said. "We survey our audiences. Did you learn something you didn't know before? Based on this program, are you more involved? Did you take action, on any level? Did you pick up a magazine and read about animals?

"What's encouraging is that eighty to ninety-five percent of our people have told us that we did provoke them to action. We want that; we want them to have open minds, to want to investigate. That's for the adults. Children are another matter. They're sponges. They have fewer fears, fewer predetermined attitudes. And there's that conditioning that predisposes them to animals."

She sat back in her chair and glanced at her collection of giraffe figurines on a nearby shelf.

"They're tall, and so am I," she said softly. "Maybe that's why I like them." Outside the building, a line of giggling children was entering the building to see a film. Judy could see them through her office window. They were evidence that she was succeeding in her job, and as she watched them, she smiled.

FIRST PERSON: JUDY KOLAR

I remember my mother not wanting animals in the house. And it stemmed from when she was fourteen years old; there was a dog in the apartment house, and all of a sudden it turned on her and bit her. I think that 'shook her up. I don't remember exactly how she communicated it to me, but I remember I found a kitten when I was a kid, a stray little baby kitten, and I brought it home and wanted it. She told me, "Oh no, we can't have it." I remember having goldfish and a turtle for a while.

I grew up in the city, on the west side of Chicago. I've always lived in apartments. And I never had kids. If I didn't live in Chicago, I'd have a dog. I absolutely would. I have had tortoises from the zoo in my apartment.

I've always loved kids. It's not that I went through school, grammar school, high school, saying I wanted to be a teacher. I didn't do that. I think my parents certainly made the suggestion along the way. I was in high school in the fifties, and there just wasn't as much exploration of your life then. I truly believe that.

I wanted to do things with people, people in need. That's what led me to look into occupational therapy, and then special education. I liked occupational therapy because it meant working with people and helping them to get functional. I was interested in learning disabilities. I decided this was another direction that I wanted to expand into. Special education is a broad category. In those years, it was called "the exceptional child"; that was the label. They've gone through ten thousand labels. Special education means anything from those who are learning disabled for whatever reason, physically, perceptually, to the gifted. The gifted were separated out, and special ed meant those that were visually impaired, hearing impaired, mentally handicapped. I came into learning disabilities when it was gaining momentum and focus and attention. I went back to school full-time, and I got very involved with diagnosis and evaluation, trying to really pinpoint what the problems were, giving diagnostic tests, and recommending remedial treatment.

In the early seventies, the Chicago public schools were going ahead with special ed. What we did was test kids in the elementary schools and set up resource rooms of kids with learning disabilities. We worked out remedial programs for them and worked with parents. Then I was asked to set up a program at the high school level. It was a self-contained classroom, and they came to me for the whole day. You can help them if you feel for the kids. Through testing, you see the results.

I was there for about five years, and we got the program

going. But in my life, two things were happening. I was starting to think, "What else is there in life?" At the same time, Chicago public schools were going through grave problems. They were going to be denied federal money because of the segregation within the schools. So I put together my résumé, I started talking to people. I was open to do anything. I was at a dinner party one night. I was sitting next to a businessman, blah blah blah blah blah blah. And he said, "You know, something's happening at the zoo." "Something's happening," he said, "but I really don't know what it is. Call Les Fisher." I said, "The zoo?" I was in gear; I followed up anything. So I called, made an appointment, and went in and talked to him. There was a fifty-thousand-dollar grant, and someone was needed to put together a program on environmental education for teachers and students.

I'm an educator, I thought, and they need me as an interpreter. I had felt very bad at the thought of leaving my profession. The zoo staff all felt strongly that the people should know; they felt strongly about education. It was always a dream of Les Fisher's to have an education department here. The commitment was strong on the part of the animal management staff. They'd take people behind the scenes and explain animal behavior. They'd do this of their own accord. They went out on the traveling zoo; they were the zoologists who gave presentations to the public. And the keepers are always in there wanting to talk to the public. So you've got a collective staff that is behind education, wanting it to happen.

I'm a Chicagoan. I grew up in the parks. I mean, that was my childhood. I did have a feel for the city, the communities, and the diverse kinds of people. That combined with teaching. We reached out to so many different audiences.

I was able to put together a program that teachers conducted in their classrooms. It's a multimedia kit. It's an approach to how to utilize the zoo. I had certain feelings on how to utilize the zoo when kids come here. They don't have to come here to do what they do in the classroom.

And that set the format for what we did later on in education.

We know we're succeeding when people come back. We know we're succeeding by evaluations we do in the workshops and the classes. We know we're succeeding nationally and internationally when people come to us for direction, and guidance, and new programs.

There was kind of a hiatus in the last couple of years. We were doing the programming, but we needed more staff to go to the next level. We had reached a plateau, and it was at that time I asked for funding for an assistant curator of education. That's when I started asking for more money for programming through the zoo society. There was no way to go on to more levels without more staff and without more support, all the way around. And so, we expanded, and now we can start reaching for another plateau.

We developed the training manual for docents, a textbook but done in a way for them to relate to better. It's stripped down to the bare essentials that they need; it's an introduction. We tell the trainees, "This is the beginning of your learning. This is a basic foundation and introduction." We have supplementary handouts; we also have some reading assignments that are in other textbooks. If the curator lectures are in the morning, then the docents do the afternoon part in taking people out to the exhibits and doing the general kind of introduction to the exhibits and the animals, and that supports the lecture.

I think there are all kinds of different levels to build on. Let's take one example: adult programs. The zoo lecture series has been terrific, it's been very successful, it's another one we won an education award for, and that's been fine. It had certain objectives. But I also know that other levels of adult programs are needed here. One thing I would like to start investigating is to have higher seminars, that go more in depth. There are a lot of people out there who want more. Seminars. Hook-ups with universities. Selected people on this staff and a university staff, giving academic credit for it. Video would be great. We're going to put video in the lion house, and we're going to have video in the learning center of the children's zoo. The video in the lion house will let us show them what they can't see there, and that's animals in the wild.

I think we're here to tell our story. We're here to give the basic facts as we know them and that we can substantiate. The animal rights people certainly come and listen, I hope with an open mind, and we tell them how we feel. We're not necessarily telling anybody else they're wrong.

I have been involved in things that I never in my life thought I'd be doing. I wrote a filmstrip. I worked with the sound people. I loved it, just loved it. The graphics element, the writing, the programming. I've put everything that I ever learned of the learning process into the materials. It's been a phenomenal opportunity and it's phenomenal because we had a small staff and I was forced to do it. I've had great satisfaction.

We're reaching the general public. We're doing what we think is best, and they're absolutely hooked up to what animal management is doing and to the direction of conservation efforts. If we place a person by the great apes, we put that person there because that's part of our programming in conservation, to help impart that knowledge. If in the amphitheatre we bring out a little European ferret, we talk about it, and it's fun, but there's a hook to everything. "By the way, this guy's kissing cousin, the black-footed ferret, is dying off." There is a thread that goes through everything that hooks up to conservation internationally, conservation that's specific to the philosophy of the zoo. And that ferret is not the only creature that's endangered; there are plenty of other ones around.

Zoo education has such potential to support conservation efforts worldwide. Zoos started out as the showcase of animals, the stamp collection. Then we got into conservation programs. In the sixties, there were the Rachel Carsons and the environmental awareness, and some zoos were realizing they are perfect places to help in that environmental education. There were some major zoos with bigger budgets, that had the staff that could do it. But many zoos didn't have budgets for education. In most zoos, volunteers really started education, because you needed unpaid staff. Many of those volunteers are highly educated people, but there's still a difference between a full-time staff on board with consistent coordination, organization, development, and a volunteer staff. So, all of a sudden, you had professional staffs getting into zoo education, and that paralleled the first endangered-species acts in the late seventies. So this momentum really started in the sixties and grew.

The European zoos have had professional education staffs for years, so there are major international conservation efforts. The U.S. zoo educators are hooking into that; we're starting to look at our programming to help support that. We're telling visitors to help conserve, help this, help that. How do you tell a kid in a starving country that he shouldn't kill an animal for food? How do you tell that to those people who have to clear land for farms because they have to grow crops? There's a big conservation education movement, and I feel part and parcel of it, because I've been very involved with international programs for eight years. What can we do to work with Third World countries? What can we do to pull together Europe, the Americas, the Third World? How can we start approaching it together?

Today, we're trying to talk about alternatives. Are there other options for the land? Are there other ways to achieve what we want to achieve without killing off the plant life that is specific for the food needs of that animal? We're looking to save species from extinction. That's the bottom line. If educators can just enlighten people, by addressing the issues, the alternatives, the options, we're addressing global conservation through education.

I think we'll win. It'll take years and years and years, but if we do our job thoroughly, with great thought and sensitivity to all concerned, I think we can achieve a thinking population of people. Which will mean it's not humans against the animals, but humans with the animals.

7

A Touch of Ginger

It was 8:30 A.M. on a midsummer Wednesday. A handful of
early risers were at the zoo. Some jogged through the zoo.
Others marched briskly to work past the awakening animals. Small children cavorted under their parents' watch-
ful eyes.

The sea lions were bellowing in their pool, asserting
their pleasure by making great sweeping arcs in the water
or sunbathing atop the rock formation. They were the
endearing comedians of the zoo, and a semicircle of their
fans stood at the rail, waving affectionately at them. In the
distance, the sound of chattering monkeys filled the air.
The lions and tigers, in their outdoor habitat, reclined
lazily, warmed by the sun.

Ginger Alexander was there, too. Ginger was a docent,
one of those zoo loyalists who volunteered four hours a
week to teach, to escort people to various parts of the zoo,
and to enlighten them about the nature of the creatures
they'd see. Ginger had been donating her time for twelve
years; few docents knew the zoo any better.

146

Ginger was a 5'5" grandmother with a blond pageboy hairdo, glasses, and a serious fondness for animals. She was wearing her khaki safari suit, looking like Miss Marple based in Kenya, wearing a badge that read: "Lincoln Park Zoo Docent/Guide, Ginger Alexander."

She was a native Chicagoan, educated in parochial schools. She was married for the second time; her first husband died, and she met her second husband at a gathering of widows and widowers. She was the mother of three daughters (one of her own, two of her current husband's), who had provided her with five grandchildren. Over the years she had been determined to get her college degree; when she was just past fifty, she got it. She'd traveled; she and her husband had lived in Italy, and they had visited the Galapagos Islands and Africa (to see the animals, of course).

Her favorite animals were the lions, the tigers, the majestic big cats. As the sun grew hotter and the zoo more crowded, she moved off briskly toward their outdoor habitat.

Behind her, a familiar dialogue was heard:

"Erwin, take him to the bathroom. Take him *now*."

"Shirley, you take him."

"He's a boy, Erwin. Take him to the men's room."

Erwin and son disappeared into the lion house. Ginger stopped in front of one of the large windows that bordered the ends of the cats' habitat. A Bengal tiger spotted Ginger at the window and approached to look at her, then began to pace back and forth, staring at her constantly.

"I don't know if she recognizes me, or if she just knows that I'm a docent," Ginger said. "She may be responding to this uniform."

She noted that the Siberians were the largest cats; they had more fur as well, for their northern clime. A second Bengal—the two were sisters—was basking in the background.

"They don't always get along," Ginger said. "See the vertical stripes. That's camouflage in tall grass. Don't

forget that they're predators. See their eyes, always looking straight ahead. Their nostrils and ears pick up the signs
ahead. They're not easily seen. The ideal hunter. Another
fact to know: tigers are solitary creatures in the wild, but
lions are not."

The Bengal had continued to pace pack and forth on its
side of the window, without taking its eyes off of Ginger.

"Some people think that they pace like that because they
are stir-crazy. Not so, not so. They're just exercising. In
the wild, they hunt, eat, sleep, and mate. That's it. They
need exercise. Pacing is exercise," she said. She did not
accept the notion that caged animals paced out of stress.

She went into the lion house.

"Do you realize that a leopard can carry its prey, even a
gazelle, into a tree?" she asked, summoning images out of a
TV nature program.

"Did you know that black leopards have spots? It's a
recessive gene, a genetic exception," she explained. "But
that's not as rare as a white tiger or a white lion." A young
couple standing next to her looked at the black leopard,
couldn't see the spots, but took her word for the fact that
they were there. Ginger spoke with authority.

She moved along, continuing her running commentary:
the jaguar is the largest cat in our hemisphere. The big cats
at the zoo are cats that roar; only the little ones purr. Lions
are the only cats with a social order; the females hunt, the
males eat first.

She paused in her monologue to collect additional facts.

"I wouldn't pet a lion," she declared. "If you touch them,
they're likely to bite. Of course, some keepers can touch
some animals. A nursery-raised animal may allow the
keeper to come close. If animals know and like the keeper,
they'll let the keeper pet them. But these aren't tame
animals. They're not pets."

She told a story: A lion cub had been raised in the zoo
nursery with some tiger cubs. When they were old enough
and were released, they were separated, lions to lions,

tigers to tigers. The lion cub wailed at the loss of its friends, the tigers. It took a female lion to calm it down, to persuade it that it wasn't a tiger.

Ginger strolled out of the lion house and into the reptile house, across the way.

A very small boy was staring at a very large snake. "Yech!" he screamed.

Reptiles had gotten a bad name, Ginger agreed. "Since the Garden of Eden," she said primly.

She walked around the hall filled with reptiles in their glassed-in cages.

"Reptiles know what to do the moment they're hatched. They're adults even when they're small. When a poisonous snake is born, it already has its venom, and it will kill with it. But that's not the only way snakes kill. They can kill by constriction—actually suffocating the prey. Or just by swallowing it.

"Sure, snakes have gotten bad press. They're always the bad guys. People look at them and think that snakes don't respond to us the way other animals do. But people who have snakes as pets they've raised, say they *do* respond. It's not like having a dog, of course. But they'll stay on your lap or approach you to be held. We've had some boas here who would cling to your waist, a living belt. I've done that. After all, snakes kill only to eat or when threatened—and I'm not threatening."

Nevertheless, she added, "I wouldn't put one around my neck."

She went from one windowed cage to another. A puff adder, from Africa. A rhinoceros viper, from Africa. An Asiatic cobra peered at her from behind a rock. A black-necked cobra, which blinds by spitting venom twelve feet, seemed to be bored. Perhaps a case of dry mouth and inactivity, Ginger theorized.

"When they feed it, they wear a mask," Ginger reported. "And before they put the food in, you can be sure they know where the snake is."

A Gila monster glared at her. Ginger pointed out that they grab, bite, hang on, and chew. And they don't let go until there's nothing left to devour.

"If it gets you, I'm told, you have to cut off its head to get it off. Or cut off your own hand, if that's what it bit. We're talking about a poisonous reptile."

An iguana sat on a tree limb, motionless, passing for weary. It looked like the ugliest of prehistoric monsters, and Ginger mentioned that it had been used as the model for them in many science fiction films.

An alligator snapping turtle was underwater munching on a small herring. It munched, rose to the waterline, stuck its nose above water, took a long, deep breath, and returned to the herring.

A ball python, from western Africa, seemed oblivious to anything but its wish to rest. "When it's attacked," Ginger explained, "it coils into a ball with its head buried, to prevent being swallowed."

The African dwarf crocodile, between four and five feet in length, seemed tired, too.

"He's very old," Ginger said. "In fact, he's the oldest animal in the zoo. We've had him since 1940, and we don't know how old he was then." As if in corroboration, the crocodile reclined in its sedentary state. It revealed nothing.

"What's *that*?" a little girl shrieked.

"An anaconda," her mother told her.

"One of the two longest snakes in the world," Ginger volunteered. "The other is the reticulated python." The anaconda was underwater (they drown their prey); it was more than twenty feet long.

"They're deaf," Ginger continued. "But they feel vibrations. Heat sensors warn them, as well, of approaching creatures. And they smell with their tongues, which transmit messages to their brains."

The reticulated python in a nearby cage was massive. It was coiled underwater, with only its neck and head out of the water, pressed tightly against the glass. It appeared to be looking up, showing off its neck.

"Never try to outstare a snake," Ginger said. "You'll lose."

She headed into the sunlight again; reptiles didn't move her as the big cats did.

She paused at the waterfowl lagoon, home for some birds and stopover for others on their migratory way. A few swans and some ducks were among the permanent residents; they had their wings pinioned (trimmed) to prevent flight, Ginger noted.

"Geese can be used as guard animals," Ginger declared. "They peck, they make noise."

The zoo was getting crowded; Ginger passed the lagoon, its sidewalk clogged with families, with kids eating popcorn. Mothers pushed strollers. The sun was hot.

Ginger marched to the farm. In the bordering neighborhood, apartment buildings dominated the skyline, and yuppie restaurants and boutiques thrived. At the zoo, however, the farm represented other values.

"You know, many city kids have never seen a cow or a pig," Ginger said. "Some of them don't know where milk comes from." At the farm, those kids could get answers.

A goat was being milked by two docents. A week-old calf was resting in a small pen. A month-old Ayrshire calf was in another pen; a sign noted its name, McHale. (There was a Boston Celtics' fan at the zoo.)

"City kids ask me, 'Are all the milk cows female, or are some male?' " Ginger said.

Nearby, a massive sow nursed six piglets; the piglets were brown and white and eager for the nourishment their mother provided.

"Pigs are the smartest of farm animals," Ginger noted. "Some people say they're even smarter than dogs or cats. And they're clean, despite what is said about them. They wallow in mud only to cool off, because they don't have sweat glands, and when the mud evaporates, it cools them.

They don't have much hair, so the sun can trouble them."

Outside the dairy barn, small children clustered to talk to the goats and sheep in their pens. "We don't tell them that some animals go back to the farmers who lent them to us. We don't tell them that they then go to market," Ginger said softly.

She headed briskly toward the primate house. It was a noisy building, with acoustics that magnified all the monkey sounds. The giddy screams of children turned into wide-ranging echoes. A wanderoo macaque, seduced by the attention from visitors, performed. When a docent he knew approached, if the docent stuck out her chin in mock defiance, so did the macaque. It had the face of a wise old Oriental man, with a gray beard. The keepers had named it the Admiral.

Back into the heat of the day, Ginger continued her walk, to the building that housed the penguins and the seabirds. For both, environments had been created that were designed to duplicate their own environments in the wild. The building was air-conditioned; one pass through it was a respite from the summer air.

Ginger emerged and headed along the path that bordered the outdoor exhibits for large mammals. Two rhinos were butting each other, like Sumo wrestlers. They seemed oblivious to the heat and to almost everything else.

"They are very nearsighted," Ginger said. "They charge first and ask questions later. If you see one charging, climb a tree or stand behind it, if the tree's fat and you're thin."

The polar bears were swimming, visible through tall windows at underwater level. "Their hair isn't white," Ginger said. "It's colorless. The light reflecting off it makes it seem white. Polar bears have black skin, and the fur funnels heat to it."

Two elephants were idling, their trunks stretched out to pluck the leaves off the trees beyond their habitat.

"Elephants must be trained. Not to do tricks, but to be managed by their keepers, to be examined. Every day there's a drill to make them respond to commands," Ginger noted.

Bozie, an elephant from Sri Lanka, appeared to be dancing, moving one foot at a time. Suti, an orphan found starving in Africa, was saved by being given a home at the zoo. She seemed to be studying Bozie.

A few yards away, several giraffes moved languorously and munched food from containers at their mouth level. A pair of giraffes were head to head, their tongues intertwined. Ginger wasn't certain if one could term that "kissing."

Her last stop was at the bird house. A tawny frogmouth from Australia peered at her from its glassed-in cage; it looked like an owl, but was more like a nighthawk. It stared in its frozen stance as she passed it. In the free-flight area, birds flew unencumbered.

"They're safe in here," Ginger said, anticipating a question she'd heard from many visitors. "Most birds won't fly out of light into darkness."

She surveyed the vast hall, with its flashes of color and its high-pitched calls.

"Parrots and parakeets like to be touched," she said, "but most birds don't. When birds are sitting in a row, they leave space between them." Next to her, a pair of Major Mitchell's cockatoos were violating the rule; they were side by side on a branch, touching, but with their heads turned away from each other. Predicting animal behavior had its risks, Ginger admitted.

It was time for Ginger to leave. She had enjoyed her stroll through the zoo, a stroll she did often, beyond her work as a docent.

"You know, there's so much personal satisfaction for me here," she said. "The friendships. I've made so many in these years at the zoo. We have a marvelous staff. I can talk to the curators and the keepers and have access to all sorts of information.

"I can touch some of the animals. I think that my biggest

thrill was when I got to play with the lion cubs at the nursery. It was pure enjoyment."

FIRST PERSON: GINGER ALEXANDER

I remember coming to Lincoln Park Zoo when I was little. I remember the lions roaring before they would get fed, and it seemed like they used to roar a lot more than they do now. Maybe it's just a child's perception. But I used to love the lion house at feeding time. I also remember the pony rides they used to have. And I loved to be able to ride the ponies. I think in those days that was about the only chance you ever had to touch an animal at the zoo.

I used to love to come here with my family. We used to have picnics in the park, and we'd always wander over to the zoo. We used to come and spend the whole day here, and of course the two things we always did were come to the zoo and ride the boats in the lagoon. Then, as I got older, we often used to come and ride horses through Lincoln Park, which you used to be able to do. Many times after we would ride, we'd have something to eat and come back. In those days the zoo was not locked with gates at night as it is now. You could walk through the zoo.

My favorites were always the lions. I admire them for the same reason I admire the housecats: the way they move. They have a very graceful way of moving. I don't think of them as slinky, as sneaky, like some people do. I think they're stealthy. They're just doing what comes natural to them when they hunt, but I love the way they look. For example, they'll see something moving, and they will freeze, or they will stalk it. I'm also very impressed with their self-composure. They are the one animal that is not afraid of anything. They are there, and that's their land. And you can see why they're called the king of the beasts, even though they are not the strongest or the biggest.

I've always liked the zoo; I've always liked animals. In 1975, I was looking for something to do. I had worked before I was married, and when I was widowed I had worked in offices and done stenographic work in research libraries, and things like that. But then I stayed home after I married John. When he started his own business, then I did all the books and all the accounting. I was the office worker, of course. I was still doing that, but when the children were all grown up, the last one was at the university, I was looking for something to do apart from my home and my husband and office, so I decided I would work with either animals or children. And just about that time, there was an ad in the paper saying the zoo was looking for volunteers, so I volunteered, and I've been here ever since.

The old philosophy of zoos was to have as many different animals as you could have, because people came to see animals. Basically, zoos were started for entertainment. The first zoos were only for royalty or for the wealthy people, and they only existed in the palaces or in big cities. By the middle 1800s, there were only twenty-nine zoos worldwide that were open to the public. There are now over nine hundred worldwide. But we started in 1868 with a pair of swans. Central Park had a lagoon with lots of swans. And someone there decided to give Chicago a pair, so we got the swans. They were so popular that other people started donating other animals, and we got deer and more birds, and some antelope, until five years later we had seventy-five different specimens.

The early zoos were built with what you now see in the lion house: the typical cages, which were small, easily cleaned, and made it easy to see the animals. They had tile walls, tile floors. But we have to remember that in those days we did not have antibiotics, we did not have a lot of the medications we now have, so that, if one animal got sick, any animal with it would also get sick, and there was nothing they could do about it. So they kept one animal in each cage. It was the logical thing to do. There were still a lot of animals in the wild. As ideas changed, it was better for the animals to be in more natural settings, so they not only removed the bars, they enlarged the animal area. They made the animal areas much more naturalistic, much more like the place the animal came from. We now have antibiotics and other ways of treating animals, so we can keep them in family groups. We have them in larger, more naturalistic settings, and we try to not have bars between them; either we have moats, or, in the case of apes, we have glass.

We're going to redo our lion house. The north side we already have redone with moats, that was done in the seventies. On the south side we have thirteen cages inside and thirteen outside, with bars. We are going to have five outside and five inside, so you can see they're going to be much larger, more than twice the width. They will also be higher and deeper. And between the indoor and outdoor cages, there will be denning areas so that the mothers will have privacy when they have their cubs. But on that side of the building, we will not have lions and tigers, which you can put behind moats; we will have probably snow leopards and possibly Afghanistan leopards and jaguars. Leopards and jaguars can jump across some moats. And they are much smaller animals, so if you had them behind a moat that would be sufficient to keep them from getting out, you would not easily be able to see them.

As I said, in the early times zoos were mainly for recreation and to satisfy people's curiosity. But now that animals are becoming endangered in almost the whole world, zoos have changed their purpose. They are still here for recreation, because it's a lot of fun to come to the zoo. But we also are very much involved in conservation, to preserve the animals that are endangered. Some animals are extinct in the wild and exist only in zoos. Tied in with this is the research that the keepers and the zoo people have to do— not experimental research like you do in laboratories, but studying the animals and their needs, because if we are to get them to reproduce, we have to know each individual species' needs, whether it's space or light or temperature or food. We have to try to duplicate their natural environment.

For example, in the penguin-seabird house, we have a

changing day length, which is exactly the way it is in the place they come from, and this is done automatically by computer. You see, their reproduction cycle is triggered by the changing day length, but you have to know this if you're going to do it. This is why the zoo people have to study the animals. And another reason for zoos is to educate the people, so that they know more about zoos.

Judy was the elephant we bought from Brookfield Zoo. And when they went to put her on the truck, she wouldn't get on the truck. They tried all day, I mean they coaxed her, they used a winch, they finally got her up on the truck, and she immediately broke the sides and got off. So they then decided that they'd make her walk. So she walked, from Brookfield to Lincoln Park Zoo. Miles. She left there at 7:30 in the evening, and she arrived here about 2:30 in the morning. She was accompanied by keepers and armed guards and a police escort. And, of course, as she started out, the children started following when they saw her. As it got to the wee hours of the morning, she surprised a lot of people who were getting out of taverns at that hour, seeing an elephant walking down the street. She only stopped twice. She stopped at a gas station to drink about six gallons of water, and then she stopped at one of the other parks and consumed two hundred pounds of hay. And then she finished walking. I think they stopped for the keepers to rest, too, because they also were walking. She was one of our most popular animals.

As far as escapes in recent years, of course, Otto the gorilla got out. I think it was in '83 or '84, in the outdoor exhibit on the south side of the ape house. They have the concrete wall, and then there's glass above it. There are electrical wires with a mild current through them at the top, and we thought the animals could not get out. Otto was out there. Now, he may have gotten upset for some reason. Usually when the gorillas were out there, keepers left the door open, so the gorillas could come in or out. They were moving some other gorillas, and they closed the door, and maybe Otto got upset because of that. Otto is quite big; he's very impressive. Anyway, a short time later the keeper in the primate house was fixing food in the kitchen. She looked up, and outside the screen door was the gorilla. Outside. In public. She called one of the other keepers. But Otto just kept moving, and he walked along the east side of the primate house and around that. Then he walked along the south side of the lion house, looking at the animals. Out in the open. There weren't a lot of people in the zoo, but a staff member announced over the loud-speakers that everyone should go in the nearest building and stay there.

Otto was looking at the animals. I mean, he had never seen them before. And he was very interested. So he walked the length of the lion house on the south side, then he walked back. Then he walked around and was watching the tigers. He was just leaning on the rail like a person would, just watching the tigers. At that point the head keeper from the ape house came along and walked up to him and said, "Come on, Otto," and Otto took his hand. They weren't sure he'd go back in the building, because he had never seen the outside of the ape house. He had a good rapport with the keeper, but he had never been loose before, and they weren't sure, so they decided the best thing to do was to tranquilize him with a dart gun.

Otto stayed there, with the keeper; they're very gentle animals, really. The vet came with the dart gun to shoot a tranquilizing dart. When the car drove up with the vet in it, and the vet got out, Otto didn't like the vet, because he didn't like shots, which he had gotten in the past. So he then broke away from the keeper and started up the ramp of the Crown-Field Center. They darted him, and he col-lapsed there. It took six or eight people to lift him onto the stretcher to carry him back to the great ape house. They have since added five feet to the wall on the outside of the great ape house. We still don't know how he managed to get out. But he did.

The high points for me are always handling the animals, helping people to understand the animals. We had a barn owl, Barney, who was an unusual bird. He was just fantastic. Very little ever fazed him. You could take him anywhere, and he didn't get upset. Most birds would get very upset with many people up close, but not Barney. He just looked at everybody. When we took Barney to schools, he knew how he was impressing the children because he'd look at all the children, and he'd stretch one wing, and the children would go aaaaaaahhhhhhh. He'd look around a little more, and then he'd stretch the other wing, and he'd wait. You just knew that somehow he was having an influence on those children. Barney the barn owl.

I handled him from the time I became a docent until he died last summer. He had been at the zoo before I came, so he probably was around fifteen when he died. And he died doing what he liked to do most, he died being handled at an exhibit. One of the docents was handling him, and all of a sudden he seemed to kind of collapse. I mean, he just seemed very weak, and she wasn't sure, you know, he wasn't sitting up right, he started to collapse, so she just took him right away over to the hospital. We don't know what he died of, but it probably was just old age. I had a very special relationship with Barney.

Years ago, when I first became a docent, the majority of weekend docents were young, single working girls who worked Monday through Friday and would volunteer on Saturday or Sunday. And the Monday through Friday docents were mainly married women who did not have outside jobs, who had some children at home or whose children were grown, and they were looking for something worthwhile to do. Now it has changed quite a bit, so that more and more professional people are becoming docents. And many of the weekday docents do have jobs. We have women who are nurses, who are doctors, who are teachers, who are real estate agents or interior decorators, flight attendants, in many different professions. And they find that docenting is the best recreation they can get.

When we advertise for docents, we have an orientation day to which we invite all the people who think they want to be docents. We tell them what it is to be a docent, what they would do, that they would be conducting tours, giving information, taking animals out. We show them a film that describes many of the docent activities, and we tell them what the requirements would be. First of all, they have to be eighteen years of age, high school graduates, and we expect them to give one day a week, four hours a day, from ten to two, every week of the year. Now, with vacations and illness and things, no one's going to be here fifty-two weeks. There is a minimum requirement of one hundred hours a year, which you must fulfill if you want to stay. Most of the docents do much more than that. We tell them they will have a training program; they have to pass a final examination. Each curator has one day with the new docents, when the curator talks about his or her animal group.

It's a very technical course. If you're going to talk about the animals, you have to know about them, so we do learn actually more than we need to know, in the sense that we learn all the taxonomy and things like that which you don't use for the average tour person. But it's a background that helps you to understand. Many drop out after orientation because they didn't realize that it would require that much training. It's not easy to become a docent.

The main thing that zoo docents do is give tours to school groups. We have tours by topics: People want all African animals or all South American animals, or they might want nocturnal animals or a tour of endangered animals. Or they might request a primate tour. We also have tours for younger children, what we call an introduction to the zoo, where we take them to one of the bird areas, one of the mammal areas, and one reptile area, so they get a touch of all three, and then we try to have one animal that they can see up close and touch.

Our direction comes from the education department. They have the professionals and have had the training in this type of thing. They develop all the classes that are taught, and they have done a lot to develop the training.

Before we had the education department, the training was done completely by docents. It is much better now; it has improved every year since we've had the education department.

Basically, we're teachers. We teach them about the zoo, and we try to show them the importance of animal life, why we have to conserve animals, besides teaching them about individual animals. For example, people want to know where animals live and what they eat, but we try to get them to understand and to care about the animals and to realize why they're important in the world.

Everything is interdependent. If you destroy all the animals, you destroy a part of our life, because we are actually tied up with the animals. Trees are important because they supply oxygen, they clean the air, besides providing homes for many things. Animals serve, too, because everything is in balance in nature. For example, in some parts of this country where we once had coyotes and wolves, people have practically eliminated all the wolves and are eliminating a lot of the coyotes. They now have an overabundance of rodents, rabbits, and other animals, which those animals used to keep limited in number. Now the rodents and the rabbits and many other smaller animals are destroying crops.

Don't mess with nature.

8

THE MERITT SYSTEM

Dennis Meritt, the assistant director of the zoo, occupied the office opposite Les Fisher's. It was a jungle of vines, hanging plants, potted plants, a pair of parakeets from Australia in a cage, two bubbling fish tanks, a pith helmet, animal carvings, photos, and paintings of animals. A computer lent the only urban touch to the setting.

However comfortable Dennis was in that jungle, or in a real one, he was, at forty-seven, a decidedly sophisticated man. As the nameplate on his desk indicated, he had a doctorate in zoology (from the University of Illinois, Chicago) acquired in 1987. He had spent the last twenty years of his life at the zoo.

He was born and raised in Rochester, New York.

"I always went to school part-time, never full-time," he remembered. The oldest of four sons, he always needed money; after high school, he went to work. He married at an early age and had to work to support his wife and two daughters.

After holding a number of research and laboratory jobs

at hospitals in Rochester, he wound up in Chicago. (Over the years, when time permitted, he completed work on his bachelor's and master's degrees in zoology.)

"I came to Chicago by default," he said. "I was interested in animals, but I didn't know about the job at the Lincoln Park Zoo. A friend of mine, the director of the zoo in Rochester, told me that a job was open at the zoo in Chicago. I followed up and got it." That job was a zoologist's. He was promoted to curator of mammals shortly after joining the zoo staff, and became assistant director in 1976.

His presence was a commanding one. Fit and tan, with dark brown hair and a dark brown, neatly trimmed beard, he spoke with a deep, resonant voice and an intense, decisive, almost theatrical manner.

His style was thoughtful and assured. Many of his associates commended him for his sense of fairness. Even his critics were left with a modest charge; as one of them said, "He tells you what he thinks you want to hear." Despite that accusation, he was successful in confronting disputes.

As he made his way through the thicket of responsibilities he had accumulated, he was comforted by the way that his fate had contradicted the prediction of his high school counselor: "Don't waste your parents' money. You'll never amount to anything."

Much of Dennis's time was spent behind his desk, but he made time for the animals. On one hot summer morning, he left his air-conditioned office and walked over to the large mammal area. Two rhinos—a male and a female— had been placed together in an outdoor habitat, in an attempt at matchmaking. They engaged in a kind of lumbering frolic. They banged horns, bounced around, raced across the habitat, with the female chasing the male, a sexist's delight. The performance, as Dennis evaluated it, was encouraging. In such attempts at mating, other emotions—fear, panic, or outright hostility—might have prevailed.

"Considering how few of these there are in the world, or

even in captivity, every introduction is important," he said to a keeper watching the rhinos with him.

He remembered the first time he had seen the massive creatures in the wild.

"I was in Africa, my first trip there, and we were in an open-sided International Harvester vehicle. I spotted a rhino in the bush. In nature, what fascinates you first is their massiveness, their latent power. Well, while I watched that rhino, he watched us. Suddenly, he rushed out of the bush and literally lifted the truck off the ground. I've never forgotten that feeling, of both danger and exhilaration. The truck bounced upright and we got away, but as I stared at that rhino, I thought that it was essentially unchanged from prehistory. Think about that."

There was little time to reflect. It was 9 A.M., time for the weekly staff meeting. Les Fisher, wearing a navy tie emblazoned with giraffes, presided.

Les had made rounds that morning and had reported the reptile house water-pressure problem to some plumbers at work in another part of the zoo. He urged Clarence Wright to camp on the plumbing foreman's door if the pressure didn't improve.

He had seen some overgrown patches of lawn.

"It looks like a little jungle here and there. Needs doing," he said.

He reported that "a guy called me to report that he was confronted by an escaped wolf. He said his wife and son had to flee into the large mammal house." It was true: The maned wolf who had escaped a few weeks earlier had done it again. As in the previous episode, the wolf had been darted with a tranquilizer and returned to its habitat.

Mark Rosenthal reminded Les that there was "a weakness in the habitat, a slight incline in the rockwork on one wall, enabling the wolf to jump down and out of the exhibit from an overhanging ledge. The wolf wasn't supposed to be in that area at all, but in another one he couldn't get out of."

The wolf was one of several that had been suffering from distemper.

"He must be fine now," Dennis noted, sarcastically. "He seems to be fully coordinated."

Les was not cheered. "Some other wolf might get out," he said. "We need a barrier, a modification. I'll call the guy who called me about it, and I'll explain it all to him," he added, with visible weariness.

One of the alcoholics on the zoo staff would be on probation for six months, Les advised. "He'll come back to work, and we'll have to monitor him. If there's a problem, we can let him go without cause during the probation period."

A woman employee had let Les know that she had been physically abused by a male worker. "It's one person's word against the other's," he said.

He reminded those present—curators, vets, and representatives of the zoo society—that the zoo functioned on a rigid budget. "Money will be tight, so be totally cost-efficient. Funding is getting tougher, not better. We must be lean, mean, hard. When we spend money, we ought to ask ourselves, how does it enhance the public's view of the zoo? What does the visitor *see* after we've spent the money? That's how to evaluate what we spend."

The meeting ended at 10 A.M., and Dennis returned to his office. He had to phone an old friend, the director of the San Antonio Zoo, to discuss a project few at the zoo knew about, but all would eventually celebrate.

He had to push twenty-six buttons on his Touch-Tone phone in order to reach the number in Texas. "The park district is economizing," he sighed. "Try that on a rotary phone, and you'll have a unique orthopedic problem."

He was phoning his friend to get him to participate in a venture that would bring the koala bear, the irresistible Australian marsupial (it was *not* a bear) to the zoo. They weren't strikingly rare in Australia, but they were seldom seen in zoos. The koalas were available from the San Diego

Zoo, which had had great success in breeding them. It was easier to get them from San Diego than directly from Australia, which imposed restrictions on exports of koalas.

Getting the koalas wasn't difficult; feeding them was. Koalas eat only eucalyptus. It could be grown in California, Puerto Rico, Trinidad, and Hawaii, Dennis had discovered. But he'd found a grower in Florida who could supply the food in large quantities, regularly. Dennis would need enough to feed three to five koalas, and for a sum not exceeding $38,000 a year, he could get the food delivered twice a week, with the air transportation funded, he hoped, by a donation from a major airline. He had the zoo society's support already; koalas would inspire more visitors to come to the zoo. Dennis hoped to get the San Antonio Zoo involved, to share expenses. The discussions would continue.

Dennis hoped to arrange a backup food supply, to be grown in one of the park district's own conservatories. If all went well, the koalas would be in residence in a habitat atop the Crown-Field Center by the spring of 1988.

After he finished his chat with his friend in San Antonio, Dennis looked up and saw Kathy Brown, the senior keeper at the bird house, standing in his doorway. Kathy walked in, bearing good news.

Over the weekend, she told Dennis, a family had come to the zoo to deposit some creatures it had collected and now wanted to get rid of; it was a common occurrence at the zoo. People who became disenchanted with their pets brought them to the zoo.

This family had delivered six ringed-neck doves and a turtle. One of the doves seemed sickly, Kathy reported, but the rest were in good condition. She brought the news to Dennis because he collected ring-necked doves. With the new arrivals, he would have thirty-two of them, in a large, walk-in cage he had put up at home three years ago.

"I've still got one with an amputated wing," he reminded Kathy. "It was hit by a car, but it's still alive and well. It climbs up a bush with its one wing." He assured Kathy that once the new doves were examined and declared to be in good health, he'd take them home.

There were risks, of course. Dennis lived in a northern suburb, and there were wild raccoons around, as there were in the city itself—and in the zoo, for that matter. He had trapped two raccoons and a neighbor's cat trying to pull doves through the mesh of the enclosure.

"A raccoon can pull a dove through a one-inch-by-one-inch opening in the wire," he told Kathy. "All that remains is a cluster of feathers on the wire."

The doves would be the latest additions to Dennis's small menagerie. He owned an "alley dog," part terrier and part beagle, that he'd cared for since 1974, when the puppy had been tossed out of a moving car near the zoo. He had a dozen tortoises. He had two large Oscars, "huge fish with definite personalities," in a large tank. He got them when he received a call at the zoo declaring, "If you don't take this fish, I'm going to flush it down the toilet." He took one, then got another call from the same person, and took the second fish. In addition, he had a Colombian rainbow boa, "just a little guy," and a dozen marine toads.

As Kathy went on her way, Dennis's phone rang.

The University of California had rescued a sea lion. But it was an epileptic and was on dilantin. No thanks, Dennis told the caller, who indicated that if Dennis didn't want the sea lion, Sea Lion Rescue International would take it.

Another call: A woman who had been calling regularly with the same message reiterated it. Every evening when she parked her car, between 2 and 4 A.M., her car was attacked by a giant anteater. It was destroying the finish on the car, she insisted.

"We'd love to have the anteater," Dennis told her. "Just let us know where it is." He put down the phone and gasped, "A lunatic!"

The phone rang again: A woman wanted to donate a one-winged great horned owl to the zoo. Again, no thanks.

He walked away from the clanging phone to the bird house, to pick up some birdseed for his doves and see the newly arrived doves, who appeared to be in good condition. A keeper told him, "Someone brought in a seagull with its feet cut off. Can you believe that? It was one of the sickest things I've ever seen." Dennis grimaced. The bird had been euthanized by one of the zoo vets.

In a nearby cage, he spotted a small gray bird, a nighthawk. It had been brought in by a family that had found it and thought it needed help.

They thought the bird was sick. It wasn't. It was just young, and its mother hadn't been around when they found the bird. Dennis examined it.

"It needs weight," Dennis told the keeper. "Wait a week. Let it eat. Then flip it out in the late afternoon. They're nocturnal. A city bird. Sleeps all day. It shouldn't have been picked up in the first place. It would have done fine out there."

Dennis's days were filled with decisions, large and small. He managed the animal collection—and the curators as well. The ongoing renovations were his concern, too. They were designed to bring the zoo and its exhibits into the twenty-first century. Some animals would be moved out on loan, some would be moved out permanently, and the entire collection would be improved as it was reduced. All of it existed as paperwork, before the construction crews ever appeared. Dennis had mastered the skill of reading blueprints and architects' renderings of the new buildings and the altered old ones. Finally, Dennis filled in for Les when the director was away, and handled any work that Les chose to pass his way.

There were rumors that Les might retire in a few years. Several of the current curators hoped to be knighted, but it was possible that a new director might come from another zoo. For most of the staff, however, Dennis appeared to be the logical heir. It was not something he thought about, at least not much, he insisted.

"I'd be happy if ten years from now, Les was still sitting there. He doesn't have to retire; it's not mandatory. But when he does, there's no question that his is a plum job.

There will be competition for it, within and without the zoo. But I haven't spent my twenty years here just waiting for his job to open up."

He changed the subject. He talked about the nature of the people who became keepers.

"There was a time when we had a huge group of old-timers who hated educated people. Some of them couldn't write their own names. Then, in the seventies, young people applied, and some of the older ones retired or died. Women came on board. They were eager to learn. They moved on, to some degree, after working here—to other jobs, to school.

"Enter the activists. They wanted answers, and if they didn't get the ones they liked, they engaged in provocation. Now, all the generations are represented here, but most of the old ones are biding their time until they retire. As it's all changed, keepers have become more professional, more visible, more accountable. There's a reason for that. It used to be that recreation was the only reason for a zoo to exist. That's gone. Now keepers must know more about animals than feeding them and cleaning their cages."

In the best of worlds, there would be a keeper perfectly suited to care for specific animals. Dennis did not antici-pate perfection.

"What we want to do," he said, "is match the person, the skills, the personality, and our need. It's impossible at times. In God's master plan, there is an ideal person for every slot. But not here."

The tribulations of coexisting with a diverse assortment of personalities were only part of Dennis's routine. He worried about the animals as well.

Every week, he chaired the animal management meet-ing, a discussion of problems and progress related to the animal collection. On one summer afternoon, he found an empty table and convened the group in a Crown-Field corridor.

Curators Mark Rosenthal and Clarence Wright were there, along with vet Tom Meehan and assistant vet Peri

Wolff; curator Kevin Bell would have been there, but he was at another meeting, with the planners of the renovated bird house.

Dennis shared with those present some of the phone calls he'd gotten: the one hoping to donate the one-winged owl and the other offering the epileptic sea lion. There were snickers around the table, and unanimous approval of Dennis's rejection of both offers.

Dennis confirmed with Mark that Bozie the elephant was set to be shipped to the zoo in Springfield, Missouri, in three months, for a stay that could last eighteen months. It was a variation on the breeding loan process. But first Bozie would have to be tested for parasites and tuberculosis. Mark would accompany the animal, along with one of the elephant keepers.

"Should her slot be taken by another elephant?" Dennis asked.

"It's a good idea," Mark replied. "For companionship, and for our keepers' professional growth. We'd take any elephant except a wild, rampaging male."

"We can test her for TB, but we have no way of knowing if that test is worth anything," Tom said. "The problem is more a matter of false positives than false negatives. But we don't have to rely on the test alone; we can do a gastric lavage."

Dennis moved on to the subject of other animals slated to leave the zoo.

"We need to move out about four to six of the Arabian oryxes by the end of the year. They're going back to the wild. In Oman."

Tom reminded Dennis of the red tape involved in shipping animals directly from the zoo to a foreign country.

"Don't worry. We'll send them to another zoo first, in preparation for the shipment overseas," Dennis said. "Oman will pay all the transportation, vet, and crating costs."

Mark told the others that the newly matched pair of

rhinos were doing fine. So was Lenore, the gorilla whose hand had to be amputated.

"She gets around," Tom added.

"Now she ought to be in a one-on-one situation, then one-on-two," Mark replied.

"I want to see if she can use her elbow to climb," Tom said.

"By the way, I've put in a work order to fix the maned wolf habitat, and we're going to relocate that wolf who got out of it," Mark said.

Tom remained concerned with the distemper that afflicted that wolf and several others. He wasn't concerned that other animals would get it, however.

"If they were going to get it, they'd have it by now," he said. "But I can't guarantee that someone won't take the virus home to a dog. There's no danger if the keepers change their shoes and use the footbath before they leave work," he added.

"But we don't have to worry about a distemper epidemic that will last ten years?" Mark asked.

"No," Tom said, smiling.

"Well, let's define that magical date when all's clear," Dennis said. "And we'll be OK. Let's do it as early as possible. And Mark, have that work order put through on an emergency basis."

"By the way, one of those wolves has a bad leg," Tom noted. "A very bad leg."

"If it can't be repaired to give that animal a normal life, we'll have to euthanize it. No choice. We can replace it," Dennis said. He was often consulted by the vets and the curators before an animal was euthanized.

"A professor in Oklahoma wants six of our king snakes. Not a loan. He wants to keep them," Clarence said.

Dennis smiled. The zoo had a surplus of king snakes.

"God love him," he said to Clarence. "Send them as a donation, and we'll pay the freight."

Tom was concerned with a problem affecting the rattlesnakes. Their spines would fuse, causing paralysis. It was a mystery and had been adding to Clarence's anxiety about plagues in the reptile house.

"We'll find out what it is," Tom assured Clarence. "Do they have a history of eating live prey?"

"Yes," Clarence said. "I've thought that whatever it is might be transmitted by mice."

"By rodent teeth. That's my guess," Tom said. "When a snake isn't hungry, it doesn't eat the mouse immediately. Then, the mouse bites the snake."

"That kind of bite could happen, and you'd never even see it," Dennis commented.

Peri had been summoned to the penguin-seabird house earlier that day by a concerned keeper who thought she had a dead penguin on her hands. The penguin had been in the pool and had appeared to be lifeless. But when Peri arrived and picked it up, it moved.

"The penguin was in poor feather condition," she said. "The insulation wasn't there. The penguin went cold. It burned up its energy, and for some reason it got stuck in the pool in a weakened state and was stressed. It may have inhaled some water. So we took it to the hospital. After a while, it started to heat up, so we took it back to penguin-seabird. It's on antibiotics now, to prevent pneumonia, and it's not in that pool now."

"Odd how animals behave," Dennis said. "I once had a dead tortoise, and I put it in a large plastic bag and tossed it into the garbage. Four hours later, I heard a scratching sound. It taught me something. Always give a reptile twenty-four hours to die."

When tamarins, small monkeys, eat roaches, as is common in the zoo, they develop parasites. Earlier that day, Peri had operated on two of them and had removed dozens of the worms from their intestines. The operation was a last resort, if antibiotics failed.

"We're doing well with our roach control in the hospital," Tom said. "But the tamarins come to us from small mammal, and over there they're loaded with roaches. Roaches are going to decimate our collection. We've got to hit them with an insecticide. If the roaches eat that and the animals eat the roaches, it's a smaller risk than the one we've got now."

Gene Brimer, the exterminator Mark had hired, would be spending time in the hospital, working on the problem, Mark said.

It was 4:30 P.M. when the discussion ended. Dennis needed some fresh air.

He went outside and stood at the railing in front of the lions' outdoor habitat. He knew that few of the majestic animals—perhaps no more than fifty—survived in captivity, and not more than two hundred were present in the only forest in India that still supported them.

A female lion was in heat. The scent she gave off could be detected by the male several miles away in the wild. In the zoo, she had tempted a male a few yards away. But she wanted to sleep, not mate.

The male approached her and attempted to nudge her out of her tranquility. She lifted her head slowly, turned it to him, and growled. He paused. She tried to return to sleep. The male approached her from behind and began to lick her genitalia. She endured the advance. He mounted her and proceeded rapidly to achieve his objective. As he did, he growled. Then, he left for a moment, paced, and returned for another episode.

She got up to avoid him. She turned her back against the cliff wall at the back of the habitat. The male was restless, pacing, growling. Then, acquiring a sense of patience that had not been evident, he crouched beside her. She did not respond. He waited for a signal. She did not acknowledge his presence.

Along the rail next to Dennis, a father held his young daughter.

"What were they doing?" the child asked.

"It's time to go," the father said.

"Yes," his wife joined in. "Let's go."

Dennis smiled.

"Usually they say, 'You don't want to watch that. They're fighting,' " he said. "Accompanied by a hooked arm around the kid who asked the question."

He moved on, passing the habitat occupied by the two Bengal tigers, the sisters. One of them was dozing in the sun. The second was propped against a cool wall at the back of the habitat. Her expression was sleepy, peaceful.

Suddenly, the sleepy tiger—in a manner familiar to owners of house cats—sat up. Her gaze fixed on something beyond the moat that separated the animals from the public. She arose and stalked toward the moat, moving slowly, deliberately, never diverting that gaze. She got to the edge of the moat and sat up, unblinking. There were people beyond the moat, floating balloons, vendors. The tiger stared for several minutes, a portrait of the predator in readiness, then turned its head, moved away from the moat, and went back to the back wall.

Something had tantalized the tiger, something had urged her on.

But Dennis did not attempt to read the minds of animals.

Only the tiger knew what had sent her on that brief dramatic prowl. For Dennis, every such mysterious moment was a part of the continuing fascination that made his job so gratifying. It was comforting for him to know that humans could know a great deal about animals. But not everything.

FIRST PERSON: DENNIS MERITT

As a teenager, I had an intense interest in animals and an intense interest in the outdoors. I had a love of nature and a love of walking across the landscape. I didn't share my family's interest in hunting, but I shared their interest in being in wild places and in seeing things and in flipping rocks and collecting squirmy, slimy things.

I had an interest in science, in pure science. Then, at age

twenty-six, I reassessed where I was and what I was doing and what I was really interested in. By that time I was intensely involved in animal things. I thought to myself, "Why not explore the possibilities of being paid for that interest?" I sought out other people who had similar interests, and those people all funneled in a zoo direction. Then I became very close with the local zoo director, actually began to spend some time as a volunteer at the zoo, began to explore what opportunities were within the zoo profession. I began a search, and the search lasted about a year and a half.

When I arrived here, I was shy, introverted, not self-assured at all. I think I compensated for all of those deficiencies with an intense desire to learn, to experience firsthand. The day that I walked into this place, and Les Fisher said, "You know what your job is, do it," and there were no constraints on it, I think that began the evolution of the person. The opportunities that I had here are largely responsible for who I am.

I had a high level of book learning, formal education. I had all of the theory, all of the principles, but I had very little real or practical experience, and that came on the job. I ate it up. As it came to me, I welcomed it. I was very much like Don Quixote; the windmills were different, but I just waded into situations here, particularly animal situations, always with the animals' best interests at heart, always knowing that we could do something more for these animals.

The first weekend that I was on—for the first twelve or fourteen years at Lincoln Park, I worked every other weekend—I was here alone. I'd probably been on the job three or four days. A camel was born. Now, I had seen a baby camel, I'd seen a mother camel, but I had never been in a position to make some kind of judgment about whether mother and baby were doing fine. And as soon as the mother started to kick the baby, I realized that all was not well. And I remember calling the then assistant director and saying, "Listen, I need some help on this, because I think I ought to pull this baby." And he said, "Don't ever call me on a day off again. Do whatever you're going to do, but make sure that you make the right decision, because if you don't, you'll pay for it on Monday morning."

So with those guidelines, I waded in to pull a baby camel, which basically meant running in and grabbing this ninety-eight-pound infant away from its mother, and running for my life. Now, what I didn't know about camels but now fully understand, and have put into my mental dictionary, is that the mother had mastitis, and it was very painful every time the baby tried to nurse, and that's why she was kicking it. She had all of the maternal instincts for that infant. Even though she didn't want it near her, she certainly didn't want me to take it away from her. And I can remember, panting, I mean panting, exhausted, running out of that field pen, with that baby camel, with mom real close to my tail. It was one of those experiences in life that you don't forget.

It actually was a very good learning experience for me, because no baby camel had ever been hand-raised here before. I went to the books, I went to other people in the zoo community and said, "How do you raise a baby camel?" We successfully raised it by hand, and it turned out to be a magnificent animal.

I believe that there is a very high level of interaction between some of the animals and some of the people at the zoo. There's no question about that. During my early years here, my office was in the lion house. There was no question in my mind that those animals responded to my presence every day, to my comings and goings, and that we could play games—hide and seek—and jump around, and that they would respond to me and I would respond to them, as I walked through that building. It was eye-to-eye contact; it was one of those mental things that happen. It clearly happens with other kinds of animals.

Take the breeding male chimp that was here for so many years, Sam. He and most of the females that formed that group came to us as juveniles. I was the person who used to check on the animals and see how they were doing and make dietary adjustments. And when they became sexually mature, I was the one who went to those females to make some judgment about how the babies were doing: Are they going to be OK? Are they strong enough? Are they big enough? Are they too small? What do we have to do? I had a very good personal relationship with the females. A lot of it came with handing out bananas or handing out peppermints. But that male, Sam, didn't like that interaction. Sam, in his mature years in the great ape house, treated me exactly like a competing male.

Jane Goodall was here, and Jane and I had known each other for a number of years. I said to her, "I want you to assess for me what happens when I walk into this building." I said, "I'm not going to say a word. You're the field biologist; you just tell me what happens." As we walked through the building, Sam took one look at me and began his hair fluffing and his foot stomping and his hooting and his swinging. And as I moved to the glass barrier, he would swing down and pound the glass and then go charging off. And she smiled and said, "Well, you're just like a competing male. If you were in nature, what you should now do, to reassure him that you have no intentions on his females, is to go in and groom him. This is the scenario that should happen, but I wouldn't advise it."

If I enjoy an interaction with an animal today, it's probably with the elephants. The elephants treat me as a neutral object. I'm not someone who trains them; I'm not someone who works them. On the other hand, I'm not a stranger, not someone to be either leery of or suspicious of or afraid of. When I'm there with the elephants, it's always under positive circumstances. That forces on me a certain responsibility, because I realize that those animals are potentially dangerous, are thinking, knowing, reasoning, testing creatures all the time. So, while I enjoy the relationship very much, and I enjoy the kind of mutual contact that we have, I have to be real careful, because I have a tendency to become too close to them in terms of trusting. And that is a real bad frame of mind to be in with any wild animal, particularly one that you're directly involved with.

The big cats still fascinate me. I think it has to do with body form, with size, and with knowing that these are predators, essentially killing machines, that they have all of the muscle and bone and form they need to carry out that task and to survive under very difficult circumstances. We know about their speed, and we know about their stealth. From my perspective, it's respect for that, and also realizing that those animals are essentially unchanged. There is very little if any difference between lions and tigers and leopards and snow leopards and cheetahs in a captive situation, as compared to nature. All of the instincts, all of the capabilities are there.

You think that an animal's changed because of a captive environment. We had a particular pair of snow leopards on the outside of the lion house. They were fed this prepared zoo mix, which looks like raw hamburger served in a sausage shape. And these two animals religiously would leave a small portion of that food, and would catnap within reaching distance of that pile, and would let starlings and pigeons come into the cage to feed off of it. And every once in a while, they would pick off a starling or pick off a pigeon. It was to me a living demonstration that that animal still has all of those instincts it was born with.

You can spot an emotional range in animals. Absolutely. It's measured in a number of things. In the higher forms of animal, here at the zoo—whether it be bird, mammal, or reptile—usually it has something to do with either body position or ear position or eyes or where the tail hangs or the way a wing is. Sometimes it's in vocalization. It's all there. After you've been here a while, you know what the usual or the normal posture or activity or appearance of an animal is, of any given species. And then without consciously knowing it, you go by or you look and you recognize, sometimes not being able to define it, that there's something different. It may be the way it's sitting or lying. It may be the luster in its eye or the lack of it. It may be the way its coat is. It may be the way the feathers lie. It's more a sixth sense than it is definable or describable.

A number of my colleagues here and elsewhere across the world see zoos as a last refuge—not a last refuge in terms of we are going to save every single animal or every endangered species in the world, but a last refuge in terms of a gene bank. If a species disappears in the wild, there will be some that survive in zoos. They will survive, not for visitor enjoyment, not for visitor viewing, but simply from a genetic standpoint, meaning that we have the potential to propagate almost anything that we set our minds to. We have the technology, we have the experience, we have the intellectual powers to be able to propagate any given species, given enough time, given enough money, given adequate facilities. So I see zoos as the last reservoir.

I also see zoos as an ambassador of wild places. Zoos are places where people can come, not only to see animals, but to learn about animals, to experience them firsthand, in a three-dimensional living, breathing, smelly, vocalizing way.

Modern zoos like Lincoln Park and others across the country have known for a number of years that they needed to change facilities to put animals into more aesthetically pleasing surroundings that allow interpretation about the animal and where it lives and how it naturally behaves. We've known that for years, but zoos have until fairly recently been poorly supported in terms of dollars. We have had the architectural skills, we've had the technological skills, we've had the interpretive skills, we've had the exhibit design skills to do it. It's just a question of money. So those things are changing. With regard to diet, you have an obligation to provide an animal with nutritionally sound, wholesome, appealing food. The only way to do that, particularly in a northern zoo on a twelve-month basis, is to substitute natural foods—foods that the animal would normally eat in nature—with other foods. In the case of carnivores, critics of zoos would have more to be critical of if we regularly released goats or sheep or gazelles into carnivore cages to provide them a meal. A small example of that is feeding day in the reptile house. We close the building, so that we do not offend anybody.

We have made a conscious attempt to reduce the number of species here in the collection—bird, mammal, and reptile, across the board. We're trying to cut down the number of kinds of animal that we have, to match species to facilities, and to show those species that we exhibit, in terms of visitor interest and international conservation, with those two priorities in mind.

If they're found in nature as a colony, they should be a colony here. If they're found as a herd, they should be a herd. If it's a family group, it should be a family group. This movement had already started twenty years ago. Fifteen years ago it really became a major emphasis. We don't show singletons. And if we show a single animal, it's because we have been unable to find a suitable mate or companion for it. For the last fifteen years, we haven't willy-nilly taken animals into this collection. I think the renovation and the reconstruction and the rebuilding here will allow us to reach that final phase of matching animals and facilities exactly. And that's what we're doing. In the lion house renovation, twenty-six cages are being reduced to ten habitats. We will show five species, and we'll show them well. We'll have backups, areas behind the scenes for sick animals, for pregnant animals, for animal introductions, for the adequate maintenance of any offspring that are produced here. In the lion house, we'll have indoor and outdoor facilities for the Afghanistan leopard and for the snow leopard, showing our long-range commitment to the international propagation programs for those animals.

We have four ways to disperse animals. One is with an outright gift. We have an animal that is surplus that someone else needs; we make some assessment of what that facility is, what their capabilities are, what their physical plant and what their staff are like, and sometimes just simply give the animal to them, because they have a need for it. We sometimes sell animals outright—this'll cost you a dollar and a half, this'll cost you ten thousand dollars, whatever the case may be; the dollar value is unimportant. But the same formula is plugged in: Who is it? What facilities do they have? What is their expertise? What are the long-range prospects for the survival of this animal? And then we have breeding loans, which also fall under the same conditions. Breeding loans are made usually because we have been so successful with an animal species that we need to move some of the animals out of here, but we still want to retain ownership of those animals and some of their offspring for our long-range propagation needs. That's basically what a breeding loan allows you to do: to choose what the satellite propagation facilities are going to be. The usual terms of a breeding loan are if we send a pair of animals out of here, we retain ownership of the adults, and we split any offspring produced equally. The fourth method is a trade—we're one of the few professions left in the world where barter still works. You trade an animal to another institution for some ballpark kind of dollar figure, or to have credit established at the other institution. We may send a particular animal to an institution that either doesn't have the finances to pay for it or wants to do it on a trade basis, and say to them, "Fine, take this. You have a need. You have a perfect match for it in terms of a mate and match in terms of facilities. We will sometime in the future get something from you of comparable value." And we don't worry about what the value is, knowing that the animal is going into a good situation.

I can't remember the last time that we went to a dealer because we needed an animal. We would always go to other zoos first, whether they be here in the States or whether they be international. The same is true for anything that is declared surplus, whether that is a sale, a trade, a gift, or a loan. The zoo community always has first refusal. And then we disperse to licensed accredited dealers. Dealers have become intermediaries or brokers. If we should be unable to find a direct institution-to-institution affiliation for the placement of an animal, there are dealers around who play that role. Basically what happens is that they act as our agent or somebody else's agent for relocating, transportation, and the actual negotiations for the relocation of the animals.

Some of the zoos I admire may surprise you. I very much enjoy going to Milwaukee. They've created a parklike setting, so that you have at least the illusion that you're in nature; lots of trees, lots of landscaping, which contribute significantly to it. In terms of surprises and a very good overall effect, particularly setting and a specific collection, go to Madison, Wisconsin, to Henry Vilas Zoo. It is a little jewel, sitting there alongside the lake, really a place to be savored. It's a retreat, in a very real sense, from city life. It's an opportunity to kind of slide into nature. One institution that has changed its image is the zoo in Pittsburgh, Pennsylvania. That zoo has undergone a tremendous evolution in the last few years; it is a very, very pleasant and enjoyable experience. San Diego has a lot of admirers. I think it isn't the San Diego Zoo at all; I think it's Southern California, the laid-back lifestyle, and the people in that community. I know its staff as well as I know my own family. And they themselves are at a loss to explain why San Diego has the image that it has. They don't care; they want it to continue. From a professional standpoint, a purely analytical devil's advocate kind of position, there are some real stinky things at San Diego that they are busily trying to take care of. There are some ancient, decrepit, outmoded facilities there. We kid our colleagues in San Diego that if they didn't have the climate, and if they didn't have the vegetation that they have at the zoo, that they would be nothing more than a concrete jungle. And that is absolutely true. That semitropical climate allows you, with planting material, on a twelve-month basis, to cover up a host of construction errors. Of course, the wild animal park that is located outside of San Diego, that very much is a model facility. But when people talk about San Diego, they aren't talking about the wild animal park, they're talking about the zoo in Balboa. And I don't know where that mystique came from.

The two zoos that people name as zoos that they want to go to, I mean that they really are impressed by, are the ones in San Diego and the Bronx. Bronx has worked very hard at its image. The Bronx has a long history of tradition. It goes back to the days of all of those wonderful early naturalists, hunters, environmentalists, whatever the right description might be. And they have built on that, and there is no question in my mind, both personally and professionally, that in terms of zoo technology, architecture, exhibit design, interpretation, the Bronx is the finest in the country. They have spent untold amounts of money to accomplish the grand illusion. They have, particularly from the standpoint of exhibit design, duplicated in a captive environment, in a northern zoo, as close as one can come to a natural environment, and have done it extremely well. They've done it not only from the visitors' standpoint, and from a maintenance standpoint, but they also have done it from the animals' standpoint, which is critical.

National in Washington is the nation's zoo. What it should mean, what it should have meant for the last twenty-five or thirty years, is that it should have been the model for all zoos within the country, let alone internationally. It isn't. It's reaching that point, but it isn't, because it didn't have the financial support it needed from the Congress and from its governing institution. It has within the last five years done some major and significant updates to bring it into the twenty-first century. They are busy making changes.

Going away and looking at other facilities energizes me, gives me a renewed sense that this is what we need to do, so let's do it. In a real sense, it's a battery charge. And there's always something to do. Twenty-plus years ago when I walked in here, it was for me a learning experience. And it still is. I learn something every day. Every time that I think that I know all there is to know, the animals show me something different. And as long as it continues to be that for me, I can't think of any better place to be.

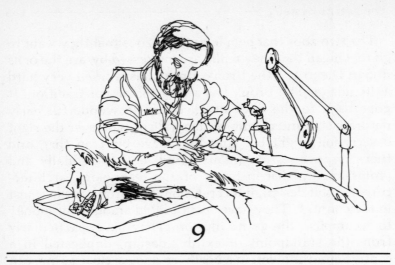

9

HOUSE CALLS

If animals could verbalize their hostility, Tom Meehan would be the most hated human at the zoo. As the zoo veterinarian, he was the one who disturbed their peace, brought pain and fright into their world, even as he saved their lives. He was not an unfeeling, sadistic man at all, but his role did not bring him gratitude from the animals whose peace he had disturbed, any more than a pediatrician won admiration from the infants he introduced to pain and fright.

When Tom approached, many animals displayed their anger and their fear openly. Fortunately, Tom accepted that reaction and did his job.

It was a job he had been prepared to do. At thirty-five, he had a bachelor's degree in animal husbandry and a D.V.M. from the University of Missouri. Born in St. Louis, he had been interested in zoos and in animals as a boy. He decided to be a vet when he was in high school and sold balloons and hot dogs at the St. Louis Zoo.

He served as a keeper at that zoo and worked there part-time while in college. He was a vet at an animal hospital in Indiana and a resident vet at the St. Louis Zoo before joining the Lincoln Park Zoo staff in 1981.

Tom lived in the northwest part of Chicago with his wife (who had been a keeper at the St. Louis Zoo), two young daughters, a dog, six doves, and two cockatiels. His work brought him to the modern bunker that housed the hospital and the commissary every weekday before 8 A.M. and often on weekends. In a dark brown, dark blue, or bright green jumpsuit, with dangling keys and a walkie-talkie attached to his belt, he was a case study in perpetual motion. At 5'9" and 185 pounds, with a full beard and thick brown hair, he had the appearance and energy of a rugged running back.

He spent most of his time treating animals, but he was in charge of the commissary as well; it had been created with a large donation from Joan and Ray Kroc, of McDonald's hamburger fame. From the commissary, food was distributed to the kitchens in the various animal houses. The quantities of food consumed were diverse and massive. Each week, the large mammals ate 200 pounds of hydroponic grass (produced at the zoo itself, it was a quick-growing oat seed grass). Birds devoured 7,500 meal worms and 850 wax worms weekly. The hoofed stock consumed 1,470 pounds of alfalfa and 1,680 pounds of timothy hay each week. The monkeys consumed 36 pounds of grapes per week and 63 pounds of sweet potatoes. The big cats dined on more than 500 pounds of horsemeat fortified with vitamins and minerals, plus 50 pounds of horse knuckles and 50 pounds of horse tails. Bananas were popular with animals in almost every house.

The commissary's keeper staff kept track of food; the keepers ordered it, and the keepers delivered it. Tom maintained control. He felt that feeding the animals properly was a part of his mission to maintain their good health.

"I had an interest in nutrition," he said. "I had contacts in the field. What I don't have now is time. Our diets have to be revamped from top to bottom. We need to bring in some zoo nutrition consultants with their computers. But when we requested that in our budget, we were turned down. So we feed the animals the same old things and handle problems as they arise. We'll shoot for those consultants in the next budget."

Time was the commodity in short supply in Tom's life.

The hospital itself was not identifiable from the zoo walk that passed above it. It was concealed from the view of passersby in its bunker reached from a metal stairway. It was not an architectural wonder. Rather, it was a utilitarian design. A long corridor from front to back doors was lined with offices, a lab, a dining area, an examining room, an operating room, an area to perform necropsies, and various holding areas for animals being held for diagnoses, animals awaiting treatment, and animals recovering from treatment. (Most animals were returned to their houses after treatment.) It was all brightly lit, immaculate. The three keepers assigned to the hospital kept the place clean and the animals cared for.

It was a quiet place, but rarely an uneventful one.

On a hot summer morning, Tom sat behind his desk, confronting a tall stack of mail, forms, and memos.

"The mornings here are always crazy," he said. "There's so much to do. There may be animals to be euthanized. Certainly there are always animals to see, to examine. We have rounds daily; we meet in my office and go over each case. We catch everyone up on what's going on, including Peri [Peregrine Wolff, the assistant vet] and Joel Pond, our lab technician. We don't specialize here. Peri doesn't just do birds, and I don't just do mammals. One of us may be away at times, so the vet on duty is *it*. Last weekend, I got eight calls on Sunday at home, and I wasn't feeling well. Fortunately, I didn't have to come in. It was my first weekend at home in months."

One of the hospital keepers, a woman, entered to interrupt Tom.

"We've got two seagulls. One may have been shot, the

other seems to have flown into a fence. Someone brought them in," she told Tom.

She reported, as well, that Lenore, the gorilla whose hand had been amputated in surgery, was showing signs of recovery. "She isn't crabby," the keeper said.

"Our lemur baby is cold, and the mother threw it out of their box," the keeper went on. The hospital was doubling as the zoo nursery while the children's zoo, where it was normally housed, was being renovated. The lemur mother had arrived from the Milwaukee Zoo, in transit to another zoo, and had been pregnant. Tom had not been warned.

"Watch it," Tom said. "Is it moving?"

"Yes."

"Keep an eye on it for a couple of hours. If I grab it and do a blood sample, I might upset it."

"Can't we just warm it up?"

"Let's put some supplemental heat in there. One of those infrared heaters. We're going to have to rethink all this. Call the primate house and find someone who knows about baby lemurs. We have to keep the mother from rejecting that baby, if we can."

The incident inspired Tom to be reflective.

"You just never know about wild animals. There's a story about a lion at the Milwaukee Zoo. It was lethargic, and the keepers were concerned. Well, they knew that lions are predatory, and they wanted to do something to stimulate that inclination. So they tossed a rabbit in with it. What happened? They became pals."

It was time for staff rounds, which included reports from a short, boyish fourth-year vet student from Iowa State University named Jeff, and a recent Michigan State University vet technician graduate, a tall blond woman named Sandy. Both were externs, putting in time at the zoo in exchange for valuable experience and a token salary. They brought up several cases for Tom to assess.

A baby chimp was upset at night and didn't eat properly. But it was fine during the day.

"Don't worry about it," Tom said. "That's common."

He told the two externs about the baby lemur.

"There's an eighty percent chance we'll have to pull that baby. My guess is that it ought to go to the primate house."

Several maned wolves had distemper. It had become a nagging problem for Tom. Distemper was a risk for all animals; it was the major killer of dogs. For dogs, there was a vaccine. But the live virus vaccine available for use on wild animals gave some animals the disease itself, instead of protecting them against it. Vaccines of lesser risk were also less effective. Zoo vets were not in agreement about which vaccines to use with various species. There were riddles in the practice of veterinary medicine. Absolute answers were not always available to Tom. The wolves presented a challenge.

One of the wolves might have gotten the disease from a wild raccoon frequenting the zoo and passed it along to the other wolves. A vaccine Tom had tried had failed.

"That's not unusual. Distemper is a virus—as mysterious in some ways as the common cold or the flu in humans. We can provide supportive care, but we can't do miracles. Still, I think that these three should make it."

The two seagulls had to be examined. "If they're not releasable, and they're hopeless, we euthanize them. If they're of value, we'll keep them or send them on to a wildlife refuge. But a bird that isn't fully flighted is in trouble. Let's find out."

He led the two externs to the treatment room, a few paces down the hall from his office. Tom opened the makeshift carrier, a large cardboard box marked "Blue Mountain Apples," and lifted one of the birds out, clutching it in one hand, examining it with the other.

"Bummed up," he muttered.

He examined the second bird.

"An old injury that's gotten debilitating. He's real skinny. Can't keep up with the other birds."

Tom made up his mind. Carefully, he sprayed alcohol on a small area where the bird's wing met its body, then injected a euthanizing solution into the bird. Its fluttering stopped instantly. The second bird took longer to die, a few seconds longer.

Tom put the dead birds back into the apple box and led the externs into an adjoining room. He snapped an x-ray onto a light box. It was a film of gorilla Lenore's wrist. Minor surgery had been attempted to cure an infection in that wrist, after antibiotics had failed, but the infection got worse. It was not possible to give a gorilla a flow of antibiotics via an IV line, so the decision was made to remove the infected bone.

"A mess," Tom said. "We tried to save the hand, but we couldn't. We had to amputate. Everybody says, how could you do that? Well, the infection would have gone systemic, and she would have died. We had to try."

He left the hospital and headed to the bear line, where the sick wolves were kept. Jeff, the extern, tagged along.

"Here's a primitive neurological exam," Tom said to Jeff. He poked a long broomstick into the wolf's cell. The wolf had appeared to be blinded by distemper.

"I think he can see," Tom commented. He moved closer to the cage. The wolf did not appear to see him.

"Maybe he can't," he said.

He visited the second wolf. The wolf's bark, normally piercing, was barely audible.

"The distemper gave him laryngitis. It's a disease that shows up everywhere, in the skin, in the respiratory system, in the nervous system. You can't tell where it will be manifested. As many as half of its victims may die. The young are particularly vulnerable."

With Jeff beside him, Tom left the bear line, got into the hospital's yellow park district van and drove over to the great ape house.

Tom looked at a chimp, Shauri, with a long history of illness, from lung infection to diabetes. She had a weight gain that needed interpretation. Tom went toward her small holding cage. She gazed at him and moved her extended lips toward his. She was one of the few animals to show friendship to him; most of them caused a commotion when he appeared.

He looked at Lenore, too, in another holding area.

One of the keepers told him, "She used her arm as she used to use it. She looks at the stump, but she hasn't been biting it."

"She *knows* it's not there," Tom said. "When you reach for something and you don't feel it, you know."

Tom stared at Lenore.

"She has a distinct individual memory of me. She doesn't like me. Even in street clothes, she'd know me. They all know me. I'm not popular."

"Are you going to knock her down again?" the keeper asked, wondering if Tom would tranquilize the gorilla.

"Not now," he answered. "But in the next three weeks, we probably will, to take care of the problems with her teeth." Lenore's troubles hadn't ended.

"I'm more and more amazed at what we can do for these apes," he said to the keeper as he moved toward the door. "They're tough, tough animals."

A gorilla nearby, behind glass, clapped loudly, cupping its hands on its vast chest. Another, nearby, stuck out a finger through the bars of its holding cage; Tom touched it briskly with one of his.

As he walked out of the great ape house, he stopped to survey a group of gorillas behind the thick glass that separated them from the public. One of the gorillas recognized him and came rushing toward the glass, leaping into it noisily in Tom's direction. Tom flinched slightly.

"Sometimes we forget just how strong that glass is," he said, smiling.

Outside, the sun was heating the zoo. Tom wiped his brow. It was summer; he'd barely noticed.

The next morning, Tom had just arrived at his desk when the phone rang. It was a keeper at the great ape house, letting him know that Shauri, the chimp, had given birth. Normally, any evidence of healthy breeding in the ape colony would have been good news, but in this case it was more than that—it was a shock.

There was little reason to believe that Shauri, a twenty-three-year-old (middle-aged for a chimp), was pregnant. It was not a planned event, and Tom did not conceal his sense of surprise. Shauri had been sickly for years.

"Given her size, you couldn't tell by looking," Tom said. "She weighs two hundred and twenty-nine pounds, and the child probably didn't weigh more than four pounds. A pregnant chimp doesn't look the way my wife did."

At one point, in trying to diagnose one of her symptoms, Shauri had been given a pregnancy test; the result had been inconclusive.

"Well, that explains her breast enlargement," Tom sighed.

At rounds in his office, Tom was joined by the two externs. He told them about Shauri.

"She's a tough animal. She was hand-reared at the zoo. And she's very intelligent. She greets us with a kind of chant-hoot, something the chimps do to each other. One day she bit my arm, then gave me a big hug. Chimps use hugs and kisses to defuse aggression. When they anticipate aggression, interpersonal contact escalates and prevents that aggression. They are demonstrative animals. They don't do anything quietly. They like to make noise. Give them sticks to throw, boxes to tear up and toss around, and they probably won't bother to attack each other.

"Shauri loves to eat. She'll even drink her own milk, instead of giving it to her child. She's lost several babies in recent years. Whatever the reason, the babies just fade out. So we might have to pull this baby. Shauri isn't well, and I didn't want her to be pregnant. The pregnancy could have exacerbated her diabetes problem. Some zoos would put her to sleep if she didn't breed. Not here. After all, she could be a kind of aunt. And we have another newborn chimp in addition to hers. It's easier to raise two of them by hand than just one. They bond."

The phone rang. A large alligator had died during the

night in the alligator exhibit in the basement of the reptile house. The keeper who called didn't seem distressed about it, and Tom wasn't either. An alligator wasn't a potential pet, even to one prone to the anthropomorphic.

Tom told Jeff and Sandy that it would take five or six people, a large tarp, and a pickup truck to move the dead alligator to the hospital.

Other animals were competing for his time. Later in the day, he told the externs, he'd have to check on one of the Major Mitchell's cockatoos in the bird house; it had sinusitis and needed medication. He alerted Jeff to help him treat the bird.

He had to find time during the day to inoculate the alpacas against tetanus. They were going to be sheared soon, and he didn't want them to get tetanus from the minor nicks and cuts involved in the shearing process.

He got up, picked up a coil of strong rope, and led Jeff and Sandy into the van for the trip to the reptile house. When he pulled up in front of it and got out, a jaguar in an outdoor cage facing the reptile house recognized him and went into a pacing frenzy, staring tensely at Tom until he disappeared into the reptile house.

"I upset that jaguar just by showing up," he said. "He remembers me."

On the door to the reptile house, one of the keepers had posted a crudely lettered sign: BUILDING CLOSED FOR RE-PAIRS. They wanted to get to the alligator exhibit before any visiting children did.

In the exhibit, which had been drained of the warm water usually there, a group of seven alligators rested lethargically on the concrete floor. In the middle of the group, a large belly-up alligator was clearly dead, legs in the air, its pale, lifeless skin peeling off.

"He was alive last night and dead this morning," a woman keeper told Tom. Sometimes it happened that way.

One of the keepers opened a small metal door at the rear of the exhibit, and seven people entered: four keepers, the two externs, and Tom. With long sticks, two keepers herded the alligators away from their dead companion. Tom jumped down into the exhibit and roped the dead animal. With help from the others, he dragged it out of the exhibit and onto the tarp. It took all seven to carry it up a flight of stairs.

As they pulled and grunted, the slightly anxious sound of a keeper's voice was heard.

"Did someone close the exhibit door?"

There was silence. Then, a soft voice said, "Yes." Finally, all seven laughed.

Four members of the group lifted the alligator, now wrapped in the tarp, into the back of the pickup truck. "Cover him up," Tom said. People were walking through the zoo in the early morning, and all zoo personnel knew that it was wise to conceal the deaths of animals from the public.

The cadaver was giving off a foul, rotting odor.

"We need to think this over before we cut this sucker open," Tom said.

A convention of flies was attracted to the dead alligator as soon as the truck pulled into the hospital driveway.

"They flew in from four states when they heard about this one," Tom said.

With help from his keepers and externs, Tom dragged the alligator into a freezer locker.

Tom had some choices. He could call the Field Museum of Natural History, and it would have a crew come out to pick up the alligator for its collection of skeletons. He could call the dead animal pickup of the sanitation department, and it would get rid of the alligator. Or he could ask that the zoo incinerator be fired up to burn the corpse. In any case, he might want to do a necropsy, because he always wanted answers to death, even when the creature involved, like the alligator, had become so singularly unattractive. But he didn't have time to decide immediately. He had to move on.

He took a medical kit and drove over to the hoofed-stock enclosure. Walking through the barn area, he passed a stall with a sable antelope in it. The antelope glared at him, a hard, antagonistic glare.

"Mean shit," Tom hissed at it.

He had come to the hoofed-stock area to take a look at a baby Arabian oryx, an antelope-like animal with long, straight horns. At first, he could see only the mother, her white body twitching to repel flies. Then, he spotted the baby—a small, awkward, beige oryx with barely developed horns. He had to get a blood sample from the baby; it hadn't been eating properly.

He conferred with two keepers whose help he would need. Sliding doors separated the stalls, and if the keepers were deft enough, they could tempt the mother out and leave the baby alone for Tom to assess.

Their deftness prevailed. They opened a door. The mother sauntered out into an adjoining stall. They closed the door behind her, and Tom and Jeff had the baby oryx to themselves. Before they entered the stall, Tom told Jeff, "The jugular on these guys is a piece of cake."

Tom grabbed the oryx, and Jeff took the blood sample, while the oryx squirmed and bleated. It was over in a few seconds, and the baby was quickly reunited with its mother.

"Maybe it's not a bad problem," Tom theorized. "The baby looks healthy. It's standing well. We noticed that its stool was yellow, but when you think about that, we see that in all nursing mammals at times. My gut feeling is that it won't develop into a problem."

The mother oryx glared at Tom again; the baby hid behind her.

"I just went in there and beat up her baby," Tom told Jeff. "That mother will remember me."

Tom headed on to the great ape house.

He picked up a supply of sliced oranges and shredded wheat and passed them out to several gorillas as he walked past their cages.

"A pretty transparent attempt at friendship," he muttered.

He stopped to visit a baby chimp in an incubator. The

setting was familiar; there were toys and small blankets in the incubator, and the tiny, appealing, vulnerable chimp was hugging its favorite blanket. Pat Sass, the senior keeper at the ape house, had worked with apes for most of her twenty-five years at the zoo. This baby chimp was one she had been taking home with her every night. She'd continue to do so until it no longer required night feedings. When it slept through the night, she'd bring it back to the zoo to stay.

Tom touched the chimp gently. It yawned widely and fingered its blanket.

Pat escorted Tom into the holding area where Shauri and her baby were resting. According to a keeper, Shauri had bred with her own son to create the child; it happened in the wild, but not often in captivity.

Vet and keeper discussed the baby chimp's fate. They could leave it with Shauri, who treated it awkwardly at best, and offer it supplementary nourishment. Or they could pull it and hand-raise it.

Close attention for forty-eight to seventy-two hours might provide some clues. Pat was closer to the apes than anyone at the zoo. Her long experience had made her an astute observer, a good judge of ape behavior. Tom would confer with her frequently; in this case, he would also confer with Mark Rosenthal, curator of mammals, and Dennis Meritt, the zoo's assistant director.

"We're talking about long-range planning," he said. "Not just what to do this week or next. That baby chimp could live for fifty years. It's important to know that when they're hand-reared, they don't make good mothers. You just perpetuate that neglect and create another inadequate mother.

"It's a big decision to pull a female chimp. If we leave the baby with Shauri, it may not make it. If we pull it, it'll survive, but for eventual breeding purposes the baby ought to learn from Shauri how to be a mother. It's a tough one."

He couldn't linger. It was time to head to the bird house, to medicate the Major Mitchell's cockatoo.

First, he weighed the bird, to determine how much

medication would be appropriate for a bird of its size. A keeper had wrapped the elegant pink and white parrot in a towel, so it wouldn't squirm, flap, bite, or hurt itself. After weighing it, Tom held it gently with one hand and gave it an injection of an antibiotic with the other. The keeper watching the procedure put the bird back in its cage, and Tom returned to the hospital.

Behind his desk, Tom shuffled through the white sheets—requests for medical services—that determined much of his schedule. When a sick animal was cured, the white sheet was discarded; the job was done. But some problems were old, chronic. Thick records—Shauri's dossier was book-length—defined sickly animals.

Tom hoped to have a sitdown lunch at one of the modest restaurants near the zoo. When he phoned the main zoo office to let the staff know that he'd be at lunch, he was told that he was needed, because most of the management team was off that day.

It didn't matter to him. He did have animals to see. A cow at the farm had an abscess on its left hock (near the heel). A rock elephant shrew had an external ear infection. A woodchuck and a porcupine were in the hospital with parasites to conquer. The last time he had treated a porcupine, the animal buried 100 of its quills in the thick glove he wore; it took plenty of time to pull them out. He hoped to return to the great ape house, to see Shauri again. If he didn't get there by day's end, he would see mother and daughter again early in the morning.

Les Fisher's weekly 9 A.M. staff meeting began without Tom, who was occupied visiting Shauri and her baby.

"We'll probably pull the baby," Dennis Meritt told the staff. "Shauri's history of neglect is crucial. As is her habit of consuming her own milk."

Les described a "vexing, troublesome, and real" problem—substance abuse among several people working at the zoo.

Another continuing issue: Some of the keepers opposed the use of volunteers in keeper areas, especially those the keepers deemed to be inadequately trained. The issue was an old one; the keepers, at times, expressed resentment about the presence of volunteers in their lives.

"It never ends," Les sighed.

The water pressure at the reptile house was "yuck," as Les put it. It was fixed, then went out again. "I have to assume that some lines got clogged with sediment," he said, wearily.

Tom arrived, to announce that he was changing the name of the great ape house to "fertility hill." Several births—two gorillas and two chimps—had occurred during the past two weeks. The breeding of apes had become a zoo specialty, for which it was widely known in the zoo world, and the current crop would enhance that reputation.

Mark Rosenthal suggested that he could locate an incubator, if Tom agreed that Shauri's baby should be pulled.

Dennis said, "Let's just do it."

Tom was not quite convinced. "We can leave it there for forty-eight hours. The baby doesn't look that bad," he said.

"We can set up a place for it today and pull it tomorrow," Mark said.

"OK," Tom agreed.

Shauri and her baby remained in Tom's mind as he conducted rounds with the externs. He told them about his visit to the chimps that morning.

"Shauri was a pain in the ass. She was covering the baby, and she wouldn't budge. We offered her a peach to get her to roll off the baby. Eventually, when she felt like it, she got up.

"The baby is long and skinny. The vocalization is less than I'd like. It hollers, but not much. The baby isn't nursing enough to get robust. It'll get weak at forty-eight hours. If we knock out the mother, the baby might get a big blast of milk. But it really does look like we'll have to pull it. I'll be happy when the new children's zoo is ready and our nursery there is back in action. We'll be able to care for all of our babies there again."

He went through his agenda:

A female black lemur, Xenobia, had a history of lumpy

legs, lesions, swelling in ankles, wrists, and elbows. "We did tests, the whole nine yards of them, and came up with nothing," Tom told the two externs.

"Then we took it to a bone radiologist at Northwestern Hospital. Nobody could figure it out. We did identify some cancerous breast tumors, but we shot down twenty or thirty diagnoses. Then, an expert came up with one—a rare, hereditary bone disease. We checked. The Toronto Zoo had put its mother to sleep; she had the same signs. Toronto may have radiographs for us to look at. I'll call them. Any hereditary disease in an endangered species is of some import.

"Suti, the elephant, has been having irregular cycles," he told the externs. "In elephants it's a three-month period, a twenty-two month gestation. We've documented that she's cycling, but we're going to take blood and send it to a lab in Oregon that specializes in elephants. The vet there knows all about elephant blood. She can't be pregnant, unless it's immaculate conception, because she hasn't been with a male in five years."

After the meeting, Tom went to the primate house to examine a newborn black and white ruffed lemur. The four-day-old monkey fit into the palm of his hand. As he held it, it urinated in his hand and passed some yellow stool. A keeper expressed his concern to Tom.

"That's what you get from an animal consuming only milk," Tom told the keeper, as he placed the tiny lemur back into its plastic box, atop a pile of towels and small blankets.

"A neat little guy," Tom said. "They're friendly to me. I guess they're too young or too stupid to know who I am."

Behind the scenes at the primate house, in a holding area, Tom found Xenobia, the sick lemur.

She bounded stiffly around the cage as Tom stared at her and contemplated her fate.

"I don't want to put her to sleep," he said, as if in response to an unpleasant suggestion from an invisible associate. "She gets around."

Early the next morning, a plea from a keeper at the hoofed-stock barn brought a number of zoo personnel on the run. Tom, assistant vet Peri Wolff, and Mark Rosenthal were all on hand before 8 A.M.

A sable antelope was giving birth. The baby's nose and forelimbs appeared first, between 7:00 A.M. and 7:40 A.M., then the process stopped. Tom and Peri, joined by the two externs, observed.

By 8:10 A.M., part of its head emerged, then the process stopped again.

The mother, a large, dark brown antelope with gracefully curved horns, was on the barn floor, on a bed of straw, rocking, rubbing against the straw, standing, reclining.

The observers were a floor above the stall, looking down from a large window designed to give visitors a clear look at the animals in the barn. A young woman keeper, watching anxiously, said, "When I see new babies, I don't want to get attached to them. They may not make it, and I don't want to suffer."

The antelope continued to strain. The baby's head and the two front legs emerged.

Peri mentioned that animals differed in the ways in which they gave birth. When a giraffe had delivered not long ago, it stood up—and the baby fell out. Then the mother urinated on it and didn't even acknowledge its presence for several minutes.

"This is a *long* birth," the keeper lamented.

By 8:34 A.M., the baby's entire head was out, just below the mother's tail. It was breathing. The mother was still, munching on the straw. Within minutes, the delivery was completed; what had been a sluggish process gathered momentum. The newborn antelope rested beside its mother.

"If the kid looks good and nurses, we'll just watch it," Tom said. "Tomorrow we'll weigh it and give it some shots that we give the newborn.

"Nature made us expendable. That's the best way. It

would have been risky to knock her down. We were ready to wait two hours before doing that. Once you intervene, you don't know what'll happen. She had it in an hour and forty-five minutes. Very good luck."

By 9 A.M., Tom was back at the hospital, collecting the equipment he'd need to tranquilize Shauri and bring her to the hospital for tests. He would pull the baby; an incubator was ready at the great ape house, and a consulting pediatrician (who treated humans, but was interested in animals as well) would drop in to look at the baby. Tom planned a series of tests for Shauri: an EKG, chest x-ray, blood analysis, urine test, and more. But first he had to hit her with a dart, from a handheld tool that resembled a grease gun attached to a foot pump. At four feet tall and 229 pounds, she was not puny, but Tom trusted her friendly manner and the effectiveness of the dart gun.

At the great ape house, Mark Rosenthal, Peri Wolff, and several keepers were ready in the kitchen area, next to Shauri's small, confining holding cell. Tom attached a long barrel to the dart gun, inserted the darted syringe, and turned to Mark.

"Mark, want a nap?"

Mark smiled.

Tom turned toward Shauri, crouched in the back of the dark cell.

"It's me, the bad guy," he said to the chimp.

Then he fired the gun. The dart struck Shauri, and she wailed once, then weakened. Tom and Pat Sass crept into the cell, and Pat picked up the baby chimp, which began to scream. She handed it to Peri, who placed it in a towel and held it on her shoulder. The baby stopped screaming. One of the externs took a blood sample from a vein in the back of the tiny chimp's leg. Peri whispered to the baby, "Oh, I know, I know. Life is so rough."

A pair of keepers, Tom and Jeff, collaborated to move Shauri onto a wheeled, metal litter for the trip to the hospital. She was numbed, on the edge of sleep, and didn't resist.

The baby, who weighed in at two pounds, fourteen ounces, remained in the ape house. Peri handed it to Pat. The baby did not cry. "Let's travel," Peri shouted, and the procession pushed the litter to the van.

In the hospital operating room, Peri placed her stethoscope on Shauri's chest. "She sounds good," Peri said, "but she smells bad."

On the table, Shauri stirred; Jeff gave her an injection to assure that she remained asleep. A keeper from the ape house held Shauri's hand. Shauri began to snore.

Tom, Peri, and Jeff hovered over Shauri. They examined her vaginal area, drew blood from her arm, attached the EKG electrodes, put an IV line in her left forearm. Peri wanted to extract urine with a catheter, but none emerged.

"Dry as a bone," she complained.

Shauri continued to snore; her lower jaw trembled from time to time, but nothing else moved.

"You know what? Think of this," Tom said. "If this were a human, all of this would be done, easily, in the doctor's office. Of course, you can't do any of this to an animal that's awake."

The ape keeper stroked Shauri's chin slowly and affectionately.

The pediatrician entered, a young, short, dark-haired woman in a proper gray suit.

"Shauri's baby looks healthy, but it's an underdeveloped, runty little baby," she said, then paused and asked, "What about her depression?"

"What depression?" Peri asked.

"Shauri's. From having her baby pulled."

"No problem," Tom said.

"She'll be a little depressed," the keeper said.

"We'll get in with her and comfort her. She's friendly. And remember, she's not that attentive a mother," Tom told the pediatrician.

Peri turned to Shauri, petted her head, and said, "You're being very, very nice about all of this."

By 11:00 A.M., Shauri was ready to be returned to the

great ape house. Tom patted her back. "Let's take her home," Peri said. By 11:12 A.M., Shauri was home. Her baby was in its incubator, in Pat Sass's care.

Down the path from the great ape house, in the hoofed-stock barn, the sable antelope baby—almost forgotten—was next to its mother.

Four hours had elapsed while Tom and associates had dealt with the two cases.

Milk extracted from Shauri's breast was mixed with formula for her baby. Assured of that, Tom left to visit the antelope. In front of the window from which he had witnessed the birth, he saw a docent assigned to keep watch. She sat in a chair, looking through the window at the mother and child below.

"She's fed, she's nursed, and she's been walking around," the docent, a middle-aged woman in familiar khaki garb, told Tom.

"Great," he said, looking down to the barn floor, where the two antelopes reclined on straw, facing each other.

It was self-indulgent to linger. Tom had other problems to deal with.

The Arabian oryx baby he'd checked the day before was being taunted, prodded by the adults in the group. There may be too many animals in that group, Tom thought; he might have to separate the baby from the aggressive older ones.

The day passed; Tom rarely glanced at his wristwatch. In late afternoon, he phoned the great ape house to find out how Shauri was doing. She was awake, eating, and moving around, he was told. Good.

Then he went to the large mammal house to take a blood sample from Suti, the elephant with the irregular menstrual cycle. When he arrived, Suti and Bozie, the other elephant, were outside with a keeper bearing an ankus and a very firm manner. She used both to lead the elephants indoors for Tom and his externs to look at Suti.

On command, both elephants knelt. Tom approached Suti, held her left ear in his hand, and showed the extern, Jeff, the network of veins visible on the back of the ear. He washed the ear, then poked the syringe into the vein.

Suti jerked.

"Steady," the keeper said.

"Good girl," Tom added.

"Steady," the keeper repeated, to be sure that Suti obeyed. An unruly elephant was a troublesome one, and a belligerent elephant was a dangerous one. There was a reason why elephants in the wild didn't have enemies except for humans.

Tom stepped in front of the elephant and patted her; she touched his shoulder delicately with the tip of her trunk.

"She doesn't trust me when she can't see me," he told the keeper. "Now she can see me."

FIRST PERSON: TOM MEEHAN

I get to put my hands on animals more than just about anybody else in this place, even the keepers to a large degree. I get to interact closely with animals. I call myself the most general of general practitioners, because it's not only every system and every disease, but every species. There's a breadth and depth to it that doesn't exist anywhere else. It can be somewhat frustrating. The main thing is you do the best you can, you try to keep up, you try not to be too hard on yourself, and if you have enough self-confidence and you do an adequate job of keeping yourself up, then you say, "I can do this as well as anybody."

Overall, I'm as good as anybody out there at doing zoo medicine. I'm better than a lot of them at some things, like the gorillas. The big trick is that it's not a big club, it's a relatively small group, of zoo veterinarians. Around sixty in North America, period. So being where I am in zoo medicine, I know most of them, and I know the ones who have a lot of elephants, I know the ones that do all birds, so I can get on the phone and call somebody who might be able to give me a hand.

We're always finding out things. Everything is kind of

out there on the edge. It's very hard. You never want to get to where you can rationalize things with yourself and explain them away. Sometimes you really did screw up, if that turns out to be the case. You should never be able to explain it away to yourself. At the very least, you ought to know that you screwed up, and make efforts to do otherwise. People who do that soul-searching and know when they make a mistake and when they don't, stand a very great risk of getting burned out because, damn, that animal had pneumonia, and if I would have known that, I could have fixed it.

It behooves animals, wild animals, to look good when they're sick. Sick animals get preyed upon or get left behind. One of the comments off the necropsy table is not why did it die, but why was it still alive? There's so much wrong inside this animal, why was it still up and around? They can have major illnesses, and you may not see them.

I had an animal one time that we immobilized, we went to bleed it. We made a stick into the carotid. It's not anything that should cause any problems, it's done all the time, single stick. The animal bled out from that stick and strangled to death, literally. Its neck filled up with blood, like a soccer ball, and it literally strangled the animal, from within. What I didn't know was the animal had a clotting disorder. I didn't know. There's no way I could have known, so you can't hold that against yourself.

If you keep looking at yourself in hindsight and saying I should have done this or I should have done that, you'll go nuts, you'll wind up leaving the field, as a lot of people have. I tell people who have been through here under me, it's OK to get down on yourself for things that you should have known better. If there was some clue that told you that this was happening and you ignored it or missed it, you screwed up, and you should make your corrections. But if there's no way you could have known, and it's just based on the fact that that's a difference between zoo animals and other animals, you can't afford to let yourself get down on yourself.

If people look sick, they don't get eaten. People do truly amazing things when they think that their life is on the line. For animals, their life is a little different. There are certain things that the animals bring with them that don't change, even after generations in captivity.

Zoo medicine is really not that old. Zoo medicine as a bona fide specialty where you could really do some good has paralleled precisely the development of anesthetics and delivery systems that allowed us to shoot them into an animal, and immobilize them, and have them wake up alive. Until vets could do that, they really couldn't do much. They weren't able to do nearly as much diagnostic work; they had to do it all over the fence.

We still do a lot of that. I sit down with the vet students when they get ready to leave here. One of them said something very interesting. She said, "I learned something here that I didn't learn in school and that I think I can use very well to my advantage on any kind of animals. I learned how to stand back and look at an animal, from a distance. Without laying my hands and feeling and listening to the lung, I learned how to stand back and look and see the whole picture, what the animal looks like, how it moves, how it breathes, how it does it." We learn how to do that because we're forced to.

Of course, we rely very heavily on the keepers. Animals react to me, to what I do. The keepers will call and say, "Oh, he's sick, he's lying on the bottom of the cage," and I go over there and the animal's bouncing off the walls. He's changed in my presence, and I can't tell. One, I don't know how the animal looks day in and day out because I don't spend that time with him, and two, he's different when I'm there than when I'm not there. So we rely heavily on the keepers.

We even go to the point of doing little tricks. For instance, in the morning we give all the marmosets a marshmallow. It helps to get their blood glucose up. That helps boost them up in the morning. But the main thing is, if they don't come up and grab that marshmallow, they're sick, and you know it. They're not normal if they don't jump on that. The most common thing is somebody calls and says, "The animal's offbeat, it's not looking good, or it's limping." Ninety-nine percent of what we get comes from the keepers, and it comes from them being observant and knowing their animals, just knowing the real subtle stuff. And we see a lot of subtle stuff.

I'm always concerned about epidemics of diseases here. The scariest one by far, because of the value of the collection and the depth of our collection, was that thing that went through our great ape house. We are pretty sure it was a respiratory virus that caused flulike symptoms in people. Great apes can get what humans can get and vice versa. A keeper brought that in, that's one of the reasons we separate all the primates from the public: basically to protect them from the public because that's where disease is likely to come from. A keeper evidently brought this disease in, and, early on, before the keeper felt sick, it had been exposed to the apes. Well, the chimps started it. It started with a cough and a severe mucous nasal discharge. You could just see it march right around the building; it left only three animals unaffected in the entire building. We lost two animals, one baby we're pretty sure died of pneumonia that was probably associated with that. The adult male chimp, Sam, who died, had pneumonia. It didn't look bad enough to kill him. He didn't have anything that looked bad enough to kill him, but he was still dead.

There's nothing you can do when you've got that sort of viral disease. We used a lot of antibiotics, to help prevent secondary bacterial infections; we drew blood samples, we did some diagnostic work and some treatment. But based on the way the thing moved around, fairly early on we thought that it was most likely to be some sort of a viral disease, for which you don't do anything but supportive care. And supportive care is often very hard to give. Peri spent an awful lot of time in there, got sick herself—she got the same thing back—and one of the other keepers became ill. Everybody had the same signs: the cough, the chest cold.

With the wolves, distemper was on the list of differential diagnoses, but not very high up. And Peri talked with probably the premier animal neurologist in the country, one of her old professors. They had it pretty well pinned down to either a brain tumor or some sort of a vascular accident. A week later, another one goes down with the same thing, and all that goes out the window. You don't have brain tumors or strokes that one animal catches from another, so then distemper moved right up to the top of the list. A few tests confirmed that.

Horse births and cattle, sheep, goats, other hoofed-stock births, are very difficult. Horses have a very quick, almost violent, birth process. If the foal hasn't been born in half an hour, it's in deep trouble. So you don't have any time on your hands. It's difficult in a zebra, too. They're like a horse in the way they give birth. The foal winds up in trouble relatively quickly if the horse hasn't given birth. The birth is violent.

One common thing in a horse is what they call a third-degree peritoneal laceration. The mother squeezes so hard that the foal puts a hoof out of the vagina and into the rectum, and when the mother gives birth, the foal tears it open, all the way to the outside. They're a real bitch to fix back up. But they happen.

Well, I got a call at home: a zebra's giving birth. The very first thing that comes to mind is that's neat, that's really neat. But by the time I get in here, it's still not out. That immediately brings you down to a certain level, because it has been more than half an hour. She's potentially in trouble, so there isn't any waiting. We got our stuff together and immobilized her. It took another fifteen minutes or so for that to take effect and for me to get all my stuff over there. Then we tried to deliver the foal. I don't even know at that point what exactly was binding everything up, but we worked. Physically, it was the most difficult thing we've ever done, because we literally dragged the zebra around for ten or fifteen minutes by the foal, because we were trying to get it out, and it was stuck.

The foal was dead by that point, and it's tremendously

exhausting to be in there all the way up to your shoulders, and fighting and trying to turn it and pulling things. Another doctor was here as well, and she and I alternated fighting. I'd just have to stop and sit down for a while and catch my breath. She'd work and I'd work and she'd work and I'd work, and we tried. We tried cutting up the animal inside the mother to bring it out in pieces, as a way of avoiding doing a C-section. We got most of the baby out, lost the rest, couldn't avoid the C-section, rolled her up, prepped her. And the surgery is a whole different thing because horses are pretty prone to infection, and we had to be relatively sterile. So it's change it into a sterile room, clean ourselves all up, go in, do the C-section, get her all sewed up. And as we were putting the last few stitches in the skin, she died.

We went from there to a necropsy, where we just took the mother and chopped her all up. The progression from being called that morning and expecting a birth, to disposing of the mother's carcass in a period of five or six hours, was certainly the most difficult time that I can recall.

You know, they say animals don't know one guy from another; people are people, they don't know who we are. The hell with that. They know who I am, and not just the great apes, not just the ones that are the sharpest. Some animals that aren't given a lot of credit for having a lot of brains, they know who the hell I am. And they know me in street clothes, and they know me when I'm with a crowd of people; they know who I am.

The first time it struck me about that drawback to zoo veterinary medicine, I was working at the St. Louis Zoo, and they were opening a section of the zoo, and they were having a big dedication. The trainer was walking up to the dedication with a little chimp in hand. The chimp was walking along, happy as a clam, holding hands with this trainer, and up walks the zoo vet. And he takes the chimp by the hand, and they're walking along and the chimp is walking between the two of them holding hands, and then he looked up and saw who it was that had come along and grabbed his hand. All the hair went up on his back, he started screaming and slapping his legs, trying to bite him and it was all the trainer could do to keep him from tearing into this veterinarian. And I realized, damn, he really hates that guy. But I've gotten used to that. You try to establish a relationship with the special animals like Shauri or animals that instead of displaying and pounding the glass will come over and let me feed them or play little games with me.

Chimps are a lot like people, in that they can be very explosive, very emotional. They have a pretty short attention span, but they're very demonstrative. They're a little bit too much for my taste. But there's no doubt that they're a very sharp animal. The gorillas, I like their attitude more. It changes a lot more. It's easier for me to see the personalities, to know the differences between them. For example, Koundu is such a character, trying to offer me a treat of some urine-soaked piece of straw off the floor, in hopes that I'm going to grab it with such relish that he's going to be able to get hold of my hand and do harm to me. But it's the kind of harm you laugh at on "The Three Stooges," typical juvenile mischief. It's kind of a crude practical joke.

Orangutans are real sharp. They're deep thinkers, and they're very manipulative. They take things apart. They'll watch you. You hear all kinds of stories about them. There was an orang at Omaha that got out repeatedly, a number of times over a relatively short span. There were a lot of keepers in danger of losing their jobs over who screwed up and left the lock open, that sort of thing. The director finally wound up spending most of a night on a level above, watching the animal, and the orang was fiddling around in his mouth, and then started working the lock. And what he had was a big long piece of wire that he kept in his lip that he would pick the lock with; you know, it was one of these old skeleton-key-type locks. He's got nothing but time, so he'd just use it as a key and work it until it came open and he could get out.

I've only felt in danger once. Shortly after we had a new arrival of an African elephant who was about three years old, weighing a thousand, eleven hundred pounds. A small elephant but a big elephant. This was a wild elephant, not trained. And we had an elephant trainer come in to train that elephant, and also to train our keepers in how to take care of it. But the elephant was not far from being very wild. She was held during this period on chains. This was, as I recall, about two or three months into this process, and she had made remarkable progress in terms of being well-behaved. I worked with the animal almost daily at that point in her training here, because it was something new to all of us, bringing an animal in from the wild at that age.

I went over there one Saturday, and something had happened, we don't to this day know what it was, but something happened to her that upset her a great deal, or just changed her, or she just decided she was going to be different that day. One of the things that she was doing was using her trunk to hit and push, things that were ill mannered, things that she wasn't supposed to do. Trunk down, back and forth, kind of pushing and shoving. She found that I had stepped away from the doorway out of this habitat, that I had my back against a wall, literally. And so she just stepped forward, wrapped her trunk around my arm and hoisted me up and slid me into a corner. She tried to pick my arm up and put it in her mouth with her trunk and bite it. I was able to keep my arm down, but she was able to pick me up and down, six inches or so off the ground. It didn't accomplish what she wanted. So she stopped that rather quickly, dropped her head, put it in my chest and started shoving me into the corner, with a big wooden beam in my back, and she was trying to smash me. You know, there are lots of ways that elephants kill people. One of the more popular ones is just pushing them into something, whether it's pushing them into the dirt, pushing them up against something.

There was one other person around, a keeper. You'd never go in with an animal without the keeper. Two keepers had been there; one had gone in to go to the bathroom. So there was one keeper there, and he had the ankus. He was flailing away at her with the ankus, trying to get her back. I think the only thing that saved me was the fact that she had a long chain on her front leg, and, in turning around, she had stretched that to its full extent and didn't have enough motion, enough freedom, to really shove me up into the wall. But she had her head right in my chest. The first time I recall feeling like I was in deep shit was when I tried to scream for the keeper but no noise came out, and I realized that she'd compressed my chest enough that I couldn't vocalize. That's when I was scared. Fortunately, when the two keepers got there, they both flailed away at her. Eventually she just turned around and quit, and I walked away.

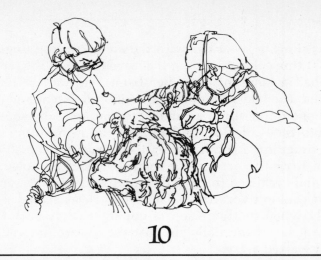

10

House Calls II:

Young veterinarian Peregrine Wolff, known to her associates as Peri, succinctly summarized her work: "Animals get sick. They get well. They love you. They hate you. It's the people who give you problems."

At twenty-eight, she had made her way to a major zoo from Middlebury, Vermont, where she was born. Before retiring, her father had been an economics professor at Middlebury College; her mother had been a physician's assistant.

Peri attended Middlebury College for a year, then spent two and a half years at the University of Vermont, where she majored in animal science. During her final semester, she worked at a zoo on the isle of Jersey, off the coast of England.

In 1984, she got her D.V.M. from Cornell University (a four-year program) and headed to Chicago. During her junior year at the University of Vermont, she served as an extern at the Lincoln Park Zoo; after she became a vet, she returned to that zoo for a year as an intern. When funding became available, she was hired as a full-time vet to work for Tom Meehan.

Peri lived in an apartment across the street from the zoo, with a dog named Bear—a shepherd-collie cross.

Her life at the zoo was an active one; she arrived at work long before most of the keepers got there. It was not unusual for her to be dashing around the zoo at 6 A.M.

In her green jumpsuit and white sneakers, she was a familiar sight. Tall (5'8") and slim, with an Ivory soap complexion and a blond ponytail, a gold chain around her neck, small earrings, and a gold bracelet on her wrist, she was a combination of the hard-working professional and the liberated woman.

One day in late summer, when the heat had faded and a cool breeze served as an indication of a less desirable season to come, she headed for the hoofed-stock area. With her in the yellow zoo van were a curly-haired young blond extern from England named David, and Joel Pond, the young, sturdy, mustached animal health technician, who ran the hospital lab.

They headed into the hoofed-stock barn. Peri had to vaccinate three zebras that were being readied for shipment to another zoo. They were being given boosters; shipment made them vulnerable, due to the stress involved. First, Peri had to tranquilize them; she would knock them down, and David would return later to give the vaccinations. She did the job quickly, pointing the long-barreled dart gun at each zebra and firing the dart with the foot pump that triggered it. The zebras twitched when hit.

By 9:15 A.M., Peri and her crew were in the lion house. Chandra, an old female lion, was down, literally; the senior keeper at the lion house had reported that the animal couldn't seem to get up.

Peri found Chandra in a holding cage. The lion spotted her and began to growl sluggishly.

"She's old, but she looks older than she is," Peri said. "She looks like hell."

"She's real shaky," the senior keeper noted.

Peri stared at the lion for several minutes, then told the senior keeper to keep the lion in the cage, give her water, obtain a urine sample if possible, and give her aspirin.

"To treat joint pain, if that's what it is," Peri explained.

"She's sore in back and in her front leg, too. She's not putting any weight on it. We may have to immobilize her," Peri said. She knew that cats were sensitive to many drugs tolerated by other animals; even aspirin had to be prescribed with care.

She wanted to assess the condition of a sickly black leopard before she returned to the hospital. The leopard—on the verge of kidney failure—was in an outside cage, sitting motionless with a glazed stare. It did not respond to Peri's presence, an indication in itself, since many animals reacted to Peri and Tom with instant rage.

Peri watched the animal for several minutes in silence.

"Why let him die this way?" she asked no one in particular. "That seems cruel to me." To euthanize the leopard, however, she would first confer with assistant zoo director Dennis Meritt and curator Mark Rosenthal.

By 9:45 A.M., she was back at the hospital to conduct rounds, an assessment of pending cases, with David, the extern, and Joel, the lab technician. Tom Meehan was out of town, so the rounds belonged to Peri.

Before the meeting could begin, the phone rang. Peri answered it.

"Butch? Walking funny? What does that mean? Dangling? No. Does he go outside? OK. I'll go look at him. Wake up? I can't. I'm tired."

Butch was one of the maned wolves; she'd check on him after rounds.

Among the cases discussed:

Two female lions, Sheila and Shelley, awaiting shipment to another zoo because of the renovation of the lion house, needed fecal and blood tests before they could be shipped out. Zoos did not seek to ship or receive sick animals.

A lame pacarana—an animal from South America that

resembled a huge rat—wasn't doing well, but it wasn't an emergency. "Her liver looks big," Peri noted.

"Who knows what a pacarana's liver is supposed to look like?" Joel asked, smiling.

"True," Peri admitted.

A group of capybaras—also large rodent-like animals—had had diarrhea for months.

Otto, a well-known gorilla, had a toe that had been gnawed by an angry female gorilla, but it was improving.

Peri was leaning toward euthanizing the black leopard; she wanted to resolve that matter promptly.

A crow with a damaged wing needed repair.

A pigeon had to be euthanized.

At 10:05, Peri stopped at the bear line to see Butch. The maned wolf was in an indoor cage and wouldn't move when Peri entered the area.

"He thinks I'm going to knock him down," Peri sighed.

The keeper opened a gate and allowed the wolf to go outside, where Peri could get a better look at him.

The wolf limped out, its left foreleg clearly damaged. It stopped and turned toward Peri.

"He sniffs vet," Peri said.

The wolf had broken its leg seven years ago and had been treated for troubles related to it ever since.

"Lock him up tonight," Peri told a keeper. "We'll do him at eight in the morning." She would arrange for an orthopedic surgeon to consult on the case, but first x-rays would have to be taken of that troublesome leg.

The morning passed quickly, as Peri moved from case to case. At lunchtime, she returned to the hospital, where she made a lunch of boiled hot dogs, a chunk of Swiss cheese, and a Diet Coke. She read her mail, which included a gift her mother had sent. It energized her for what she had to do after lunch: operate on Sam Gamgee (a name out of Tolkien), a nine-year-old cottontop tamarin, a tiny monkey plagued by worms in its intestines.

The tamarins were among Peri's favorite animals: small,

agile, animated, hardy. They came from South American rain forests, where they rarely came down to the ground, choosing to thrive in the upper reaches of the forest. Amazingly, some adjusted to the drastically different environment of the zoo.

In the wild, tamarins had a low level of parasite invasion. In captivity, where roaches thrived, the rate seemed to increase.

"They poop. The roaches eat the poop, which has parasite eggs in it. The tamarins eat the roaches. The eggs turn into adult worms in the tamarins and burrow into the wall of the gut. They make holes, causing peritonitis, which kills primates. The only way for us to fight it—if antibiotics don't work—is surgery. We've cleaned up a bunch of them. In just one procedure, we got sixty-six worms out of an animal that weighed less than a pound," Peri said.

The tamarin awaited its fate inside an animal carrier in the hospital examining room. It flicked its tongue rapidly.

"I wish I could do that," Peri said, smiling.

She put on a pair of heavy-duty gloves, leather and canvas, and grabbed the tamarin. It shrieked and tried to elude her grasp. She won. After David gave it an injection of an antibiotic, Peri put it in a weighing basket—which looked like a perforated pot with a lid—and carried it into the operating room.

The tamarin continued to shriek.

"I haven't done anything yet," Peri said to it.

In the operating room, Joel was serving as anesthetist. He placed the basket, with the tamarin in it, in a large plastic bag and piped gas (isofluorane) into it.

Joel and Peri waited; the sound of small claws against the inside of the metal basket was the only sound in the room.

Peri put on a cap and mask and whistled Brahms' "Lullaby." The tamarin slept; its little brown and white body was still. As Joel put aside the basket and used a cup on the tamarin's face, Peri shaved its belly for the incision she would make and the electrodes she would attach for the heart monitor. As she worked her way through the preliminaries, the tamarin twitched in its sleep.

"God was having an artistic day when He created these," she said, looking affectionately at the tamarin. "They look like punk rockers."

She draped the animal and gently made an incision. Suddenly, the tamarin thrashed violently, displacing the drape. It had to be replaced, and so did Peri's gloves.

Again, Peri went to work on the incision. Again, the tamarin moved.

"My God, your guts are hanging out," she shouted.

"I'm giving him twice as much gas as he might need," Joel said. He couldn't explain the tough little monkey's resistance to modern science.

"Let's tape down his legs," Peri said to David, who did the job. But the tamarin continued to jerk. Peri did not stop working; she had extracted his intestines through the incision and was examining them for parasites.

"Is there gonna be some lawsuit from this patient?" Peri said. "His gut is spastic, tight. This isn't turning out at all like I wanted it to."

She spotted several nodules and extracted three worms; she had expected to find more.

"Well, we've had them die from as few as one," Joel said, reassuringly.

Peri sutured the intestinal wall and closed the original outer incision.

"This is the most difficult one we've done, out of twenty-nine procedures," she said. "And the hardest part is getting the gut back in the hole you got it out of, especially with a nervous guy like this one."

As Peri completed her work on the tamarin, the hospital secretary, Debbie, entered unexpectedly.

"A marmoset just came walking down the hall," she said calmly. "I put it in Tom's office."

Peri and Joel stared at her, then at each other.

"Are you going to make something of that?" Joel asked Peri.

"Yes, I'm going to make something of that," Peri answered.

One of her continuing grievances was directed at keepers who were less attentive than she thought they ought to be.

She found the keeper on duty at the hospital.

"I thought I had the door locked," he appealed. "But I didn't."

The marmoset—another small, lively South American monkey—was screeching in Tom Meehan's office. The keeper grabbed a small net on a handle and entered the office.

The chase was on. It took several minutes, but man triumphed over animal. The keeper put the marmoset back in the cage in the examining room, from which it had escaped. He locked the cage.

Peri watched it all. After the marmoset had been returned to its cage, she turned to the keeper.

"They are crafty animals," she said.

The keeper did not respond.

The next morning, Peri got to work at 6:30 A.M. In a powder blue polo shirt, jeans, and sneakers, she sat at her desk before the problems of the day seized her time, and dealt with the paperwork that was inevitable in her job.

By 8 A.M., in her blue jumpsuit, she was ready for action. On the phone with curator Mark Rosenthal, she told him that if the black leopard, named Satan, after testing and examination, was found to be terminal, she felt it ought to be euthanized.

"We're going to give it a rabbit, and if it doesn't eat it, well, that means it won't go for anything," she told Mark.

She called Dennis Meritt for his view of the situation.

"He looks terrible," she told Dennis. "They're going to offer him a rabbit. We'll see." Dennis agreed with her; euthanizing the cat might be the best move.

Down the hall from her office, Sam, the cottontop tamarin she had operated on the day before, was in an incubator. He was recuperating impressively, dashing around the incubator, making beeping sounds. Peri went in to examine him; she put her gloved hand into the incubator. Sam went wild, but she managed to grasp him. David, the extern, gave him an injection of an antibiotic, and Peri placed Sam back in the incubator. He glared at her.

By 9 A.M., Peri was off on various missions around the zoo. At the bird house holding area, she examined a crow suffering from parasites. She and David collaborated; he held the bird, and she dropped liquid medication into its mouth.

"Crows are easy," she said to David. "You can see their larynx, so you make a point of missing it. Anywhere else you drop it, they swallow it."

At the reptile house, she visited a small salamander that, according to the woman keeper, was "losing weight and looking ratty." It was eight years old, old for a salamander, and it ate two crickets a day only if it was hand-fed.

"It could be dying of old age," Peri suggested, holding it in her hand and stroking it gently.

"Can we give it antibiotics?" the keeper asked.

"I can't use antibiotics if I don't know what I'm treating it for," Peri said.

The keeper was discouraged. "Do you know that there are mouse droppings in every cage in this place?" she asked.

Peri knew and didn't respond.

Clarence Wright, the curator of reptiles, was busy elsewhere in the room. And he was troubled. He reminded Peri of a memo he had sent to everyone working at the zoo, a memo titled "Disappearance of Mangrove Snake Eggs." It read:

A keeper reported the disappearance of eight Mangrove Snake Eggs that were incubating in the 'hot run' of the basement of the reptile house. The plastic shoe box that the eggs were kept in was secured with tape to hold the lid in place. The tape was removed and the eggs taken and the tape was then resecured to the box.

These eggs each measured one inch in diameter and if hatched would produce an animal that is rear-fanged and venomous. Anti-venin is NOT PRODUCED for this animal.

Eggs should be returned, with no questions asked, or the eggs should be destroyed.

According to Clarence, if the eggs were shaken, the three-week-old embryos would perish. But if the person who stole them knew enough, in three months the eggs would hatch, and the young snakes could attack. In Clarence's view, it must have been an "inside job." No locks were tampered with in getting to the eggs.

Peri noted his concern. She had to move on, however, to the great ape house. It was time to visit Otto, the burly gorilla who had attacked a female named Terra and was biting her neck when Terra decided to retaliate. Terra took a large chunk out of his toe.

Peri picked up a banana in the kitchen and, with senior keeper Pat Sass, went to visit Otto. She found him in a cage in an upstairs holding area.

"He looks healthier," she said to Pat. "How's his attitude?"

"Well, he's not chasing girls around anymore," Pat said.

"Let's keep him on antibiotics," Peri said, moving toward the door.

Back in the hospital, Peri noticed that one of the keepers was defrosting a rabbit in the microwave of the keeper dining area, for Satan, the leopard.

It was time for Peri and David to check on Butch, the lame maned wolf. At the bear line, Butch awaited them, but not eagerly. When Peri arrived at his indoor den, Butch looked right at her, snarled, and turned away.

Peri aimed her long-barreled tranquilizer dart gun at Butch. The first try didn't work; the dart didn't seem to penetrate far enough into the wolf's reddish-brown fur. Peri shot a second dart. Again, no success. Each time, she retrieved the dart with a long pole poked through the bars separating her from the wolf. The third try seemed unsuccessful as well, and Peri was baffled. But Butch began to buckle, slowly.

"I've never seen that happen before," she told the male keeper who was helping her. "And I have no idea why I wasn't getting the right force."

Finally, Butch fell. Peri and David lifted him onto a litter. Butch had his eyes open, his ears up, his tongue dangling out of the side of his mouth. His body was motionless, but he was breathing heavily. They transported him to the x-ray table in the hospital operating room. Butch reclined like a large, resting dog. He was giving off a strong, foul odor. He had defecated on the x-ray table.

While Joel cleaned the table, Peri did a conjunctiva scraping from the wolf's eyelid membrane, for a distemper test. Several of the wolves had distemper; two of them, including Butch, had been testing positive. Peri hoped that the test would now be negative. She and Tom had not been able to cure the disease; somehow the wolves had improved on their own.

Joel posted an old x-ray of Butch's bad leg; it showed a steel plate and assorted screws, the work of an orthopedic surgeon who had worked on Butch in the zoo hospital. Then Joel arranged the wolf on the x-ray table and shot several x-rays of the leg.

The wolf made a faint sound.

"I think he's snoring," Peri said. "Not growling."

When Joel was done, Peri and David moved Butch back to his den on the bear line. Peri headed for lunch.

After lunch, she went to the lion house to obtain blood samples from the two female lions being readied for shipment to another zoo. She knew that both lions disliked vets on sight.

Shelley was asleep in a holding cage when Peri arrived, with David and a keeper to help her. It was a squeeze cage, designed with a moving back wall of bars that could be brought forward to trap the animal in a narrow space, preventing it from moving, so the vet could examine and treat it. The keeper turned a wheel on the outside of the cage to bring the back wall forward.

When Peri entered, Shelley came to life in a frenzy. She

growled loudly, ran around the small cage, tried to reach through the bars to get at Peri. The second lion, Sheila, who had been in a tunnel behind the cages, entered an adjoining cage, saw Peri, and stood up on her hind feet, growling loudly.

Peri took a look at Sheila and spotted an abscess on her foot.

"I suppose no one has noticed that," she snapped at the keeper. He had a calm manner and didn't respond. Both lions continued to growl.

The keeper began to turn the wheel to trap one of the lions. As he did, the lion in the next cage tried to get at him through the bars. He flinched.

The rear bars moved forward, trapping Shelley. Peri grabbed her tail, pulled it out of the cage, and drew a blood sample from it. The keeper turned the wheel again, and the bars moved back, enabling Shelley to get out. She did, rapidly, heading for an empty cage out of reach.

The keeper moved one of the sliding panels that sealed off cages; it opened, and Sheila dashed into the squeeze cage. Soon, she was tightly encased. Peri and David repeated the procedure, adding an injection of an antibiotic for the abscess—and an instruction to the keeper to "keep her inside, so that can heal."

Sheila growled mightily.

"Be a big girl," Peri said to her. "A good kitty. Just a little blood from your tail, that's all. A good kitty."

The lion growled again, a deep, resonant roar.

Peri packed up her gear, her blood samples, and walked back to the hospital. She was exhausted. The sound of an angry lion was intimidating, even if she knew that the cat could not reach her. Once again, she was reminded that her work could not be appreciated by the animals she treated. If she were to achieve satisfaction, she would have to generate it herself.

Tomorrow, she knew, she faced another troubling test. She planned to immobilize Satan, the sick leopard, and determine whether he should live or die.

The next morning, Peri studied the x-rays of Butch's leg. The bone that had been broken in the past had not been broken again, but the plate inserted by the surgeon might be loosening. It was possible that the wolf had contracted a soft-tissue infection, and she could attack that with an antibiotic. Results of the distemper test wouldn't be ready for a week; she was hopeful that Butch would recover.

At 8:15 A.M., she phoned the lion house; she wanted to know if Satan had eaten the rabbit. He had not. The prognosis was not good. Satan had come to the zoo eighteen years ago; he was an old cat and a failing one. In a month, his weight had dropped from eighty-six pounds to sixty-eight pounds.

She was unhappy that the lion house keepers had not informed her more rapidly about the leopard's loss of appetite. If she had known earlier, she could have done a kidney function test, at least. Now, if Satan had gone into kidney failure, she would have no choice but to euthanize him.

Joel, the lab technician, would be the one to administer the fatal injection, if it came to that. It would be a lethal dose of an anesthetic, a barbiturate or T-61, literally a euthanasia solution. It was known as "blue juice," for the color added to it to prevent it from being given accidentally.

Peri, Joel, and David made their way in the van to the lion house. It was not yet open to the public. The leopard was in an indoor cage in the cavernous hall. At the front of the cage, the uneaten rabbit was a clump of flaccid white matter.

"Yech. Even if I didn't have renal disease, I wouldn't eat that," Peri commented.

Satan was prone, his head resting on his front paws, his yellow-green eyes fixed straight ahead. Peri assembled the dart gun; she had determined that what failed when she used it on Butch was the barrel. She had attached the wrong one, which permitted air to leak out around the dart.

Satan remained with his head on the floor of the cage, until he saw Peri holding the gun. He snarled at her weakly, more a hiss than a roar, and raised his head.

A lion keeper prodded Satan with a long pole to entice him to the front of the cage, giving Peri a clear shot. Satan grabbed the pole with his front paws, as if in play, and the keeper tugged, pulling the animal to the front of the cage.

Peri's dart hit Satan on his right side, and he fell. His tongue moved slowly, in and out of his mouth. He vomited. Peri guessed that was because he was toxic, in renal failure, or from the tranquilizer, probably the former.

In the next cage, a slowly pacing jaguar observed.

Within minutes, Satan was unconscious, on a metal litter on his way to the hospital.

On the table in the examining room, Satan breathed slowly, almost imperceptibly.

"Are you sure he's breathing?" Peri asked Joel.

"Yes, I'm sure. Slowly, but breathing," Joel replied.

In his incubator a few feet away, Sam, the tamarin, peered at the scene in front of him. He sat still and watched, then, seemingly in agitation, moved rapidly around the incubator.

Peri went to the phone and called Dennis Meritt.

"We have this pathetic black leopard on the table now. He is skin and bones, and his skin is dehydrated. You can pull it up and it stays there," she told Dennis. "I don't know the point of saving this animal. It's time to call it quits. It's a sad scene."

Dennis agreed with her.

Mark Rosenthal showed up, looked at Satan, patted him gently.

"We're euthanizing him," Peri told him. "It's cruel and unusual punishment to keep him alive."

"Sure," Mark said.

In his incubator, Sam pressed his face against the glass and watched in silence.

Joel injected a large syringe filled with T-61. He looked at Satan as he did. The leopard's black hair was flecked with white. His eyes were open, his teeth bared. Already tranquilized, he took a few minutes to die.

Suddenly, Sam became agitated, making a frantic, high-pitched beeping sound.

Peri, Mark, and Joel looked at the tamarin. The unspoken thought: did the tamarin understand?

No one knew, or even theorized.

"Don't worry, Sam," Peri said. "You're not next. Never."

She turned to Satan and murmured, "Poor kitty."

David and Joel carried the leopard off to the necropsy table in the back of the hospital, where two pathologists from the University of Chicago would do their work on it.

Joel returned and washed the examining table, slowly, methodically, with more dedication than was required.

"You never get used to doing that," he said, softly. "Never a pleasant thing, no matter what the circumstances are."

Behind him, Sam was seated in a corner of the incubator, silently staring out into the room.

When Joel went home to his wife and two young children that night, he would have a story to tell.

He went off to chat with the pathologists, who had just arrived. One of them looked at the leopard and said, "He looks like an old man."

Peri and David returned to the van; there was no time to consider Satan's fate. Two calves needed their attention in the dairy barn at the farm.

Peg, a brown and white Guernsey calf they had de-horned earlier in the week, needed to have a fifth teat removed. It was an "extra" teat that served no purpose and could get infected. Peri would crush it, and it would simply fall off.

Max, a black and white Holstein calf, needed to be castrated; it would end up as beef, not for breeding.

Both procedures were done with a Burdizzo, an Italian-made clamp. On the Holstein, it would crush the cord supplying blood to the testicles, which would then atrophy.

They began on the Guernsey. The Burdizzo severed the teat, instead of merely compressing it. It fell off. No harm done, Peri declared. Both animals had been given a local anesthetic. The Holstein suffered less gracefully, struggling, but eventually conceding defeat.

On the wall nearby, three signs were posted for the edification of city kids:

Heifer: female cattle that have not yet had calves.

Cow: female cattle that have had calves.

Calf: cattle under 1 year of age.

Peri and David paused to check the abscess on the hoof of the Holstein calf's mother. Peri medicated it again, and David wrapped the hoof. The massive animal, its black coat gleaming, offered no resistance.

As they walked out of the barn, Peri paused and returned to the Guernsey calf in its small pen. The calf came to the edge of the pen and stuck its face toward Peri's. She kissed it. It mooed.

On the way back to the hospital, Peri stopped at the bear line, to ask how Butch was doing. The keeper told her that Butch seemed OK, but that another maned wolf, Jocko, was limping. Peri looked at Jocko in its outdoor habitat and watched it walk. There was a visible limp, but not a serious one. She told the keeper that she would wait and see, and headed back to her office in the hospital.

She had intended to go out to lunch, to cash her paycheck at a local supermarket. When she sat behind her desk, however, she noticed a brown bag on it. She opened it. A friend had bought lunch for her, a Reuben sandwich, one of her favorites.

She smiled, exhaled loudly and sat back in her chair. She did not know what the rest of the day would bring.

FIRST PERSON: PEREGRINE WOLFF

My parents wanted unisex names, so that they wouldn't have to think up two names for the kids before they were born. My sister's name is Ashley, which goes either way. And they wanted to name me Peri, they liked that name, but they wanted something longer, so that it would be shortened to Peri. There was a very eccentric naturalist friend of my parents who was a mythology professor. And he said, "Well, why don't you call her Peregrine?" And they couldn't think of any reason why not to, so that's what they settled on.

I was talking on the phone to the head of the Chicago Veterinary Medical Association, and he asked who this was, and I said, "Well, this is Peregrine Wolff." He said, "I'd seen that name, and I saw that it was at Lincoln Park Zoo, and we thought it was a big joke. I didn't know you actually existed."

I think I can definitely attribute any animal likings to my father, because he's always been a kind person, always very gentle. We always had a dog, and we always had some birds, and things like that, nothing fanatical. But I always had an appreciation for wildlife, birds in particular. My parents sort of instilled that.

We spent fifteen months in Europe when my dad was on sabbatical when I was eight. In Germany mostly, between Berlin and Munich, and then we spent three months in Norwich, England, for the last three months of the time we were there. Mom and my sister would go shopping, and Dad and I would always go to the zoo. He liked to go, and I always wanted to see the animals. I think it was at the Berlin Zoo and the Munich Zoo, they had a great ape collection, a lot of orangutans, and I remember really being infatuated to the point of telling my parents that when I grew up, I was going to marry an orangutan. Which I think they thought was fine, you know, a nice redhead in the family. I had a little book; I would cut all the animal pictures out from the guidebooks and paste them in this book. I think it was when we were in Europe that I really got hooked on zoo animals.

I remember when I was in fifth grade, there was a veterinarian who lived just down the hill from us, and I'd go down on weekends and work with the kennel woman, and we'd clean cages. I was doing that in fifth and sixth grade. And then I was baby-sitting for a veterinarian, and he said, "Well, you can come ride on calls with us," so I started doing that. Dad once asked me how to spell rhinoceros, and I was being defeatist about it. And he said, "You can't be a veterinarian unless you know how to spell rhinoceros." So he sort of was cluing me in at that point. By the time I was in college, I pretty much knew that I wanted to be a veterinarian.

We'd traveled to England on vacation; we went to the zoo on the isle of Jersey, and we just asked, "Do you ever take students?" "Only British students," they said. When I was getting ready to apply to vet school, everybody had good grades, everybody had animal experience, everybody wanted to get in because it was right during the James Herriot craze, which really affected vet school entrance a lot. I was moaning around the house, and my mother said, "Why don't you write to them? All they can say is no." So I did. And they sent me back an application, and I applied and got accepted.

It was great. I had a wonderful time. It started out as a four-month training program where you were basically an assistant keeper. And then you did a research project. I lived with an English family, rented a room from them. Jersey is only seven miles long and two and a half miles wide, and the coastline goes from beautiful beaches to real rocky rugged coast, where they have puffins and all sorts of shore birds. They have fields and fields of irises and daffodils.

The zoo was set up as a trust by Gerald Durrell, who was an animal collector in the fifties. It's very conservation-oriented. It's about the same size as ours, about thirty-five acres.

I met Durrell. He's an absolutely charming man, overweight, old, married to a fairly glamorous young American woman. He has the most enchanting blue eyes, and if you've ever read his books, he talks the same way he writes.

I learned there, as I have here, a lot about the animals and learned much more about the different personalities, the people who were there. I stayed on for two extra months as a keeper, because I had been wait-listed for vet school, and I was going out with one of the keepers there. If I hadn't gotten into vet school, I don't know what would have happened. It was hard to leave because I was leaving not only good friends but this person that I was really fond of.

I did return home, to vet school at Cornell. I think if I could have gone back and just said, "I don't want to have anything to do with men for the whole time I'm here," it would have been a much better experience. But I did reasonably well and had a lot of fun. However, my senior year was not a good year for me emotionally. I really wanted to be in a zoo, but I didn't feel that I was brilliant enough to be in that position. I had spent the summer of my junior year as an extern at Lincoln Park. Then, during my senior year, Tom Meehan told me that there was an internship being offered. Tom knew that he could get along with me, we had worked together OK. I was an easygoing person, knew the bullshit that goes on here, and could probably handle it, although sometimes I don't think I can. He said, "I know you're not the most qualified person in the world," because I wasn't, I was fresh out of vet school. I didn't have that much experience, there were other people. But as Tom said, he didn't really want to hire somebody who was smarter than he was. So I got the job. After my first year was up, he asked the zoo society to fund the position for a second year, which it did. And then the park district said, "OK, the money's in for a second veterinarian." You really can't do this place with just one person.

I grew up with some very close friends in high school, and I just naturally assumed that all these people would be going to college. Then, when I came back, I found out that half of these people who were considered really groovy in high school were married and had two kids and never left Middlebury, Vermont. It just never occurred to me that everybody wasn't going to go the same road I was taking. I don't think there's anything wrong if you want to stay home and have children; that's fine, if that's what you want to do. But if you want to aspire to something else, then I think you should do it. I think all my views were instilled in me as a child. I've never really sat down and thought about it that much. I've never really had a desire to sit down and read *Ms.* magazine or anything like that.

I think I intimidate a lot of people. People have told me that they think that I come off differently than I think I come off. People think that I tend to exude much more confidence than I think I do, more than I personally feel. I know that I've spent time feeling incompetent. And I never think of myself as possibly threatening men, and yet I'm sure that I do. Maybe I'm just an ornery Vermonter. I'm definitely much more New England than I am midwestern. That's one of the big problems I have here. There's nobody here who I really have that much in common with, even though we all work in the same place. That was a problem at vet school, too. I don't really have any close female friends at all. Which is kind of annoying.

My favorite animals? The marmosets and tamarins, I really like them. A lot of that goes back to Jersey; the guy that I was dating at the time was the marmoset and tamarin keeper. I really enjoyed working with them. You could open the cage door and clean out the enclosure while they were in it. They would just move away, and then they'd come up and look at you. I'd wash the glass on the inside, and they'd come down and play with the soapsuds. I think they're very intelligent, even though they're really high-strung and very piercing, which I usually don't like. I don't like hyper dogs or anything like that. But they don't have diarrhea all over the place; they're not always covered in shit like mandrils. They're just fascinating little animals. I'd like to see them in a really nice environment. It would be great to have a huge aviary full of plants with marmosets running around in it.

I really do enjoy the gorillas, especially appreciating each one's individual personality. I mean, they're so individual in the way they look, and they are so civilized in the way they behave.

I've had a special relationship with just one animal. The only animal that I actually got upset about when it died was a sloth that used to be here, that was hand-raised in the children's zoo, and her name was Woolly Bully. The animal was off, just not eating and was getting bloated, and she turned out to have an infection in her chest—pus in her chest—and ended up having other problems. We brought her to the hospital, and we worked with her. She was here for months, and we were doing all sorts of tests. She was just neat. The way she used to eat oranges, or eat grapes, she'd take them with her claws and put them in her mouth, and then she'd keep poking her toenail in her mouth to eat them. And she'd kind of hang upside down and look at you with those strange little eyes that they have. I was way down at the pathology meeting the night she died. That really upset me. That was probably the only animal that I've really cried over when it died. I really liked her.

You know when the animal is sick. Unless I pick it up myself, the keepers are the first line. They're excellent judges; they know the animals. It's like the owners of dogs. You can tell when an animal's in pain. One particular incident really emphasized it to me. It was a marmoset that was sick; we'd done surgery on it. This was one that did live, even though it was sick. We gave it the usual anesthesia, and I'd just opened its belly, and I thought, "This animal's in a lot of pain." Because it was lying there all curled up, in the fetal position. So we gave it a pain-killer— after the anesthesia—and half an hour later, it was stretched out on its side asleep. The only thing I'd given it was this painkiller, and we saw such a difference between the animal before and, you know, the animal sleeping quietly. And now, since we've started using painkillers, they'll stay asleep for an hour or two after surgery. And I've done surgery without giving a painkiller, and they wake right up.

I've seen some animals that act totally normal and are dead the next day, and you open them up, and they've had pathology that's been going on for weeks. Breeding on

Friday, off food and a little bit lethargic on Saturday, dead on Sunday. You couldn't know, unless you were spending all day watching the animal, and that would be impractical. We've had marmosets die that have been totally infected, worms everywhere; you open their stomach, and the worms are out of their intestines crawling around. And you know that didn't happen last night; that's taken at least a couple of days to happen. And they were apparently fairly normal.

Parasites are a problem in all animals; they're in people, too. A lot of people in America are carrying around worms, and a lot of people in Third World countries are infested with them. But these animals are constantly reinfecting themselves. If we clean to get rid of some of the parasites the polar bears have and the lions have, we would have to either dig up a foot of dirt in their outside exhibit and change it, or else flame-throw their whole inside exhibit and kill the eggs. That's how resistant parasites are to water and soap and ammonia and all that stuff. The eggs are passed in the feces, and then they progress to a third stage, infective larvae. And then when the cat or whatever is licking the floor and licks up the infective third-stage larvae that have settled down from the feces, it reinfects itself. A lot of these animals come in from the wild with worms. And sometimes you don't get rid of the worms because sometimes they may not be passing eggs that day, so then you get a negative fecal, and well, fine, the animals go into the collection. Worms aren't necessarily lethal, because it's not really advantageous for the parasite to kill the host. Then they'd have to find a new host. But in captivity we see deaths that closely follow some sort of stress. Some animals will have been moved to a different cage, or just been weaned, or the keepers will have caught them up and done something to them, and then a week later, we'll start seeing a couple of deaths. With some parasites, the host builds up sort of an immunity, so the host kind of keeps the parasite at a dull roar rather than a raging infection, but a lot of young animals that are naive to these parasites will be overcome. They'll get so many in their intestines that the parasites starve them out basically.

Other diseases cut across this place, too. Bacterial infections. A lot of the viruses are very host-specific, like the canine distemper, which is going to hit the dogs and some of the ferrets and that sort of thing. But you're not going to have the primates dying of canine distemper. So really the only major threat is the bacterial infections that can hit a whole different realm of hosts. We had an outbreak go through our marmoset colony. If the parasites don't kill you, the bacteria will. We had animals in the basement of the primate house; it's closed down now, a horrible place. We were starting to lose animals, and I'd walk through with the keeper, Pam Dunn, and she'd say, "Well, this one's doing fine and that one's OK," and invariably one of those two would be dead the next morning. Some sort of primary stress was causing the host to be weakened, and a secondary bacteria was lurking to kill them within twelve hours. We would aspirate some blood out of the heart, and it would be loaded with bacteria.

Many diseases go back and forth between humans and animals. I've got a textbook in my office on just that subject. Parasites can be passed from animals to people. Animals donated to the zoo can bring rabies with them. It's rare, but when it occurs, it's bad news. People bring TB to primates, and the reverse can happen as well. Many animals are vulnerable, especially the great apes. They get colds, the flu from keepers, and then they give those back to us.

Apes get most of the things that humans do, and we had a very big problem with that. I think this came directly from Pat Sass, who was sick, because it started in the chimps. From a sick head keeper who happens to love chimps. It just marched right around the whole great ape building in a matter of a week. We think it was a virus, a flu type of thing, just snotty noses, coughs, lethargy. We ended up losing an adult male chimp, just bang, dead, from one day to the next. I put them on antibiotics, but whether that was helpful or not is conjecture. I think most of them cured themselves. But it was scary, because there was nothing I could do. We were getting sick, too. I got sick, a keeper got sick. I got sick because Tanga spit in my face a number of times, and she was sick. It was frightening.

Sometimes, I experience a really high level of frustration. What Tom and I tend to do a lot of is fire engine work. For zoo animals, if you're sick, someone's going to eat you, or you're going to get left behind. In the wild, that's what's going to happen, so you try to look as normal as possible, because if you look abnormal, then you're automatically picked out by something else as fair game. I think that zoo animals really hide it; that's something instinctual that is left over from the wild. So you often tend to get animals that are beyond help, that are too far gone. Like the leopard we euthanized: If that leopard had been a domestic cat, he would have been under treatment a long time ago. But what do you do if you can't give him fluids, you can't give him an IV? You know you're basically treating the symptoms, and it's not always that practical, because you can't treat the cat if he's well enough to kill you, but if he's so sick that he can't hurt you, you can help him. But then as soon as he gets better, the first thing he's going to try to do is kill you even though he may need more help.

Sometimes, I feel a sense of risk. Once, Lenore woke up ahead of schedule just outside her holding area at the great ape house. I felt that definitely there was a big risk, but it was overridden by the fact that there was a risk to the animal, who was shrieking and thrashing, surrounded by us, by people. She had an IV in her so that we might have had to knock her down again just to get it out. If she pulled out the tubing that goes to the bag, well, then she's got a perfectly open line that's dripping blood—not that she's going to bleed to death in five minutes, but it could have had potential complications. The first thing that goes through my mind in a lot of these situations is that I'm not as worried about myself getting hurt as I am about somebody else getting hurt, because we're directly responsible if anyone else gets hurt, in my opinion. We're the ones who are calling the shots. If I'm out with a vet student, I'm in control of the situation, the one who should be making the judgment call as to whether this is not a safe procedure.

With Lenore that day, Tom grabbed her, or grabbed a leg or an arm or something, was trying to turn her around so that she'd go straight up instead of out into the kitchen where people were scattering. But he said Lenore eventually did what she intended to do all along, which was to stay inside, away from the people. You can't manipulate any of the great apes. With Lenore, I didn't feel as much in danger of my life; I felt in danger of having her get out or bite somebody else. I don't think I really have ever felt in danger. I had a tapir fall on me, which was an unpleasant experience, but it happened so fast, I didn't really have time to think about it. That was the only time I've ever been really hurt here.

Many of the animals here don't want to attack. However, I think that if a lion got out, it would kill you. I think that the big cats would. I think that you could almost intimidate everybody else. The pygmy hippos are supposed to be really nasty, if you walk into their territory. I think if they were off their own turf, that they might run. Run away from you. A polar bear would probably kill you. The only other animal that I feel has the potential to do the most harm, and almost killed Tom, are the elephants. We tend to treat them like big dogs, but a lot of people have been killed by elephants. There've been more people killed by elephants than any other zoo animal. I think I have a fairly good relationship with them, but if they wanted to, it would be over so fast that I couldn't do anything about it.

I think that animals in zoos have the right to the best possible care that we can give them, and I don't think that in a lot of situations we're doing the best job possible. We can't even keep some of the animals we have here alive; I'm not even talking about breeding or doing well, I'm talking about keeping them alive. That's wrong. There are some animals that do not do well in captivity. And those are the species that are heading for extinction. There are some lemur species in Madagascar that they just can't keep alive in captivity; they live a week, they live two weeks, and then they croak. They just can't do it with today's technology. And with those animals that have probably reached such critically low population levels and are so difficult to keep, it may be better, instead of spending millions to save them, just to divide that up for species that we might be able to save.

I went up to Iceland earlier this year, and we did some necropsies on some birds up there, versus the necropsies I've done on our young birds that are only a year old, birds that are living here. They were comparable weights, but the ones from Iceland are muscle, and the ones here are fat. The animals here are flabby; they don't get a lot of exercise, they just kind of roam around and do nothing. That's not killing animals, but every animal has its territory, and we keep them in twenty-five square feet rather than two and a half square miles of territory. I think that a large part of an animal's beauty is its motion. And that's the same with people. I think that's why people like horses, because they're beautiful when they move, and like seeing giraffes. Seeing a giraffe gallop is an incredible sight; so is seeing monkeys run around.

The whole zoo population is changing now, because the percentage of animals that were born in the wild is reducing, and the percentage of animals that are born in captivity is increasing. Those animals born in captivity probably will not suffer any psychological damage, as long as certain conditions are met in captivity. That may be one reason why we have a lot of success with our great apes, because if they don't want to be looked at, they don't have to be looked at. They can go upstairs and pick their noses if they want. I think as long as they can get away and not feel threatened by the public or by whatever they feel threatened by, then that can help keep them psychologically fit.

This is probably a lot of anthropomorphism, but I'm not sure about living inside your whole life. Never having exposure to the sun. Never having exposure to anything but your own world, the smell of your own urine or feces or whatever cleansing agent the keepers are using. And to me, I can't help but think, when I see animals that are just lying outside sunbathing, or just hanging out, they seem like they're appreciating the outdoors. My dog does, so why should he have any more sense of feelings than the animals in the zoo? To live inside your whole life, that bothers me the most. That's one thing I don't like about northern zoos. And why I think that a lot of the southern zoos might have healthier animals or happier animals; at least they get out and get some sunshine.

I like San Diego's wild animal park, because it allows for natural manipulations, the herding instinct, a male standing in one spot and guarding his territory, and the females moving in and out of it. You see the same stuff out there that you see in Africa, and you don't realize that until you go to Africa and see it.

We can offer that for some animals, the smaller species that you can put in a relatively large space, so that they still can carry out a lot of their activities. But for some of the larger animals, you don't see it. I'm not sure how much the big cats suffer, but they sure look like they suffer a lot in those old cages.

The best keepers in the zoo have a lot of common sense. If I ask one to do something, she will not say, "Oh, I can't, the animal won't do it." She will say, "OK, I will figure out a way to do it," and she usually gets it done. A good keeper will call me on an animal and be able to tell me what happened the day before. She'll give me her impression of it, what she thinks, if it's normal behavior, if it's not normal behavior. I like the traits of someone who will spend extra time reading about the animal, someone I can communicate with, someone who will initiate some things on her own, someone who is keeping her eyes open.

Then there's the I-don't-give-a-damn school. I've seen animals suffer because of them, which really angers me. They suffer from neglect, pure and simple. Say an animal hasn't eaten its food for days. Now, granted, I probably should have been checking up on it, but the keeper should have come to us before that animal looked like hell. The keeper should have said, "Goddamn it, you veterinarians better get over here because this animal looks awful." I would rather have a keeper call me up ten times a day and say, "When are you going to get over here? The animal looks sick," rather than not do it. I tell a lot of people, "I'm not that organized. I tend to forget a lot of things, I'll get distracted by something else. If you want it done, call me up and bug me. I'll never hold it against you if you call me up five times and say, "Don't forget to do this tomorrow," or, "Can we do this today?" I've told a lot of people that, and they'll do it, and it helps me get things done. But, please do that rather than just assuming that you know more. And another attitude that I really don't like is that of the people who imply that they know more than I do, that I'm just a stupid veterinarian. They don't tend to think on the scientific side of things. Which is one of Tom's big bugaboos about this place; he's always trying to inject a little science into everything, rather than black magic.

I don't like holistic medicine in animals. I mean it's fine, a lot of people's problems are psychological, and I think you can believe a lot of your illnesses and problems away. Well, are you going to convince a black leopard that if he only has positive thoughts and believes that this raspberry leaf tea is going to help him, it's going to work? Give them a break.

I think that there were definitely some animals here that have died because it's our fault. There are some animals that they forgot to bring in that froze to death at night, things like that. There was one little agouti, one of those South American rodents that got left out last year. No one really thought that it might be getting cold all alone. I mean, it lived outside, but you know when it's below zero and an animal is all by itself and is from South America. His core temperature was seventy-six degrees when he came in, and four days later his little toes all turned black and fell off. He lived, but he went through a lot of pain and suffering.

We lost a bunch of saki monkeys. The reason might have been that they were getting bacterial infections from the meat. If the meat was being improperly handled and being chopped up, and then grapes and the salad were chopped up on the same cutting board with the same knife, there could be a problem. If you eat meat your whole life, that's fine; if—like sakis—you tend to eat vegetable matter and then get exposed to these horrendous bacteria that are in meat, you could get wiped out. Maybe that's how those saki monkeys died. If it was, that was our mistake, I mean that was the zoo's mistake.

I think that my next move I will make for location. Like if somebody offered me a job at the Lincoln, Nebraska, zoo as head veterinarian, I don't think I'd take it. I'd like to be a head veterinarian somewhere; I'd like a little bit more responsibility, a little bit more control. But then I know there's a lot of headaches, too. Tom does an awful lot of paperwork, and that frustrates him. I know I'll never give up exotic animals. If I had to choose today between being a small animal veterinarian and never practicing another day of veterinary medicine in my life, I'd choose the latter. If I could do field work somewhere, go off and work on some exotic animal conservation project somewhere, I would stay in the conservation field and give up the veterinary medicine field. How long I stay here, I don't know. I guess it depends on whether something better comes along. It also depends on my out-of-work life. If I'm happy, really happy in that, then this is a good job.

Tom and I have our ups and downs, but we get along. I still feel that slowly but surely we are hammering away at some of these really hard-to-change problems—getting diets settled, things like that, trying to make everything better for the animals here. And making the zoo a better place, educating the keepers. This is a good job; the place has a lot to offer. At my age and for my number of years out of school, you really couldn't ask for anything better.

11

MONKEYS' BUSINESS

When asked if she and her husband had children, primate house keeper Pam Dunn smiled and said, "No, with a capital *N* and six or seven exclamation points."

There was an intended irony in her declaration. During one three-month period in her recent past, she spent only three weeks without transporting a newborn primate between work and home.

She did it with pleasure.

"I've been doing what I want to do for as long as I can remember," she said. A powerful affection for animals had characterized her life.

Pam was born in 1952, in a Chicago suburb; she lived most of her life in Chicago. She attended the University of Illinois at Chicago and acquired a bachelor's degree in anthropology.

As a teenager, she began to volunteer her time at the zoo. She did that for ten years, then won a keeper's job. She served as a keeper, with particular interest in primates, for another ten years.

On a cool day in late summer, Pam emerged from her car carrying a familiar parcel, an animal. She wore a pink T-shirt and jeans. Her round, cheerful face was framed by curly blond hair. Her plumpness seemed less characteristic of her than her obvious energy.

The animal she carried was a DeBrazza's guenon, a small West African monkey. At birth, the monkey—which Pam had named Max (for Max Headroom)—had been neglected by his mother. A quick decision had been made in an effort to save the baby's life; the baby was pulled. That night, Pam took him home. Seventeen days later, she was still transporting him back and forth, feeding him by hand, stroking him, keeping him warm, buying toys for him. After more than two weeks, he still weighed less than one pound.

He was a tiny, squeaking creature, with a small fearful face and a delicate, spindly body. As Pam entered the primate house kitchen to begin her day, she placed Max, in his carrier, on a table in a warm corner of the room. Inside the carrier, Max was clutching a manufactured replica of himself, a stuffed monkey.

Across the room, a sign read: "Danger. No Unauthorized Personnel. Chimps Can Grab. Be Aware."

Pam had spent the previous evening worrying about Max. His early efforts to survive had been flawed. He seemed to be in teething pain. His legs seemed weak. He did not eat sufficiently.

Motivated by that concern, and affection, Pam carried Max to the zoo hospital, where vet Tom Meehan looked at him. When Tom picked him up, his squeaks became high-pitched screams. Tom extended two fingers, and the monkey grabbed them. He stroked the monkey's legs, gently.

"The legs look OK," he said. Max urinated on the examining table.

"He won't eat voluntarily," Pam told Tom. "Last night he seemed to perk up, but I had to swaddle him to get the bottle in."

"Keep an eye on him," Tom said. "Encourage him to

move around. Try to get him to climb, to cling, what he'd
do if he were still with his mother. He doesn't have much
coordination."

Pam picked up Max to return to the primate house; she
had other work to do. The monkey, wrapped in a small
blanket, went silent; only his little face was visible, wide-
eyed, staring up at Pam.

It was early morning, and the zoo was quiet except for
the occasional sound of an animal. Pam walked along,
holding Max.

Several wolves in their outdoor habitat howled. Yards
away, a dog barked, as if in response. The wolves howled
again. The dog, a rust-colored Irish terrier named Rosie,
had climbed up into a tree on the outer side of the zoo
fence, to see the wolves. Howls and barks were exchanged,
then Rosie's master coaxed her out of the tree, and the
wolves returned to their relaxed state.

Pam did not notice. She held Max and walked back to the
primate house. She was feeling reflective.

"You know what? I think of what I do as an honor," she
said. "Especially when I get to care for an endangered
species, like this one. I gear my lifestyle around raising
these little guys. Fortunately, I have Chris, the best husband in the world. We go to a party, and we have to leave
early because I have to feed Max. It's like having a kid, but
you can't get a baby-sitter who'll take care of this kind of
kid."

Pam had taken home bush babies, tiny creatures who
weighed less than three ounces at birth; Pam had remained
awake for twenty-four hours on several occasions, just to
keep them alive. There had been tamarins, marmosets,
lemurs as well. It was the part of her job that sustained her
passion for the animals and her understanding of them.

Much of her job, as it was for all keepers, was routine,
repetitious, drudgery. She kept the cages clean and the
animals fed. She hosed down the cages. She fed the monkeys early in the morning: monkey chow, which they
weren't eager to devour, and a canned primate diet (both

were nutritionally complete) that they ate with enthusiasm. After that "breakfast," they were served a meal of
fruits and vegetables later in the day.

With Max back in his carrier, Pam cut up celery in the
kitchen. A clatter arose in the cage nearest the kitchen. It
was occupied by a pair of chimps, Patsy, the female, and
Keo, the male, both in their early thirties. When the great
ape house had been opened in 1976, they were brought to
it, but they didn't tolerate the move well. They were older
than most of the other chimps and were hostile to them.
They were returned to the primate house, where they
shared a double cage just outside of the kitchen.

Keo, at times, would demonstrate his power, pound on
the steel door at the rear of the cage, cup his hands against
his chest, display his strength. He was at it again, and Pam
knew it without looking.

"He can still make plenty of noise," she said, without
looking up from the celery. "When someone out front
teases him, he takes it out on Patsy. Sometimes even when
he's not being teased. There are certain physical types that
urge him on. A guy who looks like a construction worker.
A machismo persona. A weirdo drug addict or a drunk.
They set him off, even if they're not provoking him.
There's something out there, whatever it is, that gets him
into a mood.

"Patsy used to be like that, too. She used to set you up.
She'd put her hand through an opening in the cage, in the
back, and offer a keeper a string bean. When you reached
to take it from her, she'd grab your arm and hang on.
Sneaky. But now they're both like people when they get
older. They've mellowed out."

The chimps were in a class by themselves. The other
inhabitants of the primate house fell under the broad designation of monkeys. The names were exotic: mandrills,
black and white ruffed lemurs, Celebes black apes (actually
macaques, small monkeys, not apes), black howler monkeys, squirrel monkeys, black lemurs, black and white
colobus monkeys, DeBrazza's guenons, pale-faced sakis,

wanderoo macaques, red and black ruffed lemurs, and lion-tailed macaques.

Pam hacked away at sweet potatoes and bananas. Hard-boiled eggs she sliced in half, with the shell intact; the monkeys would peel it away carefully. She chopped apples, tore lettuce, and seasoned much of it with vitamin powder.

The phone rang; it was her husband, asking how Max was doing. Pam peeked at the monkey, who was asleep, clutching the furry chest of the stuffed monkey. Pam told Chris that Max was as well as could be expected.

Pam returned to her ritual. It was part of her job to make certain that the monkeys ate a sound, satisfying diet. But she knew that her worth as a keeper went beyond being deft with a kitchen knife.

The primate house, built in 1927, was old now and slated for renovation. The renovation plan was splendid, but Pam knew it would not be completed on schedule. For her, you did what you could with what you were given.

"This is an old, crappy building," she said. "Because it's old and crappy, you try to do as much as you can to stimulate the animals, without turning into one of those animals-are-my-good-friends types. I never forget that the animals in here are capable of doing a lot of damage. Most of them can't kill you, unless you let them kill you, but I've seen lemurs in a fight, ganging up on one of them. They bite. One of them once needed two hundred stitches after-ward. But sometimes you have to let them fight, to work out their disputes. They are social animals. But there's a line. I monitor it carefully, but I don't necessarily rush to intervene."

At 10 A.M., it was time to "feed the kid." She warmed a small bottle of formula—one of the same brands used to feed human babies. She carried Max to the library, housed in the primate house, a quiet place to read or to feed a monkey.

She wrapped Max in a small blanket and sat in a chair. The monkey stared at her. She placed the nipple in its mouth; the monkey retained it but didn't suck on it. The formula dribbled into his mouth, and he swallowed. Suddenly, but without much force, it began to suck on the nipple, continuing to stare at Pam. It was a moment begging for anthropomorphic interpretation. Pam abstained.

For her, Max's survival was the main matter. It would be important to get him back with his family, even with a mother that had been less than supportive.

"At first, I'd want to sit with him in front of his family group, so he won't be frightened when we put him back in with his mother," she said. "But that's seven months to a year away—after he's on solid food. That's the time to try to reunite them."

A few minutes later, she checked the level of formula in the bottle. Some of it had been consumed. She carried Max back to the kitchen, to his carrier, to his stuffed monkey. He grabbed the monkey and curled up against it.

Pam stood at the window, looking out at the people strolling through the zoo.

"When I was a zoo volunteer years ago, they'd ask me all sorts of questions. But there was no doubt about what was the most popular question, by far," she said.

"It was, 'Where is the bathroom?' "

Late that day, when Pam was ready to take Max home, she heard that a baby saki monkey named Morgan would need her, too. The saki's mother had died suddenly in the small mammal house, but had nursed the baby for two months, and someone would have to substitute for the mother. Pam volunteered.

The next morning, Pam arrived at work with two animal carriers.

Morgan had consumed some formula at Pam's apartment, had eaten a little bit of banana, but had vomited. Pam was concerned; Tom Meehan would have to see the saki.

In the primate house kitchen, Max squeaked in his carrier and wrestled with his stuffed monkey. The saki seemed lethargic in its carrier, and as Pam looked at it, she was unhappy.

"Sakis are laid-back at best," she said. "They can even be morose in captivity. Is this one depressed, or is its behavior merely a characteristic of the species? They're rarely hyper, so it's a matter of degree."

Morgan issued a high-pitched whistle, then a howl; Max continued to play with his stuffed animal. Pam was concerned about Max, too; he had what appeared to be a blister on one leg. Tom Meehan might have to "pop it."

Last night at home, she had kept Max at one end of the apartment and Morgan at the other, running back and forth, stopping to wash her hands. Morgan might have the disease that killed its mother; she didn't want Max to become infected.

By 8:20 A. M., she had changed into her keeper uniform: dark brown slacks and khaki shirt. She filled a bowl with warm water and mild soap. She opened Max's carrier and said, "Hey, tiger, hey, tiger, come here."

She reached in and grabbed Max, who urinated. She held him in one hand easily, and gently rubbed the soapy water on him with the other. He responded with an occasional peep.

"I know, I know, life's tough," she murmured.

She washed only his bottom and his legs; he sat in the water, clutching her shirt. She dried him with paper towels and a dish towel, as he ran through a repertoire of protest sounds, stopping only to glare intently at her face.

Gene Brimer, the recently hired pest control technician, dropped in to take an inventory of the pesticides in the primate house.

Pam asked him if he'd ever conquer the pests at the zoo.

"We'll make a dent," he said. "The truth is that we'll never eliminate the problems. We don't really exterminate, although that word is still used to describe what I'm trying to do. What we do is try to control the infestation."

Pam was well aware of the problem. Roaches eaten by monkeys implanted a potentially fatal parasite. Marmosets had been particularly vulnerable, and she was fond of marmosets.

Gene was likable; his gray hair belied the presence of a youthful energy. But Pam didn't have time to chat; she had to go to the hospital to get a heating pad to warm Morgan's carrier.

On the way, she met curator of mammals Mark Rosenthal, who mentioned that a female lion had fallen into the moat that separated the lions from the public. She wasn't injured, Mark said.

A stop at the lions' outdoor habitat revealed the lioness sitting calmly at the bottom of the moat, looking up at another lioness peering down at her. An open door in the moat awaited the lioness, who chose not to enter it and make her way into the building, where the keepers could take charge.

Les Fisher had been notified and was taking in the scene.

"Over the years, maybe ten or twelve lions or tigers have fallen in, and only one even cracked a bone," he said. "Eventually, she'll come in, if only because she'll be hungry."

Pam got the heating pad from the hospital and returned to the primate house. Morgan seemed sluggish, a weariness that resembled depression in humans.

Tom Meehan called. His test on the dead saki mother revealed that she died of bacterial pneumonia, common and contagious; the baby might be in jeopardy, he told Pam. The little saki had vomited again, and Pam was concerned.

"Nothing much I can do," she sighed.

She went out into the main hall, where the public circulated, and walked along the row in front of one bank of cages. In one cage, she spotted Molly, a colobus monkey with a white face, and Puddles, a male DeBrazza's guenon, a brownish-green monkey with a white beard. Molly's mother didn't nurse her, Pam recalled, so she was pulled, and Tom Meehan took her home. Puddles was thought to be sickly at birth and was covered with sores; his mother had been urinating on him. When an attempt was made to reunite mother and son, the mother wouldn't pick him up, and he was retrieved again.

"We weren't sure that Molly would make it," she remembered. "Colobuses need a special diet, with higher greens content. She had thrush, and she had seizures. But there she is, just fine.

"Puddles was a weird cookie. He'd rock and beat his head against the wall. At first, Molly didn't like him. But slowly they got along. He likes her now, but she's more independent. Gradually, once we put them together, they grew confident in each other's company. Now, they've been OK for two weeks, so we've broken down our contact with them. We're planning to reintroduce each to its own species."

In the next cage, four colobus monkeys raced to the front of the cage when Pam appeared.

"With these monkeys—and they're all females in this group—the females are like aunts. It's called 'aunting' behavior. They take care of another's baby. It's a highly social thing. They'll go so far as to play tug-of-war with a baby, which can get scary.

"For me, they look as different as people. I know them as individuals," she said. The four colobus monkeys looked almost identical.

"Actually, all four of these will go, with Molly, to a zoo in Little Rock, Arkansas, where there's a male waiting to breed with them. Their progeny will come back here. It's a good situation."

Stopping in front of the next cage, Pam hollered, "Gracie, come in."

From the outdoor cage—connected to the indoor cage by a short tunnel and a door the keepers could open by lever— a Celebese black ape—looking like a dwarf ape but actually a monkey—entered, bared her teeth and made a lip-smacking sound. Her daughter, named Patience, followed her to the front of the cage where Pam was standing.

"When Patience sees me paying attention to her mother, she objects," Pam said. "She'll reach through the cage and try to pinch my arm. Hard."

Patience did reach, and Pam dodged her grip.

Down the row, a group of five black and white ruffed lemurs—"laid-back animals" Pam called them—were asleep. When they heard Pam's voice, they woke up.

"Sorry," she said.

A group of mandrills seemed to be waiting for Pam to visit them. The mandrills, regal members of the baboon family, had grooved facial markings that surrounded their red noses; the markings were deep enough to go all the way into their skulls. The mother of the group, called Jonesie, was, according to Pam, "bizarre, schizzy, hyper. She plucks her own hair until she looks like she's been shaved. I'd expect that of a neurotic animal low in the pecking order, but she's subordinate only to the male. She's a tense animal, a high-energy animal, but it's not all positive energy, unfortunately."

Jonesie turned her butt toward Pam.

"That's a submissive gesture," Pam said. "She's showing submissiveness to me, too."

Pam made her way back to the kitchen. She called Tom Meehan, who told her that a second saki had died, but not of the same infection that had caused the previous saki death. It was confusing, he told Pam. He would come over to see the saki baby, Morgan.

She peeked in to look at Max, still asleep beside his stuffed monkey, his slender arms around it.

"It's not that the stuffed animal is a monkey to Max," Pam said. "They have a clinging instinct. Little marmosets will clutch a stocking cap. They don't care if it looks like a monkey or not. I don't think that this little guy looked at the toy and said, 'My God, it's one of my own.' "

She had grown used to her role as a surrogate mother. She preferred to think that it made her a better keeper, rather than a woman with an anthropomorphic fixation. When nature failed, she had to be there.

"You never know if a mother knows something when she neglects her baby," she said. "First-time mothers will reject babies because the situation is stressful and they don't know what to do. That's especially true when the mother was hand-raised herself and doesn't have experience as a mother. In marmosets, the males are the ones who carry the newborn, not the mothers. And if they don't do it well, or if there's more than one baby, the mother may not be able to cope."

Tom Meehan arrived, reached into the carrier, and extracted the saki. The monkey arched its back; its eyes rolled from side to side. Tom studied it for several minutes.

"He may be hypoglycemic. We can medicate it for that," he said.

He wanted to change the formula Pam had been feeding it, in search of one it would tolerate. He wanted to give it glucose via an IV line, but, he said, "I'll have a helluva time getting an IV line in." He was prepared to insert a stomach tube, to assure that nutrition got to the saki.

Pam wrapped the saki in a dish towel and attempted to give it some Pedialyte, an oral electrolyte maintenance solution. The weary saki wasn't getting much of it, and Tom was attentive to the lack of success.

"I'll have to try to get that IV line in. The oral stuff just isn't as good. And I want to warm him up. I'll take him to the hospital," Tom told Pam.

Before Tom left, Pam wanted him to look at the blister on Max's leg. She had mentioned it to Tom earlier, but he had forgotten.

"I guess it wasn't high on my priority list today," he said, commenting on his own clogged schedule. He washed his hands and plucked Max from his carrier. Max urinated and tried to clutch his stuffed monkey. Tom ducked the flow of urine and separated real monkey from toy monkey.

Delicately holding a syringe, Tom removed fluid from the blister for the lab technician to analyze. As Tom prepared to leave, Les Fisher walked in; he had heard about the plight of the sakis, the dead and the living.

He told Pam he knew how frail sakis could be. She agreed.

"I've seen a keeper just open a cage and have a saki faint before the keeper could even grab it," she said.

Les and Tom went on their way, and Pam was alone in

the kitchen. She had chores to do. One of the primate keepers walked in and sat down. A young woman, she appreciated how seriously Pam took her job. They talked about the sick saki and the job of the involved keeper.

"Sure, after all these years, I know that this isn't Disneyland," Pam said. "An epidemic can race through here. I've seen it happen. I know when an animal can't make it. That's when I say to myself, 'I don't need this.' But then I just keep going. When they survive, and you know when they have, you're so drained that you don't feel much of anything. But the days pass and you recover, too.

"After all, it's my choice, to do what I do. And when an animal gets better, I feel proud."

Early the next morning, Pam learned that Morgan had died. The sad little saki had died in the zoo hospital shortly after arriving there the previous afternoon. Its depressed state had been a sign of things to come. Tom Meehan concluded that Morgan, like the two older sakis who had died within days of each other, had succumbed to strep pneumonia. Morgan's body was sent to the University of Chicago pathology lab for detailed analysis. The infection that had decimated the saki colony had left only one male alive; Tom was medicating it in the hope of saving it.

For Pam, the bad news only compounded her mood. Max, the DeBrazza's guenon baby, was less alert than he had been on the previous day. She was still concerned that it wasn't eating voluntarily and that its clutching instinct wasn't fully developed. Last night, she had washed its stuffed monkey but had forgotten to put it back in the carrier.

In that carrier, back in the primate house kitchen, Max seemed edgy and was scratching the back wall of the carrier in what seemed to be a display of nervous energy. Pam realized that she'd left the stuffed monkey at home and set out to replace it. She found a dish towel and rolled it into a ball as a replacement.

As Pam talked to Max, a young woman keeper prepared a potion for Patsy, the old chimp.

It contained one birth control pill—the same used by

women all over the world—which the keeper had pulver-
ized and had stirred into a paper cup filled with Tang. To
pacify Keo, the ill-mannered male chimp, another paper
cup with Tang alone was readied. Patsy had given birth to
seven children over the years, then had given birth to an
eighth and had neglected it. The decision had been made to
pull the baby and put Patsy on the Pill.

Pam went to the outside cages to check the locks; they
were intact. It was part of her routine. Then she went into
the back run and pulled the levers that opened the outside
cages to the monkeys inside. She yelled, "Good morning!"
and the monkeys, screeching excitedly, bounded down the
runways into the sunlight.

Inside, Pam paced past the glass-enclosed cages, looking
at each animal as she passed. She knew what to look for:
any sign of blood, diarrhea, bloody urine—either a sign of a
cycling female or a sign of trouble—the posture of the
animals, a tool left in a cage.

"I see them every day," she said. "I ought to know if
anything's changed."

The most obvious, and potentially most threatening,
sign was a monkey sitting silently in a corner.

"A nonmobile primate is an indication of a serious problem," she said.

She proceeded to hose down each cage thoroughly, a job
that the keepers did daily. The monkeys scrambled for a
place away from the stream of water and watched her
work.

As she passed each cage, she commented about her relationship with the animals in it.

Seven red and black ruffed lemurs struck a family pose
to greet her, as if a photographer had given them instructions. They all leaped upon a long branch in the cage, in a
perfect row. One of them leaned forward toward her.

"For a lemur, that one's aggressive," she said. "When you
feed him, he tries to nail you."

She moved along, then cried out. "Gaylord!"

Gaylord, a black male howler monkey, lumbered toward

the front of the cage. The lemurs she had passed made a loud racket, a territorial call.

"They're telling me, 'This is my territory, and I'm letting you know it is,' " she interpreted.

Gaylord peered at her. She imitated his howl, hoping to get him to respond. He didn't. Instead, he turned and gnawed some bark off a branch in his cage.

"He's responsive, interactive with people, but it's not friendly," she said. "That's a distinction that's important to make. You have to know that when he solicits attention, he may appear to be 'cute,' but he may not be friendly. It's not an invitation to play with him."

In the next cage, a group of wanderoo macaques cavorted. One of the males, Jacob, was a misogynist. He coexisted only with one female, Gertrude. All the others were in danger in his presence.

"He attacks them," Pam said. "We had to send one out of here, to the Baltimore Zoo. And another one had to have a leg amputated, thanks to him. He pulled her leg through the bars and bit her so badly the leg couldn't be saved. She survived, however. What's a little odd is that she was his daughter. Now, even though she's got only one leg, she's very aggressive, like her father."

In the cage holding the DeBrazza's guenons, Max's father sat proudly; he was a large monkey with a serious demeanor. When Max had to be pulled, his mother, Jenny, was walking along with Max on her hip. Pam had to reach in to get him. She held Jenny's tail with one hand and grabbed Max with the other. Jenny remained calm, fortunately.

In another cage, a family group of DeBrazza's guenons sat around: Lucas, the father; Olive, the mother; Mark, a son; and Kathy, a two-month-old. Pam looked at them.

"Olive rocks back and forth. Abnormal," Pam noted. "She's not very friendly, either, but she's a good mother. She's had many children. Some of them are adults now. In fact, she's a grandmother. There's some nice, loving stuff going on between brother Mark and the new little sister, too. It wasn't like that in the beginning, when she was born, but they've worked it out. Or he has."

Pam continued her stroll, out of the building to the row of outdoor cages.

"And here's my favorite animal in the entire house," she announced. It was Admiral, a male wanderoo macaque who had been caught in the wild years ago; he was now in his midtwenties. He was black with a light gray full "beard," and the hair on his head emulated a widow's peak that made him seem to be wearing an old-fashioned admiral's hat.

Pam went back to the kitchen to get Admiral his reward, a few fresh, sweet, green grapes.

"He responds to women very well," she said. "Not just to me, but to all the women keepers." She held out a grape, and Admiral reached through the bars and took it gently, put it into his mouth, but did not chew it.

He held Pam's hand, lifted his face toward hers, and opened his mouth. His teeth looked in need of repair.

"He's had a lot of dental work. Fillings. Root canals. We've got a dentist for humans who comes in and does the work," she said.

Pam continued to hand Admiral the grapes, and he kept her hand in his.

"In ten years, he's never attacked me," she said.

"You've got the worst-looking teeth," she said to him, "But you're still handsome."

Admiral offered a gesture closely resembling a salute. Then he began to chew on the grapes, which he had held in his cheek pouch.

"You're the best boy in the whole place," she said. "Yes, you are."

She invited him to reach out, beyond the bars, to hold her hand again.

"If I stuck my hand inside the bars, he probably wouldn't bite me, but why take the chance? How would I explain that in an accident report?" she asked herself.

She took a quick tour of the isolation room, where animals were held for a variety of reasons. Some were awaiting shipment to other zoos. Some were awaiting medical treatment. Single animals awaited mates or simply another of their species to serve as company.

Two red and black ruffed lemurs were in cages side by side.

"They're both males," Pam said. "We want them to hear each other, see each other, smell each other, for companionship. An all-male group can live in peace, and sometimes breeding isn't a consideration. We have enough."

When it was time for her midmorning break, Pam grabbed a Coke from the food locker in the kitchen and went to the library. She sat at a small table with the librarian, Joyce Shaw. She thought about the last twenty-four hours and the death of the saki. For several minutes, she was quiet. Then she spoke.

"I was tired and disheartened yesterday. A few weeks ago, I had a black and white ruffed lemur baby die on me, of pneumonia. The mother rejected that one, so I took it. In Morgan's case, the mother died. For that reason, until we knew why she died, I had to be cautious. Could other animals get what killed her? Could I get it? We had to find out. So when I had both babies at home, I had one in the front of the apartment and one in the back, and I was running, front to back, stopping to wash my hands in Betadine.

"What's strange is that I didn't think there was anything seriously wrong with the saki. But stress in itself can take its toll on a saki. I thought, 'Well, it never tried to bite me. It nursed.' But the cards were stacked against it, I guess. Sakis are so sensitive. And I'd never before been given an animal whose mother had died. Maybe that meant something, too."

She sipped her Coke. Two other keepers entered the room and stood nearby, listening.

"You know, one minute an animal can be hanging on the

bars. Then, it slips down. Half an hour later, it's dead," she sighed wistfully.

The others nodded.

Then all three went back to work.

FIRST PERSON: PAM DUNN

As far back as I can remember, I've always had an affinity for animals. Even before I had anything to do with the zoo, I had a lot of exotic pets. I was seven or eight years old when my father brought home rabbits for me, and ducks. I had reptiles, mainly turtles, the little dime-store turtles.

We lived in a place where they wouldn't allow dogs or cats. I was about nine years old, and I used to devour *Dog World* magazine. My parents were tolerant, and I kept begging and begging for a dog, so finally they said they'd ask the landlord if I couldn't have some sort of small innocuous dog. The landlord said no. They came back to me, and they couldn't just say the landlord was a jerk, so they said the landlord said that we couldn't have a dog because dogs bark, and they would disturb the neighbors. So I ran into my bedroom and came out with this article on basenjis, which are barkless dogs. My parents were just floored; they didn't know what to do. I sort of trapped them. They came up with some other reason why I couldn't have a dog. But we finally did move to a place where the landlady had two dogs, and I thought I'd died and gone to heaven. And that's when it really started, the animals started pouring in, and that was about the time when I began seriously exploring trying to become a volunteer at the zoo. I went there all the time.

In high school I was a good student, and I was quiet and did my work, and that didn't fit in with the basic high school party scene. By that time, I was a sophomore in high school. From that moment on, I really didn't involve myself in high school things at all; all my spare time, weekends, and during the summer, five to six days a week I was at the zoo as a volunteer.

At that point, I didn't have any interest in specific types of animals. I liked everything. I started working with the reptiles. I always tried to stay with the things that weren't real popular—reptiles and birds of prey. Then I was allowed to graduate to handling the monkeys.

At the University of Illinois, I majored in anthropology, and I was able to specialize in primates. I encountered a wonderful professor there, Dr. Reed, who encouraged me. He's still in my mind. His expectations of everyone were high, and as he got to know me more, his expectations of me got even higher. Through him I was able to realize a lot of my own potential and get a direction, and the primate thing just began to evolve. In the children's zoo, I was able to handle the monkeys. I let everything else fall to the wayside, and I spent most of my time with the monkeys.

I wanted to be a keeper at a zoo before I even went into college, though when I started at the zoo there were no women keepers. If you were female and you were an employee, you were called a zoo leader, not a keeper. I was still in college when it changed. I was beginning to get my career aspirations together once that area did open up and I could become a zoo keeper. On the test I came in number six out of over four hundred people.

I started on January 3, 1978, and it was cold and snowy, miserable, and I didn't drive at that point, so I had to take the bus, and I wanted to be prompt, because my first thing was an interview with Dr. Fisher. I had the job, but I didn't know where I was going to be working, what building, anything. I walked out, and on my way to the bus stop, I slipped on some ice and fell. I had knit slacks on, and I tore a big gaping hole. I was bleeding, but I couldn't go back and change because I was afraid I would be late. So I sat there through the whole interview with my hand over my knee trying to cover this big hole in my pants, the blood dry. It was terrible, but he sat me down and basically told me that I would be going to the primate house.

They knew my background in primates, that it was very heavy. I also had a lot of years in the children's zoo. I could have easily ended up there, and it would have been just as valid. I didn't want the children's zoo through; I was hoping that I'd get the primate house, but back then I was not the type of person who would toot my own horn and speak up. I remember Dr. Fisher stressing the safety aspects, giving me tips on how not to get killed.

So I had to deal with Sinbad, a big male gorilla, who could be nasty. I was the new person, low man on the totem pole, and all of a sudden one day I'm walking down the back run, and things start flying out of his cage. He was throwing everything, feces, food. At me, definitely. He hit me in the leg, and I said, "Oh, my God." He had this huge tractor tire that it took several people to lift if you needed to move it. It was about four feet tall, just immense. And he would take this thing, and I'd be walking down the run, and I could see him out of the corner of my eye, and he would swing it backhand into the back bars of the cage. He wanted to elicit some kind of reaction from me. He didn't care if you screamed at him; if you jumped, all the better. The more you reacted, the better he liked it. Even though it couldn't hit me, it's very hard to not react when you see a tractor tire flying at your head. I got put on that run almost right away. And I'd be cleaning the gutter, sweeping, and inevitably you have to avert your eyes. And as soon as I'd look away, something would come flying and hitting me. I went home and thought, "This animal's going to torment me forever. He's going to live forever, and his whole purpose will be to make my life miserable." Everybody else went through this with him. Some people he never let up on. The senior keeper said, "Just think of him as an old bozo with nothing better to do than to give you a bad time, and just ignore him. He'll get tired of it." So I did, and he did let up on me finally. And then we were able to develop what became a seven-year very good relationship.

I have been singled out in a positive sense, and I have been singled out in a very negative sense. In a positive sense, we had a spider monkey named Sam that I started working with in the children's zoo, and when he got older, he was sent out on breeding loan to another zoo. He was gone for several years, and I never thought I'd see him again, because rarely when you send an animal out does he come back again. This was when I was still in the children's zoo, and one day I was going outside, and they had a huge cage that went up several stories. We'd have spider monkeys, capuchins, and woolly monkeys in there, sort of a mixed group. I was heading out the back door and was a considerable distance away when I saw this black spider monkey hanging on the bars with his arms outstretched, squealing and squealing. I had no idea that Sam had come back.

It sort of reminded me of one of these movies where you see the two people running toward each other. You could almost hear the music. I realized it was Sam, and he came flying down the cage, and I came running across to him, and through the bars we just had this intensive greeting. I knew it was him, once I saw the face, I knew; there was no doubt in my mind it was him. And he had remembered me after two years of separation. Eventually, he graduated to the monkey house, and I stayed in the children's zoo. When I came to the monkey house, there he was, and it was like old home week all over again.

There are cases of bad rapport. We had a marmoset colony in the basement of the monkey house. We had a few animals who were nursery-raised, and you always have a problem with a nursery-raised animal, or any kind of hand-raised animal. They lose that little edge of fear that keeps them from attacking you. I've heard that even lion tamers prefer to work with a totally wild cat than one that's hand-raised, because that little edge is to your advantage. They may hesitate. Marmosets are small animals, but they have the potential to be very aggressive. We had these animals down there that had come from the nursery, and they became so aggressive toward us that it was almost impossible to work around them. You had to wear leather gloves, because even if they couldn't get to you to bite you, they have claws, little squirrel-type claws. So if they get your finger, they can really scratch you up. They reach through the bars, and you're trying to take the water bottle off the front, and they're going after you like crazy. Trying to take the food plate in and out, you'd be wearing your heavy leather gloves, you'd reach in, and they would just grab on. There were two of them, and you could hardly get them off. And the whole time they were just biting and biting and biting.

They alienated one person at a time. One guy bit four different keepers. And sometimes he'd get out and come after you. They're so fast that it's very hard for a human reflex to counteract that.

Marmosets are high-strung animals. They're more sensitive animals, more easily spooked. Some types of marmosets and tamarins seem to be more aggressive. There's one called a red-bellied tamarin, which seems to be exceedingly aggressive, and if you have to go in to a cage to separate out one individual, you go in looking like a snowman. I mean you have your heavy coat on, you have a hat, because the whole family is going to come after you.

Among the primates, there are different personalities. It's very hard to get an accurate measurement on gorillas because they are more introverted. I saw Sinbad over the years do some absolutely amazing things. He was known to be a thrower, so you would not allow him to have things like rocks or sticks. You had to be very selective about the play objects you gave him. So he'd go outside, in his outside cage, and invariably he'd find rocks, little stones, whatever. He'd bring them back in, and I'd be working in the kitchen, and pretty soon I'd hear this tap, tap, tap, tap. And I knew he'd gotten something. So I would go and look, and he'd show me blatantly that he'd gotten this stone. He had been taught early on to trade things. If he had something he wasn't supposed to, he learned that if he'd give it to you, you'd give him some nice treat. So I would go and get a bunch of grapes or a couple of bananas. And he'd hand me this rock. I wouldn't even have to say anything. And you had to be fair, you couldn't say, "Ah ha, you stupid animal, you gave me the rock." You had to give the treat to him;

otherwise you'd blow the whole deal. So I'd go back, and five, six minutes, later, tap, tap, tap. It turned out he had a whole pile, but he was only revealing them one at a time.

Finally I caught on. I came in and had a nice big bunch of grapes. He threw out one rock, and I said, "No, I want them all this time." He was going to snooker me out of everything I had, and we were always trying to keep him on a diet. I would talk to him just like I'd talk to a person. Not that he understood, I have no illusions that he understood everything, but he got the point. Eventually, all of a sudden, he took the back of his hand, his enormous hand, and just shoved everything out, because he knew that this was it, that I was on to his game and he had had his fun with me.

The chimps are probably, up along with the baboons, the most dangerous animals in the building. They're intelligent. They have a lot of time to sit and figure out ways of getting at the keepers, if they want to. The male chimp is very volatile. It doesn't take much to set him off, and when male chimps go into a frenzy, they are not in control. He's not a bad animal, he's not a mean animal, but when he goes into these temper tantrums, he is not in control and becomes very dangerous until it blows over. Sometimes you can almost literally see him just sit down and get it back together again.

Patsy the female chimp, on the other hand, is more of a sneak. She sets you up; she will offer you things. There's no way to interpret it but offering. She's got something in her hand, and she's holding it out through the bars and waving it at you. If you take it, she will grab your arm. I've never tried to accept the offering, but if you do, what she will do is hold on. If a chimp gets a hold of you, unless it wants to let go, you're stuck. Chimps could break your arm if they wanted to.

The hamadryas baboons, which I worked with, were probably the most volatile animals I've ever been around. I'd rank them above the chimps in terms of being dangerous to work with on a daily basis. By the way, every animal has an inventory number in this zoo. It's an identity; its medical files will have that number, it has a computer sheet. But when you're working in the building daily, giving an animal a name gives it an identity. If the animal has an identity, you're much more likely to be more keenly aware of that animal and what it's doing. And that makes you better able to determine if there is something wrong. When you're dealing with a hundred animals or more at a time, that becomes crucial.

The Celebes are a species of macaque: they're called Celebes apes, but they're not really apes. They're intelligent, they have a bright-looking face, but they are macaques, they're in the same group with the lion tails and the rhesus monkeys. Celebes are a lot of fun to work with. They're a challenge. They are very destructive, so trying to hang rope in the cage becomes the challenge of a lifetime. You can spend two hours in there tying knots that you think no one will get undone, and, sure enough, you come in twenty minutes later, everything's lying on the floor. They're very inquisitive, very aware of their surroundings, very aware of the public, more so than a lot of the other primates. They react. I see them respond to different people. They make a lot of face gestures, and they do lip smacking, which is a greeting.

They're active, but in a different sense than the squirrel monkeys. Squirrel monkeys seem to be running around aimlessly all the time. The Celebes are deliberate. They're always reaching out to check the locks to make sure you've locked them and trying to find some kind of loose screw.

The lemurs are right up there as one of my favorite animals. When I first started, I thought that my interest was going to be the great apes. Now, as much as I enjoy the great apes, it's the prosimians and the small monkeys like the marmosets that fascinate me, because the diversity is unbelievable. On the one hand, the lemurs are not very bright, so it's not a tremendously challenging, stimulating thing to work with them. But they're fascinating because they're catlike.

We have a lot of lion-tailed macaques. Lion-tails are terribly endangered. I mean, you're dealing with a very fragile captive population that is going to, at some point, be reintroduced to the wild. They've started with the golden lion tamarins, they've started putting those back in, and the lion-tails are one of the animals that are targeted for it. They come from India; the government's been working very hard to stabilize certain areas, to protect them. I was fortunate enough to attend both lion-tailed macaque symposiums, where scientists from all over the world and people from the Indian government, people from zoos, had gathered to talk about strategies for the management in captivity and in the wild.

The premise is that until an area can be stabilized, the best thing that a zoo can do is manage the captive population as best as it can, in terms of developing good blood lines, not in-breeding, trying to retain as much of the natural behavior as possible. Golden lion tamarins were probably the first primate that was reintroduced.

Our role has changed so much over the years. Just the term *keeper* in my mind applies to something from a bygone era. Where you're keeping, you're maintaining. Now it's become sort of a progressive thing where you've gone beyond just maintaining animals and trying to keep them healthy. You're actually working toward long-range plans, and there's a certain amount of decision making and input. Now it's beyond just coming in eight to five and cleaning cages, putting food out. That always will be part of my job, and I want it to be. That's all part of the continuing contact with the animals. If you lose that, you begin to lose your roots.

With zoos in general, there's so much going on that is vital. I want to continue working on a daily basis with the individual animals, but it's become such a critical thing now, with the way the environment is being so poorly managed, you get so frustrated. I belong to a lot of environmental organizations, and aside from sending in my twenty-dollar membership and writing letters, my level of frustration rises tremendously. I often feel that maybe there's more that I could do, in a positive sense, than what I'm doing now. But I wouldn't feel bad staying a keeper for the rest of my life; that wouldn't bother me.

These days, I have animals at work and at home. Pat Sass had just finished raising six tamarins at home all at one time, a tremendous amount of work, and something came along and she needed help. She asked me to help her, and that's how I started.

It's probably the most incredible learning experience I've ever had. Each animal is an individual; each has its own behavioral peculiarities. But it's also a tremendous amount of work. A lot of people say, "Well, it's just like having a kid," but if a woman has a baby, she has certain hormonal instincts that link her to the baby. The job has invaded my home. Before I got married, my husband became aware of what my life is like and that this is the way it is.

The first baby that I raised was a cotton top tamarin and is now a father; in fact, his daughter is here at the zoo. It was like the line is going to go on. But it is a trade-off. I don't want to minimize that fact. It does affect your social life. For example, we were invited to a party last Saturday, and we went but could only stay for two hours, because I had to get back. And the people that I'm friends with have come to accept this. I try to snatch a vacation between babies. Where do I go? Sometimes to other zoos. I've been to many of them.

San Diego impressed me. It's a very large facility. To me, the most impressive thing is the plants. They've done a lot of research work there, they've pioneered a lot of stuff at San Diego. It's probably the premier facility in America.

I was very impressed with the Gladys Porter Zoo in Brownsville, Texas. It's a beautiful facility. They have a lot of little lakes, so they've utilized this area to make a lot of little islands. It's a small zoo with a very nice collection. I saw some tamarins there that I'd never seen before in captivity.

Minnesota State Zoo, outside of Minneapolis is a brand-new state-run facility. They have a beautiful native American animal collection. They have other stuff, too, but it's very impressive what they've done with their North American animals. It's an impressive place to visit.

It's not just the big facilities that are impressive. We went on a tour through the Smokies and found a small zoo that I had never heard of, didn't know existed, a small private zoo called Soco Gardens, in Maggie Valley, North Carolina. This place was marvelous. The keepers were top-notch, enthusiastic. It was the most immaculate place I've ever seen.

Seeing other zoos gives me perspective. It makes it possible for me to evaluate the Lincoln Park Zoo. It's a place that has a tremendous amount of history. It's a place that has been looking forward for a long time now. I've been here long enough to see so much of the renovation and the changes and remember what it was. It used to be a classical menagerie; in the monkey house, you can see the cages were designed to exhibit as many different species in pairs as possible. That whole philosophy has changed. We have our shortcomings in that we're land-restricted, so we have to make some hard decisions about what we're going to keep. I keep saying that I want a Madagascar building, full of as many different kinds of lemurs as we can get our hands on. But the realities are that that won't happen unless I win the lottery. We are still locked in with old buildings, still living with the past, until it's all renovated, updated.

The role of the keeper is changing almost daily. There are more responsibilities, which is good. Responsibility implies competency and trust. We've changed over the years from an all-male staff of keepers and curators to a tremendously large percentage of women. Right now, in many areas, we are world-class. As long as we stay a free zoo and we're in the city environment, we are going to continue to draw tremendous numbers of people. You're going to see more and more educational programs, another thing keepers are participating in.

Sometimes I thank God for feminism. I do. I think women have a very significant role. We're proving it daily. I'm not a rabid feminist. I don't march in protests or anything like that, but I think it would have been a very sad thing indeed if the old stereotypes, that women can't do this and can't do that in terms of zookeeping, hadn't been eradicated. There were people in the field who felt that women should not work with the great apes because when women had menstruation that would agitate the social structure; the males would get bent out of shape. There was no truth to that. Not that any of us had ever known. There were all kinds of reasons why women shouldn't be keepers, and they've all become irrelevant. We've arrived.

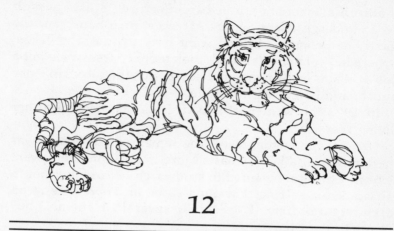

12

THE LIONS' DEN

Many animal keepers developed an infatuation for animals at an early age. Jim Campbell was not one of them. For him, being a lion keeper was a job. He had hoped to be an architect, but that didn't work out. Once he became a keeper instead, he chose to pursue matters of art and philosophy in his own time.

Jim was born in Deerfield, Illinois, in 1945, but his family moved to southern Texas when he was four. He grew up in Texas, then headed west. In 1964, he found himself at the University of California in Berkeley, then the most incendiary campus in the country. It was, as he put it, "during the free-speech movement, as the riots were called." But Jim was neither militant nor scholar.

He flunked out of Berkeley and was drafted into the navy, to serve in "the South China Sea," where he saw some combat.

"It was not active combat," he recalled. "The enemy didn't have a navy to speak of."

After that tour of duty in Vietnam, he returned to

California, where he studied architecture—still in pursuit of an undergraduate degree. After a stint at San Francisco State, he dropped out and went back to southern Texas, where he "scratched around, took more courses." He got a job at a zoo in Brownsville, Texas, but the job didn't pay much, and he got weary of small-town life.

In 1973, he went north to Chicago; he had a brother living there.

"It was a congenial place," he remembered, "and it was better than the West Coast. More important, there were jobs in Chicago. I wanted to study architecture, but not in an academic setting. I wanted to be an apprentice at an architectural firm. I talked to several of them. They weren't interested.

"Then I heard about a test being given for a keeper's job at the zoo, so I signed up."

He got the job, in 1976, and has kept it ever since, serving in the lion house. Over the years, he continued to take courses at various colleges, studied at the C. G. Jung Institute of Chicago, and got his master's in general studies at Roosevelt University. (He passed a test that conceded his bachelor's degree level.)

His master's thesis was on alcoholism.

"I knew about it," he said. "I wanted to know more."

In 1987, he enrolled in the University of Chicago's returning scholar program, as a student in the divinity school, studying "the ethical dimension of alcoholism."

"I don't like to be a regular student," he said. "I'm not a twenty-four-hour-a-day scholar."

He lived in a house he bought a few years ago, a short drive from the zoo. (In good weather, he used his bicycle.) He shared the house with a couple of cats.

Jim resembled an Old Testament prophet. He was tall (6'1") and solidly built (180 pounds). He had a full salt-and-pepper beard and thick brown hair. He wore gold-rimmed granny glasses. He spoke carefully; he rarely slurred a word. His conversation could be simple and direct or turn complex and learned, according to his mood. In matters that related to the welfare of the keepers, he was an activist and had been a spokesman for workers' rights at the zoo.

His day began at 8 A.M., at the lion house, an old dilapidated building scheduled for renovation. In the immense hall, one row of cages faced two glassed-in habitats and the kitchen across the wide tiled floor. Outside, cages lined one side of the building; two habitats—one for lions, one for tigers—bordered the other side.

On one cool summer morning, he arrived, changed into his keeper garb, and strolled past Princess, a lioness being kept in an indoor habitat.

"Hey, old Princess," he called out. He reached between the bars on a door that permitted keepers to enter the habitat, and he patted her nose.

"She's a friendly cat. Nursery-raised," he pointed out. She was twelve years old and had spent her life at the zoo.

Jim knew each animal in the lion house, in biographical detail. The collection included:

- A pair of Bengal tigers, Erica and Denise, sisters, both born at the zoo ten years ago, hand-raised.
- Ajax, a massive Siberian tiger, a male, the largest cat in the lion house.
- An Afghanistan leopard, a young female named Nouri, caught in the wild.
- Two jaguars, both born at the zoo: Jan, a female, and Junior, a male, both ten years old.
- A female black leopard named Lisa; she was between fourteen and fifteen years old. Satan, a sickly male, had been euthanized earlier in the summer.
- Five lions in the larger pride: Bernard, the male, and four females: Sister, Princess, Sheila, and Shelley. The first two were sisters; the last two also were sisters (Sister was their mother).
- In a smaller pride were Anthony, a seventeen-year-old male, and Chandra, a fifteen-year-old female.

Jim made distinctions among the big cats: leopards tend

to be solitary animals, except at breeding time. So are tigers. Lions live in prides, in families; that group atmosphere is gentle, except when the dominant male chooses to make a macho point. Tigers are excellent swimmers. A tiger will kill after a short leap or a quick chase; long pursuits are not its strong suit. The lion is the only cat that can truly roar as it does. And there is no satisfactory evidence to explain whey they do. Two theories await confirmation: roaring is simply a display of exuberance, no more than that, or it is a sound informing the "ownership" of a territory. A leopard's spots are not the same as a jaguar's; a little study reveals the difference. The leopard's are plain rosettes; the jaguar's rosettes have a center spot. The two spotted cats look alike, but the jaguar is larger, with a shorter tail.

Jim had absorbed the hundreds of details that defined the creatures in his care. He did not flaunt that knowledge. Occasionally, he was prepared to be judgmental, however: "Tigers. Leopards. Jaguars. Lions. That's the sequence, going from the most complicated animals on down to the less complicated."

Jim began his day with a stroll through the lion house basement, a dark, dirty, depressing retreat. He snapped on a light switch, and when he did, he illuminated a row of cages and awakened an assortment of owl monkeys in them. The monkeys froze and glared at him with their enormous eyes.

"They breed prolifically," he said, "but they get nervous when they're on display." The monkeys were kept in the lion house basement—there was no room for them elsewhere in the zoo—so assistant director Dennis Meritt could study them; he'd done research on them for years. In a nearby room, there were a number of South American rodents (pacas, pacaranas, and agoutis) of varying sizes, also of interest to Meritt. There were anteaters, armadillos, and sloths as well. Some were there to breed; others were awaiting shipment to other zoos. All of the animals in the basement were cared for by the lion house keepers. If one

of them wanted solitude, it did not find any in the basement, where the mingling of odors and sounds was perpetual.

Jim's first chore of the day was to hose down the cages
inside the building. As he did, the leopards, the jaguars,
and the Siberian tiger all got out of the way.

"They don't like water," Jim pointed out. "Without
stressing them or hurting them, we can direct them with a
hose if we have to."

He turned around and looked at the inside habitat occupied by the lions, Anthony and Chandra. They were not
allowed to join the larger pride outside; the two prides
would do battle. So Anthony and Chandra were kept indoors, in a warm exhibit that kept them sluggish, except
for those rare times when the larger pride was taken inside,
and they were allowed to roam outdoors.

"Discomfort on exhibit," Jim called the arrangement.

He turned pensive as he considered what he had said.

"I'm not in charge here. The senior keeper and the
curator make the decisions. I don't always agree, and I don't
always have any influence."

When he was done hosing the cages, he retrieved the
food that had been delivered for the big cats. In the distance, Ajax, the Siberian tiger, growled.

"Show-off," Jim mumbled.

He carted the food—horsemeat for the cats, and apples,
bananas, celery, carrots, and grapes for the monkeys and
the rodents—from the main floor entrance to the kitchen.

"Clean up and feed 'em," he chanted, with a faintly
mocking tone.

In the kitchen, he kneaded the horsemeat, mixed it with a
nutritionally balanced feline food, and put it in buckets.
Each cat got fed once a day, from two and a half to ten
pounds of meat. (The Siberian tiger could eat more than
that, easily, and occasionally was given more than the
allotment.) Finicky eaters might get a small supplement
later in the day. Twice a week, the cats got bones to gnaw
on, actually horse knuckles.

"Their diet used to be more complex," Jim said. "Chicken, liver, kidneys. They liked it, and it was good for them. But it was simplified three years ago. I had very little to say in it, except for the brand of food to buy.

"They were afraid of salmonella in the chickens. What the cats get instead isn't very chewy or very tasty. But they do seem to like the bones."

The offering of food was the device used to lure the lions inside from their outdoor habitat, to clean it or retrieve a lion that had fallen into the moat. When that happened, the lions above were lured inside, so another lion wouldn't be tempted to jump into the moat, and the stranded lion below was then coaxed in as well.

"Actually, they get a little lonely down there and want to know where the others are," Jim said.

At 9:20 A.M., he released Anthony and Chandra from their indoor exhibit into cages in the isolation area—it required a knowledge of the complex of tunnels and interlocking cages in the building—where he fed them, tossing the meat mixture through a narrow opening in the bars.

Chandra slopped it across the floor, trying to chew it.

"She doesn't have many teeth," Jim noted.

Anthony did better, crouching in front of the meat and licking the mound with his tongue, directing it into his mouth. While they ate, Jim hosed down their habitat. A mouse scurried away from the stream of water. Occasionally, a stray mouse had a confrontation with a lion; the lions played with mice, stomped them, but rarely killed them. Outdoors, the lions preferred pigeons, who underestimated the lions' speed of movement.

In the second indoor habitat, Princess sat at the door and peered through the bars at Jim, working in the other habitat. He spotted her looking at him.

"She's in heat, so we brought her inside to give her a chance to eat without interference from Bernard. He wouldn't permit her to go in to eat. He wouldn't let her go anywhere. Just separating them gives her a chance to eat," he said.

Princess sat in front of a pile of yesterday's food, turned rancid overnight; Jim washed it away. She was among his favorite cats, one of those who might tempt him to extend his friendship. But he wouldn't enter her habitat when she was in it.

"I don't think I'd ever play with her," he said. "I mean, really go in and play with her. She's too strong for me. Even if she were friendly, she'd be too strong a friend."

Princess was sitting against the barred door, with the tip of her nose poking through the bars. Her eyes were on Jim.

"She's waiting for something to happen. Maybe she wants to go back outside with the others. She knows that something will happen, but she doesn't know when."

He enticed her out of the habitat, into a cage area between the indoor and outdoor habitats, by calling her name and clapping. He wanted to clean her habitat; she could exit to the outdoors through a door he opened with a lever.

"You want to get their attention, but you don't want to frighten them. They get used to people's voices, what you might call the form of address. Sometimes, I even make lion noises," he said.

In the main hall, several sparrows raced and chirped in the rafters. It was 10 A.M., and the visitors had begun to arrive in numbers. The young woman who ran the lion house gift shop was counting her money before opening for the day. Outside, the lions and the tigers demonstrated one of their differences. There was a pool of water in each habitat; the lions drank the water in theirs, the tigers bathed in theirs.

For Jim, it was time to clean the outdoor cages.

While hosing down the Siberian tiger's cage, Jim heard a voice behind him. A man was leaning on the rail.

"That's a beautiful tiger," the man said to Jim.

"I have to agree with you," Jim responded.

As Jim moved down the row of cages, the animals retreated, hid, peeked at him, went indoors, as he turned the hose on their cages. Lisa, the leopard, moved her sleek black frame toward the back of the cage. When Jim finished washing it, she moved forward, sat down, and licked the wet floor.

A pair of German tourists paused, then the husband took a photo of the leopard. Lisa opened her mouth without growling; instead, she hissed.

"She's just vaguely bothered," Jim said. "If she were pushed enough, she'd growl."

At his feet, Jim discovered a penny someone had tossed at one of the cats. He picked it up and put it in his pocket. The keepers kept a collection of found coins, and with the money they bought catnip, which delighted the big cats as much as it did house cats.

The day moved along, as Jim's rituals filled the time. He finished all of the cleaning. He opened a door to entice the lions in from outside to feed them. They entered slowly, at their own pace, on their own initiative. Bernard, the male of the pride, was first, and he was hungry. He ate noisily, rapidly, and thoroughly, then relaxed and growled. In the next cage, Sheila nibbled her meat in a more delicate way, slowly. Finally, when all the lions had come in and were secured in their cages, Jim went out to clean the outdoor habitat. He washed the window that enabled the public to get a close-up view of the lions, picked up the gnawed horse bones, and collected feces from those areas the lions had designated for it. They were as determined to mark their territory in captivity as they were in the wild.

When he came in, Jim let the lions line up in the caged runway, then he opened the gate and they raced into the sunlight.

He could hear Anthony banging on the door from his indoor habitat to that runway; he knew where it led.

"He wants to get out there, to be with the females in that pride. Not a chance. Bernard would fight him. And both might lose," Jim said.

Day after day, Jim did much of his work in silence. It was either a kind of channeled brooding or a practiced introspection or a combination of the two. He rarely volunteered to speak, unless he spotted another keeper he knew and liked. When spoken to, he responded with measured replies, editing his own speech before he issued it.

Another keeper stopped him in the main hall, to ask about the death of Satan, the male black leopard who had been euthanized.

"Impaired kidney function," Jim told him. "He wasn't eating, and when he did eat, the kidneys couldn't process it. We were going to ship him out, but we had to alter that plan. We didn't want to send out a crate with a dead animal in it. It was better for him to die here."

The other keeper asked about Satan's age.

"He'd been here longer than I have," Jim said. "Everything that happened before I got here is ancient history."

When his day's cleaning chores were done, Jim went to the basement; he passed a sign that read "Have You Checked Your Locks?" In working with the big cats, safety was a factor always.

"You can make a mistake with an animal you've known well, an animal you think will be friendly," he said. "Beware. They may make a move on you. Especially males," he added. "Animals behave according to their moods, and you can never entirely predict those moods.

"Anthony does what I tell him to do, which is unusual. That's why I think he's one of the smartest. Most of the others don't do what I tell them to do. Some females respond because it's what they want to do, not because it's what I want them to do.

"Anthony wasn't hand-raised, so he doesn't like to be petted. Nevertheless, he responds. Go here. Go there. Stop doing that. He does. When Bernard gets an idea, it's *there*. You can't do anything to stop him except turn the hose on him. Most cats are like that. You can't make them go through an open door.

"Being a keeper is knowing what to do, knowing the routine as well as the animals do. But when they're excited, be careful. There's a lot of control involved in keeper work. I used to get mad when an animal didn't respond. So self-control on my part matters, too. Sometimes I spend two or three hours getting an animal out of a cage. Wait. Go away. Come back. Use the hose.

"At times, there's a reason why the animal won't do what you want it to do. If a male is behaving peculiarly, females won't enter the space that he's in, so you have to isolate him from them. A cat will skip a meal without a qualm if something else strikes it as more important. Sister won't come in to eat if Bernard is roaring.

"The Bengal tigers—at least our pair—were afraid of the dark. They wouldn't come in from outside into that dark back space, unless the lights were on. Finally, we left the door open between outdoors and indoors, so they could explore that space. After that, the darkness didn't matter to them.

"Tigers are more sensitive. They react to smaller things. Noises, subtle changes in the environment. What's normal in a tiger is neurotic in a lion. A lion may notice something, but it won't be upset by it. Not by what would upset a tiger.

"You can't read them by their faces very well either. Most animals have blank stares. Some lions seem to stare right through you, to the horizon. When they're not staring, they're probably sleeping. Cats sleep a lot, which makes it easier for them to be in captivity. Another factor is that most of the cats get used to a routine.

"We once had a leopard who couldn't adjust. She hid between the light fixture and the ceiling in her cage. All you could see was the tip of her tail. She couldn't tolerate people, so she tried to hide from them. She didn't want to be in a cage. We tried her in an outdoor cage. She wedged herself between the downspout and the wall, facing away from the public. You can't reeducate them once that attitude is fixed. A cat that appears mildly neurotic can get better, but that one never did. We sent it to another zoo."

Some of the keepers were upset about the lion that had fallen into the moat. One of them urged opposition to the zoo practice of walking elephants and camels around the zoo. When the cats spotted those large mammals, they grew excited. No one was certain about the link between the walking animals and the confined cats, but the theory persisted in the keeper circle.

Jim Campbell took the theory very seriously.

"That must be a twelve- or fifteen-foot drop," he said. "I've never actually measured it. Once two male cubs pushed their father, Bernard, into the moat. He cracked a tooth, a canine, but otherwise he was OK. Still is.

"Sometimes they just jump in or they fall in while they're chasing pigeons or they just get too close to the edge and slip in. Sure, it's possible that they can be agitated by seeing another animal walked by. The camel does resemble a lion's prey, but the elephant is too large to be prey.

"We had a female lion who fell in after the elephant walked by, but she was an aggressive one, and she might just be bold enough to attack an elephant in the wild. It's not common, but it happens.

"Of course, I remember when the lions used to get worked up when they saw a toy horse pulling a kid's cart. I've even seen them look out there, spot a child, and stalk it."

The days passed, the summer began to fade, relieving the heaviness of the air in the non-air-conditioned lion house. Jim did his job, cleaning, feeding, studying the behavior of the cats.

Late one afternoon, Sister, the female lion, was indoors. Jim approached her cage. Sister turned her massive head toward him; she looked directly at him. She moved close to the bars of the cage and turned her profile to him. He scratched her nose, her ears, her neck as she pressed against the bars, obviously permitting him to give her pleasure.

If she had purred—and lions do not purr—her behavior would have matched that of a house cat with its beloved master.

But the bars were between them, and the similarity, Jim knew, ended there.

FIRST PERSON: JIM CAMPBELL

When I was about four years old, I had an Easter bunny, a

small Easter bunny, a live Easter bunny. I remember looking at it very intently, trying to figure out what was going
on in the Easter bunny's mind. I decided that there was
absolutely nothing going on in the Easter bunny's mind.
And that was my earliest contact with animals. It bothered
me that there was nothing going on in the Easter bunny's
mind. I guess I thought it was a person because people were
treating it like a person. But it wasn't; if I had a tendency to
anthropomorphize, I was disillusioned at a rather early age.

The rootlessness of my childhood was mostly due to my
family's moving a lot. It was usually for economic reasons. I
always thought we were going to better ourselves econom-
ically somehow by making a move. Usually, it didn't work
out that way. So we'd make another one. I didn't feel
particularly rooted in the place that I grew up, which is
southern Texas. I didn't really feel like I belonged there, but
I didn't know where else I belonged. And when I got into
my college years, I think that became part of my quest for
roots, for a sort of self-identity that I didn't feel that I had.
That's probably the reason why—when I didn't do well in
school and discovered I wasn't suited to be a full-time
academic because there was too much competition for
me—I began looking for myself in other ways. Mostly
introspective ways.

About the time that I resigned from the University of
Texas, I started a course of reading on my own. I decided I
would educate myself. At the time I was a very withdrawn
and isolated person. And I knew that that was not normal.
So I spent a lot of time trying to figure out why I wasn't
normal and if it was worthwhile to become normal. I think
I've come to some of the answers, but not all of them. I'm
still searching. I don't think that I'm a career zoo keeper; I
don't think that this is my niche in life.

The military years were a turning point for me. They
provided me with a number of things I had not really
acquired when I was growing up: A sense of the limited
nature of authority or power, of discipline. That there was
a limit to how much I had to do in order to meet the

standards. Before that, I'd always been a perfectionist. The navy taught me simply that there was an objective standard that wasn't one hundred percent, maybe it was only eighty percent. You had to shine your shoes so well to pass inspection, but you didn't have to shine them perfectly.

We were an offshore bombardment unit; we went in and shot at bridges and various troop emplacements on the shore. And we rarely saw anybody, any ships or any enemy troops. I think we were fired at once or twice, from the shore, and we got hit by a shore unit, but it was very minor. We saw that we were engaged in a futile task. There was no way to win that war.

When I got out of active duty after two years, I tried going back to school in California and discovered that it was much more amenable to my temperament to take night courses. And also financially necessary, since I had to find some sort of an income in the daytime. That's when I went back to Texas. I needed to retrace where I'd been and see what that still meant to me and see if there were missed opportunities there that I could pick up on. So I went back.

When I was in California, there was a dog running across the freeway one day, and I managed to clip him, and I was never able to find the dog to find out whether or not I had injured him or whether he'd gotten away or whatever happened. I felt sort of guilty about that for years. And when that would come to my mind, I would think about the fact that I didn't really know anything much about animals at all.

The zoo that was opening in Brownsville was offering a training course for docents; they certified these people to take school groups around and give guided tours. I was working in construction at the time. I finished the course and was certified, about that same time the construction job ended, I didn't have any work, and the zoo was hiring. When I found out they were actually only paying minimum wage, not really enough for me to buy gasoline for my car, then I knew that it was a short-term engagement. But I decided to stay on for the year, get some experience, and at least take that with me when I went where I was going, which by that time I'd pretty much decided would be where I was born, which was the Chicago area. I wanted to go into architecture, but that was frustrating. Then I got the zoo job.

If there's a conflict regarding the management of an animal or a personality conflict here at work, I'll tend to brood about it until I figure out what to do about it. Occasionally, I even dream about the animals. The last dream I had I was in a pickup truck with Bernard the lion, and we were going someplace, and I was saying, "Isn't this a nice treat?" He wasn't talking much, but he seemed to be enjoying it. Other dreams have involved escape routines, where the animals would be out, and I'd have to come and put them back in their cages. I've usually managed to get them back where they're supposed to be. I've never had a dream about being injured by an animal.

There are lots of different dimensions to this type of work. I think you need a basic sensitivity and a willingness to see what the animal is telling you. The animal will usually tell you things through its behavior, which may or may not conform to your ideas about what that animal is like or what that animal is doing or wants to do. I've seen cases in which cats, even cats that are not normally friendly, will come down, approach the front of the cage or the keeper areas, when they are ill. It's not part of their normal routine. They will come down and start hanging around close to the keepers. If the area's inadequate for the animal, the animals begin to show unusual and abnormal behaviors, which may or may not be harmful to the animal. Stereotypically, these behaviors are sometimes called excessive pacing, doing strange things that they wouldn't normally do, hiding in corners all the time.

A cat should have a variety of places to go. If the presence of the public or the routine cleaning procedures didn't adversely affect the cat, and if the cat obviously had and used the various things in its enclosure for climbing, scratching, sleeping, I think that then the cat would probably be well adjusted. Zoos can help animals adjust to confinement.

Zoos can achieve that—and more. Zoos may carry a message to people, that if you like this animal that you see in the zoo and you want to see it continue to exist and flourish, then you'd better get out there and do something to save its habitat, because in the long run, without the habitat, the animal disappears.

Some keepers resist that. They pretend that this animal is like a person, is like a friend. Now, to a certain extent I think it's inevitable. I talk to my animals. I make up little nicknames for them. But I try to leave it here at work. I don't take it home. I don't put pictures of my animals on my wall; I don't regard them as the focus of my life. I think that's a danger. We can develop those sorts of relationships with animals, and they're not healthy emotionally because they interfere with the normal life outside and away from the zoo.

This profession will attract people who have the susceptibility, an emotional void in their lives which they have found that animals can fill. I think it also tends to attract people who have a penchant for collecting things, who like to control, label, classify, keep things in their place. That can be very valuable to a keeper if it means that you double-check your locks every day. People who have a lot of emotional contact with animals, a lot of emotional concern about animals, can use that in a constructive way by being very receptive to the state and condition of an animal, because they can pick up very easily on when an animal is feeling depressed or sick. Point it out to a veterinarian, and maybe something can be done about it.

On the other hand, you can become very callous as a keeper; you can become very controlling and domineering. You can become wrapped up in an illusionistic world, about the animals. And that tends to create a lot of problems. Everybody is supposed to know that we shouldn't project human characteristics onto our animals.

You learn to be a realist. I was nailed once by a black

leopard, soon after I began working the upstairs. I was routinely filling the water bowl on one of the old cages. There was a small protective grill that was supposed to prevent the animal from reaching through while you have the hose close to the water bowl, filling it. And I was trusting, blasé, and just stood there. The cat came down to the water bowl, and I thought, "Oh, well, so what, it can't reach around that thing." Well, the cat reached right around it and put a little hole in my hand. With its claw. I filled out a first aid report, put some iodine on the wound, and a Band-Aid and that was it. It was healed within two or three days. I never put my hand close to a water bowl that way again.

One of our keepers was walking in front of the tiger cage, and the tiger reached out and took her glasses off and left a little scar on her temple. I don't think the tiger was attacking her; the tiger was trying to play with her. There are times the animal will attack whoever is disturbing it. If we're trying to move it or crate it, or do something to it that it doesn't want to do, it will attack. You know in these sorts of situations that most cats will eventually charge.

They don't like to be stared at directly. If they know that they're safe, they know they're behind glass, it doesn't really bother them. But with most of them I've seen, if you come and do that, at least among leopards, they get nervous, particularly if you get something out and start pointing it at them. If they've ever had that experience before—a vet pointing a dart gun at them—they'll react.

The first six months I worked in this building, I was told that there were certain cats that I could pet, and I said, "No thank you," because I wasn't at all comfortable with the idea of petting a lion. Particularly a lion that I didn't know, and in the long run I think that's been justified. Until I know an animal on an individual basis and that animal knows me, I don't even attempt familiarities. There are certain signs. For instance, when a female lion comes in and comes over to the bars, and she rubs against them and turns her back toward me, in that situation she cannot make a move that would potentially hurt me. I know that she's asking to be petted. If she were to come in that same enclosure, stand up on her rear feet and put her front feet up on the bars and open her mouth, I'm not gonna stick my hand inside her nose.

You read their moods by their behavior. When they are feeling affectionate, they will come over and make it known, and if they're just feeling distant, then they are distant, and they walk back and forth. That's when I just do my job and open and close the doors, try not to disturb them, and we get along pretty well that way. I've found that cats really don't like loud, sudden noises. They don't like sudden moves. If you don't do them, on a consistent basis, then the cat recognizes you as somebody who doesn't disturb them. Then after a while you can develop a better relationship with the animal.

Actually, sometimes I think my own reactions are very protective. Protective of the animals. In situations in which I think they're being mistreated or are in potential danger, I get very upset. Which I guess means I have a large degree of emotional identification with some of them. We've had a lot of cats die, and there were cats that have died that I've been fond of, but I can't say that I really felt that as a loss. The only time I would feel much more severely about it is if we're responsible for it. My favorite Siberian tiger was a very nice animal, and she died of cancer, but there was no way that she could have survived. Things like that don't bother me as much as instances of an animal being injured or overly stressed or inadequately fed.

Accidents happen. And I'm not in control of everything that happens in this building. Sometimes curators or other keepers do things that I do not agree with, and sometimes I can make my position prevail and sometimes I can't. I suppose the one I still feel worst about is when the lion named Sister lost her tail. She was anesthetized for a routine operation for putting a birth control implant in. Since it was a routine operation and we were a little short in the building, I didn't stay around all the time when she was coming out of the sedation. She was in a cage that at the time had a rather large crack underneath the door. When they positioned her, unfortunately they positioned her so that her tail was close to that crack. And there was a mistake of putting an old lion, a very aggressive male, on the other side of that door. And that male lion reached through, grabbed her tail, and chewed it off. I had left another keeper there to monitor the situation who wasn't very familiar with the animals, and I was outside doing something else. By the time I got back, the tail was gone.

That is a typical example of how things can go wrong. The people that I left in charge didn't know about the possibility of using a fire extinguisher to drive an animal away. Nobody seemed to know where I was, although I was just a few feet away. They were there, but they couldn't stop it. So I still feel partly responsible for that. And that's the sort of thing that makes me feel very bad.

I've *become* a lion keeper. It was never my obsession as a youth, and it was never my ambition as a keeper. I'm still in the middle of things, I guess. When I first took this job, I took it because I wasn't able to fulfill my architectural ambitions, and this was the best type of job that I figured I was qualified for. So for me it is a job, not a career. But it's a good job. It's a job that I like and that I do well, and that I enjoy doing well. There's a lot of independence involved in being a keeper. Also, it does do some good in the world, maybe not the greatest good possible, but it doesn't do much harm. And it allows me to develop my life outside work, in a number of ways that I've never been able to do before, because it's such a secure and comfortable civil service position. There's a lot less pressure than in private employment, and lot more time off because of our particular system of comp time and working weekends. And that allows me to further my educational goals, which had been pretty well shot for years. During the years that I've been here, I've managed to learn a good deal of elementary music theory and finish a master's degree, and go on beyond that.

This job does provide opportunities, when you're hosing and doing purely routine work, to think about things, other things, in a fashion you might not be able to do with another job that demanded full attention all the time. That's one reason why I do like the job. Another is because it provides a modicum of physical exercise. I need some sort of physical exercise, or I tend to get fat. And it does provide these periods of silence or isolation from other people. If I choose to carry problems around with me, I can brood about them, which I have done, but on the other hand, it also allows me to get clear of them sometimes, just by doing something routine. I find it very, very good that I can make my living doing this sort of simple task.

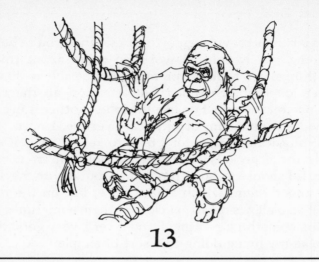

13

HOUSE OF THE APES

When the keepers themselves got around to talking about those among them whose devotion went beyond the call of duty, one name always came up: Pat Sass, the senior keeper in charge of the great ape house.

The forty-five-year-old native Chicagoan genuinely enjoyed the company of animals, at work and at home. She had never married.

"Since I first began to volunteer at the zoo, when I was nineteen, my reputation has gone from that of a promiscuous young girl to that of a lesbian. The truth is that I've never found a man who wanted to compete with the animals for my affection," she said.

The product of a working-class family and the city's public high school system (she went through one year of junior college), Pat had channeled most of her substantial energy to the animals.

She began as a volunteer, working at the children's zoo, in 1961. In 1965, she became a full-time zoo leader, the highest position available for a woman in those days; they were not eligible to work as keepers.

In 1972, a notice of a keeper exam was posted, for men only. It was time for a breakthrough, and Pat was one of the aspirants.

"We had some friendly guys pick up applications for us. We contacted some of the women's lib groups, if we needed them. Then we went down and applied," she recalled.

The bureaucracy at first resisted. A few days later, under pressure, the applications were accepted. When the exam was held, Pat finished near the top of the list. She got the job. She worked at the children's zoo at first, then went on to work in the primate house where, in those days before the great ape house was built, the chimps and the gorillas resided. For eight months, she was in charge of the children's zoo, then abruptly was shifted to the bird house. (At the zoo, keepers could be transferred without appeal.)

"I cried," she remembered.

She was moved again, to the lion house for a year, while the great ape house was being constructed. In June 1976, she joined the apes in occupying it; four years later, she had to face another frustration.

She was given the opportunity to become a senior keeper, but not at the ape house, where a senior keeper was already in residence; she had to return to the children's zoo.

"I've always had a thing for monkeys. I'd dreamed of working in the ape house. But all my friends told me to take the promotion, so I took it. I was lucky. Eventually, the senior keeper spot opened at the ape house, so I was where I wanted to be all along," she said.

By that time, her lifestyle had been established. Unable to find a landlord who shared her love for animals, she bought a house. Her pets would have a comfortable place to live. It was no small matter. Her pets included six cats, two dogs, a lemur, three turtles, a toad, several small rodents, a crow (named Edgar Allan Crow), and an assortment of transient ape babies.

Since that first day as a zoo volunteer, she spent more than twenty-five years at the zoo. She knew curator of mammals Mark Rosenthal when he was a small boy coming to the zoo to photograph the animals at the children's zoo.

At five feet tall, she was not a commanding presence. Her pageboy hairdo had turned to gray. Her eyesight required her to wear glasses, aviator-style. She did not wear makeup. She had become somewhat rounded in the years since she first appeared at the zoo; the word *plump* applied. But she had not slowed down. Her manner was pleasant, open, friendly, never overbearing.

On one typical summer day, she arrived at the great ape house—in a co-worker's car—carrying a small creature wrapped in a blanket. It was a baby chimp named Susan. Susan was two months old and weighed less than six pounds. Pat has assumed control of Susan's life since the chimp was born. In her office, which contained a pair of incubators, Pat removed the baby clothes with which she had dressed the chimp, changed the chimp's Pamper and put her in one of the incubators. By 8 A.M., the chimp was on her back, eyes closed, with her arms wrapped around a stuffed monkey her own size.

"Her mother just doesn't like her children," Pat said. "She's abusive to them, sends them to day camp on day one. So we pull them."

After making certain that the chimp was sleeping peacefully, Pat turned to her chores for the day. They would keep her busy. But unlike many keepers, she had the benefit of working in a modern building.

The great ape house, just beyond its eleventh year, was largely underground, lit by massive skylights above ground level. The apes would sleep more in winter and less in summer, thanks to that natural light. At the center of the building, within the large glassed-in areas for the apes, areas fitted with ropes and pillars holding climbing coils, was the inner service core. Visitors circulated along an outer circular pathway; the keepers worked at the center. The animals were in between.

There were three communities of apes. The chimps and

the gorillas had originated in Africa; about half of them had been born at the zoo. The orangutans were from Asia (Sumatra and Borneo).

In the chimp group there were eight animals, including the male, M'Chawi, 9; Donna, 10; June, 22; Kibala, 7; Shauri, 19; Vicki, 16; and two just months old, Akati and Susan.

The twenty-one gorillas existed in three family groups, led by males Otto, 19; Frank, 21; and Koundu, 12. Among the members were females Bassa, 10; Benga, 16; Debbie, 21; Helen, 27; Hope, 4; Makari, a few months old; Kisuma, 11; Kowali, 9; Kumba, 17; Lenore, 18; Mumbi, 24; and Terra, 8. The other males were Bebac, 3; Brooks, 4; Gino, 7; Joe, 1; Joe-Ray-K, 10; and a newborn, Mokolo.

The orangutans comprised a four-animal group: two males, Ray, 7, and Stanton, 13, and two females, Tanga, at 37 the oldest ape in the house, and her daughter, Batu, 1.

From the central kitchen, Pat could, at any moment, spot what most of the apes were doing. It was important to win their cooperation, to work out the rules with them. Male gorillas, for example, preferred women keepers; men were considered competitors. To clean a habitat, the keepers had to tempt the apes to vacate it; that was done with oranges, sweet potatoes, apples. The apes' fondness for sweets could do the trick.

Pat did not underestimate the intelligence of the apes, particularly the chimps. She knew that chimps and humans were 98.4 percent similar in their DNA; the gorillas were almost as similar, the orangutans not far behind.

"Chimps have the average intelligence of a four- to six-year-old kid," Pat noted. "Chimps are the extroverts of the lot."

In one of the holding cages just off the kitchen, Shauri, Pat's favorite chimp, was relaxing. Pat had raised her from infancy. She was a sickly animal, but when it was necessary for the vets to obtain a blood sample from Shauri, they could do it without tranquilizing her. With Pat beside her to comfort her, Shauri permitted the vets to apply a tourniquet and draw the blood. It was not a procedure the vets would even attempt with most of the zoo animals.

"Bring your cup over," Pat shouted at Shauri.

Shauri dropped off the shelf on which she had been sitting, with a plastic container in her hand. She held the container against the bars of her holding area.

Pat poured iced tea into the round plastic container. Shauri drank it, then tapped the cup against the wall of the cage. She wanted more.

Pat filled another container with canned fruit salad, unlocked the barred door and handed it to Shauri. Shauri handed Pat the empty iced tea container and took the fruit salad.

It was a special relationship. Most of the animals were fed with food placed in their habitats; bananas were handed out. The kitchen was filled with boxes of greens, carrots, potatoes, hard-boiled eggs, and more. Some animals, like Shauri, were given treats.

Shauri banged her container on the wall again. The fruit salad was gone. Pat was slicing apples for all the apes; she handed a slice to Shauri.

Everything was proceeding on schedule. Each day the cages were cleaned, hosed down, and the windows washed. Breakfast was served early in the morning, then snacks— including a monkey chow pellet food—at ten. Milk, nonfat enriched milk, was given once a day, and the main meal was served at 3 P.M.

Five keepers worked in the three-story building, including the outdoor habitat. No fewer than two keepers, no more than five, were on duty. Only a night keeper for the zoo checked the building after midnight.

While Pat worked in the kitchen, Shauri gently scratched her forehead and sat in her cage, staring at Pat. Pat cut a large slice of cantaloupe and gave it to the chimp. A few minutes later, Shauri reappeared at the front of the cage; Pat handed her a slice of potato.

"In her mind, she thinks she's getting extra goodies," Pat

said. "All that happens is that I hold it out of her feeding later."

Behind the wire mesh in a habitat on the curve of the core nearby, with a view of the kitchen, a pair of gorillas glared at Pat while she continued to slice and chop.

She smiled at them.

"They get plenty of good food. They don't have to worry about predators. They get the best medical care. Not a bad life," she said.

Caring for apes made demands on even the most zealous keeper.

"It's a bummer when you lose one of them," she said. "Even when you've done all you can." Nine years ago, when Shauri gave birth to a son, Pat had to teach her how to care for it.

"I sat in the cage with her," Pat recalled. "We go back a long way; when she first came here from Africa, she was a year old and weighed ten pounds. When she had her baby, she let me cut the cord, but she wouldn't let me touch the baby. She wasn't hostile, just protective. So we gave her a mild tranquilizer. It just made her yawn a lot. She wasn't being an attentive mother. We knew we could leave the baby with her just up to seventy-two hours, that's the limit, and it was getting close. So I went into the cage with a bottle of formula. I couldn't get it to the baby. Shauri kept reaching for it. My patience was thin. I just wanted to feed the baby, to buy time for Shauri to take charge.

"I didn't think. I just said 'no,' and I hit Shauri. I hit a hundred-and-eighty-five pound chimp. She cried. Then she put out her hand to me, for reassurance. I touched her and gave her that reassurance. It's a matter of mutual respect. In her area, you play by her rules. You let her know what you're doing.

"I picked up the baby and put it on Shauri's nipple. She tried to push the baby away. I said 'no' and held the baby while I pushed its head onto Shauri's nipple. It worked. She raised that baby herself."

In the background, as Pat told the story, Shauri began to make noises, loud, shrill, forceful. She wanted more food.

"No," Pat yelled at her.

Shauri went silent.

"She bit me once," Pat remembered. "Just a nip. I was so upset that I cried. She was upset, too. She went into a corner; I went into another. Then she came across the room to me and put her arms around me and whimpered."

At 10:15 A.M., during the keepers' morning break, Pat poured herself a cup of iced tea and took a small bottle of formula out of the kitchen refrigerator-locker for the baby chimp upstairs. She went up the spiral staircase that connected all the floors of the building.

In the keeper area (her own office adjoined it), she warmed the bottle in a microwave, picked up the chimp, and fed it. The baby clutched one of Pat's fingers in her own long, slender fingers.

"As they get older, the ones I hand-raise keep their relationship with me. They may be feisty with others, but not with me," she said. Hand-raising meant keeping the ape at home every night from as little as two weeks to as long as four months, until the animal slept through the night. At the zoo, that was not possible; there was no one on duty in the building at night.

After the hand-raising was done, however, "you have to be able to let go, and that's not easy," she added. "It makes a better animal, better adjusted. You try to give them the security and love that their mother would have given them. Their mothers cater to their every whim. Some of them are worse than I am in spoiling these kids.

"I know, too, that once they learn what 'no' means, you can discipline them. They do understand. They're very fair. I guess that trust and faith goes both ways."

As Pat sat at a table in the keepers' room, she saw a familiar face peering at her through one of the slots in the wall. On the other side were the gorilla habitats, and Debbie, one of the older gorillas, had used a rope to raise herself to that slot, from which she could peer in and spot some familiar human faces.

Debbie's large hand encircled the bar that kept her from reaching into the room; she tilted her head to get a clear view of the room. Finally, bored by her own eavesdropping, she swung away. At a nearby slot, Kumba, another female, peered in at the keepers and made a sound—smacking her lips to make a cork-popping sound—that gorillas do not make; Kumba had learned it while growing up in the children's zoo. Debbie returned to her slot, and both gorillas became spectators.

Pat had brought treats from home for Shauri: rice cakes, Cran-Raspberry juice, and a sugar-free cherry-flavored drink mix. Shauri enjoyed all of those, and there might be leftovers for a few other favored apes.

"It's all low-cal," Pat said. "Shauri likes them, and we don't have to feel guilty about giving them to her." She had brought vitamin tablets for the chimp as well.

Pat sat beside Cathy and Richard, the other keepers on duty, both young and industrious; the other full-time keeper was on vacation, and a part-time keeper had the day off. The three on duty would work hard; Pat would have to contribute as a keeper as well as the supervisor of all the keepers in the great ape house. But first, there was the usual small talk.

Pat smiled and told the others, "I had a dream last night. I dreamed that a group of young foxes were nipping at my hand until my whole hand came off. The zoo staff said it was my fault, and the staff was coming after me. Weird. Most of us dream about animals coming after us. I dream about the staff coming after us."

A hairy arm was beating at the wall slot, patting the inner wall. The three keepers took no notice; they discussed their assignments for the day, the moving of animals that enabled them to clean the habitats.

Certain apes would have to be tempted out of their habitats. Koundu, a male gorilla, resisted at times, but Pat had the solution.

"He loves the smell of pipe tobacco, so sometimes we go up there and smoke until he comes in. I don't even smoke, but we keep a pipe and tobacco around just for him. He follows the scent, tries to pull the smoke toward him. Nine out of ten times, it works. Maybe it's because he came here from England."

When the meeting ended, Pat checked the baby chimp in her office; it was asleep in its pale blue and yellow pajamas, its head resting on the stuffed monkey, its hands clutching a small blanket.

Then she made her way up to the top level of the building, where hard hats were mandatory to avoid concussions from low-hanging pipes. She went to that level to help Cathy extricate a baby orangutan, Batu, from her mother Tanga's grasp.

Batu hadn't been drinking her milk, seemed enervated, and had diarrhea; the keepers wanted a zoo vet to take a look at her. But Tanga hadn't been cooperative. In a caged tunnel used to divert apes from one location to another, Tanga, a very large, round, rust-colored mass, was determined to protect her daughter.

Within the caged tunnel, there were gates the keepers could open and close, to trap apes inside. Batu was small enough to slip under one of those gates and seemed interested in doing just that. Once under it and out the other side, she would belong to the keepers. As she attempted to slide through the low opening, Tanga grabbed her and pulled her back. Cathy and Pat tried to distract Tanga, who would not be distracted. She hated women and spat at Pat.

Cathy went down to the kitchen and returned with a treat, slices of cantaloupe, to bribe Tanga. She showed the plate of fruit to Tanga, who responded by clutching Batu. Slowly, she reached out and took a piece of the fruit, while guarding Batu at the same time. When the baby got loose momentarily and headed toward the gate, Tanga seized her and pulled her back.

"Some days you're smarter than they are, and some days you're not," Pat said.

Cathy agreed.

"With these guys you may get only one chance," Cathy said. "If you don't take it, the mother knows what you're up to. And what could have taken ten minutes takes four hours. We'll just give her a break and take it as it goes. We could stick her with a dart and send her to sleep for a few minutes, but she's pregnant again, and that might put the fetus at risk.

"Batu will sneak out. She'll know when to try, when her mother is distracted. The truth is that Tanga happens to be a great mom, and you can't punish her for doing just what she should do."

Batu was likely to respond to Pat's urging, eventually. While Tanga had raised her own child, there was a period of time when Pat had been a surrogate. Tanga had bumped the baby's head, causing a skull fracture. After that, as Cathy recalled, "Batu was poking around at the top of the orangutan habitat, and she discovered a small open space near the ceiling. The moment Batu stuck her hand through the opening into the adjoining habitat, one of the chimps grabbed her left arm, bent it backward, and bit Batu just above the wrist." The vet, Tom Meehan, sutured the wounds, but x-rays revealed the fracture of three bones in her arm; it was repaired, and a cast was placed on the arm. Pat had taken care of Batu throughout her recuperation.

Then it was determined that Tanga's milk was not sufficiently nutritious, so the baby had been pulled, and Pat took it home. After that, the mother and daughter were reunited. Batu had gotten to know Pat, so it was possible that Pat could influence her, assuming that Tanga would permit it.

"Most animals that are hand-raised don't do as well as they would have with their mothers. Primates are the exceptions. They like us. We give them an unlimited amount of nutrition. Of course, you don't want them to be obese. But you can give them what they need," Pat said.

Cathy and Pat resumed their effort to trick Tanga. She was not agitated; the large orangutan never lost control. Cathy gave her a cough drop, a treat she loved. While Tanga sucked methodically on the cough drop, Batu edged toward the gate. Tanga was not fooled; she rushed over and retrieved Batu.

The two keepers agreed that it was time for a waiting game. They were confident that they would succeed.

Back in the kitchen, Pat checked on Shauri. She opened the lock on the door to the holding area and entered it. Shauri reached out and gently put several fingers into one of Pat's pant pockets.

"There's nothing there," Pat told her. She proceeded to clean the holding cage, as Shauri watched her. "It's like going into a teenager's room and seeing all that stuff under the bed," she said.

Shauri proceeded to untie Pat's sneaker. Pat let her. Shauri removed the shoe and played with it, relacing it as a small child would. Pat hopped out, locking the gate behind her, to get another shoe; she'd retrieve the original later.

"She has a passion for buttons and zippers, too. Luckily, I don't embarrass easily," Pat said.

She handed Shauri a rice cake; Shauri devoured it.

"All this keeps Shauri from getting bored," Pat said.

Shauri retreated into a corner, holding the sneaker in her left foot while she attempted to lace it. Pat resumed her cleaning. She handed Shauri a small brush dipped in soap-suds. Shauri rubbed it against a dirty wall.

When she finished her other chores, Pat went back into Shauri's cage to get the shoe and some tools that Shauri had been playing with.

One of the tools was a window squeegee on a long handle. Using only her fingers, Shauri had unscrewed the blade of the squeegee and had removed the rubber insert. She had done it in minutes. It did not surprise Pat. Locking Shauri's cage, she looked back in admiration.

"A very sweet animal." she said, "A very special chimp."

Late that afternoon, Cathy and Pat did succeed in distracting Tanga with assorted treats. Then a long strip of burlap dragged across the cage floor tempted Batu to slip under the gate. Tom Meehan obtained a blood sample from the baby orangutan, and Batu was placed in a playpen-cage near the keepers' room, a home she had occupied before when Pat had cared for her.

The next morning when Pat got to work, she plucked Batu from the playpen and put her on her lap. Attired in her Pamper, Batu had her arms around Pat's neck and was sucking vigorously on Pat's chin. Pat pushed her away and offered her a baby bottle filled with Kool-Aid.

"What's better, kid, my chin or the Kool-Aid?" she asked Batu.

Batu looked undecided, moving from one to the other.

Eric, the part-time keeper, commented, "It looks like a miraculous recovery to me."

"I love you," Pat said to Batu, "But enough is enough."

"She's bonding with you now," Richard, the keeper, noted.

Pat extracted a chocolate chip cookie from a new package, and Batu nibbled that as well.

Downstairs, in a holding cage adjoining the kitchen, not far from Shauri's cage, Lenore, the gorilla with an amputated hand and a nasty temperament, could be heard grumbling. It was the day for her dental checkup and an x-ray of the arm. Whenever she had been tranquilized in the past, she had caused a commotion; she inspired unrest among the gorillas in the habitat when they heard her howl. The last time she had expressed her displeasure, some of the gorillas were moved to panic, and one of the young gorillas emerged with a broken arm.

This time, Pat would avoid that sort of misfortune by separating the other gorillas from where Lenore was sure to howl.

In the keepers' room, the other keepers sat around watching Pat care for Batu. Two gorillas, Kumba and Debbie, appeared again at the window slots, clutching ropes and peering in.

"Trying to mooch again," Cathy said. "They know that this is where we eat. They hear us and come up and slap the wall to let us know they're there. At lunchtime, Frank comes up, too, to see what we're eating. We'll give him a rice cake or some shredded wheat. He thinks it's special because he came up here to get it."

Pat got up and attempted to move around the room, but Batu clung to her left leg, creating a limp. She picked up the orang and carried it to her office.

"Tear up the joint. Have a good time," she told Batu, putting a box of toys beside the animal. Batu held her leg with one arm and the bottle of Kool-Aid with the other.

"OK, punk. OK, junior miss princess," Pat said to Batu. "It's time to go into your cage." She carried Batu to the toy-filled playpen-cage. "No yelling and screaming and carrying on?" Pat asked. "Good."

Pat went to the kitchen area to check on Lenore, who was sitting on a shelf in her cage. Pat cautiously opened the door and tossed straw on the floor below the cage. It was to ease Lenore's fall if she fell to the floor when she was darted later. Pat was careful; it was not like her friendship with the chimp Shauri. When she finished dumping the straw, she visited Shauri nearby.

She fed Shauri a few monkey chow pellets, which Shauri munched quickly. Pat tried to be careful in feeding Shauri; the chimp was diabetic, and the vets wanted to regulate her diet. Pat's affection for Shauri was, at times, in conflict with the vets' wishes.

When Shauri finished the pellets, Pat handed her a spoon and a container of yogurt. Shauri placed the spoon in her right hand, dipped it into the yogurt, and slowly ate it.

"You're lucky we like you," Pat said to Shauri. "They don't have yogurt in the jungle."

Tom Meehan called to say that Batu's white blood cell count was slightly elevated; a minor infection might be present. The vet prescribed antibiotics, which at the very least would prevent a secondary infection from developing.

A few minutes later, Tom and Peri and their entourage arrived. Lenore, a veteran of battles with the vets, recognized Tom. She bellowed: a declaration of fear and menace.

Tom's role was to prod Lenore with a long rod, to get her

down from the shelf; once down, she would be darted by Peri.

Tom prodded and Peri aimed. Lenore howled mightily.

Peri fired the dart gun, and the flying syringe hit Lenore in the side. She shrieked loudly, then retreated to a corner of the cage, making belching sounds. Her motions began to slow down.

Lenore had a history of being slow to react to the anesthetic, so she was given a larger than normal dose. After fifteen minutes, while the vets and the keepers stood back and watched, she remained relatively alert. Peri picked up the dart gun again. When Lenore saw it, she ducked and put an arm across her face.

The second dart went into her upper arm. It worked. Lenore went down, unconscious. The vets and two summer externs, helped by two of the keepers, got Lenore onto a litter and out of the kitchen to the hospital van parked outside. A dentist waited for Lenore at the hospital.

At the other side of the kitchen, watching it all, Shauri calmly munched a carrot.

Cleaning Lenore's cage was left to Pat. It was a mess.

"The first thing to go—at least in primates under sudden stress—is their pucker," Pat said, grimacing from the odor in the cage.

"Shit is my life. That'll be the title of my book if I ever write it," she said, laughing. "Without it, I'd be out of a job. The next time they build a building for the apes, I want flush toilets for everybody."

She resumed cleaning, as a mouse dashed across the kitchen floor, scared out of a drain by the activity.

"Every day's a routine day, right? A piece of cake. No problems," she sighed. "It never works like that."

She went upstairs and fed the baby chimp, Susan, who was wearing her pajamas. The chimp's wide-eyed, wrinkled face looked up at Pat; she fondled its thick black hair and large ears, then put a blanket in one of its hands.

"As long as she's got her blanket, she's OK," Pat said. "Take it away, and she's a problem." She carried Susan back to the incubator in her office. Next it was time to comfort Batu again.

On the wall in the keepers' room, a happy-first-birthday card to Batu was on display, signed "Mom Pat."

She opened the playpen, and Batu leaped into her arms and immediately fastened her mouth to Pat's chin. Her desire to suck would not be thwarted, and Pat did not attempt to deny her the pleasure, although Pat's chin had taken on a bright shade of red. Pat pulled her off, put her down, and removed her diaper, to discover that the orang still had diarrhea. She picked Batu up, took her to the bathroom sink, and washed her bottom, then put a new Pamper on her. She carried Batu down the stairs to the kitchen.

Batu quickly resumed sucking Pat's chin. Pat stared at her with obvious affection. "Whatever you've got, I'm gonna get," she said. "Do you care?"

Pat's respite with Batu ended abruptly. The vets and their student externs, along with the dentist, showed up with Lenore, asleep on a litter. Their work was done, and it was time to return Lenore to her cage next to the kitchen. "Where has the time gone?" Pat wondered; several hours had passed while Pat tended to her work.

The vets and a male keeper slowly slid the litter into the cage. As they did, Lenore awakened prematurely.

Both vets, the dentist, and the keeper were suddenly faced with the prospect of dealing with Lenore, who had started to behave wildly, shrieking and thrashing. A wave of anxiety passed through the room. Lenore weighed 240 pounds.

Pat, across the kitchen from the tumult, clutched Batu and froze.

The dentist fled toward an outer door. He spent most of his time treating humans, not gorillas, and was not curious about the temperament of gorillas. Peri slipped out of the cage. So did the keeper. Tom wrestled with Lenore briefly, then emerged, his face red. Lenore leaped onto her shelf.

She did not want to escape; she simply wanted to be alone.

The dentist, who had fled into an outer corridor, returned. Pat, holding Batu, sought to change the mood.

"Show the dentist your pretty teeth," she told Batu.

Batu opened her mouth and displayed her teeth.

The crowd in the kitchen laughed, including the dentist. What he didn't know was that by blowing gently on Batu's mouth, Pat got the reaction she wanted from the orang.

In the background, Shauri, unaffected by the noise, was banging her plastic container lightly on the wall of her cage. Cathy took a metal pitcher of water and moved toward the cage. Shauri didn't respond; she gazed blankly at the pitcher. Pat watched, then got a container of Kool-Aid and approached Shauri. Shauri pushed her cup beyond the bars for Pat to fill.

Slowly, the crowd vanished; the keepers went back to their work. Pat held Batu and walked up the stairway to the keepers' room. She sat down with Batu in her arms. As she did, Batu moved forward and put Pat's chin in her mouth. Pat kissed Batu's forehead; they were linked.

First Person: Pat Sass

Like the old cowboys say, I rode on a horse before I could walk. My dad was a pigeon fancier, and he raced and showed homing pigeons. When I was real little, we had a cat, her name was Tabby, a tiger-striped cat. I used to carry her everywhere with me. Back then we didn't know about spaying, so she constantly had kittens. My mother's favorite story is about the time I'm carrying this cat under my arms, and she is ready to have babies any second. I insisted I wouldn't take a nap unless Tabby went with me. Of course, while I was asleep, Tabby proceeded to have her kittens, and Mom got everything all cleaned up. And I woke up and not only was there Tabby, but there were all these little kittens, too. Then when I was about ten we got a dog, named Puddles for the obvious reason.

So I've always been interested in animals. When I was old enough to cross the streets, I used to walk about seven blocks to the veterinarian's, Dr. Higgins, who was real instrumental in getting me into this kind of work. I used to go to Dr. Higgins's animal clinic, and I would just sit in the waiting room. That's all I did. He was wonderful about it.

When I got older, when I was graduated from grammar school, I worked for him as a kennel person, cleaning up the cages where he kept the dogs. When I was in high school, I had graduated a little bit more and was the receptionist. He saw the interest that I had, and he encouraged it. My mom and dad were instrumental too, because I was one of the kids in the neighborhood who always said, "It followed me home; can I keep it?" I didn't know who the neighbors were, I didn't know them by name, but I knew where Sheep lived, and Jackie the dog, and Fluffy the cat. I ate Milk Bone dog biscuits as a kid; I thought they were pretty tasty. That's why I still have strong teeth. Never give an animal anything you wouldn't at least try yourself. That's the kind of person I was. As kids, we would come to the zoo during the summer. I had always been fascinated by monkeys, apes, and I'm sure it was Tarzan movies I used to watch as a kid.

After I graduated from high school, I started at junior college, and it must have been summer and I decided to come to the children's zoo. They had Bambi the deer, and Flower the skunk, Walt Disney–type things. I talked to one of the keepers and asked if there were summer jobs available. And he said, "It's kind of late. They're all taken, but we do have a volunteer program." And he said, "You have to talk to the director of the zoo," who was Marlin Perkins. So I stopped in at the office and made an appointment to see him. He could not have been nicer. I'm nineteen years old, very impressionable, very naive kid I guess, a late bloomer. He asked, "Besides dogs and cats, what animals have you had and what kind of success have you had with them?" He let me come in as a volunteer.

There was a lot of hard work involved. In all the years I've been here, everybody says, "Wow, do you have a nice job. Would I like to do that." Because they come in, especially in the children's zoo, they see you playing with the baby chimp or bottle-feeding a baby lion. But they don't see you at eight o'clock in the morning, when you're cleaning up diarrhea or vomit. Or you have to make up fifty plates of food, and you have to remember whose plate goes where.

On my first day in the children's zoo, I walked in, and this baby gorilla came from nowhere and sat on my foot and wrapped her arms around my leg. That was my introduction. I was a volunteer for a year, and then I became a part-time zoo leader. Now, back then a zoo leader was a woman. It was an hourly position, five days a week, six hours in summer, and then in winter they worked weekends and holidays. "Zoo leader" was just a term that was given to the women who worked in the children's zoo, because back then women did not work in the main part of the zoo. Between '61 and '72 there was one civil service exam held for keepers, and one of the qualifications was that you had to be male. Nobody really protested it then.

I was a part-time zoo leader, then I became a full-time zoo leader. I worked eight hours a day, had all the benefits that the keepers had. The keepers and zoo leaders did the same job at the children's zoo, but we were not getting as much money. What really got some of us thinking was if a new keeper, a man, came in, his very first day on the job, we taught him his job. Yet because he was a keeper and we were zoo leaders, he was our boss. That didn't make sense. It wasn't Pat against the system; it was a few of us girls against the system. I don't think it was the feminist movement. It was the fact that we felt that we could do the same if not a better job than the men. We didn't feel that just because you're a man you could do a better job.

In '72 they held another civil service exam. Again, one of the qualifications was you had to be male. Eight of us filled out applications, had the picture taken, the whole thing, and went down en masse. We had contacted a few women's groups; we were ready to contact radio, television, anyone we needed. If I can do it the easy way, I will. If we had to do it the hard way, we were willing to prove a point. After a little stalling, they accepted our applications with no problems. And when I took the exam, I think there were a hundred and eighty people who took it. And out of that, there were eighteen jobs open. Out of all of the people that took it, a woman placed number one. I was number nine, which I thought wasn't bad, and I got my job.

When I look back now, about my life with animals, sometimes I think I get a little carried away and get too involved. People have said, "I'd rather have somebody just come in and do the job than someone who comes in saying, 'I love all the animals.' " Loving all the animals doesn't cut it. You don't always think of what's best for the animal. I contradict myself a little bit because I treat a baby orang just like a person, and I treat the apes like people to a point. But I think it's more like I become one of them, than trying to make them one of me. I become the orang mother, the chimp mother, the gorilla mother, the opossum mother, the pig mother, whatever animal I'm raising at the time. Not necessarily that I'm trying to make them human. I've got scars on my body to prove that even the ones you trust the most, on occasion, will bite you.

To me, a good keeper is someone who cares. Someone who is not a clock watcher. When I worked in the monkey house, it would take me forty-five minutes to get in and scrub one cage, and scrape crap off the shelves, climb up into the runway and get in between the bars; somebody else might take the same time and do fifteen cages. Of course, it sounds good, organization sounds real good. It's a Wednesday, I know there are going to be five people, I'm at home having breakfast and think, "Well, we're going to have five people, so today we're going to hang ropes in the orang cage. We're going to scrub this particular area. We're going to make sure we do this and that." I get into work, right? First the phone rings, and it's "How many people do you have?" "Well, all of us are here today." "Well, fine. The lion house is short; we need you to send somebody over there." "Oh, OK." So we're down to four. Hey, we can still

hang ropes, we can do this and that, we'll just have to
hustle a little bit more. And then you go upstairs, and the
baby orang doesn't look too good. It's nothing we can put
our finger on, but she doesn't get up to greet us. She
doesn't try to reach for my fingers like she would normally.
Her eyes don't look as bright as they should. So you call the
vet. This is what's going on. An animal gets sick, has to be
knocked down, taken over to the zoo hospital. Again, it
isn't something that happens quickly; it takes planning.
We've got to try to separate this animal out before the vets
come over, because once the vets walk in the building, it
gets telegraphed around the entire building, from chimp to
gorilla to orang, back to gorilla again, "Hey, the vets are
here, we're all in trouble."

We have a chimp mother, Donna, that doesn't like kids.
If you leave them with her, and we've tried, she gets
abusive with them. She just doesn't want anything to do
with them. And we have to raise them. It's either that or
within three days you're going to have a dead baby. So
with Donna, when she has a baby, we know we have to pull
it. With the other ones, we'll give them the benefit of the
doubt that they'll take care of them. The ones that we
really worry about are the younger mothers, the first-time
mothers among the chimps, the gorillas, the orangs. A lot
of it is an innate behavior, but a lot of it is learned. Luckily
in this building now we can keep them in family groups, so
they see creatures being born.

The classic story that I tell is when we had Kumba, who
was the first born at the zoo, in 1970. Her mother Mumbi
took care of her for thirty-five, thirty-six days. And then
she started doing strange things to her. Mom would lie up
on the top of the bars and swing the baby. And we're
going, "She's gonna drop the kid! We're going to lose the
baby!" Now we see them do the same thing, but we've had
twenty-some births, and we know that's normal, a piece of
cake; don't worry about it, it'll be fine.

There's a story that has been going down probably since
zoos began, since Noah. If you give a screwdriver to a

group of chimps, or even one chimp, the chimp will throw it around; he'll make noise with it, he'll try to eat it, and then will throw it out of the cage. Put it in with a gorilla, and the gorilla will look at it, examine it, sniff it, maybe taste it, nyaa, doesn't do him any good, throws it out. Give it to the orang; the orang'll look at it, and all of a sudden it'll be gone. You think he threw it out, but five days later he'll be out of his cage, because he's used it to take the cage apart. They're more mechanical.

We say that the chimps, gorillas, and orangs have the average intelligence of a four- to six-year-old kid. They can do what a four- or six-year-old kid'll do. Well, they also can survive a heck of a lot more. I mean you can take a baby chimp out of the wild, away from its mother, put it in our environment, and it grows up. Granted, we're nursing it and taking care of it, but it grows up pretty well. I mean, how many humans can you take, other than Tarzan, and throw them in with a group of apes?

I talk to these animals. I think it has some effect. Years ago, way back when I first started, when I didn't know anything, I was working with the first chimp that I ever really worked with, Wesley. When I first started working with him, he would play with me. He was sent to us from the Los Angeles Zoo. He was mother-raised, and he was taken from his mother, put in a crate, and shipped here. Petrified. I would sit with him and play with him; I was his play object, I would tickle him, but he would not cling to me. I didn't know what to do about it. I was sitting in the cage with him one day, and we're playing. One of the keepers came by and as a joke pounded the side of the cage. Scared me, scared the chimp. The chimp jumped into my arms; our instinct was to just grab one another and hug. I never had any trouble handling him after that. He needed the security. I was his security. That's what I do with these guys, I play mom with them. I'm their mother; they can come to me. I have a fine line drawn—don't cross it, or I'll get mad at you—but if you need security, you need reassurance, you come to me.

I work on their mind because I'm physically not strong enough when they get older to do things with them if they didn't have the respect. With Wesley, I'm cleaning his cage one day, and he's sitting on the shelf. He's not supposed to get off the shelf. When I finally finish washing the walls and the windows, I throw the shavings in and put the straw in, and somebody comes up and starts talking to me. While I'm talking I look around, and ten, twelve feet away are the rags that I had been washing the windows with, and Wesley's still sitting on the shelf. In the same conversation, I say, "Oh, I forgot the rags. Wes, could you pick them up and bring them here?" Wes gets down off the bench, picks up all the rags, walks them over, and hands them to me. That's the first time something like that ever happened. My mouth fell open.

Now, I don't even know why I turned and said that to the chimp. It was just in passing. It wasn't like you say to a dog, "Sit down, heel, stay." Wes knew his name, he knew "rags," "come here," whatever the words he knew, but he was able to put that together, and he got down, picked up the rags, and brought them to me.

Chimps have, they claim, thirty-two different sounds that mean things. Again, you work with them. You teach them, you show them something, you say, "This is a cup, this is a pen or pencil, a rag. The chair, sit in the chair," that type of thing. Having worked with them over the years, I know that if a chimp sees something and he's looking at it and he's going, "Ooo, ooo, ooo," he's inquisitive. If chimps are upset, they have temper tantrums. When she was in the children's zoo, June the chimp had the best temper tantrums I've ever seen. Yet, to show how smart she was, if she started a temper tantrum, you could stop her just by touching her. If you moved your hand, she'd start up right where she left off. If they get what they want, they stop.

Sometimes they will point. Vicki the chimp, if she wanted something, would point to it, and if we missed it, she'd point again. Shauri, when she wants a drink, will take her cup and rattle it on the bars. You learn what the sounds mean, you learn the greeting; because you deal with them, you pick it up.

Gorillas are not as vocal. They cup their hands and beat on their chests. Males and females will do it. I do it better on my belly; I have more of a belly. Some if it is innate behavior, some of it is learned. They see the others do it, they do it. You can yell because you're mad, or you can yell because maybe you just feel good.

I can imitate chimps, I can do a few of the gorillas. The orangs have these real high-pitched sounds I can't imitate. They don't make as much noise. Chimps and gorillas live in communities, in groups. Orangs in the wild usually don't. The males are by themselves, and then they come together and breed. Females will have their offspring, maybe one or two offspring, and then as they get older, they chase them away, so they're just with an infant. Orangs tend to cling a lot more; they play mainly with their mothers, because that's all they have. The little chimps will play with each other, they have their peers, they have their brothers and sisters, their elders, they've got cousins.

When I had the orang at home, I couldn't do anything. Unless she was asleep, I couldn't get up and do anything without having her right with me, or screaming because she wanted to be where I was. Did you ever try to wash dishes when you've got a baby orang? You're trying to vacuum or dust or do anything. Get up to change the TV station, thank God for remote control. An orang is that clingy.

To clean the ape house, we hose everything down through big drains. Then we pull up a basket in each drain. We empty it and then drop it back in.

Cardinal rule number one is, if there is an animal in the habitat, you don't stick your fingers through the mesh. It's just common sense. You try to be aware of that constantly, but some days are better than others. One particular day, my mind was not where it should have been. Frank was in the habitat with the rest of the gorilla group. And, being short, I had to step down into the basket opening, and I didn't want to lose my balance. Without even thinking, I grabbed the side of the mesh on the cage. The next thing I know, I say, "Ouch!" and Frank is there. I'm convinced he could have taken three fingers off and handed them back to me if he wanted to. All he did was apply a little pressure and snicker behind his hand. He used his teeth, but it was just kind of like, "Gotcha! You weren't paying attention, but I was."

We got Shauri the chimp from Africa when she was not quite a year old. She was very, very sick. As a matter of fact, when they took her out of the crate, they thought she was dead. She was malnourished; she had roundworms that were a foot long coming out of her. She had pneumonia. She never really should have lived. And I said, "She's not going to die." I basically nourished her back to health. I had her at home with me. She's one of the nicest animals you'd ever want to meet in your life. As she got a little older, we started doing tea party. We'd bring them out, and they'd sit at the table and chairs and eat. We had anywhere from one to six chimps. This was in the outside section of the children's zoo, and it was summer.

On one particular day, we get the table set up, the dishes are there, the cereal's on the table, we've got kids, because the chimps are all real good. I know if I let the four chimps go ten feet away from the table, they'll all go sit in their chairs. The kids are sitting in a kind of semicircle on the grass. So I let all the chimps go. Three of them run up and jump in their chairs. Shauri doesn't; she goes and sits with the kids, in the grass. And I go, "Hey you!" She turns around to see who I'm talking to; it couldn't be her, you know. I go: "You—the hairy one!" She just flips back, still looking, moving backward, and sits in the second row and kind of crunches down a little. As I've always said, you could do it one of two ways: you can get mad at her, go over, spank her, make her go sit down, but then you might upset the kids. Or you make a joke out of it. And I go, "You, Shauri, we can't do tea party. After all, you're the star of the show. Could you please come up here?" With that, she got up, and she came and sat down.

You have to be emotionally involved to do what I do. The biggest problem is letting go. Batu, the baby orang, is the perfect example. I love that hairy little red kid. She's the second orang that I've worked closely with. I've worked with lots and lots of chimps, quite a few gorillas, but orangs I really hadn't had that much experience with. I know that she's an orang, I know I'm a people, and I know in order for her to be happy, she's got to be an orang. Then we decided to reintroduce her. Emotionally, it's a tough thing. Logically, I can understand that she should be with her mother, she should be an orang, this is the best thing for her. Emotionally, not being able to cling to her little body, have her suck on my chin, I had a difficult time with it. I really wasn't making her human, I was trying to be that orang mother, I was trying to do what orang mothers do.

I try to do the best for them, whatever type of animal they are. Maybe I get a little bit more emotionally involved than I should. I've cried over a lot of chimpanzees, like the first chimp that I ever worked with, Wesley, who was shipped to another place. I got really upset about that. Donna's first baby that I raised, I had at home for eleven days; it lived for three weeks and died at my house. It was real hard to take. I've had a couple of gorillas that we raised, that were doing well, they were about a year, a year and a half old. But they were hit with salmonella, and both of them died. You get upset, you cry. When we first put Batu back, I missed her. I got tears in my eyes, and my voice cracked. The people here are real supportive.

There's always the risk of being attacked. I know there's that remote chance that it will happen. I am not consciously going to do anything stupid. I'm not going to push a two-hundred-pound chimp and say, "Hey, I want you to do it because I'm telling you to." I don't. When I go in there, it's with respect and mutual affection. I don't think anything of it if I go in with Shauri and she throws her arms around me and puts her mouth on me or something. I know that that's a greeting. I will do the same thing to her. I will bite her on the neck like she's biting me. And I feel that I've been around and have read enough and have had enough experience that I know what's going on. When she was real sick, we pushed her a little. Again, her reaction nine out of ten times is to try to get up and walk away from us.

But if you're going to do something, like try to get blood from her without knocking her down, you give her an escape route. You don't stand in front of the door and say, "Well, we're going to do it, or you're going to have to go through me." I mean that's stupid. But you go in and say, "OK, look, this is gonna hurt, but this is what we have to do." I talk to her. Now, I don't know how much she understands, but nine out of ten times I've been able to get across what we want. She's known me all of her life. And there have been times I've been off and they've wanted to take blood pressure or to get blood or to do something, and they have tried, and she will not let them. Yet when I come in and sit with her, and we talk about it, and I explain what we're gonna do, she has let me do it.

When I first started as a zoo leader, I don't know that I ever thought of being a keeper. I saw myself as a ninety-year-old lady with a cane, walking toward the bunny pen: "You want to pet a bunny, little kid?" Now, I've been here half my life. I really think of doing what I'm doing. I enjoy doing what I'm doing. Sometimes people can get to me, the public will at times, but I enjoy it. I can get as much pleasure in raising a baby squirrel, a baby pig, as I can with a chimp or a gorilla. Really—if in my mind I commit to it. I've got animals coming out of my ears at home. I get up at five-thirty, and I do a whole run at home before I come here. The lemur that I've got, I hand-raised him. He was two ounces and nine and a quarter inches from the tip of his nose to the tip of his tail, and now he's full-grown. He's not as big as normal lemurs; he's a runt. But, I'm the only one now who can touch him. He's my commitment. Lemurs can live twenty-some odd years; we've got a few years to go yet.

You commit to things. I'm not married, I don't have children. These are my kids. I really do know I'm a human and that they're animals, but they're my family. I've had problems in relationships with men because they feel threatened by what I do and by my commitment to the animals. I don't know, maybe if I was ever really, as mother would say, truly in love, I would give all this up, but I don't feel I should have to give all this up. I would like to find somebody I could share it with. And I know there are people somewhere out there. But, boy, it sure beats pumping gas in a gas station. I'm dealing with living things that have emotions, that show they care. They're sometimes a lot more honest than people are. Keepers I work with, acquaintances, friends, who are nice to me to my face, as soon as I turn my back, they're talking about me to someone. The animals don't do that. They have their likes and dislikes, and they let you know exactly what those are.

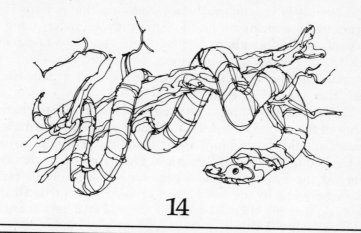

14

The Reptile Rap

Art Maraldi liked to talk: "Yeah, we've had people attack animals. We had some Galapagos tortoises in a big fenced-in area. People would climb the fence at night, probably kids with pipes and bricks. They'd smash the shells. . . .

"I remember a woman who was working as a temporary, years ago. There was a small baboon, and she'd carry it on her shoulder. It was kind of tame. Well, the baboon was a male, and he'd have an erection, and he'd stick his erection in her ear. When the director saw it one day, he screamed, 'Get that animal out of here!' . . .

"Gorillas are majestic. It's an aura. There's something about them. In the wild, they don't kill animals, they don't eat meat. Whereas chimps are much like humans; they'll kill a monkey and have a party eating it. . . .

"Elephants are intelligent. Any animal that can live in excess of fifty years has a lot going for it. . . .

"A human you've known for fifteen years, you can't predict what he'll do. How can you predict what a wild animal will do? . . .

313

"There was a true, authenticated situation where two tigers were mating in India, and they were crossing a stream, and an elephant barred their way. It was during the mating season, remember, so when the elephant wouldn't let them cross, they attacked. One got on its back, the other clawed its eyes. . . .

"Some palsied kids, with helmets on, in wheelchairs, came to the zoo. Their doctor asked if we had any animals the kids could touch. I took Henry, a chimp. We went to one of the kids, who was all excited. Henry went to the kid, hugged the kid, and kissed him on the side of his face. Then he went to the next kid. I cried. He went to all the kids and hugged them and kissed them. I still have tears in my eyes when I think about it."

Art was one of the zoo's amiable eccentrics, one of its amateur historians. He collected lore, firsthand and secondhand, polished it, and passed it on. He could be bluntly realistic, then disgress into matters of cosmic destiny, flights of mysticism, considerations of "auras" and such. Animal behavior always commanded his attention, along with the employment histories and sexual inclinations of the zoo staff.

As a keeper at the reptile house, he was conscientious, informed, and concerned.

Art began his career at the zoo in 1972, when he was thirty-six. He had tried other jobs, various exercises at paper shuffling and administrative drills that he couldn't tolerate. Compared to his years at the zoo, that part of his life seemed empty, boring, wasteful. He had a bachelor's degree in biology (from Northeastern Illinois University) and decided to put it—and his curiosity about animals—to work at the zoo.

Art was a short, 140-pound packet of energy. Whether he was at the zoo or at his modest home, which he shared with his wife, a public school administrator, and his teenage daughter, he kept busy. At home, he collected hobbies: mounting butterflies and moths, building framed insect environments, listening to music (from the Carpenters to

Bach), working with Indian beads, and gourmet cooking.

At the zoo, he spent his time with the reptiles, but he had worked in nearly every section of the zoo during his more than fifteen years there. His interest was intense enough to inspire him to spend ten years doubling as a docent, volunteering his free time to teach zoo visitors about the animals while he was a full-time keeper.

Unlike some keepers, he believed that he had an obligation to learn. He read zoological journals and every other form of information about animal behavior that he could get his hands on. In debates with curators, he had emerged victorious. He had come to grips with the role of the keeper, its rewards and its frustrations. He never thought of changing jobs.

His dark hair was thinning, and his eyesight needed the help of glasses, but his enthusiasm remained. It was not daunted by having to work in the old, decaying reptile house; he took that environment for granted.

Early one day in late September, Art was on duty on "the hot run," the area behind the main-floor exhibits that housed the poisonous snakes. As he unlocked the gate leading to the run, he noticed something.

"Someone left-handed locked the padlock," he mused. On hot run duty, he had to pay close attention; he was aware of the deadly nature of the creatures that inhabited it.

He checked the run, walking slowly from cage to cage, looking for anything that might seem suspicious. He found nothing to disturb him. On a wall, a large sign read, "You Can Be Sure! When You Are Up to Your Ass in Alligators, It Is Hard to Remember That Your Objective Was to Drain the Swamp."

He walked down to the basement of the reptile house, to change into his keeper uniform. He greeted Caryn, another keeper, who was busy feeding tortoises and a batch of doomed chicks which would become meals for reptiles.

Caryn told him that Joel Pond, the lab technician at the

zoo hospital, wanted a stool sample from a snake who had recently been donated to the zoo. Art phoned Joel.

"Another stool sample on that snake? The eastern indigo? You've had two already. Well, he just defecated in his water bowl. You want that stool sample? Yes. OK."

"He's looking for parasites," Art told Caryn. "You know, as long as people explain things to you, you don't mind going out of your way to help them."

He walked up the stairs to the main hall, where visitors would gather later in the day. He blocked the view of the Gila monster cage with a large wooden board; he would be feeding them later, and he didn't want visitors to see him do it.

He stopped to peer at the African rock python.

"He doesn't like rats or chickens," he said. "I'd better find him a rabbit." Other snakes would eat minnows, mice, even dead snakes; a king cobra would eat any kind of snake. The python preferred rabbits.

Art went downstairs again and found a frozen rabbit in a food locker. He carried it to the hot run, to permit it to defrost by the end of the day.

His first order of business was to clean the case that held a puff adder, a potentially dangerous snake in a cage marked in red, HOT.

The adder had defecated, and the newspaper that lined the heavy fiberglass case was dirty and had to be replaced. Art carefully unlocked the two padlocks that held a clear acrylic panel on the front of the case and slid the panel open, exposing the snake to the outside world.

The adder's tongue flicked out rapidly, but the snake did not resist Art's effort. He used a long pole with a metal hook on the end to lift the adder out of its case and into a larger metal container. The adder hissed. It was three feet long, in shades of gray with a flat head, expressionless.

"He's upset. He's very upset," Art said. "He doesn't like being moved. I wouldn't either, if someone came in and moved me out of my house."

He put on a pair of rubber gloves and cleaned the adder's case.

"They don't shit often," he said. "Once every few months. They process a lot; they make maximum use of everything they eat. Eat a little and get the most out of it."

He put the case on the floor and hosed it, then wiped it with a nontoxic antiseptic.

"The big snakes can come off the hook. Using it on some of them is asking for trouble," he said. "But if I use the tongs instead, I have to grab them around the neck, and I could strangle them. No thanks. With the big snakes, you need two people, at least, because you never know what the son of a bitch is going to do."

He put clean newspaper on the floor of the adder's case, slid the acrylic panel into its slot, and moved it across, leaving a small opening. He hooked the adder in its metal cage, lifted it cautiously, and put it into its clean cage.

"He doesn't want to be out here. Now he's in his home. Some snakes are curious when you move them, and they want to get out. When they do, they're actually frightened by me. That's why they may strike out. Snakes will bite the hand that feeds them.

"In general, however, the animal just wants to take things easy, that's all. And I'm the one who has to disturb it. Which means I've got to be up, constantly aware. By the end of the day, I'm the one who's pooped."

The Asiatic cobra, a sleek and lethargic snake, was next on Art's list. There were several of them in a cage that Art had to clean.

"They're slow compared to rattlers," he said. "But they strike all the time. They fling themselves at you. They'll come up high and sway and get you with a face shot. Snakes don't have to be coiled before they strike. That's bullshit."

The cobras, aware of his invasion, began to hiss and make a growling sound. He disregarded their objections and hosed the cage, being careful not to intimidate them with the stream of water.

"They see me as a threat. But they're not sophisticated. Not like a gorilla, which recognizes the keeper. These snakes don't know who I am."

He had to clean an old concrete tank with a hinged wire mesh top. Inside it, three western diamondback rattlesnakes were resting. When he opened the top of the tank, the three created a loud chorus of rattles.

Art chanted to himself, "Be careful, always. Expect the unexpected."

He hosed the tank with the snakes in it, watching them. But a drain in the tank seemed to be blocked. Art attacked it with a plunger, while he continued to keep an eye on the snakes. They rattled loudly. He told them to shut up. They didn't. To work on that drain, he concluded, he had to remove the snakes from the tank and put them into a large, wheeled plastic container. Deftly, he lifted each snake out of the tank with the long hooked pole; when he had them in the plastic bucket, he put a cinder block on top of it to restrain them.

"I have no time to fuck around with you guys," he said. "You know, sometimes I wish I had an easy day. It never happens with reptiles. Something always comes up."

He spoke to the drain: "Come on, you son of a bitch, flush out. It's these minor jobs that take forever. Just a normal day on the hot run. What did you do at the zoo today, Daddy?"

The drain wasn't working, so Art had to trace the line through adjoining tanks; they were devoid of snakes but were filled with odds and ends that other keepers had stored in them. Art pried some of that out, tossed it on the floor, and went to work again with his plunger. In time, he found the point at which the drain system was clogged, and he cleared it.

"Well, at least the rattlers hadn't eaten. If I used a hook then, they'd puke. So would I, if somebody picked me up with a hook after I ate."

He was ready to put the rattlers back into their own tank.

"Here we go, kids. It's Uncle Artie. OK, boys, who wants to be first?"

He hooked one snake, and it slithered off the hook, back into the plastic bucket.

"Better than if it fell on the floor," he said to himself.

"Now, you're going to be really pissed," he said to the snake, after he had hooked it. "Who's next?"

He hooked a second snake. The third one began to crawl out of the container.

"Don't act stupid," Art shouted at it. He hooked it, and all three were back where they began the morning. Art was sweating.

"There's a certain tension in moving a snake you know can kill you," he said. "There is that tension all the time around here. But you can't panic. A rattler on a hook can strike, so you can't let it get out of control. I'm sweating. You sweat when you handle the hot stuff. One thing for sure, it's not like working with a bunch of pissy birds. When I get a little weary, I go out for a walk, a little break. You don't want to get tired and get careless."

He walked over to the case holding the newly acquired eastern indigo snake. It was lively, wriggling swiftly around its case, its head poking against the mesh on the top of the case. It was not a poisonous snake, so Art relaxed a bit, slid open the acrylic panel, and reached in. He held the snake by its neck while he removed its water bowl, with the feces in it.

"A nice snake," he said. "That's why they're endangered." He put the feces in a lab specimen container and gave the snake a bowl of fresh water.

"You never quite get used to it all," he said. "You can't because when you think you know what can happen, something you didn't expect happens. You can watch a gorilla's eyes and know what it's going to do. Or make a good guess. A snake won't tell you anything with its eyes. There is no real warning with them. So you try to think of what might happen. Think the worst and be up for it, all the time."

His nerves were a bit frayed, despite his familiarity with the work he had done. It was time for a therapeutic break.

Art picked up the stool sample and a couple of packages he wanted to deliver. He had made a mock military medal for one of the secretaries in the main zoo office; sewing was another of his hobbies. He had bought a baby gift for a park food vendor, a new father and an old friend. He strolled outdoors, through the coils of visitors clogging the zoo. He delivered the presents. He stopped at the zoo library, to collect some science magazines for his daughter's school class. He dropped off the stool sample at the hospital lab. He scrounged a few grapes at the commissary. And he exchanged mock flirtatious banter with an attractive docent he knew.

He walked back to the reptile house; it was time to feed the Gila monsters. The Gila monsters ate mice.

Art tracked down several large, flat cartons marked LIVE ANIMALS FOR RESEARCH. The cartons contained tiny, live white mice; other cartons contained rats. All could be heard scratching within the cartons.

Art opened a carton and methodically plucked out the mice, one at a time, using metal tongs.

He removed a mouse from the carton, held it at shoulder height, then threw it to the floor. Those that did not die instantly died within seconds. When enough of them were dead, he bagged them and headed for the rear of the Gila monster cage.

He opened the cage and jumped into it, along with the eight Gila monsters—medium-sized lizards and poisonous ones. It was hot in the cage; an overhead sunlamp warmed the sand and the cactus in the cage. The Gila monsters were pink-and-black or yellow-and-black. They did not move to greet Art or to escape from him.

Art began to feed them by hand; with the tongs, he reached into his bag, extracted a mouse, and tried to force it into the Gila monster's mouth. Several of the Gilas were reluctant to eat; Art held them at the neck with one hand and pushed mice into them with the hand holding the tongs.

He wanted them to eat on their own, but he had to be sure that each Gila had its fill—two or three mice each— and he couldn't be sure of that if he simply tossed the dead mice into the cage. So he proceeded from lizard to lizard, pushing mice into their mouths. Several crept through the sand with just long tails protruding from their mouths.

"You've got to wait until the tail goes down before you offer another mouse," he said. "They're not too bright."

Time passed, and Art began to sweat profusely. His glasses began to slip down his nose, and he had to push them back up repeatedly.

"At least they won't come after me," he said, commenting on the Gila monsters' deadly bite. "I'm too big." The Gilas moved sluggishly at best. Art concluded that they had eaten what they wanted to eat; further prodding would be futile. All of the Gilas seemed sleepy.

"At night, they move like greased lightning, believe it or not. They're nocturnal."

Later, he would feed rats to some snakes.

"You don't feed a snake the way you feed a Gila," he said. "Shit, it'll kill you. I just throw the rats to the snakes. Rats, mice, birds, lizards—snakes will eat any of them. We feed them chicks because chicks can't fly. We used to feed them sparrows, but they did fly, and it got out of hand."

He was sweating and tired, and the day was barely half over. It was time for lunch. He liked to cook and occasionally would bring food he had cooked at home, to be heated in the convection oven he kept in the hot run. On this day, however, he was too exhausted to cook. He walked out of the reptile house, over to one of the vending stands, and bought a packet of M&Ms. He sat on one of the benches in front of the reptile house and ate the M&Ms slowly, one at a time.

Clarence Wright, the curator of reptiles, walked by on his way to lunch and waved at Art. Art smiled.

"He's secure in his job," Art said. "And he knows the problems; he's been there. Many zoo administrators I've come in contact with don't know a damned thing. I consider Clarence to be a class act. He's willing to listen to your ideas. He'll explain to you why he wants this done. He lets you vent your frustrations. If you're a good administrator, and he is one, you know it's the keeper, the laborer, who does the work. You shine when they shine."

In his uniform, Art was recognized by visitors. They

brought their questions to him, and he answered them with courtesy and kindness. He was particularly attentive to small children.

He watched several of them race in front of the reptile house and he smiled.

"Zoos are for children," he said. "If you don't love kids, you shouldn't work in the zoo."

He got up and went off to feed the rats to the snakes.

FIRST PERSON: ART MARALDI

I've been at the zoo almost sixteen years. Crazy things have happened. People are interesting. In the early part of my work at the zoo, we had experiences right outside the gate and even on the grounds, where people, cultists, would sacrifice goats, roosters, chickens. These are not poor people doing this, because poor people would eat the animal. Then we had two mute swans in the zoo rookery, and they were pinioned, which means they couldn't fly at all. Now the male's very aggressive during breeding season, and a big male swan can break your legs with his wings. They're very dangerous, so you have to be very careful. Yet someone climbed the fence, probably at night, and stole both birds. Stole them. Now what I find amazing, what I think is terrible, is that you have to have a market for something like that. And the only place you have a market is someone with a private lake that can accommodate swans. So we're talking about this individual who had an order for two swans. The guy who bought them is worse than the guy who took them.

Last year in September, the wolves already had their winter coats. They were full. But they had very little fur on their legs. That led me to believe that it's going to be a windy, cool kind of winter, very little snow. Because wolves in any storm situation tend to stay outside; they don't like to come into the den area. They will lie down, but in doing so they keep their legs under them. So since they're running animals, if there was going to be a lot of snow, they'd have a lot of fur, but they don't want to overheat. So it turned out last winter we had a lot of wind off the northeast and very little snow. The snow leopards will tell you how the winter's going to be. One year we got a leopard in from Buffalo, New York, for breeding. He came into Lincoln Park in October or November. His coat was twice as thick as on our snow leopards. We had a mild winter, and they had a hell of a winter in Buffalo that year. So he grew his coat based on the assumption that he was going to stay in Buffalo. He had no way of knowing he was going to be transferred. I mean, that poor guy was panting all the time.

Look at the animals. If you see the squirrels burying peanuts in November, it's going to be a terrible winter. If they eat them, it's going to be mild. So this is how you can tell some of the things about animals, what's going on. You can observe them.

You cannot always predict why an animal will do something. The record for an animal jumping in the *Guiness Book of Animal Records* is a tiger jumping eighteen feet to pull a man out of a tree. And tigers are notoriously bad jumpers compared to leopards and jaguars. So you don't know why the animal did it. Maybe the animal had a bad day; maybe it had a bad toothache or something, you just don't know.

They tell you snakes don't by and large swallow their prey headfirst. There were four guys out hunting in Sri Lanka, and a thunderstorm ensued. And they probably weighed about a hundred and twenty, a hundred and forty pounds, short-statured kind of men, and one man ran under a clump of trees, the other three ran under a group of bushes. After the storm abated, the three called the fourth, and he didn't answer. They went over to the trees, and they saw a thirty-one-foot reticulated python with a bulge in him. Their friend's hat was there, and his sandals. They killed the snake, they opened him up, and their friend had been swallowed feetfirst.

They say snakes have to coil before they strike. That's

not true. They can strike many times from any position. I've had cobras throw themselves right off the ground at me. You just can't predict. You don't know what the animal is going to do; that's only in the books. Anything can happen at any time.

There was another situation which just amazed me. It was kind of sad. A young Doberman got loose. This Doberman came running into the zoo, and the people were running after him, trying to capture him. He apparently didn't want to be captured; maybe he was going to be reprimanded, who knows, he's a puppy, you know. He came running in, and he came to the wolf compound, the outdoor area. He apparently smelled wolves, and being a young animal, not understanding the ramifications of adulthood, he thought that was a safe area. He jumped in there. It took the wolves less than a minute and a half to dismember and eat the Doberman. So to a wolf, a dog is not the same thing. With any of these predatory animals, you have to be careful.

Animals have their idiosyncracies. You have an animal who's incarcerated, you've got to help him if you can. You don't give him maid service, but on the other hand, you do what you can if you know he is a nice animal. Take the anaconda, Yolanda. You open her door, she could be hungry, but if you spray a hose on her, she'll move away. On the other hand, the reticulated python, you open his door, he may not be hungry, and he will try to grab you if he can. He'll strike at you if he has the opportunity. So he's not a nice animal. Yolanda's a nice animal. Her motives are strictly food, nothing to do with you. If you're doing something foolish like you get too close, she might just react without knowing. But if you give her an opportunity, she'll know what's going on, she won't try to do anything. That's not to say you're going to go into the cage with her, but on the other hand, the reticulated, you know, from the time you open that door, if he has a chance, he's going to try to grab you. That's what I mean by nice or not nice.

There was a story about Mike the raven. He would talk

all the time. He'd say, "Whaddya say Mike, whaddya say Mike?" One July evening, it had been very hot, and all of a sudden a high-pressure system moved through Chicago; it got very cool, and there was actually fog along the lake. And it dropped to the sixties. The zoo cop that had been here was ill, and they sent a policeman named Michael, his first name was Michael, and it was his first time at the zoo. Mike the raven was in a cage down by the old duck yard. We also had some peacocks in that yard, and it was the mating season, so the males would call, and that call in the middle of the night can scare the hell out of anybody. Well, the cop heard that—he was just walking around, he heard that noise—and he thought it was a woman being attacked. So he ran down toward the area of where he was hearing it, and he had his gun out, and it was foggy, and meanwhile the cocks had seen him and stopped calling. And as he's walking, he goes past Mike the raven's cage, and Mike is right there, and Mike says to him, "Whaddya say Mike?" And the guy nearly had a heart attack on the spot. Nearly blew away the raven. That actually happened, and it was funny as hell.

There was a tragic episode with a German shepherd. A keeper on the bear line, outside, looked behind him and saw a shepherd charging him. So he jumped over the railing. When the dog charged him again, the keeper slammed a gate, so the dog was locked between the guard railing and the bars. Mike the polar bear, who had looked like he was asleep, suddenly came to the front of the cage and stood up with his paws up on the inside of the bars. Now, all these animals know to a thirty-second of an inch how far they can reach beyond their barriers. I don't care if it's a python, a polar bear, or a tiger. They won't make a move until you're within range. The dog spying the bear standing up got real aggressive, growled with his canines bared, and went for the bear. The bear—imagine, you're talking a twelve-hundred-pound bear—can't get much of his paw through there, but with just one deft motion slapped the dog's muzzle, knocked it right off, and it went about eight

feet down the line. The dog went down in shock immediately. The bear then pulled the dog through the bars like
you pull a fat bag of potato chips through a little slit, all at
once, breaking his bones. Then he ate the dog; there wasn't
enough left to block a drain. That was early in the morning.
Then, at two-thirty I guess he ate a big pile of meat and
about twelve big fish. But the tragic thing was this guy
came looking for his dog at eight-thirty, nine o'clock. He
seemed to get a kick out of his dog out biting the hell out of
someone. Well, his dog had never met a polar bear.

A monitor is a carnivorous lizard. The biggest lizard in
the world is the Komodo dragon, a monitor from the island
of Komodo off Sumatra. They can be ten feet long, weigh
three hundred pounds. They use their tail like a whip;
they're very adept at using it, and if you got hit in the face,
you'd have a welt for a couple of weeks. They would take
the tongs right out of your hand with it. And they also have
a dirty bite; that's how Komodo dragons bite, kill their
animals. If they bite a deer, grab a deer by the leg, at dawn,
invariably the deer gets away with lacerations on the leg,
but by dusk it dies of blood poisoning. The condition clears
up once you get a Komodo dragon in captivity, because he's
fed clean meat. They eat a lot of carrion in the wild. I've
read in journals that researchers who've studied the Ko-
modos are deathly afraid of being scratched, that's how
pathogenic they are.

We had this monitor in the back tank, one of those
concrete back tanks, and he would always try to get you—
very aggressive animal, very defensive. So one day I'm
working the cage, and sure enough, he whipped his tail.
And I jumped back, recoiled, but not fast enough, and he
knocked my glasses off my face, and they fell, bounced off
the cage onto the floor and broke. I sent in an incident
report and a request for compensation for frames. The
word came back, the park district doesn't pay for frames. I
said, "It happened on the job, and it was an animal." So this
guy proceeded to tell me that for a dollar and a half I could
get this kind of cord I could put on my glasses that'd keep

my glasses from falling off. I said, "Yeah, but if you're working with an orangutan and he grabs your glasses and they don't come off, he's going to take your head with them." He said, "Oh, I didn't think of that."

We had another male polar bear, it wasn't as big as Mike, its name was Alfie. Alfie was very adept, and he loved squirrels. People used to throw popcorn and peanuts and crap like that, not realizing polar bears will go after sweet things but really they're basically meat eaters. He would lie down in the middle of the cage, with his arms stretched out, and he had his one red eye open. And in the middle where his paws were stretched around, there'd be peanuts and things. The squirrels would come in, and they'd try to go for the peanuts. As they kept coming closer and closer, each time he'd let them get closer and closer, and then all of a sudden he'd take his paw and go gwiisssh. And then he'd pick up the hairy pancake and would eat it. He was really good at it.

Keo, the chimp, had some idiosyncracies, too. One time he caught a pigeon in his cage. He meticulously plucked all the feathers out, then he was running it around like a little windup toy in the cage. While it was alive. He didn't want to kill it, he wanted a little toy.

15

BIRD WATCHING

Kathy Brown was the senior keeper in the bird house; her responsibility extended beyond that building to the water-fowl lagoon, the flamingo dome, and the zoo rookery as well. She cared about birds, understood them, and could not imagine her life without them.

It wasn't always so.

Kathy, at forty-six, looked back on a life that had taken several courses before delivering her to the zoo. She was born in Moline, Illinois, but spent her preschool years living with her family in Nebraska, before returning to Illinois, to Peoria, where she attended school.

Her parents were divorced; there were no funds for her to attend college. She got a clerical job in Chicago with Time Inc. and spent more than ten years with that publishing conglomerate. As she approached thirty, she feared being frozen in her job; she quit and "bummed around for eighteen months." After that, she got a job as a school bus dispatcher, a job she remembered as offering "no money and no future."

She heard about an exam being given for keeper jobs at the zoo. She took it, but she "didn't sit around and wait" for the results. She had never been a zoo volunteer, although she did have a fondness for animals.

"I never thought of working as a zoo keeper. It wasn't my big dream," she recalled. She continued to work as a bus dispatcher. Then she got the word that she had passed the keeper exam, and in 1975 she joined the zoo staff.

She grew to love the work. In 1987, she was promoted to senior keeper. During her twelve years at the zoo, she had spent all but seven months—working at the farm—with birds.

A short (5'1"), chubby, natural blond with blue-green eyes and a calm, reasoned demeanor, Kathy had lived with the man in her life for ten years; they shared their home with three cats. In her spare time, she took college courses at various local schools: English, Russian, art, music.

She drove to the zoo, arriving well before 8 A.M. On one cool fall morning, she began her day by visiting a pair of barn owls obtained from the Cincinnati Zoo. The owls, Alba, a female, and Spartacus, her brother, were in adjoining cages in the basement of the bird house. Kathy looked at them admiringly, but did not speak to them; she was not given to fits of anthropomorphism.

The two birds stared at her intently, moving slightly from side to side. Their feathers were brown and white; their faces were outlined with a brown line, as if drawn by a mask maker. They were members of an endangered species and had been acquired for use by the education department.

They were birds of prey. Kathy's simple definition: "Anything that hunts live food and nothing else." The owls did not look threatening; certainly, Kathy did not fear them. When she was confident that they were untroubled, she moved on.

She had to feed a seventeen-day-old Nicobar pigeon, whose mother had been found dead in the bird house ("bad kidneys," Kathy called it) when the son was only ten days old. She mixed a bowl of Gerber high-protein baby cereal and brought it to a holding area upstairs where the Nicobar, a small iridescent blue-green bird, was caged. She opened the cage, but the bird did not move. Inside the cage, she had placed a small mirror and a doll—an attempt to remind the young bird of its origins.

"The mirror is to help him retain a sense of visual identification, so when he returns to the group, he'll know who he is and who they are," she said.

She fed the bird using a syringe, simulating the way the mother—or father, because fathers feed their young, too—would have fed it. The bird accepted the meal calmly.

"At times, I wish he'd bite me and hate me, so I can be sure he'll adjust when we put him back. I want to lose him. He's not a pet, an imprinted animal. An imprinted animal is not a true member of the species. I don't appreciate having to hand-raise them. Natural parents are so much more efficient. I worry that he's going to lose a piece of his personality to us.

"I want to toss him out on the floor in our free-flight area and hope he reverts. An imprinted animal is an aberration, and it can be abused by the nonimprinted birds, with their pecking order. It has to learn the behavior that will make it compatible with the other birds."

In nearby cages, several American kestrals (also known as sparrow hawks) glared at her. Common in the city, they were federally protected birds of prey. One of them was a one-year-old male, who would be released after being retrained to return to the wild, in an area south of the city. Another, a female, had a damaged wing and would be retained for display by the education department.

It was time for Kathy to walk around the main hall of the bird house before the visitors arrived.

In one of the glass-and-tile cages, she spotted a superb starling, a beautiful blue, white, and rust-colored bird. It moved effortlessly. But it had only one leg.

"That happened eight years ago," Kathy said. "It got tangled in the foliage here and tried to break free. Its legs are fragile, and in its panic, it broke one of them. The vet amputated it. But this bird is highly adapted to flight, and it moves quite well with one leg by flapping its wings."

As Kathy watched, the bird did just that.

It was time for her to serve the insect-eating birds a snack of meal worms. With a metal pie plate filled with the small, squirming worms, she went from cage to cage, unlocking a panel in each and tossing a handful of worms to each group of birds.

"They don't have strong nutritional value, but they're useful in fending off stress. Birds that eat insects like live food. It gets them excited, entertains them. It's an early meal before the main meal," she said.

When she had distributed the worms, Kathy grabbed the long hose that ran the length of one run and began to clean the cages. The birds flew away from the steam of water, not in fright, but to observe from a distance.

"They respond to a routine," she said, "when I hose, when I feed them. Some of them can separate keepers from the public; they know the difference. When they're nesting, they're hostile to the uniform, because we invade their privacy. A few have actually tried to hit me when I encroached on their territory."

She hosed and talked. At the far end of the spacious hall, in a wide, open area, Sammy, a salmon-crested cockatoo—a large white bird with touches of salmon-colored feathers—sat sternly on his high perch, watching her.

"Hello!" she yelled at him.

There was a long pause, then the sound of the cockatoo. "Hello."

"Some of them do get to know you. Me, that is," Kathy said. "But most of them live as they do in the wild. They're not tame. They're not pets."

In one large cage, ten noisy blue-crowned conures—green parrots from South America—flew to the upper corner when Kathy intruded with her hose. They had been seized by federal authorities from an importer caught exceeding the number of birds he was authorized to bring

into the United States. The government allocated the birds
to the zoo temporarily. Kevin Bell, curator of birds, didn't
want them; soon they would be shipped to another zoo
that did want them.

As Kathy moved along the run, the birds flew away from
her and her hose, chirping at her in a language she could
not translate.

"Birds are territorial," she said. "Give them food, companionship, housing, and they don't want to get out. If
they have an appropriate flight space, they are at home."

The conures were making loud noises, summoning
Kathy's attention. She looked at them.

"You can try to train parrots, but I think that they react
reflexively. You can teach a wild bird to perch. But there's
just too much anthropomorphism with parrots. Sure, a
parrot trained to perch will perch. It may also attack the
hell out of you. A wild bird is a wild bird."

As she cleaned the cages, Eddie, one of the park district's
experts on flora and landscaping, entered with two of his
laborers. A short, balding, congenial worker, he was, at
sixty-two, a veteran of many years at the zoo and a longtime friend of Kathy's. They chatted about a plant to be
removed from the bird house and a few trees to be planted
in the free-flight area. When they were done with their
conversation, Eddie walked over to Sammy, the cockatoo.

Although Sammy preferred the company of women to
men, Eddie was an exception. He petted the bird, who
tolerated the petting.

"I'm one of the few men he likes," Eddie said proudly.

When Eddie and his crew left the building, Kathy walked
over to Sammy.

"When he's feeling nasty, he bluffs and pretends to bite
you. But he doesn't bite down, really bite. He loves attention. He'll scream and yell when he doesn't get it, when he
wants it."

She sprayed him gently with the hose. Sammy moved up
to a higher position on his hanging perch.

"Come down, baby," she urged. He came down slowly,

barely within her reach. She scratched beneath his soft, thick feathers. He stared into space, not acknowledging her affection.

"He's mad at me because I haven't talked to him lately," she said.

"Spoiled is the word for you," she said to Sammy. He shifted his position so that he was hanging upside down. She dug her fingers into his feathers to his skin. The bird remained still.

"You can achieve this kind of familiarity only with a bird that was hand-raised," she said. Sammy had been pampered by a wealthy socialite, who had donated the bird to the zoo.

"I tell people who call us about buying pets to buy a hand-raised bird from a breeder, not a wild bird. It's so much better, even if you do pay more for it," she said.

When she removed her hand from Sammy, it was covered with white powder. "Only cockatoos have this soft white powder," she said. "It's a lubricant to keep their feathers in good condition."

She walked away from Sammy, who made a loud cackling sound.

She went to the keeper area in the basement for her morning coffee and a cigarette. When she was done, she picked up a stack of pie plates with food on them—fruits and vegetables for the most part—and carried them up to the run she had cleaned earlier. Normally, another keeper would have done the feeding, but the staff was short-handed that day, and Kathy wasn't reluctant about filling in.

She put the plates in the cages; some of the birds rushed to eat, but Sammy remained on his perch, while a Nicobar pigeon sampled Sammy's plate of food. Sammy showed no sign of objecting.

"He doesn't relate to other birds," Kathy said. "Just to people."

She finished feeding the birds on one side of the hall; another keeper fed the rest. Kathy walked out into the sunlight and the cool breeze and headed for the waterfowl lagoon, to feed the flamingos, the ducks, the geese, what she called "basic work."

She took a peek into the flamingo dome, the glass bubble next to the waterfowl lagoon; it was empty. The flamingos would not be brought into their heated habitat until the rigors of winter demanded it. In the keeper service area beneath the dome, she filled containers with dry food. Outside, she dropped a trail of food along the lagoon bank and tossed some into the water. A free-for-all ensued, with a few city pigeons, ubiquitous scavengers, joining the ducks and geese.

"Most of these birds will be out here all winter," she said. "They're putting on body fat to keep them warm once winter arrives."

With a hose, she filled three tubs of water for the flamingos and added their food, "Flamingo-Fare." On the bank, away from the ravenous fowl, the tall pink birds poised gracefully on their long legs and glared, but did not acknowledge her presence.

Kathy had worked almost without interruption for four hours. It was time for lunch, for her an expedient rather than a profound pleasure. After having a bacon-cheeseburger at a nearby restaurant, she was back at work. That afternoon, she would instruct a group of docents in bird lore; it was her role in the docents' continuing education, which they would pass along to zoo visitors.

Later in the afternoon, she walked over to one of the zoo's hidden treasures, the zoo rookery. At the north edge of the zoo, bordering on the busy traffic to and from the lakefront, there was a nature preserve, a curving walk past a pond filled with ducks and geese and swans, protected from the sight of high-rise apartment buildings by arching groups of tall trees. It was a small, separate world.

The zoo rookery, built as a W.P.A. project in the 1930s, was—as a sign at its entrance announced—"a place where birds stop to feed and rest during spring and fall migrations. Some may breed, nest and hatch their young chicks in this area."

Actually, a few of the zoo's own bird collection lived in the rookery as well, but most of the birds to be found on the rookery pond were migratory mallards and Canadian geese.

Overcrowding was a problem, to be managed.

"If a bird hatches here, this is its home," Kathy said. "So we collect those eggs and destroy them. It's a form of birth control. If the mallards multiply, the cost of the food we have to provide—and making sure our own birds get some—becomes a problem."

She strolled along, listening to the shouts of small children as they encountered the ducks and the geese and the swans.

"This is one part of the zoo where the public is not discouraged from feeding the animals," she pointed out. A small boy was tossing chunks of bread to the birds.

"The migratory birds are lucky and smart," she said. "They can eat here at the rookery and then head right over to the waterfowl lagoon for more."

The rookery was a place that some keepers used, as well, for a respite in a demanding day. Kathy saw Barbara Katz, a keeper at the penguin-seabird house, pausing to appreciate the behavior of the migratory birds in the pond.

They chatted amiably for a few moments. Barbara was thirty-one, a keeper for seven years, a college graduate with a degree in biology and a special interest in hooded cranes. Short and trim, with dark brown hair cut very short, Barbara was used to being mistaken for a man; it amused her. It did not amuse her to know that any animals were being mistreated. She had a reputation as an activist, zealous in defending the rights of the penguins and the seabirds against all corner-cutting efforts by the bureaucracy. Barbara's methods, sometimes lacking in tact when an issue was at stake, were not Kathy's, but Kathy admired her tenacity, her devotion.

As Barbara saw it, "I'm here to provide the best possible care for the animals I take care of. That's my job. I couldn't live with myself if I let my animals down.

"Captivity is supposed to be the easy life. We are not reproducing natural ecosystems here. Just because an animal faces certain hardships in the wild and survives doesn't mean it's all right for us to supply anything less than luxury accommodations," Barbara said.

"The only higher-ups I'm accountable to are my penguins and seabirds," she added.

There were many reasons for her loyalty to the animals. Among them was one she would not forget. As a teenage volunteer at the children's zoo, she had been trying to conquer her own shyness. An animal had helped her win that struggle.

"I met Nicky, a two-year-old capuchin monkey at the children's zoo," she remembered. "She had been a pet, but was donated to the zoo after she became too unruly. When we first met, she was terrified of her new home, and I was a painfully shy teenager. She hid under her blanket, and I hid within myself. At first, she wouldn't even look at me when I sat in her cage. But I persisted. We sat together for days before she would come over and look at me. After several weeks, she came to trust me and enjoyed going outside to run around on the grass and climb trees.

"Of all the animals I have known and worked with, Nicky remains, to this day, the most special. We were inseparable that summer. We each did a lot of growing up. We helped each other.

"By the end of the summer, each of us was more comfortable in the company of others. I knew that I was drawn to her because of her fear and shyness. I knew that as long as I didn't pressure her, things would be OK. And they were."

It was a touching story, and there was little to comment on. Barbara headed toward the penguin-seabird house, and Kathy lingered in the rookery. She stared at a pair of elegant black swans on the pond, moving effortlessly across the water. Then she made her way slowly through the zoo back to the bird house.

She walked past the polar bears and the spectacled bears and the wolves and the giraffes, without stopping to look at them.

Suddenly she stopped, her eyes fixed on the sky. She had spotted a belted kingfisher, a bird seldom seen in Chicago, zooming overhead. She froze and followed its path, as the gray-blue and white bird headed north, to the rookery and beyond. She was sorry that she hadn't been with a birder, to share the treat.

"They're not as prolific as starlings or robins," she said. "You see just a couple every season."

It was late in the day. There was only time for one look around the bird house before she had to drive home. Still staring up at the sky, she quickened her pace.

FIRST PERSON: KATHY BROWN

I've always liked zoos. If there was a zoo around and I was on vacation, I usually went to the zoo. I liked the animals. I wasn't really motivated by any real desire to understand or relate to them at all. And here I am.

I took the keeper test because it was a lark. It wasn't a priority in my life. I didn't take seriously the fact that I passed or failed. I somehow wasn't surprised at the fact that I passed. I test well. I think at that time my perception of keepers was as a labor force, as opposed to a real profession, which it's evolving into now. It might have been after I started working here that I found out it was the first test given to women. I always have a tendency to fall in; I've done a number of things in my life that in hindsight I really shouldn't have been able to do. I wasn't looking at zoo keeping, it was really coincidental that I was called at a time I was seriously thinking of changing jobs. I simply had nothing to lose. If it didn't work out, if I didn't like it, I could go away.

I was looking for a change in direction. This was back in the very early seventies when pantsuits had just come in. Up until then, I was used to having to get into a girdle; we didn't have panty hose. I didn't like that; I wanted to be comfortable in what I did. So I was prepared; I was looking forward to a challenge.

Getting dirty didn't bother me, animal shit didn't really bother me. I'd been around animals before. I've never been scared of spiders, I've never been scared of snakes, I've never had fears of those things. When I was hired, they asked me questions like "Do you know you're going to have to pick up fifty pounds of grain? Do you know you're going to have to move hay?" I didn't know I was going to have to do that. But I've always had this attitude that I can do what everybody else can do.

I think I was a bit of a feminist before feminism actually got a name and an organization. Keep in mind that the sixties were my twenties. My parents were conservative enough to think that marriage was ultimately what I would do. You know, it wasn't too important if I made a great success of my life, as long as I got married and had children. I had a lot of problems with that. For the first time in my life at thirty I got hit with the idea that the reason I'm not married is I don't want to get married. As soon as I came to that conclusion, then I was really open to taking other directions and to being very independent.

It wasn't that I liked animals. I had no fear of working with the animals. I felt I would be competent enough to do the job, but a good part of it was getting out of that restrictive thing that women, even to this day, are in. The idea of getting up and putting on a dress, having to be immaculate. The birds don't care, you know.

Actually, it wasn't that I chose and stayed with birds. The staff usually determines personnel changes and transfers. My first seven months were on the farm. I'd proved myself there, and I was transferred to the bird house. I didn't ask for the bird house. I came in here totally blank on birds. I knew maybe four species of the common birds of North America, and that was about it. I stayed here for twelve years. I enjoyed it, and there's a tremendous amount of information to be learned here. If I was going to do my job right, I had to learn what was going on, what birds were about. And I set about doing just that, trying to understand what I was looking at, why I was looking at it, what the behavior meant, what this bird eats, what can I do to change a diet for a whole breed. It all became a challenge for me.

I've never been bored. There's just too much to do. If you're bored, there's books up here, there's books at the library, there's animals you can stand and watch. I get a lot of affection from birds by allowing them to do what they want to do. Take the Nicobar pigeons. Kevin Bell and I started about the same time back in 1976 with three pairs. He immediately saw the value and the rarity of these birds. And they were already actively breeding, so it was very important these animals be documented and detailed and records kept. This is a perfect example of spending a lot of time doing observations on what is essentially a wild animal. I got to know them a little bit individually, and their offspring, and how they related to their offspring, and how their offspring related to *their* offspring. As years go on, they peel back these layers; they're living their whole lives in front of you, they're not just hopping from a branch and then going to another branch for five minutes and coming down and eating and going to another branch. There's a pecking order, there's a community, and you see how this guy doesn't fit in well because of this problem, or all of a sudden he displaces this boss and now he's boss for the season.

I don't know what's going through their brains; I'm not a bird. Some people may think I'm a bird brain, but I don't have a bird brain. But we've had communities as large as thirty of these guys at one time, and every bird is known by the others, every bird has its place in that group. You know it's not random. It's a city, it's a village, that they've created out there, and each of them has responsibilities. I get a tremendous emotional reward from watching that.

And there's more. Yesterday was a good case. I came in, and a man was waiting for me. He'd brought in a rail, which is a small marsh bird. I understand that the cliché "thin as a rail" comes from the bird, actually. If you look at them head on, they're very narrow birds, almost like something hit them and crushed them. Anyway, I took the bird out of the bag. I looked at the bird, and I had never seen anything quite like it before. It looked to me like a juvenile sora rail, even though I'd never seen one. It certainly wasn't an adult. Anyway, the bird was perfectly healthy, it had just come down over on Clark Street instead of right here in the park and got confused by the cars and the gangways and everything. So I walked with the man down to our waterfowl area, which is an area typical for rails, and we released it there. And the man was very comfortable in our doing that. The bird ran into the bushes, which is what I expected him to do. So it was a healthy bird. He got back on track, you might say. The whole point of this, though, is that I was not real comfortable with the identification of the bird as a sora rail. So I took the time then, after the man left, to look in my bird book and check it out. Well, it was in fact a yellow rail, which is far more rare. We've only had one brought in here in the twelve years I've been here, and that was a damaged one many years ago that I don't think survived.

The public does bring in wild birds. If they're capable of recovery, even if it takes a few days—assuming we can get them to eat in captivity, which is sometimes a problem— we'll offer them those few days for recovery. We get a lot of head bashes, birds flying into glass windows, into the high rises. If a bird doesn't recover, if it's seriously damaged, it's euthanized. A few of them find their way into our collection.

In captivity, some birds have to make a lot of adjustments, some birds don't. For instance, sometimes we can have a pair of birds in the center aviary, and we can't introduce a third bird. They'll kill it, or it'll interfere with breeding behavior. In other words, their territory in the wild is so vast in terms of their own species, that they must have the whole aviary for their own territory. So then you can only have a pair of those birds. Other birds are more communal, and they might only require fifteen or twenty square feet of space, so maybe you could have two pairs. Maybe one pair will set off at one end, and maybe the other pair will go to the other end of the building, and they'll function quite well under those conditions. The Nicobars are communal and thrive in a large group.

I can think of one instance where unfortunately we were a little slow understanding what was going on. We had a baby Hartlaub's touraco. After many years of trying to breed them, we finally were successful in getting a baby touraco out of them. We had some problems with it, but ultimately they raised the baby themselves fine. And so we had the three birds up there. Well, a year went by, and we just weren't keyed in, but the touracos went back into breeding condition. The baby was a third bird. They don't want a third bird, they want that whole territory for themselves, so they killed their own baby. If we had just sensed that this was happening, we could have removed the baby from the aviary; it would have been no problem. But everything seemed to be going well, you know, mom, dad, and the kid. Under normal circumstances in the wild, that baby would have been long gone from the group, and they would have reestablished their territory. They wanted to breed again, and here's a third bird; they didn't care that it was their kid, if they even were aware that it was still their kid. So they killed him.

Among the most beautiful birds, my favorite is the paradise tanager. The tanager is a small fruit-eating bird probably no more than five inches long. They're kind of a Caribbean, South American bird. And their markings are just incredible. They have brilliant colors on this basic black velvet type of plumage, and their heads are turquoise blue. They have a big patch of turquoise blue, a big patch of orange, a big patch of red, a big patch of yellow, and it's all on this black velvet background. Absolutely beautiful. I don't think I've ever seen anything quite as beautiful as the paradise tanager.

You learn from breeding birds. And what we're doing is breeding birds to be what they are. Imprinting turns an animal into a pet. Dogs are imprinted, cats are imprinted, a couple of the birds here are imprinted. That's fine if you want a pet. But we're not in the pet business. We're in the business of taking a species of animal out of its habitat, which may be mostly gone, keeping it going and alive as a species that you hope down the road, someday, can go back. You've got to let it retain as many of its basic qualities as it can. We don't raise a bird with the intent of imprinting it. I've never taken a bird home with the intent of imprinting it. I've taken it home to keep it alive, because sometimes they're valuable enough that just having that bird alive on earth is more important than risking imprinting it. If it gets imprinted along the way, it's unfortunate, but better to have it alive and imprinted than not alive at all. You run into that situation.

Zoos started out to be displays for the public, and most of these buildings were designed to accommodate people who walked through, and the least amount of space was turned over to the animals. The animals were there to show the people what a lion or a monkey or a chimpanzee looked like. That wasn't good, so zoos began to change to at least give animals a bit more credit. But here we are, in an ecologically disastrous age, we're killing the earth and a lot of the animals with it. And so, all of a sudden, the world has come to determine that a lot of these animals, if they're going to stay alive, there is no alternative institution that's going to keep them alive. Zoos are already set up to do that, even though that's not why they were created.

Now it's my job to breed these damned things, to keep them alive and keep records and that's not something zoos set out to look for. Zoos just kind of woke up one day and said, "Wait a minute, we gotta do this, because we're the only ones around who can do it." I was vaguely aware of that when I came in here, that what I'm dealing with are wild animals.

Sure, it's very difficult to try not to relate to these birds, to try to keep from anthropomorphizing them. If I'm hand-raising a bird, I don't want to imprint him, I don't want to do it. But when I'm doing it, it's very hard. I mean, I'm not going to stand here and say, "Well, the heck with you." It's very hard for me to keep from snuggling, wanting to snuggle with a certain bird. Very hard to keep from going "cootchy cootchy cootchy coo," you know. Very hard. When you're hand-raising them, they're shifting their identification from the parent to you, because you become the parent. What I try to do is prevent that, but it's very hard for me to even draw the line sometimes. I want to just grab that bird and give it ten minutes of very intense affection. That's not good for the bird.

I've had my heart broken many times. A couple of years ago, we were breeding rose-breasted cockatoos. They're fairly common in zoos. One year a pair gave us two fine healthy chicks. The following year they went through the same behavior, but something went wrong. We recovered one chick from the nest box who was virtually starved, emaciated. The mother was not well at the time, and she was trying to starve the chicks out. That's sometimes how birds fledge; parents just stop feeding the chicks. This creates the initiative for the chick to start going out and seeking things. It's a basic pattern among birds. Well, I ended up being the person taking on the responsibility of trying to turn this emaciated baby that had been living in a little black hole, a nest box, which is normal, into some kind of a viable bird. And I didn't really care about imprinting at that point. The whole point was to keep it alive and do whatever was necessary. I named her Rosie, took her home, just to see that she got extra feedings at night, and she was getting better and better. I was going to night school that fall, and she was doing very well. I started leaving her at the zoo overnight. Three or four nights had gone by, and I came in one morning, and she was dead. She had appeared to be doing very well the night before. I thought I was doing the right thing. Her state of deterioration was so bad when she came out of the box that all I did was buy her time. But it was just coming in, knowing I left her in what I thought was good shape the night before, walking upstairs to give her her morning feeding, with a smile on my face, expecting her to respond to me, and I'd been dealing with her now for three or four weeks maybe, and there she was.

If you're dealing with an animal on a day-to-day basis, one on one, regardless of how hard you try not to imprint, there's still an affection that occurs. In many situations, regardless of whether the bird is imprinting on me or not, if I'm trying to nurse it, trying to keep it alive, sometimes by the time two or three days go by, it's too late for me emotionally. Now, if a bird dies within the first day, I can deal with that. But if I've been dealing with it for three or four days or longer, then it becomes very difficult.

Not all stories are sad. This starts with a man and a woman who came from Finland. He was quite a well-known magician in Europe, traveling with his wife as his assistant. They were retired, and how they ended up in Chicago I have no idea. Julius and Nadia, almost every keeper at the zoo knows these people. By the time I came to the bird department, Julius already had an ongoing relationship with Blackie the swan. His passion for that bird! I don't think anybody ever really understood it. I don't even know if Julius really understood it. Blackie was a black swan, actually an Australian black swan. This attachment that Julius had bordered on the obsessive. It was very passionate; the man and his wife would come almost every day. It didn't matter if it was ten degrees or five degrees, they'd put their mufflers on and their coats, and they'd come to the zoo rookery and see him anyway. So there was no way that we could take that bird away from him. Blackie stayed on. Nobody really wanted Blackie. It's not that we didn't like Blackie, but it would have been nice to have put him out with some other swans in another zoo somewhere. But Julius just wouldn't have stood for it. So we kept Blackie for a number of years alone. Nadia was very supportive of her husband, like the swan itself, but her approach was a little bit more logical.

Well, Julius had lung cancer but kept himself in very good health. Julius would bring treats, he'd bring lettuce, he'd buy watermelon out of season because Blackie loved watermelon. Blackie knew him, without a doubt. And Blackie could be aggressive; I mean, he was a male swan. But he knew Julius very well. Julius would sit down, and Blackie would come up and lay his head in Julius's lap, and he'd pet this swan. Blackie would bite the heck out of me, Blackie never liked keepers much, I can tell you that. But he loved Julius. It was my hope that Julius would pass away before Blackie did, and Blackie was not a young bird. I thought that Blackie's death would devastate him, that would be the end of Julius, that's how intense their relationship was. It's hard to say, but unfortunately Julius did die first. He was walking two days before he died.

By then we had a swan called Nadia, which is another little story in itself. I named it Nadia, even though it's a male. This black swan was brought to us by animal control, although actually the bird was very healthy; somebody was taking care of it. I named it Nadia because Julius's wife's name was Nadia. When I brought the bird in not knowing what sex it was, and knowing that this was Blackie's territory, I had three or four keepers standing around prepared to break them apart. I wasn't sure what was going to happen. It was love at first sight. Both are males, but I think they were just happy to be with one of their own kind.

You've taken this animal out of the wild. You've thrown it into this cage, and of course you get a lot of comments from the public about how inhumane this is. But these birds aren't really suffering. Nonetheless, if you're looking at a relatively rare animal that five years ago was in the wild but here it's been living in this cage for five years, it has lost quality of life. But if you've got an animal that's breeding, you've got a happy animal. I mean you're doing something right, because if it's not a happy animal, it's not going to make babies for you. You're allowing it to do something it would be doing in the wild. Maybe it's confined, granted, but you've made that animal at least comfortable within the confines of its life. It has a mate, it's got food, it may have offspring to raise. For me, that type of thing is very much a reward.

When I first took the job, I thought, "Well, I can give it five or ten years." I wasn't that serious about being a zookeeper. "I'll give it five years, then maybe I'll look around and see if there's something else I'd like to do." Well, it's twelve years now. I've learned a lot. It's been a teaching experience that I can carry over into my retired life. I toy around with the idea of getting permits to allow me to sell certain wild animals, maybe continue working with birds that are injured. It's not just a job, you know, it's kind of become a part of what I do, who I am. When I go on a vacation, I take my bird books, I find out what birds I can see while I'm on my travels. Before I worked here, it never would have occurred to me to do anything like that.

16

THE SOCIETY'S GOSPEL

The Chicago Park District owned and maintained the zoo. The 4 million visitors who came to the zoo each year to see the more than 2,000 animals it housed probably didn't care where the money came from. If they did, they would have known that the zoo would be a tattered relic without the efforts of the Lincoln Park Zoological Society.

The society had defined its mission in these words: "To provide the funding and services required to operate the zoo as a world class institution."

In practical terms, the society provided close to 50 percent of the total funding required to operate and improve the zoo. The collaboration between the park district and the zoo society enabled the zoo to sustain its reputation for excellence, to modernize its facilities, and to remain free to the public.

The zoo society, its civic-minded and influential board of directors, the park district, and the zoo director, Les Fisher, all played roles in achieving the objectives listed in the society's annual report:

- Improve zoo buildings, provide excellent animal management facilities and outstanding exhibits for visitors.
- Beautify the zoo grounds, adding gardens and sculpture.
- Make improvements to facilitate public access, and improve parking areas.
- Provide resources to acquire additional animals and to care for all the animals properly.
- Enable the zoo to participate in international efforts to breed endangered species.
- Provide free services, including information, printed matter, and a library, to the public.
- Offer free educational services to school children and visitors, at the zoo itself and in outreach programs.
- Conduct research and conservation efforts to protect endangered animals, in captivity and in the wild.
- Inspire a flow of donated revenue to accomplish all of the society's goals.

In 1986, the park district provided the zoo with funds and services worth more than $4.5 million. The zoo society provided slightly more than $4 million.

At the heart of the society's effort was Barbara Whitney, its executive director. A forty-five-year-old Chicago-born divorcée and mother of three, Barbara grew up in the Chicago area, majored in English at Denison University in Ohio, married, and moved to New York. She spent two years as a researcher in the book division of Time Inc., returned to Chicago, had her children, and spent six years in suburbia.

When she was divorced in 1973, she realized that she needed a job; she didn't have the money to be self-sustaining. She did find work and moved to the first of several apartments within walking distance of the zoo. Over the years, she had volunteered for various causes. That experience made the zoo society an appealing possibility for her. In late 1975, she became its fourth executive director. The society had been formed in 1959, but had limped along with just an executive director and a secretary for several years until Barbara arrived.

After that, things changed.

Under Barbara's direction, the society membership went from 2,200 when she arrived to 13,000 in 1987. The staff grew to forty full-time and thirty part-time (in summer). And donations to the zoo went from a trickle to a steady and substantial flow. The names of well-known local business titans began to be engraved on the walls of new zoo buildings: Pritzker on a new children's zoo; Regenstein on a large mammal house; Kroc on a new hospital-commissary; Crown and Field on the administration–zoo society building. The donations involved ranged from $500,000 to $2 million, and they highlighted the campaign to change the face of the zoo, to modernize the venerable institution.

A tall (5'8") woman, trim and fashionable, with short graying brown hair and hazel eyes, Barbara became the ruler of a substantial empire. It included the board of directors, the auxiliary board and the women's board—a total of more than 250 volunteers dedicated to the progress of the zoo. From her bright, modern, uncluttered office in the Crown-Field Center, she functioned energetically. Some of her associates saw her as "driven," an energized director locked into a single cause. Those who appreciated results didn't care how she might be defined.

She played a vital role in the renovations at the zoo, in running the docent-volunteer programs (there were more than 400 docents and volunteers at the zoo), in working with Les Fisher and his staff, in guiding her own staff— and in relating to the zoo society boards and philanthropists in the outside world.

After she had been at the zoo for six years, Barbara made a speech about her work. The message endured:

> My work at the zoo is not *with* the animals but it's *about* the animals and *for* the animals. My work is with people— literally thousands of them who make up this big family

that is called the zoo society. . . . They are investing in the future of the zoo. They are investing their money, and that equally valuable gift—their time. They are doing it so that the zoo will be here to make memories for the children of the future—memories of animals that are strange and wonderful and wild, from far-off lands they will never see.

She did not abandon that definition, but there were days when the demands of her packed schedule distracted her from such guiding abstractions. Much of her time was consumed by phone calls, meetings, dialogues with staff members, planning sessions, and more. The society's annual calendar was filled with events, mailings, publications, parties, fairs, conferences, picnics, dinners, luncheons, and zoo programs. Few pages in her desk diary were blank. She earned her $73,000 salary.

On one chilly Monday in October, she met with five staff members, one man and four women. (Men were underrepresented in the zoo society; so were minorities.) In a pink knit cardigan, trimmed in black with gold buttons, and a coordinated black knit skirt, she seemed dressed for action. But not necessarily for serious conversation, at least not immediately.

"Does anyone know what this meeting is about?" she asked, smiling. "Oh, well, it's Monday morning."

In truth, she knew quite well what the meeting was about. She wanted to talk about increasing the activity level of the committees of the board of directors. Among them: executive, architectural improvements, conservation, development, finance, programs, and visitor services. Each committee had a society staff member to depend upon. Barbara knew that much of the society's important work occurred in such committees. The staff members present were among those who worked closely with the committees.

"You must interact with them directly. We drown in details here, but they have general thoughts not obscured by such details," she said. She knew that board members—stockbrokers, industrialists, high-level executives—had an expertise that the society lacked: how to succeed in business. And the society was a business.

"Set up your own relationship with the committee chairman," she urged. "Then work with me on an agenda. I want to add my input. And remember, we need a report—a written analysis of what goes on—or there's nothing to discuss. The chairmen have full-time jobs, so they need our staff support. Keep pushing forward. Keep them moving. Make sure that meetings happen.

"Let's pay attention to the board members. They have credibility with their peers that we never have. But don't forget that they don't spend twelve hours a day thinking about the zoo, and we do. We can help them, and they can help us."

The Landmark Campaign, to renovate zoo buildings and add new exhibits, had gone along satisfactorily, given the usual delays, construction impediments, and budget restrictions. Now, it was time for the society to look beyond that major effort. Barbara knew that it took three years to get a program in place. In the nonprofit arena, one had to be patient or succumb to stomach acid.

There were plans for the future. She wanted to raise funds to rehabilitate the aged reptile house, to repair the sea lion pool. Above all, she wanted to honor the term *garden* in "zoological garden."

"A half-million dollars could work wonders," she said. "It would be easy to turn this zoo into a beautiful garden area, with gardens all over the zoo. We could have garden cafés and garden plazas. Yes, the animal areas are always our first priority, but we've been dealing with that. Now we can deal with other concerns.

"For example, we need more space for the administration. Can we solve that by renovating the basement of the reptile house? Or do we need a new administration building? Will the society pay for it? The one we have now is on valuable land. It may be too costly to house the administration, particularly when you consider that the visitors could make use of it."

Planning—and talking about planning—never ceased. When one program became a reality, it was time for another. Someday, the perfect small zoo might manifest its glory in Lincoln Park, but no one could imagine it. Work on the future went on.

Barbara knew that the society depended on the board for the success of such planning.

"Without the board, the society couldn't achieve its objectives," she said. "It's a dynamic. The board brings ideas to us, and we bring ideas to them. It's the marriage that creates good grant proposals, good presentations.

"We look ahead together. I spend an enormous amount of time thinking about five years from now."

Nonprofit organizations hoped for one or more of the three Ws from its board: wisdom, wealth, or work.

"You need a hard core—say twenty-five or thirty percent—that is active," Barbara noted. "If you have fifty percent of the board members who are active, you're lucky."

To tempt donors, the executive director had to be tactful, cautious, considerate. Donors had to be courted.

"It's not a problem for me," Barbara said. "I have a weak personality. That means I was taught to be nice, not confrontational. I've been a board member, so I can see matters from that point of view. And I like most of those people I get to know in my job. It is my job to get to people who don't even know my name, who look right through me. Effort counts. The best people in this business are those who make that extra phone call, who pay extra attention to keep our 'family' together.

"You can raise money by begging, or you can raise money by saying that a well-managed effort deserves support. We choose the latter course, a corporate image of excellence, instead of need. We demonstrate permanence, continuity, a plan—as a reality. Are we managing well? That's the greatest weight I have to bear.

"A sense of style is important in everything we market. Printed materials. Events. We want to demonstrate a new energy. Excitement. Change. Being up-to-date. It's all a conscious effort on our part."

Barbara depended upon her staff to make that effort succeed.

Chuck Harris was one of her stalwarts. The short, bearded, tweedy project manager for the society, Chuck kept her posted on all the renovation and construction at the zoo. As winter invaded, he was preparing to escape to an African safari, a common respite for zoo staff members who could afford it. But first he met with Barbara and Les Fisher.

He told Barbara what to watch out for while he was away; he had done his best to prevent a calamity from occurring during his absence, but he couldn't be certain that calm would prevail. For a few moments, their roles were reversed. Barbara took notes; she wanted to be prepared.

There was a plan to erect a souvenir stand near the small mammal house. Could it be done by next summer, Barbara wondered. Chuck wasn't sure. The stand was needed by the society, which ran it; the revenue would be useful, particularly since the society's shop in the lion house would be shut down during that building's renovation.

Chuck would contact an architect and urge him to submit a concept for the stand by the time Chuck returned.

Various projects were subject to park district approval or consultation. Implied in that was an awareness of the personalities involved—and the power they wielded. Barbara and Les shared that awareness and spoke in a kind of bureaucratic shorthand about it.

As the meeting ended, Les got up and smiled at Chuck.

"Remember, once every three years a rhino charges a vehicle," Les told Chuck. "I just wanted to keep your adrenal glands from atrophying."

Les headed back to his office; Chuck went back to his cubicle. Barbara was left alone in her office, for a few minutes of silence before going to a meeting with several members of the women's board, who were eager to discuss the future of the zoo.

It was a subject that consumed much of Barbara's time and concern. The zoo was a small zoo, just thirty-five acres, but it was a free zoo, open every day. In contrast to its 13,000 zoo society members, the San Diego Zoo had more than 120,000. And Lincoln Park had fewer personnel than most major city zoos. Those facts inspired perpetual reevaluations of goals.

No one wanted to initiate a fee to enter the zoo, but studies had indicated that zoos that did generated substantial revenue. In 1986, the San Diego Zoo had collected almost $15 million in admission revenue from its 3 million visitors. A projection of possible Lincoln Park revenues indicated that as much as $12 million might be gained from a $4 fee. What no one could know was how many people would not visit the zoo if they had to pay for it.

In the short term, Barbara had to help create and adhere to the society's annual budget. She kept it in mind. For the fiscal year ending in March 1988, the society projected revenues of more than $5 million and expenditures of more than $8 million. Fortunately, almost $5 million of the expenditures was for capital improvements and would be met by prior funding, already on hand, and pledges to be collected during the year.

In Barbara's view, there was much to be done. Suggestions, proposals, and hopes abounded.

It would be a good to convert the cramped Crown-Field Center—which housed the zoo's administrative staff and the zoo society staff, an auditorium, and a gift shop—into a public education center. That would mean that a new administration building would have to be built, or the basement of the reptile house converted to office space, not a solution guaranteed to improve staff morale. And the park district was not eager to endorse more new building at the zoo.

During the fiscal year, a number of projects would move toward fruition, and Barbara would have to attend to them, even as her thoughts headed beyond them. The children's zoo and the bird of prey area would be completed, if all went well. The lion house renovation would be 90 percent done, and the bird house 50 percent done. Architectural planning of the refurbished primate house would be completed, and the renovation of the farm would be finished.

The society hoped to begin a study of the renovation of the reptile house and the creation of a maternity area at the sea lion pool. Improvements were needed at the great ape house, and the new koala exhibit would have to be designed atop the Crown-Field Center, where a display of small mammals and a gift shop had been housed.

Barbara wanted gardens created throughout the zoo, and new sculpture added to the grounds.

Funds would be needed for education, conservation, research, graphics around the zoo, to enhance the animal collection—to purchase new animals and conduct expeditions to collect reptiles—and more. Those concerned with animal management needed a computer system; others needed new walkie-talkies. It would be useful to have a closed-circuit TV system to monitor the apes when they were in their outdoor habitat. And introducing the koalas to the zoo would cost money beyond the habitat.

The zoo's education program was wide-ranging. The society shared the cost of it with the park district. The program was essential. Barbara believed that the society had an obligation to make the zoo a satisfying place to visit, with information booths, free literature, attractive zoo merchandise, and bikes and roller skates for rent. Future plans included stroller rentals for parents with weary toddlers and operating the food service in the zoo. It was the society's intention to convert it from glorified hot dog stands to cafés and plazas offering good food in comfortable settings. In fact, the zoo society had won the bidding for the food services and planned to sublet them to a leading local restaurant chain.

For Barbara, these were the matters that kept her alert, when they weren't making her weary. With so many con-

356 ————————————————————————————— Zoo

cerns, she had learned to delegate authority. Among the
staff members reporting to Barbara were Mena Boulanger,
the director of fund-raising, and Nancy Worssam, director
of programs.

Mena, forty-six, was born in Seattle, Washington, and
had come to the zoo in 1979. A wife, mother of two, and
community activist wherever she had lived, she had a
master's degree in communication from the University of
Illinois. She was a short, neatly tailored blonde with glasses
and an understated manner that concealed a quick mind
and an ability to spot a donor on sight.

Although her office was a cramped cubicle down the
curve from Barbara's office, her role was an essential one.
She thought of what she did as "the art of persuasion."

"I studied persuasion in grad school," she said. "It involves identifying within an individual what he or she
believes in. Our challenge is to identify a commitment to
conservation, to children, to Chicago, to nature, to preservation—and to present the zoo to those people as the
effective entity to support that commitment.

"I identify the donors, then we determine which member
of the zoo family should present our case to that one
person, one company, one family. Who's best to talk to
donors? We do our research. Does Les Fisher go? Do we
prepare a grant proposal? What form does our presentation
take? We confer and we decide. It's important to talk to the
right people in the right sequence."

Looking around the society's half of the Crown-Field
Center, an observer did not have the sense of being at a
zoo; the staff, almost all women, were well dressed, well
educated, serious in their devotion. The impression was
that of an upscale women's magazine, public relations
agency, or any successful business run by women. Staffing
the society—choosing the right people—was vital. Choices
were not made casually or left to chance.

"We look for warmth, confidence, and more," Mena
pointed out. "Education is a must."

In her private life—she lived in a western suburb—she

remained the activist, the partisan; she was a township committeewoman in the Democratic Party. At the zoo, she couldn't afford to be political. The zoo was her cause.

"Actually, it's not really that I have two sides to my life these days. I want to represent the zoo and nothing else. I'm fully involved in it. It's a big commitment.

"It takes time, plenty of time. I have to get volunteers involved, board members, community leaders. The art of fund-raising is conceptualizing a plan and linking it to the people who can make it happen.

"A major gift to the zoo requires a connecting link: a fully developed idea and a rationale for it. Not simply that the zoo needs money for its good intentions. It does, and some donors know that. But most of the time we need the specific project. Les Fisher had four years of conversations about his hopes for the new children's zoo. Then the Pritzkers gave us more than a million dollars.

"You have to spend money and thought to raise money. Friends bring friends to us. We make presentations, conduct tours, send out information. There's no boilerplate when you're obtaining major gifts.

"We need funds to guarantee the quality of the zoo, to create unbridled opportunities to educate. Four million people come through the gates every year. We can educate them right here at the zoo and through video and films as well. We can sponsor conferences.

"It all comes together. I got to go to Kenya with a group from the zoo, and that gave me a sense of connectedness of it all. When you do that, all the concepts that matter to us at the zoo come to life in the wild.

"Nature, the quality of life, it's all linked at the zoo and in Africa. I know I'm sounding existential, but that's where my head is at. At least once a week, I leave my office to visit the animals. I've been a gorilla nut since I was five. I know the animals in our zoo and the keepers, and I can even conduct tours. It's essential for me to get out of my office and see the animals. I don't want to forget them."

If Mena raised the funds, Nancy Worssam was the staff

member charged with figuring out how that money ought to be spent.

The park district took care of the basics, but the zoo society had to go beyond the basics, to improve the quality of life—for animals and staff.

Tall, chic, and understated in her manner, Nancy had a bachelor's degree in history from the University of Connecticut, a master's in anthropology from New York University, and two children from a marriage that ended in divorce.

She found herself working for the National Endowment for the Humanities in Washington, D.C., but concluded that "staying with the government for too long curdles the brain." So when the man with whom she lived had an offer to move to Chicago, they made it a joint decision, and Nancy looked for a job. An exploratory chat at the zoo society led to the creation (in 1986) of the job for Nancy, directing the flow of society funds to the needs of the zoo.

In her soft-spoken way, Nancy set out to understand and appreciate the needs of the members of the zoo staff, and the programs that needed financial transfusions. She quickly realized that while some of the zoo buildings seemed dated, the attitudes were not.

"This place has changed, dramatically, from what it once was," she said. "There's been an unbelievable amount of fund-raising. Now, it's time to take on the task of getting more members. We can use that kind of added support, getting more people involved in the zoo. The society supports all sorts of programs. Conservation. Animal management. Video. Research. Staff travel. Education. It's all program money, and that's what my title—director of programs—is really all about.

"We're working toward a comprehensive plan, an effort to control our own destiny, the zoo's destiny—a kind of financial oversight. In every department, people will tell us where they want to go. Then the zoo itself will have a direction. Growth is upon us. And that means that systems have to be in place before expansion takes place. We're catching up now, and I'm a part of the system. We're after excellence, and that wouldn't be apparent without the work of the zoo society.

"Our job is to make dreams come true. Les Fisher's dreams are shared by others, by curators and by keepers. A curator wants to get something done. He tells me. I take his message to the society. I try to answer the question, 'How can we make that happen?'

"Once you know what you want to do with the money, you can raise the money. My job is to define the path we take, to define the future of the zoo. It's growth in a coherent way. That's the best course."

What Nancy defined and Mena raised funds to support lent definition to Barbara's life. But she was in charge; no one made a major decision without Barbara's voice being heard. She had gone through a period of serious trial, raising money to renovate several old buildings and the farm, and wending her way through red tape to capture the right to provide better food for zoo visitors.

She knew that all major projects were costly. She anticipated a cash squeeze down the road, and she wanted to be ready for it. She felt that the society had two years to prepare for that crunch; if it did not, important dreams would be thwarted.

It was time to create a new list of aims for the zoo, a shopping list to raise money.

In meetings with her staff, her crisp managerial stance was evident. "Impact" was one of her favorite verbs.

When she conferred with Mena, Nancy, and others, her advice surfaced again and again.

Certain maxims prevailed. Anticipate questions. Have answers ready. Plan whatever can be planned. The society's mission was not simply to raise cash for big projects. The zoo and the society were one in serving the people who came through the gates. Those people, many of them, might not be able to afford pets; their pets would reside in the cages at the zoo. The visitors' needs would have to be considered in everything the society did.

When the last meeting on a cold day had ended, Barbara sat behind her desk. She phoned one of her children to find out what was happening at home. She made a doctor's appointment. She collected a mass of paperwork to take home.

Several staff members stopped by on their way out. They clogged the doorway to her office. Barbara looked up at them and said, "It's all that, all that *stuff*, that sometimes keeps me awake at night and makes my stomach hurt." She waved an arm in the air, defining the invisible work load.

She smiled as she spoke, and everyone in the room knew that she wasn't complaining.

First Person: Barbara Whitney

I had animals when I was a kid. I had a pony, and I had a horse, and those were the important animals in my life. We always had dogs, we had cats from time to time when my mother didn't get her way, and then we had an assortment of fish and gerbils. I grew up out in the country, and I spent a lot of time during my childhood with my pony and my horse—that's what I did after school. So I spent a lot of time alone with that animal out in the fields, out in the country. That affinity was an extremely intense one, and that pony was as much a part of my life as my sisters were. But it never occurred to me to go into any kind of animal-oriented career.

However, there was a family tradition of being a volunteer. It was very strongly and directly taught by my mother, who volunteered for everything from school board to the PTA to the library board. And it was very simple. We have been given much, and we must give something in return. It probably grew out of the same streak that in my early years made me want to be Jane Addams or a nurse when I grew up. It was a belief in service, as I suppose it was for my mother, deeply rooted in the religion we grew up in. She was a genuinely Christian-oriented woman. We grew up in the Episcopal church, but it was more than going to Sunday School. I grew up believing. My mother also believed it was important to be interesting and try new things, and so she taught us that life was an avenue of experience, of learning about new things.

I'm a feminist, unofficially. I've never participated in feminist causes, in any way, shape, or form. But I am definitely a product of my time and have been for many years. I first recognized it in some things I wrote when I was maybe twenty-four or twenty-five years old. Actually I can recognize it earlier; I can recognize the anger I felt upon graduation from college that all the boys in my class could go out and get these high-paying jobs, maybe making twelve thousand dollars a year as salesman for a Fortune 500 company. And that I had to pass a typing test to get in the door anyplace. That was a very strong and visceral resentment that I remember to this day, sitting in New York City trying to speed up my typing so that I could get a job in publishing under the title of editorial assistant, which meant secretary. I resented that, and I flunked seventeen typing tests at seventeen different organizations before I got lucky and somebody overlooked the scoring.

I went into an organization in my first job where I was given enormous opportunity, and opportunity for growth very, very fast. And so the bitterness did not become deeply seated. So I never became a diehard feminist, and when I came back to Chicago, my recollection is that I still felt there was a whole world out there in which I could participate.

I really believe that what I brought with me here to the zoo, what I brought with me here that uniquely served me, were two or three things, maybe four. One thing I brought was that I was not a zoo person, I was a layperson. I was not an expert, I had not grown up next door to this zoo, and this zoo was not a household word in my life. As a matter of fact I remember bringing my kids to Lincoln Park Zoo, because after my husband left, I would try to find excursions on a Saturday morning to focus on. And I remember calling and trying to find out how you got to the zoo, and how much it cost, and that was only a couple years before I came to the zoo to work. I didn't even know whether there were gorillas at this zoo, let alone the best collection of gorillas in the world. So I think that that uninitiated vantage point served me very well.

But more directly, I think that my belief in communication skills served me, because I think I have communication skills—oral communication skills and written communication skills. I was not a marketing expert; I had not been in an ad agency, although I grew up with a Dad (and I do think that's important) who had been an advertising executive. He was the president of Leo Burnett. I grew up with that kind of conversation at the dinner table: communicate, communicate, communicate; tell them what you're going to tell, tell them, then tell them what you told them—that sort of old-fashioned American direct message stuff. And I believed it all, because I adored my father. I believed every word of it. So I was trained over the dinner table—we all were—to be communicators in one way or another.

There's another factor, an innate understanding of process. How to take an idea, something that is just ephemeral, and make it real.

We're very lucky here in that we have a product, if you will, the zoo, that sells itself. And so our job is only to make people aware of what this place is within the community, to the animals it serves, to the people it serves. Now, in fund language that's called the case statement. Uck, how dry, how awful. My experience here has been that you don't turn people into donors, that you introduce them to the zoo. The zoo turns them into donors. So my job is not fund-raising per se, it's friend-making. Get people on the premises face to face with animals; that is the best single thing we can do. Get people here, help them understand the needs of the institution, the complexity of the institution, the charm of what happens here between the visitors and the animals.

But it's very important to get them a step beyond the

visitors and the animals. This zoo was a very static experience compared to what I realized a zoo was when I saw it behind the scenes. The animals were there, and they existed in a vacuum. I didn't speak to any keepers, I didn't get to know any keepers, it was as if that didn't exist. I'd see animals munching some food, but they were just there. But the first time I came here and went behind the scenes, which was literally in conjunction with this job, and I saw the interaction of the animals and keepers back there, and walked through the commissary and realized the zillion kinds of food they need to stay alive and all the mechanics of this institution, I was blown away by them. I mean it's fascinating. People always say, "I had no idea all of this went on."

You introduce people to the zoo. Those people become converts. Converts become potential donors. But you must have a board of directors. A board of directors is not something that's just tolerated; a board of directors is an essential element in the process. I have enormous faith in the collective judgment of our board. And that's not an original quote from me; it came from Les. But it is a true statement that I often say and believe. I don't think I've ever seen our board make a bad collective judgment in the twelve years I've been here. I think the board's decisions have always been sound. And where a judgment was slow in forthcoming, it was only because the board members didn't have enough information, which is our responsibility, by the way.

One of the important functions of the board members is that they are the network into the community. It took me years before I appreciated what a strong tool that is. For years, people came up to me saying, "Well, I talked to Joe Blow—he's on your board, you know—and he was telling me this, and I didn't know that about the zoo." It works. There's much more of a sense of participating in the fate of the place here than I have discovered on boards of directors of corporations. The directors understand their role at this zoo. They know the zoo society doesn't run the zoo, and they aren't trying to run the zoo. I think they learn from us, and we learn from them.

The park district budget provides the employees who are needed to take care of the animal collection and the facility, the food for the animals, and equipment maintenance and repairs for the physical facility. We go beyond that and look at all the categories that have anything to do with travel, research, books for libraries—what we call here the frosting on the cake, but what in the past ten years has become an absolutely necessary ingredient in a zoo of the 1980s as opposed to a zoo of the 1920s. If the park district budget had to be cut 15 percent, it would be almost impossible to cut it, because you'd have to cut into diets or fire a lot of people.

Ninety percent of all the major physical changes we've made at this zoo have been on a matching basis, with public and private funds. Matching, not necessarily equal. Each campaign's been different. If Les goes to the park district and says, "The lion house is falling down. I need a new one," they won't say, "That's your problem," but because of the history that's behind us now, "Find out what you can get from the zoo society." It's almost a given now that the park district only takes on maintenance by itself. Cooperation with the zoo society is a given. There must be a tremendous temptation down at the park district to say, "Tell the zoo society to pay for that." Now with the farm, we did that. There was no money forthcoming from the park district, no money in the budget to renovate that farm. The farm, from an exhibit point of view, was in very bad shape; it was outdated and tired and run-down. And the zoo society took that on alone. The renovation of the children's zoo will cost roughly three and a half million dollars. We are paying seven hundred thousand dollars more than the park district. And all zoo society money is our donors' money.

When I first came here, I didn't understand why Les spent so much time teaching me about the history of the park district and all about the relationships with the commissioners and the staff and understanding that whole big complex chart. I came here with no understanding of that. And in the early days, there was a lot of frustration in trying to communicate. One of the beauties of being at any place long enough is that you either learn to accept that system and decide to spend your energy learning how to work within that system, or you probably wouldn't be there anymore. I genuinely believe that the park district makes every effort to support the goals of the zoo director, which are also the goals of the zoo society. There is certainly strong spiritual support for what we're all trying to achieve here. And there is financial support, as much as it can provide within reason, given its concerns, which stretch all over the city.

The zoo isn't finished being improved. We had a series of long-range planning meetings and came up with a list of probably ten to twenty million dollars' worth of additional improvements. The parking problem is going to cost millions of dollars to fix. The reptile house was not a part of this last campaign, and improvements are needed. More gardens and sculpture. And a solution to the space problem. The administration of a modern zoo simply takes more people, if you're going to go into research, conservation, all kinds of educational programming. And the facilities here are very limited.

The zoo's budget, in spite of the best efforts of the zoo society and the park district, is still severely constrained. We are probably underfinanced by three to five million dollars a year. We don't have enough people. When we did an informal survey of other zoos and the number of people they have on their staffs and the size of their budgets, what's accomplished here per dollar and per person is miraculous. The conservation and research programs could just eat money—five hundred thousand to a million dollars a year before you started scratching the surface. And that's a whole area that's going to become increasingly important, and possible, as we put behind us some of the major sums of money that had to be spent on buildings.

You must begin by spending your money on things that show for the visitors. Let them share the impact of the change. From there you can move to less visible projects, but in order to get fund-raising momentum going, you must have impact on the public so that they come in, see the results of the money, and that becomes the case for giving more money.

When you walk through the zoo now, it's turning into a beautiful place, and it was tired and run-down before. There is a real joy in seeing the animals outside against rocks and trees and in beautiful habitats. Each spring and each fall, more at the change of seasons than any other time, you walk through in the morning or in the evening when it's not crowded so you aren't looking at people, you're just looking at the place. And you say, "Not too bad; it's coming along." I guess that's what makes me proud.

Every time I've thought of giving up this job because it takes a lot out of me and makes me very tired, I try to think of anything that I could do that would be as challenging, as complex, as constantly changing as this is. I'm afraid I've become an excitement junkie or an energy junkie. There is an energy to this place, and to my task and my role in this place, that is constantly challenging. Something always needs to be done, that makes the job not finished, that makes you not want to move on. And the fact of the matter is, it will never be finished, and the day after I walk out the door, wonderful things will continue. It's not a sense of being indispensable. I have no illusions about that, I don't think any of us do around here. I mean, this place will be here, the zoo society will be here, and others will be doing what we're doing, differently but just fine.

I was recently at a park district meeting where some refinements—that's the nice word, cutbacks is the bad word—were being made to the bird of prey plans. And I looked around the table, and there were twelve men sitting around that table addressing this subject, all with goodwill, good faith, a lot of expertise, good spirit, trying to problem-solve. And it was a beautiful fall day, and I just glanced out the window, and it came over me in a flood, one of those little epiphanies that I have all the time around here: "God, am I lucky. Do you know how interesting this is, to be sitting here trying to solve this problem, a real problem that isn't ephemeral, isn't theoretical? Do you know how lucky you are? This is like going to college for the rest of your life, this is like being in a class." It's pretty exciting.

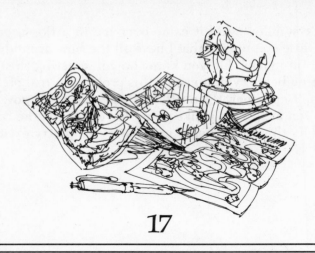

17

DOC

When those who admired zoo director Lester Fisher spoke
about him, certain words were used: good, kind, folksy,
benign, wise, compassionate, concerned. For them, he em-
bodied the qualities John Leonard had once noted: "Naturalists in general seem so kindly disposed, so full of a
sweetness of being, as to suggest that God is lucky they
enlisted in His or Her cheerful service."

When his critics defined his style—and his critics were
few in number and modest in influence—they were in-
clined to distort those virtues and term him vacillating,
wimpish, nonconfrontational, corny, the Mister Rogers of
the zoo world.

In reality, after twenty-five years as director of the zoo,
Les was in charge gently; the style and the man were
inseparable. His best dreams had been dreams about the
future of the zoo; his understated determination had transformed the zoo from a small pastoral pocket in a big city to
a perpetually revised haven for animals that required refuge in order to survive.

Les was not naive; he knew that in the best of worlds, animals would thrive in the wild. Yet he knew as well that the wild was vanishing. Human beings, who tried to protect animals in zoos, simultaneously had trashed the animals' own habitats. The critics of zoos had their reasons; so did the supporters. Les attempted to be a realist in the constant, and often abrasive debate.

To a degree, a feudal society existed at the zoo. The small kingdom was an enclave of lords and vassals, at least as perceived by the latter, the keepers.

Les was the lord of the manor, and his staff governed it. He was accessible to the keepers; when they found the curators to be too rigid in their rule, he listened. In the daily rituals of the zoo, however, the curators reigned. The keepers did not withhold their resentment. The struggle went on in subtle and nagging ways; there were no revolts to compare with the revolts of the outside world. In this sheltered society, conspiracies arose and vanished without overthrowing anyone.

It was not that Les was a despot, benevolent or otherwise. His manner was that of the concerned lord. He knew that things went wrong, that incompetence existed. He knew that there weren't enough dedicated bodies to do all the work efficiently. He tried to function, to be fair, within the system. It wasn't easy.

Les was unpretentious, diligent, and knowledgeable. His work ethic was a familiar one.

He was at his desk by 8 A.M., but he rarely spent more than a few hours behind it without heading to a meeting, a visit with keepers, or a stroll around the zoo. He was paid by the park district, and he had mastered the techniques of dealing with the bureaucracy, of getting done what must be done, and learning to avoid the delusion of instant gratification.

In discussions of the American dream, his career was a case in point.

His parents were immigrants from Czechoslovakia; his father was a butcher, and his parents raised four children on what the father could earn by selling meat. Les was born in 1921 in Chicago, the city that remained his home. As a child, he met food inspectors from the department of agriculture who visited his father's shop; in those days, food inspectors were veterinarians.

Those food inspectors had an impact on his own choice of career. He received his doctor of veterinary medicine from Iowa State University in 1943. World War II was on, and he was shipped to Europe as an army vet; he served as a food inspector as his unit moved across the continent from Brittany to Czechoslovakia. When the war ended, Les returned to Chicago, where he opened an animal hospital and became an attending vet at the zoo. In 1962, the park district board named him director, succeeding Marlin Perkins of TV's "Zoo Parade" fame. " 'Zoo Parade' put our zoo on the map nationally," Les remembered.

Over the years, he married twice, fathered two daughters, and participated in the work of countless zoological causes. Throughout the world of zoos, his name was familiar and respected.

His days at work were varied. On one winter morning, he got to work early from his lakefront high-rise apartment. He wore his typically Ivy League tweedy garb, with button-down shirt and one of his many animal motif ties. By 9 A.M., it was time to take a ride. He met curator of birds Kevin Bell and the associate executive director of the zoo society, Margo Morris, and they drove to the Hyatt Regency Hotel.

Margo had been in touch with the hotel's director of public relations, Nancy Ruth, who indicated that she and the hotel manager, Rodney Young, wanted to chat about the possibility of getting the zoo's help in erecting an aviary in the hotel's atrium.

Nancy, a chic blonde with an assured manner, and Rodney, a fastidiously tailored executive, were ready when Les, Kevin, and Margo arrived. Over coffee around a polished conference table in Rodney's office, the group discussed the project.

En route to the meeting, Les had alerted Kevin and

Margo, "We really can't get involved in the day-to-day operation in any way. Let's refer them to a veterinary practitioner and pull back and be there as a consultant." Tactfully, he repeated that message to Rodney and Nancy. They were not discouraged.

Rodney told Les that he was new to Chicago and didn't know much about the zoo.

"Well, we got started in 1868," Les said. "We might be the oldest zoo in America. In 1870 and 1872, we bought more animals and . . ."

"Is there a ranking of zoos?" Rodney interrupted.

"Sure, we're the best," Les said.

Rodney explained that a metal worker who had worked for Hyatt before was prepared to build a brass bird cage two stories tall. The hotel chain had such a cage in Atlanta, he pointed out. It was next to a bar, and the drinkers could feed their lemon peels and limes to the birds. On Sunday, when the bar was closed, the birds, suffering from alcohol deprivation, screamed for the handouts.

Les smiled.

"We are a public zoo," he said. "We can't directly run the exhibit. We can advise you. You really ought to know that, unlike years ago, when animals could be obtained easily, the movement of animals is difficult these days. And once you set it up, you'll probably have a bunch of agencies looking over your shoulder. Also, you should know that the availability of birds is limited, and the costs are high. So if it does come to be, it'll be your exhibit, not ours. If you do things right, fine. If you don't, you'll hear from someone for sure."

Rodney suggested that the cage might house macaws.

Kevin engaged in some cautious edification.

"Macaws can chew through most wire," he told Rodney. "Some birds can chew off fingers as well. Parrots chew up plants. But we can direct you to sources of birds for you to buy. What about doves? They're easier to manage, easy to get. And they're not loud. Of course, they're not as color-ful, either."

"Whatever we get, it's got to be unique," Rodney said. "I

want people to say, 'Look at those birds, aren't they great?' "

Nancy interrupted. "How can Hyatt help the zoo?"

It was a moment familiar to Les, used to courting potential donors. The zoo could use Hyatt funds, but Les didn't appear to be aggressive about it.

"You ought to get together with the zoo society," he suggested. "We're not here with hat in hand, but anything you can do to help us would be nice." He knew that the Pritzker family, which controlled the Hyatt chain, had already donated large sums to the zoo.

The group left Rodney's office to visit the atrium. A gray-haired, dapper pianist was playing florid music on a white Yamaha grand piano in the lobby.

Rodney pointed out the area that could be converted to an aviary.

"You'll need something relatively hardy," Les said. "There are considerations here. Temperature changes. Air currents. Traffic. Animals live in cycles every day, so the lighting would have to relate to their cycles."

"It could promote a lot of business for the zoo," Rodney said.

"Well, you are just a ten-minute cab ride from us," Les responded. "We'll go back home and do our homework. The challenge is real. It's interesting."

After the appropriate good-byes, back in the car heading to the zoo, Les turned to Kevin, smiled, and said, "Kevin, I give you seventy-two hours to come up with a master plan."

Kevin smiled reluctantly.

"You know, what we want is something the public enjoys that works for the birds, too," Les added.

"Yes," Kevin said stoically.

Les was in his office by 10 A.M. but didn't stay there long. He strutted out into the zoo grounds.

He walked toward the primate house, passing a young woman keeper, who waved at him.

"She had a relationship with a guy who works here that

wasn't too good for her," Les commented. "It's over, and I'm glad. She's a dedicated worker."

Inside the primate house, he went into a holding area. A young woman keeper was at work. He greeted her pleasantly and then asked her when the wire mesh on a cage would be repaired; it was ragged and might injure the monkey in the cage. The keeper assured Les that she'd follow up. He walked across the primate house to the kitchen to talk with keeper Pam Dunn.

Les told Pam that he was going to appear on a local children's TV show that afternoon and needed a well-behaved animal to appear with him. Pam took him to a cage containing a woolly opossum. She put on a pair of leather gloves and plucked the opossum out of the cage. The animal defecated but otherwise passed the test. Les would pick it up later for the show, which he did every other week.

At the great ape house, Les greeted senior keeper Pat Sass and several other keepers. One of them, Richard, was on his morning break, digging into a box of Ding Dongs.

"Want a Ding Dong?" Richard asked Les.

"I don't even know what a Ding Dong is," Les laughed.

Assistant vet Peri Wolff arrived, and the group went into a room off the keeper area, the room Pat devoted to young apes she was hand-raising. They gathered around an incubator-turned-crib for a small baby gorilla. The baby had been bitten by another gorilla and had been retrieved, treated, and returned to the gorilla exhibit. Then its mother neglected it, and another gorilla injured it, so it was pulled again for Pat to care for.

Pat noted, "There are some runny noses among the apes."

"Do we have that viral bug around again?" Les asked. On one occasion a virus, probably introduced by a human, had spread through the ape house.

"Let's hope this time it's not of the magnitude of the last outbreak," he added.

He looked at two baby chimps, happily playing with

stuffed animals. "The patients are looking good, so I feel good," he said.

He walked back to the zoo office in time for another meeting.

Months before, LuAnne Metzger, the farm curator, had been on a plane and had met the president of the National Livestock and Meat Board; he told her that he was interested in the farm. It occurred to her that the board could be helpful in funding the renovations at the farm.

The official and one of his aides would be arriving at the zoo for a tour of the farm. Getting ready for them involved Les, Barbara Whitney, and several other members of the zoo society, as well as LuAnne. They met in the Crown-Field conference room.

The entire visit had been outlined in a memo, and Les was ready. He was often pressed into service as lecturer, tour guide, and fund-raiser.

He pointed out that the National Livestock and Meat Board had been involved with the zoo before.

"We've often pursued them," he said.

"Fine, then it's time to forge a partnership," Barbara said.

Les had a few minutes before he had to join that effort. He went back to his office. A veteran keeper was standing at the door. He had been injured by a reindeer, he told Les. He had entered the yard to check the animal but had failed to carry a broom or a shovel, standard operating procedure. The animal attacked him. He grabbed its horns and held on. Eventually, the animal turned away, but the keeper did suffer a few minor bruises. He told Les that he was OK and would be back at work.

Les scowled, unhappy that an experienced keeper had put himself in a vulnerable position, but his words were consoling.

"Safety for the animals. Safety for the staff. Safety for the visitors. That's my main job," Les said.

The next morning, Les—his face reddened by the cold

wind—was at work early. He stood facing the stinging breeze, in the middle of the zoo, surveying his domain for a moment.

At 6'1", and 176 pounds, he was a conspicuous presence, wearing his dark green parka with ZOO imprinted on the back, and an expression of severe determination. He was on a mission.

He went to the power house, the massive building constructed decades before by the park district to house the heating system for the zoo, the electrical distribution network for the area, and electricians' offices. The building was so old that over the years it had gone from burning coal to burning oil to burning gas.

At 8:15 A.M., he tracked down one of the electricians; he made a point of knowing all of them, calling each by their first name, being cordial and polite with them. He knew that the zoo depended upon the cooperation of the trade workers who serviced the vital systems.

In this case, Les needed help. A new copying machine was going to be delivered to the zoo society. It would need a separate power line. The electrician, a middle-aged man and a veteran of zoo service, called Les "Doc," as many of the laborers did, and assured him that the job would be done on time.

Les walked out of the power house with a faint smile on his face and moved into the chill wind. He seemed oblivious to the elements, tough in an inconspicuous way.

Back in his office, he noted that he was genuinely grateful that the electrician would be helpful. In the past, it wasn't always that easy, when the patronage system sometimes put incompetents in place and let them live out their careers to retirement without making many demands on them to be efficient. Patronage remained, but it was not as virulent as it had been.

"I try to keep the zoo neutral," Les said. "Politically neutral. I let people know, in the bureaucracy, that it would be sad, a setback, if there were people working at the zoo who didn't deserve to work here. It would diminish our professionalism. Now, of course, most of our keepers are civil service."

At 9 A.M., he met with curator of mammals Mark Rosenthal, the zoo society's Margo Morris, and the park district's P.R. man, Don Garbarino. It was one of a periodic series of meetings to coordinate publicity for the zoo, a function shared by the park district and the zoo society.

What was newsworthy?

Bozie, one of the zoo's elephants, was being shipped to a zoo in Springfield, Missouri; the twelve-year-old, 6,000-pound female would be on a breeding loan.

A female gorilla was being transferred across town to the Brookfield Zoo for breeding purposes; the two Chicago area zoos often exchanged animals and expertise.

A University of Illinois architectural student had designed a module that would be placed in the great ape house, a module that would contain nuts and other treats and would tempt the apes to play with it and reward them for their dexterity. It was a safe form of play and intellectual stimulation for the animals.

When the meeting ended, Les attacked a small pile of phone messages and a large stack of unread mail. His office was filled with wildlife photos and drawings, framed awards, boxes of slides, family photos, animal sculptures. On one wall there was an African tribal mask from the Victoria Falls area and a spear and shield from the Masai.

That afternoon and evening, Les was set to attend a budget hearing at park district headquarters, a meeting of public library officials, and a meeting with the president of World Wildlife U.S.A. But first, he wanted to peek into the children's zoo, under construction and close to completion.

As he walked across the zoo, a group of preteenagers saw him and giggled.

"I saw him on TV," one laughed.

"Yes, that's the one. He's the man from the zoo," another said. "Should we get his autograph?"

Before they could vote on the matter, Les was into the children's zoo for a brisk walk-through.

His daily routine was a pragmatic, rather than a contemplative, one. There was much to do.

"I do try to stay abreast of medical matters, so I don't get lost," he said. "I'm not in practice now, but I take continuing education courses to keep my license. And there are dozens of institutions putting out publications that I feel I ought to scan. I still haven't figured out when I'm supposed to read a good book just for pleasure."

The meetings consumed his afternoon, and the next morning began with another.

At 9 A.M., he chaired his weekly staff meeting. Several curators were off on assignments. Present were Joan Friedman, assistant curator of education; Anne Boyle, director of graphics; Nancy Worssam, director of programs for the zoo society; reptiles curator Clarence Wright; farm curator LuAnne Metzger; and curator of education Judy Kolar.

Les consulted his notes.

He told them about the keeper who had been bruised by a reindeer. The keeper had seen Mark Rosenthal's slide presentation on safety for keepers, but hadn't been shielded from danger by it.

"Poor judgment," Les ruled. " And he paid a price. When you lose respect for an animal, you get hurt."

He announced that there had been a birth among a group of gorillas that Lincoln Park had sent to the St. Louis Zoo.

"A nice plus for us," he said. "Long-term conservation, a breeding program."

He told those present that Bozie would leave for the Springfield, Missouri, zoo within a few days, by special truck under the supervision of an elephant management specialist.

Later that day there would be a delegation from Citicorp, he announced. It would involve the "standard donor tour and lunch," and the group would be taken through the children's zoo, to which Citicorp had donated funds.

He had attended a budget hearing at park district headquarters the night before, but hadn't been called to testify. As frustrating as the experience had been, he did feel that the zoo's budget request was in "a positive mode."

There was a new memo from park district headquarters about "Employee Disciplinary Procedures."

"Not much that we don't already know," he declared.

Nancy Worssam brought up the matter of a prominent donor who wanted to provide seed money for a program to install animal sculptures in the animal houses. On the surface, it seemed like an idea to enhance the appearance of the zoo buildings, but Nancy pointed out that it would involve a long-term commitment.

"How do we protect the sculptures?" Les asked, favoring pragmatism over art for the moment. "I do have a touch of concern about that. It has to be small-scale stuff, and small-scale stuff is easy to abuse. You can't put something big in our spaces, with our crowds. You've got to plan the displays in advance." He wanted to discuss the sculpture program again when more of the curators were present.

He reported on the construction-renovation of the children's zoo: "Sadly, the contractor is slowing down. The weather is getting sloppier, wetter, colder. I think it would be good to bring in some big trees before the big freeze. The so-called dedication of the completed children's zoo is still in question."

The zoo society would sponsor three African trips next year, he announced. All staff members, those who would be going and those who would not, should adjust their schedules to consider the dates of those trips.

Clarence Wright had bad news. A baby tortoise had been stolen from the reptile house. A plastic disposable razor and a can of shaving cream had been found, inexplicably, in a tortoise pen. Clarence had begun to change the locks at various doors to the reptile house holding areas.

"More and more incidents," he muttered, unhappily. "We have to look at it closely."

"You have to assume that ninety-eight percent of it is done by 'family,' " Les said to Clarence. "You know, you can accept silliness, but something that could be calamitous is always a threat."

"So many people pass through the house," Clarence lamented. "Even volunteers, docents picking up animals to take them to schools. Maintenance people pass through all the time."

"It could be angry employees getting back at the staff," Les theorized. "We've had that in the past."

The meeting ended at 10 A.M., and Les headed with LuAnne to the farm, to check on the work being done there.

Their faces were whipped by a painful wind as LuAnne drove an open electric cart from the Crown-Field Center to the farm. Winter had arrived. A few hardy visitors walked along the paths, but the sounds of gaiety that summer brought were no longer heard. The animals as well had retreated indoors, by choice or order.

At the farm, Les could see that an attempt to match paint on an exterior wall of the main barn had not succeeded. He cornered a friendly supervisor—who called him "Doc"—and chatted about correcting the mismatch. He cajoled in a most delicate way, expressing affection and respect even as he raised his cautiously stated demand for change. In a few minutes, the supervisor had gone from reticence about such a change to believing in the possibility of it.

Les moved on to the reptile house.

The evidence had been cleaned up; the tortoises were eating in their pen, minus the razor and the shaving cream. Art Maraldi, the keeper on duty in the basement, announced to Les that there was a moral to the story: "Never go out with an unshaven tortoise."

Art's joke made Les smile. He rushed out of the building with the smile intact.

After his lunch with the delegation from Citicorp, Les lingered in the reception area. A great ape keeper, Richard, came in, saw him, and let him know that about a third of the apes looked sick, with a possible flu bug. Peri Wolff had put them on antibiotics.

Trouble with apes, any trouble, was a personal matter for Les. He had spent years winning respect and admiration for the zoo's care and breeding of the great apes.

"A year ago, we lost an old chimp and a baby gorilla," he said. "They were zapped by acute viral pneumonia. What's scary is that the great apes can get almost everything we get."

It was time for him to make rounds, to roam around the zoo, to visit the animal houses and the keepers. He began in the small mammal house, where rodents had been a problem. Gene Brimer, responsible for exterminating them, had initiated a plan.

"Any rats around?" Les asked a keeper.

"The traps are out," she replied.

"Stay with it," he urged.

He remembered, with embarrassment, a tour he had conducted of the small mammal house with a prominent member of the park district hierarchy. Les showed the executive a cage, and the cage contained the proper animal plus a lively batch of invading mice. After that, he persuaded the park district to assign a pest control specialist to the zoo.

"I try to walk around and look at the zoo as a visitor would see it," he said.

He walked to the office and warehouse for the zoo society gift shops. He had his keys in hand, a sizable collection, but when he pushed the outer door, it opened. Money was kept inside the building—the proceeds from gift shop sales—and while it was in a locked safe in a locked office, unlocked doors bothered Les. He mentioned it to a staff member.

He strolled through the building, past stacks of animal toys and other gift items—including samples of stuffed koala bear toys; the gift shops would have to be ready.

At the hospital, all was in order. In a cage in the holding

area, one of the small monkeys screeched loudly. Not far away, in another holding area, a pair of mountain lions made their high-pitched whines. It reminded Les that these were creatures in from the wild and none too happy about it.

"Stress. People have it. Animals have it, too. They get it because they're away from what's familiar to them in the wild. Birds have died in my hands from stress," he said.

He moved on to the bear line, where behind the scenes a radio blared country music. A young, attractive keeper named Diana was at work hosing down the line; a few bear noses appeared in the slots of their dens.

"Look who's here," Diana announced to the bears, "The big cheese."

Outside, the polar bears—Chukchi and Thor—splashed and swam playfully in their pool, massive figures in slow motion when seen through the underwater viewing windows.

"They're probably the most dangerous animal in the zoo," Les said. "Even trained animal people can't get a feeling for their moods. They're totally impassive. No clues. The may be happy to see you or happy to eat you. They'll eat whatever they get."

He walked to the northern edge of the zoo, where the zoo met the traffic of civilization. Between the two was the zoo rookery. Les entered it, paused, and appreciated the setting.

"It's my personal joy," he said. "Quiet. Wonderful. Removed. A very special place."

In the large mammal house, he stopped behind the scenes to peer up at the giraffes, who peered down at him.

"They have extremely sensitive circulatory systems," he said. "They knocked down two of them at Brookfield, to examine them. They never got up. When you leave a giraffe down for an hour, an animal that tall, you run a risk."

He had commissioned a kind of squeeze cage for the

giraffes, so they could be examined without tranquilizing them, a large swinging gate that would enclose each giraffe when it had to be examined.

At the bird house, he made sure that there was a keeper on duty on the main floor, watching the birds in the free-flight area. He didn't want to have a bird stolen; it had happened. In fact, two keepers were on duty.

At 3 P.M. he returned to his office; his timing was fortunate. Standing in front of the building was a zoo society staff member with a couple who might become donors. She introduced them to Les, who responded with a short, lively lecture on the history of the zoo.

"We appreciate your interest and your support," he said. "We need your help."

He walked toward the door to the Crown-Field Center, then remembered a stop he had forgotten to make. He turned around and headed for the great ape house.

The apes on exhibit seemed sluggish, but he wasn't certain if that was due to sickness or if it was their "quiet time." Inside the core of the exhibit, he checked a baby chimp in a keeper's arms. For a moment, he was a vet again.

"Sounds nice and clean," he said, after tapping the chimp's back with his finger.

He spotted Pat Sass and walked over to her. They were standing in the inner core of the exhibit, with only wire mesh between them and the apes.

A large male gorilla, Koundu, slowly came over to where Les was standing. Koundu pushed a banana through the mesh, without bruising it, offering it to Les. It was an act of sharing, a wish for interaction, and Les recognized it. He took the banana, turned away pretending to take a bite out of it, then returned it to Koundu.

"I used to be able to tickle his tongue," Les said. "Now, he'd take my hand off."

He returned to his office, thinking about the apes.

"The line between a head cold and pneumonia is such a

thin one at times," he muttered. "It's so difficult to treat this situation. So difficult."

The next morning, Les was at work by 7:30 A.M., dressed in a light brown sport jacket, khaki slacks, and a blue plaid sport shirt. It was not likely garb for the winter climate in Chicago. But it was logical for his destination many hours later that day: Zimbabwe.

He was one of a group of zoo directors who had been invited by the government of Zimbabwe to spend two weeks touring that country. It was an effort to tempt them to return with others, as Les might on a zoo society safari. He had not been to Zimbabwe in years; he remembered it as a place hostile to some of the white natives, and he hoped that it had improved.

But before he could board the plane to England for the first leg of the trip, he had several meetings to attend.

At 8 A.M., he headed for the auditorium in the Crown-Field Center to chair the keepers' meeting. As usual, he brought the keepers up to date on developments that he felt mattered to them.

Budget hearings were going on, he told them, and "we're going to come out of them perfectly OK for this year's budget. We've built a solid case for the zoo, and the people at the park district respect that."

He asked vet Tom Meehan to speak to the keepers about a new program to use consultants to help improve the diets of the animals in the zoo. The consultants would do an in-depth analysis of present feeding practices, Tom said, and would discern problems and make suggestions for changes. To begin, Tom said, "we'll make a list of what the animals are fed now and what they actually eat—that's what is important."

"Diets evolve. Different approaches, different ideas," Les said. "Our work will be reflected in the animals' health. What do they really need? Now we'll have a scientific basis for that."

A park district executive with a concern for detail had visited the zoo unannounced and wondered if many keepers worked while dressed in outfits that weren't their proper uniforms. In very hot and very cold weather, variations abounded. Les urged the keepers to wear their uniforms, not to deviate from them. He did not appear to be insistent.

He encouraged all present to read the new park district pamphlet on disciplinary procedures.

"It's a system to potentially protect both sides, labor and management," he said. "I hope everyone understands it. See me if you have any questions."

He noted that 3,000 Girl Scouts would be visiting the zoo one day in three weeks. The audience produced a collective rumble in response to the news.

Workers were putting some finishing touches on parts of the children's zoo, he added, but completion was several months away. The main building might be opened during the winter, but opening the entire children's zoo might best be put off until the spring, when the weather would be cooperative.

Park district records indicated that zoo staff members were making a lot of long-distance calls. The bureaucrats kept their eyes—or, rather, their ears—open to such abuses.

"Don't go on for twenty or thirty minutes. Be mindful," he stressed.

The food concession at the zoo had been awarded to the zoo society, he announced. The keepers managed a mild cheer.

"It'll mean real good food at a fair price," he said. "It'll phase in during a two-year period. But by spring we'll have the new food available."

Mark Rosenthal, curator of mammals, was summoned to the podium by Les, to talk about the elephant shipment later in the week. Mark pointed out that Bozie would be in heat in two weeks, so "we'll see what happens when she gets there."

"We pay for any pregnancy that results, and a board fee," Les noted. "We continue to try. This is a long-term preservation program."

Les asked Kevin Bell, the curator of birds, to make an announcement. Kevin told the keepers that a pair of king penguins—larger, at four feet tall, than any of the penguins in the zoo—would be on loan from the Milwaukee Zoo while their habitat was being renovated. He was delighted.

The meeting ended just before 9 A.M., and Les went directly to the conference room for a staff meeting.

Assistant director Dennis Meritt, back from a trip to Africa, was there, along with education curator Judy Kolar, vets Tom Meehan and Peri Wolff, farm curator LuAnne Metzger, assistant education curator Joan Friedman, Mark Rosenthal, and the zoo society's Nancy Worssam.

Les ran down his agenda.

"The zoo food is number one in excitement," he said. "The zoo society got it. Very meaningful. Now we can get rid of those crappy signs and stands. The society has committed more than four million dollars to the project. A whole new world. The quality will change dramatically."

Joan Friedman filled in the others on the details of the Girl Scout walk through the zoo. It would indeed involve 3,000 girls, in seventy buses. Three zoo tours had been arranged for them, and it would all be done in about two hours.

Les ran down his stint at the budget hearings. "We're still in reasonably OK shape," he said. "Of course, they question every line item in our budget."

He repeated his message about phone abuse. "You can get a call done in five minutes," he implored. "I'm sure we're going to hear about it, so be helpful."

He talked about the keeper who had been careless with the reindeer. Something had to be done, some discipline imposed, he said. But what? He didn't want to suspend the keeper, who had been injured, though not severely. The point had to be made—that he knew better than to enter the pen without an implement, a broom or a rake or a shovel, to defend himself. Some reprimand was necessary, Les felt.

"He could have been dead potatoes," Dennis said. "He was lucky. Reindeer bash, but they really aren't fighters."

Mark suggested that a written reprimand might be enough. Mark had discussed safety with the keeper before; he would do so again.

"Well, there was no escape and no threat to the public, or anyone else injured," Les sighed. "I'll look into a written reprimand."

By 10 A.M. Les had gotten to the bottom of his pile of notes. It was time to go. By the end of the day, he would be flying east, to London and on to Zimbabwe, for two weeks without decisions about reckless keepers, bureaucrats, and hordes of Girl Scouts. As he left the conference room, his pace quickened.

First Person: Lester Fisher

I wasn't certain I wanted to be a vet. I had a high school chum, and he was going to go out to Ames, Iowa, to Iowa State to study animal husbandry. I had an interest in some such field. I had met a few veterinarians, some of the veterinarians who worked in the meat-packing plants. They were the food inspectors, then as now. When I decided to go to Ames, I thought that I would enroll in a preveterinary course, to see what it was like.

I had a unique exposure. There was a rooming house on the edge of town, a big old three-story green house, and one of the people living in it was a faculty man, Walter Anderson, who was in charge of the ambulatory clinic of the veterinary college. Whenever he had a call and I was home, he'd knock on my door and say, "Les, do you want to come along?" And after spending many months with him, I was pretty well convinced that I'd like to try for vet school.

I'm sure that he was a deciding person in my life because

at first I was an anachronism at college. I was the city kid; they were all country boys. Even though my grades were solid, I have to assume that Walter Anderson probably said a positive thing for me, and that must have helped me get into vet school.

While in vet school, I did what everyone did—took all four years of general courses, which included everything. Emphasis was on farm animals, certainly not on dogs and cats; the horse was our anatomy animal. It wasn't any secret that I was interested in small animals, but people couldn't quite understand that. I finished school, filled in for a vet for three months until he got called in the service, and then I went in the service.

When I got out of the army, Northwestern University was looking for a veterinarian to help their animal care program, someone who might be interested in further schooling. I came on board as head of the animal care program there, and took some graduate courses in physiology. It was there that I got the zoo connection. I met Marlin Perkins. I had bought a sheet metal shop that was for sale, and set up my practice. It was then that Marlin and I talked a bit about the possibility of my doing something with the zoo, and we agreed to an arrangement whereby half a day a week, every Wednesday morning, I'd come down and make rounds and take care of what needed doing, and emergencies. And so that started and kept on for fifteen years.

I thought zoo work would be fun. But I was thinking more in terms of zoo medicine, not being a zoo director. I enjoyed my practice, and I was very successful in my practice. So, up until the day that Marlin said, "Les, I'm leaving. I'm going back to St. Louis," I hadn't seriously thought about the possibility of zoo administration.

I had to think about it for a few months. It was one of the tougher decisions of my life. It was a great financial hardship; the job paid very little then, relatively speaking, and I was doing three to four times better than that in practice. But practice had lost its edge for me. Once you accomplish a goal, it's a little hard to get yourself up a bit. The zoo just seemed like a fresh challenge. I certainly had had enough years to get a feel for it. In fact, I even remember telling Marlin that I was going to apply. He said, "You must be nuts." He said, "You mean you want to put up with all this bureaucracy and take a cut in pay and everything?" And I said, "Well, I think so. I've thought and thought and thought and finally decided that I may want to apply." And so I finally went down to the district and put in an application.

I went down one time for an interview, and I remember very clearly, it was in June that one day I was making rounds here and got a phone call to go to the park district headquarters. So I finished up what I was doing. I went down there in my shirt sleeves; it was hot, and I'd been dirty and working, and all of a sudden, the man in charge said, "You're the new zoo director." I gulped; he already had alerted the media, and they were down there, and it was really an overwhelming kind of silliness the way it evolved.

Also, Marlin was still here. Marlin had served notice that he was going to leave in September. But there were some stresses between some of the commissioners and Marlin, and I think somehow they might have thought that it was a way to get him, to appoint the replacement zoo director. For me it was fine because it gave me a chance to work with Marlin more closely for a few months. We always got along great. He never tried to treat an animal, tell me medically what to do, and I repaid that kindness—I never told him how to run a zoo.

Marlin didn't have any degree. Marlin was one of these self-made naturalists. He started sweeping floors in the reptile house at St. Louis. He became a keeper and decided not to go back to school. He put Lincoln Park on the national map. He put the zoo on television. They started with a regular Sunday show here, and the NBC people would bring a trailer out, park it next to the reptile house, and the basement of the reptile house was a studio. After two, three years of local programming, they somehow got NBC to consider doing it on the network, and "Zoo Parade" was off and running. Marlin did some wondrous things.

I got to do some television work. But I think from day one when I took over the zoo, everyone kept saying, "Well, are you going to do TV like Marlin?" And I said, "No, I'm not Marlin. He's one of a kind, and he is television." For the first two years, I tried not to get involved with television. I wanted to do Les Fisher's thing and not Marlin Perkins's thing. But then I had a Saturday morning TV show, more of a kids' show. I did that for about a year and a half, two years. And one day they called me and said, "Les, sorry, we're going to bump you. Flash Gordon's coming on to take your spot." I said, "Well, that's too bad, but I like Flash," and that ended my brief solo show. Then they put me on with Ray Rayner on his morning show, and twice a week for about ten years we did the "Ark in the Park." Today I'm happy continuing my work here at the zoo and doing some TV spots. There's plenty to accomplish at the zoo.

I feel very fortunate, truly, that I've never been seriously injured at the zoo in all my years here. I have always been a very conservative doctor and very much aware of not underestimating an animal. And in the zoo, especially in those early years when I was awed by them all anyway, I wasn't about to go in with a bear or a lion or anything unless there was a reasonable method to handle it. In the lion house, we used to take a long pole, and we'd put a lariat on the end of it. We'd put it through the bars and drop it over the animal's head. The secret was not to just put it over the head, you had to get it under one or the other front leg, because when you went to pull the lariat, if it was just around the neck, the animal would choke before you could safely loosen it. You could do that in five minutes or an hour, it depended on how the luck went. And with some of the hoofed animals, we would get them in a stall, and we'd get a group of good people, keepers, and say, "You take the horn, you take the head, you take a hind leg, you take a front leg, and when I say 'go, one-two-three' "—we all grabbed hold of something and hoped that it worked. We had different tools then, and we stressed animals and took some chances, but I didn't bravely go into a cage with a dangerous animal.

Today, we have our missions. The primary one is to save the animals' habitats. There is no substitute for that. If it's at all possible to preserve the wildlife in their home, that's objective number one. Conservation. You preserve not an individual animal but the whole ecosystem, the land, the plants, the animals, you name it. And I think truly that the zoo is a part of, or a supplement to, that. When you realize that if you put all the zoos in the world together, their total physical plant would still be a tiny space, you can see there's only a certain number of animals that we can handle. It'd be wrong to say the zoo breeding programs are going to save x animals. To me, national parks, animal reserves, and zoos are the main backup to the wild, to the habitat. There are individual cases where the zoos have saved some species, no question. And the classic American buffalo, the bison story, is dramatic. The Bison Society and the Bronx Zoo helped turn that program around when hundreds of bisons were left, out of tens of millions. That is a positive thing.

I think the zoo breeding program's important. The importance of it is varied. First of all, the zoo loves to have babies; it's very exciting for our visitors to see youngsters. Second, it's always been a historic benchmark for us, a sign that maybe we're doing something right if we can breed these animals in captivity. It's kind of a barometer of the care we give. If you get down a second, third, fourth generation of captive breeding, then you know you're doing something right. I think the breeding programs in great part hinge on a slowly evolving professionalism in the management of the zoo animal.

And nutrition has to be one of the keys. Years ago we fed what we thought was right, but there was no basis for it; we fed meat eaters meat. Meat is not a balanced diet, especially horse meat, which we fed to our cats. We started adding some calcium powder to the meat and cut a little pocket in there and put some powder in, and we started getting healthier animals. We were feeding frozen fish to a lot of animals, especially the seals and sea lions and that. And no one ever really researched what happens when you freeze a fish. We were feeding a thiamin-deficient diet to our seals, and we were losing some of them with neurological problems, and we didn't know why. And finally we did some research and now we put the B1, the thiamin tablets, down the mouth of the fish. We started balancing rations. Instead of the old days when we gave the hoofed stock a little ground corn and some hay and stuff like that, we now feed them grain rations that are nutritionally balanced, in addition to the hay and the rest. That probably did as much for the reproductive results as the other things.

The long-term hope for the survival of animals on earth is through education, there's no question about it. We have to get to the urban masses who are not able to personally experience the wild. We have to tell them the story, and that is one of the major justifications of a zoo. When you speak about the wild and a zoo and all the other things, there are people who say it's wrong to take an animal from the wild and put it in a zoo. Is the animal happier here? Who's to say? All I know is that if you just do today what we used to do—take an animal from the wild and put it in a cage and someone came and looked at it—and commented that it was either exciting or fun or silly or funny or whatever, it is not really a good justification.

We lost a lot of animals because we didn't have the facilities, we didn't have diets, we didn't have care, we didn't have a lot of things. But it seemingly wasn't serious because there was another animal out there that you could get and put in its place. So if a monkey died, you could contact someone and get another monkey. If it weren't for the long-term breeding programs, the conservation effort, if it weren't for the education department and its work here, if it weren't for some of the research we do to help the animals, I think the so-called recreation factor would be a weak one to justify taking these animals and putting them in a zoo. The fight that we wage to help animals in the world—and that comes through in our publications, our programs, our graphics—is to get people to be aware. Zoos don't do it alone, but they're a good part.

One has to try to separate emotionalism from realism. We in the animal world know that there is a balance of seals and so on in the world, and that if you don't harvest any, you may be creating a different situation than if you do. Everything ends up in a balance. Nature does balance things out, and that's one reason why in many wild animals there are multiple births. If you have thirty rattlesnakes hatched, maybe two are going to survive. Otherwise, you take thirty and keep multiplying them, and pretty soon you've got a world full of rattlesnakes.

We have more white-tailed deer in this country than we can handle. There's an annual hunt, and people pay to get a license, and that money goes into the conservation fund. Some hunters shoot deer for kicks; many shoot them for food. If we didn't hunt now, I think there'd be a tremendous die-off, due to the lack of food supply. The available food supply is what governs the number of animals that an area can hold. I am saying that I am comfortable with the fact that there is an annual hunt for deer. But there are people who say it's terrible to shoot a deer. And I can empathize with them; I understand why they say it. I'm not a hunter, I can't go out and shoot a deer. If I were starving and my family's life depended on my hunting and I had a chance to shoot a deer, I probably would do it. But I am saying that there are balances, and the business of all these save-the-whatevers, some of them make sense and some of them may not. It's an unending dialogue, and there are no easy answers.

When we say one of our justifications in these breeding programs is to have animals to reintroduce in the wild, in some places, there's no wild to reintroduce them to. Especially the large mammals and especially the predators and the more dangerous animals. You couldn't send a tiger back to India today. Where are you going to release it? There are a limited number of national parks there, and they are full to the carrying capacity of tigers. But in theory, sure, if there were some wipeout, for whatever reasons, the animals are still in a captive breeding program, and we could send them back.

Most of the animal releases that have been done have been reasonably successful, because they're done by professionals who know what they're doing, and they know where, how, and when to release them. Do they all survive? No. In a classic story about freedom in the wild, Joy Adamson wrote one of the world's great books. On the other hand when she gave it the name she did, *Born Free*, that was a tough title to those of us who are professional animal people, because the implication is that animals in the wild are free. They are and they're not. They have the same constraints that humans do. Consider their certain territories and certain available food supplies and certain natural disasters and certain predators and certain whatever, and the animal in the wild has relative freedom, primarily spatial. But beyond that, the *Born Free* syndrome is a tough one. It is and it ain't, and Joy's animals weren't in a sense free. Sure, she had a unique situation where they still could run around and do what they wanted and come back to her. I think Joy got carried away in the later years of her life; she was always out there looking for generations of Elsa, and people started questioning whether she was even being totally rational about her search.

My philosophy has always been to go ahead and treat people as adults. There's a job to do; I let them know what the job is and let them do it. I try to delegate, and I accept responsibility for the joys and the sorrows of whatever they do. I don't always agree with how they do it, and I might do it differently, but I can't do it. So I have to rely on staff, and I'm a great believer in that. I am very pleased with my staff because they are committed people, they are good people, they know their work, they are probably doing more than their counterparts in other zoos because of the small size of our staff.

I feel that I've been kind of privileged. I watched many of the young men that Marlin had when he was director; at that time Lincoln Park was one of the true training grounds for a zoo staff. Many zoologists came from college and spent a few years here with Marlin and moved on to other zoos. And that process continued after I became director. I'm always here and ready to encourage any of my staff who want to move on in their profession, because I believe in that. My door has always been open to anybody, whether it's the secretary, the keeper, the curator, the assistant director. I have great faith in people. I believe that I have to allow that kind of dialogue because that's part of the opportunity for me to be aware of what's happening in the zoo. As I make rounds or as I talk to people, I feel it's important that they're comfortable, that they can share things with me. And I tell them they can share it in two ways: they can share it in public or they can share it in private.

Dealing with people is the toughest part of anyone's life. It doesn't matter what the business is, it's the human factor. I try to listen to all sides, and I try to end up deciding what I believe is the right course. I never demean anyone in public; I always mediate in private. I try to resolve differences, because it's rare that something is totally black and white. I have to back my staff. I have to back the senior keeper over the keeper, I have to back the curator over the senior keeper and so on, but only if things are fair and correct. If there are animal things going on here—and it never ceases to be a source of concern, hopefully not contention—does the veterinarian pass judgment on a certain animal management matter, or does the curator or the animal management curator team do it? I don't favor anyone. If each staff member acts in a positive way, the animals benefit in every way. If they don't, then you have stress. The other extreme is a zoo where the curator

of mammals never goes in the bird section. The bird curator never goes in the reptile section, and it's just like a
compartmentalized ship; no one really knows what's going
on in the next compartment. I don't believe in that. One
reason I think a lot of fine young people got training here
and could move on was because they learned the whole
zoo. I think that's good.

I accept the system, the bureaucracy I work for. First of
all, I never looked upon the job as something that I had to
have. I looked upon this job as something important, but if
for whatever reason it didn't work out, I wasn't going to go
in a corner and cry. I'd do something else, either go back to
practice or some other job. So I didn't have that kind of
concern. Second, I have no civil service status; I'm here at
the will of the commission, as are some of my other staff. I
found that the people that I worked with at the park district
over the years were basically good people. I found that if I
treated people with respect, whether they were or weren't
empathetic to what I needed or was doing, they were there,
and they were doing whatever it was they were going to
do. I felt that I could either fight the bureaucracy as many
people tend to, or try to get it to work for me. I learned
patience. When I was in practice I made my own decisions
and I lived by them. Here many decisions are made for me.
I guess I was able to get through to the various people in
my early years that I wanted to do the best job I could, but I
wanted to do it my way. And as long as they respected my
job, as long as I did things that they could live with, then I
could survive all this other stuff. It is frustrating to see
some work orders sit around for a period of time, it is
frustrating to get things that aren't reacted to and so on,
sure it is. But to me the big picture is what counts, and the
big picture here is the zoo. And the zoo is what matters to
me. If I can see my animals getting cared for, if I can see
my visitors being treated properly, if I can see my employees doing their work properly, I think that's what's
important. The day-to-day problems drop a touch in perspective as time moves on and if you achieve the goal. And

the goal is to get the last of these animals out of these totally antiquated facilities. It's wrong. And so we have a commitment to them.

I never played politics. I have my own personal philosophy, and people that I respect more than others in the political scene. But I have always felt that the zoo is everybody's. Administrations come and go, and the zoo's had a long, proud history.

I travel and I look at other zoos. I react to them. I think the Basel, Switzerland, zoo is one of my personal joys. It's as small and compact as we are, beautifully landscaped, fine animal collection. The National Zoo's always been a source of concern and interest to me. I feel it's part of my zoo. I keep reminding people at the National Zoo it ain't their zoo, it's our zoo. It's the *National* Zoo. And the nice thing is that by happy coincidence, our congressman helped that zoo. Sid Yates from the Ninth District here sits on the budget committee of Interior. Sid and I have known each other twenty-five years, and Sid has an interest in Lincoln Park Zoo; he's become very aware of the role of zoos. And whenever the hearings would come up in Washington for the Smithsonian, of which the National Zoo is part, I think Sid looked out very strongly and kindly for them. So I'd like to think that whatever it is, twenty to fifty million dollars' worth of work that's gone on there in the last fifteen or twenty-five years, is in part due to that man's help, and I'd like to think I had a little piece of it. The National Zoo's very important, and like ours, it's come from pretty sad to real good.

The Bronx I've always had great respect for, not only because of the zoological job they do, but because they're concerned with international and national conservation and wildlife. They have historically done more than all the other zoos in America combined in that area. There are two major zoos in the world that have done that, Frankfurt and the Bronx. San Diego is a great zoo, and everyone mentions it. Part of it is the mystique of marketing. They sold that zoo. After the war there was this zoo, and it was a relatively small one, in some ways analogous to Lincoln Park, but it was in a lovely site, with a lot of topography and terrain. The thing that made San Diego great in its earlier years was the fact that it had the best climate in America, and everything there would grow in terms of flowering plants. Therefore you could take a facility perhaps no different from some of mine here, antiquated, outmoded, you name it, but you put flowers, plants in front of it, in back of it, on top of it, around it. So it really became a true zoological garden, and about ten, fifteen years ago they did an inventory, and I think the plants were worth ten times what the animals were worth.

The other thing that happened was Los Angeles, its closest neighbor, had literally no zoo up to fifteen years ago. There was a little collection, a dozen cages, on the side of Griffith Park, nothing to promote. San Diego wisely started marketing: "Come to our zoo." And people did, and do, and so the mystique developed. And then when they did the wild animal park on top of it, two thousand acres, thirty-five miles out, they proceeded to use the "Johnny Carson Show." Their budget for marketing and PR at one time was almost the same as my whole direct zoo operating budget, several million dollars. Well if you tell a story often enough and do it well and have good reason, people will accept it. So the mystique started and kept on that San Diego was America's number one zoo. And I accept that, with their combined collections, but once Los Angeles got into the business, and once they became good and professional at it, they're on the same level professionally as San Diego. At first, all the things that could go wrong did go wrong there. They had so many mistakes they brought in consultants on top of consultants to try to straighten things out, in terms of animal habitats and so on. It took some years, but finally it's a lovely landscaped garden of its own, much more compact than some zoos, not one of these two-hundred-acre things.

It would be wrong not to say Brookfield's one of my

favorite zoos. My kids were brought up in Brookfield, and I
took care of some of their animals and got to know the
people well. When it opened, it was one of the state-of-the-
art zoos with open space and so on. Brookfield's always
had a strong commitment to science, and I've always respected them for that. That's one of the things that we are
playing a little bit of a slower role in, because our board, the
park district, is park commissioners; they're not necessarily interested in research and academic things. Whereas
some of the Brookfield board historically has been scientists, and so they've been able to do that.

There are other zoos. I think San Francisco is coming
along. The Detroit Zoo was built by a landscape architect;
at one time it was one of the prettiest zoos in America. It
had its bad days, and now I think it's coming back strongly.
I think a lot of zoos are changing. I think the Minnesota
State Zoo and the North Carolina State Zoo are two important collections in our country. St. Louis and Cincinnati
are meaningful collections that I have respect for. Denver's
come a long way in recent years.

I think you have to have Regent's Park in London in
there; it's one of the meaningful zoos. Antwerp has to rate
as one of the fine collections in Europe. Amsterdam and
Rotterdam are very good collections. Cologne. Berlin certainly, the old tiergarten, even though the wall split it, and
they have two zoos in Berlin now, East and West. But West
Berlin is one of the early great zoos of the world. They're
one of the collectors, very interested in diversity of species.

The naturalistic setting isn't necessarily good for the
animal. After all, no one's ever really figured out what the
animal thinks on the other side of the bars. The tendency
is to provide better spaces, give animals what is biologically
important to their needs. But in my old monkey house, for
example, for forty, fifty years on the west side of the
building there were outside cages, and on the east side
there were none. From a health standpoint, I never saw any
difference if the animals got outside or not. As long as we

had ultraviolet lights, as long as we balanced the diet, from the standpoint of health, longevity, reproduction, I saw no difference. Sure, sunshine is important. But that convinced me that you could do a good job of maintaining animals inside, if you gave them a total proper environment. Animals make peace with their cages, because that's their home.

When animals escape in a zoo, unlike a human escaping from a jail, they don't want to get away from anything. They're out, and once they're out, they're perplexed and concerned and excited as to what's what, because they've lost the security of their home. And more often than not, if wild animals are given a chance in a zoo, they'll go back to the place they escaped from. The problem is that it's hard for them to ever do that because people are after them. And it'd be kind of simplistic to say, "Well, if everyone just sits back, you know, that tiger's going to go back into his cage." You worry where that tiger might go, and therefore you'd better catch it, before it gets in trouble. But it is a fact that animals look upon their cage as their home; they're secure in there. And part of the secret of good cage design is to know the needs of the kind of animal. Some animals need space, some animals don't need a lot of space. One animal has to literally touch the walls of its cage; for others, the more space the better. That's part of good cage design. We always keep the animals in mind.

The great cats have a certain beauty to them that is special, because it isn't just that they're pretty in the usual sense of the word, but it's a fabulous machine that nature has evolved—the way that animal can have the ability to hunt, the way it can move around. There's just something about a cat, the great cats especially, that's very special.

Antelope, you look at those sable antelope, you look at the adra gazelles, you look at the zebra. They are all wondrous creatures, with a dignity befitting them. And the primates—I guess most people relate to them because we anthropomorphize, and if I go through the monkey house and the wanderoo macaque will sort of grimace when I grimace at him, and there's a recognition factor, that's special. When they get excited when you come, it makes you feel good.

You can go to a circus and see a pig doing certain tricks, and someone will say it's an intelligent animal. You can see a horse doing certain tricks, or a dog, but regarding total true intelligence, I think there's no question that at the top of the heap in the animal collection in the zoo are the three great apes, the chimp, orang, and gorilla. You just have to observe them a while, and you start wondering, "What are they thinking about?" And you get eye contact, and you know that there's something going on there.

When I make rounds, especially with a lot of the mammals, certainly more than the birds or reptiles, and then with some of the primates and great apes more than other mammals, there's no question that most of them tell me they're kind of glad to see me, as I am to see them. But there are times when I sense they're not at all happy with whatever it is that's going on at that particular moment. You can see it in the way they walk around, the way they sit, the way they look.

Many times the great apes will come to whatever the barrier is, the wire mesh, the glass, and try to interact. Many times they'll pick up things in their cage and hand them to me through the wire. I think it's one of the tricks that has both pleased me and saddened me that Koundu would do for years. He and I played games through the wire mesh. I'd hand him something, he'd hand me something, I'd reach through and touch him, tickle his tongue. That went on for years. One day all of a sudden I realized he's getting in his terrible teens, and he was ready to nail me. And now he sets you up. He'll start handing you something through that wire mesh, and if you're not careful his fingers are there to grab you. Most of the animals in the great ape house would not hurt people they knew, unless there was some reason for it. But with the adult males—it doesn't matter if it's chimp, orang, gorilla—

I think potentially they could do something untoward.

I've had emotional attachments to animals. The massive gorilla, Bushman, was one of a kind during his time. I was privileged to know him and to care for him during the last three, four years of his life. He's the only animal I think that I ever used to dream about. Occasionally when I'd make night calls to the old monkey house at two in the morning, I would open the doors and look to see if Bushman was out there waiting for me somewhere. There were all kinds of thoughts and feelings in those early years that if he really wanted to, he could get out of that cage. I'd dream about the old guy, in there, waiting.

Judy, the elephant, was one of my special animals. She was here forty, fifty years. She was a big, wonderful creature, and I was awed by this mass and the fact that she was basically a reasonably good animal. She had some tricks, and if you ever got between her and a wall, she'd just slowly lean and get you in there. I had a couple of close calls until I learned that. Once someone hollered in time, and I dropped down as she hit the wall.

Sinbad, the gorilla, was a special animal to me because I took care of him when he first came and he was just a little tyke, about a year old. So I interacted with him all those years. He wasn't necessarily friendly to me, but I guess I was honored because I was one of the few people that he never threw anything at. With most people, over a period of time, he'd throw anything from food to feces to you-name-it at them. That was one way he expressed displeasure. I never had that. He was around a long time and was a cornerstone animal.

Mike, the polar bear, also had been here many years. I got a mate for Mike, and she came as a little polar bear, and I thought, "Well, she's going to grow," but she never did. She remained about one-third or one-fourth the size of Mike. And I remember when the day came that I had to decide to get rid of one of them or try them together. And with great trepidation, I had them pull the transfer door, and big Mike walked into her cage, and I thought, "With

one swipe of the paw, he could heave her right out of the
whole cage." And she just barked at him and put a paw in
his face, and he backed down. From that moment on, they
got along just great. He never bothered her, and she got
along with him. That was a classic case where I said, "Wow,
am I lucky. That worked." We've been fortunate with most
of our introductions in the zoo. We've had very few trage-
dies. It's not unusual in the zoo world for animals that are
introduced to hurt each other or kill each other. And it's a
worry we always have. But we've been lucky here.

I have great respect for animals and love them, but I still
look upon them as animals. Even my family pets at home
over the years—I've had wonderful dogs and I had a few
cats—I don't look upon them as my children. I don't look
upon one of the zoo animals on the same level that I would
equate with a human. I still am able somehow to put it in
perspective.

Millions of people in metropolitan Chicago might never
have had a firsthand experience with these wild creatures
if they weren't in a zoo. I don't care what you say about
films and TV and slides and you name it, they're no substitute for being able to see, to smell, to hear, to be near this
animal, to look at a giraffe firsthand and to be close and
look up at it and see it. Even though I'd love to have enough
space for all the animals to be in their natural homes, some
specimens have to become goodwill ambassadors to tell
their story.

I think this zoo will get more involved in conservation
around the country and the world. I think this zoo will get
more involved in research with its animals, continuing
behavioral research, nutritional research, reproductive biology. I think these are important things, and this zoo
should be doing more. I think as we get more financial
support and get more staff, that's going to be the future for
the zoo. I think its education programs will continue to
grow, as they tie in more with the school systems. I think
that people will take it for granted, finally, that the zoo is a
classroom.

Once I get the last of these kids out of their inadequate facilities, the zoo is fixed, the plan—down the road, when and where and how we can do it—is to have a farm somewhere, some space out in the country, where, for example, we can maintain a small herd of zebras and bring one or two in for exhibition. I don't envision a two-thousand-acre thing. I'm thinking of a one- to two-hundred-acre space somewhere that would be a supplement to the zoo. There's no possibility that the zoo itself would or should expand. I think the collection should scale down to the zoo size rather than the zoo trying to expand.

I think we have a moral responsibility to these animals, and I believe that very strongly. On the other hand, part of the joy to me is to see the public use this place. I can't tell you what great inner satisfaction I get watching people visit the zoo, and watching them interact with the collection and watching them have fun or learn or whatever. As each generation of young people comes along, you see it all over again. Watching parents with their kids here, and watching the kids and listening to the conversation and seeing all segments of society here is to me a great, great source of contentment. It's not an achievement, because I didn't bring it about. Maybe I helped. I feel strongly about that. It's part of my inner satisfaction about being here.

Within a few years, if everything goes well and I retain my health, I probably will retire. I'm not certain what I'll do. I'll probably want to visit some parts of our country. Believe it or not, I've been to very few national parks; I've always flown over them or gone around them or something, I've never made time to enjoy them. There are a lot of wonderful books that I want to read. I'll keep busy. The old zoo and the collection here are part of an extended family, and to just cut them off would probably be hard. I used to think about doing things in other parts of the country. I always travel and come back and make peace. Chicago is my home.

By 5 P.M., *many of the animals have come in. Some are eager to retreat from the advancing night. Some, like the lions, move at their own pace. Inside, at night, they are safe from that occasionally nasty predator, the human, who may taunt them with rocks. The gates to the zoo are locked; it is possible to leave through a turnstile, but not to enter.*

The keepers have gone for the day; the buildings close at five, and the grounds are secured fifteen minutes later. Only a few night keepers patrol the zoo after hours. They walk around, from building to building, checking on the animals, making sure that everything that should be locked is locked. By the time the sun sets, there are no joggers, no businesspeople, no giggling children in the zoo. Only the animals and the night keepers. The nocturnal animals come alive in their cages; those that thrive in sunlight wind down.

A curator may work late. A zoo society worker may stay on at a desk until the sun is gone, and beyond. By late evening, all of them are gone, and the place is quiet. The sounds of animals—roars, growls, howls, whines, chattering, the secret vocabulary of the zoo—punctuate the sounds of the city itself.

Those who live in the nearby high-rise apartments wonder, "Was that sea lion calling out to someone?"

No one knows.

ACKNOWLEDGMENTS

I want to thank all of those mentioned in this book, for their candor and their patience. They permitted me to be a part of their daily lives at the zoo. There are others to thank as well: Keeper Norm Andresen, in particular, and all the other keepers who tolerated my presence with goodwill. All of the zoo's administrative staff, including Lois Stanley, Marybeth Gilchrist, Teresa Duffy, Kathleen Marshall, and Joanne Earnhardt. The zoo society staff members who were helpful, including Marge Morra, Lynn James, Maggie Schmid, Tina Koegel, Jennifer Marx, Susie Reich, and Lynne Yamaguchi. Volunteer coordinators Susan Young and Lois Wagner and all the docents and volunteers I encountered. John Fennessey of the park district power house staff.

Special gratitude goes out to Lucy Bukowski, who transcribed my tapes and made sense out of my editing with accuracy, speed, and good cheer; Karen Schenkenfelder, a gifted and supportive copyeditor; and thanks to Bernard Shir-Cliff, an amiable, caring, and skilled editor.

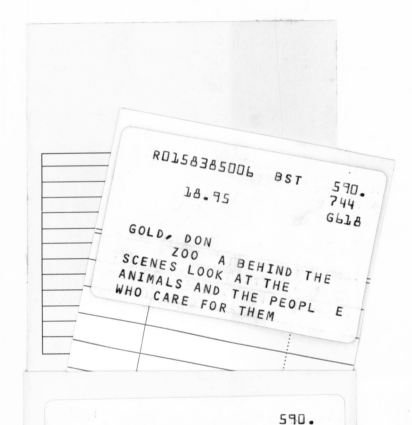

RO158385006   BST   590.
                          744
    18.95   G618

GOLD, DON
      ZOO   A BEHIND THE
SCENES LOOK AT THE
ANIMALS AND THE PEOPL E
WHO CARE FOR THEM

                          590.
RO158385006   BST   744
                          G618

HOUSTON PUBLIC LIBRARY

CENTRAL LIBRARY
500 MCKINNEY

THE BLUE CLIFF RECORD

The Blue Cliff Record

Translated from the Chinese *Pi Yen Lu* by
Thomas and J. C. Cleary

Foreword by Taizan Maezumi Roshi

PRAJÑĀ PRESS
Boulder 1978

Prajñā Press
1123 Spruce Street
Boulder, Colorado 80302

ISBN 0-87773-706-1
LCC 76-14202

Printed in the United States of America.

Contents

Biographical Supplement

Foreword

Boundless wind and moon—the eye within eyes,
Inexhaustible heaven and earth—the light beyond light,
The willow dark, the flower bright—ten thousand
houses;
Knock at any door—there's one who will respond.

This verse is known as the Preface to *The Blue Cliff Record.*
Although the name of the book is taken from the place where it
was written, all heaven and earth is nothing but the mass of
this Blue Cliff. The hundred cases selected by Hsueh Tou for
The Blue Cliff Record are as ten thousand and eighty-four
thousand, which are the numbers of dharmas expounded by
Shakyamuni Buddha. The innumerable dharmas revealed by
him are to be found in each case of *The Blue Cliff Record.*

There are numerous ways to read a book: skimming,
memorizing, careful study, quiet reading, reading aloud, reading with the body, reading with the mind, and reality-reading.
It is this last kind of reading which *The Blue Cliff Record*
requires. In this mode, you yourself become the case, and in so
doing, the Blue Cliff of ancient China stands revealed as your
very life, right here in this time and place.

Since the translators have already ably discussed the form
and compilation of the book in their introduction, it is unneces-
sary for me to cover the same ground. But I should like to
mention one thing: that the first person to introduce this text
to Japan was Kigen Dōgen Zenji, founder of the Soto School of
Japanese Zen. In 1227, at age 26, Dōgen Zenji had completed
five years of study in China and was preparing for his return to
Japan. But shortly before leaving, he discovered a copy of *The
Blue Cliff Record,* and was so impressed that he spent his entire last night in China sitting up and hand-copying it. The
hand-copied manuscript, known as the *Ichiya Hekigan* or
"One-Night Blue Cliff Record," is now treasured and housed at
Daijoji Monastery in Japan.

As mentioned in the Introduction, around 1140 Ta Hui

burned the original, published by his teacher Yuan Wu in 1128. The familiar version of the present day is the edition of 1300, based upon remaining handwritten copies and two previously published versions. The manuscript Dōgen Zenji brought back to Japan some seventy years earlier was probably based on one of the two previous versions, or on a handwritten copy of the day.

The Blue Cliff Record has become almost uniquely revered among Zen Buddhists as a model koan text, especially noted for its subtlety and profundity in both form and content. Interestingly enough, another koan collection, the *Book of Equanimity* (J.: *Shōyō Roku*) parallels it in form and level of sophistication. Unlike *The Blue Cliff Record*, which was compiled and refined by masters of the Rinzai and Ummon Schools, the *Book of Equanimity* is a product of the Soto lineage, and is primarily associated with that school. Nonetheless, *The Blue Cliff Record* appears to have been widely appreciated by Soto masters, although the *Book of Equanimity* failed to gain much prominence among teachers of the Rinzai School.

It is noteworthy that Dōgen Zenji selected twenty-four cases from *The Blue Cliff Record*, nearly a fourth of the total number of cases, for inclusion in his own three-hundred-case collection of koans entitled the *Shinji Shōbōgenzō ("The Shōbōgenzō in Chinese")*. This is not to be confused with the *Kaji Shōbōgenzō ("The Shōbōgenzō in Japanese")*, which most modern readers think of when they mention the *Shōbōgenzō*. This latter work is heavily based upon koan interpretations and commentaries by Dōgen Zenji.

We mention this because of an unfortunately widespread impression nowadays that Dōgen Zenji and the Soto School represent a non-koan or even anti-koan orientation within Zen. In fact, nothing could be further from the truth. Like Ta Hui of the Lin Chi School, Dōgen Zenji was critical of the abuses of koan study common in his day. These abuses, which essentially involved a stereotyped and overly intellectual use of koans, led Dōgen Zenji to express his concern lest the clarity and vigor of Zen students fall into deeper decline. Similarly, Ta Hui's burning of *The Blue Cliff Record* was an expression of his concern over the misuse of koans, rather than any fundamental objection to the use of koans, verses, or commentaries as such.

Avoiding sectarian prejudice, misunderstanding, or biased
views of koans, I sincerely wish that *The Blue Cliff Record*, one
of the most wonderful dharma-treasures of the world's Eastern
heritage, will at last be fully appreciated by, and benefit, its
Western readers.

This tremendous work of translating *The Blue Cliff Record*
has not previously been done by American scholars and is to be
highly appreciated and praised. Western Zen Buddhists have
waited a long time for a competent translation of this major
text; they need wait no longer.

Moreover, I appreciate the extra effort expended to translate
Master Tung Shan's *Five Ranks* and Master Fen Yang's *Eighteen Categories of Questions*. While it is true that Hsueh Tou
was the first to append appreciatory verses to *The Blue Cliff
Record*, nonetheless it was Fen Yang who first began the practice of composing such verses for koans in general. So readers
may find these appended works of some special interest.

Regarding actual practice, I firmly believe that this translation is a milestone and will immensely benefit those who are
sincerely engaged in the practice and enlightenment of the
Buddha-way. Since Zen students must deal with these cases
meticulously and in great detail, it can be seen how indispensable is a translation such as this. These cases are, after all, more
than mere anecdotes of historical or philosophical interest.
They are the living record of generations of enlightened practice. It is my sincere hope that, in appreciating these cases
along with the verses, commentaries, and capping-phrases, the
reader will be enriched in his understanding of the practice and
accomplishment of *Anuttara Samyak Sambodhi*, the Supreme
and Unexcelled Enlightenment.

A famous expression comes to mind:

"Before attaining enlightenment,
  mountains are mountains, rivers are rivers.

At the moment of enlightenment,
  *mountains are no longer mountains, nor are rivers riv-
  ers.*

But after accomplishing enlightenment,
  mountains are mountains, rivers are rivers."

This expression deals with three stages of practice. It is vital that the reader understand that the "mountains are mountains, rivers are rivers" experience *after* enlightenment is not at all the same as *before* such a realization. We cannot dispense with the "mountains are no longer mountains, nor are rivers rivers" aspect, which requires that the individual clearly realize his own true nature.

Although we know that all animate and inanimate beings are intrinsically buddhas, mere knowing is not enough. Dōgen Zenji says, "This dharma, (enlightened life) is abundantly inherent in each individual; nevertheless, without practice it will not be revealed, and without enlightenment it will not be realized."

The Blue Cliff Record reveals to us what enlightenment is, what the enlightened life is, how the patriarchs and masters of old struggled with it, attained it, actualized it, and accomplished it.

Penetrating the Blue Cliff, you will open ". . . the eye within eyes," and realizing life through the Blue Cliff, you yourself will become a torch, ". . . the light beyond light."

Being so, you will find no door at which to knock, nor any door to be opened.

Taizan Maezumi Roshi
Zen Center of Los Angeles
September, 1976

Preface

The introductory essay in this volume is intended to introduce some aspects of the tradition behind the classic Ch'an Buddhist *kung an* collection *Pi Yen Lu* which is presented here in English translation as *The Blue Cliff Record,* in the first of three parts.

The Chinese and Japanese pronunciations Ch'an and Zen are used in this volume because they are most familiar to Westerners, and it has been the Chinese and Japanese traditions of Ch'an which have thus far indirectly and directly most affected the early growth of Zen in the West. Ch'an also existed and exists in Korea and Vietnam, and contacts between these traditions and Western students have begun; for all of these, however, Chinese Ch'an is the ancestral tradition, and this will be our focus in the introduction to this volume.

Our primary aim is not historical record or doctrine as they are conventionally understood. Some books have touched on the subject, but there is as yet hardly any information in Western languages about Ch'an Buddhist teaching and history, and there are not enough authentic Ch'an texts translated to make a modern historiography practical or clearly show what Ch'an may mean in the present day.

When Buddhism crossed civilization boundaries in the past, translation, study, and practice were carried on for centuries before native schools of Buddhism emerged to present the teachings in new, currently useful forms. Western civilization has pretensions to objective scholarship and knowledge, with advanced techniques of information retrieval, but with all this has been slow to find out anything much about the Buddhist teachings, a part of the human heritage which cannot be claimed or relegated to any particular culture or time. An old description of five kinds of ch'an, or meditation, depicts the lowest as that of those seeking heavenly states; the next is that of the ordinary person who sees cause and effect and practices for the betterment of mental and physical health. Without going on to speak of the rest, it is obvious that these first two are with us now, and we can no longer be content with crude generalities, sectarian claims, or impressionistic accounts of the nature of Ch'an Buddhism. The aim of this volume is to present an authentic Ch'an text unencumbered by attempted explanations based on preconceptions regarding the text itself or the mental state of the reader.

Though we have sketched an outline of early to medieval Chinese Ch'an, since Ch'an is not a doctrinal school, generalizations about its historical forms are of limited usefulness; in an attempt to amend the shortcomings of a general approach, therefore, this volume includes excerpts from the lives and sayings of the Ch'an masters appearing in the main cases of volume one, based on materials from several collections of sayings, biographies, and "transmission of the lamp" records. Though the introduction is in the beginning, the reader may find it as interesting or useful to begin anywhere in the book.

Ch'an expression is usually very concentrated, and most recorded sayings of Ch'an masters come from people in special communities where the level of effort would be more intense than that of much of ordinary life in society. The reader must see through whatever cultural peculiarities are inevitable in an eight hundred and fifty year old book from another civilization; in doing so the reader must also see through present cultural peculiarities of thought and action, an effort which is itself a task of meditation. This book is not presented as a fossil embedded in the dust of a distant past, for the essence of Ch'an, the essence of mind, is timeless and placeless.

Introduction

The Blue Cliff Record is a translation of the Chinese Ch'an Buddhist classic *Pi Yen Lu*,[1] a collection of one hundred anecdotes of sayings and doings mainly from traditional accounts of Ch'an teachers and disciples, illustrated in verse and prose by outstanding Ch'an masters of later times. This set of one hundred *kung an*, "public cases"[2] of ancient events, was compiled by the eminent Sung dynasty Ch'an master Hsueh Tou Ch'ung Hsien (980–1052); Hsueh Tou pointed out the import of each story with verses and additional remarks of his own, as aid and guidance for observation and contemplation. About sixty years after Hsueh Tou's death, another excellent Ch'an teacher, Yuan Wu K'e Ch'in (1063–1135), gave a series of talks elucidating the original anecdotes and the verses of Hsueh Tou's collection. The anecdotes, Hsueh Tou's verses, and Yuan Wu's introductions, remarks, and commentaries all together form *The Blue Cliff Record*, named after the abode on Mt. Chia in Hunan where Yuan Wu once delivered his talks. This book has long been considered as one of the finest works of Ch'an literature, and defies adequate description short of its own presentation.

The Buddha Gautama, Shakyamuni, whom all Buddhists regard as their ancestor, invented and adapted various teachings and techniques to liberate people; he was likened to a skilled physician giving specific medicines to cure certain diseases. It is said, therefore, that there is no fixed teaching. Yet in spite of outward differences resulting from necessary adaptation to different situations, capacities of understanding and personality configurations, the real Buddha Dharma, the teaching of the enlightened ones, is of one uniform flavor, the flavor of liberation. Just as many streams lead to the ocean, where they merge into the uniform flavor of salt, goes the ancient metaphor, so do the teachings of enlightenment lead to the ocean of enlightenment and merge into the uniform flavor of liberation. When this essence is lost, and people enshrine relics of past method for a sense of personal satisfaction, righteousness, or comfort, then it is said that the medicine has become a disease. It is the practice of Ch'an and all real Buddhism to cut through all ploys of egoism in all its guises, "holy" or "profane," to break up stultifying material and intellectual idolatry.

A Ch'an master once wrote that the wise enshrine the miraculous bones of the ancients within themselves; that is, they do not regard teachings of ways to enlightenment as an external body of knowledge or information to be possessed as an acquisition or believed or revered as inflexible dogma, but rather apply it as far as possible to themselves and their situations, vivifying the way of enlightenment with their own bodies and lives, not just in their thoughts. It is therefore a matter of course that new Buddhist literature has been produced; for the Buddhist canon is not closed, as long as people continue the search for enlightenment. This is where a consideration of Buddhist history has some meaning: to help us see what ages and what is ageless.

As many Buddhist texts and practitioners entered Chinese civilization during the first millennium A.D., overtly representing different trends of thought and action, Chinese Buddhists developed, through study and practical application and experimentation, systems of organization, analysis, interpretation, meditation, and ritual. Several Buddhist schools arose in China between the fifth and seventh centuries, including the four major schools known as T'ien T'ai, Hua Yen, Pure Land (Ching T'u), and Ch'an. The schools based on specific scriptures and treatises and commentaries by Indian and Chinese masters were referred to in Ch'an jargon as "doctrinal schools" or "teaching schools."

The principal scriptures of the T'ien T'ai school are the *Saddharmapundarika* ("Lotus of Truth") and *Mahaparinirvana* ("Great Decease"); of the Hua Yen, the *Avatamsaka* ("Garland"); of the Pure Land, the *Sukhavativyuha* ("Lay of the Land of Bliss"). Ch'an students generally read these scriptures, as well as others such as the *Vajracchedika* ("Diamond Cutter"), *Surangama* ("Heroic Going"), *Vimalakirtinirdesa* ("Teaching of Vimalakirti"), and *Lankavatara* ("Descent into Sri Lanka"); thus, the study of classical Buddhist scriptures and treatises and the practice of various meditation methods were in the background of Ch'an studies, directly or indirectly, whether or not living masters of the other schools were in existence. Later followers of the teaching schools often concentrated on the works of the Chinese founders, who analyzed, synthesized, and organized the numerous and extensive Buddhist teachings, presenting them in a crystallized form for current use. Ch'an students did likewise, concentrating on the great Ch'an masters, but kept contact with other forms of Buddhist teaching, ancient and contemporary.

Ch'an was referred to by its followers as the "school of the patriarchs" because it was transmitted by a living succession of human exemplars; not a school of doctrine, or philosophical or scholastic interpretation, it was not based on any particular scripture, but on the direct experience of the enlightened mind, by whatever means currently necessary. There were many professional lecturing monks who specialized in certain texts or groups of texts, but Ch'an teachers originally did not make systematic explanations of Buddhist texts or traditional teachings; many students learned about Buddhism in the lecturing halls before coming to Ch'an study. Ch'an teachers drew freely on the ancient "Teachings," using quintessential passages from the scriptures to illustrate points in the course of their talks to students, much in the same way as they came to use sayings and anecdotes of earlier Ch'an masters. One of the attachments that Ch'an teachers had to deal with when doctrinal Buddhism became too institutionalized and formally traditionalized was the attachment of externalists and intellectuals to names and forms which had come to be hallowed.

During the fifth and sixth centuries meditation studies developed considerably in China, especially in the northern kingdoms. Early meditation adepts were generally ascetics and strict disciplinarians, often living in secluded mountain areas or in monasteries surrounding distinguished teachers or practicing alone. Recitation of scriptures, spells, and devotional formulas was carried to great lengths by some early meditators, and has been used to a greater or lesser extent throughout Ch'an history.

Ch'an tradition recognizes Bodhidharma (4–6 c. A.D.) as its first patriarch in China. He came to China in the late fifth or early sixth century[3] and traveled around for over fifty years, teaching when the occasion arose. Bodhidharma is said to have used the *Lankavatara* scripture in his teaching; this scripture represents teachings of the Yogacara, or "yoga practice" school, which says that reality as we conceive it is only mental, and uses meditational techniques of yoga to break mental attachments to mental processes which cause our discomfort and confusion. Shakyamuni Buddha used ancient techniques of yoga, but only to break concrete and abstract attachments and realize *moksha*, freedom, not to attain supposedly higher states. We have several documents purported to record teachings of Bodhidharma; the standard slogan of later times was that he pointed directly to the human mind, and undoubtedly used various methods to accomplish this. Bodhidharma is said to have had four adept disciples in China, and by the seventh century was recognized as one of the few meditation teachers of early times who inspired a continuing living succession.

Bodhidharma's principal heir Hui K'e (486–593), the second patriarch, and his successor Seng Ts'an (d. 606), the third patriarch, still living in a time of disunity and strife in what had been the Chinese empire, seem to have wandered around, engaging in local activity but never establishing any fixed abode as teaching centers. Hui K'e spent many years in Yeh, a metropolis in the northeast quarter of China, and is said to have met ten enlightened students over the years. After large numbers of monks and nuns were made to return to lay life, and monastic properties were taken by the governments in northern China around 577, Hui K'e spent the last sixteen years of his life dressed as a layman, even though the bans were later lifted, and the Buddhist communities resumed their growth and prosperity. He was opposed by an established Buddhist teacher, as Bodhidharma had been opposed by both Indian and Chinese lecturers, for unorthodox teachings and methods, and eventually killed. Seng Ts'an, of whom almost nothing is known, was also a layman when he met Hui K'e, who was his teacher for ten years in the mountains of Anwei, evidently near the close of the sixth century. He is said to have written the long poem *Hsin Hsin Ming*[4] which has always been popular and is considered the first classic of Chinese Ch'an.

The fourth patriarch of Ch'an, Tao Hsin (580–651), settled down on a mountain in central China for over thirty years, and a community of five hundred people eventually gathered around him. This community maintained its own livelihood, and Tao Hsin ignored the invitations of the T'ang imperial court, which usually richly patronized Buddhists. Tao Hsin is said to have spent two years on a journey to south China in later life. He wrote a book about standards of conduct for bodhisattvas, those following the path of knowledge of reality; he also wrote a book on meditation, outlining various methods and their effects, referring to various scriptural sources.[5] Ch'an had not been widespread during the times of the earlier patriarchs, but with Tao Hsin it came to be known all over China.

Tao Hsin was a strict teacher and only approved of one successor out of his many disciples; this was Hung Jen (602-675), the fifth patriarch. Hung Jen was with Tao Hsin from the age of seven until his late thirties, working by day and meditating by night. Among Hung Jen's eleven enlightened successors were Shen Hsiu (602–706) and Hui Neng (638–713): Shen Hsiu, a learned monk as well as a meditation master, was considered the sixth patriarch in the tradition of the so-called northern school of Ch'an; Hui Neng, an illiterate wood-cutter, was considered the sixth patriarch in the tradition of the so-called southern school. Teachers of the northern school worked mostly in or near urban areas of north China, especially the western capital of T'ang, Ch'ang An. These lineages died out by the end of the T'ang dynasty. There is a saying in Ch'an that each generation must go beyond its predecessors for the transmission to continue.

Some documents of the northern school were brought to Japan by the pilgrim Saicho in the early ninth century; Saicho had actually met Ch'an people of the so-called ox head (Niu T'ou) and northern schools, and included several texts documenting the inclusion of Ch'an as the Bodhidharma Sect in the four transmissions or heritages claimed by Tendai Buddhism in Japan, along with the philosophy and cessation of thought and observation of reality practices of T'ien T'ai, esoteric ritual, art, spells, and scriptures of tantric Buddhism, and precepts for bodhisattvas. The Bodhidharma Sect was brought to life for a time by Dainichi Nonin and some dedicated students and successors. Nonin was a Tendai student who specialized in Ch'an meditation and had such profound realization that he began to teach with effect. Many of the students of his successors and their successors eventually joined the Zen master Dogen (1200–1253), who returned from China in 1227 and gradually began to write and teach. Criticized for not having a teacher's bequest, Nonin sent two disciples to China with a statement of his realization, and was acknowledged by a Lin Chi master, of the southern school; so the reality behind Ch'an is not sectarian.

Hui Neng had become enlightened in his mid-twenties while a poor woodcutter in the frontier lands of south China. He later traveled north to see Hung Jen, and became a workman in Hung Jen's community at Huang Mei. Hung Jen recognized Hui Neng's enlightenment and after a short time passed on to him the robe and bowl of Bodhidharma as symbols of the patriarchate; he did this in secret, it is said, and sent Hui Neng away, fearing the jealous wrath of the monks because Hui Neng was a peasant from the uncivilized far south with no formal training in Buddhism. After fifteen years of wandering, Hui Neng reappeared in south China, became ordained as a Buddhist monk, and began to teach at Pao Lin monastery near the source of Ts'ao Ch'i, the Ts'ao Valley River. He awakened many people, and most of the teachers who appear in *The Blue Cliff Record* were descended from Hui Neng.

Little is known of most of Hui Neng's immediate disciples, but in the succeeding generation there appeared two great masters, Shih T'ou Hsi Ch'ien (700–790) and Ma Tsu Tao Yi (709–788), under whom Ch'an began to flourish in China as never before. From these two masters were descended the so-called "Five Houses and Seven Sects" of Ch'an which arose from the ninth to eleventh centuries. Descended from Ma Tsu were the Kuei-Yang and Lin Chi houses, named after *Kuei* Shan Ling Yu (771–854), *Yang* Shan Hui Chi (813–890), and *Lin Chi* Yi Hsuan (d. 867); during the eleventh century two great masters of Ch'an in the Lin Chi house, Huang Lung Hui Nan (1002–1069) and Yang Ch'i Fang Hui (d. 1049), were so influential and produced so many enlightened successors that their lineages became known as the Huang Lung and Yang Ch'i sects, or streams. From Shih T'ou were descended the Ts'ao-Tung, Yun Men, and Fa Yen houses, named after *Tung* Shan Liang Chieh (807–869), *Ts'ao*-Shan Pen Chi (840–901), *Yun Men* Wen Yen (d. 949), and *Fa Yen* Wen Yi (885–958). Referred to as schools, sects, houses, or clans of Ch'an, they were not sects in the sense of membership, but were terms of respect given later to successions of living masters, called after the reference names of their distinguished ancestors.

The five houses era was the most original and creative period of Ch'an teaching, source of much illustrative material and symbolic method used in later times. A considerable body of sayings and writings of the patriarchs and eminent heirs of the five houses and seven sects has been preserved. The living succession of the Kuei-Yang, the earliest house, died out in the tenth century, after five generations; Kuei Shan's *Admonitions*, a short treatise for Ch'an students, was used in Ch'an communities for over a thousand years. Te Kuang, a Lin Chi master in the second generation after Yuan Wu, sent this book over to Dainichi Nonin in Japan, and it was the first Ch'an book to be printed in that country.

The Fa Yen house also lasted about a century, while the Yun Men house, extremely effective for several generations after Hsueh Tou, lasted for some three hundred years and preserved and transmitted a great deal of Ch'an literature. The Lin Chi house, especially the Yang Ch'i branch, eventually became the most powerful and long lived Ch'an succession in China, while the Ts'ao Tung, not as prominent, nevertheless continued to exist and play a part in the Ch'an work for many centuries.

The Kuei-Yang and Lin Chi houses were both descended from Ma Tsu's great heir Pai Chang Huai Hai (720–814), who wrote the "Pure Rules for Ch'an Gardens" and uttered the famous dictum "One day without working is a day without eating." Pai Chang is known for having formally established a unique Ch'an monastic system. By the time of Kuei Shan, the monasteries were so wealthy and populous and so many monks were lazy and decadent that Kuei Shan wrote his little book warning about the deception of abundant offerings and supplies, criticizing the "rice bags" and "clothes hangers" who joined monastic life for food, clothing, and shelter without seriously trying to awaken to reality.

The Yun Men and Fa Yen houses were descended from the powerful master Te Shan Hsuan Chien (d. 867) and his successor Hsueh Feng Yi Ts'un, a great teacher of over sixty enlightened disciples. Te Shan was famous for his use of the staff to strike students; Hsueh Feng once had a major insight when struck by Te Shan. Te Shan's contemporary Lin Chi was equally famous for his shouting, and the "staff of Te Shan and the shout of Lin Chi" is a standard Ch'an expression to be met frequently in *The Blue Cliff Record*.

With the proliferation of Ch'an teaching throughout China, sincere Ch'an students usually made extensive journeys to call on various enlightened masters; some continued their travels after enlightenment, to deepen their experience, test their realization and that of established teachers, and familiarize themselves with methods currently in use. Aside from encounter with living examples of enlightenment, travel also was a means of learning to reduce needs to a minimum, live as efficiently as possible with nothing fixed to rely on, and become immersed in the contemplation of impermanence. In this way, Ch'an monks came to be called "foot travelers"; emulating the ancient Buddhists as poor wayfarers, they were also known as "patchrobed monks."

By the end of the T'ang dynasty, Ch'an was the major form of Buddhism in China, but was beginning to become rigid with age and formality. Far more is recorded of the words of distinguished masters of the Sung dynasties (960–1276) than of those of T'ang, especially as they were often teaching in large official public monasteries. Ch'an teaching became more geographically concentrated, generally speaking, in Sung times, and many enlightened Ch'an adepts stayed for years as functionaries in the public monasteries without forming communities of their own, assisting the work of teaching masters among large groups of students.

The practice of reciting and recording sayings and stories had been in evidence since early T'ang, and a number of large collections of anecdotes of many generations of Ch'an masters were made in Sung times. Students sometimes carried a puzzling remark with them on their travels seeking resolution, or recorded and studied sayings or conversations of teachers they had met or had heard of. From the early masters of the five houses we have not only original sayings, but remarks, replies, and alternative sayings for stories of other masters conveyed by traveling students. Yun Men Wen Yen, patriarch of the Yun Men house, and Fen Yang Shan Chao (947–1024), a master influential in the revival of Lin Chi Ch'an, were among the first to use quotations extensively in their teaching, giving replies and posing questions about the sayings of the old masters. Eventually it became an established practice to use old sayings to test students' insight, and for students to focus their attention on some sayings during still and active meditation.

Ch'an is based on the actual experience of enlightenment, and though Ch'an students generally still studied major great vehicle Buddhist scriptures, the sayings and doings of enlightened Ch'an masters came to supplant the Indian Buddhist scriptures as guides, indications and inspiration for their conduct, meditation, and knowledge. The production of such books as *The Blue Cliff Record* was an outgrowth of the "recollections of the Buddhas" which was part of the practice of Ch'an. Although it seems from the sayings of Yuan Wu that many students wasted Ch'an literature by remaining in conceptual or aesthetic views, it seems that the use of "public cases" of the ancients was instrumental in revivifying the inspiration of Ch'an practice, especially as contact between teacher and disciple became more ritualized. In later Ch'an literature there are many stories of people awakening under the impact of a phrase or event, a sight or a sound, after becoming engrossed in a story or saying through contemplation and observation.

The practice of observation of sayings seems to have been applied with great effect by some masters in Sung times, and the literature which grew up around it concentrated the rich legacy of the highly original T'ang and Five Dynasties (906–960) masters and provided "grammars," as it were, of Ch'an idiom, and methods of describing Ch'an history and meditation states. Eventually traditional modes of expression and transformation became widely used as a medium for question and discussion of Ch'an, though there is a virtually endless variety of detail. A good deal of Zen literature of medieval Japan also consists of recorded sayings and poems in terse symbolic style like the Sung masters who founded several streams of Ch'an in Japan; part of the reason for this was the need to communicate in writing between Chinese teachers and Japanese students. Japanese masters inherited this style somewhat, and continued to write in Chinese for over five hundred years, but also produced a parallel literature in Japanese which came to be quite different in style from the Chinese.

Hsueh Tou Ch'ung Hsien, fourth patriarch and reviver of the Yun Men school, visited the lecturing halls after his ordination and was unmatched in the study of the Buddhist scriptures and treatises; he was considered a "vessel of the Dharma" by his teachers and urged to study Ch'an. When he met Chih Men

Kuang Tso, the outstanding Yun Men master of the time, he asked, "When one does not produce a single thought, how can there be any fault?" Chih Men called him closer: as Hsueh Tou approached, Chih Men hit him on the mouth with his whisk; as Hsueh Tou was about to open his mouth, Chih Men hit him again, whereupon Hsueh Tou awoke. Hsueh Tou became a great teacher, and is said to have had eighty-four enlightened successors; through his living heirs and his great literary ability his brilliance shone and reached many people.

Yuan Wu K'e Ch'in was a master in the tenth generation of the Lin Chi succession, descendent of Fen Yang Shan Chao and Yang Ch'i Fang Hui. He studied with teachers of the Yun Men and Ts'ao-Tung as well as both branches of the Lin Chi school before he finally succeeded to Wu Tsu Fa Yen (d. 1104). Yuan Wu, "Perfect Enlightenment," was one of the titles bestowed on him by the Sung emperor Hui Tsung; he served as abbot and teaching master in several major temples by imperial request, and is said to have had seventy-five enlightened disciples. Besides *The Blue Cliff Record*, there are extensive records of Yuan Wu's sayings, as well as a large collection of letters, many to his enlightened disciples. All of the Rinzai Zen schools in modern Japan are descended from Yuan Wu.

Hsueh Tou and Yuan Wu were from the schools of Ch'an which seem to have most emphasized work with *kung an*; as is usual in the doings of Ch'an teachers, there were different ways of using the stories and sayings of the ancients. In general it may be said that contemplation and gradual application as well as complete concentration without thought were used, and we have both discursive and abrupt comments on the cases from various masters. The method of concentration without thinking, used to stop mind wandering without letting it sink into oblivion, generally focused on a word or phrase, called a *hua tou*, and was used a lot by later Lin Chi masters. *The Blue Cliff Record* gives excellent insight into what the stories point to, and advice on how to apply them in life.

The Blue Cliff Record gained great popularity in a short time, so much so that Ta Hui, an influential successor of Yuan Wu sometimes called the second coming of Lin Chi, destroyed the printing blocks because he observed that enthusiasm for eloquence and beauty of expression was hindering people from directly experiencing enlightenment on their own. In Ta Hui's

time there were still numerous enlightened teachers, and a
long tradition; Ta Hui wrote and spoke a great deal, especially
denouncing repetitious imitation Ch'an without enlightenment. One of his techniques was to reject all answers to *kung
an;* his dynamic methods were very effective in his time, and
he produced over ninety enlightened disciples, but his lineage
died out after a few generations.

We in the West are lacking even in information about Ch'an,
and many of the accounts we have been given in the last fifty
years or so are quite confused and confusing, engendering mis-
conceptions about Ch'an, if not about reality. These *The Blue
Cliff Record* seriously challenges and can help us to see
through if we do not insist upon our customary habits of
thought. There are at least four books on the same model as
The Blue Cliff Record made by Ts'ao-Tung masters after Yuan
Wu's time, and innumerable other books related to Buddhism
from all ages: instructions on conduct and meditation, recorded sayings, collections of incidents, remarks, conversations, poetry, general and specific treatises in prose and poetry
on various aspects of Ch'an history, symbolism, contemporary
situations, psychology, practice and realization. Certain communities in the present may find particular books useful and
ignore others, but for the common human heritage over a
longer period of time, individual communities or scholars cannot canonize only certain aspects of Buddhism. The publication of *The Blue Cliff Record* in English will help to open new
vistas in the study of Buddhism in the West, but is only part of
a larger task. Though even one story in this volume can reveal
infinite implications to those of profound insight, for a larger
audience the dimensions of the impact of *The Blue Cliff Record* will expand through long contemplation facilitated by the
mirrors of other Ch'an and Buddhist texts as they become
available.

Ultimately, the appreciation and usefulness of this book is
in the hands of the reader. Its literary expressiveness is so rich
that it can hardly fail to make an impression, even though the
book was not translated as a literary work. Even the manifest
content of this work provides a certain sustenance: the univer-
sality of the message beckons us on, and its immediate challenge can inspire us to profounder levels of insight. Even Hakuin, considered the greatest Zen master in Japan in the last

five hundred years, said that he still had new insights on certain sayings after having lectured on *The Blue Cliff Record* for thirty years. Ch'an masters tell us to look right where we stand and step: they ask what is there, is there anything, who are you and where do you come from, what did you see and hear when you were there?—in a hundred ways they try to make us wake up, clear our minds, and face reality directly. While people pursue various paths, the inexorable laws of cause and effect will be their inconceivable partner on every turn of every path, regardless of the conceptions we may have about what is going on. The effort of the student is an essential ingredient in Ch'an, so explanation is minimal.

The format of this translation of *The Blue Cliff Record* is as follows:

POINTER: introduction by Yuan Wu, missing in some cases.

CASE: the *kung an,* public case record from Ch'an tradition or Buddhist scripture.

NOTES: remarks by Yuan Wu at certain points in each case; in Chinese texts, notes are put right in the text, but we have separated them out and listed them in Western footnote style after each case, to preserve the continuity of the original story for ease of reading.

COMMENTARY: by Yuan Wu on each case.

VERSE: by Hsueh Tou, interspersed with remarks by Yuan Wu; the lines of the verses are more individual units in form and content than prose sections, so the notes, though visually distinguished, are left between the lines of verse. Cases and verses should be read both as wholes all at once, and with notes at every step.

COMMENTARY: by Yuan Wu, on verse and its relation to the case.

Volume one of this translation presents the first thirty-five cases of *The Blue Cliff Record:* following these are excerpts from classical biographies of the Ch'an masters who appear in the main cases of volume one, presented in order of their appearance.

Due to the burning of the book, some parts of the commentaries and remarks are thought to have been lost or replaced. Fortunately, this is not a presentation of a system, and while the happenings reflect on each other, they do so by their own coherence; southern Ch'an was known as the "abrupt school," and its expression tends to be concise and quintessential. It is said that if one thoroughly penetrates one phrase, one penetrates innumerable phrases at the same time.

Monks' names consist of two two-syllable names; a place name, epithet, or title, and an individual initiatory name. Exceptions to this custom are self-evident and do not need special treatment. Of famous monks, usually only the first name of two syllables (generally the place name—of the mountain, monastery, or city, etc., where the master lived and taught) is used, or, when already mentioned in the context, the second syllable of the first name. In the case of later monks teaching in the same places as famous ancient masters, the whole first name and the second name or second syllable of the second name are used. We have generally followed this custom. Diacritical marks are omitted from Sanskrit names as well as from Japanese names and terms. Translator's notes are marked by letters of the alphabet and listed after the end of each case.

NOTES TO INTRODUCTION

1. Japanese *Hekiganroku*; also called *Pi Yen Chi*, Japanese *Hekigan-shu.*

2. The term "public cases" or "public records" *(kung an; koan)* likens the Ch'an stories to law cases, legal precedents, according to which a determination—here, the understanding of a student—is made.

3. According to the *Hsu Kao Seng Chuan* (ca. 645), Bodhidharma arrived in China during the Liu Sung dynasty (420–479); according to the *Ching Te Ch'uan Teng Lu* (1004), a Ch'an history, he arrived in 520.

4. "Seal of Faith in the Heart." The heart is the enlightened mind; faith is in the enlightened mind inherent in all sentient beings, the potential of Buddhahood; the seal is an impression or inscription, also a name of a form of poem.

5. This book is lost, but a good deal of material quite probably excerpted from it is to be found in the *Leng Chia Shih Tzu Chi*, "Record of Masters and Disciples of the Lankavatara," a short Ch'an history written by a member of the northern school.

The Highest Meaning of the Holy Truths

POINTER

When you see smoke on the other side of a mountain, you already know there's a fire; when you see horns on the other side of a fence, right away you know there's an ox there. To understand three when one is raised, to judge precisely at a glance— this is the everyday food and drink of a patchrobed monk. Getting to where he cuts off the myriad streams, he is free to arise in the east and sink in the west, to go against or to go with, in any and all directions, free to give or to take away. But say, at just such a time, whose actions are these? Look into Hsueh Tou's trailing vines.

CASE

Emperor Wu of Liang asked the great master Bodhidharma,[1] "What is the highest meaning of the holy truths?"[2] Bodhidharma said, "Empty, without holiness."[3] The Emperor said, "Who is facing me?"[4] Bodhidharma replied, "I don't know."[5] The Emperor did not understand.[6] After this Bodhidharma crossed the Yangtse River and came to the kingdom of Wei.[7]

Later the Emperor brought this up to Master Chih and asked him about it.[8] Master Chih asked, "Does your majesty know who this man is?"[9] The Emperor said, "I don't know."[10] Master Chih said, "He is the Mahasattva Avalokitesvara, transmitting the Buddha Mind Seal."[11] The Emperor felt regretful, so he wanted to send an emissary to go invite (Bodhidharma to return).[12] Master Chih told him, "Your majesty, don't say that you will send someone to fetch him back.[13] Even if everyone in the whole country were to go after him, he still wouldn't return."[14]

NOTES

1. This dull fellow speaks up.
2. What a donkey-tethering stake this is.
3. Wu considered this answer rather extraordinary. The arrow has flown past Korea. Very clear.
4. Wu is filled with embarrassment, forcing himself to be astute. As it turns out, he gropes without finding.
5. Bah! His second reply isn't worth half a cent.
6. Too bad! Still, he's gotten somewhere.
7. This wild fox spirit! He can't avoid embarrassment. He crosses from west to east, he crosses from east to west.
8. A poor man thinks about an old debt. The bystander has eyes.
9. Wu should chase Master Chih out of the country too; Chih should be given thirty blows. Bodhidharma has come.
10. After all this is Emperor Wu's understanding of Bodhidharma's public case.
11. Chih explains haphazardly. The elbow doesn't bend outwards.
12. After all, Bodhidharma couldn't be held. As I said before, Wu is dull.
13. When someone in the eastern house dies, someone of the western house joins in the mourning. Better they should be all driven out of the country at once.
14. Again Master Chih deserves thirty blows. He doesn't know that the great illumination shines forth from under his own feet.

COMMENTARY

From afar Bodhidharma saw that this country (China) had people capable of the Great Vehicle, so he came by sea, intent on his mission, purely to transmit the Mind Seal, to arouse and instruct those mired in delusion. Without establishing written words, he pointed directly to the human mind (for them) to see nature and fulfill Buddhahood. If you can see this way, then you will have your share of freedom. Never again will you be turned around pursuing words, and everything will be completely revealed. Thereafter you will be able to converse with Emperor Wu and you will naturally be able to see how the Second Patriarch's mind was pacified.[a] Without the mental defilements of judgement and comparison, everything is cut off, and you are free and at ease. What need is there to go on distinguishing right and wrong, or discriminating gain and loss? Even so, how many people are capable of this?

Emperor Wu had put on monk's robes and personally expounded the *Light-Emitting Wisdom Scripture;* he experienced heavenly flowers falling in profusion and the earth turning to gold. He studied the Path and humbly served the Buddha, issuing orders throughout his realm to build temples and ordain monks, and practicing in accordance with the Teaching. People called him the Buddha Heart Emperor.

When Bodhidharma first met Emperor Wu, the Emperor asked, "I have built temples and ordained monks; what merit is there in this?" Bodhidharma said, "There is no merit." He immediately doused the Emperor with dirty water. If you can penetrate this statement, "There is no merit," you can meet Bodhidharma personally. Now tell me, why is there no merit at all in building temples and ordaining monks? Where does the meaning of this lie?

Emperor Wu held discussions with Dharma Master Lou Yueh, with Mahasattva Fu, and with Prince Chao Ming about the two truths, the real and the conventional. As it says in the Teachings, by the real truth we understand that it is not existent; by the conventional truth we understand that it is not nonexistent. That the real truth and the conventional truth are not two is the highest meaning of the holy truths. This is the most esoteric, most abstruse point of the doctrinal schools. Hence the Emperor picked out this ultimate paradigm to ask Bodhidharma, "What is the highest meaning of the holy truths?" Bodhidharma answered, "Empty, without holiness." No monk in the world can leap clear of this. Bodhidharma gives them a single swordblow that cuts off everything. These days how people misunderstand! They go on giving play to their spirits, put a glare in their eyes and say, "Empty, without holiness!" Fortunately, this has nothing to do with it.

My late Master Wu Tsu once said, "If only you can penetrate 'empty, without holiness,' then you can return home and sit in peace." All this amounts to creating complications; still, it does not stop Bodhidharma from smashing the lacquer bucket[b] for others. Among all, Bodhidharma is most extraordinary. So it is said, "If you can penetrate a single phrase, at the same moment you will penetrate a thousand phrases, ten thousand phrases." Then naturally you can cut off, you can hold still. An Ancient said, "Crushing your bones and dismembering your body would not be sufficient requital; when a single phrase is clearly understood, you leap over hundreds of millions."

Bodhidharma confronted the Emperor directly; how he indulged! The Emperor did not awaken; instead, because of his notions of self and others, he asked another question, "Who is facing me?" Bodhidharma's compassion was excessive; again he addressed him, saying, "I don't know." At this, Emperor Wu was taken aback; he did not know what Bodhidharma meant. When you get to this point, as to whether there is something or there isn't anything, pick and you fail.

Master Shou Tuan had a verse which said,

> Ordinarily a single arrow fells a single eagle;
> Another arrow is already too many.
> Bodhidharma goes right back to sit before Few
>   Houses Peak;
> O Lord of Liang, speak no more of going to summon
>   him.

He also said, "Who wants to summon him back?"

Since Emperor Wu did not understand, Bodhidharma secretly left the country; all this old fellow got was embarrassment. He crossed the Yangtse River into Wei; at the time, the Hsiao Ming Emperor of Wei was reigning there. This emperor belonged to a northern tribe named Toba, who were later to call themselves Chinese. When Bodhidharma arrived there, he did not appear for any more audiences, but went directly to Shao Lin Monastery, where he sat facing a wall for nine years, and met the Second Patriarch. People thereabouts called him "The Wall-Gazing Brahmin."

Emperor Wu of Liang later questioned Master Chih. Chih said, "Does your majesty know who this man is?" The Emperor said, "I don't know." Tell me, is this ("I don't know") the same as what Bodhidharma said, or is it different? In appearance it indeed seems the same, but in reality isn't. People often misunderstand and say, "Before, when Bodhidharma said 'I don't know' he was replying about Ch'an; later, when Emperor answered Master Chih, this referred to the 'knowledge' of mutual acquaintance." This is irrelevant. Tell me, when Master Chih questioned him, how could Wu have answered? Why didn't he strike Chih dead with a single blow and avoid being seen as a fool? Instead Emperor Wu answered Master Chih sincerely and said, "I don't know." Master Chih saw his chance and acted; he said, "This is the Mahasattva Avalokitesvara transmitting the Buddha Mind Seal." The Emperor felt regret and was going to send an emissary to bring Bodhidharma back. How stupid! When Chih said, "This is Mahasattva Avalokitesvara transmitting the Buddha Mind Seal," if Wu had driven him out of the country, this would have amounted to something.

According to tradition, Master Chih died in the year 514, while Bodhidharma came to Liang in 520; since there is a seven year discrepancy, why is it said that the two met? This must be a mistake in the tradition. As to what is recorded in tradition, I will not discuss this matter now. All that's important is to understand the gist of the matter. Tell me, Bodhidharma is Avalokitesvara, Master Chih is Avalokitesvara, but which is the true Avalokitesvara? Since it is Avalokitesvara, why are there two? But why only two? They are legion.

Later in Wei, Bodhidharma debated with the Vinaya Master Kuang T'ung and the canonical master Bodhiruci. The Master Bodhidharma eliminated formalism and pointed to mind; because of their biased judgments, (the other two) would not put up with this, and instead developed feelings of malevolence and tried to poison Bodhidharma several times. On the sixth attempt, since his mission was completed and he had found someone to succeed to the Dharma, Bodhidharma made no further attempt to save himself, but sat upright and passed on. He was buried at Tinglin Temple on Bear Ear Mountain. Afterwards, while Sung Yun of Wei was on a mission, he met the Master in the Ts'ung Ling Range (in Sinkiang), carrying one shoe in his hand, returning (to India).

Emperor Wu mourned Bodhidharma's death and personally wrote an inscription for his monument. It read, "Alas! I saw him without seeing him, I met him without meeting him, I encountered him without encountering him; now as before I regret this deeply." He further eulogized him by saying, "If your mind exists, you are stuck in the mundane for eternity; if your mind does not exist, you experience wondrous enlightenment instantly."

Tell me, where is Bodhidharma right now? You've stumbled past him without even realizing it.

VERSE

The holy truths are empty;
        **The arrow has flown past Korea. Ha!*

How can you discern the point?
        **Wrong. What is there that's hard to discern?*

"Who is facing me?"
        **The second try isn't worth half a cent. So you too go on
        like this.*

Again he said, "I don't know."
        **A third man, a fourth man hits the mark. Bah!*

Henceforth, he secretly crossed the river;
        **He could not pierce another's nostrils, but his own
        nostrils have been pierced by someone else.*ᶜ *What a
        pity! He sure isn't a great man.*

How could he avoid the growth of a thicket of brambles?
        **The brambles are already several yards deep beneath
        his feet.*

*Though everyone in the whole country goes after him, he will
        not return;*
        **A double case. What's the use of pursuing him? Where
        is he? Where is the spirit of a great man?*

(Wu) goes on and on vainly reflecting back.
        **He wrings his hands and beats his breast, addressing a
        plea to the sky.*

Give up recollection!
        **What are you saying? You are making a living in a
        ghost cave.*

What limit is there to the pure wind circling the earth?
        **After all, the great Hsueh Tou is rolling around in the
        weeds.*

*The Master Hsueh Tou looked around to the right and left and
        said,*

"Is there any patriarch here?"
        **So you want to retract your statement? You still act
        like this?*

He answered himself, "There is."
  * *Too much trouble.* *

"Call him here to wash this old monk's feet."
  * *Give him thirty more blows and drive him away–this*
    wouldn't be more than he deserves. Though he acts
    like this, he still amounts to something. *

COMMENTARY

Now as for Hsueh Tou's verse on this case, it is like skillfully
doing a sword dance; sure and relaxed in mid-air, he naturally
does not run afoul of the sharp point. If he lacked this kind of
ability, as soon as he picked it up we would see him run afoul
of the point and wound his hand. For those who have the eye to
see, Hsueh Tou offers, takes back, praises, and deprecates,
using only four lines to settle the entire public case.

Generally, eulogies of the Ancients express Ch'an in a
roundabout way, picking out the main principles of the old
story, settling the case on the basis of the facts, and that is all.
Hsueh Tou gives a thrust and says right off, "The holy truths
are empty—how can you discern the point?" Beneath that first
phrase, he adds this one, which is quite extraordinary. Tell me,
after all how will you discern the point? Even if you have an
iron eye or a copper eye, still you will search without finding.

When you get here, can you figure it out by means of emo-
tive consciousness? This is why Yun Men said, "It is like flint
struck sparks, like flashing lightening." This little bit does not
fall within the scope of mental activity, intellectual consciousness, or emotional conceptions. If you wait till you open
your mouth, what good will it do? As soon as judgement and
comparison arise, the falcon has flown past Korea.

Hsueh Tou says, "How will all you monks distinguish the
real point? Who is facing the Emperor?" He adds the line,
"Again he said, 'I don't know.' " This is where Hsueh Tou is
excessively doting, redoubling his efforts to help people. Now
tell me, are "empty" and "I don't know" the same or different?
If you are someone who has personally understood completely,
you will understand without anything being said. Someone

who has not understood completely will undoubtedly separate them into two. Everywhere everyone always says, "Hsueh Tou (merely) brings up (the case) again." They are far from knowing that (the first) four lines of the verse complete the case entirely.

For the sake of compassion, Hsueh Tou versifies what happened: "Henceforth (Bodhidharma) secretly crossed the river; how could he avoid the growth of a thicket of brambles?" Bodhidharma originally came to this country to melt the sticking points, untie the bonds, pull out the nails and draw out the pegs, to cut down brambles for people: why then say that he gave rise to a thicket of brambles? This is not confined to those times; today the brambles under everyone's feet are already several yards deep. "Though everyone in the whole country goes after him, he will not come back; (Wu) goes on and on vainly reflecting back." Obviously Wu is not a powerful man. Tell me, where is Bodhidharma? If you see Bodhidharma, then you see where Hsueh Tou helps people in the end.

Hsueh Tou feared that people would pursue intellectual views, so he swung open the gate and brought out his own understanding, saying, "Give up recollecting; what limit is there to the pure wind circling the earth?" Once you give up recollection, what will become of the affairs you busy yourselves with? Hsueh Tou says, here and now the pure wind is circling the earth. Throughout heaven and earth, what is there that is limited? Hsueh Tou picks up the numberless concerns of all ages and throws them down before you. This is not confined to Hsueh Tou's time. What limit is there? All of you people—what limit is there on your part?

Again Hsueh Tou feared that people would grab ahold at this point, so again he exposed his skill; in a loud voice he asked, "Is there any patriarch here?" And he answered himself, "There is." Hsueh Tou doesn't hesitate to bare his heart entirely here for the sake of others. Again he spoke up himself: "Call him here to wash this old monk's feet." He certainly diminishes the man's dignity, but at the same time he properly offers his own hands and feet as well. Tell me, where does Hsueh Tou's meaning lie? When you get here, can you call it an ass? Can you call it a horse? Can you call it a patriarch? How can it be named or depicted? The frequently expressed opinion that Hsueh Tou is employing the Patriarch fortunately has nothing to do with it. But tell me, after all what's going on here? "I only allow that the old barbarian knows; I don't allow that the old barbarian understands."

TRANSLATOR'S NOTES

a. Bodhidharma, the first Patriarch of Ch'an in China, was asked by Hui K'e (Shen Kuang), the future Second Patriarch, to pacify his mind for him; Bodhidharma said, "Bring me your mind and I will pacify it for you." Hui K'e said, "When I search for my mind, I cannot find it." Bodhidharma said, "I have pacified your mind for you." At this Hui K'e was enlightened.

b. A lacquer bucket, pitch black, is a Ch'an metaphor for ignorance; to have "the bottom fall out of the bucket" is to become suddenly enlightened. To smash the bucket means to become enlightened or to enlighten others.

c. To pierce someone's nostrils, as in putting a ring through a bull's nose, means to master, to take control, to seize the advantage and have the upper hand. When one's nostrils are in another's hands, it means that one has been "caught," even be it metaphysically, so to speak.

The Ultimate Path is Without Difficulty

POINTER

Heaven and earth are narrow; sun, moon, and stars all at once go dark. Even if blows of the staff fall like rain and shouts roll like thunder, you still haven't lived up to the task of the fundamental vehicle of transcendence. Even the Buddhas of the three times can only know it for themselves; the successive generations of patriarchs have not been able to bring it up in its entirety. The treasury of teachings of the whole age cannot explain it thoroughly; clear eyed patchrobed monks cannot save themselves completely. When you get here, how will you ask for more instruction? To say the word "Buddha" is trailing mud and dripping water; to say the word "Ch'an" is a face full of shame. Superior people who have studied for a long time do not wait for it to be said; latecoming beginners simply must investigate and apprehend it.

CASE

Chao Chou, teaching the assembly, said,[1] "The Ultimate Path is without difficulty;[2] just avoid picking and choosing.[3] As soon as there are words spoken, "this is picking and choosing," "this is clarity."[4] This old monk does not abide within clarity;[5] do you still preserve anything or not?"[6]

At that time a certain monk asked, "Since you do not abide within clarity, what do you preserve?"[7]

Chao Chou replied, "I don't know either."[8]

The monk said, "Since you don't know, Teacher, why do you nevertheless say that you do not abide within clarity?"[9]

Chao Chou said, "It is enough to ask about the matter; bow and withdraw."[10]

NOTES

1. What's the old fellow doing? Don't create complications!
2. Not hard, not easy.
3. What's in front of your eyes? The Third Patriarch is still alive.
4. Two heads, three faces. A little boasting. When a fish swims through, the water is muddied; when a bird flies by, feathers fall.
5. His thieving intent already shows; where is the old fellow going?
6. He's defeated. Still there's something, or a half.
7. The monk presses him well; his tongue is pressed against the roof of his mouth.
8. (The monk) crushed this old fellow dead; he has to fall back three thousand miles.
9. Look! Where is he going? He's chased him up a tree.
10. Lucky thing he has this move; the old thief!

COMMENTARY

Chao Chou always used to bring up this saying; that is, "Just avoid picking and choosing." This is from the Third Patriarch's *Seal of Faith in the Heart*, which says,

> *The Ultimate Path is without difficulty;*
> *Just avoid picking and choosing.*
> *Just don't love or hate,*
> *And you'll be lucid and clear.*

As soon as you have affirmation and negation, "this is picking and choosing," "this is clarity." As soon as you understand this way, you have already stumbled past. When you're riveted down or stuck in glue, what can you do? Chao Chou said, "This is picking and choosing, this is clarity." People these days who practice meditation and ask about the Path, if they do not remain within picking and choosing, then they settle down within clarity. "This old monk does not abide within clarity; do you still preserve anything or not?" All of you people tell me, since he is not within clarity, where is Chao Chou? And why does he still teach people to preserve?

My late master Wu Tsu often would say, "I reach my hand down to show you, but how do you understand?" But tell me, where does he reach down his hand? Perceive the meaning on the hook; don't stick by the zero point of the scale.

This monk coming forth was undeniably extraordinary; he got ahold of Chao Chou's gap and proceeded to press him: "Since you do not abide within clarity, what do you preserve?" Chao Chou never used the staff or the shout; he just said, "I don't know either." When being pressed by that (monk), anyone but this old fellow would time and again be at a loss. Fortunately this old fellow Chao Chou had freedom to turn himself around in, so he answered him like this. Many followers of Ch'an these days will also say when asked, "I don't know either; I don't understand." Nevertheless, though they are on the same road, they are not in the same groove.

There was something special about this monk; only thus could he ask, "Since you don't know, Teacher, why do you nevertheless say that you do not abide within clarity?" Another good rejoinder! If it had been someone other than Chao Chou, he never would have been able to explain. But Chao Chou is an adept; he just said to him, "It's enough to ask about the matter; bow and withdraw." As before, the monk had no way to cope with this old fellow; all he could do was suck in his breath and swallow his voice.

This is a very capable teacher of our clan; he does not discuss the abstruse or the mysterious, he does not speak of mentality or perspectives[a] with you—he always deals with people in terms of the fundamental matter. Thus he would have said, "When we're reviling each other, I let you clamp beaks with me; when we're spitting at each other, I let you spew me with slobber." It is hardly known that while Chao Chou ordinarily never used beating or shouting to deal with people, and only used ordinary speech, still no one in the world could handle him. It was all because he never had so many calculating judgements: he could pick up sideways and use upside-down, go against or go with, having attained great freedom. People today do not understand this, and just say that Chao Chou did not answer the question or explain it to the man. How little you realize that you've stumbled past it.

VERSE

The Ultimate Path is without difficulty:
  **A triple case. A mouthful of frost. What is he saying?*

The speech is to the point, the words are to the point.
   **When the fish swims through, the stream is muddied.*
   A profusion of confusion; he smeared it.

In one there are many kinds;
   **You should open it up; what end will there be in just*
   one kind!

In two there's no duality.
   **How could it sustain four, five, six, seven!*
   Why create complications!

On the horizon of the sky the sun rises and the moon sets;
   **It's presented right to your face; above the head*
   and beneath the feet it extends boundlessly. Don't
   lift or lower your head.

Beyond the balustrade, the mountains deepen, the waters
   grow chill.
   **Once dead, you don't return to life again. Do you feel*
   the hairs on your body stand on end in a chill!

When the skull's consciousness is exhausted, how can joy re-
   main!
   **He twinkles his eyes within his coffin. Workman Lu*
   (Hui Neng, the Sixth Patriarch) is a fellow student of
   his.

In a dead tree the dragon murmurs are not yet exhausted.
   **Bah! The dead tree blooms again. Bodhidharma*
   travels through the eastern land.

Difficult, difficult!
   **A false teaching is hard to uphold.*
   An upside-down statement. What place
   is this here, to speak of difficulty or ease!

Picking and choosing! Clarity! You see for yourself!
   **Blind! One might have thought it depended on some-*
   one else, but luckily (he says) 'See for yourself.' It's
   none of my business.

COMMENTARY

Hsueh Tou knows where Chao Chou comes down; therefore
he versifies like this: "The Ultimate Path has no difficulties."
Then immediately following this, he says, "The speech is to
the point, the words are to the point." He raises one corner, but

doesn't come back with the other three; when Hsueh Tou says, "In one there are many kinds; in two there's no duality," this is like three corners returning to one. But tell me, where is it that words are to the point, and speech is to the point? In one, why are nevertheless many kinds, yet in two there is no duality? If you don't have eyes, where will you seek?

If you can penetrate these two lines, this is the basis of the ancient saying, "Fused into one whole, as of old you see that mountains are mountains, rivers are rivers, long is long, short is short, sky is sky, and earth is earth." But sometimes we call sky earth and earth sky, sometimes we say that mountains are not mountains and rivers are not rivers. Ultimately, how to attain imperturbable tranquility? When the wind comes, the trees move; when the waves swell, the boats ride high. In spring it sprouts, in summer it matures, in fall it is harvested, in winter it is stored; with uniform equanimity, everything disappears of itself.

Thus this four-line verse abruptly cuts off; but Hsueh Tou has extra ability, so he opens up the closed bag and gives a summary account. As he said at first,

> *The Ultimate Path is without difficulty;*
> *Speech is to the point, words are to the point.*
> *In one there are many kinds;*
> *In two there is no duality.*

Though there aren't so many things, when the sun rises over the horizon the moon goes down, and when the mountains beyond the balustrade deepen, the waters grow cold. When you get here, speech is indeed to the point, words are indeed to the point, everything is the Path and all things are completely real. Isn't this where mind and objects are both forgotten, fused into one whole? At the beginning of the verse Hsueh Tou was too solitary and steep; at the end, though, he is quite indulgent. If you can bore right through and see and penetrate, naturally it will be like the excellent flavor of ghee. If you don't forget your emotional interpretations, then you'll see a profusion of confusion, and you definitely won't understand this kind of talk.

"When the skull's consciousness is exhausted, how can joy remain? In the dead tree, dragon murmurs are not yet ended." This is just a bit of combination. These are from public cases of ancient questions about the Path, which Hsueh Tou has drawn

out, pierced through and strung on the same thread to use in
versifying "The Ultimate Path is without difficulty; just avoid
picking and choosing." People these days don't understand the
Ancient's meaning, and only chew on the words and gnaw on
the phrases; when will they ever be done? If you are an adept
who is a master of technique, only then can you understand
this kind of talk.

Haven't you read how a monk asked Hsiang Yen, "What is
the Path?" Hsiang Yen said, "In a dead tree, dragon murmurings." The monk asked, "What is a man of the Path?" Hsiang
Yen said, "Eyeballs in a skull." Later the monk asked Shih
Shuang, "What are 'dragon murmurings in a dead tree'?" Shih
Shuang said, "Still having joy." The monk asked, "What are
eyeballs in a skull?" Shih Shuang said, "Still having consciousness." The monk also asked Ts'ao Shan, "What are
'dragon murmurings in a dead tree'?" Ts'ao Shan said, "The
blood line is not cut off." The monk asked, "What are 'eyeballs
in a skull'?" Ts'ao Shan said, "Not dried up." The monk asked,
"Who can hear this?" Ts'ao Shan said, "In the whole world,
there is no one who does not hear it." The monk asked, "What
book is 'dragon murmurings' taken from?" Ts'ao Shan said, "I
don't know what book it's from, but all who hear it die." He
also had a verse which said,

> In a dead tree the dragon murmurs and truly sees
>   the Path;
> When the skull has no consciousness, only then are
>   the eyes clear.
> When joy and consciousness come to an end, all
>   happenings are ended;
> How can such a one discriminate the pure in the
>   midst of impurity?

Hsueh Tou can be said to possess great skill in combining all
this at once in his verse. Though he has done this, there's been
no duality at all.

Hsueh Tou had help for people at the end of the verse when
he added "Difficult, difficult!" It's exactly this "difficult, difficult," that you must penetrate through in order to attain.
Why? Pai Chang said, "All words and speech, mountains, rivers, and the great earth, each come back to oneself." Whatever
Hsueh Tou offers and takes back must ultimately be returned

to oneself. Tell me, how did Hsueh Tou help people when he said, "Picking and choosing? Clarity? See for yourself!"? He had already created this complicated verse; why then did he say "See for yourself"? Tell me, what was his true meaning? Don't say you can't understand. At this point, even I simply cannot understand either.

TRANSLATOR'S NOTES

a. *Chi* and *ching*, rendered in this instance as 'mentality and perspective,' are very common technical terms, to be met with many times in this book, used individually and as a pair. Both are used in referring to both subjective and objective phenomena; in Ch'an meditation they sometimes speak of 'forgetting' or 'merging' subject and object; likewise, as 'turning words' or 'pivotal words,' these terms produce, individually and together, an effect which cannot be rendered conveniently in a single English expression.

    Chi is used for 'potential' (as of a student, or a situation), 'capability,' or a 'device' used to illustrate a point or state; it also means mental activity or state in general. Sometimes the first, or primary *chi* is contrasted to the secondary *chi*; this is like 'cognition' followed by 'recognition.'

    Ching is a mental object, an object, a state, a realm or sphere, a perspective (or perception). A common question is what a master's *ching* is like (i.e. what does he 'see,' what is his sphere or state of realization), and what the person in that 'realm' is like. When Ch'an students experienced purity or bliss, or perceived Buddhas and bodhisattvas in their meditations, they were told these were merely *ching*, mental objects or 'states' which should not be acknowledged as desirable or approved as real attainments, lest one become intoxicated by one's state. Similarly, all kinds of hallucinations were called *mo ching* or 'demon states,' illusory objects or perceptions caused by 'demons' or 'devils' (whether these are inside or outside the mind is a pointless question here), obstructing the path of meditation.

    As examples of *chi-ching*, Japanese commentaries conventionally refer to such things as 'twinkling the eyes,' 'raising the eyebrows,' 'raising the staff, the whisk, or the gavel,' gestures frequently met with in Ch'an records as replies to questions, or teaching devices of the masters. *Chi-ching* thus means the mentality, or mental working, and the perspective, or object it embraces; an act and the state it manifests, a device and the object(ive) it intends to convey. Ultimately, it seems that these terms can refer to any action or speech and the implication or impression it presents or represents, especially the intentional gesture or remark of the teaching master.

Master Ma is Unwell

POINTER

One device, one object; one word, one phrase—the intent is that you'll have a place to enter; still this is gouging a wound in healthy flesh—it can become a nest or a den. The Great Function appears without abiding by fixed principles—the intent is that you'll realize there is something transcendental; it covers the sky and covers the earth, yet it cannot be grasped.

This way will do, not this way will do too—this is too diffuse. This way won't do, not this way won't do either—this is too cut off. Without treading these two paths, what would be right? Please test; I cite this for you to see:

CASE

Great Master Ma was unwell.[1] The temple superintendent asked him, "Teacher, how has your venerable health been in recent days?"[2] The Great Master said, "Sun Face Buddha, Moon Face Buddha."[3,a]

NOTES

1. This fellow has broken down quite a bit. He's dragging in other people.
2. Four hundred and four diseases break out all at once. They'll be lucky if they're not seeing off a dead monk in three days. (This question) is in the course of humanity and righteousness.
3. How fresh and new! Sustenance for his fledgeling.

COMMENTARY

The Great Master Ma was unwell, so the temple superintendent asked him, "Teacher, how has your venerable health been

18

in recent days?" The Great Master replied, "Sun Face Buddha, Moon Face Buddha." If the patriarchal teachers had not dealt with others on the basis of the fundamental matter, how could we have the shining light of this Path? If you know what this public case comes down to, then you walk alone through the red sky; if you don't know where it comes down, time and again you'll lose the way before the withered tree cliff. If you are somebody in your own right, when you get here you must have the ability to drive off the plowman's ox and to snatch away the hungry man's food before you will see how Great Master Ma helps people.

These days many people say that Master Ma was teaching the superintendent; fortunately, this has no connection. Right now in this assembly there are many who misunderstand; they put a glare in their eyes and say, "It's here; the left eye is the Sun Face, and the right eye is the Moon Face." What relevance does this have? Even by the (non-existent) Year of the Ass, you won't have seen it even in a dream. You just stumble past, missing what the Ancient was about.

So when Master Ma spoke like this, where was his meaning? Some say (he meant) "Fix some stomach medicine and bring me a bowl of it." What grasp has this got on it? Having gotten to this point, how would you attain tranquility? This is why it is said, "The single road of transcendence has not been transmitted by a thousand sages; students trouble themselves with forms like monkeys grasping at reflections."

This "Sun Face Buddha, Moon Face Buddha" is extremely difficult to see; even Hsueh Tou finds it difficult to versify this. But since he has seen all the way through, he uses his life's work to the full to make his comment. Do you people want to see Hsueh Tou? Look at the text below.

VERSE

Sun Face Buddha, Moon Face Buddha;
> ***When he opens his mouth you see his guts.*
> *(Ma and Hsueh Tou) are like two facing mirrors;*
> *in between there's no image or reflection.* *

What kind of people were the Ancient Emperors?
> ***Too lofty. Don't belittle them. They*
> *can be valued high or low.* *

For twenty years I have suffered bitterly;
    **This is your own fall into the weeds—*
    it's none of my business. Here's a mute
    eating a bitter melon. *

How many times I have gone down into the Blue Dragon's
        cave for you!
    **How was it worth this? Don't misuse your mind.*
    Don't say there isn't anything extraordinary here. *

This distress
    **He saddens people to death.*
    Sad man, don't speak to sad people. *

Is worth recounting;
    **To whom would you speak of it?*
    If you speak of it to sad people,
    you will sadden them to death. *

Clear-eyed patchrobed monks should not take it lightly.
    **You must be even more thoroughgoing. Bah! Fall*
    back three thousand miles. *

COMMENTARY

When (the Sung Emperor) Shen Tsung was on the throne
(1068–1085) he thought that this verse ridiculed the state, so
he wouldn't let it be included in the (Buddhist) canon.

First Hsueh Tou quotes: "Sun Face Buddha, Moon Face
Buddha." Having brought this up, then he says, "What kind of
people were the Ancient Emperors?" Tell me, what is his
meaning? I just finished telling you a minute ago; Hsueh Tou is
commenting directly (on Master Ma). So it is said, "Letting
down his hook in the four seas, he only fishes for terrible dragons." This one line has already been completed (the verse);
afterwards, Hsueh Tou versifies how he concentrated on study
and search all his life.

"For twenty years I have suffered bitterly; how many times
I've gone down into the Blue Dragon's cave for you!" What is
he like? He's like a man going into the Blue Dragon's cave to
seize the pearl. Afterwards he broke apart the lacquer bucket.
Though this might be considered quite extraordinary, basically

it just amounts to "What kind of people were the Ancient Emperors?" Tell me, what are Hsueh Tou's words getting at? You have to take a step back on your own and look before you will see where he's at.

So what kind of people were the Ancient Emperors anyway? People mostly do not see Hsueh Tou's meaning, but only say that he is ridiculing the state. To understand in this way is merely an emotional view. This (line) comes from Ch'an Yueh's poem on "The behavior of barons," which says,

> Clothes in brocades and fine embroidery, with falcons on their wrists,
> They go about at leisure, their manner scornful.
> They know nothing of the difficulties of sowing and harvesting;
> What kind of people were the Ancient Emperors?

Hsueh Tou says, "This distress is worth recounting; clear eyed patchrobed monks must not take it lightly." How many people make their livelihood within the Blue Dragon's cave? Even if you're a clear eyed patchrobed monk with an eye on your forehead and a talisman under your arm, shining through the four continents, when you get here you still must not take it lightly; you must be thoroughgoing.

TRANSLATOR'S NOTES

a. According to the *Buddha Name Scripture*, a Sun Face Buddha lives in the world for eighteen hundred years, whereas a Moon Face Buddha enters extinction after a day and a night. Tenkei Denson says, "But is everyone's own Sun Face Buddha Moon Face Buddha something long or short?"

Te Shan Carrying His Bundle

Under the blue sky, in the bright sunlight, you don't have to point out this and that anymore; but the causal conditions of time and season still require you to give the medicine in accordance with the disease. But tell me, is it better to let go, or is it better to hold still? To test, I cite this: look!

CASE

When Te Shan arrived at Kuei Shan,[1] he carried his bundle with him into the teaching hall,[2] where he crossed from east to west and from west to east.[3] He looked around and said, "There's nothing, no one." Then he went out.[4]

Hsueh Tou added the comment, "Completely exposed."[5] But when Te Shan got to the monastery gate, he said, "Still, I shouldn't be so coarse."[6] So he reentered (the hall) with full ceremony to meet (Kuei Shan).[7] As Kuei Shan sat there,[8] Te Shan held up his sitting mat and said, "Teacher!"[9] Kuei Shan reached for his whisk,[10] whereupon Te Shan shouted, shook out his sleeves, and left.[11]

Hsueh Tou added the comment, "Completely exposed."[12]

Te Shan turned his back on the teaching hall, put on his straw sandals, and departed.[13] That evening Kuei Shan asked the head monk, "Where is that newcomer who just came?"[14] The head monk answered, "At that time he turned his back on the teaching hall, put on his straw sandals, and departed."[15]

Kuei Shan said, "Hereafter that lad will go to the summit of a solitary peak, build himself a grass hut, and go on scolding the Buddhas and reviling the Patriarchs."[16]

Hsueh Tou added the comment, "He adds frost to snow."[17]

NOTES

1. The board-carrying fellow,[a] the wild fox spirit![b]
2. Unavoidably he causes people to doubt. He has suffered defeat.
3. He has a lot of Ch'an, but what for?
4. He deserves thirty blows of the staff. Indeed his spirit reaches the heavens. A real lion cub can roar the lion's roar.
5. Wrong. After all. Check!
6. Letting go, gathering in. At first too high, in the end too low. When one realizes one's fault one should reform, but how many people can?
7. As before, he acts like this. It's already his second defeat. Danger!
8. (Kuei Shan) watches this fellow with cold eyes. It takes this kind of man to grab a tiger's whiskers.
9. He changes heads, switches faces; he stirs up waves where there's no wind.
10. Only that fellow could do this; he sets his strategy in motion from within his tent. Nothing can stop him from cutting off the tongues of everyone in the world.
11. This is the understanding of a wild fox spirit. This one shout contains both the provisional and the real, both the illumination and the function. They're all people who can grab the clouds and grasp the fog, but he is outstanding among them.
12. Wrong. After all. Check!
13. The scenery is lovely, but the case is not yet completed. (Te Shan) won the hat on his head but lost the shoes on his feet. He's already lost his body and his life.
14. He lost his interest in the east, and loses his principal in the west. His eyes look southeast, but his mind is in the northwest.
15. The sacred tortoise is dragging his tail;[c] he deserves thirty blows. How many blows to the back of the head would it take for this kind of fellow?
16. He draws his bow after the thief is gone. No patchrobed monk in the world can leap out of this.
17. Wrong. After all. Check!

COMMENTARY

Three times I added the word "check." Do all of you understand? Sometimes I take a blade of grass and use it as the sixteen-foot golden body (of Buddha); sometimes I take the sixteen-foot golden body and use it as a blade of grass.

Originally Te Shan was a lecturing monk, expounding the *Diamond Cutter Scripture* in western Shu (Szechuan). According to what it says in that teaching, in the process of the knowledge attained after diamond-like concentration, one studies the majestic conduct of Buddhas for a thousand aeons and studies the refined practices of Buddhas for ten thousand aeons before finally fulfilling Buddhahood. On the other hand, the "southern devils" at this time were saying "Mind itself is Buddha." Consequently Te Shan became very incensed and went travelling on foot, carrying some commentaries; he went straight to the South to destroy this crew of devils. You see from how aroused he got what a fierce keen fellow he was.

When he first got to Li Chou (in Hunan), he met an old woman selling fried cakes by the roadside; he put down his commentaries to buy some refreshment to lighten his mind. The old woman said, "What is that you're carrying?" Te Shan said, "Commentaries on the *Diamond Cutter Scripture*." The old woman said, "I have a question for you: if you can answer it I'll give you some fried cakes to refresh your mind; if you can't answer, you'll have to go somewhere else to buy." Te Shan said, "Just ask." The old woman said, "The *Diamond Cutter Scripture* says, 'Past mind can't be grasped, present mind can't be grasped, future mind can't be grasped': which mind does the learned monk desire to refresh?" Te Shan was speechless. The old woman directed him to go call on Lung T'an.

As soon as Te Shan crossed the threshold he said, "Long have I heard of Lung T'an ('Dragon Pond'), but now that I've arrived here, there's no pond to see and no dragon appears." Master Lung T'an came out from behind a screen and said, "You have really arrived at Lung T'an." Te Shan bowed and withdrew. During the night Te Shan entered Lung T'an's room and stood in attendance till late at night. Lung T'an said, "Why don't you go?" Te Shan bade farewell, lifted up the curtain, and went out; he saw that it was dark outside, so he turned around and said, "It's dark outside." Lung T'an lit a paper lantern and handed it to Te Shan; as soon as Te Shan took it, Lung T'an blew it out. Te Shan was vastly and greatly enlightened. Immediately he bowed to Lung T'an, who said, "What have you seen that you bow?" Te Shan answered, "From now on I will never again doubt what's on the tongues of the venerable teaching masters of the world."

The next day Lung T'an went up into the teaching hall and said, "There is one among you with teeth like a forest of swords and a mouth like a bowl of blood; even if you hit him with a staff, he wouldn't turn back. Another day he will ascend to the summit of a solitary peak and establish my path there." Then Te Shan took all his commentaries in front of the teaching hall and raised a torch over them, declaring, "Even to plumb all abstruse locutions is like a single hair in the great void; to exhaust the essential workings of the world is like a single drop of water cast into a vast valley." Then he burned the commentaries.

Later he heard that Kuei Shan's teaching was flourishing, so he traveled to Kuei Shan to meet him as an adept. Without even untying his bundle, he went straight to the teaching hall, where he walked back and forth from east to west and west to east, looked around, and said, "Nothing, no one." Then he went out. Tell me, what was his meaning? Wasn't he crazy? People misinterpret this as 'establishment,' but that is simply irrelevant. See how extraordinary that Te Shan was; this is why it is said, "To stand out from the crowd, you must be a brave spirited fellow; to defeat enemies is a matter for a lion's son. If you try to become Buddha without an eye like this, how will you ever do it, even in a thousand years?"

When you get here, you must be a thoroughly competent adept before you will be able to see. Why? In the Buddha Dharma there are not so many complications; where can you bring intellectual views to bear? This is the action of (Te Shan's) mind; where is there so much toil? This is why Hsuan Sha said, "Even if you're like the moon reflected in an autumn pond, which when striking the waves is not scattered, or like the sound of a bell on a quiet night, which when hit never fails to resound, this is still an affair on this shore of birth and death." When you arrive here there is no gain or loss, no affirmation or negation, nor is there anything extraordinary or mysterious. Since there is nothing extraordinary or mysterious, how will you understand (Te Shan's) going back and forth from east to west and west to east? Tell me, what was his meaning?

This old fellow Kuei Shan still was not taken in by that (Te

Shan); anyone but Kuei Shan would have been crushed by him. Look at how the old adept Kuei Shan meets him; he just sits there and observes the outcome. If he did not profoundly discern the 'oncoming wind,' how could he have been like this? Hsueh Tou adds the comment "Completely exposed." This is like an iron spike. In the assembly this is called an added comment: although it goes for both sides, it does not remain on either side. How will you understand his statement, "Completely exposed"? Where does the complete exposure take place? Tell me, is Te Shan completely exposed, or is it Kuei Shan who is completely exposed?

On his way out Te Shan got as far as the monastery gate, but then he said to himself, "Still, I shouldn't be so coarse." He wanted to bring out his guts, his innermost heart, in a Dharma battle with Kuei Shan; so he went back in with full ceremony to meet him. As Kuei Shan sat there, Te Shan lifted up his sitting mat and said, "Teacher!" Kuei Shan reached for his whisk; Te Shan then shouted, shook his sleeves, and left. How extraordinary!

Many in the assembly say that Kuei Shan was afraid of him. What has this got to do with it? Kuei Shan was not flustered at all. This is why it is said, "One whose wisdom surpasses a bird's can catch a bird, one whose wisdom surpasses an animal's can catch an animal, and one whose wisdom surpasses a man's can catch a man." When one is immersed in this kind of Ch'an, even if the multitude of appearances and myriad forms, heavens and hells, and all the plants, animals, and people, all were to shout at once, he still wouldn't be bothered; even if someone overthrew his meditation seat and scattered his congregation with shouts, he wouldn't give it any notice. It is as high as heaven, broad as earth. If Kuei Shan did not have the ability to cut off the tongues of everyone on earth, at that time it would have been very difficult for him to test Te Shan. If he weren't the enlightened teacher of fifteen hundred people, at this point he wouldn't have been able to explain anything. But Kuei Shan was setting strategy in motion from within his tent that would settle victory over a thousand miles.

Te Shan turned his back on the teaching hall, put on his straw sandals, and departed. Tell me, what was his meaning? You tell me, did Te Shan win or lose? Acting as he did, did Kuei

Shan win or lose? Hsueh Tou commented, "Completely exposed." Here he makes an effort and sees through the Ancients' ultimate riddle; only thus could he be so extraordinary. Hsueh Tou added "Completely exposed" twice, making a three part judgement; only then had he revealed this public case. He was like a bystander judging those two men.

Afterwards, this old fellow (Kuei Shan) was unhurried; when evening came he finally asked the head monk, "Where is that newcomer who just came?" The head monk replied, "At that time, he turned his back on the teaching hall, put on his straw sandals, and left." Kuei Shan said, "Hereafter that lad will go up to the summit of a solitary peak, build himself a grass hut, and go on scolding the Buddhas and reviling the Patriarchs." But say, what was his meaning? Old man Kuei Shan was not being good hearted; in the future Te Shan could scold the Buddhas and revile the Patriarchs, pummel the wind and beat the rain, yet he would still never get out of that cave. Te Shan's whole lifetime's methods have been seen through by this old fellow. Should we say that Kuei Shan has given him a prophecy here? Or should we say that when the marsh is wide it can hide a mountain, that reason^d can subdue a leopard? Fortunately this has nothing to do with it.

Hsueh Tou knows what this public case comes down to, so he can dare to settle it for them by further saying, "He adds frost to snow." Once again he offers it up for people to see. If you do see, I'll allow that you're a fellow student of Kuei Shan, Te Shan, and Hsueh Tou. If you don't see, beware of vainly producing intellectual interpretations.

VERSE

One "completely exposed"
    **The words are still in our ears. Gone.*

A second "completely exposed"
    **A double case.*

"Adding frost to snow"–(Te Shan) has had a dangerous fall.
    **The three stages are not the same. Where (did Te Shan fall)?*

The General of the Flying Cavalry enters the enemy camp;
   **Danger! No need to trouble to slash again at the
   general of a defeated army. He loses his body and life.*

How many could regain their safety?
   **(Te Shan) gained life in the midst of death.*

(Te Shan) hurriedly runs past—
   **He acts like no one is around him.
   Although you exhaust the thirty-six
   strategems of your supernatural powers,
   what is the use?*

(But Kuei Shan) doesn't let him go.
   **The cat can subdue the leopard.
   (Kuei Shan) pierced his nostrils.*

On the summit of the solitary peak, he sits among the weeds;
   **After all. To pierce his nostrils isn't out of the
   ordinary. But why is he (Te Shan) sitting among the
   weeds?*

Bah!
   **Understand? Two blades cut each other.
   Two by two, three by three, they walk the
   old road. Singing and clapping go together.
   I strike!*

COMMENTARY

When Hsueh Tou composed verses on one hundred public
cases, with each case he burned incense and offered it up;
therefore (his verses) have circulated widely throughout the
land. In addition he mastered literary composition. When he
had penetrated the public cases and become easily conversant
with them, only then could he set his brush to paper. Why so?
It is easy to distinguish dragons from snakes; it is hard to fool a
patchrobed monk. Since Hsueh Tou immersed himself in this
case and penetrated through it, he puts down three comments
at those impenetrable, misleading places, then picks them up
to make his verse.

"Adding frost to snow"—almost a dangerous fall. What is
Te Shan like? He is just like Li Kuang, by innate talent a skilled

archer, whom the Emperor (Wu of Han) commissioned as the General of the Flying Cavalry (Imperial elite corps). Li Kuang penetrated deep into enemy territory, where he was captured alive by the King of the Huns. Kuang was weak from wounds; they tied him prone between two horses. Kuang played dead, but stealthily observed that there was a Hun near him riding a good mount. Kuang suddenly sprang up and leaped on the horse, throwing down the Hun rider and seizing his bow and arrows. Whipping the horse, he galloped off towards the South; drawing the bow and shooting back at the riders pursuing him, he thus made good his escape. This fellow had the ability to wrest life from the midst of death; Hsueh Tou alludes to this in the verse to make a comparison with Te Shan, who re-entered (the teaching hall) to meet (Kuei Shan), and was able to leap out again, as before.

Look at how that Ancient (Te Shan) sees all the way, speaks all the way, acts all the way, and functions all the way; he's undeniably a brave spirit. Only if you possess the ability to kill a man without blinking an eye can you then become Buddha right where you stand. Someone who can fulfill Buddhahood right where he stands naturally kills people without blinking an eye; thus he has his share of freedom and independence.

When some people these days are questioned, at first they seem to have the qualities of a patchrobed monk, but when they're pressed even slightly, their waists snap and their legs break; they come all to pieces. They totally lack the slightest continuity. That is why an Ancient said, "Continuity is indeed very difficult." Look at how Te Shan and Kuei Shan acted; were theirs stammering, halting views?

"How many could regain their safety? (Te Shan) hurriedly runs past." Te Shan shouted and left; this is just like Li Kuang's strategy after he was captured, seizing a bow to shoot and kill his guard, and making good his escape from enemy territory. Hsueh Tou's verse at this point has great effect.

Te Shan turned his back on the teaching hall, put on his straw sandals and left. Some say he gained the advantage; how far they are from realizing that this old fellow (Kuei Shan), as before, still doesn't allow (Te Shan) to appear. Hsueh Tou says, "He doesn't let him go." The same evening Kuei Shan asked the head monk, "Where is that newcomer who just came?" The head monk said, "Back then, he turned his back on the teaching hall, put on his straw sandals and left." Kuei Shan said, "Hereafter that lad will go up to the summit of a solitary peak, build himself a grass hut, and go on scolding the Buddhas and reviling the Patriarchs." When did he ever let him go? Nevertheless, he's outstanding.

At this point, why does Hsueh Tou say, "On the summit of the solitary peak, he sits among the weeds," and then add an exclamation? Tell me, what does this come down to? Study for thirty more years!

TRANSLATOR'S NOTES

a. Someone carrying a board can only see one side, vision being obstructed by the burden.

b. A wild fox spirit is usually an expression of blame, referring to someone who indulges in cleverness. According to an old story, someone once became a wild fox because he said that an accomplished yogi is not subject to cause and effect. However, like all 'turning words,' this expression also has a positive side, meaning one who has complete freedom of action.

c. That is, he is leaving a trail. Some commentators explain the general metaphor by saying that when a tortoise lays eggs in the sand it covers them to hide them, but as it leaves its tail makes a track, after all revealing the whereabouts of the eggs. This expression is thus similar to the Ch'an saying about hiding the body but revealing the shadow.

d. The alternate version of this saying is that "a cat can subdue a leopard," meaning that the weaker can subdue the stronger. Confusion arose from the similarity between the Chinese characters used for "cat" and for "reason."

Hsueh Feng's Grain of Rice

POINTER

Whoever would uphold the teaching of our school must be a brave spirited fellow; only with the ability to kill a man without blinking an eye can one become Buddha right where he stands. Therefore his illumination and function are simultaneous; wrapping up and opening out are equal in his preaching. Principle and phenomena are not two, and he practices both the provisional and the real. Letting go of the primary, he sets up the gate of the secondary meaning; if he were to cut off all complications straightaway, it would be impossible for late-coming students of elementary capabilities to find a resting place. It was this way yesterday; the matter couldn't be avoided. It is this way today too; faults and errors fill the skies. Still, if one is a clear eyed person, he can't be fooled one bit. Without clear eyes, lying in the mouth of a tiger, one cannot avoid losing one's body and life. As a test, I cite this; look!

CASE

Hsueh Feng, teaching his community, said,[1] "Pick up the whole great earth in your fingers, and it's as big as a grain of rice.[2] Throw it down before you:[3] if, like a lacquer bucket, you don't understand,[4] I'll beat the drum to call everyone to look."[5]

NOTES

1. One blind man leading a crowd of blind men. It's not beyond him.
2. What technique is this? I myself have never sported devil eyes.
3. I'm afraid it can't be thrown down. What skill do you have?
4. Hsueh Feng relies on his power to deceive people. Take what's coming to you and get out!
5. Blind! The beat of the drum is for the three armies.

COMMENTARY

Ch'ang Ch'ing asked Yun Men, "When Hsueh Feng spoke like this, was there any place where he wasn't able to appear?" Men answered, "There is." Ch'ing asked, "How so?" Men said, "One can't always be making wild fox spirit interpretations."

Yun Feng said, "Compared to above, not enough; compared to below, too much. I am making up more complications for you." He raised his staff and said, "Do you see Hsueh Feng? Where the King's rule is a little more strict, it's not permitted to plunder the open markets."

Che of Ta Kuei said, "I'll add more mud to dirt for you." He raised his staff and said, "Look! Look! Hsueh Feng has defecated right in front of you all. Come now, why don't you even recognize the smell of shit?"

Hsueh Feng, teaching his assembly, said, "Pick up the whole great earth in your fingers, and it's as big as a grain of rice." There was something extraordinary in the way this Ancient guided people and benefited beings. He was indefatigably rigorous; three times he climbed (Mount) T'ou Tzu, nine times he went to Tung Shan. Wherever he went, he would set up his lacquer tub and wooden spoon and serve as the rice steward, just for the sake of penetrating this matter.

When he arrived at Tung Shan, he served as the rice steward; one day Tung Shan asked Hsueh Feng, "What are you doing?" Hsueh Feng said, "Cleaning rice." Shan asked, "Are you washing the grit to get rid of the rice, or are you washing the rice to get rid of the grit?" Feng said, "Grit and rice are both removed at once." Shan said, "What will everybody eat?" Feng then overturned the basin. Shan said, "Your affinity lies with Te Shan," and he directed Feng to go see him.

As soon as he got there, Hsueh Feng asked, "Does this student have any share in this matter handed down from antiquity as the fundamental vehicle?" Te Shan struck him a blow and said, "What are you saying?" Because of this, Hsueh Feng had an insight.

Later Hsueh Feng was snowed in on Tortoise Mountain (in Hunan). He told Yen T'ou, "When Te Shan hit me, it was like the bottom falling out of a bucket." Yen T'ou shouted and said, "Haven't you heard it said that what comes in through the gate isn't the family treasure? You must let it flow out from your own breast to cover heaven and earth; then you'll have some small portion of realization." Suddenly Hsueh Feng was greatly enlightened; he bowed and said to Yen T'ou, "Elder brother, today on Tortoise Mountain I have finally attained the Path."

People these days only say that the Ancient (Hsueh Feng) made something up specially to teach people of the future fixed precepts that they can rely on. To say this is just slandering that ancient master; this is called "spilling Buddha's blood." The Ancients weren't like people today with their spurious shallow talk; otherwise, how could they have used a single word or half a phrase for a whole lifetime? Therefore, when it came to supporting the teaching of the school and continuing the life of the Buddhas, they would spit out a word or half a phrase which would spontaneously cut off the tongues of everyone on earth. There's no place for you to produce a train of thought, to make intellectual interpretations, or to grapple with principles. See how Hsueh Feng taught his community; since he had seen adepts, he had the hammer and tongs of an adept. Whenever he utters a word or half a phrase, he's not making his livelihood within the ghost caves of mental activity, ideational consciousness and calculating thought. He just surpasses the multitudes and stands out from the crowd; he settles past and present and leaves no room for uncertainty. His actions were all like this.

One day Hsueh Feng said to his community, "On South Mountain there's a turtle-nosed snake; all of you should take a good look at it." Thereupon Wayfarer Leng (Ch'ang Ch'ing) came forward from the assembly and said, "If so, then there are a lot of people in this hall today who lose their bodies and lives."

On another occasion Hsueh Feng said, "The whole great earth is the single eye of a monk; where will you people go to defecate?" Another time he said, "I have met with you at Wang Chou Pavilion; I have also met with you in the Black Rock Range, and I have also met with you in front of the monks' hall." At the time Pao Fu asked E Hu, "Leaving aside 'in front of the monks' hall,' what about the meetings at Wang Chou Pavilion and Black Rock Range?" E Hu hurried back to his room. Hsueh Feng was always bringing up this kind of talk to instruct his community.

As for "Pick up the whole great earth in your fingers, and it's as big as a grain of rice"—tell me, at this juncture, can you figure it out by means of intellectual discrimination? Here you must smash through the net, at once abandon gain and loss, affirmation and negation, to be completely free and at ease; you naturally pass through his snare, and then you will see what he's doing. Tell me, where is Hsueh Feng's meaning?

People often make up intellectual interpretations and say, "Mind is the master of myriad things; the whole great earth is all at once in my hand." Fortunately, this has no connection. Here you must be a true and genuine fellow, who penetrates the bone through to the marrow, and sees all the way through as soon as he hears it brought up, yet without falling into emotional considerations or conceptual thinking. If you are a genuine foot-traveling patchrobed monk, you will see that in acting this way, Hsueh Feng was already indulging to help others.

Look at Hsueh Tou's verse, which says,

VERSE

An ox head disappears,
  **Like a flash of lightening.*
  You've already stumbled past it.

A horse head emerges.
  **Like sparks struck from flint.*

In the mirror of Ts'ao Ch'i,[a] *absolutely no dust.*
  **Come smash the mirror and I will meet with*
  you; you must first smash it.

He beats the drum for you to come look, but you don't see:
  **He pierces your eyes. Don't take it lightly. In the*
  lacquer bucket, where is it hard to see?

When spring arrives, for whom do the hundred flowers bloom?
  **Things don't overlap. What a mess! He sticks his head*
  out from within a cave of tangled vines.

COMMENTARY

Naturally Hsueh Tou sees that other Ancient; he only needs to go to his lifeline, and in one spurt produces a verse for him.

"An ox head disappears, a horse head emerges." Tell me, what is he saying? If you see all the way through to the bottom, it is like eating gruel early in the morning and eating rice at midday—just this ordinary. Out of compassion, Hsueh Tou shatters (everything) with one hammer blow at the outset, and settles (everything) with a single phrase. He is just undeniably solitary and steep, like a flint-struck spark or a flash of lightning. He doesn't reveal his sword point; there's no place for you to linger over. Tell me, can you search it out in your intellectual faculty? These first two lines have said it all.

In the third line, instead Hsueh Tou opens a pathway and displays a little bit of formal style—already he has fallen into the weeds. If you produce words on top of words, phrases on top of phrases, ideas on top of ideas, making up explanations and interpretations, you will not only get me bogged down, but you'll also turn your backs on Hsueh Tou. Although old man Hsueh Tou's verse is this way, his intention is not like this. He has never made up principles to bind people.

"In the mirror of Ts'ao Ch'i, absolutely no dust." Quite a few people say that a stilled mind is the mirror itself. Fortunately, this has nothing to do with it; if you're only concerned with judging and comparing principles, what end will there be to it? Hsueh Tou has spoken clearly; it's just that people do not see. Therefore Hsueh Tou, being such a dotard, says in verse, "He beats the drum for you to come look, but you don't see." Do ignorant people see? He says more to you: "When spring arrives, for whom do the hundred flowers bloom?" One could say he's opening the doors and windows, throwing them wide open all at once for you. When spring comes, in the hidden valleys and wild ravines, in places where there are no people, a hundred flowers burst forth in profusion. Tell me, who else do they bloom for?

TRANSLATOR'S NOTES

a.   Ts'ao Ch'i was the abode of the great Sixth Patriarch of Chinese Ch'an, Hui Neng (also known as 'workman Lu'), and is used to refer to him, as well as to his inspiration and lineage. According to tradition, when the Fifth Patriarch Hung Jen wanted to appoint a successor, he told his students to each compose a verse expressing his understanding. All deferred to the senior disciple, Shen Hsiu, a man of great learning and accomplishment in discipline and meditation. Shen Hsiu wrote,

> The body is the tree of enlightenment,
> The mind like a bright mirror-stand;
> Time and again polish it diligently,
> Do not let there be any dust.

Hui Neng, however, then a workman in the temple, composed the following verse:

> Enlightenment is basically not a tree,
> And the mind-mirror not a stand;
> Originally there is not a single thing—
> What is the use of wiping away dust?

An alternate version has the last line, "Where is there any dust?" Hung Jen accepted Hui Neng as his successor.

Yun Men's Every Day is a Good Day

CASE

Yun Men said, "I don't ask you about before the fifteenth day;[1] try to say something about after the fifteenth day."[2]

Yun Men himself answered for everyone, "Every day is a good day."[3]

NOTES

1. Half south of the river, half north of the river. We don't keep old calendar dates here.
2. Inevitably it will go from dawn to sunset; just don't say that the next day is the sixteenth. Days and months seem to flow by.
3. He's gathered it up. Though the frog jumps, he can't get out of the basket. Whose house has no bright moon and pure wind? But do you know it? The sea god knows its value, he doesn't know its price.

COMMENTARY

Yun Men first called on Mu Chou. Mu Chou spun devices that turned like lightning, so it was difficult to approach and linger. Whenever he received someone, he would grab him as soon as he crossed the threshold and say, "Speak! Speak!" If he couldn't attempt a reply, he would push him out, saying, "Antique drill turning in a rut!"

When Yun Men went to see Mu Chou, on the third time, as soon as he knocked on the door, Mu Chou said, "Who's there?" Yun Men answered, "(Me,) Wen Yen."[a] As soon as (Mu Chou) opened the door a little, (Yun Men) immediately bounded in; Mu Chou held him fast and said, "Speak! Speak!" Yun Men hesitated, and was pushed out; he still had one foot inside when Mu Chou slammed the door, breaking Yun Men's leg. As Yun Men cried out in pain, he was suddenly greatly enlightened. Subsequently, the trend of his words in dealing with people, his whole style, emerged from Mu Chou. After this, Yun Men stayed for three years in the home of the ministry president Ch'en Ts'ao.[b]

Mu Chou directed Yun Men to go to Hsueh Feng; when he arrived there, he came forth from the assembly and said, "What is Buddha?" Hsueh Feng said, "Don't talk in your sleep." Yun Men then bowed. He dwelt there for three years. One day Hsueh Feng asked him, "What is your perception?" Yun Men said, "My view doesn't differ in the slightest from that of all the sages since antiquity."

For twenty years Ling Shu did not appoint a head monk. He used to say, "My head monk is born," and "My head monk is tending oxen," and he would say, "My head monk is traveling on foot." Suddenly one day he ordered the bell to be struck (for everyone to assemble) to receive the head monk at the gate. The congregation was dubious about this, but Yun Men actually arrived. Ling Shu immediately invited him into the head monk's quarters to unpack his bundle. People called Ling Shu the Knowing Sage Ch'an Master, since he knew of all past and future events in advance.

Once King Liu, the Lord of Kuang (-tung), was going to mobilize his army; he intended to go to the monastery personally to ask the master (Ling Shu) to determine whether conditions were auspicious or not. Ling Shu, knowing of this beforehand, sat down and peacefully passed away. The Lord of Kuang said angrily, "Since when was the master sick?" The attendant answered, "The master hadn't been sick. He had just entrusted a box (to me), which he ordered me to present to your majesty when you arrived." The Lord of Kuang opened the box and took out a card which said, "The Eye of Humans and Gods (a living Buddha) is the head monk in the hall." Having understood Ling Shu's inner meaning, the Lord of Kuang thereupon dismissed his soldiers and invited Yun Men to appear in the world at Ling Shu Monastery. Only later did he dwell at Yun Men.

As the master was expounding the Dharma, the royal attendant Ju posed a question; "Is the fruit of Ling Shu ('Spiritual

Tree') ripe yet, or not?" Yun Men said, "When have you ever heard it said that it was unripe?"

One day King Liu summoned the master to spend the summer in the palace. Together with several other venerable abbots, he was to receive the questions of the courtiers and expound the Dharma. Only one man, the master Yun Men, did not speak, and there was no one on familiar terms with him. One of the palace functionaries wrote a verse and posted it in the Green Jade Hall:

> *Cultivation of the great wisdom—only that is Ch'an;*
> *Silence, not clamor, is in order for the Ch'an school.*
> *Ten thousand kinds of clever talk—how can they be as good as reality?*
> *They lose to Yun Men's total not speaking.*

Yun Men usually liked to teach three word Ch'an:[c] observing, "Reflect!" "Ha!" He also taught one word Ch'an: a monk asked, "When you kill your father and mother, you repent before the Buddha; when you kill the Buddha and Patriarchs, where do you turn to repent?" Yun Men said, "Exposed." Again a monk asked, "What is the treasury of the eye of the true Dharma?" Yun Men said, "Universal." It just doesn't allow any attempts to explain. In ordinary situations, even, Yun Men would still revile people. When he uttered a phrase, it was like an iron spike.

Later Yun Men produced the Four Sages: Tung Shan Shou Ch'u, Chih Men Shih Kuan, Te Shan Yuan Mi, and Hsiang Lin Teng Yuan. They all were great masters of the school. Hsiang Lin served as Yun Men's attendant for eighteen years; whenever Yun Men dealt with him, he would just call out, "Attendant Yuan!" Yuan would answer, "Yes?" Yun Men would say, "What is it?" It went on like this for eighteen years, when one day Hsiang Lin finally awakened. Yun Men told him, "From now on I won't call you any more."

In Yun Men's usual dealings with people, he would often use the methods of Mu Chou; though it was hard to approach him, he had the hammer and tongs to pull out nails and wrench out pegs. Hsueh Tou said of him, "I like the fresh devices of Shao Yang;[d] he spent his life pulling out nails and pegs for people."

Yun Men set down a question to instruct his community, "I

don't ask you about before the fifteenth day; try to say something about after the fifteenth day." He cuts off the thousand
distinctions, and doesn't let either ordinary or holy pass. He
himself answered for everyone, "Every day is a good day." The
words "before the fifteenth day" already cut off the thousand
distinctions; the words "after the fifteenth day" also cut off the
thousand distinctions. The fact is that Yun Men did not say
that the next day is the sixteenth day. People coming after him
merely followed his words to produce interpretations; but
what relevance has this? Yun Men established a protean style;
he surely had a way to benefit people. Having spoken some
words, he then answered himself in everyone's behalf: "Every
day is a good day." These words pervade past and present, from
before until after, and settle everything at once.

I too am following his words to produce interpretations
when I talk like this. Killing others is not as good as killing
yourself. As soon as you make a principle, you fall into a pit.
Three phrases are inherent in every one phrase of Yun Men;
since the source inspiration of his family is like this, when Yun
Men utters a phrase, it must be returned to the source. Anything but this will always be phony. The affair has no multitude of arguments and propositions, though those who have
not yet penetrated want (me as commentator) to go on like
this. If you do penetrate, then you will immediately see the
essential meaning of the Ancient.

Take a look at the complications Hsueh Tou creates:

VERSE

He throws away one,
    **Seven openings, eight holes.
    Where has it gone? He lets up
    a little.*

Picks up seven.
    **He can't pick them up, yet
    he doesn't let them go.*

Above, below, and in the four directions, there is no compari-
    son.
    **What's it like? Above is the sky, below is the earth.

East, west, south, north; what comparison is there?
Nevertheless, the staff is in my hand. *

Placidly walking along, he treads down the sound of the flow-
        ing stream;
        * *Don't ask what's right under your feet. It's difficult to*
    investigate it thoroughly. He's gone into the nest of en-
    tangling vines. *

His relaxed gaze descries the tracks of flying birds.
        * *In the eye, there is no such happening. A wild*
    fox spirit view; as before, he's just inside the
    same old den. *

The grasses grow thick,
        * *He pulls the arrow out of the back*
    of his head. What's going on here?
    He is fallen into equanimity. *

The mists overhang.
        * *He hasn't come out of this nest yet.*
    Beneath his feet clouds arise. *

'Round Subhuti's cliff, the flowers make a mess;
        * *Where is he? The stupid fellow! He's*
    been completely exposed. *

I snap my fingers;[e] *how lamentable is Shunyata!*
        * *The four quarters and eight directions,*
    the whole cosmos; inside Shunyata's nostrils,
    try to say something. Where is (Shunyata)? *

Don't make a move!
        * *How come your previous words?*
    When you move, then what? *

If you move, thirty blows!
        * *Take what's coming to you*
    and get out. I strike! *

COMMENTARY

Hsueh Tou's eulogies of the Ancients were always accomplished like this: at first he takes the jewel sword of the
Diamond King and brings it down at once; then afterwards he

reveals a little bit of formal style. Although it's like this, ultimately there are not two understandings.

"He throws away one, picks up seven." People often make an understanding based on the numbers and say, "'He throws away one' refers to 'before the fifteenth day'." Having abruptly put down two lines and sealed it up, Hsueh Tou then instead reveals it to let people see; "He throws away one, picks up seven." You must avoid turning to the words for your subsistence. Why? What moisture is there in unleavened bread? People often fall back into conceptual consciousness. You must obtain your understanding before the words arise; then the great function will become manifest and you will naturally see it.

This is why after old man Shakyamuni had attained the Path in the land of Magadha, he spent three weeks contemplating this matter: "The nature of all things being quiescent extinction cannot be conveyed by words; I would rather not preach the Dharma, but quickly enter nirvana." When he got to this point, even Shakyamuni couldn't find any way to open his mouth. But by virtue of his power of skill in technique, after he had preached to the five mendicants, he went to three hundred and sixty assemblies and expounded the teachings for his age. All these were just expedients. For this reason he had taken off his bejewelled regal garments and put on rough dirty clothing. He could not but turn towards the shallows within the gate of the secondary meaning in order to lead in his various disciples. If we had him face upwards and bring it all up at once, there would hardly be anyone in the whole world (who could understand).

But tell me, what is the supreme word? At this point Hsueh Tou reveals a little of the meaning to let people see. Just don't see that there are any buddhas above, don't see that there are sentient beings below; don't see that there are mountains, rivers, and earth without, and don't see that there are seeing, hearing, discernment, or knowledge within: then you will be like one who has died the great death and then returned to life. With long and short, good and evil, fused into one whole, though you bring them up one by one, you'll no longer see them as different. After that, you'll be able to function responsively without losing balance. Then you will see the meaning of his saying, "He throws away one, picks up seven; above, below, and in the four directions, there is no comparison." If you pass through at these lines, then and there above, below, and in the four directions, there is no comparison. The myriad forms and multitude of appearances—plants, animals, and people—everything everywhere completely manifests the way of your own house. Thus it was said,

> Within myriad forms, only one body is revealed;
> Only when one is sure for himself will he then be
>   near.
> In past years I mistakenly turned to the road to
>   search;
> Now I look upon it like ice within fire.

"In the heavens and on earth, I alone am the honored one." Many people pursue the branches and don't seek the root. First get the root right, then naturally when the wind blows the grass bends down, naturally where water flows a stream forms. "Placidly walking along, he treads down the sound of the flowing stream." As he goes along placidly, he can tread down and cut off even the roar of a vast swelling torrent. "His relaxed gaze descries the tracks of flying birds." Even if it's the tracks of flying birds, allow the eye one look, and it is like tracing them out. When you get here, you will not consider it difficult to blow out the fires under the cauldrons of hell, or to shatter sword forests and knife mountains with a shout.

Because of his compassion, at this point Hsueh Tou feared that people would settle down within the realm of unconcern, so he went on to say, "The grasses grow thick, the mists overhang." But tell me, whose world is this? Can it be called "Every day is a good day"? Fortunately, there's no connection. In fact, "Placidly walking along, he treads down the sound of the flowing stream" isn't it; "His relaxed gaze descries the tracks of flying birds" isn't it either; nor is "The grasses grow thick," nor "The mists overhang." But even something entirely different would just be "'Round Subhuti's cliff, the flowers make a mess." It is still necessary to turn beyond That Side. Haven't you read how as Subhuti was sitting in silent meditation in a cliffside cave, the gods showered down flowers to praise him. The venerable Subhuti said, "Flowers are showering down from the sky in praise; whose doing is this?" A god said, "I am Indra, king of the gods." Venerable Subhuti asked, "Why are you offering praise?" Indra said, "I esteem the Venerable One's skill in expounding the transcendence of wisdom." Subhuti said, "I have never spoken a single word about wisdom; why are you offering praise?" Indra said, "You have never spoken and I have never heard. No speaking, no hearing—this is true wisdom." And again he caused the earth to tremble, and showered down flowers.

Hsueh Tou once made up another verse about this:

> The rain has passed, the clouds are shrinking, dawn
>   has halfway broken through;
> The multiple peaks are like a drawing of blue-green
>   rocky crags.
> Subhuti did not know how to sit upon a cliff;
> He brought on the heavenly flowers and the shaking
>   of the earth.

When the king of gods is shaking the earth and raining down flowers, at this point where else will you go to hide? Hsueh Tou also said,

> I fear Subhuti won't be able to escape him;
> Even beyond the cosmos all is filled to the brim.
> What end will he know to his frantic turmoil?
> From all sides the pure wind tugs at his clothes.

Though you be clean and naked, bare and purified, totally without fault or worry, this is still not the ultimate. In the end though, what is? Look carefully at this quote; "I snap my fingers; how lamentable is Shunyata!" The Sanskrit word "Shunyata" in our language means the spirit of emptiness. Empty space is her body; she has no physical body to be conscious of contact. When the Buddha's brilliance shines forth, then she manifests her body. When you get to be like Shunyata, then Hsueh Tou will rightly snap his fingers in lament.

Again Hsueh Tou says, "Don't make a move!" What's it like when you move? (Like) sleeping with your eyes open under the bright sun in the blue sky.

TRANSLATOR'S NOTES

a.   Wen Yen was Yun Men's personal initiatory name: see the biographical supplement.

b. Ch'en Ts'ao was an enlightened disciple of Mu Chou and lived in the same area.

c. When Yun Men encountered someone, he would look at him and say, "Reflect!" and "Ha!" (a laugh of derision or scorn); later the word describing Yun Men's action was included by a compiler as one of the "three words" he is supposed to have used.

d. Shao Yang is the name of the region where Yun Men monastery was located, and so according to the custom of referring to Ch'an masters by the name of their abode, this is another name for Yun Men.

e. Snapping the fingers is used for alerting, warning, and for warding off filth or taboo. Abiding in subjective emptiness is referred to as intoxication in Ch'an, considered onesided, incomplete, and narrow-minded; hence it is taboo.

Hui Ch'ao Asks about Buddha

POINTER

The thousand sages have not transmitted the single word before sound; if you have never seen it personally, it's as if it were worlds away. Even if you discern it before sound and cut off the tongues of everyone in the world, you're still not a sharp fellow. Therefore it is said, "The sky can't cover it; the earth can't support it; empty space can't contain it; sun and moon can't illumine it." Where there is no Buddha and you alone are called the Honored One, for the first time you've amounted to something. Otherwise, if you are not yet this way, penetrate through on the tip of a hair and release the great shining illumination; then in all directions you will be independent and free in the midst of phenomena; whatever you pick up, there is nothing that's not it. But tell me, what is attained that is so extraordinary?

Does everyone understand? No one knows about the sweating horses of the past; they only want to emphasize the achievement that crowns the age. Leaving this matter aside for the moment, what about Hsueh Tou's public case? Look into what's written below.

CASE

A monk (named Hui Ch'ao) asked Fa Yen,[1] "Hui Ch'ao asks the Teacher, what is Buddha?"[2]
Fa Yen said, "You are Hui Ch'ao."[3]

NOTES

1. What is he saying? He's wearing stocks, giving evidence of his crime.
2. What is he saying? His eyeballs pop out.

3. He comes out with this according to his pattern. Iron scrap stuffing. He goes right up to him and takes him.

COMMENTARY

Ch'an Master Fa Yen had this ability of breaking in and crashing out at the same time,[a] and also the use of this ability; thus he could answer like this. This is what is called passing beyond sound and form, achieving the great freedom, letting go or taking back as the occasion requires, where killing or bringing life rests with oneself. He is undeniably extraordinary. Nevertheless, people from all over who deliberate over this public case are many, and those who make intellectual interpretations to understand it are not few. They do not realize that whenever the Ancients handed down a word or half a phrase, it was like sparks struck from flint, like a flash of lightning, directly opening up a single straight path.

People of later times just went to the words to make up interpretations. Some say, "Hui Ch'ao is himself Buddha; that is why Fa Yen answered as he did." Some say, "It's much like riding an ox searching for an ox." Some say "The asking is it." What relevance has any of this? If you go on understanding in this fashion, not only do you turn against yourself, but you seriously demean that man of old.

If you want to see the whole of (Fa Yen's) device, you must be a fellow who doesn't turn his head when struck, a fellow with teeth like sword trees and a mouth like a blood bowl, who knows outside the words what they refer to; then you will have a small portion of realization. If one by one they make intellectual interpretations, everyone on earth would be an exterminator of the Buddha's race. As for Ch'an traveller Hui Ch'ao's awakening here, he was constantly engrossed in penetrating investigation; therefore under the impact of one word, it was as if the bottom fell out of his bucket.

It's like Superintendent Tse: he had been staying in Fa Yen's congregation, but had never asked to enter (Fa Yen's) room (for special instruction). One day Fa Yen asked him, "Why haven't you come to enter my room?" Tse replied, "Didn't you know, Teacher, when I was at Ch'ing Lin's place, I had an entry." Fa Yen said, "Try to recall it for me." Tse said, "I asked, 'What is

Buddha?' Lin said, 'The Fire God comes looking for fire.'" Fa
Yen said, "Good words, but I'm afraid you misunderstood. Can
you say something more for me?" Tse said, "The Fire God is in
the province of fire; he is seeking fire with fire. Likewise, I am
Buddha, yet I went on searching for Buddha." Fa Yen said,
"Sure enough, the Superintendent has misunderstood." Containing his anger, Tse left the monastery and went off across
the river. Fa Yen said, "This man can be saved if he comes
back; if he doesn't return, he can't be saved." Out on the road,
Tse thought to himself, "He is the teacher of five hundred
people; how could he deceive me?" So he turned back and
again called on Fa Yen, who told him, "Just ask me and I'll
answer you." Thereupon Tse asked, "What is Buddha?" Fa Yen
said, "The Fire God comes looking for fire." At these words Tse
was greatly enlightened.

These days there are those who just put a glare in their eyes
and interpret that as understanding. As it is said, "Since this
has no wounds, don't wound it."[b] With this kind of public case,
those who have practiced for a long time know where it comes
down as soon as it's brought up. In the Fa Yen succession this is
called "arrowpoints meeting."[c] They don't employ the five
positions of prince and minister,[d] or the four propositions;[e]
they simply talk of arrowpoints meeting. The style of Fa Yen's
family is like this; one word falls and you see and immediately
directly penetrate. But if you ponder over the words, to the end
you will search without finding.

Fa Yen appeared in the world and had a congregation of five
hundred. At this time the Buddha Dharma flourished greatly.
At this time the (future) National Teacher Te Shao had spent a
long time with Su Shan, and he considered himself to have
attained Su Shan's meaning. So he had gathered together the
writings made by Su Shan in the course of his lifetime, and
a portrait of him (to symbolize his succession to Su Shan), and
led a band of followers travelling on foot. When they got to Fa
Yen's community, he himself did not go to enter the Master's
room, but just ordered his followers to go along with the others
to enter the room.

One day when Fa Yen had ascended his seat, there was a
monk who asked, "What is one drop from the fount of Ts'ao
Ch'i?" Fa Yen said, "It's one drop from the fount of Ts'ao Ch'i."
The monk was dumbfounded and withdrew; Shao, who was in

the assembly, was suddenly greatly enlightened when he heard this. Later he appeared in the world as one of Fa Yen's successors. Shao had a verse which he presented, saying,

> *The summit of the peak of the mystic crossing*
> *Is not the human world;*
> *Outside the mind there are no things—*
> *Blue mountains fill the eyes.*

Fa Yen gave his seal of approval and said, "This one verse alone can perpetuate my school. In the future kings and lords will honor you. I am not equal to you."

Look at those Ancients; when they awaken like this, what truth is this? It won't do just to have me tell you; you yourself must tune your spirit all day long. If you can attain fulfillment the way these people did, then someday you will let down your hand for people in the crossroads, and won't consider it a difficult thing, either.

Thus, when the monk asked Fa Yen, "What is Buddha?" Fa Yen said, "You are Hui Ch'ao." Is there any contradiction here? Haven't you read what Yun Men said—"When it is brought up, if you don't take heed, then you'll miss it; if you try to assess it by thinking, in what aeon will you awaken?" Hsueh Tou subsequently versified it with unmistakable clarity. I'll bring it up: Look!

VERSE

In the river country the spring wind isn't blowing;
> ***Where in the world do you find this scene?*
> *The pattern is already showing.* *

Deep within the flowers partridges are calling.
> ***What's the use of this chatter? He is*
> *blown by the wind into a different tune.*
> *How can there be such a thing?* *

At the three-tiered Dragon Gate, where the waves are high,
> *fish become dragons,*
> ***Traverse this one road. Don't fool the great congregation. Tread upon the dragon's head.* *

Yet fools still go on scooping out the evening pond water.
    Leaning on a fence, groping along a wall;*[f]* next to the gate, standing by the door;*[g]* what use is this for a patch-robed monk? This is standing by a stump waiting for a rabbit.*[h]

COMMENTARY

Hsueh Tou is an adept: where the Ancients are hard to gnaw on and hard to chew, hard to penetrate and hard to see, an impenetrable riddle, he produces it in verse to let people see. He is indeed extraordinary. Hsueh Tou knew Fa Yen's key device, and he also knew where Hui Ch'ao was at. Still, he feared that people in the future would turn to Fa Yen's words and mistakenly conceive an understanding, so he came out with this verse.

This monk's asking like this, Fa Yen's answering like this—this is "In the river country the spring wind isn't blowing; deep within the flowers partridges are calling." These two lines are just one line. But say, where is Hsueh Tou's meaning?

In Kiangsi and Chiangnan many people make a two-part interpretation; they say that "In the river country the spring wind isn't blowing" is used to versify "You are Hui Ch'ao." (They say that) this scene—even if the spring wind doesn't blow in the river country, still "deep within the flowers partridges are calling"—is used to compare the endless haggling over these words everywhere to the partridges crying deep in the flowers. But what relevance has this? How far they are from knowing that these two lines of Hsueh Tou's are but a single line. Do you want to have no seam or gap? Clearly I tell you, his speech is to the point, his words are to the point; they cover heaven and earth.

(Hui Ch'ao) asked, "What is Buddha?" Fa Yen answered, "You are Hui Ch'ao." Hsueh Tou says, "In the river country the spring wind isn't blowing; deep within the flowers partridges call." If you can make the grade here, you will be able to walk alone through the red skies; if you make intellectual interpretations, (you'll go on through) past, present, and future lives for sixty aeons.

Hsueh Tou is extremely compassionate in the third and

fourth lines; all at once he explains completely for people. Ch'an Master Ch'ao's great awakening is likened to fish becoming dragons where the waves are high at the three-tiered Dragon Gate, while fools still go on dragging through evening pond water. (The Dragon Gate is a gorge through which the Yellow River passes at the border of Shensi and Shansi; according to tradition,) King Yu cut it (through the mountains) forming a three-level (passage for the river). Nowadays, on the third day of the third month, when the peach blossoms bloom, and heaven and earth are ready, if there is a fish that can get through the Dragon Gate, horns sprout on his head, he raises his bristling tail, catches hold of a cloud, and flies away. Those who cannot leap through fail and fall back.[i] Fools who gnaw on the words are like scooping out the evening pond water looking for fish; how little they realize that the fish have already turned into dragons! Old Master Tuan had a verse which said,

> *A copper of bright money*
> *Buys a fried cake;*
> *He gobbles it down into his belly,*
> *And from then on no longer feels hunger.*

This verse is very good, only it's too crude. Hsueh Tou's verse is very clever, and he doesn't cut his hand on its sharp point.

In the old days Librarian Ch'ing liked to ask people, "What is 'Fish turn into dragons at three-tiered Dragon Gate where the waves are high'?" For me, it's not necessary, but now I'm asking you: having turned into a dragon, where is he now?

TRANSLATOR'S NOTES

a.   Breaking in and crashing out at the same time symbolizes the action of the teacher and student encounter: the student is likened to a chick still inside the shell of his ego, trying to crash its way out, while the teacher, as the 'parent,' breaks through from the outside to help the chick out. See the sixteenth case.

b.   This saying is taken from the *Vimalakirtinirdesa* scripture, in which context it should be read, "Since they have no wounds, don't wound them," meaning that the lesser vehicle of revulsion should not be taught to those who have the capacity for the greater vehicle of tolerance. We have not used "they" because of the preceding sentence in the context; "they" would cause confusion here. Yuan Wu's intent seems to be don't impute any flaw to the flawless Buddha-essence by intellectual, emotional interpretations. Tenkei Denson says, "Fa Yen's answer 'You're Hui Ch'ao,' breaking in and crashing out at the same time, has no gap or flaw, so don't you people ruin it with intellectual judgements."

c.   This represents question and answer meeting, like two arrows meeting head on in midair, stopping each other at once; the meeting of minds.

d.   This was an illustrative device of the Ts'ao-Tung tradition of Ch'an: the Prince, or Lord, symbolizes emptiness, while the Minister, or Vassal, symbolizes the world of matter, or form. The five positions are: minister turning towards prince (emptiness within matter), prince looking at minister (matter within emptiness), prince alone (emptiness as such), minister alone (matter as such), and prince and minister in harmony (simultaneous inter-identification of emptiness and matter).

e.   This was a device of the Lin Chi tradition of Ch'an: the four propositions involve conceding or taking away person and/or environment, taking away the person but not the environment, taking away the environment but not the person, taking away both, and leaving both. See the appendix on teaching devices.

f.   This depicts the blind groping their way along.

g.   This means not yet having entered.

h.   This refers to a story of a man who saw a running rabbit happen to collide with a tree stump and die; the man took the rabbit for food, and, thinking to obtain another rabbit, he foolishly stood by the stump, waiting for it to 'catch' another rabbit for him. This is used to describe those who cling to words or images, thinking them to be a source of enlightenment.

i.   This simile of passing through the Dragon Gate was also used to refer to the Chinese civil service examinations; those who passed could become government officials.

Ts'ui Yen's Eyebrows

POINTER

If you understand, you can make use of it on the road, like a dragon reaching the water, like a tiger in the mountains. If you don't understand, then the worldly truth will prevail, and you will be like a ram caught in a fence, like (a fool) watching over a stump waiting for a rabbit. Sometimes a single phrase is like a lion crouching on the ground; sometimes a phrase is like the Diamond King's jewel sword. Sometimes a phrase cuts off the tongues of everyone on earth, and sometimes a phrase follows the waves and pursues the currents.

If you make use of it on the road, when you meet with a man of knowledge you distinguish what's appropriate to the occasion, you know what's right and what's wrong, and together you witness each other's illumination. Where the worldly truth prevails, one who has the single eye can cut off everything in the ten directions and stand like a mile high wall. Therefore it is said, "When the great function appears it does not keep to any fixed standards." Sometimes we take a blade of grass and use it as the sixteen foot golden body (of Buddha); sometimes we take the sixteen foot golden body and use it as a blade of grass. But tell me, what principle does this depend upon? Do you really know? To test, I cite this; Look!

CASE

At the end of the summer retreat Ts'ui Yen said to the community, "All summer long I've been talking to you, brothers;[1] look and see if my eyebrows are still there."[2,a]

Pao Fu said, "The thief's heart is cowardly."[3]

Ch'ang Ch'ing said, "Grown."[4]

Yun Men said, "A barrier."[5]

NOTES

1. If you open your mouth, how can you know it to be so?
2. All he's achieved is that his eyes have fallen out too, along with his nostrils, which he's already lost. He enters hell fast as an arrow shot.
3. Obviously. This is a thief recognizing a thief.
4. His tongue falls to the ground; he adds error to error. After all.
5. Where is there to run to? No patchrobed monk in the world can leap out. He's defeated.

COMMENTARY

The Ancients had morning study and evening inquiry; at the end of the summer retreat Ts'ui Yen turned around and spoke to the community like this, and he was undeniably solitary and steep—nothing could stop him from startling the heavens and shaking the earth. But tell me, in the whole great treasury of teachings, in the five thousand and forty-eight volumes of the canon, whether they talk of mind or nature, whether they preach the sudden or the gradual, has there ever been this happening? They're all this kind of occasion, but among them Ts'ui Yen is outstanding. Look at the way he talks; tell me, where is his true meaning?

When the Ancients let down a hook, it was never an empty manoeuvre; they invariably had some truth to benefit people. Many people misunderstand and say, "Under the bright sun in the blue sky, Ts'ui Yen spoke aimless talk producing concern where there was none; at the end of the summer he spoke of his own faults and examined himself first to avoid others criticizing him." Fortunately this has nothing to do with it. Such views are called exterminators of the Buddha's race. The appearance in the world of the successive generations of teaching masters would have been entirely without benefit if they hadn't reached down to instruct people. What would have been the purpose? When you get here, if you can see all the way through, then you will know that the Ancients had the method to drive off a plowman's ox and to snatch away a hungry man's food.

People today, when questioned, immediately turn to the words to chew on them, making a living on Ts'ui Yen's eyebrows. Look at how the people of his house naturally know where he is operating: through a thousand changes and ten thousand transformations, amidst impenetrable complications, everywhere they have ways to show themselves; hence they are able to chime in with him like this in response. If there is nothing extraordinary about these words of Ts'ui Yen's, why then would these three men, Yun Men, Pao Fu, and Ch'ang Ch'ing, have replied to him so profusely?

Pao Fu said, "The thief's heart is cowardly." How much intellectual interpretation these words have provoked lately! But say, what about Pao Fu's meaning? You must avoid searching for that Ancient in his words. If you give rise to feelings and arouse your thoughts, then he'll snatch your eyeballs away. Above all, people don't realize that when Pao Fu utters one turning word, he cuts off Ts'ui Yen's footsteps.

Ch'ang Ch'ing said, "Grown." Many people say, "Ch'ang Ch'ing turns along following Ts'ui Yen's footsteps, therefore he says (that Ts'ui Yen's eyebrows have) grown." But this has nothing to do with it. They don't know that Ch'ang Ch'ing brings out his own view when he says, "Grown." Each has a place to appear in person, but I ask you, where is the growth?

It's just like being face to face with an adept brandishing the Diamond King's jewel sword. If you can smash the views of the ordinary current and cut off gain and loss, affirmation and negation, then you will see where Ch'ang Ch'ing responded to Ts'ui Yen.

Yun Men said, "A barrier." This is undeniably outstanding, but hard to penetrate. The great master Yun Men often taught people with one word Ch'an, though in the one word the three phrases were always present. Look how this Ancient replied to suit the occasion; naturally he was far removed from the people of this day and age. This then is the way to utter a phrase. Although Yun Men spoke like this, his meaning is definitely not here. Since the meaning is not here, tell me, where is it? If you are a clear eyed man with the ability to illumine heaven and earth, just be crystal clear in every respect. For his single word "barrier" and the words of the other three, Hsueh Tou has strung them together in one verse:

VERSE

Ts'ui Yen teaches the followers;
　**The old thief! He's corrupting
　other people's children.**

For a thousand ages, there is no reply.
　**In a thousand or ten thousand,
　still there's one or a half. He
　divides a tally.**

The word "barrier" answers him back;
　**Didn't you believe what I said?
　He is undeniably extraordinary.
　Only if you're such a person can
　you understand such talk.**

He loses his money and suffers punishment.[b]
　**He gulps down his breath and swallows
　his voice. Hsueh Tou too has done quite
　a bit of this. I'd strike while he's still
　talking.**

Decrepit old Pao Fu—
　**You're fellow travelers on
　the same path; and still you
　act this way. Two, three.**

Censure or praise are impossible to apply.
　**Letting go, holding still. Who is born
　the same and dies the same? Don't slander
　him. Luckily there's no connection.**

Talkative Ts'ui Yen
　**Wild fox spirit!
　Shut your mouth!**

Is clearly a thief.
　So it may be said. He's been caught!

The clear jewel has no flaws;
　Can you tell? No one in the world knows its price.

Who can distinguish true from false?
　**Many are just false. I myself have never had the eye
　(for this); (what about) the blue-eyed foreign monk
　(Bodhidharma)?**

Ch'ang Ch'ing knows him well;
       ***This is a spirit recognizing a spirit; only*
       he could do this. Yet he still hasn't gotten
       (the other) half.*

His eyebrows are grown.
       ***Where? From head to foot there isn't a single blade of*
       grass.*

COMMENTARY

How could Hsueh Tou be called a Good Friend if he hadn't been this compassionate, making a verse to enable people to see? When the Ancients acted like this, it was all something they couldn't but do. Because later students become attached to their words and more and more give rise to intellectual interpretations, therefore they do not see the Ancients' message. If someone suddenly came forward right now to overturn the meditation seat and scatter the great assembly with shouts, we shouldn't be amazed at him. Though someone acted like this, you yourself would still have to really arrive in this realm in order to attain this.

When Hsueh Tou says, "For a thousand ages there is no reply," he is just telling you to see if Ts'ui Yen's eyebrows are there. What's so extraordinary that there is no reply for a thousand ages? You must realize that when the Ancients spat out a word or half a phrase, it wasn't blurted out; one must have the eye to judge heaven and earth before this is possible.

When Hsueh Tou writes a word or half a phrase it's like the Diamond King's jewel sword, like a lion crouching on the ground, like sparks struck from stone, like the brilliance of a lightning flash. If he didn't have the eye on his forehead, how could he have seen where that man of old (Ts'ui Yen) comes down? This lesson that Ts'ui Yen gave the people was such that "for a thousand ages there is no reply." It goes beyond Te Shan's staff and Lin Chi's shout. But say, where is Hsueh Tou's meaning for us? And how will you understand his statement, "For a thousand ages there is no reply"?

"The word 'barrier' answers him back; he loses his money and suffers punishment." What is the meaning of this? Even if you have the eye to pass through the barrier, when you get here you still must be most thoroughgoing before you are done. Tell me, is it Ts'ui Yen who loses his money and suffers punishment, or is it Hsueh Tou, or is it Yun Men? If you can penetrate this, I'll allow that you have the eye.

"Decrepit old Pao Fu; censure or praise are impossible to apply." Does he censure himself? Does he praise the Ancients? Tell me, where does Pao Fu censure? Where does Pao Fu praise?

"Talkative Ts'ui Yen is clearly a thief." Tell me, what has he stolen, that Hsueh Tou says he's a thief? You must avoid being whirled around following after the stream of his words; when you get here you must have your own accomplishment before you'll understand.

"The clear jewel has no flaws." Hsueh Tou says that Ts'ui Yen is like a clear jewel without any flaws or cloudy patches. "Who can distinguish true from false?" It can be said that rarely is there anyone who can make this distinction.

Hsueh Tou has great talent, so he can string together the whole case from beginning to end on the single thread of this verse. Only at the very end does he then say, "Ch'ang Ch'ing knows him well; his eyebrows are grown." Tell me, where are they growing? Hurry up, take a look!

TRANSLATOR'S NOTES

a.   Teaching is said to be an act of 'facing downwards' since the transcendental cannot be spoken of directly; hence it is said in Ch'an that if one speaks too much, tries to explain too much, his eyebrows may fall out. Similarly, when one has, so to speak, 'Said everything,' it is said that he isn't anxious for, or does not spare, his eyebrows.

b.   That is to say, he loses the bribe money he has offered, and suffers the punishment he was due anyway. This is a common phrase in Ch'an.

Chao Chou's Four Gates[a]

POINTER

When the bright mirror is on its stand, beauty and ugliness are distinguished by themselves. With a sharp sword in his hand, one can kill or bring life to fit the occasion. A foreigner goes and a native comes; a foreigner comes and a native goes. In the midst of death he finds life; in the midst of life he finds death. But tell me, when you get to this point, then what? If you don't have the eye to penetrate barriers, if you don't have any place to turn yourself around in, at this point obviously you won't know what to do. Tell me, what is the eye that penetrates barriers, what is a place to turn around in? To test, I cite this; look!

CASE

A monk asked Chao Chou, "What is Chao Chou?"[1]
  Chao Chou replied, "East gate, west gate, south gate, north gate."[2]

NOTES

1. North of the river, south of the river, no one can say. There are thorns in the soft mud. If it's not south of the river, then it's north of the river.
2. They're open. "When we're reviling each other, I let you lock lips with me; when we're spitting at each other, I let you spew me with slobber." The public case is obviously complete; but do you see? I strike!

COMMENTARY

When you immerse yourself in meditation and inquire about the Path, it is in order to clearly understand yourself; just avoid picking and choosing among verbal formulations. Why? Haven't you read what Chao Chou said—"The ultimate path has no difficulties; just avoid picking and choosing." And haven't you read what Yun Men said—"These days whenever followers of Ch'an gather in threes and fives their mouths chatter on and on; they say 'these are words of high ability, those are words uttered in reference to the self.'" They don't realize that within the gate of expedient means the Ancients couldn't help but establish expedient verbal formulae for latecoming students of elementary capacities who had not yet clarified their mind ground nor seen their fundamental nature. In the Patriarch's coming from the West for the sole transmission of the mind seal, directly pointing to the human mind for the perception of nature and fulfillment of Buddhahood, where were there any such complications? It is necessary to cut off words, to see the truth outside of any pattern. When you penetrate through to liberation, this can be compared to a dragon reaching the water or a tiger at home in the mountains.

To have seen but not yet penetrated, or to have penetrated but not yet become illumined—among the worthies of the past who investigated for so long, this was called seeking more instruction. To ask for more instruction when you have seen and penetrated, you then must still turn round and round on the words so there will be no doubtful sticking points. When one who has investigated for a long time asked for more instruction, this would be giving a ladder to a thief. In reality this matter does not lie in words; that is why Yun Men said, "If this matter were in words, are there no words in the twelve part canon of the three vehicles? What need would there have been for Bodhidharma's coming from the West?"

Within Fen Yang's eighteen categories of questions,[b] this question (in the case) is called a question to examine the host; it's also called a seeking out question. The monk posing this question is undeniably extraordinary; anyone but Chao Chou would have found it hard to reply to him. The monk asked, "What is Chao Chou?" Chao Chou is an adept in his own right, so he immediately replied, "East gate, west gate, south gate, north gate." The monk said, "I wasn't asking about that Chao Chou." Chao Chou said, "What Chao Chou were you asking about?"

Later people said this was "no-nothing Ch'an" cheating quite a few people. What was their reason? When the monk asked about Chao Chou, Chao Chou answered, "East gate, west gate, south gate, north gate"; therefore (these people say) he was just answering about the other Chao Chou (i.e. the city). If you understand in this fashion, then any rustic from a village of three families understands more about the Buddha Dharma than you do. Such an interpretation destroys the Buddha Dharma. It's like comparing a fish eye to a bright pearl; in appearance they are alike, but actually they are not the same. As I said, if it's not south of the river, then it's north of the river. But say, is there something or is there nothing? This does indeed require you to be thoroughgoing before you understand.

Yuan "The Jurist"[c] said, "The very last word finally reaches the closed barrier; the inner essence of pointing out the Way is not in words and explanations:

> *In ten days, one breeze;*
> *In five days, one rain.*
> *In the peaceful countryside enjoying their tasks,*
> *Drumming their full bellies and singing hallelujah."*

This is called the season of great peace. When I call this having no concerns, it is not a matter of covering your eyes with your hands and saying "I have no concerns." You must penetrate through the barrier, emerge from the forest of brambles, clean and naked, bare and untrammelled: as before you will resemble any ordinary person, but now it's all right whether there is anything of concern or there is nothing; it's up to you. Free in all directions, you will never cling to nothingness and establish it as something.

Some people say, "Fundamentally there isn't the slightest bit of anything, but when we have tea we drink tea, and when we have rice we eat rice." This is big vain talk; I call this claiming attainment without having attained, claiming realization without having realized. Basically since they haven't bored in and penetrated through, when they hear people speaking of mind or nature, of the mysterious or the abstruse, they say, "This is just mad talk; fundamentally there isn't anything to be concerned with." This could be called one blind man leading many blind men. They are far from knowing that before the Patriarch came, people scarcely called the sky earth, or called mountains rivers; why did the Patriarch still come from the West? Everyplace where they "go up into the hall"d and "enter the room"e what do they speak of? It is all judgements of intellectual consciousness; when the feelings of judgements of intellectual consciousness are ended, only then can you see through. And when you see through, then as of old sky is sky, earth is earth, mountains are mountains, rivers are rivers.

An Ancient said, "Mind is the sense faculty, things are the objects; both elements are like flaws on a mirror." When you get to this realm you will naturally be clean and naked, bare and untrammelled. Even the ultimate principle of theory is not yet the place of peace and security. People often misunderstand this point; they stay within the realm of unconcern and neither pay homage to the Buddhas nor burn incense. They do indeed seem to be right, but in spite of that they're totally wrong. When questioned, their replies do resemble the ultimate principle, but as soon as they are pressed, they're shattered, confused; they sit there with an empty belly and a proud heart, but when they get to their last day they'll wring their hands and beat their breasts, but it'll already be too late.

This monk asked this way, Chao Chou answered this way; tell me, how will you look for them? This way won't do, not this way won't do either; ultimately, how is it? This bit is a hard one, so Hsueh Tou has brought it out in front of you to show you people.

One day while Chao Chou was sitting, his attendant reported to him, "The great king has come." Chao Chou looked surprised and said, "Myriad felicitations, O great king!" The attendant said, "He has not yet come to you, Master." Chao Chou said, "And you said he's come." He penetrated this far, he saw this far; undeniably extraordinary. Ch'an Master Hui Nan of Huang Lung commented on this, saying,

> The attendant only knew how to announce a guest,
> He did not know that he himself was in the imperial city.

Chao Chou went into the weeds to look for the man,
Heedless of getting his whole body soaked in muddy water.

Do all of you people know the truth of this? Look into Hsueh Tou's verse:

VERSE

In their words they show their ability in direct confrontation:
   ***Echoing. When fish swim through, the water is muddied.*
   Better not slander Chao Chou. *
The Adamantine Eye is completely void of dust.
   ***Scattering sand, scattering dirt: don't drag Chao Chou into this. Why search the sky and grope over the earth?* *
East, West, South, North—the gates face each other;
   ***They're open. Where are there so many gates? If you turn your back on Chao Chou city, where will you go?* *
An endless series of hammer blows can't smash them open.
   ***Your revolving hammer won't reach. They are open.* *

COMMENTARY

Chao Chou faces situations just like the Diamond King's jewel sword: hesitate, and immediately he cuts your head off; time and time again he will go on and snatch your eyeballs right away. Nevertheless, this monk dares to grab the tiger's whiskers and pose a question. It's like giving rise to something where there's nothing; yet nevertheless in his words there is ability. Once the monk had shown his ability, Chao Chou did not turn his back on his question; thus he too showed his ability in answering. It wasn't that he acted like this out of whimsy; because he was a man who had penetrated through, naturally he fit in the same groove with the monk, as if it were all arranged.

Haven't you heard? There was an outsider who came to question the World Honored One holding a sparrow in his hand. He said, "Tell me, is this sparrow in my hand dead or alive?" The World Honored One then went and straddled the threshold and said, "You tell me, am I going out or coming in?" (One version has it that the World Honored One raised his fist and asked, "Open or closed?") The outsider was speechless; then he bowed in homage. This story is just like the main case; ever since then the bloodline of the Ancients has been unbroken. Thus it is said, "The question is where the answer is, the answer is where the question is."

Since Hsueh Tou can see through things like this, he says, "In their words they show their ability in direct confrontation." There is skill in the monk's words, which seem to bear two meanings; he seems to ask about the man and he also seems to ask about the place. Without stirring a single hairsbreadth Chao Chou immediately replies to him, "East gate, west gate, south gate, north gate."

"The Adamantine Eye is completely void of dust." This praises Chao Chou snatching away both person and environment, and in his words showing his ability, giving him an answer. This is called having ability, having perspective. The moment the monk turns around, Chao Chou sees through his innermost heart. If he couldn't do this, it would have been difficult for Chao Chou to parry the monk's question. Chakra[f] Eye is a Sanskrit expression that means an adamantine eye, a diamond eye, which illumines and sees everywhere without obstruction. Not only can it clearly make out a tiny hair a thousand miles away, but also it can determine what's false and decide what's true, distinguish gain and loss, discern what's appropriate to the occasion, and recognize right and wrong.

Hsueh Tou says, "East, west, south, north—the gates face each other; an endless series of hammer blows can't smash them open." Since the hammer blows continue without limit, why can't they smash the gates open? It's that Hsueh Tou's vision is like this. How will all of you people get these gates open? Please examine this thoroughly.

TRANSLATOR'S NOTES

a. Chao Chou was the name of the city and the province where the Ch'an master Ts'ung Shen lived, and is hence the name by which he is usually known, according to Ch'an custom.

b. Fen Yang Shan Ch'ao (947-1024), a great master of the Lin Chi sect, commented on many of the devices of earlier Ch'an masters and attempted to synthesize the teachings of the various Ch'an sects; for an enumeration of his 'eighteen questions,' see the appendix on the Lin Chi sect.

c. Fu Shan Fa Yuan (10-11c.) was accredited by several masters, including Fen Yang; his nickname 'The Jurist' was on account of his great knowledge of history and legal cases, which he once had to display to free himself and his traveling companions from the clutches of a corrupt magistrate in western China.

d. This refers to masters addressing students in the teaching hall.

e. This refers to masters interviewing disciples in the master's room.

f. Chakra in Sanskrit actually means wheel or disc, whence it means a disc-shaped weapon, especially that of Vishnu, the maintainer in Hindu cosmology. The sense of adamantine, or diamond-like, in which it is used here, is a common Ch'an metaphor for wisdom which cuts through all obscurity and confusion, like 'the jewel sword of the Diamond King.' As the destroyer of all opinion and doubt, the image of the weapon cutting through fits in with this usage. The diamond is also used in classical Buddhist metaphor to symbolize the ultimate meditative concentration, which nothing can destroy, whence emerges the sharp wisdom whose function cuts off all afflictions, removes all obstacles to knowledge of things as they are.

Mu Chou's Thieving Phoney

POINTER

So, so; not so, not so. In battle, each occupies a pivotal position. That is why it is said, "If you turn upwards, then even Shakyamuni, Maitreya, Manjusri, Samantabhadra, and the myriad sages, together with all the masters in the world, all suck in their breath and swallow their voices: if you turn downwards, worms and maggots and everything that crawls, all sentient beings, each and every one emits great shining light, each and every one towers like a wall miles high." If, on the other hand, you neither face upwards nor downwards, how would you deal? If there is a principle, go by the principle; if there is no principle, go by the example. To test, I cite this; look!

CASE

Mu Chou asked a monk, "Where have you just come from?"[1] The monk immediately shouted.[2] Mu Chou said, "I've been shouted at by you once."[3] Again the monk shouted.[4] Mu Chou said, "After three or four shouts, then what?"[5] The monk had nothing to say.[6] Mu Chou then hit him and said,[7] "What a thieving phoney you are!"[8]

NOTES

1. A probing pole; a reed shade.
2. An adept Ch'an traveller! But don't pretend to be enlightened. Still, he does know how to act like this.
3. A trap to fell a tiger. Why is he making a monkey of the man?
4. Look for the horns on his head: he seems to be (a real 'dragon'), but actually isn't yet. I'm afraid he has a dragon's head but a snake's tail.

5. A wave against the current. There's never been anyone who could stick his head out (in front of Mu Chou). Where will (the monk) go?
6. After all, he searched without finding.
7. If we let Mu Chou carry out his mandate to the full, then all the plants and trees on earth would be cut into three pieces.
8. He lets go the first move and falls back into the secondary.

COMMENTARY

Whoever would uphold and establish the teaching of our school must have the eye of a true master of our school, and must have the functional ability of a true master of our school. Mu Chou's mental acuity is like a flash of lightening. He liked to put lecturers[a] to the test; he would usually utter a word or half a phrase like a thicket of brambles that can't be stepped on or touched. As soon as he saw a monk coming, he would say, "The case is complete; I let you have thirty blows of the staff." Or he would see a monk and call out "Elder!" If the monk turned his head, Mu Chou would say, "You board-carrying fellow!" Again, when he was teaching his community, he would say, "If you don't have a place to enter,[b] you must find a place to enter; once you have gained entry, you still must not turn your backs on me." Mu Chou's efforts for people were mostly like this.

This monk was also well polished and prepared, but nevertheless he had a dragon's head but a snake's tail. At the time anyone but Mu Chou would have been thrown into confusion by this monk. Like when Mu Chou asked him, "Where have you just come from?" and the monk immediately shouted: tell me, what was his meaning? The old fellow wasn't at all flustered; calmly he replied, "I've been shouted at by you once." He seems to take that shout and put it to one side, and he also seems to test him; he leans over to see how he is. Again the monk shouted; he seems to be right, but isn't yet really right—his nostrils were pierced by the old fellow, who immediately asked, "After three or four shouts, then what?" After all, this monk was speechless. Mu Chou then hit him and said, "What a thieving phoney you are!"

The aim of testing people is to know them intimately the

minute they open their mouths. Too bad this monk was speechless, provoking Mu Chou to call him a thieving phoney. If it had been any of you people who had been asked by Mu Chou, "After three or four shouts, then what?" how should you have replied in order to avoid his calling you a thieving phoney? Here if you can discern survival and destruction and distinguish right and wrong, if your feet tread the ground of reality, then who is concerned with "After three or four shouts, then what?"? But since this monk was speechless, his case was decided by old Mu Chou on the basis of the facts.

Listen to Hsueh Tou's verse:

VERSE

Two shouts and a third shout:^c
  **The sound of thunder is tremendous,
  but there isn't even a drop of rain.
  From ancient times up till now, there's
  rarely been anyone like this.*

Adepts recognize the opportune moment to change.
  **If he weren't an adept, how could (Mu Chou)
  have tested (the monk)? I'm just afraid that
  you aren't this way.*

If you call that riding the tiger's head,
  **Unh! Blind man! How can you ride
  a tiger's head? Quite a few people
  have understood in this way, and there
  are still people who entertain this view.*

The two of them would both turn out to be blind men.
  **An intimate comment from the mouth of an intimate.
  Why only two? Take what's coming to you and get out!*

Who is a blind man?
  **Who would you have decide?
  Fortunately there is a last word:
  (Hsueh Tou) is on the verge of
  cheating people completely.*

I bring it out for everyone to see.
  **When you look, it's not that it's

not there, but if you stare at it,
you'll go blind. If you set your eyes
to look, then you are grabbing empty space
with both hands. When you bring it up this
way, what level of activity is it? *

COMMENTARY

Nothing can prevent Hsueh Tou from being able to help people. If he weren't an adept, he would just be shouting wildly at random. Therefore it is said, "Sometimes a shout isn't used as a shout; then again, sometimes a shout is used as a shout. Sometimes a shout is like a lion crouching on the ground; sometimes a shout is like the Diamond King's jewel sword."

Hsing Hua said, "I see all of you shouting in the east hall and shouting in the west hall. Don't shout at random. Even if you shout me up to the heavens, break me to pieces, and I fall back down again without even a trace of breath left in me, wait for me to revive and I'll tell you it's still not enough. Why? I have never set out real pearls for you inside the Purple Curtains. As for all of you here, what are you doing when you just go on with wild random shouting?"

Lin Chi said, "I've heard all of you imitate my shouting. But I ask you, if a monk comes from the east hall and another monk comes from the west hall, and they both shout at once, which one is the guest and which one is the host? If you can't distinguish host and guest, then you must not imitate me any more after this."

Therefore Hsueh Tou says in his verse, "Adepts recognize the opportune moment to change." Although the monk in the case was taken in by Mu Chou, still he could perceive the opportune moment to change. Tell me, where did he do this? Ch'an Master Chih of the Deer Gate graded this monk by saying, "One who knows the Law fears it." Yen T'ou said, "In battle, each man occupies a pivotal position." Master Hsin of Huang Lung said, "When you reach an impasse, change; having changed, then you get through." This is where the patriarchs cut off the tongues of everyone in the world. If you recognize the opportune moment to change, then when something is raised, you immediately know what it comes down to.

Some people say, "Why worry about Mu Chou saying, 'After three or four shouts, then what?'?" and just go on shouting. Let them give twenty or thirty shouts, even go on shouting until Maitreya (the future Buddha) comes down to be born, and call this riding the tiger's head: if you understand in this fashion, it's because you don't know Mu Chou. Even if you want to see the monk, you're still too far away. To ride a tiger's head one must have a sword in his hand and versatility too before he can succeed.

Hsueh Tou says, if you call this riding the tiger's head, "The two of them would both turn out to be blind men." Hsueh Tou is like a long sword leaning against the sky, stern and awesome in full majesty. If you understand Hsueh Tou's meaning, you will naturally understand everything at once. Then you will see that the latter part of Hsueh Tou's verse is just making footnotes.

Hsueh Tou goes on to say "Who is a blind man?" Tell me, is it the guest who's blind, or is it the host who's blind? Aren't guest and host both blind at the same time? "I bring it out for everyone to see." This is the living place, where Hsueh Tou finishes the verse all at once. Yet why does he say, "I bring it out for everyone to see"? Tell me, how will you see it? Open your eyes and you can; shut your eyes and you can too. Is there anyone who can avoid it?

TRANSLATOR'S NOTES

a. These were professor-monks of the scholastic schools, specializing in various Buddhist texts and philosophies and expounding them in temples devoted to the study of the written teachings. They are sometimes derided in Ch'an literature for being too attached to doctrines and theories, or full of self-importance and pride in their learning, but without real accomplishment.

b. A place to enter the Path; this is the true initiation, disentanglement from the bonds of egoism. Beyond this is the phase of 'getting oneself out' or 'showing onself,' which means to transcend the state of quiescence and nothingness, so to speak, to go beyond the point of entry and absorption into the Path, and bring out the active function of illumination. As an Ancient said, "A sage has no self, but there is nothing that is not his self." Although the phase of getting out or showing has attributes and is personal in the sense that the nirvana of the Great Vehicle is personal, it is beyond the concept of ego and personal possession, and is like the revelation of the adamantine being spoken of in esoteric Buddhism.

c.   "Two shouts" refers to the monk; "a third shout" refers to Mu Chou.

Huang Po's Gobblers of Dregs

POINTER

The great capacity of Buddhas and Patriarchs is completely within his control; the lifeline of humans and gods is entirely subject to his direction. With a casual word or phrase he astounds the crowd and stirs the masses; with one device, one object, he smashes chains and knocks off fetters. Meeting transcendental potential, he brings up transcendental matters. But tell me, who has ever come on like this? Are there any who know where he is at? To test, I cite this: look!

CASE

Huang Po, instructing the community, said,[1] "All of you people are gobblers of dregs; if you go on travelling around this way,[2] where will you have Today?[3] Do you know that there are no teachers of Ch'an in all of China?"[4]

   At that time a monk came forward and said, "Then what about those in various places who order followers and lead communities?"[5]

   Huang Po said, "I do not say that there is no Ch'an; it's just that there are no teachers."[6]

NOTES

1. Drawing water, he's limited by (the size of) the bowl. He swallows all in one gulp. No patchrobed monk in the world can leap clear.
2. He's said it. You'll wear out your straw sandals.
3. What's the use of Today? Nothing can stop him from astounding the crowd and stirring up the community.
4. I hadn't realized. He swallows all in one gulp. He too is a cloud-dwelling saint.

5. He too gives a good thrust; confronting the situation, he couldn't but do so.
6. He just can't explain. The tiles are scattered, the ice melts. He's a fellow with a dragon's head but a snake's tail.

COMMENTARY

Huang Po was seven feet tall; on his forehead there was (a lump like) a round pearl. He understood Ch'an by nature. It's also said that he once travelled in the company of a saint: once when the master was travelling to Mount T'ien T'ai, he met a monk on the way. They talked and laughed together like old acquaintances. Huang Po looked him over carefully; the light in his eyes pierced people, and his appearance was extremely unusual. As they thus travelled along together, when they came to a swollen valley stream, Huang Po planted his staff (in the ground), took off his hat, and stopped there. The other monk tried to take the master across with him, but the master said, "Please cross over yourself." The other one then gathered up his robes and walked upon the waves as though treading on level ground. He looked back and said, "Come across! Come across!" The master upbraided him, saying, "You self-perfected fellow! If I had known you would concoct wonders, I would have broken your legs!" The other monk sighed in admiration and said, "You are a true vessel of the teaching of the Great Vehicle." As his words ended, he disappeared.

When Huang Po first met Pai Chang, Pai Chang said, "Magnificent! Imposing! Where have you come from?" Huang Po said, "Magnificent and imposing, I've come from the mountains." Pai Chang asked, "What have you come for?" Huang Po said, "Not for anything else." Pai Chang esteemed him deeply as a vessel (of Dharma).

The next day he took leave of Pai Chang. Pai Chang asked, "Where are you going?" Huang Po replied, "To Kiangsi to pay my respects to the Great Master Ma." Pai Chang said, "The Great Master Ma has already passed on." Huang Po asked, "What did he have to say when he was alive?" Pai Chang then related the circumstances of his second encounter with Ma Tsu:

"When Ma Tsu saw me approach, he raised his whisk. I asked, 'Do you identify with this action or detach from this action?' Ma Tsu then hung the whisk on the corner of the meditation seat. There was a long silence; then Ma Tsu asked me, 'Later on, when you're flapping your lips, how will you help people?' I took the whisk and held it up. Ma Tsu said, 'Do you identify with this action or detach from this action?' I took the whisk and hung it back on the corner of the meditation seat. Ma Tsu drew himself up and gave a shout that left me deaf for three days."

Huang Po unconsciously stuck out his tongue in awe. Pai Chang said, "After this, won't you be a successor of the Great Master Ma?" Huang Po said, "No. Today, because of the master's recital, I've gotten to see the Great Master Ma's great capacity and its great function; but if I were to succeed to Master Ma, in the future I would be bereft of descendants." Pai Chang said, "It is so, it is so. If your view equals your teacher, you have less than half your teacher's virtue; only when your wisdom goes beyond your teacher are you worthy to pass on the transmission. As your view is right now, it seems that you have ability which transcends any teacher." You must see for yourself how father and son act in that house before you begin to understand.

Again one day Huang Po asked Pai Chang, "How has the vehicle of the school that comes down from ancient times been demonstrated and taught?" Pai Chang was silent for a long time; Huang Po said, "You shouldn't let posterity be cut off." Pai Chang said, "I thought you were the man." Then he got up and went into his abbot's quarters.

Huang Po was an informal friend of prime minister P'ei Hsiu; he explained the essence of mind[a] to him. When P'ei was commander of Wan Ling, he invited the master to come to the district capital. He showed the master a book (expressing) his understanding. The master took the book and put it down on the seat without even opening it to look through it. After a long silence, the master asked, "Do you understand?" P'ei said, "I don't understand." Huang Po said, "If you had understood this way, you still would have gotten somewhere; if you're still trying to describe it with paper and ink, where would there still be room for my school?" At this P'ei offered a verse of praise:

From the great man he has inherited the mind seal;
There's a round jewel on his forehead, his body is
seven feet tall.
He hung up his staff and stayed ten years by the
River Shu;
Today his floating coracle has crossed to the banks
of the Chang.
Eight thousand dragons and elephants follow his
giant strides;
Over ten thousand miles fragrant flowers join in his
excellent cause.
I hope to serve the master as his disciple;
I do not know to whom he will entrust his teaching.

The master made no sign of being pleased, but said,[b]

My mind is like the boundlessness of the great
ocean;
My mouth spews red lotuses to nurse a sick body.
I myself have a pair of hands with nothing to do;
I have never received an idle man.

After Huang Po was dwelling (in a temple as a teacher), his active edge was sharp and dangerous. When Lin Chi was in his community, Mu Chou was the head monk. (Mu Chou) asked (Lin Chi), "How long have you been here? Why don't you go ask (Huang Po) a question?" Chi said, "What would you have me ask?" The head monk said, "Why don't you go ask what is the essential meaning of the Buddha Dharma?" Chi then went and asked (Huang Po); three times he was beaten and driven out. He took leave of the head monk, saying, "I have been bidden to ask the question three times by you, and have been beaten and driven out. Perhaps my affinity is not here; for now I will leave the mountain." The head monk said, "If you're going, you should bid farewell to the master (Huang Po) first." The head monk went beforehand and said to Huang Po, "The questioning monk is a very rare one; why don't you work on him to make him into a tree to provide cool shade for people of later times?" Huang Po said, "I already know."

When Chi came to take leave, Po said, "You don't need to go anyplace else; just go to the riverbank at Ta An and see Ta Yu."

When Chi got to Ta Yu, he related the preceding story and said, "I do not know where my fault was." Ta Yu said, "Huang Po was so kind, he exerted himself to the utmost for you; why do you go on speaking of fault or no fault?" Chi was suddenly greatly enlightened: he said, "There's not much to Huang Po's Buddha Dharma." Ta Yu grabbed and held him and said, "You just said you were at fault; now instead you say there's not much to the Buddha Dharma." Chi hit Ta Yu in the side three times with his fist; Yu pushed him away and said, "Your teacher is Huang Po; it has nothing to do with me."

One day Huang Po, instructing his community, said, "The Great Master Fa Jung of Ox Head Mountain^c spoke horizontally and spoke vertically, but he still didn't know the key of transcendence. These days the Ch'an followers after Shih T'ou and Ma Tsu speak of Ch'an and speak of the Way most voluminously." But why did Huang Po talk this way? It was because of this that he taught the community by saying, "All of you are gobblers of dregs; if you travel around like this, you'll get laughed at by people. As soon as you hear of a place with eight hundred or a thousand people, you immediately go there. It won't do just to seek out the hubbub; if you always take things this easy here, then where else would there be this matter of Today?"

In T'ang times they liked to revile people by calling them "gobblers of dregs," so many people say that Huang Po was reviling the people. Those with eyes see for themselves what he was getting at. The whole idea is to let down a hook to fish out people's questions. In the assembly there was a Ch'an man who didn't fear for his body or life, so he could come forth this way from the crowd to question Huang Po, saying, "Then what about those in various places who order followers and lead communities?" And he makes a good point, too. After all the old fellow Huang Po couldn't explain, so instead he broke down and said, "I don't say there is no Ch'an, just that there are no teachers." But tell me, where does his meaning lie?

That essence of the school that has come down from ancient times—sometimes holding, sometimes letting go, sometimes killing, sometimes giving life, sometimes releasing, sometimes gathering up—I dare to ask all of you, what would be a teacher of Ch'an? As soon as I speak this way, I've already lost my head. People, where are your nostrils? (A pause) They've been pierced through!

VERSE

His cold severe solitary mien does not take pride in itself;
   **He himself doesn't know he has it. He too is a cloud-
   dwelling saint.*

*Solemnly dwelling in the sea of the world, he distinguishes
      dragons and snakes.*
   **It is still necessary to distinguish initiate and unin-
   itiate, and it is also necessary that black and white be
   clearly distinguished.*

Ta Chung the Son of Heaven has been lightly handled;
   **What Ta Chung the Son of Heaven are you talking
   about? However great, he too must get up from the
   ground; and even higher, there's still the sky—what
   about that?*

Three times he personally felt those claws and fangs at work.
   **A dead frog. Why so talkative? It's not yet anything
   extraordinary; it's still a minor skill. When his great
   capacity and great function become manifest, then the
   whole world in all ten directions, the mountains and
   rivers and the great earth, all are at Huang Po's place
   begging for their lives.*

COMMENTARY

This verse by Hsueh Tou seems just like praise on a portrait of
Huang Po, yet you people mustn't understand it as "praise on a
portrait." Right in his words there's a place to get oneself out.[d]
Hsueh Tou clearly says, "His cold severe solitary mien does
not take pride in itself." When Huang Po instructed the community this way, he wasn't contesting others or asserting
himself, displaying himself or boasting of himself. If you understand what happened here, you are free in all directions:
sometimes you stand alone on a solitary peak, sometimes you
stretch out in the bustling market place. How could you one-
sidedly hold fast to a single corner? The more you abandon, the
more you aren't at rest; the more you seek, the more you don't
see; the more you take on, the more you sink down. An Ancient said, "Without wings, fly through the sky; with fame,
become known throughout the world." Wholeheartedly dis-

card the marvelous wonders of the principle of Buddha Dharma; let it all go at once, and then you will after all have gotten somewhere, and wherever you are it will naturally become manifest.

Hsueh Tou says, "Solemnly dwelling in the sea of the world, he distinguishes dragons and snakes." Is it a dragon or is it a snake? As soon as anyone comes in through the door, he puts him to the test; this is called the eye to distinguish dragons and snakes, the ability to capture tigers and rhinos. Hsueh Tou also said, "Judging dragons and snakes—how is that eye correct? Capturing tigers and rhinos—that skill is not complete."

Hsueh Tou also says, "Ta Chung the Son of Heaven has been lightly handled; three times he personally felt those claws and fangs at work." Huang Po is not just acting bad right here (in this case); he's always been like this. As for Ta Chung the Son of Heaven (Emperor), it is recorded in the *Continued Biographies of the Hsien T'ung Era* that the T'ang Emperor Hsien Tsung (r. 806–820) had two sons, one called Mu Tsung and the other called Hsuan Tsung. This Hsuan Tsung (r. 847–860) was the Ta Chung Emperor.

When Hsuan Tsung was thirteen years old, though still young, he was keen and clever, and always liked to sit in the lotus posture. During the reign of Mu Tsung (821–824), one time when the morning audience was over, Hsuan Tsung playfully mounted the (Imperial) Dragon Throne and went through the motions of saluting the assembled officials. One of the great ministers saw this and thought that Hsuan Tsung was demented, so he reported this to Mu Tsung. When Mu Tsung saw Hsuan Tsung, he rubbed his head and sighed, saying, "My younger brother is indeed a valiant son of my clan."

Mu Tsung died in 824, leaving three sons, called Ching Tsung, Wen Tsung, and Wu Tsung. Ching Tsung succeeded to his father's throne and reigned for two years until the inner court plotted against him and removed him. Wen Tsung succeeded to the throne and reigned for fourteen years. When Wu Tsung came to the throne, he always spoke of Hsuan Tsung as an imbecile. One day, filled with hatred for Hsuan Tsung because long ago he had playfully climbed up on his father's throne, he finally had Hsuan Tsung beaten almost to death, thrown out into the back gardens, and drenched with filthy water to revive him.

After this Hsuan Tsung went into hiding in the community of the Master Chih Hsien of Hsiang Yen. Later he had his head shaved as a novice, but had not yet received full ordination. He travelled around with Chih Hsien; when they got to Mount Lu, Chih Hsien made up a poem about a waterfall:

> Piercing the clouds, penetrating rock, never declin-
>   ing the work;
> When the land is distant, you know how high is the
>   place it appears.

Having intoned these two lines, Chih Hsien remained a long time in thought; he wanted to draw out a stream of words from Hsuan Tsung to see what he was like. Hsuan Tsung continued the verse, saying,

> How can the mountain torrent be held back?
> Eventually it must return to the great ocean to be-
>   come waves.

At this Chih Hsien knew that Hsuan Tsung was no ordinary man, and he silently acknowledged him.

Later Hsuan Tsung went into the community at Yen Kuan, where he was asked to be the temple scribe. Huang Po was there serving as head monk. One day as Huang Po was paying respects to (an image of a) Buddha, Hsuan Tsung saw him and asked, "If you don't seek from Buddha, don't seek from Dharma, and don't seek from the Sangha, then what are you seeking by bowing in respect?" Huang Po replied, "I don't seek from Buddha, I don't seek from the Dharma, and I don't seek from the Sangha; I always pay my respects this way." Hsuan Tsung said, "What's the use of paying respect?" Immediately Huang Po slapped him. Hsuan Tsung said, "Too coarse." Huang Po said, "What place is this to talk of coarse and fine?" and slapped him again. Later, when Hsuan Tsung succeeded to the throne of the nation, he bestowed on Huang Po the title, "Coarse-acting Ascetic." When prime minister P'ei was at court later, he proposed that Huang Po be given the title Tuan Chi Ch'an Shih, "Boundless Ch'an Master."

Hsueh Tou knew where his bloodline appeared, so he could use it cleverly. Right now is there anyone to use his claws and fangs? If so, then I'll strike!

TRANSLATOR'S NOTES

a. This refers to the *Ch'uan Hsin Fa Yao,* the "Essential Method of the Transmission of Mind," a collection of Huang Po's sermons for P'ei Hsiu.

b. According to Tenkei Denson, the following verse is probably not really Huang Po's; it does not appear in the version of this story given in the *Ching Te Ch'uan Teng Lu.* Tenkei also says that the following story of Lin Chi's enlightenment also has no particular use in this commentary, and is probably a later insertion.

c. 593–657; he was later claimed to be a successor of Tao Hsin, the Fourth Patriarch of Ch'an after Bodhidharma. A distinguished meditation master, Fa Jung is known as the first patriarch of the so-called Ox Head sect of Ch'an, which continued for ten generations and produced numerous distinguished masters. Although historically of independent origin, this sect later developed close relations with the streams of the Ts'ao Ch'i succession.

d. This means a place which reveals Huang Po's state, and the way a student must go to realize his sphere of attainment. To 'get oneself out' has the meaning of 'appearing in the world' (though this latter expression usually has the specific meaning of accepting leadership of a community as the spiritual guide, it can have the more inclusive meaning of actively revealing enlightened knowledge and conduct). The Zen master Dogen, in his *Fukanzazengi,* says, 'Although one may roam freely in the realm of entry, one may lack a living road to get himself out on.'

Tung Shan's Three Pounds of Hemp

POINTER

The sword that kills people, the sword that brings people to life: this is the standard way of high antiquity and the essential pivot for today as well. If you discuss killing, you don't harm a single hair; if you discuss giving life, you lose your body and life. Therefore it is said, "The thousand sages have not transmitted the single transcendental path; students toil over appearances like monkeys grasping at reflections." Tell me, since it is not transmitted, why then so many complicated public cases? Let those with eyes try to explain.

CASE

A monk asked Tung Shan, "What is Buddha?"[1]
Tung Shan said, "Three pounds of hemp."[2]

NOTES

1. Iron brambles; no patchrobed monk on earth can leap clear.
2. Clearly. Worn out straw sandals. He points to a pagoda tree to scold a willow tree.

COMMENTARY

So many people misunderstand this public case. It really is hard to chew on, since there's no place for you to sink your teeth into. What is the reason? Because it's bland and flavorless. The Ancients had quite a few answers to the question "What is Buddha?" One said, "The one in the shrine." One said, "The thirty-two auspicious marks." One said, "A bamboo whip on a mountain covered with a forest grown from a staff."

81

And so on, to Tung Shan, who said, "Three pounds of hemp." He couldn't be stopped from cutting off the tongues of the Ancients.

Many people base their understanding on the words and say that Tung Shan was in the storehouse at the time weighing out hemp when the monk questioned him, and therefore he answered in this way. Some say that when Tung Shan is asked about the east he answers about the west. Some say that since you are Buddha and yet you still go to ask about Buddha, Tung Shan answers this in a roundabout way. And there's yet another type of dead men who say that the three pounds of hemp is itself Buddha. But these interpretations are irrelevant. If you seek from Tung Shan's words this way, you can search until Maitreya Buddha is born down here and still never see it even in a dream.

What's the reason? Words and speech are just vessels to convey the Path. Far from realizing the intent of the Ancients, people just search in their words; what grasp can they get on it? Haven't you seen how an Ancient said, "Originally the Path is wordless; with words we illustrate the Path. Once you see the Path, the words are immediately forgotten." To get to this point, you must first go back to your own original state. Just this three pounds of hemp is like the single track of the great road to the Capital; as you raise your feet and put them down, there's nothing that is not this. This story is the same as Yun Men's saying "Cake"[a] but it's unavoidably difficult to understand. My late teacher Wu Tsu made a verse about it:

> The cheap-selling board-carrying fellow
> Weighs it out, three pounds of hemp.
> With a hundred thousand years of unsold goods,
> He has no place to put it all.

You must clean it all up; when your defiling feelings, conceptual thinking, and comparative judgements of gain and loss and right and wrong are all cleared away at once, then you will spontaneously understand.

VERSE

> The Golden Raven[b] hurries;
> **In the left eye, half a pound.

The swift sparrowhawk can't overtake it.
Lay the body down in flames of fire. *

*The Jade Rabbit*ᶜ *is swift.*
　　**In the right eye, eight ounces.*
　　He makes his nest in the palace of Heng O, the Moon
　　Lady. *

Has there ever been carelessness in a good response?
　　**As the bell when struck, as the valley embracing the*
　　echo. *

To see Tung Shan as laying out facts in accordance with the
　　situation
　　**Mistakenly sticking by the zero point of the scale; it's*
　　just Your Reverence who sees things this way. *

Is like a lame tortoise and a blind turtle entering an empty
　　valley.
　　**Take what's coming to you and get out. In the same*
　　pit, there's no different dirt. Who killed your sparrow-
　　hawk? *

Flowering groves, multicolored forests;
　　**A double case; he handles all crimes with the same*
　　indictment. As before, they're the same. *

Bamboo of the South, wood of the North.
　　**A quadruple case. He puts a head on top of his head.* *

So I think of Ch'ang Ch'ing and Officer Lu:
　　**A leper drags his companions along with him.*
　　I am this way, and Hsueh Tou is this way too. *

He knew how to say he should laugh, not cry.
　　**Ha ha. By day and by night he adds to the suffering.* *

Ha!
　　**Bah! What is this? I strike!* *

COMMENTARY

Hsueh Tou can see all the way through, so he immediately
says, "The Golden Raven hurries; the Jade Rabbit is swift."
This is of the same kind as Tung Shan's reply "Three pounds of
hemp." The sun rises, the moon sets; every day it's like this.
People often make up intellectual interpretations and just say,

"The Golden Raven is the left eye and the Jade Rabbit is the right eye." As soon as they're questioned, they put a glare in their eyes and say, "They're here!" What connection is there? If you understand in this way, the whole school of Bodhidharma would be wiped off the face of the earth. That is why it is said,

> Letting down the hook in the four seas
> Just to fish out terrible dragons;
> The mysterious device outside conventions
> Is for seeking out those who know the self.

Hsueh Tou is a man who has left the heaps and elements;[d] how could he make up this sort of interpretation? Hsueh Tou easily goes to where the barriers are broken and the hinges are smashed to reveal a little something to let you see; there he adds a footnote, saying, "Has there ever been carelessness in a good response?" Tung Shan does not reply lightly to this monk; he is like a bell when struck, like a valley embracing an echo. Great or small, he responds accordingly, never daring to make a careless impression. At once Hsueh Tou has brought out his guts and presented them to all of you. Hsueh Tou had a verse on being tranquil but responding well:

> Presented face to face, it's not a matter of multiplicity;
> Dragons and snakes are easily distinguished, but a patchrobed monk is hard to deceive.
> The golden hammer's shadow moves, the jewel sword's light is cold;
> They strike directly; hurry up and take a look!

When Tung Shan first saw Yun Men, Yun Men asked him, "Where have you just come from?" Tung Shan said, "From Cha Tu." Yun Men said, "Where did you spend the summer retreat?" Tung Shan said, "In Hunan, at Pao Tz'u." Yun Men asked, "When did you leave there?" Tung Shan said, "August twenty-fifth." Yun Men said, "I should let you have three score blows of the staff; go meditate in the hall."

That evening Tung Shan entered Yun Men's room; drawing near, he asked, "Where was my fault?" Yun Men said, "You rice bag! From Kiangsi to Hunan, and still you go on this way." At these words Tung Shan was vastly and greatly awakened. After a while he said, "Another day I'll go to a place where there are no human hearths and build myself a hut; I won't store even a single grain of rice or plant any vegetables. There I'll receive and wait upon the great sages coming and going from the ten directions; I'll pull out all the nails and pegs for them, I'll pull off their greasy caps and strip them of their stinking shirts. I'll make them all clean and free, so they can be unconcerned people." Yun Men said, "Your body is the size of a coconut, but you can open such a big mouth."

Tung Shan then took his leave and departed. His enlightenment at the time was a direct complete breakthrough; how could it have anything in common with small petty views? Later when he appeared in the world to respond to people's various potentialities, the words "Three pounds of hemp" were understood everywhere merely as a reply to the question about Buddha; they just make their reasoning in terms of Buddha. Hsueh Tou says that to understand Tung Shan's reply as expressing facts in accordance with the situation is like a lame tortoise or a blind turtle going into an empty valley; when will they ever find a way out?

"Flowering groves, multicolored forests." When a monk asked Master Hsien of Fu Teh,ᵉ "What is the mind of the Buddhas of antiquity?" The master replied, "Flowering groves, multicolored forests." The monk also asked Ming Chiao, "What is the inner meaning of 'three pounds of hemp'?" Ming Chiao said, "Bamboo of the South, wood of the North." The monk came back and recounted this to Tung Shan, who said, "I won't explain this just for you, but I will explain it to the whole community." Later he went into the hall and said, "Words do not express facts, speech does not accord with the situation. Those who accept words are lost, and those who linger over phrases are deluded."

To smash people's intellectual views, Hsueh Tou purposely draws these together on a single thread to produce his verse. Yet people of later times still give rise to even more intellectual views and say, " 'Three pounds of hemp' is the robe of mourning; bamboo is the staff of mourning: that's why he said, 'Bamboo of the South, wood of the North.' 'Flowering groves, multicolored forests' is the flowers and plants painted on the coffin." Do these people realize their disgrace? How far are they from realizing that "bamboo of the South, wood of the North" and "three pounds of hemp" are just like "daddy" and "poppa." When the Ancients answered with a turn of words, their intention was definitely not like these (interpretations). It's just like Hsueh Tou's saying, "The Golden Raven hurries; the Jade Rabbit is swift"—it's just as broad. It's just that real gold and fool's gold are hard to tell apart; similar written characters are not the same.

Hsueh Tou has the kind heart of an old woman; he wants to break up your feelings of doubt, so he brings in more dead men. "So I think of Ch'ang Ch'ing and Officer Lu; he knew how to say he should laugh, not cry." To discuss the verse itself, the first three lines by themselves have already completed the verse. But I ask you, since the whole universe is just this three pounds of hemp, why does Hsueh Tou still have so many complications? It's just that his compassion is excessive, therefore he is like this.

When Officer Lu Hsuan was Inspector of Hsuan Chou, he studied with Nan Ch'uan. When Nan Ch'uan passed on, Lu heard the (sound of) mourning so he entered the temple for the funeral. He laughed aloud a great laugh. The temple director said to him, "The late master and you were teacher and disciple; why aren't you crying?" Officer Lu said, "If you can say something, I'll cry." The temple director was speechless. Lu gave a loud lament; "Alas! Alas! Our late master is long gone." Later Ch'ang Ch'ing heard of this and said, "The officer should have laughed, not cried."

Hsueh Tou borrows the essence of this meaning to say that if you make up these kinds of intellectual interpretations, this calls for laughter, not crying. This is so, but at the very end there's a single word which is unavoidably easy to misunderstand, when he goes on to say "Ha!" Has Hsueh Tou washed himself clean?

TRANSLATOR'S NOTES

a. Asked, "What is talk that goes beyond buddhas and patriarchs?" Yun Men said, "Cake."
b. The Golden Raven is the sun.
c. The Jade Rabbit is the moon.
d. The heaps (Sanskrit *skandha*) are form (matter), sensation, perception, synergies, and consciousness; the elements (Sanskrit

dhatu) are the six sense faculties (eye, ear, nose, tongue, body, and mind), the six sense fields (form, sound, smell, taste, feeling, and entity), and the six associated consciousnesses. While the five heaps are often used to refer specifically to the human being, in which context the synergies include all sorts of mental activities such as emotion and volition, functional relations not connected with mind are also classified as synergies. It is obvious in this context that to leave the five heaps and eighteen elements does not mean annihilation, but refers to being free from attachment to them, having died the esoteric death, sloughed off the claims of egoism, under whose sway emotion and intellect, thought and habit, had been in fact inseparable.

e. The names of Chien and Ming Chiao are used after the critical edition of Ito Yuten, in accord with the One Night Book, which also accords with tradition from other sources; the Chang version has it that both these questions were posed to Chih Men, Hsueh Tou's teacher, but this poses a contradiction in time.

Pa Ling's Snow in a Silver Bowl

POINTER

Clouds are frozen over the great plains, but the whole world is not hidden. When snow covers the white flowers, it's hard to distinguish the outlines. Its coldness is as cold as snow and ice; it fineness is as fine as rice powder. Its depths are hard for even a Buddha's eye to peer into; its secrets are impossible for demons and outsiders to fathom. Leaving aside "understanding three when one is raised" for the moment, still he cuts off the tongues of everyone on earth. Tell me, whose business is this? To test, I cite this: look!

CASE

A monk asked Pa Ling, "What is the school of Kanadeva?"[1]
Pa Ling said, "Piling up snow in a silver bowl."[2]

NOTES

1. A white horse enters the white flowers. What are you saying? Check!
2. He blocks off your throat. A profuse outburst![a]

COMMENTARY

People often misunderstand and say this is a heretical school. What does this have to do with it? The fifteenth Patriarch, the honorable Kanadeva, was indeed (at one time) numbered among the outsiders; but when he met the fourteenth Patriarch, the honorable Nagarjuna (who presented a bowl of water to him), he put a needle into the bowl: Nagarjuna esteemed his capacity, transmitted the Buddha Mind School to him, and invested him as the fifteenth Patriarch.

In doctrinal disputes in India the winner holds a red flag in his hand, while the loser turns his clothes inside out and departs through a side door. Those who wanted to hold doctrinal disputes in India were required to obtain royal permission. Bells and drums would be sounded in the great temples and afterwards the debates could begin. In Kanadeva's day the heretics impounded the bell and drum in the (Buddhist) community temple in a purge. At this time the honorable Kanadeva knew that the Buddhist Teaching was in trouble, so he made use of his supernatural powers to ascend the bell tower and ring the bell, for he wanted to drive out the heretics.

Soon one of the heretics called out, "Who is up in the tower ringing the bell?" Kanadeva said, "A deva." The heretic asked, "Who is the deva?" Kanadeva said, "I." The heretic said "Who is 'I'?" Kanadeva said, " 'You' is a dog." The heretic asked, "Who is the dog?" Kanadeva said, "The dog is you." After seven go-rounds like this, the heretic realized he was beaten, so he submitted and himself opened the door of the bell tower, whereupon Kanadeva came down from the tower holding a red flag. The heretic said, "Why do you not follow?" Kanadeva said, "Why do you not precede?" The heretic said, "You're a knave." Kanadeva said, "You're a freeman."

Over and over Kanadeva would respond to questions like this, using his unobstructed powers of argument to overcome heretics, who would therefore submit. At such times the honorable Kanadeva would hold a red flag in his hand, and the one who had been defeated would stand beneath the flag. Among the heretics, to have their hands cut was generally the punishment to expiate the fault (or defeat in argument), but at this time Kanadeva put a stop to this; he only required his defeated adversaries to shave off their hair and enter the Buddhist path. Therefore the school of Kanadeva flourished greatly. Later on Hsueh Tou uses these facts to versify this.

Ma Tsu said, "The *Lankavatara* scripture says that Buddha's words have mind as their source and the gate of nothingness as the gate of the Dharma." Ma Tsu also said, "Whenever there are words and phrases, this is the Kanadeva school; just this he considered to be principal."

All of you are guests in the school of the patchrobed monks; have you ever thoroughly comprehended the school of Kanadeva as well? If you have thoroughly comprehended it, then the ninety-six kinds of heretics are all vanquished by you all at once. If you have not been able to comprehend it thoroughly, then you can't avoid going off with your clothes on inside out. Tell me, what about this? If you say words are it, this has no connection; if you say words are not it, this has no connection either. Tell me, where does Great Master Ma's meaning lie?

Later Yun Men said, "Great Master Ma spoke good words, but no one asks about it." Thereupon a monk asked, "What is the school of Kanadeva?" Yun Men said, "Of the ninety-six kinds of heretics, you are the lowest."

Formerly there was a monk who was taking leave of Ta Sui. Ta Sui asked, "Where are you going?" The monk said, "To do homage to Samantabhadra." Ta Sui raised his whisk and said, "Manjusri and Samantabhadra are both here." The monk drew a circle and pushed it towards Ta Sui with his hand; then he threw it behind him. Ta Sui said, "Attendant, bring a spot of tea for this monk."

Yun Men also said, "In India they cut off heads and arms; here you take what's coming to you and get out." He also said, "The red flag is in my hand."

In the community (of Yun Men) Pa Ling was called Mouthy Chien. When he was travelling around he always sewed sitting mats.[b] He had attained deeply into the great matter upon which Yun Men tread: thus he was outstanding. Later he appeared in the world as a Dharma successor to Yun Men. Formerly he dwelt at Pa Ling in Yueh Chou (in Hunan). He didn't compose any document of succession to the teaching, but just took three turning words to offer up to Yun Men: "What is the Path? A clear eyed man falls into a well." "What is the sword (so sharp it cuts) a hair blown (against it)? Each branch of coral upholds the moon." "What is the school of Kanadeva? Piling up snow in a silver bowl." Yun Men said, "Later on, on the anniversary of my death, just recite these three turning words, and you will have repaid my kindness in full." Thereafter, as it turned out, he did not hold ceremonial feasts on the anniversaries of his death, but followed Yun Men's will and just brought up these turning words.

Although people from all over have given answers to this question ("What is the school of Kanadeva?"), mostly they have turned to events to make up their answers; there is only Pa Ling who speaks as he does—he's extremely lofty and unique, unavoidably difficult to understand. Then too, without revealing a trace of his sharp point, he takes on enemies on all sides, and blow by blow finds a way to get himself out. He has the skill to fell tigers; he strips off human emotional views. As for the matter of One Form,[c] to get here you must have penetrated all the way through on your own, but after all you must meet another (enlightened) person before you are done. Therefore it is said, "When Tao Wu brandished his sceptre, one who was his equal would understand;[d] when Shih Kung bent his bow, an adept would tacitly comprehend."[e] For this truth, if you have no master to seal and instruct you, what teaching can you use to carry on the esoteric conversation?

Afterwards Hsueh Tou picked things out and brought them up for people in this verse:

VERSE

Old Hsin K'ai
> **A thousand soldiers are easy to get, but one general is hard to find. Talkative teacher!*

Is truly something else:
> **What truth is this? Have you ever felt his single knock on your head, even in a dream?*

He knows how to say, "Piling up snow in a silver bowl."
> **The frog can't leap out of the basket. A double case. Quite a few people will lose their bodies and lives.*

The ninety-six each must know for themselves;
> **You're included too; but do you know, Reverend? All are buried in the same pit.*

If you don't know, then ask the moon in the sky.
> **It's farther than far. Take what's coming to you and get out. Address your plea to the sky.*

The school of Kanadeva, Kanadeva's school;
> **What are you saying? I'm here. A mouthful of frost.*

Beneath the red flag, arouse the pure wind.
> **Shattered in a hundred fragments. Having struck, I'll say I've already hit it. Just cut off your heads and arms, and I'll speak a phrase for you.*

COMMENTARY

"Old Hsin K'ai." Hsin K'ai is the name of a monastery (in Pa Ling, Hunan, where the master Pa Ling stayed, hence a name for him). "Is truly something else." Hsueh Tou has ample praise for him. But tell me, how is Pa Ling special? "All words are the Buddha Dharma." When I talk like this, what's the reason for it? Hsueh Tou subtly reveals a little of his meaning when he says it's just that Pa Ling is truly something else.ᶠ Afterwards he opens up and says, "He can say, 'Piling up snow in a silver bowl.'"

Hsueh Tou goes on to provide you with further footnotes: "The ninety-six must each know for themselves." Before they can do so, they must acknowledge defeat. If you don't know, ask the moon in the sky. The Ancient used to give this answer, "Ask the moon in the sky."

Hsueh Tou's eulogy being finished, at the end there must be a living road, a phrase where the lion rears. He raises it higher for you and says, "The school of Kanadeva, the Kanadeva school; beneath the red flag, arouse the pure wind." Pa Ling said he piled up snow in a silver bowl; why then does Hsueh Tou say he roused the pure wind beneath the red flag? Do you know that Hsueh Tou kills people without using a sword?

TRANSLATOR'S NOTES

a. This obscure phrase is interpreted by commentators (hence translated) in various ways. It means the question is cracked and shattered, the answer is piercing and penetrating. Hence it can mean profusion, confusion, or it can mean opened up, clearly distinct (this latter includes the manifold, that everything is revealed in all its multiplicity). One commentator says that in this case it refers to the profuse discourse of the Kanadeva school, represented by Pa Ling's answer. Tenkei says that it means here burst open, clear and distinct, not hard to see.

b. This is interpreted in two ways; one, that Pa Ling travelled around with his sitting mat folded up, meaning that he did not prostrate himself before the teachers he visited (one rolls out one's mat to bow in full prostration). It is also interpreted to mean that he used to sew others' sitting mats for them.

c.   Or, 'One Color'; unity, or equanimity. In Tung Shan Liang Chieh's *Pao Ching San Mei Ke*, 'Song of the Jewel Mirror Concentration' (9th century), it says 'Piling up snow in a silver bowl, hiding a heron in the bright moonlight; when you array them they are not the same, when you mix them you know where they are.' Silver and snow, moonlight and the white heron, are all white, but when associated, they are not identically the same; this symbolizes the sameness within difference, the difference within sameness. Sameness and difference correspond to the 'heart of nirvana' (equanimity) and the 'knowledge of differentiation,' sometimes referred to as successive stages on the Ch'an path. It is this latter that is in the sphere of 'meeting another.'

d.   Kuan Nan Tao Wu, while on his foot travels, once heard a shamaness in a village spirit shrine take up her sceptre and intone her pledge to the spirit; at one point she said, 'Do you know the spirit or not?' whereupon Tao Wu was greatly enlightened. After travelling around to various places, he came to Kuan Nan Tao Ch'ang; to show his realization, Tao Wu flourished a sceptre, whereupon Tao Ch'ang recognized his enlightenment.

e.   Shih Kung, a successor of Ma Tsu, was formerly a hunter. Later, he used to draw his bow on those who came to ask about Ch'an. When San P'ing came to him, he drew his bow; San P'ing bared his breast and said, 'Is this a killing arrow or a life-giving arrow?' Shih Kung threw away his bow and said that after thirty years he had finally managed to shoot half a sage.

f.   This phrase also conveys the sense, 'his real point is distinct.'

Yun Men's Appropriate Statement

CASE

A monk asked Yun Men, "What are the teachings of a whole lifetime?"[1]

Yun Men said, "An appropriate statement."[2]

NOTES

1. Even up till now they're not finished with. The lecturer does not understand; he's in the cave of entangling complications.
2. An iron hammerhead with no handle-hole. A profuse outburst. A rat gnawing on raw ginger.

COMMENTARY

Members of the Ch'an family, if you want to know the meaning of Buddha-nature, you must observe times and seasons, causes and conditions. This is called the special transmission outside the (written) teachings, the sole transmission of the mind seal, directly pointing to the human mind for the perception of nature and realization of Buddhahood.

For forty-nine years old Shakyamuni stayed in the world; at three hundred and sixty assemblies he expounded the sudden and the gradual, the temporary and the true. These are what is called the teachings of a whole lifetime.[a] The monk (in this case) picked this out to ask, "What are the teachings of a whole lifetime?" Why didn't Yun Men explain for him in full detail, but instead said to him, "An appropriate statement"?

As usual, within one sentence of Yun Men three sentences are bound to be present. These are called the sentence that encloses heaven and earth, the sentence that follows the waves, and the sentence that cuts off the myriad streams. He lets go and gathers up; he's naturally extraordinary, like cutting nails or shearing through iron. He makes people unable to comprehend him or figure him out. The whole great treasure-house of the teachings just comes down to three words ("An appropriate statement"); there is no facet or aspect in which you can rationalize this.

People often misunderstand and say, "Buddha's preaching was appropriate to the conditions of one time." Or they say, "The multitude of appearances and myriad forms are all the impressions of a single truth,"[b] and call this "an appropriate statement." Then there are those who say, "It's just talking about that one truth." What connection is there? Not only do they not understand, they also enter hell as fast as an arrow flies. They are far from knowing that the meaning of that man of old is not like this.

Therefore it is said, "Shattering one's bones and crushing one's body is still not sufficient recompense; when a single phrase is understood, you transcend ten billion." Undeniably extraordinary: "What are the teachings of a whole lifetime?" just boils down to his saying, "An appropriate statement." If you can grasp this immediately, then you can return home and sit in peace. If you can't get it, then listen humbly to the verdict:

VERSE

An appropriate statement;
  ***Leaping with life.*
  The words are still in our ears.
  Undeniably unique and lofty. *

How utterly unique!
  ***The onlooker has some part in it.*
  Why only stand like a mile high wall?
  Is there any such thing? *

He wedges a stake into the iron hammerhead with no hole.
  ***He misunderstands the words. Old Yun Men too is*
  washing a lump of dirt in the mud; Hsueh Tou also
  is just pasting on ornaments. *

Under the Jambu Tree I'm laughing; ha, ha!
  ***This fellow has never been seen anywhere.*

Only those on the same path would know.
How many people could there be who know? *

Last night the black dragon had his horn wrenched off:
    * *It's not just the black dragon who gets twisted
    and broken. Has anyone seen? Do you have proof?
    Dumb!* *

Exceptional, exceptional—
    * *Ample praise; it takes Hsueh Tou to do this.
    Where is he exceptional?* *

The old man of Shao Yang got one horn. ᶜ
    * *Where is it? To whom is the other
    horn given? Te Shan and Lin Chi too
    must fall back three thousand miles.
    Again, what about that other horn? I strike!* *

COMMENTARY

"An appropriate statement; how utterly unique!" Hsueh Tou cannot praise him enough. These words of Yun Men are independent and free, unique and lofty, prior to light and after annihilation. They are like an overhanging cliff ten thousand fathoms high. Then, too, they are like a million man battle line; there is no place for you to get in. It's just that it's too solitary and perilous.

An Ancient said, "If you want to attain intimacy, don't use a question to ask a question; the question is in the answer and the answer is in the point of the question." Of course it's solitary and steep, but tell me, where is it that it's solitary and steep? No one on earth can do anything about it.

This monk (in the case) was also an adept, and that is why he could question like this. And Yun Men too answered this way, much like "wedging a stake into the iron hammerhead with no hole." Hsueh Tou employs literary language so artfully! "Under the Jambu Tree I'm laughing; ha, ha!" In the *Scripture on the Creation of the World* it says, "On the south side of Sumeru a crystal tree shines over the continent of Jambu, making all in between a clear blue color. This continent takes its name from this great tree; hence it is called Jambudvipa. This tree is seven thousand leagues high; beneath it are the golden mounds of the Jambu altar, which is twenty leagues high. Since gold is produced from beneath the tree, it is called the Jambu tree."

Thus Hsueh Tou says of himself that he is under the Jambu tree laughing out loud. But tell me, what is he laughing at? He's laughing at the black dragon who last night got his horn wrenched off. He's just looking up respectfully; he can only praise Yun Men. When Yun Men says, "An appropriate statement," what's it like? It's like breaking off one of the black dragon's horns. At this point, if there were no such thing, how could he have spoken as he did?

Hsueh Tou has finished his verse all at once, but he still has something to say at the very end: "Exceptional, exceptional—the old man of Shao Yang got one horn." Why doesn't Hsueh Tou say he got them both? How is it that he just got one horn? Tell me, where is the other horn?

TRANSLATOR'S NOTES

a. According to the analysis of Chih I, founder of the T'ien T'ai school of Chinese Buddhism, Buddha's teaching was divided into five periods: first, the period of the Hua Yen (Avatamsaka) scripture, where the Buddha directly expressed his own realization under the tree of enlightenment. Second, since no one at the time could understand the first, he expounded the Agamas for twelve years to suit elementary capacities. Third, he preached a transitional stage from this lesser to the greater vehicle, known as the extensive, or universally equal scriptures. Fourth, he preached the transcendence of wisdom. Fifth, he preached the Lotus of Truth (Saddharmapundarika) and Great Decease (Mahaparinirvana) scriptures. The teaching is divided by the Hua Yen school into the lesser vehicle, the elementary greater vehicle, the final greater vehicle, the sudden teaching, and the round, or complete teaching.

b. This saying comes from the *Dhammapada*; Yun Men's reply can be read as 'teaching in reference to one.'

c. The old man of Shao Yang is Yun Men. The horn is the stake driven into the holeless hammerhead. A hammerhead without a hole is an image used for something into which the 'handle' of logic and reason cannot be fit.

Yun Men's Upside-Down Statement

POINTER

The single-edged sword that kills people, the double-edged sword that brings people to life; the customary rule of high antiquity is still the pivotal essential for today. But tell me, right now, which is the sword that kills people, which is the sword that brings people to life? To test, I cite this; look!

CASE

A monk asked Yun Men, "When it's not the present intellect and it's not the present phenomena, what is it?"[1,a]
　　Yun Men said, "An upside-down statement."[2]

NOTES

1.　Why the leaping about? Fall back three thousand miles.
2.　They come out even. Truth comes out of the convict's mouth; he can't be let go. He stretches out his body in the wild weeds.

COMMENTARY

This monk is unquestionably an adept, to know how to pose questions like this. The question by the monk in the previous case is called "asking for more instruction"; in the present case it is a question to demonstrate understanding, and it can also be called a question with a concealed barb. For anyone but Yun Men, there would have been no way to cope with this monk. Yun Men possesses such ability that he cannot but reply once the question is raised. Why? An expert teaching master is like a bright mirror on its stand; if a foreigner comes a foreigner is reflected, and if a native comes a native is reflected.

An Ancient said, "If you want to attain intimate under-standing, don't use a question to ask a question. Why? Because the answer is where the question is." Since when have the sages from past times ever had anything to give to people? Where is there Ch'an or Tao that can be given to you? If you don't do hellish deeds, naturally you will not bring on hellish results. If you don't create heavenly conditions, naturally you won't receive heavenly rewards. All circumstances of activity are self-made and self-received. The Ancient Yun Men clearly tells you, "When we discuss this affair, it's not in the words and phrases. If it were in words and phrases, doesn't the twelve part canon of the three vehicles have words and phrases? Then what further use would there be for the Patriarch's coming from the West?"

In the previous case Yun Men said, "An appropriate state-ment." Here, on the other hand, he says, "An upside-down statement." Since there's only a difference of a single word, why then are there a thousand differences, ten thousand dis-tinctions? Tell me, where is the confusion? This is why it is said, "The Teaching is carried out according to facts; the ban-ner of the Teaching is set up according to the situation."

"When it's not the present intellect and it's not the present phenomena, what is it?" is just worth a nod of agreement. Since Yun Men is a fellow with eyes, he can't be fooled one little bit. Since the point of the question was abstruse and misleading, the answer too had to be this way. In fact Yun Men is riding the thief's horse in pursuit of the thief.

Some people mistakenly say, "Basically these are words of a host, but it was a guest who spoke them; therefore Yun Men said, 'An upside-down statement.'" What relevance does this have?

This monk asked well; "When it's not the present intellect and it's not the present phenomena, what is it?" Why didn't Yun Men answer him with some other words? Why instead did he just say to him, "An upside-down statement"? Yun Men at once demolished him utterly. Still, to say "an upside-down statement" at this point is to gouge out a wound in healthy flesh. Why? "The emergence of tracks of words is the source from which divergent opinions are born." Suppose there never were words and phrases; have this pillar and lamp right here ever had any words or phrases? Do you understand? If you don't understand at this point, you still need to turn over before you will know where the ultimate point of this is.

VERSE

An upside-down statement:
> **Can't let it go. Mixed up. He wraps up all five thousand and forty-eight volumes of the canon.*

Dividing one token,
> **Part on your side, part on my side.
> Half south of the river, half north of the river.
> Walking together holding hands.*

Dying with you, being born with you, to give you certainty.
> **Washing a lump of dirt in the mud. For what reason?
> He won't let you go.*

The eighty-four thousand disciples of Buddha were not
> *phoenix feathers;*
> **They looked like feathers. He diminishes these people's grandeur too much. Lacquer buckets are as plentiful as hemp and millet.*

Thirty-three men entered the tiger's den.
> **Only I can know. A single general is hard to find.
> A band of wild fox spirits.*

Distinctly outstanding—
> **How is it exceptional? A little boasting. Skip and leap as you will.*

The moon in the churning rushing water.
> **Under the blue sky and bright sun, he mistakes the reflection for the head. Why so busy?*

COMMENTARY

Hsueh Tou too is undeniably an adept. Right under the first line he immediately says, "Dividing one token." Clearly he lets go of the ultimate and joins hands with Yun Men to walk along together with him. Hsueh Tou has always had the technique of letting go; he dares to enter the mud and water for your sake, to die and be born together with you. This is the reason Hsueh Tou praises Yun Men this way. In reality he has no other purpose than to melt the glue and untie the bonds for you, to pull out the nails and wrench out the pegs.

These days, however, people base themselves on his words to spin out intellectual interpretations. Just as Yen T'ou said, "Although Hsueh Feng was born of the same lineage as me, he does not die of the same lineage as me." If Yun Men were not someone whose whole capacity had penetrated through to liberation, how could he die with you and be born with you? Why can he do this? Because he is free from the many leaking points of gain and loss, of is and is not.

Thus Tung Shan said, "If you would judge whether one going beyond is genuine or false, there are three kinds of leakage: emotional leakage, leakage of views, and verbal leakage. If there is leakage of views, the intellect does not stir from its fixed position and falls into the poisonous sea. If feelings leak, knowing always turns towards and against, and one's view is biased. Verbal leakage embodies the marvel but loses the fundamental; the intellect confuses beginning and end. You should know these three leaks for yourself."

There are also three mysteries; the mystery within the essence, the mystery within the phrase, and the mystery within the mystery.[b] When the Ancients came into this realm, their whole capacity was fully used: if you happened to be born, they would be born together with you; if you happened to die, they would die with you. They stretched out their bodies in the tiger's mouth; letting go their hands and feet, they would follow your lead for a thousand miles, for ten thousand miles. Why? You must go back with them to get this one realization before you'll understand.

As for "Eighty-four thousand disciples of Buddha were not phoenix feathers," this is the assembly of eighty-four thousand holy people on Vulture Peak of Spirit Mountain—they were not phoenix feathers.[c] The *Southern History* relates that in Sung times (420-479) there lived Hsieh Ch'ao-tsung ("surpassing his clan"), a man of Yang Hsia in Ch'en prefecture, the son of Hsieh Feng ("phoenix"). He had studied widely and his literary talent was superlative. At court there was no one to equal him; his contemporaries considered him unique. Since he was skilled in the written word, he served as permanent attendant at the capital. For the funeral ceremonies of the king's mother Yinshu, Ch'ao-tsung composed a eulogy and presented it at court. Emperor Wu saw what he had written and praised him highly, saying, "Ch'ao-tsung does indeed have phoenix feathers!" An old poem says,

> Audiences over, the incense smoke fills his billow-
> ing sleeves;
> In the perfection of a poem, the perfect jewel lies in
> the stroke of his brushtip.
> If you want to know the excellence of the hereditary
> managers of Imperial decrees,
> On the pond right now there's a phoenix feather
> floating.

In ancient times, at the assembly on Spirit Mountain, the four groups (monks, nuns, men and women devotees) had gathered like clouds. The World Honored One held up a flower; Kashyapa alone changed his expression with a smile. The others did not know his meaning. Taking this, Hsueh Tou says, "The eighty-four thousand were not phoenix feathers; thirty-three men entered the tiger's den."

Ananda asked Kashyapa, "The World Honored One bequeathed to you his golden robe; what special teaching did he transmit besides?" Kashyapa called out "Ananda!" Ananda responded. Then Kashyapa said, "Take down the banner pole in front of the gate."[d] Thereafter it was handed on from patriarch to patriarch, in India and this country, through thirty-three men. All had the ability to enter the tiger's den. The Ancients said, "If you don't enter the tiger's den, how can you catch a tiger cub?" Yun Men is this kind of man, well able to accompany people through birth and death. To help people, a teacher of our school must get to be like this, to sit in the carved wood seat of the teachers; abandoned, he makes you break open and lets you grab the tiger's whiskers. He must have reached such a realm to be able to teach. He has the seven things[e] always with him, so he can accompany (beings) through life and death. The high he presses down, the low he uplifts; to those who lack he gives. Those on the solitary peak he rescues and sends them into the wild weeds; if they have fallen into the wild weeds, he rescues them and puts them on the solitary peak. "If you enter a molten cauldron or a fiery furnace, I too will enter the molten cauldron and the fiery furnace." In reality there is no other purpose, just to melt the sticking points and release the bonds for you, to pull out nails and draw out pegs, to strip off the blinders, to unload the saddle bags. Master P'ing T'ien had a most excellent verse:

> *Spiritual light undimmed,*
> *Ages of good advice.*
> *Once it comes through this door,*
> *Don't keep any intellectual understanding.*

"Distinctly outstanding—the moon in the churning rushing water." Hsueh Tou unfailingly has a way to show himself, and also the skill to bring people to life. Hsueh Tou has picked this out to get people to go themselves to awaken their living potential. Don't follow another's words; if you follow them, that indeed would be the moon in the churning rushing water. Right now, how will you find peace and security? Let go!

TRANSLATOR'S NOTES

a. The monk in this case is supposed to be the same as in the fourteenth; the teachings of the age are devised and established according to the state of the intellect and total capacity of the hearers, in terms of the phenomenal situation. In an immediate sense, the present intellect and phenomena mean perceiver and perceived; according to Tenkei, the monk had seen that there is nothing outside of mind, and that all things are empty.

b. Also translated as three profundities, this was a classification of the Lin Chi school, interpreted variously through the ages. The mystery within the essence corresponds to the phrase that encloses heaven and earth; the mystery within the phrase corresponds to the phrase that follows the waves; the mystery within the mystery corresponds to the phrase that cuts off myriad streams. Yun Men's replies are said to contain all three of these aspects.

c. Phoenix feather is a metaphor for someone of outstanding talent, and also for a worthy successor.

d. The banner in front of a monastery in India signaled that teaching and debate were going on therein (see the commentary to case 13).

e. The seven items of a teacher are 1) great capacity and great function 2) swiftness of intellect 3) wondrous spirituality of speech 4) the active edge to kill or give life 5) wide learning and broad experience 6) clarity of mirroring awareness 7) freedom to appear and disappear.

Ching Ch'ing's Man in the Weeds

POINTER

The Path has no byroads; one who stands upon it is solitary and dangerous.[a] The truth is not seeing or hearing; words and thoughts are far removed from it. If you can penetrate through the forest of thorns and untie the bonds of Buddhahood and Patriarchy, you attain the land of inner peace, where all the gods have no way to offer flowers, where outsiders have no gate to spy through. Then you work all day without ever working, talk all day without ever talking; then you can unfold the device of 'breaking in and breaking out' and use the double-edged sword that kills and brings to life, with freedom and independence.

Even if you are this way, you must also know that within the gate of provisional expedients, there is 'one hand uplifting, one hand pressing down'; yet this still only amounts to a little bit: as for the fundamental matter, this has nothing to do with it. What about the fundamental matter? To test, I cite this; look!

CASE

A monk asked Ching Ch'ing, "I am breaking out; I ask the Teacher to break in."[1]
Ching Ch'ing said, "Can you live or not?"[2]
The monk said, "If I weren't alive, I'd be laughed at by people."[3]
Ching Ch'ing said, "You too are a man in the weeds."[4]

NOTES

1. Why raise waves where there's no wind? What do you want with so many views?

104

2. A jab. He buys the hat to fit the head. He adds error to error. Everyone can't be this way.
3. He drags others into it. He's holding up the sky and supporting the earth; the board-carrying fellow!
4. After all. Take what's coming to you and get out. He can't be let go.

COMMENTARY

Ching Ch'ing was a successor of Hsueh Feng, and a contemporary of the likes of Peṇ Jen, Hsuan Sha, Su Shan, and Fu of T'ai Yuan. First he met Hsueh Feng and understood his message. Thereafter he always used 'breaking in and breaking out' devices to instruct later students. He was well able to expound the teaching according to the potentialities of his listeners.

Once Ching Ch'ing taught the community saying, "In general, foot-travelers must have the 'simultaneous breaking in and breaking out' eye and must have the 'simultaneous breaking in and breaking out' function; only then can they be called patchrobed monks. It's like when the mother hen wants to break in, the chick must break out, and when the chick wants to break out, the mother hen must break in."

Thereupon a monk came forward and asked, "When the mother hen breaks in and the chick breaks out, from the standpoint of the teacher, what does this amount to?" Ching Ch'ing said, "Good news." The monk asked, "When the chick breaks out and the mother hen breaks in, from the standpoint of the student, what does this amount to?" Ching Ch'ing said, "Revealing his face." From this we see that they did have the device of 'simultaneous breaking in and breaking out' in Ching Ch'ing's school.

This monk (in the case) was also a guest of his house, and understood (Ching Ch'ing's) household affairs; therefore he questioned like this: "I am breaking out; I ask the Teacher to break in." Within the Ts'ao-Tung tradition this is called using phenomena to illustrate one's condition. How so? When the chick breaks out and the mother breaks in, naturally they are perfectly simultaneous.

Ching Ch'ing too does well; we could say his fists and feet are coordinated, his mind and eye illumine each other. He answered immediately by saying, "Can you live or not?" The monk too does well; he also knows how to change with the circumstances. In this one sentence of Ching Ch'ing's there is guest and there is host, there is illumination and there is function, there is killing and there is giving life.

The monk said, "If I weren't alive, I'd be laughed at by people." Ching Ch'ing said, "You too are a man in the weeds." He's first class at going into the mud and water, but nothing stops his wicked hands and feet. Since the monk understood enough to question in this way, why did Ching Ch'ing nevertheless say, "You too are a man in the weeds"? Because the eye of an adept must be this way, like sparks struck from stone, like flashing lightning. Whether you can reach it or not, you won't avoid losing your body and life. If you are this way, then you see Ching Ch'ing calling him a man in the weeds.

Therefore Nan Yuan taught his assembly saying, "In the various places they only have the eye of simultaneous breaking in and breaking out, but they don't have the function of simultaneous breaking in and breaking out." A monk came forward and asked, "What is the function of simultaneous breaking in and breaking out?" Nan Yuan said, "An adept does not break in and break out; breaking in and breaking out are both at once error." The monk said, "This is still doubtful to me." Nan Yuan said, "What are you in doubt about?" The monk said, "Error." Thereupon Nan Yuan struck him; the monk did not agree, so Nan Yuan drove him out.

Later this monk went to Yun Men's community, where he brought up the previous conversation. There was a monk who said, "Did Nan Yuan's staff break?" The first monk was greatly awakened. But tell me, where is the meaning? This monk returned to see Nan Yuan, but since Nan Yuan had already passed on, he saw Feng Hsueh instead. As soon as he bowed, Feng Hsueh asked, "Aren't you the monk who was asking our late teacher about the simultaneous breaking in and breaking out?" The monk said, "That's right." Feng Hsueh asked, "What was your understanding at that time?" The monk said, "At first it was as if I were walking in the light of a lamp." Feng Hsueh said, "You've understood." But say, what principle is this? This monk came and just said, "At first it was as if I were walking in the light of a lamp." Why did Feng Hsueh immediately tell him, "You've understood"?

Later Ts'ui Yen commented, "Although Nan Yuan puts his

plans into operation from within his tent, nevertheless the country is vast, the people are few, and sympathizers are rare." Feng Hsueh commented, "At the time Nan Yuan should have hit him right across the back the moment he opened his mouth, to see what he would do." If you see this public case, then you see where the monk and Ching Ch'ing met each other. How will all of you avoid Ching Ch'ing calling you a man in the weeds? For this reason Hsueh Tou likes his saying "man in the weeds," so he presents it in verse:

VERSE

The Ancient Buddhas had a family style;
     ***The words are still in our ears. The model for all time.
     Don't slander old Shakyamuni.**

Responsive preaching comes to scornful detraction
     ***Why are your nostrils in my hand? Eight blows pays for
     thirteen. What about you? He lets the initiative go, so I'll
     strike.**

Chick and mother hen do not know each other;
     ***Since they don't know each other, why then
     do they naturally break in and break out?**

Who is it that breaks in and breaks out together?
     ***Shattered in a hundred fragments. (Hsueh Tou) has the
     kindness of an old granny; but don't misunderstand.**

A peck, and he awakens;
     ***What are you saying? You've fallen into the second-
     ary.**

But he's still in the shell.
     ***Why doesn't he stick his head out?**

Once again he receives a blow;
     ***Wrong! I strike! A double case; triple, quadruple.**

*All the patchrobed monks in the world name and describe it
     in vain.*
     ***He has let go; he needn't bring it up. Is there anyone
     who can name or describe it? If there is, he too is a
     man in the weeds. From remote antiquity, the dark-
     ness is vast and boundless; it fills the channels and
     clogs the gullies. No one understands.**

COMMENTARY

With the one line "The Ancient buddhas had a family style," Hsueh Tou has completed his verse. Whoever sticks his head out simply won't be able to approach. If you do approach, you'll fall off a cliff ten thousand miles high. As soon as you come out, you've fallen into the weeds. Even if you can go freely in all directions, it wouldn't be worth a pinch.

Hsueh Tou says, "The Ancient buddhas had a family style." It's not just right now that this is so; when old Shakyamuni was first born, he pointed to the sky with one hand and to the earth with the other hand, scanned the four directions and said, "In the heavens and on earth, I alone am the Honored One." Yun Men said, "If I had seen him then, I would have struck him dead with one blow and fed him to the dogs, hoping that there would be peace in the world." Only by being like this can one reply appropriately. Thus, devices of breaking in and breaking out are all in the family tradition of the Ancient Buddhas.

If you can attain to this Path, then you'll be able to knock down a mountain fortress with one blow of your fist, you'll be able to topple a cliff-top temple with a single kick. It's like a great mass of fire; approach it, and it will burn off your face. It's like the T'ai Ya Sword; fool around with it and you lose your body and life. For this one, only those who have penetrated through and gained the great liberation will be able to act like this. Otherwise, if you miss the source and get stuck in the words, you definitely won't be able to grasp this kind of talk.

"Responsive preaching comes to scornful detraction." This then is 'one guest, one host, one question, one answer.' Right in the asking and answering, there's the scornful detraction. It's called "responsive preaching comes to scornful detraction." Hsueh Tou has deep knowledge of this matter, so he can complete his verse in only two lines.

At the end it's just Hsueh Tou going down into the weeds to explain things thoroughly for you. "Chick and mother hen do not know each other; who is it that breaks in and breaks out together?" Although the mother hen breaks in, she cannot cause the chick to break out; although the chick breaks out, he cannot cause the mother hen to break in. Neither is aware of the other. At the moment of breaking in and breaking out, who is it that breaks in and breaks out together?

If you understand this way, you still haven't been able to get beyond Hsueh Tou's final line. Why? Haven't you heard Hsiang Yen's saying,

> *The chick breaks out, the mother hen breaks in—*
> *When the chick awakens, there is no shell.*
> *Chick and hen both forgotten,*
> *Response to circumstance is unerring.*
> *On the same path, chanting in harmony,*
> *Through the marvelous mystery, walking alone.*

Nevertheless Hsueh Tou comes down into the weeds and creates entangling complications by saying, "A peck." This one word praises Ching Ch'ing's answer, "Can you live or not?" "He awakens" praises the monk's reply, "If I weren't alive, I'd be laughed at by people." Whey then does Hsueh Tou go ahead and say, "He's still in the shell"? Hsueh Tou can distinguish initiated from uninitiated in the light of a stone-struck spark; he can discern the clue to the whole thing in the flash of a lightening bolt.

Ching Ch'ing said, "You too are a man in the weeds." Hsueh Tou says, "Once again he receives a blow." This difficult part is correct. Ching Ch'ing said, "You too are a man in the weeds." Can this be called snatching the man's eyeballs away? Doesn't this line mean he's still in the shell? But this has nothing to do with it. How so? If you don't understand, you can travel on foot all over the world and still not be able to requite your debt. When I talk like this, I too am a man in the weeds.

"All the patchrobed monks in the world name and describe it in vain." Who doesn't name and describe? At this point, Hsueh Tou himself cannot name or describe it, yet he drags in others, the patchrobed monks of the world. But tell me, how did Ching Ch'ing help this monk? No patchrobed monk in the world can leap out.

TRANSLATOR'S NOTES

a.   Expressions such as 'solitary and steep,' 'solitary and dangerous (high)' are used to describe the method of an adept who is bringing up 'the true imperative,' likened to a steep and precipitous mountain peak which is unapproachable, offering no hand or foot hold, nothing to grasp. It is dangerous because if you approach you may lose your life.

Hsiang Lin's Meaning of the Coming from the West

POINTER

Cut through nails and shear through iron, then you can be a genuine master of our school. If you run away from arrows and avoid swords, how could you possibly be a competent adept? The place where even a needle cannot enter, I leave aside for now; but tell me, what's it like when the foamy waves are flooding the skies? To test, I cite this; look!

CASE

A monk asked Hsiang Lin, "What is the meaning of the Patriarch's coming from the West?"[1]

Hsiang Lin said, "Sitting for a long time becomes toilsome."[2,a]

NOTES

1. There have been many people with doubts about this; there is still news of this around.
2. When a fish swims through, the water is muddied; when a bird flies by, feathers drop down. Better shut that dog's mouth. The eye of an adept. A saw cutting apart a scale beam.[b]

COMMENTARY

Hsiang Lin says, "Sitting for a long time becomes toilsome." Understand? If you do understand, then you can put down your shield and spear on the hundred grasses. If you don't understand, then listen humbly to this treatment.

When the Ancients travelled on foot, forming associations with chosen friends to travel together as companions on the Path, they would pull out the weeds and look for the way. At the time Yun Men was causing the teaching to flourish throughout Kuang Nan. Hsiang Lin had made his way by stages out of Shu (Ssuchuan). He was contemporary with E Hu and Ching Ch'ing. He first went to Pao Tz'u Temple in Hunan; only later did he come to Yun Men's congregation, where he was an attendant for eighteen years.

At Yun Men's place he personally attained and personally heard; though the time of his enlightenment was late, nevertheless he was a man of great faculties. He stayed at Yun Men's side for eighteen years; time and again Yun Men would just call out to him, "Attendant Yuan!" As soon as he responded, Yun Men would say, "What is it?" At such times, no matter how much (Hsiang Lin) spoke to present his understanding and gave play to his spirit, he never reached mutual accord (with Yun Men). One day, though, he suddenly said, "I understand." Yun Men said, "Why don't you say something above and beyond this?" Hsiang Lin stayed on for another three years. Yun Men's eloquent elucidations of states uttered in his room were mostly so that Attendant Yuan could enter in actively wherever he was. Whenever Yun Men had some saying or remark, they were all gathered by Attendant Yuan.[c]

Later Hsiang Lin returned to Shu, where he stayed at the Crystal Palace Temple on Ch'ing Ch'eng Mountain.

Master Chih Men Tso was originally from Chekiang. Filled with what he had heard of Hsiang Lin teaching the Path, he came especially to Shu to meet him and pay homage. Tso was Hsueh Tou's master. Though Yun Men converted people without number, of all the wayfarers of that generation, Hsiang Lin's stream flourished most. After he came back to Shu, he lived in temples (teaching) for forty years; he didn't pass on until he was eighty. He once said, "Only when I was forty did I attain unity."

Ordinarily he would teach his assembly saying, "Whenever you go travelling on foot to search for men of knowledge, you must bring along the eye to distinguish initiate from uninitiate, to tell shallow from deep, then you'll be all right. First you must establish your resolve, just as old man Shakyamuni did when he was in the causal ground; wherever he thought or spoke, it was always to set his resolve."

Later a monk asked, "What is the saucer-lamp within the room?"ᵈ Lin said, "If three people testify that it's a turtle, then it's a turtle." Again he asked, "What is the affair underneath the patched robe?" Lin said, "The conflagration of the end of time burns up the mountain."

Since the old days, very many answers have been given for the meaning of the Patriarch's coming from the West. Only Hsiang Lin, right here in this case, has cut off the tongues of everyone on earth; there is no place for you to calculate or make up rationalizations. The monk asked, "What is the meaning of the Patriarch's coming from the West?" Lin said, "Sitting for a long time becomes toilsome." This could be called flavorless words, flavorless phrases; flavorless talk blocks off people's mouths and leaves you no place to show your energy. If you would see, then just see immediately. If you don't see, it's urgent you avoid entertaining intellectual understanding.

Hsiang Lin had encountered an adept; consequently he possessed Yun Men's technique and harmonious mastery of the 'three phrases' (of Yun Men). People often misunderstand and say, "The Patriarch came from the West and sat facing a wall for nine years; isn't this sitting for a long time and becoming weary?" What is there to hold on to? They don't see that the Ancient Hsiang Lin had attained the realm of great independence, that his feet tread upon the real earth; without so many views and theories of Buddha Dharma, he could meet the situation and function accordingly. As it is said, "The Teaching is carried on according to facts; the banner of the Teaching is set up according to the situation."

Hsueh Tou uses this wind to fan the fire, and from his position as a bystander points out one or a half:

VERSE

One, two, a thousand, ten thousand;
  **Why not practice accordingly?
  As plentiful as hemp and millet;
  why are they congregating into a crowd?*
Strip off the blinders, unload the saddle bags.
  **From today on, you must be purified, clean
  and at ease. Can you rest yet, or not?*

Turning to the left, turning to the right, following up behind;
  **You still can't let yourself go. Reflections upon reflec-*
  *tions, echoes upon echoes. I strike!**

Tzu Hu had to hit Iron Grindstone Liu.
  **I'd break the staff and no longer carry*
  out this order. He draws his bow after
  *the thief has gone, so I strike. Danger!**

COMMENTARY

Hsueh Tou strikes directly, like sparks struck from stone, like
the brilliance of a flash of lightening; he presses out and releases to get you to see, which you can do only if you understand it immediately as soon as you hear it being brought up.

Undeniably Hsueh Tou is a descendant of Hsiang Lin's
house; thus he is able to talk this way. If you can directly and
immediately understand in this way, then nothing can stop
you from being extraordinary.

"One, two, a thousand, ten thousand; strip off the blinders,
unload the saddle bags." Purified, clean and at ease, they are
not stained by birth and death, they are not bound by emotional interpretations of sanctity and profanity. Above, there's
nothing to look to for support; below, they've cut off their
personal selves. They're just like Hsiang Lin and Hsueh Tou;
how could there be just a thousand or ten thousand? In fact all
the people in the world, each and every one, are all like this.
The past and future Buddhas are all like this too.

If you make up interpretative understandings on the words,
then this is like "Tzu Hu had to hit Iron Grindstone Liu." In
fact, as soon as (such interpretations) are raised, Hsueh Tou
strikes while you are still speaking. Tzu Hu studied under Nan
Ch'uan; he was a fellow student of Chao Chou and Tiger Ts'en
(Ch'ang Sha). At that time Iron Grindstone Liu had set up a hut
on Mt. Kuei. People from all over couldn't cope with her. One
day Tzu Hu came proudly to call on her; he asked, "You're Iron
Grindstone Liu, aren't you?" The Grindstone said, "I don't
presume (to say so)." Hu asked, "Do you turn to the left or turn
to the right?" The Grindstone said, "Don't tip over, Teacher."
Hu struck her while her words were still in the air.

Answering the monk who asked, "What is the meaning of
the Patriarch's coming from the West?" Hsiang Lin said, "Sit-

ting for a long time becomes toilsome." If you understand this way, you are "turning to the left, turning to the right, following up behind." But tell me, what is Hsueh Tou's meaning in versifying like this?

TRANSLATOR'S NOTES

a. Hsiang Lin's reply could also be glossed as "sitting for a long time becomes tiring," or "sitting for a long time becomes hard work." Tenkei said, "When you sit for a long time your legs hurt: it's nothing special—the eyes are horizontal, the nose vertical; though everyone knows, because they are not aware of it (Hsiang Lin) just lets everyone know that they breathe through their noses. Is there any patriarch's meaning in there? If you call it an answer as to the meaning of the coming from the West, it's a worthless bag, a worn-out loincloth." A popular legend has it that Bodhidharma's legs crumbled to dust as he sat still for nine years facing a wall at the Shao Lin monastery. Dogen said that the Way is actually realized by the body. This *kung an* should not be applied to person only, but also to things. The "ground of reality" which one must tread to see this case could also be glossed as "real earth" from a certain point of view.

b. According to commentators, this means that it is hard to penetrate.

c. It is said that Yun Men forbade the recording of his words; however, Hsiang Lin stealthily wrote them down on his paper robe. They were compiled by Shou Chien, another of Yun Men's successors.

d. The lamp symbolizes wisdom; the room symbolizes stability. Without the stability of meditation, the flame of wisdom is blown by the wind of passion.

National Teacher Chung's Seamless Monument

CASE

Emperor Su Tsung[1] asked National Teacher Hui Chung, "After you die, what will you need?"[2]

The National Teacher said, "Build a seamless monument for me."[3]

The Emperor said, "Please tell me, Master, what the monument would look like."[4]

The National Teacher was silent for a long time; then he asked, "Do you understand?"[5]

The Emperor said, "I don't understand."[6]

The National Teacher said, "I have a disciple to whom I have transmitted the Teaching, Tan Yuan, who is well versed in this matter. Please summon him and ask him about it."[7]

After the National Teacher passed on,[8] the Emperor summoned Tan Yuan and asked him what the meaning of this was.[9] Tan Yuan said,

> South of Hsiang, north of T'an;[10]
> Hsueh Tou added the comment, "A single hand does not make random sound."[11]
> In between there's gold sufficient to a nation.[12]
> Hsueh Tou added the comment, "A rough-hewn staff."[13]
> Beneath the shadowless tree, the community ferryboat;[14]
> Hsueh Tou added the comment, "The sea is calm, the rivers are clear."[15]
> Within the crystal palace, there's no one who knows.[16]
> Hsueh Tou added the comment, "He has raised it up."[17]

NOTES

1. This is a mistake; actually it was Tai Tsung.
2. He scratches before it itches. As it turns out, (Hui Chung) will create a model and draw a likeness; though great and venerable, he acts this way—he shouldn't point to the east as the west.[a]
3. It can't be grasped.
4. He gives (Chung) a good poke.
5. Confined in prison, he increases in wisdom. After all he points to the east as the west and takes the south as the north. All he can do is frown.
6. It's fortunate that he doesn't understand; if he had pressed (Chung) further at this time and made him gulp a mouthful of frost, then he would have gotten somewhere.
7. He's lucky that the Emperor did not overturn his meditation seat; why didn't (Chung) give him some of his own provisions? Don't confuse the man. (Chung) let the initiative go.
8. What a pity! After all (the Emperor) will mistakenly go by the zero point of the scale.
9. The son takes up the father's work. He too falls into the second level, into the third level.
10. This too can't be grasped. Two by two, three by three—what are you doing? Half open, half closed.
11. One blind man leading a crowd of blind men. After all (Hsueh Tou) is following his words to produce interpretations. Why follow falsehood and pursue evil?
12. Above is the sky, below is the earth. I've had no such news. Whose concern is this?
13. It's been broken. This too is creating a model and drawing a likeness.
14. The Patriarch has perished. What are you saying, Reverend?
15. When vast swells of expansive white waves flood the skies, this still only amounts to a little bit.
16. Bah!
17. He draws his bow after the thief has gone. The words are still in our ears.

COMMENTARY

Su Tsung and Tai Tsung were both descendants of Hsuan Tsung. When they were princes, they were always fond of studying meditation. Because there was a great upheaval in his realm,[b] Hsuan Tsung finally fled to Shu. The T'ang dynasty originally had its capital at Ch'ang An; but because it was occupied by An Lu Shan, later (the capital) was moved to Lo Yang.

When Su Tsung came to power, National Teacher Chung was dwelling in a hut on White Cliff Mountain in Teng Chou (in Hunan). Today this is the Fragrant Cliff (Hsiang Yen) monastery. Though he did not come down from the mountain for more than forty years, word of his practice of the Way reached the Imperial precincts. In 761 the Emperor Su Tsung sent his personal emissary to summon Chung to enter the Imperial palace (to teach). The Emperor treated Chung with the etiquette due a teacher, and greatly honored him. Chung once lectured on the Supreme Path for the Emperor. When the Master departed from court, the Emperor himself escorted his carriage and saw him off. The courtiers were all angry at this and wanted to make their displeasure known to the Emperor. But the National Teacher had the power to know the minds of others, so he saw the Emperor first and told him, "In the presence of Indra, I have seen Emperors scattered like grains, evanescent as a flash of lightening." The Emperor respected him even more after this.

When Tai Tsung succeeded to the throne (in 762) he again invited (Chung) to come to the Abode of Light Temple. Chung stayed in the capital for sixteen years, expounding the Dharma according to the occasion, until he passed on in 776.

Formerly the Master of Blue File Mountain in Shan Man Fu had been the National Teacher's travelling companion. The National Teacher once asked the Emperor to summon him to court, but he did not rise to three Imperial commands; he would always upbraid the National Teacher for being addicted to fame and fortune, and for liking the company of people.

Chung was National Teacher under two emperors, father and son. In that family father and son studied meditation at the same time. According to the *Record of the Transmission of the Lamp*, it was Tai Tsung who asked the questions in the present case. When the National Teacher was asked, "What is the Ten-Body Controller?" (case 99), this on the other hand was Su Tsung's question.

When the National Teacher's life was over and he was about to enter nirvana, he was taking leave of Tai Tsung. Tai Tsung asked, "After your death,ᶜ what will you need?" This is just an ordinary question. The old fellow (Chung) stirred up waves where there was no wind and said, "Build a seamless monument for me." Under the bright sun and blue sky, why answer like this? It should have been enough to build a monument; why then did he say to build a seamless monument? But Tai Tsung too was an adept: he pressed him and said, "Please tell me, Master, what the monument would look like?" The National Teacher remained silent for a long time, then said, "Do you understand?" How extraordinary this little bit is; it's most difficult to approach. When pressed by the Emperor, the National Teacher, supposedly so great, could only frown. Although this is so, anyone but this old fellow (Chung) would probably have been bowled over.

Quite a few people say that the National Teacher's not speaking is itself what the monument is like. If you understand in this fashion, Bodhidharma and all his family would be wiped off the face of the earth. If you say that keeping silent is it, then mutes too must understand Ch'an.

Haven't you heard how an outsider asked the Buddha, "I don't ask about the spoken, I don't ask about the unspoken." The World Honored One remained silent. The outsider bowed in homage and sighed in praise; he said, "The World Honored One's great mercy and great compassion has dispersed the clouds of my delusions and caused me to gain entry." After the outsider had left, Ananda asked the Buddha, "What did the outsider witness, that he said he had gained entry?" The World Honored One said, "In worldly terms he's like a good horse; he goes when he sees the shadow of the whip." People often go to the silence for their understanding. What is there to grasp?

My late teacher Wu Tsu brought up (the 'seamless monument') and said, "In front it is pearls and agate, in back it is agate and pearls; on the east are Avalokitesvara and Mahasthamaprapta, on the west are Manjusri and Samantabhadra;ᵈ in the middle there's a flag blown by the wind, saying 'Flap, flap.'"

The National Teacher asked, "Do you understand?" The Emperor said, "I don't understand," yet he had attained a little bit. But tell me, is this "I don't understand" the same as Emperor Wu's "I don't know" (case 1), or is it different? Although they seem the same, actually they're not.

The National Teacher said, "I have a disciple to whom I have transmitted the Teaching, Tan Yuan, who is well versed in this matter. Please summon him and ask him about it." Putting aside Tai Tsung's not understanding for the moment, did Tan Yuan understand? All that was needed was to say, "Please, Teacher, what would the monument look like?"—no one in the world can do anything about it. My late teacher Wu Tsu commented by saying, "You are the teacher of a whole nation; why is it that you don't speak, but instead defer to your disciple?"

After the National Teacher died, the Emperor summoned Tan Yuan, to ask about the meaning of this. Tan Yuan then came on behalf of the National Teacher and explained the principle with foreign words and native speech; naturally he understood what the National Teacher had said, and just needed a single verse (to explain):

> South of Hsiang, north of T'an:[e]
> Within there's gold sufficient to a nation.
> Beneath the shadowless tree, the community fer-
> ryboat;
> Within the crystal palace, there's no one who
> knows.

Tan Yuan, whose name was Ying Chen, served as an attendant at the National Teacher's place. Later he dwelt at Tan Yuan Temple in Chi Chou (in Kiangsi). At this time Yang Shan came to see Tan Yuan. Tan Yuan's words were severe, his nature harsh and unapproachable. It was impossible to stay there, so at first Yang Shan went and saw the Ch'an master Hsing K'ung. There was a monk who asked Hsing K'ung, "What is the meaning of the Patriarch's coming from the West?" Hsing K'ung said, "It's as if a man were down in a thousand foot deep well; if you could get this man out without using even an inch of rope, then I would tell you the meaning of the Patriarch's coming from the West." The monk said, "These days Master Ch'ang of Hunan is talking this way and that for people too." Hsing K'ung then called to Yang Shan, "Novice, drag this corpse out of here!"

Later Yang Shan took this up with Tan Yuan and asked, "How can you get the man out of the well?" Tan Yuan said, "Bah! Ignoramus! Who is in the well?" Yan Shan didn't understand. Later he asked Kuei Shan. Kuei Shan immediately called out (Yang Shan's name) "Hui Chi!" When Yang Shan responded, Kuei Shan said, "He's out." At this Yang Shan was greatly enlightened. He said, "At Tan Yuan's I attained the essence; at Kuei Shan's I attained the function."

As for this little verse of Tan Yuan's, it has led not a few people into false interpretations. People often misunderstand and say, "*Hsiang* is the *hsiang* of 'meet' (*hsiang-chien*); *T'an* is the *t'an* of 'discuss' (*t'an-lun*). In between there's a seamless memorial tower, hence the verse says, 'In between there's gold sufficient to a nation.' 'Beneath the shadowless tree, the community ferryboat' is the interchange between the National Teacher and the Emperor. The Emperor did not understand, so the verse says, 'Inside the crystal palace there's no one who knows.'"

Again, some say, "The first line means south of Hsiang Chou and north of T'an Chou; 'In between there's gold sufficient to a nation' praises the Emperor." Then they blink their eyes, look around, and say, "This is the seamless monument." If you understand in such a way, you have not gone beyond emotional views.

As for Hsueh Tou's four turning words, how will you understand them? People today are far from knowing the Ancient's meaning. Tell me, how do you understand "South of Hsiang, north of T'an"? How do you understand "Within there's gold sufficient to a nation"? How do you understand "Beneath the shadowless tree, the community ferryboat"? How do you understand "Within the crystal palace, there's no one who knows"? If you can see this as Hsueh Tou and I do, nothing can prevent a whole life of joy and happiness.

"South of Hsiang, north of T'an." Hsueh Tou says, "A single hand does not make a random sound." He couldn't but explain for you. "Within there's gold sufficient to a nation." Hsueh Tou says, "A rough-hewn staff." An Ancient said, "If you know the staff, the work of your whole life's study is complete." "Beneath the shadowless tree, the community ferry." Hsueh Tou says, "The sea is calm, the rivers are clear." Open the windows and doors all at once—on all sides gleaming clarity. "Inside the crystal palace, there's no one who knows." Hsueh Tou says, "He's raised it." After all he's gotten somewhere. Hsueh Tou has spoken clearly all at once; afterwards he simply eulogizes the seamless monument.

VERSE

The seamless monument—
　　***How big is this one seam?*
　　What are you saying?*

To see it is hard.
　　***It's not something eyes can see.*
　　Blind!*

A clear pool does not admit the blue dragon's coils.
　　***Do you see? Great waves, vast, gigantic. Where*
　　will the blue dragon go to coil up? Here it just
　　cannot be found.*

Layers upon layers.
　　***No optical illusions! What are you doing,*
　　seeing optical illusions?*

Shadows upon shadows—
　　***Your whole body is an eye. You*
　　fall into sevens and eights. Two by
　　two, three by three, walking the old
　　road; turning to the left, turning
　　to the right, following up behind.*

For ever and ever it is shown to people.
　　***Do you see? How will blind people see?*
　　Can you catch a glimpse of it, Reverend?*

COMMENTARY

Right off Hsueh Tou says, "The seamless monument—To see it is hard." Though it stands alone revealed with nothing hidden, when you want to see it, it's still hard to do so. Hsueh Tou is exceedingly compassionate, and tells you more: "A clear pool does not admit the blue dragon's coils." My late master Wu Tsu said, "In Hsueh Tou's whole volume of eulogies on the ancients, I just like the line, 'A clear pool does not admit the blue dragon's coils.'" Still, this amounts to something.

Quite a few people go to the National Teacher's silence for their sustenance; if you understand in this way, you at once go wrong. Haven't you heard it said, "Reclining dragons aren't to be seen in stagnant water; where they are not, there's moonlight and the ripples settle, but where they are, waves arise without wind." Again, it was said, "Reclining dragons always fear the blue pool's clarity." As for this fellow Hsueh Tou, even if vast swelling billows of white waves flooded the sky, he still wouldn't coil up in there.

When Hsueh Tou gets to this, his verse is finished. Afterwards he applies a little bit of eye and carves a seamless monument. Following up behind he says, "Layers upon layers, Shadows upon shadows—For ever and ever it is shown to people." How will you look upon it? Where is it right now? Even if you see it clearly, don't mistakenly stick by the zero point of the scale.

TRANSLATOR'S NOTES

a. The three clauses of this sentence can be taken in reference to the Emperor or to Hui Chung. In the original these notes of Yuan Wu's are inserted right in the text; though they usually refer to the preceding passage, occasionally they apply to the succeeding sentence. The pronoun 'he'—absent in the original but added by the translator for grammatical English—normally refers to the same subject as the clause noted. Commentators frequently point out that it applies to you too.

b. In 755 the military man An Lushan, commander of powerful border armies on China's northern frontier, began a revolt aimed at supplanting the T'ang dynasty with his own regime. The fighting dragged on for more than five years, even after An Lushan himself had died, ravaging much of northern China, and dealing the ruling house of T'ang a blow from which it never fully recovered. Thereafter the sufferings of the people increased as rival military commanders struggled with each other and with the Imperial court for control of the revenues of the land. Hsuan Tsung fled from the capital Ch'ang An to the city of Ch'eng Tu in Szechuan (ancient Shu) in western China—a traditional route of flight before northern invaders.

c. The polite expression used is "after a hundred years."

d. Avalokitesvara represents compassion, Mahasthamaprapta represents empowerment, Manjusri represents wisdom and knowledge, and Samantabhadra represents goodness in all actions.

e. Hsiang-T'an was a district in Hunan, south of Ch'ang Sha. "South of Hsiang and north of T'an" can mean everywhere, or nowhere.

Chu Ti's One-Finger Ch'an

POINTER

When one speck of dust arises, the great earth is contained therein; when a single flower blooms, the world arises. But before the speck of dust is raised, before the flower opens, how will you set eyes on it? Therefore it is said, "It's like cutting a skein of thread: when one strand is cut, all are cut. It's like dyeing a skein of thread: when one strand is dyed, all are dyed."

This very moment you should take all complications and cut them off. Bring out your own family jewels and respond everywhere, high and low, before and after, without missing. Each and every one will be fully manifest. If you're not yet like this, look into the text below.

CASE

Whenever anything was asked,[1] Master Chu Ti would just raise one finger.[2]

NOTES

1. What news is there? Dull-witted teacher!
2. This old fellow too would cut off the tongues of everyone on earth. When it's warm, all heaven and earth are warm; when it's cold, all heaven and earth are cold. He snatches away the tongues of everyone on earth.

COMMENTARY

If you understand at the finger, then you turn your back on Chu Ti; if you don't go to the finger to understand, then it's like cast iron. Whether you understand or not, Chu Ti still goes on this way; whether you're high or low, he still goes on this way;

whether you're right or wrong, he still goes on this way. Thus it is said, "As soon as a speck of dust arises, the great earth is contained therein; when a single flower is about to open, the world immediately comes into being. The lion on the tip of a single hair appears on the tips of ten billion hairs."

Yuan Ming said, "When it's cold, all throughout heaven and earth are cold; when it's warm, all throughout heaven and earth are warm." The mountains and rivers and the great earth reach down through the Yellow Springs (Hades); the myriad images and multitude of forms penetrate upward through the heavens. But tell me, what is so extraordinary? For those who know, it's not worth taking hold of; for those who don't know, it blocks them off utterly.

Master Chu Ti was from Chin Hua in Wu Chou (in Chekiang). During the time he first dwelt in a hermitage, there was a nun named Shih Chi ('Reality') who came to his hut. When she got there she went straight in; without taking off her rain hat she walked around his meditation seat three times holding her staff. "If you can speak," she said, "I'll take off my rain hat." She questioned him like this three times; Chu Ti had no reply. Then as she was leaving Chu Ti said, "The hour is rather late: would you stay the night?" The nun said, "If you can speak, I'll stay over." Again Chu Ti had no reply. The nun then walked out. Chu Ti sighed sorrowfully and said, "Although I inhabit the body of a man, still I lack a man's spirit." After this he aroused his zeal to clarify this matter.

He meant to abandon his hermitage and travel to various places to call on teachers to ask for instruction, and had wrapped up his things for foot-travelling. But that night the spirit of the mountain told him, "You don't have to leave this place. Tomorrow a flesh and blood bodhisattva will come and expound the truth for you, Master. You don't have to go." As it turned out, the following day Master T'ien Lung actually came to the hermitage. Chu Ti welcomed him ceremoniously and gave a full account of the previous events. T'ien Lung just lifted up one finger to show him; suddenly Chu Ti was greatly enlightened. At the time Chu Ti was most earnest and single-minded, so the bottom of his bucket fell out easily. Later, whenever anything was asked, Chu Ti just raised one finger.

Ch'ang Ch'ing said, "Delicious food is not for a satisfied

man to eat." Hsuan Sha said, "If I had seen him then, I would have broken the finger off." Hsuan Chueh said, "When Hsuan Sha spoke this way, what was his meaning?" Hsi of Yun Chu said, "When Hsuan Sha spoke this way, was he agreeing with Chu Ti or not? If he agreed with him, why did he speak of breaking off the finger? If he didn't agree with him, where was Chu Ti's mistake?" The Former Ts'ao Shan said, "Chu Ti's realization was crude: he only recognized one device, one perspective. Like everyone else, he claps his hands and slaps his palms, but I look upon Hsi Yuan as exceptional."[a] Again, Hsuan Chueh said, "But say, was Chu Ti enlightened or not? Why was Chu Ti's realization crude?" If he wasn't enlightened, how could he say, "My whole life I've used one-finger Ch'an without ever exhausting it"? Tell me, where is Ts'ao Shan's meaning?

At that time, Chu Ti actually did not understand. After his enlightenment, whenever anything was asked, Chu Ti would just raise one finger; why couldn't a thousand people, even ten thousand people, entrap him or break him apart? If you understand it as a finger, you definitely won't see the Ancient's meaning. This kind of Ch'an is easy to approach but hard to understand. People these days who just hold up a finger or a fist as soon as they're questioned are just indulging their spirits. It is still necessary to pierce the bone, penetrate to the marrow, and see all the way through in order to get it.

At Chu Ti's hermitage there was a servant boy. While he was away from the hermitage, he was asked, "What method does your master usually use to teach people?" The servant boy held up a finger. When he returned, he mentioned this to the Master. Chu Ti took a knife and cut off the boy's finger; as he ran out screaming, Chu Ti called to him. The boy looked back, whereupon Chu Ti raised his finger; the boy opened up and attained understanding. Tell me, what truth did he see?

When he was nearing death, Chu Ti said to his assembly, "I attained T'ien Lung's one-finger Ch'an and have used it all my life without exhausting it. Do you want to understand?" He raised his finger, then died.

The One-Eyed Dragon of Ming Chao asked his 'uncle,' Shen of Kuo T'ai, "An Ancient said that Chu Ti just recited a three line spell and thereby became more famous than anyone else.

How can you quote the three line spell for someone else?" Shen also raised one finger. Chao said, "If not for Today, how could I know this borderlands traveller?" Tell me, what does this mean?

Mi Mo just used a forked branch all his life. The Earth-Beating Teacher would just hit the ground once whenever anything was asked. Once someone hid his staff and then asked, "What is Buddha?" The Teacher just opened his mouth wide. These (methods) too were used for a whole lifetime without ever being exhausted.

Wu Yeh said, "The Patriarch (Bodhidharma) observed that our country had people with the potential to be vessels of the Great Vehicle. He transmitted only the mind seal, in order to instruct those on the paths of illusion. Those who attain it do not choose between ignorance and wisdom, between worldly and holy. Much falsehood is not as good as a little truth. Anyone who is powerful will immediately rest right this moment and abruptly still the myriad entanglements, thus passing beyond the stream of birth and death and going far beyond the usual patterns. Though you have family and estate, if you do not seek, it is attained of itself." Throughout his whole lifetime, whenever anything was asked, Wu Yeh would just say, "Don't think falsely!" Thus it is said, "Penetrate one place, and at once you penetrate a thousand places, ten thousand places. Clearly understand one device, and at once you clearly understand a thousand devices, ten thousand devices."

Generally people these days are not this way; they just indulge in conceptual and emotional interpretations, and don't understand what is most essential with these Ancients. How could Chu Ti have had no other devices to switch to? Why did he just employ one finger? You must realize that here is where Chu Ti helps people so profoundly and intimately.

Do you want to understand how to save strength? Go back to Yuan Ming's saying, "When it's cold, all throughout heaven and earth is cold; when it's warm, all throughout heaven and earth is warm." Mountains, rivers, and earth, extending upward to the solitary heights; myriad forms in profuse array penetrate down through dangerous precipices. Where will you find one finger Ch'an?

VERSE

For his appropriate teaching I deeply admire old Chu Ti;
    ***A leper drags along his companions. Only those on*
    the same path know. Nevertheless it's (only) one
    device, one perspective.*

Since space and time have been emptied, who else is there?
    ***Two, three—there's still one more. He too should*
    be struck dead.*

Having cast a piece of driftwood onto the ocean,
    ***It's all this. So it is, but it's too*
    inaccessible. Worn out straw sandals; what
    use does it have?*

Together in the night waves we take in blind turtles.
    ***Dragging the sky, searching the earth; what end*
    will there be? When we take them in, what are they
    good for? We act according to what is imperative.
    I'd drive them towards a world where there is no
    Buddha. I've taken you in, Reverend, one blind man.*

COMMENTARY

Hsueh Tou has mastered literary composition; he's consummately accomplished. He especially likes to make up verses for obscure and unusual public cases. For students of today he censures and praises the Ancients; as guest or host, with a question or an answer, he holds them up before you—this is how he helps people. Thus he says, "For his appropriate teaching I deeply admire old Chu Ti." Tell me, why does Hsueh Tou admire him? Since heaven and earth began, who else has there ever been? Just this one, old Chu Ti. If it had been anyone else, inevitably he would have been inconsistent; only Chu Ti just used one finger up until his old age and death.

People often interpret this wrongly and say, "Mountains, rivers, and the great earth are empty; man is empty; the Dharma is empty too. Even if time and space were emptied out all at once, it's just this one, old Chu Ti." But this has nothing to do with it.

"Having cast a piece of driftwood onto the ocean." Nowadays they call this the ocean of birth and death. Within the ocean of doing, sentient beings appear and disappear without understanding themselves clearly, without hope of getting out. Old Chu Ti extends his mercy to take people in; in the ocean of birth and death he uses one finger to rescue others. It's like letting down a piece of driftwood to rescue a blind turtle. He enables all sentient beings to reach the Other Shore.

"Together in the night waves we take in blind turtles." The Lotus Scripture says, "It's like a one-eyed turtle sticking his nose through a hole in a floating board."[b] When a great man of knowledge receives a fellow who is like a dragon or a tiger, he directs him towards a world where there is Buddha to act in turn as guest and host, and in worlds without Buddhas to cut off the essential way across. Having taken in a blind turtle, what use is it?

TRANSLATOR'S NOTES

a.   Once when Ch'an master T'an Tsang of Hsi Yuan, a successor of Ma Tsu, was making the fire to heat the bath, one of his disciples told him that such menial tasks should be done by one of the novices. The Master said nothing, but clapped his hands three times.

b.   The metaphor: a blind turtle surfacing at the precise moment a piece of driftwood with a hole in it is passing by; the turtle can climb through the hole up out of the sea. This symbolizes the rare opportunity of hearing the Buddhist Teaching while in human form, itself a rare opportunity.

Lung Ya's Meaning of the Coming from the West

POINTER

Piled in mountains, heaped in ranges, up against walls, pressed against barriers; if you linger in thought, holding back your potential, you'll be bitterly cramped.

Or else, a man may appear and overturn the great ocean, kick over Mount Sumeru, scatter the white clouds with shouts, and break up empty space; straightaway, with one device, one object, he cuts off the tongues of everyone on earth, so that there is no way for you to approach. Tell me, since ancient times, who has ever been this way? To test, I cite this; look!

CASE

Lung Ya asked Ts'ui Wei, "What is the meaning of the Patriarch's coming from the West?"[1]

Wei said, "Pass me the meditation brace."[2]

Ya gave the meditation brace to Wei;[3] Wei took it and hit him.[4]

Ya said, "Since you hit me I let you hit me. In essence, though, there is no meaning of the Patriarch's coming from the West."[5]

Ya also asked Lin Chi, "What is the meaning of the Patriarch's coming from the West?"[6]

Chi said, "Pass me the cushion."[7]

Ya took the cushion and handed it to Lin Chi;[8] Chi took it and hit him.[9]

Ya said, "Since you hit me I let you hit me. In essence, though, there is no meaning of the Patriarch's coming from the West."[10]

NOTES

1. It's an old public case known everywhere; still he wants to put it to the test.
2. What will he use the meditation brace for? (Ts'ui Wei) almost let (Lung Ya) go. Danger!
3. He can't hold on to it; (Lung Ya) is given a fine steed, Green Dragon, but he doesn't know how to ride it. What a pity that he doesn't take charge right away.
4. Got him! What is accomplished by hitting a dead man? He too has fallen into the secondary.
5. This fellow's talk is in the secondary; he draws his bow after the thief has gone.
6. Again he inquires into the commonplace old public case; it's not worth half a cent.
7. If the waves of Ts'ao Ch'i resembled each other, endless numbers of ordinary people would get bogged down. One punishment for all crimes; they're buried in the same pit.
8. As before, he can't hold on to it; as before he's not very clever. What's like the land of Yueh is like Yang Chou.[a]
9. Got him! What a pity to be hitting this kind of dead man. Lin Chi comes out of the same pattern as Ts'ui Wei.
10. Obviously. He's making a living inside the demon cave. He thinks he's gained the advantage.

COMMENTARY

Master Chih of Ts'ui Yen said, "It was so at that time, but do patchrobed monks these days still have blood under their skin?"

Che of Mt. Kuei said, "Ts'ui Wei and Lin Chi can be called genuine masters of our sect."

Lung Ya was first rate at pulling out the weeds seeking the way; there's no reason why he shouldn't serve as a model for people of later times. After he had a fixed abode, a monk asked him, "Teacher, at that time did you agree with those two venerable adepts?" Ya said, "I agree, as far as agreement goes; it's just that there is no meaning of the Patriarch's coming from the West." Lung Ya looks carefully in front and behind, and dispenses medicine to suit the disease.

Ta Kuei, however, is not this way; when asked whether Lung Ya had agreed with the two venerable adepts, whether he understood or not, he would have brought his staff down across the back (of the questioner). This not only supports Ts'ui Wei and Lin Chi, but also doesn't turn away from the questioner.

Ts'ung of Shih Men said, "Lung Ya is still all right if there's no one to press him, but when he's pressed by a patchrobed one, he loses one eye."

Hsueh Tou said, "Lin Chi and Ts'ui Wei only knew how to hold still; they didn't know how to let go. If I had been Lung Ya at that time, when they asked for the cushion and meditation brace, I would have picked it up and immediately thrown it down right in front of them."

Wu Tsu Shih Chieh said, "The Teacher has such a long face!" He also said, "The patriarchal masters' star of ill-omen is over his head."

Hsin of Huang Lung Mountain said, "Lung Ya drove off the ploughman's ox, he snatched away the hungry man's food. Once he's clear, he's clear; why then is there no meaning of the Patriarch's coming from the West? Do you understand? On the staff there is an eye bright as the sun; to tell whether gold is real, see it through fire."

To extol the wonder of the essential, to advocate the fundamental vehicle, if you can understand it the very first instant, then you can cut off the tongues of everyone on earth. But if you vacillate, you fall into the secondary. These two old fellows Lin Chi and Ts'ui Wei, though they beat the wind and hit the rain, startle heaven and shake the earth, have never really hit a clear eyed fellow.

When the Ancients immersed themselves in meditation, they suffered some pains; having established powerful resolve, they would traverse mountains and rivers to call on venerable adepts. First Lung Ya met Ts'ui Wei and Lin Chi; later he called on Te Shan. There he asked, "How is it when a student holding a sharp sword tries to take the teacher's head?" Te Shan stretched out his neck and uttered a grunt. Ya said, "The teacher's head has fallen." Te Shan smiled slightly and let it go at that.

Next Lung Ya went to Tung Shan. Tung Shan asked, "Where did you come here from?" Ya said, "From Te Shan." Tung Shan said, "What did Te Shan have to say?" Ya then recounted the preceding story. Tung Shan asked, "What did he say?" Ya said, "He had no words." Tung Shan said, "Don't say that he had no words. Instead try to take Te Shan's fallen head and show it to me." At this Ya had insight; thereupon he burned incense and gazed far off towards Te Shan; he prostrated himself and repented.

When he heard of this, Te Shan said, "Old man Tung Shan can't tell good from bad; this fellow has been dead so long, what's the use of saving him? Let him wander over the earth carrying my head."

Lung Ya's basic nature was intelligent and acute. He went foot travelling carrying a bellyfull of Ch'an. As soon as he got to Ts'ui Wei in Ch'ang An he immediately asked, "What is the meaning of the Patriarch's coming from the West?" Wei said, "Pass me the meditation brace," Ya took the meditation brace and gave it to Wei. Wei took it and hit him. Ya said, "Since you hit me I let you hit me; in essence, though, there is no meaning of the Patriarch's coming from the West." He also asked Lin Chi, "What is the meaning of the Patriarch's coming from the West?" Lin Chi said, "Pass me the cushion." Ya took the cushion and gave it to Lin Chi; Chi took it and hit him. Ya said, "Since you hit me I let you hit me; in essence, though, there is no meaning of the Patriarch's coming from the West."

When Lung Ya posed the question, he not only wanted to see the old fellows up on the carved wood seats, he also wanted to illumine the great concern of his own self. We can say that his words were not spoken in vain, that his effort was not expended haphazardly; they issued from his doing his work.

Haven't you heard? Wu Hsieh went to see Shih T'ou. He had made an agreement with himself beforehand saying, "If there's accord at the first word I'll stay; otherwise, I'll go." Shih T'ou just sat on his seat; Hsieh shook out his sleeves and went out. Shih T'ou knew that Wu Wsieh was a vessel of the truth, so he had extended his teaching to him. But Hsieh hadn't understood his meaning; he had announced his departure and gone out. When he got to the gate Shi T'ou called out to him, "Reverend!" When Hsieh looked back, Shih T'ou said, "From birth to death it's only this; don't seek anymore for anything else by turning your head and revolving your brain." At these words Hsieh was greatly enlightened.

Also, Ma Ku came to Chang Ching carrying his ring-staff; he

walked three times around the meditation seat, shook his staff once, and stood there upright. Ching said, "Right, right." He also went to Nan Ch'uan; as before he walked three times around the seat, shook his staff and stood there. Nan Ch'uan said, "Wrong, wrong. This is what the power of the wind can whirl around; in the end it decomposes." Ma Ku said, "Chang Ching said right; why do you say wrong?" Nan Ch'uan said, "Chang Ching was right; it is you who are wrong."[b]

Inevitably the Ancients had to take up and penetrate through this one matter. People today, as soon as they are questioned, have not made the slightest application of effort; they're this way today, and they'll be this way tomorrow too: if you just keep on like this, even into the endless future you will never have a day of completion. You must arouse and purify your spirit; only thus will you have some small share of realization.

Look at Lung Ya coming out with one question, saying, "What is the meaning of the Patriarch's coming from the West?" Ts'ui Wei said, "Pass me the meditation brace." When Ya gave it to him, he took it and immediately hit Ya. When Ya picked up the meditation brace, how could he have not known that Wei was going to hit him? And it won't do to say that Ya didn't understand, for why then did he pass the meditation brace to Wei? But tell me, at the moment he understood, how should Ya have acted? He didn't go to the living water to function, but took himself into the dead water for his sustenance. Acting as master throughout, he said, "Since you hit me I let you hit me; in essence, though, there is no meaning of the Patriarch's coming from the West."

Lung Ya also went to Hopeh to call on Lin Chi. He asked his question as before. Lin Chi said, "Pass me the cushion." When Ya gave it to him, he took it and immediately hit Ya. Ya said, "Since you hit me I let you hit me; in essence, though, there is no meaning of the Patriarch's coming from the West." Tell me, these two venerable adepts were not of the same lineage; why did their answers resemble each other, why was their functioning of one kind? You must realize that the one word, one phrase of the Ancients was not uttered at random.

Later when Lung Ya dwelt in a temple, a monk asked him, "Teacher, at that time, when you saw the two worthies, did you agree with them or not?" Ya said, "As far as agreement

goes, I agreed; but there is no meaning of the Patriarch's coming from the West." There are thorns in the soft mud. To let go
for people is already falling into the secondary; this old fellow
(Lung Ya) held steady—he only acted as an adept in the Tung
succession.[c] To be a disciple of Te Shan or Lin Chi, he would
have had to realize that there is a living side besides. As for me,
I am not this way; I would have told the monk, "As far as
agreement is concerned, I don't agree; in essence, though, there
is no meaning of the Patriarch's coming from the West."

Haven't you heard how a monk asked Ta Mei, "What is the
meaning of the Patriarch's coming from the West?" Mei said,
"The coming from the West has no meaning." Yen Kuan heard
of this and said, "One coffin, two dead men." Hsuan Sha heard
of this and said, "Yen Kuan is indeed an adept!" (To which)
Hsueh Tou said, "There are even three (dead men)." The monk
asked about the meaning of the Patriarch's coming from the
West; though Ta Mei told him that the coming from the West
has no meaning, if you understand in this way, you fall into the
realm of unconcern. Therefore Te Shan (Yuan Mi) said, "You
must study the living word; don't study the dead word. If you
can understand at the living word, you will never forget it; if
you understand at the dead word, you won't even be able to
save yourself."

When Lung Ya spoke this way, he had undeniably done his
best. The Ancient Tung Shan said, "Continuity is very difficult." The other Ancients, Ts'ui Wei and Lin Chi, were not
acting at random with their one word, one phrase; before and
after mutually illuminating, with both temporal and true, with
both illumination and function, guest and host obvious, interchanging vertically and horizontally.

If you want to discern the inside story, since Lung Ya was
not ignorant of the vehicle of our sect, how could he have fallen
into second place? At the time when the two venerable adepts
asked for the meditation brace and cushion, Ya could not have
but known their intention. It was just that he wanted to make
use of that which was within his own breast. Although he was
right, nevertheless his use of it was too extreme. Since Lung Ya
asked this way, and the two old ones answered this way, why
then is there no meaning of the Patriarch's coming from the
West? When you get here you must know that there's something else extraordinary. Hsueh Tou picks it up to show
people:

VERSE

In Dragon Tusk Mountain the dragon has no eyes;[d]
    **He's blind. He can fool other people all*
    right, (but not me.) This is washing a clod
    of earth in the mud. Everyone on earth knows. *

When has dead water ever displayed the ancient way?
    **Should it suddenly come to life, nothing can*
    be done. He drags in everyone on earth so that
    they can't get out. *

If you can't use the meditation brace and cushion,
    **Who would you have say this? What do you want*
    to do with the meditation brace and cushion?
    Didn't he hand them over to you, Reverend? *

You should just give them over to Mr. Lu.
    **But they can't be given over. You*
    lacquer bucket, don't entertain such
    views! *

COMMENTARY

Hsueh Tou settles the case according to the facts. Though he versifies this way, tell me, where is his meaning? Where does the dragon lack eyes? Where is he in dead water? At this point you must have the power to transform before you realize. That is why it is said, "In a clear pool there's no place for the blue dragon to coil up." Has there ever been a fierce dragon in stagnant water? Haven't you heard it said, "Stagnant water cannot conceal a dragon"? If it is a live dragon, it must go to where vast swelling billows of foamy waves flood the heavens. This is to say that Lung Ya went into the dead water and was hit by the others. Yet he did say, "Since you hit me I let you hit me; in essence, though, there is no meaning of the Patriarch's coming from the West." This prompted Hsueh Tou to say, "When has dead water ever displayed the ancient way?" Although this is so, tell me, was Hsueh Tou upholding (Lung Ya), or was he diminishing his dignity?

People often misunderstand and ask, "Why did Hsueh Tou say, 'You should just give them over to Mr. Lu'?" They are far from knowing that Lung Ya did indeed give them to the others.

Whenever you visit masters to ask for instruction, you must discriminate in the midst of the action; only then will you see where those Ancients met.

"If you can't use the meditation brace and cushion." Ts'ui Wei said, "Pass me the meditation brace," and Lung Ya gave it to him; isn't this making a living within dead water? Clearly Lung Ya has been given a fine steed; it's just that he doesn't know how to ride it, that he is unable to make use of it.

"You should just give them over to Mr. Lu." People frequently say that Mr. Lu is the Sixth Patriarch; this is wrong. Hsueh Tou has called himself Mr. Lu previously in a verse called "Anonymous Bequest"—

> I saw its picture that year and loved Tung T'ing;[e]
> In the waves, seventy-two peaks of blue.
> Now, resting on high, I think back to what was before,
> To the picture, I've added Mr. Lu leaning against a wall.

Hsueh Tou wanted to walk on Lung Ya's head, but he still feared that people would misunderstand, so he made up another verse to cut away people's doubtful interpretations. Again he picks it up and says,

VERSE

Since this old fellow couldn't yet put an end to it, again he makes a verse:
    **Obviously. How many people could there be who would know? He knew himself that he had attained only a half; luckily he has a final word.*

Once Mr. Lu has accepted them, why depend on them?
    **Even if you search the whole world, such a man is still hard to find. Who would you have comprehend your words?*

Sitting, leaning—cease taking these to succeed to the lamp of the Patriarchs!

**A man in the weeds; he goes in to sit beneath the black mountain. He has fallen into the ghost cave. *

It's worth replying: the evening clouds, returning, have not yet
     come together;
     **One, a half. Bring it up and already you're wrong. After
all he can't get out. *

Distant mountains without end, layer upon layer of blue.
     **They block off your eyes, they block off your ears.
You sink into a deep pit. Study for thirty more years. *

COMMENTARY

"Once Mr. Lu has accepted them, why depend on them?" What is there to depend on? Here you must understand things directly this way; don't go on guarding a stump waiting for a rabbit. Smash what's before your skull all at once, so that there isn't the slightest bit of concern within your breast. Let go and become clean and at ease. Then what more need is there for something to rely on? Whether sitting (on the cushion) or leaning (on the brace), it's not worth considering it the principle of the Buddha Dharma. That is why Hsueh Tou said, "Sitting, leaning—cease to take these to succeed to the lamp of the Patriarchs." At once, Hsueh Tou has brought it up completely; he has a place to turn around in, and at the end reveals this scene where there's a bit of a nice place. He says, "It's worth replying: the evening clouds, returning, have not yet come together." Tell me, where is Hsueh Tou's meaning? When the evening clouds have returned and are about to join together but have not yet done so, tell me, how is it then? "Distant mountains without end, layer upon layer of blue." As before he's gone into the ghost cave. When you get here, when gain and loss, right and wrong, are cut off all at once, and you are clean and at ease, only then do you amount to something. "Distant mountains without end, layer upon layer of blue." Tell me, is this Manjusri's realm? Is this Samantabhadra's realm? Is this Avalokitesvara's realm? When you get here, tell me, whose affair is this?

TRANSLATOR'S NOTES

a. "What's like the land of Yueh is like Yang Chou" in that these two names refer to the same area of China: broadly speaking, the coastal plain river country north and south of the mouth of the Yangtse River, especially the modern provinces Chekiang and Kiangsu.

b. This story, quoted here in a somewhat different form, is the main example of the thirty-first case; Kato Totsudo thinks that it may have been inserted into this commentary by a later hand.

c. In Sung times some Lin Chi masters criticized the Ts'ao-Tung masters for being too fond of quiescence, abiding in extinction, absorbed by the vastness of the universe; the fifth rank of the Ts'ao-Tung's five ranks was symbolized by a solid black circle, which the Lin Chi masters often took to mean *nirvana* as extinction. Tenkei Denson sometimes remarked that Yuan Wu was not thoroughly familiar with the devices of the Tung lineage, and did not realize that there is a turning point, a pivot, in each rank. The Lin Chi masters emphasized the experience of *wu* (*satori*), enlightenment or awakening, and its active expression; they were foremost in the use of contemplation themes, upon which they would focus with a force known as 'doubt' or 'great doubt'. The tension of the doubt was used to rid the mind of wandering thought, unify the attention, and break mental habit patterns; the sudden dissolution of the 'mass of doubt' was sometimes brought about by blows or shouts, by a gesture, a word or phrase. After dying 'the great death' and entering the Path, one is supposed to return to life, awake and free; but it is said that many do not return, being absorbed by the peace of death, forsaking forever the clamor of life. Lung Ya is being 'criticized' for not showing his own initiative.

d. This refers to Lung Ya; the name Lung Ya means dragon's tusk, and is the name of the mountain on which the Ch'an master Chu Tun lived. As is customary, he is usually referred to by the name of the place where he lived.

e. This refers to Tung T'ing mountain in Su Chou (Soochow), Chekiang, eastern China, where Hsueh Tou lived at one time, on Ts'ui Feng (Green Peak). Hsueh Tou added a little picture of himself to a painting of Tung T'ing; this poem is just cited to show that 'Mr. Lu' refers to Hsueh Tou himself.

Chih Men's Lotus Flower, Lotus Leaves

INTRODUCTORY INSTRUCTION

Setting up the banner of the Teaching, establishing the essential meaning—this is adding flowers to brocade. Strip off the blinders, unload the saddle pack—this is the season of the great peace. If you can discern the phrase outside of patterns, then when one is raised you understand three. Otherwise, if you're not yet this way, as before humbly listen to this treatment.

MAIN CASE

A monk asked Chih Men, "How is it when the lotus flower has not yet emerged from the water?"[1] Chih Men said, "A Lotus flower."[2]

The monk said, "What about after it has emerged from the water?"[3] Men said, "Lotus leaves."[4]

NOTES

1. The hook is on the doubt-free ground. Washing a lump of dirt in the mud. How did he get this news?
2. One, two, three, four, five, six, seven. He stumps everyone on earth.
3. Don't go inside the ghost cave to make a living. Again the monk goes on this way.
4. Yu Chou (up north) is still alright: the worst suffering is south of the River. Two heads, three faces. He kills everyone on earth with laughter.

COMMENTARY

As for dealing with people in accordance with their potentials, Chih Men has attained a little. When it comes to cutting off the myriad streams, he's a million miles away. But say, is this flower before and after it emerges from the water the same or different? If you can see this way, I'll grant that you've had an entry. Nevertheless, if you say it's the same, you confuse your buddha-nature and becloud true thusness. If you say it's different, mind and environment are not yet forgotten, and you descend to travel the road of interpretation. When will you ever cease?

Tell me, what is the ancient's meaning? In reality there aren't so many concerns. That is why T'ou Tzu said, "Just don't attach names and words, classification and phrasing. If you have understood all things, naturally you won't be attached to them. Then there is no multiplicity of gradations of differences; you take in all things; but all things won't be able to take you in. Fundamentally there is no gain or loss, no illusions or dreams, no multiplicity of names. You should not insist on setting up names for them. Can I fool all of you people? Since all of you ask questions, therefore there are words. If you didn't ask, what could you have me say that would be right? All concerns are what you take up: none of it is any of my business." An ancient said, "If you want to know the meaning of the buddha nature, you must observe times and seasons, causes and conditions."

Haven't you seen Yun Men cite this story: A monk asked Ling Yun, "How was it before the Buddha appeared in the world?" Ling Yun raised his whisk. The monk asked, "What about after he appeared in the world?" Again Ling Yun raised his whisk. Yun Men said, "The first time he hit, the second time he missed." He also said, "Without speaking of appearing and not appearing, where would there be the time of his asking?"

With one answer for one question the ancients accorded with the time and season without a multitude of concerns. If you pursue words and follow after phrases, there will never be any connection. If in the midst of words you can penetrate through words, if in the midst of meanings you can pass through meanings, if within a device you can penetrate through the device, and if you let go and let yourself be at ease, only then will you see Chih Men's answer.ᵃ

Yun Men said, "From ancient times till today, it's just been one thing. There is no right or wrong, no gain or loss, no born or not born." When they got here the ancients laid down one single path where there's an entrance and an exit. If it's a man who hasn't yet understood, then he's pressing against a fence, running his hands over a wall,ᵇ (like a ghost) haunting the weeds and trees. If you make him let go, he still goes into the wild vast desolation. If it is a man who has attained, then twenty-four hours a day he won't depend on a single thing. While he doesn't depend on a single thing, when he reveals one device, one object, how will you search him out?

This monk asked, "How is it when the lotus flowers have not yet emerged from the water?" Chih Men said, "A Lotus flower." This then is just an answer that blocks the question, nevertheless it's exceptional. All over it's called "upside-down words." How so? Haven't you heard: Yen T'ou said, "I always hope you would attain a little before you open your mouths."

Where the ancient one Chih Men revealed his mind, he was already leaking and tarrying. Students these days don't wake up to the ancient's meaning: they just go on talking theoretically of "emerged from the water" and "not yet emerged from the water." What connection is there?

Haven't you heard: A monk asked Chih Men, "What is the body of Wisdom?" Men said, "An oyster enclosing the bright moon." The monk asked, "What is the functioning of Wisdom?" Men said, "A rabbit becomes pregnant." Look at him responding like this: no one on earth can search out the stream of his words.

If someone asked me, "How is it when the lotus flowers have not yet emerged from the water?" I would just answer him by saying, "The pillar and the lamp."ᶜ Tell me, is this the same as the lotus flowers or different? If I were asked, "What about after they've emerged from the water?" I would answer, "The staff upholds the sun and moon, underfoot how muddy and deep!" You tell me, is this right or wrong? And don't mistakenly stick by the zero point of a scale.

Hsueh Tou is extremely compassionate, breaking up people's emotional interpretations, so he comes out with his verse:

VERSE

Lotus flower, lotus leaves—he reports for you to know
**Grandmotherly kindness. A manifest public case. Its
    pattern is already revealed. *
How can emerging from the water compare to when it has not
    yet emerged?
**Washing a lump of dirt in the mud. Dividing them is
    alright, but you can't lump them together. *
North of the river, south of the river, ask Old Wang
**Where is the master? Why ask Old Master Wang?
    You're just wearing out your straw sandals. *
Fox-doubt after fox-doubt
**I bury them in one hole. It's you who doubt. You won't
    avoid feelings of doubt without respite. Having struck
    I say, "Do you understand?"*

COMMENTARY

Originally Chih Men was from Chekiang. He made his way by
stages to Szechuan to call on Hsiang Lin. After he had penetrated (this affair under Hsiang Lin's guidance), he returned to
dwell at Chih Men in Sui Chou.

Hsueh Tou was Chih Men's true successor: he saw well
Chih Men's most hidden, most subtle point and says directly,
"Lotus flower, lotus leaves—he reports for you to know/How
can emerging from the water compare to when it has not yet
emerged?" Here he wants people to understand directly and
immediately.

I say, "How is it when they've not yet emerged from the
water? The pillar and lamp. What about after they've emerged?
The staff upholds the sun and moon, underfoot how muddy
and deep!" But don't mistakenly abide by this as the zero point
of a scale. What limit is there to people these days chewing
over the words and phrases of others?

But tell me, when they emerge from the water, what time
and season is this? When they've not yet emerged from the
water, what time and season is this? If you can see to this
point, I'll allow that you've seen Chih Men personally.

Hsueh Tou says, if you don't see, "North of the river, south of the river, ask Old Wang." Hsueh Tou means that you should just go north of the river and south of the river to ask the venerable adepts about "emerged from the water" and "not emerged from the water." If you add two phrases south of the river, add two phrases north of the river, add one load upon another load, creating doubts over and over, just tell me, when will you get so that you don't doubt? You're like wild foxes, full of doubt, walking on river ice: they listen for the sound of the water (below); if it doesn't make a sound, then they can cross the river. If students have "fox-doubt after fox-doubt," when will they attain peace and tranquility?

TRANSLATOR'S NOTES

a. Following this, the Chang book inserts, "'How is it before the Buddha appeared in the world?' 'How was it before Niu T'ou saw the fourth patriarch?' 'How is it when a conglomerate stone is still undifferentiated inside?' 'How was it before your parents bore you?'" These are supposed to be in the same category as 'How is it before the lotus emerges from the water?' The lotus is a traditional symbol for enlightenment.

b. Pressing against a fence, running his hands over a wall, as a blind man would.

c. "The pillar and the lamp": Physical reality, the world of objects, such as the pillar and the lamp that would have been present in the Dharma Halls right in front of the eyes of Yuan Wu's listeners.

Hsueh Feng's Turtle-Nosed Snake

POINTER

There's nothing outside the great vastness; it's as fine as atomic dust. Holding on and letting go are not another's (doing): rolling up and rolling out^a rest with oneself. If you want to free what is stuck and loosen what is bound, you simply must cut away the traces (of thought) and swallow the sounds (of words). All people occupy the essential crossing place; each and every one towers up like a thousand fathom wall. But tell me, whose realm is this? To test, I'm citing this old case: look!

CASE

Hsueh Feng taught the assembly saying, "On South Mountain there's a turtle-nosed snake.[1] All of you people must take a good look."[2]

Ch'ang Ch'ing said, "In the hall today there certainly are people who are losing their bodies and their lives."[3]

A monk related this to Hsuan Sha.[4] Hsuan Sha said, "It takes Elder Brother Leng (Ch'ang Ch'ing) to be like this. Nevertheless, I am not this way."[5] The monk asked, "What about you, Teacher?"[6] Hsuan Sha said, "Why make use of 'South Mountain'?"[7]

Yun Men took his staff and threw it down in front of Hsueh Feng, making a gesture of fright.[8]

NOTES

1. If you see something strange as not strange, it's strangeness disappears by itself. What a strange thing! Unavoidably it causes people to doubt.
2. Aha! A case of over-indulgence.

3. The man from P'u Chou (Ch'ang Ch'ing) escorts the thief. He judges others on the basis of himself.

4. There's no different dirt from the same hole. When the manservant sees the maidservant he takes care. Those with the same disease sympathize with each other.

5. He doesn't avoid forming a wild fox spirit view. What news is this? His poison breath afflicts others.

6. He too presses the old fellow well.

7. On a boat fishing, the third son of the Hsiehs (Hsuan Sha). Only this wild fox spirit has attained a little. He's lost his body and his life and doesn't even realize it.

8. Why be afraid of it? One son has intimately attained. All of them are giving play to their spirits. All of you try to discern this.

COMMENTARY

If you spread it out evenly, I let you spread it out evenly; if you break it up, I let you break it up.

Hsueh Feng travelled with Yen T'ou and Ch'in Shan. In all, he went to Mt. T'ou Tzu three times, and climbed Mt. Tung nine times. Later he called on Te Shan, and only then did he smash the lacquer bucket.

One day he went along with Yen T'ou to visit Ch'in Shan. They got as far as an inn on Tortoise Mountain (in Hunan) when they were snowed in. Day after day Yen T'ou just slept, while Hsueh Feng constantly sat in meditation. Yen T'ou yelled at him and said, "Get some sleep! Every day you're on the meditation seat, exactly like a clay image. Another time, another day, you'll fool the sons and daughters of other people's families." Feng pointed to his breast and said, "I am not yet at peace here; I don't dare deceive myself." T'ou said, "I had thought that later on you would go to the summit of a solitary peak, build a hut of straw, and propagate the great teaching: but you're still making such a statement as this." Feng said, "I am really not yet at peace." T'ou said, "If you're really like this, bring forth your views one by one; where they're correct I'll approve them for you, and where they're wrong I'll prune them away for you."

Then Hsueh Feng related, "When I saw Yen Kuan up in the

hall bringing up the meaning of form and void, I gained an entry." Yen T'ou said, "Henceforth for thirty years avoid mentioning this." Again Feng said, "When I saw Tung Shan's verse on crossing the river,[b] I had an insight." T'ou said, "This way, you won't be able to save yourself." Feng went on, "Later when I got to Te Shan I asked, 'Do I have a part in the affair of the vehicle of the most ancient sect, or not?' Shan struck me a blow of his staff and said, 'What are you saying?' At that time it was like the bottom of the bucket dropping out for me." Thereupon Yen T'ou shouted and said, "Haven't you heard it said that what comes in through the gate is not the family jewels?" Feng said, "Then what should I do?" T'ou said, "In the future, if you want to propagate the great teaching, let each point flow out from your own breast, to come out and cover heaven and earth for me." At these words Hsueh Feng was greatly enlightened. Then he bowed, crying out again and again, "Today on Tortoise Mountain I've finally achieved the Way! Today on Tortoise Mountain I've finally achieved the Way!"

Later Hsueh Feng returned to Min (Fukien) and lived on Elephant Bone Mountain. He left behind this verse about himself:

> Human life so hectic and hurried is but a brief instant;
> How can you dwell for long in the fleeting world?
> As I reached thirty-two I emerged from the mountains;
> Already over forty, I return to Min.
> No use bringing up the faults of others again and again;
> One's own mistakes must be cleared away continually.
> I humbly report to the purple-clad nobles who fill the court:
> The King of Death has no awe of the golden emblems of rank you wear.

Usually Hsueh Feng would go up into the hall and teach the assembly by saying, "In every respect cover heaven and cover earth." He talked no more of mystery or marvel, nor did he speak of mind or nature. He appeared strikingly, alone, like a great fiery mass; approach and he burns off your face. Like the T'ai Ya sword, fool around with him and you lose your body and your life. If you linger in thought, holding back your activity, then you lose contact.

Pai Ching asked Huang Po, "Where are you coming from?" Po said, "I've been at the foot of Mt. Ta Hsiung picking mushrooms." Chang said, "See any tigers?" Po then made a tiger's roar. Then Chang picked up an axe and made a chopping motion; Po then slapped him. Chang chuckled and went back and ascended his seat and told the assembly, "There's a tiger on Mt. Ta Hsiung; all of you should watch out for him. Today I myself was bitten by him."

Whenever Chao Chou saw a monk, right away he would say, "Have you ever been here?" Whether the monk said he had or he hadn't, Chou would always say, "Go drink some tea." The temple overseer asked, "The teacher always asks monks if they've been here or not, then always says, 'Go drink some tea.' What is the meaning?" Chou said, "Overseer!" When the overseer responded, Chou said, "Go drink some tea."

Beneath the gate at Tzu Hu stood a signboard; the writing on the plaque said, "At Tzu Hu there's a dog: on top he takes people's heads, in the middle he takes people's midsections, and below he takes people's legs; hesitate and you're lost." As soon as he saw any newcomer, the Master of Tzu Hu would immediately give a shout and say, "Look at the dog!" The moment the monk turned his head, the master would return to his abbot's room.

(These examples) are just like Hsueh Feng's saying, "On South Mountain there is a turtle-nosed snake; all of you people should watch it carefully." At just such a time, how would you reply? Without following in your former tracks, try to say something for me to see. When you get here, you must understand the phrase outside of patterns; then, when all the public cases are brought up, you will immediately know where they come down. See how Hsueh Feng teaches the assembly this way, without speaking to you of practice or understanding. Can you figure him out by means of intellectual discrimination?

Since Ch'ang Ch'ing, Hsuan Sha, and Yun Men are sons of his house, what they say is exactly appropriate. This is why the Ancient said, "On hearing words, you must understand the source; don't set up standards on your own." Words must have that which is beyond patterns; phrases must penetrate the barrier. If your words don't leave their nest of cliché, you fall into the poison sea.

Hsueh Feng's teaching the assembly this way can be called flavorless talk that blocks off people's mouths. Ch'ang Ch'ing and Hsuan Sha are both men of his family, thus they understand when he speaks this way.

What about "On South Mountain there's a turtle-nosed snake"? Do all of you know what this really means? Here you must be possessed of the all-pervasive eye in order to understand. Haven't you seen Chen Ching's verse which says,

> Beating the drum, strumming the lute,
> Two men of understanding meet.
> Yun Men is able to harmonize—
> Ch'ang Ch'ing knows how to follow his vagaries;
> The ancient song has no rhyme.
> South Mountain's turtle-nosed snake;
> Who knows this meaning?
> Truly it's Hsuan Sha.

When Ch'ang Ch'ing replied as he did, tell me, what was his meaning? To get here you must be like a stone-struck spark, like a lightning flash; only then will you be able to reach. If there's as much as a fine hair that you can't get rid of, then you won't be able to reach his depths. It's a pity that people mostly make intellectual interpretations of Ch'ang Ch'ing's words. They say, "As soon as anything is heard in the hall, then this is 'losing body and life.'" Some say, "Fundamentally there's not the slightest speck of anything; to say this kind of thing on even blank ground makes people doubt. People hear him say, 'On South Mountain there's a turtle-nosed snake,' and immediately they have doubts." If you understand in such ways, you have no contact; you just go on making a living on the words. If you don't understand this way, then how will you understand?

Later a monk related this to Hsuan Sha. Hsuan Sha said, "It takes Elder Brother Leng (Ch'ang Ch'ing) to be like this; nevertheless, I am not thus." The monk asked, "What about you, teacher?" Hsuan Sha said, "Why make use of 'South Mountain'?" Just observe how within Hsuan Sha's words there is a place where he shows himself. Immediately he said, "Why make use of 'South Mountain'?" If it hadn't been Hsuan Sha, it would have been very difficult to reply. When Hsueh Feng speaks this way, "On South Mountain there's a turtle-nosed snake," tell me, where is it? To get here you must be a transcendent person; only then will you be able to understand such talk. The man of old Hsueh Tou said, "Up on the boat fishing, the third son of the Hsieh doesn't like South Mountain; he prefers the turtle-nosed snake."

Then again we get to Yun Men; he took his staff and threw it down in front of Hsueh Feng, making a gesture of fright. Yun Men has the ability to handle snakes, and doesn't run afoul of the sharp point. He strikes home in light, and he strikes home in darkness too. As he helps people it's always like doing a sword dance; sometimes he flies onto people's eyebrows and eyelashes, sometimes he flies three thousand miles away and snatches people's heads. His throwing down his staff and making a gesture of fright—isn't this giving play to his spirit? Doesn't he lose his body and life too? Expert teaching masters never go to a word or phrase to make a living. Just because he likes the way Yun Men accorded perfectly with Hsueh Feng's meaning, therefore Hsueh Tou makes his verse on it:

VERSE

Elephant Bone Cliff is so high no one goes there;
    **A thousand, ten thousand, search but cannot
find. It's not your realm, sir.*

Those who get there must be master snake handlers.
    **This is a spirit recognizing a spirit, a thief
recognizing a thief. Why gather in crowds?
Still, you must be of the same group to make it.*

Master Leng and Master Pei can't do anything—
    **Their crimes are listed on the same indictment.
They passed up the first move.*

How many lose their bodies and their lives?
    **A crime is not judged twice. He drags
in common people.*

Shao Yang knows:
* *He's just attained a little.
This old fellow has just one single
eye. The old fellow is just
being clever.*

Again he searches the weeds—
* *He's a fellow fallen in the weeds;
what is the use? After all, where
is (the 'snake')? I strike!*

South, north, east, west; no place to search.
* *Is there? Is there? Your eyes are
blind, Reverend.*

Suddenly he thrusts out his staff,
* *Look! Set your eyes high. I strike!*

And throws it down before Hsueh Feng; it opens wide its
mouth.
* *Self-contrived, self-experienced. It swallows a
thousand, ten thousand, but what is accomplished?
No one on earth can find it.*

The gaping mouth is like a lightning flash;
* *A double case. After all. Fortunately
there is a final word.*

Raise your eyebrows (to look) and you won't see.
* *It's already gone by. Search all over for
such a man, and still it's hard to find one.
Right now where is (the snake)?*

Right now it's hidden here on Ju Peak;
* *Where has it gone? Even the
great Hsueh Tou acts this way
too. Today I too have been bitten.*

Those who come, one by one observe expedient methods.
* *Blind! Don't look under his feet; look under
your own feet. He's shot an arrow.*

The Master (Hsueh Tou) shouted loudly and said, "Look right
under your feet!"
* *He draws his bow after the thief has gone. Secondary,
tertiary. Repeated words are not worth enduring.*

COMMENTARY

"Elephant Bone Cliff is so high that no one goes there; those who get there must be master snake handlers." On Hsueh Feng Mountain there is an Elephant Bone Cliff. Hsueh Feng's active edge is lofty and steep; rarely is there anyone who reaches his place. Hsueh Tou is a man of his house; they're birds of a feather. Answering each other with the same voice, seeking each other with the same spirit; it takes all-competent adepts to join in the mutual witness of enlightenment.

Still, this turtle-nosed snake is unavoidably hard to handle; you must know how to handle it before you can do so. Conversely, if you don't know how to handle it, you'll be bitten by the snake. My late teacher Wu Tsu said, "With this turtle-nosed snake, you must have the ability not to get your hands or legs bitten. Hold him tight by the back of the neck with one quick grab. Then you can join hands and walk along with me."

Ch'ang Ch'ing and Hsuan Sha had this kind of ability. When Hsueh Tou says that Master Leng and Master Pei couldn't handle it, people often say that Ch'ang Ch'ing and Hsuan Sha couldn't do anything about it, and thus Hsueh Tou only praises Yun Men. But this has nothing to do with it. How far they are from knowing that among the three men there is no gain or loss in ability; it's just that there is close and far away. Now I ask all of you people, where is it that Master Leng and Master Pei couldn't manage?

"How many lose their bodies and their lives?" This praises Ch'ang Ch'ing's saying, "In the hall today there certainly are people who lose their bodies and lives." To get here, first you must be thoroughly versed in snake handling.

Hsueh Tou is descended from Yun Men, so he brushes the others away all at once and just keeps one, Yun Men: Hsueh Tou says, "Shao Yang knows; again he searches the weeds." Since Yun Men knew the meaning of Hsueh Feng's saying, "On South Mountain there's a turtle-nosed snake," therefore "Again he searches through the weeds."

After Hsueh Tou has taken his verse this far, he still has more marvels. He says, "South, north, east, west; no place to search." You tell me where the snake is. "Suddenly he thrusts out his staff." From the beginning the snake has been right here. But you must not then go to the staff for sustenance. Yun Men took his staff and threw it down in front of Hsueh Feng, making a gesture of fright. Thus Yun Men used his staff as the turtle-nosed snake. Once, though, he said, "The staff changed into a dragon and has swallowed the universe; where are mountains, rivers and the great earth to be found?" Just this one staff—sometimes it's a dragon, sometimes it's a snake. Why is it like this? Only when you get here will you know (the meaning of the) ancient saying, "Mind revolves along with myriad phenomena; the turning point is truly mysterious."

The verse says, "He throws it down before Hsueh Feng; it opens wide its mouth. The gaping mouth is like a lightning flash." Hsueh Tou has extra talent; he picks up Yun Men's poisonous snake and says, "Just this gaping mouth is like a flash of lightning." If you hesitate, then you lose your body and life. "Raise your eyebrows (to look), and you won't see." Where has it gone?

His verse finished, Hsueh Tou must go to a living place to help others; he takes Hsueh Feng's snake and picks it up and plays with it himself. Nothing can stop him from killing or bringing to life in accordance with the occasion. Do you want to see? He says, "Right now it's hidden here on Ju Peak." Ju Peak is a name for Hsueh Tou Mountain.

Though Ch'ang Ch'ing, Hsuan Sha, and Yun Men can handle the snake, they don't see. After all Hsueh Tou says, "Right now it's hidden here on Ju Peak; those who come, one by one observe expedient methods." Hsueh Tou is still too subtle; he doesn't say, "Use it right away," but instead shouted loudly and said, "Look right under your feet!" Since ancient times how many people have picked up the snake and played with it? Tell me, has the snake ever wounded anyone or not?

Then the Master Yuan Wu struck.

TRANSLATOR'S NOTES

a.   In the *Chueh Kuan Lun* by Master Fa Jung of Ox Head Mountain it says: Q: What is 'rolling out'? A: Illumination and action is 'rolling out.' Q: What is 'rolling up'? A: Mind quiescent and extinct (nirvana) is 'rolling up.' When rolling out he travels everywhere throughout the universe; when rolling up even the traces of his concentration are impossible to look for.

b. See the biography of Tung Shan Liang Chieh. After leaving his teacher Yun Yen, he happened to see a reflection of himself as he crossed a river, and thereupon was greatly enlightened and composed the verse.

Pao Fu's Summit of the Mystic Peak

POINTER

Jewels are tested with fire, gold is tested with a stone; a sword is tested with a hair, water is tested with a pole. In the school of the patchrobed monks, in one word, one phrase, one act, one state, one exit, one entry, one encounter, one response, you must see whether someone is deep or shallow, you must see whether he is facing forwards or backwards. But tell me, what will you use to test him with? I bring this up: look!

CASE

Once when Pao Fu and Ch'ang Ch'ing were wandering in the mountains,[1] Pao Fu pointed with his hand and said, "Right here is the summit of the mystic peak."[2]

Ch'ang Ch'ing said, "Indeed it is. What a pity!"[3]

Hsueh Tou added a word, saying, "Today what is the purpose of travelling the mountains together with these fellows?"[4] He also said, "Hundreds of thousands of years hence, I don't say there are none, just that they will be few."[5]

Later this (dialogue between Pao Fu and Ch'ang Ch'ing) was quoted to Ching Ch'ing.[6] Ching Ch'ing said, "If it hadn't been Mr. Sun (Pao Fu), then you would have seen skulls covering the fields."[7]

NOTES

1. These two fellows have fallen into the weeds.
2. He raises a pile of bones on level ground. Just avoid speaking of it. Dig a hole and bury it deep.
3. If you don't have iron eyes or brass eyes, you'll probably be confused. Those with the same disease sympathize with each other. The two men are buried in the same hole.

4. Inevitably Hsueh Tou diminishes people's worth. Still it amounts to something. The bystander wields the double-edged sword.
5. A petty boast; here's another cloud-dwelling saint.
6. There's good, there's bad.
7. Only those on the same path know. The great earth is so vast and desolate it kills people with sadness. When the manservant sees the maidservant, he takes care. Even if Lin Chi and Te Shan appeared, they too would have to take a beating.

COMMENTARY

Pao Fu, Ch'ang Ch'ing, and Ching Ch'ing were all successors of Hsueh Feng; these three men attained alike and realized alike, saw alike and heard alike, picked up alike and used alike. With one exit and one entrance, they pressed back and forth one after the other. Since they were men born of the same lineage, as soon as one raised something the others knew where it came down. In Hsueh Feng's congregation it was just these three who always engaged in questioning and answering. Whether walking, standing, sitting, or lying down, the ancients were mindful of this path; that is why as soon as it is brought up, they know where it comes down.

One day when he was wandering in the mountains Pao Fu pointed with his hand and said, "Right here is the summit of the mystic peak." When Ch'an men these days are questioned this way, then they only frown; fortunately it was Ch'ang Ch'ing who was asked. Tell me, when Pao Fu spoke this way, what was his purpose? When the ancient Pao Fu acted like this, he wanted to test whether Ch'ang Ch'ing had eyes or not.

Ch'ang Ch'ing was a man of his house, so naturally he knew what Pao Fu was getting at; thus he replied to him by saying, "Indeed it is. What a pity!" But tell me, when Ch'ang Ch'ing spoke this way, what was his meaning? You can't always go on this way. Though there are those who seem so, (actually) there is rarely anyone at ease without the slightest concern. Fortunately Ch'ang Ch'ing understood Pao Fu completely.

Hsueh Tou added a word saying, "Today, travelling the mountains with these fellows, what is the purpose?" Tell me, where does this come down? Again he said, "Hundreds of thousands of years hence, I don't say there are none, just that they will be few." Hsueh Tou knows how to point to himself. This is just like Huang Po's saying, "I don't say that there is no Ch'an, just that there are no teachers." Hsueh Tou speaking this way is also undeniably dangerous and steep. If Hsueh Tou hadn't answered back with the same voice, how could it have been this unique and marvelous? This is called an added comment; it comes down on both sides, but though it comes down on both sides, it doesn't remain on either side.

Later this was quoted to Ching Ch'ing. He said, "If it hadn't been Mr. Sun, then you would have seen skulls covering the fields." Sun is Ch'ang Ch'ing's lay surname. Haven't you heard how a monk asked Chao Chou, "What is the lone summit of the mystic peak?" Chou said, "I won't answer this question of yours." The monk asked, "Why won't you answer this question?" Chou said, "I fear that if I answered you, you would fall onto the level ground."

In the teachings it says that the mendicant Meghasri always stayed on the lone summit of the peak of wonder; he never came down from the mountain. Sudhana went to call on him and searched for seven days without encountering him. But then one day they met on a separate peak. When he had seen him, Meghasri explained for Sudhana that the three worlds are a moment of thought and the wisdom and illumination of all the Buddhas, the gate of Dharma that appears everywhere. Given that Meghasri never came down from the mountain, why then did they meet on a separate peak? If you say Meghasri must have come down from the mountain, yet in the teachings it says that he never did come down from the mountain, that he was always on the solitary summit of the peak of wonder. At this point, where are Meghasri and Sudhana really?

Later, Elder Li created some complications, and made up a verse quite well:

> The lone summit of the mystic peak
> Is the teaching of one-flavor equanimity.
> Each and every one—they're all real;
> Each and every one—they're all complete.
> Where there's no gain and no loss,
> No affirmation and no negation,
> There it stands alone revealed;
> Therefore Sudhana couldn't see him.

When you get to the point of merging with nature, it's like "the eye does not see itself, the ear does not hear itself, the finger does not feel itself; it's like a sword doesn't cut itself, fire does not burn itself." At this point there are many instances of compassionate assistance in the teachings; this is why they let down a single path, and in methods of the secondary truth set up host and guest, devices and objects, questions and answers. Thus it is said, "The Buddhas have not appeared in the world, nor is there any nirvana. They manifest such things as expedient means to rescue sentient beings."

But tell me, in the end, how will you avoid Ching Ch'ing and Hsueh Tou talking as they did? If they hadn't been able to clap along in unison at that time, that would have been why "human skulls cover the fields all over the world." Ch'ang Ch'ing comes up with this testimony, and both Pao Fu and Ch'ang Ch'ing use it this way. Afterwards, Hsueh Tou comes out with a verse even more brilliant. The verse says,

VERSE

On the lone summit of the mystic peak, weeds grow in profusion;
    **You lose your body too. (The weeds) are already several fathoms deep beneath your feet.*

Clearly it is brought up—to be given to whom?
    **And used for what? There's no one on earth who knows. A dry piece of shit; what is it good for? You've got your nostrils, but lost your mouth.*ᵃ*

If it hadn't been Mr. Sun discerning the real point,
    **Wrong! Watch the arrow! He's caught the thief Without even realizing it.*

Skulls would cover the ground, but how many people would know?
    **They won't live again. They're numerous as hemp or millet seeds. You've got the nostrils but lost the mouth, Reverend.*

COMMENTARY

"On the lone summit of the mystic peak, weeds grow in profusion." If you roll around in the weeds, when will you ever have done? "Clearly it is brought up—to be given to whom?" Where is the clarity? This praises Pao Fu saying, "Right here is the summit of the mystic peak."

"If it hadn't been Mr. Sun discerning the real point." What truth did Mr. Sun see that he could say, "So it is. What a pity!"? As for "Skulls would cover the ground, but how many people would know?" Do all you people know? Blind!

TRANSLATOR'S NOTES

a.   "Getting the nostrils, but losing the mouth" connotes getting something vital but at the same time losing something else equally necessary by focussing exclusively on the first objective.

Kuei Shan and Iron Grindstone Liu

POINTER

Stand on the summit of the highest peak, and demons and outsiders cannot know you; walk on the bottom of the deepest sea, and even the Buddha's eye cannot catch sight of you. Even if your eyes are like shooting stars and your intellect is like flashing lightning, still you won't avoid (being like) the spirit tortoise dragging his tail (leaving traces.) At this point, what is proper? To test, I'm citing this: Look!

CASE

Iron Grindstone Liu arrived at Kuei Shan.[1] Kuei Shan said, "Old cow, so you've come!"[2]

The Grindstone said, "Tomorrow there's a great communal feast on T'ai Shan; are you going to go, Teacher?"[3]

Kuei Shan relaxed his body and lay down;[4] the Grindstone immediately left.[5]

NOTES

1. Unavoidably it'll be hard to stay there. This old lady is out of her depth.
2. Check! A probing pole, a reed shade. Where should you look to see the obscurity?
3. The arrow is not shot to no purpose. In China they beat the drum, in Korea they dance. The letting go was too fast, the gathering in is too slow.
4. The arrow got him. Where will you see Kuei Shan? Who realizes that in the far-off misty waves there is another more excellent realm of thought?
5. She's gone. She saw the opportunity and acted.

COMMENTARY

The nun 'Iron Grindstone' Liu was like a stone-struck spark, like a lightening flash; hesitate and you lose your body and your life. In the path of meditation, if you get to the most essential place, where are there so many things? This meeting of adepts is like seeing horns on the other side of a wall and immediately knowing there's an ox, like seeing smoke on the other side of a mountain and immediately knowing there's a fire. When pushed they move, when pressed they turn about.

Kuei Shan said, "After I die, I'll go down the mountain to an alms-giver's house and be a water buffalo. On my left flank five words will be written, saying, 'A Kuei Shan monk, me.' At that time, would it be right to call it a Kuei Shan monk, or would it be right to call it a water buffalo?" When people these days are questioned about this, they are stymied and can't explain.

Iron Grindstone Liu had studied for a long time; her active edge was sharp and dangerous. People called her "Iron Grindstone Liu." She built a hut a few miles from Kuei Mountain. One day she went to call on Kuei Shan. When he saw her coming, he said, "Old cow, so you've come." The Grindstone said, "Tomorrow there's a great communal feast on Mt. T'ai; are you going to go, Teacher?" Kuei Shan relaxed his body and lay down, whereupon the Grindstone left. All of you look—throughout they seemed to be conversing, but this is not Ch'an, neither is it Tao. Can it be understood by calling it unconcern?

Kuei Shan is over six hundred miles from Mt. T'ai; how then did Iron Grindstone Liu want to have Kuei Shan go to the feast? Tell me, what was her meaning? This old lady understands Kuei Shan's conversation: fiber coming, thread going, one letting go, one gathering in; they answer back to each other like two mirrors reflecting each other, without any reflection image to be seen. Action to action, they complement each other; phrase to phrase, they accord.

People these days can be poked three times and not turn their heads, but this old lady couldn't be fooled one little bit. By no means is this an emotional view based on mundane truth; like a bright mirror on its stand, like a bright jewel in the palm of the hand, when a foreigner comes, a foreigner is reflected, and when a native comes a native is reflected. It's that she knows there is something transcendent; that's why she acts like this.

Right now you are content to understand this as unconcern. Master Yen of Wu Tsu said, "Don't take having concerns as not having concerns; time and time again concern is born of unconcern." If you can immerse yourself in this and penetrate through, you will see that Kuei Shan and Iron Grindstone Liu acting in this way is the same sort as ordinary people's conversation. People are often hindered by the words, that's why they don't understand. Only an intimate acquaintance can understand them thoroughly.

It's like Ch'ien Feng teaching his assembly saying, "If you raise one, you shouldn't raise two; let the first move go and you fall into the secondary." Yun Men came forward and said, "Yesterday there was a monk who came from T'ien T'ai and returned to Nan Yueh." Ch'ien Feng said, "Chief cook, don't participate in the general labor today."

Observe these two, Liu and Kuei Shan; when letting go, both let go, and when gathering in, both gather in. In the Kuei-Yang tradition, this is called "merging of perspectives."

In the wind-blown dust the grasses move; thoroughly comprehend the whole from the surface. This is also called "a phrase which hinders one"—the meaning is conveyed but the words obstruct. When you get here, you must be able to sweep to the left and turn to the right; then you are an adept.

VERSE

Once riding an iron horse she entered the fortress;
*   **An adept accustomed to battle. Beyond the borders*
*   is the general's place. She's equipped with the*
*   seven items.* [a]*

The edict comes down reporting that the six nations are
*   cleared.*
*   **A dog carries the amnesty in its mouth. In the heart of*
*   the realm is the emperor's place. What about (the fact*
*   that) the sea is calm, the rivers clear?**

Still holding the golden whip, she questions the returning
*   traveller;*

**What's the news? Two people are supported by a single staff. They call to each other, going together and coming together. *

In the depths of the night, who will go along to walk the royal road?
    **You're headed southeast, I'm headed northwest. But tell me, why go?*

COMMENTARY

Hsueh Tou's verses are universally considered the best of their kind. Among the hundred verses this one verse is the most logical, among them it is the most wondrously arrayed and clearly set out.

"Once, riding an iron horse, she entered the fortress." This praises Iron Grindstone Liu coming as she did to Kuei Shan. "The edict comes down, reporting that the six nations are cleared." This praises the way Kuei Shan questioned her. "Still holding the golden whip, she questions the returning traveller." This praises the Grindstone saying, "Tomorrow there's a great communal feast on T'ai Shan; are you going to go, Teacher?" "In the depths of the night, who will go along to walk the royal road?" This praises Kuei Shan relaxing his body and the Iron Grindstone immediately leaving.

Hsueh Tou has this kind of ability: where they hurry he praises their hurrying, and where they are easygoing he praises their being easygoing. Feng Hsueh too once commented on this case, and his meaning was the same as Hsueh Tou's; people all over praise this verse:

> Standing on the summit of the highest peak,
> Unknown to demons and outsiders;
> Walking on the bottom of the deepest sea,
> Unseen even by Buddhas' eyes.

Look at Kuei Shan and Liu: one relaxed his body and lay down, one immediately left. If you go on wandering around, you won't ever be able to find the road. The meaning of Hsueh Tou's verse is most excellent. If he didn't have the same attainment and the same realization, how could he be capable of this? But say, what meaning was attained?

Haven't you heard how a monk asked Feng Hsueh, "When Kuei Shan said, 'Old cow, so you've come!' what was his inner meaning?" Feng Hsueh said, "In the depths of the white clouds the golden dragon leaps." The monk asked, "When Iron Grindstone Liu said, 'Tomorrow there's a great communal feast on T'ai Shan; are you going to go, Teacher?' what was her inner meaning?" Hsueh said, "In the heart of the blue waves the Jade Rabbit bolts." The monk asked, "When Kuei Shan immediately lay down, what was his inner meaning?" Hsueh said, "Old and worn-out, decrepit and lazy, days without concern; lying idly deep in sleep, facing the blue mountains." This meaning too is the same as Hsueh Tou's.

TRANSLATOR'S NOTES

a.   The seven items of a teacher are: 1) great capacity and great function; 2) swiftness of wit and eloquence; 3) wondrous spirituality of speech; 4) the active edge to kill or bring life; 5) wide learning and broad experience; 6) clarity of mirroring awareness; and 7) freedom to appear or disappear. In light of the military metaphor of the verse, it should also be noted that "the seven items" can also refer to a warrior's equipment.

The Hermit of Lotus Flower Peak Holds up His Staff

POINTER

If your potential does not leave (its fixed) position, you tumble down into the poison sea. If your words don't startle the crowd, you fall into the streams of the commonplace.

Suddenly, if you can distinguish initiate from lay in the light of sparks struck from stone, if you can decide between killing and giving life in the light of a flash of lightning, then you can cut off the ten directions and tower up like a thousand fathom wall.

But do you know that such a time exists? To test I'm citing this old case: look!

CASE

The hermit of Lotus Flower Peak held up his staff and showed it to the assembly saying,[1] "When the ancients got here, why didn't they consent to stay here?"[2]

There was no answer from the assembly,[3] so he himself answered for them, "Because they did not gain strength on the road."[4]

Again he said, "In the end, how is it?"[5] And again he himself answered in their place, "With my staff across my shoulder, I pay no heed to people—I go straight into the myriad peaks."[6]

NOTES

1. Look! He has the one eye on his forehead. Still, this is a nest for people these days.
2. You can't drive stakes into empty space. Provisionally the hermit sets up an illusionary city (to teach).

3. A thousand, ten thousand, (numerous as) hemp and millet. They've attained a little, though. What a pity! Swift falcons on a roost.

4. If you go to the road to discern this, you'll still be struggling for half a month's journey. Even if you gain strength, what's it good for? How could there be none at all?

5. A thousand people, ten thousand people, are sitting right here. Among a thousand or ten thousand people, one or two will understand.

6. Still, he deserves thirty blows, because he's carrying a board on his shoulder. If you see cheeks on the back of his head, don't go along with him.

COMMENTARY

Can all of you judge the hermit of Lotus Flower Peak? His feet still aren't touching the ground. Early in Sung times he built a hut on T'ien T'ai's Lotus Flower Peak. After they had attained the Path, the ancients would dwell in thatched huts or stone grottos, boiling the roots of wild greens in broken legged pots, passing the days. They didn't seek fame and fortune: unconcerned, they accorded to conditions. They would impart a turning word, wanting to repay the benevolence of the buddhas and patriarchs and transmit the Buddha Mind Seal.

As soon as he saw a monk coming, the hermit would hold up his staff and say, "When the ancients got here, why didn't they consent to stay here?" For more than twenty years, there was never even one person who could answer. This one question has both provisional and true, both illumination and function. If you know his snare, it isn't worth taking hold of.

But tell me, why did he ask this question for twenty years? Since this is the action of a master of the school, why did he just keep to one peg? If you can see here, naturally you won't be running in the dusts of the senses.

During the course of twenty years, there were quite a few people who laid out their remarks to the hermit to present their views, trying all their clever devices. Even if someone could speak of it, still he did not reach the place of the hermit's ultimate point. Moreover, although this matter is not in words and phrases, if not for words and phrases, it could not be distinguished. Haven't you heard it said: "The Path is fundamentally without words. We use words to reveal the Path"? Therefore the essential point in testing others is to know them intimately the minute they open their mouths.

The ancient man let down a word or half a phrase for no other purpose than to see whether or not you know that 'this matter exists.' He saw that the people did not understand; that is why he himself answered for them, "Because they did not gain strength on the road." See how what he says spontaneously accords with principles and meshes with the circumstances. When did he ever lose the essential meaning? The ancient Shih T'ou said, "When you receive words you must understand the source: don't set up standards on your own."

When people these days bump into it, they think that's enough. Though they get to it, what can be done about their fat headedness and confusion? When they come before an adept, he uses the three essential seals[a]—sealing space, sealing water, sealing mud—to test them. Then the adept sees whether the square peg is stuck in the round hole with no way to come down.

When the time comes where, will you search to look for one here with the same attainment and realization? If it's a person who knows that 'this matter exists,' then open your heart and convey the message. What is there that can be wrong? If you don't meet with such a person, then keep it to yourself for the time being.

Now I ask all of you: the staff is something patchrobed monks ordinarily use; why then does the hermit say that they didn't gain strength on the road? Why does he say that when the ancients got here, they didn't consent to stay here? In truth, though gold dust is precious, when it falls into your eyes it becomes a blinding obstruction.

Master Shan Tao of the Stone Grotto, when he was subject to the persecution (of 845) would always take his staff and show it to the assembly saying, "All the buddhas of the past are thus, all the buddhas of the future are thus, all the buddhas of the present are thus."

One day in front of the monk's hall Hsueh Feng held up his staff and showed it to the crowd saying, "This one is just for people of medium and low faculties." At the time there was a monk who came forward and asked, "When you unexpectedly encounter someone of the highest potential, then what?" Feng picked up his staff and left. Yun Men said, "I'm not like Hsueh Feng when it comes to breaking up confusion." A monk asked, "How would you do it, Teacher?" Yun Men immediately hit him.

Whenever you study and ask questions, there aren't so many things to be concerned with. (Concerns arise) because outside you perceive that mountains and rivers and the great earth exist; within you perceive that seeing, hearing, feeling, and knowing exist; above you see that there are various buddhas that can be sought; and below you see that there are sentient beings who can be saved. You must simply spit them all out at once: afterwards, whether walking, standing, sitting, or lying down, twenty-four hours a day, you fuse everything into one. Then, though you're on the tip of a hair, it's as broad as the universe; though you dwell in a boiling cauldron or in furnace embers, it's like being in the land of peace and happiness; though you dwell amidst gems and jewels in profusion, it's like being in a thatched hut. For this kind of thing, if you are a competent adept, you get to the one reality naturally, without wasting any effort.

The hermit saw that no one could reach his depths, so again he pressed them saying, "In the end, how is it?" Again they couldn't deal with him. He himself said, "With my staff across my shoulder, I pay no heed to people—I go straight into the myriad peaks." Again, what is the meaning of this? Tell me, what place is he pointing to as his whereabouts? Undeniably, there are eyes in his words, but his meaning is outside the words. He gets up by himself, he falls down by himself; he lets go by himself, he gathers up by himself.

Haven't you heard: The venerable Yen Yang met a monk on the road. He raised his staff and said, "What's this?" The monk said, "I don't know." Yen Yang said, "You don't even recognize a staff?" Again he took his staff and poked the ground saying, "Do you recognize this?" The monk said, "No, I don't." Yen Yang said, "You don't even recognize a hole in the ground?" Again, he put his staff across his shoulder and said, "Do you understand?" The monk said, "I don't understand." Yen Yang said, "With my staff across my shoulder, I pay no heed to people—I go straight into the myriad peaks." When the ancients got here, why didn't they agree to stay here?

Hsueh Tou has a verse which says:

> Who,
> Confronting the situation,
> Brings it up without deception;
> Such a person is rare:
> He destroys the steep lofty peaks,
> He melts down the mysterious subtlety.
> The double barrier has been wide open:
> Adepts do not return together.
> The Jade Rabbit—now round, now partial
> The Golden Raven seems to fly without flying.[b]
> Old Lu doesn't know where he's going—
> To go along together as before with white clouds
>   and flowing streams.

Why did I say, "If you see cheeks on the back of his head, don't go along with him"? As soon as you make a comparative judgment, you're in the demon cave of the mountain of darkness making your living. If you can see all the way through and your faith is thoroughgoing, then naturally a thousand or ten thousand people won't be able to trap you or do anything about you. When pushed or pressed, you will kill or give life spontaneously.

Hsueh Tou understood the hermit's meaning when he said, "I go straight into the myriad peaks." At that point he begins to make his verse. If you want to know where this is at, look at Hsueh Tou's verse.

VERSE

Dust and sand in his eyes, dirt in his ears,
    **Blocked up with tons of dirt. What limit is there to the
        confusion? There are other such people.*

He doesn't consent to stay in the myriad peaks.
    **Where will you go? But say, what scene is this?*

Falling flowers, flowing streams, very vast.
    **A good scene. With the lightning flash intellect, if you
        vainly toil tarrying in thought, look to the left—a

thousand lives; look to the right—ten thousand eons. *

Suddenly raising my eyebrows (to look)—where has he gone?
**Right beneath your feet another pair of eyes is given to
you. From the beginning he's just been right here.
Have you cut off the hermit's footsteps? Although it's
like this, it's still necessary to get to this realm to
begin to attain. I'll hit, saying, "Why is he just right
here?"

COMMENTARY

Hsueh Tou versifies very well: he has a place to turn around in
and doesn't stick to one corner. Immediately he says, "Dust
and sand in his eyes, dirt in his ears." This one line praises the
hermit of Lotus Flower Peak. When patchrobed monks get
here, they have nothing above to cling to or venerate, and
below they have no personal selves: at all times they are like
fools and dunces. Haven't you read of Nan Ch'uan saying,
"Among men of the Path, those that are like fools and dullards
are hard to come by." Ch'an Yueh's poem says, "I often recall
Nan Ch'uan's fine words/Such fools and dullards are indeed
rare." Fa Teng said, "What man knows the meaning of this? He
makes me think back to Nan Ch'uan." Nan Ch'uan also said,
"The seven hundred eminent monks (at the Fifth Patriarch's
place) were all men who understood the Buddhist Teachings.
There was only Workman Lu who didn't understand the Buddhist Teachings. He just understood the Path: that's why he
obtained the Patriarch's robe and bowl." Tell me, how far apart
are the Buddhist Teachings and the Path?

Hsueh Tou brought up this saying of Nan Ch'uan's and said,
"Sand can't get in his eyes, and water can't get in his ears. If
there is a fellow whose faith is thoroughgoing and who can
hold fast, he isn't deceived by others. (For such a man) what a
bunch of meaningless noises are the verbal teachings of the
buddhas and patriarchs! So I invite you to hang up your bowl
and bag, break your travelling staff, and just become an unconcerned man of the Path."

Hsueh Tou also said, "Mount Sumeru can be put in his eyes,
the waters of the great ocean can be put in his ears. There is a
kind of fellow who accepts people's haggling discussions and

the verbal teachings of the buddhas and patriarchs like a dragon reaching the water, like a tiger taking to the mountains. He must pick up his bowl and bag and put his staff across his shoulder. He too is an unconcerned man of the Path."

Hsueh Tou also said, "Neither way will do; after all, there is no connection."

Among the three unconcerned men of the Path (that Hsueh Tou has described), if you would choose one man to be your teacher, the correct choice is this kind of cast iron fellow. Why? Whether he encounters environments of evil or of wonders, to him what he faces is all like a dream. He doesn't know there are six senses, nor does he know there is sunrise and sunset. Even if you get to this realm, you must not cling to the cold ashes of a dead fire, you must not plunge into the flood of darkness. You still must have a way to turn around before you attain. Haven't you read of an ancient saying, "Don't cling to the greenness of the strange plants on the cold cliff. If you cut off the white clouds, the source is not marvellous."

Thus the hermit of Lotus Flower Peak said, "It's because they didn't gain strength on the road." To get it you simply must go into the myriad peaks. But say, what is being called "the myriad peaks"?

Hsueh Tou just likes him saying, "With my staff across my shoulder, I pay no heed to people—I go straight into the myriad peaks." Therefore he comes out with the verse. But tell me, where does he go? Is there anyone who knows where he goes?

"Falling flowers, flowing streams, very vast." Falling flowers in profusion, flowing streams vast, endless. For the lightning flash mind, what is before the eyes?

"Suddenly raising my eyebrows to look—where has he gone?" Why doesn't Hsueh Tou know where he's gone either? It's just like me raising my whisk just now: tell me, where is it now? If all of you people can see, you're studying with the hermit of Lotus Flower Peak. If not, go back to your places and try to investigate and observe carefully.

TRANSLATOR'S NOTES

a.   The three seals: Sealing mud, for the lower sort, who considers that something has been attained and leaves traces. Sealing water, for the middling sort, for whom there is something attained and the understanding mind still remains, but who leaves no traces. Sealing space, for the superior ones, who attain without attainment and leave no traces.

b.   The Jade Rabbit is the moon; the Golden Raven is the sun.

Pai Chang's Sitting Alone on Ta Hsiung Mountain

CASE

A monk asked Pai Chang, "What's the extraordinary affair?"[1] Chang said, "Sitting alone on Ta Hsiung Mountain."[2] The monk bowed;[3] Chang thereupon hit him.[4]

NOTES

1. There's an echo in the words. He demonstrates his ability in a phrase. He flabbergasts people. Though this monk has eyes, he's never seen.
2. His awesome majestic air extends over the whole country. The one standing and the one sitting both are defeated.
3. A clever patchrobed monk! There still is such a man who wants to see such things.
4. Chang is a competent teacher of our school: why does he not speak much? The imperative is not carried out vainly.

COMMENTARY

He has the eye to face situations and not heed danger or death. Thus it is said, "How can you catch tiger cubs without entering the tiger's lair?" Pai Chang was ordinarily like a tiger with wings. Nor does this monk shun birth and death: he dares to grab the tiger's whiskers and asks, "What's the extraordinary affair?" This monk too has eyes. Pai Chang immediately took up the burden with him saying, "Sitting alone on Ta Hsiung Mountain." The monk then bowed. Patchrobed monks must be able to discern the meaning before the question.

172

This monk's bowing was not the same as ordinary bowing: he had to have eyes before he could do this. He didn't spill all his guts to others. Though they knew each other, they acted like they didn't.

As for "A monk asked Pai Chang, 'What's the extraordinary affair?' Chang said, 'Sitting alone on Ta Hsiung Mountain.' The monk bowed; then Chang hit him": observe how when they let go, they both do so at once, and when they gather back, they wipe away the tracks and obliterate the traces. But say, when the monk bowed right then, what was his meaning? If you say it was good, then why and for what did Pai Chang then hit him? If you say it was no good, what was wrong about his bowing? When you get here, you must be able to tell right from wrong, distinguish initiate from outsider, and stand on the summits of a thousand peaks, to begin to understand.

This monk's bowing was like grabbing the tiger's whiskers: he was just contending for a pivotal position. Fortunately there's an eye on Pai Chang's forehead and a talisman behind his elbow, shining through the four quarters and profoundly discerning oncoming winds. Therefore he immediately hit the monk. If it had been someone else, he wouldn't have been able to handle the monk. The monk met mind with mind, conveyed intention with intention: that is why he bowed.

Nan Ch'uan said, "Last night at midnight, Manjusri and Samantabhadra came up with views of Buddha and Dharma. I gave them each twenty blows and sentenced them to be hemmed in by twin iron mountains." At the time Chao Chou came forward and said, "Who should take your beating, Teacher?" Nan Ch'uan said, "Where was my fault?" Chou bowed.

Masters of our school do not idly observe how the other takes action. The moment they are in charge of the situation and bring it into play, they are naturally leaping with life.

My late teacher Wu Tsu would often say, "It's like coming to grips in the front lines." I'm always telling you simply to cut off seeing and hearing, form and sound, all at once—then you'll be able to hold fast and act with mastery. Only then will you see Pai Chang. But tell me, how about when letting go? Look at Hsueh Tou's verse:

VERSE

In the realm of the patriarchs gallops the heavenly colt.
        ** *(Such a man) is born once in five hundred years.*
        Among a thousand or ten thousand people there's one
        or a half. The son (Pai Chang) takes up the father's (Ma
        Tsu's) work. *

Among expedients rolling out and rolling up are not the same
        path—
        ** *Already so before the words. Pai Chang gains inde-*
        pendence: it's a matter of his adepts' methods. *

In a flash of lightning or sparks struck from stone he retains
        the ability to change with circumstances.
        ** *He came head-on, turning to the left, turning to the*
        right. Do you see where Pai Chang helps people or
        not? *

How laughable—a man comes to grab the tiger's whiskers!
        ** *He deserves thirty blows. Where there's a great re-*
        ward, there must be a valiant man. He doesn't avoid
        losing his body and his life. I leave this move to
        you . . . *

COMMENTARY

Hsueh Tou can see all the way through: thus he can come out
with the verse. The heavenly colt runs a thousand miles in a
day, runs back and forth and up and down, gallops as though
flying: thus he is called the heavenly colt. Hsueh Tou is praising Pai Chang—in the territory of the patriarchs he runs from
east to west and from west to east, a single coming, a single
going, free in all directions, totally without the slightest hindrance, just like the heavenly colt. He was well able to gallop:
only thus can we see how free he is. This is because he attained
Ma Tsu's great ability and great function.

Haven't you heard? A monk asked Ma Tsu, "What is the
great meaning of the Buddhist Teachings?" Tsu then hit him
and said, "If I didn't hit you, all the people in the world would
be laughing at me." Again, the monk asked, "What is the

meaning of the Patriarch's coming from the West?" Tsu said, "Come here and I'll tell you." The monk approached and Tsu boxed his ears saying, "Six listeners don't draw the same conclusions (as to what was said.)" Observe how Ma Tsu attained the great independence in such fashion: within the gate of expedients, sometimes he rolls out, sometimes he rolls up. Sometimes the rolling out isn't in the rolling up, sometimes the rolling up isn't in the rolling out. Sometimes rolling out and rolling up both aren't there. Hence the saying, "On the same path but not in the same groove."

Hsueh Tou says, "In a flash of lightning or sparks struck from stone he retains the ability to change with circumstances." This praises the monk for being like sparks struck from stone, like the brilliance of a flash of lightning— it's just a matter of a bit of changing with the situation. Yen T'ou said, "Turning away from things is superior; pursuing things is inferior. In battle each man occupies a pivotal position." Hsueh Tou said, "The wheel of potential has never turned. If it turns, it surely must go both ways." And if it can't be turned, what's the use? Even powerful men must know a little of changing with circumstances. People these days just offer (their teacher) their true feelings and get their nostrils pierced by him. What end will there be?

This monk was able in the midst of lightning flashes and sparks to retain the ability to change with the situation, so he bowed. Hsueh Tou says, "How laughable—a man comes to grab the tiger's whiskers!" Pai Chang was like a tiger—how laughable that this monk went to grab the tiger's whiskers.

Yun Men's The Body Exposed, The Golden Wind

POINTER

Ask one, answer ten. Raise one, understand three. Seeing the rabbit he looses the falcon—he uses the wind to fan the flame—he doesn't spare his eyebrows.

This I leave aside for the moment. How is it when entering the tiger's lair? To test I'm citing this old case: look!

CASE

A monk asked Yun Men, "How is it when the tree withers and the leaves fall?"[1]

Yun Men said, "Body exposed in the golden wind."[2]

NOTES

1. What season is this? When the family breaks up, the people perish; when the people perish, the family breaks up.
2. He holds up the sky and supports the earth. He cuts nails and shears through iron. Clean and naked, bare and purified. Walking with even steps through the blue sky.

COMMENTARY

If you can comprehend here, then you begin to see where Yun Men helped people. Otherwise, if you still can't, as before you'll be pointing to a deer and calling it a horse: your eyes are blind, your ears are deaf. Who arrives at this realm?

Tell me, do you think Yun Men answered the monk's question, or do you think he was harmonizing with him? If you say he answered his question, you are wrongly sticking to the zero point of a scale. If you say he harmonized with him, this has nothing to do with it. Since it's not this way, ultimately, how is it? If you can see all the way through, patchrobed monks' nostrils are not worth a pinch. Otherwise, if you still can't, as before you'll plunge into the ghost cave.

In general, to uphold and establish the vehicle of our sect, you must take up the burden with your entire being and not fear for your eyebrows, you must stretch out in the tiger's mouth and allow others to pull you back and forth and drag you down. If you're not like this, how will you be able to help people?

This monk posed a question that was indeed dangerous and lofty. If you look at him in ordinary terms, he just seems to be a monk involved in idle concerns. If you go by the traditions of patchrobed monks, when you go into his life line and look, then he undeniably has something marvellous about him. But say, when the tree withers and the leaves fall off, whose realm is this? In Fen Yang's scheme of eighteen kinds of questions, this is called "a question to test the host." It is also called "a question that uses things."

Yun Men did not stir a hairsbreadth, but just said to him, "Body exposed in the golden wind." He answered most wondrously, and without presuming to turn his back on the monk's question either. Since his question had eyes, Yun Men's answer too was straight to the point. An ancient said, "If you want to attain Intimacy, don't ask with a question." If you really know someone, you know what he's getting at as soon as he mentions it. If you go to the vein of Yun Men's words to look, you've immediately gone wrong. It's just that in his phrases Yun Men was often wont to provoke people's emotional interpretations. If I made up emotional interpretations to understand him, I wouldn't avoid being bereft of my successors.

Yun Men liked to ride the thief's horse to pursue the thief in this way. Haven't you heard: a monk asked him, "What is that which is not within reach of thought?" Men said, "Impossible for cognition to fathom." This monk asked, "How is it when the tree withers and the leaves fall?" Men said, "Body exposed in the golden wind." In his words he unstoppably seizes and cuts off the essential bridge and doesn't let ordinary or saintly through. You must understand how Yun Men raises one and illuminates three, raises three and illuminates one. If you go to his three phrases to seek, then you're pulling an arrow out of the back of your head. In a single phrase of Yun Men's, three phrases are inevitably present: the phrase that contains heaven and earth, the phrase that follows the waves and pursues the currents, and the phrase that cuts off the myriad streams. (What he says) is naturally exactly appropriate. But tell me, of the three phrases, which one does Yun Men use to receive people? Try to discern this.

The verse says:

VERSE

Since the question has the source,
> **Hsueh Tou profoundly discerns the oncoming wind. The arrow is not shot in vain.*

The answer too is in the same place.
> **How could there be two? Yun Men is like a bell waiting to be struck. His efforts are not expended excessively.*

Three phrases should be distinguished:
> **Above, between, below. Which phrase is his answer here? First you must comprehend outside of the three phrases.*

An arrowpoint flies far into the void.
> **On target! It's gone by. Hitting, striking. The arrow flies past Korea.*

Over the great plains—chilling windblasts howling, wailing,
> **Throughout the heavens, all over the earth. Do you feel your hairs standing on end? He's let go.*

In the eternal sky—intermittent misty rains.
> **The winds are great, the waters vast. Above your heads, boundless vastness; below your feet, boundless vastness.*

Haven't you seen the traveller sitting so long at Shao Lin, who hasn't returned?
> **Here's another dunce. He's gotten others involved. The Yellow River flows turbid from its source.*

Tranquil up on Bear Ears Mountain, a single gathering.
**Open your eyes and you see, shut your eyes and you*
see too. Making a living in the ghost cave. Your eyes
are blind, your ears are deaf. Who arrives at this
realm? You don't avoid smashing your gap-teeth. *

COMMENTARY

The ancient man Shih T'ou said, "When you receive words,
you must understand the source. Don't set up standards on
your own." The ancient man's words were not empty talk.
Hence it is said, "In general to ask about this affair you must
have some knowledge of right and wrong. If you don't know
noble from base behavior, if you can't recognize pure and defiled, if you let your mouth speak at random, what will be the
gain?"

Whenever one utters words and spews out breath, it must be
like clamps, like tongs, it must have hooks and chains, it must
have unbroken continuity. This monk's question had the
source meaning: Yun Men's answer was also this way. Yun
Men always taught people with three phrases (in one): this is
his ultimate pattern.

Hsueh Tou's verse on this case is similar in kind to his verse
on the (eighty-second) case, about Ta Lung. "Three phrases
should be distinguished." Three phrases are inevitably present
in each phrase of Yun Men's. If you can distinguish them, then
you penetrate beyond the three phrases. "An arrowpoint flies
far into the void." He shot it so far that you must set your eyes
on it quickly to catch sight of it. And if you can see it clearly,
you can open out the universe in a single phrase.

At this point the verse is completed, but Hsueh Tou has
extra talent so he opens out and says, "Over the great plains—
chilling windblasts howling, wailing/In the eternal sky—
intermittent misty rains." Tell me, is this mind or is this object? Is this mysterious or is this wondrous? An ancient said,
"The truth of things is not hidden—from ancient times till
now it's always been obvious."

The monk asked, "What's it like when the tree withers and
the leaves fall?" Yun Men said, "Body exposed in the golden
wind." Hsueh Tou's intent was just to create a single environment. What's in front of your eyes right now, the whistling

wind, is either the southeast wind or the northwest wind. It will be all right only if you understand Hsueh Tou's meaning this way. If you go further and understand it as Ch'an or Tao, this has nothing to do with it.

"Haven't you seen the traveller sitting so long at Shao Lin, who hasn't returned?" Before he returned to the West Bodhidharma sat facing a wall for nine years, utterly silent. But say, is this "the tree withers, the leaves fall"? Is this "body exposed in the golden wind"? If here all past and present fools and sages, sky, earth, and the great world are all fused into one, then you will see how Yun Men and Hsueh Tou really helped people.

"Tranquil up on Bear Ears Mountain, a single gathering." Bear Ears Mountain is Shao Lin on Sung Shan near the Western Capital. In front and behind, the mountains are clustered thickly by the thousands. Where will all of you people see? Do you see where Hsueh Tou helps people? Even if you do, this is still the spirit tortoise dragging his tail (leaving traces).

Nan Ch'uan's Truth That's Never Been Spoken

CASE

Nan Ch'uan went to see Master Nirvana of Pai Chang (Mountain.)

Chang asked, "Have all the sages since antiquity had a truth that they haven't spoken for people?"[1]

Ch'uan said, "They have."[2]

Chang said, "What is the truth that hasn't been spoken for people?"[3]

Ch'uan said, "It's not mind, it's not buddha, it's not any thing."[4]

Chang said, "You said it."[5]

Ch'uan said, "I am just thus. What about you, Teacher?"[6]

Chang said, "I am not a great man of knowledge either: how would I know whether it has been spoken or not?"[7]

Ch'uan said, "I don't understand."[8]

Chang said, "I've already spoken too much for you."[9]

NOTES

1. A master should know. It stands like a wall ten thousand fathoms high. Does Chang feel his teeth falling out?
2. He's fallen into the weeds. Why so brash? Then there is such a thing!
3. Look how his hands are flustered, his feet frantic. He adds error to error. Just try and ask!
4. As it turns out he suffers defeat. After all he indulges quite a bit.
5. Don't explain it all for him: Let him go wrong his whole life. Chang shouldn't speak this way to him.
6. Fortunately he has a place to turn around. With the long, he's long; with the short, he's short. When the reasoning is superior, he goes to it.

7. Look how his hands are flustered, his feet frantic. He hides his body but reveals his shadow. He acts totally dead. There are thorns in the soft mud. Though he acts like this, how could he swindle me?

8. He can only act this way. Luckily he doesn't understand. If you understand I'll immediately break your head open! Fortunately this fellow is just this way.

9. Adding frost on top of snow. Why the dragon's head and snake's tail?

COMMENTARY

At this point he doesn't use "it's mind" or "it's not mind," nor does he use "not mind" or "not not mind." Even though from head to foot he doesn't have one hair of his eyebrows, still, he's gotten somewhere. Meditation Master Shou calls "it's mind" a revealing-explanation and "it's not mind" a concealing-explanation.

This Master Nirvana is Meditation Master Fa Cheng. Formerly he dwelled as retired abbot in the western hall at Pai Chang: (he had the monks) clear fields for him and (in return) he preached the great meaning for them.

At this time Nan Ch'uan had already seen Ma Tsu, but he was going around to various places to settle (what's right) and pick out (what's wrong.)

When Pai Chang posed this question it was indeed very difficult to respond to. He said, "Have all the sages since antiquity had a truth that they haven't spoken for people?" If it had been me, I would have covered my ears and left. Look at this old fellow's scene of embarrassment. If an adept had seen him asking this way, he would have been able to see through him immediately. But Nan Ch'uan just went by what he had seen, so he said, "They have." This was indeed brash.

Pai Chang then added error to error and followed up behind saying, "What is the truth that hasn't been spoken for people?" Ch'uan said, "It's not mind, it's not buddha, it's not any thing." Greedily gazing at the moon in the sky, this fellow has lost the pearl in the palm of his hand. Chang said, "You said it." Too bad—he explained in full for Nan Ch'uan. At the time I would have simply brought my staff down across his back to get him to know real pain.

Although it was like this, you tell me, where did he say it? According to Nan Ch'uan's view, it's not mind, it's not buddha, it's not any thing, it's never been spoken. So I ask all of you, why did Pai Chang nevertheless say, "You said it"? And there aren't any tracks or traces in Nan Ch'uan's words. If you say he didn't say it, then why did Pai Chang talk like this?

Nan Ch'uan was a man who could shift and get through, so after this he pressed Pai Chang and said, "I am just thus. What about you, Teacher?" If it had been anyone else, he wouldn't have been able to explain. But Pai Chang was an adept: his answer is undeniably extraordinary. Immediately he said, "I am not a great man of knowledge either: how would I know whether it has been spoken or not?" Nan Ch'uan then said his "I don't understand." He said "I don't understand" while actually he did understand: this is not genuine not understanding. Pai Chang said, "I've already spoken too much for you." But tell me, where did he speak?

If they had been two fellows playing with mud balls, both would have been covered with slime. If both were adepts, they were like bright mirrors in their stands. In fact in the beginning both were adepts; in the end they both let go. If you're a fellow with eyes, you'll judge them clearly. But say, how will you judge them?

Look at Hsueh Tou's verse:

VERSE

Patriarchs and Buddhas never helped people.
   **Each guards his own territory. If you have standards,
   hang onto standards. If you keep even a single word in
   your mind, you go to hell fast as an arrow.***

Patchrobed monks present and past running neck and neck.
   **Having worn out your straw sandals, break your staff
   and hang up your bowl and bag.***

When the bright mirrors are on their stands, the range of im-
ages differs.

*They've fallen, they've broken. Come smash the mirror and I'll meet with you. *

One by one they all face south and see the northern dipper.
*Do you see me astride the buddha hall going out through the mountain gate? In Korea they've gone up to the hall; in China they haven't yet beaten the drum. *

The dipper handle is hanging down.
*You still don't know where it comes down. Where is it? *

There's no place to seek.
*Blind men! Too bad! The cup falls to the ground, the plate shatters to pieces. *

When you pick up your nostrils, you lose your mouth.
*Where did you get news of this? After all, it's so, so I strike! *

COMMENTARY

Old Shakyamuni appeared in the world and in forty-nine years never said a single word. Beginning from the Land of Brilliance, ending at the river Hiranyavati, and for all the time in between, he never spoke a single word. Tell me, was such talk speaking or not? Right now it fills the Dragon Palace and fills the Oceanic Treasurehouse—how can this not be speaking? Haven't you heard Lord of the Mountain Hsiu say:

> The buddhas have not appeared in the world:
> Forty-nine years of talk.
> Bodhidharma didn't come from the West:
> Shao Lin has a wondrous secret.

Again it's said:

> The buddhas have not appeared in the world,
> Nor is there any truth to be given to people.
> They just were able to observe the hearts of living
>   beings,
> Responding to their ills according to circumstances,
> Giving medicines and dispensing prescriptions.

*Thus we have the twelve part teaching of the Triple
Vehicle.*

In fact from ancient times till now, the patriarchs and buddhas have never spoken for people. This very not helping
people deserves thoroughgoing investigation. I always say,
though I were to add a phrase as sweet as honey, when properly
viewed it's just poison. If you bring down your staff across their
backs and strike as soon as they blurt something out and push
them away, only then are you helping people on an intimate
level.

"Patchrobed monks present and past running neck and
neck." Everywhere they go they ask questions about is and is
not, about buddhas and patriarchs, about facing upwards and
facing down. Though they act like this, if they haven't arrived
at this realm, they can't do without this questioning.

"When the bright mirrors are on their stands, the range of
images differs." With just this one line you can distinguish
clearly. An ancient said, "The myriad forms are all the impression of the single truth." Again it's said, "The myriad forms are
all perfect within this." The great teacher Shen Hsiu said:

*The body is the tree of enlightenment,
The mind is like a bright mirror.
Constantly take care to wipe it clean:
Don't let it be defiled with dirt and dust.*

(The Fifth Patriarch) said that Shen Hsiu was still outside the
gate.[a] When Hsueh Tou talks this way, tell me, is he inside or
outside the gate?

You people, each of you has an ancient mirror. All the
myriad forms—long, short, square, round—each and every one
appears in it. If you go to the longness or shortness to understand, in the end you'll never be able to find it. This is why
Hsueh Tou said, "When the bright mirrors are on their stands,
the range of images differs."

Instead you must "All face south and see the northern dipper." When you're facing south why are you nevertheless to
look at the northern dipper? You'll see where Pai Chang and
Nan Ch'uan met only if you can understand this way. These
two lines (the third and fourth of the verse) praise Pai Chang
pressing and pressing again. Chang said, "I am not a great man

of knowledge either: how would I know whether it has been spoken or not?"

At this point Hsueh Tou's verse has come down into dead water. Fearing people would misunderstand he turned around and picked it up himself, saying, "The dipper handle is hanging down right now before your eyes: where else will you go to look for it? As soon as you pick up your nostrils you lose your mouth." Hsueh Tou has picked up the nostrils and lost the mouth.[b]

TRANSLATOR'S NOTES

a.   The Fifth Patriarch Hung Jen asked the members of his congregation to submit verses demonstrating their attainment, so that he could choose his successor and pass on the robe and bowl. Of the more than seven hundred disciples, none felt he could outdo Shen Hsiu, who was considered the foremost among them: thus only Shen Hsiu offered a verse. The Fifth Patriarch praised his verse and had it written on a wall for the congregation to learn and recite. Hui Neng, an illiterate workman in the congregation, happened to hear Shen Hsiu's verse being recited: knowing that Shen's verse reflected a lack of true understanding, he had a boy write another verse on the wall:

Fundamentally enlightenment is not a tree,
Nor is the mind-mirror a mirror.
From the beginning there hasn't been a single thing—
What's the use of wiping away dust?

When the Fifth Patriarch saw this, he made as if to disapprove, so that the monks of his congregation would not become jealous of Hui Neng, a layman and a barbarian. He came secretly to Hui Neng and handed on the robe and bowl to him, sealing him as the Sixth Patriarch.

b.   This means to gain one thing, but at the same time to lose something else equally vital.

Ta Sui's It Goes Along with It

POINTER

When fish swim through, the water is muddied; when birds fly by, feathers drop down. He clearly discriminates host and guest, he penetratingly distinguishes initiate and outsider, just like a bright mirror in its stand, like bright pearl in the palm of the hand. When a native comes, a native is reflected; when a foreigner comes, a foreigner is reflected. The sound is obvious, the form is evident. But say, why is it like this? As a test I'm citing this old case: look!

CASE

A monk asked Ta Sui, "The conflagration at the end of the eon sweeps through and the universe is totally destroyed. I wonder, is this one destroyed or not?"[1]
Sui said, "It is destroyed."[2]
The monk said, "If so, then this goes along with it."[3]
Sui said, "It goes along with it."[4]

NOTES

1. What thing is "this one"? No one on earth can get ahold of this phrase. He scratches in advance, anticipating the itch.
2. An iron hammer head with no handle-hole is thrown down in front of him. He's lost his nostrils. Before he opens his mouth, he's already thoroughly exposed.
3. Immeasurably great men whirl around in the stream of words. After all he misunderstands.
4. The first arrow was still light but the second arrow was deep. Just this is what so many people cannot find. When the water rises, the boats ride high; with a lot of mud, the buddha image is big. If you say "It goes along with that," where is it? If you say that it doesn't go along with that, then what? I'll hit!

COMMENTARY

Master Fa Chen of Ta Sui was a successor of Meditation Master Ta An. He was from Yen T'ing county in Tung Ch'uan (in Szechuan). He called on more than sixty men of knowledge.

Formerly he was the keeper of the fire in Kuei Shan's congregation. One day Kuei Shan asked him, "You have been here several years, yet you still don't know how to pose a question, so I can see what's what with you." Sui said, "What questions would you have me ask to be right?" Kuei Shan said, "Since you don't understand, ask, 'What is buddha?'" Sui covered Kuei Shan's mouth with his hand. Shan said, "Later you will not even find anyone to sweep the ground."

Later Ta Sui returned to Tung Ch'uan. At first he stayed by the road on P'eng K'ou Mountain, making tea and waiting on travellers for about three years in all. Only later did he finally appear in the world and open a mountain monastery, dwelling at Ta Sui.

There was a monk who asked him, "The conflagration at the end of the eon sweeps through and the universe is totally destroyed. I wonder, is this one destroyed or not?" This monk just came up with a question based on an idea in the Teachings. In the Teachings it says, "Formation, abiding, destruction, emptiness.ª When the age of the triple cataclysm occurs, the destruction reaches to the third meditation heaven." Basically this monk did not know the meaning of this statement.

Tell me, what is "this one"? People often make emotional interpretations and say, "'This one' is the fundamental nature of sentient beings." Sui said, "It is destroyed." The monk said, "If so, then this goes along with it." Sui said, "It goes along with it." As for "this one," so many people make emotional interpretations and are unable to find it. If you say that it goes along with it, where is it? If you say it doesn't go along with it, then what? Haven't you heard it said: "If you want to attain Intimacy, don't ask with questions"?

Later there was a monk who asked Master of the Mountain Hsiu, "The conflagration at the end of the eon sweeps through and the universe is totally destroyed. I wonder, is this one destroyed or not?" The Master of the Mountain said, "It's not destroyed." The monk said, "Why isn't it destroyed?" The Master said, "Because it's the same as the universe." Both "it's destroyed" and "it's not destroyed" obstruct people fatally.

Since the monk didn't understand what Ta Sui said, he inevitably had this matter on his mind. He took this question straight to Mt. T'ou Tzu in Shu Chou. T'ou Tzu asked him, "Where did you come here from?" The monk said, "From Ta Sui in western Szechuan." T'ou Tzu said, "What did Ta Sui have to say?" The monk then recounted the former conversation. T'ou Tzu burned incense and bowed and said, "In western Szechuan there's an ancient buddha who has appeared in the world. As for you, hurry back to him!" The monk returned to Ta Sui but Sui had already passed on. What an embarrassment for this monk!

Later there was a monk at the T'ang court named Ching Tsun who said of Ta Sui:

> *Clearly there is no other truth—*
> *Who says (the Fifth Patriarch) approved the south-*
> * erner Neng?*
> *The one phrase "it goes along with it"*
> *Makes a patchrobed monk run over a thousand*
> * mountains.*
> *A cricket who's cold cries in the piled up leaves;*
> *By night a ghost bows to the lamp before a crypt.*
> *The humming stops outside the lonely window,*
> *He wanders back and forth, unable to overcome his*
> * regret.*

Hence Hsueh Tou draws on two of these lines afterwards to make his verse.

Right now, you shouldn't make the understanding that it is destroyed, and you shouldn't make the understanding that it is not destroyed. In the end, how will you understand? Quick, set your eyes on it and look!

VERSE

In the light of the conflagration ending the age he poses his
*   question—*
  What is he saying? He's already gone wrong.
The patchrobed monk is still lingering within the double bar-
*   rier.*
  If you squash this man how can he be saved? A
  *hundred layers, a thousand levels.**

How touching—for a single phrase, "going along with that,"
   **The world's patchrobed monks all make this sort of
      judgment. It's not even worth it for a thousand
      phrases, for ten thousand phrases. What's hard about
      cutting off his footsteps?*
*Intently he travelled out and back alone for ten thousand
      miles.*
   **His active consciousness is very chaotic. He stumbled
      by without knowing it. He's just wearing out his
      straw sandals.*

COMMENTARY

Hsueh Tou takes charge of the situation and comes out with
his verse: in his words there's a place where he shows himself.

"In the light of the conflagration ending the age he poses his
question/The patchrobed monk is still lingering within the
double barrier." From the first this monk's question was concerned with "it is destroyed" and "it is not destroyed"—this is
the double barrier. A person who has attained has a place to
show himself whether he is told "it is destroyed" or he is told
"it is not destroyed."

"How touching—for a single phrase, 'going along with
that,'/Intently he travelled out and back alone for ten thousand
miles." This versifies this monk taking the question to T'ou
Tzu, then returning again to Ta Sui—this can indeed be called
being intent for ten thousand miles.

TRANSLATOR'S NOTES

a.   According to traditional Buddhist cosmology, these are the four
     phases an eon goes through.

Chao Chou's Big Turnips

CASE

A monk asked Chao Chou, "Teacher, I have heard that you have personally seen Nan Ch'uan. Is this true or not?"[1]

Chou said, "Chen Chou produces big turnips."[2]

NOTES

1. A thousand hearings are not as good as one seeing. He's pressing him. Everyone has a pair of eyebrows.
2. He holds up the sky and supports the earth. He cuts nails and shears through iron. The arrow flies past Korea.

COMMENTARY

This monk too is one who has studied for a long time: inevitably, there's an eye in his question. Nevertheless, Chao Chou is an adept: he immediately says to him, "Chen Chou produces big turnips." This can be called flavorless talk that blocks off people's mouths. This old fellow Chao Chou greatly resembles a thief who steals in broad daylight. As soon as you open your mouth he immediately plucks your eyes out.

If you are an exceptional brave-spirited fellow, then amidst sparks struck from stone and the brilliance of a lightning flash, as soon as you hear it raised, you immediately get up and go. Otherwise, if you linger in thought and hold back your potential, you won't avoid losing your body and your life.

In judging this case the wild sage Ch'eng of Kiangsi called it "asking about the east, answering about the west." He said that Chao Chou didn't answer and didn't climb into his trap. If you understand this way, how will you get it?

Jurist Yuan said, "These are words (affording) a glimpse from the side." This is contained in the *Nine Belts*. If you understand this way, you haven't even seen it in dreams, and, moreover, you're dragging Chao Chou down.

Some say, "Chen Chou has always produced big turnips, as everyone in the country knows. Chao Chou had called on Nan Ch'uan: everyone in the country knows this. That's why, when this monk nevertheless still asked whether or not Chao Chou had personally seen Nan Ch'uan, Chao Chou said to him, 'Chen Chou produces big turnips.'" But this has nothing to do with it.

If you don't understand in any of these ways, in the end, how will you understand? Chao Chou has his own road through the skies.

Haven't you heard: A monk asked Chiu Feng, "Teacher, I have heard that you personally saw Yen Shou. Is this true or not?" Feng said, "Is the wheat in front of the mountain ripe yet or not?" This matches exactly what Chao Chou said to the monk: both are like iron hammer heads with no handle holes.

Old man Chao Chou is an unconcerned man. If you question him carelessly he immediately snatches your eyes out. If you're a man who knows what is, you'll chew it carefully and swallow it. If you're a man who doesn't know what is, it will be like swallowing a date whole.

VERSE

Chen Chou produces big turnips—
> **Everyone knows. Just avoid saying so. Each time it's brought up it's brand new.* *

All the patchrobed monks in the country seize upon this as a principle;
> **Nevertheless, it isn't so. Who has a use for these idle words, this long-winded speech?* *

They only know it as extending from past to present:
> **Half open, half closed. (They're as numerous) as hemp or millet. In ancient times it wasn't so; right now it isn't so either.* *

How can they discern that the swan is white and the crow is black?
> **The whole capacity comes through. What's long is long

of itself; what's short is short of itself. Those who can recognize this are precious. Still, it's not worth discerning. *

Thief! Thief!
 ***Bah! It's none other: Hsueh Tou himself is wearing stocks, giving evidence of his crime.* *

He has snatched patchrobed monks' nostrils.
 ***He's pierced them, snapped them around.* *

COMMENTARY

"Chen Chou produces big turnips." If you seize upon this as the ultimate principle, you've already gone wrong. When the ancients joined hands and ascended high mountains, they couldn't avoid the laughter of onlookers. People all know that this answer of Chao Chou's is a statement of the ultimate principle, though in the end they don't know where the ultimate principle is. That's why Hsueh Tou says, "All the patchrobed monks in the country seize upon this as a principle/They only know it as extending from past to present/How can they discern that the swan is white and the crow is black?"

Though they know that both ancient people and modern people have answered this way, when have they ever been able to distinguish expert from naive? Hsueh Tou says, "To really understand you must discern the swan's whiteness and the crow's blackness within the sparks Chao Chou strikes from stone, within the brilliance of Chao Chou's lightning flash."

At this point the verse on this case is completed, but Hsueh Tou brings out his own opinion and goes to the place leaping with life to tell you more: "Thief! Thief!/He has snatched patchrobed monks' nostrils." All the buddhas of past, present, and future are thieves too; the successive generations of patriarchs are thieves too. They were well able to snatch away people's eyes. As for the skill not to blunder, I only approve Chao Chou. But tell me, how does he make a good thief? "Chen Chou produces big turnips."

Ma Ku Carrying his Ring-Staff

POINTER

Move, and a shadow appears; become aware, and ice forms. Yet if you don't move and are not aware, you will not avoid entering into the wild fox cave.

If you can penetrate thoroughly, trust completely, without a hair of blinding obstruction, you'll be like a dragon finding water, like a tiger taking to the mountains. Let go, and even tiles and pebbles emit light; hold still, and even real gold loses its color.

The ancients' public cases could not avoid being roundabout, but tell me, what were they discussing? To test, I cite this. Look!

CASE

Ma Ku, carrying his ring-staff,[a] went to Chang Ching. He circled the meditation seat three times, then shook his staff once and stood there upright.[1] Chang Ching said, "Correct. Correct."[2] (Hsueh Tou added a word, saying "Wrong!")[3]

Ma Ku also went to Nan Ch'uan: he circled the meditation seat three times, shook his staff once and stood there upright.[4] Nan Ch'uan said, "Incorrect. Incorrect."[5] (Hsueh Tou added a word, saying, "Wrong!")[6]

Ma Ku then said, "Chang Ching said 'Correct'; why do you say 'Incorrect,' Master?"[7]

Nan Ch'uan said, "Chang Ching is correct; it's you who are incorrect.[8] This is what is turned about by the power of the wind; in the end it breaks down and disintegrates."[9]

NOTES

1. He bursts forth in the same fashion as (Yung Chia did at) Ts'ao Ch'i; he startles the heavens and stirs the earth.

2. He's washing a clod of earth in the mud. He completely fools everyone. What talk is this? A donkey-tethering stake.
3. It won't do to let him go. There's still a move to go.
4. As before, he's washing a clod of earth in the mud: again he bursts forth; but though the frog leaps, he can't get out of the basket.
5. Why not accept it? He kills the man without blinking an eye. What is this talk?
6. It won't do to let the error go.
7. Where is the master? This fellow from the beginning grasps people's words; he has broken down considerably.
8. Good! When one kills someone, one must see blood; when one helps someone, he should do his utmost for them. How many people has he deceived?
9. After all, Ma Ku is trapped by Nan Ch'uan.

COMMENTARY

When the ancients travelled on foot to visit the monasteries everywhere, they only had this matter on their minds: they wanted to discern whether the old teacher on the carved wood seat possessed eyes or did not possess eyes. The people of old would stay if there was mutual agreement in a single word, and would leave if they did not agree in one word.

Observe how that Ma Ku went to Chang Ching, circled the meditation seat thrice, shook his staff once, and stood there upright. Chang Ching said, "Correct. Correct." (To use) the sword that kills people, the sword that brings people to life, one must be a master in his own right.

Hsueh Tou says "Wrong!" This falls on both sides, but if you go to either side to understand, you will not see Hsueh Tou's meaning. Ma Ku stood there upright, but tell me, what did he do it for? Why does Hsueh Tou then say "Wrong"? Where is it that he is wrong? Chang Ching said "Correct. Correct." Where is it that he is wrong? Hsueh Tou seems to be sitting there reading the judgment.

Ma Ku, carrying this word "correct," then went to see Nan Ch'uan. As before, he circled the meditation seat thrice, shook his staff once, and stood there upright. Ch'uan said, "Incorrect. Incorrect." For the sword that kills people, the sword that gives people life, one must be a master of the school in his own right. Hsueh Tou says "Wrong!" Chang Ching said, "Correct. Correct." Nan Ch'uan said "Incorrect. Incorrect." Are these the same or different? The first says "Correct": why is he also wrong? The latter says "Incorrect": why is he too wrong? If you attain understanding at Chang Ching's saying, you will not even be able to save yourself: if you attain understanding at Nan Ch'uan's saying, you can be the teacher of Buddhas and Patriarchs. Even so, patchrobed monks must prove it themselves before they will understand; do not just accept other people's verbal explanations.

Since Ma Ku's question was the same, why did one say "correct" and one say "incorrect"? If one is a thoroughly competent master, a man who has attained great liberation, he must have a life apart (from "correct" and "incorrect"). One who has not forgotten mind and objects will certainly be stuck over these two sides. If you want to clearly understand past and present, and cut off the tongues of everyone in the world, first you must clearly apprehend these two "wrongs." This is so because Hsueh Tou wants to bring up the livingness. If you are a fellow with blood under your skin, you will naturally not go to the words and phrases to create interpretations; you will not go to a donkey-tethering stake to make up theories. Some people say that Hsueh Tou utters these two "wrongs" on behalf of Ma Ku, but what has that got to do with it? They are far from knowing that the ancient's added comments lock off the essential gate; this side is correct, and that side is also correct, but ultimately they do not remain on either of the two sides. The librarian Ch'ing said, "Holding his staff, circling the meditation seat, 'correct' and 'incorrect' are both wrong. The reality of it does not lie herein."

Have you not read how Yung Chia came to Ts'ao Ch'i and saw the Sixth Patriarch? He circled the meditation seat three times, shook his staff once, and stood erect. The Patriarch said, "A monk is to have three thousand modes of dignity, and eighty-four thousand refinements of conduct; where have you come from, O Worthy, that you bear such great self-conceit?" Why did the Sixth Patriarch say that he bore great self-conceit? This one did not say "correct" or "incorrect"; "correct" and "incorrect" are both donkey-tethering stakes. There is only Hsueh Tou who, pronouncing two "wrongs," has thus attained something.

Ma Ku said, "Chang Ching said 'correct'; why do you say

'incorrect,' Master?" This old fellow didn't spare his eyebrows; he indulged considerably—Nan Ch'uan said, "Chang Ching is correct; it's you who are incorrect." One might say that Nan Ch'uan, seeing a rabbit, released a falcon. Librarian Ch'ing said, "Nan Ch'uan was excessively doting; whereas he might have let the matter rest with 'incorrect,' still he went on to bring out the other's fault for him, saying, 'This is what is turned around by the power of the wind; eventually it breaks down and disintegrates.'" The *Sutra of Complete Enlightenment* says, "This here body of mine is a combination of four major elements. The so-called defiled form of hair, nails, teeth, skin, flesh, sinews, bone, marrow, and brains, all return to earth. Saliva, tears, pus, and blood, all return to water. Warm breath returns to fire, and movement returns to wind. When the four major elements each separate, where could this illusory body be?"[b] When that Ma Ku circled the meditation seat holding his staff, already this was what is turned around by the power of the wind; eventually it breaks down and disintegrates. Then tell me, ultimately where does the matter of discovering the source of mind lie? When you get here, you must be a man made of cast iron in order to realize it.

Have you not read how the scholar Chang Ch'o called on the Ch'an Master Tsang of Hsi T'ang? He asked, "Do the mountains, rivers, and earth exist or not? Do the Buddhas of the three times exist or not?" Tsang said, "They exist." Chang Ch'o the scholar said, "Wrong!" Tsang said, "Who have you seen?" Ch'o said, "I have seen the Master of Ching Shan: whatever I asked about, Ching Shan said it doesn't exist." Tsang said, "What family do you have?" Ch'o said, "I have a wife and two children." Tsang then asked, "What family does Ching Shan have?" Ch'o said, "Ching Shan is an Ancient Buddha; you should not slander him, Master." Tsang said, "Wait till you are like Ching Shan; then I'll tell you everything doesn't exist." Chang Ch'o just bowed his head. A competent teacher of the sect always wants to melt the sticking points, remove the bonds, pull out the nails and draw out the pegs for people; he should not just hold to one side, but sweep to the left and turn to the right, sweep to the right and turn to the left.

Just observe how Yang Shan went to Chung Yi's place to thank him for ordination. When Yi saw him coming, he beat his hand on the meditation seat and said, "Wa wa." Yang Shan thereupon stood to the east; then he stood to the west, and then stood in the middle. After that, once he had finished giving thanks for ordination, he then retreated and stood there. Chung Yi said, "Where did you get this concentration?" Yang Shan said, I took it off the Seal of Ts'ao Ch'i." Chung Yi said, "You tell me, whom did Ts'ao Ch'i use this concentration to receive?" Yang Shan said, "To receive the Overnight Enlightened Guest (Yung Chia)." Yang Shan too asked Chung Yi, "Master, where did you get this concentration?" Chung Yi said, "I got this concentration at Ma Tsu's place." Isn't such conversation by fellows who raise one and understand three, see the root and pursue the branches?

Lung Ya said to his community, "Those people who penetrate the study must pass beyond buddhas and patriarchs. (Tung Shan) the Master of Hsin Feng said, 'If you see the verbal teachings of the buddhas and patriarchs as if they were your mortal enemies, only then will you have the qualifications for penetrating the study.' If you can't pass beyond them, then you will be deceived by the patriarchs and buddhas." At the time there was a monk who asked, "Do the patriarchs and buddhas have any intention to deceive people or not?" Lung Ya said, "Tell me, do rivers and lakes have any intention to obstruct people or not?" He went on to say, "Although rivers and lakes have no intention to obstruct people, it's just that people now can't cross them. Therefore, rivers and lakes after all become barriers to people. You cannot say that rivers and lakes do not obstruct people. Although the patriarchs and buddhas have no intention to deceive people, it's just that people now cannot pass beyond them. So patriarchs and buddhas after all deceive people. Again, you cannot say that patriarchs and buddhas do not deceive people. If one can pass beyond the patriarchs and buddhas, this person surpasses the patriarchs and buddhas. Still, one must completely realize the intent of the patriarchs and buddhas: only then can one be equal to those transcendent people of old. If you have not yet been able to pass through, if you study the Buddhas and study the Patriarchs, then you'll have no hope of attaining even in ten thousand aeons." The monk also asked, "How can I be able to avoid being deceived by the Patriarchs and Buddhas?" Lung Ya said, "You must be enlightened yourself." When you get here, you must be like this.

Why? When you help someone, you should do your utmost for them; when you kill someone, you must see their blood. Hsueh Tou is such a man, so he dares to pick up and play.

VERSE

This "wrong" and that "wrong"—
    **Be careful of your eyebrows! Still, this is acting*
    according to the imperative. 'In heaven and on earth,
    *I alone am the sole honored one.'**
It is important not to take them away.
    **A pair of hammerheads without holes; even the great*
    Compassionate One with a thousand hands cannot lift
    them up. If you take them away, Reverend, you'll
    *receive thirty blows.**
Then the waves are calm in the four seas,
    **No one in the world dares to move. East, West, South,*
    North, all have the same family style. Recently there
    *has been much rain and water.**
The hundred rivers return to the ocean tide.
    **Clean and naked, peace and tranquility in one's own*
    house is realized; the sea being at rest, the rivers
    *are clear.**
The standard of the ancient rod is lofty, with twelve gates;
    **How does it compare with this one? There is no eye on*
    the staff. It is important to avoid going to the staff
    *to make a living.**
In each gate there is a road, empty and desolate.
    **There's not a single thing. It belies your everyday*
    *life. If you look, you'll go blind.**
Not desolate—
    **After all. Luckily there's a place to turn around in.*
    *Already blind—so I strike!**
The adept should seek medicine without disease.
    **Once having died, you won't come back to life again.*
    Why are you fast asleep all day long? Why search
    *through the heavens and grope over the earth?**

COMMENTARY

This verse resembles the case of Te Shan seeing Kuei Shan: first (Hsueh Tou) adds two turning words, piercing it through on one string; then he produces his verse. "This 'wrong' and that 'wrong'—it is important not to take them away." Hsueh Tou's meaning is that the "wrong" here and the "wrong" there should absolutely not be taken away; if you take them away, you're mistaken. It is necessary to add this double "wrong" like this, and thus you realize right away: "The waves are calm in the four seas, the hundred rivers return to the ocean tide." How pure the wind, how bright the moon! If you gain understanding at these two "wrongs," you will no longer have the slightest concern: mountains are mountains, rivers are rivers, what is long is of itself long, and what is short is of itself short; one breeze every five days, one rainfall every ten days. That is why he said, "The waves are calm in the four seas; the hundred rivers return to the ocean tide."

The latter part eulogizes Ma Ku carrying his staff; "The standard of the ancient rod is lofty, with twelve gates." The people of old used a whip for a rod; patchrobed monks use the staff as a rod. The "ancient rod" is the staff; the pure wind is higher than the twelve vermillion gates. If you can understand this two-fold "wrong," then your staff will emit light; even the ancient rod can't be put to use. An Ancient said, "If you know the staff, your life's study is finished." It is also said, "This is not displaying form and vainly holding to things; the Tathagata's precious staff has personally left its traces." This is in the same category. When you get here, through all upsets and downfalls, throughout all times, you attain great freedom.

"In each gate there is a road, empty and desolate." Although there is a road, it is just that it's empty and desolate. At this point Hsueh Tou feels that he has indulged, so he goes on to strike a smashing blow for you; although it is so, still there is a place which is not desolate. Even if you are an adept, when you have no illness, still you must seek a bit of medicine to take.

TRANSLATOR'S NOTES

a. Monks' travelling staffs were often adorned with six or twelve rings at the top; these symbolize the causal chain: ignorance—

volition—consciousness—name and form—the six senses—contact — sensation — love — grasping — existence — birth — old age and death. The jingling of the rings is supposed to constantly remind the travelling monk of his condition. The "twelve gates" mentioned in the verse also may be taken to refer to these.

b. Fugai regards this passage from the *Sutra of Complete Enlightenment* as a later addition; in the Chinese style, it was customary to insert "footnotes" right into a text.

Elder Ting Stands Motionless

POINTER

The ten directions cut off, a thousand eyes abruptly open; when one phrase cuts off all streams, myriad impulses cease. Are there after all any who will die together and be born together? The public case is completely manifest, but if you cannot get it together, please look at the Ancients' trailing vines:

CASE

Elder Ting asked Lin Chi, "What is the great meaning of the Buddhist Teaching?"[1]

Chi came down off his meditation seat, grabbed and held (Ting), gave him a slap, and then pushed him away.[2] Ting stood there motionless.[3] A monk standing by said, "Elder Ting, why do you not bow?"[4] Just as Ting bowed,[5] he suddenly was greatly enlightened.[6]

NOTES

1. So many people are at a loss when they get here. There is still this here. Oh, why is he so feeble-minded?
2. Today he caught him. He's kind as an old woman. No patchrobed monk in the world can leap clear.
3. He's already fallen into the ghost's cave. He's already stumbled past. He can't avoid losing his nostrils.
4. On neutral ground there is a man who can see through it all. He has completely attained the other's power. When someone dies in the eastern house, the people of the western house help them mourn.
5. He uses diligence to make up for his incompetence.

6. Like finding a lamp in the darkness; like a poor man finding a jewel. (Still, this is) adding error upon error. But tell me, what did Elder Ting see, that he bowed?

COMMENTARY

See how he was; directly leaving, directly entering, directly going, directly coming—this indeed is the True School of Lin Chi, to have such dynamic function. If you can go all the way through, then you can overturn the sky and make it into earth, attaining the use of the endowment yourself.

Elder Ting was such a fellow; slapped once by Lin Chi, as he bowed and rose he immediately understood the ultimate. He was a man of the North, extremely simple and direct. Once he had attained this, he did not appear in the world thereafter. He thenceforth made complete use of the ability of Lin Chi; unavoidably his sharpness came through. One day on the road he met Yen T'ou, Hsueh Feng, and Ch'in Shan. Yen T'ou asked, "Where do you come from?" Ting said, "Lin Chi." T'ou said, "Is the teacher in good health?" Ting said, "He has already passed on." T'ou said, "We three were going especially to pay him our respects; our good fortune is shallow and thin, that we find he has 'returned to silence.' When the teacher was living, what did he have to say? Elder, please cite one or two examples for us." Ting then cited one day when Lin Chi instructed the assembly by saying, "In the lump of red flesh there is a true man with no station: he is always going in and out through the gates of your senses; those who have not witnessed proof of this, look! Look!" At the time there was a monk who came forth and asked, "What is the true man with no station?" Lin Chi immediately grabbed him and said, "Speak! Speak!" The monk hesitated, whereupon Lin Chi pushed him away and said, "The true man of no station: what a piece of crap he is!" Then Lin Chi returned to the abbot's room.

(Hearing this,) Yen T'ou unconsciously stuck out his tongue (in awe). Ch'in Shan said, "Why did he not say, 'Not a true man of no station'?" Ting grabbed him and said, "How far apart are 'a true man of no station' and 'not a true man of no station'? Speak quickly! Speak quickly!" Ch'in Shan did not speak; his face turned yellow and green. Yen T'ou and Hsueh Feng approached and bowed and said, "This novice does not know good from bad; he has offended you, Elder: we hope you will be merciful and forgive his error." Ting said, "If not for you two old fellows, I would have choked this bed-wetting sprite to death."

Again, once in Chen Chou, as he was returning from a vegetarian feast, he rested on a bridge. There he met three lecturing monks. One of them asked, "What is the meaning of 'Where the river of Ch'an is deep, you must plumb the very bottom'?" Ting grabbed him and was about to throw him off the bridge, when the other two lecturers frantically tried to rescue him, saying, "Stop! Stop! He has offended you, Elder, but we hope you will be merciful." Ting said, "If not for you two, I would have let him plumb the very bottom."

Observe such methods of his. This is wholly the dynamic function of Lin Chi. Also take a look at Hsueh Tou's verse:

VERSE

Tuan Chi's entire ability continues in his footsteps;
    **The Yellow River is muddy from the very source. The
    son inherits the father's work.*

Brought forth, why should it remain at ease?
    **Where is it? What can be done about the fact that
    there is such a man? Can a man without feet or hands
    attain that, or not?*

The great spirit lifted his hand without much ado
    **He scares people to death. A little boasting. Striking
    once with a whisk, I will not test any further.*

And split apart Flower Mountain's ten million layers.
    **The whole world appears at once. It's fallen.*

COMMENTARY

Hsueh Tou eulogizes, "Tuan Chi's entire ability continues in his footsteps; brought forth, why should it remain at ease?" Only Lin Chi alone continued in the footsteps of Huang Po's[a] great ability and great function. Once it is brought forth, it does not admit of any attempt to discuss it; if you hesitate, you'll immediately fall into the realm of ignorance.[b]

The *Surangama Sutra* says, "Just as when I put my finger on it, the Ocean Seal emits light, if you arouse your minds even momentarily, anxiety over the material world will come up first."

"The great spirit lifted his hand without much ado, and split apart Flower Mountain's ten million layers." The great spirit (of the Yellow River) had great supernatural powers; with his hand he broke open Mt. T'ai Hua and let the water of the Yellow River run through. Elder Ting's feeling of doubt was like a massive mountainous heap; struck once by Lin Chi, immediately he found the tiles had scattered, the ice had melted.

TRANSLATOR'S NOTES

a. Tuan Chi was a posthumous title of Huang Po Hsi Yun, Lin Chi's teacher.

b. "Realm of ignorance" is used here to translate "the heaps and the elements"; that is, form, feeling, perception, volition, and consciousness (the five heaps), and the six sense organs, their objects, and their associated consciousnesses (the eighteen elements). These are considered identical to fundamental ignorance.

Ministry President Ch'en Sees Tzu Fu

POINTER

He does not discriminate east from west, nor distinguish south from north, from morning till evening, evening till morning; but can you say he is fast asleep? Sometimes his eyes are like comets, but can you say he is wide awake? Sometimes he calls south north; but tell me, is he mindful or mindless? Is he a man of the Way or an ordinary man? If you can pass through here, for the first time you will know the ultimate, and then you will know how the ancients were so or not so. But tell me, what time is this? To test, I cite this. Look!

CASE

Ch'en Ts'ao, ministry president, went to see Tzu Fu. When Fu saw him coming, he immediately drew a circle.[1] Ts'ao said, "My coming here like this has already missed the point; how much more so, to go on and draw a circle!"[2] Fu thereupon closed the door of his room.[3]

Hsueh Tou said, "Ch'en Ts'ao has just one eye."[4]

NOTES

1. This is a spirit recognizing a spirit, a thief recognizing a thief. If he were not relaxed and at ease, how could he discern this fellow? But do you see the adamantine cage?[a]
2. Today he has encountered a man who's fast asleep. This old thief!
3. A thief does not break into a poor man's house. He has already entered the other's cage.
4. Hsueh Tou has an eye on his forehead. But tell me, where does his meaning lie? He should give him another circle. Clearly. Ch'en

Ts'ao has a dragon's head, but a snake's tail; at that time he should have given Tzu Fu such a thrust that he would have had no gate to advance through, and no road to retreat upon. But tell me, what further pressure could he bring to bear on him?

COMMENTARY

Ministry president Ch'en Ts'ao was a contemporary of P'ei Hsiu and Li Ao.[b] Whenever he saw a monk come, he would first invite him to a meal, and would give him three hundred cash, wishing thereby to test the monk. One day Yun Men came; seeing him, Ch'en Ts'ao immediately asked, "I do not ask about what is in the Confucian books, and the twelve part teachings of the three vehicles have their own professors: what is the purpose of a patchrobed monk's journey on foot?" Yun Men said, "How many people have you asked?" Ts'ao said, "I am asking you right now." Yun Men said, "Leaving aside 'right now' for the moment, what is the meaning of the teachings?" Ts'ao said, "Yellow scrolls on red rollers." Yun Men said, "These are written words and letters: what is the meaning of the teachings?" Ts'ao said, "When the mouth wishes to speak of it, words flee; when the mind seeks affinity with it, thought vanishes." Yun Men said," 'When the mouth wishes to speak of it, words flee' is to refer to maintaining verbalization; 'when the mind seeks affinity with it, thought vanishes' is to refer to false conceptualization. What is the meaning of the teachings?" Ts'ao was speechless. Yun Men said, "I have heard it said that you read the *Lotus of Truth* scripture; is this true or not?" Ts'ao said, "True." Yun Men said, "In that scripture it says that all livelihood and productive labor are not contrary to the characteristics of reality. But tell me, in the heaven that is beyond thought and thoughtlessness,[c] right now how many people fall back from that position?"[d] Ts'ao again was speechless. Yun Men said, "Do not be so careless. A real monk abandons the three scriptures and five discourses[e] to enter a monastery; after ten or twenty years, he still can do nothing himself. So how could you, ministry president, be able to understand?" Ts'ao bowed and said, "I am at fault."

Also one day as (Ch'en Ts'ao) had climbed up in a tower with a group of officials, they looked out and saw several monks coming. One of the officials said, "Those people approaching are all Ch'an monks." Ts'ao said, "No, they're not." The official said, "How do you know they're not?" Ts'ao said, "Wait till they come near, and I will put them to a test for you." When the monks reached the foot of the tower, Ts'ao suddenly called out, "O Elders!" The monks raised their heads. Ts'ao said to the group of officials, "Didn't you believe what I said?" There was only one man, Yun Men, whom Ch'en Ts'ao could not expose.

Ch'en Ts'ao had seen Mu Chou. One day he went to call upon Tzu Fu. When Fu saw him coming, he immediately drew a circle. Tzu Fu was an honorable adept in the Kuei-Yang lineage; he always liked to use the meeting of perspectives[f] to deal with people. When he saw the ministry president Ch'en Ts'ao coming, he thereupon drew a circular figure. But what could he do? Ts'ao was after all an adept, and didn't submit to the deceit of others; he knew himself how to make a test—he said, "My coming here like this has already missed the point; how is it worth going on to draw a circle?" Fu closed the door. This kind of public case is called "discerning the target within the words, concealing ability within a phrase." Hsueh Tou says, "Ch'en Ts'ao has just one eye." Hsueh Tou may be said to have an eye on his forehead. But tell me, where does his meaning lie? (Tzu Fu) should have produced another circular figure; but if he always acted like this, how could a patchrobed monk benefit others? Now I ask you, if you were Ch'en Ts'ao at that moment, what could you have said in order to avoid Hsueh Tou's saying that he has just one eye? Thus Hsueh Tou kicks over everything and versifies:

VERSE

Round and round the jewel turns, ringing like jade—
  ***With a three foot pole he tries to stir the Yellow River.*
  Only the Blue-eyed Barbarian (Bodhidharma) could do it. Made of cast iron. *

Horses carry it, asses bear it; load it on an iron ship;
  ***Why do you need so many for? What limit is there?*
  I give it to you. *

Share it with an unconcerned traveller of sea and mountain.
　　**There is someone who has no need of it. If one is a real
　　unconcerned traveller, he has no use for it. But you must
　　be a traveller without concern before you will get it.**

When fishing for a tortoise, he lets down a cage-trap.
　　**Coming this way, going this way; none can escape.
　　If it is a frog, what is the use of it? What's to
　　be done about prawns, mussels, snails, and oysters?
　　It is necessary to hook a tortoise.**

Hsueh Tou also said, "No patchrobed monk in the world can
　　jump out."
　　**You too are inside it. All are buried in the same hole;
　　but can you manage to jump out, your reverence?**

COMMENTARY

"Round and round the jewel turns, tinkling like jade: horses
carry it, asses bear it; load it on an iron ship." The beginning of
Hsueh Tou's poem just eulogizes the circle. If you can merge
with it, you'll be like a tiger with horns. This bit requires you
to have the bottom fall out of your bucket, your mental machinations to come to an end; throw away gain and loss, right and
wrong all at once, do not make your understanding in terms of
principle anymore, and do not understand it as a mysterious
wonder. Ultimately, how to understand? This must be carried
by horses, borne by asses, loaded on an iron ship. You will only
get it if you see it here. Anyplace else, it cannot be imparted: it
must be taken and shared with an unconcerned traveller of sea
and mountain. If you have the slightest bit of concern in your
belly, you will not be able to take it up properly. Here you must
be a person who is not affected by concerns or absence of concerns, by unpleasant feelings or pleasing situations, or by Buddhas or Patriarchs: only then can you take it up properly. If
there is any Ch'an to seek, any measure of profane or holy
feelings, you will certainly not be able to fully attain mastery.
But once you have attained mastery, how will you understand
his saying, "When fishing for a tortoise, he lowers a cage-trap"?
In fishing for tortoises, only a cage will do. That is why Feng
Hsueh said, "Used to fishing for whales, I scour the great

ocean; instead I'm disappointed by a frog crawling in the muddy sand." He also said, "O great tortoise, do not carry away the three mountains! I want to walk on the summit of P'eng Lai." Hsueh Tou also said, "No patchrobed monk in the world can leap out." If one is a great tortoise, he will not entertain the view of a patchrobed monk; if one is a patchrobed monk, he will not entertain the view of a great tortoise.

TRANSLATOR'S NOTES

a. The word for cage also means circle.
b. Like Ch'en Ts'ao, P'ei Hsiu and Li Ao were laymen who were adept at Ch'an. P'ei Hsiu was a student of Huang Po; Li Ao was a student of Yao Shan.
c. Or: "neither perception nor non-perception," *naivasamjnana-samjnanayatana,* the highest of the "four trances" which were cultivated by Buddhist mendicants since ancient times.
d. According to the Lotus Scripture, five thousand monks and nuns who thought they had attained nirvana got up and left when the Buddha began to preach the Lotus. They represent the lesser vehicle, whose devotees abide in detachment, without being able to detach from detachment itself.
e. According to the *Hekigan-Sho,* the three scriptures are the Hua Yen ("Flower Garland"), the Fa Hua ("Flower of Dharma," the Lotus), and the Nieh Pan (Nirvana) Scriptures; its list of the five discourses is redundant and thus incomplete, but it included the Wei Shih ("Consciousness Only"), Chi Hsin ("Arousal of Faith"), and the Ta Chih Tu Lun ("On the Great Perfection of Wisdom") Discourses.
f. Or: "meeting at objects," "concentration on objects." This refers specifically to circular figures, with or without characters added. Yan Shan especially is known for his use of these figures. The perspective of teacher and student meet in the object, and there's a special series of circular figures to represent this. Also, various phases and processes of Buddhist Teaching were represented symbolically in circles, figures, and words; no doubt at times these were used as meditation objects.

Yang Shan Asks "Where Have You Come From?"

CASE

Yang Shan asked a monk, "Where have you just come from?"[1]
    The monk said, "Mount Lu."[2]
    Yang Shan said, "Did you visit Five Elders Peak?"[3]
    The monk said, "I didn't get there."[4]
    Yang Shan said, "You never visited the mountain at all."[5]
    (Later,) Yun Men said, "These words were all for the sake of compassion; thus they had a conversation in the weeds."[6]

NOTES

1. Everyone in the world is the same. Still it is necessary to ask. (The monk) will inevitably construe it in the ordinary way.
2. A truthful man is hard to find.
3. He uses the wind to fan the fire. How could he have ever passed it by?
4. Take a step. A red face is not as good as honest speech. He seems to be at a loss.
5. Too much ado! He should be careful of his eyebrows. What is this old fellow's hurry?
6. The sword that kills people, the sword that gives people life. Two, three. If you want to know the mountain road, you must be the man who travels on it.

COMMENTARY

The point of testing someone is to know him intimately as soon as he opens his mouth. An Ancient said, "Immeasurably great people are turned about in the stream of speech." If you are one who has the eye on your forehead, as soon as it is being brought up, you immediately know where it comes down. See their one question, one answer; each is distinctly clear. Why did Yun Men then say that these words were all for the sake of compassion, so they had a conversation in the weeds? When that man of old gets here, he is like a clear mirror on its stand, like a bright jewel in the palm of the hand: when a foreigner comes, a foreigner is reflected, and when a native comes, a native is reflected. Not even a single fly could get past his scrutiny. But tell me, how is it that there was a conversation in the weeds for the sake of compassion? It was nevertheless dangerously steep; getting to this realm, only this fellow could hold up. This monk had personally come from Mount Lu; why did (Yang Shan) then say, "You have never visited the mountain"?

Kuei Shan one day asked Yang Shan, "When there are monks coming from various places, what do you use to test them?" Yang Shan said, "I have a way of testing." Kuei Shan said, "Try to show me." Yang Shan said, "Whenever I see a monk coming, I just lift up my whisk and say to him, 'Do they have this in other places?' When he has something to say, I just say to him, 'Leaving this aside for the moment, what about That?'" Kuei Shan said, "This has been the tooth and nail of our sect since time immemorial."

Haven't you read how Ma Tsu asked Pai Chang, "Where do you come from?" Chang said, "From down the mountain." Tsu said, "Did you meet anyone on the road?" Chang said, "Not at all." Tsu said, "Why did you not meet anyone at all?" Chang said, "If I had met anyone, I would mention it to you, teacher." Tsu said, "How could this have been happening?" Chang said, "I am at fault." Tsu said, "On the contrary, I am at fault."

Yang Shan's questioning the monk was just like these examples. At that time, when he said, "Did you ever get to Five Elders Peak?" if that monk had been a man, he would simply have said, "A disaster." Instead, he said, "I never got there." Since this monk was not an adept, why did Yang Shan not act according to the rule, so as to avoid the many complications that subsequently appeared? Instead he said, "You never visited the mountain." That is why Yun Men said, "These words were all for the sake of compassion, thus they had a conversation in the weeds." If it were a talk outside the weeds, then it would not be like this.

VERSE

Leaving the weeds, entering the weeds;
    ***Above the head, vast expanse; below the feet,*
    vast expanse. Half open, half closed. He is
    so, and I too am so.*

Who knows how to seek them out?
    ***He has a single eye on his forehead. You do not*
    know how to seek them out?*

White clouds, layer upon layer;
    ***A thousand levels, a hundred layers. He puts*
    another head on top of his head.*

Red sun, clear and bright.
    ***It has broken through. Blind! If you lift up*
    your eyes, you'll miss it.*

Looking to the left, there are no flaws;
    ***Blind fellow! As before, there's nothing to*
    be concerned about. Why are you displaying so
    much cleverness?*

Looking to the right, already old.
    ***One thought, ten thousand years. Gone past.**

Have you not seen the man of Cold Mountain?
    ***A leper drags his companion along.**

He travelled so swiftly;
    ***Still he's not fast.**

Ten years he couldn't return,
    ***Where is he right now? It's obvious.**

And forgot the road by which he came.
    ***He has attained freedom. (Hsueh Tou) passes up*
    the initiative, so (I'll) strike. Better not to
    act so lost.*

COMMENTARY

"Leaving the weeds, entering the weeds; who knows how to seek them out?" Hsueh Tou after all knows where they are at; when he gets there, with one hand he upholds, and with the other hand he pushes down. "White clouds, layer upon layer; red sun, clear and bright." This is much like "Grasses in profusion, mist overhanging." At this point there is not even so much as a single hair that belongs to the ordinary, nor so much as a single hair that belongs to the holy. The whole world has never concealed it; each particular cannot cover it. This is what is called the realm of no-mind; when cold, it doesn't feel cold, and when hot it doesn't feel hot—the whole thing is one great gate of liberation. "Looking to the left, there are no flaws; looking to the right, already old."

Master "Lazy" Ts'an dwelt in seclusion in a stone grotto on Mount Heng. Emperor Su Tsung of T'ang heard of his name and sent an emissary to summon him. The emissary went to his grotto and made the announcement, "The Emperor has a command; you should rise and give thanks for his favor, Reverend." Just then Ts'an poked into his ox-dung fire, took out a baked yam and ate it; cold nose-water dripped from his chin. He did not answer at all. The emissary laughed and said, "I suggest that you wipe off that snot, Reverend." Ts'an said, "What leisure time do I have to wipe snot for a worldly man?" After all he never arose. The emissary returned and reported this to the Emperor. Su Tsung praised him highly. Someone so pure and calm, so clear and direct as this, is not at the disposal of others; he just holds still, as though made of cast iron. It is just like the case of Master Shan Tao, who after the purge never again became a monk; people called him "the stone-grotto worker." Whenever he tread the pestle, he forgot the movement of his footsteps. A monk asked Lin Chi, "What is the essential meaning of the stone grotto worker's forgetfulness of the movement of his footsteps?" Chi said, "Sunken in a deep pit."

Fa Yen's verse on Completely Perfect True Nature reads,

> When reason is exhausted, feelings and considerations are forgotten:
> How could there be any adequate comparison?
> Wherever I go there's the frosty night's moon;
> It falls as it may into the valley ahead.
> When the fruits are ripe, they are heavy with monkeys;
> The mountains go on so long, it seems I have lost my way;

When I raise my head, there is some light remain-
ing—
Actually this is west of my dwelling place.

Hsueh Tou said, "Have you not seen the man of Cold Mountain? He travelled so swiftly: for ten years he couldn't return,
and forgot the road by which he came." In one of the Cold
Mountain Man's poems it says, "If you want a place to rest
your body, you can preserve it long on Cold Mountain. The
gentle wind blows in the dense pines; heard from nearby, the
sound is even better. Underneath there is a man with half-grey
hair furiously reading Huang-Lao.[a] For ten years he couldn't
return, and forgot the road he took when he came." Yung Chia
also said, "Mind is the organ, phenomena are the objects: both
are like flaws in a mirror. When the defilement of the flaws is
gone, only then does the light appear; when mind and
phenomena are both forgotten, nature is identical to reality."
When you get here, be like a fool, like a blockhead, and then
you will perceive this public case. If you do not reach this
realm, you will just be running around in the words; what end
will there ever be?

TRANSLATOR'S NOTES

a. That is, the Taoist teachings: a book on internal medicine by the
    Yellow Emperor (Huang Ti) and the Tao Te Ching of Laotzu,
    explaining the way to long life.

The Dialogue of Manjusri and Wu Cho

POINTER

Determining dragons and snakes, distinguishing jewels and stones, separating the profound and the naive, to settle all uncertainty: if you haven't an eye on your forehead and a talisman under your elbow, time and again you will miss the point immediately. Right at this very moment seeing and hearing are not obscured; sound and form are purely real. Tell me, is it black? Is it white? Is it crooked? Is it straight? At this point, how will you discriminate?

CASE

Manjusri asked Wu Cho, "Where have you just come from?"[1]
Wu Cho said, "The South."[2]
Manjusri said, "How is the Buddhist Teaching being carried on in the South?"[3]
Wu Cho said, "Monks of the Last Age have little regard for the rules of discipline."[4]
Manjusri said, "How numerous are the congregations?"[5]
Wu Cho said, "Some three hundred, some five hundred."[6]
Wu Cho asked Manjusri, "How is it being carried on hereabouts?"[7]
Manjusri said, "Ordinary people and sages dwell together; dragons and snakes intermingle."[8]
Wu Cho said, "How numerous are the congregations?"[9]
Manjusri said, "In front, three by three; in back, three by three."[10]

216

NOTES

1. It is necessary to pose the question. There is still this news.
2. He sticks his head up from his nest in the weeds. Why should he hoist it on to his eyebrows? There is nothing outside the great vastness; why is there nevertheless a South?
3. If he asked someone else, a disaster would happen. It still lingers on his teeth and lips.
4. A truthful man is hard to find.
5. At that moment I would immediately give him a shout. With one nudge he pushes him over.
6. They are all wild fox spirits. After all he's let slip.
7. He's pushed! Immediately he turns the spear around and comes back with it.
8. He's suffered quite a loss. In fact his feet are frantic, his hands in confusion.
9. Give me back the words. Still he can't be let go.
10. Crazy words, insane talk. But tell me, how many are they? Even the Great Compassionate One with a thousand hands could not count them all.

COMMENTARY

When Wu Cho was visiting Mt. Wu T'ai, when he came to a place on the way where it was wild and rough, Manjusri produced a temple to take him in for the night. So he asked, "Where have you just come from?" Cho said, "The South." Manjusri asked, "How is the Buddhist Teaching being carried on in the South?" Cho said, "Monks of this Last Age have little regard for the rules of discipline." Manjusri asked, "How numerous are the congregations?" Cho said, "Some three hundred, some five hundred." Wu Cho then asked Manjusri, "How is it being carried on hereabouts?" Manjusri said, "Ordinary people and sages dwell together; dragons and snakes intermingle." Cho asked, "How numerous are the congregations?" Manjusri said, "In front, three by three; in back, three by three."

Then they drank tea; Manjusri held up a crystal bowl and

asked, "Do they also have this in the South?" Cho said, "No." Manjusri said, "What do they usually use to drink tea?" Cho was speechless. After all he took his leave and departed. Manjusri ordered Ch'un T'i the servant boy to see him to the gate. When they got to the portals of the gate, Wu Cho asked the boy, "Before, he said, 'In front three by three; in back, three by three'; how many is this?" The boy said, "O Worthy!" Cho responded "Yes?" The boy said, "How many is this?" Cho also asked, "What temple is this?" The boy pointed beyond the Vajrasattva; when Cho turned his head, the illusory temple and the boy had vanished completely out of sight: it was just an empty valley. Later that place was called the Vajra (Adamantine) Cave.

Later on a monk asked Feng Hsueh, "What is the Master of Ch'ing Liang Mountain?"[a] Hsueh said, "One phrase did not settle Wu Cho's question; to this very day he is still a monk who sleeps in the fields."

If you want to penetrate the peaceful equanimity of actual truth, so that your feet tread upon the real earth, go to Wu Cho's words to get attainment; then naturally though you stay in a cauldron of hot water or the embers of a stove, still you would not feel hot, and though you stay on cold ice, neither would you feel cold.

If you want to go through to use the solitary peril, the steep and sharp, like the Jewel Sword of the Diamond King, go to Manjusri's words to get attainment; then naturally water poured will not wet, and wind blowing cannot enter.

Have you not seen how Ti Tsang of Cheng Chou asked a monk, "Where have you just come from?" The monk said, "The South." Tsang said, "How is Buddhism there?" The monk said, "There is much deliberation." Tsang said, "How can that compare with us here sowing fields and having a lot of rice to eat?" Now tell me, is this the same as Manjusri's answer, or is it different? Some say that Wu Cho's answers were wrong, while in Manjusri's answers there is both snake and dragon, there is both the ordinary and the sage. What bearing does this have on it? Can you clearly discern three by three in front, three by three in back? The first arrow will still light; the second arrow went deep. Now tell me, how many is this? If you can pass through here, then a thousand phrases, ten thousand phrases, are only one phrase. If at this one phrase you can cut off and hold still, in the next moment you will reach this realm.

VERSE

The thousand peaks twist and turn, the color of indigo.
    But do you see Manjusri?
Who says Manjusri was conversing with him?
    **Even if it were Samantabhadra, I wouldn't pay any
    attention. He's already stumbled past.**
It is laughable, "How many the people?" on Ch'ing Liang:
    **Tell me, what is he laughing at? It's already there
    before speaking of it.**
In front three by three, and in back three by three.
    **Please observe it under your feet. There are thorns
    in the soft mud. The tea bowl falls to the ground, the
    dish breaks in seven pieces.**

COMMENTARY

"The thousand peaks twist and turn, blue as indigo; who says Manjusri was conversing with him?" Some say that Hsueh Tou is just reciting it a second time, without ever eulogizing it. It is just like a monk asked Fa Yen, "What is a drop of water from the source of the Ts'ao stream?" Yen said, "A drop of water from the source of the Ts'ao stream." Also a monk asked Master Hui Chueh of Lung Ya, "How does fundamental purity and clarity suddenly give rise to mountains, rivers, and earth?" Chueh said, "How does fundamental purity and clarity suddenly give rise to mountains, rivers, and earth?" You cannot say either that these were just repetitions.

The One-Eyed Dragon of Min Ch'ao also versified the meaning of this, with the ability to cover heaven and earth; he said,

> Extending throughout the world is the beautiful
>   monastery:
> The Manjusri that fills the eyes is the one conversing.
> Not knowing to open the Buddha-eye at his words,

(Wu Cho) turned his head and saw only the blue mountain crags.

"Extending throughout the world is the beautiful monastery." This refers to the illusory temple nestled in the weeds. This is what is called having the ability to carry out both the provisional and the real together. The Manjusri which fills the eyes is talking; if you don't know how to open the Buddha-eye at his words, when you turn your head you'll only see the blue mountain crags. At such a time, could you call it the realm of Manjusri, Samantabhadra,[b] or Avalokitesvara?[c] In essence it is not this principle. Hsueh Tou just changes Ming Ch'ao's usage; instead he has a needle and thread—"Ten thousand peaks twist and turn, blue as indigo." He does not run afoul of the point and hurt his hand. Within the phrase there is the provisional, there is the real; there is principle, there are phenomena. Who says Manjusri was conversing with him? They talked all night, but he didn't know it was Manjusri.

Later Wu Cho stayed on Mt. Wu T'ai and worked as a cook. Every time Manjusri appeared on the rice pot, Wu Cho lifted the rice stirrer and hit him. Still, this is drawing the bow after the thief has left.

This time, as soon as he said, "How is the Buddhist Teaching being carried on in the South?" he should have hit him right on the spine; then he would have gotten somewhere.

"It's laughable, 'How many are the people?' on Ch'ing Liang." There is a sword in Hsueh Tou's laughter. If you can understand what he's laughing about, you will see the other's saying, "In front three by three; in back three by three."

TRANSLATOR'S NOTES

a. Ch'ing Liang ("Pure and Cool") was another name for Mt. Wu T'ai. One of the five holy mountains of China, it was traditionally thought to be the abode of Manjusri, who symbolizes wisdom and knowledge. The Vajra, or Diamond, is also a symbol of wisdom, because it can cut through everything, while itself being firm and indestructible.

b. Samantabhadra, universal goodness, is the bodhisattva representing the ultimate principle.

c. Avalokitesvara is the bodhisattva representing compassion.

Biographical Supplement

The following excerpts from the lives and sayings of the eminent Ch'an masters appearing in the main cases of *The Blue Cliff Record* are taken mostly from the classic Ch'an history *Ching Te Ch'uan Teng Lu* (briefly, *Ch'uan Teng Lu*, hereafter referred to as CTL), the "Record of the Transmission of the Lamp (compiled in) the Ching Te era (of the Sung dynasty, 1004)." Containing information on over six hundred Ch'an masters, the CTL usually gives only a few bare biographical facts such as birth, death, and enlightenment stories; most "biography" consists of dialogues, sayings and doings of the teachers. The CTL also includes three chapters of sermons, poems, and short writings. It is a standard Ch'an book and a primary source of many *kung an*.

Some material is also taken from the *Tsu T'ang Chi*, "Collection from the Halls of the Ancestors"; *Wu Teng Hui Yuan*, "Five Lamps Merged in the Source"; and *Ku Tsun Su Yu Lu*, "Records of Sayings of Ancient Venerable Adepts." (These will hereafter be referred to as TTC, WT, and KTS, respectively.)

The TTC antedates the CTL by about fifty years; though a much smaller collection, it contains a number of stories not found in CTL or later collections. The WT, a later and more extensive compilation, draws on five so-called "Lamp" records, including the CTL and its continuation, plus the *Kuang Teng Lu*, *Lien Teng Hui Yao*, and *P'u Teng Lu*. The title "Five Lamps" refers to these five source collections, but is also sometimes taken to refer to the five houses of classical Ch'an. The WT covers a longer period of time than CTL, and often contains more material on individual masters than does the former. Tenkei Denson, one of the main commentators consulted on *The Blue Cliff Record*, usually cites the WT as most detailed and authoritative.

The KTS contains extensive records of sermons and sayings of numerous Ch'an masters, and includes whole volumes which have been published as individual books, such as the *Lin*

221

Chi Lu, "Record of Lin Chi"; and the *Yun Men Kuang Lu,* "Extensive Record of Yun Men."

The order of the biographies is as follows:
Bodhidharma (case 1)
Pao Chih (cases 1, 67)
Chao Chou Ts'ung Shen (cases 2, 9, 30)
Ma Tsu Tao I (case 3)
Te Shan Hsuan Ch'ien (case 4)
Kuei Shan Ling Yu (cases 4, 24, 70)
Hsueh Feng I Ts'un (cases 5, 22, 49, 51)
Yun Men Wen Yen (cases 6, 8, 14, 15, 22, 27, 34)
Fa Yen Wen I (case 7)
Ts'ui Yen Ling Ts'an (case 8)
Pao Fu Ts'ung Chan (cases 8, 22, 23, 95)
Ch'ang Ch'ing Hui Leng (cases 8, 22, 23, 95)
Mu Chou Tao Tsung (case 10)
Huang Po Hsi Yun (case 11)
Tung Shan Shou Ch'u (case 12)
Pa Ling Hao Chien (cases 13, 100)
Ching Ch'ing (cases 16, 23, 46)
Hsiang Lin Teng Yuan (case 17)
Nan Yang Hui Chung (cases 18, 99)
Lung Ya Chu Tun (case 20)
Ts'ui Wei Wu Hsueh (case 20)
Lin Chi I Hsuan (cases 20, 32)
Chih Men Kuang Tso (cases 21, 90)
Hsuan Sha Tsung I (cases 22, 88)
Lotus Flower Peak Hermit (case 25)
Pai Chang Huai Hai (cases 26, 53, 70, 71, 72, 73)
Nan Ch'uan P'u Yuan (cases 28, 31)
Ta Sui Fa Chen (case 29)
Ma Ku Pao Che (case 31)
Chang Ching Huai Hui (case 31)
Tzu Fu Ju Pao (case 33)
Yang Shan Hui Chi (cases 34, 68)

LINEAGE OF MASTERS

Those appearing in the main examples of volume one of *The Blue Cliff Record* are marked by asterisks.

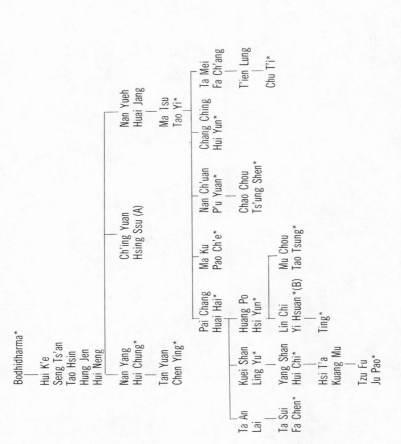

(A) Ch'ing Yuan Hsing Ssu

Shih T'ou
Hsi Ch'ien

T'ien Huang   Tan Hsia   Yao Shan
Tao Wu   T'ien Jan   Wei Yen

Lung T'an   Ts'ui Wei   Yun Yen
Ch'ung Hsin   Wu Hsueh*   Tan Ch'eng

Te Shan   Tung Shan
Hsuan Chien*   Liang Chieh

Hsueh Feng   Lung Ya
Yi Ts'un*   Chu Tun*

Yun Men   Ts'ui Yen   Pao Fu   Ching Ch'ing   Ch'ang Ch'ing   Hsuan Sha
Wen Yen*   Ling Ts'an* Tao Fu*   Tao Fu*   Hui Leng*   Shih Pei*

Feng Hsien Pa Ling   Tung Shan   Hsiang Lin   Lo Han
Chen   Hao Ch'ien* Shou Ch'u* Teng Yuan   Kuei Ch'en

Lotus Peak Hermit*   Chih Men   Fa Yen
                                     Kuang Tso*   Wen Yi*

                                     Hsueh Tou   Hui Ch'ao*
                                     Ch'ung Hsien

(B) later Lin Chi masters

Lin Chi Yi Hsuan

Hsing Hua Ts'un Chiang

Nan Yuan Hui Yung

Feng Hsueh Yen Chao

Shou Shan Hsing Nien

Fen Yang Shan Chao   Yeh Hsien Kuei Shen

Yang Ch'i   Huang Lung   Ts'ui Yen   Fu Shan
Fang Yui   Hui Nan   K'e Chen   Fa Yuan ("the jurist")

Pai Yun   Huan Lung   Ta Kuei
Shou Tuan   Tsu Hsin   Mu Ch'e

Wu Tsu
Fa Yen

Yuan Wu
K'e Ch'in

BODHIDHARMA (4–6 cent. A.D.)
CASE 1

Bodhidharma was a meditation master from southern India; by the time of *The Blue Cliff Record* his life was veiled in legend. Regarded as the first patriarch of Ch'an in China, most stories of Bodhidharma popular in Ch'an circles are what may be called illustrative history, and are used as teaching materials or guides to contemplation.

Bodhidharma did not associate with kings, did not translate any scriptures or found any temples, and transmitted his bequest to only a few successors. Though his immediate impact on the Buddhist world in China was not very great, he was influential enough locally to be opposed and assassinated. Although there were many meditation teachers in China in Bodhidharma's time, the Buddhist historian Tao Hsuan (7th century A.D.) wrote that Bodhidharma was one of only two teachers who founded continuous transmission lines.

Bodhidharma claimed to be over one hundred and fifty years old when he died. Many stories are told of him: popular legend has it, for example, that his legs fell off after sitting still for nine years; that tea plants first grew from his eyelids, which he cut off in anger after falling asleep during his nine year vigil; and that he introduced *kung-fu* combat techniques to the monks in Shao Lin monastery, to bridle aggressive tendencies and tone otherwise inactive bodies.

Bodhidharma's meeting with Emperor Wu of Liang (r. 502–549) may be part of the legend which grew up around the great teacher. In his youth Wu had mastered many branches of learning, and in 498 was appointed Inspector of Ying Chou (in Hunan); he later took advantage of internal disputes over the authority of the Ch'i dynasty, his employer, to rebel and set up his own kingdom in southern China, called Liang. Turning from warfare to culture, Wu lavishly patronized Confucianism, Taoism, and especially Buddhism, hiding from the responsibilities of sovereignty under the cloak of personal piety. Bodhidharma's blunt deflation of Emperor Wu's pretensions to sanctity and merit is emblematic of the independence of the Ch'an school; because Wu was deceived by outward forms and the concept of holiness, it is said that he did not understand Bodhidharma.

PAO CHIH (417/421–514)
CASES 1, 67

Pao Chih is recognized as a master of Ch'an; thus he is said to have "seen" Bodhidharma even though the two never met.* The *Chuan Teng Lu* (27) says,

"Meditation master Pao Chih was a man from Chin Ling (the area of Nanking, the southern capital). His surname was Shu. As a youth he left home and stayed in Tao Lin monastery and cultivated meditative concentration.

"In the beginning of the T'ai Shih era of Sung (465–472), suddenly he no longer dwelt in any fixed abode. He ate and drank without consideration of the hour of the day. His hair was several inches long. He walked barefoot, holding a staff; the staff was armed with dagger, scissors, and a mirror."

Scissors are a conventional Chinese metaphor for appointment and dismissal, promotion and demotion; a mirror is a Buddhist metaphor for clear awareness without biased views—like a mirror that reflects anything that comes before it. The record continues:

"Sometimes he wore one or two feet of silk. Even when not eating for several days, he had no appearance of hunger. Sometimes he might sing songs; his words seemed to be prophecies. The gentry and peasants alike did things for him.

"During the Yung Ming era of Ch'i, the Martial Emperor (r. 483–493) declared that the master was deluding the masses; so he had him captured and bound over to the prison at Chien K'ang.

"When it was morning, the people saw him going into the market place; but when an investigation was made, they found him in prison as before. The prefect of Chien K'ang reported the matter to the Emperor, who invited the master to dwell in the rear hall within the palace.

"The master stayed at the Flower Forest Manor. Suddenly one day he put on three cloth caps: it was not known where he had gotten them. All of a sudden the Prince of Yu Ch'ang, Wen Hui, and the Crown Prince died in succession. The Ch'i dynasty too was now at its last. Due to this, they imprisoned the master.

"When the Exalted Ancestor of Liang (the Emperor Wu of ex. I) assumed that rank, he sent down an imperial rescript stating,

'Master Chih's tracks are within the province of the defilements of the Dusts, but his spirit wanders in hidden tranquility. Water or fire could not burn or wet him; snakes or tigers could not bother him or cause him fear. To speak of his enlightenment into the Principle, he is higher than a disciple of Buddha; to talk about his mysterious obscurity, he is a lofty one among the Escaped Immortals. How could we regulate him according to the empty forms of the ordinary feelings of uninitiated people? Henceforth do not censor him again.' "

A few cryptic answers to imperial questions are attributed to Pao Chih; they are recorded along with the interpretations of "those who knew" among the court. In this case, his recognition of Bodhidharma as the bodhisattva of compassion is symbolic of the eye of the source.

"In the winter of 514, when his life was about to end, he suddenly ordered the community to move the temple's statue of the Adamantine Being and place it outside. And he said privately to people, 'A bodhisattva is about to leave.'

"Before ten days had passed he died without illness."

*It was believed that Bodhidharma came to China around 520—after Pao Chih had already died; internal evidence in *Hsu Kao Seng Chuan* suggests that Bodhidharma arrived in China during the latter part of the Liu Sung dynasty (420–479) and was already in northern China well before the end of the fifth century.

TS'UNG SHEN of Chao Chou (778–897)
CASES 2, 9, 30

Known as Chao Chou, after the place in northern China where he lived and taught for the last forty years of his long life, Ts'ung Shen was one of the most famous and revered Ch'an masters of all time. He claimed to have seen over eighty of Ma Tsu's successors during his long travels on foot; it was Nan Ch'uan to whom he succeeded.

One day Chao Chou asked Nan Ch'uan, "What is the Way?"

Nan Ch'uan said, "The ordinary mind is the Way."

Chou said, "Is it still possible to aim for it?"

Ch'uan said, "If you attempt to turn towards it, then you are turning away from it."

Chou said, "When I make no attempt, how do I know this is the Way?"

Ch'uan said, "The Way is not in the realm of knowing or not knowing; knowing is false consciousness, and not knowing is insensibility. If it is true arrival on the Way where there is no doubt, it is like the great void, like a vacant hall, empty and open; how could one insist on affirming or denying it?"

At these words Chao Chou awakened to the Way. After Nan Ch'uan's death Chao Chou resumed his travels for over twenty years more; only at the age of eighty did he settle down at the Kuan Yin Temple in Chao Chou, where he taught until his death at the age of one hundred and twenty.

Chao Chou was also known for his asceticism: "It was the Master's will to emulate the ancients, and his abbacy was austere. In the monks' hall there were no shelves in front or rear. Vegetarian food was prepared. When one leg of his rope chair broke, he tied on a leftover piece of firewood with rope to support it. There were repeated requests to make a new leg for it, but the Master would not allow it." (This and subsequent citations are taken from the record of Chao Chou's sayings in *Ku Tsun Su Yu Lu* 13–14.)

As abbot, Chao Chou upheld the custom of universal labor in the community of monks, a practice of the Ch'an school initiated by the Fourth Patriarch Tao Hsin and established as a rule by Pai Chang Huai Hai. (In older Chinese Buddhist monastic systems, only novices did manual labor.) One day when he encountered a monk behind the monks' hall, he asked, "Where have all the virtuous ones gone?" That monk said, "They have all gone to work." The master then took a knife out of his sleeve and handed it to the monk, saying, "My tasks as abbot are many; I ask you, Elder, please cut off my head for me." Then he extended his neck; the monk ran off.

Chao Chou's manner of teaching was called "Lip Ch'an," and it was said that light issued from his lips when he spoke. Many sayings of his are recorded, and his repeated appearance in *The Blue Cliff Record* is evidence of their currency. In the closing decades of the ninth century Chao Chou, Hsueh Feng, and Yun Chu (Tao Ying, Tung Shan's great disciple) were the most eminent Ch'an masters in China, but Chao Chou used to say, "Even if you come from Hsueh Feng or Yun Chu, you are still board-carrying fellows." Chao Chou's teaching style was lofty indeed, and he produced thirteen enlightened successors, but there were few who could match, let alone surpass him, so his transmission line died out after a few generations.

A monk asked, "In the aeon of emptiness, is there still someone cultivating practice?" The Master said, "What do you call the aeon of emptiness?" The monk said, "This is where not a single thing exists." The Master said, "Only this can be called real cultivation."

A monk asked, "The Buddha Dharma is remote; how should I concentrate?" The Master said, "Observe how the Former Han and Latter Han dynasties held the whole empire; yet when the end came, they hadn't a farthing."

MA TSU TAO I (709–788)
CASE 3

(Ma Tsu, "Ancestor Ma," also called Great Master Ma, was one of the most illustrious Ch'an masters of all time, the teacher of one hundred and thirty-nine enlightened successors. His teacher was Huai Jang of Nan Yueh, one of the foremost heirs of the Sixth Patriarch Hui Neng. The following is the account of Ma Tsu's meeting with Huai Jang told in the *Ching Te Ch'uan Teng Lu:*)

During the K'ai Yuan era (713–741)* an ascetic named Tao I was dwelling in the Ch'uan Fa Temple; all day he sat meditating. Huai Jang knew that he was a vessel of Dharma, and went to question him; "Great Worthy, what are you aiming at by sitting meditation?" Ma replied, "I aim to become a Buddha." Jang then took a tile and began to rub it on a rock in front of the hermitage; Ma asked him what he was doing rubbing the tile. Jang said, "I am polishing it to make a mirror." Ma said, "How can you make a mirror by polishing a tile?" Jang said, "Granted that rubbing a tile will not make a mirror, how can sitting meditation make a Buddha?" Ma asked, "Then what would be right?" Jang said, "It is like the case of an ox pulling a cart: if the cart does not go, would it be right to hit the cart, or would it be right to hit the ox?" Ma didn't reply.

Jang went on to say, "Do you think you are practicing sitting meditation, or do you think you are practicing sitting Buddhahood? If you are practicing sitting meditation, meditation is not sitting or lying. If you are practicing sitting Buddhahood, 'Buddha' is not a fixed form. In the midst of transitory things, one should neither grasp nor reject. If you keep the Buddha seated, this is murdering the Buddha; if you cling to the form of sitting, this is not attaining its inner principle."

Ma heard this teaching as if he was drinking ambrosia. He bowed and asked, "How shall I concentrate so as to merge with formless absorption?" Jang said, "Your study of the teaching of the mind ground is like planting seeds; my expounding the essence of reality may be likened to the moisture from the sky. Circumstances are meet for you, so you shall see the Way."

Ma also asked, "If the Way is not color or form, how can I see it?" Jang said, "The reality eye of the mind ground can see the Way. Formless absorption is also like this." Ma asked, "Is there becoming and decay, or not?" Jang said, "If one sees the Way as becoming and decaying, compounding and scattering, that is not really seeing the Way. Listen to my verse:

> Mind ground contains various seeds;
> When there is moisture, all of them sprout.
> The flower of absorption has no form;
> What decays and what becomes?

Ma heard this and his understanding was opened up. His heart and mind were transcendent. He served his master for ten years, day by day going deeper into the inner sanctum.

*This meeting probably took place in the mid 730's. Huai Jang had six adept pupils, but he said it was Ma Tsu who realized his "heart."

HSUAN CH'IEN of Te Shan (781–867)
CASE 4

(Among Te Shan's nine successors were Yen T'ou Ch'uan Huo and Hsueh Feng I Tsun; he was the ancestor of both the Yun Men and Fa Yen sects of Ch'an. *Ching Te Ch'uan Teng Lu 15* gives the following account of him:)

Ch'an master Hsuan Ch'ien of Te Shan in Liang Chou was a man of Chien Nan; his surname was Chou. In his youth he left home, and when he came of age he was fully ordained as a monk. He made a thorough study of the collection of regulations, and penetrated the essential import of the various scriptures expounding nature and its phenomenal expressions. He frequently lectured on the Diamond Wisdom Scripture; his contemporaries called him Diamond Chou.

Later he inquired into the Ch'an sect, whereat he said to his fellow students, "A single hair embraces the sea, yet the sea's nature is not diminished; a minute mustard seed falls upon a sword blade—the sharpness of the sword does not move. Whether there is something to learn or nothing more to learn, only I know that." Then he went to Ch'an master Hsin of Lung T'an. . . .

(After the events narrated in case 4, he dwelt in obscurity for some thirty years in Hunan. In 845, when the emperor Wu Tsung of T'ang tried to do away with Buddhism, Te Shan escaped to a stone grotto on a mountain.)

In the beginning of the Ta Chung era (847–860), Hsueh Yen Wang, the governor of Wu Ling (in Hunan), restored the monastery on Te Shan and called it the Meditation Abode of Ancient Worthies. He was going to look for a man of knowledge to dwell there, when he heard of the master's practice of the Way. Though he repeatedly invited him, the master did not come down from the mountain. Yen Wang then fabricated a ruse, sending a runner to falsely accuse the master of having violated the laws regarding tea and salt. Having taken the master into his domain, he looked up to him with reverence and insisted that he dwell there, and reveal the way of the sect.

In the hall, the master said, "There is nothing in the self, so do not seek falsely; what is attained by false seeking is not real attainment. You just have nothing in your mind, and no mind in things; then you will be empty and spiritual, tranquil and sublime. Any talk of beginning or end would all be self-deception. The slightest entanglement of thought is the foundation of the three mires (hell, animality, hungry ghosthood); a momentarily aroused feeling is a hindrance for ten thousand aeons. The name 'sage' and the label 'ordinary man' are merely empty sounds; exceptional form and mean appearance are both illusions. If you want to seek them, how can you avoid trouble? Even if you despise them, they still become a great source of anxiety. In the end there is no benefit."

Hsueh Feng asked, "In the immemorial custom of the sect, what doctrine is used to teach people?" The master said, "Our sect has no words; in reality there is no doctrine to be given to mankind."

Yen T'ou heard of this and said, "The old man of Mount Te has a spine as strong as iron; it cannot be broken. Even so, when it comes to the way of expounding the teaching, he still lacks something."

Before his death he said to his disciples, "Grasping emptiness and pursuing echoes wearies your mind and spirit. When awakened from a dream, you realize it was false; after all, what matter is there?" When he finished speaking, he died sitting at rest.

(Te Shan is perhaps most famous for his use of the staff to strike students.)

LING YU of Kuei Shan (771–854)
CASES 4, 24, 70

(Kuei Shan was the foremost successor of Pai Chang Huai Hai; the whisk which he showed to Te Shan in case 4 was given to him by Pai Chang as a symbol of the transmission. Perhaps the most famous teacher of his time in southern China, Kuei Shan's community numbered fifteen hundred persons, and he produced forty-three enlightened disciples. Among them, the best known were Hsiang Yen Chih Hsien and Yang Shan Hui Chi. Very little is known of Hsiang Yen's successors, but Yang Shan's teaching line remained active for three or four more generations; hence it came to be called the Kuei-Yang Sect, the earliest of the so-called 'Five Houses' of classical Ch'an. The following sermon of Kuei Shan is taken from Ching Te Ch'uan Teng Lu 9:)

The mind of a man of the Way is straightforward, without falsehood; there is no turning away nor turning towards, no deceitful false mind. At all times his seeing and hearing are normal; there are no further details or subtleties beyond this. He does not close his eyes or block his ears; it is enough that feelings do not attach to things.

Since time immemorial all the sages have only spoken of the faults of impurity; if there is no such perverted consciousness, opinion and thought habits, then it is like an autumn pond, limpid and clean. Pure and clear, without contrivance, quiescent and still, without hindrance; such is called a man of the Way. He is also called an unconcerned man.

[Kuei Shan also wrote a short book called the *Ching Ts'e*, or 'admonishing stick,' in which he points out the degeneracy of Buddhists in his time, and speaks of the true aim of leaving home. This book gained wide circulation in China, and was the first sectarian Ch'an work to be published in Japan, in the year 1198; it is still current in Rinzai Zen circles.]

I TS'UN of Hsueh Feng (822–908)
CASES 5, 22, 49, 51

Hsueh Feng first wanted to abandon home at the age of nine, but he was prevented from doing so by his parents. At the age of twelve, he went with his father to Yu Chien temple in Fu T'ien (in Foochow): there he saw the preceptual master Ch'ing Hsuan; he said, "This is my teacher," and remained at that temple to serve Ch'ing Hsuan. At age seventeen, he had his head shaved and changed his name to I Ts'un.

When Hsueh Feng was twenty-four, Buddhism was suppressed by the command of the Emperor. In Confucian dress, Hsueh Feng called on the Ch'an teacher Ling Hsun, spiritual grandson of Ma Tsu. The following year, when the suppression had been lifted, Hsueh Feng returned to Ling Hsun as a disciple. Later, when he himself began to teach on Hsueh Feng (one of the names of the mountain where he lived, after which he is usually called, according to Ch'an custom), he modeled the organization of his community after that of Ling Hsun.

At twenty-eight, Hsueh Feng was officially ordained at Pao Ch'a temple in Yu Chou. Two years later his teacher Ling Hsun died; after two more years had passed, at the age of thirty-two Hsueh Feng resumed his travels. He was with Yen T'ou in the community of Huan Chung (780–862, a successor of Pai Chang) at Mt. Ta Tzu in Hang Chou, where they met Ch'in Shan Wen Sui, an outstanding student of Huan Chung. The three of them left Ta Tzu and travelled together to visit other enlightened teachers.

Once in the course of their journey, Ch'in Shan stopped to wash his feet in a stream, when he saw a vegetable leaf floating by. He rejoiced and said, "There must be a man of the Way in

these mountains; let us follow the stream and seek him out."
Hsueh Feng said, "Your eye of wisdom is cloudy; later on, how
will you judge others? His carelessness about material blessings is such as this; what is he doing, dwelling in the mountains?"

Eventually, as the commentary states, Hsueh Feng went to
T'ou Tzu three times and nine times to Tung Shan. The master
Ta T'ung of Mt. T'ou Tzu (819–915) was a successor in the
fourth generation of the Shih T'ou line. Tung Shan Liang
Chieh, patriarch of the Ts'ao-Tung sect, a later branch of the
Shih T'ou (or Ch'ing Yuan) line, was one of the most famous
masters of the time; Ch'in Shan eventually remained and suc-
ceeded to the teaching of Tung Shan, whereas Hsueh Feng and
Yen T'ou succeeded to Te Shan.

Hsueh Feng was already forty years old when he met Te
Shan, who was then over eighty. Although he stayed there for
several years and is reckoned as a successor to Te Shan, in
reality it was by Yen T'ou's exhortation that he was thoroughly
liberated. Later he became a great teacher, a classic illustration
of the Ch'an proverb that "a superior vessel takes a long time
to complete."

After his enlightenment, at the age of forty-five Hsueh Feng
parted company with Yen T'ou and went back to Min
(Foochow): two years later he returned to Mt. Fu Jung ('Lotus
Mountain', where Ling Hsun had taught) and dwelt at ease
there in a stone grotto. Several followers who had sought him
out, especially one Hsing Shih Shih Po, who had been a fellow
student of his long before under Ling Hsun, urged him to "appear in the world" and teach. Finally, at the age of forty-nine,
he went to Hsiang Ku Shan, "Elephant Bone Mountain," where
two donors vied to provide for him. Because the mountaintop
was always covered with snow, it was called Hsueh Feng,
"Snowy Peak"; and at the age of fifty Hsueh Feng went to live
there and spent the next several years with his followers building a place to live and work.

Within ten years, the size of his community had reached
fifteen hundred people; so rapidly did his following increase in
the early years that there was not enough room or ample provisions for them all. Under Hsueh Feng's guidance, the community was exemplary for its industry and austerity. The renown
of Hsueh Feng spread all over China, and in 882 he was given

an honorific purple vestment by the Emperor I Tsung, along with the title Chen Chiao Ta Shih, "Truly Enlightened Great Teacher." By the time of his death at the age of eighty-seven, he had fifty-six enlightened disciples teaching in various places; among them, several who figure in *The Blue Cliff Record* were Hsuan Sha, E Hu, Ch'ang Ch'ing, Ching Ch'ing, Yun Men, Sui Yen, and Pao Fu. Hsueh Feng's teaching line flourished exceedingly through the Fa Yen and Yun Men sects, and lasted about three hundred years in China.

WEN YEN of Yun Men (?—949)
CASES 6, 8, 14, 15, 22, 27, 34

(Successor to Hsueh Feng, Yun Men taught in Kuangtung, southern China; he produced over sixty enlightened disciples, and was known as the founder of the Yun Men school of Ch'an, which lasted into the thirteenth century, and whose masters were responsible for the preservation of a great deal of Ch'an literature. Noted for his wondrous and often abstruse sayings, Yun Men forbade his disciples to record what he said; one of his attendants stealthily wrote down his sayings on a paper robe, preserving in this way an incredibly rich record of Yun Men's words. The practice of reciting and investigating sayings of earlier Ch'an masters seems to have been growing over a long period of time, but Yun Men was one of the first classical masters to make extensive use of the words of Ch'an ancients in guiding his own disciples. He is said to have originated the form of *tai-yu*, or "substitute sayings," in which he answers a question posed by himself, in behalf of his audience, or else supplies an answer to a question or saying of an earlier master, substituting for a speechless monk in a story; he also originated *pieh-yu*, or "alternative saying," a reply or remark given as an alternate to another in a story, or an alternate reply to one of his self-posed self-answered questions. Other members of Hsueh Feng's congregation were known to have discussed ancient and contemporary Ch'an sayings and doings extensively; the Lin Chi school of Ch'an became well known for its use of *k'an-hua ch'an*, or "meditation contemplating sayings," during the Sung dynasty, but the overt recommendation of this practice is in early evidence in Yun Men's sayings. Remember also that Hsueh Tou, who collected the sayings and wrote the poems which are the kernel of *The Blue Cliff Record* was a master of the Yun Men school. The following excerpt from one of Yun Men's speeches recorded in *Ching Te Ch'uan Teng Lu* 19 illustrates his approach to this technique:)

O brethren! You have all called on teachers in various places to settle life and death. Where you went, did not the venerable adepts abiding there utter some compassionate words of help to you? Are there still any phrases you did not penetrate? Come forth and cite them and let's see. This old fellow will haggle with you all. . . .

Ordinary thieving cowards slurp up the spittle of others, memorizing a bunch of miscellaneous trash: wherever they go they run off at the mouth; with asses' lips and horses' chops they boast, 'I know how to pose ten or five pivotal questions.' Even if you go on like this morning to night until the end of time, will you after all have ever seen anything, even in dreams? What use has this in imparting strength to others? Whenever anyone stakes the patchrobed monks to a meal, people like this also say, 'I have food to eat.' How are they even worth talking to? On another day, before the King of Death, he will not accept your verbal explanations.

O brethren, if you have attained, you may spend your days following the crowd in another house; but if you have not attained, just do not pass the time taking it easy. You must be most thoroughgoing.

The Ancients had a lot of problems to help you. These are such as Hsueh Feng's saying, "The whole earth is you." Chia Shan said, "Pick me out in the hundred grasses; recognize the emperor in a bustling market place." Lo P'u said, "As soon as a mote of dust arises, the entire earth is contained therein; on the tip of a hair, the whole body of the Lion is all there." You take hold, and contemplate them over and over again; over long days and many years, you will naturally find a way of entry. In this task, no one can substitute for you; it rests with each individual, without exception.

(The following examples are taken from the *Yun Men Kuang Lu,* to illustrate something of Yun Men's commentary style:)

Quoting Chia Shan's saying, "Find me in the hundred grasses," the master joined his palms and said, "How are you? How are you?" Then he pointed at a pillar with his staff and said, "Chia Shan has turned into a pillar—look! Look!"

Quoting Hsueh Feng's saying, "The Buddhas of past, present, and future turn the Great Wheel of Dharma upon flames of fire," the master said, "The flames of fire expound the Dharma; the Buddhas of past, present, and future stand there and listen."

(The 'three phrases' of Yun Men is a descriptive term first used by Yun Men's successor Te Shan Yuan Mi; the following verses by Yuan Wu describing the three phrases are taken from the *Jen T'ien Yen Mu:*)

Fundamental reality, fundamental emptiness;
One form, one flavor—it is not that a subtle
*   entity does not exist.*
It is not a matter for hesitating over; clear and lucid,
This contains the whole world.

It is fundamentally not a matter of interpretation
*   or understanding;*
When you sum it all up, it's not worth a single let-
*   ter.*
When myriad activities abruptly cease,
That is cutting off the myriad streams.

When you allow the presence of another,
Follow the sprouts to descry the ground,
Understand the person by means of his words;
This is going along with the ripples, following the
*   waves.*

FA YEN WEN I (885–958)
CASE 7

Revered as the founder of the Fa Yen sect of Ch'an, he was a successor of Lo Han Kuei Ch'en.* Kuei Ch'en's teacher had been Hsuan Sha, and the compiler of the *Ching Te Ch'uan Teng Lu* refers to Fa Yen as a reviver of the Hsuan Sha sect.

Fa Yen had his head shaved at the age of seven, and subsequently studied both Buddhist and Confucian teachings. Later he gave up these pursuits and headed for southern China to seek sudden enlightenment. First he went to the congregation at Ch'ang Ch'ing in Fu Chou, under the master Hui Leng.

It is said that he was highly esteemed there in spite of the fact that his clinging mind was not yet at rest.

Resuming his travels with several companions, at one point Fa Yen was stopped in his tracks by weather conditions and put up at the Ti Ts'ang temple, where the master Kuei Ch'en was abiding at the time. Kuei Ch'en asked him, "Where are you going?" He replied, "I am going to continue wandering around on foot." Ch'en asked, "What is the purpose of your travel?" He replied, "I do not know." Kuei Ch'en said, "Not knowing is closest to it."

According to the *Ch'uan Teng Lu*, Fa Yen was enlightened at these words, and remained at Ti Ts'ang along with three companions, seeking absolute certainty. The record in the *Wu Teng Hui Yuan* states that they went on to discuss the *Chao Lun*, a fourth century Chinese Buddhist treatise; when they got to the point where it says, "Heaven and earth and I have the same root," Ch'en asked Fa Yen, "Are the mountains, rivers, and earth identical to your own self, or separate?" Fa Yen said, "Separate." Kuei Ch'en held up two fingers; the master said, "Identical." Ch'en again held up two fingers, then got up and left.

When Fa Yen was about to depart, Kuei Ch'en saw him to the gate, whereupon he asked, "You always say that the three worlds are only mind, and myriad things are only consciousness;" then he pointed to a rock in the garden and said, "But tell me, is this rock inside your mind or outside your mind?" Fa Yen said, "It is inside my mind." Kuei Ch'en said, "What reason does a traveller have to put a rock in his head?" Fa Yen was stumped and had no reply. So he put down his bundle and stayed by Kuei Ch'en to seek certainty.

For over a month he daily expressed his understanding and spoke of the principle. Ch'en said to him, "The Buddha Dharma is not like this." Fa Yen said, "My words are exhausted, my reason come to an end." Kuei Ch'en said, "If one were to discuss the Buddha Dharma, all things would appear in full." At these words, Fa Yen was greatly enlightened. (*Wu Teng* 10)

Later, he dwelt in the Ch'iung Shou Temple in Lin Ch'uan, where he began to teach. When Tzu Fang, an elder monk from the Ch'ang Ch'ing community came to call on him, Fa Yen quoted Hui Leng's verse and said, "What is the unique body revealed in the midst of myriad forms?" Tzu Fang raised his whisk; Fa Yen said, "How can you understand it thus?" Tzu Fang said, "What is the master's honorable opinion?" Fa Yen said, "What do you call myriad forms?" Tzu Fang said, "The Ancients did not eliminate myriad forms." Fa Yen said, "In myriad forms there is a single body revealed; why talk about eliminating or not eliminating?" At these words, Tzu Fang was greatly awakened; he expressed himself in verse and submitted in sincerity.

Henceforth, people in congregations everywhere who were conscious of their understanding came in droves; at first they were unyielding, but the Master subtly aroused and awakened them, so that all of them eventually submitted to him. His ocean of followers was never less than one thousand persons. (*Ch'uan Teng Lu* 24)

(Fa Yen, the name by which Wen I is usually known to posterity, is an abbreviation of his posthumous title Ta Fa Yen Ch'an Shih, 'Meditation Master with the Great Eye of Reality.' He was also entitled Ch'ing Hui, 'Pure Wisdom,' and Ta Chih Tsang Ta Tao Shih, 'Great Guide, Repository of Great Knowledge.' His writings were said to have amounted to several tens of thousands of words; much, however, has been lost to posterity. Still extant, however, are a number of poems, and a treatise entitled *Tsung Men Shih Kuei Lun*, 'Ten Guidelines for the School,' an elegant treatise on Ch'an and a denunciation of the decadence of Ch'an schools in his time. Fa Yen had sixty-three enlightened disciples, including Te Shao, National Teacher of Wu-Yueh, Wen Sui, National Guide of Chiang Nan, and Hui Ch'u, National Teacher of Koryo, a Korean kingdom. The Fa Yen school flourished greatly into the third generation, but died out by the fifth, after about one hundred years. Te Shao also did much to revive the T'ien T'ai teachings in China; his disciple Yen Shou was also considered a patriarch of the Pure Land school, and was a great scholar and prodigious author.)

---

*In some books he is referred to as Ti Ts'ang, in others, Lo Han; he lived for a while in Ti Ts'ang temple, where Fa Yen met him. Later he moved to Lo Han temple in Chang Chou.

TS'UI YEN LING TS'AN (9–10c)
CASE 8

Almost nothing is known of this master, beyond that he was a successor of Hsueh Feng. The compilers of the *Tsu T'ang Chi* state, "We have never seen any record of his doings. King Ch'ien respected him, and bestowed on him a purple vestment and the title Yung Ming Ta Shih, 'Great Teacher of Eternal Brilliance.' "

King Ch'ien* was Ch'ien Liu, entitled King of Yueh in 902, and later became the King of Wu and Yueh in 907, under the new Liang dynasty.

There was a saying that one's eyebrows will fall out if one talks too much; in the version of this example recorded in the *Tsu T'ang Chi,* Ts'ui Yen says 'for the last thirty years' rather than 'this summer.' Judging from the paucity of his record, he died with his eyebrows on. There are, however, one or two sayings left:

A monk once asked, "When the ancients lifted the gavel or stood up the whisk, what was the inner meaning?"

Ts'ui Yen said, "A false teaching is hard to maintain."

The other characters in example 8 were also disciples of Hsueh Feng, and this is, no doubt, where this incident took place. Later on, Ts'ui Yen had two enlightened successors, of whom equally little is known as of their master.

---

*The titular head of the empire being the Emperor, the term *wang* is translated as king, although these were regional titles and there were many such kings.

PAO FU TS'UNG CHAN (?–928)
CASES 8, 22, 23, 95

A man of Fu Chou, his lay surname was Ch'en. At the age of fifteen he went to Hsueh Feng and received instruction from him. At eighteen he was fully ordained at Ta Chung. After traveling in Wu and Chu (southern China), he later returned to Hsueh Feng and served as his attendant.

One day Hsueh Feng suddenly called him and said, "Do you understand?"

Pao Fu was about to approach, when Hsueh Feng poked him with his staff. At that moment, Pao Fu realized the ultimate; he bowed and withdrew. He also always used to ask Master Leng of Ch'ang Ch'ing about the expedient teachings of past and present; Leng deeply approved of him.

A monk asked, "If one wants to arrive on the Birthless Road, he must know the Basic Source; what is the basic source?"

The Master was silent for a long time. Then he asked his attendant, "What did that monk just ask?" When that monk quoted it again, the Master shouted at him and drove him out, saying, "I am not deaf."

Pao Fu's enlightened disciples numbered twenty-five.

CH'ANG CH'ING HUI LENG (864–932)
CASES 8, 22, 23, 95

According to the *Ch'uan Teng Lu* (18),

"He was a man of Yen Kuan in Hang Chou; his lay surname was Tsun. As a child, he was of pure and peaceful nature. When he was thirteen years old he left home and received the precepts at T'ung Hsuan temple in Su Chou; then he traveled around visiting the Ch'an 'shops'.

"In 878 he went into Min and called on Hsi Yuan; then he visited Ling Yun, but he still had lingering doubts. Later he went to Hsueh Feng, and his feelings of doubt melted like ice."

According to the *Tsu T'ang Chi* (10),

"When he first went to study under Hsueh Feng, his tasks in the study were bitterly painful; he was not too brilliant. Hsueh Feng saw him going on like this and stopped him, saying, 'I am giving you a prescription for medicine for a dead horse; do you find it sweet?'

"He said, 'I will abide by the Master's judgement.'

"Hsueh Feng said, 'You do not need to come up here three or five times every day: just know how to be like a wooden pillar in a blazing fire in the mountain; put your body and mind at rest, for maybe as many as ten years, perhaps seven, or at least three years, and you will surely have understanding.'

"He followed Hsueh Feng's direction for two and a half years; one night his mind was active and he could not sit still, so he went outside the temple building, walked three times around the tea garden, and sat down under a tree. Suddenly, as he was falling asleep, he awoke and returned to the temple. Going up from the eastern hall, the moment he entered the monks' hall he saw the lamp loom large and immediately had understanding. Thereupon he went to the Master Hsueh Feng's place, but before the master got up, he went away instead; leaning on the pillar of the teaching hall, he unconsciously let out a cry.

"The Great Teacher heard it and asked, 'Who is it?'

"Hui Leng called out his name; the Great Teacher said, 'What are you doing, coming here in the middle of the night?'

"He said, 'I have had an extraordinary perception.'

"The Great Teacher himself got up and opened the gate; he grabbed Hui Leng's hand and asked him about his inner condition. The latter, expressing his inner feeling, said in a verse,

> *Wonder of wonders!*
> *Rolling up a bamboo blind, I see the whole world* *
> *If anyone asks me what sect I understand,*
> *I would lift up my whisk and hit them right in the*
>   *mouth!"*

According to *Wu Teng Hui Yuan* (7),

"He asked Ling Yun** 'What is the big idea of the Buddhist teaching?'

"Ling Yung said, 'Before the business with the donkey is over with, a problem comes up with the horse.'

"The master went back and forth between Hsueh Feng and Hsuan Sha like this for a period of twenty years, and wore out seven sitting mats, but still did not clearly understand this matter. One day as he rolled up a bamboo blind, he was suddenly greatly awakened; thereupon he had a verse . . . (same as above).

"Hsueh Feng quoted this to Hsuan Sha and said, 'This lad has finished.' Hsuan Sha said, "Not yet; this is an expression of conscious knowledge. He should be tested again.'

"In the evening, when the community of monks appeared to ask questions, Hsueh Feng said to the master, 'Ascetic Pei (Hsuan Sha) does not approve of you. If you really have correct realization, bring it up before the community.' The master again had a verse, saying,

'Within myriad appearances, a solitary body is revealed:
Only when a person experiences it personally can
  he be acquainted with it.
In former times I wrongly looked to the road in
  search—
Now I look upon it like ice in fire.'

Hsueh Feng looked at Hsuan Sha and said, 'This can't still be
an expression of conscious knowledge.'"

The master asked Hsueh Feng, "All sages from antiquity
have transmitted and received a single path; please point it out
to me."

Hsueh Feng remained silent; the master bowed and withdrew. Hsueh Feng smiled.

The master entered the abbot's quarters; Hsueh Feng said,
"What is it?"

The master said, "Today the weather is clear, good for asking everyone to work." After this, his replies to questions were
never out of accord with the mysterious meaning.

Ch'ang Ch'ing became a distinguished teacher, producing
twenty-six successors.

*Corrected according to *Wu Teng Hui Yuan;* the earlier version is
somewhat garbled.

**A successor of Kuei Shan Ling You.

TAO TSUNG of Mu Chou (780–877)
CASE 10

Master Ch'en (his lay surname was Ch'en) succeeded to Huang
Po; he lived in Lung Hsing Temple in Mu Chou (in Chekiang).
The master usually carried out his activities in secret; he al-
ways made straw sandals and sent them secretly to people.
Because of this they called him "Ch'en the straw sandal
monk." *(Tsu T'ang Chi* 19)

He first dwelt in Lung Hsing Temple in Mu Chou: he hid his
traces and concealed his activity. He made straw sandals and
secretly placed them on the street; after many years people
came to know of this, so they called him "straw-sandal
Ch'en." At the time, when there were students who sought his

inspiration, he would reply instantly to their questions, and his words were sharp; since he didn't follow a rut, therefore the shallow often derided him. Only profound students who were naturally bright respected and submitted to him; because of this, people from all quarters sought refuge with him and called him Reverend Ch'en. (*Ching Te Ch'uan Teng Lu* 12)

HSI YUN of Huang Po (?–850)
CASE 11

(Huang Po was a successor of Pai Chang, and produced thirteen enlightened disciples, among whom was Lin Chi I Hsuan, founder of the Lin Chi sect of Ch'an. The following sermon is excerpted from the *Ch'uan Hsin Fa Yao*, 'Essential Method of Transmission of Mind,' recorded by prime minister P'ei Hsiu; this version is taken from *Ching Te Ch'uan Teng Lu* 9:)

The Buddhas and all sentient beings are only one mind; there is nothing else. This mind, since beginningless past, has never been born, never perished; it is not green, not yellow; it has no shape or form. It is not subject to existence or non-existence, and is not to be considered new or old. It is not long or short, nor is it large or small; it transcends all limitation, measurement, names, words, traces or oppositions. This very substance is it; stir your thoughts and you miss it. It is like empty space; it has no bounds, and cannot be measured. Just this one mind itself is Buddha. Buddha and sentient beings are no different; it's just that sentient beings grasp appearances— seeking outwardly, they become more and more lost. If you employ Buddha to seek Buddha, use mind to grasp mind, you may go on all your life until the end of time, but will never succeed. Don't you realize that if you cease thinking and forget thought, Buddha will spontaneously appear?

SHOU CH'U TSUNG HUI of Tung Shan (n.d.)
CASE 12

(Not the more famous progenitor of the Ts'ao-Tung School, but one of Yun Men's disciples: the circumstances of his meeting with Yun Men are told in the Commentary to the Verse of Case 12. The following anecdotes are recorded in the *Ching Te Ch'uan Teng Lu* 23:)

A monk asked, "When you're far far on the one road, what's it like?" The master said, "Not agreeing to go while the sky is clear, ending up waiting for the rain to soak your head." The monk said, "What about all the sages?" The master said, "They enter the mud and water."

A monk asked, "Before mind arises, where are things?" The master said, "With no wind, the lotus leaves move: certainly there's a fish swimming through."

A monk asked, "What are the three jewels (Buddha, Dharma, and Sangha, the community of monks)?" The master said, "Impossible to discuss."

A monk asked, "What is the seamless memorial tower?" The master said, "A stone lion at the crossroads."

A monk asked, "What is the proper business of patchrobed monks?" The master said, "Up in the clouds on Mt. Chu, there's certainly a lot of wind and rain."

A monk asked, "What is buddha?" The master said, "Obviously true."

A monk asked, "A great multitude has gathered thick to beg the Master to take hold of the pivotal essentials and reveal a little of the great design." The master said, "A bubble floating on the water displays the five colors; at the bottom of the sea a frog is croaking, 'The moon is bright!'"

Great Master HAO CHIEN of Hsin K'ai in Pa Ling, Yueh Chou (n.d.)
CASES 13, 100

(Pa Ling was a successor of Yun Men; there is no record of his enlightenment story. His nickname 'Mouthy' was because of his eloquence. He had two enlightened disciples.)

A monk asked, "Are the Patriarchal meaning and the meaning of the Teachings the same or different?" He said, "When chickens are cold, they roost in trees; when ducks are cold, they enter the water."

A monk asked, "I do not doubt the twelve part teachings of the three vehicles; what is the business of the Ch'an sect?" He said, "This is not the business of a patchrobed monk." The monk asked, "What is the business of a patchrobed monk?" He said, "If you indulge in watching the foaming waves, you lose the oar in your hands."

He sent a whisk to someone. That person said, "It is fundamentally pure and clean; what is the use of a whisk?" The master said, "If you know it is pure and clean, don't forget it."

CHING CH'ING (863–937)
CASES 16, 23, 46

(The following is from *Tsu T'ang Chi* 10:)

Master Ching Ch'ing succeeded to Hsueh Feng. He lived in Yueh Chou (Fukien). The master's name was Tao Fu; he was (originally) a man of Wen Chou (in Chekiang). When the master first went into Min (Fukien) he called on Ling Yun (a successor of Kuei Shan) and asked, "How do you point out the truth of the great concern of foot travelling?" Yun said, "What is the price of rice in Chekiang?" The master said, "I almost understood it as the price of rice." Then he continued on to Hsiang Ku (Hsueh Feng).

Hsueh Feng asked him, "Where are you from?" He replied, "I'll never say I was born and raised in Wen Chou." Feng said, "Then the Enlightened Overnight Guest (Yung Chia, a successor of the Sixth Patriarch) is a fellow villager of yours." He said, "Where was the Enlightened Overnight Guest from?" Feng said, "This lad deserves to be given a score of blows, but I'll let it go."

The master also asked, "Since antiquity, the ancestral worthies have spoken of the simile of an entry road; is this right or not?" Feng said, "Right." He said, "I am a beginner, only lately come to study; I request you, teacher, to point out an entry road." Feng said, "Just enter from here." The master said, "I am enshrouded with ignorance; again I ask you to point it out." (*n.b.* Hsueh Feng's answer is not too clear; one character in the text is indistinct. Both the *Ching Te Ch'uan Teng Lu* and the *Wu Teng Hui Yuan* omit this story altogether. Hsueh Feng's answer seems to be, "I don't have many today; why sprawl out and fall right over?" Or it may read, "Hsueh Feng said, 'Today I am not too steady,' and he sprawled himself out and fell over.")

According to *Wu Teng Hui Yuan* 7, at the age of six he didn't eat meat; when his parents force fed him with dried fish, he would immediately vomit it out. Eventually he sought to leave home, and received ordination at the state K'ai Yuan Temple in his native Wen Chou. Then he went foot travelling.

(The following is from *Ching Te Ch'uan Teng Lu* 18; it accords with the *Tsu T'ang Chi* except for slight vocabulary differences:)

One day the Master asked, "Did the ancient worthies not transmit mind by mind?" Hsueh Feng said, "And they did not set up written words or spoken phrases." He said, "If you don't set up written words or spoken phrases, how will you transmit it, teacher?" Hsueh Feng remained silent. The master bowed in thanks. Hsueh Feng said, "Shouldn't you ask something further?" He said, "I ask you for a question, teacher." Hsueh Feng said, "Is it just so, or do you think there is some other consideration besides?" He said, "For you teacher, just so is all right." Hsueh Feng said, "What about for you?" He said, "Turning completely away from people." (The *CTL* stops here; the *TTC* continues,) Hsueh Feng said, "What is the business of not turning away?" The master immediately bade fare-thee-well.

Hsueh Feng once said to the assembly, "Splendidly refined." The master came forth and said, "What splendid refinement is this?" Hsueh Feng got up and said, "What did you say?" The master then retreated and stood there.

Hsueh Feng said, "This matter is so noble, so refined." The master responded by saying, "In the years since (I) Tao Fu has been here, I have never heard the teacher instruct like this." Hsueh Feng said, "Although I hadn't before, now I already have; there's nothing wrong, is there?" He said, "I do not dare (to say so). This is only what the teacher cannot avoid." Hsueh Feng said, "Let me be like this." The master gained true entry by this, but for a while he still followed the congregation. In Min he was called 'Cloth-robed Little Fu.'

As they were working, Hsueh Feng quoted Kuei Shan's saying about seeing mind upon seeing form and asked the master, "Is there any fault or not?" The master said, "What was the ancient concerned about?" Hsueh Feng said, "Although you are right, I still want to deliberate with you." The master said, "Then it would be better if I went on hoeing."

One day Hsueh Feng asked the master, "Where have you come from?" He said, "From outside." Hsueh Feng said, "Where did you meet Bodhidharma?" He said, "Where else?" Hsueh Feng said, "I still don't believe you yet." He said, "Teacher, don't vilify me so." Hsueh Feng approved of him. Later he travelled all over to various places, adding more to his temporal wisdom.

(First he dwelt at Ching Ch'ing, then at T'ien Lung and Lung Ts'e temples; King Ch'ien of Min greatly respected him, and requested him to teach in these places. The *Ch'uan Teng Lu* says that mystic studies flourished in Wu-Yueh during his teaching there.)

Someone asked, "An Ancient (Tung Shan) had a saying, 'A man who is mindless unites with the Way'; how does a man without mind unite with the Way?" The master said, "Why do you not ask about 'The Way is mindless of union with man'?" "How is it that The Way is mindless of union with man'?" The master said, "Though the white clouds may come to the blue mountain peak, how can the bright moon descend from the blue sky?"

(According to the *Tsu T'ang Chi*,) a monk asked, "What is 'leaping high'?" The master said, "Your eyes look upon the (most rare) Udambara (flower) as like a yellow leaf." "What is the Udambara like?" The master said, "It appears once in an aeon." "What is the yellow leaf?" The master said, "This is not yet real." The monk said, "Then there must still be something yet more transcendental." The master said, "Obviously." "What is the transcendental thing?" The master said, "When you drink the water of the Mirror Lake in one gulp, then I'll tell you."

"What is the single straight path to the spiritual source?" The master said, "The water of Mirror Lake is exceedingly deep."

(Ching Ch'ing had five successors.)

TENG YUAN of Hsiang Lin Temple on Ch'ing Ch'eng Mountain in I Chou (n.d.)

CASE 17

(Hsiang Lin succeeded to Yun Men, and himself produced three successors. He taught in western China. The following is from *Wu Teng Hui Yuan* 15:)

A monk asked, "Why does delicious ghee turn into poison?" The master said, "Tao Chiang paper is expensive." He asked, "How is it when one sees mind upon seeing form?" The master said, "Just then where were you going and coming?" He said, "How is it when mind and objects are both forgotten?" The master said, "Sitting sleeping with your eyes open."

Someone asked, "What is the meaning of 'hiding one's body in the north star (big dipper)'?" The master said, "The moon resembles a drawn bow; little rain and much wind."

Someone asked, "What is the mind of all Buddhas?" The master said, "If it is pure, it is pure from beginning to end." He said, "How can I attain understanding of it?" The master said, "Don't be fooled by people."

Someone asked, "What is the meaning of the Patriarch's coming from the West?" The master said, "Who is the one walking?"

Someone asked, "What is the master's marvelous medicine?" The master said, "It is not apart from the myriad flavors." He said, "How is the one who takes it?" The master said, "Sip some and see."

Someone asked, "What is the one wellspring of Hsiang Lin?" The master said, "Mindfulness without interruption." He said, "How is the one who drinks from it?" The master said, "He measures it out according to his means."

National Teacher HUI CHUNG of Nan Yang (?–776)

CASES 18, 99

(The following biography is from *Tsu T'ang Chi*, 3:)

Hui Chung, the National Teacher, succeeded to the Sixth

Patriarch. His lay surname was Jan; he was a man of Chu Chow district in Yueh Chou (Fukien). When he was a child at home, he never spoke, nor did he ever cross the bridge in front of his house, up until the time he was sixteen years old, when a certain Ch'an master came; as soon as the boy saw him from afar, he ran out and over the bridge to greet him and pay obeisance. . . . His father, mother, relatives and neighbors from far and near all came and discussed this in amazement; they said, "How imponderable it is that since his infancy till his sixteenth year we have never once seen this boy speak, nor have we ever seen him cross the bridge in front of the house. But the moment he saw the monk, he acted like this. Perhaps this boy is different from ordinary people."

The boy then asked the Ch'an master, "I beg the master's compassion, to receive and ordain one of the living. I earnestly wish to take refuge in meditation and leave home."

The Ch'an master said, "The fact is that in the school of our sect, only the crown prince of a silver wheel-turning king, the grandson of a gold wheel-turning king, is able to continue the way of this school without letting it decline; you are a kid reared on a buffalo's back by a man and woman in a village of three families; how could you enter the gate of this sect? It is not something for which you are suited."

The boy said, "I submit to the Ch'an master that this teaching is of equanimity; there is no high or low. How can you speak so as to hinder my good intention? I ask the master again to extend your compassion and admit me."

The Ch'an master observed the boy's state, and said, "You shouldn't leave home like this to follow me."

The boy said, "Then to whom should I resort to leave home? Ch'an teacher, direct me to a master of the sect."

The Ch'an master said, "Have you ever heard of Ts'ao Ch'i?"

The boy said, "I do not even know what region Ts'ao Ch'i is in."

The Ch'an master said, "On Mt. Ts'ao Ch'i in Kuang Nan (Canton) there is a Good Friend; he is called the Sixth Patriarch, and his community is as large as six hundred. You go there to leave home. I am travelling to Mt. T'ien T'ai; you just go by yourself."

The boy then went into the bush and hid; avoiding his parents, he immediately went. Three days' journey he traveled in two days; when it rained, he made a day's journey in one day. When he reached Ts'ao Ch'i, he luckily came at a time when the Patriarch was just about to expound the teaching. Immediately he bowed to the Patriarch. The Patriarch asked him, "Where do you come from?"

He replied, "I have just come near."

The Patriarch said, "Where were you born?"

The boy said, "Since having gotten the five skandhas, I have forgotten."

The Patriarch said, "Come near." The boy approached. The Patriarch said, "Tell me truly where you are from."

The boy said, "I am from Che Chung."

The Patriarch said, "You have come a long way to get here; what did you come for?"

The boy said, "For one thing, an enlightened teacher is difficult to encounter, and the true teaching is hard to hear. Secondly, I want to submit to you and abandon home. I beg the master's compassion to admit me."

The Patriarch said, "I tell you, don't abandon home."

The boy said, "Why do you say this?"

The Patriarch said, "You are a Sovereign; without moving shield or spear, for sixty years the Son of Heaven will be you. Just become an Emperor, and Buddhism will be principal."

The boy said, "I submit to the master that I would not want to be Son of Heaven for one hundred years, let alone sixty. I beg the master's compassion to accept me and let me abandon home."

The master then touched his head and gave him a prediction; "If you abandon home, you will be a Buddha standing alone in the world." Then he took him in and accepted him. He was on Mt. Pai Ya of Nan Yang cultivating his practice for forty years.

In 761 on the sixteenth day of the first month, he obeyed the summons of Emperor Su Tsung calling him to the capital, where he stayed in the western meditation hall of the Temple of a Thousand Blessings. Later he returned to the Abode of Light Temple. Both emperors Su Tsung and Tai Tsung personally accepted the bodhisattva precepts from him, and respectfully entitled him National Teacher.

(The two emperors are usually listed as successors to Hui

Chung; the master had three other successors, but Tan Yuan Ying Chen, who also appears in case 18, is the only one on whom any information is available. Perhaps the most famous dialogue recorded between these two is when Hui Chung called to Ying Chen three times, and three times Ying Chen responded; Chung said, "I had thought that I had turned my back on you, but it is you who have turned your back on me." Hui Chung was one of the last surviving successors of the Sixth Patriarch, and was greatly revered by later generations; see also case 69.)

CHU TUN of Lung Ya Mountain in Hunan (834–920)
CASE 20

Lung Ya succeeded to Tung Shan Liang Chieh, and produced five successors. The story of his first awakening is told in the commentary to the twentieth case; according to the *Tsu T'ang Chi* and later records, he finally asked Tung Shan, "What is the meaning of the Patriarch's coming from the West?" Tung Shan said, "When the Tung River reverses its flow, then I'll tell you." At this Lung Ya was enlightened. He stayed with Tung Shan for seven or eight more years. Later he had a following of five hundred disciples, and was entitled Great Master Witness to Voidness. Some of his sayings are to be found here and there in Yuan Wu's commentaries.

WU HSUEH of Ts'ui Wei Temple on Chung Nan Mountain, Ch'ang An (n.d.)
CASE 20

Ts'ui Wei was the successor of Tan Hsia T'ien Jan (738–824); among Ts'ui Wei's five enlightened successors was the great Ch'an Master Ta T'ung of Mount T'ou Tzu. The Emperor Hsi Tsung (r. 874–889) summoned him to the imperial precincts (Ch'ang An) to teach, and bestowed upon him the honorific purple robe, and the title Great Master Illumining Everywhere.

According to the *Ching Te Ch'uan Teng Lu* (14), he first

asked Tan Hsia, "What is the teacher of all Buddhas?" Tan Hsia upbraided him, saying, "Fortunately you are fine on your own; why do you want to hold onto a wiping cloth?" The master retreated three steps; Tan Hsia said, "Wrong!" The master then moved forward; Tan Hsia said, "Wrong! Wrong!" The master lifted one leg, turned his body around, and left; Tan Hsia said, "You've got it, all right, but you're turning away from those Buddhas." The master realized the inner truth from this.

I HSUAN of Lin Chi (?—867)
CASES 20, 32

(The story of Lin Chi's enlightenment given in the *Tsu T'ang Chi* 19 is quite different from that in the *Lin Chi Lu*, the 'Record of Lin Chi,' compiled by his distinguished disciple San Sheng Hui Jan. The latter version is given, with some variation, in the commentary to case 11; the *Tsu T'ang Chi* version is as follows:)

Master Huang Po said to his community, "In the old days I had a companion in the Way, a fellow student of Ta Chi (Ma Tsu), named Ta Yu (according to the *Ch'uan Teng Lu*, Ta Yu was actually a successor of Kuei Tsung Fa Ch'ang, who was a successor to Ma Tsu). This man travelled on foot all over, and his Dharma eye was clear all the way through. Now he is at Ta An; he does not like to dwell among crowds, but lives alone in a mountain hut. When we parted, he made a covenant with me, saying, 'Later on, if you should meet a spiritually sharp person, send one to call on me.'"

At that time the master (Lin Chi) was in the community; after he heard this, he immediately went to call (on Ta Yu). Once he got there, he told (Ta Yu) all of what (Huang Po) had said. In the evening, in the presence of Ta Yu he spoke of the treatise on Yoga and discussed 'only consciousness.' He also asked questions on difficult points, but Ta Yu remained aloof all night and did not answer. When dawn came, (Ta Yu) said to the master (Lin Chi), "This old monk lives alone in a mountain hut; considering that you came a long way, I let you stay for a night. Why have you been shamelessly spewing filth before me all night?" When he had spoken, (Ta Yu) beat (Lin Chi) several times with his staff, pushed him out the door and shut it.

The master returned to Huang Po and told him what had happened. When Huang Po heard this, he lowered his head and said, "An adept is like a blazing fire. It is lucky that you met a man; why then did you go in vain?"

The master again went to see Ta Yu. Ta Yu said, "Before you had no shame; what is your reason for coming again today?" When he finished speaking, he drove him out the door with his staff.

The master again returned to Huang Po and said to him, "This time I have not come back empty." Huang Po said, "Why?" The master said, "At one blow of the staff I entered the realm of Buddhas: even if I had my bones shattered and my body smashed for a hundred aeons and circled Mount Sumeru countless times carrying it on my forehead, I could never requite this profound debt of gratitude."

Huang Po, hearing this, rejoiced exceedingly in it; he said, "You know how to rest, and even assert yourself on your own."

After ten days, the master again took leave of Huang Po and went to Ta Yu's place. As soon as Ta Yu saw him, he immediately went to strike him: the master grabbed the staff and immediately pushed Ta Yu down; then he struck him on the back several times with his fist. Ta Yu then nodded repeatedly and said, "Dwelling alone in a mountain hut, I thought I had spent my whole life in vain; I never expected that today I would after all find a son." . . . Henceforth the master served Ta Yu for over ten years.

(Lin Chi had twenty-one successors, but not very much is known about them. Four of them, including the main figure of case 85, were hermits. One of his successors, Chih Kuan of Kuan Ch'i (cf. verse, case 52), also studied for three years under the nun Mo Shan, who was a disciple of the aforementioned Ta Yu. He served as the gardener in her community; later he said, 'I got half the ladle from poppa Lin Chi and half the ladle from mama Mo Shan; together they made the whole ladle, and having partaken, to this day I've been full, never hungry.' Hsing Hua Tsun Ching, whose line continued longest, also worked with San Sheng, Lin Chi's successor, and Wei Fu Ta Hsueh, another successor of Huang Po, after Lin Chi's death, before he was fully enlightened to Lin Chi's meaning, but he considered Lin Chi his teacher. San Sheng compiled the *Lin Chi Lu*, but the original version is lost, and this text, one of the most important documents of T'ang Ch'an, exists in a compilation made by a later master of the Yun Men sect. The disturbed conditions in Northern China, where the early Lin Chi sect was mainly based, probably contribute to the gaps in our knowledge of this school in the ninth and early tenth centuries. The Lin Chi sect almost died out after the fourth generation, but was greatly revived by the disciples of Shou Shan Hsing Nien (925–993), the successor of Feng Hsueh Yen Chao (896–973; cases 38, 61). During the eleventh century, in the eighth generation of the sect, two outstanding masters appeared, Yang Ch'i Fang Hui and Huang Lung Hui Nan, from whom flowed what came to be known as the Yang Ch'i and Huang Lung branches. It was in the former lineage that Yuan Wu K'o Ch'in, the commentator of *The Blue Cliff Record*, appeared; this branch endured longer than the Huang Lung branch, and flourished exceedingly during the Southern Sung dynasty, with Yuan Wu producing more than one hundred successors, among whom Ta Hui also produced more than fifty. Many streams of Lin Chi Ch'an were introduced to Japan during the twelfth, thirteenth, and fourteenth centuries; by that time contemplation of the *kung an* was firmly established in the Lin Chi sect as a principal method, and this is true in the derivative Japanese Rinzai schools today.)

Teaching Designs of LIN CHI (from the *Lin Chi Lu*)

FOURFOLD HOST AND GUEST

Followers of the Way, according to the understanding of the Ch'an school, death and life are successive. Students, you must be very thorough-going. When host and guest see each other, then there is discussion back and forth. One may show his form to adapt to the person, or one may make use of the entire body: one may use situational strategy with joy or anger, or one may show half of himself; one may ride on a lion, or one may ride on an elephant.

If there is a true student, he will immediately shout, first setting forth a bowl of glue. If the teacher doesn't discern this as an object, then he goes to that object and acts in various ways. The student then shouts, but the former will not agree to let go. This is a mortal disease, and cannot be cured; it is called a guest looking at a host.

Or it may be that the teacher doesn't bring anything out, but just follows the student's questions to dispossess him. The student, being dispossessed, won't let go till the death. This is host looking at guest.

Or there may be a student who comes before the teacher in a state of purity. The teacher, discerning that this is an object, takes it and throws it into a pit. The student says, 'Good teacher!' Then the teacher says, 'Bah! You do not know good from bad.' The student then bows. This is called host looking at host.

Or there may be a student who comes before the teacher wearing stocks and bound with chains. The teacher adds another layer of stocks and chains, and the student rejoices; neither of them are discerning. This is called guest looking at guest.

Worthies, what I have raised here is all to discern demons and pick out heretics, to know their falsehood or verity.

FOURFOLD ILLUMINATION AND FUNCTION

Sometimes I first illumine and then function; sometimes I first function and then illumine. Sometimes illumination and function are at the same time, and sometimes illumination and function are not at the same time.

I first illumine and then function when there is still person (subject). I first function and then illumine when there are still phenomena (object). Illumination and function at the same time is 'driving away the plowman's ox, taking away the hungry man's food, smashing bone and taking the marrow, pressing needle and awl into the sore spot.'

When illumination and function are not at the same time, there are questions, there are answers, guest and host are established; it is mingling with the mud and water, responding to potential in dealing with people.

If one is a man beyond measure, he will immediately get up and go before it is mentioned, and still will get somewhere.

FOUR PROPOSITIONS

Sometimes I take away the subject (person), but not the object (environment); sometimes I take away the object but not the subject. Sometimes subject and object are both taken away, and sometimes neither subject nor object is taken away.

A monk asked, "What is 'taking away subject but not object'?"

The master said, "The warm sun bursts forth, spreading the land with brocade; an infant's hair hangs down white as silk."

"What is 'taking away object but not subject'?"

The Master said, "The king's command is already in effect all over the land; the general beyond the borders is free from smoke and dust."

"What is 'subject and object both taken away' like?"

The master said, "The regions of Fen and P'ing have cut off communication—they occupy one region alone." (*N.b.* Fen and P'ing were two regions which had seceded from the control of the T'ang dynasty.)

"What is 'neither subject nor object taken away' like?"

The master said, "The king ascends his jewel palace, old peasants sing hallelujah."

THE FOUR SHOUTS

The Master asked a monk, "Sometimes a shout is like the Diamond King's jewel sword, sometimes a shout is like a golden haired lion crouching on the ground; sometimes a shout is like a probing pole or reed shade; sometimes a shout does not function as a shout: how do you understand?" The monk hesitated, whereupon the Master shouted.

KUANG TSO of Chih Men in Sui Chou (Ssuchuan) (n.d.)
CASES 21, 90

(Known as Chih Men, he succeeded to Hsiang Lin Teng Yuan, and was the teacher of Hsueh Tou, the poet of *The Blue Cliff*

Record. Besides Hsueh Tou, he had 29 other enlightened successors. The two examples given here are from *Wu Teng Hui Yuan* 15:)

"I remember that in my mother's womb I had a saying: today I quote it for everyone; you can't evaluate it rationally. Is there anyone who can evaluate it? If you can't evaluate it, thirty years hence do not quote it wrongly."

Hsueh Tou asked Chih Men, "When one doesn't arouse a single thought, how can there be any fault?" Men called Hsueh Tou to approach; as soon as Hsueh Tou came near, Chih Men hit him right on the mouth with his whisk. As Hsueh Tou was about to open his mouth, Chih Men hit him again; Hsueh Tou was opened up and enlightened.

Li Tsun Hsu, a military governor under the Sung dynasty and an enlightened lay student of Ch'an, petitioned the Emperor to honor Chih Men with a purple robe, symbolic of highest rank. The Emperor Jen Tsung (r. 1023–1063) granted the purple vestment, but Chih Men refused to accept it. The Emperor, however, did not admit the master's refusal, and finally Chih Men was obliged to accept; he said to his community, "Although this old monk's original intention is to cover this illusory body with shabby garments and fend off the pangs of hunger with coarse food, I can do nothing about the fact that the military governor has asked the Emperor to regale me with a purple robe; if I put it on, it will go against my original intent, yet if I don't put it on, it will go against the will of the Emperor. But leaving aside the issue of putting it on or not for the moment, you tell me: what robe did the patriarchs wear? If you really know, though you wear clothes all day, you have never put on so much as a single thread, and though you eat all day, you have never chewed so much as a single grain of rice. If you don't really know, watch this old monk put on this robe today." (This incident is cited by Kato Totsudo in his *Hekiganrok Daikoza,* vol. 4, page 267.)

GRAND MASTER TSUNG I of Hsuan Sha in Fu Chou (n.d.)
CASES 22, 88

(Hsuan Sha was the spiritual grandfather of Fa Yen Wen I, and the Fa Yen Sect is referred to in the *Ch'uan Teng Lu* as the

Hsuan Sha Sect. He was a successor of Hsueh Feng, and produced thirteen enlightened disciples.)

His Dharma name was Shih Pei; he was a man of Min district in Foochow. His lay surname was Hsieh. When he was
young he liked to fish, and used to go out in a little boat on the
Nan T'ai river, associating with the fishing folk.

In the beginning of the Hsien T'ung era of the T'ang dynasty
(869–873), when he was thirty years old, he suddenly wanted
to abandon the world. So he gave up his fish hook and boat, and
submitted to Ch'an master Ling Hsun of Lotus Mountain (a
successor of Kuei Tsung Fa Ch'ang, also Hsueh Feng's original
teacher), who shaved his head. He went to the K'ai Yuan Temple at Yu Chang and received full ordination from preceptual
master Tao Hsuan.

He wore a patched robe of coarse cloth and sandals made of
straw. He always sat peacefully all day long; the entire community considered him unusual.

He was a later come fellow student with Hsueh Feng I Tsun
in their original school (under the teacher Ling Hsun); and he
associated with (Hsueh Feng) like master and disciple. Because
of his painful practice, Hsueh Feng called him the ascetic.

One day Hsueh Feng asked, "Which one is Ascetic Pei?" He
replied, "I would never dare to deceive anyone."

Another day Hsueh Feng called him and said, "Ascetic Pei,
why do you not travel to study at other places?" He said,
"Bodhidharma did not come to China; the second patriarch did
not go to India." Hsueh Feng approved of this. (According to
Tsu T'ang Chi 10, Shih Pei started off on his journeys, but was
suddenly enlightened when he happened to stumble on a rock.
Afterwards he shouted and said, "Bodhidharma did not come
over; the second patriarch did not obtain the transmission.")

(When Hsueh Feng went to Elephant Bone Mountain in 872,
Hsuan Sha accompanied him and helped to build a monastery
there. He 'clearly discovered the mindground' when he read the
Surangama Sutra, and 'students of the mystery who had some
uncertainty would always seek further help from him.')

HERMIT HSIANG of Lotus Flower Peak
CASE 25

After enlightenment, before accepting a request to dwell in a
monastery as the guide of a community, Ch'an adepts usually

spent years travelling and/or living in seclusion or semi-seclusion, "maturing the holy embryo." Some, like Hsiang, the hermit of Lotus Flower Peak (on Mount T'ien T'ai, one of the five holy mountains of China), remained in humble circumstances as hermits all their lives, though small groups of seekers would come to live near them and call on them for instruction. The following brief sermon of hermit Hsiang, taken from the *Chih Yueh Lu*, "Finger Pointing at the Moon," is the greater part of the very little information we have about this Ch'an master:

"This matter is most urgent: you must clearly apprehend it; once you get it clear, at all times you will avoid being bound up and will be at ease wherever you are. Yet don't use your mind to overcome by force; you must fit into the ancient groove naturally. As soon as you get to study and analysis, you are eager to make some principle into a standard for the Buddhist teaching; (if you go on this way,) when will you ever attain to rest of the mind ground? Elders, I ask you to be thoroughgoing in this way."

The saying in case 25 was spoken by the hermit just before he died.

HUAI HAI of Pai Chang (720–814)
CASES 26, 53, 70, 71, 72, 73

(Pai Chang was one of the foremost successors of Ma Tsu; the circumstances of his enlightenment are told in case 53. Pai Chang compiled the so-called 'pure standards' for Ch'an monasteries, and is thus known as the founder of the independent Ch'an monastic institution in China. From Pai Chang's successors emerged the Kuei-Yang and Lin Chi sects of Ch'an. The following sayings, excerpted from the extensive record of his sermons, are in answer to a question about the essential method for sudden enlightenment in the great vehicle:)

You should all first put an end to all ties, and lay to rest all concerns; whether good or bad, mundane or transmundane, anything at all—do not remember, do not recollect, do not engage your thoughts with them. Abandon body and mind, letting them be free. With mind like wood or stone, mouth makes no object of distinction, mind pursues no activity; then the mind ground becomes like space, wherein the sun of illumination spontaneously appears. It is as though clouds had opened and the sun emerged.

Just put an end to all fettering connections; feelings of greed, anger, love, grasping, defilement and purity, all come to an end: unmoved in the face of five lusts and eight winds, not entangled by seeing, hearing, awareness, or knowledge, not confused by various objective realms, naturally endowed with the wondrous use of paranormal powers, this is a liberated man.

In the presence of all objects, mind being neither still nor disturbed, neither concentrated nor scattered, passing through all sound and form without lingering or obstruction, is called being a man of the Way. Not setting in motion good, evil, right, or wrong; not clinging to a single thing, not rejecting a single thing, is called being a man of the great vehicle. Not bound by any good, evil, emptiness, existence, defilement, purity, doing, non-doing, mundane, supramundane, blessings, virtue, knowledge or wisdom, is called Buddha wisdom.

Once affirmation and negation, like and dislike, approval and disapproval, all various opinions and feelings come to an end and can't bind, then one is free wherever he may be; this is called a bodhisattva with a newly aroused mind immediately ascending to the stage of Buddhahood.

P'U YUAN of Nan Ch'uan (747–834)
CASES 28, 31

The Master's lay surname was Wang, and he often referred to himself as "Old Teacher Wang." In 757, at the age of ten, he received instruction from the meditation master Ta Hui of Mt. Ta Wei; at thirty, he went to Mt. Sung in Honan, one of the five holy mountains of China, where he was formally ordained as a Buddhist monk. He learned the doctrines of the Fa Hsiang school, which analyzes existence into one hundred elements and maintains that the world is created and maintained as it is by the force of mental habit, giving a detailed account of the workings of the mind. He also made a thorough study of the Vinaya, monastic rules of conduct inherited from Indian Buddhism. Then he travelled around, hearing the *Lankavatara* "Entrance (of the Great Vehicle) into Ceylon" and *Avatam-*

saka (*Hua Yen*) "Flower Garland" scriptures expounded. The former scripture maintains that all that can be known of the world is purely subjective, and distinguishes three levels of reality; pure mental construction; relative coexistence—of sense, sense consciousness, and sense data—or interdependent co-production; and perfectly real, which is emptiness: mental construction is projected on relative coexistence, which, being purely relative, has no ultimate basis in fact and is in reality empty. The Flower Garland scripture also speaks of the relative co-production of all things in the cosmos, which means that everything is inherent in everything else; this is expressed symbolically by the net of Indra, made of jewels which each reflect all the other jewels, as well as the reflections of all the jewels in each jewel, and so on, ad infinitum to the power of infinity to an infinite infinity of powers: the ultimate pivot of interdependence is that of mind and matter. Hence this scripture says that the cosmos is produced by the mind, yet the mind does not exist of itself. Nan Ch'uan also studied the *San Lun* or "Three Treatise" school, which teaches the Middle Way based on the works of Nagarjuna and Kanadeva; accordingly, he practiced the contemplations of emptiness, conditional existence, and the mean.

Finally, after many years of study and practice, he called on the great Ch'an Master Ma Tsu Tao I in Hung Chou (in Kiangsi), and attained complete freedom. At the time there were eight hundred people in Ma Tsu's congregation, and P'u Yuan was considered the foremost; no one would dare to debate with him. In 795 he went to Mt. Nan Ch'uan in Ch'ih Chou (in Anwei), built himself a hut, and scratched out his own subsistence from the mountainside. It is said that he didn't come down from the mountain for over thirty years. In the beginning of the Ta Ho era (827–836), he was invited by Lu Hsuan to come down and teach. After that, his followers were never less than several hundred. He had seventeen enlightened disciples, including the famous Chao Chou, Ch'ang Sha, and Tzu Hu. Among Ma Tsu's one hundred and thirty-nine enlightened disciples, Nan Ch'uan is considered along with Pai Chang Huai Hai and Hsi T'ang Chih Ts'ang as the greatest of all time. He once said, "People these days walk around with 'Buddha' on their shoulders; when you hear me say that mind is not Buddha and wisdom is not the Path, you gather together and try to figure me out. You cannot figure me out. If you could wrap empty space up into a staff and hit me with it, then you might figure me out."

FA CHEN of Ta Sui (n.d.)
CASE 29

(Ta Sui succeeded to Ta An, also known as Ta Kuei, or Kuei Shan Ho Shang, who was a disciple of Pai Chang Huai Hai, and later an assistant to Kuei Shan Ling Yu.)

Someone asked, "What happens when birth and death arrive?" The master said, "When there is tea, drink tea; when there is rice, eat rice."

Someone asked, "What is the essential of the Dharma of all Buddhas?" The master raised his whisk and said, "Do you understand?" He said, "I don't understand." The master said, "An elk-tail whisk."

(The lord of Shu summoned Ta Sui repeatedly, but the master refused each time, claiming to be old and sick. The lord bestowed on him the honorific title Spiritual Illumination.)

PAO CHE of Mt. Ma Ku (n.d.)
CASE 31

(Ma Ku was one of Ma Tsu's successors: the following is taken from *Ching Te Ch'uan Teng Lu* 7:)

One day as Ma Ku was walking along with Ma Tsu he asked, "What is great extinction?" Ma Tsu said, "Swift." Ma Ku said, "What's the hurry?" Ma Tsu said, "Look at the river."

Once when Ma Ku was wandering in the mountains with Tan Hsia,* he saw a fish in a stream and pointed to it with his hand. Tan Hsia said, "Naturally, naturally."** The next day Ma Ku again questioned Tan Hsia, "What did you mean yesterday?" Tan Hsia relaxed his body and made the motion of lying down. Ma Ku said, "Heavens!" Another time he travelled with Tan Hsia to Mt. Ma Ku. Ma Ku said, "I'm staying here." Tan Hsia said, "Well, I'll let you stay, but do you still have That One or not?" Ma Ku bade him farewell.

A monk asked, "I am not in doubt about the twelve part

teachings (of the Buddhist canon), but what is the meaning of the coming from the West?" Ma Ku stood up, circled his body once with his staff, raised one foot and said, "Understand?" The monk had no reply, so Ma Ku hit him.

Tan Yuan asked, "Is Twelve-Faced Avalokitesvara ordinary or holy?" Ma Ku said, "Holy," whereupon Tan Yuan struck him a blow. Ma Ku said, "I knew you hadn't gotten to this realm."

*Tan Hsia was a successor of Shih T'ou and also spent time in Ma Tsu's community.

**Tan Hsia's initiatory name, given him by Ma Tsu, was Tzu Jan, "Natural."

HUAI HUI of Chang Ching Temple in the Capital District (?–818)
CASE 31

(The following is taken from the Ching Te Ch'uan Teng Lu 7:)

He was from T'ung An in Ch'uan Chou (in Hopei); his surname was Hsieh. He received Ma Tsu's mind seal. First he stayed at Oak Cliff in Ting Chou (in Hopei); then he stayed on Chung T'iao Mountain. In the beginning of the Yuan Ho era (806–820) Emperor Hsien Tsung summoned him to reside at Mystic Temple: there students flocked to him.

The master went up into the Hall and taught his disciples saying, "The ultimate principle is oblivious of words. People these days have not comprehended this, so they force themselves to study extraneous matters, considering this an accomplishment. They do not know that their own nature was originally not the dusty realm (of the senses), but rather the subtle mysterious gate of great liberation. All reflection and awareness neither stains nor obstructs this. This light has never been stopped or nullified: from the primordial past up to now, it has been solid and changeless. It's like the solar disc illuminating far and near: though it touches the many colors, it doesn't mix with them all. The wondrous illumination of the spiritual lamp does not depend on tempering and refining. Since you haven't understood, you cling to the forms of things—it's just like rubbing your eyes and producing false optical illusions. Thus you vainly trouble yourselves, wasting ages of time. If you can turn the light around so that there is no second person, the activities you undertake will not lack the characteristics of reality."

JU PAO of Tzu Fu in Chi Chou (in Kiangsi) (n.d.)
CASE 33

Tzu Fu succeeded to Ch'an master Kuang Mu of the Western Pagoda on Yang Shan; a fourth generation master of the Kuei-Yang lineage, he produced four enlightened disciples. His biography is in *Ching Te Ch'uan Teng Lu* 12.

A monk asked, "What is a phrase responding to potential?" The master was silent. "What is the hidden essence?" The master said, "Close the door for me." "When Lu Tsu sat facing a wall, what was his meaning?" The master said, "Irrelevant." "What is the truly correct eye of all time?" The master struck his breast and said, "Alas! Alas!" "What is the master's family style?" The master said, "Three cups of tea after rice."

HUI CHI of Yang Shan (813–890)
CASES 34, 68

(Yang Shan was a brilliant master, nicknamed 'little Shakyamuni.' According to the *Tsu T'ang Chi*, eleven regional inspectors, officials of the civil government, paid obeisance to him as their teacher. Before he was twenty years old, he had already called on successors of Nan Ch'uan, National Teacher Hui Chung, Ma Tsu, and Pai Chang; he was fully enlightened with Kuei Shan, and stayed there for fifteen years. There are various stories of his awakening. According to the *Jen T'ien Yen Mu*, after he had received the teaching of ninety-seven circular figures from Tan Yuan, who got it from Hui Chung, when he came to Kuei Shan, the latter showed him the figure of the empty circle—the 'full moon,' whereat he was enlightened. According to Dogen, the thirteenth century Japanese master, Kuei Shan first set Yang Shan to work herding buffalo for three years. The following is from the *Ch'uan Teng Lu* 10:)

Yang Shan asked Kuei Shan, "What is the abode of the real Buddha?"

Kuei Shan said, "With the subtlety of thinking the thoughtless, return thought to the boundlessness of the spiritual effulgence; when thought is exhausted, return to the source, where nature and appearances always abide, phenomena and principle are not two; the true Buddha is thus."

At these words Yang Shan was suddenly enlightened.

(Besides the use of circular figures, the dialogues of Kuei Shan and Yang Shan are known as hallmarks of the Kuei-Yang sect; Yang Shan once said that the essence of the sect was 'two mouths without a single tongue,' symbolizing the meeting of minds. The ninety-seven circular symbols handed down from Hui Chung are now lost; it is said that Yang Shan burned the book which contained them after he had read it once. Tan Yuan, who had given it to him, lamented this, so Yang Shan made another copy from memory and returned it to him. In the twelfth century, a master of the Yun Men sect named P'u Liang made a compilation containing forty or fifty examples, but this work too is lost; it is known, however, that he arranged them into six rubrics: 'circle,' 'merging of personality,' 'ocean of meaning,' 'ocean of characters,' 'speech,' and 'silent discourse.')

Bibliography

I. TEXTS AND COMMENTARIES FOR *Pi Yen Lu*

Hekiganroku Daikoza by Kato Totsudo. Tokyo, Heibonsha, 1940.

Hekiganshu Kogi by Imazu Kogaku, incorporating remarks by Zen Master Shoyaku (1572–1650). Tokyo, Mugazanbo, 1912.

Hekiganshu Shudensho by Daichi Jitto (1656–1735). Kyoto, Bunkyudo.

Hekiganshu Teidokusho by Tenkei Denson (1648–1735), edited as *Hekiganroku Kogi* by Matsuzaki Kakuhon. Tokyo, Koyukan, 1903.

Hekiganshu Teihon edited by Ito Yuten. Tokyo, Risosha, 1963.

Pi Yen Lu Chiang I by Wang Chin Jui. Tainan, 1972.

II. BIOGRAPHIES AND SAYINGS OF CH'AN MASTERS

Ching Te Ch'uan Teng Lu compiled by Tao Yuan, 1004. Taisho Shinshu Daizokyo, vol. 51, no. 2076.

Jen T'ien Yen Mu compiled by Chih Shao, 1188. Taisho Shinshu Daizokyo, vol. 48, no. 2006.

Ku Tsun Su Yu Lu compiled by Yuan Chiao, 1144. Dai Nihon Man Zokuzokyo 2.23.2.

Hsu Ch'uan Teng Lu compiled by Yuan Chi, 14th cent. Taisho Shinshu Daizokyo, vol. 51, no. 2077.

Tsu T'ang Chi compiled by Ching and Ch'un, 952. Kyoto, Chubun Shuppansha, 1972.

Wu Teng Hui Yuan compiled by P'u Ch'i, 1232. Taipei, Kuang Wen Shu Ch'u, 1971.

III. DICTIONARIES AND PHRASE BOOKS

Katto Gosen by Dochu Muchaku (1653–1745). Tokyo, Koma-
zawa Daigaku Jiten Hensansho, 1959.
Zengaku Jiten by Jimbo Nyoten and Ando Bun'ei. Tokyo,
Mugazanbo, 1927.
Zengo Ji'i by Nakagawa Shuan. Tokyo, Koshokai Shuppanbu,
1935.
Zenrin Kushu by Toyo Eicho (1429–1504), translated and an-
notated by Shibayama Zenkei. Kyoto, Kichudo, 1955.

IV. RELATED WORKS

The Zen Koan by Isshu Miura and Ruth Fuller Sasaki. New
York, Harcourt, Brace and World, 1965.

Contents

Biographical Supplement

Introduction

Zen stories and *koan* are not unique in form or content, nor in their use as processes of concentration and transmission of ways to enlightenment. The style and symbolism of *koan* do, however, vary in different cultures where Chinese-derived Zen existed, as well as from those of analogous Sufi, magical, and mystical tales. The application of traditional lore in practice seems to vary not only among 'religious traditions' but among individual communities and students; this is only to be expected in light of the Zen emphasis on suiting the teachings to the needs and capacities of those to be liberated.

In the introduction to volume one of *The Blue Cliff Record*, a number of points in the history of Zen in China were touched upon. There we emphasized the importance of the tenth and eleventh century masters Yun Men Wen Yen and Fen Yang Shan Chao in the development of the use of the *koan*, 'public records' of sayings of ancient and contemporary teachers. It should be pointed out that the quotation and elaboration of Zen sayings is in evidence in the records of all the classical masters who came to be regarded as the patriarchs of the five schools and seven streams of Zen in China.

It was several centuries before Zen took root and grew in Japan after its initial introduction; by the time of the numerous Chinese emigrants and Japanese pilgrims who firmly established Zen in Japan in the second phase of its introduction in the thirteenth and fourteenth centuries, the science of *koan* use was well developed in China and was in fact an outstanding feature of Ch'an at that time. Emphasis on *koan* was new to Japanese Buddhism but soon became a mainstay of Rinzai Zen in particular. In sifting the vast repository of Zen literature for hints on the nature and use of *koan*, therefore, it is reasonable to turn to the medieval Japanese Zen masters who were experts in this matter.

Daio Kokushi (Nanpo Jomyo 1235–1309), a famous Japanese Zen master who traveled to China and was enlightened with the guidance of Hsu T'ang Chih Yu (1185–1269), a master of the lineage of Fen Yang and Yuan Wu, introduced the *koan* as he learned and experienced it in Sung China. He once said,

> *Although there are seventeen hundred* koan *in all, everything we see and hear—mountains, rivers, earth, plants, trees and forests—all are* koan, *the public matter.*
>
> *There are three levels of meaning in our school; merging with principle, working of activity, and transcendence.*[1] *The first, merging with principle, refers to the expressions of principle such as mind, nature, etc., spoken of by the Buddhas and ancestral teachers of Zen. Next, the workings of action refers to the Buddhas and ancestors really expressing compassion, 'twisting their noses' and 'blinking their eyes,' as it were, saying things like 'a clay ox flies through the sky, a stone horse plunges into the river.'*
>
> *After that, transcendence refers to the direct speech of the Buddhas and ancestors, the real character of all things, etc., where nothing is different; 'sky is sky, earth is earth, mountains are mountains, rivers are rivers'; 'the eyes are horizontal, the nose is vertical'—such sayings refer to this.*
>
> *However, to pass through these three phrases is hard. Some may stop in principle and produce interpretation and understanding, knowledge and opinion, to understand the principle elucidated in the written and spoken teachings.*
>
> *Some may go along with workings of action in a flurry and not completely cut off doubt. They stay one-sidedly in the exercise of possibilities. Some abide in transcendence, maintain the view that everything is actually so; they thus fall into the realm of unconcern.*[2]

The ancient model of this 'classification' of *koan* and stages of practice could be said to be Pai Chang's 'three phases' (or 'phrases'), summarized in the biographical extract on Pai Chang in volume one of *The Blue Cliff Record*, these three phases, or phrases—referring to phases of expression as a method of teaching—are stages of practice and realization; detachment, calm, and personal liberation in the first phase, not abiding in detachment in the second phase, and having no understanding of nonabiding in the third phase. Pai Chang said that all the teachings of Buddhism have these three stages, and they represent a historical scheme, not only of the personal experience of people working on Zen, but of communities and constellations of communities, including their verbal and written expressions. Moreover, Pai Chang says that Buddhahood is beyond these stages and even refers to a saying in a scripture likening this to a deer leaping thrice getting out of the net.

Later Lin Chi spoke of three essentials and three mysteries; what exactly this meant in terms of Lin Chi's dealings with his disciples is one of those issues which remains obscure in spite of a number of verses by later teachers alluding to meditative states, but it should be clear that each of Pai Chang's three phases apply to each of the other phases; none of the succeeding ones can be reached without realizing the preceding one, but in each stage there are one-sided and integrated realization both. That is, for example, at the first level of detachment, a tacit negation of everything by cultivation of indifference and equanimity, utter dispassion. Detachment from detachment does not see the world as hateful or personal extinction as desirable; not dwelling on anything, even detachment, therefore, is real detachment; but unless one has actually realized detachment in (what is now seen as) the one-sided way, in the 'relative within the absolute,' or relative absolute way, so-called detachment from detachment is a feeble excuse at best. Without belaboring this point further, it can be seen that each phase must ultimately integrate with the others in the development of Zen practice.[3]

Centuries later Hakuin (1686–1769) and his disciples and heirs further developed systematic *koan* form and use. The principal type *koan* were referred to as Dharmakaya, or body of reality *koan*; they concentrated on the formless aspect first, to rid the mind of all preconceptions based on long accumulation of habit. The next stage was called workings of activity, referring to re-emergence into life after the great death, with the mind clean and mirrorlike. Ultimately the 'mirror' can function in a multifaceted way, each facet reflecting the other

facets of the essential unity of the jewel-mirror, but originally
it does not discriminate and define anything in a fixed way,
coming into the realm of 'one state, one object,' seeming both
unique and differentiated, constantly changing, one object now
encompassing the universe, the universe now appearing as one
object.

It would seem that the earlier 'workings of action' stage was
refined by Hakuin into the 'workings of action,' 'verbal expression,' and 'difficult to pass through.' Just as the study of verbal
expression is the third phase of study in the Hakuin school, the
ancient Ts'ao Shan said of the third of the five ranks of Tung
Shan, "coming from within the absolute is words within the
wordless." Ts'ao Shan also said, however, "in each phrase there
are no words; they do not set up what is precious, and do not
fall into either side—that is why it is called coming from the
absolute." This is coming from the absolute state to express it
in relative terms which do not violate the absolute, thus allowing one to discern the unspoken message without clinging to
partial views about the overt meanings of the words, but rather
using those meanings only as a channel of attention.

Hakuin's fourth stage, 'difficult to pass through,' corresponds to Tung Shan's 'attainment within the relative,' the
stage of the 'lotus blooming in the fire,' one adept in darkness
and adept in light, the tantric master who balances wisdom and
compassion.

The fifth stage of Hakuin's system, working with Tung
Shan's five ranks of relative and absolute interrelating, corresponds to Daio's 'transcendence,' and Tung Shan's simultaneous
arrival within both (relative and absolute), what Ts'ao Shan
called mutual integration. In the modern system, the five ranks
include certain specific koan, especially Tung Shan's verses,
but are also a mirror in which all the experiences one has
realized can be seen. It is that, as Hakuin said, which smashes
the twin void (of the 'lotus' and the 'fire'); that is why it is
called transcendence.

But then, as it is said, there is an impassable gate at the final
barrier; it is also said there is a road going beyond of which
none of the sages have told. Therefore a discussion of the mortal life, of living a life of cause in spite of the fact that one has
seen everything, of discipline that is efficiency in action and
strength of body and intent in the struggle for enlightenment of

all beings, is given after the student's eyes have been opened, as it had been given in the beginning to instill the mind with the spirit of enlightenment.

Regarding the matter of self-help and helping others as it relates to *koan* study, in Zen it is sometimes said that one who has not yet penetrated should seek the meaning, while one who has penetrated should seek the phrase, or expression. Someone asked Zen master Muso (1275–1352), who was also a kokushi, or Teacher of the Nation, about the difference between investigating the meaning, or intent, and investigating the expression, or phrase. Muso said,

> *Meaning and phrase are terms which come from poetry. When discussing Japanese poems, for example, it is like saying that a verse has nice phraseology but the sentiment it conveys is crude. In Zen we have gates of teaching called meaning and phrase, borrowing those terms; though the words are the same, the meaning is different.*
>
> *In Zen, there are various teachings such as transcendence and return, That Side (the 'other side') and This Side, holding still and letting go, capturing and releasing, killing and reviving, three mysteries, three essentials, five positions of lord and minister; these are phrases. Among students of trivia, there are those who think that to clearly know the distinctions among these teachings is called attainment of meaning and to be able to explain and discuss them with others freely is what is called attainment of expression. What these people think is meaning is still in the sphere of the phrase.*
>
> *Discussing principles of holding still and letting go, assessing the transcendent or the imminent within the spoken phrase, is called investigating the phrase; even when sitting silently facing a wall, if you harbor various mixtures of knowledge and understanding in your heart, figuring and calculating, this is still investigating the phrase.*

*Therefore, the method of having people investigate
the meaning is to have them cast off all understanding and emotional assessments and look at
a koan directly. Even while reading the records of
words of the ancients or hearing the teachings of
a guide, if you directly forget what is on your
mind and do not create an intellectual understanding about sense or principle, this is investigating the meaning.*

*Once a student has clearly awakened to the mean-
ing of the ancestors, then a teacher may discuss
with him the differences in style of the five
schools of Zen, and deal with the methods and
modes of holding still, letting go, capturing, releasing, killing, giving life, praising and censuring, etc.—if one does not successfully investigate
these expressions, he cannot teach people; that is
why an ancient who had realized the truth was
told that not to doubt verbal expressions is a
great illness.*

The practice of intense concentration on a *koan*, complete absorption in the so-called 'mass of doubt' generated while gazing
at the saying, seems to have become widely used in Rinzai Zen.
Muso said, "If a student has any seeking for enlightenment in
his mind, he is not really keeping a *koan* before him." Another
great Rinzai master, Shoitsu Kokushi (1202–1280) said,

*In the direct teaching of the ancestral teachers there
are no special methods; cast off all entanglements, lay to rest all affairs, and for three hours
in the morning and three hours at night keep
watch over the tip of your nose. When you drift
into distinctions among things, just call a saying
to mind—do not think in terms of Buddhism, or
of getting rid of anything; don't consciously
await understanding, don't let feelings or intellect create doubtful unrest. With no road of reason, no taste, like an iron bun, cut directly in
with a single stroke without getting involved in
various ideas. After a long time like this you will*

*naturally be like awakening from a dream, like a
lotus flower blooming. At this moment the saying you have been concentrating on is like a piece
of tile used to knock on a door; throw it away on
the 'other side,' and then look at the words of the
Buddhas and ancestors illustrating the workings
of active capacity. These are all only to stop a
child's crying. The one road of transcendence
going beyond does not let anything more
through, but cuts off the essential pass of ordinary and holy.*

Simply sitting, with ultimate if tacit faith in the inherent enlightenment of the original mind, transcending the forces of
habitual illusion by attrition, is usually associated with Soto
Zen, especially as taught by the famous Dogen, but the same
'art' was also taught by Rinzai masters like Shoitsu. The use
of *koan* concentration as a 'secondary' measure, to focus the
wandering mind as described by Shoitsu here, was also taught
by such leading Zen masters as Keizan and Meiho, who greatly
influenced the development of Soto Zen in the fourteenth century. However, intense concentration in this way evidently can
have negative results if improperly tuned, according to the Soto
Zen master Gesshu, who like Hakuin was a powerful force in
the premodern revival of Zen in Japan:

*When I was staying in Choenji in Mikawa a long
time ago, I gave various koan to the students and
made them work on them, but very few people
got koan totally solidly in their grasp to reach the
realm of great awakening and great penetration.
Most people just carried the koan around—for
some this brought about pain in the chest, some
became depressed and consumptive; or else they
produced all sorts of conceptualizations to make
rational understanding, just going further and
further from the fundamental meaning of the
koan, and got bored besides.*

*When the real true overwhelming doubt arises,
keeping one koan constantly whether awake or
sleeping for even seven days, not affected by any-*

*thing, it just becomes one solid state—then joy
rises ceaselessly in your mind. As soon as this
state of mind arises, it already becomes a seed of
wisdom, and you will not regress in your determination for enlightenment.*

From the sayings of these Zen masters we can see that 'this
side' and 'that side,' rational understanding and the ordinary
world, reflections of reflections, and, engulfing all that, the
mirror itself, inconceivable in light as well as darkness, all
have a place in Zen expression and experience. The observation
of some *koan* involves 'looking back' into the source of consciousness and thought, until all impulses are ended or overcome; this is supposed to lead to *nirvana,* the 'great death,'
leaving one equanimous by experiencing relative equanimity,
indifference, as nothingness itself, the opposite of existence in
thought and deed.

Forms of asceticism, standards of conduct, ritual remember-
ance, various auxiliary practices, as well as *zazen,* sitting meditation, the main practice of Zen monasteries, are not only intentional approaches to this extinction of personal egoism and
the concomitant experience of pure clarity, wishlessness,
openness, without any design. These are also, after all, expressions of solidarity with the human world, even as a bequest for
some unforseen future; hence they are not necessarily connected or disconnected from knowledge and vision of reality
only by tradition in the purely social or conventional institu-
tional sense.

The unity of body and mind is often emphasized by Buddhists, but the famous 'body-mind duality' of Western
philosophy is indeed sadly borne out by many of the social,
intellectual, economic, and animal habits of human beings,
especially among certain socio-strategic groups in times of
plenty and little. So on a personal level the search of the renun-
ciant for peace in having few desires and being content is a
prelude to experiences truly beyond mundane knowledge or
cares, but as an outward feature it stands for civilization in the
human community, even if it be embryonic compared to the
worlds of Mahayana, the great vehicle, or of the scenes of the
tantric *mandalas* or Zen *koan.* These pure lands are already

there, here within us, awaiting discovery; to pull out the weeds and cut through the brambles, *koan* like the word 'No' or 'Who' or 'What' are often repeated.

Once the person seeking reality has experienced the overwhelming death and complete stillness and calm, it is necessary 'to know not only that the needle is sharp, but also that the chisel is square,' to have both wisdom and knowledge, so that 'each branch of coral holds the moon.' This is a way of translating what one has realized into active expression to help others become enlightened with what means are available while deepening one's knowledge in and for that very task. The 'one road going beyond, which the sages didn't transmit' mentioned so many times in *The Blue Cliff Record* is a classic 'turning word' illustrating the 'multiplicity within one' and 'nonduality in two' of Zen; it does not refer only to the inexpressible absolute, host within host, the experience of the absolute state as the extinction of the sense of self, life, and so forth, resulting in the end of self-conscious suffering. The word for transcendence also means, in vernacular, progress; here it is in the sense of the need for the successor to go beyond the teacher for the teaching to really be handed on, to provide 'a beacon for future generations.' Here they say that there is nothing to be transmitted, but to approach that nothing is difficult and deadly, virtually impossible to survive without what we might call the compassion of the Buddhas, enlightened ancestors.

Sadaparibhuta, an ancient bodhisattva whose story is told in the *Saddharmapundarika*, or Lotus of the Truth scripture, used to say to people that he did not dislike them or hold anything against them, because they would all eventually become Buddhas. After a while people began to dislike him for saying this, so he had to learn more. An ancient Zen master in China used to say 'this mind is Buddha,' until people stopped awakening and began to think they 'had' Buddha; then the master said, 'not mind, not Buddha.' These Ch'an sayings compiled in *The Blue Cliff Record* are means which the ancients devised to offset this bewildering bluntness, to help us find the inconceivable infinite right before us without being bogged down in customary doubts and considerations on one hand or being burnt to a cinder in the fire of trascendent wisdom without properly preparing the vessel.

NOTES

1. In the book *The Zen Koan* (or *Zen Dust*) by Isshu Miura and Ruth F. Sasaki can be found different translations of the terms used here and a discussion of *koan* practice in the Hakuin school of Rinzai Zen. (see *The Blue Cliff Record* vol. I)

2. This and other quotes in the introduction are translated from sermons of famous Japanese Zen masters compiled by Kuruma Takudo in his *Zenshu Seiten*, or Zen Bible (Kyoto, Heiryakuji Shoten, 1961).

3. Pai Chang's three phases could be understood as being applied to themselves, as three phases of each of the same three phases; Lin Chi's three mysteries and three essentials seem to be developments of this; detachment, nonabiding, and nonintellectualization are each an aspect of detachment, nonabiding, and nonintellectualization. The later definition of three stages of realization of principles, active application, and transcendence, also comes from this.

Ch'ang Sha Wandering in the Mountains

CASE

One day Ch'ang Sha went wandering in the mountains. Upon returning, when he got to the gate,[1] the head monk asked, "Where are you coming from, Master?"[2]

Sha said, "From wandering in the mountains."[3]

The head monk asked, "Where did you go?"[4]

Sha said, "First I went pursuing the fragrant grasses; then I returned following the falling flowers."[5]

The head monk said, "How very much like the sense of springtime."[6]

Sha said, "It even surpasses the autumn dew[a] dripping on the lotuses."[7] Hsueh Tou added the remark, "Thanks for your reply."[8]

NOTES

1. Today, one day. He has only fallen into the weeds; at first he was falling into the weeds; later he was still falling in the weeds.
2. He still wants to try this old fellow. The arrow has flown past Korea.
3. Don't fall in the weeds. He's suffered quite a loss. A man in the weeds.
4. A thrust. If he had gone anywhere, he couldn't avoid falling into the weeds. They drag each other into a pit of fire.
5. He's let slip quite a bit. From the beginning he's just been sitting in a forest of thorns.
6. He comes following along, adding error to error; one hand uplifts, one hand presses down.
7. He adds mud to dirt. The first arrow was light; the second arrow was deep. What end will there ever be?
8. A group of fellows playing with a mud ball. The three have their crimes listed on the same indictment.

COMMENTARY

Great Master Chao Hsien of the Deer Park at Ch'ang Sha succeeded to the Dharma of Nan Ch'uan; he was a contemporary of Chao Chou and Tzu Hu. The point of his wit was sharp and swift. If anyone asked about the Teachings, he would then give him an explanation of the Teachings; if someone wanted a verse, he would then give a verse. If you wanted to have a meeting of adepts, then he would have a meeting of adepts with you.

Yang Shan was usually considered foremost in having a sharp intellect. Once as he was enjoying the moon along with Ch'ang Sha, Yang Shan pointed at the moon and said, "Everyone has this; it's just that they can't use it." Sha said, "Quite true. So, shall I have you use it?" Yang Shan said, "Try to use it yourself." Sha kicked him over with one blow. Yang Shan got up and said, "Respected Uncle, you are just like a tiger." Hence, people later called Ch'ang Sha "Ts'en the Tiger."

One day as Sha returned from a stroll in the mountains, the head monk, who was also a man of Sha's congregation, asked him, "Where are you coming from, Master?" Sha said, "I come from a stroll in the mountains." The head monk asked, "Where did you go?" Sha said, "First I went following the fragrant grasses; then I returned pursuing the falling flowers." Only a man who had cut off the ten directions could be like this. The Ancients, in leaving and entering, never ever failed to be mindful of this Matter. See how the host and guest shift positions together; confronting the situation directly, neither overlaps the other. Since he was wandering in the mountains, why did the monk ask, "Where did you go?" If he had been one of today's followers of Ch'an, he would have said, "I came to the inn on Mount Chia." See how that man of old did not have even the slightest hair of reason or judgement, and that he had no place to abide: that is why he said, "First I went following the fragrant grasses; then I returned pursuing the falling flowers." The head monk then followed his idea and said to him "How very much like the sense of springtime!" Sha said, "It even surpasses the autumn dew dripping on the lotuses." Hsueh Tou says on behalf (of the monk), "Thanks for your reply," as the final word. This too falls on both sides but ultimately does not remain on either side.

In the past there was a scholar, Chang Ch'o, who upon reading the *Sutra of the Thousand Names of Buddha*, asked, "Of
the hundreds and thousands of Buddhas, I have only heard their
names; what lands do they dwell in, and do they convert beings
or not?" Ch'ang Sha said, "Since Ts'ui Hao[b] wrote his poems in
the Golden Crane Pavillion, have you ever written or not?"
Ch'o said, "No." Sha said, "When you have some free time,
you should write one."

Ts'en the Tiger's usual way of helping people was like jewels
turning, gems revolving; he wanted people to understand immediately on the face of it. The verse says,

VERSE

The earth is clear of any dust—
   Open wide the doors and windows—who is under the
   eaves? None can miss this. The world is at peace.

Whose eyes do not open?
   One must emit a great radiant light from his forehead
   before this is possible. Why scatter dirt and sand?

First he went following the fragrant grasses,
   He's slipped quite a bit. It's not just one instance of falling
   into the weeds. Fortunately it happens that he already
   said this before.

Then he returned pursuing the falling flowers.
   Everywhere is completely real. Luckily he came back.
   Under his feet the mud is three feet deep.

A weary crane[c] alights on a withered tree,
   Accompanying him left and right, he adds a phrase. Still
   there are so many idle concerns?

A mad monkey cries on the ancient terrace.
   After all it depends on personal application of effort. It is
   impossible either to add a phrase or to take a phrase away.

Ch'ang Sha's boundless meaning—
   I strike. What does the final phrase say? Bury them all in
   one pit. He's fallen into the ghost cave.

Bah!

> A man in the weeds; this is drawing the bow after the
> thief has gone. Still, he can't be let go.

COMMENTARY

Take this public case along with Yang Shan's asking a monk,
"Where have you just come from?" The monk said, "Mount
Lu." Yang Shan said, "Did you visit the Five Elders Peak?" The
monk said, "I didn't get there." Yang Shan said, "You never
visited the mountain at all." Distinguish the black and white,
and see if they are the same or if they are different. At this
point, mental machinations must come to an end, and conscious knowledge be forgotten, so that over mountains, rivers,
and earth, plants, people, and animals you have no leaking at
all. If you are not like this, the Ancients called that "still remaining in the realm of surpassing wonder."

Haven't you seen how Yun Men said, "Even if you realize
that there is no trouble at all in the mountains, rivers, and
earth, still this is a turning phrase: when you do not see any
forms, this is only half the issue. You must further realize that
there is a time when the whole thing is brought up, the single
opening upward; only then can you sit in peace?" If you can
pass through, then as before mountains are mountains, rivers
are rivers; each abides in its own state, each occupies its own
body. You will be like a completely blind man. Chao Chou
said,

> The cock crows in the early morning;
> Sadly I see as I rise how worn out I am;
> I haven't a kilt or a shirt,
> Just the semblance of a robe.
> My loincloth has no seat, my pants no opening—
> On my head are three or five pecks of grey ashes.
> Originally I intended to practice to help save others;
> Who would have suspected that instead I would
>   become an idiot!

If one can truly reach this realm, whose eyes would not open?
Though you go through upsets and spills, all places are this
realm, all places are this time and season. "The ten directions

are without walls, and the four quarters are without gates."
That is why he said, "First I went following the fragrant grasses; then I returned pursuing the falling flowers." Skillful indeed, Hsueh Tou just goes and adds a phrase to his left and a
phrase to his right, just like a poem. "The weary crane alights
on a withered tree. The mad monkey cries on an ancient terrace." When Hsueh Tou has drawn it out this far, he realizes
how he has indulged himself: suddenly he says, "Ch'ang Sha's
boundless meaning—Bah!" This was like having a dream but
suddenly awakening. Though Hsueh Tou gave a shout, he still
didn't completely finish the matter. If it were up to me, I would
do otherwise: Ch'ang Sha's boundless meaning—dig out the
ground and bury it deeper.

TRANSLATORS' NOTES

a. According to Tenkei Denson, the head monk thought there was
    still some warmth, but Ch'ang Sha is saying No, it's clear and
    cool, colder than the autumn dew.

b. Ts'ui Hao was a statesman of the Northern Wei dynasty, noted for
    his sagacity, who also composed literary works. Golden Crane
    Pavillion was in Hupeh west of Wu Ch'ang, so situated as to look
    out over a vast vista.

c. The crane is associated with longevity.

P'an Shan's There Is Nothing in the World

POINTER

It is futile effort to linger in thought over the action of a lightning bolt: when the sound of thunder fills the sky, you will hardly have time to cover your ears. To unfurl the red flag of victory over your head, whirl the twin swords behind your ears—if not for a discriminating eye and a familiar hand, how could anyone be able to succeed?

Some people lower their heads and linger in thought, trying to figure it out with their intellect. They hardly realize that they are seeing ghosts without number in front of their skulls.

Now tell me, without falling into intellect, without being caught up in gain or loss, when suddenly there is such a demonstration to awaken you, how will you reply? To test, I cite this to see.

CASE

P'an Shan imparted the words which said, "There is nothing in the triple world;[1] where can mind be found?"[2]

NOTES

1. Once the arrow has left the bowstring, it has no power to come back. The moon's brightness shines, revealing the night traveller. He has hit the mark. One who knows the law fears it. He ought to have been hit before he finished talking.
2. Best not fool people! It's not worth bringing up again. Examine for yourself. Immediately striking, I would say, "What is this?"

COMMENTARY

Master Pao Chi of Mount P'an in Yu Chou in the far north was a venerable adept succeeding to Ancestor Ma. Later he produced one man, P'u Hua. When the Master was about to pass on, he said to the community, "Is there really anyone who can depict my true likeness?" The people all drew likenesses and presented them to the Master. The Master scolded every one of them. P'u Hua came forth and said, "I can depict it." The Master said, "Why do you not show it to me?" P'u Hua immediately turned a somersault and left. The Master said, "Later on, this guy will appear crazy to teach others."

One day, he said to the community, "There is nothing in the triple world; where can mind be found? The elements are basically empty; how can a Buddha abide? The polar star does not move; quiet and still, without traces, once presented face to face, there is no longer anything else."

Hsueh Tou takes up two phrases and eulogizes them; this here is raw gold, a rough jewel. Have you not heard it said, "Curing illness does not depend on a donkey-load of medicine." Why do I say I would have hit him before he finished speaking? Just because he was wearing stocks, giving evidence of his crimes.

An Ancient said, "When you hear mention of the phrase beyond sound, do not go seeking it in your mind." But tell me, what was his meaning? Just like a rushing stream crossing a sword; thunder rolls, a comet flies. If you hesitate and seek it in thought, even though a thousand Buddhas appeared in the world, you would grope around without finding them. But if you are one who has deeply entered the inner sanctum, pierced the bone and pierced the marrow, seen all the way through, then P'an Shan will have suffered a loss. If you are smeared with mud and dripping with water, turning about on the pile of sound and form, you have still never seen P'an Shan even in a dream. My late master Wu Tsu said, "Pass beyond the Other Side, and only then will you have any freedom."

Have you not seen how the Third Patriarch said, "Grasp it, and you lose balance and surely enter a false path. Let go naturally; there is neither going nor abiding in essence." If here you say that there is neither Buddha nor Dharma, still you have gone into a ghost cave. The Ancients called this the Deep Pit of Liberation. Originally it was a good causal basis, but it brings on a bad result. That is why it is said that a non-doing, unconcerned man is still oppressed by golden chains. Still, you must have penetrated all the way to the bottom before you will realize it. If you can say what cannot be said, can do what cannot be done, this is called the place of turning the body. There is nothing in the triple world; where can mind be found? If you make an intellectual interpretation, you will just die at his words; Hsueh Tou's view is piercing and penetrating. Thus he versifies:

VERSE

There is nothing in the triple world;
   The words are still in our ears.

Where can mind be found?
   It is not worth the trouble to mention again. See for yourself. I strike and say, "What is this?"

The white clouds form a canopy;
   Adding a head to a head. A thousand layers, ten thousand layers.

The flowing spring makes a lute—
   Do you hear it? They come along with each other. Each hearing is enough to lament.

One tune, two tunes; no one understands.
   It does not fall into A or B; it has nothing to do with D or E. He is going by a side road. The five sounds and six notes are all distinctly clear. Take what's yours and get out. When you hear it, you go deaf.

When the rain has passed, the autumn water is deep in the evening pond.
   The thunder is so swift, there's no time to cover the ears. After all he's dragging in mud and dripping with water. Where is he? Immediately I strike.

COMMENTARY

"There is nothing in the triple world; where can mind be found?" Hsueh Tou makes a verse which resembles the Flower Garland Cosmos.[a] Some people say he sings it out from the midst of nothingness, but anyone with his eyes open would never understand in this way. Hsueh Tou goes to (P'an Shan's) side and drapes two phrases on him, saying, "The white clouds form a canopy; the flowing spring makes a lute."

When Su Tung P'o, scholar of the Imperial Han Lin Academy, saw Chao Chueh, he made a verse which said,

> *The sound of the valley stream is itself the Vast*
> *Eternal Tongue;*
> *Are not the colors of the mountains the Pure Body?*
> *Since evening, eighty-four thousand verses;*
> *Another day, how could I quote them to others?*

Hsueh Tou borrows the flowing spring to make a long tongue; that is why he says, "No one understands." The harmony of this tune requires you to be a connoisseur before you can appreciate it. If you are not such a person, it is useless to take the trouble to incline an ear to it. An Ancient said, "Even a deaf man can sing a foreign song; good or bad, high or low, he doesn't hear at all." Yun Men said, "When it is raised, if you do not pay attention, you will miss it; if you want to think about it, in what aeon will you ever awaken?" Raising is the essence, paying attention is the function; if you can see before it is brought up, before any indications are distinguishable, then you will occupy the essential bridge; if you can see at the moment when the indications are distinguishable, then you will have shining and function. If you see after the indications are distinct, you will fall into intellection.

Hsueh Tou is exceedingly compassionate, and goes on to say to you, "When the rain has passed, the autumn water is deep in the evening pond." This verse has been discussed and judged by someone who praised Hsueh Tou for having the talent of a Han Lin scholar.[b] "The rain passed, the autumn water is deep in the evening pond." Still you must set eyes on it quickly; if you tarry in doubt, then you will look without seeing.

TRANSLATORS' NOTES

a. The Flower Garland Cosmos, where all are in each and each is in all, as set out in the *Hua Yen Sutra*.
b. During T'ang times the dynasty established the Han Lin "Academy" to draw on the services of talented literary men. To have the ability of a Han Lin scholar means to have superlative talent.

Feng Hsueh's Workings of the Iron Ox[a]

POINTER

If we discuss the gradual, it is going against the ordinary to merge with the Way: in the midst of a bustling market place, seven ways up and down and eight ways across.

If we discuss the sudden, it doesn't leave a hint of a trace; a thousand sages cannot find it.

If, on the other hand, we do not set up sudden or gradual, then what? To a quick person, one word; to a quick horse, one blow of the whip. At such a time, who is the master? As a test, I cite this to see.

CASE

At the government headquarters in Ying Chou, Feng Hsueh entered the hall and said,[1] "The Patriarchal Masters' Mind Seal is formed like the workings of the Iron Ox:[2a] when taken away, the impression remains;[3] when left there, then the impression is ruined.[4] But if neither removed nor left there,[5] is sealing right or is not sealing right?"[6]

At that time there was a certain Elder Lu P'i who came forth and said, "I have the workings of the Iron Ox:[7] please, Teacher, do not impress the seal."[8]

Hsueh said, "Accustomed to scouring the oceans fishing for whales, I regret to find instead a frog crawling in the muddy sand."[9]

P'i stood there thinking.[10] Hsueh shouted and said, "Elder, why do you not speak further?"[11] P'i hesitated;[12] Hsueh hit him with his whisk.[13] Hsueh said, "Do you still remember the words? Try to quote them."[14] As P'i was about to open his mouth,[15] Hsueh hit him again with his whisk.

The Governor said, "The Buddhist Law and the Law of Kings are the same."[16]

Hsueh said, "What principle have you seen?"[17]

The Governor said, "When you do not settle what is to be settled, instead you bring about disorder."[18]

Hseuh thereupon descended from his seat.[19]

NOTES

1. He explains Ch'an in public; what is he saying?
2. Thousands of people, ten thousands of people cannot budge it. Where is the impenetrable difficulty? The seal of the three essentials opens, without running afoul of the point.
3. The true imperative must be carried out. Wrong!
4. A second offense is not permitted. Observe the time when the imperative is being carried out. A thrust! Immediately I strike.
5. See how there is no place to put it. How difficult to understand!
6. The heads of everyone in the world appear and disappear. The design is already showing. But I only ask that you turn over the meditation seat and disperse the great assembly with shouts.
7. He's fished out one who's "awakened in the dark." Nevertheless, he's unusual.
8. Good words; nevertheless, he's wrong.
9. Like a falcon catching a pigeon. His jewel net extends throughout space. The wonder horse runs a thousand miles.
10. What a pity! Still, there's a place for him to show himself; what a pity to let it go.
11. He captures the flag and steals the drum. The boiling turmoil has come.
12. Three times he has died. A double case.
13. Well struck! This order requires such a man to carry it out.
14. What is the need? He adds frost upon snow.
15. Once having died, he won't come to life again. This fellow makes others out to be fools. He has run into (Feng Hsueh's) poison hand.
16. Clearly. After all, they've been seen through by a bystander.
17. He too gives a good thrust; he has turned the spearpoint around and come back with it.
18. He seems to be right, but he's not really right. (Still,) you must realize that the bystander has eyes. When someone of the eastern house dies, someone of the western house helps in the mourning.
19. He adds error to error. Seeing the situation, he adjusts. Now the task of study is completed.

COMMENTARY

Feng Hsueh was a venerable adept in the lineage of Lin Chi.

First Lin Chi was in Huang Po's community. As he was planting pine trees, Huang Po said to him, "Deep in the mountains here, why plant so many pine trees?" Chi said, "For one thing, to provide scenery for the monastery; second, to make a signpost for people of later generations." Having spoken, he hoed the ground once. Po said, "Although you are right, you have already suffered twenty blows of my staff." Chi struck the ground one more time and whistled under his breath. Po said, "With you, my school will greatly flourish in the world."

Che of Ta Kuei said, "Lin Chi in his way seemed to invite trouble in a peaceful area; nevertheless, only when immutable in the face of danger can one be called a real man."

Huang Po said, "My school, coming to you, will greatly flourish in the world." He seems to be fond of his child, unaware of being unseemly.

Later, Kuei Shan asked Yang Shan, "Did Huang Po at that time only entrust his bequest to Lin Chi alone, or is there yet anyone else?" Yang Shan said, "There is, but the age is so remote that I do not want to mention it to you, Master." Kuei Shan said, "Although you are right, I still want to know; just mention it and let's see." Yang Shan said, "One man will point south; in Wu-yueh the order will be carried out, and coming to a great wind, then it will stop." This foretold of Feng Hsueh ("Wind Cave").

Feng Hsueh first studied with Hsueh Feng for five years. As it happened, he asked for help with this story: "As Lin Chi entered the hall, the head monks of both halls simultaneously shouted. A monk asked Lin Chi, 'Are there guest and host, or not?' Chi said, 'Guest and host are evident.'" Feng Hsueh asked, "What is the inner meaning of this?" Hsueh Feng said, "In the past I went along with Yen T'ou or Ch'in Shan to see Lin Chi; on the way, we heard he had already passed on. If you want to understand his talk about guest and host, you should call upon venerable adepts in the stream of his school."

One day he finally saw Nan Yuan. He recited the preceding story and said, "I have come especially to see you personally." Nan Yuan said, "Hsueh Feng is an Ancient Buddha."

One time he saw Ching Ch'ing. Ch'ing asked him, "Where have you just come from?" Hsueh said, "I come from the East." Ch'ing said, "And did you cross the little (Ts'ao) river?" Hsueh said, "The great ship sails alone through the sky; there are no little rivers to cross." Ch'ing said, "Birds cannot fly across mirror lake and picture mountain; have you not merely overheard another's remark?" Hsueh said, "Even the sea fears the power of a warship; sails flying through the sky, it crosses the five lakes." Ch'ing raised his whisk and said, "What about this?" Hsueh said, "What is this?" Ch'ing said, "After all, you don't know." Hsueh said, "Appearing, disappearing, rolling up and rolling out, I act the same as you, Teacher." Ch'ing said, "Casting auguring sticks, you listen to the empty sound; fast asleep, you are full of gibberish." Hsueh said, "When a marsh is wide, it can contain a mountain; a cat can subdue a leopard." Ch'ing said, "I forgive your crime and pardon your error; you better leave quickly." Hsueh said, "If I leave, I lose." Then he went out; when he got to the Dharma Hall, he said to himself, "Big man, the case is not yet finished; how then can you quit?" Then he turned around and went into the abbot's room. As Ching Ch'ing sat there, Hsueh asked, "I have just now offered my ignorant view and insulted your venerable countenance; humbly favored by the Teacher's compassion, I have not yet been given punishment for my crime." Ching Ch'ing said, "Just awhile ago you said you came from the East: did you not come from Ts'ui Yen?" Hsueh said, "Hsueh Tou actually lies east of Pao Kai." Ching Ch'ing said, "If you don't chase the lost sheep, crazy interpretations cease. Instead you come here and recite poems." Hsueh said, "When you meet a swordsman on the road, you should show your sword; do not offer poetry to one who is not a poet." Ch'ing said, "Put the poetry away right now and try to use your sword a little." Hsueh said, "A decapitated man carried the sword away." Ch'ing said, "You not only violate the method of the teaching; you also show your own fat-headedness." Hsueh said, "Unless I violate the method of the teaching, how could I awaken to the mind of an Ancient Buddha?" Ch'ing said, "What do you call the mind of an Ancient Buddha?" Hsueh said, "Again you grant your allowance; now what do you have, Teacher?" Ch'ing said, "This patch-robed one from the East cannot distinguish beans from wheat. I have only heard of ending without finishing; how can you finish by forcing an end?" Hsueh said, "The immense billows rise a thousand fathoms; the clear waves are not other than water." Ch'ing said, "When one phrase cuts off the flow, myriad impulses cease." Hsueh thereupon bowed. Ch'ing tapped him three times with his whisk and said, "Exceptional indeed. Now sit and have tea."

When Feng Hsueh first came to Nan Yuan, he entered the door without bowing. Yuan said, "When you enter the door, you should deal with the host." Hsueh said, "I ask the Teacher to make a definite distinction." Yuan slapped his knee with his left hand. Hsueh immediately shouted. Yuan slapped his knee with his right hand. Hsueh again shouted. Yuan raised his left hand and said, "This one I concede to you." Then he raised his right hand and said, "But what about this one?" Hsueh said, "Blind!" Yuan then raised his staff. Hsueh said, "What are you doing? I will take that staff away from you and hit you, Teacher; don't say I didn't warn you. Yuan then threw the staff down and said, "Today I have been made a fool of by this yellow-faced riverlander." Hsueh said, "Teacher, it seems you are unable to hold your bowl, yet are falsely claiming you're not hungry." Yuan said, "Haven't you ever reached this place?" Hsueh said, "What kind of talk is this?" Yuan said, "I just asked." Hsueh said, "Still I can't let you go." Yuan said, "Sit awhile and drink some tea."

See how an excellent student naturally has a sharp and dangerous edge to his personality. Even Nan Yuan couldn't really handle him. The next day, Nan Yuan just posed an ordinary question, saying "Where did you spend this summer?" Hsueh said, "I passed the summer along with Attendant Kuo at the Deer Gate." Yuan said, "So really you had already personally seen an adept when you came here." Yuan also said, "What did he say to you?" Hsueh said, "From beginning to end he only taught me to always be the master." Yuan immediately struck him and drove him out of the abbot's room; he said, "What is the use of a man who accepts defeat?"

Hsueh henceforth submitted. In Nan Yuan's community he worked as the gardener. One day Nan Yuan came to the garden and questioned him; he said, "How do they bargain for the staff in the South?" Hsueh said, "They make a special bargain. How do they bargain for it here, Teacher?" Nan Yuan raised his staff and said, "Under the staff, acceptance of birthlessness; facing the situation without deferring to the teacher." At this Feng Hsueh opened up in great enlightenment.

At this time the five dynasties were divided and at war. The governor of Ying Chou invited the Master (Feng Hsueh) to pass the summer there. At this time the one school of Lin Chi greatly flourished. Whenever he questioned and answered, or gave out pointers, invariably his words were sharp and fresh; gathering flowers, forming brocade, each word had a point.

One day the governor requested the Master to enter the hall to teach the assembly. The Master said, "The Patriarchal Teacher's Mind Seal is formed like the workings of the Iron Ox. Removed, the impression remains; left, the impression is ruined. But if you neither take it away nor keep it there, is it right to use the seal or not?"

Why is it not like the workings of a stone man or a wooden horse, only like the workings of an Iron Ox? There is no way for you to move it: wherever you go the seal remains; as soon as you stop, the seal is broken, causing you to shatter into a hundred fragments. But if you neither go nor stay, should you use the seal or not? See how he gives out indications; you might say there is bait on the hook.

At this time there was an Elder Lu P'i in the audience. He also was a venerable adept in the tradition of Lin Chi. He dared to come forth and reply to his device; thus he turned his words and made a question, undeniably unique; "I have the workings of an Iron Ox; I ask you, Master, not to impress the seal." But what could he do? Feng Hsueh was an adept; he immediately replied to him, saying, "Accustomed to scouring the oceans fishing for whales, I regret to find instead a frog crawling in the muddy river sand." And there is an echo in the words. Yun Men said, "Trailing a hook in the four seas, just fishing for a hideous dragon; the mysterious device beyond convention is to seek out those who understand the self."

In the vast ocean, twelve buffalo carcasses are used as bait for the hooks; instead he has just snagged a frog. But there is nothing mysterious or wonderful in these words; and neither is there any principle to judge. An Ancient said, "It is easy to see in the phenomenon: if you try to figure it out in your mind, you will lose contact with it." Lu P'i stood there thinking: "Seeing it, if you don't take it, it will be hard to find again even in a thousand years." What a pity! That is why it is said, "Even if you can explain a thousand scriptures and commentaries, it is hard to utter a phrase appropriate to the moment."

The fact is that Lu P'i was searching for a good saying to answer Feng Hsueh; he didn't want to carry out the order, and suffered Feng Hsueh's thoroughgoing use of his ability to "capture the flag and steal the drum." He was unremittingly pressed back, and simply couldn't do anything. As a proverb says, "When an army is defeated, it cannot be swept up with a grass broom." In the very beginning it is still necessary to seek a tactic to oppose the adversary, but if you wait till you've come up with one, your head will have fallen to the ground.

The governor too had studied a long time with Feng Hsueh; he knew to say, "The Law of Buddhas and the Law of Kings are one." Hsueh said, "What have you seen?" The governor said, "If you do not settle what should be settled, instead you bring on disorder." Feng Hsueh was all one whole mass of spirit, like a gourd floating on the water; press it down and it rolls over; push it and it moves. He knew how to explain the Dharma according to the situation; if it did not accord with the situation, it would just be false talk. Hsueh thereupon left the seat.

VERSE

Having caught Lu P'i, he makes him mount the Iron Ox:
   Among a thousand people, ten thousand, still he wants to show his skill. The general of a defeated army need not be decapitated a second time.

The spear and armor of the Three Profundities have never been easily opposed;
   The one whose move it is, is confused. He accepts disaster like receiving good fortune and accepts submission like encountering opposition.

By the castle of the King of Ch'u, the tidal water—
   What tidal water are you talking about? Vastly extensive, it fills heaven and earth. Even were it the four seas, he would still reverse their flow.

Shouting once he caused its flow to turn back.
>   This one shout not only cuts off your tongue; oh! it star-
>   tles the Iron Ox of Shensi into a run and frightens the
>   Great Colossus of Chia Chou[b] to death.

COMMENTARY

Hsueh Tou knew Feng Hsueh to have such a style, so he
eulogized him by saying, "Having caught Lu P'i, he mounts
him on the Iron Ox; the spear and armor of the three profundities have never been easily opposed." In the tradition of Lin
Chi there are three profundities and three essentials: within
any one phrase there must be inherent three profundities; in
one profundity there must be inherent three essentials. A
monk asked Lin Chi, "What is the primary phrase?" Chi said,

>   *When the seal of the three essentials is lifted, the*
>   *red mark is narrow;*
>   *Without admitting hesitation, host and guest are*
>   *distinct.*

"What is the secondary phrase?"

>   *How can subtle discernment admit of no question-*
>   *ing?*
>   *Expedients do not go against the ability to cut off*
>   *the streams.*

"What is the third phrase?"

>   *Just observe the playing of puppets on the stage:*
>   *The pulling of the strings depends on the man be-*
>   *hind the scenes.*

In Feng Hsueh's one phrase, he is immediately equipped with
the spear and armor of the three profundities; with seven accoutrements[c] at his side, it is not easy to oppose him. If he were
not so, how could he have handled Lu P'i?

Finally, Hsueh Tou wants to bring out the active edge of the
Lin Chi line: do not speak only of Lu P'i—even by the castle of
the King of Ch'u, the great waves, vast and extensive, the white
breakers flooding the sky, all return to the source; just using a
single shout is all that's needed to make them reverse their
course.

TRANSLATORS' NOTES

a. The Iron Ox is supposed to have been built by the legendary King Yu to stem the flood of the Yellow River some four thousand years ago; its head is in Honan, and its tail is in Hopei.

b. A huge stone image of Maitreya, said to be three hundred sixty feet high.

c. The seven items that make up the teacher's accoutrements: 1) great capacity and great function; 2) swiftness of wit and eloquence; 3) wondrous spirituality of speech; 4) the active edge to kill or bring to life; 5) wide learning and broad experience; 6) clarity of mirroring awareness; 7) freedom to appear or disappear. "The seven accoutrements" can also refer to a warrior's set of equipment.

Yun Men's Flowering Hedge

POINTER

One who can take action on the road is like a tiger in the mountains; one immersed in worldly understanding is like a monkey in a cage. If you want to know the meaning of buddha-nature, you should observe times and seasons, causes and conditions. If you want to smelt pure gold which has been refined a hundred times, you need the forge and bellows of a master. Now tell me, when one's great function appears, what can be used to test him?

CASE

A monk asked Yun Men, "What is the Pure Body of Reality?"[1]

Yun Men said, "A flowering hedge."[2]

The monk asked, "What is it like when one goes on in just such a way?"[3]

Yun Men said, "A golden-haired lion."[4a]

NOTES

1. He sees the sixteen-foot golden body (of Buddha) in a heap of dust. Mottled and mixed up; what is it?
2. If the point of the question is not real, the answer comes across crude. Striking, resounding (everywhere). The bent does not hide the straight.
3. He swallows the date whole. Why indulge in stupidity?
4. He is both praising and censuring; two faces of one die. He adds error to error—what is going on in his mind?

COMMENTARY

People, do you know the point of this monk's questions and the point of Yun Men's answers? If you do know, their two mouths are alike without a single tongue. If you do not know, you will not avoid being fatheaded.

A monk asked Hsuan Sha, "What is the Pure Body of Reality?" Sha said, "Dripping with pus." He had the adamantine eye: as a test, I ask you to try to discern it.

Yun Men was not the same as others. Sometimes he held still and stood like a wall ten miles high, with no place for you to draw near. Sometimes he would open out a path for you, die along with you and live along with you.

Yun Men's tongue was very subtle; some people say he was answering him figuratively; but if you understand it this way, then tell me where Yun Men is at. This was a household affair; do not try to figure it out from outside. This was the reason Pai Chang said, "Manifold appearances and myriad forms, and all spoken words, each should be turned and returned to oneself and made to turn freely." Going to where life springs forth, he immediately speaks; if you try to discuss it and seek it in thought, immediately you have fallen into the secondary phase. Yung Chia said, "When the Body of Reality awakens fully, there is not a single thing; the inherent nature of the original source is the natural real Buddha."

Yun Men tested this monk; the monk was also a member of his household and was himself a longtime student. He knew the business of the household, so he went on to say, "What is it like to go on like this?" Men said, "A golden-haired lion." But tell me, is this agreeing with him or not agreeing with him? Is this praising him or censuring him? Yen T'ou said, "If you engage in a battle, each individual stands in a pivotal position." It is also said, "He studies the living phrase; he does not study the dead phrase. If you get understanding at the living phrase, you will never ever forget; if you get understanding at the dead phrase, you will be unable to save yourself."

Another monk asked Yun Men, "Is it true or not that 'the Buddha Dharma is like the moon in the water'?" Yun Men said, "There is no way through the clear waves." The monk went on to say, "How did you manage?" Yun Men said,

"Where does this second question come from?" The monk said, "How is it when going on in just this way?" Yun Men said, "Further complications block the mountain path."

You must realize that this matter does not rest in words and phrases: like sparks from struck flint, like the brilliance of flashing lightning, whether you reach it or not, you still will not avoid losing your body and life. Hsueh Tou is someone who is there: so he produces his verse from that very place.

VERSE

A flowering hedge:
    The words are still in our ears.
Don't be fatheaded!
    Such people are numerous as hemp and millet seeds. Still,
    there are some who are not.
The marks are on the balance arm, not on the scale pan.
    Too complicated! Everyone should go to his own place
    and introspect. He hasn't avoided talking about principle.
"So just be like this"—
    He swallows the date whole.
How pointless!
    Take what's yours and get out. Clearly. You should not
    mistakenly blame Yun Men.
A golden-haired lion—everybody look!
    He lets out one or a half. Still they are dogs. Yun Men is
    also a man from P'u Chou escorting a thief.

COMMENTARY

Hsueh Tou sizes up the audience to give his order; he makes the harpstring move and distinguishes the tune. With each phrase he continues the judgement. This one verse is not at variance with the form for quoting the Ancients: "A flowering hedge"; then he says, "Don't be fatheaded." People all say that Yun Men was responding figuratively; they all make up emotional interpretations to understand him. Hsueh Tou therefore

gives his own fodder and says, "Don't be fatheaded." All in all,
Yun Men's meaning does not lie where the flowering hedge is;
that is why Hsueh Tou says, "The marks are on the balance
arm, not on the scale pan." This one phrase is excessively
indulgent. In the water there is originally no moon; the moon
is in the sky. This is like the marks being on the balance arm,
not on the scale pan. But tell me, which is the balance? If you
can discern it clearly, you will not turn away from Hsueh Tou.

When that man of old got to this point, he was undeniably
compassionate. Clearly he says to you, "It's not here; it's over
there." But tell me, what place is that "over there"? This
finishes the eulogizing of their first statements; afterwards he
versifies the monk's saying, "What is it like when just going on
like this?" Hsueh Tou says that this monk still has no point.
But tell me, is this meeting in the light or meeting in darkness?
Did he speak this way from understanding, or did he speak thus
without understanding? "A golden-haired lion—everyone
look!" Do you see the golden-haired lion? Look!

TRANSLATORS' NOTES

a. The Golden-haired Lion is used in the Hua Yen school to sym-
    bolize the cosmos as the mutual interpenetration of the universal
    and the particular, of principle (relativity, emptiness of inherent
    fixed reality) and phenomena (the myriads of things and events).
    The Lion's whole body is reflected in each and every hair: thus
    there is an infinity of infinities within the whole, with each par-
    ticular hair reflected in and reflecting the others ad infinitum. In a
    general way the Golden-haired Lion represents reality, or the em-
    bodiment of reality. Manjusri, the bodhisattva who stands for
    wisdom and knowledge, is depicted as riding the Golden-haired
    Lion.

Nan Ch'uan's It's like a Dream

POINTER

Cease and desist; then an iron tree blooms with flowers. Is there anyone? Is there? A clever lad loses his profits; even though he is free in seven ways up and down and eight ways across, he cannot avoid having another pierce his nostrils. But tell me, where is his error? To test, I quote this to see.

CASE

As the officer Lu Hsuan was talking with Nan Ch'uan, he said, "Master of the Teachings Chao said, 'Heaven, earth, and I have the same root; myriad things and I are one body.' This is quite marvelous."[1]

Nan Ch'uan pointed to a flower in the garden.[2] He called to the officer and said, "People these days see this flower as a dream."[3]

NOTES

1. He's making a living in a ghost cave. A picture of a cake cannot satisfy hunger. This is also haggling in the weeds.
2. What is he saying? Bah! The scriptures have teachers of scriptures, the treatises have teachers of treatises: it's no business of a patchrobed monk. Bah! A powerful man in that instance would have uttered a turning word, and not only cut off Nan Ch'uan, but thereby cause all the patchrobed monks to show some energy.
3. When the mandarin duck embroidery is done, you may look at them, but do not give the golden needle away to anyone. Don't talk in your sleep! You have drawn the golden oriole down from his willow branch.

COMMENTARY

The officer Lu Hsuan studied for a long time with Nan Ch'uan. He always kept his mind on essential nature, and he immersed himself in the *Discourses of Chao*. One day as they sat, he happened to bring up these two lines, considering them remarkable. He questioned, "Master of the Teachings Chao said, 'Heaven, earth, and I have the same root; myriad things and I are one body.' This is quite marvelous." Master of the Teachings Seng Chao was an eminent monk of Chin times (latter 4th–early 5th centuries A.D.); he was together with Tao Sheng, Tao Jung, and Seng Jui in the school of Kumarajiva. They were called the Four Sages.

When (Seng Chao) was young, he enjoyed reading Chuang Tzu and Lao Tzu. Later, as he was copying the old translation of the Vimalakirti Scripture, he had an enlightenment. Then he knew that Chuang and Lao still were not really thoroughgoing. Therefore he compiled all the scriptures and composed four discourses.

What Chuang and Lao intended to say was that "heaven and earth are greatness of form; my form is also thus; we are alike born in the midst of empty nothingness." Chuang and Lao's overall meaning just discusses equalizing things; Seng Chao's overall meaning says that nature all returns to self. Have you not seen how his discourse says, "The ultimate man is empty and hollow, without form; yet none of the myriad things are not his own doing. Who can understand that myriad things are his own self? Only a sage, I wot."

Although there are spirits and there are humans, there are the wise and the sage, each is distinct, but all alike have one nature and one substance.

An Ancient said, "Heaven and earth, the whole world, is just one self; when cold, it is cold throughout heaven and earth; when hot, it is hot throughout heaven and earth. When it exists, all throughout heaven and earth exists; when it doesn't exist, heaven and earth do not exist. When affirmed, all throughout heaven and earth is; when denied, all throughout heaven and earth is not."

Fa Yen said,

He he he I I I
South north east west, everything is all right.
All right or not all right,
Only for me there is nothing not all right.

That is why it was said, "In the heavens and on earth, only I alone am honorable." As Shih T'ou read the *Discourse of Chao*, when he got to this place, "Understand myriad things as oneself," he was vastly and greatly enlightened. Later he composed the book *Ts'an T'ung Ch'i* ("Merging of Difference and Sameness"), which also does not go beyond this meaning.

See how (Lu Hsuan) questioned; tell me, what root do they share? Which body do they have in common? When he got here, still he was undeniably unique: how could this be the same as an ordinary man's ignorance of the height of the sky or the breadth of the earth? How could there be such a thing?

Lu Hsuan's questioning in this manner was indeed quite exceptional, but he did not go beyond the meaning of the Teachings. If you say that the meaning of the Teachings is the ultimate paradigm, then why did the World Honored One also raise the flower?[a] What did the Patriarchal Teacher come from the West for?

Nan Ch'uan's way of answering used the grip of a patch-robed monk to pull out the painful spot for the other, and broke up his nest; he pointed at a flower in the garden and called to the officer, saying, "People these days see this flower as though it were a dream." This is like leading the man to the edge of a ten thousand fathom cliff and giving him a push, causing his life to be cut off. If you were pushed over on level ground, even till Maitreya Buddha was born in the world, you still would simply be unable to accomplish the cutting off of life.

It is also like a man in a dream; though he wants to awaken, he cannot wake up; called by another, he awakens. If Nan Ch'uan's eyes were not true, he would certainly have been befuddled by Lu. See how he talks; yet undeniably he is difficult to understand. If the action of your eyes is alive, you will experience it like the superb flavor of ghee; if you are dead, you will hear it and turn it into poison. An Ancient said, "If you see it in phenomena, you'll fall into ordinary feelings; if you go to your intellect to figure it out, after all you will seek without finding." Yen T'ou said, "This is the livelihood of a transcendent man; he just reveals the bit before the eyes, just like a flash of lightning."

Nan Ch'uan's great meaning was like this; he has the capability to capture rhinos and tigers, to judge dragons and snakes. When you get here, you must understand on your own: have you not heard it said, "The single transcending road has not been transmitted by a thousand sages; students toil over forms like moneys grasping at reflections." See how Hsueh Tou brings it out in verse:

VERSE

Seeing, hearing, awareness, knowledge; these are not one and the same—
  In the multitude of forms and myriad appearances, there is not a single thing. Seven flowers, eight blooms.[b] Eye, ear, nose, tongue, body and mind are all at once a hammerhead without a hole.

Mountains and rivers are not seen in a mirror.
  There is no such scenery here where I am. What is long is of itself long; what is short is of itself short; green is green and yellow is yellow. Where do you see them?

The frosty sky's moon sets, the night nearly half over;
  He has led you into the weeds. The whole world has never concealed it. I only fear you will go sit inside a ghost cave.

With whom will it cast a shadow, cold in the clear pool?
  Is there anyone? Is there? If they did not sleep on the same bed, how could they know the cover is worn out? Someone who is sad should not speak of it to another who is sad; if he speaks to a sad man, it would sadden him to death.

COMMENTARY

Nan Ch'uan's little sleep talk, Hsueh Tou's big sleep talk: although they are dreaming, they are having a good dream. At first there was talk of 'one body'—here he says that they are not the same: "Seeing, hearing, awareness, and knowledge are not one and the same— / Mountains and rivers are not seen in a mirror." If you say that they are seen in a mirror, and only then illumined, then they are not apart from where the mirror is. Mountains, rivers, and the great earth; plants, trees, and forests —do not use a mirror to observe them. If you use a mirror to observe, then you make it into two parts. Just let mountains be mountains and rivers be rivers. "Each thing abides in its normal state; the mundane aspect always remains."

"Mountains and rivers are not seen in a mirror." Then tell me, where can you see them? Do you understand? When you get here, turn towards: "The frosty sky's moon sets, the night nearly half over"—This Side he has summed up for you; That Side, you must cross by yourself.

But do you realize that Hsueh Tou uses his own thing to help others? "With whom will it cast a shadow, cold in the clear pool?" Do you think he is reflected himself, or do you think he is reflected together with anyone?^c It is necessary to cut off mental activity and cut off understanding before finally reaching this realm.

Right now, we don't need a clear pool, and we don't have to wait for the moon to set in the frosty sky. Right now, how is it?

TRANSLATORS' NOTES

a. This incident marks the beginning of the 'separate transmission' of Ch'an: at the assembly on Vulture Peak, the Buddha raised a flower. No one in the crowd understood his meaning but Mahakasyapa, who gave a slight smile. Thus Buddha recognized Mahakasyapa as the heir to the treasury of the eye of the true teaching.

b. 'Seven flowers, eight blooms' is one literal translation of a phrase that bears multiple meanings. It can mean profusion, confusion in multiplicity, 'cracked and shattered.' It can also mean opened up, clearly distinct, everything revealed in all its multiplicity.

c. According to the *Shudensho*, the moon's setting can be interpreted as 'descending,' or shining into the pool, casting a reflection: is it just the moon alone, or is anyone there? The ambiguity of the subject makes this passage difficult to translate, while the ambivalence itself underscores the unity of self and world.

Chao Chou's Man Who Has Died the Great Death

Where right and wrong are mixed, even the sages cannot know; when going against and with, vertically and horizontally, even the Buddhas cannot know. One who is a man detached from the world, who transcends convention, reveals the abilities of a great man who stands out from the crowd. He walks on thin ice, runs on a sword's edge. He is like the unicorn's horn, like a lotus flower in fire. When he sees someone beyond comparison, he knows they are on the same path. Who is an expert? As a test I'm citing this old case: look!

CASE

Chao Chou asked T'ou Tzu, "How is it when a man who has died the great death returns to life?"[1]

T'ou Tzu said, "He must not go by night: he must get there in daylight."[2]

NOTES

1. There are such things! A thief doesn't strike a poor household. He is accustomed to acting as guest, thus he has a feel for guests.
2. Seeing a cage, he makes a cage. This is a thief recognizing a thief. If he wasn't lying on the same bed, how would he know the coverlet is worn?

COMMENTARY

Chao Chou asked T'ou Tzu, "How is it when a man who has died the great death returns to life?" T'ou Tzu answered him

saying, "He must not go by night: he must get there in daylight." But say, what time and season is this? A flute with no
holes strikes against a felt-pounding board. This is called "a
question to test the host"; it is also called "an intentional
question." All over they praised T'ou Tzu and Chao Chou for
having outstanding eloquence. Though the two old men succeeded to different masters, observe how their active edges
accord as one.

One day T'ou Tzu spread the tea setting to entertain Chao
Chou. T'ou Tzu himself passed some steamed cakes to Chao
Chou, but Chou paid no attention. T'ou Tzu ordered his attendant to give the sesame cakes to Chao Chou. Chou bowed to
the attendant three times. But say, what was his meaning?
Observe how he always went right to the root to uphold this
fundamental thing for the benefit of others.

There was a monk who asked T'ou Tzu, "What is the Way?"
T'ou Tzu answered, "The Way." The monk asked, "What is
Buddha?" T'ou Tzu answered, "Buddha." Again he asked,
"How is it before the golden lock is open?" T'ou Tzu answered,
"Open." He asked, "How is it before the golden rooster has
crowed?" T'ou Tzu answered, "This sound does not exist."
The monk asked, "How is it after he crows?" T'ou Tzu an-
swered, "Each knows the time for himself." His whole life
T'ou Tzu's questions and answers were all like this.

Look: when Chao Chou asked, "How is it when a man who
has died the great death returns to life?" T'ou Tzu immediately
said, "He must not go by night: he must get there in daylight."
Direct as sparks struck from stone, like the brilliance of a
lightning flash. Only a transcendental man like him could do
this.

A man who has died the great death has no Buddhist doctrines and theories, no mysteries and marvels, no gain and loss,
no right and wrong, no long and short. When he gets here, he
just lets it rest this way. An Ancient said of this, "On the level
ground the dead are countless; only one who can pass through
the forest of thorns is a good hand." Yet one must pass beyond
that Other Side too to begin to attain. Even so, for present day
people even to get to this realm is already difficult to achieve.

If you have any leanings or dependence, any interpretative
understanding, then there is no connection. Master Che called

this "vision that is not purified." My late teacher Wu Tsu called it "the root of life not cut off." One must die the great death once, then return to life. Master Yung Kuang of central Chekiang said, "If you miss at the point of their words, then you're a thousand miles from home. In fact you must let go your hands while hanging from a cliff, trust yourself and accept the experience. Afterwards you return to life again. I can't deceive you—how could anyone hide this extraordinary truth?"

The meaning of Chao Chou's question is like this. T'ou Tzu is an adept, and he didn't turn his back on what Chao Chou asked: it's just that he cut off his feelings and left no traces, so unavoidably he's hard to understand. He just showed the little bit before the eyes. Thus an Ancient said, "If you want to attain Intimacy, don't ask with questions. The question is in the answer, and the answer is in the question." It would have been very difficult for someone other than T'ou Tzu to reply when questioned by Chao Chou. But since T'ou Tzu is an expert, as soon as it's raised he knows where it comes down.

VERSE

In life there's an eye—still, it's the same as death.
> The two don't know of each other. Back and forth, coming and going. If Chao Chou wasn't well provided, how could he discern whether T'ou Tzu was monk or lay?

Why use antiserum to test an adept?
> If you don't test how can you discern the truth? Having met, try to give an examination—what's the harm? I too want to question him.

Even the Ancient Buddhas, they say, have never arrived.
> Luckily they had companions. Even the thousand sages haven't transmitted it. I don't know either.

I don't know who can scatter dust and sand.
> There is quite a bit of this right now. (The dust and sand) gets in your eyes whether they're opened or closed. When you bring it up this way, Your Reverence, where does it come down?

COMMENTARY

"In life there's an eye—still, it's the same as death." Hsueh
Tou is a man who knows what is, therefore he can dare to
make up verses. An Ancient said, "He studies the living
phrase; he doesn't study the dead phrase." Hsueh Tou says that
to have ·eyes within life is still to be just the same as a dead
man. Has he ever died? To have eyes within death is to be the
same as a live man. An Ancient said, "Utterly kill a dead man,
then you will see a live man. Bring a dead man fully to life,
then you will see a dead man."

Though Chao Chou is a live man, he intentionally made up
a dead question to test T'ou Tzu. It was like taking a substance
that vitiates the character of a medicine in order to test him.
That's why Hsueh Tou said, "Why use antiserum to test an
adept?" This versifies Chao Chou's questioning.

Afterwards he praises T'ou Tzu: "Even the Ancient Buddhas, they say, have never arrived." Even the ancient Buddhas
never got to where the man who has died the great death returns to life—nor have the venerable old teachers ever gotten
here. Even old Shakyamuni or the blue-eyed barbarian monk
(Bodhidharma) would have to study again before they get it.
That is why Hsueh Tou said, "I only grant that the old barbarian knows; I don't allow that he understands."

Hsueh Tou says, "I don't know who can scatter dust and
sand." Haven't you heard: a monk asked Ch'ang Ch'ing, "What
is the eye of a man of knowledge?" Ch'ing said, "He has a vow
not to scatter sand." Pao Fu said, "You mustn't scatter any
more of it." All over the country venerable old teachers sit on
carved wood seats, using blows and shouts, raising their
whisks, knocking on the seat, exhibiting spiritual powers and
acting as masters—all of this is scattering sand. But say, how
can this be avoided?

Layman P'ang's Good Snowflakes

POINTER

Bringing it out unique and alone (is still) dripping with water, dragging through mud. When knocking and resounding occur together (it's still like) a silver mountain, an iron wall.

If you describe and discuss, you see ghosts in front of your skull. If you seek in thought, you sit beneath the black mountain. The bright shining sun lights up the sky. The pure whispering wind circles the earth.

But say, do the Ancients have any obscurities? To test I'm citing this old case: look!

CASE

When Layman P'ang took leave of Yao Shan[1], Shan ordered ten Ch'an travellers to escort him to the gate.[2] The Layman pointed to the snow in the air and said, "Good snowflakes—they don't fall in any other place."[3]

At the time one of the Ch'an travellers named Ch'uan said, "Where do they fall?"[4] The Layman slapped him once.[5] Ch'uan said, "Even a layman shouldn't be so coarse."[6] The Layman said, "Though you call yourself a Ch'an traveller this way, the King of Death still won't let you go."[7] Ch'uan said, "How about you, Layman?"[8] Again the Layman slapped him[9] and said, "Your eyes see like a blind man, your mouth speaks like a mute."[10]

Hsueh Tou said besides, "When P'ang first spoke I just would have made a snowball and hit him with it."[11]

NOTES

1. This old fellow is acting strange.
2. Yao Shan does not take him lightly. What realm is this? Only a

patchrobed monk who knows the whole thing could (give P'ang this treatment).

3. He stirs up waves where there's no wind. The finger (he points with) has eyes. There's an echo in this old fellow's words.

4. On target. He comes on following after P'ang. Of course he climbed onto P'ang's hook.

5. A hit! As it turns out, the thief that Ch'uan pulled in ransacked his house.

6. Staring eyes inside a coffin.

7. The second ladleful of foul water has been poured over him. Why only the King of Death? Here I wouldn't let him go either.

8. His coarse mind hasn't changed. Again he's asking for a beating. From beginning to end this monk is at a loss.

9. Of course. Adding frost on top of snow. Having taken a beating, reveal the truth.

10. He has another conciliatory statement. Again he reads the verdict for him.

11. Hsueh Tou is right, but he draws the bow after the thief has gone. This is still quite indulgent. Nevertheless, I'd like to see their arrowpoints meet. But what can we do?—Hsueh Tou has fallen into the ghost cave.

COMMENTARY

Layman P'ang called on Ma Tsu and Shih T'ou: at both places he had verses (to express his realization).

When he first saw Shih Tou he asked, "What man doesn't keep company with the myriad things?" Before he stopped talking, he had his mouth covered by Shih T'ou and had an awakening. He made up a verse saying,

> My everyday affairs are no different:
> Only I myself naturally harmonize.
> No place is grasped or rejected,
> Nowhere do I go for or against.
> Who considers crimson and purple honorable?
> The green mountains have not a speck of dust.
> Spiritual powers and their wondrous functioning—
> Hauling water and carrying firewood.

Later P'ang called on Ma Tsu. Again he asked, "What man doesn't keep company with the myriad things?" Tsu said, "Wait till you can swallow all the water in West River in one gulp, then I'll tell you." The Layman emptied out in great enlightenment. He made up a verse saying,

> *The ten directions, a common gathering—*
> *Everyone studies not-doing.*
> *This is the place where Buddhas are chosen—*
> *Minds empty, they return successful.*

Since P'ang was an adept, all the various monasteries later welcomed him, and wherever he went they vied to praise him. After he had gotten to Yao Shan and stayed around there quite a while, he went to take leave of Yao Shan. Shan held him in the highest esteem, so he ordered ten Ch'an travellers to see him off. It happened to be snowing at the time: the Layman pointed to the snow and said, "Good snowflakes—they don't fall in any other place."

When Ch'an traveller Ch'uan asked, "Where do they fall?" the Layman immediately slapped him. Since Ch'uan was unable to carry out the order, the Layman ordered him to carry out half. Although the order was put into effect, when Ch'an traveller Ch'uan responded in this way, it was not that he didn't know what P'ang was getting at. They each had a point to their activity, but their rolling up and rolling out were not the same. Even so, in some respects he didn't come up to the Layman. That is why he fell into his trap and found it difficult to get out of the Layman's range.

After the Layman had hit him, the Layman went on to explain the reason to him saying, "Your eyes see like a blind man, your mouth speaks like a mute." Besides the previous words Hsueh Tou said, "When he first spoke I just would have made a snowball and hit him with it." Hsueh Tou talked this way, not wanting to turn his back on the question: it's just that his action was tardy. Librarian Ch'ing said, "The Layman's mind is like a lightning bolt. If we waited for you to grab a snowball, how long would it take? Only if you hit him while he's still speaking can you cut him off completely."

Hsueh Tou versifies his own hitting and says:

VERSE

The snowball hits! The snowball hits!
> What will he do about falling into a secondary action? It's not worth the trouble to bring it forth. Overhead vastness, underfoot vastness.

Old Pang's ability cannot grasp it.
> Again and again there are people who don't know this. I only fear it's not so.

Gods and humans do not know for themselves:
> What scene is this? Does Hsueh Tou know?

In eyes, in ears, absolutely clean.
> The arrowpoints meet. Your eyes see like a blind man, your mouth speaks like a mute.

Absolutely clean—
> How? Where will you see Layman P'ang and Hsueh Tou?

Even the blue-eyed barbarian monk Bodhidharma would find it hard to discriminate.
> Bodhidharma comes forth: what does he say to you? I'll hit saying, "What are you saying?" They're buried in the same pit.

COMMENTARY

"The snowball hits! The snowball hits! / Old P'ang's ability cannot grasp it." Hsueh Tou wanted to walk on the Layman's head. The Ancients used "snow" to illustrate the matter of Uniformity. Hsueh Tou meant: "If at that time I had made a snowball and hit him with it, no matter what abilities the Layman had, it would have been hard for him to reach (me.)" Hsueh Tou praises his own hitting, far from knowing where he's lost his profit.

"Gods and men do not know for themselves: / In eyes, in ears, absolutely clean." In the eyes is snow, in the ears is snow too—just at that moment they are dwelling in Uniformity. This is also called "the realm of Samantabhadra." The phenomenon of Uniformity is also called "becoming solid."

Yun Men said, "Even 'having not the slightest worry in the world' is still a turning phrase." When you don't see a single form, this finally is half the issue. If you want the whole issue, first you must know that there is a single road going beyond; when you get here your great function must become manifest (with no gap) for even a needle to enter, and you don't accept the judgments of other people.

Thus it was said, "He studies the living phrase; he doesn't study the dead phrase." An Ancient said, "An appropriate statement is a stake at which to tether a donkey for ten thousand eons." What's the use?

When he gets to this point Hsueh Tou has finished the verse. But he turns around again and says, "But this cleanness is absolute—even Bodhidharma would find it hard to discriminate." Since even Bodhidharma finds it hard to discern, what more would you have me say?

Tung Shan's No Cold or Heat

POINTER

Ten thousand ages abide by the phrase that determines heaven and earth. Even the thousand sages cannot judge the ability to capture tigers and rhinos. Without any further traces of obstruction, the whole being appears everywhere equally.

If you want to understand the hammer and tongs of transcendence, you need the forge and bellows of an adept.

But say, since ancient times has there ever been such a family style or not? To test I'm citing this old case: look!

CASE

A monk asked Tung Shan, "When cold and heat come, how can we avoid them?"[1]

Shan said, "Why don't you go to the place where there is no cold or heat?"[2]

The monk said, "What is the place where there is no cold or heat?"[3]

Tung Shan said, "When it's cold, the cold kills you; when it's hot, the heat kills you."[4]

NOTES

1. It's not this season. (Cold and heat) are right in your face, right on your head. Where are you?
2. The world's people can't find it. He hides his body but reveals a shadow. A con man sells a bogus city of silver.
3. Tung Shan swindles everyone utterly. The monk turns around following him. As soon as Tung Shan lets down his hook the monk climbs onto it.
4. The real does not conceal the false, the crooked does not hide the straight. Looking out over the cliff he sees tigers and rhinos—this

is indeed an occasion to be sad. Tung Shan overturns the great ocean and kicks over Mt. Sumeru. But say, where is Tung Shan?

COMMENTARY

Master Hsin of Huang Lung picked this out and said, "Tung Shan puts the collar on the sleeve and cuts off the shirtfront under the armpits. But what could he do?—This monk didn't like it." Right then a monk came forward and asked Huang Lung, "How are they to be dealt with?" After a long silence Huang Lung said, "Peaceful meditation does not require mountains and rivers: when you have extinguished the mind, fire itself is cool."

Tell me all of you, where is Tung Shan's trap at? If you can clearly discern this, for the first time you will know how the five positions of the Tung Shan tradition of interchanging correct and biased[a] handle people in an extraordinary way. When you reach this transcendental realm, then you'll be able to be like this without needing any arrangements, and you'll spontaneously accord perfectly.

Thus it is said:

The biased within the correct:
In the middle of the first night, before the moon
*   shines,*
No wonder, when they meet, they don't recognize
*   each other:*
Each is hidden, still embracing the aversion of
*   former days.*

The correct within the biased:
At dawn an old woman encounters an ancient mir-
*   ror;*
Clearly she sees her face—there is no other reality.
Don't go on mistaking the image for the head.

Coming from within the correct:
Within nothingness there's a road out of the dust.
If you can just avoid violating the present taboo
*   name,*
You'll still surpass the eloquent ones of former
*   dynasties who silenced every tongue.*

Arrival within the biased:
When two swords cross points, there's no need to
    withdraw.
A good hand is like a lotus in fire—
Clearly he naturally has the energy to reach the
    heavens.

Arrival within both at once:
He does not fall into being or non-being—who dares
    to associate with him?
Everyone wants to get out of the ordinary flow,
But after all he returns and sits in the ashes.

Jurist Yuan of Fu Shan considers this case as being in the pattern of the five positions. If you understand one, then the rest are naturally easy to understand. Yen T'ou said, "It's like a gourd (floating) on the water: push it, and it rolls over without making any effort at all."

Once there was a monk who asked Tung Shan, "How is it when Manjusri and Samantabhadra come to call?" Shan said, "I'd drive them into a herd of water buffalo." The monk said, "Teacher, you enter hell fast as an arrow." Shan said, "I've got all their strength."

When Tung Shan said, "Why don't you go to the place where there is no cold or heat?" this was the correct within the biased. When the monk said, "What is the place where there is no cold or heat?" and Shan said, "When it's cold the cold kills you; when it's hot the heat kills you," this was the biased within the correct. Though it's correct, still it's biased; though it's biased, nevertheless it's complete. This is recorded in full detail in the Records of the Ts'ao Tung School. Had it been the Lin Chi tradition, there wouldn't have been so many things. With this kind of public case you must understand directly as soon as it is uttered.

Some say, "I like no cold no heat very much." What grasp do they have on the case? An Ancient said, "If you run on a sword's edge, you're fast. If you see with emotional consciousness, then you're slow."

Haven't you heard: A monk asked Ts'ui Wei, "What is the meaning of the Patriarch coming from the West?" Wei said, "When no one comes, I'll tell you," then went into the garden. The monk said, "There's no one right here: please, Teacher, tell me." Wei pointed to the bamboo and said, "This stalk is so tall, that stalk is so short." Suddenly the monk was greatly enlightened.

Again: Ts'ao Shan asked a monk, "When it's so hot, where will you go to avoid it?" The monk said, "I'll avoid it inside a boiling cauldron, within the coals of a furnace." Ts'ao Shan said, "How can it be avoided in a boiling cauldron or among the coals of a furnace?" The monk said, "The multitude of sufferings cannot reach there." See how the people of the Ts'ao Tung house naturally understood the conversation of people of their house.

Hsueh Tou uses the affairs of their house to produce his verse:

VERSE

He lets down his hand, but still it's the same as a ten thousand fathom cliff:
Who can discern this without being an adept? Where are correct and biased not perfectly merged? Once the imperial edict is on its way the nobles get out of the road (to let it pass).

Why must correct and biased be in an arrangement?
If you do arrange them, where will you have Today? How will you not become involved in dualism? When the wind moves, the grasses bend down; where the water runs, streams form.

The ancient crystal palace reflects the bright moon,
Round and full. Just don't grasp the reflection, and don't run right in.

The sly hound of Han vainly runs up the stairs.
It isn't just this time. He's stumbled past. Why is he running after dirt? I'll hit and say you are a fellow student of this monk.

COMMENTARY

In the Ts'ao Tung tradition there is appearing in the world and not appearing in the world; there is letting down a hand and not letting down a hand. If you don't appear in the world, your eyes gaze at cloudy skies. If you appear in the world, then your head and face are covered with ashes and dirt.

"Eyes gazing at cloudy skies" is "on top of a ten thousand fathom peak." "Head and face covered with ashes and dirt" refers to the business of letting down a hand. Sometimes "head and face covered with ashes and dirt" is "on top of a ten thousand fathom peak." Sometimes "on top of a ten thousand fathom peak" is "head and faces covered with ashes and dirt." In reality, going into inhabited areas to let down a hand and standing alone on a solitary peak are the same. Having returned to the source and comprehended nature, it is no different from discriminating intelligence. You must avoid understanding them as two parts.

Thus Hsueh Tou said, "He lets down his hand, but still it's the same as a ten thousand fathom cliff." There's simply no place for you to approach. "Why must correct and biased be in an arrangement?" When it comes time to function, they are naturally like this, they are not in any arrangement. This praises Tung Shan's answer.

Afterwards he said, "The ancient crystal palace reflects the bright moon / The sly hound of Han vainly runs up the stairs." This just versifies this monk running after Tung Shan's words. In the Ts'ao Tung tradition they have "the stone woman," "the wooden horse," "the bottomless basket," "the pearl that shines (of itself) at night," "the dead snake," and so on, eighteen kinds. Their general purpose is to illustrate the position of the correct.

When Tung Shan answered, "Why not go to where there is no cold or heat?" this was like the moon shining in the ancient crystal palace, seeming to have a round reflection. The monk asked, "What is the place where there is no cold or heat?" This is just like the hound of Han chasing a clod of dirt: he runs frantically up the stairs to catch the moon's reflection. Tung Shan said, "When it's cold, the cold kills you; when it's hot, the heat kills you." This monk was like the hound of Han running up the stairs but not seeing the image of the moon.

"The hound of Han" comes out of *Essays on the Warring States* where it says, "He was a swift black dog belonging to the Han clan. The rabbits in the mountains were clever; only he could catch these rabbits." Hsueh Tou draws on this to make a comparison for this monk.

What about all of you—do you know where Tung Shan helped people?

After a long silence, Yuan Wu said, "What rabbits are you looking for?"

TRANSLATORS' NOTES

a. 'Correct' symbolizes emptiness, nirvana; 'biased' symbolizes matter-energy, samsara. The intrinsic identity of emptiness and matter-energy, nirvana and samsara, and hence the complementary unity of wisdom and compassion, is basic to Mahayana, or Great Vehicle Buddhism.

Ho Shan's Knowing How to Beat the Drum

CASE

Ho Shan imparted some words saying, "Cultivating study is called 'learning.' Cutting off study is called 'nearness.'[1] Going beyond these two is to be considered real going beyond."[2]

A monk came forward and asked, "What is 'real going beyond'?"[3] Shan said, "Knowing how to beat the drum."[4]

Again he asked, "What is the real truth?"[5] Shan said, "Knowing how to beat the drum."[6]

Again he asked, "'Mind is Buddha'—I'm not asking about this. What is not mind and not Buddha?"[7] Shan said, "Knowing how to beat the drum."[8]

Again he asked, "When a transcendent man comes, how do you receive him?"[9] Shan said, "Knowing how to beat the drum."[10]

NOTES

1. The world's patchrobed monks can't leap clear of this. An iron hammerhead with no handle hole. An iron spike.
2. What are you doing with the one eye on your forehead?
3. What is he saying? I'd blot it out with a single brush stroke. There's an iron spike.
4. An iron spike. Iron brambles. Hard, hard.
5. What is he saying? A doubled case. There's another iron spike.
6. An iron spike. Iron brambles. Hard, hard.
7. What is he saying? This garbage heap! The three sections are not the same. There's another iron spike.
8. An iron spike. Iron brambles. Hard, hard.
9. What is he saying? This monk encounters a fourth ladleful of his foul water. There's another iron spike.
10. An iron spike. Iron brambles. Hard, hard. But say, what does this really mean? In the morning he goes to India, in the evening he returns to China.

COMMENTARY

Ho Shan imparted some words saying, "Cultivating study is called 'learning.' Cutting off study is called 'nearness.' Going beyond these two is to be considered real going beyond." The words of this case come from the *Jewel Treasure Treatise*. To study till there is nothing to study is called "cutting off study." Thus it is said, "Shallow learning, deep enlightenment; deep learning, no enlightenment." This is called "cutting off study." Yung Chia, who was enlightened in one night at Ts'ao Ch'i, said, "Years ago I accumulated learning, consulted the commentaries, and searched scriptures and treatises. Once one's cultivation of studies is completed and exhausted, he is called a non-doing, free man of the Path, beyond study. When he reaches the point of cutting off study, only then for the first time is he near to the Path. When he manages to go beyond these two (aspects of) study, this is called 'real going beyond.'"

The monk too was undeniably bright and quick, so he picked up on these words to question Ho Shan. Shan said, "Knowing how to beat the drum." This is what is called flavorless words, flavorless speech. If you want to understand this case, you must be a transcendent man. Only then will you see that these words have nothing to do with inherent nature, nor is there anything about them to discuss. Understand directly like the bottom falling out of a bucket: only this is where a patchrobed monk rests easy and begins to be able to accord with the meaning of the Patriarch coming from the West. Thus Yun Men said, "Hsueh Feng's rolling a ball, Ho Shan's beating the drum, the National Teacher's bowl of water, Chao Chou's 'Drink some tea,'—all these are indications of the absolute."

Again the monk asked, "What is the real truth?" Shan said, "Knowing how to beat the drum." In the real truth not one other thing is set up. As for the worldly truth, the myriad things are all present. That there is no duality to real and conventional is the highest meaning of the holy truths.

Again the monk asked, " 'Mind is Buddha'—I'm not asking about this. What is not mind and not Buddha?" Shan said, "Knowing how to beat the drum." "What's mind is Buddha" is easy to seek. But when you get to that which is not mind and not Buddha, it's hard and there are few people who arrive.

Again the monk asked, "When a transcendent man comes, how do you receive him?" Shan said, "Knowing how to beat the drum." A transcendent man is a man who has passed through, who is free, purified, and at ease.

All over they consider these four phases as a message from the source: they are called Ho Shan's four beating the drums. This is just like the following:

A monk asked Ching Ch'ing, "At the beginning of a new year, is there any Buddha Dharma or not?" Ch'ing said, "There is." The monk said, "What is the Buddha Dharma at the beginning of a new year?" Ch'ing said, "Initiate good fortune on new year's day and the myriad things are all renewed." The monk said, "I thank the Master for the answer." Ch'ing said, "Today I lost the advantage." He had six kinds of losses like this answer.

Again: A monk asked the great teacher Ching Kuo, "How is it when a crane perches upon a lone pine?" Kuo said, "Beneath its feet, an embarrassing situation." He also asked, "How is it when snow covers the thousand mountains?" Kuo said, "After the sun comes out, an embarrassing situation." Again the monk asked, "Where did the spirits who protect the Teaching go during the purge of 845?" Kuo said, "For the two guardians outside the triple gate, an embarrassing situation." All over, these are called Ching Kuo's three embarrassments.

Again: Pao Fu asked a monk, "What Buddha is the one in the temple?" The monk said, "Try to decide for sure, Teacher." Fu said, "It's old Shakyamuni." The monk said, "Better not deceive people." Fu said, "On the contrary, it's you who are deceiving me." Fu also asked the monk, "What's your name?" The monk said, "Hsien Tse." (which means "all wet") Fu said, "How is it when you encounter withering dryness?" The monk said, "Who is the withering dry one?" Fu said, "I am." The monk said, "Better not deceive people, Teacher." Fu said, "On the contrary, it's you who are deceiving me." Again Fu asked the monk, "What work do you do that you eat till you're so big?" The monk said, "You're not so small yourself, Teacher." Fu made a crouching gesture. The monk said, "Better not deceive people, Teacher." Fu said, "On the contrary, it's you who are deceiving me." Fu also asked the bath keeper, "How wide is that cauldron (you heat the water in)?" The bath keeper aid, "Please, Teacher, measure and see." Fu went through the motions of measuring. The bath keeper said, "Better not deceive people, Teacher." Fu said, "On the contrary, it's you who are deceiving me." All over they call this Pao Fu's four deceptions of people.

This main case is also like Hsueh Feng's four tubs of lacquer:[a] all were masters of our ancient sect. Each produces profound and marvelous teachings and devices to receive people.

Afterwords Hsueh Tou draws out a single continuous line based on Yun Men's teachings to his assembly, and versifies this public case.

VERSE

One hauls rock;
> In the heart of the realm the emperor commands. A leper drags along his companions. A transcendent man comes this way.

A second moves earth.
> Outside the passes the general gives orders. Both have their crimes covered by the same indictment. Those with the same disease sympathize with each other.

To shoot the bolt requires a ten-ton crossbow.
> Even if it's got a ten-ton pull, it still won't be able to penetrate. It should not be used against light opposition; how could it be used for a dead frog?

The old master of Elephant Bone Cliff (Hsueh Feng) rolled balls—
> There's another man who has come this way. He had an iron hammer head with no handle hole. Who doesn't know?

How could this equal Ho Shan's "Knowing how to beat the drum"?
> An iron spike. It takes this old fellow to understand. One son has attained intimately.

I report for you to know:
> Even Hsueh Tou hasn't seen it in dreams. He's adding frost on top of snow. Do you know?

Don't be careless!
> Again there's a bit of utter confusion.

The sweet is sweet, the bitter is bitter.
> Thanks for the answer. Hsueh Tou wrongly adds a footnote: he should be given thirty blows. Has he ever taken a beating? As before, dark vastness. I'll hit!

COMMENTARY

One day Kuei Tsung gave the general call to labor (summoning everyone) to haul rock. Tsung asked the Duty Distributor where he was going. The Duty Distributor said, "I'm going to haul rock." Tsung said, "For now I'll let you haul rock, but don't move the tree in the middle."

Whenever a newcomer arrived (at his place) Mu P'ing would first order him to move three loads of earth. Mu P'ing had a verse which he showed to his assembly saying:

> East Mountain Road is narrow, West Mountain is
>   low:
> New comers must not refuse three loads of mud.
> Alas, you've been traversing the roads so long,
> It's so clear, but you don't recognize it and instead
>   get lost.

Later there was a monk who asked Mu P'ing, "I don't ask about what is included in the three loads. What about what's outside the three loads?" P'ing said, "The Iron Wheel Emperor commands in his realm." The monk was speechless, so P'ing hit him.

This is why Hsueh Tou said, "One hauls rock / A second moves earth."

"To shoot the bolt requires a ten-ton crossbow." Hsueh Tou uses the ten-ton pull crossbow to explain this case: he wants you to see how Ho Shan helped people. If it's a monstrous dragon or tiger or some other fierce beast, then you use this crossbow. If it's a tiny bird or a creature of little consequence, of course you mustn't use the crossbow lightly. Hence a ten-ton crossbow does not shoot its bolt for a rat.

"The old master of Elephant Bone Cliff rolled balls." That is: one day Hsueh Feng saw Hsuan Sha coming and rolled out three wooden balls together. Hsuan Sha made a smashing gesture. Hsueh Feng profoundly approved of him.

Although all of these stories are instances of the great functioning of their entire capacities, none equal's Ho Shan's "Knowing how to beat the drum." How direct this is—but it's hard to understand. Thus Hsueh Tou said, "How could this equal Ho Shan's 'Knowing how to beat the drum'?"

Again he feared that people would just make their living on the words without knowing their source, (and thus be) careless.

Therefore he said, "I report for you to know: don't be careless!" You too must really get to this realm before you can understand. If you don't want to carelessly confuse things, "The sweet is sweet, the bitter is bitter." Though Hsueh Tou picked it up and played with it like this, in the end he can't leap clear of Ho Shan either.

TRANSLATORS' NOTES

a. "Hsueh Feng's four tubs of lacquer" refers to some incidents between Hsueh Feng and T'ou Tzu, recorded in the *Record of the Transmission of the Lamp:*

Hsueh Feng was attending on T'ou Tzu, who pointed to a piece of rock in front of his hut and said to Hsueh Feng, "All the Buddhas of past, present, and future are right here." Feng said, "One must know that there is one who is not here." T'ou Tzu then returned to his hut to sit, saying, "You dull tub of lacquer!"

Feng followed T'ou Tzu to call on the hermit of Lung Yen. Feng asked, "Where does the road of Lung Yen go to?" T'ou Tzu took his staff and pointed before them. Feng said, "Does it go east or go west?" T'ou Tzu said, "You tub of lacquer!"

Another day Feng asked, "How is it when 'immediately completed with a single stroke'?" T'ou Tzu said, "It's not someone of unsettled temperament." Feng said, "How is it when not using a single stroke?" T'ou Tzu said, "You tub of lacquer!"

One day when T'ou Tzu was in his hut sitting, Feng asked, "Master, is there anyone who comes here to study or not?" T'ou Tzu took a hoe from under his bed and threw it down in front of him. Feng said, "If so, then I'll dig right here." T'ou Tzu said, "This tub of lacquer is not quick."

Chao Chou's Seven-Pound Cloth Shirt

POINTER

When he must speak, he speaks—in the whole world there is no match for him. When he should act, he acts—his whole capacity doesn't defer (to anyone). He is like sparks struck from stone, like the brilliance of a flash of lightning, like a raging fire fanned by the wind, like a rushing torrent crossing a sword edge. When he lifts up the hammer and tongs of transcendence, you won't avoid losing your point and having your tongue tied.

He lets out a single continuous road. To test I'm citing it: look!

CASE

A monk asked Chao Chou, "The myriad things return to one. Where does the one return to?"[1]

Chou said, "When I was in Ch'ing Chou I made a cloth shirt. It weighed seven pounds."[2]

NOTES

1. He's pressing this old fellow. Piled in mountains, heaped up in ranges. He should avoid going to the ghost cave to make his living.

2. After all Chou goes in all directions, drawing a net that fills the sky. But do you see Chao Chou? He has picked up the nostrils of patchrobed monks.

COMMENTARY

If you understand "going immediately at one stroke," then you've pierced the nostrils of the world's old teachers all at once, and they can't do a thing about you. Naturally where water goes, a channel forms. But if you vacillate and hesitate, the old monk Chao Chou is under your feet. The essential point of the Buddhist Teaching is not a matter of many words or verbose speech.

A monk asked Chao Chou, "The myriad things return to one. Where does the one return to?" Yet Chou answered him saying, "When I was in Ch'ing Chou I made a cloth shirt; it weighed seven pounds." If you go to the words to discriminate you are mistakenly abiding by the zero point of a scale. If you don't go to the words to discriminate, what can you do about it that he did nevertheless speak this way? This case, though hard to see, is nevertheless easy to understand; though easy to understand, it's still hard to see. Insofar as it's hard, it's a silver mountain, an iron wall. Insofar as it's easy, you are directly aware. There's no place for your calculations of right and wrong.

This story is the same kind as the story of P'u Hua saying, "Tomorrow there's a feast at the Temple of Great Compassion."[a]

One day a monk asked Chao Chou, "What is the meaning of the Patriarch coming from the West?" Chou said, "The cypress tree in the garden." The monk said, "Don't use objects to teach people with, Teacher." Chou said, "I've never used objects to teach people." Observe how, at the ultimate point, where it is impossible to turn, he does turn, and spontaneously covers heaven and earth. If you can't turn, wherever you set foot on the road you get stuck.

But say, did Chao Chou ever have discussions of Buddhist doctrine or not? If you say he did, when has he ever spoken of mind or of nature, of mysteries or of marvels? If you say he didn't have the source meaning of the Buddhist Teaching, when has he ever turned his back on anyone's question?

Haven't you heard: a monk asked Mu P'ing, "What is the great meaning of the Buddhist Teaching?" P'ing said, "This winter melon is so big." Again: a monk asked an ancient worthy, "Deep in the mountains on an overhanging cliff, in a remote, inaccessible, uninhabited place, is there any Buddhist Teaching or not?" The ancient worthy said, "There is." The monk said, "What is the Buddhist Teaching deep within the mountains?" The ancient worthy said, "The large rocks are large, the small ones small."

When you look at such a case, where are the obscurities? Hsueh Tou knows what they come down to: thus he opens up a road of meaning and comes out with a verse for you:

VERSE

He wraps everything up and presses against the ancient old awl.
     What's the need to press this old fellow? They push and push back—to where?
How many people know the weight of the seven-pound shirt?
     To bring it out again is not worth half a cent. All I can do is frown. Still, Chou has done the monk one better.
Right now I throw it down into West Lake;
     Only with the ability of Hsueh Tou could this be done. I don't want it either.
The pure wind of unburdening—to whom should it be imparted?
     From the past through the present. Tell me, is Hsueh Tou harmonizing with Chao Chou, or is he putting down footnotes for him? One son attains intimately.

COMMENTARY

Of Fen Yang's eighteen kinds of questions, this one in the Case is called a "wrapping-up question." Hsueh Tou says, "He wraps everything up and presses against the ancient old awl." He wraps up everything and makes it return to unity.

This monk wanted to press Chao Chou, but Chou too was an adept. Where it was impossible to turn, he had a way to show himself: daring to open his big mouth he immediately said, "When I was in Ch'ing Chou I made a cloth shirt that weighed seven pounds." Hsueh Tou says, "How many people can there be who know the weight of this seven-pound shirt?"

"Right now I throw it down into West Lake." Myriad things return to one, but he doesn't even need the one. Since he doesn't need the seven-pound cloth shirt either, all at once he throws it down into West Lake. When Hsueh Tou dwelt on Tung T'ing's green peak, there was a West Lake (nearby).

"The pure wind of unburdening—to whom should it be imparted?" This refers to Chao Chou teaching his assembly, saying, "If you're coming north I'll load up for you. If you're coming south I'll unload for you. Even if you're coming from Hsueh Feng or Yun Chu, you're still a fellow carrying a board." Hsueh Tou says, "To whom should a pure wind like this be imparted?" "Loading up" means speaking for you of mind and nature, of mysteries and marvels—all sorts of expedient methods. If it's unloaded, there are no longer so many meanings and hidden wonders.

Some people carried a load of Ch'an to Chao Chou's place, but when they got there they couldn't make use of it at all. He would set them straight all at once, making them free and easy, without the slightest concern. We say of this, "After awakening it's the same as before awakening."

People these days all make unconcern an understanding. Some say, "There is no delusion or enlightenment: it's not necessary to go on seeking. Even before the Buddha appeared in the world, before Bodhidharma ever came to this country, it could not have been otherwise. What's the use of the Buddha appearing in the world? What did the Patriarch still come from the West for?" All such views—what relevance do they have? You must have greatly penetrated and greatly awakened: then as before, mountains are mountains, rivers are rivers, in fact all the myriad things are perfectly manifest. Then for the first time you can be an unconcerned person.

Haven't you heard Lung Ya say:

> To study the Path, first you must have a basis of
>   enlightenment:
> It's like having vied in a boat race:
> Though you relax on idle ground as before,
> Only having won can you rest.

As for this story of Chao Chou's seven-pound cloth shirt, look how this man of old talks this way, like gold and jade. Me talking like this, you listening like this—all of this is "loading up." But say, what is unloading? Go back to your places and look into this.

TRANSLATORS' NOTES

a. The story is told as follows in the *Ch'uan Teng Lun* 10:

When (his master) P'an Shan died, P'u Hua carried on his teaching in the north, sometimes in city markets, sometimes in isolated villages. He would ring his bell and say, "I hit whether you're coming from light or coming from darkness."

One day Lin Chi sent a monk to catch him by saying, "How is it when neither light nor dark?" P'u Hua answered, "Tomorrow there's a feast at the Temple of Great Compassion."

Ching Ch'ing's Sound of Raindrops

POINTER

With a single stroke he completes it and passes beyond ordinary and holy. His slightest word can break things up, untying what is bound and releasing what is stuck. As if walking on thin ice or running over sword blades, he sits within the heaps of sound and form, he walks on top of sound and form.

For the moment I leave aside wondrous functioning in all directions. How is it when he leaves that very instant? To test I'm citing this old case: look!

CASE

Ching Ch'ing asked a monk, "What sound is that outside the gate?"[1] The monk said, "The sound of raindrops."[2]

Ch'ing said, "Sentient beings are inverted. They lose themselves and follow after things."[3]

The monk said, "What about you, Teacher?"[4]

Ch'ing said, "I almost don't lose myself."[5]

The monk said, "What is the meaning of 'I almost don't lose myself'?"[6]

Ch'ing said, "Though it still should be easy to express oneself, to say the whole thing has to be difficult."[7]

NOTES

1. He casually lets down a hook. He doesn't suffer from deafness: what is he asking?
2. He's undeniably truthful. It's good news too.
3. A concern is born. Ch'ing is used to getting his way. He rakes the monk in. He depends on his own abilities.
4. As it turns out the monk suffers a defeat. He's turned the spear around: inevitably it will be hard for Ch'ing to stand up to it.

Instead (of Ch'ing, the monk) grabs the spear and stabs the man back.

5. Bah! He just can't explain.

6. He presses this old fellow and crushes the man. His first arrow was still light, the second arrow was deep.

7. Provisions to nourish a son. Although it's like this, where have Te Shan and Lin Chi gone? If he doesn't call it the sound of raindrops, what sound should he call it? It simply can't be explained.

COMMENTARY

You too should understand right here. When the Ancients imparted their teaching, with one device, one object, they wanted to guide people. One day Ching Ch'ing asked a monk, "What is that sound outside the gate?" The monk said, "The sound of quail." Ch'ing said, "If you wish to avoid uninterrupted hell, don't slander the Wheel of the True Dharma of the Tathagata." Another time Ch'ing asked, "What is that sound outside the gate?" A monk said, "The sound of a snake eating a frog." Ch'ing said, "I knew that sentient beings suffer: here is another suffering sentient being." These words are the same as the Case. If patchrobed monks can penetrate here, nothing can block their independence within the heaps of sound and form. If you can't penetrate then you are constrained by sound and form.

In various places they call this "tempering words." If it were tempering, it would only amount to mental activity. (Those with this view) do not see where the ancient man Ching Ch'ing helped people. (Ch'ing's words in the Case) are also called "penetrating sound and form," "explaining the eye of the Path," "explaining sound and form," "explaining the mind source," "explaining forgetting feelings," "explaining preaching." Though (such interpretations) are undeniably detailed, nevertheless they still are stuck in clichés.

When Ch'ing asked this way, "What is that sound outside the gate?" the monk said, "The sound of raindrops." But then Ch'ing said, "Sentient beings are inverted. They lose themselves and follow after things." People all misunderstand and call this intentionally upsetting the man, but this has nothing to do with it. How little they realize that Ch'ing has the skill to help people. Ch'ing is so brave he isn't bound by a single device and a single object. Above all he doesn't spare his eyebrows.

How could Ching Ch'ing not have known that it was the sound of raindrops? Why was it still worth asking? You must realize that the Ancient was using his probing pole and reed shade (to see into the depths) to examine this monk. The monk too pressed back well, immediately saying, "What about you, Teacher?" What happened then was that Ching Ch'ing went into the mud and water to say to him, "I almost don't lose myself." The reason (for saying this) was that the monk was losing himself, pursuing things. Why did Ching Ch'ing lose himself too? You must realize that Ch'ing had a place to get out himself within the phrase he used to test the monk.

This monk was very dull—he wanted to beat this statement into the ground, so he asked, "What is the meaning of 'I almost don't lose myself'?" If it had been the school of Te Shan or Lin Chi the blows and shouts would already have been falling. But Ching Ch'ing put through a single continuous path and followed him creating complications: he went on to say more to him, "Though it still should be easy to express oneself, to say the whole thing has to be difficult." Nevertheless, as an Ancient said, "Continuity is indeed very difficult." Ching Ch'ing illuminated for this monk the great affair under his feet.

Hsueh Tou's verse says:

VERSE

An empty hall, the sound of raindrops. . .
> Never ever interrupted. Everyone is here.

Hard to respond, even for an adept.
> Of course he doesn't know how. I have never been an adept. There's provisional and real, there's letting go and gathering in, there's killing and bringing to life, there's catching and releasing.

If you say he's ever let the streams enter,
> You stick your head into a bowl of glue. If you don't call it the sound of raindrops, what sound will you call it?

As before you still don't understand.
> How often I've asked you! You tubs of lacquer! Give me back my holeless iron hammer.

Understanding or not understanding—
>Cut off the two ends. The two are not separate. It's not on these two sides.

On South Mountain, on North Mountain, more and more downpour.
>Above our heads and under our feet. If you call it the sound of raindrops, you're blind. If you don't call it the sound of raindrops, what sound will you call it? Your feet must be treading the ground of reality before you can get here.

COMMENTARY

"An empty hall, the sound of raindrops / Hard to respond, even for an adept." If you call it the sound of raindrops, then this is "losing oneself, following after things." If you don't call it the sound of raindrops, then how will you turn things around? At this point even if you're an adept, it's still hard to respond. Therefore an Ancient said, "If your view equals your teacher's, you have less than half the teacher's merit. Only if your view goes beyond your teacher's are you fit to receive and carry on the transmission." And as Nan Yuan said, "With acceptance of birthlessness under the cudgel, he faces situations without deferring to a teacher."

"If you say he ever let the streams enter, / As before you still don't understand." In the *Surangama Sutra* it says, "First, in the midst of hearing, (Avalokitesvara) let the streams enter, but was mindless of what was there. Since what he let in was quiescent, the two forms, motion and stillness, were ultimately not produced." If you say it's the sound of raindrops, it's not right, and if you say it's not the sound of raindrops, it's not right either. If you say he lets the streams of sound and form enter, that's not right either. If you call it sound and form, as before you don't understand his meaning. It is compared to pointing at the moon with one's finger: the moon is not the finger.

Understanding and not understanding, "On South Mountain, on North Mountain, more and more downpour."

Yun Men's Six Do Not Take It In

POINTER

What does the sky say? The four seasons go on there. What does the earth say? The myriad things are born there. Where the four seasons go on, he can see the essence; where the myriad things are born, he can see the action.

But say, where can you see a patchrobed monk? Having abandoned words and speech and active functioning, having blocked off your throat when walking, standing, sitting, and lying down—can you still discern him?

CASE

A monk asked Yun Men, "What is the Body of Reality?"[1a] Men said, "Six do not take it in."[2]

NOTES

1. So many people have doubts about this. The thousand sages can't leap out of it. He's indulged quite a bit.
2. He cuts nails and shears through iron. "An eight-corner mortar flies through the air." The spirit tortoise is dragging his tail.

COMMENTARY

Yun Men said, "Six do not take it in." This is indeed hard to understand: even if you reach it before the first indications are distinct, this is already the secondary. If you understand after the first indications arise, then you've fallen into the tertiary. If you go to the words and phrases to discern (his meaning), you will search without ever being able to find it.

But ultimately, what do you take as the Body of Reality? Those who are adepts immediately get up and go as soon as they hear it raised. If on the other hand you linger in thought and hold back your potential, you should listen humbly to this treatment.

The senior monk Fu of T'ai Yuan was originally a lecturer. One day when he had gone up to his seat to lecture, he spoke of the Body of Reality saying, "Vertically it reaches through the three times, and horizontally it extends through the ten directions." There was a Ch'an traveller in the audience who let out a laugh as he heard this. Fu came down from his seat and said, "What was my shortcoming just now? Please, Ch'an man, explain so I can see." The Ch'an man said, "Lecturer, you only lecture on that which pertains to the extent of the Body of Reality—you don't see the Body of Reality." Fu said, "After all, what would be right?" The Ch'an man said, "You should temporarily stop lecturing and sit in a quiet room. You have to see it for yourself."

Fu did as he said and sat quietly all night. Suddenly he heard them hitting the bell for the fifth watch: suddenly he was greatly enlightened. So he went and knocked on the Ch'an man's door saying, "I've understood." The Ch'an man said, "Try to say something so I can see." Fu said, "From today onwards I'll no longer twist these nostrils born of my parents."

Again: in the scriptures it says, "The Buddha's true Body of Reality is like empty space. It manifests shapes in response to things like the moon (reflected) in the water."

Again: a monk asked Chia Shan, "What is the Body of Reality?" Shan said, "The Body of Reality has no form." The monk asked, "What is the Eye of Reality?" Shan said, "The Eye of Reality has no flaws."

Yun Men said, "Six do not take it in." Some say of this case, "This is just the six sense-organs, the six sense-objects, the six consciousnesses. These sixes all arise from the Body of Reality, so the six faculties cannot take it in." Intellectual interpretations such as this, though, are irrelevant. Moreover, they drag down Yun Men. If you want to see, then see: there's no place for your attempts to rationalize. Haven't you seen how it says in the scripture: "This Truth is not something that calculating thought and discrimination can understand."

Yun Men's answers have often provoked people's intellectual interpretations. Thus in every phrase of Yun Men's there are inevitably three phrases present. Nor does he turn his back

on your questions: responding to the time, adapting to the
season, with one word, one phrase, one dot, one line, he indeed
has a place to show himself. Thus it is said, "When a single
phrase is penetrated, a thousand phrases, ten thousand phrases,
are penetrated all at once."

But say, is "Six do not take it in" the Body of Reality? Is it
the Patriarchs? I give you thirty blows!

Hsueh Tou's verse says:

VERSE

One, two, three, four, five, six—
>   Go all the way through, then start again at the beginning.
>   For every drop of water, a drop of ice. Why expend so
>   much effort?

The blue-eyed barbarian monk can't count up to it.
>   Past, present, and future lives for sixty eons. Have you
>   ever seen Bodhidharma even in a dream? Why do you
>   deliberately transgress?

Shao Lin deceptively said he passed it on to Shen Kuang—
>   When one man transmits a falsehood, ten thousand
>   transmit it as truth. From the start it was already wrong.

He rolled up his robe and said he was returning to India.
>   He utterly swindled ordinary people. How embarrassing!

India is vast, there's no place to look for him—
>   Where is he? This at last is the Great Peace. Right now,
>   where is he?

He comes back by night to stay here at Ju Peak.
>   He pokes out your eyes. Still, he's raising waves where
>   there's no wind. But say, is it the Body of Reality or the
>   Body of Buddha? I'll give you thirty blows!

COMMENTARY

Hsueh Tou is well able to show his eye where there is no seam
or crack and come out with a verse to make people see. Yun
Men said, "Six do not take it in." Why does Hsueh Tou

nonetheless say, "One, two, three, four, five, six"? In fact not even the blue-eyed barbarian monk can count up to it. That is why it is said, "I just allow that the old barbarian knows—I don't allow that he understands." Only a descendant of Yun Men's house (like Hsueh Tou) could do this. I just said that Yun Men responds to the time and adapts to the season with one word, one phrase. Only if you can penetrate through will you know that the Path is not a matter of words and phrases. But if you're not yet this way, you won't avoid making up intellectual interpretations.

My late master Wu Tsu said, "Shakyamuni Buddha was a lowdown hired worker. The cypress trees in the garden: one, two, three, four, five." If you can manage truly to see under Yun Men's words, you'll reach this realm instantly.

"Shao Lin deceptively said he passed it on to Shen Kuang." The Second Patriarch's initial name was Shen Kuang. Later he said that Bodhidharma had returned to India. Bodhidharma had been buried at the foot of Bear Ears Mountain. At that time the (Liu) Sung emissary Yun Feng was returning from the West. In the Western Mountains he saw Bodhidharma carrying one shoe in his hand going back to India. The emissary returned and reported this to the Emperor. When Bodhidharma's tomb was opened they only saw a single shoe left behind.

Hsueh Tou says, "How can this matter really be imparted?" Since there was no imparting it, Bodhidharma rolled up his robe and said he was returning to India. But then tell me, why has this country nevertheless had six patriarchs handing it on in succession this way? Here it's unavoidably obscure. You must be able to comprehend before you can enter and act.

"India is vast, there's no place to look for him— / He comes back by night to stay here at Ju Peak." But tell me, where is he right now?

Master Yuan Wu then struck saying, "Blind men!"

TRANSLATORS' NOTES

a.   The Body of Reality (Dharmakaya) is called the real true body of all Buddhas, the most essential and most inclusive aspect of Buddhahood. Different elaborations on the nature of Dharmakaya have been made in the various schools of Buddhist thought and practice. Sometimes it is said to comprise two complementary aspects, knowledge and principle, meaning realization of the inherent pattern that matter-energy is one with a void like empty space. The infinite universe or cosmos itself can be seen as the Dharmakaya of True Suchness, represented in the esoteric schools as the manifestation of Vairocana Buddha, the universal illuminator, the so-called Adibuddha or Primordial Buddha. According to esoteric Buddhist teaching, the exoteric schools regard the Dharmakaya as being unmanifest and inexpressible, whereas the esoteric schools see that it is also manifest and expressive. As in the present case, Ch'an Buddhism sees both sides of this. Seng Chao, the great sage of the Middle Path school, quoted several times in this case, said that the Dharmakaya is uncompounded and is not contained in sets of classification or enumeration. See also Cases 39 and 82.

Turning Over the Tea Kettle at Chao Ch'ing

CASE

When Minister Wang entered Chao Ch'ing, they were making tea.[1] At the time Elder Lang was holding the kettle for Ming Chao.[2] Lang turned the tea kettle over.[3] Seeing this, the Minister asked the Elder, "What's under the tea stove?"[4] Lang said, "The spirit who holds up stoves."[5] The Minister said, "If it's the spirit who holds up stoves, why then did you turn over the tea kettle?"[6] Lang said, "Serve as an official for a thousand days, lose it in a single morning."[7] The Minister shook out his sleeves and left.[8]

Ming Chao said, "Elder Lang, you've eaten Chao Ch'ing food, but still you go beyond the river to make noise gathering charred wood."[9] Lang said, "What about you, Teacher?"[10] Ming Chao said, "The spirit got the advantage."[11]

Hsueh Tou said, "At the time I just would have kicked over the tea stove."[12]

NOTES

1. A gathering of adepts: there's bound to be something extraordinary. Casual and unconcerned. Everyone set one eye on them. Wang has invited trouble.
2. A bunch of fellows playing with a mud ball. Lang doesn't know how to make tea, so he drags in someone else.
3. Something's happened after all.
4. As it turns out, it's trouble.
5. After all he runs into Wang's arrow. Nonetheless, it's extraordinary.
6. Why doesn't he give him some real provisions? Something's happened.

7. A mistaken indication. What kind of talk is this? Phoney Ch'an men are (as numerous) as hemp seeds, as millet grains.
8. Obviously an adept. I allow that he has one eye.
9. I would go on to give him thirty blows. This lone-eye dragon only has one eye. Still, it takes a clear-eyed man to examine thoroughly.
10. He presses him—he too deserves to be pressed. Never make up such dead senile views!
11. After all, he only has one eye. He was able to speak half. One hand presses down, one hand lifts up.
12. What can be done about it? He draws his bow after the thief has gone. Nonetheless, he still can't be called a member of Te Shan's school. The lot of them, (Wang, Lang, and Ming Chao) are rascals, scoundrels—among them Hsueh Tou is the stand-out.

COMMENTARY

Minister Wang was in charge of Ch'uan Chou. He had studied at Chao Ch'ing for a long time. One day he went into the temple while Elder Lang was making tea, and Lang turned over the tea kettle. The Minister too was an adept. As soon as he saw him turn over the tea kettle he immediately asked the Elder, "What is under the tea stove?" When Lang said, "The spirit who holds up stoves," inevitably there was an echo in his words. But what could he do about his head and tail contradicting each other, so that he lost the source meaning and blundered with the sharp point, cutting his own hand? Not only did he wrong himself, but he also offended the other man.

Though this is an affair without gain and loss, if we bring it up, as before there is near and far, initiate and outsider. If you discuss this matter, though it's not in words and phrases, nevertheless you must discern what's alive in the words and phrases. Thus it is said, "He only studies the living phrase; he doesn't study the dead phrase."

When Elder Lang talked this way he was like a mad dog chasing a clod of dirt. The Minister shook out his sleeves and left, appearing to disapprove of him.

Ming Chao said, "Elder Lang, you've eaten Chao Ch'ing food, but still you go beyond the river to make noise gathering charred wood." This charred wood is sticks of wood burnt by fire in the wild. Ming Chao used this to illustrate how Elder Lang didn't go to the correct place to walk, but instead ran off outside. Lang pressed him saying, "What about you, Teacher?" Ming Chao said, "The spirit got the advantage." Naturally Ming Chao had a place to show himself without turning his back on Lang's question. Thus it is said, "A good dog bites in without showing his teeth."

Master Che of Kuei Shan said, "Minister Wang was like Hsiang Ju[a] carrying off the jewel—in fact his sideburns were sticking out from under his hat." Since Ming Chao couldn't contain his feelings, it was difficult for him to do what was proper. If I had been Elder Lang, as soon as I saw the Minister shake out his sleeves and go, I would have let go of the tea kettle and laughed out loud. Why? If you see him but don't grab him, it's hard to meet with him even in a thousand years."

If you wish to know the meaning of the Buddha-nature, you must observe times and seasons, causes and conditions. Haven't you heard? Pao Shou asked Nail Cutter Hu, "For a long time I've heard of Nail Cutter Hu—aren't you him?" Hu said, "I am." Shou said, "Can you drive nails into empty space?" Hu said, "I invite the Master to come smash it." Shou then hit him. Hu did not agree, so Shou said, "Another day there will be a talkative teacher who will examine this thoroughly for you." Later Hu saw Chao Chou and related the previous conversation. Chou said, "Why were you hit by him?" Hu said, "I don't know where the fault was." Chou said, "You couldn't even do anything about this one crack, yet you went on to tell him to break up empty space." At this Hu was stopped—Chou spoke for him, "Well, nail up this one crack." At this Hu had an awakening.

When Seven Masters Mi of Ching Chao returned from his foot travels, an old adept asked him, "A piece of well-rope on a moonlit night—people all called it a snake. I wonder what you call it, Seven Masters, when you see the Buddha." Seven Masters said, "If there is something seen, then it's the same as sentient beings." The old adept said, "This is a peach pit that sprouts once in a thousand years."

National Teacher Chung asked the purple-clad Imperial Attendant Monk, "I hear tell that you have (written a commentary) explaining the 'Consideration of Benefit' Scripture. Is this so or not?" The Imperial Attendant said, "It is so." The National Teacher said, "One must first understand the Buddha's meaning to be fit to explain the scriptures." The Imperial Attendant said, "If I didn't understand the meaning, how could I dare to say I've explained the Scripture?" The National Teacher then ordered the servant to bring a bowl of water, seven grains of rice, and a single chopstick. Putting them in the bowl, he passed it to the Imperial Attendant and asked, "What meaning is this?" The Imperial Attendant said, "I don't understand." The National Teacher said, "You don't even understand my meaning: how can you go on talking of Buddha's meaning?"

(So we see) Minister Wang and Elder Lang were not the only ones to have conversations like this.

At the end Hsueh Tou turns around and says, "At the time I just would have kicked over the tea stove." Though Ming Chao was like this, he never equalled Hsueh Tou. Hsueh Feng was the cook in Tung Shan's congregation. One day when he was sifting rice, Tung Shan asked, "What are you doing?" Feng said, "Sifting rice." Shan said, "Do you sift the rice to get rid of the grit, or do you sift the grit and get rid of the rice?" Feng said, "Grit and rice are both removed at once." Shan said, "What will the great congregation eat?" Feng turned the bowl over. Shan said, "The right conditions for you are not here." Though he acted this way, how can this compare with Hsueh Tou saying, "At the time I just would have kicked over the tea stove"? What time and season was it for them? Their action naturally stands out in the present and shines through the ages: they had a place of living liberation.

The verse says:

VERSE

(Wang) poses a question like creating a wind—
  His arrow was not shot in vain. He happens to be artful yet quintessential.

(Lang's) responsive action was not skillful.
  Fellows playing with a mud ball—what end is there to it? A square peg stuck in a round hole. Indeed, he ran into an adept.

How lamentable! the lone-eyed dragon (Ming Chao)
> He only has one eye. He only gets one part.

Didn't display his teeth and claws.
> Indeed he had no teeth and claws that could have been displayed. What teeth and claws are you talking about? Don't cheat them.

Teeth and claws open
> Do you see? After all Hsueh Tou has gotten somewhere. If you have such ability, kick over the tea stove!

Producing clouds and thunder.
> All the world's people take a beating at once. The world's patchrobed monks have no place to put themselves. Crashing thunder in a parched sky.

How many times I've gone through the waves of adverse currents!
> Seventy-two blows turns into a hundred and fifty.

COMMENTARY

"Posing a question like creating a wind— / The responsive action was not skillful." The Minister's question was not skillful." The Minister's question was like swinging an axe (so swiftly that) it creates a wind. This comes from (a story in) *Chuang Tzu*: a man of Ying was plastering a wall. Only one small gap remained, so he threw a gob of plaster on to fill it in, whereupon a bit of plaster splashed down onto the tip of his nose. Nearby was an axeman who said, "You filled that hole very skillfully. I'll wield my axe and take that plaster off the tip of your nose for you." Though the plaster on his nose was (as small as) a fly speck, he let him remove it. The axeman swung his axe so fast he created a wind and removed the plaster entirely without cutting his nose. The man of Ying stood there without losing his composure. This is what is called wondrous skill on the part of both. Though Elder Lang did respond to Minister Wang's actions, his words were without excellent skillfulness. That's why Hsueh Tou said, "(Wang) poses a question like creating a wind / (Lang's) responsive action was not skillful."

"How lamentable: the lone-eyed dragon / Didn't display his teeth and claws." Ming Chao speaking was indeed very outstanding. Nevertheless, he didn't have the teeth and claws to grasp clouds and hold onto fog. The bystander Hsueh Tou didn't approve. Not containing his feeling, he showed some energy on behalf of Ming Chao.

Hsueh Tou secretly goes to merge with Minister Wang's meaning. He versifies his own statement about kicking over the tea stove: "Teeth and claws open / Producing clouds and thunder / How many times I've gone through the waves of adverse currents!" Yun Men said, "I don't expect you to have waves that go against the current. Just have the mind that goes along with the current and you'll be all right too." Thus it is said, "If you comprehend at the living phrase, you'll never forget." The words and phrases of Elder Lang and of Ming Chao seem dead. If you want to see the living place, just look at Hsueh Tou kicking over the tea stove.

TRANSLATORS' NOTES

a. "Hsiang Ju carrying off the jewel"—During the Warring States Period, Lian Hsiang Ju was a minister of the state of Chao, sent to Ch'in to exchange a precious jewel for fifteen cities. Suspecting that the King of Ch'in didn't intend to keep the bargain to turn over the fifteen cities, Hsiang Ju managed to get out of Ch'in and return the jewel safely to his master the King of Chao.

San Sheng's Golden Fish Who Has Passed through the Net

POINTER

Piercing, penetrating, one takes the drum and captures the flag. Fortified, entrenched, one inspects the front and oversees the rear.

One who sits on the tiger's head to take the tiger's tail is not yet an adept. Though an ox head disappears and a horse head returns, this too is not yet extraordinary.

But say, how is it when a man who has passed beyond measurements comes? To test I'm citing this old case: look!

CASE

San Sheng asked Hsueh Feng, "I wonder, what does the golden fish who has passed through the net use for food?"[1]

Feng said, "When you come out of the net I'll tell you."[2]

Sheng said, "The teacher of fifteen-hundred people and you don't even know what to say!"[3]

Feng said, "My affairs as abbot are many and complicated."[4]

NOTES

1. (The golden fish) is free in all ways. This question is too lofty. You must just know for yourself—then what need is there to ask any further?
2. He diminishes the other man's reputation quite a bit. An expert teacher of our sect is naturally independent.
3. The crashing noise of sudden thunder really startles the crowd. Let him leap about.
4. It's not a matter of victory and defeat. Hsueh Feng lets his move go. This statement is most poisonous.

COMMENTARY

With Hsueh Feng and San Sheng, though there's one exit and one entry, one thrust and one parry, there is no division into victory and defeat. But say, what is the eye that these two venerable adepts possess?

San Sheng received the secret from Lin Chi. He travelled all over and everyone treated him as an eminent guest. Look at him posing a question. How many people look but cannot find him! He doesn't touch on inherent nature or the Buddha Dharma: instead he asks, "What does the golden fish who has passed through the net use for food?" But say, what was his meaning? Since the golden fish who has passed through the net ordinarily does not eat the tasty food of others, what does he use for food?

Hsueh Feng is an adept: in a casual fashion he replies to San Sheng with only ten or twenty percent. He just said to him, "When you come out of the net, I'll tell you." Fen Yang would call this "a question that displays one's understanding." In the Ts'ao Tung tradition it would be called "a question that uses things." You must be beyond categories and classifications, you must have obtained the use of the great function, you must have an eye on your forehead—only then can you be called a golden fish who has passed through the net. Nevertheless, Hsueh Feng is an adept and can't help but diminish the other man's reputation by saying "When you come out of the net, I'll tell you."

Observe how the two of them held fast to their territories, towering up like ten thousand fathom walls. With this one sentence of Hsueh Feng's anyone other than San Sheng would have been unable to go on. Yet San Sheng too was an adept: thus he knew how to say to him, "The teacher of fifteen hundred people and you don't even know what to say!" But Hsueh Feng said, "My affairs as abbot are many and complicated." How obstinate this statement is!

When these adepts met, there was one capture and one release—(each) acted weak when encountering strength and acted noble when encountering meanness. If you form your understanding in terms of victory and defeat, you haven't seen Hsueh Feng even in dreams. Look at these two men: initially both were solitary and dangerous, lofty and steep; in the end both were dead and decrepit. But say, was there still gain and loss, victory and defeat? When these adepts harmonized with each other, it was necessarily not this way.

San Sheng was the Temple Keeper at Lin Chi. When Lin Chi was about to pass on he directed, "After I'm gone you mustn't destroy the treasure of the eye of my correct teaching." San Sheng came forward and said, "How could we dare destroy the treasure of the eye of your correct teaching, Master?" Chi said, "In the future, how will you act when people ask questions?" San Sheng then shouted. Chi said, "Who would have known that the treasure of the eye of my correct teaching would perish in this blind donkey?" San Sheng then bowed in homage. Since he was a true son of Lin Chi's, he dared to respond like this.

Afterwards Hsueh Tou just versifies the golden fish who has passed through the net, revealing where these adepts saw each other. The verse says:

VERSE

The golden fish who has passed through the net—
    A thousand soldiers are easy to get, but one general is hard to find. What is the golden fish like? The thousand sages can't do anything about it.

Stop saying he tarries in the water.
    He stands beyond the clouds, leaping with life. But better not make him out to be a fool.

He shakes the heavens and sweeps the earth,
    An adept! An adept! This still isn't where he's extraordinary. Let him come out (of the net)—what's to prevent it?

He flourishes his mane and wags his tail.
    Who would presume to judge the whole from the surface? He's performed a clever trick and startled the crowd.

When a thousand-foot whale spouts, vast waves fly,
    San Sheng revolved over to That Side: he is indeed outstanding! He's swallowed everyone in the world in a single gulp.

At a single thunderclap, the pure wind gusts.
    Having eyes and ears, but being like blind and deaf. Who is not frightened?

The pure wind gusts—
   Where? Bah!

Among gods and humans, how many know? How many?
   Hsueh Feng holds down the front lines, San Sheng holds
   down the rear. Why scatter dust and sand? I'll hit and say,
   "Where are you?"

COMMENTARY

"The golden fish who has passed through the net— / Stop saying he tarries in the water." Wu Tsu said that just this one
couplet alone completes the verse. Since it's the golden fish
who has passed through the net, how could he linger tarrying
in the water? He must be where the vast swelling floods of
white foamy waves tower up to the skies. But say, during the
twenty-four hours of the day, what does he use for food? All of
you go back to your places and try to see for sure.

   Hsueh Tou said, "This matter is picked up and played with
according to one's capacity." When something like the golden
fish "flourishes his mane and wags his tail," he does in fact
shake heaven and earth.

   "When a thousand-foot whale spouts, vast waves fly." This
versifies San Sheng saying, "The teacher of fifteen hundred
people and you don't even know what to say!" He was like a
whale spouting out giant waves. "At a single thunderclap, the
pure wind gusts." This versifies Hsueh Feng saying, "My affairs as abbot are many and complicated." He was like the pure
wind gusting when a thunderclap sounds. The overall meaning
is to praise the two of them for both being adepts.

   "The pure wind gusts— / Among gods and humans, how
many know? How many?" But say, what do these lines come
down to? When the pure wind arises, among gods and humans
how many can there be who will know?

Yun Men's Every Atom Samadhi

POINTER

Passing beyond stages, absolutely transcending expedient means, mind to mind in mutual accord, each phrase harmonizing with the other. If you haven't entered the gate of great liberation and attained great liberty of action, how can you measure the Buddhas and Patriarchs, or be a mirror and guide for the Essential Vehicle?

But say, when taking charge of a situation directly, whether going with or going against, whether vertically or horizontally, how will you be able to speak a phrase to express yourself? To test, I'm citing this old case: look!

CASE

A monk asked Yun Men, "What is every atom samadhi?"[1] Men said, "Food in the bowl, water in the bucket."[2]

NOTES

1. All the monks under heaven make their nests here. His whole mouth is filled with frost. Why is he scattering sand and dirt?
2. A cloth bag filled with awls. Gold dust and sand intermingled. He adds error to error. Inside the palace, they don't ask about the capital.

COMMENTARY

Can you settle this case properly? If you can, then Yun Men's nostrils are in your hands. If you are unable to settle it properly, then your nostrils are in Yun Men's hands. Yun Men has phrases that cut nails and shear through iron. In this one phrase three phrases are present.

When questioned about this case, some say, "Each grain of the food in the bowl is round; each drop of the water in the bucket is wet." If you understand in this fashion, then you don't see how Yun Men really helped the man.

The verse says:

VERSE

"Food in the bowl, water in the bucket"—
> It's obvious. Why scatter sand and dirt? You must wash your mouth out for three years before you'll get it.

The talkative teacher can hardly open his mouth.
> He draws in his tongue. Those who know the law fear it. Why then bring it up this way?

Northern Dipper, Southern Star—their positions are not different:
> Why call east west? Sitting, standing, still and solemn. What's long is the long Body of Reality; what's short is the short Body of Reality.

White foamy waves flooding the skies arise on level ground.
> Several fathoms deep underfoot. Guest and host interchange. Suddenly they're on top of your head—what will you do? I hit.

Trying or not trying,
> Heavens! Bah!

Stopping or not stopping,
> What are you saying, Hsueh Tou? You are adding more hatred and bitterness.

Each and every one is a rich man's son with no britches.
> Quite decrepit! The onlooker laughs at them.

COMMENTARY

Previously, in his verse on (Case 14) 'Yun Men's An Appropriate Statement,' Hsueh Tou said, "An appropriate statement / How utterly unique! / He wedges a stake into the iron hammer head with no handle hole." Later, in his verse on (Case 73) 'Ma

Tsu's Beyond All the Permutations of Assertion and Denial,'
he says, "Tsang's head is white, Hai's head is black / Clear-eyed
patchrobed monks cannot understand." If you are able to penetrate these cases, then you will see this present verse.

At the start Hsueh Tou immediately says, "Food in the
bowl, water in the bucket." There's an echo in his words; he
shows his capacity in the line. "The talkative teacher can
hardly open his mouth." With this he adds footnotes for you. If
you demand rational calculations here of the mysterious and
the wondrous, it will be even harder to open your mouths.

At the beginning he holds fast. Fearing that there would be
someone with eyes in the assembly who would see through
him, later he had to forego the primary and bend down to open
it up for beginners, coming out with a verse to make people see.
As before the Northern Dipper is in the north and the Southern
Star is in the south. Thus he says, "Northern Dipper, Southern
Star—their positions are not different."

"White foamy waves flooding the skies arise on level
ground." When waves suddenly arise on level ground, what
will you do? If you catch sight of it in the phenomena, then it's
easy. If you seek for it in your conceptual faculty, then you will
never be able to find it. This line is like an iron spike: it can't
be pulled out, and you can't get your beak into it. If you try to
discuss it, though you wish to understand, you won't understand; though you wish to stop, you won't stop wildly displaying your load of ignorance. This is precisely (what is meant by)
"Each and every one is a rich man's son with no britches."

Han Shan's poem says:

> Everywhere constantly suffering pain,
> All over vainly discussing themselves,
> Though they have talent, it's abandoned in the
>   weedy swamps;
> Having no power, they shut their reed doors.
> The sun comes up over the cliff, but still it's dark,
> The mist melts away, but the valley is still dim.
> The rich men's sons there
> Are all without britches.

Hsueh Feng's What Is It?

POINTER

As soon as there is affirmation and denial, you lose your mind in confusion. If you don't fall into grades and stages, then there is no seeking.

But say, is letting go right, or is holding fast right? At this point, if you have any trace of an interpretative route, you are still stuck in verbal explanations. If you're still involved with devices and objects, then all of this is haunting the fields and forests.ᵃ

Even if you arrive immediately at the point of solitary liberation, you haven't avoided looking back to the village gate from ten thousand miles away. Can you reach it? If you can't, just comprehend this perfectly obvious public case. To test I am citing it: look!

CASE

When Hsueh Feng was living in a hut, there were two monks who came to pay their respects.¹ Seeing them coming, he pushed open the door of the hut with his hand, popped out, and said, "What is it?"² A monk also said, "What is it?"³ Feng lowered his head and went back inside the hut.⁴

Later the monk came to Yen T'ou.⁵ T'ou asked, "Where are you coming from?"⁶ The monk said, "I've come from Ling Nan."⁷ T'ou said, "Did you ever go to Hsueh Feng?"⁸ The monk said, "I went there."⁹ T'ou said, "What did he have to say?" The monk recounted the preceding story.¹⁰ T'ou said, "What did he say?"¹¹ The monk said, "He said nothing; he lowered his head and went back inside the hut."¹² T'ou said, "Alas! It's too bad I didn't tell him the last word before;¹³ if I had told him, no one on earth could cope with old Hsueh."¹⁴

At the end of the summer the monk again brought up the preceding story to ask for instruction.¹⁵ T'ou said, "Why didn't you ask earlier?"[16] The monk said, "I didn't dare to be casual."[17] T'ou said, "Though Hsueh Feng is born of the same lineage as me, he doesn't die in the same lineage as me.[18] If you want to know the last word, just this is it."[19]

NOTES

1. What for? Their crimes are listed on the same indictment.
2. Ghost eyes. A flute with no holes. He raises his head, wearing horns.
3. A mud ball. A felt-pounding board. The arrow points meet.
4. There are thorns in the soft mud. Hsueh Feng is like a dragon without feet, like a snake with horns. This is the hardest of all to handle.
5. He had to ask before he could understand. Only one on the same path would know.
6. It takes an adept to be able to be this way. This (monk) suffers defeat again and again. If Yen T'ou wasn't a fellow student of Hsueh Feng he probably would have let him go.
7. What news does he bring? He must convey the news. Did he see Hsueh Feng?
8. He already exposed him a while ago. He mustn't say he didn't go there.
9. A truthful man is hard to find. He breaks it in two.
10. So he goes on this way. Again and again he suffers defeat.
11. He should have hit the monk in the mouth, (but instead) he's lost his nostrils.
12. Again he suffers defeat. But tell me, what is he?
13. Vast swelling billows of white foamy waves flooding the skies.
14. A leper drags along his companions. Not necessarily. Even Mt. Sumeru would be shattered to bits. But say, where is his trap?
15. Already this monk is not alert. When the real thief has already been gone for quite a while, he draws his bow.
16. He deserves to have his meditation seat overturned. He's gone by.
17. This staff was originally for the monk to be beaten with. Yen T'ou pierced his nostrils. An imprisoned man increases in wisdom. It's already a double case.
18. He fills the heavens and covers the earth.
19. Though he utterly swindles ordinary people, I don't believe him. He almost couldn't complain.

COMMENTARY

Whoever would uphold the teaching of our school must discern how to take charge of the situation; he must know advance and retreat, right and wrong; he must understand killing and giving life, capturing and releasing. If one's eyes suddenly blur and go sightless, everywhere he goes, when he encounters a question, he questions, and when he encounters an answer, he answers, scarcely realizing that his nostrils are in the hands of others.

As for Hsueh Feng and Yen T'ou, they were fellow students under Te Shan. When these monks called on Hsueh Feng their views only reached to such a place (as seen in the case); when the monk saw Yen T'ou, he still didn't complete his business. He troubled these two worthies to no purpose. One question, one answer, one capture, one release—right up till today this case has been impenetrably obscure and inexplicable for everyone in the world. But tell me, where is it impenetrable and obscure?

Though Hsueh Feng had travelled all over through the various localities, at last it was at Tortoise Mountain because Yen T'ou spurred him on that he finally attained annihilation of doubt and great penetration.

Later, due to a purge, Yen T'ou became a ferryman by the shores of Lake O Chu (in Hupeh). On each shore hung a board: when someone wanted to cross, he would knock on the board. T'ou would call out, "Which side are you crossing to?" Then he would wave his oar and come out from among the reeds.

(After his enlightenment with Yen T'ou) Hsueh Feng returned to Ling Nan and lived in a hut. These monks were people who had studied for a long time. When he saw them coming, Hsueh Feng pushed open the door of the hut, popped out and said, "What is it?" Some people these days when questioned in this way immediately go and gnaw on his words. But these monks were unusual too; they just said to him "What is it?" Feng lowered his head and went back into the hut. This is frequently called "wordless understanding;" hence, these monks couldn't find him. Some say that, having been questioned by these monks, Hsueh Feng was in fact speechless, and so he returned to the hut. How far they are from knowing that there is something deadly poisonous in Hsueh Feng's intention. Though Hsueh Feng gained the advantage, nevertheless while he hid his body, he revealed his shadow.

Later one monk left Hsueh Feng and took this case to have Yen T'ou decide it. Once he got there, Yen T'ou asked him, "Where are you coming from?" The monk said, "I've come from Ling Nan." T'ou said, "Did you get to Hsueh Feng?" If you want to see Hsueh Feng, you better hurry up and look at this question. The monk said, "I went there." T'ou said, "What did he have to say?" This question was not posed to no purpose. But the monk did not understand: he just turned around following the trend of his words. T'ou said, "What did he say?" The monk said, "He lowered his head and went back into the hut without saying anything." This monk was far from knowing that Yen T'ou had put on straw sandals and had already walked around inside his belly several times.

Yen T'ou said, "Too bad I didn't tell him the last word before; if I had told him, no one on earth could cope with old Hsueh." Yen T'ou too supports the strong but doesn't help the weak. As before the monk was flooded with darkness and didn't distinguish initiate from naive. Harboring a bellyful of doubt, he really thought that Hsueh Feng did not understand.

At the end of the summer he again brought up this story and asked Yen T'ou for more instruction. T'ou said, "Why didn't you ask earlier?" This old fellow was crafty. The monk said, "I didn't dare to be casual." T'ou said, "Though Hsueh Feng is born of the same lineage as me, he doesn't die in the same lineage as me. If you want to know the last word, just this is it." Yen T'ou indeed did not spare his eyebrows! In the end, how will all of you people understand?

Hsueh Feng was the cook in Te Shan's community. One day the noon meal was late; Te Shan took his bowl and went down to the teaching hall. Feng said, "The bell hasn't rung yet, the drum hasn't been sounded—where is this old fellow going with his bowl?" Without saying anything, Te Shan lowered his head and returned to his abbot's quarters. When Hsueh Feng took this up with Yen T'ou, T'ou said, "Even the great Te Shan doesn't understand the last word."

Te Shan heard of this and ordered his attendant to summon Yen T'ou to the abbot's quarters. Shan said, "So you don't approve of me?" T'ou tacitly indicated what he meant. The next day Shan went up to the hall and taught in a way which was different from usual; in front of the monks' hall T'ou clapped his hands and laughed loudly saying, "Happily the old fellow does understand the last word! After this no one on earth will be able to do anything about him. Nevertheless, he's only got three years."

When Hsueh Feng saw Te Shan speechless, he thought that he had gained the advantage. He certainly didn't know that he had run into a thief. Since he had met a thief, later Feng too knew how to be a thief. Thus an Ancient said, "At the final word, one first reaches the impenetrable barrier."

Some say that Yen T'ou excelled Hsueh Feng; they have misunderstood. Yen T'ou always used this ability; he taught his community saying, "Clear-eyed folks have no clichés to nest in. Spurning things is considered superior, pursuing things is considered inferior. As for this last word, even if you've personally seen the Patriarchs, you still wouldn't be able to understand it rationally."

When Te Shan's noon meal was late, the old fellow picked up his bowl himself and went down to the teaching hall. Yen T'ou said, "Even great Te Shan doesn't understand the last word." Hsueh Tou picked this out and said, "I've heard that from the beginning a lone-eyed dragon has only one eye. You certainly didn't know that Te Shan was a toothless tiger. If it hadn't been for Yen T'ou seeing through him, how could we know that yesterday and today are not the same? Do all of you want to understand the last word? An Ancient said, 'I only allow that the old barbarian knows; I don't allow that he understands.'"

From ancient times up till now, the public cases have been extremely diverse, like a forest of brambles. If you can penetrate through, no one on earth can do anything about you, and all the Buddhas of past, present, and future defer to you. If you are unable to penetrate, study Yen T'ou saying, "Though Hsueh Feng is born in the same lineage as me, he doesn't die in the same lineage as me." Spontaneously, in just this one sentence, he had a way to express himself.

VERSE

The last word
>   It's already present before any words. You think it's real.
>   If you look right now at it, you'll go blind.

Is spoken for you;
> The tongue falls to the ground. It can't be spoken. It has a head but no tail; it has a tail but no head.

The time of light and dark pair by pair:
> Hsueh Tou is an old fellow who's full of complications. Like an ox without horns, like a tiger with horns. This one and that one are this way.

Born of the same lineage, they share the knowledge,
> What clan is this? There's no connection between this one and that one. You're headed southeast, I'm headed northwest.

Dying of different lineages, they're utterly separated.
> The staff is in my hand. How can you blame me? Why are your nostrils in someone else's hands?

Utterly separated—
> Do you want to take a beating? Where is there to search?

Even Yellow Head (Buddha) and Blue Eyes (Bodhidharma) have yet to discern.
> Everyone on earth loses his point and is tongue-tied. I too am this way; nevertheless, others are not. "I only allow that the old barbarian knows; I don't allow that he understands."

South, North, East, West, let us return—
> Hsueh Tou has gathered everyone in. His trail is still following the Five-Color Thread (leading to paradise). I ask you for a staff.

And in the depths of the night together look at the snow on the thousand crags.
> They still have half a month's journey. Let the world be covered with snow, filling the channels and gullies. There is no one who understands. You too are just blind people: do you know the last word? I'll hit!

COMMENTARY

"The last word is spoken for you." When Hsueh Tou made up his verse on this last word, he intentionally went to extremes falling into the weeds to help people. His verse was thoroughgoing as a verse, but he only versified a little of the fine detail. If you want to see all the way through, this is still not enough.

Daring to say even more, Hsueh Tou opened his big mouth and said, "The time of light and dark pair by pair" to open a road for you and also to finish it off for you in one line. Then at the end he provided even more explanations for you. Just as Chao Ch'ing one day asked Lo Shan, "When Yen T'ou says, 'So, so, not so, not so,' what is his meaning?" Lo Shan called out, "Great Master," and Master Chao Ch'ing responded. Shan said, "Both light and both dark." Ch'ing bowed in thanks and left. Three days later he again questioned Lo Shan, "A few days ago I received your compassionate instruction; it's just that I couldn't see through it." Shan said, "I've told you the whole thing already." Ch'ing said, "Master, please light the way." Shan said, "If so, Great Master, go ahead and ask about what you are in doubt over." Ch'ing said, "What is 'both light and both dark'?" Shan said, "Born the same and dying the same." Then Ch'ing bowed in thanks and left.

Later there was a monk who asked Chao Ch'ing, "How is it when being born the same and dying the same?" Ch'ing said, "Shut your dog mouth." The monk said, "Try to eat food with your mouth closed, Great Master." This monk then came to ask Lo Shan, "How is it when being born the same and dying the same?" Shan said, "Like an ox without horns." The monk asked, "How is it when being born the same but not dying the same?" Shan said, "Like a tiger with horns." The last word is precisely this truth.

There was a monk in Lo Shan's congregation who used this idea to put a question to Chao Ch'ing. Ch'ing said, "This one, this one, they all know. Why? If I spoke a phrase on the eastern continent, they would know it on the western continent too. If I spoke a phrase in heaven, in the human world they would also know it. All minds know each other, all eyes shine on each other."

Born of the same lineage, they're still easy to see. Not dying in the same lineage, they're utterly separate, and not even Shakyamuni or Bodhidharma can find them.

"South, North, East, West, let us return." There's something of a good world. "And in the depths of night together look at the snow on the thousand crags." But say, is this "both light and both dark" or is it "born of the same lineage" or is it "dying in the same lineage"? Patchrobed monks who have eyes should try to discern.

TRANSLATORS' NOTES

a. The image here is of ghosts clinging to trees and grasses, likened to people clinging to things, especially to words and expressions.

Chao Chou Lets Asses Cross, Lets Horses Cross

CASE

A monk asked Chao Chou, "For a long time I've heard of the stone bridge of Chao Chou, but now that I've come here I just see a simple log bridge."[1]
    Chou said, "You just see the log bridge; you don't see the stone bridge."[2]
    The monk said, "What is the stone bridge?"[3]
    Chou said, "It lets asses cross, it lets horses cross."[4]

NOTES

1. Here's another man who comes to grab the tiger's whiskers. This is the proper business of patchrobed monks.
2. Chou is accustomed to getting the advantage. This old fellow is selling off his body.
3. He's climbed up onto Chou's hook, after all.
4. A single net cast over "asses" and "horses." In fact all the people in the world have no place to breathe; once dead they don't come back to life again.

COMMENTARY

In (the place) Chao Chou there's a stone bridge; ever since it was built (in the Latter Han dynasty) by Li Ying, it has been famous throughout the country. A simple log bridge is a bridge (made of) a single log.
    Intentionally downgrading (Chao Chou's) grandeur, this monk questioned him saying, "For a long time I've heard of the stone bridge of Chao Chou, but now that I've come here I just see a simple log bridge." Chou immediately said, "You just see

353

the log bridge, but you don't see the stone bridge," based on the other man's question. This seems just like ordinary conversation, but Chao Chou used it to hook him. This monk after all climbed onto the hook; he followed up behind and asked, "What is the stone bridge?" Chou said, "It lets asses cross, it lets horses cross." Inevitably Chao Chou naturally has a place to show himself in his words. Chao Chou is not like Lin Chi or Te Shan, carrying on with blows and shouts—he just uses words and speech to kill and bring to life.

Take a good look at this case. It seems to be an ordinary battle of wits; it is nevertheless hard to approach.

One day Chao Chou was with the head monk looking at the stone bridge when he asked the head monk, "Who built this?" The head monk said, "Li Ying built it." Chou said, "When he built it, where did he start?" The head monk had no reply. Chou said, "You're always talking about the stone bridge, but when you're asked about where it was started, you don't even know."

Also one day when Chao Chou was sweeping the floor, a monk asked, "Teacher, you are a man of knowledge—why is there dust?" Chou said, "It's something that comes from outside." Again the monk asked, "In a pure and clean monastery, why is there dust?" Chou said, "There's another little bit."

Also a monk asked, "What is the Path?" Chou said, "It's outside the wall." The monk said, "I'm not asking about that path, I'm asking about the Great Way." Chou said, "The Great Way runs through the capital."

Chao Chou was partial to using such devices; he would go to the safe secure place of ordinary reality to help people. He never cut his hand on the sharp point; naturally he was solitary and lofty, using these devices most wondrously.

Hsueh Tou's verse says,

VERSE

He doesn't set up the solitary and dangerous; in that his path is lofty.
  You must get to this realm before you realize. The words are still in our ears. This goes back to his own provisions.

Entering the ocean, he must hook a giant tortoise.
> He cuts off the essential crossing place and doesn't let profane or holy pass. Shrimps or clams, snails or oysters aren't worth asking about. People of power don't come by twos and threes.

His contemporary the Elder of Kuan Hsi is worth a laugh;
> There's been another such man who's come this way, who had such ability to use active devices.

Though he knew how to say "Whistling Arrow," his effort was in vain.
> He still has half a month's journey. He seems to resemble, but isn't really.

COMMENTARY

"He doesn't set up the solitary and dangerous; in that his path is lofty." Hsueh Tou is praising Chao Chou's usual way of helping people. Chou doesn't establish mysteries or marvels, and doesn't set up the solitary and dangerous. He isn't like those in various places who say that only breaking up empty space, smashing Mount Sumeru to bits, producing dust on the bottom of the ocean and pounding waves on Mount Sumeru can be called the Path of the Patriarchal Teachers. Thus Hsueh Tou says, "He doesn't set up the solitary and dangerous; in that his path is lofty." Others may tower up like ten-mile-high walls to display the extraordinary spiritual effects of the Buddha Dharma—but though they're solitary and dangerous, lofty and steep, this is not as good as not setting up the solitary and dangerous, and simply acting ordinary, naturally turning smoothly. Chao Chou doesn't establish anything, yet he is established himself; he doesn't make anything high, yet he is high himself. When capacity goes beyond solitary and dangerous, only then do we see profound wonders.

Thus Hsueh Tou says, "Entering the ocean, he must hook a giant tortoise." Look at Chao Chou: a master of our school with eyes, he is perfectly at ease as he imparts a word and employs a device. He doesn't hook shrimps or clams, snails or oysters—he only hooks giant tortoises. Indeed he is an adept! This one line is used to illustrate the Case.

"His contemporary the Elder of Kuan Hsi is worth laughing at." Haven't you heard—a monk asked Kuan Hsi, "I've long heard of Kuan Hsi ('Pouring Mountain Stream'). Now that I've come here I only see a hemp-soaking pool." Hsi said, "You just see the hemp-soaking pool; you don't see the pouring mountain stream." The monk said, "What is the pouring mountain stream?" Hsi said, "Swift as a whistling arrow."

Also a monk asked Huang Lung, "I've long heard of Huang Lung ('Yellow Dragon'), but now that I've come here I only see a red striped snake." Lung said, "You just see the red striped snake; you don't see the yellow dragon." The monk said, "What is the yellow dragon?" Lung said, "Slithering along." The monk said, "How is it when he suddenly encounters the (dragon-eating) Garuda bird?" Lung said, "Difficult to stay alive." The monk said, "If so, then he'll get eaten up by the bird." Lung said, "Thank you for feeding me."

These are both cases of setting up the solitary and dangerous. Though Kuan Hsi and Huang Lung are both right, nevertheless they did waste effort. They never equalled Chao Chou's ordinary action. That's why Hsueh Tou says, "Though he knew how to say 'Whistling Arrow,' his effort was in vain."

Leaving Kuan Hsi and Huang Lung aside for the moment, how will you understand when Chao Chou says, "It lets asses cross, it lets horses cross"? Try to do it.

Pai Chang's Wild Ducks

POINTER

The whole world does not hide it—his entire capacity stands alone revealed. He encounters situations without getting stuck—with every move he has the ability to assert himself. In his phrases there's no partiality—everywhere he has the intention to kill people.

But say, in the end, where do the Ancients go to rest? To test I'm citing this old case: look!

CASE

Once when Great Master Ma and Pai Chang were walking together they saw some wild ducks fly by.[1] The Great Master asked, "What is that?"[2] Chang said, "Wild ducks."[3] The Great Master said, "Where have they gone?"[4] Chang said, "They've flown away."[5] The Great Master then twisted Pai Chang's nose.[6] Chang cried out in pain.[7] The Great Master said, "When have they ever flown away?"[8]

NOTES

1. Two fellows in the weeds. They're rolling around in the weeds. Why suddenly notice the ducks?
2. You should know, Teacher. This old fellow doesn't even know his nostrils.
3. Chang's nostrils are already in the hands of the other man. He just offers the actual facts. The second ladleful of foul water will be even more poisonous.
4. His first arrow was still light, but the second arrow is deep. A second enticing peck. Here too Ma Tsu should know for himself.
5. He just rolls along behind Ma Tsu. He's stumbled past what's right in front of him.

357

6. The nostrils born of his parents are in the hands of someone else. Ma Tsu turned the spear around and twisted Chang's nostrils around.
7. It's right here. Can it be called wild ducks? Are you conscious of pain?
8. Better not deceive people. From the beginning this old fellow has been making his living inside a ghost cave.

COMMENTARY

If you observe this case with the correct eye, unexpectedly it's Pai Chang who has the correct basis, whereas Great Master Ma is creating waves where there is no wind. If all of you want to be teachers of Buddhas and Patriarchs, then study Pai Chang. If you want to be unable to save even yourselves, then study the Great Master Ma. Observe how those Ancients were never absent from Here, twenty-four hours a day.

At a young age Pai Chang left behind the dusts of wordly life and became well versed in the three studies (discipline, meditation, and wisdom). When Ma Tsu (known as) Ta Chi was teaching at Nan Ch'ang, Pai Chang set his heart on joining him. For twenty years he served as Ma Tsu's attendant, until the time of his second calling (on Ma Tsu, as related in the commentary to Case 11), when he was finally greatly enlightened at Ma Tsu's shout.

But these days some say, "Where there is fundamentally no enlightenment, they construct the gate of 'enlightenment' and establish this affair." If you view it in this way, you are like a flea on a lion's body feeding itself on the lion's flesh. Haven't you seen where an Ancient said, "If the source is not deep, the stream is not long; if the wisdom is not great, the vision is not far-reaching." If you entertain the understanding that enlightenment is a construct, how could the Buddhist Teaching have come down to the present?

Look: once when Great Master Ma and Pai Chang were walking together they saw some wild ducks fly by. How could the Great Master not have known they were wild ducks? Why did he nevertheless ask like this? Tell me, what does his meaning come down to? When Pai Chang merely followed up behind him, Ma Tsu then twisted his nose. Chang cried out in pain and Ma Tsu said, "When have they ever flown away?" At this Pai Chang had insight. But these days some people misunderstand: as soon as they're questioned, they immediately make a cry of pain. Fortunately they can't leap out of it.

When teachers of our school help people, they must make them penetrate through. You see that Pai Chang didn't understand, that he didn't avoid cutting his hand on the point. Ma Tsu just wanted to make him understand this matter. Thus it is said, "When you understand, you can make use of it wherever you are; if you don't understand, then the conventional truth prevails." If Ma Tsu hadn't twisted Pai Chang's nose at that time, the conventional truth would have prevailed. It's also necessary when encountering circumstances and meeting conditions to turn them around and return them to oneself; to have no gaps at any time is called "the ground of nature bright and clear." What's the use of one who just haunts the forests and fields, accepting what's ahead of an ass but behind a horse?[a]

Observe how Ma Tsu and Pai Chang act this way; though they seem radiant and spiritual, nevertheless they don't remain in radiance and spirituality. Pai Chang cried out in pain; if you see it as such, then the whole world does not hide it, and it is perfectly manifest everywhere. Thus it is said, "Penetrate one place, and you penetrate a thousand places, ten thousand places all at once."

When Ma Tsu went up to the hall the next day, as soon as the congregation had assembled, Pai Chang came forward and rolled up the bowing mat. Ma Tsu immediately left his seat. After he had returned to his abbot's quarters, he asked Pai Chang, "I had just gone up to the hall and had not yet preached; why did you roll up the mat right away?" Chang said, "Yesterday I had my nose twisted by you, Teacher, and it hurt." Tsu said, "Where were you keeping your mind yesterday?" Chang said, "Today the nose no longer hurts." Tsu said, "You have profound knowledge of Today's affair." Chang then bowed and returned to the attendants' quarters, crying. One of his fellow attendants asked, "Why are you crying?" Chang said, "Go ask our Master." The attendant then went to ask Ma Tsu. Tsu said, "Go ask Pai Chang." When the attendant returned to their quarters to ask Pai Chang, Chang laughed loudly. The attendant said, "You were just crying—now why are you laughing?"

Chang said, "I was crying before, now I'm laughing." Look at Pai Chang after his enlightenment; turning smoothly, he can't be trapped. Naturally he's sparkling clear on all sides.

VERSE

Wild ducks—
Gathering in flocks. Here's another one.

Who knows where they are?
Why use wild ducks? They're as numerous as hemp or millet seeds.

Ma Tsu saw them coming and they had words with each other—
What end is there to creating complications? What did they say? Ma Tsu alone recognizes the outstanding one.

He told all about the scene of the clouds on the mountains and the moon over the sea.
The ladle handle of the eastern house is long; the ladle handle of the western house is short. Who knows how many complications he created?

As before Chang didn't understand, but said, "They've flown away."
Gaa! Don't say he didn't know how to speak. Where did they fly off to?

Pai Chang wanted to fly away,
His nostrils were in the other man's hands. This is already adding footnotes for others.

But Ma Tsu held him fast.
With grandmotherly kindness. What else did he say?

Speak! Speak!
What is there to say? Don't make me speak too. Don't make a wild duck cry. Heavens! Right where you are you deserve thirty blows. Who knows where they went to?

COMMENTARY

Directly and immediately, Hsueh Tou makes his verse saying, "Wild ducks—who knows where they are?" But say, how many are there? "Ma Tsu saw them coming and they had words with each other." This versifies Ma Tsu asking Pai Chang, "What is that?" and Chang saying, "Wild ducks." "He told all about the scene of the clouds on the mountains and the moon over the sea." This versifies Ma Tsu again asking, "Where have they gone?" The teaching which Great Master Ma conveyed to Pai Chang spontaneously revealed everything. As before Chang did not understand; instead he said, "They've flown away." Twice he missed it.

With "Pai Chang wanted to fly away, but Ma Tsu held him fast," Hsueh Tou settles the case on the basis of the facts. He also says, "Speak! Speak!" This is where Hsueh Tou turns himself around. But say, how will you speak? If you make a cry of pain, then you're wrong. If you don't make a cry of pain, then how do you understand it? Though Hsueh Tou versifies most wondrously, no matter what he does he can't leap out either.

TRANSLATORS' NOTES

a.   "What's ahead of an ass but behind a horse" is often referred specifically to the "radiant spirituality," a designation of the conscious radiance of the mind temporarily cleared or halted by meditation, which is beyond unregenerate ignorant people, but is not yet thorough realization of personal and phenomenal emptiness, still in the realm of subjectivity.

Yun Men Extends Both Hands

POINTER

Having penetrated through and out of birth and death, he sets his devices in motion. Perfectly at ease, he shears through iron and cuts through nails. Wherever he goes he covers heaven and covers earth.

But say, whose behavior is this? To test I'm citing this old case; look!

CASE

Yun Men asked a monk, "Where did you come here from?"[1] The monk said, "Hsi Ch'an."[2] Yun Men said, "What words and phrases are there at Hsi Ch'an these days?"[3] The monk extended both hands;[4] Yun Men slapped him once.[5]

The monk said, "I'm still talking."[6] Yun Men then extended his two hands.[7] The monk was speechless,[8] so Yun Men hit him.[9]

NOTES

1. Don't say Hsi Ch'an. A probing pole, a reed shade. Don't say east, west, north or south.
2. As it turns out, he's too literal. At that moment the monk should have given him some of his own provisions.
3. "I want to bring it up, but I fear that it would startle you, Teacher." Yun Men profoundly discriminates among oncoming winds. "Hsi Ch'an was like you, Teacher, talking in your sleep."
4. He's been defeated. He took in a thief and got his house ransacked. This will inevitably cause people to doubt.
5. He acts according to the imperative. The monk should be hit. A fleeting chance is hard to meet with.
6. So you want to change your plea? Nevertheless, he seems to have the ability to capture the flag and carry off the drums.

7. Danger! The monk is being given an excellent mount, but he doesn't know how to ride it.
8. What a pity!
9. Don't let him go. It should be Yun Men who takes this beating. Why? When you don't settle what should be settled, instead you invite disorder. How many blows should you receive? Yun Men let up on him a little. If he hadn't let up, what should he have done?

COMMENTARY

Yun Men asked this monk, "Where did you come here from?" The monk said, "Hsi Ch'an." This is direct face to face talk, like a flash of lightening. Men said, "What words and phrases are there at Hsi Ch'an these days?" This too is just ordinary conversation. This monk, however, is also an adept; contrary to expectations, he goes to test Yun Men—he immediately extended his two hands. If it had been an ordinary person who met with this test, we would have seen him flustered and agitated. But Yun Men has a mind like flint struck sparks, like flashing lightening; immediately he slapped him.

The monk said, "You may hit me all right, but nevertheless I'm still talking." This monk had a place to turn around, so Yun Men opened up and extended his two hands. The monk was speechless, so Yun Men hit him.

Look—since Yun Men is an adept, whenever he takes a step he knows where the step comes down. He knows how to observe in front and take notice behind, not losing his way. This monk only knows how to look ahead; he's unable to observe behind.

VERSE

At once he takes the tiger's head and the tiger's tail—
  The single-edged sword that kills people, the double-edged sword that brings people to life. Only this monk can handle it. A thousand soldiers are easy to get, but one general is hard to find.

His stern majesty extends everywhere.
>He cuts off the tongues of everyone on earth. He covers heaven and covers earth.

I ask back, "Didn't you know how dangerous it was?"
>You shouldn't blindly fetter and beat them. From the beginning Hsueh Tou himself didn't know. You are speaking carelessly, Reverend.

Hsueh Tou says, "I leave off."
>If he hadn't left off, then what? Everyone on earth loses out all at once. I hit the meditation seat once.

COMMENTARY

Hsueh Tou's verse on this story is very easy to understand—its overall meaning is to praise the sharp point of Yun Men's ability. Thus he says, "At once he takes the tiger's head and the tiger's tail." An Ancient said, "Occupy the tiger's head, take the tiger's tail, then at the first phrase you'll understand the source meaning." Hsueh Tou just settles the case on the basis of the facts. He likes the way Yun Men is able to occupy the tiger's head and also take the tiger's tail. When the monk extended his two hands and Yun Men immediately hit him, this was occupying the tiger's head. When Yun Men extended two hands and the monk was speechless so that Yun Men hit him again, this was taking the tiger's tail. When head and tail are taken together, the eye is like a shooting star.

Yun Men is naturally like stone-struck sparks, like flashing lightning; in fact, "His stern majesty extends everywhere." The wind whistles all over the world.

"I ask back, 'Didn't you know how dangerous it was?'" Unavoidably there was danger. Hsueh Tou says, "I leave off." But say, right now as I don't leave off, what will you do? Everyone in the world will have to take a beating.

Followers of Ch'an these days all say that when Yun Men extended his two hands, the monk should have repaid him with some of his own provisions. This seems correct, but in reality isn't. Yun Men can't just get you to stop this way—there must be something else besides.

Tao Wu's Condolence Call

POINTER

Secure and intimate with the whole of reality, one obtains realization right there. In contact with the flow, able to turn things around, one assumes responsibility directly.

As for cutting off confusion in the light of a stone-struck spark or a flash of lightning, or towering up like a mile-high wall where one occupies the tiger's head and takes the tiger's tail—this I leave aside for the moment. Is there a way to help people by letting out a continuous path or not? To test, I cite this: look!

CASE

Tao Wu and Chien Yuan went to a house to make a condolence call. Yuan hit the coffin and said, "Alive or dead?"[1] Wu said, "I won't say alive, and I won't say dead."[2] Yuan said, "Why won't you say?"[3] Wu said, "I won't say."[4] Halfway back, as they were returning,[5] Yuan said, "Tell me right away, Teacher; if you don't tell me, I'll hit you."[6] Wu said, "You may hit me, but I won't say,"[7] Yuan then hit him.[8]

Later Tao Wu passed on. Yuan went to Shih Shuang and brought up the foregoing story.[9] Shuang said, "I won't say alive, and I won't say dead."[10] Yuan said, "Why won't you say?"[11] Shuang said, "I won't say, I won't say."[12] At these words Yuan had an insight."[13]

One day Yuan took a hoe into the teaching hall and crossed back and forth, from east to west and west to east.[14] Shuang said, "What are you doing?"[15] Yuan said, "I'm looking for relics of our late master."[16] Shuang said, "Vast waves spread far and wide, foaming billows flood the skies—what relics of our late master are you looking for?"[17]

Hsueh Tou added a comment saying, "Heavens! Heavens!"[18]

Yuan said, "This is just where I should apply effort."[19]

Fu of T'ai Yuan said, "The late master's relics are still present."[20]

NOTES

1. What is he saying? He sure isn't alert. This fellow is still lingering in duality.
2. When a dragon puffs, fog gathers; when a tiger roars, wind rises. He buys the hat to fit the head. He's kind-hearted.
3. He's stumbled past. As it turns out, he misunderstands.
4. He pours foul water right on Yuan's head. The first arrow was still light, but the second arrow goes deep.
5. Not very alert.
6. If he hits, then he'll be getting somewhere. It's rare to meet with the pierced-ear traveller (Bodhidharma); you often encounter travellers who cut a notch in the boat (thinking to mark the spot on the water which the boat is going over at a given time).[a] If you are like this latter kind of fool, you'll enter hell as fast as an arrow.
7. Again and again he must repeat this. He gets in close to take him. This old fellow's whole body is covered with muddy water. His original attitude is unchanging.
8. He should be hit. But say, why does he hit him? From the beginning there have been people who have received unjust beatings.
9. He knows, yet deliberately offends. He doesn't know whether he's right or wrong—if he's right, that would be wonderful.
10. How fresh and new! Yet there have always been people who eat this kind of food and drink.
11. Though his words are the same, his intent is different. But say, is this the same as or different from his asking before?
12. In the heavens and on earth. If the waves of Ts'ao Ch'i resembled each other, innumerable ordinary people would get bogged down.
13. The blind man! Better not fool me.
14. Within death he has found life. He should show some life for his late master. Don't question him—but observe this fellow's embarrassment.
15. He just follows along behind.
16. He hangs a medicine bag on the back of a hearse. Too bad that he was not so careful at first. What are you saying, Yuan?
17. Only that adept could do this. Why gather in crowds?

18. Too late. Hsueh Tou draws his bow after the thief has gone. He should be buried in the same pit.

19. But tell me, what does this really mean? What has the late master ever said to you? From beginning to end, and even up till now, this fellow has been unable to get himself out.

20. Does everyone see them? They're like flashing lightning. What worn out straw sandals are these? Fu has realized a little bit.

COMMENTARY

Tao Wu and Chien Yuan went to a house to make a condolence call. Yuan hit the coffin and said, "Alive or dead?" Wu said, "I won't say alive, and I won't say dead." If you can immediately enter at these lines, if at these words you immediately know what they come down to, then this is the key to penetrating beyond life and death. Otherwise, if you can't, then you will miss it over and over again even though it's right in front of you.

Observe how these Ancients, whether walking, standing, sitting, or lying down, were always mindful of this matter. As soon as they got to the house to offer condolences, Chien Yuan hit the coffin and asked Tao Wu, "Alive or dead?" Without stirring a hairsbreadth, Tao Wu answered him saying, "I won't say alive, and I won't say dead." Chien Yuan was face to face with it, but he stumbled past, running after the other man's words. He went on to say, "Why won't you say?" Wu said, "I won't say, I won't say." This can be called Wu meeting an error with an error, his heart bared entirely.

Yuan was still not awake himself: halfway back as they were returning he again said, "Tell me right away, Teacher; if you don't tell me, I'll hit you." What does this fellow know of good and bad? This is what is called "a good intention not getting a good reward." With tender kindness as before, Tao Wu said more to him; "You may hit me, but I won't say." Yuan then hit him. Even so, Tao Wu nevertheless won the point. Tao Wu was dripping with blood like this to help him, but Chien Yuan could be so unseeing!

After being hit, Tao Wu then said to Chien Yuan, "You should go away for a while. I fear that if the monastery's director of affairs finds out, he would make trouble for you." He secretly sent Chien Yuan away. Yuan later came to a small temple where he heard a workman reciting the Avalokitesvara scripture, where it says, "To those who would attain salvation as monks, he appears as a monk to expound the Dharma for them." Suddenly Yuan was greatly enlightened and said, "At that time I was wrongly suspicious of my late teacher. How was I to know that this affair isn't in words and phrases?" As an Ancient said, "Even someone great beyond measure can be whirled around in the stream of words."

Some interpret intellectually and say that when Tao Wu said, "I won't say, I won't say," he had thereby already said something, that this is what is called "turning a back-flip, making people unable to get ahold of you." If you understand in this fashion, how will you attain tranquility? If your feet tread the real earth, you aren't even a hairsbreadth away.

Haven't you heard? Seven women sages were travelling through the Forest of Corpses. One of the women pointed to a corpse and asked her sisters, "The corpse is here—where is the person?" The eldest sister said, "What? What?" and all seven together experienced the tolerance of birthlessness. But say, how many are there like this? In a thousand or ten thousand, there's just one.

Later Chien Yuan went to Shih Shuang and related his previous conversation with Tao Wu. Same as before, Shih Shuang said, "I won't say alive, and I won't say dead," and Yuan said, "Why won't you say?" When Shih Shuang said, "I won't say, I won't say," Yuan was immediately enlightened.

One day Yuan took a hoe into the teaching hall and crossed back and forth, from east to west and west to east. He intended to display his insight. Sure enough Shuang asked him, "What are you doing?" Yuan said, "I'm looking for relics of our late master." Shuang then cut off his footsteps, saying, "Vast waves spread far and wide, foaming billows flood the skies—what relics of our late master are you looking for?" Since Yuan was looking for relics of the late master, why did Shih Shuang nevertheless talk to him this way? At this point, if you can comprehend the words, "I won't say alive, and I won't say dead," then you will know that from beginning to end the entire capacity is put to use. If you make up rationalizations, hesitate and ponder, then it will be impossible to see.

Chien Yuan said, "This is just where I should apply effort."

See how after his enlightenment he can speak spontaneously so extraordinarily.

Tao Wu's skull bone was golden-hued; when struck it sounded like metal.

Hsueh Tou commented, "Heavens! Heavens!" His meaning comes down on both sides.

Fu of T'ai Yuan said, "The late master's relics are still present." Naturally what he said was fitting—at once he put this loose end in place.

But tell me, what is the most essential place? How is effort applied? Haven't you heard it said that if you penetrate in one place you penetrate in a thousand, ten-thousand places all at once." If you can penetrate "I won't say, I won't say," then you cut off the tongues of everyone on earth. If you can't penetrate this, then you must study for yourself and awaken yourself. You mustn't take it easy and let the days go by—you must value the time.

VERSE

Rabbits and horses have horns—
Chop them off. How extraordinary! How fresh and new!

Oxen and Rams have no horns.
Chop them off. What pattern is being formed? You may fool others.

Nary a hair, nary a wisp—
"In the heavens and on earth, I alone am the honored one." Where will you search?

Like mountains, like peaks.
Where are they? Waves arising on level ground clog your nostrils.

The golden relics still exist right now—
Cutting off tongues, blocking throats. I put them to one side; I only fear that there won't be anyone who can recognize them.

With white foaming waves flooding the skies, where can they be put?
Hsueh Tou lets his move go. They're right under your feet but you miss them. They can't be put in your eyes or ears.

There's no place to put them—
> After all. Yet Hsueh Tou has managed somewhat. But as
> it turns out he's sunk in a deep pit.

*Even the one who returned to the West with one shoe has lost
        them.*[b]
> If the ancestral shrine is not completed, the trouble ex-
> tends to the descendants. I'll hit, saying, "Then why are
> they here?"

COMMENTARY

Hsueh Tou understands how to add footnotes exceptionally
well. He is a descendant of Yun Men, with the hammer and
tongs to have three phrases present in every single phrase.
Where it's hard to express, he explains thoroughly; the un-
openable he opens up. He goes to the most crucial and essential
place and produces it in verse, immediately saying, "Rabbits
and horses have horns—oxen and rams have no horns." Tell
me, why do rabbits and horses have horns? Why then do oxen
and rams have no horns? Only if you can penetrate the preceding story (in the case) will you realize that Hsueh Tou has a
way to help people.

Some mistakenly say, "Not saying is saying; having no
phrases is having phrases. Though rabbits and horses have no
horns, yet Hsueh Tou says they have horns. Though oxen and
rams have horns, nevertheless Hsueh Tou says they don't." But
this has nothing to do with it. They are far from knowing that
the Ancient's thousand changes and ten thousand transformations, which manifest such supernatural powers, were just to
break up the ghost cave of your spirit. If you can penetrate
through, it's not even worth using the word "understand."

> *Rabbits and horses have horns—*
> *Oxen and rams have no horns.*
> *Nary a hair, nary a wisp—*
> *Like mountains, like peaks.*

These four lines are like the wish-fulfilling jewel. Hsueh Tou
has spit it out whole right in front of you.

The last part of the verse is all settling the case according to
the facts. "The golden relics still exist right now—with white

foamy waves flooding the skies, where can they be put?" This versifies the statements of Shih Shuang and Fu of T'ai Yuan. Why is there no place to put them? "Even the one who returned to the West with one shoe has lost them." The sacred tortoise is dragging his tail—this is where Hsueh Tou turns around to help people. An Ancient said, "He just studies the living phrase; he doesn't study the dead phrase." Since the relics are lost, why is that bunch still struggling with each other over them?

TRANSLATORS' NOTES

a. Once someone riding in a boat happened to drop his sword overboard; he marked the spot on the boat, but as it is also said in reference to this story, "the sword was long gone."

b. After Bodhidharma was supposed to have died and been interred, he was allegedly seen walking back to India with one shoe in hand. When his coffin was exhumed, nothing but a single shoe was found inside. Hence this refers to Bodhidharma, the first patriarch of Ch'an in China.

Ch'in Shan's One Arrowpoint Smashes Three Barriers

POINTER

The Buddhas never appeared in the world—there is nothing to be given to people. The Patriarch never came from the West— he never passed on the transmission by mind. Since people of these times do not understand, they frantically search outside themselves. They are far from knowing that the One Great Matter right where they are cannot be grasped even by a thousand sages.

Right now, where do seeing and not seeing, hearing and not hearing, speaking and not speaking, knowing and not knowing come from? If you are unable to apprehend clearly, then try to understand inside the cave of entangling vines.[a] To test, I cite this: look!

CASE

Ch'an traveller Liang asked Ch'in Shan, "How is it when a single arrowhead smashes three barriers?"[1]

Shan said, "Bring out the lord within the barriers for me to see."[2]

Liang said, "So then knowing my fault I must change."[3]

Shan said, "Why wait any longer?"[4]

Liang said, "A well-shot arrow doesn't hit anywhere," and (started to) leave.[5] Shan said, "Come here a minute."[6] Liang turned his head;[7] Shan held him tight and said, "Leaving aside for the moment a single arrowhead smashing three barriers, let's see you shoot an arrow."[8] Liang hesitated,[9] so Shan hit him seven times and said, "I'll allow as this fellow will be doubting for thirty more years."[10]

NOTES

1. Danger! Undeniably Liang is extraordinary—he is a fierce general.
2. He comes on directly. He wants everyone to know; Mt. Chu is high, Mt. An is low.
3. He sees his opportunity and acts. He's already fallen into the secondary.
4. There's capture, there's release. When the wind moves the grass bends.
5. After all. So Liang is trying to change his plea. He strikes his second blow, but Ch'in Shan feels no pain.
6. Summoning him is easy, dispatching him is hard. What good is someone who turns his head when called?
7. As it turns out Liang couldn't hold fast. He's hit.
8. Ch'in Shan lies down in the tiger's mouth. Waves against the current. Having seen one's duty but not doing it is lack of courage.
9. As it turns out, he searches without finding. I'll hit, saying, "Too bad."
10. The imperative must be so. There's a beginning, there's an end. Ch'in Shan is correct at the beginning and correct at the end. It's Ch'in Shan who should receive this beating.

COMMENTARY

Ch'an traveller Liang was undeniably a battle-tested general. In Ch'in Shan's hand he turned to the left and revolved to the right, bringing down his whip and flashing his stirrups. In the end, what a pity—his bow is broken, and his arrows are used up. Even so, "General Li Kuang, though he had a glorious reputation, was never enfeoffed as a noble, so it was useless."

This public case has one exit and one entry, one capture and one release. "Taking charge of the situation, he brings it up face to face; face to face, taking charge of the situation is swift." Throughout there is no falling into existence and nonexistence or gain and loss. This is called "mysterious activity." If one lacks strength, then he will stumble.

This monk too was a brave and spirited patchrobed one; he posed a question that really startles the crowd. Being an expert teacher of our school, Ch'in Shan immediately knew where his question came down. How is it when a single arrowhead smashes the three barriers? Ch'in Shan's reply meant, "For the moment leave aside your shooting through; try to bring out the lord within the barriers for me to see." Liang's saying, "So then knowing my fault I must change," was undeniably extraordinary. Ch'in Shan said, "Why wait any longer?" See how he replied—this question of Ch'in Shan's has no gaps.

Finally Ch'an traveller Liang just said, "A well-shot arrow doesn't hit anywhere." He shook out his sleeves to go away. As soon as he saw him talking this way, Ch'in Shan immediately called out to him, "Come here a minute, Reverend."[b] As it turned out Liang couldn't hold fast; he turned his head back then. Ch'in Shan held him tight and said, "Leaving aside for the moment a single arrowhead smashing three barriers, let's see you shoot an arrow." When Liang hesitated, Ch'in Shan immediately struck him seven blows. After this he went on to pronounce a curse on Liang saying, "I'll allow this fellow will be doubting for thirty more years."

Followers of Ch'an these days all say, "Why didn't he hit him eight times or six times? Why just seven times? Or else why didn't he hit him immediately as he was asking him to try to shoot an arrow?" Though this seems right, in reality it isn't. For this case you must not cherish the least bit of rational calculation in your heart; you must pass beyond the words. Only then will you be able to have a way to smash the three barriers[c] at a single phrase and to shoot an arrow. If you keep thinking of right and wrong, you will never be able to get a grasp on it.

At that time, if this monk had been a real man, Ch'in Shan would have been in great danger too. Since Liang could not carry out the imperative, he couldn't avoid it being carried out on him. But say, after all, who is the lord within the barriers? Look at Hsueh Tou's verse:

VERSE

I bring out the lord within the barriers for you—
    On target. Face to face, still you miss it. Retreat! Retreat!

You disciples who would shoot an arrow, don't be careless!
    Once dead, one doesn't come back to life again. Very
    obscure. Gone by.

Take an eye and the ears go deaf;
    In the left eye half a pound. Hsueh Tou lets his move go.
    On the left not advancing, on the right not retreating.

Let go an ear and the eyes both go blind.
    In the right eye eight ounces. There's only one road. Ad-
    vance and you fall into a pit; retreat and a ferocious tiger
    will bite your leg.

I can admire a single arrowpoint smashing three barriers—
    How is it when the entire capacity comes forth this way?
    What is he saying? The barriers have been smashed, the
    barriers have fallen.

The trail of the arrow is truly clear.
    Dead man! Bah! I'll hit, saying, "Do you see it?"

You don't see!
    A leper drags along his companions. He's creating com-
    plications.

Hsuan Sha had words for this:
    Who isn't Hsuan Sha?

"A great adept is the primordial ancestor of mind."
    With one line he cuts off the flow and puts myriad
    impulses to rest. The nostrils of the great adept are in my
    hands. Before heaven and earth and the world existed,
    where would you rest your body and establish your life?

COMMENTARY

Several of the lines of this verse draw on the words of a verse of
Kuei Tsung. Since Kuei Tsung made up this verse in the old
days, he was given the name Kuei Tsung ('return to the
source'). Within the gate of our school this is called "talk of the
source meaning."

Later Tung An heard of this case and said, "Mr. Liang was
well able to shoot arrows, but in essence he didn't know how to

hit the target." There was a monk then who asked, "How can one hit the target?" An said, "Who is the lord within the barriers?" Later there was a monk who cited this to Ch'in Shan. Shan said, "Even if Mr. Liang had been this way, he still wouldn't have avoided Ch'in Shan's mouth. Although this is so, T'ung An is not good-hearted."

Hsueh Tou says, "I bring out the lord within the barriers for you." Open your eyes and you can see, close your eyes and you can see too. With form, without form—all is cut into three sections. "You disciples who would shoot an arrow, don't be careless." If you are able to shoot well, you won't be careless. If you don't shoot well, then it's obvious that you are careless.

"Take an eye and the ears go deaf; let go an ear and the eyes both go blind." Tell me, when an eye is taken, why is it nevertheless the ears that go deaf? When an ear is let go, why then is it the eyes that both go blind? You can penetrate these words only if you have no grasping or rejection; if you are grasping and rejecting, then it will be impossible to see.

"I can admire a single arrowpoint smashing three barriers— the trail of the arrow is truly clear." Ch'an traveller Liang asked, "How is it when a single arrowpoint smashes the three barriers?" and Ch'in Shan said, "Bring out the lord within the barriers for me to see." These statements and everything down to T'ung An's case at the end are all "the trail of the arrow." In the end, what is it?"

"You don't see? Hsuan Sha had words for this: 'A great adept is the primordial ancestor of mind.' " It is commonplace to take mind as the ultimate principle of the school of the Patriarchs; here though, why is the great adept still the ancestor of this mind even before heaven and earth were born? If you can thoroughly understand this time and season, only then will you be able to recognize the lord within the barriers.

"The trail of the arrow is truly clear." If you want to hit the target, there clearly is a trail behind the arrow. But say, what is the trail behind the arrow? Before you'll understand, you must apply concentrated mental effort on your own.

"A great adept is the primordial ancestor of mind." Hsuan Sha often taught his community with these words. This is from a verse of Kuei Tsung's which Hsueh Tou has wrongly attributed to Hsuan Sha. Students of today who take this mind as the ancestral source can study until Maitreya Buddha comes down to be born here and still never understand. For one who is a great adept, even mind is still just the descendant.

"Heaven and earth not yet distinct" is already the secondary. Tell me, at just such a time, what is "before heaven and earth"?

TRANSLATORS' NOTES

a. Tangled or entangling vines is an expression colloquially meaning complications, and has been so translated. In Ch'an talk it is often used on one level to refer specifically to words, hence the public cases (*kung an*) themselves.

b. "Reverend" used here was used sometimes by Ch'an teachers as a term of direct address, hence is not always necessary to translate, except for emphasis. In formal usage it really means teacher, so it is possible that there can be some irony in the Ch'an usage. The original Sanskrit word, *Acarya*, was transliterated into Chinese syllables instead of semantic translation; the connotations of teacher, exemplar, and guide tended in common usage to fade into a general term of respect.

c. Nothing is specifically said about what the three barriers are; since the point seems to be the lord within the barriers, perhaps it is pointless to say anything. The form of Liang's question need not be considered totally arbitrary, however; we have seen mention, for example, of Yun Men's three phrases within a phrase, cutting off the stream, covering heaven and earth, and going along with the waves. Pai Chang said that the Buddhist Teachings all had three phases (expressed verbally and metaphorically as phrases): detachment from everything, not abiding in detachment (not seeing that there is anything really real to either grasp or reject), and not having any understanding of non-abiding (no awareness of knowledge of non-duality as such, no more delusion of subtle and extremely subtle knowledge). In the Lin Chi Ch'an school of the Southern Sung dynasty, after Yuan Wu, when the use of *kung an* as meditation themes was popular, there also was reference to three phases of "understanding" a *kung an*; seeing its intent, practical application, and transcendence. All of these designated states of attainment could be called "barriers"; probably "three barriers" means all barriers.

Chao Chou's Stupid Oaf

POINTER

Before you have penetrated, it all seems like a silver mountain, like an iron wall. When you have been able to penetrate, from the beginning it was your self that was the silver mountain, the iron wall.

If someone asks me, "So what?" I would just say to him, "Here, if you can reveal an action and observe an environment, occupy the essential bridge without letting profane or holy pass, this would not be beyond your inherent capacity."

If, on the other hand, you are not yet thus, observe the look of an Ancient.

CASE

A monk asked Chao Chou, " 'The Ultimate Path has no difficulties—just avoid picking and choosing.' What is not picking and choosing?"[1]

Chou said, " 'In the heavens and on earth I alone am the Honored One.' "[2]

The monk said, "This is still picking and choosing."[3]

Chou said, "Stupid oaf! Where is the picking and choosing?"[4] The monk was speechless.[5]

NOTES

1. So many people cannot swallow these iron brambles. There are many people who have doubts about this. His whole mouth is filled with frost.

2. He heaps up a pile of bones on level ground. All at once he has pierced the nostrils of patchrobed monks. A talisman hard as cast iron.

3. As it turns out he's rolled along after Chao Chou. He challenges this old fellow.
4. Mountains crumble, rocks shatter.
5. I forgive you thirty blows. His eyes open wide, his mouth is agape.

COMMENTARY

The monk questioned Chao Chou about (the saying) "The Ultimate Path has no difficulties—just avoid picking and choosing." The Third Patriarch's *Inscription of the Believing Heart* starts off directly with these two lines. There are quite a few people who misunderstand. How so? (According to them,) the Ultimate Path is fundamentally without difficulties, but also without anything that's not difficult; it's just that it's only adverse to picking and choosing. If you understand in this fashion, in ten thousand years you won't even see it in dreams.

Chao Chou often used this saying to question people. This monk reversed this by taking this saying to question him. If you look to the words, then this monk does after all startle heaven and shake the earth. If it is not in the words, then what? You must be able to turn this little key before it will open. To grab the tiger's whiskers, you must be able to do it on your own abilities. Heedless of the mortal danger, this monk dared to grab the tiger's whiskers, so he said, "This is still picking and choosing." Chao Chou immediately blocked off his mouth by saying, "Stupid oaf! Where is the picking and choosing?" If the monk had asked someone else, he would have seen him flustered and confused. But what could he do about this old fellow who was an adept? Chao Chou moved where it was impossible to move, turned around where it was impossible to turn around.

If you can penetrate all evil and poisonous words and phrases, even down to a thousand differences and ten thousand forms, then all conventional fabrications will be the excellent flavor of purified ghee. If you can get to where you touch reality, then you will see Chao Chou's naked heart in its entirety.

"Stupid oaf" is a country expression of the people of Fu Chou, to revile people for being without intelligence. When the monk said, "This is still picking and choosing," Chao Chou said, "Stupid oaf! Where is the picking and choosing?" The eye

of teachers of our school must be thus, like the golden winged
Garuda bird parting the ocean waters to seize a dragon directly
and swallow it.

VERSE

Deep as the ocean,
>What measure is this? The abyssal source is impossible to
fathom. This still hasn't got a half of it.

Firm as a mountain.
>Who can shake him? This is still only halfway there.

A mosquito sports in the fierce wind of the sky,
>There are others like this. After all, he didn't assess his
strength; he certainly didn't measure himself.

An ant tries to shake an iron pillar.
>There's no different dirt in the same hole. He's out of
touch. You're a fellow student with him.

Picking, choosing—
>Carrying water to sell at the river. What is he saying?
Chao Chou has come.

A cloth drum under the eaves. [a]
>It is already present before any words. They're buried in
the same pit, as numerous as hemp and millet seeds. I hit,
saying, "I'll block off your throats."

COMMENTARY

Hsueh Tou explains Chao Chou's two lines in the case by
saying, "Deep as the ocean, firm as a mountain." The monk
said, "This is still picking and choosing," so Hsueh Tou says
that this monk is just like a mosquito playing in a gale, like an
ant trying to shake an iron pillar. Hsueh Tou praises this
monk's great bravery. Why? This "the ultimate path has no
difficulties" is something superior people use, yet this monk
dared to talk in this way. Chao Chou did not let him go; he
immediately said, "Stupid oaf! Where is the picking and choosing?" Isn't this a fierce wind, an iron pillar?

"Picking, choosing—a cloth drum hung under the eaves." At the end Hsueh Tou picks this up to bring you to life. If you recognize it clearly, then you are carrying the whole thing yourself. What's the reason? Haven't you heard it said that if you want to attain intimate understanding, don't use a question to ask. That is why "the cloth drum under the eaves".

TRANSLATORS' NOTES

a. A cloth drum makes no sound when beaten; just so, Tenkei explains, asking questions ('beating the drum') will never yield the real answer. Ultimately all discrimination, even between discrimination and clarity, is beating a cloth drum; the sound disappears in the emptiness of space.

Chao Chou Can't Explain

CASE

A monk asked Chao Chou, " 'The Ultimate Path has no difficulties—just avoid picking and choosing'—isn't this a cliché for people of these times?"[1]

Chou said, "Once someone asked me, and I really couldn't explain for five years."[2]

NOTES

1. A double case. This too is a point which makes people doubt. Treading on a scale beam, hard as iron. There's still this one. Don't judge others on the basis of yourself.
2. Honest speech is better than a red face. A monkey eats a caterpillar, a mosquito bites an iron ox.

COMMENTARY

Chao Chou usually didn't use blows or shouts; his action went beyond blows and shouts. This monk's question was also very special; it would have been hard for anyone but Chao Chou to answer him. Since Chao Chou was an adept, he just said to him, "Once someone asked me, and I really couldn't explain for five years." The question towered up like a mile-high wall, and the answer didn't make light of it. Just understand it this way and it's right here. If you don't understand, then don't make rational calculations.

Haven't you heard how when the man of the Path Tsung of T'ou Tzu was the scribe in Hsueh Tou's community, Hsueh Tou had him immerse himself in "The Ultimate Path has no difficulties; just avoid picking and choosing." Thereby Tsung had an awakening. One day Hsueh Tou asked him, "What is the meaning of 'The Ultimate Path has no difficulties; just avoid picking and choosing'?" Tsung said, "Animal, animal." Later he dwelt in seclusion on Mt. T'ou Tzu. Whenever he went to serve as an abbot, he wrapped his straw sandals and his scriptural texts in his robe. A monk asked him "What is your family style, Wayfarer?" Tsung said, "Straw sandals wrapped in a robe." The monk said, "What does this mean?" Tsung said, "T'ung Ch'eng (the neighboring city) is under my bare feet."

Thus it is said, "Making offerings to the Buddha is not a matter of a lot of incense." If you can penetrate through and escape, then letting go or holding on rest with oneself. Since this case is one question and one answer, clear and perfectly obvious, why then did Chao Chou say that he couldn't explain? But tell me, is this a cliché for people of these times or not? Did Chao Chou answer him inside or outside the nest of cliché.[a] You must realize that this matter isn't in words and phrases. If there's a fellow who penetrates the bone and penetrates the marrow, whose faith is thoroughgoing, then he's like a dragon reaching the water, like a tiger taking to the mountains.

VERSE

The Elephant King trumpets
> Noblest of the noble, richest of the rich. Who isn't awed? Good news.

The Lion roars.
> An expert among experts. The hundred beasts' brains burst. A good route to enter by.

Flavorless talk
> When we're reviling each other, I'll let you lock jaws with me. It's like an iron spike; what place is there to bite into? He couldn't explain for five years and more; carrying all China in a single-leaf boat, far in the distant flats, waves are rising; who knows that there is yet another, better realm of thought?

Blocks off people's mouths.
> When we're spitting on each other, I'll let you spray me with slobber. Ha! What are you saying, Reverend?

South, north, east, west—
   Is there? Is there? In the heavens and on earth. Heavens!
   Heavens!
The raven flies, the rabbit runs.
   From past and from present. Buried alive all at once.

COMMENTARY

Chao Chou said, "Once someone asked me, and I really
couldn't explain for five years." This is like "The Elephant
King trumpets, the Lion roars. Flavorless talk blocks off
people's mouths. South, north, east, west—the raven flies, the
rabbit runs." If Hsueh Tou didn't have the last word, where
else would he have come from? Since "the raven flies, the
rabbit runs,"[b] tell me, where do Chao Chou, Hsueh Tou, and I
end up?

TRANSLATORS' NOTES

a.   In literary Chinese, the word 'nest' is used to refer to a cliché; that
     is, something people stick to. It is used in the same way in Ch'an
     to refer to words and sayings which have become cliché, and
     generally to any rut or habit in which one 'nests' complacently,
     any point on which one depends.
b.   The raven and rabbit also refer to the sun and moon; their flight is
     the passage of terrestrial time.

Chao Chou's Why Not Quote It Fully?

POINTER

He includes the heavens and encompasses the earth, going beyond holy and profane. On the tips of the hundred weeds he points out the wondrous mind of nirvana; within the forest of shields and spears he decisively establishes the lifeline of patchrobed monks.

But tell me, endowed with whose power, can one get to be this way? As a test I cite this: look!

CASE

A monk asked Chao Chou, " 'The Ultimate Path has no difficulties—just avoid picking and choosing.[1] As soon as there are words and speech, this is picking and choosing.'[2] So how do you help people, Teacher?"[3]

Chou said, "Why don't you quote this saying in full?"[4] The monk said, "I only remember up to here."[5]

Chou said, "It's just this: 'This Ultimate Path has no difficulties—just avoid picking and choosing.' "[6]

NOTES

1. Again it's hauled out. What is he saying?
2. He takes a mouthful of frost.
3. He presses this old fellow. Gaa!
4. The thief is a small man, but his wisdom surpasses a lord's. Chao Chou is a thief who steals in broad daylight. He's riding the thief's horse in pursuit of the thief.
5. Two fellows playing with a mud ball. The monk has encountered a thief. When immobile it's hard to be a worthy opponent for Chao Chou.

6. In the end it's up to this old fellow. The monk has his eyes snatched away; he's been overtaken.

COMMENTARY

Chao Chou saying, "It's just this: 'The Ultimate Path has no difficulties—just avoid picking and choosing,' " is like a stone-struck spark, like a flash of lightning. Capturing and releasing, killing and giving life—he has such independent mastery. All over they said that Chao Chou had eloquence beyond the common crowd.

Chao Chou often taught his community with this speech, saying, "The Ultimate Path has no difficulties—just avoid picking and choosing. As soon as there are words and speech, 'this is picking and choosing,' 'this is clarity.' This old monk does not abide within clarity; do you still preserve anything or not?" Once there was a monk who asked, "Since you do not abide in clarity, what is to be preserved?" Chou said, "I don't know either." The monk said, "Since you don't know, Teacher, why do you say you don't abide in clarity?" Chou said, "It's enough just to ask about this matter. Now bow and withdraw."

Later a monk picked on his gap and went to question him; this monk's questioning was undeniably extraordinary, but nevertheless it was just mental activity. Someone other than Chao Chou would have been unable to handle this monk. But what could he do? Chao Chou was an adept and immediately said, "Why don't you quote this saying in full?"

This monk too understood how to turn himself around and show his mettle; he said, "I only remember up to here." It seems just like an arrangement. Directly after the monk spoke, Chao Chou immediately answered him; he didn't need any calculations. An Ancient said of this, "Continuity is indeed very difficult." Chao Chou distinguished dragons from snakes and differentiated right from wrong; this goes back to his being an adept in his own right. Chao Chou snatched this monk's eyes away without running afoul of his sharp point. Without relying on calculations, he was spontaneously exactly appropriate.

It's wrong to say either that he had words or didn't have words; nor will it do to say that his answer neither had nor didn't have words. Chao Chou left behind all the permutations of logic. Why? If one discusses this matter, it is like sparks struck from stone, like flashing lightning. Only if you set your eyes on it quickly can you see it. If you hesitate and vascillate you won't avoid losing your body and life.

VERSE

Water poured on cannot wet,
> What are you saying? Too deep and far off. What is there to discuss?

Wind blowing cannot enter.
> It's like empty space. Hard, impervious. Address your plea to the sky.

The tiger prowls, the dragon walks;
> He gains independence; he's outstanding.

Ghosts howl, spirits wail.
> Everyone cover your ears! When the wind moves, the grasses bow. Are you not a fellow-student of theirs, Reverend?

His head is three feet long—I wonder who it is?
> A strange being. A sage from where? Do you see? Do you see?

Standing on one foot, he answers back without speaking.
> Bah! He draws back his head and lets his move go. Mountain ghost? He shouldn't be let go, so I strike.

COMMENTARY

"Water poured on cannot wet, wind blowing cannot enter. The tiger prowls, the dragon walks; ghosts howl, spirits wail." There's no place for you to chew on. These four lines versify Chao Chou's answer, which is indeed like a dragon galloping, like a tiger charging. This monk just got an embarrassing situation. Not only this monk; even the ghosts howl, even the spirits wail. It's like when the wind moves, the grasses bow down.

Of the final two lines, it could be said, "One son has intimately understood." "His head is three feet long—I wonder who it is? Standing on one foot, he answers back without speaking." Haven't you heard how a monk asked an Ancient Worthy, "What is the Buddha?" The Ancient Worthy said, "His head is three feet long, his neck two inches long." Hsueh Tou draws on this to use in the verse. I wonder, do you people recognize him? Not even I know him. All at once Hsueh Tou has fully depicted Chao Chou. The real one has always been within: all of you must investigate carefully and try to see it.

Yun Men's Staff Changes into a Dragon

POINTER

Buddhas and sentient beings—fundamentally there is no difference between them. Mountains and rivers and one's own self—how could there be any distinction? Why then is it all divided into two sides?

Even if you can set words turning and occupy the essential bridge, it still won't do to let go. If you don't let go, the whole great earth isn't worth grasping. But what is the place to set words turning? To test, I cite this: look!

CASE

Yun Men showed his staff to the assembly and said,[1] "The staff has changed into a dragon[2] and swallowed the universe.[3] Mountains, rivers, the great earth—where are they to be found?"[4]

NOTES

1. He exposes or transforms according to the occasion. The single-edged sword that kills people, the double-edged sword that brings people to life. He's snatched your eyeballs away.
2. What's the use of so much talk? What's the use of changing?
3. The world's patchrobed monks cannot preserve their lives. Did he block off your throats? Reverend, where will you go to settle your body and establish your life?
4. In the ten directions there are no walls, on the four sides there are no gates. East, west, south, north, the four intermediate points, above, below. How will you handle this one?

389

COMMENTARY

As for Yun Men's saying, "The staff has changed into a dragon and swallowed the universe. Where are the mountains, rivers, and earth to be found?" If you say it exists, then you are blind; if you say it doesn't exist, then you are dead. Do you see where Yun Men helped people? Bring the staff back to me!

People these days do not understand where Yun Men stood alone and revealed. Instead they say that he went to form to explain mind, that he relied on things to reveal principle. But old Shakyamuni couldn't have not known this theory as he taught the Dharma for forty-nine years; why then did he also need to hold up the flower for Kashyapa's smile? This old fellow caused confusion saying, "I have the treasury of the eye of the correct teaching, the wondrous mind of nirvana—these I pass on to MahaKashyapa." Why was there still a need for the specially transmitted mind seal? Given that all of you are guests in the house of the ancestral teachers, do you understand this specially transmitted mind?

If there is a single thing in your breast, then mountains, rivers, and the great earth appear in profusion before you; if there isn't a single thing in your breast, then outside there is not so much as a fine hair. How can you talk about principle and knowledge fusing, about objective world and mind merging? What's the reason? When one is understood, all are understood; when one is clear, all are clear.

Ch'ang Sha said, "People studying the Path don't know the real, because they've always given recognition to their cognizing mind; this, the basis of countless aeons of births and deaths, fools call the original person." If you suddenly smash the shadowy world of the heaps and elements of life so that body and mind are one likeness and there is nothing else outside your body, you still haven't attained the other half. How can you talk about going to form to reveal the mind, using things to demonstrate principle?

An Ancient said, "As soon as one atom of dust arises, the whole world is contained therein." But say, which atom of dust is this? If you can know this atom of dust, then you can know the staff. As soon as Yun Men picks up his staff, we immediately see his unconfined marvelous activity. Such talk is already a mass of entangling vines, complications; how much the more so is transforming the staff into a dragon! Librarian Ch'ing said, "Has there ever been such talk in the five thousand and forty-eight volumes of the canon?" Every time he turned to his staff, Yun Men brought out the great function of his whole capacity and helped people in a way that was leaping with life.

Pa Chiao said, "If you have a staff, I'll give you a staff; if you have no staff, I'll take your staff away."

Yung Chia said, "This is not an empty exhibition displaying form; it is the actual traces of the Tathagata's precious staff."

Long ago in the time of Dipamkara Buddha, the (future) Tathagata (Shakyamuni) spread his hair to cover some mud for that Buddha. Dipamkara said, "A temple should be built here." Also present then was an elder who thereupon set up a blade of grass right there and said, "The temple has been built." All of you tell me, where is this scene to be found?

The ancestral teacher Hsueh Tou said, "At a blow, experience it; at a shout, receive it rightly." But tell me, receive what rightly? Supposing there's someone who asks, "What is the staff?" Shouldn't you turn a backflip? Shouldn't you clap your hands? All of this would be giving play to your spirits, and has nothing to do with it.

VERSE

The staff swallows the universe—
　　What is he saying? The staff is only used for beating dogs.
He vainly talks of peach blossoms floating on the rushing
　　waves.
　　Make an opening upwards and all the thousand sages will stand downwind. It's not a matter of grasping clouds and seizing fog. Being able to say it a thousand or ten thousand times isn't as good as catching it in your hand once.
For those with tails burnt off, it's not a matter of grasping
　　clouds and seizing fog;
　　I just look to the right and to the left of this. It's just a stick of dry firewood.

Why should the exhausted ones necessarily lose their courage and spirit?
Everyone's temper is like a king's. It's just that you are far far away. What will you do about being scared?

I have picked it up—
Thanks for being so compassionate; you're kindhearted as an old lady.

Do you hear or not?
You can't avoid falling into the weeds. Why hear?

One simply must be completely free and at ease—
Part-eaten soup, spoiled food. Where does the universe come from?

Stop any further mixed up confusion.
One who quotes this rule has already broken it. It's already on your head. I strike and say, "It won't do to let go."

With seventy-two blows I'm still letting you off easy—
I've never carried out this imperative, but if you are going to act according to the imperative, it's lucky you found me.

Even with one hundred and fifty it's hard to forgive you.
A just order must be carried out. How could it only be this many? Even if he gave three thousand blows in the morning and eight hundred blows in the evening, what good would it do?

Master Hsueh Tou suddenly picked up his staff and came down from his seat; all at once the great assembly scattered and fled.
Why does Hsueh Tou have a dragon's head but a snake's tail?

COMMENTARY

Yun Men helps people by a circuitous path; Hsueh Tou helps people by a direct shortcut. That's why Hsueh Tou discards the transformation into a dragon; he doesn't need such talk, just "the staff swallows the universe." Hsueh Tou's great intent is to have people avoid fanciful interpretations. He goes on to say,

"He vainly talks of peach blossoms floating on the rushing waves." There's no further need for transformations into dragons. At the Gate of Yu there's a three-level rapids; every year by the third month when the peach blossoms bloom and the waves rise, those fish who can go against the current and leap past the rapids change into dragons. Hsueh Tou says even though they change into dragons, this too is still vain talk.

"For those with tails burnt off it's not a matter of grasping clouds and seizing fog." When fish pass through the Gate of Yu a celestial fire burns their tails; they grab the clouds, seize the fog, and depart. Hsueh Tou means that though they change into dragons, it still isn't a matter of grabbing clouds and seizing fog. "Why should the exhausted ones necessarily lose their courage and spirit?" The introduction to Ch'ing Liang's commentary on the Avatamsaka scripture says, "Even bodhisattvas who have accumulated virtuous conduct gasp for breath at the Gate of Yu." His overall meaning is to explain that the realm of the Avatamsaka Flower Garland Cosmos[a] is not something mastered by small virtue or small knowledge; it's like the fish trying to pass through the Dragon Gate of Yu, where those who cannot pass through fail and fall back. They lie in the sand shoals of the dead water, exhausted and gasping. Hsueh Tou means that once they fail and fall back, they always lose their courage and spirit.

"I have picked it up—do you hear or not?" Again he adds footnotes; all at once he's swept it clean for you. All of you "simply must be completely free and at ease—stop any further mixed up confusion." If you go on with mixed up confusion, you have lost the staff.

"With seventy-two blows I'm still letting you off easy— even with a hundred and fifty it's hard to forgive you." Why has Hsueh Tou discarded the heavy for the light? An Ancient said, "Seventy-two blows doubled makes one hundred and fifty." These days people misunderstand and just calculate numerically and say, "It should be seventy-five blows; why is it instead just seventy-two blows?" How far they are from knowing that the Ancient's meaning was beyond the words. Thus it is said, "This matter is not in words and phrases." Hsueh Tou drew on this to use in order to avoid people later on trying to rationalize. Even if you're truly free and at ease, you still rightly deserve to be given seventy-two blows—this is still letting you off easy. Even if you're not free and at ease like this at all, it would be hard to let you go with one hundred and fifty.

Hsueh Tou had completed his verse all at once, yet he picked up his staff again to help some more. Nevertheless, there wasn't even one with blood under his skin.

TRANSLATORS' NOTES

a. The Avatamsaka (Hua-Yen, Kegon) scripture is a major Greater Vehicle Buddhist scripture. The name, which means flower garland or ornament, refers to myriad religious practices, likened to flowers, adorning the realm which is produced as a result of practices in the causal state. It also refers to the representation of myriad qualities and states of being 'adorning' the worlds and universes of the cosmos. In this cosmos, all realms contain infinite realms, ad infinitum, all mutually reflecting and dependent on each other and a moment of thought. Many Ch'an masters were familiar with the Avatamsaka scripture; Tsung-mi, a successor of the Ho-tse line of Southern Ch'an, was also considered the Fifth Patriarch of the Hua-Yen school of Buddhism in China.

Feng Hsueh's One Atom of Dust

POINTER

To set up the Banner of the Teaching and establish its fundamental message is a matter for a genuine master of the school. To judge dragons and snakes, distinguish the initiate from the naive, one must be an accomplished teacher. As for discussing killing and giving life on the edge of a sword, discerning what is appropriate for the moment with a staff, this I leave aside for the moment; just tell me in one phrase how you will assess the matter of occupying the heartland singlehandedly. To test, I cite this:

CASE

Feng Hsueh, giving a talk, said,[1] "If you set up a single atom of dust,[2] the nation flourishes;[3] if you do not set up a single atom of dust,[4] the nation perishes."[5]

Hsueh Tou raised his staff and said,[6] "Are there any patch-robed monks who will live together and die together?"[7]

NOTES

1. He rouses clouds and brings rain. He wants to be host and be guest.
2. "I am king of all things and the autonomous master of all things." Clusters of flowers, clusters of brocade.[a]
3. This is not the business of his house.
4. He sweeps away the tracks and obliterates the traces; having lost his eyes, his nostrils are gone too.
5. Everywhere light shines. What is the use of the nation? This is entirely the business of his house.
6. One must stand like a mile-high wall to accomplish this. Bodhidharma has come.

7. Return the words to me. Although they are right, he wants to even out what is not even. It is necessary to deal with Hsueh Tou to accomplish it. But do you know? If you know, I admit that you are autonomous and free. If you do not know, you get hit three thousand times in the morning, eight hundred times in the evening.

COMMENTARY

As Feng Hsueh said to his assembly, "If you set up a single atom of dust, the nation flourishes; if you don't set up a single atom of dust, the nation perishes." Now tell me, is it right to set up an atom of dust, or is it right not to set up an atom of dust? When you get here, your great function must become manifest before you'll understand. That is why (Feng Hsueh) said, "Even if you can grasp it before it is spoken of, still this is remaining in the shell, wandering in limitation; even if you thoroughly penetrate it at a single phrase, you still won't avoid insane views on the way."

He was a venerable adept in the lineage of Lin Chi; he directly used his own provisions; "If you set up a single atom of dust, the nation flourishes, and the old peasants frown." The meaning lies in the fact that to establish a nation and stabilize the country, it is necessary to rely on crafty ministers and valiant generals; after that, the Unicorn appears, the Pheonix soars—these are the auspicious signs of great peace. How could the people of three-family villages know there are such things? When you do not set up a single atom of dust, the nation perishes, the wind blows chill; why do the old peasants come out and sing hallelujah? Just because the nation has perished. In the (Ts'ao-) Tung lineage, they call this the point of transformation: there is no more Buddha, nor sentient beings; no affirmation, no negation, no good, no bad—it is beyond sound and echo, track or trace. That is why it is said, "Although gold dust is precious, in the eye it obstructs vision."[b] And it is said, "Gold dust is a cataract on the eye; the jewel in one's robe is the defilement of the Dharma.[c] Even one's own spirit is not important; who are the Buddhas and Patriarchs?" Piercing and penetrating supernatural powers and their wondrous action would not be considered exceptional; when he gets here, with his patched robe covering his head, myriad concerns cease—at this time, the mountain monk does not understand anything at all. If one were to speak any more of mind, speak of nature, speak of the profound, speak of the wondrous, it would not be any use at all. What is the reason? "He has his own mountain spirit realm."

Nan Ch'uan said to his community, "The seven hundred eminent monks on Huang Mei were all men who understood the Buddha Dharma. They did not get his Robe and Bowl; there was only workman Lu who did not understand the Buddha Dharma—that is why he got his robe and bowl."[d]

He also said, "The Buddhas of the past, present, and future do not know what is; but cats and oxen do know what is." The old peasants either frown or sing, but tell me how you will understand? And tell me, what eye do they possess, that they are like this? You should know that in front of the old peasants' gates no ordinances are posted.

Hsueh Tou, having raised both sides, finally lifts up his staff and says, "Are there any patchrobed monks who will live together and die together?" At that time, if there had been a fellow who could come forth and utter a phrase, alternately acting as guest and host, he would have avoided this old fellow Hsueh Tou's pointing to himself in the end.

VERSE

The old peasants may not unfurrow their brows,
> There is someone three thousand miles away. Delicious food is not for a satisfied man to eat.

But for now I hope that the nation establishes a sturdy foundation.
> The one song of great peace, everyone knows. When you want to go, go; when you want to stay, stay. Heaven, earth, the whole world is one gate of liberation. How will you establish it?

Crafty ministers, valiant generals—where are they now?
> Are there any? Are there? The land is broad, the people are few, and rarely is anyone met with. But do not point to yourself.

Ten thousand miles' pure wind, only I know.
     If there is no one by your side, who will you have sweep
     the ground? Here's another cloud-dwelling saint.

COMMENTARY

Previously he quoted both sides; here, instead, he just raises
one side and lets the other go. He cuts down the long and adds
to the short, abandons the heavy and goes along with the light.
That is why he says, "The old peasants may not unfurrow their
brows, but for now I hope the nation establishes a sturdy foundation; where are the crafty ministers and valiant generals
now?" When Hsueh Tou lifted up his staff and said, "Are there
any patchrobed monks who will live together and die together?" This was just like saying, "Are there still any crafty
ministers and valiant generals?" In one gulp he has swallowed
everyone completely. That is why I say that the land is broad,
the people few, and rarely is anyone met with. Are there any
who know? Come forth and be buried in the same pit. "Ten
thousand miles' pure wind, only I know." This is where Hsueh
Tou points to himself.

TRANSLATORS' NOTES

a.   Clusters of flowers and brocade refer to spring and autumn, which
     in turn symbolize birth and death.
b.   Gold dust in the eyes symbolizes attachment to the Buddha
     Dharma, the teaching of enlightenment; the Diamond Cutter
     scripture says that even the Dharma should be abandoned, let
     alone what is not Dharma.
c.   The jewel in one's robe symbolizes Buddha-nature, the potential
     of enlightenment inherent in everyone; the defilement of the
     Dharma means attachment to the Dharma, maintaining a sense
     of attainment; pride, however subtle, in one's faith, practice, or
     accomplishment.
d.   Huang Mei was the mountain abode of Hung Jen, the Fifth Pa-
     triarch of Ch'an in China; workman Lu was an illiterate woodcut-
     ter who came to the community of Hung Jen and was later chosen
     as the latter's successor. After fifteen years travelling anony-

mously with a band of hunters, he "appeared" in south China, with the robe and bowl, signifying the inheritance of the Dharma, of the Fifth Patriarch. He was known as Hui Neng (his name), Ts'ao Ch'i (the name of the place he lived as a teacher), and workman Lu; he was the sixth and perhaps most illustrious patriarch of Ch'an.

Yun Men's Within There Is a Jewel

POINTER

By means of the knowledge that has no teacher, he produces the marvelous function of non-doing; by means of unconditional compassion, he acts unasked as an excellent friend. In one phrase there is killing, there is giving life; in one act there is releasing, there is holding. Tell me, who has ever been like this? To test, I cite this to see.

CASE

Yun Men said to the community, "Within heaven and earth,[1] through space and time,[2] there is a jewel,[3] hidden inside the mountain of form.[4] Pick up a lamp and go into the Buddha-hall;[5] take the triple gate[a] and bring it on the lamp."[6]

NOTES

1. The land is broad, the people few. The six directions cannot contain it.
2. Stop making your living in a ghost cave. You already missed it.
3. Where is it? Light is produced. I only fear that you'll seek it in a ghost cave.
4. A confrontation. Check!
5. It still can be discussed.
6. Great Master Yun Men is right, but nevertheless difficult to understand. He seems to have gotten somewhere. If you examine thoroughly, you will not avoid the smell of shit.

COMMENTARY

Yun Men says, "Within heaven and earth, through space and time, there is a jewel, hidden in the mountain of form." Now tell me, is Yun Men's meaning in the "fishing pole,"ᵇ or is the meaning in the lamp? These lines are paraphrased from a treatise of Seng Chao, Master of the Teachings, called *Jewel Treasury*; Yun Men brought them up to teach his community.

In the time of the Latter Ch'in, Seng Chao was in the Garden of Freedom composing his treatise. When he was copying the old *Vimalakirtinirdesa* scripture he realized that Chuang-tzu and Lao-tzu had still not exhausted the marvel; Chao then paid obeisance to Kumarajiva as his teacher. He also called on the bodhisattva Buddhabhadra at the Tile Coffin Temple, who had transmitted the Mind Seal from the Twenty-seventh Patriarch (Prajnatara) in India. Chao entered deeply into the inner sanctum. One day Chao ran into trouble; when he was about to be executed, he asked for seven days' reprieve, during which time he composed the treatise *Jewel Treasury*.

So Yun Men cited four phrases from that treatise to teach his community. The main idea is "how can you take a priceless jewel and conceal it in the heaps and elements?" The words spoken in the treatise are all in accord with the talk of our school. Have you not seen how Ching Ch'ing asked Ts'ao Shan, "How is it when in the principle of pure emptiness ultimately there is no body?" Ts'ao Shan said, "The principle being like this, what about phenomena?" Ch'ing said, "As is principle, so are phenomena." Shan said, "You can fool me, one person, but what can you do about the eyes of all the sages?" Ch'ing said, "Without the eyes of all the sages, how could you know it is not so?" Shan said, "Officially, not even a needle is admitted; privately, even a cart and horse can pass."

That is why it was said, "Within heaven and earth, in space and time, there is a jewel, hidden in the mountain of form." The great meaning of this is to show that everyone is fully endowed, each individual is perfectly complete. Yun Men thus brought it up to show his community; it is totally obvious—he couldn't go on and add interpretations for you like a lecturer. But he is compassionate and adds a footnote for you, saying, "Pick up a lamp and go into the Buddha-hall; bring the triple gate on the lamp."

Now tell me, when Yun Men speaks this way, what is his meaning? Have you not seen how an Ancient said, "The true nature of ignorance is identical to Buddhahood; the empty body of illusion is identical to the body of reality." It is also said, "See the Buddha mind right in the ordinary mind."

The "mountain of form" is the four gross elements and five heaps (which constitute human life).ᶜ "Within there is a jewel, hidden in the mountain of form." That is why it is said, "All Buddhas are in the mind; deluded people go seeking outside. Though within they embosom a priceless jewel, they do not know it, and let it rest there all their lives." It is also said, "The Buddha-nature clearly manifests, but the sentient beings dwelling in form hardly see it. If one realizes that sentient beings have no self, how does his own face differ from a Buddha's face?" "The mind is the original mind; the face is the face born of woman—the Rock of Ages may be moved, but here there is no change."

Some people acknowledge this radiant shining spirituality as the jewel; but they cannot make use of it, and they do not realize its wondrousness. Therefore they cannot set it in motion and cannot bring it out in action. An Ancient said, "Reaching an impasse, then change; having changed, then you can pass through."

"Pick up a lamp and head into the Buddha-hall"; if it is a matter of ordinary sense, this can be fathomed—but can you fathom "bring the triple gate on the lamp"? Yun Men has broken up emotional discrimination, intellectual ideas, gain, loss, affirmation, and negation, all at once for you. Hsueh Tou has said, "I like the freshly established devices of Shao Yang (Yun Men); all his life he pulled out nails and drew out pegs for others." He also said, "I do not know how many sit on the chair of rank; but the sharp sword cutting away causes others' admiration." When he said, "Pick up a lamp and go into the Buddha-hall," this one phrase has already cut off completely; yet, "bring the triple gate on the lamp." If you discuss this matter, it is like sparks struck from stone, like the flash of a lightning bolt. Yun Men said, "If you would attain, just seek a way of entry; Buddhas numerous as atoms are under your feet, the three treasuries of the holy teachings are on your tongues; (but) this is not as good as being enlightened. Monks, do not think falsely; sky is sky, earth is earth, mountains are mountains, rivers are rivers, monks are monks, lay people are lay people." After a long pause he said, "Bring me the immovable mountain before you." Then a monk came forth and asked, "How is it when a student sees that mountains are mountains and rivers are rivers?" Yun Men drew a line with his hand and said, "Why is the triple gate going from here?" He feared you would die, so he said, "When you know, it is the superb flavor of ghee; if you do not know, instead it becomes poison."

This is why it is said, "When completely thoroughly understood, there is nothing to understand; the most abstruse profundity of the mystery is still to be scorned."

Hsueh Tou again brought it up and said, "Within heaven and earth, through space and time, therein is a jewel; it lies hidden in the mountain of form. It is hung on a wall; for nine years Bodhidharma did not dare to look at it straight on. If any patch-robed monk wants to see it now, I will hit him right on the spine with my staff."[d] See how these self-possessed teachers of our school never use any actual doctrine to tie people up. Hsuan Sha said, "Though you try to enmesh him in a trap, he doesn't consent to stay; though you call after him, he doesn't turn his head. Even though he is like this, still he is a sacred tortoise dragging his tail."

VERSE

Look! Look!
　　Set your eyes on high. Why look? A black dragon admires a gem.

On the ancient embankment, who holds the fishing pole?
　　Alone, quite alone; stolid, quite stolid. Hsueh Tou draws his bow after the thief has gone. If you see jowls on the back of someone's head, don't have anything to do with him.

Clouds roll on.
　　Cut them off. A hundred layers, a thousand levels. A greasy hat and stinking shirt.

The water, vast and boundless—
　　Left and right it goes, blocking in front and supporting in back.

The white flowers in the moonlight, you must see for yourself.
　　When you see them, you'll go blind. If you can comprehend Yun Men's words, then you will see Hsueh Tou's last phrase.

COMMENTARY

If you can comprehend Yun Men's words, then you will see how Hsueh Tou helps people. He goes to the last two phrases of Yun Men's address to the community and there gives you a footnote saying, "Look! Look!" If you thereupon make raising your eyebrows and glinting your eyes your understanding,[e] you are out of touch.

An Ancient said, "The spiritual light shines alone, far transcending the senses; the essential substance is manifest, real and eternal. It is not captured in written letters. The nature of mind has no defilement; it is basically naturally perfectly complete. Just get rid of delusive clingings and merge with the Buddha that is as is." If you just go to raising your eyebrows and glinting your eyes and sit there forever, how will you be able to transcend the senses?

Hsueh Tou is saying, "Look! Look!" Yun Men appears to be on an ancient embankment holding a fishing pole; the clouds are rolling and the water is vast and boundless. The bright moon reflects white flowers, and white flowers reflect the bright moon. At this moment, tell me, what realm is this? If you can perceive it immediately and directly, the former and the latter phrases are just like one phrase.

TRANSLATORS' NOTES

a. The triple gate is the main gate of a monastery; usually it comprises three gates, hence the name, but it is called the triple gate even if there is only one. It is also called the "mountain gate," since monasteries were referred to as "mountains" even if they were not actually so situated. Many Ch'an monasteries, especially in the earlier days, were actually in the mountains, hence the name.

b. See Hsueh Tou's verse; Yun Men's saying is likened to a "fishing pole." The idea of "fishing" as one of the strategies of a teaching Ch'an master has been met with several times in this book.

c. The four gross elements are earth, air, fire, and water; the five heaps are form, sensation, perception, synergies, and consciousness. These classifications represent the elements of existence in general, of human life in particular. The analysis of the human being into five 'heaps' is to show that there is no real self or soul, no individual self-subsistent entity.

d. This is from the *Hsueh Tou Hou Lu*, "Later Record of Hsueh Tou".

e. Tenkei says this means making a show of meditational effort.

Nan Ch'uan Kills a Cat

POINTER

Where the road of ideation cannot reach, that is just right to bring to attention; where verbal explanation cannot reach, you must set your eyes on it quickly. If your thunder rolls and comets fly, then you can overturn lakes and topple mountains. Is there anyone in the crowd who can manage this? To test, I cite this to see.

CASE

At Nan Ch'uan's place one day the (monks of) the eastern and western halls were arguing about a cat.[1] When Nan Ch'uan saw this, he then held up the cat and said, "If you can speak, then I will not kill it."[2] No one in the community replied;[3] Nan Ch'uan cut the cat into two pieces.[4]

NOTES

1. It's not just today that they're haggling together. This is a case of degeneracy.
2. When the true imperative goes into effect, the ten directions are subdued. This old fellow has the capability to distinguish dragons from snakes.
3. What a pity to let him go. A bunch of lacquer tubs—what are they worth? Phoney Ch'an followers are as plentiful as hemp and millet.
4. How quick! How quick! If he hadn't acted like this, they would all be fellows playing with a mud ball. He draws the bow after the thief has gone. Already this is secondary; he should have been hit before he even picked it up.

COMMENTARY

An accomplished master of our school: see his movement, stillness, his going out and entering in. Tell me, what was his inner meaning? This story about killing the cat is widely discussed in monasteries everywhere. Some say that the holding up is it; some say it lies in the cutting. But actually these bear no relation to it at all. If he had not held it up, then would you still spin out all sorts of rationalizations? You are far from knowing that this Ancient had the eye to judge heaven and earth, and he had the sword to settle heaven and earth.

Now you tell me, after all, who was it that killed the cat? Just when Nan Ch'uan held it up and said, "If you can speak, then I won't kill it," at that moment, if there were suddenly someone who could speak, tell me, would Nan Ch'uan have killed it or not? This is why I say, "When the true imperative goes into effect, the ten directions are subdued." Stick your head out beyond the heavens and look; who's there?

The fact is that at that time he really did not kill. This story does not lie in killing or not killing. This matter is clearly known; it is so distinctly clear. It is not to be found in emotions or opinions; if you go searching in emotions and opinions, then you turn against Nan Ch'uan. Just see it right on the edge of the knife. If it exists, all right; if it does not exist, all right; if it neither exists nor doesn't exist, that is all right too. That is why an Ancient said, "When at an impasse, change; when you change, then you can pass through." People nowadays do not know how to change and pass through; they only go running to the spoken words. When Nan Ch'uan held up (the cat) in this way, he could not have been telling people they should be able to say something; he just wanted people to attain on their own, each act on their own, and know for themselves. If you do not understand it in this way, after all you will grope without finding it. Hsueh Tou versifies it directly:

VERSE

In both halls they are phoney Ch'an followers:
> Familiar words come from a familiar mouth. With one phrase he has said it all. He settles the case according to the facts.

Stirring up smoke and dust, they are helpless.

Look; what settlement will you make? A completely obvious public case. Still there's something here.

*Fortunately, there is Nan Ch'uan, who is able to uphold the
command:*

Raising my whisk, I say, "It's just like this." Old Master
Wang (Nan Ch'uan) amounts to something. He uses the
fine jewel-sword of the Diamond King to cut mud.

*With one stroke of the knife he cuts into two pieces, letting
them be lopsided as they may.*

Shattered into a hundred fragments. If someone should
suddenly hold his knife still, see what he would do. He
can't be let go, so I strike!

COMMENTARY

"In both halls they are phoney Ch'an followers." Hsueh Tou
does not die at the phrase, and he also does not acknowledge
that which is ahead of a donkey but behind a horse. He has a
place to turn, so he says, "Stirring up smoke and dust, they are
helpless." Hsueh Tou and Nan Ch'uan walk hand in hand; in
one phrase he has said it all. The leaders of the two halls have
no place to rest their heads; everywhere they go, they just stir
up smoke and dust, unable to accomplish anything. Fortunately there is Nan Ch'uan to settle this public case for them,
and he wraps it up cleanly and thoroughly. But what can be
done for them, who neither reached home nor got to the shop?
That is why he said, "Fortunately there is Nan Ch'uan, who is
able to uphold the command; with one stroke of the knife he
cuts into two pieces, letting them be lopsided as they may." He
directly cuts in two with one knife, without further concern as
to whether they'll be unevenly lopsided. But tell me, what
command is Nan Ch'uan enforcing?

Nan Ch'uan Questions Chao Chou

CASE

Nan Ch'uan recited the preceding story to question Chao Chou.[1] Chou immediately took off his straw sandals, placed them on his head, and left.[2] Nan Ch'uan said, "If you had been here, you could have saved the cat."[3]

NOTES

1. They must be of like hearts and like minds before this is possible. Only one on the same road would know.
2. He does not avoid trailing mud and dripping water.
3. Singing and clapping, they accompany each other; those who know the tune are few. He adds error to error.

COMMENTARY

Chao Chou was Nan Ch'uan's true heir; when Nan Ch'uan spoke of the head, Chao Chou understood the tail; when it is brought up, he immediately knows where it comes down.

In the evening Nan Ch'uan repeated the preceding story and asked Chao Chou about it. Chou was an old adept; he immediately took off his straw sandals, put them on his head, and left. Ch'uan said, "If you had been here, you could have saved the cat." But tell me, was it really like this or not? Nan Ch'uan said, "If you can speak, then I won't kill it." Like a flint-struck spark, like a flash of lightning. Chao Chou immediately took off his sandals, put them on his head, and left; he studied the living word, not the dead word—each day renewed, each moment renewed; even the thousand sages could not stir a hairsbreadth. You must bring forth your own family treasure; only then will you see the great function of his total capacity. He is saying, "I am King of Dharma, free in all respects."[a]

Many people misunderstand and say that Chao Chou temporarily made his sandals into the cat. Some say he meant, "When you say, 'If you can speak, then I won't kill it,' I would then put my sandals on my head and leave. It's just you killing the cat—it is none of my business." But this has nothing to do with it; this is just giving play to the spirit. You are far from knowing that the Ancient's meaning was like the universal cover of the sky, like the universal support of the earth.

That father and son conformed with each other; the edges of their activity met with each other. When Nan Ch'uan raised the head, Chao Chou immediately understood the tail. Students these days do not know the turning point of the Ancients, and vainly go to the road of ideation to figure them out. If you want to see, just go to Nan Ch'uan's and Chao Chou's turning points and you will see them well.

VERSE

The public case completed, he questions Chao Chou:
    The words are still in our ears. No use to cut any more. He
    hangs a medicine bag on the back of a hearse.
In the city of Ch'ang An, he's free to wander at leisure.[b]
    He has attained such joyful liveliness; he has attained
    such freedom. He lets his hands pick the plants. I cannot
    but let you go on this way.
His straw sandals he wears on his head—no one understands;
    Yet there is one or a half. This is a special style. Light is
    fitting, darkness is also fitting.
Returning to his native village, then he rests.
    You should be given thirty blows right where you stand.
    But tell me, where is the fault? It's just that you are rais-
    ing waves where there is no wind. They let each other off.
    I only fear you will not be thus; if so, it's quite unusual.

COMMENTARY

"The public case completed, he questions Chao Chou." The librarian Ch'ing said, "It is like a man settling a case; eight strokes of the staff is eight strokes; thirteen is thirteen. Already he has settled it completely. Yet he then brings it up to ask Chao Chou."

Chao Chou was a man of his household and understood the essence of Nan Ch'uan's meaning. He was a man who had thoroughly passed through; struck, he resounds and immediately rolls. He possesses the eyes and brain of a genuine adept; as soon as he hears it mentioned, he immediately gets up and acts.

Hsueh Tou says, "In the city of Ch'ang An, he is free to roam at leisure." He is quite a dotard. An Ancient said, "Although Ch'ang An is pleasant, it is not a place to stay for long." It has also been said, "Ch'ang An is quite noisy; my province is peaceful." Still, you must recognize what is appropriate to the situation and distinguish good and bad before you will understand.

"His grass sandals he wears on his head—no one understands." When he put the sandals on his head, this bit, though without so much ado, is why it is said, "Only I myself can know, only I myself can experience it." Then you will be able to see how Nan Ch'uan, Chao Chou, and Hsueh Tou attained alike and acted alike.

But tell me, right now, how will you understand? "Returning to his native village, then he rests." What place is his native village? If he didn't understand, he surely wouldn't speak this way. Since he did understand, tell me, where is the native village. I strike immediately.

TRANSLATORS' NOTES

a. This phrase is taken from the *Saddharmapundarika* scripture, where it refers to the Buddha's independent mastery in the use of teachings, provisional or true, in a manner appropriate to the time, situation, and capacities of the hearers.

b. Commentaries explain variously that this second line refers to Nan Ch'uan, to Chao Chou, or to both. Ch'ang An, which name means "eternal peace," was at various times a capital of the Chinese empire. As "the capital," it was used in Ch'an to refer to enlightenment; that one should not dwell forever in Ch'ang An is a re-statement of the admonition to transcend all sense of attainment, not to be attached to the Dharma.

An Outsider Questions the Buddha

POINTER

Appearing without form, filling the ten directions of space, expanding everywhere equally; responding without mind, extending over lands and seas without trouble; understanding three when one is raised, judging grains and ounces at the glance of an eye. Even if the blows of your staff fall like rain and your shouts are like thunder rolling, still you have not yet filled the footsteps of a trancendent man. But tell me, what is the business of a transcendent man? Try to see.

CASE

An outsider asked the Buddha, "I do not ask about the spoken or the unspoken."[1] The World Honored One remained silent.[2] The outsider sighed in admiration and said, "The World Honored One's great kindness and great compassion have opened up my clouds of illusion and let me gain entry."[3]

After the outsider had left, Ananda asked the Buddha, "What did the outsider realize, that he said he had gained entry?"[4] The Buddha said, "Like a good horse, he goes as soon as he sees the shadow of the whip."[5]

NOTES

1. Although he is not a member of the household, still he has a bit of a fragrant air. Twin swords fly through space. It's lucky he doesn't ask.
2. Do not slander the World Honored One; his voice is like thunder. No one sitting or standing here could move him.
3. A sharp fellow—one push and he rolls, a bright pearl in a bowl.
4. He can't avoid making others doubt; still he wants everyone to know. He is trying to repair a pot with cold iron.

5. Tell me, what do you call the shadow of the whip? Striking with my whisk, (I say) on the staff there is an eye bright as the sun. If you want to know if it is real gold, see it through fire. Having gotten a mouth, eat.

COMMENTARY

If this matter were in words and phrases, do not the twelve parts of the Teachings of the Three Vehicles contain words and phrases? Some say it is right just not to speak. Then what would have been the use of the Patriarch's coming from the West? As for so many public cases which have come down from ancient times, after all how will you see what they are getting at?

This one public case is understood verbally by quite a few people. Some call it remaining silent, some call it remaining seated, and some call it silently not answering. But fortunately none of this has anything to do with it; how could you ever manage to find it by groping around? This matter really isn't in words and phrases, yet it is not apart from words and phrases. If you have the slightest bit of hesitation, then you are a thousand miles, ten thousand miles away. See how after that outsider had intuitively awakened, only then did he realize that it is neither here nor there, neither in affirmation nor in negation. But tell me, what is this?

Master I Huai of T'ien I made a verse which said,

> *Vimalakirti was not silent, did not remain that*
> *   way;* [a]
> *Sitting on his seat engaged in deliberation, he made*
> *   an error.*
> *Though the sharp sword is in its scabbard, its chill*
> *   light is cold;*
> *Outsiders and celestial demons all fold their hands*
> *   helplessly.*

When Master Tao Ch'ang of Pai Chang was studying with Fa Yen, Yen had him contemplate this story. Fa Yen one day asked him, "What incident are you contemplating?" Ch'ang said, "The outsider questioning the Buddha." Yen said, "Stop! Stop! You're about to go to his silence to understand, aren't you?" At these words Ch'ang was suddenly greatly enlightened. Later, in teaching his community, he said, "On Pai Chang there are three secrets; 'drink tea,' 'take care,' and 'rest.' If you still try to think any more about them, I know you are still not through."

"Breast-beater Chen" of Ts'ui Yen cited (this case) and said, "In the six directions and nine states, blue, yellow, red, and white each intermingle."

The outsider knew the four Vedas and told himself he was omniscient; everywhere he was, he drew people into discussions. He posed a question, hoping to cut off old Shakya Buddha's tongue. The World Honored One did not expend any energy, yet the outsider was immediately awakened. He sighed in admiration and said, "The World Honored One's great kindness and great compassion have opened up the clouds of my confusion and allowed me to gain entry."

But tell me, where are the World Honored One's great kindness and compassion? The World Honored One's single eye sees through past, present, and future; the outsider's twin pupils penetrate the Indian continent.

Chen Ju of Kuei Shan brought this up and said,

> The heretic had the most precious jewel hidden
>   within;
> The World Honored One kindly lifted it on high for
>   him.
> Forests of patterns are clearly revealed,
> Myriad forms are evident.

But after all, what did the outsider realize? It was like chasing a dog towards a fence: when he gets as far as is possible, when there is no way to get by, he must turn around and come back; then he will be leaping lively. If you cast away judgement and comparison and affirmation and negation all at once, your emotions ended and your views gone, it will naturally become thoroughly obvious.

After the outsider had left, Ananda asked the Buddha, "What did the outsider realize, that he said he had gained entry?" The Buddha said, "Like a good horse, he goes as soon as he sees the shadow of the whip." Since then, everywhere it has been said that at this point even he was blown by the wind into a different tune. It has also been said that he had a dragon's head but a snake's tail. Where is the shadow of the World Honored One's whip? Where is the seeing of the shadow of the whip? Hsueh Tou said, "False and true are not separate; the fault comes from the shadow of the whip."

Chen Ju said, "Ananda's golden bell is rung twice, and everyone hears it together. Even though this is so, it is very much like two dragons fighting for a jewel. It matured the majestic dragon of that other wise one."

VERSE

The wheel of potential has never turned;
    It is here. After all it doesn't move a bit.

If it turns, it will surely go two ways.
    If it doesn't fall into existence, it will surely fall into
    nonexistence; if it doesn't go east, then it will go west.
    The left eye is half a pound, the right eye eight ounces.

A clear mirror is suddenly leaned on a stand,
    But do you see old Shakyamuni? One push and it turns.
    Broken! Broken! Scattered! Scattered!

And immediately distinguishes beautiful and ugly.
    The whole world is the gate of liberation. I should give
    you thirty blows of the staff. But do you see old
    Shakyamuni?

Beautiful and ugly distinct, the clouds of illusion open.
    He lets out a pathway. I allow as you have a place to turn
    your body, but nevertheless you're just an outsider.

In the gate of compassion, where is any dust produced?
    The whole world has never concealed it. Retreat;
    retreat—Bodhidharma has come.

Thus I think of a good horse seeing the whip's shadow:
    I have a staff; there's no need for you to give me one. But
    tell me, where is the shadow of the whip, and where is the
    good horse?

Gone a thousand miles in pursuit of the wind, I call him back;
    Riding on the Buddha-hall, I go out the main gate. If he
    turns around, he goes wrong. He shouldn't be let go, so I
    strike.

Calling, if I get him to return, I'd snap my fingers thrice.
He neither reaches the village nor gets to the shop. With your staff broken, where will you go? The sound of Hsueh Tou's thunder is great, but there is no rain at all.

COMMENTARY

"The wheel of potential has never turned; if it turns it will surely go two ways." The "potential" is the spiritual potential of the thousand sages; the "wheel" is the original lifeline of all people. Have you not read Hsueh Tou's saying,

> *The spiritual potential of the thousand sages is not*
> *   easily approached;*
> *Dragon's sons born of dragons, do not be irresolute.*
> *Chao Chou has stolen a gem worth many cities;*
> *The King of Ch'in and Hsiang Ju both lose their*
> *   lives.* [b]

The outsider, after all, was able to hold it still and be the master; he never moved at all. How so? He said, "I do not ask about the spoken or the unspoken." Is this not the entirety of potential?

The World Honored One knew how to observe the wind to set the sail, how to give medicine in accordance with the disease; that is why he remained silent. The entire potential uplifted, the outsider merged with it completely; his wheel of potential then turned freely and smoothly: it neither turned towards existence nor nonexistence; it did not fall into gain or loss, was not bound by the ordinary or the holy—both sides were cut off at once. Just as the World Honored One remained silent, the other bowed. Many people nowadays fall into nonexistence, or else they fall into existence; they only remain within being and non-being, running either way.

Hsueh Tou says, "A clear mirror is suddenly leaned on a stand, and immediately distinguishes beautiful and ugly." This has never moved; it just calls for silence, like a clear mirror leaning on its stand—myriad forms cannot avoid their appearance.

The outsider said, "The World Honored One's great kindness and compassion have opened my clouds of illusion and allowed me to gain entry." Tell me, where is the outsider's point of entry? At this point, you must each seek on your own, investigate on your own, awaken on your own, and understand on your own before you will find it. Then in all places, walking, standing, sitting, and lying, without question of high or low, all at once it is completely manifest and does not move at all anymore. The moment they make judgements and comparisons, or have the slightest hair of rationalization, then this blocks people up completely, and there is no more ability to enter actively.

The last part versifies, "The World Honored One's great kindness and great compassion have opened up the clouds of my illusion and allowed me to gain entry." Right away he abruptly distinguishes beautiful and ugly; "Beautiful and ugly distinct, the clouds of illusion open; in the gate of compassion, where is any dust produced?" The whole world is the door of the World Honored One's great compassion. If you can pass through, it's not worth grasping. This also is an open door. Have you not read how the World Honored One contemplated this matter for twenty-one days—"I would rather not explain the truth, but quickly enter extinction."

"So I think of a good horse seeing the shadow of the whip; gone a thousand miles in pursuit of the wind, I call him back." A "wind-chasing" horse, seeing the shadow of a whip, immediately goes a thousand miles; if you make it return, it returns. Hsueh Tou intends to praise him by saying, "If you find an excellent breed, then you can give one push, and he immediately rolls; one call, and he immediately comes back. Calling, if I get him to return, I'd snap my fingers thrice." But tell me, is this criticism, or is it scattering sand?

TRANSLATORS' NOTES

a. In the scripture spoken by Vimalakirti (*Vimalakirtinirdesasutra*), after hearing a number of bodhisattvas give eloquent explanations of non-duality, the enlightened layman Vimalakirti gave his explanation of non-duality by not saying anything; Manjusri, the embodiment of wisdom, praised this explanation as most eloquent. (See Case 84.)

b.   Hsiang Ju was a minister of the King of Chao in the early third century B.C., during the "Warring States" period; he was sent to offer a rare gem to the king of Ch'in (a neighboring state in what is now northern China) in exchange for dominion over fifteen cities. After presenting the gem, Hsiang Ju perceived that the king of Ch'in was reluctant to keep his part of the bargain; so he used a ruse to get the gem back, and had it returned secretly to the kingdom of Chao. In this poem from his *Tsu Ying Chi* ("Collection on Outstanding Ancestors"), Hsueh Tou constructs a simile based on the name of Chao Chou, the place where the great Ch'an master Ts'ung Shen (778-897) lived. He was called by the name of the place, which had been in the ancient Kingdom of Chao. The King of Ch'in and Hsiang Ju represent opposition; the Buddha, represented by Ch'an master Chao Chou, cuts off opposition by taking away the object of contention.

Yen T'ou's Getting Huang Ch'ao's Sword

POINTER

Meeting the situation head-on, setting a pitfall for a tiger; attacking from front and side, laying out strategy to capture a thief. Adapting in light and adapting in darkness, letting both go or gathering both in, knowing how to play with a deadly snake—all this is a matter for an adept.

CASE

Yen T'ou asked a monk, "Where do you come from?"[1]
    The monk said, "From the Western Capital."[2]
    Yen T'ou said, "After Huang Ch'ao had gone, did you get his sword?"[3]
    The monk said, "I got it."[4]
    Yen T'ou extended his neck, came near and said, "Yaa!"[5]
    The monk said, "Your head has fallen, Master."[6] Yen T'ou laughed out loud.[7]
    Later that monk went to Hsueh Feng.[8] Feng asked, "Where did you come from?"[9] The monk said, "From Yen T'ou."[10] Hsueh Feng said, "What did he have to say?"[11] The monk recounted the preceding story.[12] Hsueh Feng hit him thirty blows with his staff and drove him out.[13]

NOTES

1. He is defeated before he even opens his mouth. (Yen T'ou) is boring into a skullbone. If you want to know where he's coming from, it's not hard.
2. After all, he's a petty thief.
3. Yen T'ou has never been a petty thief. He doesn't fear losing his head, so he asks such a question: he's very courageous indeed!

4. He's defeated, but doesn't know where to turn. Ignoramuses are as plentiful as hemp and millet.

5. He must know what's appropriate to the moment, to do this. This is a pitfall to catch a tiger. What is going on in his mind?

6. He only sees the sharpness of the awl; he does not see the squareness of the chisel. What good or bad does he know? He's struck!

7. No patchrobed monk in the world can do anything to him. He completely fools everyone in the world. No one can find out where this old fellow's head has fallen.

8. As before, he is fatheaded and stupid. This monk is thoroughly defeated time and again.

9. He cannot but tell where he comes from; but still Hsueh Feng wants to try him.

10. After all he is defeated.

11. If he can recite it, he won't avoid getting hit.

12. Right then he should be driven out.

13. Although it is true that he cuts nails and shears through iron, why does he only strike thirty blows with his staff? He hasn't yet gotten to the point where his staff breaks. This is not yet the real thing. Why? "Three thousand blows in the morning, eight hundred blows in the evening." If (Hsueh Feng) were not a fellow student (with Yen T'ou), how could he discern the point? Although this is so, just tell me, where do Hsueh Feng and Yen T'ou abide?

COMMENTARY

Whenever you carry your bag and bowl, pulling out the weeds seeking the Way, you must first possess the foot-travelling eye. This monk's eyes were like comets, yet he was still thoroughly exposed by Yen T'ou, and pierced all the way through on a single string. At that time, if he had been a man, whether it were to kill or to enliven, he would have made use of it immediately as soon as it was brought up. But this monk was a rickety dotard and instead said, "I got it." If you travel on foot like this, the King of Death will question you and demand you pay your grocery bill. I don't know how many straw sandals he wore out until he got to Hsueh Feng. At that time, if he had had a little bit of eye power, then he would have been able to get a glimpse; wouldn't that have felt good?

This story has a knotty complication in it. Although this matter has neither gain nor loss, the gain and loss are tremendous: although there is no picking and choosing, when you get here, you after all must possess the eyes to pick and choose.

See how when Lung Ya was travelling on foot, he posed this question to Te Shan: "How is it when the student wants to take the Master's head with a sharp sword?" Te Shan stretched out his neck, approached, and said, "Yaa!" Lung Ya said, "The Master's head has fallen." Te Shan returned to the abbot's room. Lung Ya later recited this to Tung Shan. Tung Shan said, "What did Te Shan say at the time?" Lung Ya said, "He said nothing." Tung Shan said, "His having nothing to say, I leave aside for the moment: just bring Te Shan's fallen head for me to see." Lung Ya at these words was greatly awakened; later he burned incense, and gazing far off towards Te Shan, he bowed and repented. A monk repeated this to Te Shan. Te Shan said, "Old man Tung Shan does not know good from bad; this fellow has been dead for so long, even if you could revive him, what would be the use?"

This public case is the same as that of Lung Ya: Te Shan returned to the abbot's room; thus in darkness he was most wonderful. Yen T'ou laughs loudly—in his laugh there is poison: if any one could discern it, he could travel freely throughout the world. If this monk had been able to pick it out at that moment, he would have escaped critical examination for all time. But at Yen T'ou's place, he had already missed it. Observe that old man Hsueh Feng; being a fellow student (with Yen T'ou), he immediately knew where he was at. Still, he didn't explain it all for that monk, but just hit him thirty blows of the staff and drove him out of the monastery. Thereby he was "before light and after annihilation." This is the method of holding up the nostrils of an adept patchrobed monk to help the person; he doesn't do anything else for him, but makes him awaken on his own.

When genuine teachers of our school help people, sometimes they trap them and do not let them come out; sometimes they release them and let them be slovenly. After all, they must have a place to appear. Yen T'ou and Hsueh Feng, supposedly so great, were on the contrary exposed by this rice-eating Ch'an follower. When Yen T'ou said, "After Huang Ch'ao had gone, did you get his sword?" People, tell me, what could be said here to avoid his laughter, and to avoid Hsueh Feng's brandishing his staff and driving him out? Here it is difficult to understand; if you have never personally witnessed and personally awakened, even if your mouth is swift and sharp to the very end, you will not be able to pass through and out of birth and death. I always teach people to observe the pivot of this action; if you hesitate, you are far, far away from it. Have you not seen how T'ou Tzu asked a monk from Yen Ping, "Have you brought a sword?" The monk pointed at the ground with his hand. T'ou Tzu said, "For thirty years I have been handling horses, but today I have been kicked by a mule." Look at that monk; he too was undeniably an adept—neither did he say he had it, nor did he say he did not have it; he was like an ocean away from the monk from the Western Capital. Chen Ju brought this up and said, "Those Ancients; one acted as the head, the other as the tail, for sure."

Hsueh Tou's verse says,

VERSE

After Huang Ch'ao's passing, he had picked up the sword.
    What is the usefulness of an impetous fellow? This is just
    a tin knife.

The great laughter after all needs an adept to understand it.
    One son is familiar with it. How many could be?

Thirty blows of the mountain cane is still a light punishment;
    Born of the same lineage, they die of the same lineage. In
    the morning, three thousand; in the evening, eight
    hundred. When someone in the eastern house dies, some-
    one of the western house helps in the mourning. But can
    they bring him back to life?

To take advantage is to lose the advantage.
    He settles the case according to the facts. It is regrettable
    not to have been careful in the very beginning.

COMMENTARY

"After Huang Ch'ao's passing, he had picked up the sword. The great laughter needs an adept to understand it." Hsueh Tou immediately versifies this monk and Yen T'ou's great laughter. This little bit cannot be grasped by anyone in the world. But tell me, what was he laughing at? You must be an adept in order to know. In this laughter there is the provisional, there is the real; there is illumination and there is function; there is killing and there is giving life.

"Thirty blows of the mountain cane is still a light punishment." This versifies this monk later coming into the presence of Hsueh Feng: the monk was as crude as before, so Feng thereupon acted as was imperative, and hit him thirty times with his staff and drove him out. But tell me, why did he act like this? Do you want to understand this story fully? "To take the advantage is to lose the advantage."

TRANSLATORS' NOTES

a.   In 874 a rebellion against the T'ang dynasty broke out, and under the leadership of Wang Hsien-chih overthrew government forces in many parts of China. Huang Ch'ao was a follower of Wang, and when the latter was killed in the fifth year of the rebellion, Huang Ch'ao took over the leadership of the rebel forces. Eventually they occupied Ch'ang An, the western capital, and slew all the members of the Imperial family who were still there. Huang Ch'ao proclaimed himself Emperor and intended to start a new dynasty, but in 881 he was finally driven out of Ch'ang An, and in 884 he was at last defeated and killed. This great rebellion, which brought about the ultimate downfall of the T'ang dynasty, is usually known as the Huang Ch'ao rebellion. Huang Ch'ao himself had earlier failed the government civil service examinations several times and had taken up salt-selling. According to legend, one day he suddenly obtained a sword which was inscribed, "Heaven gives this to Huang Ch'ao," and this inspired him to join the rebel forces of Wang Hsien-chih. In Ch'an terminology, a sword is a metaphor for *prajna*, or transcendent wisdom; Yen T'ou used the fact that the monk came from Ch'ang An to pose his question in this way. Yen T'ou died in 887, so the Huang Ch'ao rebellion was a current event.

Mahasattva Fu Expounds the Scripture

CASE

Emperor Wu of Liang requested Mahasattva Fu to expound the Diamond Cutter Scripture.[1] The Mahasattva shook the desk once, then got down off the seat.[2] Emperor Wu was astonished.[3]

Master Chih asked him, "Does Your Majesty understand?"[4] The Emperor said, "I do not understand."[5] Master Chih said, "The Mahasattva Fu has expounded the scripture."[6]

NOTES

1. Bodhidharma's brother has come. This is not unheard of in fish markets and wineshops, but in the school of the patchrobed monks, it is inappropriate. This old fellow Fu is supposedly so venerable and great, yet he acts like this.
2. He's like a comet bursting out then disappearing. He seems to be right, but is not yet really right. He doesn't bother to create any entangling complications.
3. Twice and three times he's been fooled by someone. Fu too makes him unable to get a grasp.
4. He sides with principle, not with emotion. The elbow does not bend outward. He too should be given thirty blows.
5. What a pity!
6. He too should be driven from the country. Only if Emperor Wu at that time had at once driven Master Chih out of the country along with Mahasattva Fu would he have been an adept. (Chih and Fu) are two fellows in the same pit, where the dirt is no different.

COMMENTARY

Emperor Wu, the founder of the Liang Dynasty, was of the Hsiao clan. His name was Yen and his nickname was Shu Ta. By the deeds he accomplished, he came to secure the abdication of the Ch'i Dynasty.ᵃ After he had assumed the throne, he made new commentaries on the Five Confucian Classics, to expound them. He served Huang-Lao (Taoism) very faithfully, and his nature was most filial.

One day he thought of attaining the transmundane teaching in order to requite (his parents') toil. At this point he abandoned Taoism and served Buddhism. Then he received the Bodhisattva precepts from the Dharma Master Lou Yueh. He put on Buddhist vestments and personally expounded the Light-emitting Wisdom Scripture to recompense his parents.

At the time, the Mahasattva Master Chih, because he manifested wonders and confused people, was confined in prison. Master Chih then reproduced his body and wandered around teaching in the city. The emperor one day found out about this and was inspired. He esteemed Chih most highly. Master Chih time and again practiced protective concealment; his disappearances and appearances were incomprehensible.

At that time there was a Mahasattva in Wu Chou, dwelling on Yun Huang Mountain. He had personally planted two trees and called them the "Twin Trees." He called himself the "Future Mahasattva Shan Hui." One day he composed a letter and had a disciple present it to the emperor. At the time, the court did not accept it because he had neglected the formalities of a subject in respect to the ruler.

When the Mahasattva Fu was going to go into the city of Chin Ling (Nanking, the capital of Liang) to sell fish, at that time the emperor Wu happened to request Master Chih to expound the Diamond Cutter Scripture. Chih said, "This poor wayfarer cannot expound it, but in the market place there is a Mahasattva Fu who is able to expound the scripture." The emperor issued an imperial order to summon him to the inner palace.

Once Mahasattva Fu had arrived, he mounted the lecturing seat, shook the desk once, and then got down off the seat. At that moment, if (Wu) had pushed it over for him, he would have avoided a mess; instead he was asked by Master Chih, "Does Your Majesty understand?" The emperor said, "I do not understand." Master Chih said, "The Mahasattva has expounded the scripture thoroughly." This too is one man acting as the head and one man acting as the tail. But when Master Chih spoke in this way, did he after all see Mahasattva Fu, even in a dream? Everyone gives play to their spirits, but this one is outstanding among them. Although it is a deadly snake, if you know how to handle it, you'll still be alive. Since he was expounding the scripture, why then did he not make the general distinction into two aspects, just as ordinary lecturers say— "The substance of the Diamond is hard and solid, so that nothing can destroy it; because of its sharp function, it can smash myriad things." Explaining like this could then be called expounding the scripture. People hardly understand: the Mahasattva Fu only brought up the transcendental mainspring and briefly showed the swordpoint, to let people know the ultimate intent, directly standing it up for you like a mile-high wall. It was only appropriate that he should be subject to Master Chih's ignorance of good and bad in saying, "The Mahasattva has expounded the scripture thoroughly." Indeed, he had a good intent but didn't get a good response. It was like a cup of fine wine, which was diluted with water by Master Chih; like a bowl of soup being polluted by Master Chih with a piece of rat shit.

But tell me, granted that this is not expounding the scripture, ultimately what can you call it? The verse says,

VERSE

He does not rest this body by the Twin Trees:
>It's just because he can't hold still. How could it be possible to hide a sharp awl inside a bag?

Instead, in the land of Liang he stirs up dust.
>If he did not enter the weeds, how could we see the point? Where there is no style, there is still style.

At that time, if it weren't for old Master Chih,
>To be a thief, one does not need capital. There is a leper dragging a companion along.

He too would have been a man hastily leaving the country.
His crime should be listed on the same indictment; so I
strike.

COMMENTARY

"He does not rest this body by the Twin Trees; instead, in the
land of Liang he stirs up dust." Mahasattva Fu and that old
gap-toothed fellow (Bodhidharma) met (Emperor Wu) in the
same way. When Bodhidharma first arrived at Chin Ling and
saw Emperor Wu, the emperor asked, "What is the highest
meaning of the holy truths?" Bodhidharma said, "Empty,
without holiness." The emperor said, "Who is here in my presence?" Bodhidharma said, "I don't know." The emperor did not
understand, so Bodhidharma eventually crossed the river into
Wei. Emperor Wu mentioned this to Master Chih and asked
him about it. Chih said, "Does Your Majesty recognize this
man, or not?" The emperor said, "I do not recognize him."
Master Chih said, "This is the Mahasattva Avalokitesvara,
transmitting the seal of the Buddha-mind." The emperor felt
regret and so sent an emissary to get (Bodhidharma). Master
Chih said, "Don't tell me Your Majesty is going to send an
emissary to get him: even if everyone in the country went, he
would not return." That is why Hsueh Tou says, "At that time,
if not for Master Chih, he too would have been a man hastily
leaving the country." At the time, if it hadn't been for Master
Chih exerting energy on behalf of Mahasattva Fu, he too would
surely have been driven out of the country. Since Master Chih
was so talkative, Emperor Wu after all was fooled by him.

Hsueh Tou's intent is to say that there is no need for him to
come to the land of Liang to expound the scripture and shake
the desk. That's why he says, "Why does he not rest this body
by the Twin Trees, eating gruel and eating rice, passing the
time according to his means? Instead he comes to the land of
Liang, and comments in this way—shaking the desk once, he
immediately gets down off the seat." This is where he stirs up
dust.

If you want the marvelous, then look at the cloudy skies;
above you do not see that there is any Buddha, and below you
do not see that there are any sentient beings. If you discuss the

business of appearing in the world, you cannot avoid ashes on your head and dirt on your face, taking the non-existent and making it exist, taking the existent and making it not exist; taking right and making it wrong, taking coarse and making it fine; in the fish markets and wineshops, holding it sideways and using it upside down, making everyone understand this matter. If you do not let go in this way, then even until Maitreya is born, there will not be one or a half (who will understand). Mahasattva Fu was already dragging in mud and dripping with water; fortunately he had a sympathizer. If not for old Master Chih, he would probably have been driven out of the country. But tell me, where is he now?

TRANSLATORS' NOTES

a. Murderous fighting within the ruling Liu clan gave the local commander Hsiao Tao Cheng the chance to overthrow the Sung and set up his new Ch'i Dynasty in 479. Within fifteen years a collateral branch of the Hsiao clan had usurped the throne, leading to new strife and inner turmoil and giving an opportunity for a local commander to repeat the scenario. This man, Hsiao Yen, became Emperor Wu of the Liang Dynasty.

Yang Shan's What's Your Name?

POINTER

He overthrows the polar star and reverses the earthly axis; he captures tigers and rhinos, distinguishes dragons from snakes—one must be a lively acting fellow before he can match phrase for phrase, and correspond act to act. But since time immemorial, who could be this way? Please bring him up for me to see.

CASE

Yang Shan asked San Sheng, "What is your name?"[1]
  Sheng said, "Hui Chi."[2]
  Yang Shan said, "Hui Chi? That's me."[3]
  Sheng said, "My name is Hui Jan."[4]
  Yang Shan laughed aloud.[5]

NOTES

1. His name is about to be stolen. He brings in a thief, who ransacks his house.
2. (San Sheng) cut off (Yang Shan's) tongue; took his flag and stole his drum.
3. Each guards his own territory.
4. He steals in the noisy market place. That one and this one guard their own portion.
5. It can be said that this is the season; he spreads flowers on brocade.

COMMENTARY

San Sheng was a venerable adept in the Lin Chi succession. Since youth he possessed abilities that stood out from the crowd: he had great capacity and had great function; while still in the community, he was in full vigor, and his name was known everywhere.

Later he left Lin Chi and travelled throughout Huai Nan and Hai Chou[a]; the monasteries everywhere he went all treated him as a distinguished guest. He went from the north to the south; first he went to Hsueh Feng and asked, "What does a golden carp who has passed through the net take for food?" Feng said, "Wait till you've come out of the net; then I'll tell you." Sheng said, "The teacher of fifteen hundred people doesn't even know what to say." Feng said, "My tasks as abbot are many." As Hsueh Feng was going to the temple manor, on the way he encountered some macaques, whereupon he said, "Each of the macaques is wearing an ancient mirror." San Sheng said, "For aeons it has been nameless; why do you depict it as an ancient mirror?" Feng said, "A flaw has been created." Sheng said, "The teacher of fifteen hundred people does not even know what to say." Feng said, "My fault. My tasks as abbot are many."

Later he came to Yang Shan. Shan very much admired his outstanding acuity and seated him under the bright window.[b] One day an official came to call on Yang Shan. Shan asked him, "What is your official position?" He said, "I am a judge." Shan raised his whisk and said, "And can you judge this?" The official was speechless. All the people of the community made comments, but none accorded with Yang Shan's idea. At that time San Sheng was sick and staying in the Life-Prolonging Hall; Yang Shan ordered his attendant to take these words and ask him about them. Sheng said, "The Master has a problem." (Yang Shan) again ordered his attendant to ask, "What is the problem?" Sheng said, "A second offense is not permitted." Yang Shan deeply approved of this.

Pai Chang had formerly imparted his meditation brace and cushion to Huang Po, and had bequeathed his staff and whisk to Kuei Shan; Kuei Shan later gave them to Yang Shan. Since Yang Shan greatly approved of San Sheng, when one day Sheng took his leave and departed, Yang Shan took his staff and whisk to hand them over to San Sheng. Sheng said, "I already have a teacher." When Yang Shan inquired into his reason for saying this, it was that he was a true heir of Lin Chi.

When Yang Shan asked San Sheng, "What is your name?"

he could not have but known his name; why did he then go ahead and ask in this way? The reason is that an adept wants to test people to be able to know them thoroughly. He just seemed to be casually asking, "What is your name?", and spoke no further judgement or comparison. Why did San Sheng not say "Hui Jan," but instead said, "Hui Chi"? See how a man who has the eye is naturally not the same (as others). This manner of San Sheng's was still not crazy, though; he simply captured the flag and stole the drum. His meaning was beyond Yang Shan's words. These words do not fall within the scope of ordinary feelings; they are difficult to get a grasp on. The methods of such a fellow can bring people to life; that is why it is said, "He studies the living phrase—he does not study the dead phrase." If they followed ordinary feelings, then they couldn't set people at rest.

See how those men of old contemplated the Path like this: they exerted their spirits to the utmost, and only then were capable of great enlightenment. Once they were completely enlightened, when they used it, after all they appeared the same as people who were not yet enlightened. In any case, their one word or half a phrase could not fall into ordinary feelings.

San Sheng knew where Yang Shan was at, so he said to him, "My name is Hui Chi." Yang Shan wanted to take in San Sheng, but San Sheng conversely took in Yang Shan. Yang Shan was only able to make a counterattack and say, "I am Hui Chi." This is where he let go. San Sheng said. "My name is Hui Jan." This too is letting go. This is why Hsueh Tou later says, "Both gather in, both let go—which is fundamental?" With just one phrase he has completely versified it all at once.

Yang Shan laughed aloud. "Ha,ha!" There was both the provisional and the real, there was both illumination and function. Because he was crystal clear in every respect, therefore he functioned with complete freedom. This laugh was not the same as Yen T'ou's; in Yen T'ou's laugh there was poison, but in this laugh, for all eternity the pure wind blows chill.

VERSE

Both gather in, both let go—which is fundamental?
    I don't know how many of them there are. Crystal clear in every respect. I thought that there really was such a thing.

To ride a tiger always requires absolute competence.
If you don't have the eye on your forehead and a talisman under your elbow, how could you get here? Ride you may, but I only fear you won't be able to get down. If you are not such a man, how could you understand such a thing?

His laughter ended, I do not know where he's gone;
Even if you seek throughout the country for such a man, he would be hard to find. His words are still in our ears. For ever and ever there is the pure wind.

It is only fitting eternally to stir the wind of lament.
Right now where is he? Bah! Since it is great laughter, why (does it) stir a piteous wind? The whole earth is flooded with darkness.

COMMENTARY

"Both gather in, both let go—which is fundamental?" Letting go, alternately they act as guest and host. Yang Shan says, "What is your name?" San Sheng says, "My name is Hui Chi." This is both letting go. Yang Shan says, "I am Hui Chi." Sheng says, "I am Hui Jan." This is both gathering in. In reality, this is the action of interchange: when gathering up, everyone gathers up; when letting go, everyone lets go. Hsueh T'ou has all at once completely versified it. What he means to say is that if we don't let go and gather up, if we don't interchange, then you are you and I am I.

The whole thing is just four characters (Hui Chi, Hui Jan): why is there after all emergence and disappearance, spreading out and rolling up therein? An Ancient said, "If you stand, I then sit; if you sit, I then stand. If we both sit or both stand at the same time, we'll both be blind men." This is both gathering, both releasing, which can be considered the fundamental essential.

"To ride a tiger always requires absolute competence." When you have such a lofty manner, the highest essential of active potential, when you want to ride, you ride; when you want to dismount, you dismount. You can sit on the tiger's head and also hold the tiger's tail. San Sheng and Yang Shan both had this style.

"His laughter ended, I do not know where he's gone." Tell me, what did he laugh at? He was just like the pure wind blowing chill and severe. Why does (Hsueh Tou) after all say in the end, "It is only fitting eternally to stir the wind of lament"? This too is death without mourning; all at once he has finished adding explanations for you, but nevertheless no one in the world can bite in, and they do not know where (Yang Shan) is at. Even I do not know where he is at; do you people know?

TRANSLATORS' NOTES

a. Central eastern and southeastern China; there were many monasteries in these regions where Ch'an flourished in the late T'ang and Five Dynasties eras.

b. This means the first seat in the monks' hall, seat of the "chief monk," highest rank in the hall.

Nan Ch'uan's Circle

POINTER

There is no place to bite into: the Patriarchal Teacher's Mind Seal is formed like the works of the Iron Ox.ᵃ Having passed through the forest of thorns, a patchrobed monk is like a snowflake in a red hot furnace. As for piercing and penetrating on level ground, this I leave aside for the moment. Without falling into entangling ties, how will you act? To test, I cite this: look!

CASE

Nan Ch'uan, Kuei Tsung, and Ma Ku went together to pay respects to National Teacher Chung. When they got halfway there,¹ Nan Ch'uan drew a circle on the ground and said, "If you can speak, then let's go on."² Kuei Tsung sat down inside the circle;³ Ma Ku curtseyed.⁴ Nan Ch'uan said, "Then let's not go on."⁵
Kuei Tsung said, "What's going on in your mind?"⁶

NOTES

1. "Among three people travelling together, there must be a teacher of mine." What is so special? Still, they want to discern the truth.
2. He rouses waves where there is no wind. Still he wants people to know. He casts off a boat that's foundered on solid ground. Without posing a test, how could he discern the truth?
3. When one man strikes the cymbal, his companions join in.
4. When one man strikes the drum, all three prove able.
5. The one who can extricate himself halfway along is a good man. A good tune! An adept! An adept!

6. A lucky thing he understood him completely. At the time he should have given him a slap. Brash fellow!

COMMENTARY

At that time Ma Tsu's teaching was flourishing in Kiangsi, Shih T'ou's Way was current in Hu-Hsiang (Hunan), and National Teacher Chung's Way was influencing Ch'ang An. The latter had personally seen the Sixth Patriarch; at the time, of those in the South who held up their heads and wore horns, there was none who did not want to ascend his hall and enter his room; otherwise, they would be shamed by others.

These three old fellows wanted to go pay respects to National Teacher Chung; when they got half-way, they enacted this scenario of defeat. Nan Ch'uan said, "Then let's not go." Since they had each been able to speak, why did he instead say he wouldn't go? Tell me, what was the intention of that man of old? At that time, when he said, "Then let's not go," I would have slapped him right on the ear, to see what trick he would pull; what eternally upholds the all-embracing source is just this little bit of active essence. That is why Tz'u Ming said, "If you want to restrain him, just grab the rein and yank." Hit and he turns, like pushing down a gourd on the water. Many people say that (Nan Ch'uan's) words are words of disagreement, but they are far from knowing that in this matter, when you get to the ultimate point, it is necessary to leave the mud, get out of the water, draw out the wedges, and pull out the nails. If you make an intellectual interpretation, then you've missed it. The Ancients could turn and shift well; at this point they could not be otherwise—there must be killing and giving life: see how one of them sat inside the circle, and one curtseyed. That too was very good. Nan Ch'uan said, "Then let's not go." Kuei Tsung said, "What is going on in your mind?" Brash fellow! He too goes on like this. His whole idea was that he wanted to test Nan Ch'uan. Nan Ch'uan always said, "Call it thusness, and already it has changed." Nan Ch'uan, Kuei Tsung, and Ma Ku—after all they were people of one house. One holds, one releases; one kills, one enlivens: undeniably they are exceptional.

Hueh Tou's verse says:

VERSE

You Chi's arrow shoots the monkey:
>Who would dare to advance on the road facing
>him? Whenever he hits, he is marvelous; he hits the mark
>before he shoots.

Circling the tree, how exceedingly direct!
>Without attaining mastery, how could one presume to be
>thus? North, south, east, west—one family style. They
>have already been going around for a long time.

A thousand and ten thousand—
>Plentiful as hemp and millet. A pack of wild fox spirits.
>What about Nan Ch'uan?

Who has ever hit the mark?
>One or a half. Not even one. Even one would still be no
>use.

Calling them together, he beckons them, "Come, let's go
>   *back;"*
>They're a bunch of fellows playing with a lump of mud.
>This is not as good as having gone back; then they would
>have gotten somewhere.

He stops climbing on the road of Ts'ao Ch'i.
>Too much trouble. It seems to me that he is not a member
>of Ts'ao Ch'i's school. Level off the lowest of places, and
>there is too much; view the highest of places, and there is
>not enough.

(Hsueh Tou) also said, "The road of Ts'ao Ch'i is level and
>   *even; why stop climbing?"*
>Not only Nan Ch'uan extricates himself halfway along;
>Hsueh Tou also extricates himself halfway along. Even a
>good thing is not as good as nothing. Hsueh Tou too suf-
>fers from this kind of illness and pain.

COMMENTARY

"You Chi's arrow shoots the monkey; circling the tree, how
exceedingly direct!" You Chi was a man of Ch'u times; his
surname was Yang, his name was Shu and his nickname was

You Chi. Once when King Chuang of Ch'u went out hunting, he saw a white monkey and had someone shoot it. That monkey grabbed the arrow and played with it. The King ordered his entourage of courtiers to shoot it, but none could hit it. The King then asked his courtiers, and they said to him, "The man You Chi is a good shot." So he ordered him to shoot it. As You Chi drew his bow, the monkey immediately hugged the tree and howled piteously. When the arrow was shot, the monkey went around the tree to avoid it. The arrow also circled the tree, and struck and killed the monkey. This was a supernatural arrow. Why does Hsueh Tou say it was exceedingly direct? If it had been too direct, it wouldn't have hit; since it went around the tree, why instead does Hsueh Tou say it was exceedingly direct? Hsueh Tou borrows the idea and indeed uses it well. This even appears in the *Ch'un Ch'iu:*[b] some people say that "circling the tree" is the circle; if they really think so, they do not know the basic import of the words— they do not know where the directness is. These three old fellows are on different roads but return to the same place. They are uniformly and equally exceedingly direct. If you know where they're going, then you are free in all directions without leaving your heart. A hundred rivers flow separately but alike return to the great sea. That is why Nan Ch'uan said, "Then let's not go." If you look at this with the true eye of a patchrobed monk, this is just giving play to the spirit: but if you call it giving play to the spirit, then it is not giving play to the spirit. My late Master Wu Tsu said, "Those three men were absorbed in the Lamp of Wisdom, absorbed in the King of Adornment." Although (Ma Ku) curtseyed in this way, he never understood it as curtseying; although (Nan Ch'uan) made a circle, he never understood it as a circle. Without understanding in this way, then how will you understand? Hsueh Tou says, "A thousand and ten thousand—who has ever hit the mark?" How many could there be who hit the mark a hundred times out of a hundred?

"Calling them together, he beckons them, 'Come, let us go back.'" This is versifying Nan Ch'uan's saying, "Then let's not go on." Nan Ch'uan did not go on from here, so it is said, "He stops climbing on the road of Ts'ao Ch'i." He destroys the forest of thorns. Hsueh Tou cannot hold still, and again says, "The road of Ts'ao Ch'i is level and even; why stop climbing?"

The road of Ts'ao Ch'i is dustless and trackless, openly exposed, naked and clean, level, even, and smooth: why, after all, stop climbing? Each of you should observe your own footsteps.

TRANSLATORS' NOTES

a.   See Translators' Note a, Case 38.
b.   The *Ch'un Ch'iu* is a classic book of historical annals of the state of Lu, said to have been composed by Confucius himself, covering the period 722–481 B.C., before the first unification of China. This eminent chronicle became a model for later histories.

Biographical Supplement

The order of the biographies is as follows:

LINEAGE OF MASTERS APPEARING IN VOLUME II

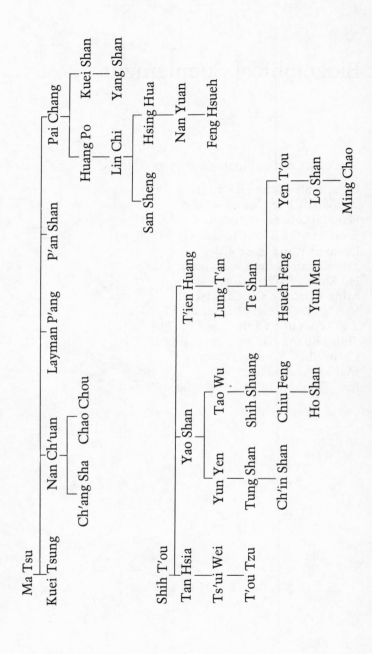

CHING TS'EN, 'Great Master Chao Hsien' of Ch'ang Sha in Hunan (n.d.)
CASE 36

(Known as Ch'ang Sha, he was a distinguished successor of Nan Ch'uan; the following is taken from *Ching Te Ch'uan Teng Lu* 10)

He first dwelt at the Deer Park, where he was the first generation; after that he dwelt in no fixed abode, but just went along with circumstances and expounded the Dharma as was appropriate to the occasion. At the time he was called 'The Teacher of Ch'ang Sha.'

> In the hall he said, If I were to thoroughly uphold the teaching of our sect, there would be weeds a fathom deep in the teaching hall; (but) I am unable to avoid facing all of you people and saying that the entire cosmos is the eye of a monk; the entire cosmos is the whole body of a monk; the entire cosmos is one's own light; the entire cosmos lies within one's own light; in the whole cosmos there is no one who is not oneself.
>
> I always tell you people that the Buddhas of the triple world, the cosmos, and the mass of living beings, are the light of great perfect wisdom. When the light has not yet shone forth, where can you people turn to become intimately acquainted with it? Before the light shines forth, there isn't even any news of Buddhas or sentient beings; where do we get the mountains, rivers, and earth?

At that time a monk asked, "What is the monk's eye?"

The master said, "Never, ever can one depart from it; (those who) attain Buddhahood and become patriarchs cannot depart from it; the six paths of transmigration cannot depart from it."

The monk said, "What is it that they cannot depart from?"

The master said, "In daytime, seeing the sun; at night, seeing stars."

The monk said, "I don't understand."

The master said, "Marvelous towering mountains, their color blue upon blue."

A monk asked, "Who is the teacher of all Buddhas?"

The master said, "By whom has he been concealed ever since beginningless aeons?"

A monk asked, "How is it when the student does not depend on the ground?"

The master said, "Where will you rest your body and live?"

He asked, "Then how is it when he does depend on the ground?"

The master said, "Drag this corpse away!"

He asked, "What are 'different kinds'?"

The master said, "A foot is short, an inch is long."

The master sent a monk to ask Teacher Hui, a former fellow student, "How is it after the teacher had seen Nan Ch'uan?" Hui was silent. The monk said, "How about before the teacher had seen Nan Ch'uan?" Hui said, "There could not be another besides." The monk returned and quoted this to the master. The master spoke a verse, saying,

> The unmoving man atop the hundred-foot pole:
> Though he has gained entry, he is not yet real.
> Atop the hundred-foot pole, he should step
>   forward—
> The whole universe in the ten directions is his
>   whole body.

The monk then asked, "Atop the hundred-foot pole, how to advance?" The master said, "Mountains of Liang, rivers of Li." The monk said, "I don't understand." The master said, "The whole country is under the imperial sway."

(Many more sayings are attributed to Ch'ang Sha; he had two enlightened successors.)

PAO CHI of P'an Shan in Yu Chou (n.d.)
CASE 37

(P'an Shan was a successor of Ma Tsu; his abode was in northern China, near modern-day North Korea. He was one of the few early Ch'an masters to teach in this region. Of his two successors, P'u Hua is the only one about whom anything is known; P'u Hua later assisted the great Lin Chi in his teaching. The story of P'an Shan's enlightenment is given in *Wu Teng Hui Yuan* 3)

As the master was walking through a market place, he saw a customer who was buying some pork say to the butcher, "Cut me a pound of the fine stuff." The butcher put down his cleaver, folded his hands and said, "Inspector, which isn't fine?" At this, the master had insight.

Again one day when he had gone out of the monastery, he saw people in mourning, singing and ringing bells: "The red disc inevitably sinks into the west; we don't know where the ghost will go." Inside an enclosure, a filial son was crying, "Alas! Alas!" The master's body and mind leaped; he returned and told Ma Tsu about it. Ma Tsu gave him his seal of approval.

(The saying which forms case 37 is taken from a longer sermon of P'an Shan, other parts of which are repeatedly quoted in Yuan Wu's commentaries throughout the text. The following version is from *Ching Te Ch'uan Teng Lu* 7; given in parentheses are significant variants from the version given in *Tsu T'ang Chi* 15:)

If there is no concern in the mind, myriad forms are unborn. When the mind is devoid of subtle activity, where can a trace of dust remain? The Way fundamentally has no substance; because of speaking, a name is established. The Way fundamentally has no name; because of naming, an epithet is found. If you say the very mind itself is identical to Buddha, still people these days have not yet entered the profound subtlety; if you say it is not mind, not Buddha, this is still the ultimate example of pointing to the traces. The one road going upwards, the thousand sages did not transmit; students toil over forms like monkeys grasping at reflections. The Great Way has no middle; who then goes forward or back? The eternal void is without bound; how could it be measured? Since the void is like this, how could the Way be spoken of? The mind-moon solitary and full, its light engulfs myriad forms: the light is not shining on objects, and the objects also do not remain; when light and objects are both gone, then what thing is this? Ch'an worthies, it is like hurling a sword into the sky; do not speak of reaching or not reaching: then the wheel of the void is without a trace, the sword's blade is without a flaw. If you can be like this, mind and mental conditions are without knowledge. The whole mind is identical to Buddha; the whole Buddha is identical to man. When mind and Buddha are not different, then this is the Way. Ch'an worthies should study the middle path: like the earth supporting a mountain, unaware of the mountain's steep height; like a stone containing a gem, without knowing the gem is flawless. If you can be like this, this is called Leaving Home. Thus the Guide said, "Things fundamentally do not hinder each other; the three times are also the same." A nondoing, unconcerned man still has the problem of the golden chains; therefore an Ancient said, "The spiritual source shines alone; the Path is fundamentally birthless." Great wisdom is not clarity; the true void is trackless. In true thusness, "ordinary" and "holy" are all dream talk; "Buddha" and "Nirvana" are both excess words. Ch'an worthies, you must see for yourselves; no one can substitute for you. There is nothing in the triple world; where can mind be found? The four elements are originally void; how can a Buddha abide? The turning potential doesn't move (The oracle doesn't move); it is silent and rootless (it is silent and speechless). Once it is presented right to your face, there is nothing else. Farewell.

YEN CHAO of Feng Hsueh (896—973)
CASES 38, 61

Feng Hsueh originally studied Confucianism; he sat for the civil service examination once, but failed. After that, he abandoned home to become a Buddhist. First he studied the 'stopping and observing' methods of T'ien T'ai Buddhist meditation; he then turned to Ch'an. He finally succeeded to Nan Yuan Hui Yung, a third generation Lin Chi master. He first taught at Feng Hsueh in Ju Chou (in Honan), at the request of the community there. He spent a summer in the Yamen at Ying Chou because the local army had revolted and the area was in danger. Later he was requested to return to Ju Chou, where he spent the last twenty-two years of his life teaching a congregation of over a hundred students.

Hsing Nien of Shou Shan, who was a latecomer to Feng Hsueh's community, served as the receiver of guests there: according to the *Wu Teng Hui Yuan* 11, one day as he was standing by, Hsueh wept and said to him, "Unfortunately, the way of Lin Chi, having reached me, is about to fall to the ground." Hsing Nien said, "As you look upon this whole community, is there no one at all?" Hsueh said, "There are many who are intelligent, but few who perceive nature." Nien said, "What about me?" Hsueh said, "Though I've had hopes for you for a long time, I still fear you are addicted to this sutra and can't let it go." (Hsing Nien constantly recited the Lotus Sutra to himself.) Nien said, "This too should be served: but I beg to hear its essence." Hsueh then went into the hall and cited the World Honored One's looking over the great crowd with his blue lotus eyes, then said, "Tell me, at that time, what did he say? If you say he spoke without speaking, this is still burying that former sage. Tell me, what did he say?" Nien then shook out his sleeves and left.

Hsueh threw down his staff and returned to the abbot's room; his attendant followed him and asked for further instruction, saying, "Why did Nien not answer you, master?" Hsueh said, "Nien understands."

The next day as Hsing Nien went along with gardener Chen to inquire (into the master's health), Hsueh asked Chen, "What is the World Honored One's unspoken speech?" Chen said, "A dove calling in a tree." Hsueh said, "Why do you make so much abundance of folly? Why don't you thoroughly investigate the spoken phrases?" He also asked Hsing Nien about it; Nien said, "Activity upholds the ancient road, without falling into passivity." Feng said to Chen, "Why don't you observe Nien's comment?"

After Hsing Nien had received Feng Hsueh's seal of approval, he obliterated his tracks and concealed his light.

(Shou Shan Hsing Nien (925-992) later appeared to teach, as the first patriarch of Shou Shan; this was in the beginning of the Sung dynasty, when the country was more stable. Shou Shan had sixteen successors, among whom was Fen Yang Shan Chao (947-1024), said to be an originator of poetic commentary to ancient *kung an*. Fen Yang is said to have seen seventy-one teachers, and attempted to synthesize the various illustrative schemes of the Ch'an schools; the Lin Chi branch of Ch'an flourished greatly with his successors and descendants, becoming the dominant school of Buddhism in China.)

TA T'UNG of Mt. T'ou Tzu (845—914)
CASES 41, 79, 80, 91

(The following is taken from the *Ching Te Ch'uan Teng Lu* 15)

He was a man from Huai Ning in Shu Chou (in Anhui); his surname was Liu. He left home at an early age . . . . He first practiced breath-contemplation; next he investigated the Hua Yen teachings and discovered the ocean of nature. He visited the Dharma assembly on Mt. Ts'ui Wei and was suddenly awakened to Ts'ui Wei's source meaning. (This is told in the *Ch'uan Teng Lu* 14:)

T'ou Tzu asked Ts'ui Wei, "I wonder, when the Second Patriarch first saw Bodhidharma, what was really attained?" Ts'ui Wei said, "What is attained right now when you see me?" One day as Ts'ui Wei was walking inside the Dharma Hall, T'ou Tzu approached him, bowed, and asked, "Teacher, how do you show people the secret message of the coming from the West?" Ts'ui Wei stopped for a moment. T'ou Tzu again said, "Please, Teacher, instruct me." Ts'ui Wei said, "Do you want a second ladleful of foul water besides?" T'ou Tzu bowed in thanks and withdrew.

(After this) T'ou Tzu wandered all over as he pleased, returning to frequent his native territory. He concealed himself on Mt. T'ou Tzu (which is in Shu Chou), built a grass hut, and lived there.

(The following story leads up to the dialogue between Chao Chou and T'ou Tzu that makes the Main Case 41:) One day Master Shen of Chao Chou came to (a nearby district); T'ou Tzu too had come down from the mountain that day. They encountered each other on the road without recognizing each other. Chao Chou privately asked a lay gentleman and found out it was T'ou Tzu. Then he turned back (to go after him). He asked, "Aren't you the master of Mt. T'ou Tzu?" T'ou Tzu said, "I beg you for a coin for the tea and salt tax." Chao Chou then went up onto Mt. T'ou Tzu first and sat there in his hut, (waiting for T'ou Tzu to return.) Later T'ou Tzu returned to his hermitage, bringing along a jar of oil. Chao Chou said, "I've long heard of T'ou Tzu, but now that I've come here I just see an old man selling oil." T'ou Tzu said, "You just see an old man selling oil, but you don't know T'ou Tzu." Chao Chou

said, "What is T'ou Tzu?" T'ou Tzu said, "Oily oil." Chao
Chou said, "How is it when gaining life amidst death?" T'ou
Tzu said, "One must not go by night; one must get there by
daylight." Chao Chou said, "I'm a swindler, yet you swindled
me."

Henceforward T'ou Tzu's Path was heard of all over the
country, and "cloud and rain" folk (traveling Ch'an students)
flocked to him. The master told the assembly, "All of you have
come here trying to find fresh new sayings and beautiful verses.
I am an old man whose strength has dwindled, my way of
talking is slow and blunt. If you question me, I'll follow you
and give my reply. I have no hidden marvels that can be conveyed to you. . . .Here there is nothing that can be given to you,
there is no outside or inside that can be related to you. Do all of
you realize this?" . . .The master lived on Mt. T'ou Tzu for
over thirty years. He dealt with and aroused those who came
seeking instruction who constantly filled his room.

The Huang Chao revolt broke out in 881 and there was
chaos throughout the country. A madman came up the mountain carrying a blade; he asked T'ou Tzu what he was living
there for, so the master expounded the Dharma in accordance
with the situation to the man. When he heard this, the man
bowed and submitted; then he stripped off his clothes and gave
them to T'ou Tzu and went away.

In 914 the master showed a slight illness: the congregation
wanted to call a doctor, but the master told them, "The activity of the four elements is a continual process of assembly and
dissolution. Don't you worry: I'll preserve myself." When he
finished talking, he sat cross-legged and died.

LAYMAN P'ANG (8–9 cent.)
CASE 42

(Layman P'ang succeeded to both Shih T'ou and Ma Tsu, the
foremost teachers of the eighth century. He had been a minor
civil official, but later he took all his wealth and sank it in a
river. His family of a wife, son, and daughter split up, and he
went from place to place with his daughter, weaving bamboo
baskets and selling them to make a living. In his travels he

visited many of the Ch'an masters who had succeeded to Ma Tsu. The following account is excerpted from *Ching Te Ch'uan Teng Lu* 8)

His name was Tao Hsuan: in the world, Confucianism was his business; yet the layman somewhat understood the toil of passion, and aspired to seek the real truth. In the latter 780's he visited Master Shih T'ou; he forgot the words and comprehended the inner meaning. He also was a friend of Ch'an Master Tan Hsia (a successor of Shih T'ou).

One day Shih T'ou asked him, "Since you've seen me, how are your daily affairs?" He responded, "If you ask about my daily affairs, I have no way to open my mouth." He also presented a verse which said,

> In my daily affairs there's nothing different;
> Only I myself am in harmony.
> Nothing do I grasp or reject,
> Nowhere do I insist or turn away.
> Who regards crimson and purple as honorable?
> The hills and mountains are void of any dust.
> Supernatural powers and their marvelous function—
> Fetching water and carrying firewood.

Shih T'ou approved of this; he said, "Will you be a monk or a layman?" The layman said, "I want to follow my wish," and after all did not shave his head or wear the dark (garment of a monk).

Later he went to Kiangsi and asked Ma Tsu, "Who is he who is not the companion of myriad things?" Tsu said, "When you swallow all the water of the West River in one gulp, then I'll tell you." At these words the layman suddenly apprehended the abstruse essence; subsequently he stayed to learn for two years. He had a verse which said,

> I have a son who does not marry
> And a daughter who does not wed:
> The whole family gathered 'round,
> Together we speak birthless talk.

Henceforth his eloquence was swift; he was heard of everywhere. . . . He had three hundred and more poems which circulated in the world.

LIANG CHIEH of Tung Shan (806—869)
CASE 43

(The following account is taken from *Wu Teng Hui Yuan* 13)

In youth he followed a teacher and recited the Perfection of Wisdom Heart Sutra; coming to where it says, 'There is no eye, ear, nose, tongue, body, or mind,' he suddenly felt his face and asked the teacher, "I have eyes, ears, nose, tongue, and so forth; why does the sutra say there are none?" The teacher was surprised at this and said, "I am not your teacher." Then he directed him to go to Mt. Wu Hsieh (in Chekiang) to pay obeisance to Ch'an master (Ling) Mo (746–818; reckoned as one of Ma Tsu's successors, he was actually enlightened under Shih T'ou and was his attendant for twenty years), by whom he had his head shaved. At twenty-one he went to Sung Shan and received the precepts in full.

Travelling around, he first called on Nan Ch'uan; as it happened, it was the anniversary of Ma Tsu's death, so they were preparing a ceremonial feast. Ch'uan asked the community, "Tomorrow we will set out a feast for Ma Tsu; do you think Ma Tsu will come, or not?" No one replied; the master (Tung Shan) came forth and answered, "If he has a companion, he'll come." Ch'uan said, "Though this lad is young, he is quite suitable for carving and polishing." The master said, "Teacher, don't oppress a freeman (Liang, Tung Shan's personal name) and make him a slave." (The *Tsu T'ang Chi* says that after this he began to be known as an adept.)

Next he called on Kuei Shan and asked, "I recently have heard that the National Teacher Chung of Nan Yang had a saying about inanimate objects expounding the Dharma, but I have not thoroughly comprehended its subtlety." Kuei Shan said, "Do you not remember it?" The master said, "I remember." Kuei Shan said, "Try to recite it for me." The master then recited, "A monk asked, 'What is the mind of an ancient Buddha?' The National Teacher said, 'Walls, tiles, and pebbles.' The monk said, 'Aren't walls, tiles, and pebbles inanimate?' The National Teacher said, 'That's right.' The monk said, 'And can they expound the Dharma, or not?' The National Teacher said, 'They are always expounding it clearly, without interruption.' The monk said, 'Why don't I hear it?' The National Teacher said, 'You yourself don't hear it, but you shouldn't hinder the one who does hear it.' The monk said, 'Who can hear it?' The National Teacher said, 'All the saints can hear it.' The monk said, 'Can you hear it too, Master?' The National Teacher said, 'I don't hear it.' The monk said, 'Since you don't hear it, how do you know that inanimate objects can expound the Dharma?' The National Teacher said, 'It's lucky I don't hear it; if I heard it, then I'd be equal to the saints and you wouldn't hear me expound the Dharma.' The monk said, 'Then sentient beings have no part in it.' The National Teacher said, 'I explain for sentient beings, not for the saints.' The monk said, 'How are sentient beings after they have heard it?' The National Teacher said, 'Then they are not sentient beings.' The monk said, 'What scripture is the "inanimate expounding the Dharma"based on?' The National Teacher said, 'Obviously if the words do not accord with the classics, it is not the talk of a gentleman: you have not read how the Avatamsaka Sutra says, "Lands expound it, sentient beings expound it, everything in the three times expounds it"?'"

When the master had finished reciting, Kuei Shan said, "I too have something here, but a suitable man is hard to come across." The master said, "I'm still not clear; please point it out to me." Kuei Shan raised his whisk and said, "Do you understand?" The master said, "I don't understand. Please explain." Kuei Shan said, "The mouth born of my father and mother will never explain it to you." The master said, "Is there another who sought the Way in the same time as you?" Kuei Shan said, "From here go to Yu district in Li Leng, to where there is a row of stone grottoes; there is a man of the Way there, Yun Yen; if you can pull out the weeds to find his way, he will be of value to you." The master said, "How is this man?" Kuei Shan said, "He once asked me, 'When I want to serve you, how can I do so?' I told him, 'You must just absolutely cut off all leakage before you can.' He said, 'And would I be able to not go against your teaching or not?' I said, 'Above all, don't say that I'm here.'"

The master took leave of Kuei Shan and went right to Yun Yen; having quoted the preceding incident, he asked, "Who can hear inanimate objects expounding the Dharma?" Yun Yen said, "The inanimate can hear it." The master said, "Can you hear it, teacher?" Yun Yen said, "If I heard, you would not hear my expounding of the Dharma." The master said, "Why wouldn't I hear?" Yen raised his whisk and said, "Do you hear?" The master said, "No." Yen said, "You do not even hear my expounding of the Dharma; how could you hear the inanimate expounding the Dharma?" The master said, "What scripture contains the inanimate expounding the Dharma?" Yen said, "Haven't you read how the Amitabha Sutra says, 'Rivers, birds, trees, and forests all commemorate Buddha and Dharma.'" At this the master had insight; thereupon he uttered a verse:

> *How wonderful! How wonderful!*
> *The inanimate expounding of Dharma is inconceiv-*
> *   able;*
> *If you use your ears to listen, you'll never under-*
> *   stand—*
> *Only when you hear in your eyes will you know.*

The master asked Yun Yen, "I have leftover habits which are not yet exhausted." Yun Yen said, "What have you ever done?" The master said, "I have not even practiced the holy truths." Yen said, "And do you rejoice, or not?" The master said, "I am not without joy; it is like finding a bright jewel in a dungheap."

When he was about to go, he asked Yun Yen, "After your death, if someone should suddenly ask me if I can depict your true likeness, how shall I answer?" Yen remained silent for a good while, then said, "Just this is it." The master was sunk in contemplation; Yen said, "Reverend Chieh, now that you have taken up this matter, you must be very careful and thoroughgoing."

The master still had some doubt; later, as he was crossing a river, he saw his reflection and was greatly awakened to the inner meaning of what had happened before. He made a verse which said,

> *Just avoid seeking from others,*
> *Or you will be far estranged from yourself.*
> *I now go on alone; I meet Him everywhere—*
> *He is now just I, but I now am not He:*
> *One must understand in this way*
> *In order to unite with thusness.*

From the end of the Ta Chung era (847–859) of T'ang, the master received and guided students at Hsin Feng Mountain; after this, he caused the teaching to flourish at Tung Mountain (Tung Shan) in Kao An in Yu Chiang (in Kiangsi). He provisionally opened up the five ranks, and skillfully handled the three potentials (high, middling, low); he greatly opened up the One Sound, and widely spread it through the myriad classes. He drew his precious sword sideways and cut off the forest of various views: his wondrous harmony spread widely, cutting off myriad rationalizations.

He also found Ts'ao Shan, who was deeply enlightened into the real essence, and wonderfully extolled the felicitous way, the harmony of the ways of lord and vassal, biased and true interdepending. Because of this the mystic breeze of the Tung succession spread throughout the land. Therefore, the masters of Ch'an everywhere all esteemed it and called it the Ts'ao-Tung Sect.

(Tung Shan had twenty-six successors; among them, Tao Ying of Yun Chu (d. 903) was one of the greatest masters of the time, who led a community of fifteen hundred people and produced twenty-eight enlightened disciples. Su Shan K'uang Jen (n.d.) was another distinguished successor to Tung Shan, with twenty enlightened disciples. The most enduring line of the Tung succession was that which came down through Yun Chu; he and Hsueh Feng, who is said to have called on Tung Shan nine times, were the foremost masters of their age in southeastern and southern China. The Ts'ao Tung sect trickled down in China until the seventeenth century; it was transmitted to Japan in the thirteenth century, over three hundred years after the founders, and still continues there in a modified form until present times.)

WU YIN of Ho Shan (—960)
CASE 44

(The following is from the *Ching Te Ch'uan Teng Lu* 17)

The master was a man from Fu Chou; his surname was Wu. At age seven he left home under the Great Master Hsueh Feng; when he came of age he was ordained.

The master travelled around till he come to Chün Yang and visited Chiu Feng. Feng permitted the master to enter his private room. One day Feng said to him, "You have come from far, far away to join the assembly. Have you seen any realm that can be cultivated? What shortcut can you get out by?" The master replied, "In the dark empty clearing, the blind are blind of themselves." At first Chiu Feng didn't approve: because of this the master discovered his intent and suddenly forgot his knowledge and views.

Previously the master had received an invitation to stay at Great Wisdom Temple on Ho Shan in Chi Chou (in Kiangsi). There students flocked around him. The master imparted ten booklets of admonitions which were received joyously all over. All said that Ho Shan was a suitable standard for the communities of monks.

Around this time the Li Clan (in power) south of the (Yangtse) River summoned the master. He was asked, "Where have you come from, Teacher?" The master said, "From Ho Shan." "Where is the mountain?" The master said, "The man has come for an audience at the Imperial Palace, but the mountain has never moved." The Lord esteemed him and ordered him to dwell at Lucky Light Temple in Yang Chou. The master requested (to be allowed) to go back into the mountains.

In 960 the master showed a slight illness. He ordered his attendants to open up the abbot's quarters and assemble everyone there. He bade them farewell saying, "Hereafter students won't know Ho Shan: better get acquainted right now. Take care of yourselves!"

MING CHAO TE CHIEN (n.d.)
CASE 48

(The following account is from *Ching Te Ch'uan Teng Lu* 23)

He received the seal and testimonial of Lo Shan (a successor of Yen T'ou). He did not linger in one corner (but) powerfully extolled the mystic teaching. All the elders were in awe of his genius; there were rarely any latecoming students who dared to confront his 'swordpoint.'

When the master was in the great hall of Chao Ch'ing in Ch'uan Chou (in Fukien), he pointed to a wall painting and asked a monk, "What spirit is that?" (The monk) said, "The good spirit who guards the Dharma." The master said, "Where did it go at the time of the persecution?" The monk had no reply.

The master then had the monk go ask attendant Yen. Yen said, "In what aeon did you meet with this calamity?" The monk returned and quoted this to the master; the master said, "Even if attendant Yen later on gathers a following of a thousand people, what would be the use?" The monk then bowed and asked the master for an alternate saying; the master said, "Where did it go?"

Elder Ch'ing brought up the story of Yang Shan sticking the hoe in the ground and asked the master, "Was the Ancient's meaning where he folded his hands, or is the meaning where he stuck the hoe in the ground?" The master said, "Elder Ch'ing!" Ch'ing responded; the master said, "Have you ever seen Yang Shan even in a dream?" Ch'ing said, "I don't want a comment; I just want you to discuss it." The master said, "If you want discussion, there are fifteen hundred old teachers in the hall."

The master came to Shuang Yen; the elder of Shuang Yen observed the master's appearance, then said, "I will pose a question to ask you; if you can speak, then I will abandon this temple; if you cannot speak, then I won't abandon it. The Diamond Sutra says, 'All Buddhas and all the Buddhas' teachings come forth from this sutra.' Tell me, who expounds this sutra?" The master said, "Putting 'expounding' and 'not ex-pounding' aside for the moment, just what do you call 'this sutra'?" Shuang Yen had no reply. The master cited the sutra, saying, "All wise ones and sages rely on the uncontrived way, yet there are distinctions; this is because the uncontrived way is the ultimate law—on what basis are there distinctions? But are distinctions faults or not? If they're faults, all wise ones and sages have faults; if they're not faults, just what is to be called 'distinctions'?" Shuang Yen again had nothing to say. The master said, "What Hsueh Feng said."

When the master was in Chih Che temple in Wu Chou (in Chekiang), he sat in the first seat (as a 'head monk'). He never would take clean water. The monk who was superintendent of affairs asked him, "Why are you not conscious of defilement, that you won't take clean water?" The master got down from the platform, picked up the pure water pitcher, and said, "This is pure." The superintendent said nothing; the master then broke the water pitcher. Henceforth the master's repute in the Way spread afar.

The congregation on Mt. Ming Chou (also in Wu Chou, Chekiang) asked him to abide there and open up the teaching. Ch'an folk from all quarters filled the halls and rooms.

Someone asked, "Who can face the smokeless fire?"

The master said, "One who isn't anxious for his eyebrows."

He asked, "Can you face it, Master?"

The master said, "Tell me, how many eyebrow hairs do I have left?"

A certain monk who had been in the master's audience took his leave and went to live in a hut for a year. Later he came back and paid obeisance; he said, "A man of old said 'If you haven't met for three days, do not look upon someone as before.'" The master then exposed his chest and said, "Tell me, how many hairs do I have on my chest?" The monk had no reply. The master then asked, "When did you leave your hut?" He said, "This morning." The master said, "When you came, to whom did you give your broken-legged pot?" The monk again had nothing to say. The master then shouted him out.

(The master dwelt on Ming Chao for forty years, and 'his words were circulated everywhere.' He had five enlightened successors.)

CH'UAN HUO of Yen T'ou (827—887)
CASES 51, 66

(Yen T'ou was a successor of Te Shan and "brother" of Hsueh Feng: see Cases 5, 21, and 51. The following account is from the *Ching Te Ch'uan Teng Lu* 16)

The master was a man of Ch'uan Chou (in Hopei); his surname was K'o. In his youth he paid homage to Master Yi of (the district town) Ch'ing Yuan and had his head shaved. He went to Pao Shou Temple in (the capital) Ch'ang An and was ordained. He studied all the sections of the Sutras and Vinaya Texts.

Yen T'ou made the rounds of the Ch'an monasteries with Hsueh Feng I Ts'un and Ch'in Shan Wen Sui as his companions. From Mt. Ta Tz'u in Yü Hang he made his way to Lin Chi, but it was just after Lin Chi himself had died. Then he visited Yang Shan. As soon as he entered the gate, Yen T'ou picked up his sitting mat and said, "Teacher!" Yang Shan took his whisk and made as if to hold it up. T'ou said, "An undeniable expert."

Later Yen T'ou called on Te Shan: holding his sitting mat, he went into the Dharma Hall and looked up (at Te Shan). Te Shan said, "Well?" T'ou snorted at him. Shan said, "Where was my fault?" T'ou said, "A doubled case," then left the hall. Shan said, "This master looks a little like a foot-travelling man." The next day when Yen T'ou went up to inquire after him, Te Shan said, "Didn't you just arrive here yesterday, Reverend?" T'ou said, "That's right." Shan said, "Where did you learn this empty-headedness?" T'ou said, "I never deceive myself." Shan said, "After this you shouldn't turn your back on me." Another time Yen T'ou went to visit Te Shan: entering the abbot's quarters, T'ou contorted his body and asked, "Ordinary or sage?" Te Shan shouted, and Yen T'ou bowed in homage. (Further incidents involving Yen T'ou, Hsueh Feng and Te Shan are contained in the Commentary to Case 51.)

Yen T'ou said, "The intent of my teaching is like a poison-smeared drum: one beat and all who hear it, near and far, perish."

Later whenever anyone asked about Buddha, asked about Dharma, asked about Tao, or asked about Ch'an, Yen T'ou would always sigh.

During the 880's the central plain (i.e., the area around the capital, the heart of the realm) was infested with plundering armies: the master's congregation all fled the area. Yen T'ou himself (remained) sitting solemn and calm. One day bandits came in force. Accusing the master of not offering them any gifts, they slashed him with their blades. His countenance calm and collected, the master gave a loud shout, then died. The sound could be heard for several dozen miles.

YUAN CHIH of Tao Wu Shan (768—835)
CASES 55, 89

(The following is from the Ching Te Ch'uan Teng Lu 14)
He was originally from Hai Hun in Yü Chang (modern Nan Ch'ang); his surname was Chang. At an early age he received

instruction from Master Nie'h-p'an and was ordained. He joined Yao Shan's Dharma assembly and gained intimate accord with the Mind Seal. One day Yao Shan asked him, "Where are you coming from?" Tao Wu said, "From wandering in the mountains." Yao Shan said, "Speak quickly without leaving from this room." Tao Wu said, "The ravens on the mountain are white as snow; the fish swimming in the pond are hurrying ceaselessly."

Tao Wu and Yun Yen were attending Yao Shan. Yao Shan said, "Better not speak where your wisdom doesn't reach. If you do, then horns sprout on your head. What about it, Ascetic Chih?" Tao Wu immediately left. Yun Yen asked Yao Shan, "Why did Elder Brother Chih not answer you, Teacher?" Yao Shan said, "I have a back ache today—(despite his leaving,) he does understand: go ask him." Yun Yen immediately went and asked Tao Wu, "Why didn't you reply to our Teacher, Elder Brother?" Tao Wu said, "Go back and ask our Teacher."

When Yun Yen was about to die, he sent someone to deliver his farewell letter to Tao Wu. Tao Wu opened it, glanced through it and said, "Yun Yen knows no shame: I shouldn't have spoken to him that time. Nevertheless, in essence he was a (faithful) 'son' who didn't go against Yao Shan."

Yun Yen asked, "What is your family style, Elder Brother?" Tao Wu said, "What would be the use of having you point it out?"

(Ho was asked,) "What is the place to apply effort in these times?" Tao Wu said, "If a thousand people call you, and you don't turn your head, only then will you have some small portion (of attainment.)"

He was asked, "What is your family style, Teacher?" Tao Wu got down from the meditation seat and curtseyed saying, "Thanks for coming from so far away."

In 835 Tao Wu showed sickness: he was in pain. The monks of his congregation came to offer condolences and inquire about his health. Tao Wu said, "There is an experience which is not repaid: do you realize that?" The congregation were all sorrowful. When he was about to go, Tao Wu said to them. "I am crossing over to the west, but Principle has no eastward movement." As he finished speaking, he showed the stillness of death.

CH'ING CHU of Shih Shuang Shan (807—889)

CASES 55, 91

(The following is taken from the *Ching Te Ch'uan Teng Lu* 15)

He was originally from Hsin Kan in Lu Ling (in Kiangsi); his surname was Ch'en. At age thirteen he had his head shaved by Ch'an Master Shao Luan; at twenty-three he was fully ordained on (the holy mountain) Sung Yueh.

The master came to the Dharma assembly on Mt. Kuei: there he served as the rice steward. One day he was in the rice room sieving rice, when Kuei Shan said to him, "You shouldn't throw away what the donor gave us." Shih Shuang said, "I'm not throwing anything away." Kuei Shan picked up a grain of rice off the floor and said, "You said you didn't throw anything away: where did this come from?" Shih Shuang had no reply. Kuei Shan also said, "Don't slight this one grain of rice: a hundred thousand grains are born from this one grain." Shih Shuang said, "A hundred thousand grains arise from this one grain, but where does this one grain come from?" Kuei Shan laughed loudly and returned to his abbot's quarters. That night he went up to the hall and said, "(Attention) everybody! There's a worm in the rice."

Later Shih Shuang studied with Tao Wu. He asked, "What is enlightenment right before the eyes?" Tao Wu called to a novice, and the novice responded. Wu said, "Fill the water pitcher." Wu then asked Shih Shuang, "What did you just ask?" Shuang then repeated his question. Wu immediately got up and left. From this Shuang had an awakening. Tao Wu said, "I'm sick: I am about to leave the world. I have something on my mind that has been bothering me for a long time—who can clear it up?" Shuang said, "Mind and things are both wrong; trying to clear them away increases the affliction." Tao Wu said, "How sage!"

In order to shun the world, the master mixed with lay people in the Liu Yang Pottery works in Ch'ang Sha. In the mornings he wandered, in the evenings he rested. No one could become acquainted with him. Later, because Tung Shan Liang Chieh sent a monk to search him out, his talents began to be revealed, and he was chosen to reside on Shih Shuang Shan ("Stone Frost Mountain.") Later when Tao Wu was about to abandon his congregation and die, he considered Shih Shuang his true successor, and personally went to Shih Shuang to be near him. Shih Shuang served him scrupulously, with all the etiquette due a teacher. After a while Tao Wu died, and disciples flocked to Shih Shuang, forming a congregation of five hundred.

A monk asked, "What is the meaning of the coming from the West?" The master said, "A piece of rock in empty space." When the monk bowed, the master said, "Do you understand?" The monk said, "I don't understand." The master said, "Luckily you don't understand. If you did it would have smashed your head."

The master stayed at Shih Shuang for twenty years' time. His students always sat, they never lay down. All over the country they were known as the "dead tree congregation." The T'ang emperor Hsi Tsung heard of the fame of the master's Path and sent emissaries to bestow purple robes on him. The master steadfastly refused to accept them. In 889 he showed sickness and died at the age of eighty-two; he had been a monk for fifty-nine years.

WEN SUI of Ch'in Shan
CASE 56

(The following is from the *Ching Te Ch'uan Teng Lu* 17)

The master was originally from Fu Chou. While still young he was ordained by Ch'an Master Huan Chung at the Temple of Great Compassion in Hang Chou. At the time Yen T'ou and Hsueh Feng were in the congregation: when they saw Ch'in Shan express his opinions, they knew he was a vessel of the Dharma. They took him along with them as they went travelling. The affinities of these two worthies meshed with Te Shan: each received his seal; but though Ch'in Shan was aroused many times, in the end he was still frozen and stuck. One day he asked Te Shan, "T'ien Huang spoke this way; Lung T'an spoke this way; (Lung T'an was Te Shan's master; T'ien Huang was Lung T'an's) I wonder, how does Te Shan speak?" Te Shan said, "Try to cite what T'ien Huang and Lung T'an said." As Ch'in Shan was about to put forward some words, Te Shan herded him into the Nirvana Hall (i.e., the infirmary). Ch'in Shan said, "You may be right, but you beat me too much."

Later Ch'in Shan awoke at Tung Shan's words: hence he was Tung Shan's successor. At age twenty-seven he settled at Ch'in Shan. To his congregation he related that when he first visited Tung Shan, Tung Shan asked, "Where did you come here from?" The master said, "From Great Compassion." Tung Shan said, "And did you see the master of Great Compassion?" The master said, "I did." Tung Shan said, "Did you see him before form or after form?" The master said, "It was not seeing before or after." Tung Shan was silent, so the master then said, "Having left my master too soon, I didn't get to the bottom of his meaning."

A monk asked, "What is the meaning of the coming from the West?" Ch'in Shan said, "The Lord of Liang's (Emperor Wu's) T-square, Master Chih's cutting knife."

A monk asked, "What is your family style, Teacher?" The master said, "Brocade curtains and a silver incense box: when the wind blows, the whole road is filled with perfume." Another monk asked, "How do you teach people, Teacher?" The master said, "If I taught people, I'd be the same as you lot." The monk said, "I've come especially to visit you, Teacher: you should reveal the style of the sect." The master said, "If you came specially, I'll have to." The monk said, "Please do." The master then struck him. The monk was speechless. Ch'in Shan said, "You're guarding a stump, waiting for a rabbit,* falsely using your mental spirit."

---

*A man who happened to see a rabbit collide with a tree stump and drop down dead foolishly sticks by the stump, waiting for it to "catch" another rabbit.

MAHASATTVA FU (497-569)
CASE 67

Mahasattva Fu, also called Shan Hui, was a layman and a small farmer; in his middle twenties he retired to a mountain with his wife and two children, where he worked during the day and practiced the Way at night. In the course of time he gave up all of his possessions three times, sold his wife and children, and hired himself out as a laborer, spending the proceeds to feed the poor and hungry. Throughout his life he continued to work, assisted by his family (who, out of respect for the Mahasattva, were not actually enslaved by their purchasers) and disciples; he fasted and gave the food saved thereby to the needy. The time during which he lived was especially bitter for great masses of peasants, and Mahasattva Fu is exemplary for his continued generosity in almsgiving, not only of Dharma, but also of material goods. He went into the capital of Liang several times to preach, hoping to spread the Dharma more widely than was possible from his mountain abode. The following is a summary of three levels of goodness, to which Fu enjoined Emperor Wu of Liang in his first letter to the monarch:

> *The highest good has an empty heart as its basis,*
> *and non-attachment as its source; abolishment of*
> *formality is the cause, and nirvana is the result.*

> *The middling good has government of oneself as its*
> *basis, and government of the nation as its source;*
> *the fruits experienced by gods and humans will be*
> *peace and happiness.*

> *The least good is to protect and nourish living*
> *beings,*
> *to overcome cruelty and abolish murder, and to*
> *have all*
> *the farmers receive free food six times a month.*

Mahasattva Fu was thought to be a manifestation of Maitreya, the future Buddha.

CHIH CH'ANG of Kuei Tsung Temple
CASE 69

(The following is taken from the *Ching Te Ch'uan Teng Lu* 7)

The master went up into the Hall and said, "The ancient worthies of antiquity were not without knowledge. Those most high great men were not the same as the common sort. Right now, if you can't establish yourself independently, you're wasting your time. All of you: don't misuse your minds—there's no one to take your place, nor is there any way for you to use your minds. Don't go to others to seek. Since you've always just relied on others to understand, when they spoke you always got stuck. The fact that your light doesn't penetrate through is just because there are things before your eyes."

A monk asked, "What is the hidden meaning?" The master said, "There is no one who can understand." "What is turning towards it?" The master said, "If there is turning towards, this immediately goes against it." "What is not turning towards it?" The master said, "Who is looking for the hidden meaning?" He also said, "Go away! There's no place for you to use your mind." The monk said, "How is it you have no expedient means to enable this student to gain entry?" The master said, "The Sound-Seer's* wondrous wisdom-power can save you from the suffering of the world." "What is Kuanyin's wondrous wisdom—power?" asked the monk. The master knocked three times on the lid of the three-legged cauldron and said, "Do you hear that or not?" The monk said he did hear. The master said, "Why didn't I hear it?" The monk was speechless, so the master drove him out with blows of his staff.

Yun Yen came calling. The master made the motions of drawing a bow. Yun Yen, after a pause, made the gesture of drawing a sword. The master said, "Too late."

The master went up into the Hall and said, "Today I'm going to talk Ch'an: all of you come closer." Everyone approached, and the master said, "Listen to Kuanyin's conduct, responding well in all the various places." A monk asked, "What is Kuanyin's conduct?" The master then snapped his fingers and said, "Do all of you hear or not?" The monks said, "We hear." The master said, "What is this bunch of guys looking for here?" and drove them out with blows. Laughing loudly, he returned to his abbot's quarters.

* "Sound-Seer" is a translation of the name of Kuanyin, the bodhisattva of unlimited compassion, who "observes the sounds of the world."

Traditional Teaching Devices

THE THREE ROADS OF TUNG SHAN

(The following explanation is taken from Shigetsu Ein's *Funogo san ro, da, shi i rui,* a 'Non-talk on the three roads, (three) falls, and four different kinds' (1761). Shigetsu was a Soto Zen master, a Japanese descendant of Ts'ao-Tung Ch'an.)

For innumerable aeons, since there has been self, this stinking skinbag has been changed from time to time, transformed from place to place, in a thousand conditions, ten thousand forms; who can reach the realm of our fundamental quiescence?

If you get here, you must know this road. 'This road' means while dwelling in the present heap of sound and form, first getting rid of clinging to self, and attaining our former original state of selflessness. And furthermore, you must know that all things have no self. Once person and things are selfless, in your daily activities you walk in the void. This life basically has an undefiled practice and experience; thus would we practice and experience nondefilement. Today you must diligently walk in the void. Walking in the void is not some special art; each day when you go into the hall, you should not chew through a single grain of rice. Not chewing through a single grain of rice means that there is no breaking of the fast or violation of discipline by arousing mindfulness of tasting flavor. This is called traveling the bird's path.

Travel on the bird's path is trackless; when you don't leave your body in the realm of tracklessness, this is the turning point of an ascetic. After you have arrived here and settled here, there is still one road going beyond. This road is not in going or coming; it is what is called 'moss growing in the jade palace.' All the names of the Other Side are temporary names for this. In reality, it is the one road that cannot be touched upon. That is why we say 'hidden.' And 'hidden' is not a matter of giving a name as its meaning; the realm called the hidden road is the realm of no name or meaning. This is why it is said, 'He has no country; he does not abide, dwells in no home.'

To know this and yet be able to not remain here, to be an example for beings, to inspire and lead them, unify and teach them, is called 'extending the hands.' In extending the hands, there is no separate road; it does not transgress the bird's path. Traveling the bird's path by yourself, yet you extend your hands. In the bird's path there is no separate road; knowing the hidden road yourself, you still don't transgress it. Dwelling in the bird's path, you don't sprout horns on your head but always extend your hands.

Thus the three roads are the cause and effect of the great practice; and the cause and effect spreads vast and wide throughout the whole universe.

THREE KINDS OF FALL

(The following sayings are attributed to Ts'ao Shan Pen Chi, a great desciple of Tung Shan, also known as the Former Ts'ao Shan; the remarks in parenthesis may be those of Ts'ao Shan Liao Wu, known as Great Master Hui Hsia, a successor of Pen Chi, known as the second generation Ts'ao Shan. There is a certain amount of confusion as to the authorship of some early Ts'ao-Tung works, but this is totally irrelevant to our purpose.)

An ascetic taking food has three kinds of fall: being a water buffalo is the fall of an ascetic; not accepting food is the fall of the precious; not cutting off sound and form is the fall according to kind. Just fall; whose business is this?

(If you want to know, this is going in among different kinds, not approving the business of asceticism, purification, and tranquilization. Therefore the Ancients provisionally used the water buffalo to represent different kinds. But these are different kinds in terms of phenomena, not speech.)

As for different kinds of speech, all speech back and forth is of a kind; that is why Nan Ch'uan said, "Where knowledge cannot reach, just don't speak of it; if you speak of it, then horns will grow on your head. Even if you call it 'thus,' already it has changed. You should just go work among different kinds of beings." Right now you must go into differentiation and speak of the phenomena in differentiation; only when there are no words in your words will you be able to do so. When Nan Ch'uan was ailing, someone asked, "Master, after you die, where will you go?" Ch'uan said, "I'll be a water buffalo at the house of the patron down the mountain." His questioner said, "I want to accompany you, master, but can I?" Ch'uan said, "If you follow me, come with a blade of grass in your mouth."

(These are words of an ascetic transforming himself; therefore he says, 'If you want to approach, come with a blade of grass in your mouth.' To approach intimately is called 'Only nonattachment is worthy of offering.')

He also said, "As for the fall according to kind, right now in the midst of all sounds and forms, to turn oneself around on everything and not fall into gradations is called falling according to kind."

He also said, "As for the fall of the precious, the body of reality and nature of reality are precious things; they too must be turned around—this is the fall of the precious. Right now, the White Ox on Open Ground is the ultimate model of the body of reality; it too must be turned around, so that one may avoid sitting in the region of uniformity with no discrimination. This is also called the business of cutting off offering. If you want to use offerings, you must obtain this food. Thus it is called flavorless flavor, and it is called nonattachment being worthy of offering. All the rest is defiled food; it is not the food of nonattached liberation. Someone asked Pai Chang, 'What is used for food?' Pai Chang said, 'Nonattachment is used for food.' Yun Yen said, 'Do not use flavor for offerings.' Tao Wu said, 'Knowing there exists something to maintain, all is offering.'"

Those who take food from correct livelihood must have all three kinds of fall.

At the time, a monk asked, "Wearing fur and horns—what fall is this? Not accepting food—what fall is this? Not cutting off sound and form—what fall is this?" I said, "Wearing fur and horns is the fall of the ascetic. Not cutting off sound and form is the fall according to kind. Not accepting food is the fall of the precious—this is the fundamental thing; one knows it exists, yet does not grasp it, so it is said, 'fall of the precious.' As for wearing fur and horns, the fall of an ascetic, this is not clinging to the business of asceticism, nor to the states of rewards of all saints. As for not cutting off sound and form, the fall according to kind, because a beginner knows he has his own fundamental thing, when he turns back the light he gets rid of all form, sound, smell, flavor, feel, and ideas, and attains stillness. Thus after he perfects this accomplishment, he does not cling to the six sense fields; falling among them, he is not befuddled, going along with them without hindrance. Therefore it is said, 'The six teachers of outside paths are your teachers; when those teachers fall, you also fall along with them, and thereby can eat.' The food is the food of right livelihood; it is also the fundamental thing. It is just that not being defiled by the perceptive awareness in your six senses is called 'falling'—it is not the same as former fears. One does not even grasp his own concern, the fundamental thing, much less anything else."

THE FIVE STATES OF LORD AND VASSAL

(The germ of the five states—or positions, ranks—is in the *Ts'an T'ung Ch'i*, 'Merging of Difference and Identity,' written by Shih T'ou (700–790), ancestor of the Ts'ao-Tung house. Tung Shan exposed the five states in his *Pao Ching San Mei Ke*, 'Song of the Jewel Mirror Meditation,' and composed a set of poems on the five states of the interrelation of the true/ absolute and biased/relative. Ts'ao Shan, who seems to have used the five ranks more than Tung Shan's other disciples, had been a scholar of Confucianism until the age of nineteen and expressed the five states in terms of lord and vassal, or prince and minister. The following is Ts'ao Shan's explanation.)

The absolute state is the realm of emptiness, where there has never been a single thing; the relative state is the realm of form, with myriad forms. The relative within the absolute is turning away from principle and going to phenomena; the absolute within the relative is indifference to phenomena, entering principle. Mutual integration is subtly responding to myriad circumstances without falling into various existences. It is not defiled, not pure, not true, not biased; therefore it is called the empty mysterious great way, the non-grasping true source. The past worthies since time immemorial have esteemed this rank (state of integration) as the most wondrous and most mysterious. You must discern it clearly and thoroughly. The lord is the absolute state, the vassal is the relative state. The vassal turning towards the lord is the absolute within the relative; the lord looking upon the vassal is the relative within the absolute. The way of lord and vassal in harmony is an expression of mutual integration.

A monk asked, "What is the lord like?"

The master said, "His wondrous virtue is honored throughout the world; his lofty illumination shines through the great void."

"What is the vassal like?"

"His spiritual activity spreads the holy way; true wisdom benefits living beings."

"What is the vassal turning towards the lord?"

"Without falling into various dispositions, freezing his feelings he gazes upon the holy countenance."

"What is the lord looking at the vassal?"

"Although his wondrous countenance doesn't move, the shining of his light is fundamentally without bias."

"What is the way of lord and vassal in harmony?"

"Comingling, without inside or outside; merging harmoniously, with upper and lower equal."

FEN YANG ON THE FIVE STATES

(Fen Yang Shan Chao, 947–1024, was one of the great ancestors of the Lin Chi house of Ch'an, noteworthy for his development of the *kung an* as a tool in Ch'an study; one of his points was to show the unity of the essence of Ch'an in the midst of the various methods which had evolved in the streams of Ch'an teaching over the preceding three hundred years.)

Coming from within the absolute

> *The jewel sword of the diamond king*
> *Sweeps the skies with a spiritual light;*
> *It shines freely throughout the world, like a crystal,*
> *Its clear radiance free of dust.*

The relative within the absolute (biased within the true)

> *The thunderous roar of cutting dynamism—*
> *To watch for the sparks and lightning*
> *Is still dull thinking;*
> *Hesitate and you are a thousand mountains away.*

The absolute within the relative (true within the biased)

> See the wheel-turning king;
> Enforcing the true imperative, with seven regal
>   treasures and a thousand sons.
> Everything accompanies him on the road,
> Still he seeks a golden mirror.

Arriving in both (in old tradition, this is arriving in the relative/biased)

> A three year old golden lion;
> His teeth and claws are all there—
> All demons and apparitions
> Faint at the sound of his roar.

Simultaneous realization of both

> Great glory is effortless;
> Quit making a wooden ox walk.
> The real one goes through the fire—
> The wonder of wonders of the King of Dharma.

Coming from within the absolute is lotus flowers blooming on parched ground—their golden calyxes and silver stems are bathed in jade dewdrops. The eminent monk does not sit on the phoenix pedestal. The relative within the absolute—the moon is bright at midnight, the sun must greet the dawn. The absolute within the relative—a hair tip becomes a huge tree, a drop of water becomes a river. Arriving in both—spirit does not come from heaven or earth; how can heroism depend on the four seasons for its impulse? Simultaneous realization—the jade woman casts the shuttle on the whirring loom, the stone man beats the drum, boom boom.

FEN YANG'S EIGHTEEN TYPES OF QUESTIONS

(This list is taken from the *Jen T'ien Yen Mu*, 'Eye of Humans and Gods,' and it seems that the examples given are not necessarily chosen by Fen Yang Shan Chao himself.)

asking for instruction—a monk asked Ma Tsu, "What is Buddha?" Ma Tsu said, "Mind is Buddha." Chao Chou said, "The one in the shrine."

presenting one's understanding—a monk asked Lung Ya, "How is it when 'sky cannot cover, earth cannot hold'?" Lung Ya said, "People of the way should be like this."

investigating and discerning—someone asked Lin Chi, "The student has a question; how is it when it is on the part of the teacher?" Lin Chi said, "Say it quickly! Tell me right away!" As the student hesitated to speak, Lin Chi struck him.

meeting of minds—a monk asked T'ien Huang, "What about when the feeling of doubt has not subsided?" T'ien Huang said, "Sticking to one is not real."

wrapping up (focusing)—a monk asked Pa Chiao, "The whole earth is an eye; I ask the teacher's guidance." Pa Chiao said, "A poor man comes upon a feast."

mental activity—a monk asked Hsing Hua, "I cannot distinguish black from white; I ask the teacher to help me." Hua hit him as he spoke.

seeking out—someone asked Feng Hsueh, "Why does someone who does not understand not doubt?" Hsueh said, "When the sacred tortoise crawls overland how can it avoid leaving tracks in the mud?"

not understanding—a monk asked Hsuan Sha, "The student has just entered the monastery; please show me an entry road." Hsuan Sha said, "Do you hear the sound of the valley stream?" "Yes," answered the monk. Sha said, "Enter from there."

lifting up—someone asked an old adept, " 'Wordly knowledge and brilliant intellect should not be brought out at all'— return the words to me." The adept immediately hit him.

posing a question—someone asked Yun Men, "What about when you don't see any boundaries when looking directly?" Yun Men said, "Reflect."

intentional question—someone asked Shou Shan, "All sentient beings have the Buddha nature—why don't they know it?" Shou Shan said, "They know."

using things/events—someone asked Feng Hsueh, "There is a pearl in the sea; how can I get it?" "When Wang Hsiang arrives, the light shines; where Li Lou goes, the waves flood the skies." (Wang Hsiang and Li Lou were legendary men of supernormal eyesight: the former once found a lost pearl for the Yellow Emperor of high antiquity.)

real question—someone asked San Sheng, "I only see that you are a monk; what are the Buddha and the Teachings?" San Sheng said, "This is Buddha, this is the Teaching; do you know it?"

fabricated question—someone asked Ching Shan, "This here is the one in the shrine—what is the Buddha?" Ching Shan said, "This is the one in the shrine."

making sure—someone asked one of the ancestral teachers, "All things fundamentally are existent—what is nonexistent?" The Patriarch said, "Your question is quite clear; why bother to ask further of me?"

eliciting—someone asked Mu Chou, "What did the ancestral teacher Bodhidharma come from India to China for?" Mu Chou said, "You tell me what it's for." The monk did not reply, so Mu Chou hit him.

clarifying (the example given is the main case of *The Blue Cliff Record* 65)

silent question—an outsider came to the Buddha and stood there silently in his presence. The Buddha said, "So much." The outsider said, "World Honored One, your great mercy and compassion have allowed me to enter."

Contents

Biographical Supplement

Original Preface to The Blue Cliff Record

The lifeline of the perfect sages, the great capacity of the successive Patriarchs, the miraculous method of changing the bones, the wondrous art of nourishing the spirit—the Ch'an Master Hsueh Tou had the true eye which transcends any sect and goes beyond patterns; he upheld the true imperative and did not reveal a customary standard. He took up the hammer and tongs to smelt and forge Buddhas and Patriarchs, and versified the transcendental noses of the patchrobed monks. A silver mountain, an iron wall; who could dare try to bore in? A mosquito trying to bite an iron ox cannot manage to penetrate. If you do not meet a great Master, how can you thoroughly comprehend the abstruse subtleties?

Here there is an old man, Yuan Wu; when he was dwelling at the Blue Cliff, students were confused and asked him for instruction. The old man pitied them and therefore extended his compassion; he dug out the profound source and elucidated the underlying principles. Directly pointing at the ultimate, how could he have set up any opinionated understanding? The hundred public cases are pierced through on one thread from the beginning; the whole crowd of old fellows are all judged in turn.

You should know that the jewel of Chao was flawless to begin with; Hsiang Ju brazenly fooled the king of Ch'in. The ultimate path is in reality wordless; masters of our school extend compassion to rescue the fallen. If you see it like this, only then do you realize their thoroughgoing kindness. If, on the other hand, you get stuck on the phrases and sunk in the words, you won't avoid exterminating the Buddha's race.

P'u Chao was fortunate to be close to the Master's seat and was able to hear what he had never heard before. Companions in the Way compiled it into a volume, and this stupid oaf has reported the root and branches of the matter.

At the time it is the last day of the month in late spring,

1128. The monk P'u Chao, a participant in the study and successor to the Patriarchs, humbly writes this preface.

*   *   *   *   *   *   *

A long time ago a king offered to trade fifteen cities to another king in exchange for a single jewel. When the emissary came with the jewel and handed it over, he saw that the first king was reluctant to part with his cities; he then recovered the jewel by claiming it was flawed and threatened to smash it unless the king honored his part of the bargain, whereat the king relented. Unless we are willing to give up our attachments, we cannot appreciate the priceless jewel of our true nature. Each case of the Blue Cliff Record shows us not only where to find the jewel, but also how to dig it out and cut and polish it to bring out its inherent beauty and magnificence.

Kuei Shan Attends on Pai Chang

POINTER

For a fast man, a single word; for a fast horse, a single stroke of the whip. Ten thousand years, one thought; one thought, ten thousand years. You must know directly before it is raised.

But say, before it is raised, how will you search for it? I'm citing this old case: look!

CASE

Kuei Shan, Wu Feng, and Yun Yen were together attending on Pai Chang.[1] Pai Chang asked Kuei Shan, "With your throat, mouth, and lips shut, how will you speak?"[2]

Kuei Shan said, "Please, Teacher, you speak instead."[3]

Chang said, "I don't refuse to speak to you, but I fear that (if I did) in the future I would be bereft of descendants."[4]

NOTES

1. Haha! From beginning to end obscure and hard to understand. You're headed west, I'm going east.
2. One general is hard to find.
3. Kuei Shan proceeds by Pai Chang's road.
4. He doesn't avoid grandmotherly kindness. The skin on his face is three inches thick. He mingles and mixes with mud and water. He goes right up and takes him.

COMMENTARY

Kuei Shan, Wu Feng, and Yun Yen were together attending on Pai Chang. Pai Chang asked Kuei Shan, "With your throat, mouth, and lips shut, how will you speak?" Shan said, "Please, Teacher, you speak instead." Chang said, "I don't refuse to speak to you, but I fear that (if I did) in the future I would be bereft of descendants." Although Pai Chang acted like this, his pot had already been carried off by someone else. He also asked Wu Feng (this same question). Feng said, "Teacher, you too should shut up." Chang said, "Where there's no one, I shade my eyes with my hand and gaze out towards you." He also asked Yun Yen. Yen said, "Teacher, do you have (any way to speak) or not?" Chang said, "I have lost my descendants." Each of these three men was a Master.

An Ancient said, "On the level ground there are dead people without number. Those who can pass through the forest of brambles are the skillful ones." Therefore teachers of our school use the forest of brambles to test people. Why? They couldn't test people if they stuck to phrases based on ordinary feelings. Patchrobed monks must be able to display their ability in phrases and discern the point within words. As for board-carrying fellows, they often die within the words and say, "If throat, mouth, and lips are shut, there's no longer a way to say anything." As for those who can adapt successfully, they have waves which go against the current, they have a single road right in the question. They don't cut their hands blundering against its sharp point.

Kuei Shan said, "Please, Teacher, you speak instead." Tell me, what did he mean? Here he was like sparks struck from stone, like a flash of lightning: pressing back against Pai Chang's question, he answered immediately. He had his own way to get himself out, without wasting the slightest effort. Thus it is said, "He studies the living phrase; he doesn't study the dead phrase."

Nevertheless, Pai Chang did not take him up on it, but just said, "I don't refuse to speak to you, but I fear that (if I did) in the future I would be bereft of descendants." Whenever teachers of our school help people, they pull out nails and extract pegs. As for people these days who say that this answer doesn't approve of Kuei Shan and doesn't comprehend his words, how far they are from knowing that right here is the one path of his living potential, towering up like a thousand-fathom wall, interchanging guest and host, leaping with life.

Hsueh Tou likes these words of Kuei Shan's, likes his freedom to revolve around and maneuver elegantly while still being able to hold fast to his territory. Therefore his verse says:

VERSE

"Please, Teacher, you speak instead."
> This contains the universe. He's already cut his hand
> against the sharp point.

*The tiger's head sprouts horns as he emerges from the wild
weeds.*
> Very startling indeed. Undeniably, he's extraordinary.

*On the ten continents spring ends and the flowers fade and
   wither—*
> Everywhere is pure and cool. No praise is sufficient.

Over the coral forest the sun is dazzling bright.
> (In the coral branches the light is reflected) a hundred-
> fold, a thousand-fold. Nevertheless, he can't be found on
> the tips of the hundred weeds. Kuei Shan's answer covers
> heaven and earth.

COMMENTARY

The answers of these three men (to Pai Chang's question) are
all different from each other. There's (Kuei Shan's) towering up
like a thousand-fathom wall; there's (Wu Feng's) shining and
functioning at the same time; and there's (Yun Yen's) who
can't even save himself.

   "'Please, Teacher, you speak instead.'" Immediately in this
one line Hsueh Tou has displayed his device. He goes farther
into it and presses ever so lightly to make it easy for people to
see by saying, "The tiger's head sprouts horns as he emerges
from the wild weeds." Kuei Shan's answer seems to be placing
horns on the head of a ferocious tiger—is there any way to
approach it?

   Haven't you heard? A monk asked Lo Shan, "How is it when
they are born together and die together?" Shan said, "Like an
ox without horns." The monk asked, "How is it when they are
born together but don't die together?" Shan said, "Like a tiger
wearing horns."

   Though Hsueh Tou has completed the verse in one couplet,
he has ample talent to turn around and change. He goes on and
says, "On the ten continents spring ends and the flowers fade

and wither.'' On the ocean there are ten continents where one hundred years make one spring. Hsueh Tou's words have graceful elegance, turning freely with great ease. When the spring is over, hundreds of thousands of myriad flowers fade and wither all at once. Only the coral tree forest doesn't fade and wither— it takes the light of the sun and reflects it back and forth (among the branches). At just such a time it is amazing indeed! Hsueh Tou uses this to illuminate Kuei Shan's saying, ''Please, Teacher, you speak instead.''

Wu Feng's Shut Up, Teacher

CASE

Pai Chang also asked Wu Feng, "With your throat, mouth, and lips shut, how will you speak?"[1]

Feng said, "Teacher, you too should shut up."[2]

Chang said, "Where there's no one, I shade my eyes with my hand and gaze out towards you."[3]

NOTES

1. Hahaha! The arrow has gone past Korea.
2. He captures the banner and carries off the drum. With a single phrase he cuts off the flow and puts to rest myriad impulses.
3. Where the land is broad and the population sparse, those met with are few.

COMMENTARY

Kuei Shan held fast to his territory—Wu Feng cut off the myriad streams. For this bit one must be a fellow who takes it up directly, like a head-on clash in the front lines. There's no room for hesitation. Wu Feng functions directly and immediately: (his reply) is urgent and swift, perilous and steep. He's not like Kuei Shan who is so relaxed and easy-going and exuberant.

Followers of Ch'an these days just move under the shelf, unable to go beyond him. Thus it is said, "If you want to attain Intimacy, don't ask with questions."

Wu Feng's answer cut him off immediately; undeniably it was fast and brilliant. Pai Chang said, "Where there's no one, I shade my eyes with my hand and gaze out towards you." But say, is this approving of Wu Feng or not? Is it killing or bringing to life? Seeing him turn so smoothly, Pai Chang just was giving him a check.

Hsueh Tou's verse says:

VERSE

"Teacher, you too should shut up."
>   Already present before the words. It cuts off the myriad
>   streams.

Observe Wu Feng's strategy on the dragon and snake battle
>   *lines—*
>   It takes the golden drum and serrated banner (of a great
>   general) to be able to do this. He's fully equipped: he's an
>   expert accustomed to battle.

He makes people think of General Li Kuang.
>   There aren't many with such marvelous skill. With his
>   horse and spear (he covers) a thousand miles, ten
>   thousand miles, and (defeats) a thousand men, ten
>   thousand men.

Over the ten-thousand-mile horizon a single kingfisher hawk
>   *soars.*
>   Does everyone see? But say, where does it alight? On
>   target. I'll hit saying, "It's flown past."

COMMENTARY

"'Teacher, you too should shut up.'" In one line Hsueh Tou
gives a push and says, "Observe his strategy on the dragon and
snake battle lines." It is as though Wu Feng set out two battle
lines to burst out and to burst in. He has the ability of a battle
commander, unrestrained in all directions. A man with a grand
strategy is free to appear and disappear with his horse and spear
up on the dragon and snake battle lines. How would you be
able to surround him? If you're not this kind of person, how
will you know that there is this kind of strategy?

In all these three verses (70, 71, and 72) of Hsueh Tou's,
what he describes within them is like this, like Li Kuang's
miraculous arrows.[a] "Over the ten-thousand-mile horizon a
single kingfisher hawk soars." That one arrow fells one eagle is
certain: there's no more (chance of) escape. In Hsueh Tou's

verse, Pai Chang's question is like a kingfisher hawk—Wu Feng's answer is like an arrow. I have been so occupied with praising Wu Feng that without realizing it my whole body has been immersed in mud and water.

TRANSLATORS' NOTES

a. A renowned archer and great general, Li Kuang had a long career fighting the Huns on the northern frontiers for the Western Han Dynasty in the middle of the second century B.C. See the commentary to the verse in case 4.

Pai Chang Questions Yun Yen

CASE

Pai Chang also asked Yun Yen, "With your throat, mouth, and lips shut, how will you speak?"[1]

Yen said, "Teacher, do you have (any way to speak) or not?"[2]

Chang said, "I have lost my descendants."[3]

NOTES

1. "Come out of your hole, frog." What is he saying?
2. Sticking to his skin, clinging to his bones. Mud and water is streaming off him. Ahead he doesn't reach the village, behind he doesn't get to the shop.
3. Obviously with an answer like this, half is in front and half is left behind.

COMMENTARY

Yun Yen was an attendant for twenty years at Pai Chang. Later he went along with Tao Wu to Yao Shan. Shan asked him, "When you were in Pai Chang's congregation, what was your purpose?" Yen said, "To escape birth and death." Shan said, "Have you escaped yet or not?" Yen said, "There's no birth and death for this one." Shan said, "Twenty years at Pai Chang and your force of habit still hasn't been cleared away yet." Yen took his leave and went to see Nan Ch'uan. Later he returned to Yao Shan and at last understood and was enlightened.

Look how the ancient man Yun Yen studied and investigated for twenty years and still was half green and half yellow (unripe). He stuck to his skin and clung to his bones, and couldn't break through. He was indeed this way; in fact, ahead he didn't reach the village, behind he didn't get to the shop. Haven't you heard it said:

If your words do not leave the old clichés,
How will you be able to get out of what covers and
   binds you?
White clouds lie athwart the valley mouth,
Making so many people miss the source.

In the Ts'ao Tung tradition this is called "transgression."
Thus they say, "Throw open the well-guarded phoenix tower
but avoid transgressing (the prohibition against saying) the
present emperor's name." Hence it is said, "To attain it is first
necessary to pass beyond the forest of brambles. If you do not
pass beyond it, then from beginning to end you will get stuck
in subtleties without being able to cut them off."

As I just said, "Ahead he didn't reach his village, behind he
didn't get to his shop." Yun Yen just went to test the other
man's depths. When Pai Chang saw him acting like this, he
immediately held him and struck him dead.

Hsueh Tou's verse says:

VERSE

"Teacher, do you have (any way to speak) or not?"
   The case is perfectly manifest. Yun Yen was following the
   waves, pursuing the ripples, mixing with mud, mingling
   with water.

The golden-haired lion is not crouching on the ground.
   Obviously. What's the use? Too bad!

Two by two, three by three, travelling the old road—
   "With your throat, mouth, and lips shut, how will you
   speak?" Turn around and show some spirit! Though it
   was right under his feet, he missed it.

On Ta Hsiung Mountain Pai Chang snapped his fingers in
   vain.[a]
   Once dead Yun Yen did not come back to life again. Too
   bad! Too sad! Hsueh Tou adds more grief to his cry of
   woe.

COMMENTARY

" 'Teacher, do you have (any way to speak) or not?' / The golden-haired lion is not crouching on the ground." Hsueh Tou concludes the case on the basis of the facts. Yun Yen is indeed one, but this golden-haired lion nevertheless is not crouching on the ground (ready to spring). When a lion captures its prey, it conceals its teeth, hides its claws, and crouches on the ground to rear back (and leap). Whether the prey is large or small, a lion always uses his whole power, wanting to complete his deed.

When Yun Yen said, "Teacher, do you have (any way to speak) or not?" he was just travelling on his former road. That's why Hsueh Tou says that Pai Chang snapped his fingers in vain on Ta Hsiung Mountain.

TRANSLATORS' NOTES

a.   One snaps one's fingers at someone to make him wake up.

Ma Tsu's Permutations of Assertion and Denial

POINTER

In explaining the Dharma, there is neither explanation nor teaching; in listening to the Dharma, there is neither hearing nor attainment. Since explanation neither explains nor teaches, how can it compare to not explaining? Since listening neither hears nor attains, how can it compare to not listening? Still, no explaining and no listening still amount to something.

As for all of you right here, listening to me explain here, how will you avoid this mistake? For those with the eye to pass through the barrier, as a test, I'm citing this old case: look!

CASE

A monk asked Grand Master Ma, "Please, Teacher, going beyond the permutations of assertion and denial, directly point out to me the meaning of the coming from the West."[1]

Master Ma said, "I'm tired today and can't explain for you. Go ask Chih Tsang."[2]

When the monk asked Chih Tsang,[3] Tsang said, "Why didn't you ask the Teacher?"[4] The monk said, "The Teacher had me come here to ask you."[5] Tsang said, "I have a headache today and can't explain for you. Go ask Elder Brother Hai."[6] When the monk asked Elder Brother Hai (Pai Chang),[7] Hai said, "At this point, after all, I don't understand."[8]

When the monk related this to Grand Master Ma,[9] Master Ma said, "Tsang's head is white, Hai's head is black."[10]

NOTES

1. Where did he get this question from? Where did he get this news?
2. He retreats three paces. The monk has stumbled past without

realizing it. Ma hides his body but reveals his shadow. Undeniably this old fellow Ma has passed the buck to someone else.

3. He should have pressed Ma. He's stumbled past without realizing it.

4. The scorched-tail tiger has come out of the weeds. What is he saying? In fact, the monk is binding himself with straw ropes—he's totally dead.

5. He's at the disposal of someone else. The first arrow was still light, but the second arrow is deep.

6. It seems that the eighty-four men of knowledge (produced by Ma Tsu) all suffer from this kind of sickness.

7. Again the monk passes it to someone else. Clutching the loot, he cries out that he's been wronged.

8. He doesn't make a fuss. At any rate, the obscurity extends endlessly, forever and ever.

9. Despite everything, this monk does have a little eyesight.

10. In the heart of the realm, the emperor commands; outside the passes, the generals give orders.

COMMENTARY

In the old days when I studied with Chen Chueh in Ch'eng Tu (in Szechuan), Chueh said of this case, "You just need to look at Ma Tsu's first line and you will naturally understand all at once." Tell me, did this monk understand when he asked, or did he ask not understanding? This question of his is undeniably profound and far-reaching.

As for going beyond the permutations of assertion and denial, the four basic propositions are: 'it exists,' 'it doesn't exist,' 'it neither exist nor doesn't exist,' and 'it both exists and doesn't exist.' When you depart from these four propositions, you cut off their hundred negations. But if you just occupy yourself making up theories, you won't recognize the point of the story—you'll be looking for your head without seeing it.

If it had been me, I'd have waited until Ma Tsu had spoken, then unrolled my mat and bowed three times, to see how he would have responded. If I had been Ma Tsu at that time, when I saw this monk come up and ask, "Please, Teacher, going beyond the permutations of affirmation and denial, directly point out to me the meaning of the coming from the West," I would have brought my staff down across his back and driven him out with blows, to see if he would awaken or not.

Grand Master Ma just created complications for him. When this fellow was right in front of it and stumbled past missing it, Ma Tsu still directed him to go ask Chih Tsang. The monk really didn't know that Grand Master Ma profoundly discerns oncoming winds. The monk went in ignorance to ask Chih Tsang. Tsang said, "Why didn't you ask the Teacher?" The monk said, "The Teacher had me come here to ask you." Watch this bit of his: when pressed, he immediately turns without wasting any more time. Chih Tsang said, "I have a headache today and can't explain for you. Go ask Elder Brother Hai."

This monk went to ask Elder Brother Hai, who said, "At this point, after all, I don't understand." But say, why did one man say he had a headache and one man say he didn't understand? In the end, what's what? This monk then came back and related this to Grand Master Ma. The Master said, "Tsang's head is white, Hai's head is black."

If you figure this by way of intellectual interpretation, then you would say that they were fooling the monk. Some say that is was all just buck-passing. Some say that all three knew the monk's question, and therefore they didn't answer. All such interpretations amount to clapping your hands over your eyes and putting poison into the excellent-flavored pure ghee of the Ancients.

Thus Ma Tsu said (to Layman P'ang), "When you swallow all the water in West River in one gulp, then I'll explain to you." This is the same as the present case. If you can understand "Tsang's head is white, Hai's head is black," then you can understand this talk about West River's water.

This monk took his load of confusion and exchanged it for uneasiness: he went on troubling these three adepts, making them enter the mud and water. In the end this monk didn't catch a glimpse of it. Although it was like this throughout, nevertheless these three masters of our school were exposed by a board-carrying fellow.

People these days just go to the words to make their living. They say that white refers to merging in brightness, while black refers to merging in darkness. Just occupying themselves with pursuing their calculations, such people are far from knowing that the ancient Ma Tsu cuts off their intellectual faculties with a single line. You must go to the true lifeline and look for yourself before you can gain firm accord. Therefore Ma Tsu said, "With the last word you finally get to the impenetrable barrier." If you cut off the essential crossing place, you don't let profane or holy pass. If you discuss this matter, it's like having a sword pressing against your forehead—hesitate and you lose your body and your life. Again, it's said, "It's like hurling a sword into the sky—it's not a question of whether it reaches or not." Just go to the place of glistening clarity to understand.

Haven't you heard of the Ancients saying "You tub of lacquer!" or "Wild fox spirit!" or "Blind man!"? Tell me, is this the same as, or different from, a blow or a shout? If you know that the myriad differences and distinctions are all one, then naturally you will be able to take on opponents on all sides. Do you want to understand "Tsang's head is white, Hai's head is black"? My late teacher Wu Tsu said, "Mr. Dustsweeper."

Hsueh Tou's verse says:

VERSE

"Tsang's head is white, Hai's head is black."
> Half closed, half open. One hand lifts up, one hand presses down. The sound of gold bells, the flourish of jewel chimes.

Clear-eyed patchrobed monks cannot understand.
> Go travel for thirty more years. It ends with your nostrils being pierced by someone else. Because of this, my mouth seems to be in a frown.

The Colt has trampled everyone on earth to death—
> Among all the monasteries, only this old fellow Ma could do this. Bring this old fellow out!

Lin Chi isn't yet a thief who can steal in broad daylight.
> A leper drags along his companions. Even though Ma Tsu and Lin Chi are experts, they've been caught by another person, Hsueh Tou.

*Going beyond the four propositions and cutting off their
    hundred negations—*
>   What is he saying? You too must check into this and see
    for yourself. "Poppa" resembles "daddy."

Among gods and humans only I know.
>   Why use "I"? I'll snatch away your staff. If there's no self
    and no others, no gain and no loss, what will you use to
    know?

COMMENTARY

"'Tsang's head is white, Hai's head is black.'" But say, what
does this mean? The world's patchrobed monks can't leap clear
of this little bit. Look at how well Hsueh Tou closes up tight at
the end: he says that even if you're a clear-eyed patchrobed
monk you still won't be able to understand. This bit of news is
called the hidden secret of the spiritual immortals which is not
passed on from father to son. After old Shakyamuni had
preached the teachings of his entire lifetime, at the end he
specially transmitted the mind seal. It is called the Diamond
King's jewel sword;[a] it is called the Rank of the Correct.[b] Such
complications were a matter that couldn't be avoided—(with
them) the Ancients showed a little of their sharp point. If you
are a person who can pass through, then you will pierce and
penetrate to attain the great independence. If you can't pass
through, then as before there is no place for you to awaken and
enter, and the more you talk the farther away you are.

"The Colt has trampled everyone on earth to death." Back in
India Prajnatara prophesied to Bodhidharma (of Ma Tsu) saying,
"Though China is vast, there is no other road: it will run in the
footsteps of your descendants. A golden rooster will know how
to take a grain of millet in his beak and offer sustenance to the
arhats of the ten directions."[c] In addition, the Sixth Patriarch
said to (Ma Tsu's teacher) Master Jang, "Hereafter the Buddha
Dharma will go forth from you. In the future you will produce a
colt who will trample everyone on earth to death." After this
he did spread the teaching over the whole country as the
Dharma successor in Kiangsi—at the time he was called Ma

Tsu. Thus both Bodhidharma and the Sixth Patriarch predicted Ma Tsu in advance. Look how his way of doing things was, as it turned out, special—he just said, "Tsang's head is white, Hai's head is black." This is where to see how he tramples everyone on earth to death. A thousand men, ten thousand men can't bite through this one line about black and white.

"Lin Chi isn't yet a thief who can steal in broad daylight." One day Lin Chi taught his assembly saying, "In this red lump of flesh there is a true man without station. He's constantly going in and out through all of your senses. Those who haven't yet experienced this—look! look!" At the time there was a monk who came forward and asked, "What is the true man without station?" Lin Chi came down from the meditation platform and grabbed the monk tightly saying, "Speak! Speak!" The monk was speechless. Lin Chi pushed him away and said, "The true man without station—what a dry piece of shit he is!" Later Hsueh Feng heard of this and said, "Lin Chi greatly resembles a thief who steals in broad daylight."

Hsueh Tou wants to meet that Lin Chi, but in observing Ma Tsu's active edge, it is certainly superior to Lin Chi's. Ma Tsu is truly a thief who steals in broad daylight; Lin Chi is not yet one. Hsueh Tou has pierced them both at once.

Turning to versify this monk, Hsueh Tou says, "Going beyond the four propositions and cutting off their hundred negations—/Among gods and humans only I know." But don't go into the ghost cave to make your living! An Ancient said, "The question is in the answer, the answer is in the question." This monk was already extraordinary—how will you be able to go beyond the four propositions and cut off their hundred negations? Hsueh Tou says, "Only I know this matter." Even the Buddhas of past, present, and future cannot catch sight of it. Since each one must know for himself alone, what are all of you looking for when you keep on coming up here (to listen to me)?

Chen Ju of Ta Kuei commented, "This monk asking this way and Ma Tsu answering this way went beyond the permutations of assertion and denial. Chih Tsang and Elder Brother Hai didn't realize it at all."

Want to understand? Haven't you heard it said?—"The Colt has trampled everyone on earth to death."

TRANSLATORS' NOTES

a. The Diamond King's jewel sword is a symbol of *prajna,* transcendent wisdom.

b. The Rank of the Correct symbolizes emptiness, *nirvana;* see the appendix on the devices of Tung Shan.

c. Prajnatara was Bodhidharma's teacher, the Twenty-Seventh Indian Patriarch. "There is no other road" refers to Ma Tsu, whose Dharma name was Tao I, "The Path is one." "A golden rooster" refers to Ma Tsu's teacher, Master Huai Jang of Nan Yueh, a man from Chin Chou ("Gold Prefecture"); like a rooster who naturally knows how to crow at the right time, Huai Jang knew when to appear in the world to cause the Dharma to flourish. The "grain of millet" means the specially transmitted mind seal. The colt in Hsueh Tou's verse and in the Sixth Patriarch's prediction to Huai Jang, of course, means Ma Tsu: in Chinese, "Ma" means horse.

Chin Niu's Rice Pail

POINTER

Wielding a sharp sword horizontally, he cuts off the nest of trailing vines in front of his point. Hanging a clear mirror on high, he brings forth Vairocana's seal within a phrase. Where one's state is secure within, one wears clothes and eats food. Where spiritual powers wander at play, how can one linger? Have you fully mastered it? Look at what's written below:

CASE

Every day at mealtime, Master Chin Niu would personally take the rice pail and do a dance in front of the monks' hall: laughing aloud, he would say, "Bodhisattvas, come eat!"[1]

Hsueh Tou said, "Though he acted like this, Chin Niu was not good-hearted."[2]

A monk asked Ch'ang Ch'ing, "When the man of old said, 'Bodhisattvas, come eat!' what was his meaning?"[3] Ch'ing said, "Much like joyful praise on the occasion of a meal."[4]

NOTES

1. "You may play with the fishing line as you will—without disturbing the clear waves, its meaning is naturally distinct." He applies pure ghee and poison at the same time—and he's right! Jewels and gems he arrays all at once, but what can he do?—those he meets with are few.
2. This is a thief recognizing a thief, a spirit recognizing a spirit. If someone comes to talk of right and wrong, then he's a right and wrong person.
3. Indeed, anyone would have doubts about this. From the beginning, he hasn't known where Chin Niu is at. What will Ch'ang Ch'ing say?

4. He sizes up the audience to give his order, and wraps up the case on the basis of the facts.

COMMENTARY

Chin Niu was a venerable adept descended from Ma Tsu. Every day at mealtime he would personally take the rice pail and do a dance in front of the monks' hall: laughing aloud, he would say, "Bodhisattvas, come eat!" He did this for twenty years. Tell me, where was his intent? Was he just summoning the others to eat? He always struck the (wooden) fish and beat the drum (for mealtimes) and also personally announced it. So what further need was there for him to take the rice pail and do so many tricks? Wasn't he crazy? Wasn't he "expounding by design"? If he was expounding this matter, why didn't he mount the jewel flower throne to "knock on the seat and hold up the whisk"? Why did he need to act like this?

People today are far from knowing that the Ancients' meaning was outside of words. Why not then take a brief look at the stated purpose for the Patriarchal Teacher's first coming here? What was it? It was clearly explained: for a separate transmission outside the verbal teachings, to transmit individually the mind seal. The ancient man Chin Niu's expedient methods too were just to make you directly receive this. Later people would vainly calculate on their own and say, "Why so many concerns? When cold, turn toward the fire; when hot, take advantage of the cool shade; when hungry, eat; when tired, get some sleep." If we interpreted meanings this way, on the basis of ordinary feelings, to explain and comment, then the whole school of Bodhidharma would have been wiped off the face of the earth. Don't you realize that twenty-four hours a day, from moment to moment, the Ancients never gave up wanting to understand This Matter?

Hsueh Tou said, "Though he acted like this, Chin Niu was not good-hearted." Many people misunderstand this line. That which is called the supreme flavor of pure ghee is converted, on encountering such people, into poison. Since Chin Niu descended into the weeds to help people, why did Hsueh Tou say that he wasn't good-hearted? Why did he talk this way? Patch-robed monks must have living potential to begin to understand this.

People today don't get to the Ancient's realm—they just say, "What mind is there to see? What Buddha is there?" If you construct such views you have destroyed the old adept, Chin Niu. It takes thorough observation to begin to understand. If today and tomorrow you go on with such facile explanations, you'll never be finished.

Later when Ch'ang Ch'ing had gone up to his seat, a monk asked, "When the ancient man said, 'Bodhisattvas, come eat!' what was his meaning?" Ch'ing said, "Much like joyful praise on the occasion of a meal." The honored worthy Ch'ang Ch'ing was extremely compassionate—he leaked and tarried quite a bit. In truth it was "joyful praise on the occasion of a meal." But you tell me, rejoicing over what?

Look at Hsueh Tou's verse which says:

VERSE

Laughing aloud in the shadow of the white clouds,
In his laugh, there's a knife. Why the enthusiasm? The world's patchrobed monks don't know where he comes down.

He lifts it up with both hands to give to them.
How can there be such things? Better not slander Chin Niu! Can it be called a rice pail? If you are a legitimate patchrobed monk in your own right, you don't eat this kind of food.

If they were sons of the golden-haired lion,
They must first be beyond patterns. I'll allow that they had eyes, but I only fear that their eyes were not true.

They would have seen the deception from three thousand miles away.
It wasn't worth half a cent. A scene of leaking and tarrying. Where was the deception? Blind men!

COMMENTARY

"Laughing aloud in the shadow of the white clouds." Ch'ang Ch'ing says, "Joyful praise on the occasion of a meal." Hsueh

Tou says, "He lifts it up with both hands to give to them." But say, was he just giving them food to eat, or do you think that there must have been something special besides? If you can know the true point here, then you're a son of the golden-haired lion. If they had been sons of the golden-haired lion, then there would have been no more need for Chin Niu to take the rice pail, do a dance, and laugh aloud—in fact they would have known his mistake immediately from three thousand miles away.

An Ancient said, "Perceive before the act and you won't have to use the least bit of effort." Thus patchrobed monks must always function outside of patterns before they can be called genuine Masters of our school. If they just base themselves on words and speech, they won't avoid leaking and tarrying in indulgent attachments.

Wu Chiu's Unjust Beating

POINTER

The subtle point, the jewel sword, perpetually revealed, present in front of us. It can kill people and it can bring people life. It's there and it's here, gaining and losing together with us. If you want to pick it up, you're free to pick it up; if you want to put it down, you're free to put it down.

But say, what's it like when not falling into guest and host, when interchanging without getting stuck? To test, I'm citing this old case: look!

CASE

A monk came to Wu Chiu from the congregation of the Master of Ting Chou. Wu Chiu asked, "How does Ting Chou's Dharma Path compare to here?"[1] The monk said, "It's not different."[2] Chiu said, "If it's not different, then you should go back there," and then hit him.[3] The monk said, "There are eyes on the staff: you shouldn't carelessly hit people."[4] Chiu said, "Today I've hit one," and hit him again three times.[5] The monk thereupon went out.[6]

Chiu said, "All along there's been someone receiving an unjust beating."[7] The monk turned around and said, "What can I do? The handle is in your hands, Teacher."[8] Chiu said, "If you want, I'll turn it over to you."[9] The monk came up to Chiu, grabbed the staff out of his hands, and hit him three times.[10] Chiu said, "An unjust beating, an unjust beating!"[11] The monk said, "There's someone receiving it."[12]

Chiu said, "I hit this fellow carelessly."[13] Immediately the monk bowed.[14] Chiu said, "Yet you act this way."[15] The monk laughed loudly and went out.[16] Chiu said, "That's all it comes to, that's all it comes to."[17]

NOTES

1. There's an echo in his words. He must distinguish shallow from deep. (The question is like) a probing pole, a reed shade. He's really deceiving the man!
2. Among the dead men there's a live one. One or a half. ("Not different") is the same as an iron spike. He's treading upon the ground of reality.
3. Obviously. The correct imperative must be carried out.
4. Only this adept could do this. After all, he's a lion cub.
5. What one is he talking about? (Why not hit) a thousand, ten thousand?
6. All along the monk's been a man of our house. In fact he has been wronged. He just sees his opportunity and goes.
7. A mute eating a bitter melon. Chiu both lets go and gathers in. What good is someone who turns back around when hit?
8. It's this way three hundred and sixty-five days a year. After all he is a clever patchrobed monk.
9. Who knows which of them is the prince and which is the minister? Chiu dares to lie down in the tiger's mouth. He really doesn't know good from evil.
10. Here again, only an adept Ch'an traveller could do this. Guest and host interchange, releasing or capturing according to the occasion.
11. Check! Why is this old fellow in such a rush?
12. Haha! How many handles are now in this monk's hands?
13. It doesn't come down on either side. Who knows who he is?
14. Only one who doesn't flinch when faced with danger is a man of power.
15. Check!
16. An adept Ch'an traveller naturally has (such ability). A fierce tiger must have a pure wind following him. Now we know that he finished the beginning and finished the end. No one on earth can get a grasp on him.
17. Too bad he let the monk go. Why didn't he bring his staff down across his back? Where do you think the monk went?

COMMENTARY

A monk came to Wu Chiu from the congregation of the Master of Ting Chou. Chiu was also an adept. If here all of you people can realize that there was a single exit and a single entry for these two men, then a thousand or ten thousand is in fact just one. It is so, whether acting as host or as guest: in the end the two men merge together into one agent for one session of careful investigation. Whether as guest or host, whether asking or answering, from beginning to end both were adepts.

Look at Wu Chiu questioning this monk: "How does Ting Chou's Dharma Path compare to here?" The monk immediately said, "It's not different." At the time, if it hadn't been Wu Chiu, it would have been hard to cope with this monk. Chiu said, "If it's not different, then you should go back there," and then hit him. But what could he do? This monk was an adept and immediately said, "There are eyes on the staff: you shouldn't carelessly hit people." Chiu carried out the imperative thoroughly saying, "Today I've hit one," and hitting him again three more times. At this the monk went out. Observe how the two of them revolved so smoothly—both were adepts. To understand this affair it is necessary to distinguish initiate from lay, and tell right from wrong. Though this monk went out, the case was still not finished.

From beginning to end Wu Chiu wanted to test this monk's reality, to see how he was. But this monk had barred the door, so Chiu hadn't yet seen him. Then Wu Chiu said, "All along there's been someone receiving an unjust beating." This monk wanted to turn around and show some life, yet he didn't struggle with Wu Chiu, but turned around most easily and said, "What can I do? The handle is in your hands, Teacher." Being a Master of our school with an eye on his forehead, Wu Chiu dared to lay his body down in the fierce tiger's mouth and say, "If you want, I'll turn it over to you."

This monk was a fellow with a talisman under his arm. As it is said, "To see what is right and not do it is lack of bravery." Without hesitating any longer, the monk came up to Wu Chiu, grabbed the staff out of his hands, and hit him three times. When Chiu said, "An unjust beating, an unjust beating!" tell me, what did he mean? Before, Chiu said, "All along there's been someone receiving an unjust beating." But when the monk hit him he said, "An unjust beating, an unjust beating!" When the monk said, "There's someone receiving it," Chiu said, "I hit this fellow carelessly." Chiu said before that he had hit a person carelessly. Afterwards, when he had taken a beat-

ing himself, why did he also say, "I hit this fellow carelessly"?
If it hadn't been for this monk's independent resurgence, he
couldn't have been able to handle Wu Chiu.

Then the monk bowed. This bow was extremely poisonous—it wasn't good-hearted. If it hadn't been Wu Chiu, he
wouldn't have been able to see through this monk. Wu Chiu
said to him, "Yet you act this way." The monk laughed loudly
and went out. Wu Chiu said, "That's all it comes to, that's all it
comes to."

Observe how all through the meeting of these adepts, guest
and host are distinctly clear. Though cut off, they can still
continue. In fact this is just an action of interchanging. Yet
when they get here, they do not say that there is an interchange. Since these ancient men were beyond defiling feelings
and conceptual thinking, neither spoke of gain or loss. Though
it was a single session of talk, the two men were both leaping
with life, and both had the needle and thread of our blood line.
If you can see here, you too will be perfectly clear twenty-four
hours a day.

When the monk (first) went out, this was both sides letting
go. What happened after that was both sides gathering in. This
is called interchanging. Hsueh Tou makes his verse just this
way:

VERSE

To summon is easy—
> Everyone on earth doubts this. Rancid meat attracts flies.
> None of the world's patchrobed monks know where this
> comes down.

To send away is hard.
> Getting rid of them thoroughly (is hard). Mirages appear
> over the sea.

Observe carefully the interchange of action points.
> One exit, one entry—both are adepts. Two men hold a
> single staff. But say, whose side is it on?

The rock of ages though solid can still crumble—
> How will you handle the golden hammer up his sleeve?
> The thousand sages haven't transmitted it.

When they stand in its depths the ocean must dry up.
> Where will this be arranged? There are eyes on the staff.
> I'll only allow that they have attained intimately.

Old Wu Chiu! Old Wu Chiu!
> What a pity that this old fellow doesn't know good from evil.

How many kinds?
> He's another fellow with no reasons (for what he does).
> Hundreds, thousands, myriads of miles.

Indeed he had no reason for giving him the handle.
> Already so before the words. Wu Chiu's life was hanging by a thread. He deserves thirty blows. But say, where was his fault?

COMMENTARY

"To summon is easy—to send away is hard." It's all falling into the weeds. With his excessive compassion, Hsueh Tou would often say, "Calling snakes is easy; sending snakes away is hard." Right now if I were to take a (dried and hollow) gourd and blow through it, it would be easy to summon snakes, but when I wanted to send them away it would be hard. Similarly, it's easy to give one's staff to someone else, but to take it back from him and send him away is hard. You must have your own ability—only then will you be able to send him away.

Wu Chiu was an adept with the skill to call snakes and also the ability to send snakes away. This monk wasn't asleep either. When Wu Chiu asked, "How does Ting Chou's Dharma Path compare to here?"—this was calling him. When Wu Chiu then hit him, this was sending him away. When the monk said, "There are eyes on the staff: you shouldn't hit people carelessly"—this is the summoning transferred over to the monk's side. When Wu Chiu said, "If you want, I'll turn it over to you," and the monk then came up to Chiu, grabbed the staff out of his hands, and hit him three times—this was the monk sending him away. As for the monk laughing loudly and going out, and Wu Chiu saying, "That's all it comes to"—this clearly is each sending the other away appropriately.

Observe how these two exchanged action points, spinning with perfect continuity, fusing into one whole. From beginning to end, guest and host are clearly distinct. Sometimes, though, host acts as guest and sometimes guest acts as host. Even Hsueh Tou cannot praise this enough. Thus he speaks of the act of interchange and has you people observe it carefully.

"The rock of ages though solid can still crumble." He speaks of this "rock of ages": it's 84,000 leagues wide and 84,000 leagues thick.ª Every five hundred years a god comes down and brushes across it with a gossamer cloth, then departs for another five hundred years. The brushing continues like this until it wears the rock away—this makes one age called the "light cloth brushing across the rock" age. Hsueh Tou says, "The rock of ages though solid can still crumble." Though the rock is strong and solid, still it can be worn away to nothing. But the action point of these two men can never be obliterated over the ages.

"When they stand in its depths the ocean must dry up." Even the ocean, with its vast swelling billows flooding the skies, even the very ocean would inevitably dry up utterly if you have these two men stand within it. At this point Hsueh Tou has completed his verse all at once.

At the end he goes on to say, "Old Wu Chiu! Old Wu Chiu!/How many kinds?" Sometimes catching, sometimes letting go; sometimes killing, sometimes giving life—in the end, how many kinds is this? "Indeed he had no reason for giving him the handle." This staff has been used by all the Buddhas of past, present, and future, and by the successive generations of Patriarchal Teachers, and by the Masters of our school, to pull out nails and extract pegs for people, to loosen what is stuck and untie what is bound. How can it be given over to someone else lightly? Hsueh Tou means that it should be used by oneself alone. Fortunately it happened that this monk then just opened up to him—if he had suddenly stirred up thunder over dry ground, we would have observed how Chiu met it. When Wu Chiu passed him the handle, wasn't this indeed without any reason?

TRANSLATORS' NOTES

a. Yojana is a unit of distance: a day's march by the king and his retinue in ancient India; maybe ten or twenty miles.

Tan Hsia's Have You Eaten Yet?

POINTER

Fine as rice powder, cold as icy frost, it blocks off heaven and earth and goes beyond light and dark. Observe it where it's low and there's extra; level it off where it's high and there's not enough. Holding fast and letting go are both here, but is there a way to appear or not? To test I'm citing this old case: look!

CASE

Tan Hsia asked a monk, "Where have you come from?"[1] The monk said, "From down the mountain."[2] Hsia said, "Have you eaten yet or not?"[3] The monk said, "I have eaten."[4] Hsia said, "Did the person who brought you the food to eat have eyes or not?"[5] The monk was speechless.[6]

Ch'ang Ch'ing asked Pao Fu, "To give someone food to eat is ample requital of the debt of kindness: why wouldn't he have eyes?"[7] Fu said, "Giver and receiver are both blind."[8] Ch'ang Ch'ing said, "If they exhausted their activity, would they still turn out blind?"[9] Fu said, "Can you say that I'm blind?"[10]

NOTES

1. It's truly impossible to have no place at all you've come from. If he wants to know where he's come from, it won't be hard.
2. He has put on his straw sandals and walked into your belly. It's just that you don't understand. There's an echo in his words, but he keeps it to himself. Is he yellow or green?
3. A second ladleful of foul water douses the monk. Why just the zero point of a scale? He wants to know the real truth.
4. As it turns out, he's collided with the pillar. After all, he's had his nostrils pierced by a bystander. From the beginning it's been an iron hammer head with no handle hole.

500

5. Although he is relying on his power to mystify the man, he is also wrapping up the case on the basis of the facts. At the time he deserved to have his meditation seat overturned. Why is there no reason for what he did?

6. After all, he couldn't run. If this monk had been an adept he would have said to him, "The same as your eyes, Teacher."

7. He's still only said half. Is it "throughout the body" or is it "all over the body"? One cut, two pieces. One hand lifts up, one hand presses down.

8. He acts according to the imperative. With one line he says it all. Such a man is rarely encountered.

9. What does he know of good and evil? He still isn't settled himself: what bowl is he looking for?

10. The two of them are both in the weeds. Fu has a dragon's head but a snake's tail. At the time when he said, "If they had exhausted their activity, would they still turn out blind?" I would have just said to him, "You're blind." Since they're both adepts, why is it that "ahead they didn't reach the village, behind they didn't get to the shop"?

COMMENTARY

"Tan Hsia" was Ch'an Master T'ien Jan of Tan Hsia in Teng Province of Honan—I don't know what locality he was from. At first he studied Confucianism, intending to go to Ch'ang-an to take part in the examinations for official posts. Then unexpectedly while he was staying over at a travellers' lodge, he dreamed that a white light filled the room. A diviner said, "This is an auspicious omen of understanding emptiness." There happened to be a Ch'an traveller there who asked him, "Good man, where are you going?" He said, "To be chosen to be an official." The Ch'an traveller said, "How can choosing an official career compare to choosing Buddhahood?" Tan Hsia asked, "What place should I go to to choose Buddhahood?" The Ch'an traveller said, "At the present time Grand Master Ma has appeared in the world in Kiangsi. This is the place to choose Buddhahood—you should go there, good man."

After this Tan Hsia went directly to Kiangsi. The moment he saw Grand Master Ma he lifted up the edge of his turban (to look at Ma). Master Ma observed him and said, "I am not your

Teacher—go to Shih T'ou's place in Nan Yueh." Tan Hsia hastened to Nan Yueh where he submitted to Shih T'ou with the same idea as before (at Ma Tsu's place). Shih T'ou told him to go to the stable, and Tan Hsia bowed in thanks. He entered the workmen's hall and worked along with the congregation for three years.

One day Shih T'ou announced to the assembly, "Tomorrow we're going to clear away the weeds in front of the Buddha's shrine." The next day everyone equipped himself with a hoe to cut down the weeds. Tan Hsia alone took a bowl, filled it with water, and washed his head; then he knelt in front of Master Shih T'ou. Shih T'ou saw this and laughed at him, then shaved his head for him. As Shih T'ou began to explain the precepts for him, Tan Hsia covered his ears and went out.

Then Tan Hsia headed for Kiangsi to call again on Ma Tsu. Before meeting with Ma Tsu to pay his respects, he went into the monks' hall and sat astride the neck of the holy statue (of Manjusri). At the time everybody became very perturbed and hurried to report this to Ma Tsu. Tsu personally went to the hall to have a look at him and said, "My son is so natural." Hsia immediately got down and bowed saying, "Thank you, Master, for giving me a Dharma name." Because of this he was called T'ien Jan (which means natural). This man of old Tan Hsia was naturally sharply outstanding like this. As it is said, "Choosing officialdom isn't as good as choosing Buddhahood." His sayings are recorded in the *Records of the Transmission of the Lamp*.

His words tower up like a thousand-fathom wall. Each and every line has the ability to pull out nails and extract pegs for people, like when he asked this monk, "Where have you come from?" The monk said, "From down the mountain," yet he didn't communicate where he had come from. It seemed that he had eyes and was going to reverse things and examine the host. If it hadn't been Tan Hsia, it would have been impossible to gather him in.

But Tan Hsia said, "Have you eaten yet or not?" At first he hadn't been able to see this monk at all, so this is the second attempt to examine him. The monk said, "I have eaten." From the beginning this confused and ignorant fellow hadn't understood. Hsia said, "Did the person who brought you the food to eat have eyes or not?" and the monk was speechless. Tan Hsia's meaning was, "What's the use of giving food to such a fellow as you?" If this monk had been a fellow (with eyes) he would have given Tan Hsia a poke to see what he would do. Nevertheless, Tan Hsia still didn't let him go, so the monk was (left standing there) blinking stupidly and speechless.

When Pao Fu and Ch'ang Ch'ing were together in Hsueh Feng's congregation, they would often bring up the public cases of the Ancients to discuss. Ch'ang Ch'ing asked Pao Fu, "To give someone food is ample requital of kindness: why wouldn't he have eyes?" He didn't have to inquire exhaustively into the facts of the case; he could take it all in using these words to pose his question. He wanted to test Pao Fu's truth. Pao Fu said, "Giver and receiver are both blind." How direct! Here he just discusses the immediate circumstances—inside his house Pao Fu has a way to assert himself.

When Ch'ang Ch'ing said, "If they had exhausted their activity, would they still turn out blind?" Pao Fu said, "Can you say that I'm blind?" Pao Fu meant, "I have such eyes to have said it all to you—are you still saying I'm blind?" Nevertheless, it's half closed and half open. At that time if it had been me, when he said, "If they had exhausted their activity, would they still turn out blind?" I would have just said to him, "You're blind." What a pity! If Pao Fu had uttered this one word "blind" at that time, he would have avoided so many of Hsueh Tou's complications. Hsueh Tou too just uses this idea to make his verse:

VERSE

(Ch'ang Ch'ing) exhausts his activity, (Pao Fu) doesn't become
   blind—
   They've only said half. Each wanted to test the other. The
   words are still in our ears.

(Like) holding down an ox's head to make it eat grass.
   They lose their money and incur punishment. Half south
   of the river, half north of the river. Without realizing it,
   they've run afoul of the point and cut their hands.

Twenty-eight and six Patriarchs—
> If you have a rule, hold on to the rule. Hsueh Tou is dragging down the former sages; he doesn't just involve one man.

Their precious vessel is brought forth, but it turns out to be an error.
> Everyone on earth beats his breast (in sorrow). Give me back my staff. They've dragged me down so that I can't even show my face.

The error is profound—
> Extremely profound. The world's patchrobed monks cannot leap clear of it. But tell me, how profound?

There's no place to look for it.
> Though it's right beneath your feet, it can't be found.

Gods and humans sink down together on dry land.
> The world's patchrobed monks are all buried in one pit. Is there anyone alive? I let my move go. Heavens! Heavens!

COMMENTARY

"(Ch'ang Ch'ing) exhausts his activity, (Pao Fu) doesn't become blind." Ch'ang Ch'ing said, "If they exhausted their activity, would they still turn out blind?" Pao Fu said, "Can you say that I'm blind?" This was all like "Holding down an ox's head to make it eat grass." To get it right you must wait till he eats on his own: how can you push down an ox's head and make him eat? When Hsueh Tou versifies like this, naturally we can see Tan Hsia's meaning.

"Twenty-eight and six Patriarchs—/Their precious vessel is brought forth, but it turns out to be an error." Not only does Hsueh Tou drag down Ch'ang Ch'ing, but at the same time he buries the twenty-eight Patriarchs of India and the six Patriarchs of this country. In forty-nine years, old man Shakyamuni preached the whole great treasurehouse of the Teachings; at the end he only transmitted this precious vessel. Yung Chia said, "This is not an empty exhibition displaying form: it's the actual traces of the Tathagata's jewel staff." If you adopt Pao Fu's view, then even if you bring forth the precious vessel, it all turns out to be an error.

"The error is profound—/There's no place to look for it."
This can't be explained for you: just go sit quietly and inquire
into his lines and see. Since the error is profound, why then is
there no place to look for it? This is not a small mistake: he
takes the Great Affair of the Buddhas and Patriarchs and sub-
merges it entirely on dry land. Hence Hsueh Tou says, "Gods
and humans sink down together on dry land."

Yun Men's Cake

POINTER

Turning upwards, he can pierce the nostrils of everyone on earth, like a falcon catching a pigeon. Turning downwards, his own nostrils are in the hands of other people, like a turtle hiding in its shell.

Here if someone suddenly comes forth and says, "Fundamentally, there is no upwards and downwards—what use is turning?" I simply say to him, "I know that you are going inside the ghost cave to make your living."

But say, how will you distinguish initiate from naive? After a silence, Yuan Wu said, "If you have precepts, go by the precepts; if you have no precepts, go by the example."

CASE

A monk asked Yun Men, "What is talk that goes beyond Buddhas and Patriarchs?"[1] Men said, "Cake."[2]

NOTES

1. He opens up. Suddenly there's thunder over the parched earth. He presses.
2. The tongue is pressed against the roof of the mouth. It's gone by.

COMMENTARY

This monk asked Yun Men, "What is talk that goes beyond Buddhas and Patriarchs?" Men said, "Cake." Do you feel your hairs standing on end with the chill? Patchrobed monks have asked about Buddhas and asked about Patriarchs, asked about Ch'an and asked about Tao, asked about facing upwards and facing downwards—there's nothing more that can be asked,

yet this one posed a question and asked about talk that goes
beyond Buddhas and Patriarchs. Yun Men was an adept: thus,
when the water rises, the boats ride high, and when there is
much mud the Buddha-image is big. So he answered saying
"Cake." It can be said that the Way is not carried out in vain,
that his effort is not wasted.

Yun Men also taught the assembly saying, "Without any
understanding, when you see people talking about the intent of
the Patriarchal Teachers you immediately ask for theories of
talk that goes beyond Buddhas and Patriarchs. But what do you
call 'Buddhas,' what do you call 'Patriarchs,' that you immediately speak of talk that transcends Buddhas and Patriarchs? Then you ask about escape from the triple world, but
you take hold of the triple world to see. What seeing, hearing,
feeling, and knowing are there to hinder you? What
phenomena of sound and form are there that you can be made
to understand? What 'bowl' do you know how to use? On what
basis do you entertain views of differentiations? Those ancient
sages can't do anything for you, though they extend themselves
to help living beings. Even if they say that the whole Body is
entirely real, that in everything we see the Essence—this is
ungraspable. When I say to you, 'In fact, what concerns are
there?' this has already buried it." If you can understand this
statement, then you can recognize the "Cake."

Wu Tsu said, "Donkey shit is like horse shit." This is what
Yung Chia called "Going direct to the root source, as the Buddhas have sealed—picking through leaves and searching
through twigs I cannot do." When you get to this point, if you
want to attain Intimacy, don't ask with questions.

Observe how this monk asked, "What is talk that goes beyond Buddhas and Patriarchs?" and Yun Men said, "Cake."
Does Yun Men know shame? Is he aware of indulging? There's
a type of phoney person who says, "Yun Men saw the rabbit
and released the hawk; thus he said 'Cake.'" If you take such a
view, that "Cake" is talk that goes beyond Buddhas and Patriarchs, how can there be a living road? Don't understand it as
cake and don't understand it as going beyond Buddhas and
Patriarchs—this, then, is the living road. (Yun Men's "Cake")
is the same as (Tung Shan's) "Three pounds of hemp" (Case 12)
and (Ho Shan's) "Knowing how to beat the drum" (Case 44):
though he just said "Cake," its reality is hard to see.

Later people often made up rationalizations and said, "Coarse words and subtle talk all come back to the primary truth." If you understand in this fashion, just go be a lecturer and spend your life collecting much knowledge and many interpretations. Followers of Ch'an these days say, "When you go beyond the Buddhas and Patriarchs you are trampling both Buddhas and Patriarchs underfoot—that's why Yun Men just said to him, 'Cake.'" Since it's "Cake," how does this explain going beyond the Buddhas and Patriarchs? Try to investigate thoroughly and see.

In the various places the verses about this case are extremely numerous, but they all go to the side of the question to make their comment. Hsueh Tou alone has versified it the best—naturally he's outstanding. The verse says:

VERSE

Ch'an travellers asking about transcendent talk are especially numerous.
> One after another they come forth and make up this kind of view, (numerous as) hemp or millet.

His gap opens—see it?
> Already open before the words. Hsueh Tou doesn't notice the smell of his own shit.

Even the cake stuffed in doesn't stop him.
> He's replaced your eyes with wooden beads.

Up till now there has been confusion all over the world.
> I'll draw a circle and say, "Haven't you been understanding this way?" What end is there to chewing over the words of others? The great earth is desolate, killing people with sadness, so I'll hit.

COMMENTARY

"Ch'an travellers asking about transcendent talk are especially numerous." Followers of Ch'an are especially fond of asking about this saying ("talk that goes beyond Buddhas and Patriarchs"). Haven't you heard? Yun Men said, "All of you carry

a staff across your shoulders and say, 'I am immersed in meditation, I am studying the Path,' and then go looking for a truth
that goes beyond the Buddhas and Patriarchs. But I ask you,
during the twenty-four hours of the day, when walking, standing, sitting, and lying down; when shitting and pissing among
the vermin in a roadside privy; when at the counter of the
butcher's stall in the market; is there still any truth that goes
beyond the Buddhas and Patriarchs? Let those who can speak of
it come forward. If there isn't anyone (who can), then don't stop
me from acting this way and that as I please." Then Yun Men
went down from his seat.

Some can no longer tell right from wrong—they draw a circle, adding mud to dirt, putting on chains while wearing
stocks. "His gap opens—see it?" What a big gap there is in this
monk posing his question! Yun Men saw it opening up in his
question, so he said "Cake" to block it up tight. But this monk
still wouldn't agree to stop—instead, he went on asking. Thus
Hsueh Tou says, "Even the cake stuffed in doesn't stop him."

"Up till now there has been confusion all over the world."
Followers of Ch'an these days just go to "Cake" to understand,
or else they go to "beyond Buddhas and Patriarchs" to make up
theories. Since it's not in these two places, in the end, where is
it? Thirty years from now, when I've exchanged my bones, I'll
tell you.

Sixteen Bodhisattvas Go In to Bathe

CASE

In olden times there were sixteen bodhisattvas.[1] When it was time for monks to wash, the bodhisattvas filed in to bathe.[2] Suddenly they awakened to the basis of water.[3] All of you Ch'an worthies, how will you understand their saying, "Subtle feeling reveals illumination,[4] and we have achieved the station of sons of Buddha"?[5] To realize this you too must be extremely piercing and penetrating.[6]

NOTES

1. What's the use of forming a crowd? This bunch of idiots!
2. They've collided with the pillar. Why such lacquer tubs?
3. Suddenly their heads are soaked with foul water.
4. It's no longer anyone else's business. How will you understand them? "Having knocked it down, it's nothing else."
5. Here the world's patchrobed monks seek but cannot find. Why two heads, three faces?
6. One blow with the staff, one welt. Better not turn your back on me! You're colliding with it, you're bumping into it. Have you ever seen Te Shan and Lin Chi?

COMMENTARY

At the Surangama Assembly, Bhadrapala and the sixteen bodhisattvas all practiced pure conduct and each related the basis on which he had experienced the Dharma gate of perfect pervasiveness. This is numbered as one among twenty-five (kinds of) perfect pervasiveness. (They related that) when it was time for monks to bathe they had filed in to bathe and suddenly awakened to the basis of water. Since they didn't wash off the dirt, and they didn't wash their bodies, tell me, what did they wash? If you can understand, then, at peace within, you realize the absence of anything existing. Then a thousand or ten thousand will no longer be able to get near you. As it is said, "Absence of attainment is true wisdom; if there is something which is attained, this is just semblance wisdom."

Haven't you heard? Bodhidharma said to the Second Patriarch, "Bring out your mind and I will pacify it for you." The Second Patriarch said, "When I search for my mind, I can't find it." This little bit here is the basic root of patchrobed monks' lives. There's no more need at all for so many complications: all that's needed is to speak of suddenly awakening to the basis of water, and you spontaneously understand properly.

Since they didn't wash off the dust, and they didn't wash their bodies, tell me, what did they awaken to? When you get to this realm, nothing at all is applicable—even the word "Buddha" must be avoided. They said, "Subtle feeling reveals illumination, and we have achieved the station of sons of Buddha." "Reveals" means "makes apparent." The subtle feeling is illumination. Once you awaken to the subtle feeling, then you achieve the station of sons of Buddha, that is, you are in the stage of Buddhahood.

People these days also go in to bathe, they also wash in water and feel it this way. Why then don't they awaken? They are all confused and obstructed by the objects of the senses: they stick to their skins and cling to their bones. That's why they can't wake up immediately then and there. Here, if there's nothing attained in washing or feeling or in the basis of water, then tell me, is this "Subtle feeling reveals illumination" or not? If here you can see directly, then this is "Subtle feeling reveals illumination, and we achieve the station of sons of Buddha." People these days feel too, but do they perceive its subtlety? Subtle feeling is not ordinary feeling and feeler, where contact is considered feeling and separation is not.

When Hsuan Sha was crossing the mountains and stubbed his toe (thereupon awakening), when Te Shan hits—isn't this subtle feeling? Although it is so, to realize this you must be extremely piercing and penetrating. If you just search on your body, what connection is there? If you are extremely piercing and penetrating, then what need is there to go in and wash? You will make the jewel king's realm appear on the tip of a hair and turn the great Dharma Wheel in every speck of dust. If you can penetrate in one place, then you penetrate a thousand places, ten thousand places all at once. Don't just hold onto a single nook or den—all places are the gates by which Avalokitesvara enters the truth.

For the Ancients too there was "awakening to the Path by hearing sounds, illuminating Mind by seeing forms." If a single man awakens, this is the reason. But why did the sixteen bodhisattvas awaken at the same time? Because the Ancients practiced together and experienced together, awakened together and understood together. Hsueh Tou picks up the meaning of their teaching to make people go to where "Subtle feeling reveals illumination" to understand. But Hsueh Tou goes beyond the eye of their teaching to let people avoid being trapped within the net of the teaching, half-drunk and half-sober. He wants to make people directly become clean, free, and unbound. The verse says:

VERSE

I only need one patchrobed monk who understands this matter—
  There's one right here. I'll give him three thousand blows in the morning and eight hundred blows at night. Leap out of the unbreakable trap! Not even one is needed.
Stretch out your legs on the long-bench and lie down.
  After all he's a sleepyhead. For eons he never discusses Ch'an.
In a dream you once spoke of awakening to perfect pervasiveness—
  Already asleep, he goes on to speak of dreams. Yet I'll allow that he has seen it in dreams. Why the talking in his sleep?
Though you've washed in fragrant water, I'll spit right in your face.
  Bah! He adds another layer of mud on top of the dirt. Don't come and shit on the clean ground!

COMMENTARY

"I only need one patchrobed monk who understands this matter." But say, understands what matter? Once they hear it mentioned, adept Ch'an travellers immediately go carry it out. It just takes one such patchrobed monk—what's the use of forming a crowd?

"Stretch out your legs on the long-bench and lie down." An Ancient said, "In clear illumination, there is no such thing as awakening. (The concept of) 'having awakened' turns around and deludes people. When you stretch out both feet and sleep, there's no false and there's no true—thus, there isn't a single concern in one's heart. When hungry, one eats; when tired, one sleeps."

Hsueh Tou means that if you speak of going in to wash and awakening to "Subtle feeling reveals illumination," from the standpoint of this kind of unconcerned patchrobed monk, this is just like speaking of a dream in a dream. That's why Hsueh Tou says, "In a dream you once spoke of awakening to perfect pervasiveness—Though you've washed in fragrant water, I'll spit right in your face." Though it seems like fragrant water, in fact it's foul water suddenly soaking your head. What "perfect pervasiveness" can you go on talking about? Hsueh Tou says that this sort of fellow quite rightly gets his face spattered with spit. I say that this is adding another layer of mud on top of dirt.

T'ou Tzu's All Sounds

POINTER

When his great function manifests before you it doesn't keep to patterns and rules. He captures you alive without exerting superfluous effort. But say, who has ever acted this way? To test I'm citing this old case: look!

CASE

A monk asked T'ou Tzu, "All sounds are the sounds of Buddha—right or wrong?"[1] T'ou Tzu said, "Right."[2] The monk said, "Teacher, doesn't your asshole make farting sounds?"[3] T'ou Tzu then hit him.[4]

Again the monk asked, "Coarse words or subtle talk, all returns to the primary meaning—right or wrong?"[5] T'ou Tzu said, "Right."[6] The monk said, "Can I call you an ass, Teacher?"[7] T'ou Tzu then hit him.[8]

NOTES

1. This monk too knows how to grab the tiger's whiskers. Crashing thunderclaps in a clear sky. He doesn't notice the bad smell of his own shit.
2. He's utterly swindling ordinary people. He's sold his body to you. He's put it over on one side. What's going on in your mind?
3. He just sees that the awl point is sharp; he doesn't see that the chisel edge is square. What is he saying? After all, he suffers defeat.
4. A hit! He should be hit—it won't do to let him go.
5. Grabbing the tiger's whiskers a second time. He's clutching the loot crying out that he's been wronged—why? East, west, south, north—the reflections and echoes are still present.

6. Again he's sold his body to you. A pitfall to trap tigers. What's going on in your mind?
7. He just sees that the awl point is sharp; he doesn't see that the chisel edge is square. Though he has waves that go against the current, yet he has no horns on his head. With a mouth full of blood, he spits out at people.
8. A hit! It won't do to let him go. He should be hit—why does T'ou Tzu stop before his staff is broken?

COMMENTARY

T'ou Tzu was plain and truthful; he had the eloquence which stood out from the crowd. Whenever a question was put to him, you saw his guts as soon as he opened his mouth. Without expending superfluous effort, he would immediately cut off the questioner's tongue. It could be said that, setting his plans in motion from within his headquarters tent, he decided victory beyond a thousand miles. This monk had taken his views of sound and form Buddhism and stuck them to his forehead: whenever he met someone, he would immediately ask about it. But T'ou Tzu, an adept, profoundly discerns oncoming winds.

Knowing that T'ou Tzu was truthful, this monk from the start was making a trap for him to go into—hence his subsequent remarks. Nevertheless it was T'ou Tzu who used the tiger trap to fish out the monk's subsequent words. This monk received T'ou Tzu's answer by saying, "Teacher, doesn't your asshole make farting sounds?" As it turned out, as soon as T'ou Tzu set his hook, the monk immediately climbed onto it. Anyone else would have been unable to handle this monk, but T'ou Tzu had the eye and followed up behind and hit him. Such "hound biting a boar" ability is only possible for an adept. Whether he turned to the left or to the right, T'ou Tzu followed him, turning smoothly. When this monk made a trap, wanting to grab the tiger's whiskers, he was far from knowing that T'ou Tzu was above his trap and would hit him. Too bad for this monk—he had a head but no tail. As soon as T'ou Tzu picked up his staff, the monk should have overturned his meditation seat. Then even if T'ou Tzu had used his full capacity, he still would have had to fall back three thousand miles.

The monk also asked, "Coarse words or subtle talk, all returns to the primary meaning—right or wrong?" Again T'ou Tzu said, "Right." This is just like his previous answer; there is no difference. When the monk said, "Can I call you an ass, Teacher?" T'ou Tzu again hit him. Although this monk was making himself a nest, nevertheless he was still exceptional. If the old fellow up on the carved wood seat had been without an eye on his forehead, it would have been impossible for him to crush this monk. But T'ou Tzu did have a place to turn around. When this monk made up a theory, he wanted to plunder T'ou Tzu's shop; but in the end, as before, he couldn't cope with the old fellow.

Haven't you seen Yen T'ou's saying? "In battle each one occupies a pivotal position." T'ou Tzu let go very slowly and gathered in very swiftly. At the time, if this monk had known how to turn himself around and show some life, wouldn't he have been able to act as a man with a mouth like a bowl of blood? A patchrobed monk either doesn't act or (once he begins) doesn't quit. Since this monk was unable to spring back, his nostrils were pierced by T'ou Tzu. The verse says:

VERSE

T'ou Tzu! T'ou Tzu!
> Obviously there's no one on earth like this truthful old fellow. He spoils the sons and daughters of other people's families.

The wheel of his ability is unobstructed.
> What difficulty is there to handling him? There is a bit indeed.

He releases one and gets two—
> He snatches your eyes. Where will you see T'ou Tzu?

The same for that and the same for this.
> Act this way and you'll get a beating; don't act this way and you'll still get a beating. If you take this monk's place, I'll hit you.

How pitiful: innumerable people playing in the tide,
> The monasteries produce one or a half: they produced this fellow. The world's patchrobed monks act this way.

In the end fall into the tide and die.
> Too bad! What can they do? They can't get out of the trap.
> A sad person shouldn't talk to sad people.

If they suddenly came to life,
> My meditation seat shakes—he's startled me. I too fall
> back three thousand miles.

The hundred rivers would reverse their flow with a rushing
> *roaring noise.*
> Danger! It is useless to stop and think. I wouldn't dare
> open my mouth. Old man T'ou Tzu, too, must break his
> staff before he's all right.

COMMENTARY

"T'ou Tzu! T'ou Tzu!/The wheel of his ability is unobstructed." T'ou Tzu often said, "You always say that T'ou
Tzu is truthful, but if you suddenly went three steps down the
mountain and someone asked you, 'What is T'ou Tzu's truth-
fulness?' how would you respond?" The man of old Hsueh Tou
said, "Where the wheel of his ability turns the actor is still
deluded." The wheel of T'ou Tzu's ability turns so smoothly,
entirely without obstructions.

Thus Hsueh Tou says, "He releases one and gets two."
Haven't you heard? A monk asked, "What is Buddha?" T'ou
Tzu said, "Buddha." Again he asked, "What is the Path?" T'ou
Tzu said, "The Path." Again he asked, "What is Ch'an?" T'ou
Tzu said, "Ch'an." He also asked, "How is it when the moon is
not yet full?" T'ou Tzu said, "Swallowing three or four." Again
he asked, "How is it after the moon is full?" T'ou Tzu said,
"Spitting out seven or eight." When T'ou Tzu received people
he always used this ability.

When he answered this monk (in the main case) he just used
the one word "Right." This monk got hit both times. Hence
Hsueh Tou says, "The same for that and the same for this."
The first four lines have all at once completed Hsueh Tou's
praise of T'ou Tzu.

At the end Hsueh Tou versifies the monk saying, "How
pitiful: innumerable people playing in the tide." This monk
dared to seize T'ou Tzu's banner and drums saying, "Teacher,
doesn't your asshole make farting sounds?" and "Can I call you

an ass, Teacher?" This then is where he played in the tide. When this monk had exhausted his clever maneuvers, as before he died amidst T'ou Tzu's words, so T'ou Tzu then hit him. Thus this monk "In the end falls into the tide and dies."

Hsueh Tou releases this monk and says that if he suddenly came to life and overturned the meditation seat, then even T'ou Tzu would have to fall back three thousand miles, and then "The hundred rivers would reverse their flow with a rushing roaring noise." Not only does my meditation seat shake, but the mountains and rivers quake and heaven and earth are abruptly blacked out. If each and every one of you were like this, I'd be beating the drums of retreat. Where will all of you go to secure your bodies and establish your lives?

Chao Chou's Newborn Baby

CASE

A monk asked Chao Chou, "Does a newborn baby also have the sixth consciousness?"[1] Chao Chou said, "(Like) tossing a ball on swift-flowing water."[2]

The monk also asked T'ou Tzu, "What is the meaning of 'Tossing a ball on swift-flowing water'?"[3] T'ou Tzu said, "Moment to moment, nonstop flow."[4]

NOTES

1. With a lightning flash intellect, what newborn baby is he talking about?
2. It's gone by. Even a swift hawk cannot overtake it. You still must check it out.
3. This too is adepts investigating together. Understand? It's gone by.
4. He's a fellow who creates complications.

COMMENTARY

In the school of the Teachings, this eighth consciousness is set up as the true basis. Mountains, rivers, and the great earth, sun, moon, and stars come into being because of it. It comes as the advance guard and leaves as the rearguard. The Ancients say that "The triple world is only mind—the myriad things are only consciousness." If one experiences the stage of Buddhahood, the eight consciousnesses are transformed into the four wisdoms.[a] In the school of the Teachings they call this "Changing names, not changing essence."

Sense-faculties, sense-objects, and consciousness of sensation are three. Originally we are unable to discriminate among the sense-objects before us. But the subtle inner faculties can produce consciousness, and consciousness can reveal discrimination of forms. This is the sixth consciousness—conceptual thinking. The seventh consciousness is Manas. It can go take hold of the imaginary things of the world and cause a person to be vexed and troubled so that he doesn't attain freedom and independence. As for the eighth consciousness, it's called the Alayavijnana and it's also called the Storehouse Consciousness. It contains all the seeds of good and evil.

This monk knew the ideas of the verbal teachings, so he used them to question Chao Chou by saying, "Does a newborn baby also have the sixth consciousness or not?" Although a newborn baby is equipped with the six consciousnesses, though his eyes can see and his ears can hear, he doesn't yet discriminate among the six sense-objects. At this time he knows nothing of good and evil, long and short, right and wrong, or gain and loss. A person who studies the Path must become again like an infant. Then praise and blame, success and fame, unfavorable circumstances and favorable environments—none of these can move him. "Though his eyes see form, he is the same as a blind man; though his ears hear sound, he is the same as a deaf man." He is like a fool, like an idiot—his mind is motionless as Mt. Sumeru. This is the place where patchrobed monks really and truly acquire power.

An Ancient said, "My patched garment covering my head, myriad concerns cease: at this time I don't understand anything at all." Only if you can be like this will you have a small share of attainment. Though an adept is like this, nevertheless he can't be fooled at all—as before, mountains are mountains and rivers are rivers. He is without artifice and without clinging thoughts. He is like the sun and moon moving through the sky without ever stopping and without saying, "I have so many names and forms." He is like the sky everywhere covering, like the earth everywhere supporting: since they have no mind, they bring up and nurture myriad beings without saying, "I have so many accomplishments." Since sky and earth are mindless, they last forever—what has mind has limits. A person who has attained the Path is like this too. In the midst of no activity, he carries out his activities, accepting all unfavorable and favorable circumstances with a compassionate heart.

When they got to this point the Ancients still upbraided themselves and said, "When you've completely perfectly comprehended, there's nothing to comprehend; in the dark, abstruse, hidden place, you still must be rebuked." They also said, "All things are thoroughly comprehended and all beings are clearly understood—when one who has Arrived senses this, he's startled in the darkness." Again it was said, "Without making a sound he goes beyond the ordinary and enters sagehood. The reclining dragon deeply fears the blue pool's clarity." If human beings can be like this always, how can a single name remain in the world? Though it's this way, they must go on to leap out of their nest before they attain.

Haven't you seen where it says in the (Hua Yen) sutra,[b] "A bodhisattva of the eighth stage, Immovability, turns the great Dharma Wheel in an atom of dust, using the wisdom of non-activity. At all times, whether walking, standing, sitting, or lying down, he doesn't cling to gain and loss, but lets himself move and flow into the sea of All-Knowledge." When patch-robed monks get here they still must not become attached: they follow the occasion freely. When they have tea, they drink tea; when they have food, they eat food. Neither the words "concentration" nor "not concentration" can be applied to this transcendental matter.

Master Shan Tao of the Stone Grotto taught his congregation saying, "Haven't you seen a little one when it's just emerged from the womb? Has a baby ever said, 'I know how to read the scriptures'? At that time it does not know the meaning of having the Buddha nature or not having the Buddha nature. As he grows up he learns all sorts of knowledge; then he comes forth saying 'I am able' and 'I understand,' without knowing that this is troubling over illusory dusts. Among the sixteen contemplation practices, the baby's practice is the best. When he's babbling he symbolizes the person studying the Path, with his detachment from the discriminating mind that grasps and rejects. That's why I'm praising infants. I can make a comparison by taking the case of a baby, but if I say that the baby is the Path, people of these times would misunderstand."

Nan Ch'uan said, "After eighteen, I was able to make a living." Chao Chou said, "After eighteen, I was able to break up the family and scatter the household." He also said, "I was in the South for twenty years: only the two mealtimes of gruel and rice were points of mixed application of mind."

Ts'ao Shan asked a monk, "'In his concentration the bodhisattva smells the fragrant elephant crossing the river very clearly.' What scripture does this come from?" The monk said, "From the *Nirvana* scripture." Shan said, "Does he smell it before or after his concentration?" The monk said "You've flowed, Teacher." Shan said, "Receive it on the river bank."

Again: the *Surangama* scripture says, "The fullness (of the six consciousnesses) enters to merge in the fullness (of the Storehouse Consciousness), going into the realm of consciousness."

Again: the *Lankavatara* scripture says, "Birth of signs— being obstructed by grasping. Birth of conception—false thinking. Birth of flow—pursuing falsehood, revolving and flowing. You must get out of the third aspect, 'birth of flow'; only then will you be joyfully alive and independent."c

Thus Kuei Shan asked Yang Shan, "How is it with you Disciple Chi?" Yang Shan said, "Are you asking about his perceptive understanding or his active understanding? If you ask about his active understanding, I don't know. If you ask about his perceptive understanding, it's like a pitcher of water being poured into a pitcher of water." If you can be like this you can be the teacher of a region.

When Chao Chou said, "Tossing a ball on swift-flowing water," he was already turning smoothly. When you toss it onto swift-flowing water, in a blink of an eye it's gone. As the *Surangama* scripture says, "Looked upon from afar, swift-flowing water is tranquil and still." An Ancient said, "In a fast-flowing river the currents of water never stop and they are unaware of each other—all things are like this too." The meaning of Chao Chou's answer is completely similar to these (quotations).

The monk also asked T'ou Tzu, "What is the meaning of 'Tossing a ball on swift-flowing water'?" T'ou Tzu said, "Moment to moment, nonstop flow," spontaneously matching the monk's question perfectly. The practice of these Ancients, Chao Chou and T'ou Tzu, was so thoroughgoing that they answered as one. They no longer make use of calculations—as soon as you question them they already know where you come down.

Although a baby's sixth consciousness is inactive, nevertheless from moment to moment it doesn't stop, but flows on like a hidden river. Of T'ou Tzu's answering this way we can say that he profoundly discerns oncoming winds.

Hsueh Tou's verse says:

VERSE

Sixth consciousness inactive—he puts forth a question.
    Though he has eyes, he is like a blind man; though he has
    ears, he is like a deaf man. The bright mirror is in its
    stand; the bright pearl is in the palm of his hand. In one
    line Hsueh Tou has said it all.

The adepts have both discerned where he's coming from—
    What's the need? Still, one must distinguish initiated
    from naive. Just experience it, then you'll know.

On the boundless swift-flowing water, tossing a ball:
    Consistent from beginning to end. It's gone. What is he
    saying?

Where it comes down, it doesn't stay—who can watch it?
    Watch it and you'll go blind. It's gone. "Receive it on the
    river bank."

COMMENTARY

"Sixth consciousness inactive—he puts forth a question."
When the Ancients studied the Path they brought themselves
to this point: this is called "achievement of non-activity."
They were the same as a newborn baby: though possessed of
eyes, ears, nose, tongue, body, and mind, they didn't discriminate among the six sense-objects. In sum, they were non-
active. When you get to this realm, then you can overcome
dragons and subdue tigers, die sitting or die standing up. Right
now people should just take the myriad phenomena before
their eyes and put them to rest at once. What need is there to
get above the eighth stage (of a bodhisattva) before you can be
like this? Although there's no activity, as of old mountains are
mountains and rivers are rivers.

    In a previous verse (about Chao Chou and T'ou Tzu, in Case
41) Hsueh Tou said, "In living there's an eye—still, it's the
same as death/Why use anti-serum to test an adept?" Since
Chao Chou and T'ou Tzu were adepts he says, "The adepts

have both discerned where he's coming from—/On the boundless swift-flowing water, tossing a ball." T'ou Tzu said, "Moment to moment, nonstop flow." Do all of you people know what this really means? At the end Hsueh Tou has people set eyes on it for themselves and watch. Hence he says, "Where it comes down, it doesn't stay—who can watch it?" This is Hsueh Tou's living line. But say, what does it really mean?

TRANSLATORS' NOTES

a. The eight consciousnesses are transformed into four knowledges as follows: The first five consciousnesses (associated with seeing, hearing, tasting, smelling, and touching) are transmuted into the Knowledge of Accomplishment. The sixth consciousness becomes the Wondrous Observing Knowledge, the seventh becomes the Knowledge of Equality, and the eighth becomes the Great Perfect Mirror Knowledge.

b. The ten stages of a bodhisattva's career, as described in the Hua Yen (*Avatamsaka*) scripture, are called: 1) Joy; 2) Freedom from Defilement; 3) Emanating Light; 4) Radiant Wisdom; 5) Impossible to Surpass; 6) (True Thusness) Becoming Manifest; 7) Far-reaching; 8) Immovability; 9) Good Wisdom; 10) Clouds of Dharma.

c. Kuei Shan said to Yang Shan, "I consider the Mirror Knowledge to be the source of the school. It produces three kinds of birth: birth of conception, birth of signs, birth of flowings. The *Surangama* scripture says, 'Concepts and signs constitute the dusts; conscious feelings constitute defilement. Detach from both and your Dharma Eye will be clear and pure at all times: how could you fail then to realize unexcelled correct awakening?' The birth of conception is fragmentation and confusion of the mind which thinks; the birth of signs is the manifestation of the object thought of. Together with the subtle flowings, they constitute the dusts and defilements. If you can clear them completely, only then will you be free." (*Jen T'ien Yen Mu*, 3)

Yao Shan's Shooting the Elk of Elks

POINTER

He captures the banner and seizes the drums—the thousand sages cannot search him out. He cuts off confusing obscurities—ten thousand devices cannot get to him. This is not the wondrous functioning of spiritual powers, nor is it the suchness of the basic essence. But tell me, what does he rely on to attain such marvels?

CASE

A monk asked Yao Shan, "On a level field, in the shallow grass, the elk and deer form a herd: how can one shoot the elk of elks?"[1] Shan said, "Look—an arrow!"[2] The monk let himself fall down.[3] Shan said, "Attendant, drag this dead fellow out."[4] The monk then ran out.[5] Shan said, "This fellow playing with a mud ball—what end will there be to it?"[6]

Hsueh Tou commented saying, "Though he lived for three steps, after five steps he had to die."[7]

NOTES

1. He enters enemy headquarters with his helmet off. He raises his head wearing horns. He pulls an arrow out of the back of his head.[a]
2. He goes right up and takes him. If you're not running downhill fast, it's hard to meet him. A hit!
3. Obviously this monk is unusual, but once dead he doesn't come to life again. He's a fellow giving play to his spirit.
4. He acts according to the imperative. He doesn't bother to test the monk again. The first arrow was still light; the second arrow was deep.

5. Inside the coffin, he opens up his eyes—within death he finds life. He still has some breath left.

6. Too bad Yao Shan let him go. He acts according to the imperative, but he's adding frost on top of snow.

7. One hand lifts up, one hand presses down. Even if he ran a hundred steps he would still have to lose his body and his life.

COMMENTARY

In the Ts'ao Tung tradition this case is called "a question that uses things." It's also called "a question testing the host," used in order to illustrate his present state of mind.

Ordinarily deer and elk are easy to shoot. Only the elk of elks, that is, the king among deer, is very difficult to shoot. This (king) elk always sharpens his horns on the rocks of the cliffs (where it lives,) so that they become sharp as sword blades. He defends the herd of deer with his own body so that even tigers cannot come near.

Likewise, this monk seems intelligent and alert as he draws on this to question Yao Shan to reveal what he would do first. Shan said, "Look—an arrow!" An expert Teaching Master, he is undeniably marvellous, like sparks struck from stone, like a flash of lightning.

Haven't you heard (about what happened) when San P'ing first called on Shih Kung? As soon as Kung saw him coming, he immediately went through the motion of bending a bow and said, "Look—an arrow!" San P'ing opened his breast (to the "arrow") and said, "This is the arrow that kills the man—what is the arrow that brings the man life?" Kung plucked the bowstring three times, whereupon San P'ing bowed in homage. Kung said, "After thirty years with a single bow and two arrows, today I've finally managed to shoot half a sage." Then he broke his bow and arrows.

Later San P'ing took this up with Ta Tien. Tien said, "Since it is the arrow that brings people life, why draw it on a bowstring?" an P'ing was speechless. Tien said, "Thirty years hence it will still be hard to find someone to raise these words."

Fa Teng had a verse saying:

In the old days we had Master Shih Kung—
Setting his bow and arrows, he sat.
He went on like this for thirty years—
Not a single one understood (until)
San P'ing came and hit the target,
And father and son reached harmony.
Thinking back carefully, (I see that)
From the beginning, they were shooting the mound
*   (instead of the target on it.)*

Shih Kung's strategy was the same as Yao Shan's. San P'ing
had an eye on his forehead, so he hit the target immediately
given a single phrase. It was just like Yao Shan saying,
"Look—an arrow!" and this monk then letting himself fall
down, playing the elk. This monk seemed to be an adept too,
but it's just that he had a head but no tail. Once he had set his
trap, he wanted to make Yao Shan fall in. But what could he
do? Yao Shan was an adept and kept on pressing relentlessly.
When Shan said, "Attendant, drag this dead fellow out," it was
as if he was extending his battle lines forward. This monk then
ran out: he may have been right, but nonetheless he wasn't free
and clean, his hands and feet were stuck. That's why Yao Shan
said, "This fellow playing with a mud ball—what end will
there be to it?" If Yao Shan hadn't had the final word at that
time, he would have been criticized by others down through
the ages.

Shan said, "Look—an arrow!" whereupon this monk fell
down. Tell me, was this understanding or not? If you say it was
understanding, why then did Yao Shan speak of him this way,
as a fellow playing with a mud ball? This was extremely evil,
just like (the following):

A monk asked Te Shan, "How is it when a student holding a
sharp sword tries to take the Master's head?" Te Shan extended
his neck forward toward him and shouted. The monk said,
"The Master's head has fallen." Te Shan lowered his head and
returned to his abbot's quarters. Again: Yen T'ou asked a
monk, "Where have you come from?" The monk said, "From
the Western Capital." Yen T'ou said, "After Huang Ch'ao
passed by, did you take his sword?" The monk said, "I did."
Yen T'ou extended his neck forward toward him and shouted.
The monk said, "The Master's head has fallen." Yen T'ou

laughed loudly. Cases of this kind are all traps to fell tigers, just like the present main case. Fortunately Yao Shan wasn't taken in by this monk—since he saw through him, he just kept on pressing.

Hsueh Tou says, "Although this monk lived for three steps, after five steps he had to die." Although this monk knew very well how to look at the arrow, he immediately let himself fall down—when Yao Shan said, "Attendant, drag this dead fellow out," he immediately ran out. Hsueh Tou says, "I'm afraid he won't live beyond three steps." If the monk had leaped beyond five steps at that time, no one in the world would have been able to handle him.

In a meeting of adepts, from beginning to end there must be an uninterrupted interchange of guest and host; only then is there a share of freedom and independence. Since at that time the monk wasn't able to continue from beginning to end, consequently he meets with Hsueh Tou's censure. But at the end Hsueh Tou himself uses his words for his verse saying:

VERSE

The elk of elks—
> Set your eyes high and look! He raises his head wearing horns.

You should take a look.
> What sort of thing is it? He's running in the secondary level. If you want to shoot, then shoot, but why look?

(Yao Shan) releases one arrow—
> On target. You must realize that Yao Shan is an expert.

(The monk) runs three steps.
> He's leaping with life, but only for three steps. He's been dead a long time.

If he had lived for five steps,
> What for? He leaps a hundred steps. How is it when unexpectedly finding life in the midst of death?

He would have formed a herd and chased the tiger.
> The two reflect each other. You should fall back three thousand miles. The world's patchrobed monks let the tiger get away.

The correct eye has always been given to a hunter.
> What can you do? Yao Shan doesn't consent to acknowledge these words. It's so for Yao Shan—what about Hsueh Tou? It doesn't concern Yao Shan, it doesn't concern Hsueh Tou, it doesn't concern me, and it doesn't concern you.

In a loud voice Hsueh Tou said, "Look—an arrow!"
> One punishment for all their crimes. You must fall back three thousand miles from them before you're all right. I hit, saying, "He's already blocked off your throats."

COMMENTARY

"The elk of elks—you should take a look." Patchrobed monks must have the eye of the elk of elks and the horns of the elk of elks, they must have devices and strategy. Even if it's a fierce tiger with wings or a great cat with horns, the elk of elks can still preserve his body and keep harm at a distance. At that time when this monk let himself fall, he was saying of himself, "I am the elk of elks."

"Yao Shan releases one arrow—the monk runs three steps." When Yao Shan said, "Look—an arrow!" the monk then fell down. When Yao Shan said, "Attendant, drag this dead fellow out," the monk then ran out. He did very well, but nevertheless he was only able to run three steps.

"If he had lived for five steps,/He would have formed a herd and chased the tiger." Hsueh Tou said, "I'm afraid that after five steps he had to die. If he had been able to leap beyond five steps at that time, then he would have been able to gather his herd and gone to chase the tiger." The horns of the elk of elks are sharp as spears—when a tiger sees him, even he becomes afraid and flees. This elk is the king among the deer: he always leads the herd in driving the tiger to another mountain.

Finally Hsueh Tou praises Yao Shan for having a way to assert himself in that situation. "The correct eye had always been given to a hunter." Yao Shan is like a hunter who knows how to shoot and this monk is like (his quarry) the elk. Then, having gone up to the hall and related this story, Hsueh Tou wrapped it up into a single bundle, speaking a single line in a loud voice: "Look—an arrow!" At once those who had been sitting and standing (listening to him) were unable to stir.

TRANSLATORS' NOTES

a.   "He pulls an arrow out of the back of his head": the arrow pierces his head from the front; he pulls it all the way through and out the back.

Ta Lung's Hard and Fast Body of Reality

POINTER

Only those with eyes can know the fishing line. Only adepts can handle devices outside of patterns. But say, what is the fishing line? What are devices beyond patterns? To test I'm citing this old case: look!

CASE

A monk asked Ta Lung, "The physical body rots away: what is the hard and fast body of reality?"[1]

Lung said, "The mountain flowers bloom like brocade, the valley streams are brimming blue as indigo."[2]

NOTES

1. His statement makes them into two. Still, it's all right to separate them.
2. A flute with no holes hitting against a felt-pounding board. The whole cannot be broken apart. When someone comes from one end of the province, I go to the other end.

COMMENTARY

If you go to the words to search for this thing, it's like trying to hit the moon by waving a stick—you won't make any connection. An Ancient clearly stated, "If you want to attain Intimacy, don't ask with questions. Why? Because the question is in the answer and the answer is in the question."

This monk picked up a load of crudeness and exchanged it for a load of confusion: in posing this question, his defeat was not slight. How could anyone other than Ta Lung manage to cover heaven and cover earth? The monk asking this way and Ta Lung answering this way is a single whole. Ta Lung didn't move a hair's breadth: it was like seeing a rabbit and releasing a falcon, like seeing a hole and putting in a plug. Is this time and season in the twelve-part canon of the Triple Vehicle? Undeniably his answer was extraordinary, it's just that his words have no flavor and he blocks up people's mouths. Thus it is said, "When white clouds lie across the valley mouth, many birds returning by night can't find their nests."

Some say that this was just answering glibly. Those who understand in this fashion are nothing but exterminators of the Buddha's race. They are far from knowing that with one device and one objective, the Ancients broke fetters and smashed chains, that every word and phrase were pure gold and raw gems.

If one has the eye and brain of a patchrobed monk, sometimes he holds fast and sometimes he lets go. Shining and functioning at the same time, with both persons and objects taken away, both sides let go and both sides gather in. Facing the situation, he changes accordingly. Without the great function and great capacity, how would he be able to enclose heaven and earth like this? Much as a bright mirror on its stand: when a foreigner comes, a foreigner appears, and when a native comes, a native appears.

This case is the same as the story (case 39) of the Flower Hedge, though the meaning is not the same. Here the monk's question was ignorant, so Ta Lung's answer was exactly appropriate. Haven't you heard (this story, case 27)? A monk asked Yun Men, "How is it when the tree withers and the leaves fall?" Men said, "The body exposed in the golden wind." This is called "arrowpoints meeting." Here the monk asked Ta Lung, "The physical body rots away: what is the hard and fast body of reality?" Ta Lung said, "The mountain flowers bloom like brocade, the valley streams are brimming blue as indigo." This is just like "you go west to Ch'in, I go east to Lu": since he acts this way, I don't act this way. Matching Ta Lung's answer with Yun Men's, they're opposites. It's easy to see Yun Men

acting thus, but it's hard to see Ta Lung acting otherwise.
Nevertheless, Ta Lung's tongue is very subtle.

VERSE

Asking without knowing.
> East and west not distinguished. Playing with the thing
> without knowing its name. He buys the hat to fit the
> head.

Answering, still not understanding.
> South and north not differentiated. He switched the
> monk's skull around. South of the river, north of the river.

The moon is cold, the wind is high—
> What is it like? Today is precisely this time and season.
> The world's people have eyes but have never seen, have
> ears but have never heard.

On the ancient cliff, frigid juniper.
> Even better when it's not raining. A flute with no holes
> hitting against a felt-pounding board.

*How delightful: on the road he met a man who had attained
>   the Path,*
> You too must get here personally before you're all right.
> Give me back my staff. They come like this, forming a
> crowd.

And didn't use speech or silence to reply.
> Where will you see Ta Lung? What would you use to
> answer him properly?

His hand grasps the white jade whip.
> It should be broken to pieces.

And smashes the black dragon's pearl.[a]
> It remains for future people to look at. Too bad!

If he hadn't smashed it,
> Letting his move go. Again you go on like this.

He would have increased its flaws.
> What is he doing, playing with a mud ball? He seems
> more and more decrepit. His crimes fill the sky.

The nation has a code of laws—
>   Those who know the law fear it. "In the morning three
>   thousand blows, at night eight hundred blows."

Three thousand articles of offenses.
>   He's only told the half of it. There are eighty-four
>   thousand. Countless eons of uninterrupted hell wouldn't
>   make up for half of it.

COMMENTARY

Hsueh Tou versifies here with much skill. Before when he was
versifying Yun Men's words ("body exposed in the golden
wind") he said, "Since the question has the source/The answer
too is in the same place." Since it's not so with this case,
Hsueh Tou instead says, "Asking without knowing/
Answering, still not understanding." Ta Lung's answer was a
glimpse from the side that was simply amazing. His answer
was so clear that whoever questioned him this way had already
incurred defeat even before he asked. With his answer he was
able to bend down to the monk and match him perfectly:
adapting to his capacity he rightly said, "The mountain flowers
bloom like brocade, the valley streams are brimming blue as
indigo." How will all of you understand Ta Lung's meaning
right now? As a glimpse from the side, his answer was truly
extraordinary.

   Thus Hsueh Tou comes out with his verse to make people
realize that the moon is cold, the wind is high and still beats
against the frigid juniper on the ancient cliff. But say, how will
you understand Hsueh Tou's meaning? Thus I just said that it's
a flute with no holes hitting against a felt-pounding board.

   The verse is completed with just these first four lines, but
Hsueh Tou was still fearful that people would make up
rationalizations, so he said, "How delightful: on the road he
met a man who had attained the Path,/And didn't use speech or
silence to reply." This matter, then, is not seeing, hearing,
discernment, or knowledge; nor is it the discriminations of
calculating thought. Therefore it was said:

>   *Direct and truthful, without bringing anything else*
>   *along,*

Moving on alone—what is there to depend on?
On the road, if you meet anyone who has attained
    the Path,
Don't use speech or silence to reply.

This is a verse of Hsiang Yen's that Hsueh Tou has drawn on. Haven't you heard? A monk asked Chao Chou, "Without using speech or silence to answer, I wonder with what should one answer?" Chou said, "Show your lacquer vessel." These (sayings of Hsiang Yen and Chao Chou) are the same as Ta Lung's statement (in the main case): they don't fall within the scope of your feelings or conceptual thoughts.

What is this like? "His hand grasps the white jade whip/And smashes the black dragon's pearl." Thus the command of the patriarchs must be carried out, cutting off everything in the ten directions. This is the matter on the sword's edge, for which one must have this kind of strategy. Otherwise you turn your back on all the sages since antiquity. When you get here you must be without the slightest concern, then naturally you'll have the advantage. This, then, is how a transcendent man comports himself. "If he hadn't smashed it," necessarily "He would have increased its flaws," and thus he would have seemed broken down and decrepit.

But in the end, how can you be right? "The nation has a code of laws—/Three thousand articles of offenses." There are three thousand subdivisions of the five punishments, and none is greater than (the punishment) for not being respectful. This monk offended against all three thousand articles at once. How so? Because he didn't deal with people on the basis of his own thing. As for Ta Lung, he of course was not this way.

TRANSLATORS' NOTES

a. This precious jewel of legend is to be found in the ocean depths, right under the jaws of the black dragon.

Yun Men's Ancient Buddhas and the Pillar

CASE

Yun Men, teaching the community, said, "The ancient Buddhas and the pillar merge—what level of mental activity is this?"[1] He himself said on their behalf,[2] "On South Mountain clouds gather,[3] on North Mountain rain falls."[4]

NOTES

1. Three thousand miles away. There's no connection. Cracked open.
2. When someone in the eastern house dies, someone from the western house assists in the mourning. The single compounded form cannot be grasped.
3. Throughout heaven and earth, they can't be seen. A knife cannot cut through.
4. Not a drop falls. Half south of the river, half north of the river.

COMMENTARY

Great Master Yun Men produced more than eighty men of knowledge. Seventeen years after he passed on, when they opened his tomb and beheld him, (his body was not decomposed, but) upright and sound as formerly. The field of his vision had been bright and clear, his mentality and perspective swift. All his instructions, alternative remarks, and words spoken on behalf of others were direct, solitary, and steep. This present case is like sparks struck from stone, like flashing lightning; in fact, it's "a spirit appearing and a demon disappearing."[a] Librarian Ch'ing said, "Is there such talk in the whole great treasury of the Teachings?"

People these days make their living on emotional interpretations and say "Buddha is the guide for the three realms, the compassionate father of the four orders of living beings. Why then do the ancient Buddhas merge with the pillar?" If you understand this way, you'll never be able to find it. Some call (Yun Men's saying) "calling out from within nothingness." They are far from knowing that the talk of the teaching masters of our school cuts off conceptual consciousness, cuts off emotional evaluation, cuts off birth and death, and cuts off the defilement of doctrine, enters the correct state[b] without retaining anything at all. As soon as you rationalize and calculate, you tie your hands and feet.

But tell me, what was old Yun Men's meaning? Just make mind and objects a single thusness; then good and bad, right and wrong, won't be able to shake you. Then it will be all right whether you say "there is" or "there isn't"; then it will be all right whether you have mental activity or you don't. When you get here, each and every clap of the hands is the true imperative. My late teacher Wu Tsu said, "Yun Men, supposedly so great, really didn't have much guts." If it were me, I just would have told him, "The eighth level of mental activity."

He said, "The ancient Buddhas and the pillar merge—what level of mental activity is this?" In that moment he wrapped it all up in front of you. When a monk asked him what this meant, Yun Men said, "one belt worth thirty cents." He has the eye to judge heaven and earth.

Since no one understood, afterwards he himself spoke on their behalf: "On South Mountain clouds gather, on North Mountain rain falls." Thus he opened up a route of entry for future students. That's why Hsueh Tou picks out the place where he settles heaven and earth to make people see. But as soon as you blunder into calculation, you stumble past and miss it, though it's right in front of you. You simply must go to the source of Yun Men's fundamental meaning to clearly understand his lofty mind. Thus the verse says,

VERSE

South Mountain clouds,
    Throughout heaven and earth, they can't be seen. A knife cannot cut in.

North Mountain rain—
> Not a drop falls. Half south of the river, half north of the river.

The Twenty-Eight and Six see it before them.
> Wherever I look, I can't see. Hsueh Tou is dragging in other people. The lantern is hanging from the pillar.

In Korea they've gone up into the hall,
> Surging up in the east, sinking down in the west. The east guild doesn't see the profits of the west guild. Where does he get this news?

In China they haven't yet beaten the drum.
> Fifteen minutes late. Give me back the story. At first he doesn't get there, afterwards he goes too far.

In suffering, happiness—
> Who would you have know this?

In happiness, suffering—
> A double case. Who would you have bring this up? Suffering is suffering, happiness is happiness. Where are there two heads, three faces?

Who says gold is like shit!
> Those with eyes will discern this. Try to brush it off and look. Uh-oh! What a pity! But say, is it the ancient Buddhas or the pillar?

COMMENTARY

"South Mountain clouds, / North Mountain rain." Hsueh Tou buys the hat to fit the head, watches the wind to set his sails. On the edge of a sword, he puts down footnotes for you. As for "The Twenty-eight (Indian Ch'an Patriarchs) and Six (Chinese Ch'an Patriarchs) see it before them," don't misunderstand! This simply versifies "The ancient Buddhas and the pillar merge—what level of mental activity is this?"

Afterwards, Hsueh Tou opens up a road and creates complications to make you see Yun Men's meaning. "In Korea they've gone up into the hall, / In China they haven't yet beaten the drum." Hsueh Tou goes where the thunder rolls and comets fly and says, "In suffering, happiness— / In happiness, suffering."

Hsueh Tou seems to have piled up gems and jewels and put them here.

Finally there's this little line, "Who says gold is like shit?" This line is from Ch'an Yueh's poem "Travelling the Road is Hard," which Hsueh Tou draws on here to use. Ch'an Yueh wrote,

> *People cannot fathom the ocean's depth or the mountains' height—*
> *Past and present, more and more green and blue.*
> *Don't associate with the shallow and superficial—*
> *Where the ground is low it can only produce brambles.*
> *Who says gold is like shit?*
> *No more news of Chang Er and Ch'en Yu.*[c]
> *Travelling the road is hard;*
> *The hardships of travel, see for yourself!*

And isn't the territory broad and the people few? You cloud-dwelling saints!

TRANSLATORS' NOTES

a. This term is used to describe the maneuvers of a skilled battle commander, who can direct his forces in unexpected movements that are baffling and unpredictable to the enemy.

b. In early Buddhism, the "correct state" means *nirvana*, the extinction of egoism and suffering. In the Ts'ao-Tung Ch'an tradition, the "correct state" was used to refer to emptiness as opposed (propositionally in dialectic and subjectively in meditation) to the "biased state," or the realm of myriad forms. The patriarchs of the Ts'ao-Tung school used a five step dialectic to show that the correct and biased simultaneously contain each other, and that each (defined as separate under the aforementioned conditions) has both a correct and biased, or absolute and relative, aspect. Of the correct, or absolute, Ts'ao Shan said, "This correct state does not come from illumination; it is so whether or not the Buddhas appear in the world. Thus all the thousand sages, the myriad sages, return to the correct state to attain realization" (from *Wu I Hsien Chueh*, "Revealing the Secret of the Five Ranks").

c. Chang Er and Ch'en Yu are the proverbial close friends who fell
out and turned against each other. During the period of the fall of
the Ch'in dynasty (end of the third century B.C.) Ch'en Yu's
father had occupied territory with his army and begun to revive
an independent state of Chao. (China had been unified for the first
time under the Ch'in dynasty, which had conquered the six other
major states, one of which was Chao.) Chang Er was an important
minister in Chao under the Ch'ens. Later the friendship between
Chang Er and Ch'en Yu turned to hatred, and Chang Er cooper-
ated with the forces of one of the generals of the founder of the
Han dynasty (which eventually succeeded Ch'in), which destroyed independent Chao and killed Ch'en Yu.

Vimalakirti's Gate of Nonduality

POINTER

Though you say "It is," there is nothing which "is" can affirm. Though you say "It is not," there is nothing that "is not" can negate. When "is" and "is not" are left behind, and gain and loss are forgotten, then you are clean and naked, free and at ease.

But tell me, what is in front of you and in back of you? If there is a patchrobed monk who comes forward and says, "In front is the Buddha shrine and the main gate, behind is the abbot's sleeping room and private quarters," tell me, does this man have eyes or not? If you can judge this man, I'll allow that you have personally seen the Ancients.

CASE

Vimalakirti asked Manjusri,[1] "What is a bodhisattva's entry into the Dharma gate of nonduality?"[2]

Manjusri said, "According to what I think,[3] in all things,[4] no words, no speech,[5] no demonstration and no recognition,[6] to leave behind all questions and answers;[7] this is entering the Dharma gate of nonduality."[8]

Then Manjusri asked Vimalakirti, "We have each already spoken. Now you should tell us, good man, what is a bodhisattva's entry into the Dharma gate of nonduality?"[9]

Hsueh Tou said, "What did Vimalakirti say?"[10] He also said, "Completely exposed."[11]

NOTES

1. This fellow is making quite a fuss. He should shut his mouth.
2. He knows, yet he deliberately transgresses.
3. What will he say? It simply can't be explained. He's wearing

stocks, carrying evidence of his crime, hauling himself into the magistrate's office.

4. What is he calling "all things"?

5. What is he saying?

6. He can fool others . . .

7. What is he saying?

8. What's the use of entering? What's the use of so many complications?

9. Not even the Buddhas of the past, present, and future, let alone the Golden Grain Tathagata (Vimalakirti), can open their mouths about this one support. Manjusri has turned the spear around and stabbed one man to death. The arrow hits Vimalakirti just as he was shooting at the others.

10. Bah! Hsueh Tou gathers ten thousand arrows to his breast and speaks the truth in Vimalakirti's place.

11. Not only that time, but now too, it is so. Hsueh Tou is drawing his bow after the thief has gone. Although he uses all his strength to help the congregation, what can he do—calamity comes forth from his own door. But tell me, can Hsueh Tou see where this comes down? Since he hasn't seen it even in a dream, how can he say "completely exposed"? Danger! Even the golden-haired lion is unable to search it out.

COMMENTARY

Vimalakirti had the various great bodhisattvas each speak on the Dharma gate of nonduality. At the time, the thirty-two bodhisattvas all took dualistic views of doing and nondoing, of the two truths, real and conventional, and merged them into a monistic view which they considered to be the Dharma gate of nonduality.

Finally he asked Manjusri. Manjusri said, "According to what I think, in all things, no words and no speech, no demonstration and no recognition, to leave behind all questions and answers; this is entering the Dharma gate of nonduality." Since the other thirty-two had used words to dispense with words, Manjusri used no-words to dispense with words. At once he swept everything away, not wanting anything, and considered this to be the Dharma gate of nonduality. He certainly didn't realize that this was the sacred tortoise dragging its tail, that in wiping away the tracks he was making traces. It's just like a broom sweeping away dust; though the dust is removed, the tracks of the broom still remain.

Since in the end, as before, some traces were left, Manjusri then asked Vimalakirti, "We have each already spoken. Now you tell us, good man, what is a bodhisattva's entry into the Dharma gate of nonduality?" Vimalakirti was silent. If you're alive, you'll never go sink into the dead water. If you make up such (dead) views, you're like a mad dog chasing a clod of earth.[a]

Hsueh Tou didn't say that Vimalakirti kept silent, nor did he say that he sat silently on his seat. Hsueh Tou just went to the critical point and said, "What did Vimalakirti say?" Just when Hsueh Tou spoke this way, did he see Vimalakirti? He hadn't seen him even in a dream.

Vimalakirti was an ancient Buddha of the past, who also had a family and household. He helped the Buddha Shakyamuni teach and transform. He had inconceivable intelligence, inconceivable perspective, inconceivable supernatural powers and the wondrous use of them. Inside his own room he accommodated thirty-two thousand jeweled lion thrones and a great multitude of eighty thousand, without it being too spacious or too crowded. But tell me, what principle is this? Can it be called the wondrous function of supernatural powers? Don't misunderstand; if it is the Dharma gate of nonduality, only by attaining together and witnessing together can there be common mutual realization and knowledge.

Only Manjusri was able to give a reply. Even so, was he able to avoid Hsueh Tou's censure? Hsueh Tou, talking as he did, also had to meet with these two men (Vimalakirti and Manjusri). Hsueh Tou said, "What did Vimalakirti say?" and "Completely exposed." You tell me, where was the exposure? This little bit has nothing to do with gain or loss, nor does it fall into right and wrong. It's like being up on a ten thousand fathom cliff; if you can give up your life and leap off, you may see Vimalakirti in person. If you cannot give it up, you're like a ram caught in a fence. Hsueh Tou was a man who had abandoned his life, so he produces it in verse, saying,

VERSE

Bah! to old Vimalakirti—
> Why revile him? In the morning, three thousand blows, in
> the evening, eight hundred blows. Reviling him doesn't
> accomplish anything. He deserves thirty blows.

Out of compassion for living beings, he suffers an empty afflic-
*   tion,*
> Why have compassion for them? They themselves have
> the Diamond King's jewel sword. For this idle affair Vim-
> alakirti increased their ignorance. He took the trouble but
> accomplished nothing.

Lying ill in Vaisali,
> On whose account does he do this? It involves everyone.

His whole body withered and emaciated.[b]
> Leaving aside his illness for a moment, why was his
> mouth bent into a frown? He can't eat food or draw a
> breath.

Manjusri, the teacher of seven Buddhas, comes
> When a guest comes, one must attend to him. When a
> thief comes, one must beat him. Manjusri brings along a
> crowd. It takes an adept for this.

To the single room that's been swept repeatedly;
> It still exists. From the beginning Vimalakirti has been
> making his living inside a ghost cave.

He asks about the gate of nonduality.
> If there were anything that could be said, it would have
> been said by him. I hit, saying, "You too have searched
> without finding it."

Then Vimalakirti leans and falls.
> Heavens! Heavens! What are you saying?

He doesn't lean and fall—
> He finds life in the midst of death; there's still some
> breath in him.

The golden-haired lion has no place to look.
> Bah! Do you see?

COMMENTARY

Hsueh Tou says "Bah! to old Vimalakirti!" Why does he start off at the very beginning reviling him? Right at the start Hsueh Tou takes the Diamond King's jewel sword and cuts him right off. Vimalakirti must be given three thousand blows in the morning and eight hundred blows in the evening.

In Sanskrit, Vimalakirti means "undefiled repute" or "pure name." He was also known as the Golden Grain Tathagata. Haven't you heard how a monk asked Master Chien of Yun Chu, "If he was the Golden Grain Tathagata, why then did he listen to the Dharma in the congregation of the Tathagata Shakyamuni?" Chien said, "He didn't contend over self and others. Someone who is greatly liberated has nothing to do with 'becoming Buddha' or 'not becoming Buddha.' If you say that he practices cultivation and strives to attain the Path of Buddhahood, this has even less to do with it." As the Perfect Enlightenment Scripture says, "If you use your routine mind to produce routine views, you will never be able to enter the Tathagata's great ocean of peaceful extinction."

Yung Chia said, "Whether he's right or wrong, people cannot know. Whether he goes against or goes along, the gods cannot fathom. If he goes along, then he turns toward the stage of the fruition of Buddhahood; if he goes against, then he enters the realms of sentient beings." Meditation Master Shou said, "Even if you can perfect yourself and get to this realm, you still can't follow your inclinations. Only when you have experienced the holy state without leaks can you go along or go against." Thus Hsueh Tou said, "Out of compassion for living beings, he suffers empty affliction." In the scripture Vimalakirti says, "Since sentient beings have illnesses, I also will have an illness." Hsueh Tou says, "Lying ill in Vaisali," because Vimalakirti manifested his illness in the city of Vaisali.

"His whole body withered and emaciated." Vimalakirti used his physical illness to preach the Dharma widely. He said, "This body has no permanence, no strength, no power or solidity; it's a thing that quickly decays, it can't be trusted. It produces suffering and trouble, a mass of diseases. It is something made of the heaps, elements, and sense media compounded together."

"The teacher of seven Buddhas comes." Manjusri was the teacher of seven Buddhas, but he obeyed the World Honored One's command to go to Vimalakirti and ask about his illness. "To the single room that's been swept repeatedly." Vimalakirti had cleared everything out of his room, just leaving his bench. When Manjusri arrived, he asked about the Dharma gate of nonduality, so Hsueh Tou says, "He asks about the gate of nonduality."

"Then Vimalakirti leans and falls." Vimalakirti's mouth was bent into a frown. Followers of Ch'an these days say that his speechlessness was the leaning and falling. But don't mistakenly go by the zero point of the scale.

Pushing you up onto a ten thousand fathom cliff, Hsueh Tou then says, "He doesn't lean and fall." With one hand he lifts up, with one hand he pushes down. Hsueh Tou has this kind of skill, and the way he uses it is sharp and clear. This line versifies his own previous comment, "What did Vimalakirti say?"

"The golden-haired lion has no place to look." It was not only this way at that time, but it's this way right now. Do you see old Vimalakirti? Even if the whole world, the mountains, rivers, grasses, trees, and forests all turned into a golden-haired lion (for you to ride, as does Manjusri), you still wouldn't be able to find him.

TRANSLATORS' NOTES

a. The image of a dog which, hit with a clod of dirt thrown by a man, ignores the man and chases the clod in anger, is found in the *Kasyapa-parivarta* (the old *Maharatnakuta* scripture); it symbolizes those who are afraid of the delights of the senses and seek deliverance in solitude and quiet—they never really become free because they are dependent on solitude and quiet, becoming every bit as much, and even more, miserable and confused as before when they again come in contact with the hustle and bustle of ordinary life.

b. Vimalakirti's show of disease is the setting of the *Vimalakir-tinirdesa*, the scripture spoken by Vimalakirti, a major Mahayana Buddhist scripture; at first Shakyamuni directed his great disciples one by one to go to ask after Vimalakirti, but each explained how in the past Vimalakirti had criticized their practices and shattered their views, demolishing the dualistic (*samsara* vs. *nirvana*) standpoint of Hinayana (Lesser Vehicle) Buddhism (which is also symbolized by the 'dog chasing a clod' image of asceticism noted above). So after the disciples begged off, Shakyamuni then sent a host of bodhisattvas led by Manjusri to inquire after Vimalakirti; the latter took this opportunity to edify the bodhisattvas, and the discussion of nonduality, as well as miraculous displays and profound teachings by Vimalakirti, ensued.

The Hermit of T'ung Feng Makes a Tiger's Roar

POINTER

To hold the world fast without the slightest leak, so that all the people in the world lose their points and become tongue-tied—this is the true imperative for patchrobed monks.

To release a light from one's forehead that shines through the four quarters—this is the adamantine eye of patchrobed monks.

To touch iron and turn it into gold, to touch gold and turn it into iron, to suddenly capture and suddenly release—this is the staff of patchrobed monks.

To cut off the tongues of everyone in the world so that there's no place for them to breathe out, to make them fall back three thousand miles—this is the mettle of patchrobed monks.

But tell me, when one is not this way at all, who is he? To test I cite this to see.

CASE

A monk came to the place of the hermit of T'ung Feng and asked, "If you suddenly encountered a tiger here, what then?"[1] The hermit made a tiger's roar.[2] The monk then made a gesture of fright.[3] The hermit laughed aloud.[4] The monk said, "You old thief!"[5] The hermit said, "What can you do about me?"[6] The monk gave up.[7]

Hsueh Tou said, "This is all right, but these two wicked thieves only knew how to cover their ears to steal the bell."[8]

NOTES

1. The fellow is an expert at playing with shadows. Within the nest of weeds, there's one or a half.

548

2. He adds error to error. Nevertheless he does have teeth and claws. They are born together and die together. "Hearing the words, you should understand the source."

3. Two fellows playing with a mud ball. The monk saw his opportunity and acted. He seems to be right, but in reality he isn't.

4. This still amounts to something. In his laugh there's a sword. He can let go and he can also gather in.

5. You too must see through this. The monk has been defeated. The two of them both let go.

6. I would slap him across the ear. Too bad the monk let him go. He adds another layer of frost on top of snow.

7. Thus he was stopped. Neither of them understood. Heavens! Heavens!

8. The words are still in our ears. They have been censured by Hsueh Tou. But tell me, at that time, how should they have acted to avoid Hsueh Tou's criticism? No patchrobed monk in the world arrives.

COMMENTARY

The Ta Hsiung lineage (of Pai Chang Huai Hai) produced four hermits: Ta Mei,[a] Pai Yun, Hu Ch'i, and T'ung Feng.

Look at how those two men had such knowing eyes and capable hands. Tell me, where is the place that's difficult to understand? Though produced to meet the situation, the Ancients' one device, one object, one word, one phrase, are naturally leaping with life, since their eyes are perspicacious and true. Hsueh Tou picked this case to make people know wrong from right and discern gain and loss. Nevertheless, from his standpoint as a man who has arrived, though it's handled in terms of gain and loss, after all there is no gain or loss. If you view those Ancients in terms of gain and loss, you miss the point entirely. People of the present day must each comprehend the place where there's no gain or loss. If you only apply your mind to picking and choosing among words and phrases, when will you ever be done?

Haven't you heard how Great Master Yun Men said, "Foot-travellers, don't just wander over the country idly, just wanting to pick up and hold onto idle words. As soon as some old teacher's mouth moves, you immediately ask about Ch'an and ask about Tao, ask about transcendance and accommodation, ask about how and what. You make great volumes of commentaries which you stuff into your bellies, pondering and calculating. Wherever you go you put your heads together by the stove in threes and fives, babbling on and on. These, you say, are words of eloquence; these, words in reference to the self; these, words in reference to things; these, words from within the essence. You try to comprehend the old fathers and mothers of your house. Once you have gobbled down your meal, you only speak of dreams and say, 'I have understood the Buddha Dharma.' You should know that if you go foot-travelling this way, you will never be done."

When the Ancients briefly picked it up and played with it, how could there be such views as victory and defeat, gain and loss, or right and wrong?

T'ung Feng had seen Lin Chi. At the time of the story he had built a hut deep in the mountains. This monk came there and asked, "If you suddenly encountered a tiger here, what then?" Feng then made a tiger's roar; he rightly went to the thing to act. This monk too knew how to meet error with error, so he made a gesture of fright. When the hermit laughed aloud, the monk said, "You old thief!" Feng said, "What can you do about me?" This is all right, but neither of them understood. From ancient times on down, they've met with other people's criticism. Thus Hsueh Tou said, "This is all right, but these two wicked thieves only knew how to cover their ears to steal the bell." Though both of them were thieves, nevertheless they didn't take the opportunity to act; hence, they were covering their own ears to steal the bell. With these two Elders, it's as though they set up battle lines of a million troops, but only struggled over the broom (for sweeping up casualties).

To discuss this matter, it is necessary to have the ability to kill people without blinking an eye. If you always let go and never capture, if you always kill and never bring to life, you won't avoid the scornful laughter of others. Although this is so, these Ancients still didn't have so many concerns. Observe how they both saw their opportunity and acted. Wu Tsu spoke of the concentration of supernatural powers at play, the concentration of the torch of wisdom, and the concentration of the King of Adornment. It's just that people of later times don't have their feet on the ground; they just go criticize the Ancients and say there is gain and loss. Some say that the hermit clearly lost the advantage, but this has nothing to do with it.

Hsueh Tou said, "When these two men met, it was all letting go." When the monk said, "If you suddenly encountered a tiger here, then what?" and Feng made a tiger's roar, this was letting go. And when he said, "What can you do about me?" this too was letting go. In every instance they fell into the secondary level of activity. Hsueh Tou said, "If you want to act, then act." People these days hear such talk and say that at the time the hermit should have carried out the imperative for the monk. But you shouldn't blindly punish and beat the hermit.

As for Te Shan immediately hitting people when they came in through the gate, and Lin Chi immediately shouting at people when they came in through the gate—tell me, what was the intent of these Ancients? In the end Hsueh Tou makes his verse just like this. But tell me, in the end, how will you avoid "covering your own ears to steal the bell"?

VERSE

If you don't grab it when you see it,
> You've stumbled by. It's already a thousand, ten thousand miles away.

You'll think about it a thousand miles away.
> Regretting that you weren't careful from the first. Heavens! Heavens!

Fine stripes—
> Take what's coming to you and get out, Reverend. What could he do—he didn't know to act.

But he hasn't got claws and teeth.
> I only fear that his use of them will be ignorant. I'll talk to you when your claws and teeth are ready.

Haven't you seen the sudden encounter on Mt. Ta Hsiung?
> If you have a rule, go by the rule; if you have no rule, go by the example.

The vast sound and light shakes the earth—
> This tiger, after all, goes on this way. Still he amounts to something. How many sons are powerful men?

Do great men of power see or not?
　　Hsueh Tou is so kind. If you can open your eyes, you can
be born together and die together. Hsueh Tou is creating
complications.

They take the tiger's tail and grab the tiger's whiskers.
　　How will you take it when it suddenly appears? All the
patchrobed monks in the world are taken in here. If one
suddenly comes forth, I'd challenge him. I'm making you
turn around and spew out your breath. Ha! I hit, saying,
"Why didn't you say, 'You old thief!'?"

COMMENTARY

"If you don't grab it when you see it, / You'll think about it a
thousand miles away." Just at the point of danger, the monk
couldn't use it at all; when the hermit said, "What can you do
about me?" the monk should have given him some of his own
provisions. If at that time he had been able to show his skill,
the hermit would have had to have a last word. Both men only
knew how to let go; they couldn't gather in. "If you don't grab
it when you see it" is already white clouds for ten thousand
miles; why did he go on to say, "You'll think about it a
thousand miles away"?

"Fine stripes— / But he hasn't got claws and teeth." This is
so, but a tiger also knows how to conceal his teeth and hide his
claws. What could he do, though—he didn't know how to bite
people.

"Haven't you seen the sudden encounter on Mt. Ta Hsiung?
/ The vast sound and light shakes the earth." One day Pai
Chang asked Huang Po, "Where are you coming from?" Po
said, "From down the mountain." Chang said, "See any tigers?" Po then made a tiger's roar. Chang took the axe at his
side and made the gesture of chopping. Po held it fast and
slapped him. That evening Chang went up into the hall and
said, "Down Ta Hsiung Mountain there's a tiger; all of you
must watch out for him when you're going and coming. Today
I myself have been bitten by him."

Later Kuei Shan asked Yang Shan, "What about Huang Po's
tiger story?" Yang said, "What is your esteemed opinion,

Teacher?" Kuei Shan said, "At the time Pai Chang should have chopped him to death with one blow; how did it come to this?" Yang Shan said, "Not so." Kuei Shan said, "What about it then?" Yang Shan said, "Not only did he ride the tiger's head, but he also knew how to take the tiger's tail." Kuei Shan said, "You do indeed have some precipitous phrases, Chi." Hsueh Tou draws on this to illumine the main case.

"The vast sound and light shakes the earth." This bit transforms freely. Hsueh Tou wants to have a road to show himself within the words. "Do great men of power see or not?" Do you see? "They take the tiger's tail and grab the tiger's whiskers." Here again this must be one's own. Even if you take the tiger's tail and grab the tiger's whiskers, you won't avoid me instantly piercing your nostrils.

TRANSLATORS' NOTES

a. Ta Hsiung was the name of the mountain on which Ch'an Master Pai Chang Huai Hai lived and taught in the eighth and ninth centuries A.D. It was known as Pai Chang because of its precipitous heights, and the master Huai Hai was also known by that name, according to custom. Ta Mei was actually an early successor of Ma Tsu Tao I, Pai Chang's teacher; the hermit of T'ung Feng was a successor of Lin Chi, who succeeded to Huang Po, Pai Chang's great disciple. Four of Lin Chi's successors were hermits.

Yun Men's Kitchen Pantry and Main Gate

POINTER

He holds the world fast without the slightest leak; he cuts off the myriad flows without keeping a drop. Open your mouth and you're wrong; hesitate in thought and you miss. But tell me, what is the barrier-penetrating eye? To test, I cite this to see:

CASE

Yun Men imparted some words saying, "Everyone has a light;[1] when you look at it, you don't see it and it's dark and dim.[2] What is everybody's light?"[3]

He himself answered on their behalf, "The kitchen pantry and the main gate."[4] He also said, "A good thing isn't as good as nothing."[5]

NOTES

1. Black lacquer buckets.
2. When you look, you're blinded.
3. Mountains are mountains, rivers are rivers. Washing black ink in a bucket of lacquer.
4. He is very kind, but why is he creating complications?
5. He himself knew that he had only gotten halfway there; still, this amounts to something.

COMMENTARY

In his room Yun Men imparted some words to teach people: "All of you—right where you stand, each and every one of you

554

has a beam of light shining continuously, now as of old, far removed from seeing or knowing. Though it's a light, when you're asked about it you don't understand—isn't it dark and dim?" For twenty years he handed down this lesson, but there was never anyone who understood his meaning.

Later Hsiang Lin asked Yun Men to speak on their behalf. Men said, "The kitchen pantry and the main gate." He also said, "A good thing isn't as good as nothing." Usually what he said in place of others was just a single sentence; why then are there two here? The first sentence barely opens a road for you to let you see. If you're for real, as soon as you hear it mentioned, you get right up and go. Yun Men feared people would get stuck here, so he also said, "A good thing is not as good as nothing." As before, he's swept it away for you.

As soon as they hear you mention "light," people these days immediately put a glare in their eyes and say, "Where is the kitchen pantry? Where is the main gate?" But this has nothing to do with it. Thus it is said, "Perceive the meaning on the hook; don't abide by the zero point of the scale." This matter is not in the eye or in the environment. To begin to understand you must cut off knowing and seeing, forget gain and loss, and become purified, naked, and perfectly at ease; each and every one must investigate on his own.

Yun Men said, "You come and go by daylight; you distinguish people by daylight. Suddenly it's midnight, and there's no sun, moon, or lamplight. If it's some place you've been to, then of course it's possible; in a place you have never been, can you even manage to get hold of something?"

(Shih T'ou's) *Merging of Difference and Sameness* says,

> *Right within light there's darkness,*
> *But don't see it as darkness:*
> *Right within darkness there's light,*
> *But don't meet it as light.*

If you cut off light and darkness, tell me, what is it? Thus it is said, "The mind flower emits light, shining on all the lands in the ten directions." P'an Shan said, "Light isn't shining on objects, nor do the objects exist. Light and objects both forgotten, then what is this?" Also it was said,

This very seeing and hearing is not seeing and hear-
ing—
But there's no other sound and form that can be
offered to you.
Here, if you can understand that there's nothing at
all,
You are free to separate, or not, essence and action.

Just understand Yun Men's final statement thoroughly, then
you can go back to the former one to roam at play. But ultimately, you do not make a living there. The ancient Vimalakirti said, "All things are established on a non-abiding
basis." You mustn't go here to play with lights and shadows
and give play to your spirit. Nor will it do to make up an
understanding in terms of nothingness. An Ancient said, "Better you should give rise to a view of existence as big as Mt.
Sumeru, than that you produce a view of nothingness as small
as a mustard seed." People of the (lesser) two vehicles[a] often
fall onesidedly into this view.

VERSE

Spontaneously shining, ranged in the solitary light.
    The myriad forms and images. Guest and host inter-
    mingle. He snaps your nostrils around. What are you do-
    ing, blind men?

He opens a route for you.
    Why only one route? Ten suns are shining side by side. He
    has managed to set down one route.

Flowers fall, the tree has no shadow—
    What end is there to creating complications? Where will
    you seek it? He fills a black lacquer bucket with black
    ink.

When looking, who doesn't see?
    Blind! You shouldn't always hold onto fences and grope
    along walls. Two blind men, three blind men . . . .

Seeing or not seeing—
    Both ends are cut off. Blind!

Riding backwards on an ox, entering the Buddha shrine.
Inside the main gate he joins his palms. Give me back the story. I hit, saying, "Where has he gone?" Hsueh Tou too is just making his living inside the ghost cave. Do you understand? At midnight the sun comes out, at noonday the midnight watch is sounded.

COMMENTARY

"Spontaneously shining, ranged in the solitary light." Originally, right where you stand, there's this beam of light; it's just that your use of it is dark. That's why Great Master Yun Men set out this light for you right in front of your faces. But say, what is everyone's light? "The kitchen pantry and the main gate." This is where Yun Men arrays the solitary light. P'an Shan said, "The mind-moon is solitary and full; its light engulfs myriad forms." This is the true, eternal, unique revelation.

Afterwards "He opens a route for you." Yun Men still feared that people would become attached to "The kitchen pantry, the main gate." Conceding for the moment the kitchen pantry, when the morning flowers fall and the tree has no shadow, when the sun has gore down and the moon goes dark and all of heaven and earth is black vastness—do you still see? "When looking, who doesn't see?" Tell me, who is it that doesn't see? Here, where "right within light there's darkness" and "right within darkness there's light," both are "like a step forward and a step backward." You must see for yourself.

Hsueh Tou says, "Seeing or not seeing," or versifies "A good thing isn't as good as nothing." Merged with seeing, still you don't see; merged with illumination, still you don't understand.

"Riding backwards on an ox, entering the Buddha shrine." He's gone into the black lacquer bucket. You must personally ride the ox into the Buddha shrine to see what it is that he's saying.

TRANSLATORS' NOTES

a. The two vehicles refer to Buddhist disciples and self-enlightened sages, who strive only for the extinction of passion and personal suffering; they only realize the emptiness of ego and do not realize the emptiness of things as identical to the things themselves. They are apt to fall into the empty quiescence of subjective nothingness, intoxicated by trance. Bodhisattvas, however, realizing that existence itself is empty and not made so by annihilation, do not fear life or seek death, and arouse great kindness and compassion towards living beings, resolving that they all be liberated. If one clings to the idea of nothingness, this compassion is impossible.

Medicine and Disease Subdue Each Other

POINTER

A clear-eyed fellow has no nest: sometimes on the summit of the solitary peak weeds grow in profusion; sometimes he's naked and free in the bustling marketplace. Suddenly he appears as an angry titan with three heads and six arms; suddenly as Sun Face or Moon Face Buddha he releases the light of all-embracing mercy. In a single atom he manifests all physical forms; to save people according to their type, he mixes with mud and water. If suddenly he releases an opening upwards, not even the Buddha's eye could see him; even if a thousand sages appeared, they too would have to fall back three thousand miles. Is there anyone with the same attainment and same realization? To test, I cite this to see.

CASE

Yun Men, teaching his community, said, "Medicine and disease subdue each other:¹ the whole earth is medicine;² what is your self?"³

NOTES

1. A compounded form cannot be grasped.
2. Bitter gourd is bitter to the root. He's put it over to one side.
3. Sweet melon is sweet to the stem. Where did he get this news?

COMMENTARY

Yun Men said, "Medicine and disease subdue each other: the whole earth is medicine; what is your self?" Do all of you have a way to get out? Twenty-four hours a day, concentrate on "towering like a mile-high wall." Te Shan's blows fall like rain, Lin Chi's shouts roll like thunder—putting this aside for the moment, Shakymuni is himself Shakyamuni and Maitreya is himself Maitreya. Those who don't know what it comes down to frequently understand by calling it "medicine and disease merging with each other." For forty-nine years, in more than three hundred assemblies, the World Honored One adapted to potential to set up the teachings—all of this was giving medicine in accordance with the disease, like exchanging sweet fruit for bitter gourds. Having purified your active faculties, he made you clean and free.

"The whole earth is medicine." Where will you sink your teeth into this? If you can sink your teeth in, I'll grant that you have a place to turn around and show some life; then you see Yun Men in person. If you look around and hesitate, you won't be able to get your teeth into it; Yun Men is the one under your feet.

"Medicine and disease subdue each other." This is just an ordinary proposition. If you cling to existence, he speaks of nonexistence for you; if you are attached to nonexistence, he speaks of existence for you. If you are attached to neither existence nor nonexistence, he manifests the sixteen-foot golden body for you in a pile of crap and rubbish, appearing and disappearing.

Right now this whole great earth is a profuse array of myriad forms, up to and including one's own self. At once it's medicine—at such a time, what will you call your self? If you only call it medicine, even by the time Maitreya Buddha is born down here, you still won't have seen Yun Men even in dreams. Ultimately, how is it? "Perceive the meaning on the hook; don't stick by the zero point of the scale."

One day Manjusri ordered Sudhana to pick medicinal herbs. He said, "If there is something that is not medicine, bring it to me." Sudhana searched all over, but there was nothing that was not medicine. So he went back and told Manjusri, "There is nothing that is not medicine." Manjusri said, "Gather something that is medicine." Sudhana then picked up a blade of grass and handed it to Manjusri. Manjusri held it up and showed it to the assembly, saying, "This medicine can kill people and it can also bring people to life."

This talk of medicine and disease subduing each other is extremely difficult to see. Yun Men often used it in his room to guide people. One day Elder Chin O called on Hsueh Tou. Chin O was an adept, an honorable worthy of the Yun Men succession. They discussed this statement "medicine and disease subdue each other" all night until dawn before they were finally able to exhaust its excellence. At this point no learned interpretations, thought or judgment can be employed. Afterwards, Hsueh Tou made a verse to see him off which said,

> *Medicine and disease subdue each other—most difficult to see;*
> *The ten thousand locked gates indeed have no starting point.*
> *Wayfarer Chin O came calling;*
> *In one night we exhausted the waves of the ocean of learning.*

Hsueh Tou's subsequent verse is most effective. Is his meaning in the host or in the guest? You must see for yourself.

VERSE

The whole earth is medicine:
> Who would you have discern the point? Scattering sand and dirt. Put it on a high shelf.

Why have Ancients and moderns been so mistaken?
> There's an echo in the words. With one brush stroke they're all blotted out.

I don't make the carriage behind closed doors—
> Great Hsueh Tou uses all his strength to help the assembly, but misfortune comes forth from his own door. In the calm vastness, not a hair is hanging. Who has any spare time? He is making a living in a ghost cave.

The road through is naturally quiet and empty.
> Set foot on it and you enter the weeds. When you get on the horse, you'll see the road. He picks it up freely, undeniably outstanding.

Wrong! Wrong!
> Twin swords fly through space. A single arrow fells two eagles.

Though they be high as the sky, your nostrils have still been
    pierced.
    Your head has fallen. I hit, saying, "They've been
    pierced!"

COMMENTARY

"The whole earth is medicine: / Why have Ancients and moderns been so mistaken?" From ancient times till now those of
you who have understood by calling it medicine have instantly
gone wrong. Hsueh Tou said, "There's a kind of person who
doesn't know how to cut off Ta Mei's footsteps, but merely
says that (Ta Mei) was in too much of a hurry to go."ᵃ Hsueh
Tou knew how to cut off Yun Men's footsteps.

Since this one line of his had thrown everyone in the world
into confusion, Yun Men said, "When my staff is waves, you
may go freely in all directions; when the whole earth is waves,
I'll watch to see if you float or sink."

"I don't make the carriage behind closed doors—/The road
through is naturally quiet and empty." Hsueh Tou speaks to
open up a road for you: "If you build your carriage behind
closed doors, and you bring it out the gate and it fits the ruts,
what has this accomplished? I am not building the carriage
behind closed doors here. When I go out the door, naturally it's
quiet and empty." Here Hsueh Tou reveals a slight crack to let
people see.

Still hurrying on, Hsueh Tou then says, "Wrong! Wrong!"
Both Yun Men's former statement and his latter statement are
wrong. Who would know that Hsueh Tou's opening up a road
is also wrong? Since your nostrils are as high as the sky, why do
they get pierced anyway? Do you want to understand? Then
immerse yourself in this for thirty years. If you have a staff, I'll
give you a staff; if you have no staff, you won't avoid having
your nostrils pierced by others.

TRANSLATORS' NOTES

a. When Ta Mei was about to die he said, "Coming, there is nothing
    to look to; going, there is nothing to pursue." Happening to hear

the cry of a squirrel, he said, "It's just this thing, not anything else. Keep it well—I am going to go." Later Hsueh Tou said of this, "This fellow was sloppy in life and fat-headed in death. 'Just this thing, not anything else'—what thing is this? Is there anything to impart, or not? Some people do not know how to cut off Ta Mei's footsteps, and merely say that he was in too much of a hurry to be on his way."

Hsuan Sha's Guiding and Aiding Living Beings

POINTER

The established methods of our school are thus: they break two into three. For profound talk entering into principle, you too must be piercing and penetrating.

Taking charge of the situation, he hits home and smashes to pieces the golden chains[a] and the hidden barrier. He acts according to the imperative, so that he obliterates all tracks and traces.

Tell me, where is there confusion? For those who have the eye on their forehead, I bring this up to see.

CASE

Hsuan Sha, teaching the community, said, "The old adepts everywhere all speak of guiding and aiding living beings.[1] Supposing they encountered three kinds of sick person, how would they guide them?[2] With a blind person, they could pick up the gavel or raise the whisk, but he wouldn't see.[3] With a deaf person, he wouldn't hear the point of words.[4] With a mute person, if they had him speak, he wouldn't be able to speak.[5] But how would they guide such people? If they couldn't guide these people, then the Buddha Dharma has no effect."[6] A monk asked Yun Men for instruction on this.[7] Yun Men said, "Bow."[8] The monk bowed and rose.[9] Yun Men poked at him with his staff; the monk drew back. Yun Men said, "You're not blind."[10] Then Yun Men called him closer; when the monk approached,[11] Men said, "You're not deaf."[12] Next Yun Men said, "Do you understand?"[13] The monk said, "I don't understand."[14] Yun Men said, "You're not mute."[15] At this the monk had an insight.[16]

564

NOTES

1. They set up their shops according to their capacities, according to whether their houses are rich or poor.
2. He is beating the weeds just to frighten the snakes. My mouth is agape, my eyes open wide. You must fall back three thousand miles.
3. Truly blind! This is guiding and aiding living beings. One doesn't have to be blind (not to see).
4. Truly deaf! This is guiding and aiding living beings. One doesn't have to be have to be deaf (not to hear). Who hasn't heard yet?
5. Truly mute! This is guiding and aiding living beings. One doesn't have to be mute (to be unable to speak). Who hasn't spoken yet?
6. How true these words are! I fold my hands and submit, having already accepted. I'll strike!
7. He wants everyone to know too. This is pertinent.
8. When the wind blows, the grasses bend. Bah!
9. This monk has broken the staff.
10. Truly blind! Better not say this monk is blind.
11. The second ladleful of foul water douses the monk. Avalokitesvara has come. At that time the monk should have given a shout.
12. Truly deaf. Better not say the monk is deaf.
13. Why doesn't Yun Men offer his own provisions? At that time the monk shouldn't have made a sound.
14. A doubled case. Heavens! Heavens!
15. Truly mute. His mouth is babbling. Better not say this monk is mute.
16. He draws his bow after the thief has gone. What bowl[b] is he looking for?

COMMENTARY

Hsuan Sha had investigated till he reached the point of eliminating all emotional defilement and conceptual thought, where he became purified and naked, free and unfettered; only thus could he speak this way. At this time, when (Ch'an flourished) and the various monasteries all looked to one another, Hsuan Sha would often teach his community by saying, "The old adepts, all over, all speak of guiding and aiding living beings. If they should encounter three kinds of sick person, how would they guide them? With a blind person, they could pick up the gavel or raise the whisk, but he wouldn't see. With a deaf person, he wouldn't hear the point of words. With a mute person, if they had him speak, he wouldn't be able to speak. So how would they teach such people? If they couldn't guide these people, then the Buddha Dharma has no effect." If you people right now understand this as being blind, deaf, and mute, you'll never be able to find it. Thus it is said, "Don't die in the words." To attain, you must understand Hsuan Sha's meaning.

Hsuan Sha often used this statement to guide people. There was a monk who had been with Hsuan Sha for a long time. One day, when Hsuan Sha went up into the hall, this monk asked, "Will you permit me to present a theory of the story of the three kinds of sick person, Teacher?" Hsuan Sha said, "Go ahead." The monk then bade farewell and left. Sha said, "Wrong! That's not it." Did this monk understand Hsuan Sha's meaning? Fa Yen subsequently said, "When I heard Master Ti Tsang tell about this monk I finally understood the story of the three kinds of sick person." If you say this monk didn't understand, then why would Fa Yen talk like this? If you say he did understand, then why did Hsuan Sha say "wrong"?

One day Ti Tsang said to Hsuan Sha, "Teacher, I hear you have a saying about three kinds of sick person—is this so or not?" Sha said, "It is so." Tsang said, "I have eyes, ears, nose, and tongue—how will you guide me, Teacher?" Hsuan Sha immediately stopped. If you can understand Hsuan Sha's meaning, how could it be in the words and phrases? Ti Tsang's understanding was naturally outstanding.

Later a monk took this story up with Yun Men. Men immediately understood his intentions and said, "Bow." The monk bowed and rose. Men poked at him with his staff, and the monk drew back. Men said, "You're not blind." Then Men called him closer. When the monk approached, Men said, "You're not deaf." Next he said, "Do you understand?" When the monk said, "I don't understand," Men said, "You're not mute." At this the monk attained insight. At the time, if the monk had been for real, when Yun Men told him to bow he would have immediately turned over his meditation seat. Then how could so many complications have appeared? But tell me, are Yun Men's understanding and Hsuan Sha's understanding the same or different? The understanding of those two men was the same.

Look at how the Ancients appeared and created millions of kinds of expedient methods. "The meaning is on the hook." How much exertion to make each and every one of today's people understand this one matter!

My late teacher Wu Tsu said, "One man can speak, though he doesn't understand; one man, though he understands, cannot speak. If these two men came calling, how would you be able to discriminate between them? If you can't distinguish these two, in fact you will be unable to free what is stuck and untie what is bound for people. If you can distinguish them, then as soon as you see them come through the gate, you put on your straw sandals and walk around several times within their bellies. If you still haven't awakened on your own, what bowl are you looking for?[b] Go away!"

Now you better not make your understanding in terms of blind, deaf, and mute. Thus it is said, "His eyes see forms as though blind, and his ears hear sounds as though deaf." Again, it was said,

> *Though it fills his eyes, he doesn't see form;*
> *Though it fills his ears, he doesn't hear sound—*
> *Manjusri is always covering his eyes,*
> *Avalokitesvara blocks his ears.*

At this point, only if your eyes see as though blind and your ears hear as though deaf will you be able to not be at odds with Hsuan Sha's meaning. Do all of you know where the blind, deaf, and mute fellows are at? Look closely at Hsueh Tou's verse, which says,

VERSE

Blind, deaf, mute—
    Already there before it's said. The three openings (eye, ear, mouth) are all illumined. It's already been made into one piece.
Soundless, without any adjustments to potentialities.
    Where will you search? Can you make any judgments? What have they got to do with it?

In the heavens, on earth—
> With the correct principle, Hsueh Tou is on his own. I am also thus.

Laughable, lamentable.
> Laugh at what? Lament over what? Half light, half dark.

Li Lü can't discern the true form;
> Blind man! A skillful craftsman leaves no traces. Truly blind!

How can Shih K'uang recognize the mystic tune?
> Deaf man! No reward has been established for the great achievement. Truly deaf.

How can this compare to sitting alone beneath an empty window?
> You must be this way to attain. Don't make your living in a ghost cave. Instantly Hsueh Tou smashes the lacquer bucket.

The leaves fall, the flowers bloom—each in its own time.
> What time and season is it right now? You mustn't understand it as unconcern. Today goes from morning to evening and tomorrow too goes from morning to evening.

Again Hsueh Tou said, "Do you understand or not?"
> Again he speaks the words of the verse.

An iron hammer head with no hole.
> Take what's coming to you and get out! Too bad—Hsueh Tou let go, so I'll hit.

COMMENTARY

"Blind, deaf, mute— / Soundless, without any adjustments to potentialities." All your seeing and not seeing, hearing and not hearing, speaking and not speaking—Hsueh Tou has swept it all away at once for you. In fact, views in terms of blindness, deafness, and muteness, and calculations and judgments of what's right to suit potentials are at once silenced and cut off; none of them can be applied. This transcendental matter can be called real blindness, real deafness, real muteness, without potentials and without adjustments.

"In the heavens, on earth—/ Laughable, lamentable." Hsueh Tou lifts up with one hand and pushes down with one hand. But say, laugh at what? Lament over what? It's worth laughing joyously that this blindness is not really blind, that this deafness is not really deaf, that this muteness is not really mute. It's worth lamenting being clearly not blind, yet still being blind, being clearly not deaf, yet still being deaf, being clearly not mute, yet still being mute.

"Li Lü can't discern the true form." If you can't tell green from yellow or red from white, then you're really blind. Li Lü was a man of the time of the Yellow Emperor (third millennium B.C.); from a hundred paces away he could see the tip of the finest hair—his eyes were very clear. As the Yellow Emperor was crossing the Red River, he dropped a pearl down into the water; he ordered Li Lü to look for it, but he couldn't find it. He ordered Ch'i Hou to search for it, but he couldn't find it either. Finally he ordered Hsiang Wang to look, and he at last recovered it. Thus it was said, "Hsiang Wang's glory shone bright at all times; Li Lü's actions were like waves flooding the sky." Even Li Lü's eye can't discern the true form of this lofty place.

"How can Shih K'uang recognize the mystic tune?" In Chou times (first millennium B.C.) Duke Ching of Chin had a son (some say it was the music teacher of Duke P'ing of Chin) named Shih K'uang Tzu Yeh, who was well able to distinguish the five notes and six pitches. He could hear the sound of ants fighting on the other side of a mountain. At that time (the states of) Chin and Ch'u were contending for hegemony. Shih K'uang had but to strum his guitar and set the strings in motion in order to know that Ch'u would have no success in the war. Although he was like this, Hsueh Tou says that even he would be unable to recognize the mystic tune. People who, even though they are not deaf, are nonetheless still deaf, even if they were Shih K'uang, still couldn't recognize the mystic tune of this lofty place.

Hsueh Tou says, "I am not Li Lü, nor am I Shih K'uang— how can this compare to sitting alone beneath an empty window? The leaves fall, the flowers bloom—each in its own time." If you get to this realm, though you see, it's like not seeing; though you hear, it's like not hearing; though you speak, it's like not speaking. When hungry you eat and when tired you sleep. You let the leaves fall and the flowers bloom. When the leaves fall it's autumn; when the flowers bloom it's spring—each has its own time and season.

Having swept it clean for you, Hsueh Tou again puts down a single path and says, "Do you understand or not?" Hsueh Tou's strength is exhausted and his spirit wearied; he can just manage to say, "An iron hammer head with no (handle) hole." Be quick to set your eyes on this line; only then will you see. If you hesitate, you've missed it again.

(Master Yuan Wu held up his whisk and said,) Do you see? (Then he rapped once on the meditation seat and said,) Do you hear? (Then he came down from his seat and said,) Can you speak?

TRANSLATORS' NOTES

a.   "Golden chains" is a classic Buddhist metaphor for the moral code or behavioral discipline, one of the three Buddhist studies. Though one renounces society to become a monk or nun, and is thus freed from the problems of secular life, one is said to be still bound by the "golden chains" of precepts. Attachment to precepts, pride in one's way of life, or belief in the efficacy of mere morality or ritual, is called a form of bondage in Buddhist teaching. In Ch'an this is extended to refer to the whole of the Buddhist teachings, to all sense of realization or attainment, attachment to holiness, which still must be transcended before one is really free. This is like the image of "gold dust in the eyes"; though gold (Buddha Dharma) is precious, gold chains still bind and gold dust still blinds: the qualities of Buddhahood are not to be set up as external objects of attainment.

b.   The "bowl," from which one eats and drinks, symbolizes a line of reasoning or doctrine which one attempts to use to get the "nourishment" of understanding.

The Hands and Eyes of the Bodhisattva of Great Compassion

POINTER

If your whole body were an eye, you still wouldn't be able to see it. If your whole body were an ear, you still wouldn't be able to hear it. If your whole body were a mouth, you still wouldn't be able to speak of it. If your whole body were mind, you still wouldn't be able to perceive it.

Now leaving aside "whole body" for the moment, if suddenly you had no eyes, how would you see? Without ears, how would you hear? Without a mouth, how would you speak? Without a mind, how would you perceive? Here, if you can unfurl a single pathway, then you'd be a fellow student with the ancient Buddhas. But leaving aside "studying" for the moment, under whom would you study?

CASE

Yun Yen asked Tao Wu, "What does the Bodhisattva of Great Compassion use so many hands and eyes for?"[1]

Wu said, "It's like someone reaching back groping for a pillow in the middle of the night."[2]

Yen said, "I understand."[3]

Wu said, "How do you understand it?"[4]

Yen said, "All over the body are hands and eyes."[5]

Wu said, "You have said quite a bit there, but you've only said eighty percent of it."[6]

Yen said, "What do you say, Elder Brother?"[7]

Wu said, "Throughout the body are hands and eyes."[8]

NOTES

1. At that time Tao Wu should have given him some of his own

provisions. Why are you constantly running around? Why do you ask, Reverend?

2. Why didn't Tao Wu use his own provisions? One blind man leading a crowd of blind men.

3. He adds error to error. He's cheating everyone. There's no different dirt in the same hole. Yun Yen doesn't avoid running afoul of the point and cutting his hand.

4. Why bother to inquire further? He still had to ask; Yun Yen should be challenged.

5. What does this have to do with it? He's making his living in the ghost cave, washing a lump of dirt with mud.

6. There's no different dirt in the same hole. When the manservant sees the maidservant, he takes care. A leper drags along his companions.

7. How can one get it by accepting another's interpretation? Tao Wu too should be challenged.

8. The frog cannot leap out of the basket. He's snatched your eyes and made off with your tongue. Has he gotten a hundred percent or not? He's calling daddy poppa.

COMMENTARY

Yun Yen and Tao Wu were fellow students under Yao Shan. For forty years Yun Yen's side did not touch his mat. Yao Shan produced the whole Ts'ao-Tung school. There were three men with whom the Path of Dharma flourished: descended from Yun Yen was Tung Shan; descended from Tao Wu was Shih Shuang; and descended from Ch'uan Tzu was Chia Shan.

The Bodhisattva of Great Compassion (Avalokitesvara) has eighty-four thousand symbolic arms. Great Compassion has this many hands and eyes—do all of you? Pai Chang said, "All sayings and writings return to one's self."

Yun Yen often followed Tao Wu, to study and ask questions to settle his discernment with certainty. One day he asked him, "What does the Bodhisattva of Great Compassion use so many hands and eyes for?" Right at the start Tao Wu should have given him a blow of the staff across his back, to avoid so many complications appearing later. But Tao Wu was compassionate—he couldn't be like this. Instead, he gave Yun Yen an explanation of the reason, meaning to make him understand immediately. Instead (of hitting him) Tao Wu said, "It's like someone reaching back groping for a pillow in the middle of the night." Groping for a pillow in the depths of the night without any lamplight—tell me, where are the eyes?

Yun Yen immediately said, "I understand." Wu said, "How do you understand it?" Yen said, "All over the body are hands and eyes." Wu said, "You have said quite a bit there, but you've only said eighty percent of it." Yen said, "What do you say, Elder Brother?" Wu said, "Throughout the body are hands and eyes."

But say, is "all over the body" right, or is "throughout the body" right? Although they seem covered with mud, nevertheless they are bright and clean. People these days often make up emotional interpretations and say that "all over the body" is wrong, while "throughout the body" is right—they're merely chewing over the Ancients' words and phrases. They have died in the Ancients' words, far from realizing that the Ancients' meaning isn't in the words, and that all talk is used as something that can't be avoided. People these days add footnotes and set up patterns, saying that if one can penetrate this case, then this can be considered understanding enough to put an end to study. Groping with their hands over their bodies and over the lamp and the pillar, they all make a literal understanding of "throughout the body." If you understand this way, you degrade those Ancients quite a bit.

Thus it is said, "He studies the living phrase; he doesn't study the dead phrase." You must cut off emotional defilements and conceptual thinking, become clean and naked, free and unbound—only then will you be able to see this saying about Great Compassion.

Haven't you heard how Ts'ao Shan asked a monk, "How is it when (the Dharmakaya, the body of reality) is manifesting form in accordance with beings, like the moon (reflected) in the water?" The monk said, "Like an ass looking at a well." Shan said, "You have said quite a lot, but you've only said eighty percent of it." The monk said, "What do you say, Teacher?" Shan said, "It's like the well looking at the ass." This is the same meaning as the main case.

If you go to their words to see, you'll never be able to get out of Tao Wu's and Yun Yen's trap. Hsueh Tou, as an adept, no longer dies in the words; he walks right on Tao Wu's and Yun Yen's heads to versify, saying,

VERSE

"All over the body" is right—
>Four limbs, eight joints. This isn't yet the ultimate abode of patchrobed monks.

"Throughout the body" is right—
>There's half on the forehead. You're still in the nest. Blind!

Bringing it up is still a hundred thousand miles away.
>It won't do to let Tao Wu and Yun Yen go. Why only a hundred thousand miles?

Spreading its wings, the Roc soars over the clouds of the six compounds[b]*—*
>A tiny realm—I had thought it would be extraordinary. Check!

It propels the wind to beat against the waters of the four oceans.
>A bit of dust—I had thought no one in the world could cope with you. Wrong!

What speck of dust suddenly arises?
>Again he's adding footnotes for Ch'an people. Cut! He's picked it up, but where has he put it?

What wisp of hair hasn't stopped?
>Exceptional! Special! Blown away. Cut!

You don't see?
>Again this way.

The net of jewels hanging down in patterns; reflections upon reflections.
>So the great Hsueh Tou is doing this kind of thing—too bad! As before he's creating complications.

Where do the hands and eyes on the staff come from?
>Bah! He draws his bow after the thief has gone. I can't let you go. No one in the world has any way to show some life. Hsueh Tou has let go, but he still must take a beating. Again I hit and say, "Tell me, is mine right or is Hsueh Tou's right?"

Bah!
>After three or four shouts, then what?

COMMENTARY

"All over the body is right—/ Throughout the body is right."
Whether you say reaching back with the hand groping for a
pillow is it, or running the hand over the body is it, if you make
up such interpretations, you're doing nothing but making your
living in a ghost cave. In the end neither "all over the body" nor
"throughout the body" is right. If you want to see this story of
Great Compassion by means of emotional consciousness, in
fact you're still a hundred thousand miles away. Hsueh Tou
can play with a phrase—reviving, he says, "Bringing it up is
still a hundred thousand miles away."

In the subsequent lines Hsueh Tou versifies what was extraordinary about Tao Wu and Yun Yen, saying, "Spreading its
wings, the Roc soars over the clouds of the six compounds[a]—/
It propels the wind to beat against the waters of the four
oceans." The great Roc swallows dragons: with his wings he
sends the wind to beat against the waters; the waters part, then
the Roc captures the dragon and swallows it. Hsueh Tou is
saying that if you can propel the wind against the waves like
the great Roc, you would be very brave and strong indeed.

If such actions are viewed with the thousand hands and eyes
of the Bodhisattva of Great Compassion, it's just a little bit of
dust suddenly arising, or like a wisp of hair ceaselessly blown
by the wind. Hsueh Tou says, "If you take running the hands
over the body as the hands and eyes of Great Compassion, what
is this good for?" In fact this is just not enough for this story of
the Bodhisattva of Great Compassion. Thus, Hsueh Tou says,
"What speck of dust suddenly arises? / What wisp of hair hasn't
stopped?"

Hsueh Tou said of himself that an adept at once wipes away
his tracks. Nevertheless, at the end of the verse as usual he
broke down and gave a comparison—as before, he's still in the
cage. "You don't see? / The net of jewels hanging down in
patterns, reflections upon reflections." Hsueh Tou brings out
the clear jewels of Indra's net to use as patterns hanging down.
But tell me, where do the hands and eyes come to rest?

In the Hua Yen school they designate four Dharma realms:
first, the Dharma realm of principle, to explain one-flavor
equality; second, the Dharma realm of phenomena, to explain
that principle in its entirety becomes phenomena. Third, the

Dharma realm of principle and phenomena unobstructed, to explain how principle and phenomena merge without hindrance; fourth, the Dharma realm of no obstruction among phenomena, to explain that every phenomenon everywhere enters all phenomena, that all things everywhere embrace all things, all intermingling simultaneously without obstruction. Thus it is said, "As soon as a single speck of dust arises, the whole earth is contained therein; each atom contains boundless Dharma realms. That being so for each atom, it is so for all atoms."

As for the net of jewels; in front of Indra's Dharma Hall of Goodness, there's a net made of jewels. Hundreds of thousands of jewels are reflected in every individual jewel, and each jewel is reflected in hundreds of thousands of jewels. Center jewel and surrounding jewels reflect back and forth, multiplying and remultiplying the images endlessly. This is used to illustrate the Dharma realm of no obstruction among phenomena.

In the old days National Teacher Hsien Shou set up a demonstration using mirrors and a lamp. He placed ten mirrors around the circumference (of a room) and put a lamp in the center. If you observed any one mirror, you saw nine mirrors mirroring the lamp, mirrors and lamp all appearing equally and perfectly clearly.

Thus when the World Honored One first achieved true enlightenment, without leaving the site of enlightenment he ascended into all the heavens of the thirty-three celestial kingdoms, and at nine gatherings in seven places he expounded the Hua Yen scripture.

Hsueh Tou uses Indra's jewel net to impart the teaching of the Dharma realm of no obstruction among phenomena. The six aspects[b] are very clear; that is, the all-inclusive, the separate, the sameness, the difference, the formation, and the disintegration. Raise one aspect and all six are included. Because living beings in their daily activities are unaware of it, Hsueh Tou raises the clear jewels of Indra's net hanging down in patterns to describe this saying about the Bodhisattva of Great Compassion. It's just like this: if you are well able, amidst the jewel net, to understand the staff and the marvellous functioning of supernatural powers going out and coming in unobstructed, then you can see the hands and eyes of the Bodhisattva. That's why Hsueh Tou says, "Where do the hands and eyes on the staff come from?" This is to make you attain realization at the staff and obtain fulfillment at a shout.

When Te Shan hit people as soon as they came in through the gate, when Lin Chi shouted at people as soon as they came in through the gate, tell me, where were the hands and eyes? And tell me, why did Hsueh Tou go on at the end to utter the word "Bah!"? Investigate!

TRANSLATORS' NOTES

a. The six compounds are the six senses—eye, ear, nose, tongue, body, and mind, and their respective sense-fields.

b. The six aspects of all things are defined in terms of the interdependent coproduction or relative coexistence of all things. The classic metaphor is of a house: the house represents the all-inclusive aspect, its beams and such represent the separate, or distinct aspect; since the beams, etc., join to form a house and nothing else, this is their aspect of sameness, but since they depend on each other as individual parts which are not the same, this is their aspect of difference. As they collectively create a house, this is the aspect of formation, but since each part has its own position and does not individually create anything, this is the aspect of disintegration. Put another way, one compound contains many elements or qualities; this is the all-inclusive aspect. The many qualities or elements are not one; this is the separate, or distinct aspect. Many functions or meanings are not at odds with each other; this is the aspect of sameness. From these many functions or meanings, interdependent co-production takes place; this is the aspect of formation. These conditions each abide in their own nature, without moving; this is the aspect of disintegration. (This explanation is from the section on Fa Yen Ch'an in the *Jen T'ien Yen Mu*, "Eye of Humans and Gods.")

Chih Men's Body of Wisdom

POINTER

Even the thousand sages[a] have not transmitted the single phrase before sound. The single thread right before us is perpetually unbroken. Purified and naked, free and unbound, hair dishevelled and ears alert—tell me, what about it? To test, I cite this to see.

CASE

A monk asked Chih Men, "What is the body of wisdom?"[1] Chih Men said, "An oyster swallowing the bright moon."[2]
The monk asked, "What is the function of wisdom?"[3] Chih Men said, "A rabbit getting pregnant."[4]

NOTES

1. Throughout the body there are no reflected images. It cuts off the tongues of everyone in the world. What's he using "body" for?
2. Leaving aside for the moment "the light engulfs myriad forms," what is the affair of the correct eye on the staff? The crooked does not conceal the straight. Chih Men is adding a layer of frost on snow.
3. Fall back three thousand miles! What does he want "function" for?
4. Danger! A bitter gourd is bitter to the root, a sweet melon is sweet to the stem. If you make your living in the shadows of the light, then you won't get out of Chih Men's nest. If there is someone who can come out, tell me, is this the body of wisdom or the function of wisdom? In essence this is adding mud to dirt.

COMMENTARY

When Chih Men said, "An oyster swallowing the bright moon" and "A rabbit getting pregnant," in both he used a mid-autumn sense; even so, the Ancient's meaning was not in the oyster or the rabbit. As Chih Men was a venerable adept in the congregation of Yun Men,[b] each of his phrases had to contain three phrases; that is, the phrase that contains heaven and earth, the phrase that cuts off the myriad streams, and the phrase that follows the waves. Moreover, without using any prearranged maneuvers, each of his phrases is spontaneously appropriate. Thus he went to the danger point to answer this monk's questions, showing a bit of his sharp point—he was undeniably extraordinary. Nevertheless, this ancient never played with the shadows of a light, he just pointed out a bit of a road for you to make you see.

This monk said, "What is the body of wisdom?" Chih Men said, "An oyster swallowing the bright moon." Oysters contain bright pearls: (it is said that) when the mid-autumn moon comes out, the oysters float to the surface, open their mouths, and swallow the moonlight; from the effects of this, pearls are produced. If there is moonlight in mid-autumn, the pearls are many; without a moon, the pearls are few.

The monk also asked, "What is the function of wisdom?" Chih Men said, "A rabbit getting pregnant." The meaning of this is no different. The rabbit belongs to (the female, negative principle) Yin (to which the moon also belongs); in mid-autumn when the moon comes out, the rabbits open their mouths and swallow its light, thus becoming pregnant. Here too, if there's moonlight the offspring are many; without a moon, they're few.

That Ancient's answer was free from so many concerns; he just made temporary use of these meanings to answer about the light of wisdom. Although his answer was this way, his meaning wasn't in the words and phrases. It's just that later people go to his words to make a living. Haven't you heard how P'an Shan said,

> *The mind-moon is solitary and full:*
> *Its light engulfs the myriad forms.*

The light is not shining on objects,
Nor do the objects exist—
Light and objects both forgotten,
Then what is this?

People these days just stare and call this the light: from their feelings they produce interpretations, driving spikes into empty space.

An Ancient said, "Day and night all of you people release a great light from the gates of your six senses; it shines through mountains, rivers, and the great earth. It's not only your eyes that release light—nose, tongue, body and mind also all release light." To get here you simply must clean up your six sense faculties so that you're without the slightest concern, purified and naked, free and unbound—only then will you see where this story is at. Hsueh Tou does his verse just this way:

VERSE

One piece of empty solidity, beyond saying and feeling;
    Stir your mind and you err, move your thoughts and
    you're obstructed. Not even Buddha's eye can catch sight
    of it.
From this humans and gods see Subhuti.
    Subhuti should be given thirty blows. Why make use of
    this old fellow? Even Subhuti has to fall back three
    thousand miles.
The oyster swallowing, the mysterious rabbit—deep, deep
        meaning:
    You'd have to be the man himself to understand. What
    intention did he have? What further need for "deep, deep
    meaning"?
Having been given to Ch'an people, it makes them fight and
        struggle.
    When shields and spears are already at rest, then there's
    great peace under heaven. Do you understand? I hit, say-
    ing, "How many blows can you take, Reverend?"

COMMENTARY

"One piece of empty solidity, beyond saying and feeling." With a single line, Hsueh Tou has versified it well: naturally he can see the Ancient's meaning. What is it that the six senses are brimming with? It's just this one mass, empty and bright, solid and quiescent. You don't need to go to heaven to look for it. You don't have to seek it from someone else. The perpetual light spontaneously appears before us: right here in this very place it towers up like a mile-high wall, beyond verbal appellation and mental sense.

Fa Yen's verse on perfect reality says,

> When reasoning is exhausted, saying and feeling are
>   forgotten;
> How could this be properly described?
> Wherever I go, the frosty night's moon
> Falls as it may on the valley ahead.
> The fruits are ripe and heavy with monkeys,
> The mountains go on so far it seems I've lost my
>   way.
> When I raise my head, there's a remnant of illumi-
>   nation left—
> Actually this is west of my dwelling place.

Thus it is said,

> Mind is the faculty, things are the objects;
> Both are like flaws on a mirror.
> When the defilement of objects is obliterated, the
>   light first appears.
> When mind and things are both forgotten, nature is
>   real.

It is also said,

> I've always lived in a three-section reed hut;
> In the spiritual light of the one Path, myriad objects
>   are at rest.
> Don't use right and wrong to judge me—
> Fleeting life and its rationalizations have nothing to
>   do with me.

These verses too make you see "One piece of empty solidity, beyond saying and feeling."

"From this humans and gods see Subhuti." Haven't you heard how Subhuti was sitting quietly on a cliff when all the gods showered him with flowers to praise him: the venerable Subhuti said, "Who is showering down these flowers in praise?" A god said, "I am Brahma." Subhuti said, "Why are you offering praise?" The god said, "I honor you for being good at expounding the transcendance of wisdom." Subhuti said, "I have never spoken a single word about wisdom; why offer praise?" The god said, "You didn't speak and I didn't hear—no speaking and no hearing is true wisdom," and again he caused the earth to tremble and flowers to shower. See how Subhuti expounded wisdom so well, without speaking of its body or its function. If at this you can see, then you can see Chih Men's saying, "An oyster swallowing the bright moon" and "A rabbit getting pregnant."

Though the Ancient's meaning was not in the spoken phrases, nevertheless in his answer there was a deep, deep meaning. This caused Hsueh Tou to say, "The oyster swallowing, the mysterious rabbit—deep, deep meaning." Here, "Having been given to Ch'an people, it makes them fight and struggle." The followers of Ch'an in the world have haggled over Chih Men's answers profusely and noisily; there's never been a single person who has even seen him in a dream. If you want to be a fellow student with Chih Men and Hsueh Tou, you must first set your eyes on it for yourself.

TRANSLATORS' NOTES

a. In Chinese convention, multiples of ten represent infinite numbers; ten thousand especially is so used and really means "myriad." Hence "the thousand sages" means "all the sages."

b. Chih Men was a successor of the Yun Men lineage in the third generation; his teacher was Yun Men's great disciple Hsiang Lin Teng Yuan.

Yen Kuan's Rhinoceros

POINTER

To transcend emotion, detach from views, remove bonds and dissolve sticking points, to uphold the fundamental vehicle of transcendence and support the treasury of the eye of the true Dharma, you must also respond equally in all ten directions, be crystal clear in all respects, and directly attain to such a realm. But tell me, are there any who attain alike, realize alike, die alike and live alike? To test, I cite this to see.

CASE

One day Yen Kuan called to his attendant, "Bring me my rhinoceros-horn fan."[1]

The attendant said, "The fan is broken."[2]

Yen Kuan said, "If the fan is broken, bring the rhinoceros back to me."[3]

The attendant had no reply.[4]

T'ou Tzu said, "I do not refuse to bring it out, but I fear the horn on its head will be imperfect."[5] Hsueh Tou commented, "I want an imperfect horn."[6]

Shih Shuang said, "If I return it to the Master, then I won't have it."[7] Hsueh Tou commented, "The rhino is still there."[8]

Tzu Fu drew a circle and wrote the word 'rhino' inside it.[9] Hsueh Tou commented, "Why did you not bring it out before?"[10]

Pao Fu said, "The Master is aged; he should ask someone else."[11] Hsueh Tou commented, "What a pity to have worked hard without accomplishing anything."[12]

NOTES

1. He creates quite a few complications. How can it compare with the fine scene here?

2. What a pity! What is he saying?
3. He's broken down quite a bit. Yu province is still all right; the worst suffering is in Korea. What does the master want with the rhinoceros?
4. After all he's a hammerhead without a hole. What a pity!
5. This seems to be like it, but nevertheless he has two heads and three faces. He is still speaking theoretically.
6. What is it good for? He adds error to error.
7. What is he saying? It's right under his nose.
8. Danger! He almost mistook it. Pull its head back!
9. Grass that's withered isn't worth bringing out. He's a fellow playing with a shadow.
10. He doesn't distinguish gold from brass. He too is a fellow in the weeds.
11. In an out of the way place he rebukes an official. What is he doing, avoiding hardship yet speaking of his suffering?
12. You yourself are included. It would be even better to give thirty blows of the staff. Clearly.

COMMENTARY

Yen Kuan one day called to his attendant, "Bring me my rhinoceros-horn fan." Although this matter does not lie in words, yet if you want to test someone's ordinary disposition and ability, still it is necessary to be able to use words in this way to show it. On the last day of the last month of your life, if you can find strength and be the Master, even when myriad visions appear in profusion, you can look upon them without being moved: this can be called accomplishment without accomplishment, effortless power.

Yen Kuan was Ch'an Master Chi An; he used to have a fan made of rhinoceros horn. At the time, how could Yen Kuan not have known that the fan was broken? He purposely asked the attendant, and the attendant said, "The fan is broken." Observe how that Ancient was always within It twenty-four hours a day, encountering It everywhere; Yen Kuan said, "If the fan is broken, bring the rhinoceros back to me." But tell me, what did he want with the rhinoceros? He just wanted to test the man to see whether or not he knew where it was at.

T'ou Tzu said, "I do not refuse to bring it out, but I fear the head's horn will be imperfect." Hsueh Tou said, "I want the imperfect horn." He too goes to the phrase to match wits.

Shih Shuang said, "If I return it to the Master, then I won't have it." Hsueh Tou says, "The rhino is still there."

Tzu Fu drew a circle and wrote the word "rhino" inside; because he had succeeded to Yang Shan, he always liked to use objects to teach people and illustrate this matter. Hsueh Tou says, "Why didn't you bring it out before?" He pierced his nostrils too.

Pao Fu said, "The Master is aged; he should ask someone else." These words are most appropriate; the preceding three quotes are after all easy to see, but the words of this one phrase have a profound meaning. Yet Hsueh Tou has broken them up too. When I was at Librarian Ch'ing's place in the old days, I understood the reasoning; he said, "The Master is old and senile; getting the head, he forgets the tail—before he sought the fan, now he seeks the rhinoceros; it is hard to attend to him, and therefore (Pao Fu) said, 'Better ask someone else.'" Hsueh Tou said, "What a pity to work hard without accomplishing anything."

All these were in the form of remarks: the Ancients saw through this matter, so though each was different, when they spoke forth, they hit the mark a hundred times out of a hundred, always having a way to show forth; each phrase does not lose the bloodline. People these days, when they are questioned, just make up theoretical judgments and comparisons; that is why I want people to chew on this twenty-four hours a day, making every drop of water a drop of ice, seeking the experience of enlightenment. See how Hsueh Tou versified it on one thread, saying,

VERSE

The rhinoceros-horn fan has long been in use,
> In summer, cool; in winter, warm. Everyone has it; why don't they know? Who has never used it?

But when asked, actually nobody knows.
> They know, but they don't understand. Better not fool people. And you shouldn't suspect anyone else.

The boundless pure breeze and the horn on the head,
> Where are they? If you do not understand in yourself,
> where will you understand? In the heavens and on earth.
> The horn has regrown. What is it? He rouses waves with-
> out wnd.

Just like the clouds and rain, when gone, are difficult to pur-
> *sue.*
> Heavens! Heavens! Still this is losing one's money and
> incurring punishment anyway.

Hsueh Tou also said, "If you want the pure breeze to return,
and the horn to regrow,[1] I ask you Ch'an followers to each turn
a word.[2] I ask you, since the fan is broken, return the
rhinoceros to me."[3]

At that time a monk came forth and said, "Everyone, go
meditate in the hall!"[4]

Hsueh Tou said, "I cast my hook fishing for whales, but
caught a frog." Then he got down from the seat.[5]

NOTES *(cont'd.)*

1. Everyone has this fan: throughout the twenty-four hours of the
   day, they completely obtain its power; why do they not know at
   all when they are asked? Can you speak?
2. He has already spoken thrice. Yen Kuan is still alive.
3. There is yet one or a half. Bah! It would be better to overthrow his
   meditation seat.
4. He draws the bow after the thief has gone. He neither gets to the
   village nor reaches the shop.
5. He brought this about. He draws his bow after the thief is gone.

COMMENTARY

"The rhinoceros-horn fan has long been in use, / But when
asked, actually nobody knows." Everyone has this fan, and
throughout the twenty-four hours of the day is in complete
possession of its power—why is it that when asked, no one
knows where it's gone? The attendant, T'ou Tzu, all the way
down to Pao Fu—neither do any of them know. But tell me,
does Hsueh Tou know?

Have you not seen how when Wu Cho called on Manjusri, as they were drinking tea, Manjusri held up a crystal bowl and asked, "Do they have this in the South?" Wu Cho said, "No." Manjusri said, "What do they usually use to drink tea?" Wu Cho was speechless. If you know what this public case is about, then you will know that the rhinoceros-horn fan has a boundless pure breeze; you will also see the horn towering on the rhino's head.

The four old fellows speaking as they did were like the morning clouds and evening rain; once gone, they are difficult to pursue. Hsueh Tou also said, "If you want the pure breeze to return and the horn to regrow, I ask you Ch'an followers to each utter a turning word: I ask you, since the fan is broken, return the rhinoceros to me." At that moment a Ch'an follower came forth and said, "Everyone, go meditate in the hall!" This monk has usurped the Master's sceptre of authority. He certainly could speak, but he was only able to say eighty percent. If you want a hundred percent, then throw the meditation seat over for him. Now, you tell me, did this monk understand the rhinoceros or not? If he did not understand, yet he knew how to speak in this way; if he did understand, why did Hsueh Tou not approve of him? Why did he say, "I cast a hook fishing for whales, but only caught a frog."

Tell me, ultimately how is it? Everyone, there's nothing to worry about; try to hold it up to view.

The World Honored One Ascends the Seat

POINTER

One who can discern the tune as soon as the lute strings move is hard to find even in a thousand years. By releasing a hawk upon seeing a rabbit, at once the swiftest is caught. As for summing up all spoken words into a single phrase, gathering the universe into a single atom, dying the same and being born the same, piercing and penetrating in all ways, is there anyone who can stand witness? To test, I cite this to see.

CASE

One day the World Honored One ascended his seat.[1] Manjusri struck the gavel and said, "Clearly behold the Dharma of the King of Dharma; the Dharma of the King of Dharma is thus."[2]
The World Honored One then got down off the seat.[3]

NOTES

1. Guest and host both lose. This is not the only instance of indulgence.
2. One son has intimately understood.
3. Sad man, do not speak to sad people; if you speak to sad people, you'll sadden them to death. Beating the drum, playing the lute, two masters in harmony.

COMMENTARY

Before the World Honored One had raised the flower,[a] already there was this scene. From the beginning at the Deer Park[b] to

the end at the Hiranyavati River,[c] how many times did he use
the jewel sword of the Diamond King? At that time, if among
the crowd there had been someone with the spirit of a patchrobed monk who could transcend, he would have been able to
avoid the final messy scene of raising the flower. While the
World Honored One paused, he was confronted by Manjusri,
and immediately got down from his seat. At that time, there
was still this scene; Shakyamuni barred his door, Vimalakirti
shut his mouth—both resemble this, and thus have already
explained it. It is like the story of Su Tsung asking National
Teacher Chung about making a seamless memorial tower,[d] and
also like the story of the outsider asking Buddha, "I do not ask
about the spoken or the unspoken."[e] Observe the behavior of
those transcendent people; when did they ever enter a ghost
cave for their subsistence? Some say that the meaning lies in
the silence; some say it lies in the pause, that speech illumines
what cannot be said, and speechlessness illumines what can be
said—as Yung Chia said, "Speaking when silent, silent when
speaking." But if you only understand in this way, then past,
present, and future, for sixty aeons, you will still never have
seen it even in dreams. If you can immediately and directly
attain fulfillment, then you will no longer see that there is
anything ordinary or holy—this Dharma is equanimous, it has
no high or low. Every day you will walk hand in hand with all
the Buddhas.

Finally, observe how Hsueh Tou naturally sees and produces
it in verse:

VERSE

Among the assembled multitude of sages, if an adept had
known,
  Better not slander old Shakyamuni. Leave it up to Lin Chi
  or Te Shan. Among a thousand or ten thousand, it's hard
  to find one or a half.

The command of the King of Dharma wouldn't have been like
this.
  Those who run after him are as plentiful as hemp and
  millet. Three heads, two faces. Clearly. How many could
  there be who could reach here?

In the assembly, if there had been a "saindhava man,"
> It's hard to find a clever man in there. If Manjusri isn't an adept, you sure aren't.

What need for Manjusri to strike the gavel?
> What is the harm of going ahead and striking the gavel once? The second and third strokes are totally unneccesary. How will you speak a phrase appropriate to the situation? angerous!

COMMENTARY

"Among the assembled multitude of sages, if an adept had known." The great mass of eighty thousand on Vulture Peak all were ranked among the sages: Manjusri, Samantabhadra, and so on, including Maitreya; master and companions were assembled together—they had to be the skilled among the skillful, the outstanding among the outstanding, before they would know what he was getting at. What Hsueh Tou intends to say is that among the multitude of sages, there was not a single man who knew what is: if there had been an adept, then he would have known what was not so. Why? Manjusri struck the gavel and said, "Clearly behold the Dharma of the King of Dharma; the Dharma of the King of Dharma is thus." Hsueh Tou said, "The command of the King of Dharma is not like this." Why so? At the time, if there had been in the assembly a fellow with an eye on his forehead and a talisman at his side, he would have seen all the way through before the World Honored One had even ascended the seat; then what further need would there be for Manjusri to strike the gavel?

The Nirvana Scripture says, "Saindhava is one name for four actual things: one is salt, the second is water, the third is a bowl, and the fourth is a horse. There was a wise attendant who well understood the four meanings: if the king wanted to wash, and needed *saindhava*, the attendant would then bring him water; when he asked for it when eating, then he served him salt; when the meal was done, he offered him a bowl to drink hot water; and when he wanted to go out, he presented a horse. He acted according to the king's intention without error; clearly one must be a clever fellow to be able to do this."

When a monk asked Hsiang Yen, "What is the king asking for *saindhava*?" Hsiang Yen said, "Come over here." The monk went; Hsiang Yen said, "You make a total fool of others." He also asked Chao Chou, "What is the king asking for *saindhava*?" Chou got off his meditation seat, bent over and folded his hands. At this time if there had been a *"saindhava* man"* who could penetrate before the World Honored One had even ascended his seat, then he would have attained somewhat. The World Honored One yet ascended his seat, and then immediately got down; already he hadn't got to the point—how was it worth Manjusri's still striking the gavel? He unavoidably made the World Honored One's sermon seem foolish. But tell me, where was it that he made a fool of him?

TRANSLATORS' NOTES

a. This refers to the oft-repeated story of the Buddha holding a flower up before a huge assembly, whereat Mahakasyapa smiled, the only one to understand the Buddha's message. In Ch'an tradition this represents the first "heart to heart transmission" of Ch'an in India.

b. Shakyamuni Buddha gave his first sermon at the Deer Park in Benares, to five ascetics with whom he had formerly associated.

c. Shakyamuni Buddha died by the Hiranyavati River.

d. See case 18.

e. See case 65.

Ta Kuang Does a Dance

CASE

A monk asked Ta Kuang, "Ch'ang Ch'ing said, 'Joyful praise on the occasion of a meal'—what was the essence of his meaning?"[1a]

Ta Kuang did a dance.[2] The monk bowed.[3] Kuang said, "What have you seen, that you bow?"[4] The monk did a dance.[5] Kuang said, "You wild fox spirit!"[6]

NOTES

1. The light shines again. This lacquer tub! It is unavoidable to doubt; without asking, you won't know.
2. Do not deceive people completely. He acts in the same way as (Chin Niu did) before.
3. He too acts this way; he's right, but I fear he's misunderstood.
4. He still should press him; it's necessary to be discriminating.
5. He draws a cat according to a model. After all he misunderstood. He's a fellow playing with a shadow.
6. This kindness is hard to requite. The Thirty-three Patriarchs only transmitted this.

COMMENTARY

The Twenty-eight Patriarchs in India and the Six Patriarchs in China only transmitted this little bit; but do you people know what it comes down to? If you know, you can avoid this error; if you do not know, as before you will only be wild fox spirits.[b]

Some say (Ta Kuang) wrenched around the other's nostrils to deceive the man; but if it were actually so, what principle would that amount to? Ta Kuang was well able to help others; in his phrases there is a road along which to get oneself out. In general, a teacher of the school must pull out the nails, draw out the pegs, remove the sticking points and untie the bonds for people; only then can he be called "a good friend."ᶜ

Ta Kuang did a dance, the monk bowed; in the end, the monk also did a dance, and Ta Kuang said, "You wild fox spirit!" This was not turning the monk over; after all, if you do not know the real point, and just do a dance, going on one after the other like this, when will you ever find rest? Ta Kuang said, "Wild fox spirit"—these words cut off Chin Niu, and are undeniably outstanding. That is why it is said, "He studies the living word, not the dead word." Hsueh Tou just likes his saying "You wild fox spirit!" That is the basis on which he produces his verse. But tell me, is this "wild fox spirit" the same as or different from "Tsang's head is white; Hai's head is black,"ᵈ "This lacquer bucket!"ᵉ or "Good monk!"? Just tell me, are these the same or different? Do you know? You meet him everywhere.

VERSE

The first arrow was still light, but the second arrow went
        deep:
        A hundred shots, a hundred hits. Where can you go to escape?
Who says yellow leaves are yellow gold?
        Yet they'll put an end to crying; but even if you can fool a child, it's of no use.
If the waves of Ts'ao Ch'i were alike,
        What limit is there to people playing with mud balls? He draws a cat according to a model. He lets out a single road.
Innumerable ordinary people would get bogged down.
        We meet a living man! He has entangled every patchrobed monk in the world, and makes them unable to get a hold; he entangles you too, and makes you unable to appear.

COMMENTARY

"The first arrow was still light, but the second arrow went deep." Ta Kuang's dance was the first arrow. He also said,

"This wild fox spirit!" This was the second arrow. This has been the tooth and nail since time immemorial.

"Who says yellow leaves are yellow gold?" Yang Shan said to his community, "You people should each turn back your light and reflect; do not memorize my words. Since beginningless aeons you have turned your backs on the light and plunged into darkness; the roots of your false conceptions are deep, and after all are hard to pull out all at once. That is why I temporarily set up expedient methods to take away your coarse discriminating consciousness; this is like using yellow leaves to stop a little child's crying." It is like exchanging sweet fruit for bitter gourd. The Ancients provisionally established expedient methods to help people; when their crying has stopped, yellow leaves are not gold.ᶠ When the World Honored One explained timely doctrines throughout his lifetime, these too were just talks to put an end to crying. "This wild fox!"—he just wanted to transmute the other's active discriminating consciousness; within (the process) there are provisional and real, there are also illumination and function; only thus can you see the grasp of the patchrobed monk there. If you can understand, you'll be like a tiger with folded wings.

"If the waves of Ts'ao Ch'i were alike."ᵍ If suddenly all the students in all quarters did a dance like this, and only acted like this, then innumerable ordinary people would get bogged down; how could they be saved?

TRANSLATORS' NOTES

a.   See case 74; reference to that case is made several times.

b.   As a term of scorn, "wild fox spirit" connotes fakery or show; "wild fox Ch'an" is an expression used to refer to empty pretense.

c.   *Shan chih shih*, a translation of Sanskrit *kalyanamitra*, which means a good or virtuous friend, refers to a spiritual guide, teacher, benefactor.

d.   See case 73.

e.   A lacquer bucket, or lacquer tub, means an ignoramus. The blackness of lacquer symbolizes ignorance, lack of enlightenment.

f.   That is, just as yellow leaves are used to placate a crying child by pretending they are gold trinkets, various teachings and techniques are used to put an end to people's confusion and misery, though ultimately, as Te Shan said, there is nothing to give to people, no true doctrine.

g. By Hsueh Tou's time, all the living streams of Ch'an were descended from the Sixth Patriarch Hui Neng, who is also referred to by the name Ts'ao Ch'i after his dwelling place. Ts'ao Ch'i was a river; the temple where Hui Neng taught was built near its source in Shao Chou in the far south of China.

The Surangama Scripture's Not Seeing

POINTER

The one phrase before sound is not transmitted by a thousand sages; the single thread before our eyes is forever without a gap. Pure and naked, bare and clean, the White Ox on Open Ground.[a] Eyes alert, ears alert, the golden-haired lion—leaving this aside for a moment, tell me, what is the White Ox on Open Ground?

CASE

The *Surangama* scripture says, "When I do not see, why do you not see my not seeing?[1] If you see my not seeing, naturally that is not the characteristic of not seeing.[2] If you don't see my not seeing,[3] it is naturally not a thing[4]—how could it not be you?"[5]

NOTES

1. Good news! What is the use of seeing? Old Shakyamuni has broken down quite a bit.
2. Bah! What leisure time is there? You shouldn't tell me to have two heads and three faces.
3. Where are you going? It's like driving a nail into an iron spike. Bah!
4. He pushes down the ox's head to make it eat grass. What further verbal sound and form is there to speak of?
5. To say you or me is totally beside the point. Striking, I say, "Do you see old Shakyamuni?"

COMMENTARY

In the *Surangama* scripture it says, "When I don't see, why don't you see my not seeing? If you see my not seeing, naturally that is not the characteristic of not seeing. If you don't see my not seeing, it is naturally not a thing; how could it not be you?" Hsueh Tou here does not quote the entire passage of the scripture; if it is quoted in full, then it can be seen. The scripture says,[b] "If seeing were a thing, then you could also see my sight. If seeing alike were called seeing my (seeing), when I don't see, why don't you see my not seeing? If you see my not seeing, naturally that is not the characteristic of not seeing. If you don't see my not seeing, naturally it is not a thing; how could it not be you?" The words are many, and I won't record them. Ananda intended to say, "The lamps and pillars in the world all can be given names; I also want the World Honored One to point out this subtle spiritual fundamental illumination—what can you call it, to let me see the Buddha's intent?" The World Honored One says, "I see the incense stand." Ananda says, "I also see the incense stand; then this is the Buddha's sight." The World Honored One says, "When I see the incense stand, then that can be known; when I do not see the incense stand, then how will you see?" Ananda says, "When I don't see the incense stand, then this is seeing the Buddha." The Buddha says, "If I say I don't see, this is my own knowledge; when you say you don't see, this is your own knowledge—where another doesn't see, how can you know?" The ancients said that when you get here, you can only know for yourself; you can't explain to others. Just as the World Honored One said, "When I do not see, why don't you see my not seeing? If you see my not seeing, naturally that is not the characteristic of not seeing. If you do not see my not seeing, naturally it is not a thing; how could it not be you?" If you say you acknowledge sight as an existent thing, you are not yet able to wipe away the traces. "When I don't see" is like the antelope with his horns hung up—all echo of sound, traces of tracks, all breath is utterly gone; where will you turn to search for him? The sense of the scripture is total indulgence in the beginning and total restraint in the end. Hsueh Tou goes beyond the eye of the scriptural teachings to versify: he neither eulogizes things, nor seeing or not seeing; he just eulogizes seeing Buddha.

"The Whole Elephant" or *"The Whole Ox"—as blinding*
    cataracts, they're no different.
    Half-blind man! Half open, half closed. What are you do-
    ing, clinging to fences and groping along walls? One cut,
    two pieces.

Adepts of all time have together been naming and describing.
    Twenty-eight (Patriarchs) in India, six in China, all the
    old teachers in the world, numerous as hemp and millet
    seeds—yet you have still left yourself out.

If you want to see the yellow-faced old fellow right now,
    Bah! The old barbarian! Blind fellow! He's right at your
    feet.

Each atom of every land lies halfway there.
    Where you stand you've already missed him. What more
    would you have me say? Will you ever see him, even in a
    dream?

"The Whole Elephant or the Whole Ox—as blinding cataracts, they're no different." A group of blind people groping over an elephant each speaks of a different aspect; this comes from the *Nirvana* scripture. A monk asked Yang Shan, "Master, when you saw someone come and ask about Ch'an or ask about the Way, you then drew a circle, and wrote the word 'ox' inside it; where does the meaning of this lie?" Yang Shan said, "This too is an idle matter: if you immediately can understand, it doesn't come from outside; if you cannot understand immediately, you certainly don't recognize it. Now I ask you, what have the aged adepts in various places pointed out in your body as your Buddha-nature? Do you consider it that which speaks, or is it that which is silent? Is it not that which neither speaks nor is silent? Or do you consider everything to be it, or do you consider that everything is not it? If you acknowledge that which speaks as it, you are like the blind man who has grabbed on to the elephant's tail. If you acknowledge that which is silent as it, you are like the blind man grabbing the elephant's ear. If you acknowledge that which neither speaks nor is silent as it, you are like the blind man grabbing the elephant's trunk. If you say everything is it, you are like the blind man grabbing the elephant's four legs. If you say none are it, you abandon the original elephant and fall into the view of emptiness. According to what these blind men perceive, they just attribute different names and descriptions to the elephant. If you want to do right, just avoid groping over the elephant: do not say perceptive awareness is it, yet do not say that is not it."

The Sixth Patriarch said, "Enlightenment basically has no tree; the clear mirror also has no stand. Fundamentally there is not a single thing; how is it possible to be defiled by any dust?" He also said, "The Way fundamentally has no shape or form; wisdom itself is the Way. To attain this understanding is called true transcendent wisdom." One with clear eyes sees the elephant and apprehends its entire body; the seeing of Buddha nature is also like this.

The "whole ox" appears in the *Chuang-tzu:* Pao Ting, in cutting up oxen, never saw the whole ox; he followed the internal patterns to cut them apart; letting his cleaver glide freely, he did not need to add any further effort. In the time it takes to raise your eyes, head and horn, hoof and flesh were separated of their own accord. He did so for nineteen years, and his cleaver was still as sharp as though it had newly come from the whetstone. This is called the "whole ox." Although he was so excellent, Hsueh Tou says that even if you can be like this, the whole elephant and the whole ox are no different from blinding cataracts in the eyes. "Adepts of all time together name and describe." Even adepts still grope inside without finding. From Kasyapa on down through the patriarchs and masters of India and China, the old teachers all over the world are just naming and describing.

Hsueh Tou directly says, "If you want to see the old yellow-face^c right now, every atom of dust in every land lies halfway there." Usually we say that each atom is a Buddha-land, each leaf is a Shakyamuni. Even when all the atomic particles in the cosmos can be seen in one atom, you're still only halfway there; there is still another half of the way yonder. But tell me, where is he? Old Shakyamuni didn't even know himself; how would you have me explain?

TRANSLATORS' NOTES

a. The open ground symbolizes the stage of Buddhahood; the white ox symbolizes the Dharmakaya, the body of reality, the ultimate and universal body of all Buddhas. In the *Saddharmapundarika* scripture, the white ox symbolizes the unique vehicle of Buddhahood. See also the appendix on Tung Shan's three falls in volume two.

b. This passage occurs in the second volume of the *Surangama* scripture; we have translated according to the Sung dynasty commentary of Tzu Jui. This scripture, whose title means "Heroic Going," describes many psychological states and pitfalls of meditation; it was one of the favorite scriptures of Ch'an students, and numerous quotations from it are to be found in the sayings of Ch'an masters.

c. "Yellow-face" refers to Shakyamuni Buddha, who as a Buddha represents all Buddhas and Buddhahood in general; the Buddha was said to have golden skin, hence the epithet "yellow face."

Ch'ang Ch'ing's Three Poisons

POINTER

Where there is Buddha, do not stay; if you keep staying there, your head will sprout horns. Where there is no Buddha, quickly run past; if you don't run past, weeds will grow ten feet high.

Even if you are pure and naked, bare and clean, without mental activity outside of things, without things outside of mental activity, you still have not escaped standing by a stump waiting for a rabbit.[a]

But tell me, without being like any of this, how would you act? To test, I cite this to see.

CASE

Ch'ang Ch'ing once said, "Rather say that saints have the three poisons,[1] but do not say that the Tathagata has two kinds of speech.[2] I do not say the Tathagata is speechless,[3] just that he doesn't have two kinds of speech."[4]

Pao Fu said, "What is Tathagata speech?"[5]

Ch'ing said, "How could a deaf man hear?"[6]

Pao Fu said, "I knew you were talking on the secondary level."[7]

Ch'ing said, "What is Tathagata speech?"[8]

Pao Fu said, "Go drink tea."[9]

NOTES

1. Scorched grain doesn't sprout.
2. He has already slandered old Shakyamuni.
3. He is still making a fool of himself; already he has seven openings and eight holes.
4. Useless maundering. What third or fourth kind will you talk about?

601

5. He gives a good thrust; what will you say?
6. He addresses a plea to the sky. It's burst forth in profusion.
7. How can you fool a clear-eyed man? He snaps his nostrils around. Why stop at only the second level?
8. A mistake; yet he's getting somewhere.
9. Understood. But do you comprehend? Stumbled past.

COMMENTARY

Ch'ang Ch'ing and Pao Fu, while in the community of Hsueh Feng, were always reminding and awakening each other, engaging in discussion. One day casually talking like this, (Ch'ang Ch'ing) said, "Rather say that saints have the three poisons than say that the Tathagata has two kinds of speech." The Sanskrit word for saint, *arhat,* means killer of thieves;[b] by their virtue and accomplishment they illustrate their name; they cut off the nine times nine, or eighty-one kinds of passion, all their leaks are already dried up,[c] and their pure conduct is already established—this is the state of sainthood, where there is nothing more to learn. The three poisons are greed, hatred, and folly, the fundamental passions. If they have themselves completely cut off the eighty-one kinds (of passion), how much more so the three poisons! Ch'ang Ch'ing said, "Rather say that saints have the three poisons, but don't say that the Tathagata has two kinds of speech." His general idea was that he wanted to show that the Tathagata does not say anything untrue. In the Lotus of Truth scripture it says, "Only this one thing is true;[d] any second besides is not real." It also says, "There is only one vehicle of truth; there is no second or third." The World Honored One, in over three hundred assemblies, observed potentiality to set down his teachings, giving medicine in accordance with the disease: in ten thousand kinds and a thousand varieties of explanations of the Dharma, ultimately there are no two kinds of speech. His idea having gotten this far, how can you people see? The Buddha widely taught the Dharma with One Voice; this I don't deny—but Ch'ang Ch'ing actually has never seen the Tathagata's speech even in a dream. Why? It's just like a man talking about food—after all that can't satisfy his hunger. Pao Fu saw him talking about the doctrine on level ground, so he asked, "What is Tathagata speech?'' Ch'ing said, "How can a deaf man hear it?'' This fellow (Pao Fu) knew that (Ch'ang Ch'ing) had been making his living in a ghost cave for some time; Pao Fu said, "I knew you were speaking on the secondary level.'' And after all (Ch'ang Ch'ing) lived up to these words; he asked back, "Elder brother, what is Tathagata speech?'' Fu said, "Go drink tea.'' (Ch'ang Ch'ing) had his spear snatched away by someone else; Ch'ang Ch'ing, supposedly so great, lost his money and incurred punishment.

Now I ask everyone, how many (kinds of) Tathagata speech are there? You should know that only when you can see in this way, then you will see the defeat of these two fellows. If you examine thoroughly, everyone should be beaten. I'll let out a pathway, to let others comprehend. Some say that Pao Fu spoke correctly, and that Ch'ang Ch'ing spoke incorrectly; they just follow words to produce interpretations, so they say there is gain and loss. They are far from knowing that the Ancients were like stone struck sparks, like flashing lightning. People nowadays do not go to the Ancients' turning point to look; they just go running to the phrases and say, "Ch'ang Ch'ing didn't immediately act; therefore he fell into the secondary lvel. Pao Fu's saying 'Go drink tea' is the primary level.'' If you only look at it in this way, even by the time Maitreya Buddha comes down to be born here, you still won't see the Ancients' meaning. If you are an adept, you will never entertain such a view; leaping out of this nest of cliché, you'll have your own road upward.

If you say, "What is wrong with 'How could a deaf man hear?'? What is right about 'Go drink tea'?'' Then you are even further from it. For this reason it is said, "He studies the living phrase, he doesn't study the dead phrase.'' This story is the same as the story of "It is all over the body; it is all through the body"[e]—there is nowhere you can judge and compare right or wrong. It is necessary for you to be clean and naked right where you stand; only then will you see where the Ancients met. My late teacher Wu Tsu said, "It is like coming to grips on the front line.'' It requires a discerning eye and a familiar hand. In this public case, if you see it with the true eye, where there is neither gain nor loss, it distinguishes gain and loss; where there is no near or far, it distinguishes near and far. Ch'ang Ch'ing still should have bowed to Pao Fu to be proper. Why?

Because (Pao Fu) used this little bit of skill well, like thunder rolling or a comet flying. But Pao Fu couldn't help but produce tooth upon tooth, nail upon nail.

VERSE

Primary, secondary:
> In my royal storehouse, there are no such things. The standard for past and present. What are you doing, following the false and pursuing the bad?

A reclining dragon does not look to still water—
> Only one on the same road would know.

Where he is not, there is the moon; the waves settle:
> Over the four seas the solitary boat goes by itself. It is useless to trouble to figure it out. What bowl are you looking for?

Where he is, waves arise without wind.
> He threatens people ferociously; do you feel your hair standing on end in a chill? Striking, I say, "He's come!"

O Ch'an traveller Leng! Ch'an traveller Leng!
> He takes in a thief, who ransacks his house. Do not appear in a bustling marketplace. He lost his money and incurred punishment.

In the third month, at the Gate of Yü, you've got a failing mark.
> Not one in ten thousand can withdraw himself and defer to others. He can only suck in his breath and swallow his voice.

COMMENTARY

"Primary, secondary." If people only theoretically understand primary and secondary, this indeed is making a living in dead water. This active skill, if you only understand it in terms of first or second, you will still be unable to get hold of it. Hsueh Tou says, "A reclining dragon does not look to still water." In dead water, how can there be a dragon hidden? If it is "primary and secondary," this indeed is making a livelihood in dead stagnant water. There must be huge swells wide and vast, white waves flooding the sky; only there can a dragon be concealed. It is just like was said before; "A limpid pond does not admit the blue dragon's coils." Have you not heard it said, "Stagnant water does not contain a dragon." And it is said, "A reclining dragon is always wary of the clarity of the blue pond." That is why (Hsueh Tou) says that where there is no dragon, there is the moon, the waves settle—the wind is calm, the waves grow still. Where there is a dragon, waves rise without wind; much like Pao Fu's saying "Go drink tea"—this indeed is rousing waves without wind. Hsueh Tou at this point cleans up emotional interpretations for you, and has completed the verse. He has extra rhymes, so he makes the pattern complete; as before he sets a single eye on the content, and again is undeniably outstanding. He says, "O Ch'an traveller Leng! Ch'an traveller Leng!ᶠ In the third month at the Gate of Yü, you get a failing mark."ᵍ Although Ch'ang Ch'ing was a dragon who had passed through the Dragon Gate, yet he got a tap right on the head from Pao Fu.

TRANSLATORS' NOTES

a.   A fool once saw a rabbit run into a stump and die; he waited by the stump, hoping it would "catch" another rabbit for him. See case 10.

b.   *Arhat* also means "worthy"; that is, worthy of offerings.

c.   "Leaks" are passions, attachments, defilements; the flow of energy into habitual patterns of clinging, into emotional involvement with the world, draining people of their will and making them slaves of passion. The four knowledges of sainthood—*arhat*ship—are that one's leaks are dried up—that is, one is free from affectation and affliction, that pure conduct has been established, that one has done what was to be done, and that one is freed from further existence in the profane state.

d.   The main idea of this scripture is that all sentient beings will eventually realize Buddhahood, perfect enlightenment; "this one thing" is the knowledge and vision of Buddhas—the one vehicle is the vehicle of Buddhahood, within which the vehicles of discipleship, leading to sainthood, and of self-enlightenment through understanding the conditions of confusion and suffering, are shown to be provisional teachings designed for beings of lesser capacity and inspiration who are temporarily unable to bear the burdens of bodhisattvahood on the way to the unexcelled perfect enlightenment of all Buddhas.

e.   See case 89.

f.   Ch'ang Ch'ing's personal initiatory name was Hui Leng; it was standard practice to refer to someone by the second syllable of the name.

g.   According to legend, fish who can leap past the Dragon Gate (which is called the Gate of Yü because it was built under the direction of the great king Yü in the latter part of the third millennium B.C. during the time of a great flood in northern China) turn into dragons and soar off into the clouds. In Chinese literary convention this is used to symbolize the civil service examinations; those who pass and are eligible for official posts are likened to the fish who have become dragons. In Ch'an this is used to symbolize the attainment of enlightenment. This first appears in the seventh case, q.v., and recurs several times in this book.

Chao Chou's Three Turning Words

CASE

Chao Chou expressed three turning words to his community.[1]
("A gold Buddha does not pass through a furnace; a wood
Buddha does not pass through fire; a mud Buddha does not pass
through water.")

NOTES

1. What did he say? The three parts are not the same.

COMMENTARY

After Chao Chou had spoken these three turning words, in the
end he said, "The real Buddha sits within." This phrase is
exceedingly indulgent. That man of old set forth a single eye,
extended his hand to guide people; briefly making use of these
words to convey the message, he wanted to help others. If you
one-sidedly bring up the true imperative in its entirety, there
would be weeds ten feet deep in front of the teaching hall.
Hsueh Tou dislikes the indulgence of that final phrase, so he
omits it and just versifies three phrases. If a mud Buddha passes
through water it will dissolve; if a gold Buddha passes through
a furnace it will melt; if a wood Buddha passes through fire it
will burn up. What is difficult to understand about this? Hsueh
Tou's hundred examples of eulogizing the Ancients are complicated with judgments and comparisons; only these three
verses directly contain the breath of a patchrobed monk. However, these verses are nevertheless difficult to understand. If
you can pass through these three verses, I'll allow as you have
finished studying.

VERSE (1)

A mud Buddha does not pass through water:
    He's soaked it till the nose decomposes. Without wind he
    raises waves.

Spiritual Light illumines heaven and earth;
    Seeing a rabbit, he releases a hawk. What has it got to do
    with others?

Standing in the snow, if he didn't rest,
    When one person transmits a falsehood, ten thousand
    people transmit it as truth. He adds error to error. Who
    has ever seen you?

Who would not carve an imitation?
    Upon entering a temple, you see its nameplate. Running
    up and running down twenty-four hours a day—what is
    it? You are it.

COMMENTARY

"A mud Buddha does not pass through water: Spiritual Light
illumines heaven and earth." This one phrase clearly completes the verse: but tell me, why does he mention Shen Kuang
("Spiritual Light")? When the Second Patriarch was first born, a
spiritual light illumined the room, extending into the sky. Also
one night a spirit appeared and said to the Second Patriarch,
"Why remain here long? The time for you to attain the Way
has arrived: you should go South." Because of his association
with spirits, the Second Patriarch was eventually named Shen
Kuang (which means "Spiritual Light"). He lived for a long
time in the Yi-Lo area (Loyang), and widely studied many
books. He always lamented, "The teachings of Confucius and
Lao Tzu only transmit customary norms. Recently I have heard
that the great teacher Bodhidharma is dwelling at Shao Lin." So
he went there, visiting and knocking day and night; but
Bodhidharma sat still, and gave no instruction. Kuang thought
to himself, "When people of ancient times sought the Way,
they broke their bones and took out the marrow, shed their
blood to appease hunger, spread their hair to cover mud, threw
themselves off cliffs to feed tigers. Even of old they were like
this; what about me?"

That year on the night of the ninth of December there was a great snow. The Second Patriarch stood by the wall; by dawn the snow had piled up past his knees. Bodhidharma took pity on him and said, "You, standing in the snow there; what do you seek?" The Second Patriarch sighed sadly and said, "I only beg your compassion, to open up the gate of ambrosia, and save all creatures." Bodhidharma said, "The wondrous path of all the Buddhas requires zealous work over vast aeons, practicing that which is difficult to practice, enduring the unendurable; with little virtue and petty knowledge, a shallow heart and arrogant mind, how can you hope to seek the true vehicle? There is no way." The Second Patriarch, hearing this admonition, was even more earnest towards the Path; he secretly took a sharp knife and cut off his own left forearm, and placed it before Bodhidharma. Bodhidharma knew he was a vessel of Dharma, so he asked him, "You stand in the snow and cut off your arm; what for?" The Second Patriarch said, "My mind is not yet at ease. Please, Master, ease my mind." Bodhidharma said, "Bring forth your mind, and I will ease it for you." The Second Patriarch said, "When I search for my mind, ultimately I can't find it." Bodhidharma said, "I have put your mind at ease for you." Afterwards Bodhidharma changed (Shen Kuang's) name to Hui K'e. Later (Hui K'e) taught the Third Patriarch, Great Master Seng Ts'an.

So Hsueh Tou says, "Standing in the snow, if he didn't rest, who would not carve an imitation?" Slavishly fawning deceitful people would all imitate him, at once becoming mere contrived false imitations: these are the obsequious phoney followers. Hsueh Tou is eulogizing "A mud Buddha does not pass through water"—why then does he bring up this story? He had reached the absence of anything at all in his mind; clean and naked, only thus could he versify like this.

Wu Tsu always used to have people look at these three verses. Have you not seen how Master Shou Ch'u of Tung Shan had a verse which he showed his community, saying,

Atop Mount Wu T'ai, clouds are steaming rice;
In front of the Ancient Buddha Hall, a dog is pissing
    skyward.
Frying cakes atop the flagpole,
Three monkeys pitch pennies in the night.

And Master Tu Shun said,

> *When oxen in Huai province eat grain,*
> *The bellies of horses in Yi province are distended;*
> *Looking for a doctor all over the world*
> *To cauterize a pig's left arm.*

And Mahasattva Fu said,

> *Empty handed, holding a hoe,*
> *Walking, riding a water buffalo,*
> *A man is crossing over a bridge;*
> *The bridge, not the water, flows.*

It is also said,

> *If the capacity of a stone man were like you,*
> *He too could sing folk songs;*
> *If you were like a stone man,*
> *You too could join in the opera.*

If you can understand these words, then you will understand that verse of Hsueh Tou's.

VERSE (2)

A gold Buddha does not pass through a furnace;
> He burns off the eyebrows. "In the heavens and on earth, I alone am the Honored One."

Someone comes calling on Tzu Hu;
> He goes this way too? I only fear he'll lose his life.

On the sign, several words—
> An illiterate would have no way of understanding even if it were about a cat. No patchrobed monk in the world can get his teeth in.

Where is there no pure wind?
> You go this way too? Above the head it is vast and boundless; below the feet, vast and boundless. I also say, "It's arrived."

COMMENTARY

"A gold Buddha does not pass through a furnace; / A man comes calling on Tzu Hu." This one phrase has also completed the verse. Why does he bring up "someone calling on Tzu Hu"? Only with the forge and bellows of a Master is it possible. Master Tzu Hu set up a sign on his outside gate; on the sign were words saying, "Tzu Hu has a dog: above, he takes people's heads; in the middle, he takes people's loins; below, he takes people's legs. If you stop to talk to him, you'll lose your body and life." Whenever he saw a newcomer, he would immediately shout and say, "Watch out for the dog!" As soon as the monk turned his head, Tzu Hu would immediately return to the abbot's room. But tell me, why could he not bite Chao Chou? Tzu Hu also once late at night shouted in the lavatory, "Catch the thief! Catch the thief!" In the dark he ran into a monk; he grabbed him by the chest and held him, saying, "Caught him! Caught him!" The monk said, "Master, it's not me." Hu said, "It is, but you just won't own up to it." If you can understand this story, then you may chew everyone to death; everywhere the pure wind will be chill and severe. If not, you will certainly not be able to do anything about "the several words on the sign." If you want to see him, just pass through completely and then you will see what the verse is saying.

VERSE (3)

A wood Buddha does not pass through fire;
  Burned up! Only I can know.

I always think of the Oven Breaker—
  Going east, going west, what is wrong? A leper drags a companion along.

The staff suddenly strikes,
  It is in my hands. I still don't need it. Who doesn't have it in his hands?

And then one realizes he'd turned away from his self.
  Just like you. If you can't find it out, what use is it? Alas! Alas! After thirty years you'll finally get it. It is better to be sunk forever than to see the liberation of the saints. If you can seize it here, you'll still not avoid turning away. How to be able not to turn away? The staff is still in another's hands.

COMMENTARY

"A wood Buddha does not pass through fire; / I always think of the Oven Breaker." This one phrase also has completed the verse. Hsueh Tou, because of this "wood Buddha does not pass through fire," always thinks of the Oven Breaker. The "Oven Breaker Monk" of Mount Sung was not known by any surname; his speech and behavior were unfathomable. He dwelt in seclusion on Mount Sung. One day, leading a group of followers, he went among the mountain aborigines: they had a shrine which was most sacred; in its hall was placed only an oven. People from far and near sacrificed to it unceasingly; they had immolated very many living creatures. The Master entered the shrine and tapped the oven three times with his staff. He said, "What humbug! You were originally made of brick and mud compounded; where does the spirit come from, whence does the sanctity originate, that you burn living creatures to death like this?" And again he hit it three times. The oven then toppled over, broke and collapsed of itself. Momentarily there was a man in a blue robe and tall hat suddenly standing in front of the Master; bowing, he said, "I am the god of the oven; for a long time I have been subject to retribution for actions, but today, hearing the Master explain the truth of non-origination, I am already freed from this place, and living in heaven. I have come especially to offer thanks." The Master said, "It is your fundamentally inherent nature, not my forced saying so." The god again bowed, and disappeared. An attendant said, "I and others have been around the Master for a long time, but have never received instruction. What shortcut did the oven god find, that he was immediately born in heaven?" The Master said, "I just said to him, 'You were originally made of brick and mud put together; where does the spirit come from, whence does the sanctity emerge?'" The attendant had no reply. The Master said, "Do you understand?" The monk said, "I do not understand." The Master said, "Bow!" The monk bowed; the Master said, "Broken! Collapsed!" The attendant was suddenly greatly enlightened.

Later a certain monk reported this to National Teacher Hui An. The Teacher sighed in admiration and said, "This lad has comprehended thoroughly things and self as one suchness."

The oven god understood this principle, therefore he was thus: that monk was a body composed of five heaps; (the Master) also said, "Broken! Collapsed!" Both opened to enlightenment, but tell me, are the four elements and five heaps the same as or different from brick and tiles, mud and earth? Since it is so, why does Hsueh Tou say, "The staff suddenly strikes; (the oven god) then realizes he had turned away from his self"? Why does one become turned away? It is just a matter of not yet having found the staff.

And tell me, as Hsueh Tou eulogizes "a wood Buddha does not pass through fire," why does he cite the public case of the oven breaking and collapsing? I will explain it directly for you; his intention is just to cut off feelings and ideas of gain and loss; once cleaned and naked, you will naturally see his kindness.

The Diamond Cutter Scripture's Scornful Revilement

POINTER

If you take up one and let two go, you are not yet an adept; even to understand three corners when one is raised still goes against the fundamental essence. Even if you get heaven and earth to change instantly, without rejoinder from the four quarters, thunder rolling and lightning flying, clouds moving and rain rushing, overturning lakes and toppling cliffs, like a pitcher pouring, like a bowl emptying, you have still not raised up a half. Is there anyone who can turn the polar star, who can shift the axis of the earth? To test, I cite this to see.

CASE

The Diamond Cutter scripture says, "If one is scornfully reviled by others,[1] this person has done wicked acts in previous ages[2] which should bring him down into evil ways,[3] but because of the scorn and vilification by others in the present age,[4] the wicked action of former ages[5] is thereby extinguished."[6]

NOTES

1. It lets out a pathway. And what is wrong with that?
2. Assloads, horseloads.
3. He's already fallen.
4. Paying off the roots has effects that extend to the branches. He can only accept it with forbearance.
5. Where can you seek for it? Planting grain will not produce beans.
6. This is adding another layer of frost upon snow. It's like boiling water melting ice.

COMMENTARY

In the Diamond Cutter scripture[a] it says, "If one is scorned and vilified by other people, the fact is that this person has done evil actions in former ages which should bring him down into evil ways; but because of the scornful revilement of people in this age, the wicked action of former ages is thereby extinguished." According to the ordinary way of interpretation, this is the constant theme throughout the scripture. Hsueh Tou brings it up and versifies this meaning; he wants to break up the scholastic schools' livelihood in the ghost caves. Prince Chao Ming[b] singled out this part and considered it able to clear away obstruction by former deeds.

The general idea of the scripture talks about the efficacy of this scripture: someone like this in former times created hellish deeds, but because of the strength of its good power, he has not yet suffered. Because of scorn and vilification by people in the present age, the wicked action of former ages is thereby extinguished. This scripture therefore can extinguish the wicked deeds of innumerable aeons, changing the grave to become light, changing the light to being inconsequential, and furthermore bringing the attainment of enlightenment, the fruit of Buddhahood.

According to the scholastic schools, turning[c] this twenty-odd page scripture is itself called "upholding the scripture," but what connection is there? Some say that the scripture itself has spiritual power. If so, take a volume and lay it in an uncluttered place; see if there is any effect or not. Fa Yen said, "Realizing Buddhahood is called 'upholding this scripture.'" In the scripture it says, "All the Buddhas and the teaching of complete perfect awakening of all the Buddhas, all comes forth from this scripture." But tell me, what do you call "this scripture"? Is it not that with yellow scrolls on red rollers? Don't mistakenly stick by the zero point of the scale.

The Diamond is likened to the body of truth: because it is hard and solid, things cannot break it; because of its sharp cutting function, it can break anything. Apply it to a mountain, and the mountain crumbles; apply it to the sea, and the sea dries up. The name is expressed in metaphor, and so is its activity.

This wisdom is of three kinds: the first is the wisdom of the character of reality, the second is observant illumination wisdom, and the third is verbal wisdom. The wisdom of the character of reality is true knowledge: it is the one great matter where each of you stands, shining across past and present, far beyond knowledge and opinion; it is that which is clean and naked, bare and untrammelled. Observant illumination wisdom is the real world; it is that which emits light and moves the earth twenty-four hours a day, hearing sound and seeing form. Verbal wisdom is the language which can express it; that is, the present speaker and hearer. But tell me, is this wisdom or is it not wisdom? An Ancient said, "Everyone has a volume of scripture." It has also been said, "My hand does not hold a scripture scroll, but I am always turning such a scripture."

If you depend on this scripture's spiritual efficacy, why stop at just making the serious trifling, and making the trifling totally inconsequential? Even if you could match the ability of the sages, that would still not be anything special.

Have you not seen how Layman P'ang, listening to an exposition of the Diamond Cutter scripture, asked the lecturer, "A layman dares to have a small question; is that all right?" The lecturer said, "If you have a doubt, please ask." The layman said, "'There is no sign of self, no sign of others'—since there is no sign of self or others, who would you have lecture, who would you have listen?" The lecturer had no reply; instead he said, "I just interpret the meaning according to the letter; I do not know the meaning of this." The layman then said in verse,

> No self and no others; how could there be near or
>   far?
> I urge you to stop going through lectures;
> How could that be compared to seeking the real
>   directly?
> The nature of adamantine wisdom is devoid of a
>   single particle of dust;
> 'I have heard' through 'I faithfully accept'
> Are all just artificial names.

This verse is most excellent; it has clearly explained all at once.

Kuei Feng picked out a four line stanza, saying, "Whatever is seen, all is empty falsehood; if you see that various forms are not forms, then you see the Tathagata." The meaning of this four line stanza is exactly the same as "Realizing Buddhahood is called 'upholding this scripture.'"

It is also said (in the scripture), "If one sees me by means of form, if he seeks me by means of sound, this person is traversing a false path; he cannot see the Tathagata." This too is a four line stanza; we just take from among them those whose meaning is complete. A monk asked Hui T'ang, "What is the four line stanza?" Hui T'ang said, "Your talk is degenerate, yet you don't even realize it."

Hsueh Tou points out what is in this scripture. If there is someone who can uphold this scripture, then this is the scenery of everyone's original ground, the original face: but if you act according to the Patriarchs' imperative, the scenery of the original ground, the original face, would still be cut into three pieces; the twelve-part teachings of the Buddhas of the three times wouldn't be worth a pinch. At this point, even if you had the ten thousand varieties of skill, you still couldn't handle them. Nowadays people only revolve scriptures and do not know what the principle is at all. They merely say, "In one day, I have revolved so many." They only recognize the yellow scrolls on red rollers, perusing the lines and counting the ink-marks. They are far from realizing that it all arises from their own original minds, that this is only a bit of a turning point.

Master Ta Chu said, "Pile up several cases of scriptures in an empty room, and see if they emit light." It's just your own mind, inspired in a single moment of thought, that is the virtue. Why? Myriad things all come forth from one's own mind. One moment of thought is aware; once aware, it pervades; having pervaded, it transforms. An Ancient said, "The green bamboos are all true thusness; the lush yellow flowers are all wisdom." If you can see all the way through, then this is true thusness; but if you have not yet seen, tell me, what do you call true thusness? The Flower Garland scripture says, "If a person wants to know all the Buddhas of past, present, and future, he should observe that the nature of the cosmos is all just the fabrication of mind." If you can discern, then in whatever situations or circumstances you meet, you'll be the master and the source. If you cannot yet get it clear, then humbly listen to the verdict: Hsueh Tou puts forth an eye and versifies the main theme, wishing to clarify the scripture's spiritual efficacy.

VERSE

The clear jewel is in my palm;
   Above, it goes through the sky; below, it penetrates the
   Yellow Springs (Hades). What is he saying? Impenetrable
   on four sides, crystal clear on eight faces.

Whoever has accomplishment will be rewarded with it.
   Quite clear; it would go along with him. If there were no
   accomplishment, how would you reward it?

When neither foreigner nor native comes
   Inside and outside are void of happenings. Still this
   amounts to something.

It has utterly no abilities.
   More and more irrelevant. Where would you look for it?
   Come break the lacquer bucket and I'll meet with you.

Since it has no abilities,
   Stop, rest, Who is speaking this way?

The Evil One loses the way.
   Outsiders and the king of demons cannot find any tracks.

Gautama, Gautama!
   Even the Buddha-eye cannot see in. Bah!

Do you know me or not?
   Bah!

(Hsueh Tou also said,) "Completely exposed!"
   Each blow of the staff leaves a welt. It was already so
   before it was said.

COMMENTARY

"The clear jewel is in my palm; to whoever has accomplishment, I'll reward it." If there is someone who can uphold this
scripture with actual effect, then he is rewarded with the jewel.
When he gets this jewel, he will naturally know how to use it:
when a foreigner comes, a foreigner is reflected; when a native
comes, a native is reflected—myriad forms and appearances,
vertically and horizontally, are clearly reflected. This is having
actual accomplishment. These two lines have finished versifying the public case.

"When neither foreigner nor native comes, it is utterly without abilities." (Here) Hsueh Tou turns your nose around. When foreigners or natives appear, then he has you reflect them; if neither foreigner nor native comes, then what? When he gets here, even the Buddha's eye cannot see in. But tell me, is this accomplishment, or is it wicked action? Is he a foreigner? Is he a native? He's just like the antelope with his horns hung up: do not say there is any sound or trace of him—there is not even a breath; where could you go to search for him? He has gotten to where there is no road on which to have the gods offer flowers, no gate through which demons and outsiders might secretly spy. That is why the Master of Tung Shan dwelt all his life in the temple, but the earth spirit couldn't find any trace of him. One day someone spilled rice flour in the kitchen; Tung Shan aroused his mind and said, "How can you treat the communal supplies with such contempt?" So the earth spirit finally got to see him; thereupon he bowed.

Hsueh Tou says, "Since there are no abilities;" if you reach the point where there is no ability, you will make even the Evil One, the king of demons, lose the way. The World Honored One regarded all sentient beings as his children: if there is one person who rouses his mind to practice, the palace of the Evil One would tremble and split because of this, and the demons would come to torment and confuse the practitioner. Hsueh Tou says that even if the Evil One comes like this, still one must make him lose his way and have no avenue of approach.

Hsueh Tou goes on to point to himself and say, "Gautama, Gautama! / Do you know me or not?" Do not even speak of demons; even should the Buddha come, would he know me or not? Even old Shakyamuni himself couldn't see him; where will you people search for him? He also said, "Completely exposed." But tell me, is this Hsueh Tou exposing Gautama, or is it Gautama exposing Hsueh Tou? Those who have eyes, try to see for sure.

TRANSLATORS' NOTES

a. This is the *(Prajnaparamita) Vajracchedika sutra.* This was one of the most popular scriptures in China, and studied by most Ch'an students. The Sixth Patriarch of Ch'an, Hui Neng, was first enlightened when he chanced to hear a passage of this scripture being recited in a marketplace where he was selling wood; Hung Jen, the Fifth Patriarch, was said to have used it in his teaching. See also the fourth case, volume one.

b. Prince Chao Ming was the son of the Emperor Wu of Liang; he was an outstanding scholar, fond of Buddhist studies like his famous father. See the first case, in volume one.

c. "Turning" or "revolving" means recitation; usually, in the case of long scriptures, it means reciting snatches of the scripture while skipping rapidly through. Mahasattva Fu invented a revolving case for the canon, so that all of the scriptures could be "turned" at once by this device; usually memorized passages of scripture are recited while turning the whole canon.

T'ien P'ing's Travels on Foot

POINTER^a

POINTER[a]

Collecting the causes, producing the result, completing the beginning, completing the end. Face to face, there is nothing hidden, but fundamentally I have never explained. If there is suddenly someone who comes forth and says, "All summer we've been asking for instruction; why have you never explained?"—Wait till you've awakened, then I'll tell you.

Tell me, do you think that this is avoidance of direct confrontation, or do you think it has some other merit? To test, I cite this to see.

CASE

When the Master of T'ien P'ing was travelling on foot, he called on Hsi Yuan. He always would say, "Do not say you understand the Buddhist Teaching; I cannot find a single man who can quote a saying."[1]

One day Hsi Yuan saw him from a distance and called him by name: "Ts'ung Yi!"[2]

P'ing raised his head:[3] Hsi Yuan said, "Wrong!"[4] P'ing went two or three steps;[5] Hsi Yuan again said, "Wrong!"[6] P'ing approached;[7] Hsi Huan said, "These two wrongs just now: were they my wrongs or your wrongs?"[8]

P'ing said, "My wrongs."[9]

Hsi Yuan said, "Wrong!"[10] P'ing gave up.[11] Hsi Yuan said, "Stay here for the summer and wait for me to discuss these two wrongs with you."[12]

But P'ing immediately went away.[13] Later, when he was dwelling in a temple, he said to his community,[14] "When I was first travelling on foot, I was blown by the wind of events to Elder Ssu Ming's place: twice in a row he said 'Wrong!' and tried to keep me there over the summer to wait for him to deal with me. I did not say it was wrong then; when I set out for the South, I already knew that it was wrong."[15]

NOTES

1. He's let slip quite a bit. This fellow is right, but nevertheless he's like the sacred tortoise dragging his tail.
2. The hook is set.
3. Got him! A double case.
4. Still he must have been tempered in a furnace before being able. He splits his guts and wounds his heart. When the seal of the three essentials is lifted, the red spot is narrow; before any attempt to discuss it, host and guest are distinguished.
5. Already he's fallen halfway behind. This fellow is washing a clod of dirt in the mud.
6. Splits his guts and wounds his heart. Everyone calls this a double case, but they do not know it is like putting water in water, like exchanging gold for gold.
7. As before, he doesn't know where to rest. More and more he gropes without finding.
8. The first arrows were still light; this last arrow goes deep.
9. He mistakes a saddle ridge for his father's lower jaw.[b] As for such patchrobed monks as this one, even if you killed a thousand or ten thousand of them, what crime would it be?
10. He adds frost to snow.
11. He mistakenly goes by the zero point of the scale. After all he doesn't know where to rest. I knew his nostrils were in someone else's hand.
12. Hsi Yuan's spine is usually hard as iron; why did he not immediately drive (T'ien P'ing) away?
13. He still resembles a patchrobed monk; he resembles one, but isn't really.
14. A poor man thinks of his old debts. Still it is necessary to check.
15. What can he do about the two wrongs? A thousand "wrongs," ten thousand "wrongs"; nonetheless it's all irrelevant. All the more he shows his senility and saddens others.

COMMENTARY

Master Ts'ung Yi of T'ien P'ing, travelling on foot, went to see Hsi Yuan. Ssu Ming of Hsi Yuan had first called on Ta Hsueh, and later succeeded to the former Pao Shou. One day he asked, "How is it after trampling down the Temporary Citadel of

nirvana?" Shou said, "A sharp sword does not cut a dead man."
Ming said, "Cut!" Shou thereupon hit him. Ssu Ming said
"Cut!" ten times, and Shou hit him ten times and said, "What
is this fellow's big hurry to take this dead corpse and submit it
to another's painful staff?" Finally he shouted and drove Ssu
Ming out. At that time there was a monk who asked Pao Shou,
"That monk who just asked a question is quite reasonable,
Master; deal with him appropriately." Pao Shou hit him too,
driving out this monk. But tell me, when Pao Shou also drove
out this monk, can you say it was just because he was speaking
of right and wrong, or is there another reason? What was his
idea? Later they both succeeded to Pao Shou.

Ssu Ming one day went to see Nan Yuan. Yuan asked him,
"Where do you come from?" Ming said, "From Hsu Chou."
Yuan said, "What did you bring?" Ming said, "I brought a razor
from Kiangsi; I offer it to you." Yuan said, "Since you come
from Hsu Chou, how is it that you have a razor from Kiangsi?"
Ming took Yuan's hand and pinched it once. Yuan said, "Attendant! Take him away!" Ssu Ming gave a whisk of his sleeve
and left. Yuan said, "O wow!"

T'ien P'ing had once called on the Master of Chin Shan.
Because he had gone to various places and attained this
turnip-Ch'an and put it in his belly, everywhere he went he
scornfully opened his big mouth and said, "I understand Ch'an,
I understand the Way." He always said, "Do not say you understand the Buddhist Teaching; I cannot find even a single man
who can quote a saying." His stinking breath affected others,
and he only indulged in scorn and contempt.

Before the Buddha had appeared in the world, before the
Patriarch had come from the West, before there were questions
and answers, before there were public cases, was there any
Ch'an Way? The Ancients could not avoid imparting teachings
according to potentialities; people later called them "public
cases." As the World Honored One raised a flower, Kasyapa
smiled; later on, Ananda asked Kasyapa, "The World Honored
One handed on his golden-sleeved robe; what special teaching
did he transmit to you besides?" Kasyapa said, "Ananda!"
Ananda responded; Kasyapa said, "Take down the flagpole in
front of the monastery gate." But before the flower was raised,
before Ananda had asked, where do you find any public cases?
You just accept the winter melon seals of various places, and

once the seal is set, you then immediately say, "I understand the marvel of the Buddhist Teaching! Don't let anyone know!"

T'ien P'ing was just like this: when Hsi Yuan called him to come and then said, "Wrong!" twice in a row, right away he was confused and bewildered, unable to give any explanations; he "neither got to the village nor reached the shop." Some say that to speak of the meaning of the coming from the West is already wrong; they are far from knowing what these two wrongs of Hsi Yuan ultimately come down to. You people tell me, what do they come down to? This is why it is said, "He studies the living word, not the dead word." When T'ien P'ing raised his head, he had already fallen into two and three. Hsi Yuan said, "Wrong." But (T'ien P'ing) did not grasp his straightforward action, but just said, "I have a bellyful of Ch'an," and didn't pay any attention to him, and went two or three steps. Hsi Yuan again said, "Wrong!" But T'ien P'ing was as muddled as before, and approached Hsi Yuan. Yuan said, "The two wrongs just now; were they my wrongs or your wrongs?" T'ien P'ing said, "My wrongs." Fortunately, there is no connection. Already he had fallen into seventh and eighth place. Hsi Yuan said, "Just stay here for the summer and wait for me to discuss these two wrongs with you." T'ien P'ing immediately went away. He seemed to be right, but wasn't really. Then again, I don't say he wasn't right; it's just that he couldn't catch up. Nevertheless, he still had something of the air of a patchrobed monk.

When T'ien P'ing later was dwelling in a temple, he said to his community, "When I was first travelling on foot, I was blown by the wind of events to Master Ssu Ming's place. Twice he said 'Wrong!' and tried to have me pass the summer there to wait for him to deliberate with me. I did not say it was wrong then; when I set out for the South, I already knew that it was wrong." This old fellow has said quite a bit; it's just that he's fallen into seventh and eighth place, shaking his head thinking, out of touch. When people these days hear him saying, "When I set out for the South, I already knew that it was wrong," they immediately go figuring it out and say, "Before even going on foot travels, there is naturally not so much Buddhism or Ch'an; and when you go foot travelling, you are completely fooled by people everywhere. Even before foot travels, you can't call earth sky or call mountains rivers; fortunately there is nothing to be concerned about at all." If you all entertain such common vulgar views, why not buy a bandanna to wear and pass your time in the boss's house? What is the use? Buddha's teaching is not this principle. If you discuss this matter, how could there be so many complications? If you say, "I understand, others do not understand," carrying a bundle of Ch'an around the country, when you are tried out by clear-eyed people, you won't be able to use it at all. Hsueh Tou versifies in exactly this way:

VERSE

Followers of the Ch'an house
   The lacquer buckets all have their crimes listed on the same indictment.
Like to be scornful:
   Still there are some (who are otherwise). Those who scold Buddhas and revile Patriarchs are as plentiful as hemp and millet.
Having studied till their bellies are full, they cannot put it to use.
   It would be best to have use. A square peg does not fit in a round hole. You are a fellow student of theirs.
How lamentable, laughable old T'ien P'ing;
   No patchrobed monk in the world can leap out. He doesn't fear that bystanders may frown. Still he's gotten people to foolishly fret.
After all he says at the outset it was regrettable to go travel on foot.
   He was already wrong before he had gone travelling. Wearing out sandals, what is the use? He blots it out with one brush stroke.
Wrong, wrong!
   What is this? Hsueh Tou has already wrongly named it.
Hsi Yuan's pure wind suddenly melts him.
   Where is Hsi Yuan? What is it like? Do not speak only of Hsi Yuan; even the Buddhas of past, present, and future and the old masters everywhere also must fall back three thousand miles. If you can understand here, you may travel freely anywhere.

(Hsueh Tou) also said, "Suppose there is suddenly a patchrobed monk who comes out and says, 'Wrong';[1] how does Hsueh Tou's wrong compare to T'ien P'ing's wrong?"[2]

NOTES TO PROSE

1. The crimes are listed on the same indictment. He's still gotten somewhere.
2. Hsi Yuan again appears in the world. He settles the case according to the facts. Totally irrelevant. But tell me, after all, how is it? Striking, I say "Wrong!"

COMMENTARY

"Followers of the Ch'an house like to be scornful; having studied till their bellies are full, they can't put it to use." This fellow understood, as far as understanding goes; it's just that he couldn't use it. He always gazed at the cloudy sky and said he understood so much Ch'an; but when he was heated a little in the fireplace, it turned out that he couldn't use it at all. My late Master Wu Tsu said, "There is a kind of person who studies Ch'an like stuffing cakes in a crystal pitcher; it can't be turned over any more, it can't be cleaned out, and if you bump it, it immediately breaks. If you want to be lively and active, just study 'leather bag' Ch'an: even if you smash it down from the highest mountain, it still won't break, it won't burst." An Ancient said, "Even if you can grasp it before it is spoken, this is still remaining in the shell, wandering within limitation; even if you can thoroughly penetrate upon hearing a phrase, you still won't avoid crazy views on the way."

"How lamentable, laughable old T'ien P'ing; after all he says it was regrettable at the outset to go travelling." Hsueh Tou is saying that it's lamentable that he couldn't explain to others; it's laughable that he understood a bellyful of Ch'an but couldn't go on to make even the slightest use of it. "Wrong, wrong!" Some say that T'ien P'ing didn't understand, and thus was wrong; and some say his not speaking was wrong. But what connection is there? They hardly realize that these two "wrong"s are like stone struck sparks, like flashing lightning;

this is where those transcendent people tread, like using a sword to kill people, immediately grabbing people's throats, whereupon their root of life is severed. If you can travel on the sword's edge, then you will be free in all ways. If you can understand these two "wrong"s, then you can thereby see Hsi Yuan's pure wind suddenly melting (T'ien P'ing). When Hsueh Tou had finished quoting this story in the hall, he meant to say "wrong." I ask you, how does this wrong of Hsueh Tou compare to T'ien P'ing's wrong? Study for thirty more years.

TRANSLATORS' NOTES

a. According to the recommendation of Tenkei Denson, this pointer has been exchanged with that of the hundredth case, but either is suitable for both.

b. A man searching a battlefield for his father's remains finds a saddle ridge and mistakes it for his father's lower jaw.

Su Tsung's Ten-Body Controller

POINTER

When a dragon howls, mist arises; when a tiger roars, wind arises. In the fundamental design of appearing in the world, gold and jade[a] play together; in the strategic action of omnicompetence, arrowpoints meet each other.[b] The whole world is not concealed, far and near are equally revealed, past and present are clearly described.

But tell me, whose realm is this? To test, I cite this to see.

CASE

Emperor Su Tsung asked National Teacher Chung, "What is the Ten-Body Controller?"[1]

The National Teacher said, "Patron, walk on Vairocana's head."[2]

The emperor said, "I don't understand."[3]

The National Teacher said, "Don't acknowledge your own pure body of reality."[4]

NOTES

1. An adept ruler, the emperor of Great T'ang; he too should know this. On his head is the rolled lobe hat, on his feet are unworn shoes.
2. He takes his hand and walks together with him on the other side of Mount Sumeru. There is still this.
3. Why don't you understand his words? What a pity! The details are not imparted. The emperor should have immediately shouted then; what further need did he have to understand?
4. Although he makes complications, he still has a way to get himself out. Drunk and doddering, he saddens others to death.

COMMENTARY

When the Emperor Su Tsung was living in the Eastern Palace (as crown prince) he was already studying under National Teacher Chung. Later, when he succeeded to the throne, he honored him even more earnestly; when (Chung) came and went, (Su Tsung) greeted and saw him off, personally bearing the palanquin.

One day he posed a question to ask the National Teacher, "What is the Ten-Body Controller?" The Teacher said, "Patron, walk on Vairocana's head." The National Teacher's spine was usually as stiff as cast iron; but when he came into the presence of the emperor, it was like soft mud. Although he answered subtly, still he had a good point. He said, "If you want to understand, Patron, you must walk on Vairocana's head before you can understand." The emperor didn't get it; he said, "I don't understand." The National Teacher was subsequently extremely indulgent and entered into the weeds; he further commented on the preceding phrase by saying, "Do not mistakenly acknowledge your own pure body of reality." That refers to what is inherent in everyone, complete and perfect in each and every one. See how (Chung) lets go and gathers in, taking on adversaries from all sides.

Have you not heard it said that one who is good as a teacher sets up the teaching according to potential? He observes the wind to set the sail; if he just stayed in one corner, how could he interchange? Observe the Elder of Huang Po; he was well able to guide people; when he met Lin Chi, in three times he hit him sixty painful blows, and Lin Chi thereupon understood. But when he came to helping Prime Minister P'ei Hsiu, it was complicated in the extreme.[c] Was he not good as a teacher of people? National Teacher Chung skillfully used appropriate methods to teach Emperor Su Tsung; in all it was because he had the skill to take on adversaries from all sides. The "Ten-Body Controller" is the ten kinds of other-experienced body.[d] The three bodies of Reality *(dharmakaya)*, Enjoyment *(sambhogakaya)*, and Appearance *(nirmanakaya)*, are identical to the body of reality. Why? Because the enjoyment and appearance are not the real Buddha, and they are not what expounds the Dharma. When remaining in the body of reality, then as a single expanse of empty solidity, spiritual brightness quiescently shines.

When the Elder Fu of T'ai Yuan was expounding the *Nirvana* scripture in Kuang Hsiao Temple of Yang Chou, there was a wandering monk—actually it was the cook of Chia Shan—who was staying in the temple, snowed in; he took the opportunity to go listen to the lecture. When the lecture touched on the three bases of Buddha nature[e] and the three qualities of the body of reality,[f] and as Fu spoke profusely of the subtle principle of the body of reality, the cook suddenly broke out laughing. Fu then looked at him. When the lecture was over, he had someone summon the Ch'an man, and asked him, "My simple knowledge is narrow and inferior; I interpret the meanings according to the words. Just now, in the course of the lecture, I saw you break out in a laugh; I must have some shortcoming—please explain it to me."

The cook said, "If you did not ask, I dare not speak. Since you have asked, I cannot but explain. I was actually laughing because you don't know the body of reality." Fu said, "What is wrong with my explanation, such as it was?" The cook said, "Please explain it once more." Fu said, "The principle of the body of reality is like the great void: vertically, it goes through past, present, and future; horizontally it extends throughout the ten directions of the universe; it fills the eight extremities and embraces both positive and negative modes. According to conditions, it tends toward effect; there is nowhere it does not extend." The cook said, "I did not say your explanation is wrong; but you only know that which pertains to the extent of the body of reality; you do not actually know the body of reality." Fu said, "Granting that you are right, you should explain it for me." The cook said, "If you agree, then give up lecturing for ten days, and meditate correctly in a quiet room; collect your mind, gather your thoughts, give up various clingings to good and bad all at once, and investigate exhaustively on your own."

Fu did just as he had said, from the first to the fifth watch of the night; when he heard the sounding of the drum, he suddenly attained enlightenment and immediately went to knock on the Ch'an man's door. The cook said, "Who's there?" Fu said, "Me." The cook scolded him, saying "I would have you transmit and maintain the Great Teaching, explaining it in the

Buddha's stead; why are you laying in the street drunk on wine in the middle of the night?" Fu said, "Hitherto in my lectures on the scriptures I have been twisting the nostrils of the father and mother who gave birth to me; from today on, I no longer dare to be like this."

See that outstanding fellow! Did he merely go accept this radiant spirituality and fall in front of asses but behind horses? He had to have broken up his habitual active consciousness, so that there is nothing that can be apprehended; yet he has still only realized one half. An Ancient said, "If you do not give rise to any thought of practice or study, within formless light you'll always be free." Just discern that which is always silent and still; do not acknowledge sound and form; just discern spiritual knowledge, do not acknowledge false imagination. This is why it was said, "Even if an iron wheel is turning on your head, with concentration and wisdom complete and clear, they are never lost."

Bodhidharma asked the Second Patriarch, "What did you cut your arm off for, standing there in the snow?" The Patriarch said, "My mind is not yet at ease; please ease my mind for me, Master." Bodhidharma said, "Bring me your mind and I'll ease it for you." The Patriarch said, "When I seek my mind, after all I can't find it." Bodhidharma said, "I have eased your mind for you." The Second Patriarch suddenly attained enlightenment. But tell me, at just such a moment, where is the body of reality? Ch'ang Sha said,

> *Students of the Way do not know reality*
> *Just because they acknowledge the conscious spirit*
>   *as before;*
> *It's the root of countless aeons of birth and death,*
> *Yet fools call it the original man.*

People right now just acknowledge this radiant awareness, and immediately stare and glare, playing with their spirits: but what relevance does this have? As he said, "Do not acknowledge your own pure body of reality," but when it comes to your own body of reality, you have still not even seen it in a dream; how can you yet talk about not acknowledging it? In the doctrinal schools, they consider the pure body of reality to be the ultimate law; why not let people acknowledge it? Haven't you heard it said, "As long as you are acknowledging it, as before it is after all still not so." Bah! It's best to immediately strike a blow. Whoever can understand the meaning of this will for the first time understand his saying, "Don't acknowledge your own pure body of reality." Hsueh Tou dislikes his indulgent kindness, but nevertheless there are thorns in the soft mud.

Have you not seen how Master Tung Shan had three roads for teaching people? They were called the "Hidden Road," the "Bird's Path," and "Extending the Hands." Beginners in the study of the Way temporarily travelled the three roads. A monk asked the Master, "You always teach students to travel the Bird's Path: what is the Bird's Path like?" Tung Shan said, "You don't meet anyone." The monk asked, "How can I travel it?" Shan said, "There just should not be a single thread under your feet as you go."g The monk said, "If I travel the Bird's Path, is this not my Original Face?" Shan said, "Why are you upside down?" The monk said, "How am I upside down?" Shan said, "If you are not upside down, why do you take the servant to be the master?" The monk said, "What is the Original Face?" Shan said, "It does not travel the Bird's Path."

You must see as far as this realm; only then will you have a little realization. Even if you cleaned everything and made yourself cut off your tracks and swallow your voice, still in the school of the patchrobed monks this is still the view of novices and children. You must still turn your heads around to the troubles of the world and fully arouse your great function.

VERSE

"The Teacher of a Nation" is also a forced name;
    What is the necessity? A flower in the sky; the moon in
    the water. When the wind passes over, the treetops move.

Nan Yang alone may flaunt his good fame:
    After all he cuts off the essential bridge. Among a
    thousand or ten thousand, it's hard to find one or a half.

In Great T'ang he helped a real son of heaven—
    Pitiful. What is the use of teaching him? What is ac-
    complished by teaching a blind patchrobed monk?

Once he had him tread upon Vairocana's head.
    Why doesn't everybody go like this? They would find
    heaven and earth. How would you tread?

Then his iron hammer struck and shattered the golden bones;
> He's happy in everyday life. It's already thus before saying so.

Between heaven and earth, what more is there?
> Within the fast and boundless four oceans, there are few who know. The whole body bears the load. He is scattering sand and dirt.

The lands and seas of three thousand worlds by night are still and silent;
> Set your eyes high. Hold fast to your territory; are you waiting to enter a ghost cave?

I do not know who enters the Blue Dragon's cave.
> Thirty blows of the staff; not one can be omitted. He's finished bringing it up, but do you understand? Bah!
> People, your nostrils have been pierced by Hsueh Tou. Do not mistakenly acknowledge your own pure body of reality.

COMMENTARY

"The Teacher of a Nation is also a forced name; / Nan Yang alone may flaunt his good fame." This verse is just like a eulogy on a portrait. Haven't you heard it said that the ultimate man has no name? To call him National Teacher is also a case of having forcibly affixed a name. The Way of the National Teacher is incomparable. He was skillfully able to teach others in this way.

Nan Yang alone may be accepted as a Master: "In Great T'ang he helped a true son of heaven, and once had him tread upon Vairocana's head." If you have the eye and brain of a patchrobed monk who possesses the eye, you must walk upon Vairocana's head, and only then will you see this Ten-Body Controller. A Buddha is called the "Controller"; this is one of his ten epithets.[h] One body transforms into ten bodies, ten bodies transform into a hundred bodies, and so on, to a thousand hundred hundred million bodies; in their totality they are just one body. This one verse is easy to explain; the latter versifies that saying, "Do not acknowledge your pure body of reality," and versifies in sucha way that water poured on cannot wet it; it is difficult to explain.

"His iron hammer strikes, smashing the golden bones." This versifies "Do not acknowledge your own pure body of reality." Hsueh Tou praises (Chung) greatly; the golden bones have been smashed by one blow of his mallet. "Between heaven and earth, what more is there?" It is just necessary to be clean and naked, bare and untrammelled, so there is no longer anything to be apprehended; then this is the scenery of the basic ground. It is just like the lands and seas of three thousand worlds still and silent in the night. In a universe of three thousand great world systems, in the midst of the Sea of Fragrant Waters, there are infinite lands; in each land there is an ocean. Just when the night is deep and still, and heaven and earth are at once clear and calm, tell me, what is this? Just don't make an understanding of closing your eyes. If you understand in this way, then you'll fall into the poisonous sea.

"I don't know who enters the Blue Dragon's cave." Stretching out the legs, folding the legs; tell me, who is this? Everybody's nostrils have been pierced by Hsueh Tou all at once.

TRANSLATORS' NOTES

a.   "Gold" means an instrument made of metal; "jade," an instrument of stone: ancient Chinese music began with "gold" and ended with "jade"—hence "gold and jade" refers to "consummation." Also they are used to indicate excellence, so we translate literally.

b.   This refers to two master archers shooting at each other; their skill is equal, so their arrows meet each other midway and stop. This story is originally from the *Lieh-tzu*, a Taoist classic; there is also the famous passage in Shih T'ou's *Ts'an T'ung Ch'i* which says, "Phenomena's existence is like box and cover joining; principles' correspondence is like arrowpoints meeting."

c.   This refers to the *Ch'uan Hsin Fa Yao*, "Essentials of the Method of Transmission of Mind," addresses of Huang Po recorded by P'ei Hsiu. Being for a layman, they are quite different from Huang Po's dealings with monks.

d.   A Buddha is said to have two kinds of real body *(dharmakaya)*; that experienced by himself, and that experienced by others. The former is his own enlightenment, and the latter is his teaching of others, or how others experience the Buddha in their perceptions of his qualities and teachings. According to the *Hua Yen*, or Flower Garland scripture, there are the Buddha of nonattachment, the Buddha of vows, the Buddha of results of action, the Buddha of abiding maintenance, the Buddha of extinction *(nirvana)*, the Buddha of the cosmos (the *dharmadhatu*, or ultimate realm), the Buddha of mind, the Buddha of concentration, the Buddha of nature, and the magical Buddha. Vairocana, the Great Illuminator, also called the Great Sun Buddha in Chinese, is the primordial Buddha, representing the body of reality, the basis and totality of all these.

e. The three bases of Buddha nature are the true basis, the basis of understanding, and the basis of conditions. The true basis is the real nature which underlies Buddhahood, the Buddha nature inherent in everyone; the basis of understanding is wisdom, which realizes this real nature; the basis of conditions is the practices which unfold wisdom and allow one to realize one's Buddha nature.

f. The three qualities of the body of reality correspond to the three bases of Buddha nature; the quality of the pure body of reality, which corresponds to the true basis, the quality of wisdom, which corresponds to the basis of understanding, and the quality of liberation, which corresponds to the basis of conditions, cultivation of liberating practices.

g. Even the most ancient texts give an alternative reading which is homonymous; "Nothing private under your feet." For an explanation of the three roads of Tung Shan, see the appropriate appendix.

h. The ten epithets of a Buddha are, Realized One (Tathagata), Worthy (Arhat), True and Universal Knower, Perfect in Knowledge and Conduct, Blissful One, Understander of the World, Unexcelled Knight, Controller of Humanity, Teacher of Humans and Gods, Enlightened One (Buddha), World Honored One. The translations given here are based on Chinese; the Sanskrit equivalents given in parentheses are those which are frequently used in English books.

Pa Ling's Blown Hair Sword

POINTER

All summer I've been verbosely making up complications, and almost entangled and tripped up all the monks in the land. But when the Diamond Sword cuts directly, I first realize my hundred-fold incompetence. But tell me, what is the Diamond Sword like? Open your eyes and I'll reveal the swordpoint for you to see.

CASE

A monk asked Pa Ling, "What is the Blown Hair Sword?"[1a]
Pa Ling said, "Each branch of coral supports the moon."[2]

NOTES

1. Cut! Dangerous!
2. The light engulfs myriad forms, the entire land.

COMMENTARY

Pa Ling does not move his shield and spear, (but) in the land, how many people's tongues fall to the ground! Yun Men taught people just like this; (Pa Ling) was a true son of Yun Men. And each of (Yun Men's successors) had his strategy of action; that is why (Hsueh Tou) said, "I always admire Shao Yang's newly established devices; all his life he pulled out nails and drew out pegs for people."

This story is just like this; within one phrase there are three phrases naturally inherent—the phrase enclosing heaven and earth, the phrase cutting off all streams, and the phrase following the waves. His reply was undeniably outstanding. Yuan "the jurist" of Fu Shan said, "For a man who has not yet passed through, studying the meaning is not as good as studying the phrase." At Yun Men's place there were three venerable adepts who replied about the "Blown Hair Sword"; two of them said, "Complete." Only Pa Ling was able to give an answer beyond the word "complete"—this is attaining the phrase.

But tell me, are "complete" and "each branch of coral supports the moon" the same or different? Before, (Hsueh Tou) said, "The three phrases should be distinguished; one arrow flies through space." If you want to understand this story, you must cut off the defilement of feelings and conscious conceptions, and be completely purified; then you will see his saying, "Each branch of coral supports the moon." If you make up any further rationalization, all the more you'll find you're unable to grasp it.

These words are from Ch'an Yueh's poem of remembering a friend:

> *Thick as the iron on the Iron Closure Mountains,*
> *Thin as the dapples on the body of immortal Shuang Cheng.*
> *Pheonixes and fowl from the looms of Shu always make him stumble.*
> *Each branch of coral supports the moon;*
> *Stored away in the house of Wang K'ai, it is hard to dig out.*
> *Yen Hui, that hungry fellow, laments the sky's snow;*
> *The ancient cypress brush is so straight, even snow can't break it.*
> *The snow-clad stone girl's curling peach belt—*
> *Wearing it, he enters the dragon palace, his steps slow.*
> *The embroidered screen, the silver ladle; how do they differ?*
> *The jet black dragon has lost the jewel; do you know it or not?*

Pa Ling took one phrase from among these lines to reply to the "Blown Hair Sword"; he is quick. One blows a hair against the edge of a sword to test it; when the hair splits of itself, then it is a sharp sword, and it is called a blown hair sword. Pa Ling just goes to the point of his question and immediately answers this monk's words. (The monk's) head fell without him even realizing it.

When it is necessary to even the uneven,
    Tiny as an ant. A powerful man should be like this.

Even the great adept seems inept.
    He does not stir sound or form. He hides his body but reveals his shadow.

Sometimes on the finger, sometimes in the palm;
    Look! After all this is not it.

Leaning against the sky, it shines on the snow—
    Cut! If you stare at it, you'll go blind.

Even a great smith cannot hone it;
    What do you still want to forget it for? Even Kan Chiang (the legendary smith) couldn't find it.

Even a master craftsman wouldn't finish polishing it.
    No one could do it. Even if Kan Chiang came forth, he too would fall back.

It is exceptional, unique:
    Bah! What is so special about it? (Yet) there is something praiseworthy about it.

Each branch of coral supports the moon.
    In the third watch the moon descends, its image shining in the cold pond. Tell me, where does it go? Drunk and doddering, he saddens others to death.

"When it is necessary to even the uneven, the great adept seems inept." In the past there were wandering warriors; on their way when they saw inequity where the strong oppressed the weak, then they would let fly with their swords to take the heads of the strong. Thus, masters of our school hide a jewel sword in their eyebrows, and hang a golden mallet in their sleeves, whereby to settle matters of unrest. "The great adept seems inept"—Pa Ling's answer was intended to even what was uneven; because his words were exceeding skillful, instead they turn out to seem inept. What is the reason? Because he does not come attack directly: instead he goes off into a corner and with one stroke secretly beheads the man, yet the man is not aware of it.

"Sometimes on the finger, sometimes in the palm; / Leaning against the sky, it shines on the snow." If you can understand, then it is like the cold and severe spiritual grandeur of a long sword leaning against the sky. An Ancient said, "The mind moon solitary and full, its light engulfs myriad forms. The light is not shining on objects, and the objects are not existing, either. Light and objects both forgotten, then what is this?" This jewel sword is sometimes manifest on the fingertip; suddenly it appears in the palm. In the old days when Librarian Ch'ing had reached this point in his explanation, he raised his hand and said, "Do you see?" Still, it's not necessarily in the hand or the finger: Hsueh Tou just takes a shortcut to let you see the Ancient's meaning. But say, every place cannot but be the Blown Hair Sword; that is why it is said, "When the waves are high at the triple gate, the fish turn to dragons; yet foolish people still drag the evening pond water."

Hsueh Tou says this sword can lean against the sky and shine upon the snow. Usually it is said that the light of the long sword leaning against the sky can shine on the snow: this little bit of function is such that even a great smith cannot hone it, even a master craftsman could never finish polishing it. The master craftsman is such as Nan Chiang (the legendary expert smith): the old tale is self-evident.[b]

When Hsueh Tou has finished the verse, in the end he reveals (the sword), saying, "Exceptional, unique!" It is undeniably exceptional, and has special excellence; it is not like an ordinary sword. But tell me, how is it special? "Each branch of coral supports the moon." This can be said to be prior to light and after annihilation, occupying the heartland alone, without any peer.

Ultimately, how is it? People, your heads are fallen. I have one more little verse:

> *Filling a boat with ten thousand bushels, I let you*
>   *haul it away;*
> *Instead, for one grain of rice, the pot has entrapped*
>   *the snake.*
> *Having brought up one hundred old public cases,*
> *How much sand have I thrown in people's eyes to-*
>   *day?*

TRANSLATORS' NOTES

a. As usual, the sword symbolizes wisdom, cutting off confusion and attachment; uncontrived and equanimous, it sees the moon of truth everywhere in everything.

b. There is a story inserted in the text about Kan Chiang, the legendary smith, and how he made the famous sword No Yeh. All commentaries reject it as a later addition, and it serves no purpose except to identify the name of Kan Chiang.

Biographical Supplement

The order of the biographies is as follows:

CH'ANG KUAN of Wu Feng (n.d.)
CASE 70,71

(Wu Feng was one of Pai Chang's successors; the following is from the *Ching Te Ch'uan Teng Lu 9*:)

There was a monk who asked, "What is the scenery (or: perspective) of Wu Feng?" The master said, "Dangerous." The monk asked, "What is the man within the scene?" The master said, "A block."

The master said to a monk who was taking leave of him, "Where are you going, Reverend?" The monk said, "I'm going to Mt. T'ai." The master raised one finger and said, "If you see Manjusri, return here and I'll meet with you." (Traditionally, Mt. T'ien T'ai was an abode of Manjusri.) The monk had no reply.

The master asked a monk, "Have you seen the ox?" The monk said he had seen it. The master said, "Did you see the left horn or the right horn?" The monk had no reply. The master answered himself on his behalf, "I saw that there was no left or right."

641

Another monk was taking leave of the master, who said to him, "When you go all over, don't slander me (by saying that) I am here." The monk said, "I won't say you're here." The master said, "Where would you say I am?" The monk held up one finger. The master said, "You have already slandered me."

T'AN SHENG of Yun Yen (781–841)
CASE 72, 89

(The following is from the *Ching Te Ch'uan Teng Lu* 14:)

He was from Chien Ch'ang in Chung Ling; his surname was Wang. At an early age he left home. At first he studied under Ch'an Master Hai of Pai Chang, but he did not awaken to his mystic meaning. After he had served Pai Chang for around twenty years, Pai Chang died so Yun Yen visited Yao Shan and reached understanding there at his words. . . . Later the master dwelt at Yun Yen Shan ("Cloud Cliff Mountain") in T'an Chou (in Hunan).

One day Yun Yen told the assembly, "There's a son of someone's family—when questioned, there is nothing he cannot explain." Tung Shan asked, "How many scriptures were there in his house?" The master said, "Not even a single word." "Then how did he get so much knowledge?" The master said, "Day and night he never slept." "Could I still ask him about something?" The master said, "If he could say, he wouldn't say."

Once when Yun Yen was sweeping the floor, Kuei Shan said to him, "Too busy!" The master said, "You should know that there's one who isn't busy." Kuei Shan said, "If so, then there's a second moon." The master held up his broom and said "Which moon is this?" Kuei Shan lowered his head and left. When Hsuan Sha heard of this he said, "Precisely the second moon."

Once when Yun Yen was making shoes, Tung Shan asked, "If I come to you, Master, and ask for eyes, I wonder, will I get them or not?" Yun Yen said, "Who did you give yours to?" Tung Shan said, "I haven't got any." The master said, "If you had, where would you put them?" Tung Shan was speechless. The master said, "Is the one asking for eyes an eye or not?" Tung Shan said, "He's not an eye." The master scoffed at him.

In 841 in the tenth month the master showed illness. On the twenty-sixth, after he had washed, he called the Superintendent Monk and ordered him to prepare a feast. On the twenty-seventh when evening came the master returned to quiescence.

CHIH TSANG of Hsi T'ang (734–814)
CASE 73

(The following is taken from the *Ching Te Ch'uan Teng Lu* 7:)

The master was originally from Ch'ien Hua; his surname was Liao. From age eight he followed a teacher; at twenty-five he was fully ordained. Someone who met him noticed his special appearance and said to him, "Your mettle is not commonplace: you ought to be the Dharma King's helper." So the master went to Buddha's Footprint Range to visit Ma Tsu and pay his respects. There he entered Ma Tsu's room along with Ch'an Master Hai of Pai Chang: both received Ma Tsu's seal.

One day Ma Tsu sent the master to Ch'ang An to present a book to National Teacher Chung. The National Teacher asked, "What Dharma does your master expound?" Hsi T'ang crossed from east to west and stood there. The National Teacher said, "What else is there besides just this?" The master recrossed to the east and stood there. The National Teacher said, "This is Ma Tsu's; what about you, good man?" The master said, "There's already been a showing for you, Teacher."

Hsi T'ang returned to his native district: he had received Ma Tsu's patched robe. . . . One day Ma Tsu asked him, "Why don't you read sutras?" The master said, "Could sutras be any different (from this)?" Ma Tsu said, "Though this is so, later on you'll still have to help people." The master said, "I am sick and want to heal myself: how could I dare to speak for others?" Ma Tsu said, "In your last years you will inevitably (cause the Dharma to) flourish in the world." After Ma Tsu had died, the congregation in 791 asked the master to open the hall (and teach).

Hsi T'ang died in 814 at the age of 80: he had been a monk for fifty-five years. (Two T'ang emperors,) Hsien Tsung and Mu Tsung bestowed posthumous titles on him.

TING CHOU SHIH TSANG (714–800)

(The record says he was entombed in a memorial tower in 800, but it is not clear just when he died.)

CASE 75

(No biography of this master is recorded in the sectarian Ch'an histories; the information given here is taken from the *Sung Kao Seng Chuan*, 10.)

When young, the master studied Confucianism; later he entered the Buddhist order, and went to study under the renowned P'u Chi (who was known as the Seventh Patriarch in the northern Ch'an tradition; his master had been Shen Hsiu, one of the Fifth Patriarch Hung Jen's ten great disciples). There he was enlightened in Ch'an; later he came to Great Elephant Peak in the mountains of central China, where he sat alone peacefully in deep nirvanic stillness for several years. Students came seeking him out and gathered around him; eventually Li T'ao Ying, military commander of Hui Cou and member of the imperial clan, ordered him to come to the city; but Shih Tsang refused, saying that his rustic nature was impossible to bridle, and he couldn't be bothered with rules of etiquette. Li then climbed the mountain himself to talk to the Master; afterwards, he petitioned the throne to grant a title to Shih Tsang's abode, but Shih Tsang had already taken leave of his disciples, and passed on the next day.

The master Wu Chiu ('Crow's Nest'), who figures in case 75, is obscure, but it seems he was a successor of Ma Tsu (709–788).

T'IEN JAN of Tan Hsia (738–824)

CASE 76

(A successor to Shih T'ou, Tan Hsia was the "father" of Ts'ui Wei and thus the "grandfather" of T'ou Tzu. The following is related in the *Ching Te Ch'uan Ten Lu* 14:)

It is not known what locality the master was from. At first he studied Confucianism, intending to go to Ch'ang An to take part in the imperial examinations. (What happened to him on the road that made him turn to Buddhism, as well as the circumstances of his meetings with Ma Tsu and Shih T'ou, is told by Yuan Wu in Case 76.) After he returned to Ma Tsu's after having his head shaved by Shih T'ou, Ma Tsu asked, "Where did you come here from?" Tan Hsia said, "Shih T'ou." Ma Tsu said, "Shih T'ou's road is slippery: did he trip you up?" The master said, "If he had, I wouldn't have come."

Next the master went travelling to look over the various localities (where Ch'an flourished). For three years he lived on Mt. T'ien T'ai's Flower Top Peak. He went to Hang Chou's Ching Shan and payed his respects to Ch'an Master Kuo I. In the middle of the Yuan Ho years (806–821) he went to the Dragon Gate (Mountain's) Fragrant Mountain near Loyang, where he and Master Fu Niu were faithful friends. . . . He also visited National Teacher Chung. . . .

(One day during the year) 809 the master stretched out on T'ien Chin Bridge. When the governor, Lord Cheng, appeared, the master reviled him and didn't get up. One of the governor's attendants asked him his reason for doing this. The master took his time about answering and said, "(Because I am) an unconcerned monk." The governor considered him extraordinary and offered him clothes and daily provisions of food. In the spring of his fifteenth year (in Loyang) the master announced to his disciples, "I've been thinking of a place with forests and streams in which to die." Soon his disciples had a geomancer (pick a site for) a hermitage to be built on Tan Hsia Mountain in Nan Yang. Within three years time (after the master had taken up residence there) students of the mystery had gathered, forming a congregation of three hundred, so they built a monastery.

WEI YEN of Yao Shan (750–834)
CASE 81

(Yeo Shan was a successor to Shih T'ou and the ancestor of the Ts'ao-Tung School. The following comes from the *Te Ching Ch'uan Teng Lu* 14:)

Ch'an Master Wei Yen of Yao Shan in Li Chou (in Hunan) was a man from Chiang Chou (in Shansi); his surname was

Han. He left home at age seventeen and was ordained in 774 on
Heng Yueh by the Vinaya Master Hsi Ts'ao.

As soon as he visited Shih T'ou, the master intimately comprehended his esoteric message. One day as the master was
sitting, Shih T'ou saw him and asked, "What are you doing
here?" The master said, "I'm not doing anything at all." Shih
T'ou said, "If so then you're sitting idly." The master said, "If I
were sitting idly, that would be doing something." Shih T'ou
said, "You speak of not doing: not doing what?" The master
said, "Even the thousand sages do not know." Shih T'ou
praised him with a verse:

> Since we've lived together I haven't known your
>   name.
> Doing as you please, acting this way, bringing me
>   along—
> Even the sages of high antiquity don't know:
> How could the hurried common type be able to un-
>   derstand.

Shih T'ou once said, "Speech and action have nothing to do
with it." The master said, "Not speaking and non-action don't
have anything to do with it either." Shih T'ou said, "Here, not
even a needle can enter." The master said, "Here, it's like
growing flowers on stone." Shih T'ou approved of him. Later
the master dwelt on Yao Shan in Li Chou: an oceanlike congregation gathered.

A monk asked, "How can one not be confused by all
phenomena?" The master said, "If you go along with them,
how can they obstruct you?" The monk said, "I don't understand." The master said, "What phenomena are confusing
you?"

A monk asked, "What is *nirvana?*" The master said, "What
did you call it before you opened your mouth?"

A monk asked, "I have not yet understood my own thing:
please, Teacher, point it out to me." After a silence the master
said, "It wouldn't be hard for me to say something for you right
now: it would only be proper if you immediately saw at my
words—then you'd have gotten somewhere. But if you kept on
entering into calculating thought, it would become my fault.
It's not as good as both of us shutting up to avoid entangling
each other."

As Yao Shan was about to die he cried out, "The Dharma Hall is collapsing! The Dharma Hall is collapsing! Everybody prop it up!" Then he raised his hand and said, "You disciples don't understand my meaning," and died.

CH'I AN of Yen Kuan (District's) Chen Kuo Hai Ch'ang Temple

(The following is taken from the *Ching Te Ch'uan Teng Lu* 7:)

Yen Kuan was originally from Hai Men District (in Chekiang); his surname was Li. When he was born a spiritual light filled the room. Also, there was a strange monk who told him, "Will you not be the one who will establish the supreme banner and make the Buddha-sun shine back?" So he had his head shaved and was ordained by Ch'an Master Yun Tsung of his native district. Later he heard that Ma Tsu was teaching on Kung Kung Mountain, so he took his staff and went to visit him there. Yen Kuan had an extraordinary appearance: as soon as Ma Tsu saw him he considered him a profound vessel, so he ordered him to come into his room and intimately instructed him in the Correct Dharma.

A monk asked Yen Kuan, "What is one's own Vairocana Buddha?" The master said, "Bring me that brass pitcher." The monk then brought the pitcher over. The master said, "Take it back and put it where it was." Having returned the pitcher to its place, this monk came back to ask again about his previous question. Yen Kuan said, "The ancient Buddha is indeed long gone!"

A lecturing monk came calling. The master asked him, "What is your work?" The lecturer said, "I lecture on the Hua Yen sutra." The master said, "How many kinds of dharma worlds are there in the sutra?" The lecturer answered, "To explain fully, there are many many, without end; to explain briefly, there are four kinds." The master held up his whisk and said, "Which kind of dharma world is this?" The lecturer sank into thought as he slowly pondered his reply. The master said, "To know by pondering, to understand by thinking it over—

this is the way ghosts make their living. Sure enough, the lone lamp beneath the sun loses its glow."

A monk asked Ta Mei, "What is the meaning of the coming from the West?" Ta Mei said, "The coming from the West has no meaning." When Yen Kuan heard of this he said, "One coffin, two corpses."

Later, without illness, Yen Kuan sat peacefully and died.

CHÜ HUI of Ta Kuang (836–903)
CASE 93

(The following is taken from the account in the *Ching Te Ch'uan Teng Lu* 16:)

The master was a man from the capital district (Ch'ang An); his surname was Wang.

When he first visited the room of Shih Shuang (his master) he passed two years staying close by, asking for instruction. He was ordered to take charge of the North Stupa. With clothes of hemp and shoes of straw, he was on the verge of forgetting his body and consciousness. One day Shih Shuang, intending to test what Ta Kuang had attained, questioned him saying, "Every year the country sends its chosen candidates to compete in the examinations: do they get posts at court or not?" The master said, "There are people who do not seek advancement." Shih Shuang said, "Why?" The master said, "Because they do not act for the sake of fame." While he was ill, Shih Shuang again questioned the master, "Is there any other time besides Today?" The master said, "I don't even say Today is right." Shih Shuang approved of him very much. . . . The master stayed in the vicinity (of Shih Shuang) for over twenty years.

The benefactor of Buddhism, Lord Hu of Liu Yang (in Hunan), invited the master to reside on Mt. Ta Kuang, in order to propagate the teachings of the sect.

There was a monk who asked, "As for Bodhidharma, was he a Patriarch or not?" Ta Kuang said, "He wasn't a Patriarch." The monk said, "Since he wasn't a Patriarch, what did he come for?" The master said, "Because you wouldn't comprehend a Patriarch." The monk asked, "What's it like after comprehending?" The master said, "You finally know he wasn't a Patriarch."

The master was asked, "What was it like during the primordial chaos, before differentiation?" The master said, "Who can relate the Teachings of the Age?" The master also said, "The Teachings of the Age were just to straighten out the people of the age. Even if you can cut all the way through them, this is just becoming a person who has finished his task. You shouldn't then take this as the business of patchrobed ones." Thus it is said, "In forty-nine years Buddha couldn't explain it fully; in forty-nine years he couldn't wrap it all up." Whenever Ta Kuang taught students it was generally like this.

SSU MING of Hsi Yuan in Ju Chou (in Honan) (n.d.)
CASE 98

(Ssu Ming succeeded to Master Chao of Pao Chou, a disciple of Lin Chi; he had one successor. The following dialogues are taken from *Ching Te Ch'uan Teng Lu* 12:)

Someone asked, "What is a monastery?"

The master said, "A forest of thorns."

He asked, "What is the man in the monastery?"

The master said, "A boar; a badger."

Someone asked, "What is the one shout of Lin Chi?"

The master said, "A thirty-thousand-pound catapult is not shot at a rat."

He said, "Where is the master's compassion?"

The master hit him.

Tsung I of T'ien P'ing Mountain, also in Honan, who also appears in case 98, has no separate record in any of the classical histories; he was a successor of Ch'ing Ch'i Hung Chin, a disciple of Lo Han Kuei Ch'en and former travelling companion of Fa Yen Wen I.

Select Glossary of Names and Terms

alayavijnana—The so-called storehouse or repository consciousness, wherein accumulate influences of deed and habit, producing impressions which are customarily mistaken for qualities of the objective world; when all egoism and self-affirming habits of attachment are eliminated, this all embracing consciousness is 'transformed' into the so-called great perfect mirror knowledge.

Avalokitesvara—The bodhisattva representing compassion and all-sided skill in liberative technique, traditionally said to be the guardian of the compassion and love of Amitabha, Buddha of Infinite Light and Life. Known also as the Sound Seer from the image of the lord who watches the sounds of the world to rescue beings in distress; it is said in the Surangama scripture that Avalokitesvara attained enlightenment through audition by turning back to look into the source of hearing; this meditative exercise is well known and often applied in Ch'an practice.

Bodhidharma—The First Patriarch of Ch'an in China, said to have originally been of a noble Brahmin family from south India, later became the successor of Prajnatara, Twenty-seventh Patriarch of Buddhism, and spent fifty years in China after having already taught in India for sixty odd years.

bodhisattva—An enlightened being or a warrior for enlightenment, one who forgoes the repose of extinction to struggle for the enlightenment of all conscious beings, voluntarily accepting the passions and confusions of the mundane life in order to communicate with the beings involved there so as to be able to fulfill his commitment to liberate them.

Buddha—A completely enlightened one, also called one who has come to realize thusness, World Honored One, king of Dharma, teacher of humans and gods, lord.

Buddha Dharma—The teaching of the enlightened ones, the way to enlightenment; also used to refer to truth or reality.

consciousnesses—Refers to the fields and functions of consciousnesses associated with senses, intellection, judgment, and formation of habit, etc. Emotional consciousness is states of mind, emotion, and intellection, which are primarily influenced by emotions ('like' 'dislike' etc., which inevitably return to the attempt to preserve the idea or feeling of self) and thus screened by such involvements from clear perception of reality or truth.

demon—Representation of deluding or confusing forces, objects of attachment or aversion, or malevolent forces robbing people of clarity, will, and the life of wisdom.

diamond king—The awakened mind; diamond is a symbol of penetrating wisdom, indestructible as a diamond.

dragon—Someone who is enlightened or has reached an advanced spiritual degree; though 'dragons' live physically in the 'animal' world, their profound state of meditation allows them to transcend this condition and enjoy the bliss of heavenly states or complete calm. Great Ch'an adepts and students are often referred to as 'dragons and elephants'—one who looks adept at first but turns out otherwise is said to have a 'dragon's head but a snake's tail.'

Gaptooth—'He with gapped rotting teeth' is Bodhidharma (qv), also known as the Blue-Eyed Barbarian or the Red-Bearded Barbarian, the Pierced-Ear Traveller, the First Patriarch, the Ancestral Teacher; he is also referred to by place names such as Shao Lin, Few Houses (name of mountain where Shao Lin temple was), and Bear's Ear Mountain (where he is entombed).

Gautama—A Buddha, inspirator of Buddhism's historical forms and perhaps the greatest of known teachers of the way of enlightenment; also called Yellow Face and Old Shakyamuni.

jewel sword—Symbol of adamantine wisdom, transcendental knowing, which is able to cut through all confusion and delusion.

intimacy—Intimate communion with reality, personal experience of the Way.

It—The absolute (used both so as to contain the relative absolute and the absolute relative); reality, or what is. Often *It* is not specified in Chinese but needed in English to fit the sense. *This* (one, side) and *That* (one, side) are sometimes used to refer specifically to the imminent and transcendent aspects of *It*. *He* is also used similarly, like the Arabic *Hu*, a name for reality; in Ch'an usage, this can be read as personal ('there is nothing that is not the self of a saint') or impersonal ('a saint has no self').

kashaya—An upper vestment worn by monks when meditating or performing symbolic services.

Maitreya—The Loving One, the future Buddha, said to be presently living in the heaven of satisfaction, awaiting the time when he will be born on earth for the welfare of all beings. Mahasattva Fu (cf. case 67) and Pu Tai (Hotei) were both considered to be manifestations of Maitreya.

mahasattva—An enlightened bodhisattva, a great hero or great knight (the literal meaning of mahasattva) who is fully qualified for complete buddhahood, but travels endlessly in the rounds of life to liberate beings rather than abiding as the pole of a field of enlightenment. All the transhistorical bodhisattvas mentioned in the Blue Cliff Record are mahasattvas.

Mahasthamaprapta—The bodhisattva representing empowerment, depicted as the guardian of the knowledge of Amitabha Buddha.

Manjusri—The bodhisattva representing wisdom and knowledge, depicted as riding on a golden lion (symbol of the body of reality) and being the teacher of the seven Buddhas of antiquity. Manjusri's image is the conventional main icon of Ch'an meditation halls.

nirvana—Extinction of suffering, known as Peace, Liberation, Bliss, the Other Shore, the Refuge, the Uncompounded, etc. In early Buddhism *nirvana* was known as the correct, or absolute state, and is the essence of sainthood.

outsider—This is used by Buddhists to refer to non-Buddhists, but in Ch'an lingo anyone who seeks or grasps anything is called an outsider, estranged from inherent enlightened nature.

Patriarch—Ancestor; refers to living examples of enlightenment; it can refer to the leaders or founders of branches of Buddhism, and in Ch'an is also used as a term of respect for adepts of earlier generations as well as the founders of the streams.

patchrobe—An example and symbol of poverty, the clothes of Buddhist ascetics were made of patched rags. This expression is also used in Sufism, with the same basic sense.

pillar and lamp—Being present in the teaching halls, the pillar and lamp are often mentioned as examples and thus representative of the objective world.

reed shade—A bundle of reeds used to shade sun off water so as to be able to see beyond the surface into the depths—a simile for tactics of a Teaching Master to draw out or see into a student.

samadhi—One-pointed focus of mind; concentration or absorption; sometimes extended in Ch'an usage to refer to any state of mind, any activity, even phenomena.

Samantabhadra—Bodhisattva representing goodness and wisdom in all actions, the ultimate principle of union of knowledge and myriad deeds for the enlightenment of all beings; Samantabhadra is depicted as riding on an elephant. The vow of Samantabhadra closes the *Gandhavyuha*, a major scripture contained in the grand *Avatamsaka* (Hua Yen) scripture; it bespeaks the ultimate aspirations of those who conceive the will for universal enlightenment.

South—A code word for Ch'an study ('going South') or enlightened knowledge itself; the journey of Sudhana for enlightenment (which is the story of the *Gandhavyuha*) was to the South and Ch'an flourished most in southern China during its golden age in the T'ang dynasty—hence the association came to be a fixed term.

Tathagata—An epithet of Buddhas, meaning one who has come to realize thusness.

triple world—Three worlds; refers to the realms of desire, form, and formlessness or immateriality.

turning word—Word or expression occasioning or representing the transformation from delusion to enlightenment, especially a term or phrase which contains both ordinary and spiritual or transcendental meanings, both provisional and real, or both negative and positive modes.

triple vehicle—Three vehicles; refers to the careers of discipleship (following the Dharma to realize personal emptiness and sainthood), self-enlightenment (solitary liberation through understanding of the process of conditioning), and bodhisattvahood (realization of both personal and phenomenal emptiness and the conception of great compassion and commitment to the enlightenment of all beings). These three vehicles lead into the so-called unique vehicle, which is the way of complete Buddhahood.

Ts'ao Ch'i—A river and river valley in south China, where the famous Sixth Patriarch of Ch'an taught; hence it comes to be a codeword not only for that Patriarch, Hui Neng, but for all the streams of Ch'an (and hence Ch'an itself, after the ninth century) which were descended from Hui Neng's enlightened disciples.

whisk—Used for nonviolent insect dispersal, its use was a prerogative of abbots, so it came to be another symbol (and in fact was physically handed down as such) of the succession of a Ch'an lineage; it is commonly used, however, like the pillar and the lamp, as a representative symbol of This, objective reality.

Vairocana—The great Sun Buddha, the Illuminator, the so-called Adibuddha or primordial awakening, symbolizing the body of reality. As a meditation *(dhyani)* Buddha in esoteric Buddhism, Vairocana is associated with mind and may be said to represent the basic awakened intelligence or the fundamental luminous quality of awareness. The cosmos itself also may be said to be an attribute of Vairocana.

Guide to Chinese Pronunciation

According to the transcription method used in The Blue Cliff
Record, *based on the modified Wade-Giles system*

Chinese	*English approximation*
a	f*a*ther
ai	eye
ao	h*ow*
ch	j
ch'	ch
e	b*u*t (n.b. er(h) sounds like *are,* ei sounds like h*a*y)
f	f
h	h
i	p*i*n (ih sounds like h*e*r)
hs	*s*ure
k	g
k'	k
l	l
m	m
n	n
o	b*u*t (only when whole syllable consists of o; otherwise, o sounds like th*a*w); ou sounds like thr*ow*
p	b
p'	p
r	no equivalent; resembles mix of French j and English r
s	s
sh	sh (palatalized hs)
sz	s (only in szu, which resembles *ce*rtain)

t	d
t'	t
ts	dz
ts'	ts
tz	dz (these two only before u; see sz)
tz'	ts
u	put (ui=*way*, ua=*wa*, uo=*waw*, ueh=*ywe*)
w	w
y	y

This does not exhaust the intricacies of Chinese phonetics but is intended to help the reader with a reasonably comfortable and accurate way of reading Chinese names.

Bibliography

The following early modern commentaries on the *Blue Cliff Record* by Japanese Zen Masters were also consulted in addition to the commentaries cited in the bibliography appended to volume 1;

Ashahina Sōgen, *Hekiganroku kōwa*. Tokyo, Kawade shobō, 1956.
Iida Tōin, *Hekiganshū teishōroku*. Tokyo Morikawa shoten, 1932.
Imazu Kōgaku *Heikiganshū Kōgi*. Tokyo, Mugazanbō, 1913.
Ōuchi Seiran, *Hekiganroku kōwa*. Tokyo, Kōmeisha, 1906.
Shaku Sōen, *Hekiganroku kōwa*. Tokyo, Kōyūkan, 1915–16.